Dubai

Residents' Guide

there's more to life...
askexplorer.com

GET IN TOUCH WITH
WILDLIFE & NATURE
AT AL AIN ZOO.

حديقة الحيوانات بالعين
AL AIN ZOO

THE INSIDE STORY OF
EVERY BEAUTIFUL HOME.

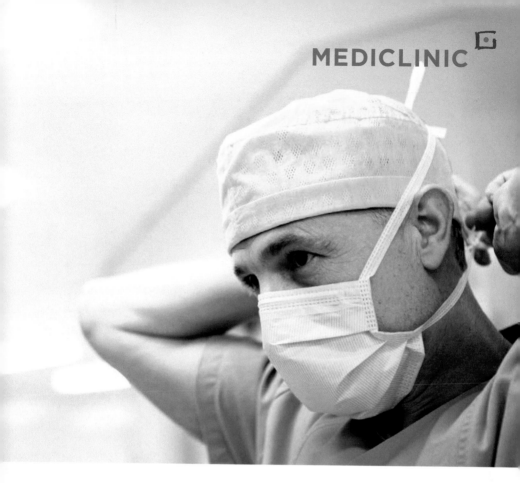

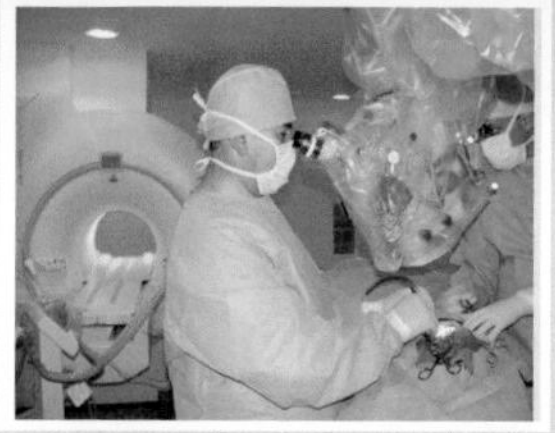

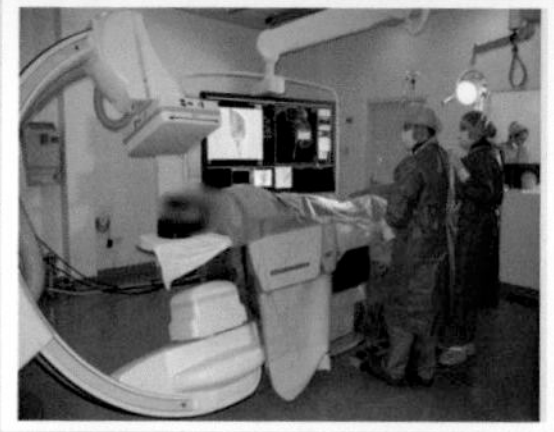

NEURO SPINAL HOSPITAL SERVICES

- Spinal Surgery
- Neuro Surgery
- Neurology
- Neurophysiology
- Joints and Bones Replacement
- General Orthopaedics
- Neurourology and Urology
- General Surgery
- Functional & Interventional Radiology
- Rehabilitation, Physiotherapy and Hydrotherapy
- Laboratory
- Pharmacy
- 24 / 7 Emergency room

NEURO SPINAL HOSPITAL SPECIALTY CLINICS

At Neuro Spinal Hospital, our expertise extends to cover all of your neurosurgical, neurological and orthopaedics needs. All under one roof:

- Back Pain
- Headache
- Brain Surgery
- Epilepsy
- Neurovascular and Stroke
- Spasticity and Cerebral Palsy
- Laproscopic
- Scoliosis
- Spinal Cord Injury
- Total Joint Replacement
- Sports Medicine and Orthopaedics
- Neurourology and Urodynamic
- Urology
- Chronic Pain

Physical Address

Jumeirah Beach Road, opposite to Jumeirah Beach Park, Dubai, United Arab Emirates.

Switchboard Number: +971 (4) 342 0000
Fax Number : +971 (4) 342 0007
Emergency Number: +971 (4) 315 7777

Online

www.nshdubai.com
info@nshdubai.com

Hours

Our emergency department is open 24 hours a day, 7 days a week to treat all critical emergency patients.

Healthcare with a human touch

Turkey's No. 1 Modern Design Furniture

Dolce Belleza living room

Korsan kids room

Natura Style dining room

Dolce Belleza dining room

Dubai Duty Free
Wonderful fragrances
Collectable cosmetics
Exquisite jewellery
One way to have it all
TRAVEL LIGHT
Shop at Dubai Duty Free
www.dubaidutyfree.com
Full of surprises.

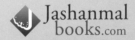

Do Something Different!
Shake up the routine and discover something new for the whole family at Ski Dubai.
Whether it's twisting and turning down the tube slides,
rolling down in a Giant Snow Ball, experiencing the thrills of a family chairlift ride
or enjoying a mug of the Avalanche Café's famous hot chocolate at minus 4 degrees,
you'll always find something new at Ski Dubai.
SKI DUBAI
سكي دبي
For more information please visit www.skidxb.com and us on facebook.com/skidxb

Hello to more wow.
With fine dining and a business class seat that transforms into one of the longest fully flat beds in the sky, Upper Class really is the most fabulous way to fly.
Discover more at **virginatlantic.com** or call **+971 4406 0600**
upperclass
to London
virgin atlantic
Virgin

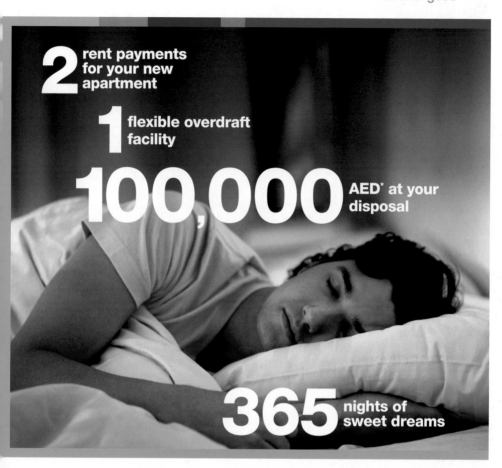

VOTED
Superbrand
UAE's Choice
2013
Our achievements
are our pride and glory.
Proudly bringing quality food and lifestyle products to the region.
Over the past 30 years, Al Maya Group has grown to touch your lives in many ways. We take pride in our success steming from a deep-rooted commitment to delivering consistent quality and great value through the best brands and products. With your support we look forward to achieving even greater success in the years to come.
Tel. +971 4 282 2555, Fax +971 4 282 6660, PO Box 8476, Dubai, United Arab Emirates
مجموعة المايا
Al Maya Group
www.almaya.ae
شركة المايا التجارية ذ.م.م
Al Maya Trading Co. L.L.C.
Bhs
mom and me
BORDERS.
Paperchase
almaya
supermarkets

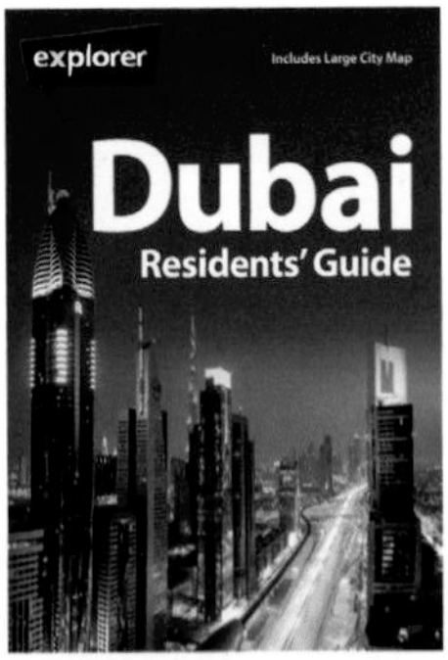

Dubai Residents' Guide 2013/17th Edition
First Published 1996
2nd Edition 1997
3rd Edition 1998
4th Edition 2000
5th Edition 2001
6th Edition 2002
7th Edition 2003
8th Edition 2004
9th Edition 2005
10th Edition 2006
11th Edition 2007
12th Edition 2008
13th Edition 2009
14th Edition 2010
15th Edition 2011
16th Edition 2012
17th Edition 2013 ISBN 978-9948-8518-4-4

Front Cover Photograph – Sheikh Zayed Road – Derrick Pereira

Printed and bound by Emirates Printing Press, Dubai, United Arab Emirates.

Explorer Publishing & Distribution
PO Box 34275, Dubai
United Arab Emirates

Phone	+971 (0)4 340 8805
Fax	+971 (0)4 340 8806
Email	info@askexplorer.com
Web	askexplorer.com

Welcome...

...to the 17th edition of the **Dubai Residents' Guide**, the ultimate insider's guide to living in and enjoying one of the world's most exciting cities.

This guide is packed with everything you need to know about life in Dubai, from red-tape procedures to restaurants, housing to hobbies, entertainment to exploring, and shopping to socialising. Whether you've just stepped off the plane or have been living in Dubai for years, this guide will help you make the most out of life. Plus, as a special gift, we're giving you a **Dubai Map** to help you locate the best attractions, hotels and shopping areas in the city.

Dubai is a modern, thriving metropolis – one that is constantly growing and changing. For more information about Dubai and the UAE, plus up-to-the-minute events and new releases, log on to ask**explorer**.com. And, if you make a great insider discovery, let us and your fellow Dubaians know all about it at ask**explorer**.com

Finally, don't forget that Explorer publishes hundreds of maps and activity guides that help to make the good life in the UAE even better. Discover more at ask**explorer**.com/shop.

In your hands, in the glove box, in your rucksack; on your laptop, tablet or smartphone. Wherever you're going and whatever you're doing, be sure to take us with you.

There's more to life...
The Explorer Team

ask**explorer**.com

Contents

Contents

Contents

UAE: A Country Profile

UNITED ARAB EMIRATES

Located in the heart of the Middle East, the United Arab Emirates (UAE) is home to more than 200 nationalities. While proud and protective of its own Islamic culture, it is also one of the most progressive, cosmopolitan and open-minded countries in the region. From the brash metropolis of Dubai to the desert wilderness of the Empty Quarter, its many landscapes lie just waiting to be explored. Whether you're new to this remarkable land or have been living here for years already, there's always something new to discover.

Location

Located on the eastern side of the Arabian Peninsula, the UAE borders Saudi Arabia and the Sultanate of Oman, with coastlines on both the Arabian Gulf and the Gulf of Oman. The country comprises seven emirates – Abu Dhabi, Ajman, Dubai, Fujairah, Ras Al Khaimah, Sharjah and Umm Al Quwain. Abu Dhabi is by far the largest of the UAE's emirate, occupying over 80% of the country, with the emirate of Dubai the second largest, although they have similar populations (p.9).

The country is best known for the modern, rapidly expanding metropolis of Dubai, but visitors may be surprised by the variety of landscapes when they venture beyond the city. The coast is littered with coral reefs and more than 200 islands, most of which are uninhabited. The interior of the country is characterised by sabkha (salt flats), stretches of gravel plain and vast areas of sand desert.

To the east rise the Hajar Mountains (hajar is Arabic for rock). Lying close to the Gulf of Oman, they form a backbone through the country, from the Musandam Peninsula in the north, through the eastern UAE and into Oman. The highest point is Jebel Yibir at 1,527 metres. The Rub Al Khali, or Empty Quarter, occupies a large part of the south of the country. Stretching into Saudi Arabia, Oman and Yemen, it's the largest sand desert in the world, covering an area roughly the same size as France, Belgium and the Netherlands. This stark desert is interrupted by salt flats and occasional oases, and its spectacular sand dunes rise to more than 300 metres.

Climate

Dubai has a subtropical and arid climate. Sunny blue skies and high temperatures can be expected most of the year. Rain falls on an average of only 25 days per year, mainly in winter (December to March). It rarely rains very heavily or for long periods. However, in the Hajar Mountains the amount of rainfall can be much higher and flash floods in the wadis are not unheard of.

Although certainly infrequent, on the rare occasion that it does come, heavy rainfall can really take its toll on the city within a relatively short period.

During winter there are occasional sandstorms when the sand is whipped up off the desert. This is not to be confused with a shamal, a north-westerly wind that comes off the Arabian Gulf and can cool temperatures down considerably. Sandstorms cover anything left outside in gardens or on balconies and can even blow inside, so make sure your doors and windows are shut.

Temperatures range from a low of around 10°C (50°F) in winter to a high of 48°C (118°F) in summer. The mean daily maximum is 24°C (75°F) in January, rising to 41°C (106°F) in August. Humidity is usually between 50% and 65%, however, when combined with the high summer temperatures, even 60% humidity can be extremely uncomfortable.

UAE Fact Box

Coordinates: 24°00' North 54°00' East
Borders with Oman and Saudi Arabia
Total land area: approx. 83,000 sq km
(Dubai land area: 3,885 sq km)
Total coastline: 1,318 km
Highest point: 1,527 m
Capital city: Abu Dhabi
Currency: UAE dirham
Time zone: UTC+4 (all year – daylight saving time not observed)

The most pleasant time to visit Dubai is in the winter months, when temperatures are perfect for comfortable days on the beach and evenings outside. For up to date weather reports, visit the National Centre of Meteorology and Seismology's website at ncms.ae/english or call 02 222 7374.

HISTORY

Although recent archaeological discoveries suggest an area that was inhabited as far back as 3000BC, Dubai's early existence is most closely linked to the arrival and development of Islam in the greater Middle East region.

Islam developed in modern-day Saudi Arabia at the beginning of the seventh century AD with the revelations of the Quran being received by the Prophet Muhammad. Military conquests of the Middle East and North Africa enabled the Arab empire to spread the teachings of Islam from Mecca and Medina to the local Bedouin tribes. Following the Arab Empire came the Turks, the Mongols and the Ottomans, each leaving their mark on local culture.

After the fall of the Muslim empires, both the British and Portuguese became interested in the area due

Modern UAE

Trade and commerce are still the cornerstones of the economy, with the traditional manufacturing and distribution industries now joined by finance, construction, media, IT and telecom businesses. With so many world-class hotels, and leisure and entertainment options, the UAE has become an increasingly popular tourist destination.

to its strategic position between India and Europe. By 1820, the British had exerted their authority and a general treaty was agreed with the local rulers. The following years witnessed a series of maritime truces, with Dubai and the other emirates accepting British protection in 1892. In Europe, the area became known as the Trucial Coast (or Trucial States), a name it retained until the departure of the British in 1971.

In the late 1800s, Dubai's leader, Sheikh Maktoum bin Hasher Al Maktoum, granted tax concessions to foreign traders, encouraging many to switch their base of operations from Iran and Sharjah to Dubai. The city's importance as a trading hub was further enhanced by Sheikh Rashid bin Saeed Al Maktoum, father of the current ruler of Dubai, who ordered the creek to be dredged, thus providing access for larger vessels. Dubai came to specialise in the import and re-export of goods, mainly gold to India, and trade became the foundation of this emirate's wealthy progression.

In 1968, the UK announced its withdrawal from the region. The ruling sheikhs of Bahrain, Qatar and the Trucial Coast realised that by uniting forces as a single state, they would have a stronger voice in the wider Middle East region. Negotiations collapsed when Bahrain and Qatar chose independence, however, the Trucial Coast remained committed to forming an alliance, and in 1971 the federation of the United Arab Emirates was born.

The new country comprised the emirates of Dubai, Abu Dhabi, Ajman, Fujairah, Sharjah, Umm Al

UAE TIMELINE

1760	The Baniyas Tribe finds fresh water in Abu Dhabi and settles on the island
1833	The Maktoum family settles in Dubai
1835	Maritime Truce signed between the Trucial States and the UK
1890s	Dubai and Abu Dhabi fall under the protection of the UK
1950s	Oil is discovered in Abu Dhabi and production begins
1963	Maktoum Bridge is built, becoming the first bridge across Dubai Creek
1966	Commercial quantities of oil discovered off the coast of Dubai. HH Sheikh Zayed bin Sultan Al Nahyan becomes ruler of Abu Dhabi. Dubai's first hotel, The Carlton (now The Riviera), is built
1967	The Shindagha Tunnel is built, providing an alternative to Maktoum Bridge for crossing the creek
1971	The UK withdraws from the Gulf and Dubai becomes independent. The United Arab Emirates is born, with HH Sheikh Zayed bin Sultan Al Nahyan as the leader. The UAE joins the Arab League
1972	Ras Al Khaimah joins the UAE
1973	The UAE launches a single currency, the UAE dirham
1981	The Gulf Cooperation Council (GCC) is formed, with the UAE as a founding member
1985	Emirates Airline is founded
1990	After the death of his father, Sheikh Rashid bin Saeed Al Maktoum, Sheikh Maktoum bin Rashid Al Maktoum becomes the ruler of Dubai
1999	The doors of the Burj Al Arab, the tallest hotel in the world, open to the public for the first time
2001	Construction starts on Palm Jumeirah
2002	The freehold property market is opened up to foreigners
2004	Sheikh Zayed bin Sultan Al Nahyan dies and is succeeded as leader of the UAE by his son, Sheikh Khalifa bin Zayed Al Nahyan
2006	Sheikh Maktoum bin Rashid Al Maktoum dies and is succeeded as ruler of Dubai and prime minister of the UAE by his brother, Sheikh Mohammed bin Rashid Al Maktoum
2007	The first residents move on to the Palm Jumeirah
2008	Atlantis on the Palm opens its doors; in the wake of global economic crisis, Dubai's property market crashes to around 50% of its peak value
2009	Abu Dhabi hosts its inaugural grand prix at Yas Marina Circuit. Dubai Metro, the region's first public mass-transit system, is launched
2010	The tallest building in the world, the Burj Khalifa, and Ferrari World Abu Dhabi open
2011	The second line of the Dubai Metro opens and the UAE celebrates its 40th anniversary
2012	Yas Waterworld in Abu Dhabi is completed; the Dubai 24 Hours Shopping initiative is launched for the Eid celebrations in October

Quwain and, in 1972, Ras Al Khaimah (each emirate is named after its main town). Under the agreement, the individual emirates each retained a certain degree of autonomy, with Abu Dhabi and Dubai providing the most input into the federation. The leaders of the new federation elected the ruler of Abu Dhabi, His Highness Sheikh Zayed bin Sultan Al Nahyan, to be their president, a position he held until he passed away on 2 November 2004. His eldest son, His Highness Sheikh Khalifa bin Zayed Al Nahyan, was then elected to take over the presidency.

The formation of the UAE came after the discovery of huge oil reserves in Abu Dhabi in 1958 (Abu Dhabi has an incredible 10% of the world's known oil reserves). This discovery dramatically transformed the emirate. In 1966, Dubai, which was already a relatively wealthy trading centre, also discovered oil.

Dubai's ruler at the time, the late Sheikh Rashid bin Saeed Al Maktoum, ensured that the emirate's oil revenues were used to develop an economic and social infrastructure, which is the basis of today's modern society. His work was continued through the reign of his son and successor, Sheikh Maktoum bin Rashid Al Maktoum and by the present ruler, Sheikh Mohammed bin Rashid Al Maktoum.

GOVERNMENT & RULING FAMILY

The Supreme Council of Rulers is the highest authority in the UAE, comprising the hereditary rulers of the seven emirates. Since the country is governed by hereditary rule there is little distinction between the royal families and the government. The Supreme Council is responsible for general policy involving education, defence, foreign affairs, communications and development, and for ratifying federal laws. The Council meets regularly throughout the year; each emirate has one single vote and the rulers of Abu Dhabi and Dubai have power of veto over decisions.

The Supreme Council elects the chief of state (the president) from among its seven members. The current president is the ruler of Abu Dhabi, Sheikh Khalifa bin Zayed Al Nahyan. He took over the post in November 2004 from his late father, Sheikh Zayed bin Sultan Al Nahyan.

Emirs Or Sheikhs?

While the term emirate comes from the ruling title of 'emir', the rulers of the UAE are actually called 'sheikhs'.

The Supreme Council also elects the vice president of the UAE, currently Sheikh Mohammed bin Rashid Al Maktoum, ruler of Dubai. The president and vice president are elected and appointed for five-year terms, although they are often re-elected time after time, as was the case with Sheikh Zayed. The president appoints the prime minister (currently Sheikh Mohammed bin Rashid Al Maktoum) and the deputy prime ministers (currently Sheikh Saif bin Zayed Al Nahyan and Sheikh Mansour bin Zayed Al Nahyan).

The emirate of Dubai is currently ruled by Sheikh Mohammed bin Rashid Al Maktoum, vice president and prime minister of the UAE (who is considered the driving force behind Dubai's exponential growth) and

DUBAI RULING FAMILY TREE

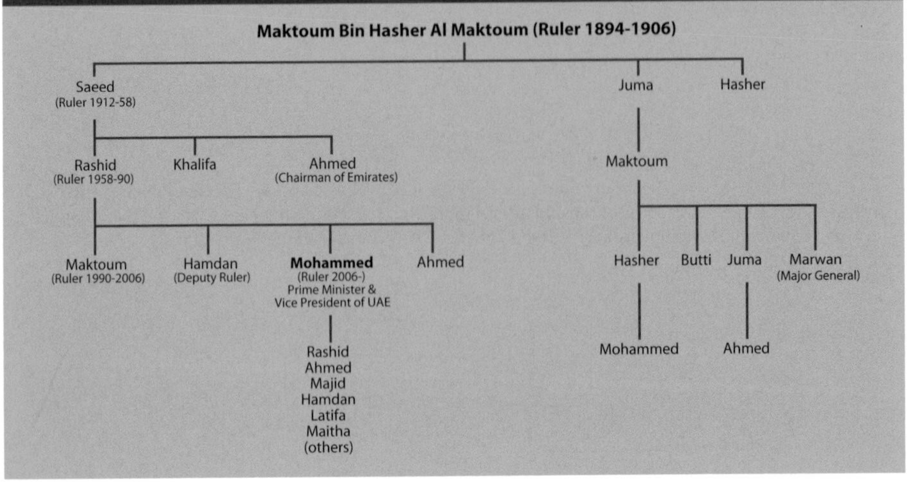

his brother Sheikh Hamdan bin Rashid Al Maktoum, the UAE minister of finance and industry.

The Federal National Council (FNC) reports to the Supreme Council. It has executive authority to initiate and implement laws and is a consultative assembly of 40 representatives. The Council currently monitors and debates government policy but has no power of veto.

Girl Power

Following elections in 2007, a number of women were voted in to government positions and, today, more than 60% of UAE government employees are women, one of the highest rates in the world.

The individual emirates have some degree of autonomy, and laws that affect everyday life vary between them. For instance, if you buy a car in one emirate and need to register it in a different emirate, you will have to export and then re-import it. Each emirate has its own police force, with a distinct uniform and car.

Downtown Dubai

INTERNATIONAL RELATIONS

The UAE remains open in its foreign relations and firmly supports Arab unity. HH Sheikh Khalifa bin Zayed Al Nahyan is very generous with the country's wealth when it comes to helping Arab nations and communities that are in need of aid.

The UAE became a member of the United Nations and the Arab League in 1971. It is a member of the International Monetary Fund (IMF), the Organisation of Petroleum Exporting Countries (Opec), the World Trade Organisation (WTO) and other international and Arab organisations. It is also a member of the Arab Gulf Cooperation Council (AGCC, also known as the GCC), whose other members are Bahrain, Kuwait, Oman, Qatar and Saudi Arabia.

All major embassies and consulates are represented either in Dubai or in Abu Dhabi, or both. See Embassies & Consulates, p.596.

SHEIKH MOHAMMED: A PROFILE

Sheikh Mohammed bin Rashid Al Maktoum is ruler of Dubai, and prime minister and vice president of the UAE. He acceded to both positions in 2006 following his brother Sheikh Maktoum bin Rashid Al Maktoum's death. Born in 1948, his children include Rashid, the deputy ruler of Dubai, and Hamdan, crown prince and future ruler of Dubai.

Widely accredited with the vision of modern day Dubai, Sheikh Mohammed has been a major driving force in the completion of some of the emirate's elaborate construction projects such as the Burj Al Arab and Palm Jumeirah. His pioneering Free Trade Zones, such as Dubai Media City, offer tax exemptions which have attracted foreign companies to set up in the emirate, helping Dubai's economy flourish and reducing its reliance on oil-based industries. He is also attributed with fostering the progressive, cosmopolitan society that exists in the emirate today.

Among Sheikh Mohammed's passions are poetry and horse racing; the latter nowhere more evident than in the emirate's hosting of the richest horse race in the world, the Dubai World Cup (p.26). Dubai's ruler is a patron of the ancient poetic form, Nabati (also known as Bedouin poetry), and has published volumes of his own verses.

To find out more about the ruler of Dubai visit sheikhmohammed.co.ae or visit his Facebook profile facebook.com/HHSheikhMohammed.

FACTS & FIGURES

Population

The UAE population has grown rapidly in recent years as expat arrivals, robust economic expansion and high birth rates have continued to push up the total number. According to the World Bank, the UAE's population stood at 4.6 million in 2009 and, in 2010, the UAE Statistics Bureau estimated that the country's population had shot up by 65% in four years to reach 8.26 million. An official census has been delayed from the scheduled April 2010 date and the results are due to be published by 2015. The latest figures do, however, reveal that Dubai's population ticked over the two million mark in 2012.

Nearly nine out of ten UAE residents are expats, with Emirates accounting for 11.5% of the population.

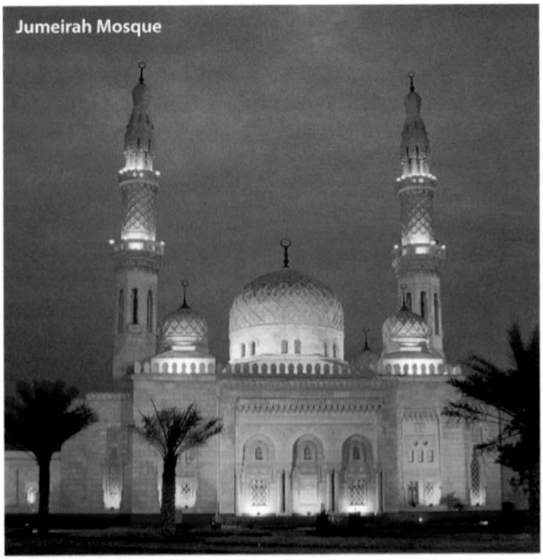

Local Time

The UAE is four hours ahead of UTC (Universal Coordinated Time – formerly known as GMT). Clocks are not altered for daylight saving in the summer, so when Europe and North America gain an hour, the time in the UAE stays the same. During this period the time difference is one hour less, so when it is 12:00 in the UAE it is 09:00 in the UK instead of 08:00 during the winter. The table below shows time differences between the UAE and various cities around the world (not allowing for any daylight savings in those cities).

Time Zones

Amman	-2	**Los Angeles**	-12
Athens	-2	**Manama**	-1
Auckland	+8	**Mexico City/Dallas**	-10
Bangkok	+3	**Moscow**	-1
Beijing	+4	**Mumbai**	+1.5
Beirut	-2	**Munich**	-3
Canberra	+6	**Muscat**	0
Colombo	+2	**New York**	-9
Damascus	-2	**Paris**	-3
Denver	-11	**Perth**	+4
Doha	-1	**Prague**	-3
Dublin	-4	**Riyadh**	-1
Hong Kong	+4	**Rome**	-3
Johannesburg	-2	**Singapore**	+4
Karachi	+1	**Sydney**	+6
Kuwait City	-1	**Tokyo**	+5
London	-4	**Toronto**	-9
		Wellington	+8

Social & Business Hours, Weekends

Working hours differ greatly in the UAE, with much of the private sector working a straight shift (usually from 08:30 to 17:30 or 09:00 to 18:00, with an hour for lunch), while a minority work a split shift (working from 09:00 to 13:00, then taking a long lunch break before returning to work from 16:00 to 19:00). It's not uncommon for working hours in private companies in the UAE to be longer than in other international cities. Government offices are generally open from 07:30 to 14:30, Sunday to Thursday. Embassies and consulates operate similar hours, but may designate specific times and days for certain tasks (such as passport applications), so it's best to call before you go. Most embassies take a Friday/Saturday weekend. All will have an emergency number on their answering service, website or office doors.

The majority of larger shops and shopping centres are open throughout the day and into the evening, generally closing at 22:00 or midnight. Traditional shops and smaller street traders often operate under split shift timings, closing for three or four hours in the afternoon. Some food outlets and petrol stations are open 24 hours a day.

Friday is the Islamic holy day and therefore a universal day off for offices and schools; most companies and schools have a two-day weekend over Friday and Saturday. Some companies still require a six-day week from their staff, while others operate on a five and a half day system. Consumer demand means that the hospitality and retail industries are open seven days a week.

Ramadan Hours

According to the labour laws, all companies are obliged to shorten the working day by two hours during Ramadan. Even though this is to assist Muslim employees who are fasting, the law makes no distinction in this regard between Muslim and non-Muslim employees. So technically, even expats are entitled to a shorter working day. However, many international companies do not follow this principle, and labour lawyers would advise you not to make a fuss if you are not given a shorter working day. Some lucky expats do get to work shorter hours during Ramadan, and many businesses, schools and shops change their hours slightly.

Dubai's traffic has a totally different pattern during Ramadan; instead of being gridlocked in the mornings and quiet in the afternoons, the mornings are almost jam-free and you'll sail through all the usual trouble spots, while in the afternoons the roads are totally clogged. Night-time activity increases during Ramadan, with many shops staying open later (until midnight or even 01:00) and the city's many shisha cafes, and some restaurants, stay open until the early hours.

Public Holidays

The Islamic calendar starts from the year 622AD, the year of Prophet Muhammad's migration (Hijra) from Mecca to Al Madinah. Hence the Islamic year is called the Hijri year and dates are followed by AH (AH stands for Anno Hegirae, meaning 'after the year of the Hijra').

As some holidays are based on the sighting of the moon and do not have fixed dates on the calendar, Islamic holidays are more often than not confirmed less than 24 hours in advance. Most companies send an email to employees the day before, notifying them of the confirmed holiday date. Some non-religious holidays are fixed according to the Gregorian calendar. It should be noted that the public sector often gets additional days off for holidays where the private sector may not (for example on National Day the public sector gets two days of official holiday, whereas private sector companies take only one day). This can be a problem for working parents, as even private schools fall under the public sector and therefore get the extended holidays, so your children will usually have more days off than you do. No problem if you have full-time home help, but if not then you may have to take a day's leave.

Lunar Calendar

The Hijri calendar is based on lunar months; there are 354 or 355 days in the Hijri year, which is divided into 12 lunar months, and is thus 11 days shorter than the Gregorian year. There are plenty of websites with Gregorian/Hijri calendar conversion tools, so you can find the equivalent Hijri date for any Gregorian date, and vice versa. Try rabiah.com/convert.

Below is a list of the holidays and the number of days they last for. This applies mainly to the public sector, so if you work in the private sector you may get fewer days per holiday.

The main Muslim festivals are Eid Al Fitr (the festival of the breaking of the fast, which marks the end of Ramadan) and Eid Al Adha (the festival of the sacrifice, which marks the end of the pilgrimage to Mecca).

Mawlid Al Nabee is the holiday celebrating the Prophet Muhammad's birthday, and Lailat Al Mi'raj celebrates the Prophet's ascension into heaven.

Public Holidays	2013	2014
New Year's Day (Fixed)	1 Jan	1 Jan
Mawlid Al Nabee (Moon)	24 Jan	13 Jan
Lailat Al Mi'raj (Moon)	6 Jun	26 May
Eid Al Fitr (2-3 days; Moon)	8 Aug	28 Jul
Eid Al Adha (2-3 days; Moon)	15 Oct	4 Oct
Islamic New Year's Day (Moon)	4 Nov	25 Oct
UAE National Day (Fixed)	2 Dec	2 Dec

Media City

UAE: Facts & Figures

The World Economic Forum's Global Competitiveness Report 2012-2013 ranks the UAE as 24th out of 144 countries globally, rising three places from 2011.

The 2012 Daman Investments GCC Economics Report places the country second in the GCC in terms of attracting foreign direct investment; non-oil foreign trade for Dubai reached a record Dhs.602bn during the first half of 2012, a 12% increase over the same period in 2011.

UAE Free Zones

There are more than 30 free zones in the UAE. Incentives for setting up business in a free zone include 100% foreign ownership, 100% repatriation of profit and 0% tax.

Dubai GDP By Sector

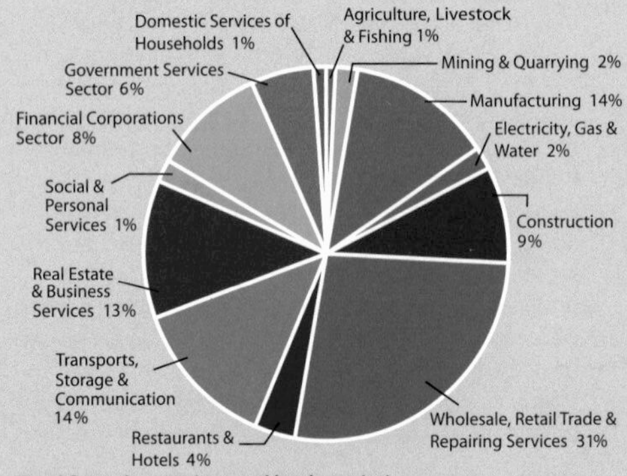

(Total figure less 7% imputed bank service)
Source: Dubai Statistics Centre, 2011

UAE GDP By Sector

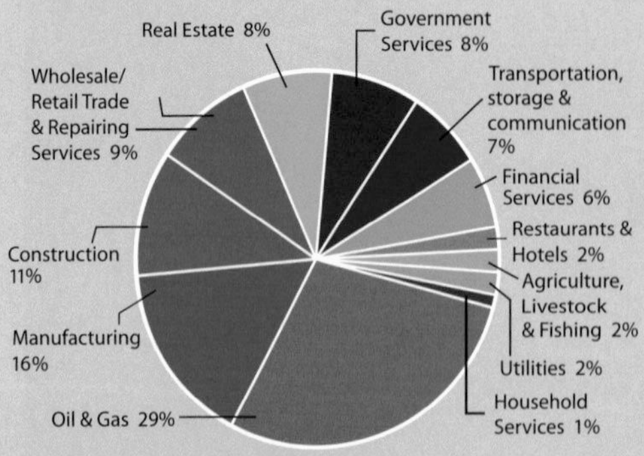

Source: UAE Economic Report 2010

UAE GDP By Emirate

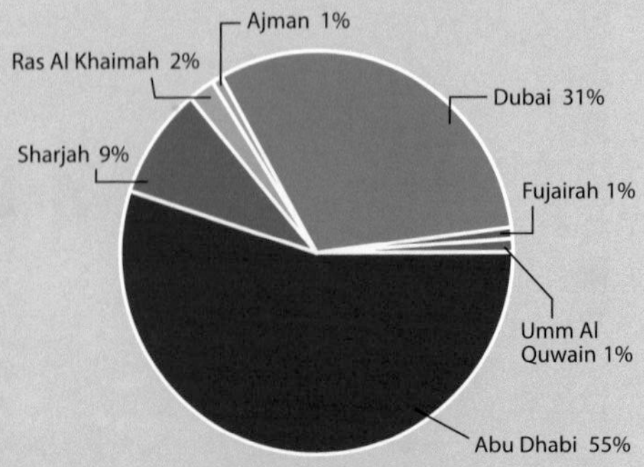

Source: Ministry of Economy, 2008

Temperature & Humidity

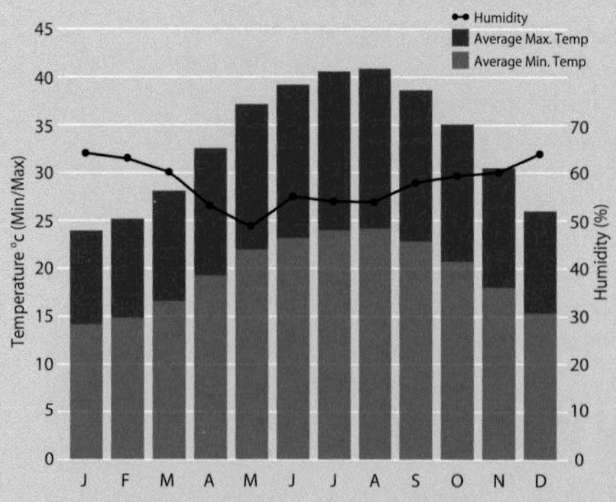

Rainfall

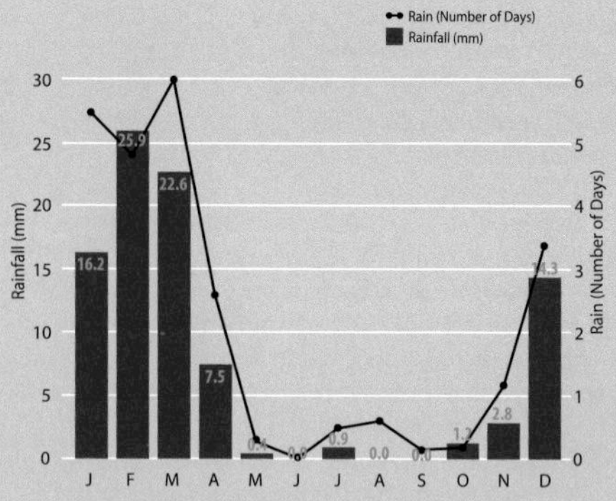

Education Levels

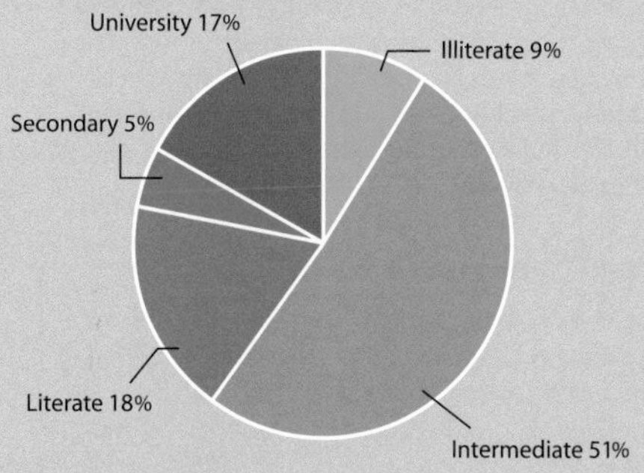

Source: Dubai Statistics Centre

Population By Emirate

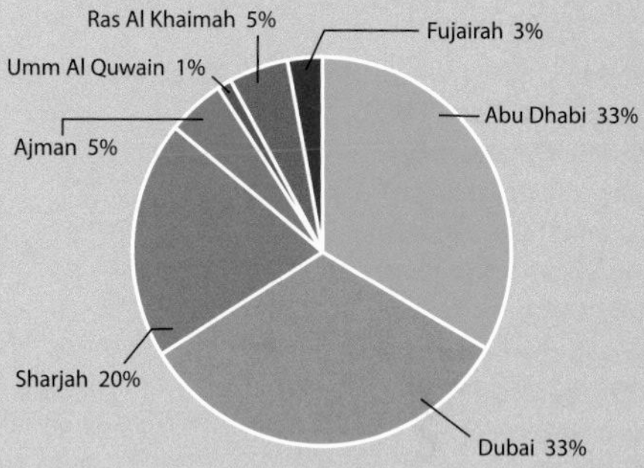

Source: Ministry of Economy, 2007

Dubai Population Age Breakdown

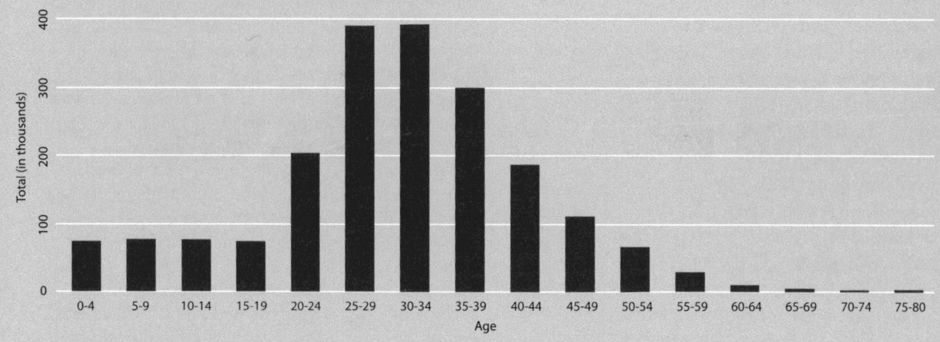

Source: Dubai Statistics Centre, 2011

Currency

The monetary unit is the dirham (Dhs.), which is divided into 100 fils. The currency is also referred to as AED (Arab Emirate dirham). Notes come in denominations of Dhs.5 (brown), Dhs.10 (green), Dhs.20 (light blue), Dhs.50 (purple), Dhs.100 (pink), Dhs.200 (yellowy-brown), Dhs.500 (blue) and Dhs.1,000 (browny-purple).

The denominations are indicated on the notes in both Arabic and English. To see examples of the UAE's banknotes, visit the website of the Central Bank of the UAE (centralbank.ae) and click on 'currency' on the left.

There are actually six coins in circulation in the UAE, although you are only ever likely to see three of them. Still, distinguishing them can be tricky because the amount is written in Arabic only. The Dhs.1 coin is the largest, the 50 fils is smaller but seven-sided, and the 25 fils is of a similar size to the 50 fils but is circular. All are silver in colour.

The dirham has been pegged to the US dollar since 1980, at a mid rate of $1 to Dhs.3.67.

Exchange Rates

Foreign Currency	1 Unit FC = x Dhs.	Dhs.1 = xFC
Australia Dollars (AUD)	3.86	0.26
Bahrain Dinars (BHD)	9.74	0.10
Bangladesh Taka (BDT)	0.05	21.67
Canada Dollars (CAD)	3.70	0.27
Denmark Kroner (DKK)	0.66	1.53
Euro (EUR)	4.89	0.20
Hong Kong Dollars (HKD)	0.47	2.11
India Rupees (INR)	0.07	14.69
Japan Yen (JPY)	0.04	24.39
Jordan Dinars (JOD)	5.19	0.19
Kuwait Dinars (KWD)	13.03	0.08
Malaysia Ringgits (MYR)	1.21	0.82
New Zealand Dollars (NZD)	3.07	0.33
Oman Rials (OMR)	9.54	0.10
Pakistan Rupees (PKR)	0.04	26.59
Philippines Pesos (PHP)	0.09	11.06
Qatar Riyals (QAR)	1.01	0.99
Saudi Arabia Riyals (SAR)	0.98	1.02
Singapore Dollars (SGD)	2.99	0.33
South Africa Rand (ZAR)	0.41	2.42
Sri Lanka Rupees (LKR)	0.03	34.48
Sweden Kronor (SEK)	0.41	2.42
Switzerland Francs (CHF)	3.93	0.25
Thailand Baht (THB)	0.12	8.11
UK Pounds (GBP)	5.83	0.17
US Dollars (USD)	3.67	0.27

Source: xe.com, Jan 2013

Local and international banks, and exchange centres are open 24 hours at Dubai International Airport.

Exchange Centres

Al Ansari Exchange 04 341 4005, *alansariexchange.com*
Al Fardan Exchange > *p.129* 04 351 3535, *alfardanexchange.com*
Al Ghurair Exchange 04 295 5697, *alghurairexchange.com*
Al Rostamani International Exchange Co. 04 353 0500, *alrostamaniexchange.com*
First Gulf Exchange 04 351 5777, *fgb.ae*
UAE Exchange 04 341 8822, *uaeexchange.com*
Wall Street Exchange Centre 04 226 9871, *wallstreet.ae*

ENVIRONMENT

Flora & Fauna

While the variety of flora and fauna in the UAE is not as extensive as in some parts of the world, a number of plants and animals have managed to adapt to a life in arid conditions. In addition, the Dubai Municipality has an extensive greening programme in place and areas along the roads are unusually colourful for a desert environment, with grass, palm trees and flowers being constantly maintained by an army of workers and round-the-clock watering. The city also boasts a large number of well-kept parks (see p.256).

See Them For Yourself

Get out of the city and into some natural habitats. In the sand dunes, mountains and wadis you'll find hardy creatures that survive despite harsh conditions. Don't forget to take a copy of the *UAE Off-Road Explorer* with you – it's the ultimate guide to the best off-road routes in the region.

The region has about 3,500 native plants, which is perhaps surprising considering the high salinity of the soil and the harsh environment. The most famous is, of course, the date palm, which is also the most flourishing of the indigenous flora. In mountainous regions, flat-topped acacia trees and wild grasses create scenery not unlike that of an African savannah. The deserts are unexpectedly green in places, even during the dry summer months, but it takes an experienced botanist to get the most out of the area.

Indigenous fauna includes the Arabian leopard and the ibex, but sightings of them are extremely rare. Realistically, the only large animals you will see are camels and goats (often roaming dangerously close to roads). Other desert life includes the sand cat, sand fox and desert hare, plus gerbils, hedgehogs, snakes and geckos. Recent studies have shown that the number of species of birds is rising each year, due in part to concerted greening efforts. This is most apparent in the parks, especially in spring and autumn, as the country lies on the route for birds migrating between central Asia and east Africa. You can also see flamingos at the Ras Al Khor Wildlife Sanctuary (wildlife.ae) at the southern end of Dubai Creek.

Off the coast of the UAE, the seas contain a rich abundance of marine life, including tropical fish, jellyfish, coral, the dugong ('sea cow') and sharks. Eight species of whale and seven species of dolphin have been recorded in UAE waters. Various breeds of turtle are also indigenous to the region including the loggerhead, green and hawksbill turtles, all of which are under threat. Sightings are not uncommon by snorkellers and divers off both coasts, particularly at places such as Snoopy Island (p.310) and Khor Kalba (p.308) on the east coast.

Environmental Issues

The UAE has been ranked with one of the highest ecological footprints in the world per capita, according to the WWF's (World Wide Fund for Nature) Living Planet Report. The energy and water consumption levels are also some of the highest in the world, and its residents are among the highest waste producers.

There is high level support for ecological issues, and the late Sheikh Zayed was awarded the WWF's Gold Panda Award in 1997 for his environmental efforts. The government is actively involved in the UAE Ecological Footprint Initiative, making it the third country in the world, after Japan and Switzerland, to embark on such in-depth research to manage its footprint.

Dolphin Friendly?

There are two dolphinariums in the emirate: Dubai Dolphinarium at Creek Park and Dolphin Bay at Atlantis the Palm. Animal welfare organisations have been critical of how the star attractions were acquired, contending that no dolphinarium could ever be big enough to house these magnificent marine creatures, who can swim up to 100 km per day in the wild. There was also huge controversy about the addition of sand tiger sharks to Dubai Aquarium and a rescued whale shark, who was found a new home in Atlantis' Ambassador Lagoon aquarium, but then released into the wild in March 2010. To find out more about dolphins in captivity, log on to wdcs.org.

Conservationists assert that the massive construction for projects in the Arabian Gulf, such as the Palm Islands and Dubai Waterfront, will destroy coral reefs and fish stocks, as well as damage breeding grounds for endangered species such as the hawksbill turtle. The developers, however, argue that the sites will attract sea life, and point to the recent increase

RECYCLING CONTACTS

Clothes
Beit Al Khair (04 267 5555)
Dubai Centre for Special Needs (04 344 0966)
Dubai Flea Market (055 452 6030)
Holy Trinity Thrift Centre (04 337 8192)
UAE Red Crescent (800 733)

Books
House of Prose, Jumeirah Plaza (04 344 9021)
Dubai Garden Centre (04 340 0006)

E-books
Feedbooks has over 3,000,000 titles (feedbooks.com)
ManyBook.net has over 29,000 titles for free (manybooks.net)
Project Gutenberg has over 40,000 free books (gutenberg.org)

Furniture
Dubai Municipality (800 900)

Computers
Dubai Municipality computer recycling (800 900)

Wood/Wooden Doors
Bee'ah's Construction & Demolition Waste Recycling Facility (06 572 9000, beeah-uae.com)

Batteries
Emirates Environmental Group (04 344 8622, eeg-uae.org)

Food
Dubai Municipality (800 900)

Paper, Cartons
Union Paper Mills (04 266 6300)

Plastic, Cans, Glass
Al Tajir Glass (04 880 1222)
Eco Plastic Industries (04 880 1167)
Lucky Recycling Ltd (04 883 5250)

General Recycling
Enviroserv recycles electronics such as televisions (04 885 2434, info@enviroserve.ae)
Take My Junk
(050 179 4045, info@takemyjunkuae.com)

Going Green

If everyone in the world was to live like the average UAE resident, calculations suggest that 4.5 planets would be needed to provide the natural resources. Indisputably, the UAE is living beyond its ecological means and habits have to change.

Responsibility

Perhaps as a result of living in a nation inhabited mainly by expatriates, the average UAE resident feels little responsibility towards the country's environment. Expats from countries where 'green' initiatives, such as household recycling, are commonplace may be surprised by the lack of awareness and facilities for similar schemes in the UAE. Government efforts, such as the ban on plastic carrier bags, are steps in the right direction but are slow to take effect. Meanwhile, there is a pressing need for all residents to start making a personal contribution to reduce the impact of their presence.

Recycling

On the recycling front, UAE residents are becoming more proactive. The Emirates Environmental Group (p.336) has reported a large increase in its schools, corporate and community recycling drives which collect paper, plastic, glass, aluminium and toner cartridges. Mobile phones, broken computers and all kinds of electronic equipment can be recycled through Enviroserve (enviroserve.ae) or at your nearest Plug-ins store (800 758 4467).

A few of Dubai's residential areas now have an official recycling collection service for glass, paper, cans and plastic bottles (800 732 9253, zenath.com). If your area doesn't have a recycling scheme, it can involve rather a lot of administrative wrangling with the developer or community management company, but it's worth bringing the issue to the attention of your residents' committee to build support and put pressure on the developers.

In the meantime, there are now a lot of recycling bins dotted around Dubai. The municipality has installed recycling bins for paper, glass and plastic at petrol stations and bus stops, while you'll find recycling bins for everything from plastic bottles to shoes and clothing outside the UAE's bigger supermarkets. In addition, large cages for collecting recyclable materials have been installed on Al Wasl Road near Safa Park, at Mirdif Recycling Centre and on the service road near to the Shangri-La on Sheikh Zayed Road. Keep your eyes peeled – your nearest bins won't be far away.

Small Efforts For Big Changes

The first step towards a greener way of life in Dubai is simply to consider the three Rs – Reduce, Reuse and Recycle. Look for a positive and practical change that you can make into a routine, like switching off the lights when you leave a room, and make it a habit. Once you've done that, don't rest on your laurels – find the next change that you can make, and the next. You'll soon find that looking for ways to use the three Rs becomes habit in itself, influencing your buying decisions, your product consumption and usage levels.

Consider the three Rs – Reduce, Reuse and Recycle. Look for a positive and practical change that you can make into a routine and make it a habit. Once you've done that, don't rest on your laurels – find the next change you can make, and the next.

Getting Started

It's easy to start making positive environmental changes in your own home which contribute to a greener Dubai. Here are a few suggestions to get you on your way:

- It is estimated that 35% of Dubai's waste is organic matter – kitchen and garden waste. Cut down on wasted produce in your own household by planning your meals for the week ahead before you make the trip to the supermarket. Write a shopping list and only buy items which are on the list so that you know you'll be able to use them up before they go bad.
- The average resident of the UAE consumes more than double the amount of energy of citizens in countries such as France and the UK, and more even than America, traditionally the worst ecological offender. Simple actions such as turning your air conditioning up by a few degrees or replacing traditional light bulbs with energy efficient ones can have a big impact on your energy usage. Find energy saving inspiration and work out your carbon and money savings at heroesoftheuae.ae.
- Opt for water coolers rather than buying bottled water – a five-gallon bottle contains nearly 19 litres, meaning you will only use a fraction of the number of plastic bottles over the course of a year – and most water companies recycle or reuse water cooler bottles as well.
- Do you really need that litre of milk right now, or can you pick one up on your way to somewhere else later? Think twice before jumping in the car for small errands, and try to combine trips to cut car usage and emissions.
- Cover your pool in the summer. An uncovered pool loses up to 3,785 litres of water per year through evaporation. Unplug your phone charger. Between 65% and 95% of the energy used by mobile phone chargers is wasted by leaving them plugged in when not in use.
- Create your own desert oasis and choose native plants for your back yard to cut down on the volumes needed for daily watering.
- Make the most of Dubai's arid climate and dry your laundry in the open air rather than using the tumble dryer.
- All non-biodegradable plastic bags are now banned across the UAE, so invest in reusable carriers or trendy jute bags for your weekly shop.
- If you've got some time on your hands, why not get involved with a volunteer environmental programme? See p.122 for more details.
- Dubai Municipality's 'Bulky Waste Collection Service' (800 900) will pick up old home appliances and dispose of them in a safe and environmentally friendly manner. If your old appliances still work, extend their useful life by selling them at the flea market (p.420) or online at dubizzle.com.
- Public transport continues to improve as more stations open on the Dubai Metro (p.54) and bus services (p.53) are increased. Ditch the car and hop on board.

in fish and marine life witnessed around the crescent on the Palm Jumeirah. One strange by-product of this development is that due to the crescent being six kilometres out to sea, certain species of shark that wouldn't normally come so close to the land have been spotted around the beaches.

Similarly, developments like Dubailand are potentially impacting the desert landscape and its wildlife. Of the animals that can survive in this naturally harsh environment, those that disappear from the area due to construction work will be very difficult to reintroduce. It remains a contentious issue though as, arguably, the greening of new residential areas has resulted in an increase in vegetation and a rise in bird and insect life in these areas.

Environmental Initiatives & Organisations

On the positive side, the UAE government and the local municipalities have started making efforts towards reducing waste and consumption and raising environmental awareness. Masdar City in Abu Dhabi is being hailed as a groundbreaking green project and will be one of the world's most sustainable places to live, powered by renewable energy sources (masdarcity.ae).

There are various green building codes in place and, in 2009, the Dubai Department of Tourism and Commerce Marketing (DTCM) announced an initiative to reduce carbon emissions in the hospitality industry.

The Change Initiative (thechangeinitiative.com) is a new flagship store in Al Barsha for environmentally-friendly services and products. The first company of its type in the region, it specialises in products including sustainable cleaning products, solar panels, household appliances and building solutions.

The government effort is being accelerated by various environmental organisations who aim to protect the environment, as well as to educate the population about environmental issues. The Environment Agency Abu Dhabi (ead.ae) assists the Abu Dhabi government in the conservation and management of the emirate's natural environment, resources, wildlife and biological diversity.

Sir Bani Yas Island, which is part of the Abu Dhabi emirate, is home to an internationally acclaimed breeding programme for endangered wildlife. Created as a private wildlife sanctuary by the late Sheikh Zayed, it is now an exclusive eco-resort (02 801 5400, anantara.com).

Emirates Wildlife Society is a national environmental NGO that operates in association with the WWF (panda.org). In addition, The Breeding Centre for Endangered Arabian Wildlife (06 531 1212) at Sharjah Desert Park has a successful breeding programme for wildlife under threat, particularly the Arabian leopard. The breeding centre is off-limits to visitors but the Arabian Wildlife Centre (06 531 1999), also at the Desert Park, is open to the public. See also Environmental Groups (p.335).

Water Usage & Desalination

Demand for water from the UAE's growing population means that natural water sources are being depleted faster than their rate of replenishment. As the water table decreases (it has dropped by an average of one metre a year for the past 30 years), saltwater moves inland to fill the gap. This contaminates fresh water, especially near the coast where the increasing salinity of the ground affects the fertility of the soil, hampering farming. It has even affected places as far inland as the Hajar Mountains, where inland freshwater wells have started to dry up in areas close to Masafi, home of the country's most famous brand of bottled water.

The UAE currently has one of the highest water consumption per capita in the world; UAE residents use an average of 550 litres per person per day compared to 85 litres in Jordan, which has a similar climate. To meet this demand, water desalination complexes have been built around the country (the biggest in the world operates in Jebel Ali), but while solving one issue, desalination creates new problems of its own. As well as the large quantities of highly saline water which are released back into the sea to the detriment of marine life, water desalination plants require vast amounts of energy to operate and are thus major contributors to the UAE's sky-high energy demands.

BUSINESS & COMMERCE

Overview

The UAE is considered the second richest Arab country, after Qatar, on a per capita basis. The country has just under 10% of the world's proven oil reserves (most of it within Abu Dhabi emirate) and the fourth largest natural gas reserves.

Prior to the crash of 2009, the UAE enjoyed the benefits of a thriving economy growing at a rate of

Capital Business District

Sowwah Square (almaryahisland.ae) is the central business district in Abu Dhabi, with the iconic new headquarters of the Abu Dhabi Securities Exchange as its centrepiece. Located on Al Maryah Island (formerly Sowwah Island), this financial hub is billed as the emirate's answer to London's Canary Wharf; its four office towers are home to tenants including top-end British law firms Clifford Chance and Norton Rose Group, and financial firms JP Morgan, Gulf Capital and Dunia Finance. A retail centre and hotels are due to open from 2013.

over 7% a year. After a temporary blip in that year, the economy reverted back to positive territory by registering 4.9% growth in 2011 (World Bank).

Successful economic diversification means that the UAE's wealth is not solely reliant on oil revenue; services alone already account for more than half of the GDP. In Dubai, the most economically diverse of the Emirates, oil revenues accounted for around half of Dubai's GDP 20 years ago, but today the oil sector contributes less than 2%.

Across the country, trade, finance, manufacturing, tourism, construction, real estate and communications are playing an increasingly important part in the national economy. Other sectors such as publishing, recruitment, advertising and IT, while not as developed in terms of size, have been steadily growing in Dubai and Abu Dhabi, aided in part by the various free zones.

However, don't be fooled by the high national income into thinking that the average expat coming to work in Dubai will automatically be on a huge salary. The wealth isn't spread evenly and even before the financial crisis, the salaries for most types of jobs, with the exception of highly skilled professionals, were dropping. This downward trend is attributed in part to the willingness of workers to accept a position at a very low wage. While the UAE GDP per capita income stands at around Dhs.170,000 (Forbes), this figure includes all sections of the community; the average labourer, of which there are many, can expect to earn as little as Dhs.600 ($165) per month.

While the unemployment level of the National population in the UAE is lower than that of many other Arab states, there are still a significant number of Emirates out of work (over 30,000, according to some estimates). This is partly due to a preference for public sector work and partly because of qualifications, and salary expectations, not matching the skills required in the private sector. However, the Dubai government is working to reduce unemployment in the local sector with a Nationalisation or 'Emiratisation' programme. The eventual goal is to rely less on an expat workforce, which will be achieved by improving vocational training and by making it compulsory for certain types of companies, such as banks, to hire a set percentage of Emirates.

Trade

A long trading tradition, which earned Dubai its reputation as 'the city of merchants' in the Middle East, continues to be an important consideration for foreign companies looking at opportunities in the region today. It is reflected not just in an open and liberal regulatory environment, but also in the local business community's familiarity with international commercial practices and the city's cosmopolitan lifestyle.

Strategically located between Europe and the Far East, Dubai attracts multinational and private

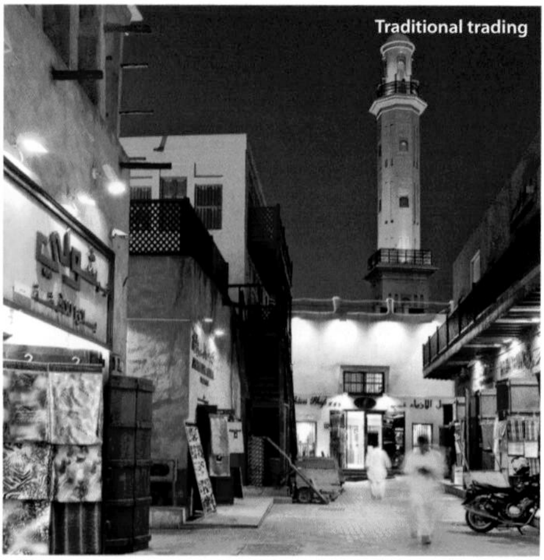
Traditional trading

companies wishing to tap into the lucrative Middle Eastern, Indian and African markets (with a combined population of over two billion). The UAE's main export partners are Saudi Arabia, Iran, Japan, India, Singapore, South Korea and Oman. The main import partners are Japan, USA, UK, Italy, Germany and South Korea.

The UAE's annual non-oil external trade hit Dhs.499 billion in the first half of 2012, of which Dubai accounts for 76%.

Tourism

The UAE is well ahead of many other cities in the Middle East in terms of travel and tourism. Boosting tourism plays a central part in the government's economic diversification plans and is a major driving force behind the array of record-breaking tourism, infrastructure and hospitality developments announced over the past few years.

The development of these high-end tourist amenities and visitor attractions, in conjunction with an aggressive overseas marketing campaign, means that Dubai's popularity as a holiday destination continues to increase. It is striving to reach its target of attracting 15 million visitors a year by 2015 and, despite tough economic conditions, the number of tourists coming to Dubai is still on the rise.

In 2011, there was a 1% increase in the number of hotels in Dubai, a 7% increase in the number of hotel rooms and apartments, and average hotel room occupancy jumped to 72%. The number of hotel guests staying in Dubai increased by around 11% to more than nine million.

Annual passenger traffic through Dubai International Airport – now ranked the world's fourth busiest in terms of international traffic – reached 51 million in 2011, an 8% increase from 2010. Passenger numbers are projected to reach 98 million by 2020.

Dubai World Central – Al Maktoum International Airport opened in 2010, in the south of Dubai, near to the Jebel Ali industrial area. At present, the airport only handles cargo; it's due to open for passenger services in 2013, and it will eventually become the world's largest airport, with a capacity of 160 million passengers and 12 million tonnes of cargo per year.

Abu Dhabi's sights are set on 3.3 million tourists by 2015 and 7.9 million tourists by 2030, and over the past few years it has followed Dubai's lead, announcing multi-billion dollar tourism developments. These include Yas Island, the venue for the Abu Dhabi F1 Grand Prix, Ferrari World and Yas Waterworld, and Saadiyat Island, soon to be home to a Louvre Gallery, a Guggenheim Museum and other cultural attractions.

In Dubai, work on some key tourism developments is still going ahead and, despite the slowdown since 2009, major projects such as Dubai Metro (p.54), the Meydan Racecourse, and the world's tallest construction, Burj Khalifa, have been completed. Work continues on some of Dubai's most ambitious ventures, including Palm Jebel Ali, the second of the three Palm Islands; Meydan, the urban community surrounding the new horse racing track; the vast Dubai Sports City; and the residential district of Al Furjan (see a list of the main developments on p.32).

Economic Growth

The pace of economic growth in Dubai over the last 20 years has been incredible. Trade alone has grown at more than 9% per annum over the past 10 years and the population has doubled since 1990.

Really Tax Free?

Do taxes exist in the UAE? Yes and no. You don't pay income or sales tax, except when you purchase alcohol from a licensed liquor store – when you'll be hit with a steep 30% tax. The main tax that you will come across is the municipality tax of 5% on rent and 10% on food, beverages and rooms in hotels. The rest are hidden taxes in the form of 'fees', such as your car registration renewal, visa/permit fees and Salik (road toll).

Over the last decade, legislation and government institutions have been honed to reduce bureaucracy and create a constructive business environment. Free zones, such as Internet City, Media City and Healthcare City, offer financial incentives to encourage international business; they have flourished and multiplied (see Free Zones, p.118) and multi-billion dollar mega project proposals such as the three Palm Island projects, Dubai Sports City and Burj Khalifa, were the result of the government's active promotion of investment in Dubai.

When the financial crisis hit in late 2008, the UAE, along with the rest of the world, seemed caught unawares. Within a few short months, the country was reeling, with Dubai feeling the full brunt of the crisis, while Abu Dhabi's oil revenues shielded it from the worst of the effects. Daily reports of mass redundancies, cancelled projects, company closures and absconding business owners sent shock waves through the economy, and the property market all but collapsed to around 50% of its peak value.

The worst, it seems, has now passed. According to the International Monetary Fund (IMF), after a small shrinkage in 2009, the UAE's economy grew 3.3% in 2011 and continued to grow by 3.8% in 2012. Inflation, which was spiralling out of control in the years running up to the global crash, reaching a bloated 12.3% in 2008, fell to 1.6% in 2009 and recorded an all-time low of below 1% in 2010, before normalising at around 2.5% in 2011. The outlook is positive: the IMF has projected steady economic growth through to 2016.

Bolstering feelings of confidence in economic recovery, a 2012 report by employment website Bayt.com revealed that more than half of employees believe that salaries in the UAE are increasing. Plus, in both Dubai and Abu Dhabi, construction work is continuing on many key projects.

On a less positive note for renters, after a significant drop in prices from 2009-2011, the property market is slowly on the up with rises of up to 5% on villa and apartment rentals. Increases in well established and popular communities such as Palm Jumeirah, Downtown Dubai and Arabian Ranches are even higher in some cases.(See Renting A Home, p.70).

With its vast oil reserves to buffer the impact, it's likely that the UAE's economy is resilient enough to recover in the long run. Popular opinion maintains that the country's unbridled ambition needed a healthy dose of realism and that the economy will ultimately be all the stronger for it.

Although Dubai was the most affected of the seven emirates by the global credit crunch, it remains part of a successful federal economy and, despite the financial downturn, the UAE is still one of the world's richest countries on a per capita basis. With its sizeable government-led projects and ongoing expansion plans, Dubai is well-placed to continue growing as a global hub and tourist destination.

CULTURE & LIFESTYLE

Culture

The UAE manages what some Arab cities fail to achieve: a healthy balance between western influences and eastern traditions. Its culture is still very much rooted in the Islamic customs that deeply penetrate the Arabian Peninsula and beyond. However, the country's effort to become modern and cosmopolitan is proof of an open-minded and liberal outlook.

Islam is more than just a religion; it is a way of life that governs even mundane everyday events, from what to wear to what to eat and drink. Therefore, the culture and heritage of the UAE is closely linked to its religion. However, the UAE is tolerant and welcoming; foreigners are free to practise their own religion, alcohol is served in hotels and the dress code is liberal. Women play an integral role in active society and are able to drive and walk around without restriction.

Cross Culture

The Sheikh Mohammed Centre for Cultural Understanding (04 353 6666, cultures.ae) was established to give visitors a clearer appreciation of the Emirati way of life. It organises tours of Jumeirah Mosque (p.250) where you can learn about Islam, and a Cultural Breakfast where you can find out about local food and customs.

The rapid economic development over the last 30 years has changed life in the Emirates beyond recognition. However, the country's rulers are committed to safeguarding their heritage. They are therefore keen to promote cultural and sporting events that are representative of their traditions, such as falconry, camel racing and traditional dhow sailing. Arabic culture in poetry, dancing, songs and traditional art and craftsmanship is encouraged.

Courtesy and hospitality are the most highly prized virtues, and visitors are likely to experience the genuine warmth and friendliness of the Emirati people. Luckily, the negative view of Islam that has affected many Muslims living abroad has not had an impact on Dubai, where you'll find people of various nationalities and religions working and living side by side without conflict. In Islam, the family unit is very important and elders are respected for their experience and wisdom. It's common for several generations to live together in the same house. Polygamy is practised in the UAE, with Islam allowing a man to have up to four wives at one time, providing he has the financial and physical means to treat each of them equally. However, a Muslim man taking more than one wife is more the exception than the norm, and most Muslim families resemble the traditional family unit: mum, dad and kids.

Weddings are important cultural occasions; the men and women celebrate separately with feasting and music. They are usually very large affairs; however, the government has placed a ceiling of Dhs.50,000 on dowries, and overly lavish weddings can result in a prison sentence or Dhs.500,000 fine. The government-sponsored Marriage Fund, based in Abu Dhabi, assists Emirates with marriage, from counselling and financial assistance (long term loans up to Dhs.70,000 for a UAE National man marrying a UAE National woman) to organising group weddings to keep costs down. With so many UAE Nationals studying abroad, and so many expats in Dubai, inter-cultural marriages are increasingly common. The Marriage Fund strongly encourages Nationals to marry fellow Nationals (in an effort to preserve the culture and reduce the number of UAE spinsters), although it is easier for a National man to marry a non-National woman than it is for a National woman to marry a non-National man.

When you first arrive, many aspects of the local culture may seem strange to you. Take time to observe and understand before you pass judgement; you'll soon realise that the many different nationalities living here make it a sometimes-frustrating but ultimately fascinating city.

Language

Arabic is the official language of the UAE, although English, Hindi, Malayalam and Urdu are commonly spoken. Arabic is also the official business language, but English is so widely used that you could conduct business here for years without learning a single word of Arabic. Most road signs, shop signs and restaurant menus are in both languages. The further out of town you go, the more you will find just Arabic, both spoken and on street and shop signs.

Arabic Family Names

Arabic names have a formal structure that traditionally indicates the person's family and tribe. Names are usually taken from an important person in the Quran or someone from the tribe. This is followed by the word bin (son of) for a boy or bint (daughter of) for a girl, and then the name of the child's father. The last name indicates the person's tribe or family. For prominent families, this has Al, the Arabic word for 'the', immediately before it. For instance, the president of the UAE is His Highness Sheikh Khalifa bin Zayed Al Nahyan. When women get married, they do not change their name.

Arabic isn't the easiest language to pick up, or to pronounce. But if you can throw in a couple of words here and there, you're more likely to receive a warmer welcome or at least a smile – even if your pronunciation is terrible. See the box on p.20 for a list of useful Arabic phrases, and p.175 for Arabic language courses.

Religion

Islam is the official religion of the UAE, and is widely practised. The Islamic holy day is Friday. The basis of Islam is the belief that there is only one God and that Prophet Muhammad is his messenger. The faith shares a common ancestry with Christianity and many of the

Arabian heritage

prophets before Muhammad can be found in Christian as well as Muslim writings. There are five pillars of Islam which all Muslims must follow: the Profession of Faith, Prayer, Charity, Fasting and Pilgrimage. Every Muslim is expected, at least once in his or her lifetime, to make the pilgrimage (Hajj) to the holy city of Mecca (also spelt Makkah) in Saudi Arabia.

Additionally, a Muslim is required to pray (facing Mecca) five times a day. The times vary according to the position of the sun. Most people pray at a mosque, although it's not unusual to see people kneeling by the side of the road if they are not near a place of worship. It is considered impolite to stare at people praying or to walk over prayer mats. The modern-day call to prayer, transmitted through loudspeakers on the minarets of each mosque, ensures that everyone knows it's time to pray.

While the predominant religion is Islam, the UAE is tolerant of other faiths, and the ruling family has, on occasion, donated plots of land for the building of churches. Christian churches of various denominations have been built in clusters on Oud Metha Road and in Jebel Ali, and there is a Hindu temple complex in Bur Dubai (see Places of Worship, p.47).

National Dress

On the whole, Emiratis wear traditional dress in public. For men this is the dishdasha or khandura: a white

BASIC ARABIC

General

Yes	*na'am*
No	*la*
Please	*min fadlak (m)* / *min fadliki (f)*
Thank you	*shukran*
Please (in offering)	*tafaddal (m)* / *tafaddali (f)*
Praise be to God	*al-hamdu l-illah*
God willing	*in shaa'a l-laah*

Greetings

Greeting (peace be upon you)	*as-salaamu alaykom*
Greeting (in reply)	*wa alaykom is salaam*
Good morning	*sabah il-khayr*
Good morning (in reply)	*sabah in-nuwr*
Good evening	*masa il-khayr*
Good evening (in reply)	*masa in-nuwr*
Hello	*marhaba*
Hello (in reply)	*marhabtayn*
How are you?	*kayf haalak (m) / kayf haalik (f)*
Fine, thank you	*zayn, shukran (m)* / *zayna, shukran (f)*
Welcome	*ahlan wa sahlan*
Welcome (in reply)	*ahlan fiyk (m) / ahlan fiyki (f)*
Goodbye	*ma is-salaama*

Introductions

My name is...	*ismiy…*
What is your name?	*shuw ismak (m) / shuw ismik (f)*
Where are you from?	*min wayn inta (m) /* *min wayn inti (f)*
I am from…	*anaa min...*
America	*ameriki*
Britain	*braitani*
Europe	*oropi*
India	*al hindi*

Questions

How many / much?	*kam?*
Where?	*wayn?*
When?	*mataa?*
Which?	*ayy?*
How?	*kayf?*
What?	*shuw?*
Why?	*laysh?*
Who?	*miyn?*
To/for	*ila*
In/at	*fee*
From	*min*
And	*wa*
Also	*kamaan*
There isn't	*maa fee*

Getting Around

Is this the road to...	*hadaa al tariyq ila...*
Stop	*kuf*
Right	*yamiyn*
Left	*yassar*
Straight ahead	*siydaa*
North	*shamaal*
South	*januwb*
East	*sharq*
West	*garb*
Turning	*mafraq*
First	*awwal*
Second	*thaaniy*
Road	*tariyq*
Street	*shaaria*
Roundabout	*duwwaar*
Signals	*ishaara*
Close to	*qarib min*
Petrol station	*mahattat betrol*
Sea/beach	*il bahar*
Mountain/s	*jabal/jibaal*
Desert	*al sahraa*
Airport	*mataar*
Hotel	*funduq*
Restaurant	*mata'am*
Slow down	*schway schway*

Accidents & Emergencies

Police	*al shurtaa*
Permit/licence	*rukhsaa*
Accident	*haadith*
Papers	*waraq*
Insurance	*ta'miyn*
Sorry	*aasif (m) /* *aasifa (f)*

Numbers

Zero	*sifr*
One	*waahad*
Two	*ithnayn*
Three	*thalatha*
Four	*arba'a*
Five	*khamsa*
Six	*sitta*
Seven	*saba'a*
Eight	*thamaanya*
Nine	*tiss'a*
Ten	*ashara*
Hundred	*miya*
Thousand	*alf*

full length shirt dress, which is worn with a white or red checked headdress, known as a gutra or sifrah. This is secured with a black cord (agal). Sheikhs and important businessmen may also wear a thin black or brown robe (known as a bisht), over their dishdasha at important events, which is equivalent to the dinner jacket in western culture.

In public, women wear the black abaya – a long, loose black robe that covers their normal clothes – plus a headscarf called a sheyla. The abaya is often of very sheer, flowing fabric and may be open at the front. Some women also wear a thin black veil hiding their face and/or gloves, and older women sometimes still wear a leather mask, known as a burkha, which covers the nose, brow and cheekbones. Underneath the abaya, women traditionally wear a long tunic over loose, flowing trousers (sirwall), which are often heavily embroidered and fitted at the wrists and ankles. However, these are used more by the older generation and modern women will often wear the latest fashions from international labels under their abayas.

Food & Drink

You can eat your way around the world in Dubai – it is home to every cuisine imaginable, from European and American to Indian and Asian. Alongside a glut of fine-dining options, you can find cheaper fare at the many street cafes, independent restaurants and fast-food chains.

In terms of food shopping, supermarkets stock a range of products from around the world to keep their multinational client base happy. Waitrose is a luxury British supermarket; Spinneys and Park n Shop stock British and South African products including Waitrose-branded items, Safestway sells more American items, and Choithrams has a mix of both. Carrefour, HyperPanda and Géant are huge and stock products from just about everywhere. Fruit and vegetables are imported from around the world, and so can be a bit more expensive than buying local produce. Look out for locally grown cucumbers, tomatoes, aubergines, courgettes, green peppers and potatoes, all of which are extremely cheap. For a more colourful food-buying experience, head to the fruit and vegetable market off Sheikh Mohammed bin Zayed Road where you can bulk buy various fruits and vegetables at bargain prices. The fish market in Deira offers a seemingly unlimited range of fresh fish and seafood at low prices, and the buzzing atmosphere is worth the trip in itself.

Arabic Cuisine

Culturally speaking, eating in the Middle East is traditionally a social affair. Whether eating at home with extended families, or out with large groups, the custom is for everybody to share a veritable feast of various dishes, served in communal bowls. Starters are generally enjoyed with flat Arabic bread, and main courses are often eaten with the fingers. The Arabic food available in Dubai is based predominantly on Lebanese cuisine. Common dishes are shawarmas (lamb or chicken carved from a spit and served in a pita bread with salad and tahina), falafel (mashed chickpeas and sesame seeds, rolled into balls and deep fried), hummus (a creamy dip made from chickpeas and olive oil), and tabbouleh (finely chopped parsley, mint and crushed wheat). Drinking Arabic coffee (kahwa) is an important social ritual in the Middle East. Local coffee is mild with a distinctive taste of cardamom and saffron. It is served black without sugar, but is accompanied by dates to sweeten the palate between sips.

Emirati Cuisine

There are also opportunities to sample Emirate food while in Dubai. The legacy of the UAE's trading past means that local cuisine uses a blend of ingredients imported from Asia and the Middle East. Dried limes are a common ingredient, reflecting a Persian influence; they impart a distinctively musty, tangy, sour flavour to soups and stews. Spices such as cinnamon, saffron and turmeric along with nuts (almonds or pistachios) and dried fruit add interesting flavours to Emirate dishes. Look out for Al Harees, a celebratory dish made from meat and wheat, slow-cooked in a clay pot or oven for hours, and Al Majboos, in which meat and rice are cooked in a stock made from local spices and dried limes. Fish is widely used in local cuisine, both freshly caught and preserved. Al Madrooba is a dish which uses local salted fish, prepared in a thick, buttery sauce. Use the Cuisine Finder on p.466 to find the pick of Arabic and Emirate restaurants.

Pork

Pork is taboo in Islam. Muslims should not eat, prepare or serve pork. In order for a restaurant to put pork on the menu, it should have a separate fridge, preparation equipment and cooking area. Supermarkets are also required to sell pork in a separate area and Spinneys, Park n Shop, Waitrose and Choithrams all have a screened-off pork section. As pork is not locally produced you will find that it's more expensive than many other meats. In restaurants, where bacon appears on a menu, you will usually be served beef or veal bacon. All meat products for Muslim consumption have to be halal, which refers to the method of slaughter.

Alcohol

Alcohol is only served in licensed outlets associated with hotels (restaurants and bars), plus a few leisure clubs (such as golf clubs and sports clubs) and associations. Restaurants outside of hotels that are not part of a club or association are not permitted to serve alcohol. For more information on liquor licences, see p.40.

Nevertheless, permanent residents who are non-Muslims can get a liquor licence (p.40) which allows them to obtain alcohol for consumption at home.

Shisha

Smoking the traditional shisha (water pipe) is a popular pastime enjoyed throughout the Middle East. It is usually savoured in a local cafe while chatting with friends. Also known as hookah or hubbly bubbly, the proper name is nargile. Shisha pipes can be smoked with a variety of aromatic flavours, such as strawberry, grape or apple, and the experience is unlike normal cigarette or cigar smoking. The smoke is 'smoothed' by the water, creating a much more soothing effect (although it still causes smoking related health problems). QD's (p.561), Chandelier (p.500) and The Courtyard (p.503) are good spots to try shisha.

Dates

One of the very few crops that thrive naturally across the Middle East, date palms have been cultivated for around 5,000 years. It's said that in some countries the Bedouin way of life was sustained primarily by dates and camel milk up until as recently as the mid 20th century. High in energy, fibre, potassium, vitamins, magnesium and iron, with negligible quantities of fat, cholesterol and salt, dates are a cheap and healthy snack. Just five dates per day provide enough nutrition for one recommended daily portion of fruit or vegetables.

Tipping

It is entirely up to the individual whether to tip for services and it is not a fixed expectation as you find in other countries. Some people in Dubai choose not to tip at all, but for those who feel that the service was worth recognising, the usual amount is 10% and tips are greatly appreciated. Some bars and restaurants automatically include a service charge on the bill, although it's not clear whether this ever sees the inside of your waiter's pockets, so many people add a little extra on top. Tips in restaurants and bars are often shared with other staff. See Going Out for more information (p.459).

For taxi drivers, it is regular practice to round up your fare as a tip, but this is not compulsory, so feel free to pay just the fare, especially if the driving standards were poor. For tipping when collecting your valet-parked car at hotels, around Dhs.5 is average. At petrol stations, especially when you get your windows cleaned, it's common practice to give a few dirhams as a tip. In beauty salons, spas and hairdressers, tipping is at your discretion but around 10% of the treatment price is an acceptable amount.

Date palm

LOCAL MEDIA

Newspapers & Magazines

The UAE has a number of daily English language broadsheets – the cream of the crop is definitely The National; arguably the region's first national newspaper offering quality journalism, intelligent editorial and meaty lifestyle pieces. Other titles include Gulf News, Khaleej Times and Gulf Today.

In most areas of Dubai, you can also pick up a free copy of 7 Days, a tabloid-size newspaper published five days a week that features local and international news, business and entertainment news, and a sports section. An international edition of British publication The Times is also printed and distributed in Dubai.

Censorship

International magazines are available in bookshops and supermarkets at greatly inflated prices. All international titles are examined by the censor to ensure that they don't offend the country's moral codes. The same is true of international films and TV shows, most of which make it over here, but must pass through the censor before hitting the big screen or appearing on TV.

There are plenty of local magazines, including a range of Middle Eastern editions of international titles that are produced here (examples include OK!, Grazia, Harpers Bazaar and Stuff). Keep an eye out for expat titles like Connector and Aquarius, as well as for listings magazines such as Time Out Dubai and What's On.

Radio

The UAE has a number of commercial radio stations broadcasting in a range of languages.

Cultural Dos & Don'ts

You'll find that, in general, people in the UAE are patient when it comes to cultural etiquette and are keen to explain their customs to you. However, there are a few cultural dos and don'ts that you should be aware of to avoid causing offence to others.

PDAs

Not a reference to a handheld gadget but to public displays of affection: these are a no-no in the UAE and anything more than an innocent peck on the cheek will, at best, earn you disapproving looks from passersby.

Appropriate Attire

While beachwear is fine on the beach or by the pool, you should dress a little more conservatively when out and about in public places. Although there's no official dress code, ensuring that your shoulders and knees are covered is a safe bet, and it's advisable to cover up in the more traditional emirates like Sharjah and Abu Dhabi, and in male-dominated areas, such as around the souks. That said, when out at bars and clubs in the evening, pretty much anything goes. Pashminas are useful for the journey home or in case the air conditioning is set to 'deep freeze'.

Photography

Dubai is full of snap-worthy sights and normal tourist photography is fine. Like anywhere in the Arab world, it is courteous to ask permission before photographing people, particularly women. In general, photographs of government and military buildings should not be taken.

Arabic Coffee

It's likely that you'll be served traditional Arabic coffee (kahwa) during formal business meetings. This is an important social ritual in the Middle East, so be polite and drink some when offered. Cups should be taken in the right hand and, if there is a waiter standing by replenishing your cup, the signal to say that you have had enough is to gently shake the cup from side to side.

Meeting People

Long handshakes and warm greetings are common when meeting people in the Middle East. It's normal to shake hands when you are introduced to someone, although if you are meeting members of the opposite sex, be aware that a handshake may not be welcome. Take your cue from the other person and don't offer your hand unless they first offer theirs. It's polite to send greetings to a person's family, but can be considered rude to enquire directly about someone's wife, sister or daughter. You may see men greeting each other with a nose kiss; this is a customary greeting between close friends and associates in the Gulf region but you should not attempt to greet someone in this way.

Out On The Town

Dubai has a good variety of nightlife and alcohol is widely available in hotel bars, pubs and clubs (see Going Out, p.550). Remember, however, that you're in a Muslim country and drunken or lewd behaviour is not only disrespectful but can lead to arrest and detention.

Business Etiquette

Business meetings in the region usually start with introductions and small talk before you get down to business. Business cards are exchanged; you should treat them with respect as an extension of the person who gave them. Punctuality to meetings is important and arriving late is considered to be bad mannered. Do not assume, however, that your meeting will start on time or that once started it will not be interrupted.

Home Values

When visiting an Emirate home it is customary to remove your shoes, however, it's best to take your cue from your host. Traditionally, men and women dine separately and meals are eaten while seated on floor cushions. When you sit, be careful not to point your feet at anyone or to show the soles of your feet. Mealtimes are long and leisurely and as a guest your plate will be heaped high. Try everything offered but if you're not sure you'll like something, take a small amount that you can finish. If you invite a Muslim to your home, you should not offer pork or alcohol, as this may cause offence.

The leading English stations operate 24 hours a day:
Dubai 92: Current music, competitions and popular DJs, 92.00 FM, dubai92.com
Dubai Eye: Quality talk radio, 103.8 FM, dubaieye1038.com
Virgin Radio: Hit music along the lines of Virgin Radio in other cities, 104.4FM, virginradiodubai.com
Channel 4: Contemporary music for a younger audience, 104.8FM, channel4FM.com
The Coast: Middle of the road and classic hits throughout the day, 103.2FM, 1032thecoast.com
Radio 1: Hit music broadcast across the country, 104.1 FM, gulfnews.com
Radio 2: Contemporary music broadcast throughout the UAE, 99.3FM, gulfnews.com

Television

Local TV is in a state of continuous improvement – gone are the days when all you could watch was early episodes of ER and Mad About You, with all kissing scenes cut out. Channels like Dubai One, MBC4 and Fox Movies, despite being free-to-air, are doing a good job of securing the rights to some fairly mainstream international shows and movies. Local programming is also improving, with new media ventures like Dubai Studio City and Abu Dhabi's twofour54 providing the infrastructure and know-how for locally-made shows. Satellite or cable TV is a staple in most expat homes – although it can be a bit hit and miss when judged by international standards. Some shows are aired just a few days later than they are in the US or UK, while others are delayed by a few months.

Always On The Box

OSN offers an HD Showbox service that lets you pause live television and record your favourite shows on a digital box. The box is loaded with over 1,000 free movies, as well more than 50 virtual boxsets of popular TV series – all available at the touch of a button. See osn.com for info.

Where you live in Dubai may affect what channels are available to you – if you live in one of the freehold residential communities, such as Emirates Living, Arabian Ranches, JBR or International City, you will have your satellite package installed and maintained by telecom provider du, which may offer a slightly different specification than if you deal directly with the satellite providers.

Internet & Directory Of Useful Websites

Although they sometimes come under criticism for being expensive and slow in comparison with what is available in other cities around the world, internet

USEFUL WEBSITES

Dubai Information	
7days.ae	Local newspaper
askexplorer.com	Essential info on living in Dubai from Explorer
dubaikidz.biz	Great site for kids' info
dubaitourism.ae	Department of Tourism & Commerce Marketing
dubizzle.com	Dubai's largest website for classifieds and community
expatwoman.com	General information on living in UAE from a woman's perspective
gulfnews.com	Local newspaper
khaleejtimes.com	Local newspaper
propertyfinder.ae	Rental and sales property portal with listings from local agents
sheikhmohammed.co.ae	Info on HH Sheikh Mohammed Bin Rashid Al Maktoum
Business/Industry	
dm.gov.ae	Dubai Municipality
dubaipolice.gov.ae	Dubai Police Headquarters
UAE Information	
ameinfo.com	Middle East business news
definitelydubai.com	UAE Government official tourism site
dha.gov.ae	Dubai Health Authority: emergency numbers and e-services
government.ae	UAE Government website with lots of practical info
gulfnews.com	National newspaper
sheikhzayed.com	A site dedicated to the life of the late UAE President
thenational.ae	National newspaper
uaeinteract.com	UAE National Media Council

services in Dubai are fairly modern and easy to install. Etisalat and du both offer a range of packages, from the practically prehistoric dial-up option to high-speed broadband solutions.

You will probably find that using the internet in Dubai has a few quirks that can take some getting used to, not least the much-despised proxy that blocks access to any sites deemed offensive. What is or isn't offensive is at the discretion of the Telecommunications Regulatory Authority (TRA), which supposedly applies the same rules to both Etisalat and du subscribers. While living in a Muslim community, you can certainly expect sites containing pornography or dubious religious content to be blocked; however, the TRA has been criticised for blocking access to VoIP sites such as Skype, meaning that you can't use the internet to make those cheap calls back home. If you do want to speak to friends and family abroad, you either have to use the actual telephone (and pay the comparatively expensive rates), or access VoIP sites such as Skype illegally with the help of a proxy blocker. It's a frustrating conundrum, made even more so by the lack of valid reason (apart from financial, of course) for blocking such sites in the first place. Being able to make a cheap internet call to wish your granny a happy birthday can hardly be classed as offending religious or moral values, but rules are rules. Other sites that you will not be able to access include online dating sites, and sites dealing with gambling, pornography or drugs.

UAE ANNUAL EVENTS

Throughout the year, the UAE hosts a wide variety of public events, some of which have been running for years. Whether you choose to chill out to international jazz performances, show off your prized pooch, raise money for charity or watch the world's best tennis stars, the country offers some unforgettable experiences.

Dhow Racing — All year round

Nr Marina Mall Abu Dhabi **02 681 5566**
adimsc.ae

This is a great traditional Arabic spectator sport. Fixed races are held throughout the year as well as on special occasions, such as National Day. Check the website for upcoming events.

Abu Dhabi HSBC Golf Championship — January

Abu Dhabi Golf Club Abu Dhabi
abudhabigolfchampionship.com

With $2.7 million in prize money and some of the biggest names in golf appearing annually, the Abu Dhabi Golf Championship is one of the UAE capital's biggest sporting events.

Standard Chartered Dubai Marathon — January

Nr Burj khalifa Downtown Dubai **04 433 5669**
dubaimarathon.org

This event attracts all types of runners, from those aiming to fundraise or work off that festive tummy in the 10km road race or 3km charity run, to dedicated pavement pounders and several of the biggest names in long distance running who tackle the full 42km.

Dubai Shopping Festival — January – February

Various locations **04 445 5642**
dubaievents.ae

Dubai Shopping Festival is a great time to be in the city, with bargains galore for shoppers as well as entertainers, prize draws and kids' shows held in participating malls.

Omega Dubai Desert Classic — January – February

Emirates Golf Club Emirates Living **04 380 2112**
dubaidesertclassic.com

This longstanding PGA European Tour fixture has been won in the past by golfing legends such as Ernie Els and Tiger Woods, and is a popular event among Dubai's golfing community.

Dubai Pet Show — February

The Sevens Dubailand
dubaipetshow.com

A popular family outing and the only show of its kind in the Middle East, with pedigree and crossbreed shows, a police dog unit demonstration and the uncanny 'Dog Most Like its Owner' competition.

Al Ain Aerobatic Show

Emirates Airline Dubai Jazz Festival — February

Festival Park Dubai Festival City **04 391 1196**
dubaijazzfest.com
The Jazz Festival, which celebrated its 10th year in 2012, attracts artists from all around the world to a stunning but chilled setting near Festival City. Courtney Pine, John Legend, James Blunt and David Gray have all performed in previous years.

Gourmet Abu Dhabi — February

Various locations, Abu Dhabi gourmetabudhabi.ae
This annual culinary and arts festival features free master classes from Michelin-starred chefs, industry insights from experts in the hospitality field, and gourmet dinners hosted by various Abu Dhabi hotels.

Wild Wadi's Swim Burj Al Arab — February

Burj Al Arab Umm Suqeim 3 **02 631 7645**
swim.msf-me.org
A charity swimming race on a 800m route around the island on which the spectacular Burj Al Arab hotel sits. Both competitive swimmers and fundraisers can take part. All proceeds go to Medecins Sans Frontieres. There is also a non-competitive social swim.

Dubai Duty Free Tennis Championships — February – March

The Aviation Club Al Garhoud **04 282 4122**
dubaidutyfreetennischampionships.com
Firmly established on the ATP and WTP circuit, the $2 million tournament attracts the world's top men's and women's seeds. Tickets for the semis and finals sell out in advance, but you can often buy tickets to the opening matches a few days before and at very reasonable prices.

Dubai Polo Gold Cup — February – March

Dubai Polo & Equestrian Club Dubai Studio City **04 343 7887**
dubaipologoldcup.com
Some of the world's best polo teams and players compete for the Silver Cup and Gold Cup in this prestigious and international week-long tournament.

Abu Dhabi Desert Challenge — March

Empty Quarter Abu Dhabi **02 296 1122**
abudhabidesertchallenge.ae
This high profile motorsport event attracts some of the world's top rally drivers and bike riders to race across Abu Dhabi emirate's challenging desert routes.

Abu Dhabi International Triathlon — March

The Corniche Abu Dhabi **02 668 8840**
abudhabitriathlon.com
Launched in 2010, this is one of the world's richest triathlons with a prize purse of $250,000 that draws some of the best pros from around the world who compete alongside all levels of amateur age groupers. The course takes in Abu Dhabi's most famous landmarks, including Yas Island.

Art Dubai — March

Madinat Jumeirah Al Sufouh 1 **04 384 2000**
artdubai.ae
An international art exhibition that sees visits from dozens of international galleries. Running alongside it is the Global Art Forum lecture and discussion board programme, plus art prizes including a people's choice award and the $1 million Abraaj Capital Art Prize.

Dubai International Boat Show — March

Dubai International Marine Club Dubai Marina **04 308 6430**
boatshowdubai.com
You don't need to have big bucks to enjoy the Boat Show. The largest marine industry exhibition in the Middle East showcases yachts and boats from both local and international builders, together with the latest innovations in marine equipment and accessories.

Dubai World Cup — March

Meydan Racecourse Nad Al Sheba **04 327 0077**
dubaiworldcup.com
The world's richest horse race takes place at the state-of-the-art Meydan race course. The huge prize fund (last year's was over $27 million), a buzzing, vibrant atmosphere, and the star-studded entertainment line-up ensure that the Dubai World Cup is one of the year's big social occasions.

Emirates Airline Festival Of Literature — March

InterContinental Dubai Festival City Dubai Festival City **04 353 4002**
emirateslitfest.com
This event draws a host of celebrated literary greats to take part in lectures, debates and panels. Past speakers have included Alexander McCall Smith, Carol Ann Duffy, Michael Palin and Margaret Atwood. Join the festival reading group to swot up on the latest releases by speakers.

Abu Dhabi International Book Fair — April

Abu Dhabi National Exhibition Centre (ADNEC) Abu Dhabi **02 657 6180**
adbookfair.com
A joint venture between Frankfurt Book Fair and Abu Dhabi Authority for Culture and Heritage, this is the Middle East's fastest-growing book fair. You can view over half a million titles, plus there are programmes for book industry professionals, publishers and kids, as well as an Illustrator's Corner and workshop.

Out & About

Bars, pubs, clubs and restaurants around town host a spectrum of annual events. For New Year's Eve and Christmas celebrations, Jumeirah Beach Hotel (p.240), Atlantis The Palm (p.236), Madinat Jumeirah (p.242) and the establishments in Downtown put on a festive show. Oktoberfest at the Grand Hyatt (p.238) is an authentic lederhosen-clad replica of the Munich original, Sir Bob Geldof's yearly St Patrick's Day performance at Irish Village (p.558) is a good excuse to raise a jar, and Chi at The Lodge's legendary Halloween fancy dress party (p.554) is enough to frighten the fiercest of fiends. Visit askexplorer.com to find out what's coming up next.

Dubai Festival City Dragon Boat Festival — April

Dubai Festival City
dubaidragonboat.com
Open to social, school and corporate groups, this is a fun, competitive and sociable team building event.

Red Bull Air Race — April

The Corniche Abu Dhabi
redbullairrace.com
Abu Dhabi is usually the starting fixture of the Red Bull Air Race World Series. The series took a break in 2011, but it is expected to return as normal in 2014.

Terry Fox Run — April

Atlantis The Palm Palm Jumeirah
dubaiterryfoxrun.org
Each year, thousands of individuals run, jog, walk, cycle and rollerblade their way around an 8.5km course to raise funds for cancer research programmes at approved institutions around the world. The run will be held at a new location for 2013, on the Palm Jumeirah; another Terry Fox event is held in Ras Al Khaimah in March.

WOMAD Abu Dhabi — April

Abu Dhabi
womadabudhabi.ae
The Abu Dhabi arm of this world music festival has become hugely popular since its inception. Held over three days on Abu Dhabi Corniche and at Al Jahili Fort in Al Ain, it is free to enter and attracts thousands of spectators to enjoy music and dance acts, plus art installations, workshops and food stalls.

International Property Show — April – May

Dubai International Convention & Exhibition Centre Trade Centre 2 **04 392 3232**
internationalpropertyshow.ae
Featuring everything to do with buying international property, this show is particularly popular among expats who are looking to invest overseas.

Summer in Abu Dhabi — May – September

Abu Dhabi **800 555**
summerinabudhabi.ae
A family carnival held in the air-conditioned comfort of ADNEC. The exhibition halls are home to a host of games, sports and educational experiences, as well as live daily character shows.

Dubai Summer Surprises — June – July

Various locations **600 54 55 55**
dubaievents.ae
Held in shopping malls around the city, with fun-packed, family-orientated activities and big shopping

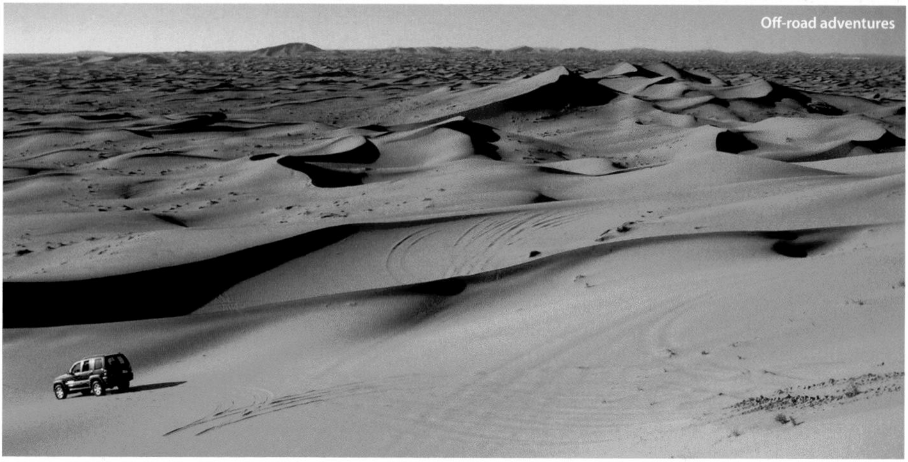
Off-road adventures

discounts, this is a popular event with Dubai residents and visitors looking to escape the heat during the summer months.

Gala Celebrations

There's always an excuse to get dressed up, with a number of annual gala events held in the UAE. Most are open to the general public and are usually attended by a round-up of international celebrities. The CNCF gala dinner, in aid of the Christina Noble Children's Foundation, kicks off the Dubai Rugby Sevens (urbanevents.ae); the Chequered Flag Ball is a key event of the Abu Dhabi F1 weekend (chequeredflagball.com); while the Oil Barons' Ball is the calendar highlight for the oil and gas sector (theoilbaronsball.com). St George's Day balls are held in both Abu Dhabi and Dubai (rssgauh.com, dsgs.org); St Andrew's Day is marked by the Scottish St Andrew's Society (adscots.com) and the annual Kiwi Ball brings New Zealand expatriates and their friends together.

Abu Dhabi Film Festival — October

Abu Dhabi **02 401 1900**
abudhabifilmfestival.ae
Having grown rapidly since its inception in 2007, ADFF brings more films, more awards, and more stars to the capital each year, giving a huge boost to the country's developing film industry.

GITEX Technology Week — October

Dubai International Convention & Exhibition Centre Trade Centre 2 gitex.com
This five-day event is renowned for Gitex Shopper, where the public can snap up some great deals on technology and gadgets.

Gulf Bike Week — October

Al Badia Golf Club By Intercontinental Dubai Festival City Dubai Festival City **04 435 6101**
gulfbikeweek.com
Over 50,000 visitors attended last year's event, enjoying stunt shows, motorbike displays, test rides and rock concerts, with previous acts including Nickelback, N.E.R.D and Megadeth.

Camel Racing — October – April

Al Marmoom Camel Racetrack, Dubai – Al Ain Rd 04 832 6526
This popular local sport is serious business, with racing camels changing hands for as much as Dhs.10 million. Races run on different days throughout October to March at 07:00 and 14.00. Admission is free. The race track is located past The Sevens on the Dubai-Al Ain E66 Road.

Abu Dhabi Classics — October – May

Emirates Palace Abu Dhabi
abudhabiclassics.com
This annual series of classical music concerts features international artists and orchestras and takes place at venues across the capital and at Al Jahili Fort in Al Ain. The festival runs from October to May and gets bigger, lasts longer, and becomes more adventurous every year.

Abu Dhabi Art — November

UAE Pavilion and Manarat Al Saadiyat, Saadiyat Island Abu Dhabi **02 657 5800**
abudhabiartfair.ae
With 2013 representing its fifth year, this international art fair is gaining international attention, with a full programme of exhibitions, lectures, debates and workshops. There is also an art zone and interactive workshops for children.

Dubai Airshow — November

Dubai World Central Jebel Ali **04 603 3300**
dubaiairshow.aero
A five-day biennial event that has been attracting visitors for the past 22 years. It began as the Arab Air Show in 1986 and over two decades later is a huge draw for all those interested in the aerospace sector, with more than 130 planes on display.

DP World Tour Championship — November

Jumeirah Golf Estates Sheikh Mohammed Bin Zayed Rd dpworldtourchampionship.com
The world's best golfers congregate in Dubai for the final fixture of the PGA European Golf Tour and a shot at a share of the $8 million prize fund. One of Dubai's great spectator events.

Dubai World Game Expo — November

Dubai International Convention & Exhibition Centre Trade Centre 2 **04 362 4717**
gameexpo.ae
A calendar highlight for all gaming fans desperate to try out the latest software and hardware in the market; the expo also plays host to the Dubai World Game Championship.

Formula 1 Etihad Airways Abu Dhabi Grand Prix — November

Yas Marina Circuit Abu Dhabi **02 659 9999**
yasmarinacircuit.com
Although no longer the season's closing race, Abu Dhabi always puts on a great show. As well as the on-track action, ticket holders can enjoy live music; in previous years, this has been served up by the likes of Kanye West, Prince and Kings Of Leon, while free concerts, exhibitions and competitions are held for the public across the capital.

Sharjah International Book Fair — November
Expo Centre Sharjah (ECS) Sharjah **06 512 3344**
sharjahbookfair.com
One of the oldest and largest book fairs in the Arab World showcases thousands of titles in Arabic, English and other languages, displayed by private collectors, publishers, governments and universities.

Whatever Floats Your Boat — November
Festival Marina Dubai Festival City **04 701 1059**
This charity race invites schools and businesses to build boats from recycled materials to raise awareness of recycling and take part in a fun day on the water. For more info email axelle.bouquet@ichdfc.ae.

Powerboat Racing — November – February
Dubai International Marine Club Dubai Marina **04 399 5777**
dimc.ae
The UAE is very well established on the world championship powerboat racing circuit – in Abu Dhabi with Formula One (Inshore), in Dubai and Fujairah with Class One (Offshore), and in Sharjah (F1H2O). Check the DIMC website for dates of Dubai races.

Horse Racing — November – March
Meydan Racecourse Nad Al Sheba
dubairacingclub.com
All horseracing in Dubai has moved to the impressive Meydan City. Racing takes place at night under floodlights (see the website for race dates) with the winning horses, jockeys and trainers taking home prizes or cash. The season ends with the spectacular Dubai World Cup in March.

Al Ain Aerobatic Show — November – December
Al Ain International Airport Al Ain **800 555**
alainaerobaticshow.com
A five-day annual air show with flying daredevils from around the world performing aerobatic displays.

Emirates Airline Dubai Rugby Sevens — November – December
The Sevens Dubailand **04 321 0008**
dubairugby7s.com
Over 130,000 spectators descend on The Sevens Stadium to watch top international teams compete for the coveted 7s trophy, as Gulf teams contest the local competitions. With friendly rivalry between competing nations and prizes for the best fancy dress, the party atmosphere carries on until the small hours.

Dubai International Film Festival — December
Various locations, Dubai
dubaifilmfest.com
A hotly anticipated annual event showcasing Hollywood and international arthouse films, as well as work from the Middle East region. Premieres are generally held at Madinat Jumeirah, while screenings take place in cinemas across the city. The red-carpet opening gala event has attracted Hollywood stars such as Cate Blanchett and Kevin Spacey. It's a great opportunity to catch non-mainstream films and do a bit of celeb spotting.

Mother, Baby & Child Show — December
Dubai International Convention & Exhibition Centre Trade Centre 2
motherbabyandchild.com
Mums and kids will love this show, featuring exhibits by child-friendly companies and lots of entertainment for the little ones, plus endless samples and giveaways.

Mubadala World Tennis Championship — December
Zayed Sports City Abu Dhabi **02 493 8888**
mubadalawtc.com
An end of year international tennis tournament featuring the world's top seeded players fighting it out for a $250,000 prize. Previous players have included Andy Murray, Novak Djokovic and Rafael Nadal.

Sharmila Dance Gala — December
Community Theatre & Arts Centre (DUCTAC) Al Barsha 1 **04 341 4777**
sharmiladance.com
More than 160 renowned dancers of all ages come together for a dancing extravaganza, with performances ranging from Latino and soul to Indian and hip hop. Last year saw the Stuttgart Ballet and locally-based dance companies Sharmila Dance and El Firulete BNF Dance Company take to the stage.

Sharjah Water Festival — December
Al Majaz Park Sharjah **800 80000**
swf.ae
Sharjah hosts an annual family extravaganza at Al Majaz Park, as part of the Powerboat Formula One Grand Prix. The festival kicks off with a parade on National Day (2 December) and, for the subsequent 10 days, kids can enjoy a variety of attractions. Entry is Dhs.5 per person, Dhs.20 per family.

Exhibitions
With its increasing emphasis on MICE (meetings, incentives, conferences, exhibitions) tourism, Dubai has two large, state-of-the-art exhibition spaces. These are the Airport Expo and the exhibition halls at the Dubai World Trade Centre. For details of exhibitions in Dubai, contact the Department of Tourism & Commerce Marketing (dubaitourism.ae) or see Exhibitionist Tendencies, p.120.

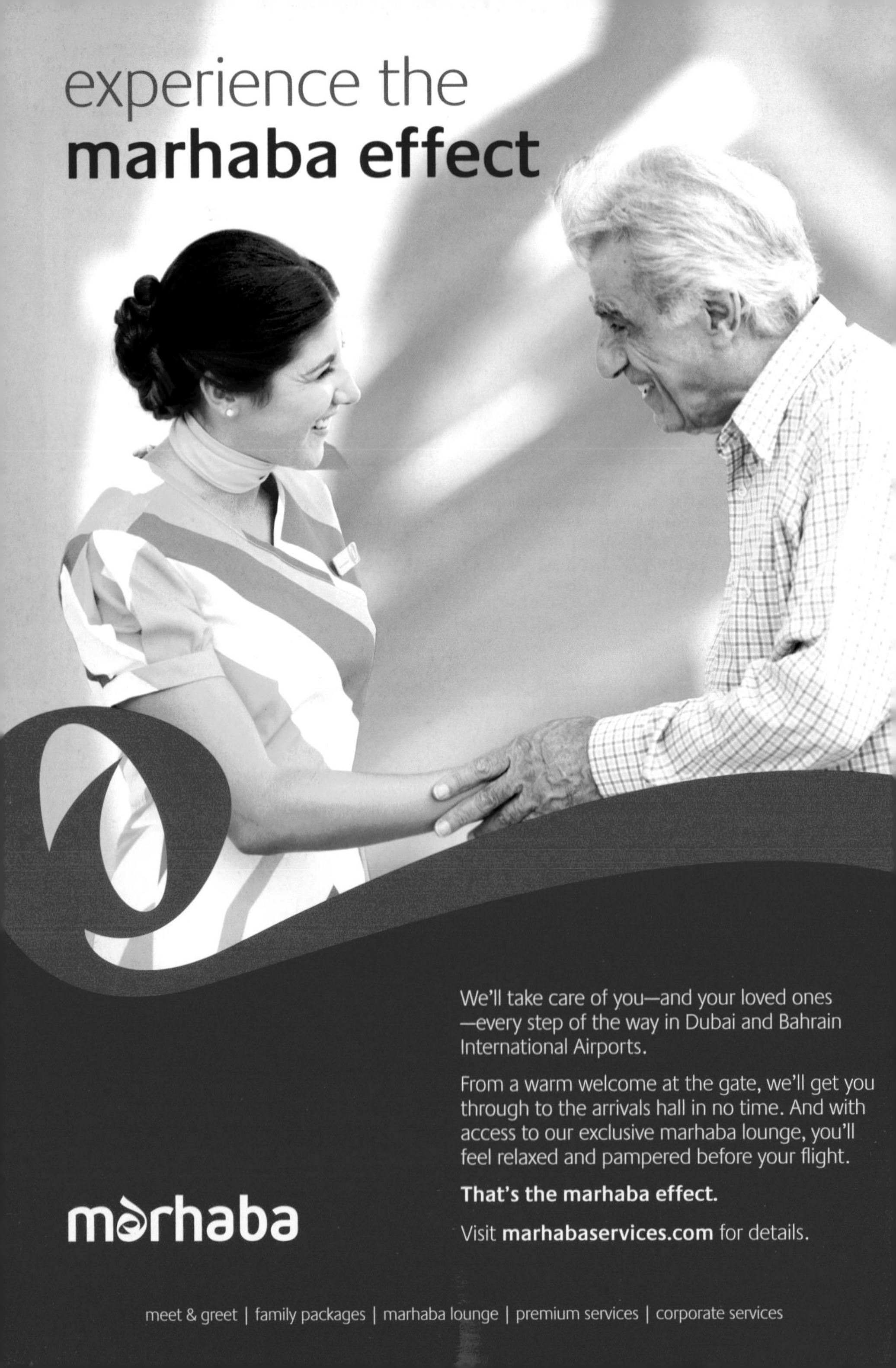
experience the
marhaba effect
We'll take care of you—and your loved ones —every step of the way in Dubai and Bahrain International Airports.
From a warm welcome at the gate, we'll get you through to the arrivals hall in no time. And with access to our exclusive marhaba lounge, you'll feel relaxed and pampered before your flight.
That's the marhaba effect.
Visit marhabaservices.com for details.
marhaba
meet & greet | family packages | marhaba lounge | premium services | corporate services

Dubai: Becoming A Resident

CITY PROFILE

There are certain descriptions of Dubai that are frequently used: pearl of the Gulf, sleepy fishing village transformed into modern metropolis, tax-free expat haven, headquarters of luxury living, and so on.

The truth is that, behind these cliches, Dubai is for most people a wonderful place to live, with some excellent career opportunities, a readily available network of social contacts, some unique activities and, apart from a few sweaty months in summer, brilliant weather. Most expats will tell you that their standard of living is better here than it was back home, they can travel more, spend more time with family, enjoy outdoor living and make more friends.

Cost Of Living

Dubai has become a more affordable city to live in, according to the 2012 Worldwide Cost Of Living survey. The emirate is ranked number 94 in the index, published by the Economist Intelligence Unit (EIU) – a drop of 16 places from 2011.

This chapter is here to help you, whether you are making the decision to move or not, you've just arrived and don't know where to start, or you find yourself faced with an overwhelming amount of red tape. Just remember, procedures and laws do change regularly, often in quite major ways. While these changes are generally announced in newspapers, they are often implemented quickly so it's a good idea to be prepared for the unexpected.

Drinking In DXB

While alcohol is forbidden for Muslims, it is served in the many bars, clubs and restaurants throughout Dubai. You won't find a booze aisle in your local supermarket, although some people have made the mistake of stocking up on the alcohol-free beers that line the shelves. Two companies operate liquor stores, but you'll need a licence to buy alcohol (see p.40).

DUBAI'S ECONOMY & TRADE

Whereas 20 years ago oil revenues accounted for around half of Dubai's GDP, today the oil sector contributes around 2% or less. Knowing that oil will eventually run out, the government has invested heavily in other industries, and trade, manufacturing, transport, tourism, construction and real estate are now the main contributors to the economy. See p.8 for a full breakdown of Dubai's GDP.

Historically, Dubai has enjoyed a long tradition of trading, and continues to be an important location for foreign companies looking at opportunities in the region. Dubai's strategic location, liberal regulatory environment and cosmopolitan population are all factors that attract foreign business. Annual domestic imports exceed $17 billion and Dubai is the gateway to over $150 billion annually in trade.

During the recent global recession, Dubai's economy took some hard knocks; some say it was one of the hardest-hit economies in the world. While this may be true when looking at the real estate market (some property values plummeted by 50%), it can be argued that Dubai had a strong trade economy before the property market opened up, and this has continued to thrive. What's more, Dubai's diverse industry base means that it is not dependent on a single, potentially vulnerable, revenue stream, but has a wider, more solid foundation on which to build its future growth. Prior to the economic crash, the cost of living increased rapidly for residents and there were serious concerns about the rate of inflation. Factors such as rising rents meant that in 2007 inflation reached its highest rate for two decades, at 11.8%. The drop in rental prices and other cost of living indicators brought inflation down as low as 1.5% a couple of years ago.

Employment levels are good, and the unemployment rate declined by 50% in Dubai from 2009-2012; there are around 5,600 unemployed people living in the emirate. However, as expatriates in the Gulf have to be employed or studying in order to have a valid residency visa, and since the workforce is heavily expatriate-dominated, the unemployment rates are not a significant economic indicator.

In 2009, there were significant redundancies made in the private sector, resulting in many expat professionals returning to their home countries or taking up employment in regional markets that were less affected by the recession, such as Qatar and Abu Dhabi. Those days have passed and many companies are hiring again. Some have even found a shortage of adequately skilled candidates.

One of the main effects of the recession was the cancellation of major projects that had been announced during Dubai's period of rapid growth. Some of the projects still going ahead include:

Al Furjan: A luxurious residential and commercial site with freshwater streams, cycle paths and a golf course designed by Greg Norman. *nakheel.com*

Business Bay: Built around an extension to the creek, this self-contained city within a city is fast becoming the commercial and business capital for the region. *dubaipropertiesgroup.ae*

Creek Crossings: Three more bridges across the creek are planned, one near Shindagha Tunnel, one between the Shindagha Tunnel and Maktoum Bridge, and the 'Dubai Smile' to replace the Floating Bridge.

Dubai Sports City: DSC will be home to a mass of sporting venues and facilities, and is set to be a key part of Dubai's 2020 Olympic bid. *dubaisportscity.ae*
Dubai World Central: This will be a self-contained urban centre based around a new airport with six runways, expected to handle 160 million passengers a year by 2050. *dwc.ae*
Meydan: Aspiring to be a 'horseracing city' with a business park, residential areas, shopping arcades and a major racecourse, Meydan will be linked to the creek by canal, and have its own marina. *meydan.ae*
Palm Islands: Work continues on the three Palm Islands, with over 70% of the Palm Jumeirah now complete and reclamation work on the Palm Jebel Ali also complete. Each island will feature villas and apartments, luxury hotels and numerous leisure attractions. *thepalm.ae*

There are also signs that the economy is picking up with new projects in the pipeline including:
Jewel of the Creek: A Dhs.3 billion mixed-use development on the banks of Dubai Creek next to Al Maktoum Bridge, with hotels, apartments, a convention centre and marina.
The Point at Palm Jumeirah: A waterfront dining and entertainment complex at the tip of The Palm.
Dubai Sustainable City: An eco-friendly city with villas, resort and spa, educational zone, a green belt with 20,000 trees, a canal and solar farms to generate electricity and heat water.
Madinat Jumeirah: The emirate's largest resort is due to be expanded with a five-star hotel, villas, restaurants, shops and an open walking area, all due to open by 2015.

CONSIDERING DUBAI

Sunny days, great shopping, outdoor living and tax-free salaries sum up the Dubai dream. Of course there are red-tape hassles and everyday annoyances, but for many expats these are far outweighed by the positives.

The cost of living in Dubai has become much more affordable following the economic crash, prior to which rents were sky-high and prices for everything were increasing at an astronomical rate. Prices have stabilised to a more normal, affordable level and, despite a slight drop in salaries, some expats even find they have greater disposable income than before.

The job market has mainly recovered; however, before you jump on the first plane, make sure you test the waters by contacting potential employers, monitoring newspaper appointments pages and scouring international recruitment websites.

You should also consider how you will enter the city and stay here. To stay in Dubai long-term, you need a residency visa, and for this you need a 'sponsor'. Your sponsor is usually your company, or your spouse if

Dubai Marina

you are not working (see p.42). If you don't have work lined up, you can enter on a visit visa, but will only be allowed to stay for a limited time (p.36).

BEFORE YOU ARRIVE

If you're coming to Dubai to work, or even just to look for work, you should have any qualification certificates and important documents (such as your marriage certificate, and kids' birth certificates) attested in your home country. This can be quite a lengthy process, and involves solicitors and the UAE foreign embassy.

Property owners may consider selling up before the move, but don't be hasty. It may be wise to test

Stare Wars

As annoying and infuriating as it is to have someone blatantly stare at you, the good news is that these stares are not really sexual in nature – they are more the result of curiosity. The bad news is that there is little you can do to stop this strange little quirk of living in the region. Your best defence is to avoid wearing tight or revealing clothing, particularly in certain areas such as the Gold Souk.

the water and give yourself a year before you commit long-term – although, increasingly, people who came for a year or two are still in the country five or 10 years later.

You also need to get your financial affairs in order, such as telling banks and building societies, and the tax office – tax rules differ from country to country, so check whether you have to inform the tax office in your home country of any earnings you accrue while in Dubai. Speak to your pension company too – moving abroad could have implications for your contributions (see Work, p.127).

If you've got kids, you should start researching schools as soon as possible. There are fortunately a lot more schools in Dubai today than there were a few years ago, although it can still be tough to get a guaranteed place at the school of your choice. The earlier you get your child's name on the waiting list, the better.

When it comes to choosing an area of Dubai to live in, take your time to explore the different residential areas (see p.84 for a head start). It's a good idea to arrange temporary accommodation for when you first arrive (try to negotiate this with your employer), so that you can look for your perfect home. Speak to shipping companies about bringing your stuff over, and try to book as far in advance as possible.

If you're coming to Dubai on a 'look-see', do your homework before you arrive. Contact recruitment agencies in advance, sign up with online job sites, and visit agencies in your home country that specialise in overseas recruitment. Check also that your qualifications or industry experience are in demand here. See Work (p.115) for more information.

Customs

Before you fly into Dubai, be aware that several prescription medications are banned, especially anything containing codeine or temazepam. The UAE maintains a strict zero-tolerance policy on recreational drugs, and even microscopic amounts could land you in jail. Your bags will be scanned on arrival to ensure you have no offending magazines or DVDs. Each passenger is allowed 400 cigarettes, 50 cigars or two kilograms of tobacco. Non-Muslims are also allowed four litres of wine or four litres of spirits.

WHEN YOU ARRIVE

As you would expect during an international move to any new city, you're very likely to find a long 'to do' list waiting for you when you arrive in Dubai. You'll be doing a lot of driving around, form filling, and waiting in queues in government departments. Just keep your sense of humour handy and soon all the boring red tape will be a distant memory.

Arrive In Style

For a hassle-free arrival into Dubai you can book the Marhaba Meet & Greet Service (marhabaservices.com). You'll be met at arrivals before immigration, assisted through airport clearance and escorted with your baggage to the exit. A Gold package offers priority buggy car transfer, and the Family service is ideal for mothers travelling alone with children.

The first thing you'll probably need to sort out is visas – you may be lucky enough to have a company PRO who does this all for you; if not, see p.36. House-hunting will also be on your agenda – see p.68 for advice on finding your ideal home, and then getting electricity, water, phones and furniture. You'll probably need a car; while the bad news is that driving seems a little scary here at first, the good news is that cars and their upkeep are cheap. See p.60. As for paperwork, you'll need to get your driving licence, and your liquor licence if you're planning on buying alcohol. See p.40.

Tax Free Shopping

Take this opportunity before you exit the airport to do any last-minute shopping at Dubai Duty Free (dubaidutyfree.com), located in Arrivals and Departures at Dubai International Airport, where you can purchase limited quantities of duty free goods such as cigarettes, cigars, tobacco, wine, spirits and perfumes.

Once you've got the administrative stuff out of the way, it's time to put your feelers out and start meeting fellow expats – a task which some find challenging, but most find easier than expected (p.46).

At The Airport

The e-Gate service allows UAE and GCC nationals, as well as people with a valid residence permit, to leave and enter Dubai International Airport without a passport. Swipe your smart card through an electronic gate and through you go. Applications for a card are processed within minutes at Dubai International Airport, in the dnata buildings (one on Sheikh Zayed Road and one in Deira near Deira City Centre), or the DNRD office on Sheikh Khalifa Bin Zayed Road. You'll need your passport, containing the valid residence permit and you will be fingerprinted and photographed. The e-Gate card costs Dhs.200 and is valid for two years; however, you can now activate the e-Gate service on your Emirates ID and pay just Dhs.150 for two years. Payment can be made by cash

Emirates ID

After a stop-start couple of years, the Emirates ID (also known as Resident Identity Card) is now becoming a reality – and a necessity.

The UAE's Emirates Identity Authority (EIDA) launched the Emirates ID (Resident Identity Card) – a mandatory identification card scheme for all Nationals and residents – in 2005; the aim is to integrate information from labour cards and visas to make all government transactions easier.

It has become increasingly difficult to deal with government departments and to complete transactions without an Emirates ID, particularly since it was announced that all expats living in Dubai need to register for the card before renewing a residency visa. Those without a card will not be able to complete the medical tests required for visa renewal. Additionally, those who fail to sign up for Emirates ID face daily fines of Dhs.20, up to a total of Dhs.1,000. Consequently, the majority of Dubai's population has now signed up for their ID.

Each card contains the holder's address, photo, date of birth and fingerprints, and is now an official source of identification in the UAE. The card will eventually replace all other cards, such as health cards and labour cards, and can already be activated with the e-Gate service for travel through Dubai International Airport.

Expat residents pay a fee that is linked to the validity of their residence visa, paying Dhs.100 per year of validity remaining (so, for example, if your residence visa expires in two years, you will pay Dhs.200 for your ID).

To register for your card, take your passport with your residency visa, ID fee and a typing fee of Dhs.30 to an authorised typing centre, where your application will be filled in and translated into Arabic. Then take the completed form to a registration centre, with your fee receipt, passport and residency visa, where you'll be fingerprinted and have your photo taken. Once it has been processed, your Emirates ID will be delivered to you (for an additional fee of Dhs.20). A fast-track service at the Al Barsha centre allows applicants to obtain their Emirates ID within just 24 hours.

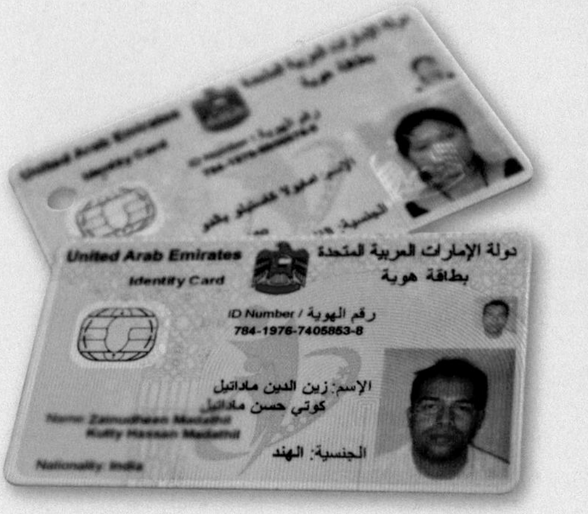

You can apply online at emiratesid.ae and pay by credit card for first-time registration, renewals and replacement ID cards. This not only speeds up the process, it saves the need to visit a typing centre. If applying for a new card, you'll then be able to reserve an appointment to visit an Emirates ID registration centre where your fingerprints and a photograph will be taken. Once it's time to renew your ID, you should be able to complete the entire process online.

A list of authorised typing and registration centres, plus up-to-date information, can be found at emiratesid.ae and dubai.ae.

or credit card. For further information, contact 04 316 6966 or see dubai.ae.

Better still, you can now check in and out through passport control without having to apply for an e-Gate card. All holders of modern passports with barcodes, including children above the age of seven, can use the new Smart e-Gate service, which has been rolled out across Dubai International Airport.

GETTING STARTED

Entry Visa

Visa requirements for entering Dubai vary greatly between different nationalities, and regulations should always be checked before travelling, since details can change with little or no warning. GCC nationals (Bahrain, Kuwait, Qatar, Oman and Saudi Arabia) do not need a visa to enter Dubai. Citizens from many other countries (including the UK, USA, Australia and many EU countries) get an automatic visa upon arrival at the airport (p.36). The entry visa is valid for 30 days, although you can renew for a further 30 days at a cost of Dhs.620.

Expats with residency in other GCC countries, who do not belong to one of the 32 visa-on-arrival nationalities but who do meet certain criteria (professions such as managers, doctors and engineers), can get a non-renewable 30 day visa on arrival – check with your airline before flying.

People of certain nationalities who are visiting the Sultanate of Oman may also enter Dubai on a free-of-charge entry permit. The same criteria and facilities apply to Dubai visitors entering Oman (although if you have Dubai residency you will pay a small charge).

All other nationalities can get a 30 day tourist visit visa sponsored by a local entity, such as a hotel or tour operator, before entry. The fee is Dhs.620 Dhs, for a long term visa of up to 90 days it is Dhs.1,120. Also, a deposit of Dhs.1,000 needs to be paid by a local sponsor, which can be reimbursed after the visit visa holder has left the country. It is valid for 60 days from the date of issue.

Visa On Arrival

Citizens of the following countries receive an automatic visit visa on arrival: Andorra, Australia, Austria, Belgium, Brunei, Denmark, Finland, France, Germany, Greece, Hong Kong, Iceland, Ireland, Italy, Japan, Liechtenstein, Luxembourg, Malaysia, Monaco, Netherlands, New Zealand, Norway, Portugal, San Marino, Singapore, South Korea, Spain, Sweden, Switzerland, United Kingdom, United States of America and Vatican City.

Canadian citizens used to be on the automatic visa list but, as from 2 January 2011, they are required to obtain a visa in advance. Citizens of eastern European countries, former Soviet Union countries, Cyprus, China and South Africa can get a 30 day, non-renewable tourist visa sponsored by a local entity, such as a hotel or tour operator, before entry into the UAE. The fee is Dhs.220, and there is a refundable deposit of Dhs.1,000 for each person being sponsored. See dnrd.ae for more details.

An entry service permit (sometimes referred to as a 14-day stay) is available to business travellers and tourists. The visa, which is non-renewable, is valid for 14 days from the date of issue and the duration of stay is 14 days from date of entry, exclusive of arrival and departure days. There is a fee of Dhs.120 plus Dhs.10 delivery charge. (This permit is not required for citizens of the countries listed above)

EMBASSY INSIGHT **Yacoob Abba Omar,** South African ambassador to the UAE

The main role of the embassy is to promote South Africa to our host country. Aside from consular services, we also deal with signing agreements, arranging for various delegations to visit SA, and meeting with industry and government representatives. Despite the current economic climate, the business ties between South Africa and the UAE have been growing from strength to strength, with bilateral trade between the two countries reaching Dhs.6.14 billion in 2008. I believe that we will be seeing more South African initiatives in the future, as South African businesses are resilient and innovative and have the reputation of adhering to high standards and quality.

We encourage South African citizens to register with the Embassy. This would come in handy especially during emergencies, but we also connect citizens with the South Africa Business Council so they can network with fellow South Africans.

Our flagship event is the Freedom Day celebration on 27 April, which is aimed at key contacts of the Embassy. We also support SABCo in hosting the South Africa Family Day, which the South African community attends in droves to celebrate Freedom Day. My advice to first timers is to begin by learning some of the culture and traditions of our host country. Use the opportunity of being here to visit many countries in the region.

For a full list of embassies in Dubai, see p.596.

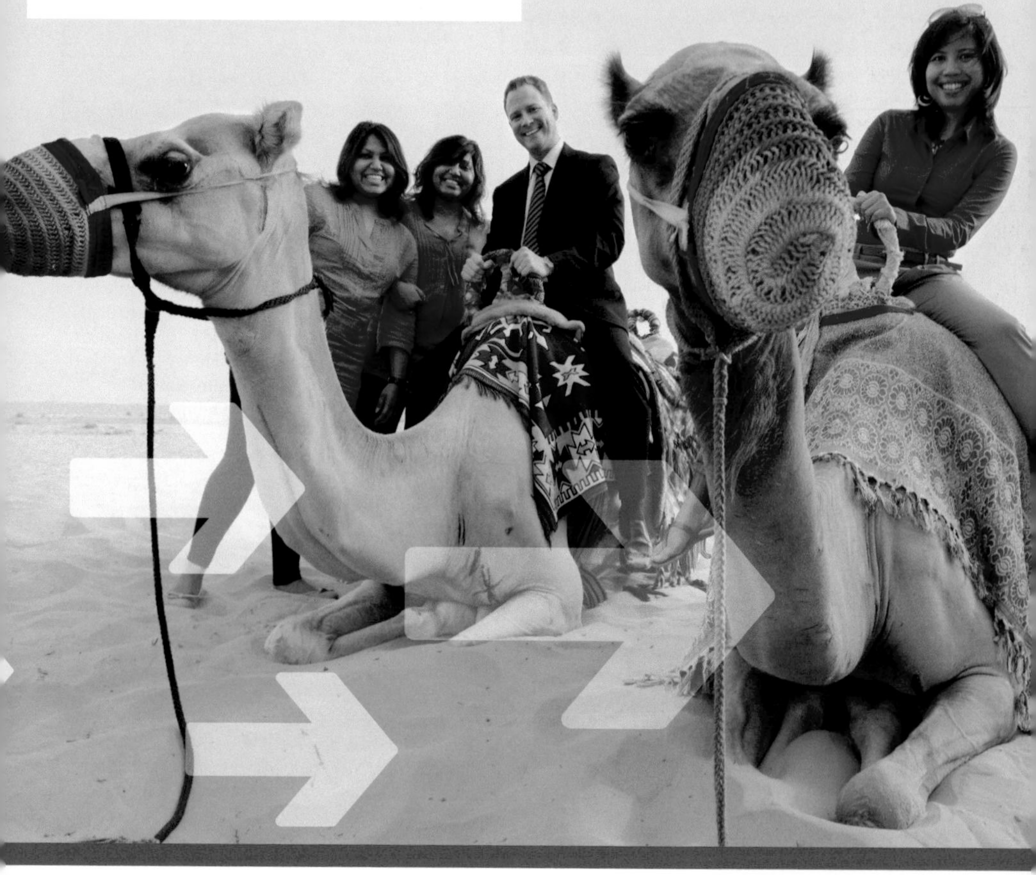

Bastakiya: traditional Dubai

A multiple-entry visit visa is available to business travellers who need to make regular visits to the UAE. Valid for visits of a maximum of 14 days each time, for six months from date of issue, it costs Dhs.2,100 and should be applied for after entering the UAE on a visit visa. For an additional Dhs.200, a multiple entry visa holder is eligible for the e-Gate service (see p.34). Cruise tourists and property investors can also apply for a multiple-entry visit visa, with varying conditions.

Companies may levy a maximum of Dhs.50 extra in processing charges for arranging visas. The dnata (Dubai National Airline Travel Agency) visa delivery service costs an extra Dhs.20. For an additional charge there are various companies who can arrange the necessary visa for you, and, here in Dubai, dnata offers a visa service for all in/outbound applications. Alternatively, for advice on any visa and naturalisation issues for any of the emirates, contact the government's toll free AMER service on 800 5111.

Fully Fledged Resident

After entering Dubai on an employment or residency visa, you have 60 days to complete all of the procedures involved in becoming a resident – although it's unlikely to take anywhere near that long. If you need to leave the country again before the process is completed, you should be able to do so as long as you have the entry visa that was stamped in your passport when you first entered. It's probably best though if you avoid booking any holidays in those first few weeks.

Sponsorship

Residence Visa

To live in Dubai, you need a residence visa. There are two types of visa, both requiring the individual to be sponsored: one is for those sponsored for employment, and the other for residence only (for example, if you are sponsored by a family member who is already sponsored by an employer). There was a property-owner visa for a while, which fell into the latter category, with the developer acting as sponsor for as long as you own the property, but without employment rights. This law ceased to exist in 2008, so buying a property no longer entitles you to a residency permit – although property owners are still able to apply for investor-based residency, and are entitled to an initial six-month multiple-entry visa (renewable for Dhs.2,000 provided the owner leaves and then re-enters the country; see dubai.ae for more details).

Older Children

For parents sponsoring children, difficulties arise when sons (not daughters) turn 18. Unless they are enrolled in full-time education in the UAE, they must transfer their visa to an employer, or the parents can pay a Dhs.5,000 security deposit (one-off payment) and apply for an annual visa. Daughters can stay on their father's sponsorship until they get married.

Recent laws changed the validity of residency visas for private sector workers from three years to two, in line with changes to the labour card. If you leave the UAE for a period of more than six months at any one time, your residency will lapse. This is particularly relevant to women going back home to give birth, or children studying abroad. If the residency is cancelled, the original sponsor can visit the Immigration Department and pay Dhs.100 for a temporary entry permit which will waive the cancellation and allow the person to re-enter Dubai. You'll need their passport copy, and will have to fax them a copy of the permit before they fly back.

Expat residents in Dubai are now required to show their Emirates ID for residence visa renewal.

Sponsoring A Maid

To sponsor a maid you must have a salary above Dhs.6,000 per month, and be able to provide the maid with housing and the usual benefits, including an airfare home at least once every two years. The process is very similar to sponsoring a family member (see p.42), and once again you will also need attested copies of your tenancy contract and a DEWA utilities bill. The main differences are the additional costs involved – you have to pay a 'maid tax' of around Dhs.5,080 per year, as well as a refundable deposit of Dhs.2,030. You may need to pay an additional fee for a compulsory Hepatitis B vaccination (Dhs.50), which is valid for 10 years. There will also be a small typing fee (see Domestic Help, p.107).

Liquor Licence 101

For many expats moving, or considering the move, to Dubai, the alcohol question is one of the first to come up. It seems to be a subject mired in rumours and misunderstandings, so let's clear a few things up.

Dubai has a relatively liberal attitude towards alcohol. You can't buy alcohol in supermarkets, but you can buy it from licensed liquor shops for home consumption if you have a liquor licence. Independent restaurants cannot serve alcohol, but hotels, sports clubs and areas with special dispensation (Festival City and Wafi, for example) are permitted to serve alcoholic drinks in their bars and restaurants. To drink in a bar or restaurant you need to be 21 years or older.

VISITORS...
...do not require a licence.

RESIDENTS...
...do not officially require a licence to buy alcohol in the UAE. This is why you won't be asked to show your licence at the likes of Barracuda Beach Resort in Umm Al Quwain (p.304) or Al Hamra Cellar in Ras Al Khaimah, or, indeed, at Duty Free as you pass through the airport. What you do require a licence for is transporting alcohol and for consuming it outside of licensed premises, such as at home. Despite regular urban myths, you'd have to be extremely unlucky to be stopped and searched while driving from the airport or a non-licensed bottle shop to your home although you should be aware that if you are discovered transporting alcohol (especially across Sharjah) you could wind up in quite a lot of trouble; equally, as long as you're not hosting or attending raucous house parties and generally staying out of trouble, you're unlikely to ever be called upon to justify that G&T or glass of wine you enjoy with dinner at the weekends.

THE LAW STATES...
...that UAE residents (i.e. anyone who has a visa) should be in possession of a liquor licence when drinking in licensed premises, such as bars, restaurants, clubs and sports clubs. In reality, it's unheard of for the police to enter a bar or sports event and start sifting through everyone present to check whether they have a liquor licence.

YOU NEED A LICENCE BECAUSE...
...there are two licensed liquor chains operating in Dubai, African + Eastern (africaneastern.com) and MMI (mmidubai.com), and you do need a licence to buy from these. They have branches throughout the city and, once you have your licence, you can buy alcohol from any branch. They can work out expensive thanks to a 30% tax but the range and service is excellent. And they're extremely convenient. Plus, it's always better to be safe than sorry.

Getting Your Licence

1. You must be 21 or older, in possession of a resident's visa and, of course, not Muslim. Head down to your local branch of African + Eastern or MMI where they'll give you the necessary forms and explain the procedure.
2. Fill out the form and have it stamped and signed by your employer and then return it with:

a. a copy of your passport and a copy of the resident's visa page

b. a copy of your residential rental or ownership contract (or a letter from your employer if you're in company accommodation)

c. copies of your official Ministry of Labour contract in both Arabic and English, or salary certificate if you work in a free zone

d. a passport photo (and a photo of your spouse along with their details and a photocopy of their visa if you want them to be able to use the licence)

e. a payment of Dhs.160, which the store typically gives you back in vouchers or credit.

3. If there is any Arabic part to fill out, they can usually do this at the off-licence. The store will then take your application to the police for processing on your behalf. This should take around 10 days. The store will contact you by phone or text message when your licence is ready and then you're all set.

Get The Red Card

There are many benefits to getting your liquor licence, and not just because it can keep you out of trouble. African + Eastern, for example, runs offers at bars and restaurants across town, or you can join up to the wine club. You'll be notified of any special events (like tastings with experts or launches of new products) and will also get regular updates on the latest offers.

THEN WHAT? When you receive your licence, you'll also receive your monthly allowance, which is based on your salary. This is usually more than enough for personal home use during the month.

However, you can't 'save up' your allowance from one month to the next; so, if you're planning a big dinner party or celebration, then you'd do well to stock up for a few months beforehand, grab a few bottles each time you or a visitor passes through the airport or, more practically, to make a trip over to Al Hamra or Barracuda.

Employer Sponsorship

If you have moved to Dubai to take up a job offer, your employer is obliged to sponsor you. Your company's PRO (Personnel Relations Officer) should handle all the paperwork, meaning you probably won't have to visit the Immigration Department yourself. They will take your passport, employment visa (with entry stamp), medical test results, attested education certificates, copies of your company's establishment immigration card and trade licence, and three passport photos. For a fee of Dhs.300 (plus typing fees), the Immigration Department will process everything and affix and stamp the residency permit in the passport. This takes up to 10 days, during which time you'll be without your passport. For an extra Dhs.100, they can do it on the same day. Your company must pay these fees for you. When arranging your residency, the company will apply directly for your labour card (see p.112). The Ministry of Labour website (mol.gov.ae) has a facility for companies to process applications and transactions online.

Labour Card

Once you have your residency permit, either through your employer or family sponsor, you need a labour card (although this may soon be phased out in favour of the Emirates ID; see p.35). If you are on a family residency and decide to work, your employer, not your visa sponsor (usually your spouse), will need to apply for a labour card. You'll need to give your employer the usual documents including a letter of no objection (NOC) from your sponsor, your passport with residency stamp, attested certificates, passport photos, and a photocopy of your sponsor's passport. The labour card must be renewed every two years. See Work, p.112.

To be accepted by the authorities here, your education certificates must be verified by a solicitor or public notary in your home country, then by your foreign office to verify the solicitor as bona fide, and finally by the UAE embassy. It's a good idea to have this done before you come to Dubai. There are private attestation companies in Dubai offering a verification service, but this is likely to take a minimum two weeks.

Family Sponsorship

If you are sponsored and resident in Dubai you should be able to sponsor your family members, allowing them to stay in the country as long as you are here. To sponsor your wife or children you will need a minimum monthly salary of Dhs.3,000 plus accommodation, or a minimum all-inclusive salary of Dhs.4,000, although there are rumours this amount may rise to as high as Dhs.10,000 – check dnrd.ae for the latest regulations. Only what is printed on your labour contract will be accepted as proof of your earnings, so make sure you're happy with this before starting the job. To apply for residency visas for your family, you'll need to take your passport, the passports of the family member(s), your labour contract, and copies of an attested tenancy contract and DEWA utilities bill in the sponsor's name to the Family Entry Permit counter at the Immigration Department. Your company PRO may help you with this process, but in most cases you will need to do it (and pay for it) on your own. After submitting all the documents, return after a couple of days to collect the visa. Once the visa is processed, all family members over the age of 18 must take a medical test.

You then return to the Immigration Department with all the essential documents as before, plus the medical test result and the attested birth certificate (if sponsoring a child) or attested marriage certificate (if sponsoring your spouse). For Dhs.300 (plus typing fee) the application will be processed and around five days later the passport – with the residency visa attached – will be ready for collection. (For an additional fee of Dhs.20 it can be couriered to you)

If the family member is already in Dubai on a visit visa you can still apply for residency as above. Once processed, the family member must exit the country and re-enter with the correct visa. If you have family sponsorship and then get a job, you don't need to change to employer sponsorship, but the company will need to apply for a labour card on your behalf.

PROs & NOCs

In Dubai, a PRO (Personnel Relations Officer) is the person in your company who liaises with various government departments and carries out admin procedures. The PRO will take care of all visa, residency, health card, and labour card applications. An NOC (No Objection Certificate) is essentially a letter stating that the person in question permits you to carry out a particular procedure. You'll find you need one of these in a variety of situations, whether it's from your employer allowing you to switch jobs, or your own NOC permitting a family member to work.

It is common to hear that women can't sponsor their husbands unless they are doctors, nurses or teachers. While this used to be the rule at one stage, today it is possible for working women to sponsor their husbands and children, provided they meet the minimum salary requirements. If you are in this situation, you should speak to the Immigration Department and present your case. The main disadvantage of a wife sponsoring her husband is that the spouse's visa must be renewed annually,

NEW TO DUBAI?
School admissions
Internet connections
who.?
how?
NATIONAL ID
Driving Licence
Bank Accounts
Navigating The City
House hunting
?
where?
Phone and TV packages
who.?
GET OFF TO AN EASY START BY APPLYING FOR YOUR BEVERAGE LICENCE WITH US!
Some things in life are sent to try us and make our life seem like hard work! We believe in making life EASY!
Whether you are applying for a new beverage licence or renewing your existing one, African + Eastern helps you get it done in 3 easy, hassle free steps! Visit any one of our stores conveniently located all over Dubai to pick up an application form, get expert advice and have all your questions answered. It's as EASY as that!
If you have any queries, please ask our staff in-store or call 800 CHEERS (243377)
Al Wasl Road* • Arabian Ranches* • Bur Dubai* • Deira • Dubai Marina Mall* • Dubai Marina Walk*
Green Community** • Jumeirah* • Karama • Le Méridien Dubai** • Mirdif • TECOM
*Stores also open on Fridays from 2:00pm - 9:00pm
**Green Community and Le Méridien Dubai stores open Saturday to Thursday from 2:00pm - 9:00pm
رخصة مشروبات كحولية
ALCOHOLIC DRINKS LICENCE
JOHN A. SMITH
1234567891010
EXP - 09/07/2
african+eastern

while if a husband sponsors his wife, the spouse's visa only needs to be renewed every two or three years (depending on whether he works in the private or public sector respectively).

There are constraints when Dubai residents want to sponsor their parents – a special committee meets to review each case on an individual basis, usually to consider the age and projected health requirements of the parents.

Medical Test

You need to pass a medical test in order to get your residence visa and labour card. To take your test, you will need the test form filled out in Arabic (there are typing offices near the government hospitals which can do this for you for around Dhs.20), two passport photos, a copy of your passport, and the test fee of Dhs.260 plus Dhs.20 for courier delivery, Dhs.470 for 24 hour service and Dhs.370 for a 48 hour service. Blood will be taken and tested for communicable diseases such as HIV. If your tests are positive you will be deported to your home country; if you are at all nervous about the possibility of testing positive it may be a good idea to get tested in your home country before you arrive in Dubai. You will also need to undergo a chest x-ray to test for TB, and female domestic workers are usually required to take a pregnancy test. All expat domestic workers, as well as those working at nurseries, salons and health clubs, are now required to complete a course of Hepatitis B vaccinations. After all your tests are finished, collect your receipt, which will tell you when to return to collect your results (usually three days later).

Health Card

Once you have passed your medical test, you are able to get a health card. If you are not covered by a company or private medical insurance, it is advisable to apply for a health card as it entitles residents to low cost medical treatment at public hospitals and clinics. The health card must be renewed each year, but you only need to take a new medical test when your visa is up for renewal. See Health, p.181, for how to get your card.

You may find the government testing centres chaotic, which can be a little bit scary if this is your first experience of Dubai's healthcare system. Rest assured that, despite appearances, medical hygiene standards are followed and test results are processed efficiently. A good tip is to go wearing a plain, pale-coloured t-shirt: this way you should not have to remove your clothes and wear a hospital gown (which may have been used by someone else before you) for your x-ray.

You can have your medical test done at a private clinic, but not all private clinics are authorised to perform government health tests, so your employer should inform you of your options and whether they will cover the extra cost.

Improved Service

The Department of Health & Medical Services is embracing the digital age; online booking is now available at government health clinics and health cards can be renewed using the Express HC service. Register at dha.gov.ae to use these services.

Driving Licence

If you are in Dubai on a visit visa and wish to drive a hire car, you will need your national licence and a valid international licence. Visitors from countries on the transfer list below are allowed to drive in the UAE with just their valid national driving licence.

Traffic Police

- **Traffic Police HQ:** Nr Galadari Roundabout, Dubai-Sharjah Rd (04 269 4444)
- **Bur Dubai Police Station:** Sheikh Zayed Rd, Junction 4 (04 398 1111)
- **Al Quoz Police Station:** Nr Dubai Police Academy, Umm Suqeim St (04 347 2222)

If you want to drive a private vehicle, you will need to get a temporary or permanent Dubai driving licence – you are not allowed to drive a privately owned Dubai car on just an international driving licence.

As soon as your residence visa comes through, then you will need to switch to a Dubai driving licence, which is valid for 10 years. If you are not a citizen of one of the licence transfer countries, then you will need to take a driving test, which is a fairly arduous process by all accounts. Obtaining a motorcycle licence follows the same procedure. For more information, see p.55.

Tests

To get your eye test certificate, go to an optician and tell them you need a driving licence eye test; most will do it there and then. It costs as little as Dhs.30, and you'll need to take along two passport photos.

Automatic Licence Transfer

Citizens with licences from the following countries are eligible for automatic driving licence transfers: Australia, Austria, Bahrain, Belgium, Canada*, Denmark, Finland, France, Germany, Greece*, Ireland, Italy, Japan*, Kuwait, Netherlands, New Zealand, Norway, Oman, Poland*, Portugal, Qatar, Romania, Saudi Arabia, South Africa, South Korea*, Spain, Sweden, Switzerland, Turkey*, United Kingdom, United States.

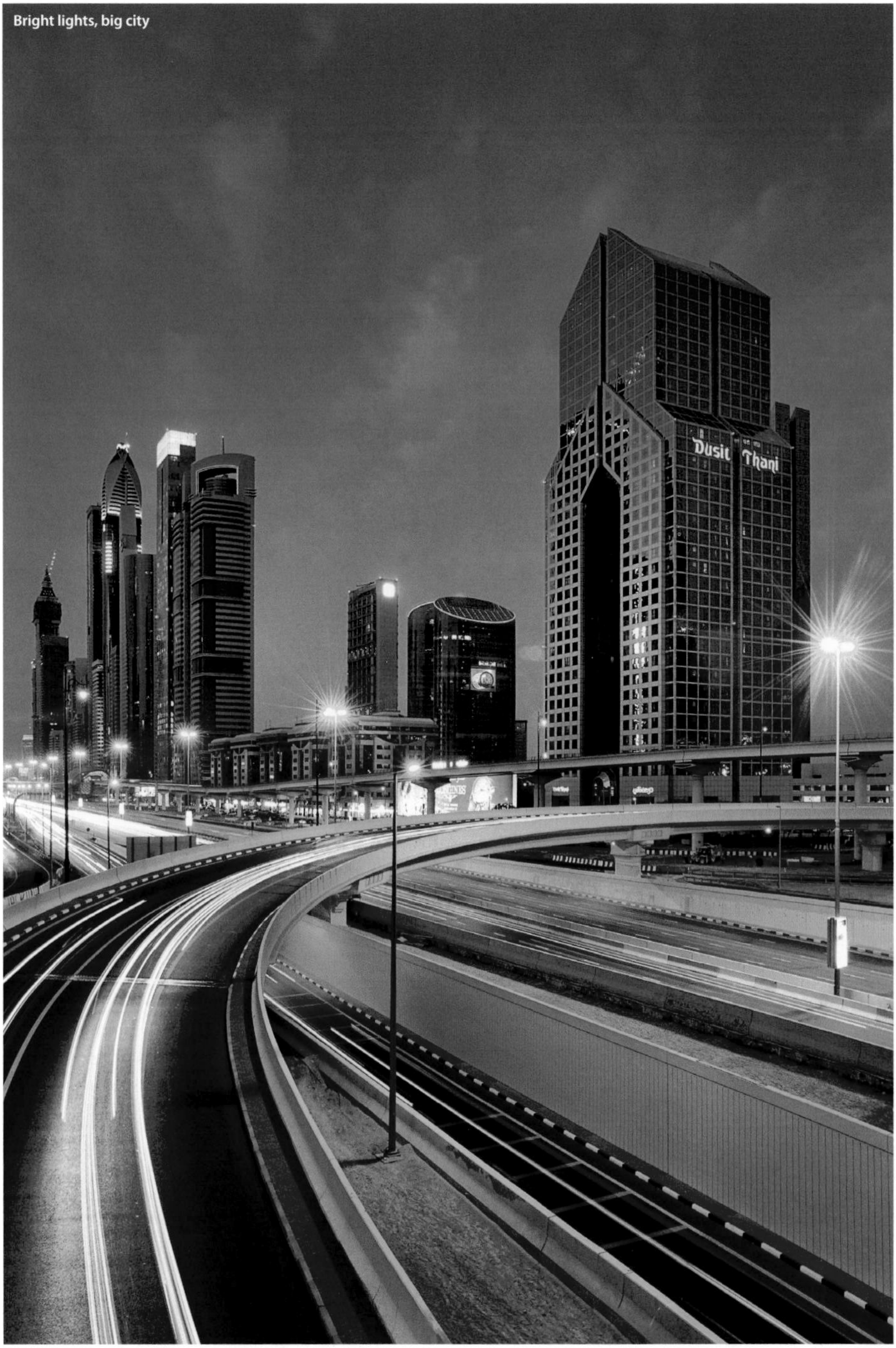

Bright lights, big city

*Citizens of these countries will require a letter of approval from their consulates and an Arabic translation of their driving licence (unless the original is in English).

MEETING NEW PEOPLE

Moving to a new country is a major upheaval in many ways, particularly if you're leaving a big network of friends and family behind. If you don't know anyone in your new home town, it's important to get out and about as soon as you can to meet people and make friends. Not only will these acquaintances be able to offer you loads of help in terms of cutting through red tape and getting word-of-mouth recommendations for a good school, doctor or hairdresser, some of them may also end up becoming life-long friends.

Dubai's transient nature means people tend to come and go more frequently than in other places, but it generally follows that expats here are more sociable, amenable and open to friendship as a consequence – and the relationships you do make could last long after you've moved on to new pastures.

National Groups

Meeting new people early on is one of the keys for dealing with culture shock and starting the settling-in process. Talking to people you meet at work and in social situations will help you discover the lie of the land a lot more quickly – you'll be able to get advice on where to live, how to get things done, and coping with the differences between your home country and the UAE.

To help you get started, there are numerous nationality-based and other social groups in Dubai, and these are handy for broadening your network of acquaintances, and ultimately your circle of friends:

American Women's Association Of Dubai: A group of volunteers offering information programmes, social functions and common interest groups to American women. *awadubai.org*

Anza UAE: This social and community group welcomes all Australians and New Zealanders living in the UAE, organising various events and functions throughout the year. *anzauae.org*

BilgiDubai: A large, sociable network for the Turkish community with regular activities and meet-ups. *bilgidubai.com*

Dubai Caledonian Society: A social network for Scottish expats with several annual events including the St Andrew's Ball in November and the Chieftain's Ball in May. *dubaicaledoniansociety.com*

Dubai Irish Society: Promotes Irish culture, social events and sporting interests, as well as organising several events throughout the year. *irishsocietydubai.com*

Dubai Toastmasters Club: The Dubai branch of this worldwide, non-profit organisation provides a supportive environment that promotes self-confidence and personal growth. *http://7492.toastmastersclubs.org*

Dubai St George's Society: Serving the British expat community, the DSGS focuses mainly on fun and social activities, but also raises money for various charities. *dsgs.org*

South African Women's Association: SAWA is dedicated to bringing together South African women in Dubai through various networking and social events. *sawa-uae.org*

There are also several web-based groups that will help you to get settled and meet new people. Expatwoman is like a permanent virtual coffee morning, where you can log on to discuss anything with fellow Dubai females from cleaning your dog to irritating husbands, as well as more serious issues. The group organises real-life get-togethers too (so just be careful what you say about other posters in case you end up meeting them face to face). There are several Dubai groups on Facebook and Twitter as well (see Websites, p.24, for more ideas).

If you're a full-time parent there are a number of friendly mother and toddler groups in Dubai, which are great to break up those long days and help both mum and junior make new friends (see p.144).

Leisure Activities

Joining a sports team is not only a fun means of staying in shape, it's also a great way to meet lots of new people and mix in new circles. Organisations such as Duplays (duplays.com) run a number of leagues and teams year-round that anybody can sign up to. See the Activities chapter (p.320) for details of some of the other clubs and societies that operate in Dubai.

Social Networks

Networking is one of the easiest ways to make new business contacts, so it makes sense that it is a good way to increase your social circle too. With strict laws against dating and matchmaking services here in Dubai, these social networking groups are purely for meeting like-minded people in a friendly, social setting.

Below is a selection of some of the social networking groups that operate in Dubai. See Work, p.116, for a list of business networking groups.

Match: Match meetings offer the opportunity to try 'speed networking' – mainly for creative professionals, at Match you get two minutes to talk to each person before the buzzer goes and you have to move on. Email match.dubai@gmail.com.

Ranches Ladies: A multinational ladies group which organises coffee mornings, social nights, activities and fundraising events. *arabianranchesladies.com*

Social Circles Dubai: A well-organised social community that focuses on meeting new people and networking for business or pleasure. *socialcirclesdubai.com*

Speak Dating: Foreign language speakers can find 'language exchange' partners who help you practise your foreign language in return for you helping them to learn your native tongue. *shelter.ae*

Places Of Worship

The UAE has a fairly liberal and welcoming attitude to other religions and, as a result, various places of worship also act as good community hubs, even if you're not a regular worshipper. In addition to the churches below, there is a popular Hindu temple complex in Bur Dubai, near Dubai Museum.

Christ Church Jebel Ali, *christchurchjebelali.com*
Dubai Evangelical Church Centre, *deccc.com*
Emirates Baptist Church International, *ebci.org*
Fellowship Of The Emirates, *fellowshipoftheemirates.org*
Holy Trinity Church Dubai, *holytrinitychurchdubai.org*
New Covenant Church Dubai, *nccuae.org*
St Francis Of Assisi Church, *stfrancisjebelali.ae*
St Mary's Catholic Church Dubai, *saintmarysdubai.com*
Well Of Life Church Dubai, *wolhome.com*

BEFORE YOU LEAVE

Whether your time in Dubai lasts a few months, a few years, or longer, there are a few things you should take care of before you jump on the plane.

Get your electricity, water and other utilities disconnected. You should remember that most providers (DEWA, Etisalat, du) will need at least two days' notice to take a final reading and return any security deposits you have paid. You'll need to settle the final bill before you get your deposit, and make sure you keep hold of the original deposit receipt to smooth the process. You'll also need to go through the official channels to close any bank accounts you have here. Banks (p.127) have been known to freeze an individual's account once they have been informed by the sponsor of a visa cancellation, so it's a good idea to get your finances in order first.

Settle your debts – you can get into serious trouble if you try to leave the country without paying off all your loans and outstanding bills, so be sure to keep on top of payments to avoid large sums complicating your exit. You should also cancel all credit cards and close bank accounts before you leave.

If you are leaving rented accommodation, make sure the place is spick and span so that you can reclaim your entire security deposit. The landlord may also require a clearance certificate from DEWA to prove you've paid all your bills, so make sure you leave enough time for all the administration involved. If you own a property you may choose to either sell or rent out your home – see Housing, p.80, and dubai.ae for more information.

Sell your car. This has been a tricky one recently, with many people owing more than they can sell the car for, but persevere and be prepared to take a financial knock if you need to offload it quickly with a dealer. See p.62.

Organise your shipping: shop around for good rates and give as much notice as possible to the shipping company. See p.100.

Sell the stuff you're not taking with you. Have a garage sale, list your items on dubizzle.com or expatwoman.com, or put photos up on supermarket noticeboards. Dubai Flea Market (p.420) is a good option for last-minute clearouts.

If you're taking pets with you, you will need to make sure their vaccinations are up to date, particularly rabies. There are other procedures to be followed when exporting pets (p.148), and ideally you need around six months to prepare. If you can't take your pets with you, find them a new family home, ask friends and family, or advertise online (p.24) – Dubai has a dreadful problem with abandoned pets.

Cancelling Your Visa

Your visa and how you cancel it will depend on the type of document you have. If you're on a residence visa that has been sponsored by your employer, as soon as your employment ends, so does your privilege to a work visa. Just as your employer would have been responsible for sorting out your paperwork, it is their responsibility to cancel it.

There's not much paperwork involved: you'll have to submit your passport and sometimes sign a waiver or a memorandum of understanding clarifying that you have received all monies owed to you and so on. Once your visa has been cancelled, you have a grace period of 30 days to leave the country, after which time you will be fined at a rate of Dhs.25 per day for the first six months, Dhs.50 per day for the next six months, and Dhs.100 per day after that.

If you are in Dubai on a spousal visa, and have, for example, separated or just need to leave, you will need the help of your husband or wife to cancel your status. Again, if your spouse's company has completed the paperwork, they will have to get their employee (your husband or wife) to sign off on the cancellation papers.

The whole process takes about five days, whichever visa you happen to be on, and is reasonably smooth sailing.

Getting Around

GETTING AROUND IN DUBAI

Private cars and taxis have long been the primary means of transportation for many of Dubai's residents, and the government has made great strides in improving the city's infrastructure to accommodate all of the drivers. Traffic is still a major problem, but Dubai's public transportation options are also getting better, especially with the expansion of the efficient Metro and a much improved bus network.

Many residents of Dubai are crazy about cars and you'll see every make and model imaginable cruising down the highway. Buying, insuring, registering and maintaining your car are all fairly easy and straightforward, but getting a driving licence can be a drawn-out nightmare for some. Dubai's roads can be dangerous if you're not careful, but if you avoid speeding, pay attention at all times and learn how to drive defensively you will gain confidence in no time.

Dubai Road Network

When you arrive, the extensive, expanding network of roads can be intimidating, but once you find your bearings things become easier. The creek divides Bur Dubai (to the south) and Deira (to the north), and has five main crossing points: Shindagha Tunnel, Maktoum Bridge, Garhoud Bridge, Business Bay Bridge and the Floating Bridge. The Floating Bridge is due to be replaced by the Dubai 'Smile' Bridge in late 2013.

The main thoroughfare through the city is Sheikh Zayed Road, which runs from Sharjah, parallel to the sea, all the way to Abu Dhabi. Three bypass roads have been constructed inland towards the desert to ease the city's congestion problems. All run parallel to the coast and Sheikh Zayed Road. Al Khail Road (E44) is the closest bypass to the coast and runs from Sports City to Ras Al Khor, where it turns east and heads towards Hatta and Oman. Sheikh Mohammed bin Zayed Road (E311), formerly Emirates Road, is the next furthest from the coast and connects Abu Dhabi directly to Sharjah and the northern emirates. The Outer Ring Road (E611) sits outside of the E311 and runs roughly from the southern border of Dubai all the way to the Sharjah-Umm Al Quwain border, although it is still being expanded. There are also a few main east-west roads, including Umm Suqeim Road (D63), the Dubai-Al Ain Road (E66), Financial Centre Road (D71), and Muscat Street (D69).

Wafi Junction

Despite all the road expansions, traffic is still a problem in Dubai, especially at the creek crossings.

Within the city, the roads in older parts of town, such as Bur Dubai and Deira, are smaller and more congested, while the road networks in newer developments such as Downtown Dubai tend to accommodate greater traffic flow.

Traffic Regulations

While the infrastructure is superb, the general standard of driving is not. You'll see drivers displaying all manner of bad, and dangerous, driving habits and, as a result, you must take extra care when driving here. The good news is that once you're behind the wheel yourself, it isn't as scary or as difficult as it looks, and you'll soon learn to drive defensively and safely.

It is important to note that you drive on the right side of the road in Dubai, and you should overtake on the left – people often ignore this rule but if you are caught you could receive a fine (see p.57).

Speed limits are usually 60 to 80km/h around town, while on main roads and roads to other emirates they are 100 to 120km/h. The limit is clearly indicated on signs. Both fixed and movable radar traps, and Dubai Traffic Police, are there to catch the unwary violator.

Parking

Most street parking in Dubai is now governed by parking meters. After feeding your coins into the machine, you get a ticket to display on your dashboard. The minimum fare is Dhs.2 for one hour. The price increases steeply the longer you park in a spot, so you'll pay Dhs.4 or Dhs.5 for two hours, Dhs.8 for three hours, and Dhs.11 for four hours (the maximum). Parking is free from 13:00 to 16:00 and 21:00 to 08:00 daily, and on Fridays and public holidays. Several areas support the mParking system (mpark.rta.ae), which allows drivers to pay parking tolls through SMS (non-Dubai registered vehicles must register online first). Areas where mParking is supported have an orange sign displaying the parking code and a guide on how to use the system. To use mParking, send an SMS to PARK (7275) with your car licence plate number (including the first letter), a space, the area parking code listed on the sign, a space, and the number of hours you wish to pay for (one to four). The system will then send you a confirmation SMS, and the parking fee plus a 30 fils service charge will be deducted from your Etisalat or du phone credit. Ten minutes before your time has expired, the system will send an SMS reminder and ask if you'd like to add more time. Commuters can also use their Nol Metro card (see p.55) to pay for parking at many machines, with the appropriate fee being deducted from the card's credit.

Maps

With new roads popping up on a weekly basis, finding your way around Dubai can be difficult and confusing. Explorer produces several of the most up-to-date street maps available, including the fully indexed *Dubai Street Atlas* and the pocket-sized *Dubai Mini Map*.

Parking at Dubai's shopping malls used to be mostly free, but since the opening of the Metro several shopping centres that are adjacent or near to Metro stations have introduced parking charges for stays over a certain length of time. Both Mall of the Emirates and Deira City Centre have free parking for the first four hours, and then charges that rise steeply from Dhs.20 for four to five hours up to Dhs.150 for eight hours or over and Dhs. 350 for overnight (Fridays and public holidays are free).

Free Zone Parking

Free parking in Dubai's free zones is coming to an end with plans to introduce paid parking at Dubai Media City, Dubai Internet City and Dubai Knowledge Village in 2013. RTA charges will apply between 08.00 and 18.00 from Saturday to Thursday – get a ticket or face a Dhs.500 fine.

Road Signs

Signposting in Dubai is generally good once you understand the system. Blue or green signs indicate the roads, exits or locations out of the city, and brown signs show heritage sites, places of interest and hospitals. Dubai's new signage system relies more heavily on street names and compass directions, compared to the older system which featured local area names. If the signage gets confusing, remember that Abu Dhabi is south of Dubai, Sharjah is north, the beach is to the west and the desert is to the east.

Address System

All roads are numbered to aid navigation, but the numbers are gradually being phased out and replaced with official road names. In Jumeira 3, where a successful pilot of this scheme was run, all of the roads are named. The District Addressing project will cover the entire city by the end of 2015, starting with areas including Umm Suqeim, Al Sufouh and Dubai Marina.

Although all roads in the city have an official name or number, many roads are referred to by a different moniker. For instance, Jumeira Road is often known as Beach Road, and Interchange One, on Sheikh Zayed Road, is invariably called Defence Roundabout. Dubai Municipality has started a more formal road-naming process to help eliminate confusion, and many of the city's main roads have been given the names of prominent Arab cities, such as Marrakech Road. Street signs now also include the direction of travel, so you know whether you are travelling north or south.

This lack of consistency makes locating an address difficult. Companies often only list their building name, road and nearest landmark when writing their address. The *Dubai Street Atlas* features an index of over 13,000 roads and building. Also, you can search for a business, product or service on localsearch.ae, which lists information for around 110,000 companies such as telephone number, email and website address.

People With Disabilities

Dubai is starting to consider the needs of disabled visitors more seriously and services for disabled residents are improving. Dubai International Airport is well equipped for disabled travellers, with automatic doors, large lifts and all counters accessible by wheelchair users, as well as several services such as porters, special transportation and quick check-in to avoid long queues. Dubai Taxi has a few specially modified taxis for journeys from the airport and around town. Some Metro stations have disabled access and trains have wider doors and are flush with the platform, making access easier for wheelchair uses. There are also talks that the Metro will be free for disabled commuters in the near future. Disabled parking spaces do exist, though there are ignorant drivers who don't need the facility; however, police do monitor these spaces and hand out fines to offenders.

Most of Dubai's five-star hotels have wheelchair access, but in general, facilities for disabled guests are limited, particularly at tourist attractions. Wheelchair ramps are often really nothing more than delivery ramps with steep angles. When asking if a location has wheelchair access, make sure it really does – an escalator is considered 'wheelchair access' by some.

Visit dubaitourism.ae for more information on disabled access in Dubai.

Cycling

Although the RTA has often talked about the benefits of cycling in the city's most congested districts, not much has been done to promote this form of transportation. You cannot cycle on Dubai's highways and even riding within city neighbourhoods can be dangerous. Also, summer temperatures can reach

45°C, which makes riding to work a very sweaty option. There are, however, a number of places where you can cycle safely for pleasure (p.328) and, if you do decide to take to two wheels, you are required to wear a helmet and a high visibility jacket, or you could face a fine of Dhs.500.

Walking

Cities in the UAE are generally very car-oriented and not designed to encourage walking. Additionally, summer temperatures of over 45°C are not conducive to spending any length of time outdoors. The winter months, however, make walking a pleasant way to get around and people can be found strolling through the streets, especially in the evenings. Most streets are lined with pavements and there are pedestrian paths either side of the creek, along the seafront in Deira and Jumeira, at The Walk JBR, and around Dubai Marina, as well as in the city's parks (see Walk This Way, p.364). There are also plans underway to build an extra 13 footbridges at key locations across Dubai, including Sheikh Rashid Street (near Deira City Centre), Umm Suqeim Street (near Mall of the Emirates), and Al Khaleej Street (near Deira Palm Metro Station).

Police are cracking down on jaywalking, and you can be fined Dhs.200 for crossing the road in an undesignated area, so always use the pedestrian crossings available.

PUBLIC TRANSPORT

In an effort to ease the city's congestion problems, the government's Roads & Transport Authority (rta.ae) has made a serious commitment to improving public transport. The Metro is the centrepiece of its efforts and, since its opening in September 2009, has helped to reduce the overall number of daily drivers. Dubai's bus system has also seen major improvements over the past few years with the introduction of air conditioned bus stops, new buses and an increase in routes. The RTA's fleet of water buses offers commuters and travellers an expanding network of routes along Dubai's waterways; alternatively, there is more costly water taxi service – operating from Deira across to Jebel Ali.

Air Travel

Currently, about 100 airlines take advantage of Dubai's open skies policy, operating to and from over 200 destinations. Dubai International Airport's three terminals are a 15 to 30 minute taxi ride apart, depending on the traffic, and there's also a shuttle bus. All terminals offer car rental, hotel reservations and exchange services. Most of the better-known airlines use Terminal 1, while Terminal 2 is used primarily by flydubai and airlines serving former Soviet countries and central Asia. Terminal 3, which opened in 2008, is the newest and most luxurious of the three and exclusively dedicated to Emirates Airlines. By comparison, Terminal 2 has limited facilities and, invariably, extensive queues, while both Terminal 1 and Terminal 3 have a vast selection of drinking and dining venues, plus a large duty free shopping section. For up-to-date flight information from Dubai International Airport, call 04 216 6666.

All three terminals have both short and long-term parking facilities, as well as busy taxi ranks. There are Metro stations at both Terminal 1 and Terminal 3 that any traveller can access. The stations are part of the Red Line, which runs throughout Deira, under the creek and along Sheikh Zayed Road all the way to Jebel Ali. Keep in mind that luggage larger than a large holdall or standard case is not permitted on the Metro. Airport buses operate to and from the airport. Call 800 9090 or visit rta.ae.

A second airport, Dubai World Central – Al Maktoum International, which is predominantly servicing cargo operations, opened in 2011 for cargo flights. The airport, which is located at the Jebel Ali end of town, will eventually be the world's largest, with five runways handling passenger flights too. Phase 2 of the airport is scheduled to open late 2013, ahead of hosting the Dubai Air Show in December 2013.

Dubai's official airline, Emirates, operates scheduled services to more than 100 destinations in over 50 countries. flydubai is a low-cost carrier based in Dubai that flies to more than 40 destinations, mainly other Arab cities such as Damascus and Alexandria, with further expansion plans underway. Both airlines use Dubai International as their hub of operations.

Other airlines include Etihad operating out of Abu Dhabi, low-cost carriers Air Arabia in Sharjah and flydubai in Dubai, and RAK Airways. Air Arabia offers a city terminal check-in at Lamcy Plaza. Rotana Jet, the UAE's first domestic airline, connects Abu Dhabi with three emirates – Sharjah, Fujairah, and Ras Al Khaimah – with flights starting from Dhs.150 a ticket.

Abu Dhabi airport is a 90 minute drive from Dubai, and Sharjah airport is 45 minutes away. For more information on travelling from Dubai, see Out Of The City on p.292.

Aeroflot Russian Airlines 04 222 2245, *aeroflot.ru*
Air Arabia 06 558 0000, *airarabia.com*
Air France 800 23 823, *airfrance.ae*
Air India 04 227 6787, *airindia.com*
Air Mauritius 04 221 4455, *airmauritius.com*
Air New Zealand 04 335 9126, *airnewzealand.com*
Air Seychelles 04 286 8008, *airseychelles.com*
Alitalia 04 221 4455, *alitalia.com*
American Airlines 04 316 6116, *aa.com*
Austrian Airlines 04 211 2538, *austrian.com*
Bahrain Air 04 239 9921, *bahrainair.net*

Biman Bangladesh Airlines 04 203 2029, *biman-airlines.com*
British Airways 800 0441 3322, *britishairways.com*
Cathay Pacific 04 204 2888, *cathaypacific.com*
China Airlines 02 626 4070, *china-airlines.com*
CSA Czech Airlines 04 294 5666, *czechairlines.ae*
Cyprus Airways 04 221 4455, *cyprusair.com*
Delta Airlines 04 397 0118, *delta.com*
EGYPTAIR 04 230 6666, *egyptair.com*
Emirates 600 55 5555, *emirates.com*
Etihad Airways 800 2277, *etihadairways.com*
flydubai 04 231 1000, *flydubai.com*
Gulf Air 04 271 6207, *gulfair.com*
IranAir 04 224 0200, *iranair.com*
Japan Airlines 04 217 7501, *jal.com*
Jazeera Airways 04 224 4464, *jazeeraairways.com*
KLM Royal Dutch Airlines 800 556, *klm.com*
Kuwait Airways 04 228 5896, *kuwait-airways.com*
Lufthansa 04 373 9100, *lufthansa.com*
Malaysia Airlines 04 325 4411, *malaysiaairlines.com*
Middle East Airlines 04 223 7080, *mea.com.lb*
Oman Air 04 351 8080, *oman-air.com*
Pakistan International Airlines 04 223 4888, *piac.com.pk*
Qantas 04 316 6652, *qantas.com*
Qatar Airways 04 231 9921, *qatarairways.com*
RAK Airways 04 228 4875, *rakairways.com*
Rotana Jet 02 444 3366, *rotanajet.ae*
Royal Air Maroc 04 286 9499, *royalairmaroc.com*
Royal Brunei Airlines 04 334 4884, *bruneiair.com*
Royal Jet Group 02 575 7000, *royaljetgroup.com*
Royal Jordanian 04 294 4288, *rj.com*
Saudi Arabian Airlines 04 229 6227, *saudiairlines.com*
Singapore Airlines 04 316 6888, *singaporeair.com*
South African Airways 04 397 0766, *flysaa.com*
SpiceJet 04 396 5186, *spicejet.com*
SriLankan Airlines 04 316 6711, *srilankan.aero*
Swiss Air 04 381 6100, *swiss.com*
Thai Airways 04 266 5498, *thaiair.com*
Tunisair 04 221 1176, *tunisair.com*
Turkish Airlines 04 211 2528, *turkishairlines.com*
United Airlines 800 0441 5492, *united.com*
Virgin Atlantic > *p.xx* 04 406 0600, *virgin-atlantic.com*
Yemen Airways 04 295 6797, *yemenia.com*

Boat

Crossing Dubai Creek by abra is a common mode of transport for many people. The fare for a single journey across the creek is Dhs.1, and the abras run from 05:00 to midnight. There are four abra stations, two on the Deira side near the souks and two on the Bur Dubai side near the Ruler's Court.

The RTA manages a fleet of air-conditioned water buses costing Dhs.4 per round trip. There are three water bus routes running along the creek, leaving every 15 to 20 minutes from stations including Dubai Old Souq, Al Seef and Al Ghubaiba. There is also the Dubai ferry service – three excellent value sightseeing trips aimed at tourists. The first Dubai ferry makes the round trip from Al Ghubaiba station in Bur Dubai to Burj Al Arab and back; the second connects the cruise terminal at Port Rashid with Al Ghubaiba; and the third goes from Dubai Marina Mall and turns around near Atlantis The Palm. Each journey lasts around an hour and cost Dhs.50 for silver class and Dhs.75 for gold class, with four trips per day.

Abra Ka Dabra

An abra is a wooden, single engine boat used to carry passengers across the creek. Abras have long been the primary method of crossing the creek. Each one can carry around 20 seated passengers. Abras don't run on a regular schedule, and tend to depart as soon as all of their seats have been filled.

The RTA launched the first phase of a new water taxi project in mid 2010. An initial five luxury 11-seater boats shuttle passengers between 25 stops, stretching from Jebel Ali Hotel to Festival City. Fares range from Dhs.50 to travel one stop, up to a hefty Dhs.570 to travel the whole route.

Tourists can also book a water taxi for an hour for Dhs.400; the number to call is 800 9090. The other 23 stops that are open are: Al Mamzar, Deira Old Souk, Al Sabkha, Bani Yas, Dubai Creek Golf & Yacht Club, Al Shindagha, Bur Dubai, Al Fheidi, Al Seef, Dubai Creek Park (A & B), Al Boom Tourist Village, Al Ghubaib, Jumeira Open Beach, Jumeira Beach Park, Jumeirah Beach Hotel, Dubai Marina, Atlantis, Mena Seyahi, One&Only Royal Mirage, One&Only Royal The Palm, Rixos The Palm Hotel, and Dubai Marina Mall.

Bus

There are currently around 70 bus routes servicing the main residential and commercial areas of Dubai. While all of the buses and most of the bus shelters are air-conditioned and modern, they can be rather crowded. However, the RTA has taken concrete steps to increase usage of the city's bus system, which now stands at roughly 6% of the population. Many of the bus stations now display better timetables and route maps, and a host of double-deck and articulated buses have helped with the crowding problem. The RTA piloted Wi-Fi on intercity bus routes from Dubai to Abu Dhabi, Fujairah and Sharjah, with plans to extend this to other routes; it now also offers on-board catering services between Bur Dubai and Abu Dhabi.

The main bus stations are near the Gold Souk in Deira and on Al Ghubaiba Road in Bur Dubai. Buses run at regular intervals, starting between 05:00 and 06:00 and running until midnight or so, and a handful of Nightliner buses operate from 23:30 till 06:00. The front three rows of seats on all buses are reserved for women and children only. Cash is not accepted so you need to purchase a Nol card (see p.55) before boarding.

Buses also go further to Khawaneej, Warsan and Hatta, for very reasonable prices – a one-way ticket to Hatta, which is 100 kilometres away, is Dhs.10. The E1 service links Dubai and Abu Dhabi. From early morning to late at night, buses operate every 40 minutes between Al Ghubaiba and Abu Dhabi Central bus stations, and the two-hour journey costs Dhs.20 each way. There is also a service to and from Al Arouba Road and Al Wahda in Sharjah to both Bur Dubai and Deira, which runs every 10 minutes and costs Dhs.7. For a complete list of the RTA's inter-emirate routes, see rta.ae.

Metro

The Dhs.28 billion Dubai Metro opened in September 2009, bringing public transport to the masses. The Red Line runs from Rashidiyah to Dubai International Airport, and down Sheikh Zayed Road – passing the financial district, Downtown, Al Barsha and Dubai Marina – before terminating at Jebel Ali. To date, 28 out of the 29 stations on the Red Line are open; 16 of the 18 stations are open on the Green Line, which runs from Al Qusais on the Sharjah border to Jaddaf. (A Blue Line has been proposed to link the current International airport with the new Dubai World Central airport at Jebel Ali.) An air-conditioned, 820m glass tunnel walkway links The Dubai Mall and the Dubai Mall Metro station.

Trains run from around 05:50 to 24:00 on weekdays, and until 01:00 during the weekend, at intervals of six to eight minutes at peak times; on Fridays, the service starts at 13:00. Each train has a section for women and children only, and a first or Gold Class cabin. The fare structure operates as a pay-as-you-go system, in which you scan your prepaid Nol card in and out of stations.

Commuters can also take advantage of du Wi-Fi at stations and on the trains themselves. Access cards are available for Dhs.20 per hour, or you can pay via credit card at a rate of Dhs.10 per hour.

Plan Your Trip

The best way to work out your public transport options is to use the Roads & Transport Authority's (RTA) online journey planner (wojhati.rta.ae). For further assistance, call the RTA on 800 9090.

There is a feeder bus system to transport passengers from stations to local destinations. The buses are free if boarded within 30 minutes of exiting the Metro. Each station also has a taxi rank outside the exit to help you reach destinations that aren't accessible by bus.

A monorail runs the length of Palm Jumeirah from the Gateway Towers station on the mainland to Atlantis hotel. Trains run daily from 10:00 to 22:00 and cost Dhs.15 for a single fare or Dhs.25 for a return. Work has also begun on the Al Sufouh Tram system which is being designed as a key link for the Dubai Metro and the Palm Monorail. The tram will run along Al Sufouh Road, linking Mall of the Emirates, Dubai Marina, and Jumeirah Lakes Towers. Construction is underway but, due to several major delays, the tramline will not be completed until 2014.

...Another World Record

In February 2012, Dubai Metro entered the Guinness World Records Book as the longest driverless metro network in the world, spanning 74.69km.

Travelling by abra

Nol

Introduced with the opening of the Metro, Nol cards are rechargeable travel cards which can be used to pay for public transport and street car parking in Dubai. The card is meant to help streamline the Metro, bus and water bus systems, and fares are calculated by the number of zones travelled through on a single journey, regardless of what form of transportation you use. Single journeys start at Dhs.1.80 for up to 3km, rising to Dhs.5.80 for travel across two or more zones. The red Nol card is a paper ticket aimed at tourists. It can be charged for up to 10 journeys, but is only valid on one type of transport – bus, Metro or water bus. The silver Nol card costs Dhs.20, including Dhs.14 credit. It can be recharged up to Dhs.500 and can be used across all forms of transport and for street parking (p.50). The gold Nol card is identical to the silver, except that holders are charged first-class prices (usually double the standard fare) and can travel in the Gold Class cabins on the Metro.

There are daily and monthly Nol passes available. A daily unlimited travel pass costs Dhs.14, while the monthly passes range from Dhs.100 to Dhs.270. Student and senior discounts are available on most ticket types.

Nol cards can be purchased and topped up at Metro and bus stations and at selected supermarkets including Carrefour and Spinneys. Information on the Nol fare structure and a map of the different zones can be found at nol.ae.

Taxi

If you don't have a car, taxis are still the most common way of getting around. There are nearly 7,000 metered taxis in Dubai with a fixed fare structure. The cars are all beige with different coloured roofs. A fleet of 'ladies taxis' with distinctive pink roofs have female drivers and are meant for women or family groups only; In-Safe Hands caters to women, children, students, families and people with special needs; and there is a luxury VIP fleet of taxis.

Taxis can be flagged down by the side of the road or you can call 04 208 0808. If you make a booking, you will pay a slightly higher starting fare. The Dubai Taxi automated phone system stores your address after the first time you call. Each subsequent time you ring from that number, listen to the prompts, hit 1, and a taxi will be dispatched automatically, (or hit 2, then enter a later time using the phone's keypad). Unfortunately, the dispatch centre never gives approximate waiting times, so the taxi could arrive in five minutes or 30. Waits are longer at weekends.

The minimum taxi fare is Dhs.10, and the pickup fare ranges from Dhs.3 to Dhs.7, depending on the time of day, and whether or not you ordered by phone. The starting fare inside the airport area is Dhs.20. Specialist services charge higher rates. Taxis are no longer exempt from Salik tolls, and crossing the border into Sharjah adds another Dhs.20 to the fare. The rate for stoppage or waiting is 50 fils per minute, so don't be surprised when the meter keeps running in standstill traffic. Taxis can be hired for six hours for Dhs.500 or for 12 hours for Dhs.800.

Driver On Call

You can now hire a driver on an hourly, daily, weekly or monthly basis for a fixed fare by booking through Dubai Taxi's Mashaweer service. Drivers can be hired for a minimum of two hours at Dhs.40 per hour, while a daily fare for a maximum of eight hours would be Dhs.250.

Stay Safe

If you've had a drink, don't even think about getting behind the wheel. Instead, call Safer Driver (04 268 8797, saferdriver.ae), which will send a driver to pick you up and drive your car home for you. Rates vary depending on distance, but the minimum charge is Dhs.120. Money well spent.

Dubai taxi drivers occasionally lack a decent knowledge of the city and passengers may have to direct them. Start with the area of destination and then choose a major landmark, such as a hotel, roundabout or shopping centre. Then narrow it down as you get closer. It's helpful to take the phone number of your destination with you, in case you and your driver get lost. As a last resort, you can ask the driver to radio his control point for instructions.

Finding a taxi in congested areas can be difficult, and in their frustration, many people are using illegal cabs. Be warned though that unlicensed taxis haven't had to meet the safety standards for their cars that legal cabs do. As these cabs are difficult to trace, there have also been cases where drivers have either been the victim of crimes or have perpetrated them.

Passenger Rights

Taxi drivers are obliged to accept any fare, no matter the distance. They are also obliged to drive in a safe manner, so don't be timid about asking them to slow down. If a driver refuses to pick you up because of your destination or refuses to drive responsibly, you can call the RTA complaint line (800 90 90).

DRIVING

Getting A Driving Licence

Once you have your residence permit you must apply for a permanent (10 year) UAE licence if you want to drive in Dubai. Nationals of the countries listed opposite can automatically transfer a valid driving licence.

Take your existing foreign licence, your passport (with residency stamp), Emirates ID, an eye test certificate (available from any optometrist), two passport photos, and a Dhs.410 fee to any of the RTA Customer Centres (rta.ae) – along with a letter of no objection from your company and a copy of the company's trading licence. This may seem like a lot to take, but the process is actually easy and you should have your licence that same day.

If your nationality is not on the automatic transfer list you will need to sit a UAE driving test to be eligible to drive in Dubai. Much of the process has been handed over to the five authorised driving institutes (see opposite), so you can apply for a learner's permit at the driving school, instead of going to the Traffic Police.

Some driving institutions insist that you pay for a set of pre booked lessons. In some cases, the package extends to 52 lessons and can cost up to Dhs.4,000. The lessons usually last 30 to 45 minutes during the week, or longer lessons can be taken at weekends.

Women are generally required to take lessons with a female instructor, a cost of Dhs.60 per hour. You will take three different tests on different dates. One is a Highway Code test, another includes parking and manoeuvres, and the third is a road test. You also have to take an assessment prior to doing the final test. Before you are issued with your permanent driving licence you will have to attend a number of road safety lectures, the cost of which is not included in the initial the price of your lessons. Currently the additional charge is Dhs.300. For more information, call 800 90 90. It is not uncommon to fail the road test multiple times. Each time you fail, you will need to attend and pay for another set of lessons before you can take the test again.

Always carry your licence and the car's registration card when driving. If you fail to produce it during a police spot check you will be fined.

The rules for riding a motorbike in Dubai are similar to driving a car. If you have a transferable licence from one of the countries listed above, you can get a six-month temporary licence or a 10-year permanent one. If you plan to hire a car overseas, the UAE now issues a one-year International Driving Licence (IDL) that is recognised in 180 countries worldwide. To apply, you will need your UAE driving licence, two passport photos and your residency visa, plus the Dhs.150 fee.

Traffic Jam Session

Avoid a traffic jam by tuning in to any of the following radio channels: Al Arabiya (98.9 FM), Al Khaleejia (100.9 FM), Dubai 92 (92.0 FM), Channel 4 FM (104.8 FM), or Emirates 1 FM (99.3FM, 100.5 FM). Regular updates about the traffic situation on main roads are provided throughout the day, forewarning you if a certain road is blocked so you can take an alternative route.

Driving Schools

Al Ahli Driving Center 04 341 1500, *alahlidubai.ae*
Belhasa Driving Center 04 324 3535, *bdc.ae*
Dubai Driving Center 04 345 5855, *dubaidrivingcenter.net*
Emirates Driving Institute 04 263 1100, *edi-uae.com*
Galadari Motor Driving Center 04 267 6166, *gmdc.ae*

Automatic Licence Transfer

Australia, Austria, Bahrain, Belgium, Canada*, Denmark, Finland, France, Germany, Greece*, Hong Kong, Ireland, Italy, Japan*, South Korea*, Kuwait, Netherlands, New Zealand, Norway, Oman, Poland*, Portugal*, Qatar, Romania, Saudi Arabia, Singapore, South Africa, Spain, Sweden, Switzerland, Turkey*, United Kingdom, United States.

*Citizens of these countries require a letter of approval from their consulates and an Arabic translation of their driving licence (unless the original is in English).

Renewing A Driving Licence

Licences can be renewed at any of the RTA Customer Centres (rta.ae). The procedure costs Dhs.110 and you will need to take your Emirates ID card (see p.35), an eyesight test and the expired driving licence. The process is usually quick if there isn't a queue. Traditionally, you have only been able to renew your licence in the emirate in which it was initially issued but, thanks to the recent federalisation of a number of services and procedures, you can now renew your licence in any of the seven emirates.

Car Pooling

In an effort to reduce rush-hour congestion, the government has introduced an online lift sharing programme (sharekni.ae). After registering, a passenger can search for a driver that lives nearby and is heading to the same destination. Drivers can also register for the programme to request passengers. The programme aims to legalise carpooling while minimising the number of illegal cabs in the city. Cash is not to be transferred from passenger to driver, but passengers can pay for petrol. Colleagues do not need to register with the programme to share rides.

Road Toll

Salik

Salik is an automated toll system for Dubai's roads. There are currently four gates: one at Garhoud Bridge, another on the Sheikh Zayed Road after Mall of the Emirates, one at Safa Park on Sheikh Zayed Road (between interchanges one and two), and another on Maktoum Bridge. There are plans to open two new Salik gates: on Al Ittihad Rd and near Dubai Airport Tunnel. The Maktoum Bridge crossing is free between 22:00 and 06:00 and 22:00 and 09:00 on Fridays, when the Floating Bridge is closed. There are no booths, and no need to stop as you drive through. Instead, drivers stick a tag to their windscreen, which is read by radio frequency as they pass through.

Drivers must initially buy a 'welcome pack' costing Dhs.100: Dhs.50 for the tag and Dhs.50 credit. It costs Dhs.4 each time you pass a toll gate, but if you travel between the Al Barsha toll gate and the Al Safa toll gate during one trip (and in the space of an hour) you will only be charged once. The maximum you will be charged in one day is Dhs.24. If your Salik card is out of credit you will be fined Dhs.50 for each gate you pass through. The Salik system will send you an SMS when your account balance runs low or when you pass through a gate without any balance. The kit can be bought from Emarat, EPPCO, ENOC, and ADNOC petrol stations, Dubai Islamic Bank and Emirates Bank. For more information about the toll gates, visit the Salik website, salik.gov.ae, or call 800 72545 (800 SALIK).

Traffic Fines & Offences

In an effort to help combat bad driving, the Dubai Police initiated a black points system to go along with the existing fines system. You are issued a certain number of black points against your licence according to the particular violation. For example, the fine for allowing a child under 10 years of age to sit in the front of a car is Dhs.400 and the driver will be given four black points. If you get 24 points you will lose your licence for a year, but any points you acquire will expire 12 months after they are issued.

A white points system, due to be introduced in 2013, will 'reward' law-abiding drivers with one white point every month; motorists will be given incentives to collect white points, ranging from raffle prizes to exemption from traffic fines.

Parking fines start at Dhs.200, and speeding fines start at Dhs.400 for driving up to 10kph over the speed limit and go up from there. Driving in a reckless manner or racing will earn you six points, as will parking in a handicapped zone or in front of a fire hydrant.

At the end of 2011, the laws relating to speeding were tightened further when Dubai Police announced that an additional 14 speed cameras had been placed on the emirate's motorways; drivers caught far exceeding the limit would be fined Dhs.900 and have six black points added to their licence, while any driver caught exceeding the limit by 60kph can expect 12 black points, a Dhs.1,000 fine and their car to be impounded immediately. An outline of the black points system can be found at dubaipolice.gov.ae.

Blood Money

By law, the family of a pedestrian killed in a road accident is entitled to Dhs.200,000 *diya* (blood) money. The money is usually paid by the insurance company unless there's any whiff of the driver having been under the influence of alcohol. However, an amendment to the law is being considered to put a stop to the terrible trend among desperate lower-income workers of killing themselves to provide for their family. This will mean blood money is not automatically due if the victim was walking across a road not intended for use by pedestrians, such as Sheikh Zayed Road.

Be careful to avoid driving in the dedicated bus and taxi lanes, which have recently been added to some major roads. The lanes are clearly marked, and you are liable to a fine of Dhs.600 if you enter one without authorisation. The only exception is if you need to cross the lane to enter or exit the thoroughfare.

Average-speed and stopping-distance traps were recently introduced to try to catch speeding drivers who only slow down when they see speed cameras, and to discourage tailgating. On-the-spot traffic fines for certain offences have been introduced, but in most cases you won't know you've received a fine until you check on the Dubai Police website or renew your vehicle registration. Most fines are paid when you renew your annual car registration. However, parking tickets that appear on your windscreen must be paid within a week, or the fine increases.

Dubai Police exercises a strict zero tolerance policy on drinking and driving. If you get into an accident, whether it is your fault or not, and you fail a blood-alcohol test, you could find yourself spending a night in a cell before a trial in Dubai Courts, after which a jail sentence will likely be applied. In addition, your insurance is automatically void. Police have increased the number of random drink-driving checks. Be aware also that alcohol still in your system from the night before will get you in just as much trouble.

Breakdowns

In the event of a breakdown, you will usually find that passing police cars will stop to help, or at least to check your documents. It's important that you keep water in your car at all times so you don't get dehydrated while waiting. Dubai Traffic officers recommend, if possible, that you pull your car over to a safe spot. If you are on the hard shoulder of a highway you should pull your car as far away from the yellow line as possible and step away from the road until help arrives.

The Arabian Automobile Association – the AAA – (04 266 9989 or 800 4900, aaauae.com) offers a 24 hour roadside breakdown service for an annual charge. This includes help in minor mechanical repairs, battery boosting, or help if you run out of petrol, have a flat tyre or lock yourself out. Mashreq Bank Visa card holders receive free AAA membership. The more advanced service includes off-road recovery, vehicle registration and a rent-a-car service. Other breakdown services that will be able to help you out without membership include IATC (iatcuae.com), Dubai Auto Towing Services (04 359 4424) and AKT Recovery (04 263 6217). Some dealers and insurance companies offer a free breakdown and recovery service for the first few years after buying a new car. Be sure to ask the dealership about this option when purchasing a new car.

Traffic Accidents

If you are involved in an accident call 999. If the accident is minor and no one has been hurt you need to agree with the other driver where the blame lies and move your cars to the side of the road to avoid obstructing the flow of traffic. You can be fined Dhs.100 for failing to do so even if the accident wasn't your fault. If blame has been clearly decided and the accident is minor, the 999 dispatcher may ask you to drive yourself to the nearest Traffic Police station to fill out the necessary paperwork. The Dubai Police Information Line (800 7777, Arabic and English) gives the numbers of police stations around the emirate.

Cash Only

In 2007, Dubai petrol stations adopted a 'cash only' policy, whereas before you could pay for your petrol by debit and credit card. So make sure you have cash before you fill up, and don't rely on there being an ATM at all petrol stations.

If blame cannot be decided without police intervention, an officer will be dispatched to assess the accident and apportion blame. The officer will then give you a copy of the accident report; if it is green then the other party is at fault but if it is pink then you are to blame for the accident and you will receive a Dhs.200 fine from the attending officer. You will need to submit the accident report to the insurance company in order to process the claim, or to the garage for repairs. Keep in mind that garages rarely repair vehicles without a police report.

Stray animals are something to avoid on desert roads. If the animal hits your vehicle and causes damage or injury, the animal's owner should pay compensation, but if you are found to have been speeding, you must compensate the animal's owner.

Petrol Stations

Petrol is subsidised in the UAE and generally inexpensive. Within Dubai, you will find Emarat, ENOC and EPPCO stations, and the price of unleaded petrol (around Dhs.1.72 per litre) is the same at all of them. The octane rating of unleaded petrol in the UAE is high – 'Special' is rated at 95 octane and 'Super' at 98 octane. Many of the stations have convenience stores and some have small cafes or fast food restaurants attached to them. Every station is manned by attendants who will pump your petrol for you.

Sheikh Zayed Road

flying elephant EVENTS

800-EVENTS (383687)
flyingelephant.ae

The region's largest supplier of corporate and family entertainment with 16 years of celebrating events.

- Corporate Family Days
- Themed Staff Parties
- Private Events
- Events Contractor

GETTING A CAR

Hiring A Car

New arrivals to Dubai often find that they have no other option than to hire a vehicle until their residency papers go though. Most leasing companies include the following in their rates: registration, maintenance, replacement, 24 hour assistance and insurance. All the main car rental companies, plus a few extra, can be found in Dubai.

It is best to shop around as the rates vary considerably. The larger, reputable firms generally have more reliable vehicles and a greater capacity to help in an emergency (an important factor when dealing with the aftermath of an accident). Find out which car hire agent your company uses, as you might qualify for a corporate rate. Most rental companies will keep track of how many times you pass through Salik gates and charge you at the end of the month, along with a Salik service charge.

Leasing is generally weekly, monthly or yearly. Monthly lease prices start at around Dhs.2,500 for a small vehicle such as a Toyota Yaris, and go up from there. As the lease period increases, the price decreases, so if you're considering keeping the car for a long period, it may not work out that much more expensive than buying.

Before you take possession of your leased car, check for any dents or bumps. To hire any vehicle you will need to provide a passport copy, credit card and a valid driving licence. Those with a residence visa must have a UAE driving licence to drive a hired car, while those on a visit visa can use a licence from their home country as long as it is at least one year old. Comprehensive insurance is essential; make sure that it includes personal accident coverage, and perhaps Oman cover if you're planning on exploring.

Car Hire Companies

Autolease Rent A Car 04 282 6565, *autolease-uae.com*
Avis 04 295 7121, *avisuae.ae*
Bettercar Rentals 04 258 6331, *bettercardubai.com*
Budget Car & Van Rental UAE > *p.61* 800 2722, *budget-uae.com*
Car Fare Rent A Car 800 22 73 273, *carfarellc.com*
Carlease Rent A Car 04 424 5944, *carlease.ae*
Diamondlease Car Rental 04 885 2677, *diamondlease.com*
DRC Rent A Car 04 338 9070, *discountcardubai.com*
Dubai Exotic Limo 800 5466, *dubaiexoticlimo.com*
EuroStar Rent A Car 04 266 1117, *eurostarrental.com*
Fast Rent A Car 04 3387 171, *fastuae.com*
German Rent A Car 04 298 0607, *germanRAC.com*
Green Car Rental 04 358 8488, *greencardubai.com*
Hertz UAE 800 43 789, *hertzuae.com*
Icon Car Rental 04 257 8228, *dubairentacar.ae*
Impala Rent A Car 04 234 5651, *impalauae.com*
Low Cost Rent A Car 04 339 6661, *lowcostcardubai.com*
National Car Rental 04 283 2020, *national-me.com*
Parklane Car Rental 04 347 1779, *parklanerental.com*
Payless Car Rental 04 384 5526, *paylesscar.com*
Shift Leasing & Car Rental 04 3393 722, *shiftleasing.com*
Thrifty Car Rental 800 4694, *thriftyuae.com*
Travel House Rent A Car 04 397 2757, *travelhouserentacar.com*
United Car Rentals & Wafi Limousine 04 285 7777, *unitedcarrentals.com*

Buying A Car

Aside from the horrendous traffic, the UAE is a motorist's dream. Petrol is cheap, big engines are considered cool and the wide highways stretching across the country are smooth and perfect for weekend drives.

Most of the major car makes are available through franchised dealerships in Dubai, with big Japanese and American brands particularly well represented. Expat buyers are often pleasantly surprised by the low cost of new cars compared to their home countries.

Tinted Windows

Currently, the government allows you to avoid the sun somewhat by tinting your vehicle's windows up to 30%. Some areas have facilities where you can get your car windows tinted but don't get carried away – remember to stick to the limit. Random checks take place and fines are handed out to those caught in the dark. Tinting in Sharjah is allowed for a fee of Dhs.100 and Ajman residents may tint for Dhs.200 per annum, but only if they are women. Company cars are banned from having tinted windows.

For many, this lower initial cost, coupled with cheaper fuel and maintenance, means they can afford something a little more extravagant than they might drive at home.

There is a large second-hand car market in the UAE. Dealers are scattered around town but good areas to start are Sheikh Zayed Road and Warsan, behind Ras Al Khor. Expect to pay a premium of between Dhs.5,000 and Dhs.10,000 for buying through a dealer (as opposed to buying from a private seller), since they also offer a limited warranty, insurance, finance and registration.

The Al Awir complex houses several smaller used-car dealers and it's easy to spend a whole day walking around the lots speaking with salesmen. Al Awir is also the location for Golden Bell Auctions (goldenbellauctions.com), with sales held each Wednesday evening. All cars up for auction have to

undergo a test at the nearby Eppco Tasjeel garage, and all outstanding fines will have been cleared. There's a Traffic Department office on the site so buyers can register their new vehicles on the spot.

For private sales, check the classifieds in Gulf News and Khaleej Times and supermarket noticeboards. Online sites such as dubizzle.com and expat forums such as expatwoman.com are also useful.

Second Opinion

When buying a used car it's well worth having it checked over by a garage or mechanic. Eppco Tasjeel, AAA and Max Garage offer a checking service. Alternatively, speak to the service department at the dealership where the car was originally bought. A thorough inspection will cost about Dhs.250.

New Car Dealers

AGMC BMW, Rolls Royce, Mini, 04 339 1555, *bmw-dubai.com*
Al Futtaim Motors Lexus, Toyota, 04 206 6000, *alfuttaimmotors.ae*
Al Ghandi Auto Fiat, Lancia, Ssangyong, 04 231 0800, *alghandi.com*
Al Habtoor Motors Aston martin, Bentley, Mitsubishi, 04 608 4000, *alhabtoor-motors.com*
Al Khoory Automobiles 04 314 6214, *subaru-uae.com*
Al Majid Motors Kia, Renault, 04 347 7999, *kia-uae.com*
Al Naboodah Automobiles Audi, 04 384 7777, *nabooda-auto.com*
Al Naboodah Automobiles VW, 04 705 3333, *nabooda-auto.com*
Al Rostamani Trading Company Suzuki, 04 295 5907, *alrostamani.com*
Al Tayer Motors Ferrari, Ford, Jaguar, Landrover, Lincoln, Maserati, Mercury, 04 201 1001, *altayermotors.com*
Al Yousuf Motors Chevrolet, Daihatsu, 04 339 0000, *aym.ae*
Arabian Automobiles Company Nissan, Infinity, 04 295 2222, *nissan-dubai.com*
The Car Zone Megastore 800 227 9663, *carzone.me*
Galadari Automobiles Mazda, 04 299 4666, *mazdauae.com*
Gargash Enterprises Mercedes Benz, 04 209 9777, *gargash.mercedes-benz.com*
Gargash Motors Alpha Romeo, Saab, 04 340 3333, *gargashme.com*
Juma Al Majid Est Hyundai, 800 498 6324, *hyundai-uae.com*
Liberty Automobiles Cadillac, Opel, Hummer, 04 282 4440, *libertyautos.com*
McLaren Dubai 04 382 7500, *dubai.mclarenretailers.com*
Porsche Centre Dubai 04 321 3911, *porschedubai.com*
Skoda Showroom 04 341 2022, *skoda-uae.com*
Swaidan Trading Co Peugeot, 04 294 8111, *swaidan.com*
Trading Enterprises Chrysler, Dodge, Honda, Jeep, Volvo, 04 295 4246, *tradingenterprises.ae*

Used Car Dealers

4x4 Motors Sells all types of used cars. Nr Oasis Centre, Shk Zayed Rd, Al Quoz 3, 04 338 4866. There's also a second branch at Al Aweer Auto Market Phase 1, Ras Al Khor Industrial 3, Dubai, 04 333 2757, *4x4motors.com*
Al Futtaim Automall Has three sites in Dubai; see website for locations. Each car comes with a 12 month warranty and a 30 day exchange policy. Nr Times Square, Shk Zayed Rd, Al Quoz Industrial 1, 04 340 8029, *automalluae.com*
Al Naboodah Automobiles Al Wasl, 04 310 5300, *nabooda-auto.com*
Auto Plus Shk Zayed Rd, Al Qusais Industrial 1, 04 339 5900, *autoplusdubai.com*
The Car Zone Megastore Nr Dubai Garden Centre, Shk Zayed Rd, Al Quoz Industrial 3, 800 227 9663, *carzone.me*
Dynatrade Shk Zayed Rd, Al Quoz Industrial 1, 04 328 5511, *dynatrade-uae.com*
Exotic Cars Shk Zayed Rd, Al Quoz 3, 04 338 4339, *exoticcarsdubai.com*

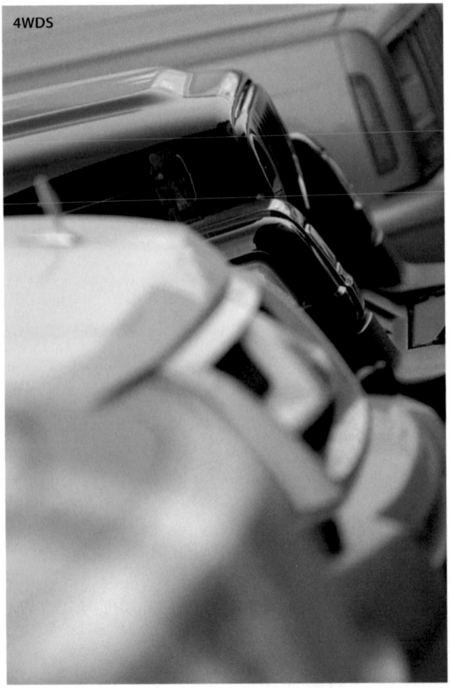
4WDS

Higer Motors Ras Al Khor Industrial 3, 04 333 1119, *higermotors.com*
House Of Cars > *p.63* Nr Mazaya Centre, Shk Zayed Rd, Al Wasl, 04 343 5060, *houseofcarsgroup.com*
Motor World Dubai Auto Market, Ras Al Khor Industrial 3, 04 333 2206, *motorworlddubai.com*
Reem Automobiles Nr Mazaya Centre, Shk Zayed Rd, Al Wasl, 04 343 6333, *reemauto.ae*
Sun City Motors Al Itihad Rd, Al Khabaisi, 04 269 8009, *suncitymotors.net*
Western Auto AW Rostamani Bldg, Al Ithihad Rd, Port Saeed, 04 297 7788, *westernauto.ae*

Vehicle Finance

Many new and second-hand car dealers will be able to arrange finance for you, often through a deal with their preferred banking partner. Previously, this involved writing out years and years worth of post-dated cheques, but most official dealers and main banks will now set up automatic transactions for your monthly repayments; be prepared to pay a deposit too, roughly 20% of the car's value. Always ask about the rates and terms, and then consider going directly to one of the banks to see if they can offer you a better deal. It's often easier to get financing through the bank that receives your salary.

Personal Loans

The interest rates for personal loans are often lower than those for car loans. Be sure to compare the two rates and to check with your bank to see if you qualify for a personal loan.

Vehicle Insurance

Before you can register your car you must have adequate insurance. The insurers will need to know the usual details such as year of manufacture, and value, as well as the chassis number. If you got a real bargain of a car and feel it's worth much more than you paid, make sure you instruct the insurance company to cover it at the market value. Take copies of your UAE driving licence, passport and the existing vehicle registration card.

Annual insurance policies are for a 13 month period (this is to cover the one-month grace period that you are allowed when your registration expires). Rates depend on the age and model of your car and your previous insurance history; however, very few companies will recognise any no-claims bonuses you have accrued in your home country.

The rates are generally 4% to 7% of the vehicle value, or a flat 5% for cars over five years old. Fully comprehensive cover with personal accident insurance is highly advisable, and you are strongly advised to make sure the policy covers you for 'blood money' (p.57). For more adventurous 4WD drivers, insurance for off-roading accidents is also recommended. Young or new drivers might need to call a few insurance companies before finding one that is willing to insure them, especially if they own a sports car. If you have made no claims for three years, you will probably qualify for a reduction in your insurance rates.

There's a wide choice of car insurance companies in Dubai, and the UAE's online car insurance comparison websites are a good starting point; try insurancemarket.ae or insureme.ae.

Registering a Vehicle

All cars must be registered annually with the Traffic Police. There is a one-month grace period after your registration has expired (hence the 13 month insurance period), but after that is a Dhs.100 fine for each month the registration has expired.

Along with the Dubai Traffic Police, both EPPCO and Emarat run full registration services under the names of Tasjeel (eppcouae.com) and Shamil (shamil.ae) respectively. Both have several locations throughout Dubai. Five major insurance firms can now also carry out the procedure: Royal & Sun Alliance (RSA), Fujairah National Insurance, Oman Insurance, AXA and Noor Takaful Insurance.

The process is relatively straightforward. You will need to take your old car registration, your driving licence, proof of car insurance for the coming year (although you can sometimes purchase the insurance on site), Dhs.50 for the car inspection and Dhs.385 for the registration. You must also pay all outstanding fines before the car can be re-registered. The fines can usually be paid at the registration centre, but try to check how much you owe beforehand (you can do so on dubaipolice.gov.ae), as some of the larger fines cannot be paid at the test centre. New cars don't need to be inspected for the first two years, but still need to be re-registered every year.

Both EPPCO Tasjeel and Emarat Shamil offer VIP pick-up and drop-off registration services for an extra charge, usually around Dhs.200. Call 800 4258 to make an appointment with Tasjeel or 800 4559 for Shamil. The RTA also recently launched a service enabling owners to carry out vehicle registration online; to sign up to the service, visit rta.ae.

Vehicle Repairs & Maintenance

By law, no vehicle can be accepted for major 'collision' repairs without an accident report from the Traffic Police, although very minor dents can be repaired without one. Your insurance company will usually have an agreement with a particular garage to which they will refer you. The garage will carry out the repair work and the insurance company will settle the claim. Generally, there is Dhs.500 deductible for all claims, but check your policy details.

If you purchase a new vehicle your insurance should cover you for 'agency repairs', that is, repairs at the workshop of the dealer selling the car, although this is not a guarantee and you may have to pay a premium. It's worth it though as your car's warranty (two to three years) may become invalid if you have non-agency repairs done on it. Even if you buy a fairly new second-hand car (less than three years old) it may be beneficial to opt for agency repairs in order to protect the value of the car.

To Oman & Back

It is wise to check whether your insurance covers you for the Sultanate of Oman as, within the Emirates, you may find yourself driving through small Oman enclaves (especially if you are off road, near Hatta, through Wadi Bih and in Dibba). Insurance for a visit to Oman can be arranged on a short-term basis, usually for no extra cost.

Besides accidents and bumps, you may also have to deal with the usual running repairs associated with any car. Common problems in this part of the world can include the air-conditioning malfunctioning, batteries suddenly giving up and tyres blowing out. With the air-con it may just be a case of having the system topped up, which is a fairly straightforward procedure. Car batteries don't tend to last too long in the hot conditions, and you may not get much warning (one day your car just won't start), so it's always handy to keep a set of jump leads in the boot.

If you do manage to get your car started then it's worth taking a trip to Satwa; before you know it, your car will be surrounded by people offering to fix anything. Haggle hard and you can get a bargain for simple repairs and spares – including a new battery.

When buying a used vehicle, many shoppers like to see a history of agency maintenance, especially for relatively new cars. It may seem ridiculous to have your oil changed at the dealership every 5,000km, but it often pays in the long run when selling your car.

Vehicle Repairs

4x4 Garage 04 323 2100, *4x4motors.com*
Al Saeedi Auto Trading 04 885 8560, *alsaeedi.com*
Al Wataniya Workshop 04 340 8546, *aww.ae*
Bosch Service Centre 04 338 6000, *cmeuae.ae*
Central Motors & Equipment 04 338 6000, *cmeuae.ae*
House Of Cars > ***p.63*** 04 339 3466, *houseofcarsgroup.com*
Icon Auto Garage 04 338 2744, *icon-auto.com*
Max Garage 04 340 8200, *maxdubai.com*
Octane > ***p.48*** 04 341 4511 *octane-me.com*
Stellar Auto Garage 04 262 9946
X Service Centre 04 339 5033, *houseofcarsgroup.com*

Deira by night

Housing

HOUSING

Apart from securing your new job, getting your accommodation satisfactorily sorted out is probably the most crucial factor in making your move to Dubai a success. The first thing to decide is what type of accommodation you want (and can afford), and in what part of town. This chapter provides a detailed look at the different residential areas in Dubai (p.84), focusing on the type of accommodation available, the amenities, and the pros and cons. There are sections on the procedures and practicalities involved in both the rental (p.70) and ownership (p.72) markets too. Once you've found somewhere to live, this chapter also tells you how to get settled in, covering everything from getting your TV and electricity connected to sprucing up the garden. Happy house hunting.

ACCOMMODATION OPTIONS

Hotel & Serviced Apartments

Hotel apartments are expensive, but ideal if you need temporary furnished accommodation. There's a large concentration in Bur Dubai, but more and more are cropping up around town, especially in Al Barsha. They can be rented on a daily, weekly, monthly or yearly basis. Water and electricity are also included in the rent.

Jumeirah Beach Residence

Al Bustan Centre & Residence Al Qusais 1, 04 263 0000, *al-bustan.com*
Al Deyafa Hotel Apartments Port Saeed, 04 295 5855, *aldeyafa.com*
Al Faris 3 Hotel Apartments Oud Metha, 04 336 6566, *alfarisdubai.com*
Al Mas Hotel Apartments Al Mankhool, 04 355 7899, *almashotelapts.com*
Arjaan By Rotana Dubai Media City Al Sufouh 1, 04 436 0000, *rotana.com*
Ascott Park Place Dubai > ***p.101*** Trade Centre 1, 04 310 8503, *the-ascott.com*
Bonnington Jumeirah Lakes Towers Jumeirah Lakes Towers, 04 356 0000, *bonningtontower.com*
Boutique 7 Hotel & Suites Tecom, 04 434 5555, *boutique7.ae*
BurJuman Arjaan By Rotana Khalid Bin Al Waleed Rd, Al Mankhool, 04 352 4444, *rotana.com*
Capitol Residence Hotel Apartments Al Rolla St, Khalid Bin Waleed Rd, Al Raffa, 04 393 2000, *capitoldubai.com*
Chelsea Tower Hotel Apartments Shk Zayed Rd, Trade Centre 1, 04 343 4347, *chelseatowerdubai.com*
City Centre Residence Deira City Centre, Port Saeed, 04 294 1333, *accorhotels.com*
Coral Al Khoory Hotel Apartments Al Barsha 1, 04 323 7777, *coral-international.com*
Desert Rose Hotel Apartments Al Mankhool, 04 352 4848, *hoteldesertrose.com*
Dusit Residence Dubai Marina Dubai Marina, 04 425 9999, *dusit.com*
Fraser Suites Dubai Al Sufouh 1, 04 440 1400, *frasershospitality.com*
Gloria Hotel Al Sufouh 1, 04 399 6666, *gloriahoteldubai.com*
Golden Sands Hotel Apartments 3 Al Mankhool, 04 355 5553, *goldensandsdubai.com*
Grand Hyatt Residence Umm Hurair 2, 04 317 1234, *dubai.grand.hyatt.com*
Grand Midwest Bur Dubai Hotel Apartments Al Mankhool, 04 351 1114, *grandmidwest.com*
Hilton Dubai Jumeirah Residences Dubai Marina, 04 399 1111, *hilton.com*
InterContinental Residence Suites Dubai Festival City Dubai Festival City, 04 701 3333, *residencesuites.intercontinental.com*
Jumeirah Living World Trade Centre Residence Trade Centre 2, 04 511 0000, *jumeirah.com*
Kempinski Hotel & Residences Palm Jumeirah Palm Jumeirah, 04 444 2000, *kempinski.com*
Khalidia Hotel Apartments Al Rigga, 04 228 2280, *khalidiahotel.ae*
Legacy Hotel Apartments Tecom, 04 430 9191, *legacyhotelsdubai.com*
Lotus Downtown Metro Hotel Apartments Al Rigga, 04 206 8888, *lotus-hospitality.com*

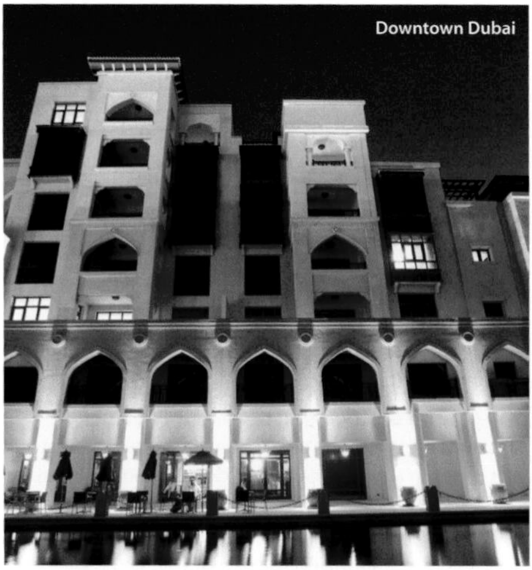

Lotus Marina & Spa Hotel Apartments Dubai Marina, 04 440 2888, *lotus-hospitality.com*
Marriott Executive Apartments Dubai Creek Al Rigga, 04 213 1000, *marriottdubaicreek.com*
Marriott Executive Apartments Dubai Green Community Green Community, 04 885 2222, *marriott.com*
Media Rotana > *p.461* Tecom, 04 435 0000, *rotana.com*
Movenpick Hotel & Apartments Bur Dubai Oud Metha, 04 336 6000, *moevenpick-hotels.com*
Nojoum Hotel Apartments Al Muraqqabat, 04 265 8888, *nojoumsuites.com*
Number One Tower Suites Trade Centre 1, 04 343 4666, *numberonetower.com*
Nuran Greens Serviced Residences The Greens, 04 422 3444, *nuran.com*
Nuran Marina Serviced Residences Dubai Marina, 04 367 4848, *nuran.com*
Oasis Beach Tower Dubai Marina, 04 8145 700, *jebelali-international.com*
The Radisson Blu Residence Dubai Marina Dubai Marina, 04 435 5000, *radissonblu.com*
Ramee Hotel Apartments Dubai Al Raffa, 04 352 2277, *rameehotels.com*
Rihab Rotana Port Saeed, 04 294 0300, *rotana.com*
Rose Rayhaan By Rotana Trade Centre 2, 04 323 0111, *rotana.com*
Savoy Central Hotel Apartments Al Mankhool, 04 393 8000, *savoydubai.com*
Savoy Crest Exclusive Hotel Apartments Al Mankhool, 04 355 4488, *savoydubai.com*
Splendid Hotel Apartments Oud Metha, 04 336 0004
TIME Crystal Hotel Apartments Tecom, 04 420 2555, *timehotels.ae*
Villa Rotana Al Wasl, 04 321 6111, *rotana.com*
Wafi Residence Wafi, Umm Hurair 2, 04 324 7222, *wafi.com*
Yassat Hotel Apartments Shk Zayed Rd, Tecom, 04 381 8888, *yassatgloria.com*

Owning A Property

Since 2002, foreigners have been allowed to purchase property in certain areas of Dubai. Property prices soared for six years until the end of 2008, when everything came crashing down and mortgages from banks dried up. Prices have now levelled out a bit, and buying a house is once again becoming a viable option for people planning on staying in Dubai for the long term. It's not a decision to be taken lightly though, and it pays to really do your research. For more information on the procedures and pitfalls involved in buying a property, see p.72.

Standard Apartments

Dubai apartments come in various sizes, from studio to four-bedroom, with widely varying rents to match. Newer apartments usually have central air conditioning (C A/C) and older ones have noisier air conditioner units built into the wall. C A/C is usually more expensive, although in some apartment buildings your air-conditioning costs are built into the rent. Many of the newest developments utilise district cooling, a system in which all of the buildings within an area receive cold water from a central cooling plant. Residents living in apartments with district cooling will need to sign an agreement with the local cooling company and pay that company monthly.

Solar Heaters A Must-Have

Although the UAE still has a long way to go to reduce its ecological footprint, it's refreshing to see that measures are being taken. Since 2012, any developer submitting plans for a new build has to integrate solar water heaters that provide for at least 75% of the building's hot water needs and 50% of any swimming pool heating, or Dubai Municipality will refuse to grant a building licence.

Top of the range apartments often come semi-furnished (with a cooker, fridge, dishwasher and washing machine), and have 24-hour security, covered parking, private gym and swimming pool.

One downside to apartment living is that you're at the mercy of your neighbours to some extent, especially those upstairs. Depending on the area, parking may be a problem too – check to see if you get a dedicated space with your apartment.

Villa Sharing

Sharing a large villa is a popular option with young professionals for economic and lifestyle reasons.

The downside is the lack of privacy and the chore of finding new housemates when someone moves out. If you're looking to share, the property classifieds in Gulf News or dubizzle.com are good places to start. See opposite for information on the legality of sharing.

Villas

The villa lifestyle doesn't come cheap, and smart villas are snapped up pretty quickly. The good news is that if you look hard enough and use the grapevine, you might find the perfect villa that won't break the budget. Depending on the location, size and age of the property it may be cheaper than some apartments, even if air-conditioning costs will be higher.

Villas differ greatly in quality and facilities. Independent ones often have bigger gardens, while compound villas are usually newer and most have shared facilities like a pool or gym.

RENTING A HOME

New residents arriving in Dubai to start a new job may be given accommodation or a housing allowance as part of their package. The allowance is often not enough to rent a place in an ideal area, so many expats choose to cover the costs out of their own pockets. If your contract provides specific accommodation but you would prefer the cash equivalent, it is worth asking as most employers are willing to be flexible.

Thanks to the economic crisis, rents in Dubai fell up to 45% in 2009, and there was a further drop in some areas in 2010. Prices have started to rise again but, unlike in recent years, renters still have the upper hand in lease negotiations. The RERA rental index (see p.72) has also brought in some regulation to a previously spiralling rental market.

Finding A Rental Home

There are a number of ways to find suitable accommodation, the most obvious of which is via a real estate agent (see p.72). Agents will be able to show you several properties, but if that agent also represents the landlord, they might not have your best interests in mind. If you have the time, it is worth checking classified ads in Gulf News and online at propertyfinder.ae and dubizzle.com, although the latter is better for shared accommodation.

Most of the listings in Dubai's classifieds are done by real estate agents. An even better bet is to drive around a few areas and look out for 'To Let' signs displayed on vacant villas; these will display the phone number of either the landlord or the letting agent.

If you find a particularly attractive apartment building, try asking the security guard on duty if there are any vacant properties. Often this extra effort when looking for a home can result in a 'real find' and many proud barbecues to come. It also helps to ask colleagues and friends to keep an eye out for vacancies in shared villas.

Sharing

There is some confusion as to the legality of villa or apartment sharing in Dubai. The topic reached its pinnacle in 2008 and 2009 when tenants of several shared villas were handed eviction notices. In some cases, the electricity and water to those villas was cut off in order to force the tenants out. Things calmed down in 2010 and the Dubai Municipality clarified its stance. According to them, the main issue was overcrowding and defiance of health codes. It is now generally understood that unrelated singles of the same sex are allowed to share a villa as long as that villa is not in a neighbourhood designated for families and is not overcrowded. Sharing villas should still be approached with caution as the rules could change at any time. Areas designated as family-only include, but are not limited to, Al Barsha and Jumeira. As a rule, villa sharing among singles is looked down upon in areas with a high concentration of local families.

The Lease

Your lease is an important document and, in addition to the financial terms, states what you are liable for in terms of maintenance as well as what your landlord's responsibilities are. Therefore, it is important that you read the contract and discuss any points of contention before you sign on the dotted line. Now that rents are dropping, negotiating power is in the hands of the tenant. Since rents are expected to keep dropping, avoid signing a multiple-year lease. This will allow you to renegotiate once the lease is up for renewal. The following points are often open to negotiation:

- Tenants usually pay rent via a number of post-dated cheques. One or two cheques are the standard, and you can use this as a bargaining chip to lower the rent.
- Make sure you agree who is responsible for maintenance. Some rents might be fully inclusive of all maintenance and repairs, while you could negotiate a much cheaper rent (particularly on older properties) if you agree to carry out any maintenance work.
- While not common, some landlords will include utility expenses in the rent.
- The security deposit can sometimes be negotiated, but Dhs.5,000 to Dhs.10,000 is standard.
- The landlord must give written notice of any rent increase at least one month in advance. If your landlord does try to increase the rent unfairly then you can raise a dispute through the government's Rent Committee (see below).

It is important to have the official lease registered with the Rent Committee (rpdubai.ae). This procedure

should be taken care of by the real estate agent. You also need to reregister your lease when you renew your contract, as your Municipality Housing Tax (also known as the 'Housing Fee' – see below) will be recalculated based on the rent. The Land Department will only work to resolve rent disputes in which the original lease was registered at the time of signing. Keep in mind that for a lease to be registered, the landowner must have an official title deed for the property. Not all properties in Dubai have title deeds.

Other Rental Costs

Extra costs to be considered when renting a home are:

- Water and electricity deposit (Dhs.2,000 for villas, Dhs.1,000 for apartments) paid directly to Dubai Electricity & Water Authority (DEWA) and fully refundable on cancellation of the lease.
- If your accommodation is in an area that uses district cooling, you will need to pay a deposit to the cooling company (usually Palm District Cooling, palmutilities.com). The deposit amount varies depending on the size and location of the property.
- Real estate commission is around 5% of annual rent and is a one-off payment.
- Maintenance charges vary, but could be around 5% of annual rent, and are sometimes included.
- A housing fee of 5% of your yearly rent is charged through your DEWA bill, spread across 12 months.
- If you're renting a villa, don't forget that you may have to maintain a garden and pay for extra water. It's worth asking the landlord what the average DEWA bills are for a particular property.

RERA & The Rent Committee

In an effort to better regulate Dubai's rental market, the Real Estate Regulatory Agency (RERA) set up the Rent Committee in 2011 to release a quarterly rental index that lists the top and bottom of the average market value of a rental property based on size and location. The index was introduced to control the huge rental increases that had been taking place in the previous years, and put a cap on them. The index also serves as a useful guideline for the sort of price you should be paying in a particular area – look for the latest releases on local media websites. The RERA website, rpdubai.ae, features a rental increase calculator to help determine whether your landlord is eligible to put your rent up at renewal time, based on the area you are in, your property size, and your current rent. Ironically, shortly after the RERA rental index was brought in, the global recession hit hard and rental prices dropped naturally. This, combined with the many new apartments and villas that are still being released, has meant that recently tenants have had few problems with increasing rents – and in fact many rental contracts have had prices reduced at renewal time, or at least frozen. Any tenants (or landlords) that have disputes with a rent increase, or evictions, can take their case to the Dubai Municipality Rent Committee (04 221 5555), and in many cases it finds in favour of the tenant.

Ejari Does It

Ejari – meaning 'my rent' in Arabic - is RERA's online portal (ejari.ae) where tenants can find information on registering their tenancy contract and the downloadable forms to do so. The process is fairly simple and painless and means that, in the event of any dispute, RERA can be called on to mediate. In the vast majority of disputes, this helps the tenant and protects them from greedy or misbehaving landlords.

Real Estate Agents

Al Futtaim Group Real Estate 04 213 6222, *afrealestate.com*
Arenco Real Estate 04 440 1144, *arencore.com*
Asteco Property Management 04 403 7700, *astecoproperty.com*
Better Homes 600 52 2212, *bhomes.com*
Cluttons 04 334 8585, *cluttons.com*
Dubai Properties Group 04 435 2117, *dubai-properties.ae*
Dubai Property Group 04 211 5266, *dubaipropertygroup.com*
ERE Homes 04 455 0800, *ere-homes.com*
Exclusive Links Real Estate Brokers 04 422 5750, *exclusive-links.com*
Flash Properties > ***p.73*** 04 376 0880, *flash-properties.com*
Hamptons International 800 4267 8667, *hamptons.ae*
Landmark Properties 04 350 2888, *landmark-dubai.com*
Power House Properties 04 347 6853, *powerhousedubai.com*
The Property Shop 04 345 5711, *propertyshopdubai.com*
Propertyfinder > ***p.71*** 04 454 8464, *propertyfinder.ae*
Sherwoods Independent Property Consultants 04 343 8002, *sherwoodsproperty.com*
The Specialists 04 329 5959, *resdubai.com*

BUYING A HOME

The UAE property buying process is unlike that of any other established market. Dramatic price inflations in 2007 and 2008 were followed by equally dramatic falls in 2009, and further, if smaller, drops in 2010. New regulations have frequently been introduced over the years. That said, RERA has done an excellent job in standardising and formalising the regulations and

DOWNTOWN
OLD TOWN
PALM JUMEIRAH
DUBAI MARINA
JUMEIRAH LAKE TOWERS
JUMEIRAH ISLAND
ACACIA AVENUES
JUMEIRAH BEACH RESIDENCES
DISCOVERY GARDENS
JUMEIRAH VILLAGE TRIANGLE
THE MEADOWS
BUSINESS BAY
THE GREENS
THE SPRINGS
SPORTS CITY
MOTOR CITY
INTERNATIONAL CITY

procedures, as well as making them as transparent as possible. Buying or selling a property here is still a complex affair, but navigating the minefield is made easier by having a clear idea of the costs, procedures, laws and expectations of all involved.

Despite the recent instability, if you choose your property carefully there is still the potential to make a sound investment, for either rental income or to live in, but it pays to be cautious. However, unless you are planning a long-term use of your property as your main home, you may need to think twice about snapping up a 'bargain', which could be difficult to sell on due to market saturation.

It is important to select your 'property partners' wisely (from agents to developers) in order to ensure that the process will run a little smoother. One key thing to note is that non-UAE nationals can only buy in areas designated specifically for expatriate freehold and leasehold sales. In some areas of Dubai, only Emiratis or other GCC nationals can purchase property, most notably Jumeira, Umm Suqeim, Al Barsha and most parts of 'old Dubai'. See the Where To Buy box, p.80, for areas where expats can purchase.

Most property in Dubai available for purchase by non-nationals is freehold, although there are some properties available on 99-year leases.

If you buy leasehold, you need to be aware that your lease will stipulate who is responsible for maintaining and repairing different parts of the property and any conditions you must meet as a resident. You must also pay a ground rent to the owner of the land (the freeholder), which is usually a small annual fee. It is important to check that the seller is up to date with ground rent payments before you take over the contract.

Within the residential apartments market, notably in areas such as Dubai Marina, Jumeirah Lakes Towers and Business Bay, there are numerous buildings constructed by sub-developers. Generally the developers are reputable; however the level of finish and facilities management capability will vary. By buying from one of the larger known developers, you are also buying the peace of mind that comes with purchasing from a reputed organisation. Since the slow-down, the off-plan property market has slowed almost to a halt. Buyers and investors are understandably far more cautious, and the preference has shifted to buying finished property. However, just because a property is finished doesn't mean moving in is immediate. Handovers are notoriously delayed and protracted, and can be costly due to extended rents or mortgage payments on properties that cannot yet be moved into.

Residential Developments

If you are buying off-plan or are the first owners of a new property, you will undoubtedly have to purchase directly from a developer. As the market matures, more properties are being sold on a secondary basis, but although you will buy from the owner via an agent, as a freeholder you are still subject to the maintenance fees, rules and regulations of the master developer.

Check Before You Buy

When buying or selling a property, always check that the real estate agent is registered with RERA, which is there to safeguard and protect your rights. Registered agents such as Flash Properties (flash-properties.com) are one-stop shops for real estate buyers, investors and sellers, and can offer accurate and up-to-date information, in-depth analysis and reliable real estate consultancy services to help you make your purchase.

There was a lot of controversy surrounding the major players in real estate development in the last couple of years, with big redundancies and rumours of financial difficulties and mergers. What will happen moving forward is anyone's guess, but what can be expected is a higher level of accountability and more major shake-ups. It pays to do your research and keep an eye on news stories concerning developers you are considering buying from. Some of the major players include the following:

Nakheel

Built, sold and is responsible for maintaining several large developments, including: Palm Jumeirah, Jumeirah Islands, International City, Discovery Gardens, Jumeirah Village, Palm Jebel Ali, Palm Deira, The World and Al Furjan Community.

Emaar

Emaar's flagship property is Burj Khalifa; its portfolio of freehold real estate projects includes: Dubai Marina, Arabian Ranches, Emirates Living (The Views, The Meadows, The Springs, The Lakes, The Greens), Emaar Towers and Downtown Dubai (Burj Khalifa, Burj Residence, Burj Views, Old Town, South Ridge).

Dubai Properties

Its flagship freehold properties are Jumeirah Beach Residence (p.88) and Business Bay. It also has a big residential development called The Villa and is the master developer behind the Dubailand project.

Union Properties

The Green Community, Uptown Mirdif and MotorCity.

Damac

Develops apartment buildings and commercial office towers, including Ocean Heights, Marina Terrace and The Waves in Dubai Marina, Palm Islands, and Lake View and Lake Terrace in Jumeirah Lakes Towers.

Dubai's Property Market

The Palm Jumeirah

Between mid 2006 and the second half of 2008, the price and scope of property developments in Dubai appeared limitless. Then the taps of freely obtainable credit were turned off globally, and the crazy, unsustainable bubble that was the local housing market burst in spectacular fashion, causing a steep price correction of an over-inflated market – good news for renters and potential purchasers, bad news for those who had already invested.

The boom was largely driven by speculators. The process of 'flipping' was so widespread it became a phenomenon. Investors would buy up individual off-plan properties, whole floors, or even the building, and immediately sell on at a profit to a new buyer before the next payment was due to the developers.

In the first quarter of 2008, it was impossible to find a villa in Dubai to buy for less than $1 million – and even then, this would only have got you a regular-sized place in a new Dubai development, usually without landscaping. Completed properties were scarce and snapped up at once by potential landlords keen to cash in on exorbitant rental rates.

The returns were good, but for many the ultimate price was high. In the second half of 2008, credit dried up affecting not only new purchases but also the ability of investors to pay subsequent instalments on off-plan properties. The industry spiralled into a panic, and property sales all but stopped. Investor confidence was non-existent, and access to funds for any potential purchasers was just as scarce. Distress sales took place with desirable homes being sold on for 50% or less of their value at the height of the bubble. By the time buyers began to dip their toes back into the market in 2009, average prices were down 30% to 40% from the 2008 peak.

In 2010, life began to slowly creep back into the property market, albeit in a tentative fashion. Some lenders began to loosen up a little on mortgages, and the crashing prices seemed to approach levelling out status, or at least where they still fell the drop was more marginal.

Dubai's property market is maturing and showing signs of polarisation, with differing prospects for property based on location, quality and management. CBRE Middle East forecasts that sales in Dubai's residential real estate sector will continue their upward trend in 2013, albeit at a slower pace than in 2012. Caution remains the watchword. Some things will remain in Dubai's favour as a place to buy: its central location, its popularity with expats, its global hub position and its tax-free status will always be appealing to property buyers. Proximity to metro stations is a new factor that has quickly begun to affect popularity and prices, as the metro transport link has established itself as a substantial variable. There are low-priced properties to be picked up in less desirable communities (studio flats of approximately 500 sq ft for around Dhs.175,000, for example) but buyers must consider their rental yield and ultimate sell-on potential.

Dubai's real estate sector will continue to experience an upturn in 2013, with the recovery extending to a wider cross-section of the property market.

Studio and one bedroom apartments start at anything from Dhs.750,000 in recently built properties in areas such as MotorCity or Jumeirah Lakes Towers, rising to Dhs.2 million and beyond for larger units in parts of Downtown and Jumeirah Beach Residence, The Palm Jumeirah, or serviced apartments within hotels. Apartment living is where prices vary massively, depending on location, developer and quality of finish.

Villa prices are affected by location, size and any cosmetic upgrades or features such as swimming pool, garden etc. Master planned communities by the major developers consist of hundreds of villas of the same style floor plan, with a few variations. If you decide on a particular area to live, regardless of an advertised price, you get a good feel for the average offer as there is guaranteed to be more than one of its kind available.

Villas on the flagship Palm Jumeirah that cost Dhs.14 million at the beginning of 2008 are now valued at Dhs.7.5 million upwards; their larger signature villa cousins advertise from Dhs.16 million as opposed to a previous Dhs.21 million. Other popular, established villa-only communities are Emirates Living, Arabian Ranches, Green Community and Victory Heights. In these places, two-bedroom houses can range from Dhs.1.6 million up to over Dhs.3 million, with three bedroom or larger villas starting at Dhs.2.2 million for a 2,000 sq ft villa and going up to more than Dhs.20 million for a 16,000 sq ft polo home.

What happens next in Dubai's property market remains to be seen, but figures from the Dubai Land Department show that Dubai property transactions grew 21% to Dhs.63 billion in the first half of 2012, compared to the third and fourth quarters of 2011. And, according to Cluttons, Dubai prices will remain relatively stable over the next six to 12 months as the completion of new residential units will increase supply and make huge price uplifts or a 'boom' scenario unlikely.

Jumeirah Beach Residence

Sama Dubai
Has retail, commercial and residential projects in the Lagoons and Dubai Towers.

One Site Fits All
Finding and contacting each developer or agent separately can be quite time-consuming, and there is an increasing number of sites popping up that combine listings from numerous agents and developers. Propertyfinder.ae, for example, has listings for thousands of commercial and residential properties from more than 3,000 brokers for sale or rent across the UAE along with buyers' guides, advice and real estate news. Its Market Price Live tool is particularly useful, letting you know exactly what you should be paying for a certain property in a given area. A good place to start your search.

Legal Issues
By law, there might be no requirement to have a solicitor act for you when buying property in Dubai, but having one provides extra peace of mind. Inheritance issues are something you must consider before buying Dubai apartments or villas too; succession is based on a number of factors, such as whether the owner is a non-Muslim and whether a will exists (see p.132).

House Hunting
Real estate agencies in Dubai are numerous. The choice may have lessened in the course of the downturn, but this is definitely a positive. All agents in Dubai now have to be registered and 'trained' via RERA (Real Estate Regulatory Authority), which, along with the Dubai Land Department, formulates, regulates, manages and licenses various real estate-related activities in Dubai.

Despite a choice of big-name agencies available, the experience you'll have usually depends on the individual agent you end up dealing with. While new laws have made processes more transparent and regulated, and levels of professionalism and service within the real estate industry have largely improved from a couple of years ago, not everything is up to perfect standards just yet. Be sure to only use a registered broker, and ask to check their Broker ID card.

An excellent government website that collates all relevant laws, fees and information related to property purchases is rpdubai.ae (Dubai Land Department).

In the UAE, the purchaser must pay a fee to the agency that finds and secures their desired property; estate agents and brokers in Dubai are not entitled to a commission or fee for service until the sale is settled and completed. The fee is usually around 2% of the purchase price of the property. To get an idea of the players on the estate agent market, see Real Estate Agents, p.72. It's worth checking the freehold section of Gulf News, as well as dubizzle.com and propertyfinder.ae. The online version of Gulf News classifieds (gnads4u.com) is also updated daily.

Going It Alone
You can, of course, always cut out the middle man and attempt to buy a property privately. Private sales are not very common in Dubai unless it is an arrangement between friends or business associates. It is very rare to see properties advertised in Dubai as private sales. When they do crop up, they are usually advertised via noticeboards in community centres or supermarkets locally, listed as classified adverts in Gulf News, or featured online at dubizzle.com or gnads4u.com.

Maintenance Fees
Maintenance fees payable by the owner encompass the costs to the developer of maintaining all the facilities and communal areas. Fees are typically paid annually, although some developers, such as Emaar, are now accepting quarterly payments.

Potential purchasers should also factor in the maintenance fees when deciding where to buy. Not only do fees vary from developer to developer but also from one development to the next. These fees are rarely mentioned in any of the developers' contracts, and if they are, the fine print will nearly always read 'subject to change.'

If you live in an apartment, communal facilities may include a gym, changing areas, and a swimming pool. Full time security and cleaning personnel will also be employed to service communal areas. In a villa, communal responsibility will extend to more security personnel manning the way to gated communities and all communal landscaping. Both will include rubbish collection, and villa communities may also enjoy pools and tennis court areas.

Strata Committees
Brought in at the beginning of 2008, Dubai Strata law requires the proper division of property according to the Strata plan. This, along with a drawing which marks out the boundaries of lots, entitlement of these lots and other required documents, should be registered with the registrar.

Strata law is designed to settle disputes over issues like parking, keeping pets that disturb other owners, privacy, and alteration or maintenance of common areas. It relates to the management of common property and shared facilities such as parking, fire services, air conditioning, lifts, pools, gyms, walkways, roadways and gardens. Under the law, an association of owners should be established as a regulatory framework to maintain the quality of shared facilities.

The law, which clearly defines the relationship between developers and owners, should help remove ambiguities about who is responsible for common property management, and aims to reduce scepticism among investors. Though Strata law cannot stop these disputes altogether, it can help in solving them before the quarrels escalate.

Mortgages

The UAE mortgage industry is still in its relative infancy compared to other countries. Dubai is home to many of the world's international finance houses, as well as local banks and lenders, but although familiar names such as HSBC, Barclays, Standard Chartered and Citibank sit alongside local entities, sophisticated borrowing structures are difficult to secure and can take significantly longer to complete than in other parts of the world.

The financial crisis that began in late 2008 also saw a lot of banks in the region suspend or severely curtail their mortgage lending activities. By 2010, most banks had begun to lend again, and there is certainly finance for property available now, but on a much more cautious basis than in the gung-ho pre-recession days.

The mortgage process is slightly more convoluted in Dubai. Banks and lenders will only provide mortgages – or home loans as they are more commonly referred to in the UAE – on a select number of developments, which vary from institution to institution. Additionally, each bank and lender has different acceptance criteria and mortgage processes, which change frequently.

Shariah Compliant

Shariah compliant or Islamic mortgages are an alternative financing option which are available to non-Muslims. The term 'home finance' is used as opposed to mortgages. Complying with Islamic beliefs, the bank purchases the asset on behalf of the buyer who then effectively leases it back from the institution. The bank owns the title deeds of the purchased property until the full amount is paid.

Interest rates can vary massively from a competitive 3.99% to 9%, and many lenders will insist on life insurance on the loan amount. This is often a stumbling block if overlooked and not addressed before the transfer date. In addition, many lenders will only finance up to 85% of the property price (100% finance mortgages do not currently exist in the UAE and are unlikely to appear anytime soon). The amount financed by the lender also varies and depends on whether the property is a villa or an apartment and where it is and who built it. The best option is to check with the major lenders, either directly or through an advisor or broker, what individual current mortgage requirements and offers are.

Equity release and mortgage transfers have recently been introduced to the market, offering investors the opportunity to release equity and secure better rates. To combat price sensitive customers moving their loans, most banks have introduced exit fees but there are still completely flexible mortgages available. New innovations also include international mortgages, which offer loans in currency denominations other than dirhams. This offers clients the ability to structure their loan in a preferred currency, with the ability to switch.

Lend Some Advice

A mortgage consultancy or broker will conduct all the legwork for you. Upon assessing your circumstances, choice of property and financial eligibility, they will gain pre-approval on your behalf and cut out the middleman of the banks and all the running around that goes with it, holding your hand until the keys are handed over. The fee will either be a percentage of the purchase price (approximately 0.5%) or a set price.

Mortgage Application

It is possible for prospective buyers to seek a mortgage pre-approval before beginning their property search, which can give the buyer confidence when entering the market. For a mortgage application you will need the original and copies of your passport, six months of bank statements, salary confirmation from your employer and six months of salary slips.

A mortgage 'approval in principle' should only take up to four working days to come through upon submitting the correct paperwork. Generally, employed applicants can borrow a higher percentage of income than self employed. Most lenders will offer mortgages of up to 50% of disposable monthly income, based on the applicant's debt burden ratio – your realistic ability to service the monthly payments from your income, minus your other financial commitments. The larger the deposit placed, the better your terms are likely to be. Mortgage terms are usually for 25 years. Age restrictions are in place and vary, but lenders will normally finance individuals up to 65 years of age.

The next step is for the lender to provide an unconditional approval on the basis that any conditions noted in the pre-approval are satisfied. This enables you to be sure that no more requirements are to be fulfilled in order for you to get your mortgage. The lender will then issue a letter of offer followed by the mortgage documentation. This will provide the terms of the mortgage and, once signed and sent back to the lender, the settlement process is started.

The process is settled when the lender has transferred the mortgage payment to either the seller or to the existing lender who has the first charge over the property. This will usually occur on the day of transfer or as per the conditions of the lender.

Other Purchase Costs

On top of the purchase cost and deposit required, charges incurred by the property purchaser securing a home with a mortgage are as follows:

- Real estate agent/broker fee: 2% of purchase price.
- Mortgage arranged via bank or lender: 1% to 1.25% mortgage processing fee based on value of loan.

Valuation

Your mortgage lender will arrange a valuation of your chosen property via an independent source. This is to determine the market worth against the selling price and the lender's loan to you. The cost to the buyer is Dhs.2,500 to Dhs.3,000. Additional obligatory costs to the mortgaged property buyer equate to approximately an extra 6% on top of the purchase price, not including any cash deposit required.

Where To Buy

The areas where expats can currently purchase property are: Discovery Gardens, Dubai Investments Park, Dubai Marina, Jumeirah Beach Residence, Jumeirah Lakes Towers, Emirates Living, The Meadows, The Springs, The Lakes, The Greens, Palm Jumeirah, Arabian Ranches, Falcon City, The Villa, Al Barari, Dubai Sports City, MotorCity, Green Community, Downtown, Old Town, Business Bay, International City, IMPZ, Jumeirah Village and Jumeirah Islands.

Optional Costs

It is not required to secure the use of a lawyer for property transactions in the UAE, but you may wish to employ legal help to see you through the process. Costs vary depending on whose services you use. If employing the services of a mortgage consultancy or broker, the typical cost is 0.5% of the property price.

Land Registry

The government of Dubai Land Department is the emirate's registry and land transactions agency. The department requires that all new real estate transactions are registered with them, and establishes legal ownership of the land or property, thus safeguarding the owner from future dispute, and provides the owner with the title deeds to their property or land. Fees levied by the Dubai Land Department are dependent on whether the property purchase is covered by a conventional mortgage, an Islamic (Shariah compliant) mortgage or a cash purchase. All fees are payable by the buyer.

Selling A Home

Contrary to many international press reports, property transactions in Dubai are steady and can be viewed at their actual selling value via rera.ae.

When selling, your first and most important task is to find yourself a preferred agent. Remember that private property sales are very rare so finding the right agent is key. Some real estate agencies charge 'marketing' fees of between 1-2% of the sale price. This is essentially to cover the costs of print and online advertising, open days and brochures. There is no legal need in Dubai for a property survey, assessment or solicitor, so all of these fees are negated.

Real Estate Law

The Real Estate Regulatory Authority (RERA) is a subsidiary agency under the Dubai Land Department. It is a government organisation that, aside from setting the rental index, regulates the real estate market and aims to maintain healthy property investment in Dubai.

The agency's responsibilities include the following: licensing all real estate activities; regulating and registering rental agreements, owners' associations, and real estate advertisements in the media; regulating and licensing real estate exhibitions; and publishing official research and studies for the sector.

RERA has imposed regulations on contractors, developers and agencies involved within Dubai's real estate industry in a bid to safeguard the investor and regulate any disputes that may occur. This is particularly important for those buyers investing in properties yet to be completed or 'handed over'.

Any potential property dispute can be taken to RERA; there are comprehensive rules on issues such as payments, escrow accounts and more. To find out more about RERA, visit rpdubai.ae or call 04 222 1112.

Dubai Marina

Residential Areas Map

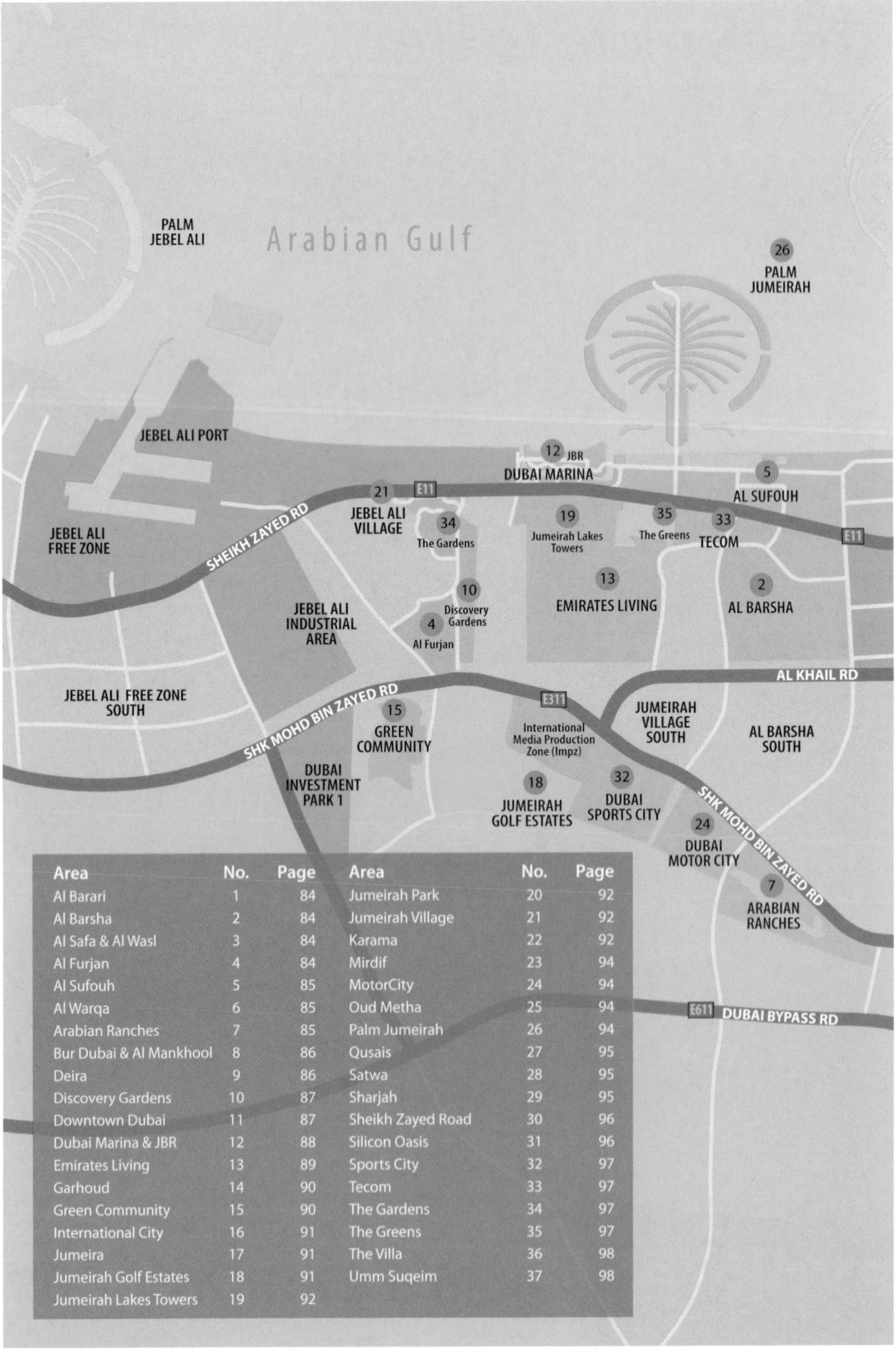

Area	No.	Page	Area	No.	Page
Al Barari	1	84	Jumeirah Park	20	92
Al Barsha	2	84	Jumeirah Village	21	92
Al Safa & Al Wasl	3	84	Karama	22	92
Al Furjan	4	84	Mirdif	23	94
Al Sufouh	5	85	MotorCity	24	94
Al Warqa	6	85	Oud Metha	25	94
Arabian Ranches	7	85	Palm Jumeirah	26	94
Bur Dubai & Al Mankhool	8	86	Qusais	27	95
Deira	9	86	Satwa	28	95
Discovery Gardens	10	87	Sharjah	29	95
Downtown Dubai	11	87	Sheikh Zayed Road	30	96
Dubai Marina & JBR	12	88	Silicon Oasis	31	96
Emirates Living	13	89	Sports City	32	97
Garhoud	14	90	Tecom	33	97
Green Community	15	90	The Gardens	34	97
International City	16	91	The Greens	35	97
Jumeira	17	91	The Villa	36	98
Jumeirah Golf Estates	18	91	Umm Suqeim	37	98
Jumeirah Lakes Towers	19	92			

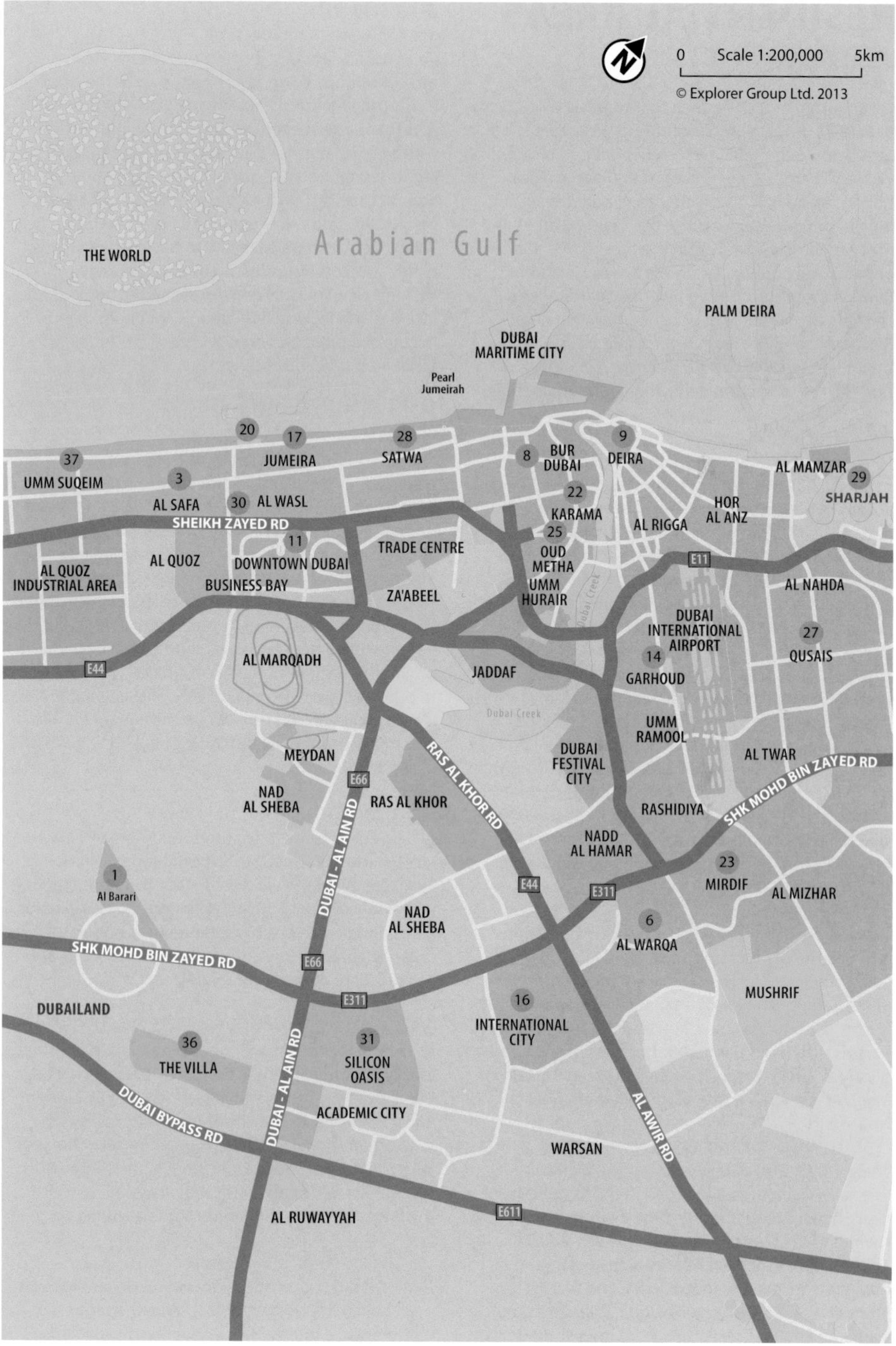

0 Scale 1:200,000 5km
© Explorer Group Ltd. 2013
Arabian Gulf
THE WORLD
PALM DEIRA
DUBAI MARITIME CITY
Pearl Jumeirah
20
17
28
9
37
UMM SUQEIM
3
JUMEIRA
SATWA
8
BUR DUBAI
DEIRA
AL MAMZAR
29
SHARJAH
AL SAFA
30
AL WASL
22
KARAMA
HOR AL ANZ
SHEIKH ZAYED RD
25
AL RIGGA
11
OUD METHA
E11
AL QUOZ INDUSTRIAL AREA
AL QUOZ
DOWNTOWN DUBAI
TRADE CENTRE
UMM HURAIR
AL NAHDA
BUSINESS BAY
ZA'ABEEL
Dubai Creek
DUBAI INTERNATIONAL AIRPORT
27
QUSAIS
E44
AL MARQADH
14
GARHOUD
JADDAF
Dubai Creek
UMM RAMOOL
MEYDAN
DUBAI FESTIVAL CITY
AL TWAR
SHK MOHD BIN ZAYED RD
E66
RAS AL KHOR RD
NAD AL SHEBA
RAS AL KHOR
RASHIDIYA
DUBAI - AL AIN RD
NADD AL HAMAR
23
1
Al Barari
E44
E311
MIRDIF
AL MIZHAR
NAD AL SHEBA
6
AL WARQA
SHK MOHD BIN ZAYED RD
E66
DUBAILAND
E311
16
MUSHRIF
INTERNATIONAL CITY
36
31
THE VILLA
SILICON OASIS
DUBAI - AL AIN RD
AL AWIR RD
DUBAI BYPASS RD
ACADEMIC CITY
WARSAN
E611
AL RUWAYYAH

RESIDENTIAL AREAS

Al Barari

Map **2 A13**

Lakes, lush plantations and gigantic villas – welcome to Dubai's utopian neighbourhood situated just off Sheikh Mohammed Bin Zayed Road (Emirates Rd). This exclusive community features magnificent private homes set in their own landscaped paradise with infinity pools, water features, entertaining areas and roof-top terraces. Set within the prestigious Nad al Sheba district, this collection of five to seven-bedroom family villas is surrounded by public gardens and there's a strong sense of eco-friendly living here. Residents have The Farm restaurant (see p.506) on their doorstep, with future plans for a health club, nursery, spa, and ultimately, a luxury boutique hotel.

Al Barsha

Map **1 Q6** Metro **Mall of the Emirates**

Al Barsha has two distinct zones, each with its own accommodation options. The main area offers large villas with big gardens and is popular with local families. Some of the older apartment blocks offer competitively priced options, while the new apartment blocks, closer to Mall of the Emirates, are popular with Media and Internet City workers.

Accommodation

Accommodation is mainly in the form of fairly new, three to five-bedroom villas. Around 75% of the houses are locally owned and inhabited. Rental prices for villas start at Dhs.130,000 for a three bedroom and go up to Dhs.300,000 for larger options. Apartments in Al Barsha 1, near the mall, rent from Dhs.44,000 a year for a one-bedroom and Dhs.75,000 for a two-bedroom, but they do get snapped up quickly.

Shopping & Leisure

The area's proximity to Mall of the Emirates means it has plenty of accessible amenities, including a Carrefour and LuLu Hypermarket, a cinema, and plenty of restaurants. The Kempinski and Pullman hotels at Mall of the Emirates have licensed restaurants and bars, as do a handful of other business hotels nearby, plus Al Barsha is just across Sheikh Zayed Road from Madinat Jumeirah and a short drive from the Marina.

Healthcare & Education

There is a GP and paediatrician at the Medical Specialist Centre (04 340 9495), in the Khoury Building near Sheikh Zayed Road, but the nearest emergency room is in the Medcare Hospital (p.184) in Al Safa.

The Dubai American Academy (p.160) and Al Mawakeb are located in Al Barsha, and Wellington International School (p.163), Dubai College (p.160) and Jumeirah English Speaking School (p.164) are nearby.

Al Furjan

Map **1 H8** Metro **Ibn Battuta**

Very much a family-style development, Al Furjan has community living at its heart. Located south of Ibn Battuta Mall and adjacent to Discovery Gardens and The Gardens, there are four communities, each with a choice of three, four and six-bedroom villas and three-bedroom terraced homes. Rents start at around Dhs.140,000 for a three-bedroom villa. Each neighbourhood will eventually have an Al Furjan Village Centre that's designed to have supermarkets, coffee shops, restaurants, open spaces and gym facilities all within walking distance from home. Future facilities also include two schools and more than 50 hectares of parks and outdoor spaces, including sports facilities, pools, and cycling trails.

Al Safa & Al Wasl

Map **2 C6** Metro **Business Bay**

These residential areas are separated from the beachside districts of Jumeira and Umm Suqeim by Al Wasl Road. Everything between Safa Park and Satwa is officially known as Al Wasl, while Al Safa 1 and 2 lie between Safa Park at the north and Al Manara Street, which comes off Interchange 3. The area is safe, well lit and popular with families. Traffic within the communities is rarely a problem, but Al Wasl Road tends to get congested during rush hours. Its proximity to Sheikh Zayed Road makes it easy to get to other places in the city quickly. The area's openness is great for evening strolls when the weather is nice, and the low traffic means kids can ride their bikes and play outside safely.

Accommodation

Al Safa consists mostly of three-bedroom villas with rents starting at Dhs.150,000, but bigger villas are available. All of the villas are locally owned, so renting is the only option. Both independent villas and older compounds with established greenery populate the areas. There are a few older bungalows to be found, but most are home to local families.

Shopping & Leisure

Its central location means shopping is a breeze. The Mazaya Centre, Spinneys Centre (with supermarket, bank, clothing stores and Starbucks), two Choithrams and a Park n Shop are all within 10 minutes by car. Wasl Square, next to Safa Park, is a new retail hotspot with a variety of shops and eateries, and there are restaurants and cafes lining Jumeira Road, as well as the licensed venues at nearby Madinat Jumeirah.

Healthcare & Education

Al Wasl Road and nearby Jumeira Road (Beach Road) have plenty of private medical centres, specialist doctors and dentists. The private Medcare Hospital (p.184) near Safa Park has an emergency room, and the excellent value Iranian Hospital (p.184) is just down Al Wasl Road towards Satwa.

This area has several schools including Jumeirah English Speaking School (p.164), Horizon School (p.164), The English College (p.162), Jumeirah College and GEMS Jumeirah Primary School (p.163), as well as an assortment of nurseries that includes Jumeirah International Nursery School (p.156) and Blossom Village (p.152). The proximity to Sheikh Zayed Road makes GEMS Wellington International School (p.163) a popular choice, and the highway provides easy access to other schools too.

Up & Coming Areas

When buildings in brand new developments are completed, shops and services, and sometimes even the gym and swimming pool within the building, tend to follow a few steps behind. But, while you may have to travel further for essential amenities, such as shops, chemists, schools and clinics, and you may find your balcony regularly inch-deep in construction dust, you may just snap up a bargain price, brand new apartment.

Some up and coming areas worth considering include: Business Bay (particularly Executive Towers), Jumeirah Islands, Dubai Sports City (p.97), Studio City, and The Crescent in International Media Production Zone. For a bargain new villa try Victory Heights on the edge of The Els Club golf course (p.339) or The Villa in Dubailand (p.98).

Al Sufouh

Map **1 N5** Metro **Dubai Internet City**

Located between Knowledge Village and Umm Suqeim, this tiny collection of compounds is in high demand and the villas, which start at Dhs.150,000 for a three-bed, are hard to come by. Some of the villas are old by Dubai standards but the area is largely finished, so construction is not a problem. The facilities within the Marina, Al Barsha and Umm Suqeim are a short drive away. There's plenty of parking and the Media City Interchange from Sheikh Zayed Road makes accessing the area a breeze. Dubai College (p.160), the International School of Choueifat (p.164) and GEMS Wellington International School (p.163) are all in Al Sufouh.

Al Warqa

Map **2 M13** Metro **Rashidiya**

Directly south of Mirdif, Al Warqa has a lot of big opulent villas belonging to local families, as well as many new apartment blocks where one-bedrooms start at around Dhs.30,000, there are many new large villas that start at Dhs.120,000. Many of the apartment blocks are still under construction, as are some of the roads, so residents will often have to drive over dirt to reach their parking space.

Aside from the tiny corner shops, there is a big Mars supermarket in the area and both Uptown Mirdif and Mirdif City Centre are within easy reach for more serious shopping. There are a few schools near Al Warqa, including Sharjah American International School (04 280 1111). Mirdif's many nurseries, including Small Steps (04 288 3347), Super Kids (p.157) and Emirates British Nursery (p.154) are also close. The Al Warqa Medical Centre (04 280 0899) has a paediatrician and GP, but the nearest government A&E unit is Rashid Hospital (p.186), near Garhoud Bridge.

Arabian Ranches

Map **1 Q13** Metro **Mall of the Emirates**

The quiet, curving, grass-lined lanes of the Arabian Ranches development are located well away from the centre of town, up off Sheikh Mohammed Bin Zayed Road near Dubai Autodrome. This is an all-villa project set among lush greenery, lakes and the Arabian Ranches Golf Course, with a range of luxury facilities that all add up to some pretty fine suburban living. It was one of the first freehold residential areas to be completed and there is certainly a homely and mature neighbourhood feel to the place.

Accommodation

Arabian Ranches villas range from two-bedroom townhouses to seven-bed mansions. The starting price for renting a two-bedroom villa is around Dhs.125,000, although most of the people who bought villas in the development still live in them, so finding one that suits your needs can be difficult.

Shopping & Leisure

There are several pools, basketball and tennis courts, barbecue pits and grassy areas throughout, plus the Village Community Centre, which houses Le Marche supermarket, a chemist, liquor store and several cafes, restaurants and takeaways. Although a bit out of town, it is still just a 15 minute drive from Madinat Jumeirah. The Arabian Ranches Golf Course (p.339) is home to a restaurant and bar. The Autodrome, Uptown MotorCity and the licensed Dubai Polo & Equestrian Club are just a couple of minutes away too.

Healthcare & Education

The Mediclinic Arabian Ranches (04 453 4020) offers general practice and a range of medical specialities, and MediCentres MotorCity (04 360 8866) is nearby. The nearest emergency room is Cedars Jebel Ali International Hospital (p.184). The Jumeirah English Speaking School (p.164) is the only school in the Ranches, but it isn't too far away from options in Al Barsha and Emirates Living.

Bur Dubai & Al Mankhool

Map **2 L5** Metro **BurJuman**

This older, traffic-laden area of Dubai is a bit of a concrete jungle, with mid-size apartment blocks and virtually no green spaces. Many of the newer apartments have excellent facilities and spacious interiors, and the area itself is always humming with activity. The dense population means traffic and parking can often be a problem. It also means the streets are always full of people, and women may feel uneasy walking the streets, especially in the evening.

One of the most popular areas is Al Mankhool (also known as Golden Sands), but there are some nice apartment blocks in the Al Hamriya area (across Khalid Bin Al Waleed Road from the BurJuman Mall). Nearer the creek and west towards the sea, the buildings are generally a lot older with fewer facilities and limited parking, although those with balconies facing in the right direction do have beautiful creek views.

Accommodation

The area is dominated by apartments in a mix of new and old medium-rise buildings, from studios to large flats with several bedrooms. Some of the larger apartments are used as company flats. Rents in the newer buildings have risen to nearly the same as in other areas of Dubai, but the older the accommodation the cheaper it gets. A two-bedroom apartment in a new building could set you back more than Dhs.100,000 but for that you should expect excellent facilities. A one-bedroom apartment in an older building starts at Dhs.45,000 while a two bedroom will be around Dhs.70,000, depending on the age of the building and range of facilities offered.

Shopping & Leisure

There are two large Spinneys supermarkets in the area, as well as a Union Co-Op on Sheikh Khalifa Bin Zayed Road, a Choithrams on Mankhool Road and a huge Carrefour in Al Shindagha near the mouth of the creek. On and around Khalid Bin Al Waleed Road, there are a number of banks and ATMs, some smaller food stores, clothing shops and sports stores. BurJuman (p.423) provides a huge range of shops too. The souk area of Bur Dubai and the markets in Karama are good for picking up funky gifts.

The hotels on and around Khalid Bin Al Waleed Road house some great dive bars and inexpensive licensed restaurants, including expat-favourite Waxy O Connor's (p.566). The Melia Hotel (melia-dubai.com) opened in 2012, bringing fine dining to the area with Marco Pierre White's Titanic restaurant and Sanjeev Kapoor's Signature venue. There are also many small independent eateries on Khalid Bin Al Waleed Road and into Bur Dubai. The central location makes it easy to find a cab to take you the short distance to Downtown Dubai and on to Sheikh Zayed Road.

Healthcare & Education

Both in Bur Dubai and in neighbouring Karama you can find a number of small medical centres. The emergency room at Rashid Hospital (p.186) is just a stone's throw away in Umm Hurair, as is the private American Hospital (p.182). If that weren't enough, Healthcare City, which is home to two hospitals and more than 100 outpatient medical centres, is only a few minutes away by car.

There's a wide choice of nurseries, and plenty of choice for schools nearby including the Dubai English Speaking School (DESS) in Oud Metha.

Deira

Map **2 M4** Metro **Baniyas Square**

Although it's not very popular with expats in higher income brackets, Deira's heavily lived-in atmosphere and traffic-laden, bustling streets have been made more accessible by the introduction of the Metro. The heart of Deira is densely built up with a mix of old apartment blocks, while nearer the creek there are several new buildings offering modern apartments, many with spectacular views across the water. Rents are relatively low in some of the more built up areas, while the creekside dwellings cost much more. Once you get past the horrible traffic and lack of parking that plagues it, Deira's best attribute is its walkability.

Deira Is Not Dead

This is the oldest and one of the most atmospheric parts of town. Many might have forgotten its charms as Dubai expands, but it's a great place to explore along the bustling corniche, through the souks, in heritage sites and creekside restaurants and bars. For more on exploring this part of the city, see p.228.

Accommodation

Although Deira does have some areas with villas (Abu Hail, Al Wuheida), they are almost exclusively inhabited by Emiratis, with the areas closer to the creek full of apartments where most expats in the area congregate. In the heart of Deira, you'll pay around Dhs.65,000 for a one-bedroom apartment and Dhs.80,000 for two bedrooms, but these are often in older buildings and are not what you might call very salubrious. This area tends to attract couples and singles, rather than families.

The creekside area just north of Maktoum Bridge offers a great standard of accommodation and is used by professional expats of all nationalities. There are many executive apartments with great views over the creek, impressive landscaping and good facilities – but prices here tend to be high, with a standard two-bedroom apartment costing upwards of Dhs.100,000.

Shopping & Leisure

Deira is home to several popular malls including Al Ghurair Centre (p.436) and Deira City Centre (p.424). Both have good supermarkets (Spinneys and Carrefour respectively) as well as many other shops. Being an older area of town, there are also plenty of smaller groceries, pharmacies, dry-cleaners and laundry services within walking distance. Close to the bus station, the fish market and fruit and vegetable market are great for fresh produce. Deira's main post office is close to Al Ghurair Centre and there are many banks on Al Maktoum Road.

Within a small area, there's also a choice of hotels, including the Intercontinental, Hilton and Sheraton Creek, the JW Marriott, Renaissance, Traders and Metropolitan Palace, all of which offer a great choice of dining outlets, bars and nightclubs.

For cheap eats, Al Rigga Street has a great range of independent restaurants, including the famed Automatic Lebanese restaurant (p.493). Al Ghurair Centre also has some particularly nice cafes on the terrace. There are some pleasant walking areas by the creek and along the corniche towards Al Mamzar Beach Park, which is great for weekends, especially with the beach chalets available for daily rental.

Healthcare & Education

Local healthcare is provided by the government-run Dubai Hospital (p.184) near the corniche, while Dubai's foremost emergency hospital, Rashid Hospital (p.186), is just across Maktoum Bridge in Umm Hurair. There are also many small private medical clinics, although the larger private hospitals tend to be located on the Bur Dubai side of the creek (p.86). Since the area tends to attract fewer families, Deira doesn't have many expat schools within its borders, so most children in Deira attend school in nearby Garhoud.

Discovery Gardens

Map **1 H7** Metro **Nakheel**

Made up of hundreds of seemingly identical low-rise apartment blocks, Discovery Gardens is surprisingly green. Rents tend to be lower here and apartments easy to come by. The buildings only contain studios and one-bedroom apartments. A one-bedroom can be found for around Dhs.50,000. Although there aren't any shops within the development, Ibn Battuta is conveniently close and contains a large Géant hypermarket, a cinema and several restaurants. Heading to the Marina and Al Barsha for a drink or a nice dinner isn't much of a hassle, and the newly opened Movenpick Ibn Battuta Gate Hotel (p.244) is a welcome addition to the immediate area's dining and bar scene. Traffic bottlenecks can be a problem during rush hours, but there is plenty of parking around the buildings. There is also a Red Line Metro stop outside Ibn Battuta, but you need to take the F43 feeder bus to access it.

Downtown Dubai

Map **2 F6** Metro **Burj Khalifa/Dubai Mall**

One of Dubai's newest residential areas, Downtown was designed to foster a community. Children's play areas, hubs of cafes and restaurants, souks and elegant swimming pools all encourage residents to spend time outside and enjoy the surroundings. On top of this, the wide promenades, Arabian passageways and palm-lined streets that link the different residential quarters encourage residents to get around on foot. The massive development is made up of high and low rise residential units, with landmark buildings – The Address (Dubai Mall and Downtown), The Palace Hotel, Emaar Square and the Burj Khalifa – as the cornerstones. At one end, near to the Burj, are the Burj Residence towers, The Lofts and 8 Boulevard Walk, while at the opposite end, on the border with

Downtown Dubai

the Business Bay development, are the South Ridge and Burj Views high-rises. In between these is the distinctive Arabian architecture of Old Town. Traffic throughout the area is constantly being improved with the opening of new roads, and the entire development sits between Sheikh Zayed Road and Al Khail Road (E44), making it very accessible. There is plenty of parking within each of the residential complexes, and the Burj Khalifa/Dubai Mall Metro stop is walking distance from some apartments and a short feeder bus ride from the others.

Accommodation

Options range from tiny studios to expansive four-bedroom townhouses, and the finishing in most buildings is of a high spec. One-bedroom apartments start at the Dhs.75,000 mark in Old Town, rising to Dhs.160,000 in Burj Khalifa. Most residential towers come with facilities including games rooms, libraries, barbecue areas, gyms, swimming pools and sports courts.

Shopping & Leisure

Downtown Dubai is a shopper's dream with both The Dubai Mall (p.426) and Souk Al Bahar (p.421) within walking distance of all residential districts. For groceries, The Dubai Mall has a Waitrose supermarket and there are several small Spinneys stores and Al Maya outlets scattered throughout the area. Pretty much all of the banks are covered on the ground floor of The Dubai Mall, along with plenty of pharmacies, money exchanges and opticians.

Right next door to The Dubai Mall is the more low-key Souk Al Bahar, which houses a few boutique shops and is fast becoming a nightlife hub with several licensed bars and restaurants, including Left Bank (p.559). The Dubai Mall has quite a few unlicensed restaurants along with two of the largest foodcourts in the city. If that isn't enough, there's also the two Address hotels, which are home to the gorgeous Neos sky bar (p.561) on the 63rd floor of the Downtown hotel, and Cabana (p.552), the funky pool bar at The Dubai Mall hotel.

Healthcare & Education

Apart from pharmacies dotted round the Old Town, The Dubai Mall and the Residences, there is the large Mediclinic Dubai Mall (p.190). The closest hospitals are Medcare Hospital (04 407 9100) in Al Safa and the Iranian Hospital (04 344 0250) on Al Wasl Road in Satwa. While there are no primary or secondary schools in Downtown Dubai, those in Jumeira and Al Quoz are an easy drive away. There are however, nursery facilities for pre-school aged kids. Old Town Nursery, part of Raffles International School, is in the Qamardeen district of Old Town. Kangaroo Kids' bright and colourful nursery is in the Burj Residences, and Cello Kids Club (04 422 1303) is located in the Al Manzil Club.

Dubai Marina & JBR

Map **1 K5** Metro **Dubai Marina**

The high-rise apartment towers of the Marina and Jumeirah Beach Residence have quickly become one of the most desirable places to live in Dubai. The many hotels that dot the area are home to numerous restaurants and bars and The Walk is packed every evening with couples and families socialising and strolling. Road access in and out of the area is fairly efficient; the main exceptions are the roads leading to The Walk which get congested in the evenings. Much of the neighbourhood is walkable so residents rarely need to venture far to access amenities. There is also a great open beach and an incredible marina to enjoy.

Dubai Marina

Accommodation
Apartments in Dubai Marina vary greatly in quality, and the rent for a studio in one of the less luxurious towers starts around Dhs.45,000 a year, while a three-bedroom in a building with great facilities and impressive finishing might go for as much as Dhs.160,000 a year. Apartments in one of JBR's many identical towers go for a bit less and a one-bedroom can be found for Dhs.70,000 a year. All of the buildings in the district are freehold, and most of the apartments are owned by expats.

Shopping & Leisure
Shopping options in the area are good if not great; Dubai Marina Mall (p.428) is not one of the city's largest malls, but it does hold a Waitrose supermarket and a few good highstreet shops. On Marina Walk, alongside all the restaurants, there's a Spinneys supermarket, a pharmacy, a bookshop, a florist and a liquor store, plus a number of ATMs. The Walk along JBR is also home to a decent shopping scene, with clothing boutiques and furniture stores as well as a regular tourist market. Both Mall of the Emirates and Ibn Battuta are only a short drive away.

Several large hotels line the beach outside JBR and each has a decent selection of bars and licensed restaurants. The Walk below JBR is teeming with places to eat, many of which are open until the early hours. Marina Walk also has a number of popular restaurants, including The Rupee Room (p.534). The hotels along the beach all have bars and restaurants too, including the popular Mai Tai bar (p.564) and Frankie's Italian restaurant (p.508) at Oasis Beach Tower.

Healthcare & Education
Medcare Hospital (p.184), near Al Safa Park, has the closest emergency room. In the other direction, the Cedars Jebel Ali International Hospital (p.184) also offers 24-hour emergency care. There's a Mediclinic Al Sufouh (04 366 1030) in nearby Knowledge Village, and Drs Nicolas & Asp (p.198) dental and medical clinics in JBR.

There are a few nurseries in the Marina, but no schools. However, Al Sufouh is only five minutes away by car and is home to Wellington International School (p.163) and the International School of Choueifat (p.164). Its location along Sheikh Zayed Road means all of the schools on this side of town are easily accessible.

Emirates Living: Meadows, Springs, Lakes & Emirates Hills
Map **1 L6** Metro **Nakheel**

Emirates Living is a desirable address with a range of villa-style houses in The Springs, The Lakes and The Meadows. Tree-lined streets and pathways, attractively landscaped lakes, gardens and recreation areas make it perfect for those who want to enjoy the peace and quiet of suburbia. Located between Sheikh Zayed Road and Al Khail Road, across from Media City, each individual zone of Emirates Living (for example Springs 6, Meadows 5) has its own gated security entrance. The gated-community feel runs throughout each neighbourhood, as kids play in the streets and parks, while adults jog the pavements. Traffic within each community is not a problem now that major roads leading to the communities are all complete. This said, the intersections near the highways can get busy at rush hour.

Accommodation
Generally, the style and quality of all houses in Emirates Living is good, although they all look the same. The smallest villas available are located in The Springs, where a two-bedroom townhouse can be rented from around Dhs.90,000. Prices go up from there, and a six-bedroom mansion in The Lakes will cost around Dhs.400,000 a year. Those looking for larger, mansion-like homes can go to the more exclusive (and expensive) Emirates Hills area.

Shopping & Leisure
There are several supermarkets within the various compounds. There's a Choithrams at The Springs end, a large Spinneys at Springs Town Centre in the middle and a Spinneys Market in the Meadows. The latter two centres each have a Fitness First club, and all have a beauty salon, a pharmacy and ATMs. Between them all, you should find everything you need, from laundry services to fast food and fine dining, or coffee shops to video rentals. Other nearby supermarkets include Spinneys and Waitrose at Dubai Marina, Géant at Ibn Battuta and Carrefour at Mall of the Emirates.

The Fitness First in the Lakes has a licensed restaurant and bar, as does the Montgomerie Golf Club for evenings where you want to stay local. Other than that, you'll have to venture to the Marina or Al Barsha for a better selection of dining venues. Both Ibn Battuta and Mall of the Emirates are only 10 minutes away in either direction.

Healthcare & Education
The Rosary Medical Centre is located at Springs Town Centre in Springs 7, while nearby facilities include a private medical centre in Al Barsha, Medical Specialist Centre (04 340 9495), the Cedars Jebel Ali International Hospital (p.184), and Mediclinic Al Sufouh in Knowledge Village (04 366 1030).

There are several education options for families based in the area, but waiting lists for a place in the most sought-after schools and nurseries are long, and it is best to sign up well in advance. Schools already open include Emirates International School in The Meadows (p.162), Dubai British School (p.160), Dubai International Academy (p.162) in The Springs, and

Dubai American Academy (p.160) at the Emirates Living entrance near The Lakes. As for nurseries, Raffles International School (04 427 1200) operates several nurseries in The Springs, Springs Town Centre, Emirates Hills and The Lakes.

Garhoud

Map **2 N8** Metro **Emirates**

With its central location, range of villas and suburban feel, it's no surprise that Garhoud is such a popular residential area. It's handy for both central Dubai and downtown Deira, although this does mean that traffic can be a problem at peak times. Finding available accommodation isn't always easy, and there's not much in the way of new construction. Being only two minutes away from the airport means it's popular with airline staff and frequent travellers. It also means there is a chance of aircraft noise depending on the wind direction. Parking is a problem and finding a spot on the street, even with the introduction of parking meters, can often be difficult.

Accommodation

Garhoud has some nice, older villas, usually with well-established gardens and plenty of character. They are also relatively cheap considering the central location. The rent for a three-bedroom ranges from Dhs.140,000 upwards, and depends on the age of the villa. The biggest problem is finding somewhere vacant. Away from the airport, there are some newer villas, predominantly in large compounds, that are similar in standard and price to villas in other areas of Dubai. The usual size is four bedrooms, which should rent for around Dhs.160,000 per year. There are also a few apartment blocks near the Aviation Club where a one-bedroom can be found for as little as Dhs.45,000.

Shopping & Leisure

There is one main shopping street in Garhoud which has two supermarkets, as well as a laundry, pharmacy and ATM. Other than that, both Carrefour in Deira City Centre (p.416) and HyperPanda in Festival City (p.416) are less than a 10 minute drive away. Garhoud may be the best location for nightlife lovers. The many licensed restaurants and bars in Al Bustan Rotana, Le Meridien Dubai, Jumeirah Creekside Hotel, Millennium Airport Hotel, Century Village and Aviation Club are all within walking distance, and a taxi to the hotels on Sheikh Zayed Road shouldn't set you back more than Dhs.30. Festival City is also just around the corner and has a large selection of shops, as well as licensed and unlicensed restaurants, to choose from.

Healthcare & Education

There are no government clinics in the area, but there are good private facilities such as Mediclinic Welcare Hospital (p.186). Two of the main government hospitals, Latifa Hospital (p.184) and Rashid (p.186), are only a short distance away across the creek.

Several schools are located on the southern edge of Garhoud including Deira International School (p.160) and Cambridge International School (p.160). Many other schools are accessible in areas like Umm Hurair, Al Twar and Festival City. Yellow Brick Road Nursery (p.157) and Montessori Nursery (p.154) are in the neighbourhood as well.

Green Community

Map **1 F9** Metro **Energy**

An oasis of green in the desert, this new development is good for families, and homes are hard to come by. The area is made up of villas with large front gardens, as well as spacious, low-rise apartment blocks set among lakes and green parks. There's plenty of room for kids to play in and the place has quietly developed a strong community feel. It's a bit out of the city, but a good choice for people working in the Jebel Ali Free Zone. At the moment, the community has only one road leading into and out of it, so rush-hour traffic is often a problem. Its location away from the rest of Dubai also means that taxis can be expensive for nights when the car needs to be left at home.

Accommodation

There is a wide variety including villas, townhouses, and apartments. The original Green Community was so well received that the developer built a new phase – Green Community West. For a four-bedroom villa you can expect to pay around Dhs.180,000 in rent, and you should be able to find a one-bedroom apartment for around Dhs.65,000. The developer, Union Properties, has a good reputation and the finishing in all of the units is high quality.

Shopping & Leisure

The area is serviced by The Market shopping centre, which houses a large Choithrams supermarket, as well as a jewellers, clothes shops, and home furnishing outlets. There's also a pharmacy, a florist, a dry cleaners, an optician, and a branch of ACE Hardware. If that's not enough, Ibn Battuta Mall is not far away.

There are a few good licensed restaurants within the Courtyard by Marriott, and The Market is home to a number of coffee shops and good unlicensed restaurants. For a better selection, Dubai Marina is about 15 minutes by car.

Healthcare & Education

The private Green Community Medical Centre (04 885 3225) is upstairs in The Market, while the nearest government-run clinic is at Jebel Ali. For emergencies, the Cedars Jebel Ali International Hospital (p.184) is nearest. For government A&E care, it's quite a trip to Rashid Hospital.

The Children's Garden (04 885 3484) offers a primary bilingual curriculum in English/German or English/French, and there are various primary and secondary schools in Emirates Living and Jebel Ali.

International City

Previously a popular place to live for budget-conscious residents, this collection of hundreds of nearly-identical low-rise apartment blocks has fallen out of favour in recent months. Crashing rents have brought the already low prices down to rock-bottom and a one-bedroom apartment can go for as little as Dhs.30,000 a year. However, poor maintenance and security have caused many budget-beaters to look elsewhere. Located at the intersection of Sheikh Mohammed bin Zayed Rd and the Dubai-Hatta Road, the development is a bit out of the way, but a trip to Festival City is close by.

Both Carrefour and Spinneys have outlets within International City and there are smaller groceries and cornershops underneath nearly every building. A few small private clinics have opened within International City, as have some pharmacies. There are no schools within the development, but options in Mirdif and Al Warqa are only 10 minutes away.

Jumeira

Map **2 G4** Metro **Business Bay**

The actual area of Jumeira occupies a prime nine-kilometre strip of coastline stretching south-west from the port area, but the name has been hijacked to such an extent that new residential and commercial developments bearing the Jumeira tag are cropping up for miles around. Even the Palm Jumeirah doesn't connect with Jumeira, but actually extends from the area of Al Sufouh. Jumeira itself is characterised by quiet streets lined with sophisticated villas, golden beaches, and good access to lots of shopping. Traffic and parking on the back streets is never a problem, but Al Wasl Road and Jumeira Road can get clogged during peak hours.

Jumeira or Jumeirah?

According to the 'official' spelling used by Dubai Municipality, it's Jumeira, so that's what we use when referring to this area. However, many hotels, parks, clubs, schools, and residential developments have added an 'h' to the end, so don't be surprised if you see the two different spellings side by side throughout the book.

Accommodation

Although prices have dropped considerably, Jumeira villas still attract some of the highest rents in the city. There's a mixture of huge 'palaces', independent villas, and villas in compounds with shared facilities. For a three-bedroom, stand-alone villa you can expect to pay rent of around Dhs.160,000 upwards depending on the age and specific location. You can, however, get the odd villa in an older compound for less.

Shopping & Leisure

Jumeira Road (also known as Beach Road) has long been home to several boutiques selling art and fashion. For groceries, there are two Spinneys, a Union Co-op and two Choithrams all within a short drive. There is also the popular Mercato (p.432) on Jumeira Road, along with several smaller shopping centres.

Jumeira Road hosts several independent restaurants and takeaways, as well as many fast-food joints. The Jumeirah Beach Hotel and Madinat Jumeirah are both packed with impressive licensed restaurants and bars and the restaurant-filled hotels that line Sheikh Zayed Road are nearby as well. Best of all, the city's most popular beaches are all within walking distance, including Jumeirah Beach Park (p.257).

Jumeirah Golf Estates

Map **1 J11**

Lots of people dream of living on a golf course. But now you can put on your Callaways, step out your front door and you're ready to sneak in a quick nine holes before dinner. Anyone looking to garner a slice of the residential golfing lifestyle could do a lot, lot worse than moving into one of the villas at Jumeirah Golf Estates, home to the DP World Tour Championship. That short walk to the first tee aside, there are many things to love about living on a golf course: the stunning vistas, an expanse of manicured grass fairways, unlimited access to first-class golf courses designed by the pros, and even the odd, hilarious sight of hackers butchering their way through a game. There's a range of villa types, from four-bedrooms upwards, all oozing style and luxury. At the heart of this exclusive development is the Norman Country Club, with a leisure centre, bar and restaurants (including one by Jamie Oliver), tennis academy, lap pool and a leisure lagoon.

Healthcare & Education

Al Safa Health Centre (04 502 1400) opposite Safa Park is the nearest government health clinic. Emirates Hospital (p.184), opposite Jumeirah Beach Park, has a 24 hour walk-in clinic, but they do not accept emergency cases. The Neuro Spinal Hospital (p.186) in the same building does have a 24 hour emergency department though. Medcare (p.184), near Safa Park, is a popular new private hospital. Jumeira is known for being home to countless beauty salons and private medical facilities, including dentists, physiotherapists and cosmetic surgery centres.

There are numerous nurseries in Jumeira, and GEMS Jumeirah Primary School (p.163), Jumeirah College (p.164) and Jumeirah English Speaking School (p.164) are all in the neighbourhood. Easy access to road networks means outlying schools are within reach.

Jumeirah Lakes Towers

Map **1 K5** Metro **Jumeirah Lakes Towers**

JLT is a high-rise community made up of 79 towers, both residential and commercial. It is located directly across Sheikh Zayed Road from the Marina, and is serviced by two Metro stations. The quality of housing is comparable to the Marina, but prices are still quite a bit less. When the lakes are completed there will be a promenade around them with cafes and shops. In the meantime there's a Carrefour Express and a handful of bars and restaurants at The Bonnington (p.236). Getting in and out of the area by car can be quite tedious due to the huge one-way loop that revolves around the development, but there's a Metro stop right on the doorstep. There is still lots of construction going on, so noise pollution can be a problem.

Jumeirah Park

Map **1 J6** Metro **Jumeirah Lakes Towers**

Its prime location – next to the popular communities of Meadows, Lakes and Springs – is definitely a draw for Jumeirah Park. Perfect for families, take your pick of one of 2,000 three, four and five-bedroom villas with an emphasis on open plan living. Rents are slightly higher here, you'll pay at least Dhs.220,000 for a three-bedroom villa, but you are getting larger living areas and established recreational facilities for your money. There's a childrens' day care centre, childrens' play area, and kindergarten through to secondary school, as well as a community centre with shops and restaurants.

Jumeirah Village

Map **1 K9**

It's a little bit out of the way and, as yet, still quite underdeveloped – but you can rent a decent sized three-storey townhouse in Jumeirah Village Circle for around Dhs.100,000. And, at Jumeirah Village Triangle, which is more developed, there are primarily smaller two-bedroom townhouses suited for couples or smaller families. So, if you don't mind living on a bit of a building site, with dust, noise, trucks and little facilities, and you're happy to drive that bit further to get into 'town', this is a great value neighbourhood – and not far from Dubai Sports City.

There's a choice of villas, townhouses, low-rise and high-rise buildings, all built in classic Arabian and Mediterranean. Residents tend to visit nearby MotorCity for groceries at Spinneys and shops along the MotorCity strip mall. Additional shopping in neighbouring communities include: Choithrams located in The Springs and Spinneys in The Meadows.

Karama

Map **2 L5** Metro **Karama**

Near the heart of old Dubai lies Karama. Its convenient location means it is a thriving commercial area with plenty of amenities. The price you pay is a lack of peace and quiet and lots of traffic. There are many low-cost restaurants, supermarkets and shops, as well as the Karama Market (p.411), which sells a wide range of goods. Reasonable rents make Karama a good choice for Dubai residents on a budget.

Accommodation

Most accommodation is in low-rise blocks with apartments ranging from studios to three-bedrooms. Rents can be as low as Dhs.40,000 for a one-bedroom in the older buildings, but those tend to get snapped up quickly through word of mouth. The most desirable buildings are along Zabeel Road or in the area along Sheikh Khalifa Bin Zayed Road, opposite Spinneys. A two-bedroom in one of those neighbourhoods can be found for around Dhs.60,000. If you can find a flat in a newer building with a full set of facilities, rent for a two-bedroom could be a lot higher.

Shopping & Leisure

Everything is on your doorstep here. On Sheikh Khalifa Bin Zayed Road there is a Spinneys and a Union Co-Op. There are plenty of small grocers, a fish market and the well known Karama Market. The BurJuman Mall (p.423) provides good shopping, while cheap-and-cheerful Avenue and Sana department stores are nearby. There are beauty salons, barbershops, laundries and independent fitness clubs all within walking distance. The central post office and several banks are also in the area. A Carrefour hypermarket and 14-screen VOX cinema complex is due to open at BurJuman in 2014.

For daytime leisure, the gorgeous Zabeel Park is within walking distance. Karama is also home to some of the finest inexpensive eateries in Dubai and you'll have access to takeaways from the many Arabic, Indian, Filipino, Sri Lankan and Pakistani restaurants that populate the area. There are several three-star hotels in the area, most of which house a dive bar which is a blast for a down-and-dirty night out. Otherwise, the licensed restaurants and bars of Downtown Dubai, Sheikh Zayed Road and Bur Dubai are only a short cab ride away.

Healthcare & Leisure

Karama is convenient for many reasonably priced medical centres, doctors and dentists and is also just a few minutes away from Rashid Hospital (p.186) for emergencies. Although there are no popular schools or nurseries in the area, there are plenty of options close by in Oud Metha, Garhoud and along Sheikh Zayed Road, and reaching them should be relatively easy.

Jumeirah Islands

Grand villas

Dubai Marina

The Springs

Mirdif

Map **2 Q12** Metro **Rashidiya**

Mirdif was, for many years, a faraway suburb where locals and expats enjoyed the quiet life (apart from those directly under the flight path) in stand alone villas. However, flashy new developments, such as the Uptown Mirdif complex, the vast Shorooq community and the low-cost apartments of Ghoroob, plus the recent opening of Mirdif City Centre (p.433), mean that the once sleepy suburb is now a bustling residential and commercial community. It's popular with families and, increasingly so, with couples and singles. Traffic in and out of the area can be annoying during rush hour, but the streets within the individual neighbourhoods are free-flowing, and there are usually enough speed-bumps to prevent speeders.

Accommodation

A decent three-bedroom villa should cost around Dhs.90,000 upwards a year and, depending on whether it's a standalone or in a compound, it may have a little garden or shared pool. Prices for a one-bed apartment can be as low as Dhs.45,000, while Dhs.140,000 could get you a new, spacious four-bedroom with a garden and pool. When searching for a place in Mirdif, be sure to take your time and see as many houses as possible, as the quality of construction and finishing varies greatly.

Shopping & Leisure

The massive Mirdif City Centre (p.433) which opened in 2010 is a welcome addition to Mirdif's shopping, dining and leisure scene. Among a host of high street stores, it houses a large Carrefour, a cinema and Playnation (p.264). Further down Airport Road is the smaller Arabian Centre shopping mall (p.436) which has a World Mart and a Cinecity cinema. There is a large Spinneys supermarket in Uptown Mirdif, along with several shops, a pharmacy, hairdressers and restaurants. Mirdif also has many small shopping areas throughout that usually contain a small convenience store and at least one cafe or takeaway.

There aren't any hotels or licensed premises within Mirdif, but Uptown Mirdif and Mirdif City Centre both have a number of sit down restaurants and fastfood outlets. There are also several independent restaurants scattered throughout the community that offer delivery. Festival City is the nearest destination for licensed restaurants and bars.

Healthcare & Education

Mediclinic Mirdif is in Uptown Mirdif and offers a wide range of medical services (04 288 1302). Drs Nicolas & Asp Dental Clinic is also in the area (04 288 4411). Rashidiya Health Centre (04 502 2300) is the nearest government health facility. The nearest government hospital is Rashid (p.186), with 24-hour emergency services. There is a choice of nurseries in Mirdif including Small Steps (04 288 3347), Super Kids (p.157) and Emirates British Nursery (p.154). Uptown Primary (p.166) is recommended. Other new schools include Star International School (p.165) in Mirdif, the Sharjah American International School (04 280 1111) in Al Warqa, Royal Dubai School (p.163) in Muhaisnah, and the American Academy in Al Mizhar (p.159).

MotorCity

Map **1 N11**

Built around the Dubai Autodrome, MotorCity is the latest part of the giant Dubailand project to reach some degree of maturity. Very reasonable rental prices – with one-bedroom apartments from Dhs.50,000 and a four-bedroom villa for Dhs.250,000 – and a good array of services make it an attractive place to live for couples and singles after a slice of suburbia. There's a Medicentres clinic (04 360 8866) in Uptown MotorCity, along with a couple of pharmacies, and a nice strip of cafes and shops. Both JESS Arabian Ranches (jess.sch.ae) and the giant GEMS World Academy (04 373 6373) are a stone's throw away. Arabian Ranches Golf Course, The Els Club and Dubai Polo Club are all close at hand, plus it's just 20 minutes to Mall of the Emirates and Dubai Marina.

Oud Metha

Map **2 L6** Metro **Oud Metha**

Oud Metha is centrally located and within easy reach of the highways. There are plenty of shops and restaurants within walking distance, as well as Lamcy Plaza (p.438) and the Wafi (p.435) complex of shops and restaurants. Accommodation is mainly in low-rise apartment blocks, which are not as densely packed as in other 'inner-city' areas. Oud Metha is quite popular and vacant apartments often get snapped up quickly. If you're lucky, you can find a one-bedroom for Dhs.60,000, but apartments in newer buildings with good facilities usually cost more. The apartments are often larger than their freehold counterparts in the Marina or JLT. A large three-bedroom can go for as much as Dhs.140,000. Wafi, the Movenpick Hotel and the Grand Hyatt all have a good selection of licensed restaurants and bars. Many of the city's best independent restaurants, including Lemongrass (p.519) and Lan Kwai Fong (p.518) are also in the area. There are many private clinics and hospitals in Healthcare City, and both the American Hospital (p.182) and the Canadian Specialist Clinics (04 336 4444) are very close. Oud Metha is also home to Dubai English Speaking School (p.162).

Palm Jumeirah

Map **1 N1** Metro **Nakheel**

The Palm Jumeirah is synonymous with Dubai's extravagance, and the rental prices on the man-made island match its reputation. The trunk of the island is made up of large one to four-bedroom apartments, and a one-bedroom goes for around Dhs.75,000 a year. The fronds are covered in nearly identical three to six-bedroom villas which range between Dhs.275,000 and Dhs.550,000 to rent. Traffic onto the island isn't a problem and there is plenty of parking underneath the apartment buildings and next to the villas. Aside from the fine-dining options at Atlantis and Rixos The Palm, there are a few licensed restaurants and bars in the Shoreline Apartments on the trunk, but as new hotels open their doors, The Palm is becoming a high-class hub for dining and partying. In the meantime, the Marina and Madinat Jumeirah are five minutes away. Nearby Al Sufouh has several popular expat schools.

Qusais

Map **2 R7** Metro **Al Qusais 1**

Right on the border with Sharjah, apartments in Qusais tend to cost much less than in the rest of Dubai. Traffic is still a problem and commutes to other parts of Dubai can be a nightmare. A one-bedroom in Al Qusais shouldn't cost more than Dhs.40,000 and large four-bedroom apartments can be found for around Dhs.90,000. The area has several larger supermarkets, including a LuLu Hypermarket and Union Co-op, as well as several smaller corner groceries, shops and pharmacies. There are plenty of inexpensive Indian, Pakistani and Arabic restaurants that deliver, but you'll have to travel closer to the centre of Dubai to find a bar or licensed restaurant. The private Zulekha Hospital (p.188) has an emergency room and is located in Al Qusais, as are a few private clinics.

Mirdif

Satwa

Map **2 G5** Metro **Trade Centre**

Despite having large sections demolished for the now-on-hold Jumeirah Garden City project, Satwa is still a desirable place to live. The main Second December Street buzzes with pedestrians and is home to several of the city's favourite Arabic restaurants as well as plenty of fast food venues. There are a number of low-rise apartment blocks on 2nd December Street and Al Hudeiba Street (Plant Street), popular with singles looking for a vibrant area. There are also villas on the outskirts of the area, in Al Bada'a that are popular with families. Rent for a two-bedroom place shouldn't cost more than Dhs.85,000 and if you can find a villa in good condition, expect to pay Dhs.100,000-140,000 for a three-bedroom. Chelsea Plaza and Jumeirah Rotana have long been nightlife hubs and there are several three-star hotels in the area that are home to intimate licensed restaurants and bars.

Shoppers will be able to find everything they need along 2nd December Street and Plant Street, and there are several supermarkets including two Carrefour Expresses and a Westzone. Traffic can be bad at rush hour and street parking is hard to come by, but once the car is parked, the large pavements and many pedestrian crossings make walking easy. In case of emergency, the Iranian Hospital (p.184) on Al Wasl Road has a very good A&E unit and Rashid Hospital (p.186) is nearby. There are no schools in Satwa, but several in neighbouring Jumeira, Al Wasl and Oud Metha.

Sharjah

Dubai's neighbouring emirate is an attractive location for many mainly due to the lower rents, which can be up to half what you'd pay in Dubai. As you'd expect in any city, there's a wide range of options, from small apartments to big villas. Unfortunately, rush-hour traffic in and out of Sharjah is a nightmare and finding a parking spot in some areas is almost impossible.

Accommodation

Downtown, it's all high-rise apartment blocks. Some have been around for a few years so facilities are a little basic. Newer, better equipped blocks command higher rents. As you venture out of town there are some big independent villas, and smaller, older villas too. For a new, large one-bedroom apartment in town with good facilities you could pay as little as Dhs.40,000, while a three-bedroom villa can be found for Dhs.100,000.

Shopping & Leisure

Sharjah City Centre, Sharjah Mega Mall, and the Sahara Centre all feature a host of international brands and stores (such as M&S and Debenhams), and there are plenty of smaller shopping centres catering to all tastes and budgets. For a slightly more traditional shopping experience, the big Central Souk (aka Blue Souk) has rows of jewellery shops and stores selling Arabian knick-knacks and pretty much anything you could imagine. The Souk Al Arsah (p.422), in the Heritage Area, is a traditional Arabian market. Sharjah also has fruit, vegetable and fish markets in Al Jubail beside the water, with many stalls offering a variety of fresh produce.

For your everyday shopping needs, there's a big Carrefour in City Centre mall and a Spinneys in the Sahara Centre. You'll also find plenty of small grocery stores dotted around the residential areas, as well as dry cleaners and laundries.

Sharjah has a reputation for being quiet and the emirate is 'dry'. That said, Sharjah has some of the country's best independent restaurants, and some top museums and attractions (see p.299). There is one licensed club in Sharjah, the Sharjah Wanderers Sports Club (sharjahwanderers.com), which is popular with expats in need of a local drink.

Healthcare & Education

Sharjah has a number of government health clinics for subsidised medical care, plus private clinics and hospitals. The two government hospitals with emergency facilities are the Qassimi (06 538 6444) and Kuwaiti (06 524 2111) hospitals, while Al Zahra (06 561 9999), Zulekha (06 565 8866), and the Central Private (06 563 9900) are the main private hospitals with 24 hour emergency care.

Sharjah English School is a primary and secondary school for English-speaking children (06 558 9304), and Wesgreen International School (06 534 6333) teaches the British curriculum. There is also The Sharjah American International School (06 538 0000), and the German School Sharjah (06 567 6014). The Australian International School (06 558 9967) is on the Sharjah-Dubai border, just five minutes from Sharjah Airport.

Sheikh Zayed Road

Sheikh Zayed Road

Map **2 J6** Metro **World Trade Centre**

The strip between Trade Centre Roundabout and Interchange One is home to some of Dubai's biggest, brightest and boldest towers, both residential and commercial, plus some of the most impressive hotels in town. Being so close to all the action it's a popular area, and rents are high as a result. A one-bedroom with a good view will cost around Dhs.70,000 a year, and a three-bedroom in a newer building could cost upwards of Dhs.125,000. With The Dubai Mall, Mazaya Centre and the supermarkets of Jumeira (p.91) nearby, residents never have to travel far to get what they need. Both sides of Sheikh Zayed Road have pharmacies and smaller shops for daily needs, and there are plenty of takeaway restaurants for when you don't want to leave the apartment.

The strip is a popular nightlife destination with several bars and licensed restaurants in the Shangri-La, Fairmont, Crowne Plaza and Towers Rotana. In other words, if you live here you should purchase a comfortable couch for friends who can't make it home after a night on the town.

Al Zahra Medical Centre (04 331 5000) in Al Safa Tower has a number of departments including family medicine and dentistry. The nearest emergency care is either Rashid Hospital (p.186) near Garhoud Bridge or the Iranian Hospital (p.184) on Al Wasl Road.

There aren't any schools in the direct area, but as Sheikh Zayed Road is the city's main thoroughfare, several schools in Jumeira and beyond are only a short drive away.

Silicon Oasis

Silicon Oasis, located off the Academic City Road, is a development containing hundreds of lovely villas with gardens and apartment blocks finished to an impressively high standard. It is considered to be quite far out of town, although it is just a 10 minute drive from Mirdif, and, as a new area, it is now starting to develop an identity and community feel of its own with supermarkets, restaurants and cafes opening regularly. The Outlet Mall is just a quick trip over the other side of the Dubai-Al Ain Road too. If you work locally, or are happy with a slightly longer commute, you can definitely find some bargains here, with well-appointed two-bed apartments with top notch communal facilities available for Dhs.65,000. For more information, check out the community forum on siliconoasis.org.

Sports City

Map **1 L10**

The world's first integrated sports city still has a long way to go before completion, but there are now a large handful of completed towers with enticing low rents. Rents are very competitive in this area, and you can bag a two-bedroom apartment from Dhs.65,000; if the budget allows though there are four and five-bed villas from Dhs.240,000. Not bad at all when you also get facilities in each tower including underground car parking, gym, barbecue area, a jacuzzi, steam room and sauna, and free internet.

Tecom

Map **1 N6** Metro **Dubai Internet City**

Next to The Greens (p.97), Tecom is made up primarily of residential towers. Since each plot in the area was sold to a different developer, there is still a lot of construction going on, and although the roads have all been finished, there are no pedestrian sidewalks. As a result, rents tend to be a bit cheaper than in neighbouring Al Barsha or The Greens, and a one-bedroom can be found for around Dhs.60,000. The quality of apartments varies, and traffic in and out of the neighbourhood can get busy during peak hours. There is a Metro stop in front of the area, which is useful for anyone working on Sheikh Zayed Road, and there are small Geant and Park n Shop supermarkets, with the Spinneys and other amenities in The Greens just a stone's throw away. Nightlife destinations such as the Marina and Al Sufouh are just across Sheikh Zayed Road and the Media Rotana in Tecom is home to local pub Nelson's (p.560).

The Gardens

Map **1 G6** Metro **Ibn Battuta**

The Gardens is somewhat of an anomaly for Dubai real estate. The entire development is fully owned by Nakheel and, unlike the rest of the city, rents here haven't really boomed since its opening. Located directly behind Ibn Battuta, the collection of low-rise apartment blocks is characterised by large trees and fully-matured gardens. If you can find an apartment here, which isn't an easy task, expect to pay around Dhs.50,000 for a decent-sized one-bedroom.

Residents of The Gardens tend to do their shopping at Ibn Battuta Mall (p.430) which has a large Geant supermarket, and they spend their nights at the licensed restaurants and bars at the nearby Marina, although there are licensed bars and restaurants now at Ibn Battuta Gate Hotel. Traffic is rarely a problem within the development and its location is great for anyone working in Jebel Ali. For emergencies, Cedars Jebel Ali International Hospital (p.184) has a 24-hour emergency room and is very close.

The Greens

Map **1 N6** Metro **Dubai Internet City**

The Greens, on the edge of Emirates Living, offers a range of one to four-bedroom apartments, which are well appointed but a bit small for the money. A one-bedroom rents for around Dhs.60,000 and a three-bedroom for around Dhs.120,000. The shopping

Emirates Living

centre in the middle of the neighbourhood has a range of shops, including Choithrams and Organic Foods & Cafe, as well as a few unlicensed restaurants. The area shares the same educational and healthcare facilities as Tecom and Emirates Living. The Greens is convenient for those working in Media or Internet City, as there is a flyover connecting the two sides of SZR.

The Villa

For luxury living at an affordable price, The Villa offers residents spacious villas, many with pools, for relatively low prices. Due to its location further out in Dubailand, and the lack of facilities as yet, most people who move to The Villa are large families who are looking for luxury and space. A Spanish-styled, five-bedroom villa rents for as little as Dhs.170,000, although be prepared to have to foot the bill for landscaping if you are the first tenant to move in. For shops, schools and other amenities, Silicon Oasis, Dubai Autodrome, International Media Production Zone and Arabian Ranches are all only a short drive away.

Umm Suqeim

Map **1 T5** Metro **Noor Islamic Bank**

This is a desirable area mainly because it is close to the beach and has all the amenities you could wish for, while still remaining relatively peaceful. There are only villas in the area. Umm Suqeim is within easy reach of the major road networks and midway between the old centre of Dubai in Deira and the New Dubai emerging further along the coast towards the marina. This is an ever-popular choice for expats with kids but the rents are on the steep side. There is hardly any traffic on the residential streets, but Al Wasl Road and Jumeira Road can get clogged in the evenings.

Accommodation

Villas range from traditional, old single-storey dwellings and smart multi-bedroom villas to palatial mansions. If you're extremely lucky you may hear about an old (perhaps run-down) villa going for Dhs.150,000, but for this price you can expect to have to pay for any maintenance and repairs. In fact, you hear stories of people spending a fair amount to make their cheap villa more liveable, only for the owner to then up the rent once they see how nice it is. For a detached four or five-bedroom villa, you'll be paying at least Dhs.250,000.

Shopping & Leisure

There are several supermarkets in the area, including a large Choithrams on Al Wasl Road, which has a dry cleaners, a good florist and a pharmacy. There is also a new Aswaaq supermarket (04 423 4431) in Umm Suqeim 3. Jumeira Road is littered with clothing boutiques and small takeaways, and Madinat Jumeirah sits right on the border between Umm Suqeim and Al Sufouh. Mall of the Emirates (p.431) is less than five minutes away by car and has a large Carrefour.

With the Burj Al Arab, Jumeirah Beach Hotel, and Madinat Jumeirah all on the doorstep, the entertainment and dining options are plentiful. There are also several independent restaurants on Jumeira Road. The nearest cinema is in Mercato (p.432) or Mall of the Emirates, and the entire community is within walking distance to the beach.

Healthcare & Education

The nearest hospital with a 24-hour emergency room is the private Neuro Spinal Hospital opposite Jumeirah Beach Park in Jumeira 2. For general medical care there is the government-run Umm Suqeim Health Centre (04 502 3100). Jumeira Road has several specialist clinics as well. The Medcare Hospital (p.184) by Safa Park is also nearby. The largest secondary school is Emirates International School (p.162). Umm Suqeim is also home to two Raffles International campuses (04 427 1200), and there are several other schools in neighbouring Jumeira and Al Sufouh. There are plenty of nurseries including Emirates British Nursery (p.154) and Alphabet Street Nursery (p.152).

SETTING UP HOME

Moving Services

When hiring from abroad, Dubai employers sometimes offer help (such as a shipping allowance or furniture allowance) but the city is also well served by relocation specialists. If you're planning to arrive with more than a suitcase, you'll need to send your belongings by air or by sea. Air freight is faster but more expensive. Sea freight takes longer but it's cheaper, and containers can hold a huge amount.

Everything you ship will need to be checked by customs and you must be present to collect your goods. Air freight must be picked up from Cargo Village in Garhoud and sea freight from Jebel Ali Port. Be sure to have your own copy of the inventory so that you know exactly what is in each box. And be patient.

Shipping goods by air can be expensive, so it may be worth only sending your bare essentials. Most of the big relocation companies will have warehouses at Cargo Village, so the entire process can be handled there. Head to the warehouse and fill out the customs information, and pay any applicable fees. You will then have to go across to Customs where you will pay any duty, plus a processing fee. Once this has been done, you can go back to the warehouse and collect your shipment. Before you can leave, you will have to head back over to Customs to have your goods x-rayed.

The process for sea freight is a little longer but some agencies will do the customs clearing for you, and arrange delivery to your home. This is also true

for some air freight companies. Once your sea freight is ready for collection (you'll get a call or letter), go to the agent's office and pay the administration and handling charges. Keep these documents. The Bill of Lading number must be marked on all paperwork and entered into the customs computer system.

Smooth Moves

- Get more than one quote – some companies will match lower quotes to get the job.
- Make sure that all items are covered by insurance.
- Ensure you have a copy of the inventory and that each item is listed.
- Don't be shy about requesting packers to repack items if you are not satisfied.
- Take photos of the packing process, to use for evidence if you need to make a claim.
- Carry customs restricted goods (DVDs, videos or books) with you: it's easier to open a suitcase in the airport than empty a box outside in the sun.

Then go to Dubai Customs House, on Al Mina Road. The staff are helpful and the procedure is fairly straightforward, so ignore the touts outside. When the papers have been stamped and the Port Clearance received (there are fees at each stage) head down to Jebel Ali Port.

Now that rents are dropping, many people are moving within Dubai. If your possessions are valuable, you will want to hire an insured company to do the packing and moving for you. If not, you may benefit from packing your belongings yourself and hiring an uninsured 'man with a van'. There are several trucks-for-hire companies in the city and the best way to find a good one is to ask a friend or colleague. Otherwise, go to large furniture places such as Dragon Mart (p.437) or IKEA (p.386) where these unlicensed movers often congregate. A quick drive through an industrial area such as Al Quoz will also turn up some results. The trucks will usually have a mobile number written on the side of the door. Call the number and try to negotiate a good price (usually around Dhs.60 an hour) for the truck, driver and moving labour.

Storage

Whether you're making the move to Dubai and haven't yet found the perfect home for all that furniture you've had shipped over, you've downsized a little and have possessions that simply won't fit between your current four walls, or you're moving on for a few months but don't want to take all your worldly goods with you quite yet, storage can be an excellent option. Stor all (storall.ae) based in Jebel Ali, for example, is a good facility with space rentable on a monthly basis and accessible seven days a week.

Sentinel Storage (sentinelme.com) is another option, while the bigger removals and deliveries firms may also be able to offer storage services.

Relocation & Removal Companies

Acorn Movers 04 323 6920, *acornmovers.com*
Ahmed Saleh Packing Worldwide Movers 04 285 4000, *ahmedsalehpacking.com*
Al Futtaim Logistics > ***p.99*** 04 881 8288, *aflogistics.com*
Allied Pickfords 04 408 9555, *alliedpickfords.com*
Crown Relocations > ***p.37*** 04 230 5300, *crownrelo.com*
Gulf Agency Company (GAC) 04 881 8090, *gac.com/dubai*
Interem > ***p.39*** 04 807 0584, *interem.ae*
ISS Worldwide Movers > ***p.66*** 04 303 8555 , *iss-shipping.com*
Move One Inc 04 438 5300, *moveoneinc.com*
Santa Fe Relocations 04 454 2724, *santaferelo.com*
StorAll 04 880 3644, *storall.ae*
Writer Relocations 04 884 9864, *writercorporation.com*

Furnishing Accommodation

Most properties, including rentals, come unfurnished, and don't even have basic white goods such as a cooker or fridge. Not all villas have fitted cupboards and wardrobes, although most apartments do. Dubai is home to a wide range of furniture shops offering different types of furnishings, from Swedish simplicity at IKEA (p.386) and modern design at Home Centre (p.385) and Dogtas (dogtasuae.com) to rich Indian teak at Marina Gulf Trading (p.388). Alternatively, head to one of the carpentry workshops on Naif Road or in Satwa. See p.385 for more information on where to buy furniture, and p.390 for white goods.

Jumeirah Lakes Towers

Second-Hand Furniture

The population of Dubai is still fairly transitory. As a result, finding second-hand furniture in good condition is quite easy. There are a number of small shops, mainly in Karama, Naif and Satwa that sell second-hand furniture, but you might find even better bargains from scouring online classifieds. Try dubizzle.com, expatwoman.com, websouq.com, dubaidonkey.com or askexplorer.com. They have quite large followings and everything from white goods to living room furniture can be picked up. The Expat Woman website will often have notices for garage sales, where it's quite often possible to buy in bulk and prices can be negotiable.

Supermarket noticeboards also carry listings for garage sales, or individual items with photos so you have a good idea what to expect before you view. Dubai Flea Market is held regularly in Safa Park, usually on the first Saturday of every month, with occasional markets also held at Al Mamzar Beach Park and at Uptown Mirdif (dubai-fleamarket.com). The markets are open between 08:00 or 09:00 and 15:00, and can draw quite a crowd of eager bargain hunters.

Furniture Leasing

Setting up a new life and home is an expensive business. Aside from rental or mortgage costs, it is unlikely that many expats will have shipped their entire home contents over here, so renting furniture is an option worth considering. Indigo Living (p.446) provides rentals on a short and long-term basis – perfect for new arrivals and those who are in town on a short working contract. Having the option of renting furniture also means it's possible to move into your new home earlier, and there is no initial rush to have the entire house furnished before you can move in.

Curtains & Blinds

Finding the right blinds or curtains can add a finishing touch to your room, ensure privacy if the house is overlooked, or stop you waking up with the sun. Some properties have windows built to standard sizes, which means you can buy ready-made options from shops such as IKEA (p.386) and THE One (p.386). If these don't measure up, there are several companies that will tailor and install curtains and blinds to fit your property. Curtain specialist Dubai Blinds can bring samples to your home to help you ensure the curtains or blinds match your decor, and they'll also take measurements for tailormade finishes.

Swanky new curtains don't always come cheap though, so if you're looking for something more affordable, try your regular tailor (p.374), or look on community noticeboards for second-hand blinds or curtains that were made to fit the strange window sizes found in many freehold developments.

Avenue Interiors 04 341 2505, *avenueinteriors.ae*
Dubai Blinds 04 368 8759, *dubaiblinds.com*
Home Centre 04 341 4441, *homecentrestores.com*
IKEA 04 203 7555, *ikea.com*
Indigo Living 04 339 7705, *indigo-living.com*
Pan Emirates 04 383 0800, *panemirates.com*
Sedar 04 345 4597, *sedaremirates.com*

Interior Design

Moving into a new, empty apartment can be a hassle if you have arrived without any furnishings – but there are several good interior design firms in the city that can make the interior decorating process easier.

3 Square 04 34 63 872, *3squareinteriors.com*
Cecilia Clason 04 362 6261, *ceciliaclason.com*
Cottage Chic 04 437 0268, *cottagechic.ae*
Élan Interiors 04 338 7417, *elaninteriorsdubai.com*
Emirates Decor & Furniture Directory 04 267 4274, *emiratesdecor.com*
Indigo Living 04 339 7705, *indigo-living.com*
Jadis Interiors 04 347 4233, *jadisuae.com*
OX Interior Design 04 257 3330, *oxinterior.com*
WA International 04 266 3050, *wa-international.com*

Household Insurance

Crime and natural disasters are not generally a big concern for Dubai's residents, but insuring your household goods against theft or damage is still wise. To create a policy, the insurance provider will need your home address, a list of household items and valuation, and invoices for anything worth more than Dhs.2,500.

Cover usually includes theft, fire and storm damage. You can also insure personal items outside the home. As a guideline you can expect to pay around Dhs.1,500 per 1.2 sq m for building insurance, Dhs.250 for up to Dhs.60,000 worth of home contents and Dhs.850 for up to Dhs.60,000 worth of personal possessions.

For complete peace of mind, register your home in the Dubai Police Home Security Programme, a free service that provides round-the-clock protection for houses while residents are away. Register at any Dubai police station.

AFIA Insurance Brokerage Services 04 337 9987, *afia.ae*
AXA Insurance (Gulf) 04 324 3434, *axa-gulf.com*
Greenshield Insurance 04 397 4464, *greenshield.ae*
HSBC Bank Middle East 800 4560, *hsbc.ae*
National General Insurance Co 04 222 2772, *ngi.ae*
Nexus Insurance 04 323 1111, *nexusadvice.com*

UTILITIES & SERVICES

Electricity & Water

Dubai Electricity and Water Authority (DEWA) provides electricity and water products and services for the entire emirate of Dubai. You can easily sign up for a new connection for your new premises at one of the 14 conveniently-located DEWA customer care centres or online at dewa.gov.ae. A deposit (calculated based on supplied load), is required when you sign up for DEWA services; this will be refundable when you close your account and leave the property.

Standard DEWA charges are applicable as per its slab system with a fixed rate (fils per kWh and fils per gallon) in each slab, and rates will change based on your consumption. There will be an additional variable fuel surcharge of fils per kWh and fils per gallon, which will be added to the bill. For more information on the slab rate and other charges, visit dewa.gov.ae/tariff/newtariff.aspx.

DEWA has an active campaign to encourage everyone to moderate their use of electricity and water. You'll find helpful advice and tips on its website, as well as a range of online services; for example, use the consumption calculator to help you manage and conserve your consumption. And, once you register, it's easy to pay your bills from your new home through one of DEWA's 17 payment methods.

Your DEWA bill also includes a housing charge from Dubai Municipality; this adds up to approximately 5% of the rental value of your property divided over the course of 12 months.

Water

Bottled water is cheap, but most people end up buying a water cooler or pump (available from most large supermarkets), or leasing one from a water supplier and using the four or five-gallon bottles of purified water to drink at home.

Prices vary per company; some charge a deposit of around Dhs.50 for each re-useable bottle, and then Dhs.7 per refill, while Masafi recycles its bottles rather than re-using them and charges Dhs.12 per new bottle. Companies will deliver the bottles to your door, and then collect your empties.

Water Suppliers

Al Shalal 800 4342 *alshalalwaters.com*
Culligan International 800 4945, *culligan.com*
Desert Springs 04 340 6504, *desertspringswateruae.com*
Falcon Spring Drinking Water 04 396 6072, *falconspringwater.com*
Masafi 04 346 5959, *masafi.com*
Nestle Waters Management & Technology 04 324 0800, *nestle-waters.com*
Oasis Water 04 884 5656, *oasiscome2life.com*

Gas

There are still no gas mains in Dubai, and therefore individual gas canisters need to be purchased and attached to the cookers. There are a number of gas suppliers that will deliver the canisters and connect up the supply. Supply companies tend to slip stickers or flyers under doors on a regular basis and they're all essentially the same in terms of both service and price. A few of the largest companies include Al Fahidi Gas (04 351 6452), Oasis Gas (04 396 1812) and New City Gas (04 351 8282).

Gas bottles come in three sizes: most houses use the medium size, the small are better in apartments and the large are really only for industrial use – they are enormous. The canisters initially cost around Dhs.350 and refills are usually Dhs.75 (keep your receipt so that you can get some of your deposit back). There is usually a gas van operating around each area at all times; chances are that if you run out of gas in the middle of cooking your chips, one call to your local gas man and he can be with you in less than 20 minutes.

Sewerage

Much of Dubai now has mains sewers but there are areas where houses and apartment buildings are still serviced by septic tanks. These are regularly emptied by municipality contractors, but should you have a problem, contact your landlord or local municipality office. All sewage has to be treated, hence the charges on the DEWA bill even for houses not on the main sewer network.

Rubbish Disposal

Dubai's per capital domestic waste rate is extremely high, with some estimates saying that each household generates over 1,000 kg of rubbish per year – one of the worst offenders in the world. Fortunately, rubbish disposal is efficient, with municipality trucks driving around each area and emptying skips daily.

Just empty your household bins into the skips (there is usually one on every street). If you don't have a skip on your street, then contact the municipality on 800 900 to request one. Certain areas, such as Emirates Living, have wheelie bins outside each house, where waste is regularly collected from. Recycling efforts are poor but slowly improving. For more information on recycling and environmental issues, see p.11.

Telephone

There are two telecommunications companies in the UAE, Etisalat and du. Both are government-owned.

To install a landline with Etisalat you must apply directly with a completed application form, the original and a copy of your passport and residence visa or Emirates ID, and Dhs.225 (inclusive of first quarterly rental). Taking the number of the landline

closest to your house can help pinpoint your location. Telephone calls between landlines in Dubai are free, but there is a nominal charge for calls to Jebel Ali. Depending on the time of day, calls to elsewhere in the UAE cost Dhs.0.30 per minute. The tariffs for international calls vary by country but there is some variation in peak timings, depending on country. For more information on phone services with Etisalat, including peak and off-peak timings, see etisalat.ae.

du's landline service offers pay-by-the-second landlines and flat rates on long-distance calls. du provides services to many Emaar and Nakheel properties, both business and residential (such as Dubai Marina, Arabian Ranches, Emirates Living, the Greens/Springs/Lakes, and International City). Villas and apartments in these areas are equipped with multiple sockets for telephone, internet and TV signals. To apply, you will need a copy of your passport including residency visa page and tenancy agreement. The fees include a one-off installation charge (Dhs.200) plus line rental of Dhs.15 per month. For more information on phone services with du, check its website, du.ae.

Area Codes & Prefixes

Abu Dhabi	02	Jebel Ali	04
Ajman	06	Ras Al Khaimah	07
Al Ain	03	Sharjah	06
Dubai	04	Umm Al Quwain	06
Fujairah	09		
Hatta	04	UAE Country Code	+971

Mobile Phones

Mobile phone users can choose between du (prefix 055 and 052) and Etisalat (prefixes 050 or 056). Both providers offer monthly or pay-as-you-go packages. You can register for a pay-as-you-go line and pick up a SIM card for either Etisalat or du from any of the company kiosks located in malls or from any of the many mobile phone shops scattered throughout the city. To get a line, you will need your passport with residency visa. A du pay-as-you-go line costs Dhs.55 including a Dhs.25 credit to get you started. An Etisalat pay-as-you-go line costs Dhs.40 and includes Dhs.5 credit. You do not need to renew the line as long as you keep using it, and for du you get lifetime validity if you recharge the phone more than 20 times in four months.

Both companies also offer monthly post-paid services. To sign up for a post-paid plan through du, you will need to bring your passport and residency visa as well as either a UAE credit card, a recent utility bill with your physical address, your tenancy agreement, or a salary certificate that shows a minimum salary of Dhs.2,500 per month. For an Etisalat post-paid mobile line you will need to bring your passport with residency visa as well as Emirates ID, and a salary certificate showing a minimum salary of Dhs.2,500 per month. A new du postpaid line costs from Dhs.25 monthly, while an Etisalat line costs from Dhs.20 per month plus a Dhs.125 connection fee (covered by a Dhs.125 welcome credit).

Cheap Calls Not Allowed

Downloading voice over internet protocol (VoIP) services such as Skype can be difficult within the UAE due to the sites being blocked here. However, if you have downloaded it in a different country, or within an area where the restriction is lifted, such as in some free zones, it will work when calling another computer, but not when calling landlines or mobiles.

Internet

Internet services in the UAE are provided by either Etisalat or du. All internet usage, however, is regulated by the Telecommunications Regulatory Authority (TRA). This means that many sites that are deemed to be offensive, either religiously, culturally or politically, are blocked and can't be accessed.

Etisalat has various packages available based on speed. For a 1mbps broadband connection with unlimited usage you pay a Dhs.180 installation fee plus Dhs.259 per month. Or, you can opt for an eLife landline, TV and internet bundle , which starts from Dhs.299 per month plus Dhs.180 installation fee. Check etisalat.ae for more details.

That's My Number!

All mobile phone customers now have to register their SIM card with Etisalat or du. Wait until you receive an SMS asking you to register, then take along your Emirates ID or a passport with your residency visa to the nearest service provider outlet. You have three months to register your details, after which any unregistered SIM cards will be cancelled. Registration is free and once only.

If you live in a new development, your internet will most likely be provided by du (du.ae). It offers a range of 'Talk and Surf' internet packages, ranging from 8mbps (Dhs.199 per month) to 24mbps (Dhs.349 per month). There is a Dhs.200 installation fee. You can also add on digital TV with packages starting from Dhs.279. Check du.ae for details.

Wi-Fi Hotspots

Surf the net at cafes and restaurants across the Dubai. There is complimentary Wi-Fi at most the main hotels and a handful of cafes including More, Caffe Nero and Caribou Coffee – you just need to buy a drink. There are also Etisalat and du Wi-Fi hotspots across the emirate – pay from Dhs.5 for 30 minutes or use the free hours' entitlement based on your internet subscription package.

du Installation

All of du's home telecommunication services, including cable TV, are routed through the same sockets. As a result, du recommends you sign up for all of your services at the same time. The installation fee for all du services is Dhs.200, regardless of how many services you have installed at one time.

Postal Services

Until very recently, there has been no postal delivery service to home addresses, and everyone has had their mail delivered to a PO box. In January 2012, Empost rolled out a new system that more closely resembles the traditional postal services in western countries. If you live in a villa, you can sign up to the My Home service which will see post delivered direct to your home three times a week – or six for an additional payment. My Building is the option for apartment residents, with post delivered to a PO box in the lobby or basement. My Box sees your mail delivered to a PO Box at a post office, and finally there's My Zone, where post is delivered to local shelters that contain a large number of boxes, with the idea that you get a box close to your place of work or home. Visit empostuae.com for more details and rates. Alternatively, many people have personal mail delivered to their company's PO box; this traditional method still works and, for many, may be the best option.

Sending Gifts Home

If you would rather not chance the post, Gift Express provides a selection of gifts that can be sent to most countries (giftexpressinternational.com).

Letters and packages do occasionally go missing and, if the item has not been registered, there's little that you can do apart from wait – some turn up months after they are expected, although this happens less and less frequently.

Empost offers a courier service, while registered mail is a relatively inexpensive alternative and can be tracked via a reference number. The major international courier services also deliver and have a presence in Dubai, including DHL (04 299 5333), FedEx (04 218 3860), UPS (800 4774) and Aramex (600 544 000). If you're expecting a package, ensure the person sending it has included your phone number, as that is often the only way for the courier to find your location.

Carpet Cleaners & Laundry Services

Wall-to-wall carpets are rare in this part of the world, but many homes do sport loose rugs and carpets. When they're looking a bit grubby, the companies listed below can pay you a visit, give you a quote, and take the carpets away to be cleaned, returning them a couple of days later. All of the carpet services listed below will also come to your house to clean upholstery.

There are no self-service launderettes, but laundry shops are everywhere. Some of the largest chains in the city include Butler's (04 347 2106) and Champion Cleaners (04 366 3359). As well as dry cleaning and laundry, they all offer ironing services. If you have specific instructions, make sure these are noted when you drop off your laundry – creases in trousers are standard, so if you don't want them, speak up.

Compensation policies for lost or damaged items vary, but losses are rare, even in the places that look most disorganised. Large chains normally have a free pick-up and delivery service. Expect to pay Dhs.16 for a shirt, Dhs.53 for a suit and Dhs.48 for a quilt.

Alpha Cleaning Services 800 2737, *alphaserves.com*
Churchill 04 323 6863, *churchill-gulf.com*
Dubai Carpet Cleaning 04 221 9800, *dubai-carpet-cleaning.com*
Modern Cleaning Methods 04 285 1668, *modernmethodsco.com*

Domestic Help

Domestic help is readily available in Dubai, whether full or part-time, and there are a number of options available. Legally, a housemaid may only be employed by the individual who sponsors her, but in practice many maids take on cleaning or babysitting for other families; if you are caught you face a hefty fine and the maid may be deported.

If you are looking for someone part time, but want to stay within the law, there are many companies in Dubai that provide cleaners and maids on an hourly basis, and for around Dhs.35 per hour they'll take care of all your sweeping, mopping, dusting, washing, and ironing. Most companies stipulate a minimum number of hours, usually two or three per visit.

City Sky Maid Services 04 332 4600, *cityskymaid.com*
Dubai Maids 04 880 4670, *dubai-maids.com*
Ecomaid Middle East 04 386 9977, *ecomaidme.com*
Home Help 04 380 5111, *homehelp.ae*
Housekeeping Co 04 221 1996, *housekeepingco.com*
Howdra 800 469372 *howdra.ae*
Molly Maid 04 339 7799, *mollymaidme.com*
Ready Maids 04 396 6779

HOME IMPROVEMENTS

Maintenance

Whether you're a homeowner or live in rental property, are responsible for your property's general maintenance or have an assigned company, housing in Dubai requires constant maintenance – not in small part thanks to the climate.

Air-conditioning units can be temperamental and need regular servicing, plumbing problems aren't uncommon, electrics can go haywire and creepy crawlies like to pay a visit.

Most homeowners and tenants employ the services of a maintenance company. Annual contracts don't come cheap, but the benefit is it will cover you for most of your maintenance needs. The contract should include regular scheduled servicing of air conditioning units and boilers, seasonal pest control protection, basic masonry works and 24 hour emergency call out services. Most companies offer extra services such as swimming pool maintenance and gardening for an add-on fee. Typical costs for maintenance contracts range from Dhs.7,000 up to Dhs.11,000 per year.

Companies that offer maintenance services include Emrill (covering Emaar Properties, emrill.com), Howdra (howdra.ae), and Hitches & Glitches (hitchesandglitches.com); Green Facilities Management (green-fms.com) prides itself on its environmental and sustainability credentials, offers a 24/7 emergency call-out service, can assess your home for energy efficiency, and sources environmentally sound maintenance products.

For more specialist services, try Under One Roof (04 323 2722, underoneroof.ae); Floorworld (800 35667, floorworld.ae) and Alomi Real Wood Flooring (04 885 8825, alomirealwoodflooringllc.ae).

Whichever community you live in, your developer will have standard rules and regulations relating to noise, parking, and general upkeep of your property. These will be detailed on the developer's website and local security guards perform regular checks. If you live in a villa, a dirty or messy garage may be frowned upon, and you could be fined for such things as parking on the street rather than in a designated bay, so it's worth making yourself aware of what is required of you as either a tenant or homeowner.

Builders

Exact regulations are constantly changing when it comes to making alterations to your property, but so far they have always been extremely restrictive. In Nakheel and Emaar developments, for example, you are not allowed to build any higher than your perimeter wall, so should you wish for the popular addition of an outside extension, conservatory or garden house, you would have had to dig down and build upwards to avoid the structure being higher than the wall.

To build an extension, you need to apply for permission via your master developer, who would need to approve the plans and receive a deposit of Dhs.5,000. An inspector will make a site visit during the works and then carry out a final assessment on completion of the building, after which your deposit will be returned if you have met all the guidelines. These guidelines are very stringent as developers seek to protect the look and feel of communities. They can determine the colour of the paint you may use on the exterior of your property and also the particular design and style of any doors, gates or decorative iron fencing.

All this may change though as the Planning & Engineering Department of Dubai Municipality is currently working to centralise all structural work carried out on residential buildings in Dubai, effectively taking the responsibility out of the hands of the developers. The anticipation is that when the new laws are passed, rules on extension plans and designs will be more lenient.

If you are intending to make some structural changes to your property you should always use a licensed and experienced contractor. Options include Kalandoor Contracting (04 884 9426), Al Baraha Land Building Contracting and General Maintenance (04 272 2999), and Danube Buildmart (800 284536278).

Painters

Once you own your property you are free to paint the insides in any style you choose. If you rent, the likelihood is that your landlord will not mind on the basis that he has your deposit, and will be happy to keep hold of it should you not leave the villa or apartment in its original state. Many Dubai landlords do not need much of a reason to hold back security deposits though, so it's worth checking and getting something in writing before you get the roller out.

An excellent range of paints can be found at Jotun Paints and ACE Hardware (800 275 223). Companies like Alpha Services (800 2737) offer painting services, and artists such as Mackenzie Art (mackenzieart.com, 04 41 9803) can be commissioned for children's murals and original artwork. The cost of internally painting a whole villa can vary between Dhs.3,000 and Dhs.8,000, depending on size.

Gardens

For a city on the edge of the desert, Dubai boasts a surprising amount of lush greenery – but, with very little annual rainfall and rapidly diminishing groundwater, plenty of artificial hydration is required if you want to create your very own little garden oasis.

Gardens need watering twice a day ideally, and you will notice a huge deterioration in the quality of your plants and lawns if this routine lessens – green can turn to brown within just a matter of days in these conditions. You can install a timed irrigation system or employ the services of a gardener, while boring a well in your garden to access natural water supplies is also an option.

For houses further in from the coast, such as villas in the Dubailand (Arabian Ranches, for example) area, you'll need to drill down approximately 25 metres before you hit groundwater, whereas houses in areas nearer to the coast, such as Al Barsha or Jumeira, will access water after just a couple of metres. The level of salt in the water can vary considerably, and it is possible to pump the water into a mixed tank to desalinate it for your domestic use. The cost for drilling and finding should be approximately Dhs.1,800 if you secure the expertise of any of the landscaping companies found in the Plant Street area of Satwa (see p.411).

If maintaining a grassy garden seems like just too much hassle, you can always opt for astroturf. Fake lawns are increasingly popular in Dubai; they stay green throughout the year and need no watering (although you do need to hose them down every few weeks). You can buy astroturf (in varying degrees of quality) in ACE Hardware, while Clearview (clearview.ae) and Cape Reed (capereed.com) both install fake lawns. Another option is to go for block paving or decking. Again, you can purchase various qualities of decking in ACE Hardware (800 275 223), while Alomi (alomirealwoodflooringllc.ae) is a wood merchant that has carpenters with experience in laying decks.

For apartment dwellers, or those who wish to add to or beautify their existing outside areas, sourcing individual plants, trees, shrubs, decorative pots, soil and composts is a relatively simple process. The Dubai Municipality Nursery recently relocated to the Jadaf area, next to Business Bay Crossing. Prices are reasonable and discounts based on quantity will be given. Dubai Garden Centre (04 340 0006) sells pretty much everything you could ever need for your outdoor space; prices here are often at the higher end of the spectrum, but you can expect excellent service and not inconsiderable expertise, as well as delivery if you have really gone to town on your plant buying. Plant Street in Satwa has a number of basic nurseries, but choice here can be limited.

Larger retailers such as Spinneys (p.417), Carrefour (p.416) and IKEA (p.386) sell plants, pots and smaller sized gardening implements, while ACE Hardware is a one-stop-shop for the outdoor enthusiast, selling everything from flora to furniture, tools to trees and plants to pergolas.

If you are buying a brand new house, the developers may have left you with no more than a sandpit plot, so you will need to start your garden from scratch, which can be somewhat challenging. Equally, landlords are not obliged to landscape the gardens of new villas before they rent them to you, so don't assume that the 'work in progress' you see upon viewing a property will be an outdoor oasis by the time you move in.

If the green-fingered DIY is not for you, Dubai Garden Centre offers a full landscaping service, while Royal Gardenscape (royalgardenscape.com) provides all you need in the way of paving and gravel. Plant Street is a great place to start for cheap labour and materials, while Terraverde (terraverde.ae), Grow Gardens (growgardens.ae), Toscana Landscaping & Pools (toscanalandscaping.com) and Bespoke Concept (bespokeconcept.com) all offer full service design and installation for gardens. For more information on garden furniture see Shopping, p.388.

Swimming Pools

A lot of properties in Dubai have private pools or access to a shared pool. If you don't have one in your villa, you can always pay to have one installed – but it doesn't come cheap. One option is to have a custom-made, free-form fibre glass and ceramic tiled pool fitted. As tough and durable as a concrete version, these are effectively portable. Delivery of one of these usually takes around four weeks, with an onsite installation period of approximately 10 days. Prices for such a pool start at around Dhs.110,000 including labour, pumps and filtration. Try Pools by Design (poolsdesign.net).

Aside from cleaning, your pool will also need the water to be changed and chemical levels balanced on a regular basis. MAK Pools (makpools.com) offers a full range of swimming pool cleaning and maintenance services. Those Pool Guys (thosepoolguys.com), Al Wasel Swimming Pools Maintenance (alwaselswimmingpools.com) and Pools r Us (poolsrusdubai.com) are also well established in Dubai. If you have a young family, then take a look at Aqua-Net (aquanet.ae), which creates custom safety netting that quickly and easily covers your pool.

Waterfront living

Work, Finance & The Law

WORKING IN DUBAI

Expat workers come to Dubai for a number of reasons: to advance their career, for a higher standard of living, to take advantage of new opportunities or, most commonly, for the lifestyle and the experience of living and working in a new culture. Whatever the reason, there are various advantages to working here.

While the biggest bonus of working in Dubai may seem to be tax-free salaries, the cost of living (or your newly acquired lifestyle) can somewhat balance out this benefit.

In addition, the instability of the world's economy has had an effect on the job market in Dubai, and there has been a shift from the fervent recruitment drive of past years. However, the situation is constantly changing. At the very senior end of the scale, there remain some idyllic opportunities and huge packages that attract the big players, and these are predominantly in the construction, aviation and finance industries.

However, for less senior positions, the image of a cushy expat life in the Gulf is changing, with much more competition in all areas of the market and an increasing number of people looking for work in Dubai. Not so long ago, foreign expats could walk into jobs that they could only dream of back home, but these days the market is much more competitive, not least because of the effects of the global economic downturn. All-inclusive packages with accommodation and education allowances are not as common, although basic benefits still apply (such as annual flights home and 22 calendar days leave).

Work-wise, Dubai is still a land of opportunities for skilled professionals. It is easier to change industries, as skill sets are less 'pigeon-holed' than in other countries and jobs in certain industries (such as construction) are more readily available.

Licensed To Work

All professionals working in the social sector, including social workers, counsellors, social therapists and special education teachers, now need a license from the UAE government. For more information about the license, which is valid for two years, visit cda.gov.ae.

One of the main differences with working in Dubai, as opposed to your country of origin, is that you need to be sponsored (see p.38) by an employer, which often leaves people feeling tied or uncomfortably obligated to their employer. If you leave the company, your current visa will be cancelled and you will have to go through the hassle of getting a new residency permit (for you and your family, if they are on your sponsorship).

Labour Card

To work in the UAE you are legally required to have a valid labour card. The labour card can only be applied for once you have residency, and is usually organised by the company PRO. If you are recruited from your home country, your company will have to get approval from the Ministry of Labour. You will then enter on an employment visa, get a health card, take the medical test, and get the residency stamp in your passport. The company PRO then takes all of the relevant paperwork to the Ministry of Labour where the actual labour card will be issued (even though it has 'work permit' printed on the back). The card features your photo and details of your employer. You're supposed to carry the card with you at all times but it is highly unlikely that you will ever be asked to produce it. The process can also be quite slow, and it's possible you may not receive your card for a few weeks, or even months, after starting work. The labour card costs Dhs.1,000 (paid by your company) and is valid for two years. It must be renewed within 60 days of expiry. Failure to do so will result in a fine (which your company will be liable for) of Dhs.5,000 for each year the card has expired.

If your employer is arranging your residency, you will need to sign your labour contract before the labour card is issued. This contract is printed in both Arabic and English. It's not necessarily your agreed

'contract' as such – most employees will sign a more comprehensive contract. Unless you read Arabic it may be advisable to have a translation made of your details, since the Arabic is the official version in any dispute. However, if there is any discrepancy, the judge would want to know why your company got the details wrong in the first place (see Employment Contracts, p.116). Note that the plan is for labour cards to be phased out in favour of the Emirates ID (p.35) but, for now, the labour card is still required.

Working Hours

Working hours differ dramatically between companies; straight shifts vary from 07:30 to 14:30 for government organisations to the common 09:00 to 18:00 for private companies. Most retail outlets tend to be open from 10:00 to 22:00 but often operate shifts. Teachers start early at around 07:30 and classes finish around 14:30, although their hours aren't as predetermined as other roles. Although less common nowadays, some offices and shops operate split shifts, which allow for a longer break in the afternoon (hours are usually 08:00 to 13:00 and 16:00 to 19:00).

The maximum number of hours permitted per week according to UAE Labour Law is 48, although some industries, such as hospitality and retail, have longer stipulated hours. Annual holiday allowance starts at one calendar month per year, or roughly 22 working days. Some employees, especially those in management, have more than this and long service usually adds to holiday allowance.

Friday is the Islamic holy day and therefore a universal day off for offices and schools. Consumer demand means that the hospitality and retail industries are open seven days a week. Saturday is the second day of the weekend; some companies work five and a half days a week and some operate a six-day week, taking only Friday as a rest day.

Public holidays (see p.7) are set by the government, while the timing of religious holidays depends on the sighting of the moon. This can mean that it is difficult to plan holidays, as confirmation of public holidays can come just days before the event. The Labour Law states that all employees (even non-Muslims) are entitled to a shorter working day during Ramadan, although labour lawyers would advise you not to insist on this if you are non-Muslim or not fasting.

Business Culture

Like anywhere in the world, doing business in the UAE has its unique idiosyncrasies. Even if you work for a western company, the chances are that some of your business transactions will be with Emiratis, whether on a customer or client basis. While you're likely to find that Emiratis are open to different styles of business and are generally keen to explain their customs,

DIFC & Jumeirah Emirates Towers

understanding some of the local business etiquette can help you keep one step ahead of the competition.

It's a good idea to dress conservatively for meetings, particularly if you are female, and it is advisable to cover your knees and arms. You may also have a meeting with a woman wearing a hijab (a veil which leaves the face uncovered), or some women choose to wear a niqab which covers the full face.

Don't be surprised if greetings are more tactile in the UAE than in your home country; long handshakes, kisses and effusive compliments are common. While it's normal to shake hands with people of the same sex, if you are meeting someone of the opposite sex it's best to take your cue from the other person and not offer your hand unless they offer theirs.

It's polite to send greetings to a person's family, but can be considered rude to enquire directly about someone's wife, sister or daughter. A nose kiss is a customary greeting in the Gulf region but is only used between close friends and associates, and you should not attempt to greet someone in this way.

Business meetings will usually start with numerous greetings and an exchange of business cards – you should take the time to read the card as a sign of respect. Punctuality is important and arriving late to meetings is considered very impolite – however, don't assume that your meeting will start at the appointed time or that it will not be interrupted.

If you're attending a business meeting at an Arab-owned company, it's likely that you'll be served traditional Arabic coffee, or kahwa. Sharing coffee is an important social ritual in the Middle East so you should drink some when offered. Cups should be taken in the right hand and if there is a waiter standing by, replenishing your cup, there are two ways to signal that you have had enough: either leave a small amount of coffee in the bottom of your cup or gently tip the cup from side to side.

While not so much a matter of etiquette, patience is the ultimate virtue for doing business in the UAE. Things may move more slowly and decisions take longer than you may be used to. Keeping in regular contact with your clients and customers helps to maintain genial relations and picking up the phone rather than relying on email can make the world of difference.

Finding Work

Until the financial crisis hit, Dubai's economy was booming and therefore the recruitment market was extremely buoyant. Things have slowed down a great deal and a large majority of companies made redundancies, forcing many expats to return home. However, the UAE remains optimistic and the outlook is more positive for 2013 onwards. Opportunities are out there but the competition for good positions is greater, which means there is a stronger focus on what skills employees will bring to the table.

There are numerous recruitment agencies in Dubai but employers also use local newspapers and headhunters to advertise job opportunities. It is undoubtedly easier to look for a job once you are in Dubai. Your first step should be to get your hands on the Gulf News appointments supplement (gnads4u.com), published every day except Fridays and Saturdays, or the Khaleej Times Appointments (khaleejtimes.com) every day except Friday – also available online. The National has a careers section that is available to those who subscribe online.

It is beneficial too to check listings on online versions of international newspapers as companies within the UAE often post jobs on these sites. Websites for The Guardian (guardian.co.uk) and The Times (timesonline.co.uk) newspapers in the UK and The Washington Post (washingtonpost.com) in the US are often a good resource. You can also upload your CV to sites like monstergulf.com, naukrigulf.com, bayt.com and gulftalent.com. Job advertisements are posted on dubizzle.com and expatwoman.com.

It is a good idea to register with a recruitment agency too (p.116) and to contact companies directly and start networking (p.116). Networking sites like linkedin.com should also be useful. Thanks to Dubai's relatively small size, the more people you meet the more likely you are to bump into someone who just happens to work somewhere that has a vacant position that you might be able to fill.

Many large Dubai-based companies have vacancy listings on their websites, so if you have a company in mind, it's up to you to keep checking its site for updated listings.

Advertisements in Dubai can be more direct than in other countries and, while it isn't always acceptable to specify candidate requirements like nationality in other countries, advertisements here will often detail whether they are looking for a 'western applicant' for example.

Most recruitment agencies accept CVs via email, but you can check whether they accept walk-ins. The agency will then set up an interview where you are usually required to fill out a form summarising your CV, you will also need a few passport photos. The agency takes its fee from the registered company once the position has been filled. It is illegal for a recruitment company to levy fees on candidates for this service, although some might try.

Headhunters (also known as executive search companies) will usually contact desirable candidates directly to discuss opportunities, but this is normally for more senior positions.

Should you be suitable for a job, a recruitment agency will mediate between you and the employer and arrange interviews. However, don't rely too heavily on the agency finding a job for you. Often, agencies depend on candidates spotting one of their advertised vacancies. Below is a list of recruitment agencies based in the UAE. Some of these specialise in certain industries, so do your research.

For external advice on changing jobs or improving your long-term employment prospects, contact Sandpiper Coaching (sandpipercoaching.com), a career coaching company based in Dubai that provides coaching programmes for people who have lost their jobs, those who are looking for a change of job, and people returning to work after a career break.

Recruitment Agencies

Akhtaboot 04 364 9419, *akhtaboot.com*
BAC Middle East 04 439 8500, *bacme.com*
Bayt.com 04 449 3100, *bayt.com*
Charterhouse Partnership > *p.117* 04 372 3500, *charterhouseme.ae*
Focus Direct Management Consultants 04 355 4134, *focusdirect.net*
Hays Specialist Recruitment 04 361 2882, *hays.ae*
Kershaw Leonard 04 422 8970, *kershawleonard.net*
Manpower Professional 04 391 0460, *manpower-me.com*
Morgan McKinley 04 324 4094, *morganmckinley.ae*
SOS Recruitment Consultant 04 358 5170, *sosrecruitment.net*
Talent Management Consultancy 04 335 0999, *talentdubai.com*

Networking & Events

With Dubai still being a relatively small city, made up of communities that are smaller still, networking is critical, even across industries. Everyone seems to know everyone and getting in with the corporate 'in-crowd' definitely has its plus points.

Business acumen here can, at times, be more important than specific industry knowledge so it pays to attend business events and trade shows. Make friends in government departments and this will often land you in the front line for opportunities.

Likewise, bad news is rarely made public here, so staying in tune with the grapevine can help prevent wrong decisions. Social networking sites like LinkedIn (linkedin.com) are a great resource when looking for new jobs or contacts, while groups like Heels & Deals (heelsanddeals.org) arrange regular meet-ups. Eleqt.com is an exclusive social networking site for high-level executives and entrepreneurs willing to pay the Dhs.18,000 joining fee.

Business Councils

American Business Council Of Dubai & The Northern Emirates 04 379 1414, *abcdubai.com*
Arab Business Club 04 358 3000, *arabbusinessclub.org*
Australian Business Council Dubai 04 367 2437, *abc-dxb.com*
British Business Group 04 397 0303, *britbiz-uae.com*
Canadian Business Council 04 359 2625, *cbc-dubai.com*
Danish Business Council Dubai 04 359 2625, *danishbusinessdubai.com*
French Business Council Dubai & The Northern Emirates 04 312 6700, *fbcdubai.com*
German Emirati Joint Council For Industry & Commerce 04 447 0100, *ahkuae.com*
Indian Business & Professional Council 04 332 4300, *ibpcdubai.com*
Iranian Business Council 04 335 9220, *ibc.ae*
Italian Business Council 04 321 3082, *italianbusinesscouncil.com*
Malaysia Business Council 04 335 5538, *mbc-uae.com*
Netherlands Business Council 050 559 2272, *nbcdubai.com*
Pakistan Business Council Dubai 04 335 9991, *pbcdubai.com*
Singapore Business Council 04 338 7336, *sbcuae.com*
South African Business Council 04 390 0433, *sabco-uae.org*
Spanish Business Council 04 427 0379, *spanishbusinesscouncil.ae*
Swedish Business Council 04 429 8600, *sbcuae.se*
Swiss Business Council 04 368 7702, *swissbcuae.com*

Employment Contracts

An employment contract should list the full details of your employment, including the name of the employer, details of your salary and a breakdown of your responsibilities. Accepting an expat posting can have its pitfalls, so before you sign, pay special attention to things such as probation periods, accommodation, annual leave, travel entitlements, medical and dental cover, notice periods, and repatriation entitlements.

Labour Your Point

If you have a complaint about any issues that occur while dealing with the Ministry of Labour, there is a special departmental hotline you can call (04 702 3333), which aims to improve the ministry's transparency.

There is often confusion over the offer letter and the contract. An offer letter should give details of the terms of the job you are being offered, such as salary, leave, hours and other benefits; if you accept the terms of this offer, it becomes a legally binding contract. You may be asked to sign an additional Ministry of Labour contract that accompanies your residency application, but the initial offer letter is, in effect, your contract. If you receive your employment

Explore further with
Charterhouse Partnership
STRATEGIC CAREER DEVELOPMENT
Banking
Finance
Human Resources
Construction
Sales and Marketing
Legal and Compliance
Information Technology
Insurance
Healthcare
Facilities Management
Professional Support
Supply Chain and Logistics
CHARTERHOUSE
PARTNERSHIP
MIDDLE EAST · AUSTRALIA · EUROPE · ASIA
www.charterhouseme.ae
info@charterhouse.ae
Dubai Office:
Tel: +971 4 372 3500
Fax: +971 4 332 8062
Abu Dhabi Office:
Tel: +971 2 406 9819
Fax: +971 2 406 9810

contract in both English and Arabic, it's a good idea to have the Arabic translated to ensure they match – the Arabic version will prevail in the UAE courts.

The UAE Labour Law allows for an end-of-service gratuity payment for employees. The rules are a bit convoluted but, basically, an employee on a fixed-term contract, who has completed one or more years of continuous service, will be entitled to 21 days pay for each of the first five years of service, and 30 days pay for each additional year. If the employee is on an 'unlimited duration' (open-ended) contract and terminates it of his own accord, he will get a third of the gratuity for a service period of between one and three years, two thirds for three to five years, and the full amount if service exceeds five years.

Leaving before the end of your fixed-term contract or being fired for breaking the UAE Labour Law could result in the loss of your gratuity payment. Gratuity payments are worked out according to your basic salary, but note that your salary will be split into various categories (basic, housing, transport and utilities). You will still get the same cash salary at the end of every month, but because your basic salary is much lower than your total salary, your gratuity payment is lower.

The UAE Labour Law states that probation periods can be set for a maximum of six months. Some companies may delay the residency process illegally until the probation period is up, which can make settling in difficult – no residency means you can't sponsor family members, buy a car or get a bank loan.

By law, employees are not entitled to paid sick leave during probation and most firms do not permit annual leave to be taken during this time – you will continue to accrue annual leave over the course of the year.

Free Zones

It was way back in 2001 when Dubai Media City first opened its doors to regional and international media companies and, since then, not only has the free zone concept expanded rapidly across several industries, but there has also been the arrival of several other creative free zones. Unique laws regarding taxation, recruitment of labour, and income apply to these areas. These benefits make free zones ideal for companies wishing to establish a distribution, manufacturing and service base for trade outside of the UAE.

Employees of companies in free zones have different sponsorship options depending on the free zone. For example, in Jebel Ali you can either be sponsored by an individual company or by the free zone authority itself. Whether you are in the Jebel Ali Free Zone, Dubai Internet City, Media City, Knowledge Village, Healthcare City or the Dubai Airport Free Zone, the respective authority will process your residency permit directly through the Immigration Department, without having to get employment approval from the Ministry of Labour. This speeds up the process significantly, and residency permits can sometimes be granted in a matter of hours. Once Immigration has stamped your residence permit in your passport, the free zone will issue your labour card – this also acts as your security pass for entry to the free zone. A big advantage of working in a free zone is the lack of red tape encountered if you move jobs to another free zone company. This is because the free zone is actually your sponsor, so when you switch jobs to another employer you won't be switching sponsors.

If you want to work as a consultant or you wish to set up a small business, free zones are the best bet. The process and fees for getting a visa varies between each free zone, and the cost of commercial property can be quite high in popular free zones, such as Dubai Media City and the Jebel Ali Free Zone.

The validity of a free zone residency permit depends on how long the labour card is valid for (either one or two years, depending on the free zone). Designed to encourage investment from overseas, free zones allow 100% foreign ownership and offer exemption from taxes and customs duties. An added attraction is the relative lack of red tape. For more information on setting up a business in a free zone, refer to Explorer's *Working In The Gulf*.

Labour Law

The UAE Federal Law Number 8 for 1980 on regulation of labour relations (otherwise known as the UAE Labour Law) outlines information on employee entitlements, employment contracts and disciplinary rules. The law is employer friendly, but it also clearly outlines employee rights. You can download a copy of the document from the Ministry of Labour website (mol.gov.ae); the document has not been fully updated for some time but amendments and additions are often posted on the site.

Maternity Leave

Under UAE Labour Law, women are entitled to 45 days maternity leave, on full pay, once they've completed one year of continuous service – fathers are not entitled to paternity leave. Maternity leave can only be used directly before and after the birth. Those who have been with their employer for less than a year can claim 45 days on half pay (see p.139 for more information).

Labour unions and strikes are illegal, although there have been protests by labourers in the past. The labourers achieved some results and the employers concerned were forced to pay wages immediately or remedy living conditions, and a hotline was set up for other unpaid workers to report their employers.

Also, an amended federal labour law looks likely to allow the formation of labour unions (trade unions have long existed in some other Gulf countries). If you find yourself in the situation where you have not been paid, you can file a case with the UAE Labour Department who will take the necessary action. You could also get a lawyer to deal with the claim on your behalf (see p.132 for a list of law firms). Although lawyers are expensive in Dubai, the employer will have to bear the cost if the case is settled in your favour.

Changing Jobs

Previously, anyone leaving a job and cancelling their visa faced the possibility of being 'banned' for six months. Fortunately, the banning rules have been relaxed, so as long as you remain on good terms with your employer, and you are given permission to leave your job (in the form of a no objection certificate or NOC), you should be able to switch to a new job without any problem.

It is important to review whether a non-compete clause was added to your contract, particularly if your new role is with a direct competitor to your current employer. This clause could mean that you are restricted to taking an unrelated role before returning to your current field.

To change sponsors, pick up the relevant forms from the Ministry of Labour and get them typed in Arabic. Get the forms signed and stamped by both your previous and new employers, and submit them along with the trade licence and establishment card of your new company. Everything goes to the Immigration Department, which will amend your visa. In most cases your new employer will take care of this procedure for you.

There are some exceptions where you can transfer your sponsorship without the approval of your current sponsor, such as death of your sponsor, change of company ownership, company closure and cancellation of your company's trade licence. If your company has closed, it is important to note that you will receive an automatic labour ban unless the company has cancelled its trade licence.

Regulations differ in the free zones, as you are technically sponsored by the Free Zone Authority (FZA) rather than the company. Therefore if you move to another company within the free zone, there is no need to transfer your visa.

Banning

The notorious 'ban' is a topic of frequent discussion in Dubai, however the details of when and for how long you can be banned change from case to case.

There are two types of ban: an employment ban that restricts employment for a period (usually six months to a year), or a visa ban (which restricts entry or departure from Dubai). A visa ban is often imposed

DIFC

if you have committed a serious criminal offence, or you have absconded (p.122). Theoretically, it is possible for your employer to ban you from working with another company for a short period of time, even if you have served the correct notice period and have left on good terms. However, this is less likely since a new fee was introduced and employers now have to pay to ban an employee.

A six-month employment ban can also be imposed by the Ministry of Labour, with no instruction from your previous employers, but this is indeterminate and can often be resolved. This ban can also apply to working women sponsored by a family member who decide to change jobs or to leave work without completing two years of employment. If you do receive a ban, all is not lost; it may be possible to pay for your ban to be lifted.

The laws regarding banning change frequently and revisions are occasionally posted online without any announcements to the general public. On the whole, recent revisions have very much favoured employees and have made it far easier to move between jobs, and much harder for companies to impose bans. Check the Ministry of Labour website (mol.gov.ae) for updates.

NOC

A No Objection Certificate is a letter of confirmation awarded by your former employer or the Ministry of Labour giving you permission to work for another employer. If you have an NOC from your previous employer, and the Ministry of Labour approves the move, your visa transfer should be hassle-free. But this is one area where laws change frequently so it's best to check with the Labour Department or a lawyer first.

Exhibitionist Tendencies

MICE – it's the one rodent that everyone wants to catch, but what is all the fuss about?

The UAE didn't waste any time in securing its reputation in the area of Meetings, Incentives, Conventions and Exhibitions (or MICE). In just a few short years, this sector has become remarkably buoyant, with Dubai and Sharjah alone organising hundreds of international events each year. The UAE is now recognised as a major player, thanks in part to initiatives by Abu Dhabi's leadership, for instance, who've recognised and backed the industry via a series of incentives and infrastructure developments.

Last year, Abu Dhabi National Exhibition Centre (ADNEC) alone staged more than 120 events, an almost ten-fold increase in just four years. ADNEC's activities are estimated to deliver an economic impact of Dhs.3.1billion each year to the UAE capital. Similarly, Dubai World Trade Centre (DWTC) brings together enterprises, people and ideas, with the goal of accelerating trade, and expertly delivers global events from its purpose-built exhibition centre. Its presence has helped to consolidate Dubai's reputation as an international destination for trade. The results of a burgeoning MICE industry are far from limited to the walls of Dubai and Abu Dhabi's giant conferencing centres. For every trade show that comes to town, there are thousands of flights booked, nights spent in hotels, meals eaten in local restaurants and, ultimately, millions of dirhams are ploughed into the local economy. In terms of showcasing a city, business travel is now every bit as important as conventional tourism – if not even more so.

The Big Three

World Future Energy Summit
Held in January, this features the latest innovations and cutting-edge technologies for sustainable energy alternatives. The summit boasts keynote presentations by leading organisations and experts, and previous events have attracted 26,200 people from 137 countries. *worldfutureenergysummit.com*

Cabsat Mena
Aimed at the region's digital media industry, this three-day event in March showcases the latest tech products and services – from broadcasters, production companies and animation houses to online game developers, computer graphics producers and multimedia retailers. The last event attracted close to 11,500 visitors from over 110 countries. *cabsat.com*

Arabian Travel Market
One of the most popular showcases of the travel and tourism industry, this event, held each May, attracts over 2,000 exhibitors from 70 countries, all keen to exhibit their destinations, routes, accommodation, attractions and more. The event also organises extravagant social functions. *arabiantravelmarket.com*

Major Exhibitions In Dubai & Abu Dhabi 2013

January		
	The Bride Show Abu Dhabi	*thebrideshow.com/abudhabi*
	Dubai Shopping Festival	*dubaievents.ae*
	World Future Energy Summit Abu Dhabi	*worldfutureenergysummit.com*
February		
	Big Boys Toys	*bigboystoysuae.com*
	Gulfood Exhibition	*gulfood.com*
	International Education Show	*educationshow.ae*
	National Career Exhibition	*nationalcareer.ae*
March		
	Cabsat Mena	*cabsat.com*
	Dubai International Arabian Horse Championship	*diahc.ae*
	Dubai International Boat Show	*boatshowdubai.com*
	Dubai International Horse Fair	*dihf.ae*
	Dubai International Humanitarian Aid & Development Conference & Exhibition	*dihad.org*
	International Jewellery & Watch Show Abu Dhabi	*jws.ae*
	25 Years of Arab Creativity	*abudhabifestival.ae*
April		
	The Bride Show Dubai	*thebrideshow.com*
	Careers UAE	*careersuae.ae*
	Cityscape Abu Dhabi	*cityscapeabudhabi.com*
	GITEX Shopper	*gitexshopperdubai.com*
	Gulf Education & Training Exhibition	*mygetex.com*
May		
	Arabian Travel Market	*arabiantravelmarket.com*
	Beauty World Middle East	*gulfbeautyexpo.com*
June		
	Dubai Summer Surprises	*mydsf.com*
	Indian Property Show	*indianpropertyshow.com*
October		
	ArabiaShop	*arabiashop.com*
	Cityscape Global	*cityscapeglobal.com*
	GITEX Technology Week	*gitex.com*
	Gifts & Premium Dubai	*giftsandpremium-dubai.com*
	Green Middle East	*green-middleeast.com*
November		
	Big Five Exhibition	*thebig5.ae*
	Dubai International Motor Show	*dubaimotorshow.com*
	SEAFEX, Middle East & Africa Seafood Exhibition	*seafexme.com*
December		
	Abu Dhabi International Motor Show	*reedexpo.com*

For further listings, visit askexplorer.com

Absconding

Anyone leaving the country without cancelling their residence visa with their sponsor will be classed as 'absconding' and may receive a ban, though employers have to wait six months to report absconders who have left the country. Anyone who leaves their employment and remains in the country without notifying their employer can be reported as having absconded after a period of seven days.

Absconders are reported to the Ministry of Labour, who then pass information on to Immigration and the Dubai police.

Under Article 120 of the Labour Law, if you leave the country or are unaccountable for seven days in a row or 20 days in total, your company can terminate your employment contract without awarding you gratuity pay or any outstanding benefits.

During the economic downturn, there were reports of residents leaving the city at short notice to avoid the ramifications of defaults on bank loans and debts. If you default on a loan and the bank files a case against you, you could receive a visa ban which restricts you from either entering or leaving the country. Details of this claim are filed with the Immigration Department, the police and the Ministry of Labour, which means you could be identified and detained when your visa is scanned at the airport on departure or arrival.

Redundancy

Redundancy can be a serious blow to your personal life and finances, particularly in a city like Dubai where you may only be here as long as you have a job. If you are made redundant, try not to dwell on feelings of self doubt about your performance or likeability and instead focus on the financial reasons for your termination.

The first thing to discuss with your employer is whether they are prepared to be flexible with your visa status. If you have a good relationship with your company, you should have room to negotiate the terms under which you are leaving, and it's a good idea to request a few months leeway so that you have the opportunity to find a new employer and sponsor. If this is not possible and your company wishes to cancel your visa immediately, you have a standard 30 day grace period within which to leave the country before incurring any fines for overstaying your visa. Similarly, if you are in company accommodation, try to negotiate the date on which you need to move out. If your company has paid for your villa or apartment up front, they may let you stay for a fixed period.

It is always a good idea to plan for every eventuality by putting money aside to act as a buffer should you lose your job; rather than incur large credit card debt, this money can help pay for key bills like rent and car loans.

Company Closure

Employees who face the unlucky situation of company bankruptcy or company closure are entitled under, UAE Labour Law, to receive their gratuity payments and holiday pay, but you will need to speak to the Ministry of Labour for the proper process as it is rather complex. An employee of a firm that has been closed is allowed to transfer sponsorship to a new employer if they are able to find a new job, but if not, their visa will be cancelled and they will have to leave the country. To transfer the visa they'll need an attested certificate of closure, issued by the court and submitted to the Ministry of Labour (04 702 3333). If your company were to close without cancelling their trade licence you could receive a short term ban from taking a new role with a new employer. Consult the appropriate government offices to get your paperwork right, or consider investing in the services of a lawyer who specialises in labour issues (see p.132 for a list of lawyers).

Voluntary & Charity Work

There are a number of opportunities to do voluntary or charity work in Dubai and the organisations listed below are always looking for committed volunteers. The Dubai Volunteering Centre, run by the Community Development Authority (CDA), regulates, promotes and encourages people to get involved in voluntary work. To register as a volunteer, call the CDA at 8002121 or visit the website at cda.gov.ae

Want to help protect the planet? Well, if it's environmental voluntary work you're after, the Emirates Environmental Group (eeg-uae.org) organises regular waste collection campaigns, encouraging people to recycle cans, paper etc. If you're not entirely sure which charity you'd like to help, or want to volunteer for more than one charity, check out volunteerindubai.com – the website matches volunteers with the needs of specific drives or events.

All As One

Fairmont Dubai Trade Centre 1 **04 311 6707**
allasone.org

A non-profit organisation that cares for abandoned, disabled, abused and destitute children of Sierra Leone at the All As One Children's Centre. Operating costs are funded through donations, child sponsorship and charity events.

Breast Cancer Arabia

055 303 5364
breastcancerarabia.com

A charity that raises money to pay for breast cancer treatment for women who cannot afford it. Monies are raised at events such as golf days organised by the Breast Cancer Arabia Foundation, as well as through donations. Email foundation@breastcancerarabia.com for further information.

Feline Friends Dubai

050 451 0058
felinefriendsdubai.com

This non-profit organisation, with volunteers who rescue and re-home stray cats and kittens, promotes the control of street cats by sterilisation and provides care and relief to sick and injured cats. Rescue volunteers and foster homes are always needed.

Gulf For Good

International Humanitarian City
Dubai Industrial City 04 368 0222
gulf4good.org

A UAE-based charitable organisation that raises funds for selected worthy causes around the world by organising sponsored expeditions and treks to locations across the globe. Challenges include hikes in the Himalayan foothills and a trek through Palestine's remote highlands, wadis and deserts.

K9 Friends > p.149

04 887 8739
k9friends.com

A group of volunteers who rescue, care for and re-home unwanted dogs from all over the UAE. Running costs are met entirely through public donations and corporate sponsors. Assistance is always welcome.

Medecins Sans Frontieres (MSF)

Al Shafar Bldg, Shk Zayed Rd Tecom 04 457 9255
msf-me.org

An international, non-profit emergency medical relief organisation. Volunteers can become involved locally with fundraising and awareness campaigns. Annual events include the Dubai Vertical Marathon, where participants climb the Emirates Towers' 1,334 steps, and Wild Wadi's Swim Burj Al Arab.

Riding For The Disabled Association Of Dubai

Desert Palm Dubai Warsan 2
rdad.ae

Launched by HH Sheikha Hassa bint Mohammed bin Rashid Al Maktoum, the association provides therapeutic benefits for children with special needs through gentle horse riding. Reliable volunteers are always needed to lead the horses and assist riders.

Women For Women International

Various locations 050 342 4949
womenforwomen.org

Informal charity events organised by a group of ladies to help Women for Women International, a charity giving aid to war survivors. Contact Julie Wilkinson for details on 050 342 4949 or at jwilkinson@valleyforge.com.

Working As A Freelancer/ Contractor

It is possible to obtain a visa to work in Dubai on a freelance basis. This kind of visa is linked to the various free zones that exist, such as Dubai Media City, Jebel Ali Free Zone and Knowledge Village. Your profession needs to be related to the free zone's activities, so artists, editors, directors, writers, engineers, producers, photographers, camera operators and technicians in the fields of film, TV, music, radio and print media can only set up in a media free zone. Previously, Dubai Media City was the only such zone, but media professionals can now also obtain freelance visas linked to Dubai Studio City and twofour54 in Abu Dhabi.

Working On The Move?

MAKE Business Hub (makebusinesshub.com) near JBR Walk offers freelancers a workspace and a cafe rolled into one; there are work stations, work pods for private meetings and a tasty menu serving breakfast through to dinner.

If you fall into one of the categories, and meet all the relevant criteria, you will get a residence visa and access to 'hot desk' facilities. There are a number of fees involved in this process, and obtaining a visa in this way will cost somewhere between Dhs.20,000 and Dhs.30,000. For more information, contact the appropriate free zone (see Free Zones, p.118). An alternative option, depending on your line of work, may be to set up or register your own company (see below). The Department of Economic Development (dubaided.gov.ae) is the place to contact for details on how to do this. See also Virtuzone (p.126).

Flying Solo

If you do decide to freelance in the media sector, here's what you need to know:

- You need to apply for a freelance permit through the appropriate free zone.
- Media professionals can apply to Dubai Media City (dubaimediacity.com), Dubai Studio City (dubaistudiocity.com), and twofour54 in Abu Dhabi (twofour54.com).
- Costs vary at each free zone, and come with different benefits. At Dubai Media City, the permit includes a residence visa, access to 10 shared workstations, and a shared PO box address and fax line. A minimum of three hours per week and no more than three hours per day must be spent at the hot desk. A business plan, CV, bank reference letter and portfolio must be submitted with your application.

Pension Planning

Many expats come to Dubai to advance their career and the city's advantageous tax climate makes it an appealing choice financially as well. But what about pensions and securing your financial future?

Ask The Expert

Robert Palmer Senior Pensions Advisor, Mondial Dubai

What should expats bear in mind when considering the impact that working in Dubai will have on their pensions?
Planning for your financial future is a topic not to be taken lightly no matter where you live; however, this is especially the case for expats and in my opinion, the answer is exceptionally straightforward: it's simply always best to take advice from an expert who specialises in pensions.

For expats in general, what's the single most important characteristic to look for in a pension plan?
The key word here is 'flexibility.' Basically, you can never know what's going to happen next. It can be amazing career prospects one minute and redundancy the next. Choose something that can take account of a sudden change in your circumstances.

Are pension products available locally or should expats look into making arrangements in their home country?
All of the large international assurance companies have offices here and offer easy-to-understand retirement planning products. Tax status can influence advice here in the UAE, but the rule of thumb is to take advantage of solutions using one of the world's traditional offshore centres. These include the Isle of Man, Jersey and Guernsey in the UK.

How about any pensions expats may have been saving for in their home countries or elsewhere before making the move here?
This is an important consideration and it's crucial to understand your options fully. For example, not everyone is aware that it's now possible to take advantage of new legislation initiated in most EU countries, which allows expats to transfer their existing pension plans with them.

Why should expats transfer their existing pension plans? What are the main benefits of doing this while working in Dubai?
Transferring your existing pension during the time you're working here in Dubai offers a number of benefits, which can be summarised under the following three areas:

1) Tax advantages
2) Investment control
3) Easy-to-understand solutions

Planning Ahead

New to Dubai? The tax-free lifestyle is a great opportunity to advance your financial standing. However, if you have a pension scheme in your home country, it may not be worth continuing your contributions once you come to Dubai, but rather to set up a tax-free, offshore savings plan. It's always advisable to speak to your financial adviser before you make any big move – after all, it may have a huge impact on your future.

Working Part-Time

In the past, it has been extremely difficult to organise part-time work. What little there is has been offered 'off the books' to those already in Dubai under their partner's sponsorship. But new legislation now allows residents to work part-time in Dubai, which is good news for everyone from mothers returning to work to teenagers wanting to earn some spending money. Part-time work is still a new concept in Dubai and it may be quite a while until there's the variety of casual work available that you'll find in most other countries, but there are an increasing number of opportunities. For more information, contact the Department of Naturalisation & Residency (04 313 9999).

Setting Up A Small Business

Since the global economic meltdown, the business climate in the UAE has quickly changed from one of hope and optimism to one of uncertainty for many. However, small and medium sized businesses are still starting up in the region and many are finding success.

Starting a business in the current economy requires meticulous market research, a strict and realistic business plan and responsive action to take advantage of fleeting openings in the market. Recent high-profile cases have also made it clear that there are serious risks involved in doing business in the country. Bankruptcy laws are not as defined as in other countries and mismanagement of funds could result in harsh repercussions, including deportation or even jail time. The rulers have passed legislation and formed organisations that aid the start-up process in the UAE. In 2009, the UAE Ministry of Economy removed the minimum capital requirements for new businesses, which used to be Dhs.300,000 in Dubai.

Good Day At The Office

If you are the head of a company or looking to set up your own concern, there are several general furnishers you can turn to for office furniture, including IKEA (p.386) and PAN Emirates (p.386), but BAFCO (bafco.com) which has showrooms in Dubai and Abu Dhabi, specialises in complete office fit-outs.

One of the main hesitations that entrepreneurs have about starting a business here is the traditional requirement of having a local sponsor control a majority stake of the company. However, there are persistent rumours that this rule is to be relaxed to let foreigners take majority ownership of new businesses, but the exact percentage – whether full ownership or just a higher slice – remains to be seen.

The exception to the above are free zones (p.118), where full private foreign ownership is already permitted. The licensing process for opening a business in a free zone is also more streamlined and helped by the free zone organisation.

Government and private-sponsored initiatives are also helping spur growth and educate potential business owners. The Mohammed Bin Rashid Establishment for SME Development (sme.ae) was set up to help entrepreneurs understand the procedures and potential costs of setting up in Dubai. The organisation provides guidance and information to Emiratis and expats hoping to start their own business. Among its varied schedule of events, arts community hub Shelter (shelter.ae) also hosts a programme of workshops for entrepreneurs, as well as providing hotdesk facilities for creatives. If you want someone to handle all of the red tape for you, companies like Sentinel Business Centres (sentinelbusinesscentres.com) can help you set up in a free zone or even help find a local sponsor for your business.

There are various business groups in Dubai that help facilitate investments and provide opportunities for networking. Some provide information on trade with their respective countries, as well as on business opportunities both in Dubai and internationally. Most also arrange social and networking events on a regular basis (see Networking & Events, p.116).

Before you set up, contact the Dubai Chamber of Commerce & Industry (dubaichamber.com) and the Ministry of Economy (economy.gov.ae). Both can offer excellent advice. Embassies or consulates (p.596) can also be a good business resource and may be able to offer contact lists for the UAE and the country of representation. For further information, refer to Explorer's *Working In The Gulf*, the Dubai Commercial Directory or the Hawk Business Pages.

Virtuzone

Until recently, setting up as a freelancer in the UAE has been a fairly difficult and costly affair, and you've also needed to be active in a field covered by one of the specific free zones. Virtuzone has provided a solution to many of these problems. Officially part of Fujairah Creative City free zone (although its physical location is unimportant), it was set up with the express aim of helping those who want to either set up a small company or relocate it to the UAE while keeping costs as low as possible. Start up costs begin at around Dhs.10,000 and Virtuzone looks after the whole process; significantly, there's no need for a UAE sponsor, companies can be 100% foreign owned and there are no corporate or income taxes. Also, there's no requirement to take a commercial premises – something that really drives up the price of setting up in other free zones. If you're looking to move your small business from your home country or are thinking about taking a skill and going solo, it's probably the easiest and cheapest way to set up. Visit vz.ae or there's a physical office on The Walk, JBR.

FINANCIAL AFFAIRS

Mobile Banking

Banks such as Standard Chartered (standard chartered.ae) now offer you the convenience of having your account information at your fingertips with SMS banking. Get your account balance and last five transactions sent to your phone, or request a chequebook, simply by sending a text.

Bank Accounts

There are several reputable banks in Dubai, including well-known names like HSBC and Standard Chartered. Banks that operate internationally rarely have connections with their counterparts in other parts of the world, so you won't be able to manage accounts held in other countries through your Dubai account.

Most banks offer online banking, so you can check your balance, transfer money and pay bills online. There are plenty of ATMs (cash points) around Dubai and most cards are compatible with the Central Bank network (some also offer global access links). You may pay a small fee for using another bank's ATM but it should never be more than a few dirhams.

To open an account in most banks, you need a residence visa or to have your residency application underway. To apply, you will need to submit your original passport, copies of your passport (personal details and visa) and an NOC from your sponsor and/or a salary certificate from your employer. Some banks set a minimum account limit – this can be around Dhs.2,000 for a deposit account and as much as Dhs.10,000 for a current account. This means that at some point in each month your balance must be above the minimum limit (normally covered by a monthly wage deposit). Banks are exercising more caution than they have in the past, due to the global credit crisis of 2008, particularly where loans are concerned.

Valuable Information

If you have some precious items that you would like to give a little extra protection to, JFT Safe Deposit Lockers, based in Al Nadha 1, offer secure storage boxes in monitored premises on a monthly or annual basis. Visit jftlockers.com or call 04 257 7427 for details.

A number of laws have been introduced to combat money laundering. The UAE Central Bank monitors all incoming and outgoing transfers, and banks and currency exchanges are required to report transfers over a certain limit. Additionally, if you need to send more than Dhs.2,000 by international transfer you may have to show a valid passport. Note that, in line with international practice, you now need to provide an IBAN number when making a transfer to or from a UAE bank.

Main Banks

ABN AMRO Bank 04 440 9400, *abnamroprivatebanking.com*
Abu Dhabi Commercial Bank 800 2030, *adcb.com*
Arab Bank 04 445 0000, *arabbank.ae*
Bank Of Sharjah 04 282 7278, *bankofsharjah.com*
Barclays Bank Plc 04 438 1038, *barclays.ae*
BNP Paribas 04 424 8200, *bnpparibas.com*
Citibank 04 507 4104, *citibank.com*
Dubai Islamic Bank 04 295 3000, *alislami.ae*
Emirates Islamic Bank 600 59 9995, *emiratesislamicbank.ae*
Emirates NBD 600 54 0000, *emiratesnbd.com*
Habib Bank AG Zurich 04 221 4535, *habibbank.com*
HSBC Bank Middle East 600 55 4722, *hsbc.ae*
Mashreq 04 424 4444, *mashreqbank.com*
National Bank Of Abu Dhabi 04 509 8500, *nbad.com*
RAKBANK 04 213 0000, *rakbank.ae*
Standard Chartered Bank – Middle East > *p.xxi* 600 52 2288, *standardchartered.ae*
Union National Bank 600 56 6665, *unb.co.ae*

Financial Planning

Many expats are attracted to Dubai for the tax-free salary and the opportunity to put a something away for the future. However, Dubai's alluring lifestyle can quickly steer you away from your goal. It is often necessary for residents to get credit cards and bank loans to finance their life in Dubai and it is easy to slip further into debt – you'll find there is little or no support if you do (see Debt p.130). It is important to plan your finances and arrange a safeguard in case your finances take a turn for the worse.

Financial Advice

There seems to be an overabundance of financial advisors in the city who may contact you over the phone and advertise their services. Most advisors won't ask for money initially; however, they may ask you for contact details of your friends and family members so that they can continue to spread the word.

When choosing a financial planner in Dubai, you should ensure that they are licensed by the Central Bank of the UAE (centralbank.ae), so that you have some recourse in the event of a dispute. You should also consider the company's international presence – you'll still want the same access to advice and your investments if you return home. It may be better to use an independent company or advisor who is not tied to a specific bank, and will objectively offer you the full range of savings products on the market.

Before leaving your home country you should contact the tax authorities to ensure that you are complying with the financial laws there. Most countries will consider you not liable for income tax once you prove you're a UAE resident (a contract of employment is normally a good starting point). However, you may still have to fulfil certain criteria, so do some research before you come (if you are already here, check with your embassy). You may be liable for tax on any income you receive from back home (for example if you are renting out your property).

If you have a pension scheme in your home country, it may not be worth continuing your contributions once you come to Dubai, but rather to set up a tax-free, offshore savings plan. It is always advisable to speak to your financial adviser about such matters before you make any big move.

Guardian Life Management 04 450 9700, *guardianwealthmanagement.com*
Holborn Assets 04 457 3800, *holbornassets.com*
KPMG 04 403 0300, *kpmg.com*
Mondial Dubai > *p.125* 04 399 6601, *mondialdubai.com*
PIC Middle East 04 343 3470, *pic-uae.com*
Prosperity Offshore Investment Consultants 04 454 2530, *prosperity-uae.com*

Insurance Companies

Abu Dhabi National Takaful Company 04 210 8700, *takaful.ae*
Aetna Global Benefits (Middle East) 04 438 7500, *aetnainternational.com*
AFIA Insurance Brokerage Services 04 337 9987, *afia.ae*
Al Ain Ahlia Insurance Company 04 272 5500, *alaininsurance.com*
Al Khazna Insurance Company 04 294 4088, *alkhazna.com*
Alfred's Insurance Market 04 337 9987, *insurancemarket.ae*
Alliance Insurance 04 605 1111, *alliance-uae.com*
Allianz SE 04 702 6666, *allianz.com*
Arab Orient Insurance Company 04 253 1300, *insuranceuae.com*
AXA Insurance (Gulf) 04 324 3434, *axa-gulf.com*
Daman National Health Insurance Company 04 436 0222, *damanhealth.ae*
Emirates Insurance Company 04 294 2949, *eminsco.com*
Gargash Insurance 04 337 9800, *gargashinsurance.com*
Greenshield Insurance Brokers 04 397 4464, *greenshield.ae*
Lifecare International 04 331 8688, *lifecareinternational.com*
MedNet UAE 800 4882, *mednet-uae.com*
MetLife Alico 04 360 0555, *metlifealico.ae*
Nasco Karaoglan 04 352 3133, *nascodubai.com*
National General Insurance Co (NGI) 04 211 5800, *ngi.ae*
Neuron 04 399 6779, *neuron.ae*
Nexus > *p.103* 04 323 1111, *nexusadvice.com*
Oman Insurance Company 04 233 7777, *tameen.ae*
Qatar General Insurance & Reinsurance Co 04 268 8688, *qgirco.com*
Qatar Insurance Company 04 222 4045, *qatarinsurance.com*
RSA 04 480 0772, *rsagroup.ae*
Zurich International Life 04 425 2300, *zurich.com*

Credit Cards

The process for obtaining a credit card is fairly straightforward and is usually offered by the bank connected to your payroll account. If you are eligible, you'll often receive calls from your bank offering credit cards. Visa and MasterCard branded cards are available through most banks; to apply for an American Express card visit americanexpress.ae or call 800 4013.

At The Pump

You are not able to use your card to buy petrol at garages in Dubai. Garages only accept cash at petrol pumps, but cards are accepted at most forecourt convenience stores for other purchases.

Banks will usually ask that you have a minimum salary (dependant on the credit amount), a salary certificate, which details your earnings (this should be provided by your employer), and a copy of your passport with your residence visa and work permit. Most shops, hotels and restaurants accept the major credit cards (American Express, Diners Club, MasterCard and Visa). Smaller retailers are sometimes less likely to accept credit cards and if they do you may have to pay an extra 5% for processing (and it's no use telling them that it's a contravention of the card company rules – you have to take it or leave it). Conversely, if you are paying in cash, you may sometimes be allowed a discount – it's certainly worth enquiring.

If you lose your credit or debit card, contact the bank as soon as possible and report the missing card. Once you have reported the loss, it is highly unlikely you will be held liable for any further transactions made on the card.

As a consequence of ATM fraud, banks have now set a limit on the amount of cash you can withdraw per day (the amount varies from card to card). In addition to these measures, banks also advise the public on how to prevent credit card crime. A frequent problem is people not changing their PIN when the card arrives. This is vital for secrecy, and banks suggest you change your PIN on a regular basis.

Offshore Accounts

While offshore banking used to be associated with the very wealthy or the highly shady, most expats now take advantage of tax efficient plans. An offshore account works in much the same way as a conventional account, but it can be adjusted specifically for you. Money can be moved where it will produce the best rewards, and cash accessed whenever and wherever you need it, in your desired currency. Offshore accounts allow for management through the internet and over the phone, in a range of currencies (most commonly in US dollars, euros or pounds sterling). If you are travelling outside the UAE, make sure your account comes with 24-hour banking, internationally recognised debit cards, and the ability to write cheques in your preferred currency.

To open an account, there is usually a minimum balance of around $10,000. Do some thorough research before opening an account, and check the potential tax implications in your home country. It is important to seek independent financial advice, and not just the opinion of the bank offering you an account. HSBC (hsbc.ae) offers good offshore services, but will of course only advise on its own products. To open your account, you may have to produce certain reports or documents from your chosen country. However, for those willing to do the research and undertake the admin, offshore banking can prove to be a lucrative investment.

Taxation

The UAE levies no personal income taxes or withholding taxes, but there are talks that income tax and VAT may be introduced in the future. There are no firm dates for implementation at present, and it would no doubt be unpopular, and could hamper attempts to attract foreign investment, but the IMF is advising Middle Eastern governments to introduce tax reforms in order to diversify their resources.

The only noticeable taxes you pay as an expat are a 5% municipality tax on rental accommodation, a 30% tax on alcohol bought at Dubai liquor stores and 50% tax on tobacco (although cigarettes are still comparatively cheap). The municipality tax is included in your DEWA bill, and if you don't pay this your utilities will be cut off. This has resulted in some complaints – the tax is meant to cover refuse collection, street lighting and community road networks, but people renting freehold properties also pay maintenance to cover these things so it's understandable why they may have objections. There is also a 10% municipality tax and a 10% service charge in hotel food and beverage outlets, but you'll find that these are usually incorporated into the displayed price. In 2007, the Salik road toll system (p.57) was introduced for the purpose of 'traffic management'. Some residents are unhappy about the system and view Salik effectively as a road tax.

Taxing Issues

You may need to register your residency in the UAE with the government in your home country to avoid paying income tax or capital gains tax. It's best to check with your consulate for exact details. British expats can visit the Inland Revenue's website at hmrc.gov.uk/international/abroad.htm for comprehensive advice on tax and National Insurance payments

UK Not OK?

Changes in tax law mean that some British expats living in the UAE need to monitor their situation and working habits closely. UK workers who work in the UK for more than 20 days per tax year and expats who spend more than 90 days per tax year in the UK could soon be liable to pay UK tax.

Cheques

Cheques aren't commonly used as a method of payment in Dubai. Most residents will only have to deal with them when organising post-dated cheques for rental agreements. The most important thing to remember is that issuing a cheque when you have insufficient funds in your account to cover the amount is considered a criminal offence. If you issue more than four bounced cheques within one year you will be blacklisted by the UAE Central Bank, and your account may be closed. When writing a post-dated cheque it is important that you are sure of your finances; you should also encourage the beneficiary to deposit the cheques as soon as possible (if that is best). A cheque cannot be cancelled, unless it is mislaid or stolen, so a cheque you wrote several months ago could land you in big trouble, if cashed unexpectedly.

Debt

In a city that seems to run on credit cards and post-dated cheques, it can be quite a shock (and a major inconvenience) when severe penalties are dealt out for late or missed payments.

While you may be forced to take large loans to purchase vehicles or for annual rent, it is important to note that if you are suddenly made redundant and your finances spiral out of control there is no safety net if you've overstretched.

Unlike some countries, where you will receive several reminders for missed payments, if you are late paying for basic household bills such as electricity or water, your services may be disconnected without much warning – even if you regularly pay your bills. Missed payments on credit cards bills will often

Top Tips For Healthy Personal Finance

Don't Neglect Your Credit Cards: They are great to bail you out in emergencies, but unless you are self-disciplined when using them, credit cards can land you in trouble. Leave them in a secure place at home where you won't be tempted and always make the minimum repayments on time to avoid late fees.

Try To Live Off Half Your Salary: Really examine your expenses and be brutal when it comes to deciding what you can live without – manicures, double lattes, fancy restaurants and gym memberships are all luxuries, and cutting them out of your budget could mean surprising savings at the end of the month.

Entertain At Home: Eating out in Dubai's lavish restaurants is so alluring, but it doesn't come cheap. Master the art of 'cocooning' – staying in and inviting friends round for dinner.

Shop Smart: Certain supermarkets may be convenient and stock all your favourites from back home, but are much more expensive than other, more basic supermarkets. You'll save much more if you buy your everyday items from a larger hypermarket (p.415). Decide on a grocery budget at the beginning of the month, and make it last.

Don't Pay Full Price For Anything: Shops in the city regularly offer promotions, sales and buy-one-get-one free promotions. Shop around to find the best bargains; you'll be amazed at what you can save.

Get Packing: There's no such thing as a free lunch, but packing your own sandwiches is the next best thing. It's healthier and the savings you'll make do add up.

Avoid Salik: No matter where you're going, there's usually a way around the Salik toll gates. If you often pass under a Salik gate on your way to and from work, avoid them for a month and you'll save nearly Dhs.200.

Take Advantage Of Exchange Rates: Certain items can work out much cheaper when buying from Amazon, even when you factor in the shipping, simply because of the exchange rate. You can get a current CD for over Dhs.10 cheaper than what you'd pay in a retail outlet here – so if you're ordering a few, you could save a bundle. If you've got visitors coming over, get your Amazon order delivered to them (most orders ship free locally), and get them to bring it with them.

Buy Second-hand: Visit Dubai Flea Market for a browse through other people's unwanted items (it is held at Al Safa Park and Uptown Mirdif from June to September; dubai-fleamarket.com). House of Prose sells a huge range of second-hand books (04 344 9021), and supermarket noticeboards are cluttered with great pre-owned items looking for new homes.

Reduce Costs Over Summer: If you are planning to be away for some time over the summer, look into downgrading your satellite TV and internet packages for a few months. That way you can usually upgrade again come September without having to pay any reconnection fees. Better yet, if you only have satellite TV so you can watch the premier league football, cancel it completely over summer. You can always resubscribe when the season kicks off again.

Cost Of Living

Bottle of wine (off-licence)	Dhs.40
Burger (takeaway)	Dhs.12
Can of soft drink	Dhs.1.5
Car rental (per day)	Dhs.100
Cigarettes (pack of 20)	Dhs.7
Cinema ticket	Dhs.30
Cleaner (per hour)	Dhs.35
Dozen eggs	Dhs.8
House wine (glass)	Dhs.35-45
Loaf of bread	Dhs.4.5
Milk (1 litre)	Dhs.5.5
Mobile to mobile call (local, per minute)	30 fils
New release DVD	Dhs.85
Newspaper (international)	Dhs.15
Petrol (litre)	Dhs.1.79
Pint of beer	Dhs.35
Six-pack of beer (off-licence)	Dhs.25
Taxi (10km journey)	Dhs.20
Text message (local)	18 fils
Water 1.5 litres (supermarket)	Dhs.1.5

incur fines or restrictions to services, and it is also considered a criminal offence to write a cheque when you have insufficient funds to cover the balance (see cheques p.130). In some cases, failure to meet payments can lead to prosecution, a visa ban (p.119) and jail time.

Don't Bank On It

There are no bankruptcy laws in the UAE, so individuals who fall into financial difficulties are fully liable for their debt. If you are unable to keep up with repayments for your bank loans, and your bank files a complaint against you, you may be faced with a visa ban or an extended term in jail.

The recent economic downturn highlighted this issue when several residents, who were made redundant, made a swift departure from Dubai to avoid prosecution (see Absconding, p.122). Banks are subsequently more cautious about who they will offer loans and credit cards to. There are also rumours that debt collectors are increasingly being employed to recover outstanding debts from residents who have returned to their home countries.

The best way to avoid any unpleasant situations is to try and avoid getting into debt in the first place – plan well, don't get carried away just because you're abroad, and always keep some money in reserve.

LEGAL ISSUES

Shariah Law

The country's constitution permits each emirate to have its own legislative body and judicial authority. Dubai has thus retained its own judicial system, including courts of appeal, which are not part of the UAE federal system. There are three primary sources of UAE law, namely federal laws and decrees (applicable in all emirates), local laws (laws and regulations enacted by the individual emirates), and Shariah (Islamic law). Generally, when a court is determining a commercial issue, it gives initial consideration to any applicable federal and/or local laws. If such federal and local laws do not address the issue, Shariah may be applied. Moreover, Shariah generally applies to family law matters, particularly when involving Muslims.

Afridi & Angell 04 330 3900, *afridi-angell.com*
Al Rowaad Advocates & Legal Consultancy 04 325 4000, *awf.ae*
Al Sharif Advocates & Legal Consultants 04 262 8222, *dubailaw.com*
Al Tamimi & Company 04 364 1641, *tamimi.com*
Bayat Legal Services 04 355 4646, *ilsgroup.com*
Bin Haider Advocates & Legal Consultants 04 358 8777, *binhaideradvocates.com*
DLA Piper Middle East LLP 04 438 6100, *dlapiper.com*
Hadef & Partners 04 429 2999, *hadefpartners.com*
Musthafa & Almana International Consultants 04 329 8411, *musthafa-almana.com*
The Rights Lawyers 04 390 3646, *therightslawyers.com*
Trench & Associates 04 355 3146, *trenchlaw.com*

Wills & Estate Law

Having a valid will in place is something that everybody should do. It is especially important to seek legal advice when drawing up your will if you become a property owner in Dubai. This is an area where the law is rather complicated – under Shariah law, the basic rules as to who inherits property after someone's death differ to 'western' rules. For example, in the event of your death, it may be the case that your sons (or brother, if you don't have any sons) are first in line for inheritance and your wife could end up with nothing. It is best to make sure that you have a clear last will and testament in place. A Dubai-based lawyer will be able to assist you with a locally viable will. See the list of law firms above, or contact The Wills Specialists (willsuae.com), which specialises in all aspects of writing wills and succession planning.

Family Law

In accordance with the constitution of the UAE, family law (governing matrimonial matters such as divorce) will either be governed by UAE law – Shariah law – or the laws of the individuals' originating country. If the parties are from different countries, the law applicable will be the law under which their marriage was solemnised. Normally, the court will look into the possibility of reconciliation before granting a divorce. This means that, before filing for divorce, you can approach the Family Guidance and Reformation Centre which functions under the Department of Justice at Dubai Courts (04 334 7777). Anyone experiencing marital problems or a family dispute is able to approach this organisation. The other party in the dispute will be called in and the counsellors will try to help you reach an amicable settlement. If the matter is not resolved, the Guidance Centre may refer the matter to the court for legal proceedings.

In deciding on the custody of any child, the court's paramount concern will be the child's welfare. In Shariah law and most other laws, the custody of the child will be the mother's right while the child is a minor, unless there are compelling reasons to decide otherwise. For more information on divorce and legal proceedings, see p.140.

Laws To Remember

Licence To Imbibe: There are several places you can go to buy alcohol if you don't have a liquor licence, but the fact of the matter is that, if you want to enjoy a few drinks in Dubai, you should really have a 'red card'. The good news is that it is easy to get a licence: just head down to any branch of MMI or A&E, fill in the form, pay Dhs.160 (which you get back as a voucher to spend on booze), and wait a few days. See Getting An Alcohol Licence, p.40.

Crimes Of Cohabitation: You would have to be pretty unlucky to get pulled up on this, but the UAE law states that men and women who are not related to each other cannot live together. If you are worried about the risk, however low it may be, the choice is to get married, or live apart.

Illegitimate Bumps: Getting pregnant if you are not married is a big no-no here. If you are having your prenatal checkups at a government hospital, you will be asked for your marriage certificate when you register. If you are at a private clinic, you won't have to show your marriage certificate until the baby is born. Either way, you need to have that crucial piece of paper before giving birth here, or you could be looking at a serious spot of bother that transcends sleepless nights and dirty nappies.

Remain Orderly: Drinking in public view (unless you are at a licensed venue or event), is illegal. Being drunk and disorderly in public is against the law no matter where you are. Be careful when you are ordering that seventh cocktail – if that's the one that's going to make you lose your decorum, think about the consequences and make sure there is someone responsible for getting you home safely (apart from the taxi driver).

Keep The PDAs In Check: Holding hands won't land you in any trouble, but think twice about kissing, hugging and other public displays of affection. It may be acceptable in some places (like in airport lounges), but it has been known to get people into trouble, particularly if the kissing and hugging is on the more amorous side. Beware in nightclubs: a seemingly innocent kiss, even between married couples, can result in a bouncer giving you a rather firm warning.

Bounce Into Jail: It is a criminal offence to bounce a cheque in the UAE and can result in jail time, so make sure you have enough money in your account to honour it.

Don't Have One For The Road: It goes without saying that drinking and driving is illegal. But what many people fail to understand is that there is no such thing as a safe, legal limit when it comes to drinking and driving here. Even a sip of wine or a strong brandy pudding can put you over the limit, because the limit is zero. If you are driving, you should stick to soft drinks, and only soft drinks, all night. If you are drinking, it's best to leave the car keys at home and get a cab.

Over The Counter But Outside The Law: Codeine is widely available in over the counter medications in countries like the UK, and temazepam is a commonly prescribed sleep aid. However, they are illegal substances in the UAE, and possessing them could result in arrest. You can't buy them here, but it's a good idea to tell your overseas visitors not to stock up on the Tylenol or Restoril before they arrive. If they do need these medications, they should carry a doctor's prescription, translated into Arabic if possible.

Respect Ramadan: In the UAE, it is illegal to eat, drink or smoke in public view during Ramadan fasting hours. 'In public view' includes your car, the beach, and even the gym. You should not chew gum either. Many restaurants have closed off sections where you can eat lunch out of sight, and most offices set up a little area where non-Muslims can eat and drink during the day. If these options are not available to you, then you should wait for iftar (the breaking of the fast) before eating, drinking or smoking.

Look Mum, No Hands: It's one of the most widely flouted laws in the history of the legal system, but it is absolutely illegal to drive while talking on your mobile handset. Apart from being dangerous, not just for you but for your fellow road users, it is punishable with hefty fines and black points. Invest in a hands-free kit, or better yet, switch your phone off while driving – it may be one of your few opportunities to enjoy some peace and quiet in the midst of a typical busy day.

Crime

Dubai is known for having a low crime rate – in fact for many expats it is still the number one benefit of living here. However, it would be naive to think that there was no crime, as there are cases of theft, rape and murder, but these occur on such a small scale that they rarely affect the quality of life of the average expat. The most common reason for expats getting on the wrong side of the law is driving under the influence of alcohol. In the UAE there is a zero-tolerance drinking and driving policy. If even a sip of alcohol has passed your lips, you are not allowed to drive. While there are few spot checks, if you have even a minor accident, and even if you were not at fault, you might be breathalysed and the consequences can be serious. Driving in the morning after a heavy night is risky, since you will still have alcohol in your system. You will be arrested and the usual penalty is a minimum 30 days in prison, although it varies from case to case. Bear in mind too that your insurance company will likely refuse to pay the claim if you were in an accident, even if you were not to blame. It's just not worth the risk – cabs are cheap and there are plenty of them. It also pays to keep your cool if you are involved in an altercation on the road as obscene gestures can result in a prison sentence or a fine and even deportation.

Neighbourhood Watch

In their efforts to maintain and promote a safe community, the Dubai Police launched Al Ameen, a confidential toll free telephone service where you can report anything suspicious. For example, if you have seen someone hanging around your property or loitering at cash points, you can pass the information on anonymously by calling 800 4888 or emailing alameen@eim.ae.

Harming others, physically or verbally, will get you into trouble – at the very least a heavy fine, but if the other person was injured a jail term may be in order. If the victim chooses to drop the charges then you will be released. If you are detained for being drunk and disorderly, you may spend a night in the cells, but if you are abusive you could be looking at a fine or longer sentence.

In a very high profile case in 2008, two Britons were charged with public indecency (after it was alleged they were having sex in public) and being under the influence of alcohol. Apart from having their exploits publicly broadcast by the world's media and being fired from work (in the case of the female), the pair received a three-month suspended sentence, fines and deportation, although legally the punishment could have been much stronger. This case should serve as a warning for all visitors and residents in the UAE, and a reminder that the authorities will extend the full arm of the law if you are caught breaking it.

Tips For Women

The following general tips are useful for women in Dubai:

- Stick to the dress code; tight, revealing clothing equals unwanted attention.
- Be careful when out alone at night, especially after a few drinks.
- Never get into a non-metered taxi; and always take down the taxi number.
- As long as you exercise due care and attention Dubai is a safe place for women.

Police

Dubai Police are generally calm and helpful – if you stay on the right side of the law. The police have a visible presence in the city, albeit not as prominent as in other large cities; you can recognise the police by their green army-style uniform and green and white saloon cars or 4WDs. You are most likely to be stopped for a traffic offence; you must always carry your driving licence and vehicle registration – failure to do so could result in a fine. If you are stopped by the police, it is important to appear helpful and co-operative at all times. Even if you are positive you are in the right, arguing your case aggressively or being impolite could help land you in further trouble. If you are being charged with a very serious offence it is advisable to contact your embassy for more advice (see p.596).

In an effort to better serve Dubai's visitors, the Dubai Police has launched the Department for Tourist Security. It acts as a liaison between you and Dubai Police, although in general police officers are extremely helpful. Its website (dubaipolice.gov.ae) is easy to navigate, helpful and has extensive information on policies and procedures. For assistance, call the toll fee number (800 4438). This is a non-emergency number that you can call for information about the Dubai Police, its services and the locations of stations.

There is a hotline for people suffering problems at the beach such as sexual harassment (04 266 1228). However, for other emergency services call 999 for the police or ambulance and 997 for the fire department.

If You Are Arrested

If you are arrested you will be taken to a police station and questioned. If it's decided that you must go to court the case will go to the public prosecutor who will set a date for a hearing. For a minor offence you may get bail, and the police will keep your passport and often the passport of a male resident who is willing to vouch for you. Police stations have holding cells, so if you don't get bail you'll be held until the hearing. All court proceedings are conducted in Arabic, so you should secure the services of a translator. If sentenced, you'll go straight from court to jail.

Upon being arrested you are advised to contact your embassy or consulate. They can liaise with family, advise on local legal procedures and provide a list of lawyers, but they will not pay your legal fees. The consulate will try to ensure that you are not denied your basic human rights, but they cannot act as lawyers, secure bail, or get you released.

If You Are Detained

Most prisoners will be detained in the new Central Jail near Al Awir, which was moved from its old location in Al Wasl. Short-term or temporary male prisoners may be held in an 'Out Jail', while long-term prisoners are likely to go to the main Central Jail.

Conditions inside the old jail were described as basic but bearable, but the new complex has much improved conditions, with the reported overcrowding in the old jail a thing of the past. Inmates are given three meals a day, and there's a small snack shop with limited opening hours. Prisoners are allowed occasional access to payphones, so if you are visiting an inmate a few phone cards will be appreciated.

Prisoners are generally allowed visits once a week. Thursdays are reserved for visits to Arab detainees, and Fridays are for other nationalities. Men and women are not allowed to visit together – men can visit from 10:00 to 11:00 and women from 16:00 to 17:00. If you are a woman you may not be allowed to visit a man who is of no family relation to you.

Visiting times are subject to change so it's best to check by calling the Department of Punitive Establishments (04 213 8888).

Victim Support

There are some support services available to those who have been victims of crime. Women and children who are victims of domestic violence can seek shelter at Dubai Foundation for Women and Children (800 111, dfwac.ae); the organisation also offers counselling and advice for women and their partners. The National Committee to Combat Human Trafficking (02 404 1000, nccht.gov.ae) assists those who are the victim of sexual abuse. Its website also provides information on other support services in the UAE.

Dubai Police (dubaipolice.gov.ae) offers a victim continuity service that offers support and provides updates on the progress of cases.

Prohibited Items

Taking illegal narcotics is an absolute no-no – even the smallest amounts of marijuana or hashish could earn you a prison sentence of four years or more. This will almost certainly be followed by deportation. If you are found guilty of dealing or smuggling, you could be looking at a life sentence, or even the death penalty (although this is uncommon).

Medications that are legal in your home country, such as codeine, temazepam and Prozac, may be banned here – check with the UAE embassy in your home country before you leave and, if you are in any doubt, find an alternative.

If you must bring the medication, keep a copy of the prescription with you and obtain a medical report from your doctor – this may help explain your case if questioned. You are not permitted to bring more than three months' supply of medicine. You can see a list of approved drugs on the Ministry of Health website (moh.gov.ae), although it is not known how frequently this list is updated or how reliable it is.

Dubai Marina

Family & Education

FAMILY

Family is a huge part of life in Dubai, as well as an integral part of Emirati culture. From birth to higher education, bringing up your family here is a rewarding and enjoyable experience. The facilities, from the practical to the pleasurable, are world class and Dubai has much to offer families of all nationalities. However, while the nurseries, play centres and facilities for babies and toddlers are very good, and the primary and secondary schools of a high standard, older children may have more of a struggle settling into life in the Emirates. With improved education facilities, especially at university level, and an ever-expanding leisure industry, teens have a lot to keep them occupied. The challenges are transport – although Dubai Metro has alleviated this slightly – as driving your teenagers to and from malls can be a bit of a chore. Also, chores need to be enforced for older kids in order to avoid 'expat brat' syndrome. In spite of recent changes in regulations pertaining to part time work, there is still little in the way of Saturday jobs in Dubai, but you may want to encourage your older children to volunteer (p.122).

Children are rarely expected to be seen and not heard in Dubai, and many restaurants are abuzz with kids running around. (There are however many places where kids will be less welcome so you should always call before you turn up). Cinemas also seem to have a pretty open door policy – although often to the annoyance of other patrons. Parks (p.256), beaches (p.258) and amusement centres (p.262) keep families happy and childcare options are available, although more in the form of paid babysitters than parent-run babysitting circles.

Whether you come with your family or have a family here, Dubai is a great place to call home.

Getting Married

A few years ago, organising a wedding in Dubai could be a bit of a challenge, but thanks to the trusty rules of supply and demand, weddings are now big business.

While many hotels offer wedding packages, they only extend to the reception – The One&Only Royal Mirage (04 399 3999) and The Ritz-Carlton (04 399 4000) are the hot favourites, but the Radisson Blu also offers a tailored wedding service (04 205 7047) as does the Park Hyatt (04 602 1234). Most Dubai hotels will offer a wedding service (see p.234 for a list of hotels).

A wedding planner could be your fairy godmother (especially when your family support network is miles away); check out Royal Events & Weddings for bespoke weddings (royalevents.com). Sarah Feyling is an expert wedding planner based in Dubai who will help you every step of the way – from the paperwork to the seating plan (theweddingplanner.ae). Upscale & Posh offers a tailored service for flowers and wedding reception decorations (upscaleandposh.com). Brides needn't worry about missing out on the princess treatment since most spas offer tailor-made services for them; see p.213 for a list of spas. For more information on wedding dresses and accessories, as well as cakes and invitation cards, see p.409 in the Shopping section.

The Paperwork

Before going ahead with a wedding you should consult your embassy or consulate for advice, especially regarding the legality of the marriage back home. In nearly all cases, a marriage that is performed in Dubai will be legally recognised elsewhere in the world, but it's always best to check. In addition, you may need to inform your embassy of your intention to marry. The British Embassy in Dubai, for example, will display a 'notice of marriage' in the embassy waiting room for 21 days prior to the marriage (along the same lines as 'the banns' being published in a parish newsletter for three successive Sundays). Afterwards, providing no one has objected, they will issue a 'certificate of no impediment' that may be required by the church carrying out your ceremony.

Shotgun Weddings

It is illegal to have a baby out of wedlock in the UAE. If you are unmarried and fall pregnant, you have two choices: march down the aisle ASAP or leave Dubai. You'll be asked for your marriage certificate when you give birth (and even earlier if you are having your prenatal checks at a government hospital). If there is a significant discrepancy in the dates, you will probably face many questions and a lot more paperwork.

Christ Church Jebel Ali can offer further assistance regarding marriage between two Christians (christchurchjebelali.com).

A Muslim marrying another Muslim can apply at the marriage section of the Dubai Courts, next to Maktoum Bridge. You will need two male witnesses and the bride should ensure that either her father or brother attends as a witness. You will require your passports with copies, proof that the groom is Muslim, and Dhs.50. You can marry there and then. A Muslim man can marry a non-Muslim woman, but a non-Muslim man cannot marry at the court. The situation is more complicated for a Muslim woman wishing to marry a non-Muslim man and this may only be possible if the man first converts to Islam. Call the Dubai Courts (04 334 7777) or the Dubai Court Marriage Section (04 303 0406) for more information.

Christians can either have a formal church ceremony with a congregation, or a small ceremony that must take place in a church, followed by a blessing at a different location, such as a hotel. Your church may require that you have someone to witness you signing a 'legal eligibility for marriage' document (a legal paper signed under oath) at your embassy or consulate. You may also need to attend at least three sessions of premarital counselling.

At the official church ceremony, you will need two witnesses to sign the register and the church will then issue a marriage certificate. You will need to get the certificate translated into Arabic by a court-approved legal translator. Take this, and the original, along with your essential documents to the Notary Public Office at the Dubai Courts. They will certify the documents for a fee of about Dhs.80. Next you will need to go to the Ministry of Justice (ejustice.gov.ae) to authenticate the signature and the Notary Public seal. Just when you think it's all over, you still have to go to the Ministry of Foreign Affairs (behind the distinctive Etisalat building in Deira) to authenticate the seal of the Ministry of Justice. Now you just need to pop back to your embassy for final legal verification.

Catholics must also undertake a marriage encounter course, which usually takes place at the busy St Mary's Church in Oud Metha (04 337 0087) on a Friday. At the end of the course, you are presented with a certificate. You should then arrange with the priest to undertake a pre-nuptial ceremony (which will require your birth certificate, baptism certificate, passport and passport copies, an NOC from your parish priest in your home country and a donation, and the filling out of another form). If you are a non-Catholic marrying a Catholic, you will need an NOC from your embassy/consulate stating that you are legally free to marry. A declaration of your intent to marry is posted on the public noticeboard at the church for three weeks; after this time, if there are no objections, you can set a date for the ceremony.

Wedding Photographers

Rates vary depending on where your wedding is located and how long you will require a photographer for. Try the following photographers for your big day: Sue Johnston (imageoasisdubai.com), Charlotte Simpson (hotshotsdubai.com), or Darrin James (djphotography.net).

Anglicans should make an appointment to see the chaplain at Holy Trinity Church (04 337 0247). You will need to fill out forms confirming that you are legally free to marry and take your essential documents along (passport, passport copies, passport photos, residence visa). If you have been married previously, you will need to produce either your divorce certificate or the death certificate of your previous partner. Fees differ depending on nationality and circumstances but are around Dhs.1,500 for the ceremony and an additional Dhs.1,000 if you wish to hold the ceremony outside the church. You'll pay Dhs.50 for any additional copies of the marriage certificate that you want. If you're not overly concerned about sticking to a particular doctrine, but want a church wedding, the Anglican ceremony is simpler to arrange and less time consuming than the Catholic equivalent.

These marriages are recognised by the government of the UAE but must be formalised. To make your marriage 'official', get an Arabic translation of the marriage certificate and take it to the Dubai Court. Hindus can be married through the Hindu Temple and the Indian Embassy Consulate (04 397 1222). The formalities take a minimum of 45 days.

Having A Baby

In many ways, having a baby while you are living in Dubai as an expat is very easy. The standard of maternity healthcare, whether you choose to go private or government, is excellent. As long as you have insurance or the means to pay for healthcare, there is absolutely no reason to return to your home country to give birth (more on maternity healthcare on p.194). There is a greater likelihood that you can get away with one income in Dubai, meaning that many mothers get to stay at home with their new babies, rather than having to return to work. And you will have access to cheap childcare and babysitting services here, so you may find that you can be a little more independent than your counterparts back home.

Of course, there are some disadvantages too. If you are pregnant and working, then you've got some pretty paltry maternity leave to look forward to: just 45 days paid leave, and absolutely nothing for dads (public sector employees are entitled to three days' paternity leave). You can take another month unpaid, as long as your employer agrees, and if you need some extra time for medical reasons, you can take up to 100 days, although this is only granted upon production of a medical certificate from your doctor. Having an understanding employer can obviously result in maternity leave rules being slightly more flexible.

Another big disadvantage of living here and having a baby is the absence of the family support network you may have had back home – grandparents and other family members, who would normally muck in to help you with mundane tasks like cooking, cleaning and babysitting are now thousands of miles away. Fortunately, many people who have babies here find themselves a strong network of other parents who meet up regularly and offer plenty of support to each other.

Pregnant Out Of Wedlock

If you fall pregnant but are not married then there is no reason to panic, but there are several decisions that you will need to make fairly quickly. It is illegal to have a baby out of wedlock while you are a resident in the UAE and if you deliver your baby at any hospital here, private or public, and can't produce a marriage certificate, you will most likely face a prison sentence. Therefore, as soon as you see the blue lines on the pregnancy test, you need to sort a few things out. The easiest solution is to have a quick wedding, after which you can go on to have antenatal care in a government or private hospital without any fear of punishment. If this is not an option, you can stay in Dubai until a reasonable time before you are due to give birth, and even have your antenatal check-ups in a private hospital, but you will need to ensure that you return to your home country to actually deliver the baby. Once you have delivered you can return to Dubai with the baby: there are no rules against being a single mother here (see p.140 for more information on single parents).

Birth Certificate & Registration

The hospital that delivers the baby will prepare a 'notification of birth' (which will be in Arabic) upon receipt of hospital records, photocopies of both parents' passports, your marriage certificate, and a fee of Dhs.50.

To get the actual birth certificate, take the birth notification to the Birth Certificate Office at Al Baraha Hospital (04 271 0000).

Every expat child born in the UAE should be registered with their parents' embassy. If the parents are from different countries, you will probably be able to choose which nationality your child adopts, and in some cases he or she may be able to take on dual nationality. Check with your embassy for additional information and details.

Babies Born Back Home

Babies born abroad to expatriate mums with UAE residency are required to have a residence visa or a visit visa before entering the UAE. The application should be filed by the father or family provider, along with the essential documents, a salary certificate and a copy of the birth certificate.

The important thing to remember is that your baby needs to get a UAE residency visa within 120 days of birth, and in order to do this you need to have received his or her passport, so you should start the process as soon as possible. If you don't get the residency within that time, you will have to pay a fine of Dhs.100 for every day that you go over the limit.

If you feel like you've got enough on your hands with your new arrival, MEDI-Express offers a service, for a fee, that will take much of the administration and hassle out of arranging the birth certificate for your baby. The firm is based at Al Baraha Hospital. See mediexpressuae.com or call 04 272 7772 for more details.

Adoption

While you can't adopt a UAE National baby, many couples in Dubai adopt children from Africa, Asia and Far Eastern countries. Adoption regulations vary according to which country the child comes from, but once you clear the requirements of that country, and complete the adoption process, you will have no problems bringing your new child into the UAE on your sponsorship. Check with your embassy about the procedure for applying for citizenship of your home country for your new child.

If you are considering adopting a child, a good place to start is the Adoption Support Group Dubai. Join the Yahoo group (groups.yahoo.com/group/asgdubai), or email asgdubai@yahoogroups.com.

Getting Divorced

Statistics show that the UAE has one of the highest divorce rates in the Arab world. To counter this, bodies such as the State Marriage Fund have launched schemes offering education and counselling services to National couples. Expats can get divorced in Dubai, and in some cases the procedure can be relatively straightforward. Expat couples can now choose to get divorced according to the laws of the UAE or their home country (if the couple has mixed nationalities, the home country of the husband applies), and it is advisable to seek legal advice. A husband who sponsors his wife has the right to have her residence visa cancelled in the event of divorce. See p.132 for a list of law firms.

If you do decide to get divorced while living in Dubai and are an expat couple, you will most likely be governed by the law of the country that issued your marriage licence. It can be challenging getting divorced whilst living abroad, especially if the situation isn't amicable. If you are the one filing for divorce, and you have legal representation in your home country, it is likely that you will also need a solicitor here to serve the divorce papers to your spouse. In addition, while you may be living in Dubai and therefore think custodial issues are not relevant, it may still be a good idea to arrange for a residence and access order or similar through the courts in your home country, in order to clarify your parental rights for when you do intend to return. If the relationship between you and your spouse has deteriorated, it is a good idea to try and meet with a mediator; Dr Ruth McCarthy at the Counselling & Development Clinic Dubai (drmccarthypsychologyclinic.com) specialises in marriage counselling.

Single Parents

It is possible to live in Dubai and sponsor your children as a single parent, even if you are a woman. There will be extra requirements that you need to meet, including a minimum salary level and a letter of no objection from the other parent (or a death certificate, in the case of a deceased spouse). You may also need to show your divorce certificate but it is best to visit the Immigration Department to find out the exact requirements, as these may change from time to time. Being a working single parent in Dubai may seem daunting for a number of reasons. Firstly, as an expat, your support system may not be as great as back home, where friends and family can help out, and, secondly, in a country where marriage and family are so important you may feel a little like the 'odd one out'. However, once you get used to people enquiring where your husband is (if you have a child with you people assume you're married), there are actually lots of advantages of living in Dubai as a working single parent. The nurseries (p.150) in Dubai are very good and a few offer full day care; they are generally much more affordable than in your home country. There is also the option of having a live-in nanny (see Sponsoring a Maid, p.38), which means that you cannot only work as a single parent but also still have a social life.

Babysitting & Childcare

Dubai may be a great place to raise children, but it can be a challenging task to find reliable childcare here. Many families choose to hire live-in, full-time maids (nannies) to assist them with childcare and babysitting; however, this can work out to be quite expensive due to the sponsorship fees, and you also need to have an apartment or villa with suitable accommodation.

If both you and your spouse work full time then a live-in maid is really your best option as there is no official network of childminders, although you will find the occasional expat mum offering her services underneath the radar, so to speak.

Finding the right live-in person can certainly be a challenge. There are a number of agencies around Dubai but they don't have the greatest reputations, so it is best to speak to them before you interview any of their candidates. It is preferable to recruit someone who is already in the country, and therefore your best bet would be to find an expat who is leaving the country and no longer needs their maid. Speak to other parents and check/put up notices on Spinneys and community noticeboards, as well as on expatwoman.com and dubizzle.com.

Depending upon the nationality of your live-in maid (the majority of whom are Sri Lankan and Filipina) you may have to visit their local embassy to get a contract drawn up before beginning the sponsorship process (see Sponsoring A Maid, p.38).

Domestic help agencies (p.107) can provide part-time babysitters, although there is no guarantee that you will get the same babysitter every time.

Ask around your neighbourhood to see if any of the local maids or teenagers are available for ad hoc evening babysitting, or try your child's nursery, as

Enjoy family time in Safa Park

classroom assistants are often up for a bit of extra work and they will already know your children.

If you do manage to find someone for part-time babysitting, the rate ranges from Dhs.15 to Dhs.30 per hour. Western childminders are most likely to charge more than this.

Activities For Kids

During the cooler months (October to May), kids can enjoy the many parks (p.256) and beaches (p.258) around Dubai, which house playgrounds for varying ages (Safa Park, Zabeel Park and Dubai Creek Park have excellent play areas for both toddlers and older kids; see Parks, p.256), as well as tennis and basketball courts. There are also a number of waterparks (p.258) in and around the city; however, while swimming is obviously popular, there are few public pools. Mushrif Park (p.257) has separate women's and men's pools but, outside the hotels and health clubs, the only other options are villa compound pools or the beach. Unless your child is an extremely strong swimmer, it is unwise to let them swim unsupervised at the public beaches as there are undercurrents.

During the warmer months (June to September) the many amusement centres (p.262) and kids' play areas keep your brood from getting bored. Fun Corner is a soft play centre with a few arcade games and small rides located in Bin Sougat Centre (p.436), Al Ghurair City (p.436), and the Spinneys Centre on Al Wasl Road. Fun City (funcity.ae) offers similar facilities, plus scheduled classes, and can be found in the Arabian Center (p.436), Oasis Centre (p.438), Reef Mall (p.439), Ibn Battuta (p.430), Mercato (p.432), Lamcy Plaza (p.438) and BurJuman (p.423). Located near Dubai Garden Centre along Sheikh Zayed Road, Mini Monsters (minimonsters.ae) is the UAE's largest indoor soft play venue.

There are various sports and activity clubs that run after-school activities (p.146) and summer camps (p.146), plus some great kids' attractions such as Kidzania (p.264). The Activities chapter (p.319) covers a range of hobbies that children may be interested in. Visit dubaikidz.biz for up to date information on family events and activities.

Active Sports Academy

Various locations
050 559 7055
activeuae.com

In operation for 13 years, Active Sports Academy organises various sports coaching classes in multiple venues around Dubai, including at various campuses after school. It teaches tennis, soccer, cricket, basketball, swimming and gymnastics and runs various tournaments, as well as holiday camps through all school break periods, including spring, Eid, Christmas and summer.

Apple Seeds

Gold & Diamond Park Al Quoz Industrial 3
04 380 6064
appleseedsdubai.com
Map **1 S6** Metro **First Gulf Bank**

This New-York themed indoor playground features an NYC taxi cab and apartment, yoga block skyscraper, shape sorter garden, deli with play foods, Lego table, magnet wall and more. There are also classes covering everything from science to ballet, cooking to art – so lots to keep the little ones amused. New for 2013 are character and confidence building programmes for four to 13 year olds.

Desert Sport Services

Palace Tower 2 Dubai Silicon Oasis **04 326 2822**
desertsportservices.com

Desert Sport Services runs swimming programmes for all ages, from parent & baby/toddler through to learn to swim and stroke development; sessions are held at various sites including Emirates International School, English College Primary, Jebel Ali Club and Horizon School. The club also organises pool parties for children, staffed by fully qualified lifeguards.

DuGym Gymnastics Club

Various locations **050 553 6283**
dugym.com

DuGym offers gymnastics and trampoline coaching to children of all ages and abilities. Established by Suzanne Wallace in 2000, the club now operates at 15 locations including Wellington International School, Jumeirah English Speaking School and Emirates International School. Classes are held from Sunday to Thursday. Contact Suzanne on the above number for more details.

Favourite Things

Dubai Marina Mall Dubai Marina **04 434 1984**
favouritethings.com
Map **1 K5** Metro **Jumeirah Lakes Towers**

The perfect place to leave your kids happily playing for an hour or two, Favourite Things, in Dubai Marina Mall, has more than enough activities to keep the rug rats happy. There's everything from toddlers' soft play area to a mini race track, jungle gym and dressing up area. Parents can join in, watch from the comfort of the cafe, or even leave the tots in the centre's capable hands while they go shopping.

Kids' Theatre Works

Dubai Community Theatre & Arts Centre (DUCTAC)
Al Barsha 1 **04 341 4777**
kidstheatreworks.com
Map **1 R6** Metro **Mall of the Emirates**

Running classes in creative drama, musical theatre, acting, dance, youth theatre, music and scene work for ages three and up; if your kids are budding superstars, Kids' Theatre Works is a good start. It runs classes at DUCTAC, Uptown Mirdif Primary, Jebel Ali, DESS and American School of Dubai.

Kidville

The Walk, Jumeirah Beach Residence Dubai Marina
04 440 1220
mykidville.ae
Map **1 K5** Metro **Dubai Marina**

Based on an innovative concept pioneered in New York, Kidville offers newborns to six year olds a unique range of classes that include musical journeys on the Rockin' Railroad, building 3D art projects in Construction Junction, and exploring a variety of paints, dough, crayons, chalk and collage in My Big

Weekend fun in the dunes

Messy Art Class. There's also the Kidville University, an alternative programme for pre-schoolers. Other branches include MotorCity (04 454 2760) and Uptown Mirdif (04 236 3648).

Kidz Venture

Ibn Battuta Mall The Gardens **04 368 4130**
kidzventure.ae
Map **1 G5** Metro **Ibn Battuta**
Open seven days a week, from 07:00 to 22:00, Kidz Venture offers a variety of childcare options as and when you need them. From nursery and after-school programmes, to drop 'n' shop babysitting, birthday parties, and arts and crafts activities, there is always something to keep your little one amused.

Little Explorers > *p.145*

Playnation Mirdif **800 386**
theplaymania.com/little-explorers
Map **2 P12** Metro **Rashidiya**
Little Explorers at Playnation Mirdif City Centre is a mix of education and entertainment for children from two to seven years old. Focused on acquiring skills in a fun and safe environment, this edutainment centre is set out in five distinctly-themed zones that give the centre plenty of variety to keep kids interested; there's everything from seeing how fast you can run to scientific experiments that investigate the natural environment. With games and activities spanning over 97 different exhibits that get the brain ticking and stimulate the senses, children can discover hidden talents and new skills. There are also a couple of birthday party packages available.

My Gym UAE

Villa 520, Jumeira Rd Jumeira 3 **04 394 3962**
mygymuae.com
Map **2 C4** Metro **Noor Islamic Bank**
Offering a wide range of programmes for kids up to 13 years old, the expert staff lead classes that combine increases in strength, agility, coordination and flexibility with the development of social skills and self-esteem.

Peekaboo Creative Play Centre

The Village Jumeira 1 **04 344 7122**
peekaboo.ae
Map **2 H4** Metro **Emirates Towers**
This children's play centre offers a packed schedule of organised activities, which aim to develop children's creativity and provide an educational experience at the same time as letting the kids have fun. Children aged 0 to seven can join in with cooking, nursery rhymes, yoga, arts, crafts and much more. Children under three and a half must be accompanied by an adult. The centre operates an hourly fee structure with memberships also available. Also at Mall of the Emirates and Ibn Battuta.

Quay Skillz Youth Facility

Madinat Jumeirah Al Sufouh 1 **050 480 7670**
skillz.ae
Map **1 R4** Metro **1 R4 Mall of the Emirates**
Dedicated children's gym with secure entry and specialised trainers who provide an environment for kids aged seven to 16 to exercise, while adults can use the extensive club facilities. Includes running machines, spinning bikes, cross trainers, fitness trampolines and rowing machines all tailored to the needs and interests of the younger gym-goer.

Tickles & Giggles

The Walk, Jumeirah Beach Residence Dubai Marina **04 432 8681**
ticklesandgiggles.com
Map **1 K5** Metro **Dubai Marina**
Tickles and Giggles has a kids' salon and spa, and offers unique classes such as baby yoga, etiquette classes, arts and crafts and nursery rhymes. It also hosts ultra trendy parties for kids (no bears or tank engines in sight), and will match decorations and the menu to your chosen theme. You can become a member on the website, where you can order party supplies as well as make online bookings.

Mother & Toddler Activities

Dubai is a great place for young families, and while you may not have the helpful hand of family close by, there are lots of mother and baby groups, as well as support groups (p.146), to keep you and your baby happy. There are of course also the city's parks (p.256) which make great spots for mothers to meet, and many of them have walking tracks which are excellent for a bit of pram pushing exercise. As pavements are rare in Dubai, going for a stroll with your pushchair may be a challenge – malls are of course an option, The Walk at Jumeirah Beach Residence (p.413) has nice wide walkways and Uptown Mirdif's pedestrianised area provides traffic-free space, as does much of the Downtown Dubai area. For more on places to walk see p.364.

Dubai Mums Club

Various locations
dubaimumsclub.com
This group operates via its online site and through meet ups. Registered members have access to the club forum, as well as special discounts and can consult an online paediatrician and fitness instructor.

Mirdif Mums Dubai

Mirdif **055 735 4759**
mirdifmums.webs.com
As Mirdif has a strong family population it is only fitting that the mums get together to share coffee mornings, afternoons in the park and various activity

days. The group also has some social outings without the kids, which is a great way to make new friends.

Mumcierge

Various locations **050 640 8322**
mumcierge.ae
A complete club for mums that showcases clubs and activities for tots, while also making sure that mum stays sane and can chat with other mothers at themed coffee mornings. A great resource for all parents. Membership is just Dhs.200 per month which allows free attendance at all coffee mornings, or you can pay as you go too.

Summer Camps

With more and more kids in Dubai during the summer holidays, many hotels, clubs and organisations have added summer camps and activities to their annual schedule. Most language schools run summer courses for kids (see Language Courses, p.175), if you want your kids to put their time off to good use. If you'd rather see them having fun over the holidays, many leisure clubs offer summer camps that focus on sports, arts and crafts, so if you have a leisure club in your area, contact them to see what they have on offer. Alternatively, contact Active Sports Academy (p.142), which arranges sporty summer camps at various venues around the city.

After-School Activities

Many schools will run ECAs (Extra Curricular Activities) from kindergarten upwards. Generally, the younger years only have one ECA a week for around 30-60 minutes directly after school, while the older years may have multiple classes at various times. School-run ECAs are often included in the school fees, however, independent companies also hold classes at schools during the afternoons and evenings and charge term fees (which are far from cheap). Many school campuses are utilised by various sports academies and dance schools in the afternoons, at weekends and during school holidays, and you are likely to receive a multitude of flyers in your kids' school bags from such companies.

Turning Pointe (p.332) runs ballet classes for all ages in various schools around Dubai, as does Kids' Theatre Works (p.142), and Kids Active has a range of sports classes. If your kids are sports players (or you want them to be) there are a number of academies that can develop their talents – would-be Federers should sign up with the Clark Francis Tennis Academy (p.361), budding Beckhams can hone their skills with the International Football Academy (p.338) or UAE English Soccer School of Excellence (p.338), wanna-be Olympic gold medallists should dive in with Australian International Swim Schools (p.360) and potential Bruce Lees can kick it with various clubs around Dubai (see Martial Arts, p.345). Many parents get together in the parks (in the winter) and play centres (in the summer) around Dubai for their own impromptu after-school activities, so new families shouldn't worry about long afternoons and bored kids.

Support Groups

Starting a new life in a different country away from your normal support network of family and friends can be challenging, but there are a number of support groups to help you through the difficult patches. In addition to the groups listed below, the Human Relations Institute offers a range of support group workshops (p.210), and Dubai Community Health Centre (p.210) provides space for support group meetings.

Adoption Support Group

Various locations **04 360 8113**
groups.yahoo.com/group/asgdubai
Meetings are held once a month for parents who have adopted children or who are considering adopting. For more information on the meetings, call Carol on the number listed above.

Alcoholics Anonymous

Various locations **056 788 1416**
This organisation spans the GCC and wider Middle East with regular AA meetings held in various locations. It also offers a 12 step programme that allows AA members to join a 'closed' workshop. Check out the website for the classes and workshop schedule.

All 4 Down Syndrome Dubai

Various locations **050 880 9228**
downsyndromedubai.com
All 4 Down Syndrome provides support to families whose lives have been affected by Down Syndrome. The group is part of an awareness-raising campaign, and offers advice on health, education and care for people with Down's. Social mornings are held every Sunday between 10:00 and 12:00.

Dubai Dyslexia Support Group

Various locations **04 344 6657**
This group holds occasional meetings for people with dyslexia and may be able to assist you if you suspect that your child is suffering from dyslexia.

Dubai Foundation For Women & Children

Al Awir **04 606 0300**
dfwac.ae
The first licensed, non-profit shelter in the UAE for women and children who are the victims of domestic violence, abuse or human trafficking. Established in July 2007 to offer immediate protection and support services in accordance with international human rights obligations, the foundation provides a helpline,

emergency shelter, and support services to women and children victims.

Friends Of Cancer Patients (Pink Caravan)
Sharjah **06 506 5542**
focp.ae
One of the leading cancer organisations in the UAE, this volunteer-run group offers advice, information and support to cancer sufferers and their families.

Mothers Of Children With Special Needs
Various locations **050 659 1707**
A support group run by parents of special needs children offering support and information, as well as get togethers with their children. Call Lilly for details of monthly meetings.

UAE Down Syndrome Association
Villa 5, Nr Dubai Marine Beach Resort & Spa, Jumeira Rd Jumeira 1 **04 344 4471**
uaedsa.ae
This active group organises day trips and events and offers support to people with Down Syndrome in the UAE and their families. The organisation also runs conferences and workshops and publishes a regular newsletter for members. Call Dr Eman Gaad on the above number.

Death
In the event of the death of a friend or relative, the first thing to do is to notify the police by dialling 999. The police will fill out a report and the body will be taken to Rashid Hospital (p.186) where a doctor will determine the cause of death and produce a report. The authorities will need to see the deceased's passport and visa details. Dubai Police will investigate in the case of an accidental or suspicious death, and it's likely that an autopsy will be performed at a government hospital. If you're unhappy with the outcome of an investigation you could hire a private investigator, but this is a bit of a grey area so seek advice from your embassy or consulate.

Clearly, this can all be a tricky – not to mention unpleasant – process, especially given the circumstances; Middle East Funeral Services (mefs.ae) is a private company that can be employed to look after some or all of the details on your behalf.

Certificates & Registration
On receipt of the doctor's report, the hospital will issue a death certificate declaration, for a fee of Dhs.60. Take the declaration and original passport to the nearest police department, which will issue an NOC addressed to Al Baraha (Kuwaiti) Hospital (p.182). You should also request NOCs addressed to the mortuary for embalming, the airport for transportation and the hospital for the release of the body. This letter, plus death declaration, original passport and copies should be taken to Al Baraha Hospital, Department of Preventative Medicine, where an actual death certificate will be issued. You will also need to cancel the deceased's visa at the Department of Naturalisation and Residency.

If you are sending the deceased home you should request a death certificate in English (an additional Dhs.100) or appropriate language – check this with your embassy. Since Islam requires that the body be buried immediately, the death certificate and registration procedures for deceased Muslims can be performed after the burial.

Local Burial
A local burial can be arranged at the Muslim or Christian cemeteries in Dubai. The cost of a burial is Dhs.1,100 for an adult and Dhs.350 for a child. You will need to get a coffin made, as well as transport to the burial site. Cremation is also possible, but only in the Hindu manner and with the prior permission of the next of kin and the CID.

Returning The Deceased To Their Country Of Origin
To return the deceased to his or her country of origin, you will need to book your own ticket with the airline of your choosing as well as make shipping arrangements through dnata (04 211 1111), which will handle the body at Cargo Village and process any required documentation. The deceased will need to be embalmed before reaching Cargo Village, and you will need the original death certificate, the NOC from Dubai Police, an NOC from the embassy of the deceased (which must be the same as the destination to which they are being sent), the cancellation or the passport and visa and a copy of the air tickets specifying flight details. You will also need to purchase a coffin in accordance with the size of the deceased. Embalming can be arranged through the Dubai Health Authority and will cost around Dhs.1,000, which includes the embalming certificate. The body must be identified before and after embalming, after which it should be transferred to Cargo Village for shipping. Cargo fees will range from Dhs.1,000 to Dhs.10,000 and a coffin costs about Dhs.750. When preparing the documentation, remember that dnata will require seven copies of each document and the translation.

Local Burial Or Cremation
Before the deceased can be buried or cremated locally, you will need the following documentation: passport (cancelled from the embassy), death certificate, proof that the visa was cancelled and a non objection certificate (NOC) from the sponsor stating that all debts have been settled. For Hindu cremation, you

must also provide written permission from the next of kin, as well as that person's passport. The procedure for local cremation and burial can be complicated and changes often, so you will need to contact the Dubai Municipality (04 221 5555, dm.gov.ae), the Christian Cemetery (04 337 0247), or the Hindu Temple in Bur Dubai (04 353 5334) for the latest information.

Pets

The attitude (both socially and legally) towards pets in Dubai is mixed so it's sensible to keep your pet under control. Pets are prohibited from parks and beaches, but aside from the streets the desert is also a good place to take a dog for a walk or run. In addition to having dogs on leads at all times when walking, certain dogs have to be muzzled in Dubai when walked in public (see dkc.ae for details). All dogs must be registered, microchipped and vaccinated. Fines and confiscations are the consequences of not doing so. While uncommon, animal abuse is a problem in the city, and can be reported to the municipality. See dm.gov.ae or call 04 289 1114.

You should check with your landlord what the pet policy is before you move in. In many cases it is not permitted to keep a pet, particularly in apartments. Some landlords will be amenable if you negotiate, but it is advisable to get any permission in writing to avoid difficult situations further down the line.

When walking your dog, keep it on a short leash, as many people are frightened of them. Be sure to keep your pet indoors or within your garden to avoid contact with strays and to prevent any problems with frightened neighbours. Dubai has a significant problem with strays, although both Feline Friends (050 451 0058) and K9 Friends (04 887 8739) are hard-working animal charities that take in as many as they can. The Dubai Municipality is also hard at work fixing the stray problem.

Cats & Dogs

K9 Friends (04 887 8739) helps to rehome stray and injured dogs, many of which are abandoned family pets looking for a second chance. See k9friends.com for more information. Another useful website for pet owners in the Emirates is petdubai.com.

Feline Friends (050 451 0058) is a non-profit organisation, aiming to improve the lives of cats by rescuing and rehoming stray cats and kittens. It has a 24 hour telephone answering service as well as a useful website, felinefriendsdubai.com.

You should inoculate your pet annually against rabies, distemper, canine hepatitis, leptospirosis and parvovirus. Cats have to be vaccinated against rabies, feline rhinotracheitis, calicivirus and panleukopnia.

Register your pet with the Dubai Municipality (04 289 1114), which will microchip cats and dogs and provide plastic neck tags. If the Municipality picks up an animal without a tag and chip, it is treated as a stray and there is a strong chance it will be put down.

Sleek Salukis

The saluki is a breed of dog most commonly associated with the region; they are used in traditional forms of hunting. The Arabian Saluki Center (02 575 5330) can provide information on all aspects of the care of these animals. Many 'desert dogs' descend from the saluki. If you'd like to adopt your own desert dog, contact K9 Friends (k9friends.com).

While rare, there have been reports of dogs being stolen, either to be sold to unscrupulous pet shops, or for dog fighting. Ensure your garden is secure and don't let your dog roam around on the street.

Bringing Your Pet To Dubai

Pets may be brought into the UAE without quarantine as long as they are microchipped and vaccinated with verifying documentation, including a government health certificate from the country of origin; however, you'll need an import permit. You cannot import cats and dogs under four months old and all pets must arrive as manifest cargo with a valid rabies vaccination more than 21 days before their arrival. Imports from some countries will also be subjected to a rabies test. For more information visit petimport.moew.gov.ae and create an account.

There are certain breeds of dog that are banned from being imported into the UAE: pit bull terriers, Argentinean and Brazilian mastiffs, Japanese tosa inu, American Staffordshire terriers, and any wolf hybrids; the UAE also bans any dogs crossed with any of the banned breeds listed. There are other breeds which, while not banned outright, have restrictions on them too. Make sure you check with the Municipality before you embark on the process. Dubai Kennels & Cattery provides a detailed guide to importing and exporting pets.

Taking Your Pet Home

A pet can be sent out of Dubai either accompanied by their owner on the same flight or unaccompanied as cargo depending on the airline and destination, but you need to contact the airline cargo department to find out the regulations. Many boarding facilities and vets offer an export service, including Dubai Kennels & Cattery and The Doghouse (dubaidoghouse.com). You need to check the laws of the country you are exporting your pet to as they each have varying

quarantine stipulations. It is advisable to check with a pet relocation specialist here or in the country you are going to.

Pet Grooming & Training

Standards of care at Dubai's veterinary clinics are reasonably high. Prices do not vary dramatically, but the Deira Veterinary Clinic and Al Barsha Veterinary Clinic are a little cheaper than the rest. Dubai Municipality has a veterinary services department (04 289 1114) next to Mushrif Park that only vaccinates animals. The Nad Al Shiba Veterinary Hospital (04 323 4412) also treats more exotic animals and birds.

Kennels are generally of a good standard, although spaces are limited during peak times (summer and Christmas). An alternative is to use an at-home pet-sitting service – someone will come into your house at least once a day to feed and exercise your pet for a reasonable fee (for a bit extra they might even water your plants). For further information on pet shops see p.404.

There are a number of firms that offer a variety of grooming treatments from the basic (shampooing, medicated baths and nail clipping) to the more indulgent, like fashion advice.

Pet Boarding, Training & Clinics

Al Barsha Veterinary Clinic Al Barsha 1, 04 340 8601, *abvc.ae*
Al Safa Veterinary Clinic Umm Suqeim 2, 04 348 3799, *alsafavetclinic.com*
Animal Care Centre Various locations, 050 646 7792, *animalcarecentre.biz*
Deira Veterinary Clinic Al Qusais Industrial 5, 04 258 1881, *dr-azziz.com*
Doggies Palace Al Quoz 1, 04 339 3737, *doggiespalace.com*
Dubai Kennels & Cattery > *p.151* Umm Ramoul, 04 285 1646, *dkc.ae*
Energetic Panacea Jumeira 2, 04 344 7812, *energetic-panacea.com*
European Veterinary Center Trade Centre 2, 04 343 9591
Homely Petz Dubai Marina, 04 399 4223, *homelypetz.com*
Jumeirah Veterinary Clinic Jumeira 3, 04 394 2276
Modern Veterinary Clinic Al Safa 2, 04 395 3131, *vetdubai.com*
Nad Al Shiba Veterinary Clinic Nad Al Sheba 1, 04 323 4412, *nadvethosp.com*
Noble Veterinary Clinic Green Community, 04 885 4848, *noblevetclinic.com*
Pampered Pets Dubai Marina, 04 447 5330, *pamperedpets.ae*
Paws Pet Planet Dubai Investment Park 2, 04 884 8894, *pawspetplanet.com*
The Pet Palace Of Dubai Al Quoz Industrial 4, 04 323 6993, *petpalace.ae*
PetZone Al Wasl, 04 321 1424, *petzoneonline.com*
Poshpaws Kennels & Cattery Sharjah, 050 273 0973, *poshpawsdubai.com*
Positive Paws Al Barsha 1, 04 379 0996, *positivepaws.ae*
Shampooch Mobile Pet Grooming Various locations, 04 344 9868, *shampooch.ae*
Snoopy Pets Al Barsha 1, 04 420 5348, *snoopypets.com*
Tail-Waggin' – Mobile Pet Spa Various locations, 050 366 6622
Urban Tails Pet Resort Dubai Investment Park 2, 04 884 8847, *urbantailsdubai.com*
The Veterinary Hospital Al Quoz Industrial 1, 04 338 7726, *vet-hosp.com*
World Of Pets Jumeira 3, 04 395 5701, *worldofpetsme.com*
Zabeel Veterinary Hospital Za'abeel 1, 04 334 0011, *zabeelvet.com*

EDUCATION

There is no cause for concern that your child's education will suffer as a result of going to school in Dubai; on the contrary, many parents report satisfaction with the way a multicultural upbringing results in well-rounded, worldly wise children.

Something you can't escape, unfortunately, is paying high school fees – as an expat, your child will have to go to private school, and it will cost you a pretty penny, with fees seemingly permanently on the increase from year to year.

So, before you hand over wads of your hard-earned cash, it really is worth doing your research and picking a school that best suits the needs of your child. Have a chat with other parents for word-of-mouth recommendations, or ask your company's HR departments which schools they are used to dealing with. And, as Dubai traffic can be a nightmare, it makes sense to look at schools near your home or office as a starting point. School terms run to a similar calendar to education systems in the UK and USA, with the academic year starting in September after a long summer holiday.

Nurseries & Pre-Schools

Some nurseries accept babies from as young as three months, although most prefer to take on children who are at walking age (around 12 months). Fees and timings vary dramatically so it's best to call around and visit a few nurseries to get an idea of what's available. As a general rule of thumb, most nurseries are open for four or five hours in the morning and charge anything from Dhs.3,000 to Dhs.12,000 per year.

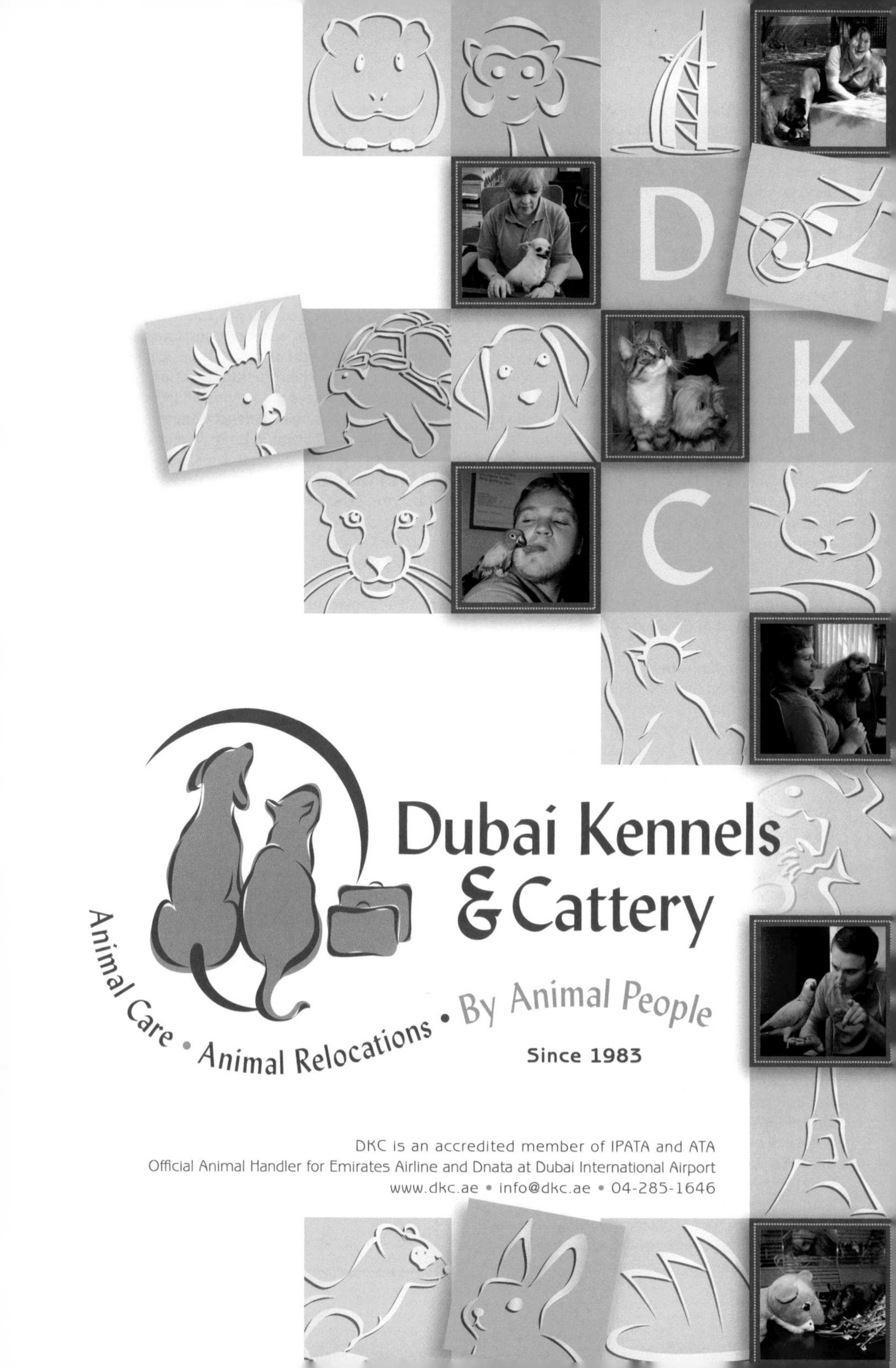
D
K
C
Dubai Kennels
& Cattery
Animal Care • Animal Relocations • By Animal People
Since 1983
DKC is an accredited member of IPATA and ATA
Official Animal Handler for Emirates Airline and Dnata at Dubai International Airport
www.dkc.ae • info@dkc.ae • 04-285-1646

The more popular nurseries have long waiting lists so you should enrol your child before he or she is even born. Some of the bigger primary schools also have nursery sections – if you've got a primary school in mind for your child, it's worth checking to see if they have a nursery as this may help you secure a place a few years down the line.

There are a number of factors to consider when you are looking for a nursery and it is always a good idea to take your time to visit a number of schools, and ask as many questions as you can.

Try to drop in during the day so that you can have a look at the facilities while there are children in school. Some of the nurseries in Dubai operate morning hours only which may rule them out if you are working. However, many also run late classes for an extra fee, while a number of them have early-bird drop-offs as well as running holiday classes and summer schools. Another factor worth considering when selecting your child's nursery is whether or not the school provides meals – having to make a packed lunch every morning when you're trying to get ready for work may not be suitable for you.

Al Khaleej National School

Nr Emirates Post Al Garhoud **04 282 2707**
gemsakns.com
Map **2 N9** Metro **Emirates**
From Kindergarten through to Grade 12, this GEMS school features an American syllabus with regular assessments. Facilities for nursery-aged children include an outdoor play area, well-stocked library, gym and swimming pool.

Alphabet Street Nursery

Villa 11, Al Manara St Al Manara **04 348 5991**
alphabetstreetnursery.com
Map **1 U5** Metro **First Gulf Bank**
Alphabet Street employs a mix of the Montessori teaching method and the Early Years Foundation Stage Programme (UK), to develop each child's communication, control and coordination. It offers a flexible early morning drop off, with the possibility of a 07:30 start, and also provides holiday care outside of term time. A late class is available until 17:30. Age range: 14 months to four-plus years.

Baby Land Nursery

Nr Choithrams, Al Wasl Rd Al Manara
04 348 6874
babylandnursery.com
Map **1 T5** Metro **First Gulf Bank**
Baby Land uses Montessori methods to encourage learning through play and exploration. Children participate in a series of practical activities specially designed to improve independence, concentration, hand-eye coordination, fine motor skills, patience and judgement. Baby Land offers late classes until 16:00 and a summer school. Age range: 12 months to 4.5 years.

Blossom Children's Nursery

Villa 37, 10A St Umm Al Sheif **04 348 6275**
theblossomnursery.com
Map **2 B5** Metro **First Gulf Bank**
Blossom Children's Nursery focuses on all-round development of children through varied methods of learning. Based on the International Early Years Curriculum, structured play programmes include dance, drama, music, water play and foreign languages. A 'smartbook' record keeps parents informed of their child's development, and there's a high priority placed on parent-staff interaction and sensory learning experiences. There is a second branch, Blossom Village, in Umm Suqeim (04 394 883).

British Orchard Nursery

Villa 20A, Street 33 Al Mankhool **04 398 3536**
britishorchardnursery.com
Map **2 K5** Metro **Al Karama**
This nursery follows the British national curriculum and the guidelines of Ofsted. Timings are from 08:00 to 12:30 and there are two out-of-school daycare clubs, Little Apples and Breakfast Club, which run from 07:30 to 17:00. Parents can also log on to a secure website to see their children through the in-class CCTV. There's another branch in Jumeira (04 395 3570).

Building Blocks

Apex Atrium Dubai MotorCity **04 453 4363**
building-blocks.ae
Map **1 N11**
Building Blocks follows the Early Years Foundation Stage curriculum (UK) framework, which concentrates on helping babies and toddlers to learn and grow through play. The nursery has an 'enrichment centre' where children can learn the basics in dance, music, sport, language and cooking.

The Montessori Way

Montessori is a popular teaching method that encourages a flexible approach to learning than a strict academic curriculum. Children are encouraged to discover new things through imaginative play, social interaction and physical activity. The method encourages children to develop their own instinct to learn, and is a good foundation for the International Baccalaureate curriculum. Montessori nurseries in Dubai including: Baby Land (p.152), Gulf Montessori Dubai (p.154), Yellow Brick Road (p.157), Tiny Home (04 349 3201), First Steps (p.154), Ladybird Nursery (p.156), and Little Land (04 394 4471).

Children's City

KHDA, Academic City

Dubai International Academic City

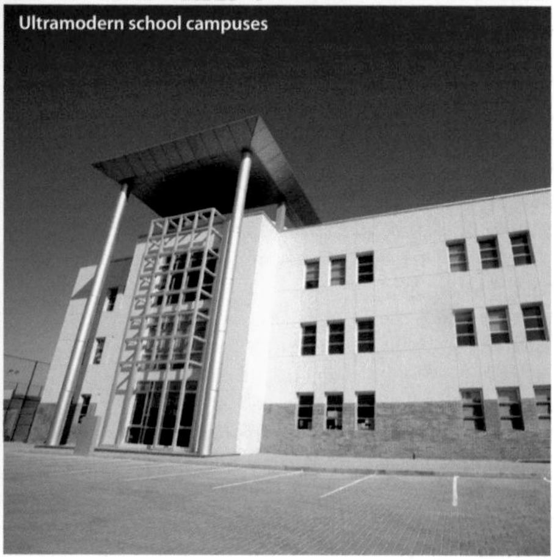
Ultramodern school campuses

Burj Daycare Nursery
Burj Khalifa Downtown Dubai **04 431 8320**
burjdaycarenursery.com
Map **2 F6** Metro **Burj Khalifa/Dubai Mall**
Open 08:00 until 14:00, this one-classroom nursery follows the UK's Early Years Foundation Stage programme, including classes in music and movement, Kidzart and French. There's a dedicated outdoor space, which includes a wave pool and 'splash maze', as well as an area for bikes and push-along toys.

The Children's Garden
Nr Courtyard Marriott Hotel Green Community
04 885 3484
childrensgarden.ae
Map **1 G10** Metro **Danube**
Offering early years education for two to five year olds, Children's Garden features an innovative curriculum which focuses on the attainment of knowledge through creativity. Languages form an integral part of this and children will be taught in at least two languages, becoming fluent in both after three years. There are other branches in Jumeira 2 (04 349 2985) and in Al Barsha 2 (04 385 6605).

Chubby Cheeks Nursery
Gardens Furnished Apartments Bldg 5 The Gardens
04 435 6598
chubbycheeksnursery.com
Map **1 H6** Metro **Ibn Battuta**
Well located for parents living in any of the main New Dubai communities (Emirates Living, Dubai Marina, The Greens, etc.), this nursery adopts a caring and fun approach to learning within a multinational, multicultural environment.

Cooper Nursery
Street 29B Al Safa 2 **04 380 9077**
coopernursery.com
Map **2 A6** Metro **Noor Islamic Bank**
Cooper Nursery adopts the Reggio Emilia Philosophy, teaching children from birth through to five years through play-based activities. Facilities include a sensory room, art studio, gym area and learning resource centre, and there is a special needs programme that gives children their own ILP (Individual Learning Programme) drawn up by practitioners.

Emirates British Nursery
Al Wasl Rd Umm Al Sheif **04 348 9996**
emiratesbritishnursery.com
Map **1 S6** Metro **First Gulf Bank**
This nursery regards playtime as an important factor in a child's early development. Both locations (the other is in Mirdif, 04 288 9222) are spacious and well planned, with multilingual staff and an in-house nurse. A summer school (a lifesaver for working mums) is available during July and August. Late class available until 15:00. Age range: three months (Mirdif only) and upwards.

First Steps Nursery School
Villa 10, Nr Burj Al Arab Umm Suqeim 3 **04 348 6301**
firststepsdubai.com
Map **1 S5** Metro **Mall of the Emirates**
This Montessori nursery opens from 07:30 to 18:00 and caters for ages 18 months to five years. It encourages child development through arts and crafts, reading, educational videos and indoor and outdoor play areas. It's open on Saturdays when it also accepts children up to the age of 10. In addition, it runs summer camps.

GEMS Modern Nursery > *p.155*
Dubai Modern High School Nad Al Sheba
04 326 3339
gemsmhs.com
Map **2 H13**
Dubai Modern High School in Nad Al Sheba offers a one year pre-kindergarten programme for children aged two to three years. This nursery follows the self-directed learning principles of both Reggio Emilia and Montessori.

Golden Beach Nursery
Villa 24, St 17A Umm Suqeim 3 **04 380 9336**
goldenbeachnursery.com
Map **1 S5** Metro **Mall of the Emirates**
Follows the British EYFS curriculum, with a focus on qualified staff and healthy, hygienic meals. Facilities include two indoor play areas and a large outdoor shaded play area, and the curriculum includes water play, music, French and art classes. Open 50 weeks a year from Sunday to Thursday (07:00-18:00). Age range: six months to four years.

Gulf Montessori Nursery
Nr Choithrams Al Garhoud **04 282 7046**
gulfmontessori.com
Map **2 N8** Metro **Airport Terminal 1**
This Gulf Montessori Nursery has fully equipped Montessori classrooms, a dedicated art room, swimming pool and large outdoor play area. Children are required to wear a uniform. Age range: two to five years.

Home Grown Children's Eco Nursery
Villa 33, Street 9 Umm Suqeim 2 **04 330 7008**
homegrownnursery.ae
Map **1 U5** Metro **Noor Islamic Bank**
Billed as Dubai's first 'eco-nursery', Home Grown follows the British Early Years Foundation Stage curriculum, uses eco-friendly resources and equipment, and many of the activities are focused on outdoors and nature.

Hopscotch Nursery

Villa 48, Street 15 Al Manara **04 328 2226**
hopscotchnursery.net
Map **1 U6** Metro **Noor Islamic Bank**
Using the British Early Years Foundation Stage curriculum for children aged 18 months to four years old, this nursery aims to care for, develop, motivate and educate kids in equal measures, with the help of some excellent facilities and a broad range of sporting activities.

Jumeirah International Nursery School

Villa 8, Street 13 Al Wasl **04 349 9065**
jinschools.com
Map **2 F5** Metro **Burj Khalifa/Dubai Mall**
One of the oldest in Dubai, this nursery follows the UK's Ofsted standards, and individual attention is given in a safe and balanced environment. Classes run from 08:00 to 12:30. Another branch, off Al Wasl Road, offers early drop-offs at 07:30 and late classes until 17:00 (04 394 5567). Age range: 18 months to four years.

The Kensington Nursery

Umm Al Sheif Rd Umm Suqeim 1 **04 394 4473**
thekensingtonnursery.com
Map **2 B4** Metro **Noor Islamic Bank**
With locations in Umm Sequim and Dubai Silicon Oasis, this nursery follows the British Early Years Foundation Stage curriculum. It is open 07:30-18:00 with full and half day options, operates a transport service, and runs holiday camps outside of term time.

Kid's Island Nursery

Al Hamra St Jumeira 3 **04 394 2578**
kidsislandnursery.com
Map **2 B4** Metro **Business Bay**
This British curriculum nursery is open all year round. There are large, shaded outdoor play areas, an activity room and playroom. Late class until 13:30. Age range: 13 months to three years. Also in Jumeira 3 is Cocoon Nursery, 04 394 9394.

Kids Cottage Nursery

Street 12 Umm Suqeim 1 **04 394 2145**
kidscottagenursery.com
Map **2 B5** Metro **Noor Islamic Bank**
This cheerful nursery with good facilities offers an activities-based curriculum for children over the age of 12 months. Parents can check up on their kids via a live webcam (access is password protected).

Kids Zone Nursery

The Villa Community Dubailand **04 452 6474**
kidszonenursery.com
Follows the British EYFS curriculum for children aged 12 months to four years, and also adopts the Reggio Approach to teaching.

Kidz Venture

Ibn Battuta Mall The Gardens **04 368 4130**
kidzventure.ae
Map **1 G5** Metro **Ibn Battuta**
Children are free to experiment and imitate through multiple activities like gardening, music, drama, cooking and games at this nursery for infants aged six months and above through to pre-school, aged two to three years. Offers a Montessori programme as well as the Early Years Foundation Stage curriculum.

Ladybird Nursery

Villa 8, Street 25A Al Wasl **04 344 1011**
ladybirdnursery.ae
Map **2 E5** Metro **Business Bay**
Ladybird strikes an interesting balance between a traditional nursery and a Montessori school, by providing a bright and cheerful environment, toys, dressing up clothes and soft play. Late class available until 13:30. Age range: 18 months to four years.

The Little Discoverers Nursery > *p.143*

Nr Dubai English College Primary Safa 1 **04 394 6066**
littlediscoverers.com
Map **2 B6** Metro **Noor Islamic Bank**
Open between 07:00 and 18:00, this nursery follows the British Early Years Foundation Stage to care for children aged three months to four years. Facilities include a jungle gym, herb garden and bike tracks.

Little Panda's Nursery

Villa 6, Street 51, Off Jumeirah Rd Jumeira 1 **04 344 6371**
littlepandasnursery.com
Map **2 G4** Metro **World Trade Centre**
Open 07:00 to 18:30, the nursery's Early Years Foundation Stage programme cares for children aged six months to four years. Home cooked meals are provided, outdoor facilities include a large sand-pit and an organic garden, and there is a bus service.

Little Woods Nursery

Villa 82, Street 4C Al Safa 2 **04 394 6155**
littlewoodsnursery.com
Map **2 A5** Metro **Noor Islamic Bank**
This well-equipped Safa nursery has a strong emphasis on child learning through interaction and individual development, all within a structured framework.

Mulberry Tree Nursery

Villa 5, Safeena St Jumeira 3 **04 394 9909**
mulberrytreenurseryuae.com
Map **2 C5** Metro **Business Bay**
Offers both the Montessori and British curriculum to ages 12 months to four years. The nursery welcomes children with special educational needs; facilities include an indoor gym and puppet theatre.

My Nursery

Street 2B, Al Wasl Rd Jumeira 1 **04 344 1120**
mynursery.ae
Map **2 H4** Metro **Financial Centre**
This nursery takes children between the ages of two and four, and delivers a bilingual English-Arabic curriculum aimed at educating children to the same level of proficiency in both languages. After-school care and school transport are available, and the nursery will soon be opening a class for children aged one year and eight months and upwards.

Palms Nursery

Al Meedaf St Jumeira 3 **04 394 7017**
palmsnurserydubai.com
Map **2 C5** Metro **Business Bay**
Now in its new spacious home, Palms Nursery has six classrooms and seven outdoor play areas. The curriculum is intended to help children acquire the skills that enable them to develop socially, physically and emotionally. An early birds session starts at 07:30, and a late class is available until 13:30. Age range: 22 months to four years.

Raffles Nursery

Various locations rafflesis.com
Raffles operates nine nurseries at various locations in Dubai including Arabian Ranches, Dubai Marina, Springs, Lakes, Emirates Hills and Umm Suqeim. Nursery timings are 08:00 to 14:00, and there is a choice of two curriculums: the British Early Years Foundation Stage and Montessori. A healthy lunch is served every day. Visit the website for contact details of each branch.

Safa Kindergarten Nursery

Nr Shangri-La, Off Sheikh Zayed Rd Trade Centre 1 **04 344 3878**
Map **2 F6** Metro **Burj Khalifa/Dubai Mall**
This British curriculum nursery uses the popular Montessori learning principles. Activities include educational play, singing, and water play. Arabic or French as a second language is introduced to children at three years.

Seashells Nursery

Nr Mall of the Emirates Al Barsha 2 **04 341 3404**
seashellsnursery.com
Map **1 R7** Metro **Mall of the Emirates**
Seashells follows the British curriculum, has two indoor playrooms, an indoor gym, a project room for cooking and fun experiments, and outdoor shaded play areas. The children can join in library, show and tell, and recycling activities, and there are organised field trips. After-school activities include soccer, gym and languages, and a school holiday programme is also available. Age range: 18 months to four years.

Small World Nursery

Nr Archaeological Site Jumeira 2 **04 349 0770**
smallworldnurserydubai.com
Map **2 H4** Metro **Business Bay**
Small World combines academic learning with physical education. Facilities include a discovery garden, swimming pool and outside play area. There is a late class until 13:30. Another branch in Umm Suqeim (Child's Play, 04 348 0788) offers a mixture of the UK curriculum and Waldorf-Steiner philosophy, a swimming pool, and a late class until 15:00. Age range: one to four years.

Super Kids Nursery

Villa 99, Street 23C Mirdif **04 288 1949**
superkidsnursery.com
Map **2 Q13** Metro **Rashidiya**
Super Kids is a small but popular nursery in Mirdif. The focus is on providing a warm, cosy 'home away from home' environment. Facilities include a large, shaded outside play area, an activity gym and a music room. Hot lunch and transport are optional extras. Early bird class from 07:30 and late class available until 17:00.

Tender Love & Care

Dubai Media City Al Sufouh 1 **04 367 1636**
tenderloveandcare.com
Map **1 M5** Metro **Nakheel**
A popular option for people working in Internet and Media Cities, this nursery has weekly activity plans and parents are notified of the monthly theme. Facilities include a gymnasium and garden. The nursery has a daily 'drop in' service, and a late class until 17:00.

Willow Children's Nursery

Villa 75, Off Al Wasl Rd Umm Suqeim 2 **050 472 5890**
willownurserydubai.com
Map **1 U5** Metro **Noor Islamic Bank**
This bright and pleasant nursery, with large gardens and play areas, is run by British staff teaching the Early Years Foundation Stage curriculum. Flexible hours are offered and a home-cooked lunch can be provided. There is also a dedicated baby area, Little Willow.

Yellow Brick Road Nursery

Nr Irish Village Al Garhoud **04 282 8290**
yellowbrickroad.ws
Map **2 N8** Metro **GGICO**
This huge and very popular nursery (with a long waiting list) accommodates 180 children in nine classes and a dedicated baby room. Children are taught the British nursery curriculum as well as enjoying outdoor play and swimming in the paddling pool. A cooked breakfast and lunch are provided. Late class available until 18:00. Another branch, Emerald City Nursery (04 349 0848), is in Jumeira 2. Age range: four months to four and a half years.

Primary & Secondary Schools

As an expat in Dubai, you most likely have no choice but to enrol your child in private education – government schools are for UAE Nationals and Arab expats only. When planning your child's education, there are several golden rules to help ease the process.

Firstly, if you have a school in mind, get your child's name on the waiting list as soon as possible, since the demand for spaces at the more popular schools is high. Secondly, consider the 'school run' when choosing your school – Dubai's rush-hour traffic can turn a short journey into a tedious hour-long trek every morning. Thirdly, pick a school that offers the best curriculum for your child: if you are British and are planning to return home after a couple of years, it might be best to find a school that offers the English National Curriculum; similarly, if you think you might end up elsewhere on another expat assignment after you leave Dubai, it might be better to choose the International or American Curriculum, which will help your child slot into a wide range of curriculums.

Kids here start school as early as three years old (in schools that offer a foundation or reception year), and usually graduate from secondary school at around 18 years. Most schools are open from 08:00 to 13:00 or 15:00, from Sunday to Thursday. Ramadan hours are shorter – usually starting an hour or so later and finishing an hour earlier.

School fees are a contentious issue: private education doesn't come cheap. For a good school, you can expect to pay Dhs.30,000 plus per year for KG years, Dhs.38,000 and up for the middle primary years, and as much as Dhs.65,000 per year for secondary school. Ouch. If you're lucky, your company may offer school fees as part of your package. On top of this, you will usually need to pay around Dhs.500 to put your child's name on a school's waiting list, and a registration fee (around Dhs.2,000), which comes off your fees. There is talk of the government putting an official cap on how much schools can hike their fees in order to prevent some establishments springing nasty surprises on parents, but nothing concrete has been confirmed yet.

Be prepared to accept that there are a lot of school holidays here in Dubai. The summer holidays stretch for 10 long weeks over the hottest months of July and August, when many kids return to their home countries for extended holidays, or attend summer camps. There are also holidays in April and December. Schools close for at least a week twice a year for Eid Al Fitr and Eid Al Adha, and will most likely also open for reduced hours during the month of Ramadan. If one of you is a stay at home parent then this poses few problems in terms of childcare; however, if both of you work, you will need to make sure that you have alternative arrangements for childcare during school holidays and random days off.

Homeschooling

One of the main reasons for homeschooling in the UAE is to avoid the hefty private school fees. There are very few private schools in Dubai that offer homeschooling curriculums; K12 in Knowledge Village offers some online courses (k12.com/int/arabian_gulf). The Ministry of Education offers homeschooling for all nationalities but the curriculum is only in Arabic.

Schools in your home country will be able to provide you with the curriculum, materials and online testing, for a fee. Many expats with multiple children find that whilst nurseries tend to be more affordable than in their home countries, when it comes to schooling it makes more financial sense to return home where free public education is often available.

School Inspections

Education standards in private schools are high. The Knowledge and Human Development Authority (KHDA) has been set up to ensure that education in Dubai is delivered consistently and to an acceptable standard. In the 2011-2012 academic year, the KHDA conducted a fourth round of annual school inspections, in which a team of international inspectors visited all Dubai private schools and rated them on a number of issues. Of four possible results (Outstanding, Good, Acceptable and Unsatisfactory), 11 schools received an outstanding rating. The results achieved by each school determined the amount by which that school could raise its fees, with those schools rated outstanding raising their fees the most, and those rated unsatisfactory raising their fees the least. See khda.gov.ae for more information and for a breakdown of each school's result.

British schools can now apply for inspection and British School Overseas certification by the British government; the KHDA plans to make this compulsory and also to introduce a similar quality assurance scheme for US curriculum schools.

Which Curriculum?

Choosing the right curriculum for your child can be obvious – for example, if you're planning on being here for a year or two before returning to your home country, it makes sense to pick the curriculum that is offered back home, such as the English National Curriculum or the American Curriculum. However, if you are not sure what your future plans are, you may want to consider the International Baccalaureate Programme (IB), which is compatible with most curriculums worldwide. There are distinct differences between each curriculum; it is a good idea to do plenty of research before deciding which one is best for your child.

School Uniforms
Most private schools here in Dubai will insist on students wearing the official school uniform. Each school will use a particular uniform supply shop, and this will be the only place where you can buy official school items. Before heading out and spending a fortune on uniforms, check with the school and with other parents which items are compulsory and which are not: a sturdy pair of black school shoes and a pair of non-marking trainers are usually essential items, whereas a branded school bag is often not.

Uniforms bought from the official suppliers are usually priced very highly, and can often be of poor quality, so if your school offers any flexibility on the uniform issue (such as your child wearing a plain white collared shirt as opposed to a white shirt with the school badge on the pocket), you may want to take it. A final word on uniforms: if you leave your uniform shopping until the last few days before the beginning of term, chances are you'll get to the uniform shop to find several items have sold out. This is definitely one task where it pays to shop in advance. Find out from your school who their uniform supplier is, and stock up on uniforms as early as possible.

School Transport
If for whatever reason you are not able to do the school run every morning and afternoon, you can make use of the bus services offered by most schools. The advantages are that the bus driver gets to deal with the traffic every day, and, since school transport has to abide by some strict regulations, you can rest assured that your child will reach school safely. The disadvantages are that it can be a very expensive option: you will pay the same fee whether you live 500 metres or 10 kilometres from the school. Also, if your child is one of the first on the pick-up roster, it will mean a very early start and then a very long ride on the bus as it drives round to pick up all the other kids.

Still, for parents who work or don't drive, school transport really is a godsend, and you should speak to your child's school directly about the costs and travel arrangements.

Al Mizhar American Academy
Nr 11A & 4A Streets, Al Mizhar 1 **04 288 7250**
americanacademy.ae
Map **2 S13** Metro **Etisalat**
An American curriculum, all-girls' school in Mizhar (near Mirdif) for pupils from Kindergarten to Year 12. The school is equipped for a range of activities including swimming, basketball, football, volleyball and drama. A gymnasium, well-resourced library, computer labs, interactive whiteboards, art studios, music studios, science labs, and a mini auditorium are all present. KHDA inspection rating: Good.

American International School
Nr LuLu Hypermarket Al Qusais 1 **04 298 8666**
aisch.net
Map **2 R7** Metro **Stadium**
Established almost a decade ago, AISCH follows a curriculum that leads to both US and UAE High School Diplomas, making this school a popular choice for Americans, Canadians and Emiratis. There are almost 2,000 students in total with buses running all over Dubai. KHDA inspection rating: Acceptable.

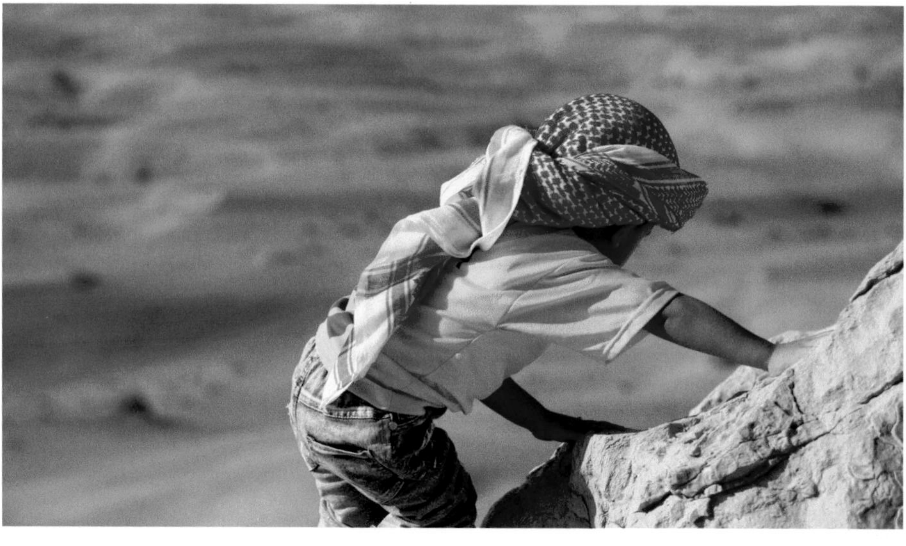

American School Of Dubai
Nr Saudi German Hospital, Al Mafraq Rd & Hessa St Al Barsha 1 **04 395 0005** asdubai.org
Map **1 P6** Metro **Dubai Internet City**
Founded in 1966, the school serves over 1,600 students pre-kindergarten (K1) through to Grade 12. The school recently expanded and in 2011 moved to its new 23-acre site, with three main academic buildings, 100 classrooms, two libraries, two multi-purpose gyms and a purpose built 700-seat performing arts theatre. The campus also offers a 1:1 laptop programme from Grade 6 onwards. Sporting facilities include a fitness centre with indoor climbing wall, two 25-metre swimming pools, and a well-equipped elementary playground. KHDA inspection rating: Good.

Australian International School
Nr Sharjah University, Maliha- Kalba Rd Sharjah
06 558 9967
ais.ae
This school is run in partnership with the State of Queensland, offering the Australian curriculum to primary school children. Facilities include large activity rooms, teaching areas for art and music, computer labs, a comprehensive library, conference rooms, a swimming pool and a multi-purpose hall and gym area.

Bradenton Preparatory Academy > *p.161*
Dubai Sports City Dubailand **04 449 3600**
bradentonprepdubai.com
Map **1 M12**
An innovative curriculum (based on the American Common Core standards) from pre-KG to Grade 12 at a colourful campus with venues for art, music, drama, laboratory sciences, as well as a library and full-sized gym. Located in Dubai Sports City, the academy boasts small class sizes – Kindergarten is 15:1 and Grades 1 to 11 are 18:1. KHDA inspection rating: Acceptable

Cambridge International School Dubai
Nr American College Of Dubai Al Garhoud
04 282 4646
gemscis-dubai.com
Map **2 N9** Metro **Emirates**
This school follows the National Curriculum of England. Set in a spacious campus, the school is divided into two sections: Primary (Kindergarten to Year 6) and Secondary (Year 7 to Year 13). There's a variety of opportunities and good facilities, preparing students for the International General Certificate of Secondary Education (IGCSE) course, the Advanced Subsidiary (AS) and A-level Examinations of the Universities of Cambridge and London (UK). KHDA inspection rating: Good.

Collegiate American School
Street 34 Umm Suqeim 2 **04 427 1400**
casdubai.com
Map **1 U5** Metro **Noor Islamic Bank**
This American school, from pre-KG to Grade 8, centres on a technology-enabled learning environment that focuses on digital learning. Facilities include library, art rooms, dance studio, music rooms, swimming pools and sports hall.

Deira International School
Nr Al Badia Residence Dubai Festival City
04 232 5552
disdubai.ae
Map **2 M9** Metro **Emirates**
DIS offers GCSE/IGCSE, A-levels and the International Baccalaureate programme. There are primary, middle and secondary levels, including a foundation year. Facilities within the school include a gymnasium, a full-size track and football field, music rooms, computer and science labs, libraries, a large auditorium and a swimming pool. KHDA inspection rating: Good.

Dubai American Academy
Nr LuLu Hypermarket, Al Mafraq Rd Al Barsha 1
04 347 9222
gemsaa-dubai.com
Map **1 R7** Metro **Mall of the Emirates**
DAA offers the International Baccalaureate Diploma and an enriched American curriculum. It takes both primary and secondary students, and there is an extensive after-school programme. Facilities include computer and science labs, gymnasium, library, pool, athletics track and an auditorium. KHDA inspection rating: Outstanding.

Dubai British School
Off Interchange 5, Springs 3 Emirates Living
04 361 9361
dubaibritishschool.ae
Map **1 K7** Metro **Nakheel**
Offering good facilities and convenient for residents in the Emirates Living area, DBS offers the English National Curriculum at primary and secondary levels, including a foundation year. Facilities at the school include a swimming pool, gymnasium and library. KHDA inspection rating: Good.

Dubai College
Off Al Sufouh Rd Al Sufouh 1 **04 399 9111**
dubaicollege.org
Map **1 P5** Metro **Dubai Internet City**
Offering the English National Curriculum and a diverse range of facilities and activities, Dubai College accepts students from Year 7 (around 11 years of age). Specialist facilities include a science

block with 13 laboratories, and a music centre with a recording studio. Sporting activities include athletics, rugby, football, netball, tennis and swimming. KHDA inspection rating: Outstanding.

Dubai English Speaking College

Nr Al Ghurair University Dubai International Academic City **04 360 4866** descdubai.com

This English curriculum secondary school opened in 2005, offering Year 7 to Year 13 (A-level). There's a dedication to sport with good facilities (a 25m pool, several pitches and double sports hall). The school offers rugby, football, netball, basketball, badminton and volleyball. KHDA inspection rating: Good.

Dubai English Speaking School

Nr St Mary's Church Oud Metha **04 337 1457**
dessdubai.com
Map **2 L7** Metro **Oud Metha**

DESS first opened in a single room of a villa in 1963, and has grown into a highly respected school offering the English National Curriculum from reception to Year 6. Facilities and activities include IT labs, music, swimming, dance and a library, and the school is regionally successful at sport. KHDA Inspection rating: Good.

Dubai International Academy

Nr Jebel Ali Race Course Emirates Living
04 368 4111
diadubai.com
Map **1 M7** Metro **Nakheel**

DIA follows the International Baccalaureate curriculum including the Primary Years Programme (PYP), the middle years programme (MYP) and the diploma programme (DP). The school has more than 80 classrooms, as well as music, art, dance and drama rooms, science and computer labs, libraries, swimming pools, playing fields, basketball and tennis courts. KHDA inspection rating: Good.

Cultural education

Dubai Modern High School

Nad Al Sheba **04 326 3339**
gemsmhs.com
Map **2 H13**

Affiliated to the Council for the Indian School Certificate Examinations, Dubai Modern High School teaches the ICSE & IB syllabus admissions to pupils from elementary through to high school. Part of the GEMS group, the school offers a unique Day Boarding System, which incorporates academics in the morning, followed by lunch and then Activities for Curriculum Enrichment (ACE) that includes a supervised study-session with clubs and games. KHDA inspection rating: Outstanding.

Emirates International School Jumeirah

Al Thanya Rd Umm Al Sheif **04 348 9804**
eischools.ae
Map **1 T6** Metro **First Gulf Bank**

EIS-Jumeirah was first opened in 1991 as a community service of the Al Habtoor Group, and was the first school in Dubai to be authorised to offer the International Baccalaureate Diploma Programme. It accepts children at primary, middle school and senior school levels and runs an alumni programme for graduates. KHDA inspection rating: Good.

Emirates International School Meadows

Meadows Drive Emirates Living **04 362 9009**
eischools.ae
Map **1 L7** Metro **Dubai Marina**

The Meadows campus of the Emirates International School offers the International Baccalaureate curriculum to both primary and secondary students. Facilities include large classrooms, computer and science labs, a library and a theatre. The school offers a comprehensive, free after-school activity programme with sporting, artistic, cultural and social activities for students from KG2 through to Grade 13. KHDA inspection rating: Good.

The English College Dubai

Off Shk Zayed Rd Al Safa 1 **04 394 3465**
englishcollege.ac.ae
Map **2 B6** Metro **Business Bay**

The English College Dubai (EC) offers the English National Curriculum and a varied extra-curricular programme to primary and secondary level students. The school has a long tradition of academic and sporting excellence and a varied extra-curricular programme offers activities such as chess, rugby, tennis, trampolining, and even rock climbing. KHDA inspection rating: Good.

GEMS Jumeirah Primary School

Nr Park n Shop, Off Al Wasl Rd Al Safa 1 **04 394 3500**
jumeirahprimaryschool.com
Map **2 C5** Metro **Business Bay**
GEMS Jumeirah Primary School teaches the National Curriculum for England to students from Foundation Stage to Year 6. The school is a full member of British Schools in the Middle East (BSME) which provides teachers with training and networking opportunities, as well as support. The school has excellent facilities, including a Library and Discovery Centre and 25-metre swimming pool, and is set on a modern campus in the heart of Jumeira. The whole campus and its facilities are bright, spacious and comfortable. KHDA inspection rating: Outstanding.

GEMS Royal Dubai School > *p.155*

Street 11A, Off Al Khawaneej Rd Al Mizhar 1
04 288 6499
royaldubaischool.com
Map **2 S13** Metro **Rashidiya**
GEMS Royal Dubai School offers high quality education from Foundation Stage to Year 6 in line with the National Curriculum for England. The school employs British-trained and experienced teachers, chosen for their abilities to create a motivational learning environment for the kids. The spacious building provides cutting-edge facilities and the school is especially convenient for those living in Mirdif or Sharjah. KHDA inspection rating: Good.

GEMS Wellington Academy > *p.155*

Dubai Silicon Oasis **04 342 4040**
gemswellingtonacademy-dso.com
Metro **Rashidiya**
GEMS Wellington Academy – Silicon Oasis is based on the National Curriculum for England from Foundation Stage to Sixth Form. Students in Key Stage 4 follow GCSE examination courses and students in the Sixth Form prepare for AS and A2 examinations. Key skills identified in the National Curriculum that underpin success in education, employment, lifelong learning and personal development are embedded in planning. Students also benefit from excellent, purpose-built facilities at this well-designed Silicon Oasis campus, including swimming pool and visual arts suite.

GEMS Wellington International School > *p.155*

Shk Zayed Rd Al Sufouh 2 **04 348 4999**
wellingtoninternationalschool.com
Map **1 Q5** Metro **Sharaf DG**
Following the National Curriculum of England and the International Baccalaureate Diploma Programme in Years 12 and 13, students benefit from a state of the art IT infrastructure, classrooms fitted with interactive whiteboards, and access to digital editing suites and multimedia presentations. There is also a television studio and radio station onsite, a first for UAE schools. The school's Blue Frog Cafe serves healthy refreshments to students. KHDA inspection rating: Outstanding.

GEMS Wellington Primary School > *p.155*

Nr Shangri-La Hotel Trade Centre 1 **04 343 3266**
gemswps.com
Map **2 G5** Metro **Financial Centre**
The curriculum at GEMS WPS complies with the National Curriculum in England, and is underpinned by the GEMS core values of World Citizenship, Leadership Qualities, Universal Values and Forward Thinking. It has well-equipped music, art and IT departments, as well as a library, gymnasium, shaded play areas and two swimming pools. KHDA inspection rating: Good.

GEMS Winchester School, Dubai > *p.155*

Nr American Hospital Oud Metha **04 337 4112**
gemswinchesterschool-dubai.com
Map **2 L6** Metro **Oud Metha**
The latest addition to the GEMS network of international schools. The school follows the Early Years Foundation Stage followed by the National Curriculum for England. The curriculum lays the foundation so that students can pursue university levels of education or professional career paths suited to their abilities, talents and interests. KHDA inspection rating: Good.

GEMS World Academy, Dubai > *p.155*

Al Khail Rd Al Barsha South 1 **04 373 6373**
gemsworldacademy-dubai.com
Map **1 Q9** Metro **Mall of the Emirates**
An international school providing an IBO program delivery for students aged three to 18, the GWA Discovery World – with its large and impressive library and study zones – is at the heart of this school, giving students access to computer rooms, science rooms, robotics lab, design and technology studios and the curriculum resource centre. There is also a planetarium, rooftop peace garden and symphony centre for music. KHDA inspection rating: Good.

Greenfield Community School

Green Community Market Green Community
04 885 6600
gcschool.ae
Map **1 F12** Metro **Jebel Ali**
Located in Dubai Investments Park just beyond the Green Community, Greenfield Community School teaches the IB curriculum to primary and middle years children, as well as to students in the diploma programme. GCS has excellent facilities and a progressive special needs policy. KHDA inspection rating: Acceptable.

Horizon School

Nr Safa Park, Off Shk Zayed Rd Al Wasl **04 342 2891**
horizonschooldubai.com
Map **2 D5** Metro **Business Bay**
Horizon opened in 1992 with just 15 pupils, and has expanded to a large complex complete with top-class facilities, offering the British curriculum to children from reception to Year 6. They have an additional campus at Safa Horizon School (04 394 7879). KHDA inspection rating: Good.

The International School Of Choueifat Dubai

Nr Dubai College Al Sufouh 1 **04 399 9444**
iscuae-sabis.net
Map **1 D5** Metro **Dubai Internet City**
Choueifat offers the rigorous SABIS curriculum – a unique method of education allowing students to learn more in a shorter time. The school accepts primary and secondary level children; new students take placement tests to check whether they have attained certain standards in English and maths. KHDA inspection rating: Acceptable.

Jebel Ali Primary School

Jebel Ali Village **04 884 6485**
jebelalischool.org
Map **1 F6** Metro **Ibn Battuta**
Opened in 1977, JAPS teaches the English National Curriculum as well as offering an excellent range of after-school activities, with separate sites for infants and juniors. Activities include football, netball, golf, gymnastics, swimming, squash, drama, dance, cooking, music and computers. KHDA inspection rating: Outstanding.

Jumeira Baccalaureate School

53B Street, Off Al Wasl Rd Jumeira 1 **04 344 6931**
jbschool.ae
Map **2 G4** Metro **Financial Centre**
This co-educational school is one of the newest in Dubai, having opened in 2010. It offers the English Early Learning Goals at kindergarten level, the International Primary Curriculum, and the International Baccalaureate Middle Years and Diploma programmes. The middle and high school (grades 6-11) became operational in September 2011. KHDA inspection rating: Good.

Jumeirah College

Nr Park n Shop, Off Al Wasl Rd Al Safa 1 **04 395 5524**
gemsjc.com
Map **2 C5** Metro **Business Bay**
Jumeirah College is a Year 7 to Year 13 school that has earned a reputation for providing premium education. Using the National Curriculum for England, and offering a wide range of GCSE and A-level courses, the student body is multicultural with members from more than 59 countries represented. The school has a reputation for high academic standards. KHDA inspection rating: Outstanding.

Jumeirah English Speaking School

Street 16, Nr Safa Park Village Al Safa 1 **04 394 5515**
jess.sch.ae
Map **2 C5** Metro **Business Bay**
JESS teaches the English National Curriculum from Foundation Stage 1 up to Year 6 and it is one of the most in-demand British schools and therefore has a long waiting list. The campus has a gymnasium, music rooms, two playing areas, a football pitch and a swimming pool. KHDA inspection rating: Outstanding.

Jumeirah English Speaking School

Arabian Ranches **04 361 9019**
jess.sch.ae
Map **1 R13** Metro **Mall of the Emirates**
A second branch of the successful JESS school, this offers the English National Curriculum to primary school students aged three and upwards, alongside a wide range of excellent facilities. Sports facilities include a nine-lane shaded swimming pool, plus four tennis and three netball courts. Naturally, the majority of the pupils live within the Arabian Ranches complex, making it a close-knit community of parents and pupils. KHDA inspection rating: Outstanding.

Kings' Dubai

Nr 26th & 17C Streets Umm Suqeim 3 **04 348 3939**
kingsdubai.com
Map **1 S5** Metro **First Gulf Bank**
Kings' Dubai opened in 2004 and teaches the English National Curriculum through an innovative, creative approach; the school accepts primary age children and offers a foundation year. The facilities include a gymnasium, swimming pool, games court and sports field. KHDA inspection rating: Outstanding.

Lycee Francais International Georges Pompidou

Nr American Hospital Oud Metha **04 337 4161**
lfigp.org
Map **2 L7** Metro **Oud Metha**
Also called the 'Dubai French School', the school educates 1,677 students from pre-Kindergarten through to secondary, based on a French curriculum. KHDA inspection rating: Good

Raffles International School

Nr Burj Al Arab Umm Suqeim 3 **04 427 1200**
rafflesis.com
Map **1 S5** Metro **First Gulf Bank**
The South Campus follows the Cambridge Curriculum (UK-based) at primary and secondary level, and offers

the Montessori programme at Nursery and KG1. All classrooms are equipped with the latest instructional audio-visual facilities, and there is a theatre, art rooms, dance studio, swimming pools, tennis courts and sports hall. KHDA inspection rating: Good

Raffles World Academy

Street 22 Umm Suqeim 3 **04 427 1351**
rafflesis.com
Map **1 S5** Metro **First Gulf Bank**
Established in 2008, this is an authorised World School for the International Baccalaureate Diploma Programme (IBDP), along with offering the Primary Years Programme (PYP),the Cambridge Secondary 1(CS1) and the International General Certificate of Secondary Education (IGCSE). The school admits pupils from Kindergarten through to Grade 12 with a range of sporting, science, art, music and IT facilities. KHDA inspection rating: Good

Regent International School

The Greens Emirates Living **04 360 8830**
risdubai.com
Map **1 N6** Metro **Nakheel**
Regent International School offers the English National Curriculum at primary and secondary levels, including a foundation year, on its campus in the Greens. Facilities include state-of-the-art technology, multimedia zones, library, computer, science and language labs, as well as a football pitch, playing fields and gymnasium and a swimming pool. KHDA inspection rating: Good.

Repton School

Nad Al Sheba 3 **04 426 9393**
reptondubai.org
Map **2 H13**
This prestigious school offers the English National Curriculum to primary and secondary level students and has premium educational and sporting facilities on its custom-built campus. It also offers an extensive list of extra-curricular activities. Repton is also the first school in Dubai to offer boarding – students can board on a weekly or per-term basis. KHDA inspection rating: Good.

The Sheffield Private School

Doha Rd Al Nahda 2 **04 267 8444**
sheffield-school.com
Map **2 T7** Metro **Al Nahda**
Currently accepting primary school students, including foundation year, Sheffield Private School offers the English National Curriculum. Facilities include music and art studios, an ICT lab, covered play areas, plus pools for swimming and wading. There are plans to eventually offer schooling up to Year 13. KHDA inspection rating: Acceptable.

St Mary's Catholic High School

Nr Iranian Club Oud Metha **04 337 0252**
stmarysdubai.com
Map **2 L7** Metro **Oud Metha**
St Mary's retains the discipline of a convent education but welcomes all religions. The school teaches the English National Curriculum to primary and secondary students. In addition to various sports activities, other activities include drama, music, debating, cookery and chess. KHDA inspection rating: Acceptable.

Star International School

Nr New Airport Terminal Al Twar 2 **04 263 8999**
starschoolaltwar.com
Map **2 R9** Metro **Al Qusais**
Star International School Al Twar offers the English National Curriculum and a day boarding facility, so that you can leave your child at the school under full supervision until 16:30. There are primary and secondary levels. KHDA inspection rating: Acceptable.

Star International School – Umm Al Sheif

Nr 9A & 10A Streets Umm Al Sheif **04 348 3314**
starschoolummsheif.com
Map **1 S6** Metro **First Gulf Bank**
One of three Star International schools in Dubai teaching the Early Years Foundation Stage and the National Curriculum of England. A bright and modern campus with great facilities for primary years including splash pools, a large indoor play area with 'desert', ICT Suite with programmable robots, and sports hall. KHDA inspection rating: Good.

Star International School Mirdif

Uptown Midrif Mirdif **04 288 4644**
starschoolmirdif.com
Map **2 R13** Metro **Rashidiya**
This new school offers the English National Curriculum from Foundation to Year 6, and will phase in secondary school levels over the next few years. With a 700 seat auditorium the school aims to be an important location for the promotion and teaching of arts and culture in the community. KHDA inspection rating: Acceptable.

Universal American School

Nr Al Badia Residences Dubai Festival City
04 232 5222
uasdubai.ae
Map **2 U9** Metro **Emirates**
UASD follows a full American curriculum culminating with the American high school diploma. The school accepts primary and secondary level students. The campus has a gymnasium, Olympic size track and football field, music rooms, art rooms, computer and science labs, libraries, a large auditorium and a swimming pool. KHDA inspection rating: Good.

Uptown Primary School

Uptown Mirdif Mirdif **04 288 6270**
uptownprimary.ae
Map **2 Q13** Metro **Rashidiya**
Uptown Primary follows the International Baccalaureate programme and accepts children from the age of four for its Primary Years Programme (PYP), and houses an early learning centre developed specifically for the under six year olds. Facilities include a swimming pool, gymnasium, library, computer labs, art studios, music rooms, safe play areas and science labs. Students can remain here into the Middle Years Programme (MYP). All Primary students will move to the new Uptown School campus on the corner of Algeria and Tripoli Streets in September 2013. KHDA inspection rating: Good.

The Westminster School

Al Ghusais School Zone Al Qusais 1 **04 298 8333**
gemsws-ghusais.com
Map **2 S7** Metro **Al Nahda**
Prepares students to take the International General Certificate of Secondary Education (IGCSE) course and the Advanced Subsidiary (AS) Level Examinations and A Level Examinations of the Universities of Cambridge and London (UK). The spacious, purpose-built premises provide separate facilities for boys and girls from Year 5 onwards. With students from over 72 nationalities, The Westminster School has an international character and a culturally rich environment. The school is scheduled to close in 2014. KHDA inspection rating: Acceptable.

The Winchester School

The Gardens Jebel Ali **04 882 0444**
thewinchesterschool.com
Map **1 G5** Metro **Ibn Battuta**
Founded in 2003, The Winchester School provides a quality and relatively affordable education to students of all nationalities but following the National Curriculum for England. Its classrooms are cutting-edge while the spacious, air-conditioned, multi-purpose auditorium is a superb indoor facility for students to play indoor games in, when they're not developing their musical and theatrical talents. KHDA inspection rating: Good.

University & Higher Education

Upon leaving school, children of expat families have traditionally returned to their home country to continue with higher education, but Dubai does have a growing number of internationally recognised universities and colleges offering degree and diploma courses in the arts, sciences, business and management, and engineering and technology. There are also a number of opportunities for post-graduate study here in the UAE.

Many institutions are based at Knowledge Village near Media and Internet Cities – for more info visit kv.ae. Dubai International Academic City, on the outskirts of Dubai, will house a number of tertiary institutions when it is finally completed (see below). Several business schools have also opened recently, offering MBAs and other professional qualifications for those looking to advance their careers. A number of UK institutions have shown enthusiasm in tapping in to this potentially lucrative market. The London Business School (london.edu) is based in DIFC, as is Cass (cass.city.ac.uk, formerly City University Business School). The latter specialises in energy and Islamic finance. Warwick Business School (wbs.ac.uk) has been offering MBAs in Dubai since 2003.

Destination Education

Academic City (diacedu.ae) is a dedicated tertiary development that hosts international universities including: American University in the Emirates, Cambridge College International Dubai, Dubai English Speaking College, EHSAL, French Fashion University Esmod, Hamdan Bin Mohamed e-University (HBMeU), Heriot-Watt University Dubai Campus, Hult International Business School, Institute of Management Technology, Islamic Azad University, JSS Education Foundation, Mahatma Gandhi University, MAHE, Manipal-Dubai Campus, Manchester Business School Worldwide, Michigan State University Dubai, Middlesex University, Murdoch University International Study Centre Dubai, PIM International Center, S P Jain Center of Management, SAE Institute, Saint-Petersburg State University of Engineering and Economics, Shaheed Zulfikar Ali Bhutto Institute of Science and Technology (SZABIST), Syrian Virtual University, The British University in Dubai, The University of Exeter, The University of Wollongong in Dubai (UOWD), Universitas 21 Global Pte Ltd, University of Bradford and University of Phoenix.

Knowledge Village

Knowledge Village prides itself on creating an environment conducive to education, the business of

Education UK Exhibition

Organised annually by the British Council, Education UK Exhibition (EDUKEK) is part of an initiative to enhance educational relations between the UK and the Middle East. Students from across the region can attend the event to gather information on UK universities, whether they have campuses in the UAE or in the UK. The event usually takes place in January at the Dubai International Convention and Exhibition Centre. See britishcouncil.org.

education and networking. The operating rules and regulations are relatively straightforward and they simplify the application process for a one-year student's resident visa, too. Some of the tertiary institutions to be found here are: European University College Brussels, Institute of Management Technology, Islamic Azad University, Mahatma Ghandhi University, UAE University, Royal College of Surgeons and the University of New Brunswick in Dubai. Find out more at kv.ae.

Public Universities & Colleges

The Higher Colleges of Technology and Zayed University are the two most prominent local universities in Dubai. The HCT is the largest, with around 16,000 students (all UAE Nationals) studying at 16 campuses across the UAE; it offers Higher Diplomas, Bachelor's and Master's across over 80 different programmes. Prior to 2009, Zayed University only offered its degree programmes to UAE Nationals, however it now invites all UAE residents and international students to apply. The university also accepts male students at both its Dubai and Abu Dhabi campuses; see p.174.

American College Of Dubai

Al Rebat St Al Garhoud **04 282 9992**
acd.ac.ae
Map **2 N8** Metro **Airport Terminal 1**
The American College of Dubai offers courses that will provide students with university-level credits allowing them to transfer to institutions in the US, UK, UAE, Canada, Europe, India, or elsewhere around the world. Additionally, associate degrees in the liberal arts, business and information technology are also available.

American University In Dubai

Shk Zayed Rd Al Sufouh 1 **04 399 9000**
aud.edu
Map **1 M5** Metro **Nakheel**
With its impressive main building that is something of a landmark along Sheikh Zayed Road, the American University in Dubai is a well-established institution with over 2,000 students of various nationalities. Courses offered include business, engineering, information technology, visual communication, interior design and liberal arts.

American University Of Ras Al Khaimah

Shk Saqr Bin Khalid Rd, Seih Al Hudaibah
Ras Al Khaimah **07 221 0900**
aurak.ae
Set up in 2009, the American University of Ras Al Khaimah offers a number of degree courses including BScs in biotechnology, business administration, computer engineering, and electronics and communications engineering. There are also BAs in English Language and Communication.

American University Of Sharjah

Sharjah **06 515 5555**
aus.edu
The university offers a wide range of undergraduate programmes in areas such as language, literature, communications, business, finance and engineering. Postgraduate courses are also offered from the schools of Arts and Sciences, Architecture and Design, Business and Management, and Engineering.

Amity University

Block 10 Dubai International Academic City
04 455 4900
amityuniversity.ae
With campuses in Dubai and India, Amity offers a wide range of MBA, BBA and B Tech courses in subjects as wide-ranging as hospitality, tourism, real estate, civil engineering and aerospace. Open evenings are held every Thursday.

The British University In Dubai

Block 11 Dubai International Academic City
04 391 3626
buid.ac.ae
The British University In Dubai, established in 2004, is the region's first postgraduate research based university. BUID offers postgraduate degrees including MSc Environmental Design of Buildings, MSc Information Technology and PhD programmes.

Canadian University Of Dubai

Shk Zayed Rd Trade Centre 1 **04 321 9090**
cud.ac.ae
Map **2 G5** Metro **Financial Centre**
CUD strives to create an international academic experience for its students with credit transfer if you wish to continue your studies in Canada. They offer various accredited degrees including business

Fashion: An Opportunity

If you're interested in studying anything relating to the fashion industry, keep an eye out for the latest short courses offered by the London School Of Fashion in Dubai. Programmes last between one and five days, and cover a whole range of subjects including: fashion journalism, fashion communication and PR, luxury brand management, fashion marketing, design and styling, and starting your own fashion label. The courses are all led by tutors who have extensive experience in the fashion world, including designers, journalists and image consultants. The programmes are held throughout the year, so check the website (fashion.arts.ac.uk) for up to date news and how to register.

and marketing, human resource management, interior design and architecture, telecommunication engineering and health management.

Cass Business School City University London

Dubai International Financial Centre (DIFC) Trade Centre 2 **04 401 9316**
cass.city.ac.uk
Map **2 H6** Metro **Financial Centre**
Part of City University London, the Cass Executive MBA is targeted towards Middle East business executives, with a focus on Islamic Finance or Energy. It boasts elite status amongst EMBA programmes around the world. The two-year course (with lectures over the weekends to avoid disruption to the working week) is accredited by both the Association of MBAs (AMBA) and the European Quality Improvement System (EQUIS). Students have direct access to City of London contacts and can take electives at the London campus. Degrees include accounting, business studies, and actuarial science.

Dubai School Of Dental Medicine > *p.199*

Dubai Healthcare City Umm Hurair 2
04 424 8777
dsdm.ac.ae
Map **2 L7** Metro **Dubai Healthcare City**
This home-grown dental institution was launched in 2013 to support the UAE community with the finest quality of dental care services and education. Located within District 5, the postgraduate school offers students a three-year MSc degree in a range of specialisations such as endodontics, oral surgery, orthodontics, paediatric dentistry, periodontology, and fixed and removable prosthodontics. DSDM's students will have the opportunity to sit a membership examination in their dental specialty from The Royal College of Surgeons of Edinburgh.

Dubai School Of Government

Dubai World Trade Centre Trade Centre 2
04 329 3290
dsg.ae
Map **2 J5** Metro **World Trade Centre**
Established under the patronage of His Highness Sheikh Mohammed Bin Rashid Al Maktoum, the DSG is a research and teaching institution that focuses on Arab world politics, public policy and administration, economics, energy, history and operations management. It offers two graduate programmes, the Master of Public Administration (MPA), in cooperation with Harvard Kennedy School, and the Executive Diploma in Public Administration (EDPA). DSG's executive education programs provide courses in public policy, leadership and management for government and non-government leaders.

EMDI Institute Of Media & Communication

Dubai Knowledge Village Al Sufouh 1 **04 367 1145**
emdiworld.com
Map **1 N5** Metro **Dubai Internet City**
EMDI specialises in providing education and qualifications in media and communications. Full time and part time courses are available in everything from journalism and PR, through advertising and graphic design, to DJing, events and wedding planning.

The Emirates Academy Of Hospitality Management

Bldg 69, Street 10 Umm Suqeim 3 **04 315 5555**
emiratesacademy.edu
Map **1 S5** Metro **First Gulf Bank**
As part of the Jumeirah Group, this school offers highly respected hospitality management degree courses including a BSc in International Hospitality Management, Associate of Science Degree in International Hospitality Operations or MSc in International Hospitality Management. Internships are available in Dubai or at a Jumeirah hotel overseas.

Esmod Dubai

Dubai International Academic City **04 429 1228**
esmod-dubai.com
The French Fashion University is the only university in the Middle East fully dedicated to fashion. Accredited by the French Ministry of Education it offers three-year BA courses, fashion workshops, trend forecasting masterclasses, merchandising training sessions, and an MBA in Fashion Management.

European University College

Dubai Healthcare City Umm Hurair 2 **04 362 4787**
dubaipostgraduate.com
Map **2 L7** Metro **Dubai Healthcare City**
Formerly Nicholas & Asp University College, this is the first postgraduate dental institution to offer international training programmes in the UAE, including masters degrees, specialty training, certificates, diplomas, and CPD courses. As well as general dentistry, areas covered include oral implantology, paediatric dentistry, endodontics, and orthodontics. There is also an associate degree in dental assisting.

Heriot-Watt University Dubai Campus

Block 2 Dubai International Academic City
04 435 8700
hw.ac.uk/dubai.htm
One of the UK's oldest universities, Heriot-Watt offers undergraduate and postgraduate courses in business, management, finance, accounting, and IT at its purpose-built campus in the heart of Dubai International Academic City. Comprehensive English language programmes are also available.

Hult International Business School > *p.173*

Dubai Internet City Al Sufouh 1 **04 427 5800**
hult.edu/explorer
Map **1 J5** Metro **Dubai Internet City**
This highly-ranked global business school offers US accredited further education. Courses offered at the Dubai campus include a one-year, full time MBA programme, a part-time Executive MBA programme, and a Master's degree in International Marketing and International Business. There is also a Project Management Specialisation course. Students can choose to take electives at the school's campuses in London, Boston, San Francisco and Shanghai.

International House Dubai > *p.171*

Addiyar Bldg, Nr Safa Park Al Wasl **04 321 3121**
ihdubai.com
Map **2 D6** Metro **Business Bay**
With a team of teachers speaking 16 different languages, including Arabic, English, Spanish, Hindi, Farsi and Japanese, IH Dubai specialises in teaching languages, teacher training and industry-specific professional qualifications. It also delivers the National Development Programme, with tailormade induction courses to help Emirati Nationals to enter the workforce.

Lotus Educational Institute

Dubai Knowledge Village Al Sufouh 1 **04 391 1718**
lotus.ae
Map **1 N5** Metro **Dubai Internet City**
Located in Knowledge Village, Lotus Education Institute provides professional training in arts and design subjects, development programmes in business studies and holistic self development, as well as preparatory classes in English and IT.

Manchester Business School

Dubai Knowledge Village Al Sufouh 1 **04 446 8664**
mbs.ac.uk
Map **1 N5** Metro **Dubai Internet City**
Affiliated to the UK's Manchester University, this business school was established in Knowledge Village in 2006, and offers a range of MBAs in subjects including engineering, construction, sports and finance, plus doctoral programmes and executive education courses.

Manipal University Dubai Campus

Dubai International Academic City **04 429 1214**
manipaldubai.com
A branch of Manipal University in India, this campus offers certificate programmes and Bachelor's and Master's degree programmes in a range of subjects including information systems, engineering, biotechnology, media and communications, and fashion and interior design.

Michigan State University Dubai

Dubai Knowledge Village Al Sufouh 1 **04 446 5147**
dubai.msu.edu
Map **1 N5** Metro **Dubai Internet City**
This non-profit institution offers UAE and international students Bachelor's and Master's degree programmes in line with those at MSU in the US. Programmes covered include business administration, computer engineering, construction management, media management, human resources and family community services. The university encourages a combination of teaching methods including lectures and seminars, online classes, and internships/study abroad options.

Middlesex University Dubai

Dubai Knowledge Village Al Sufouh 1 **04 367 8100**
mdx.ac
Map **1 N5** Metro **Dubai Internet City**
The UK's Middlesex University recently opened a campus at Knowledge Village. Students have the option of studying for single or joint honours degrees in subjects including accountancy, business studies, tourism, human resource management, journalism, advertising, public relations and media, marketing and computing science.

Murdoch University International Study Centre Dubai

Block 10 Dubai International Academic City
04 435 5700
murdoch.edu.au
Murdoch University offers undergraduate degrees in business, environmental management, information technology and media, and postgraduate degrees in business and media. Their impressive campus houses a fully professional HD TV studio, a sound recording studio, two control rooms, an editing suite, a video editing suite, an advanced editing suite and three radio studios. Students can transfer all credits to Murdoch in Australia if they wish to continue their studies there.

New York University Abu Dhabi

Nr ADIA Tower, Off Al Nasr St Abu Dhabi
02 628 4000
nyuad.nyu.edu
Bringing NYU to the Emirates, this research university's arts and science undergraduate programmes are affiliated with the US campus. The university aims to give students the full, traditional college experience and its approach is firmly set on creating a campus where students will learn and develop not just in the lecture halls and libraries, but also in residences, clubs and campus events. Students across the arts, humanities, social sciences, science and engineering programmes will choose from 18 majors and five

HULT International Business School
GET PLUGGED IN TO THE WORLD
CLINTON GLOBAL INITIATIVE
Join the world's most International Business School
U.S.-accredited One-Year MBA, Executive MBA, Master Programs, and International Bachelor of Business Administration
Top-ranked by The Economist and Financial Times
Seven global locations - Boston, San Francisco, London, Dubai, Shanghai, New York, and São Paulo
Extraordinary student diversity – over 135 nationalities
Executive Speaker Series featuring Bill Clinton (42nd President of the U.S.), Jimmy Wales (Wikipedia), Biz Stone (Twitter), etc.
Contact us at hult.edu/explorer or call +971 4 427 5800
Hult International Business School
Dubai Internet City, United Arab Emirates
hult.edu/explorer
HULT PRIZE

multidisciplinary concentrations in addition to the required classes in their core curriculum.

Paris-Sorbonne University Abu Dhabi

Abu Dhabi **02 656 9555**
sorbonne.ae
The legendary Sorbonne arrived in Abu Dhabi in 2006. This French-speaking university focuses on a wide range of majors in humanities and law, with undergraduate degrees and Master's degrees in archaeology and history of arts, economics and management, French and comparative literature, geography and urban planning, history, international business and languages, law and political sciences, philosophy and sociology. Classes are either in French (with translation) or in English.

Overseas Study

For students looking to travel further afield within the Middle East, there are several higher education institutions in Qatar. Virginia Commonwealth University (qatar.vcu.edu) specialises in research and education in art and design; UCL Qatar (ucl.ac.uk) is the first British university to open a campus in Qatar, offering postgraduate degree programmes in archaeology, conservation, cultural heritage and museum studies; and Carnegie Mellon University (qatar.cmu.edu) offers full-time, coeducational, English-language undergraduate degree programmes in business administration and computer science in Doha.

Rochester Institute Of Technology

Techno Point Bldg Dubai Silicon Oasis **04 371 2000**
rit.edu
Currently RIT Dubai mirrors the degree programmes of RIT in the United States, offering Master's degrees in Business Administration (MBA), engineering (electrical and mechanical), fine arts, architecture, science, service leadership and innovation and networking and systems administrations. An undergraduate programme has also been offered since 2010, in subjects as diverse as accounting to ceramics, 3D digital graphics to woodworking and furniture design.

SAE Institute Dubai

Dubai Knowledge Village Al Sufouh 1 **04 361 6173**
sae.edu
Map **1 N5** Metro **Dubai Internet City**
This large, well-known and respected Australian film institute, which has branches on every continent, has an impressive multimedia training facility in Dubai's Knowledge Village. SAE offers degree courses specialising in audio engineering, digital animation, filmmaking and web development, with short courses teaching everything from how to build an iPhone app to becoming a digital DJ. Online courses in music, film, 3D animation, games and business, where you can study at your own pace, are also available through the SAE.

University Of Wollongong In Dubai

Dubai Knowledge Village Al Sufouh 1 **04 367 2400**
uowdubai.ac.ae
Map **1 N5** Metro **Dubai Internet City**
The University of Wollongong offers a number of undergraduate and postgraduate programmes in business and IT, in addition to certificates and awards in accounting, banking and management. This Australian university used to be situated along Jumeira Road, but moved its campus in 2005 making it one of the more established unis in the city.

Zayed University

Dubai International Academic City **04 402 1111**
zu.ac.ae
While Zayed University has traditionally been a UAE National only institution, its campuses in Academic City and Abu Dhabi Khalifa City now accept female and male students from all nationalities, whether international or UAE residents. It offers both Bachelor's degrees and Master's programmes in the arts, sciences, business, communication and media, education and IT.

Special Needs Education

Al Noor Training Center For Children With Special Needs

Nr Emirates NBD, Off Al Mafraq Rd Al Barsha 1
04 340 4844
alnoorspneeds.ae
Map **1 R6** Metro **Mall of the Emirates**
This centre provides therapeutic support and educational and vocational training to special needs children from three to 18 years of age. Its new facility has allowed the centre to expand its services to more than 300 children. The centre is also extremely active in the community with fundraisers, special events such as swimming galas, programmes to help parents learn to best support their children, and a summer camp.

All 4 Down Syndrome Dubai

Various locations
050 880 9228
all4downsyndrome.com
This support group is open to families whose lives have been affected by Down Syndrome. The group is part of an awareness-raising campaign, and offers advice on health, education and care for people with Down's. Social mornings are held every Sunday.

Dubai Autism Centre
6B Street Hudaiba **04 398 6862**
dubaiautismcenter.ae
Map **2 J4** Metro **Al Karama**
This educational centre offers diagnostic, intervention, family support, training and school services for children with autism.

A Lending Hand

All parents want the best education for their child, and kidsFIRST Medical Center provides answers for parents and help for kids with both ordinary and special needs. kidsFIRST (kidsFIRSTmc.com, 04 348 5437) works hand-in-hand with teachers and learning support staff to assist and educate children with learning difficulties and behaviour issues.

This parent resource centre also has educational consultants to help you find the right school for your child, and it offers a variety of parenting skills courses covering child development and how to manage behaviour problems.

Dubai Center For Special Needs
Nr Gulf News, Off Shk Zayed Rd Al Wasl **04 344 0966**
dcsneeds.ae
Map **2 B5** Metro **Business Bay**
A learning institution offering individualised therapeutic and educational programmes to its 130 students. A pre-vocational programme is offered for older students, including arranging work placements.

Rashid Paediatric Therapy Centre
Nr Mall of the Emirates Al Barsha 1 **04 340 0005**
rashidc.ae
Map **1 R6** Metro **Mall of the Emirates**
An educational centre offering classes for students with learning difficulties aged between three and 15, and a senior school offering functional academic and practical, life skills education for 13 to 17 year olds. Classes are taught in both Arabic and English.

Riding For The Disabled Association Of Dubai
Desert Palm Dubai Warsan 2
rdad.ae
A unique and therapeutic riding programme designed to help children with disabilities and special needs such as autism, cerebral palsy and spina bifida to develop their abilities through interaction with horses. Having fun also plays a large role, however. Sessions usually take place at Desert Palm Dubai (p.266). For more information on lesson schedules, volunteer requirements, rider applications and other general programme details, please contact the instructors at Lessons@rdad.ae

Special Needs Future Development Centre
Karama Centre Al Karama **04 337 6759**
snfgroup.com
Map **2 L5** Metro **Al Karama**
An educational and vocational training centre for children and young adults with special needs. The centre also aims to help the families and communities of children with special needs.

Language Courses

Alliance Française Dubai Umm Hurair, 04 335 8712, *afdubai.org*
Arabic Language Centre Trade Centre 2, 04 331 5600, *arabiclanguagecentre.com*
Berlitz Language Center Jumeira 1, 04 344 0034, *berlitz.ae*
British Council Umm Hurair 2, 600 529 995, *britishcouncil.org/uae*
Confucius Institute Al Rigga, 04 207 2678
Dar El Ilm School Of Languages Trade Centre 2, 04 331 0221, *dar-el-ilm.com*
Eton Institute Al Sufouh 1, 04 360 2955, *eton.ac*
Goethe-Institut German Language Center Dubai Al Raffa, 04 325 9865, *goethe.de*
Inlingua Oud Metha, 04 334 0004, *inlingua.com*
International House Dubai > *p.171* Nr Safa Park, Al Wasl 04 321 3121, *ihdubai.com*
Lotus Educational Institute Al Sufouh 1, 04 391 1718, *lotus.ae*

Libraries

Al Ras Public Library Al Ras, 04 226 2788, *dubaipubliclibrary.ae*
Al Rashidiya Public Library Al Rashidiya, 04 285 8065, *dubaipubliclibrary.ae*
Al Twar Public Library Al Twar, 04 263 0013, *dubaipubliclibrary.ae*
Alliance Française Dubai Umm Hurair, 04 335 8712, *afdubai.org*
Archie's Library Al Karama, 04 396 7924
The Archive Gate 5, Safa Park, 04 349 4033 *thearchive.ae*
Dubai Public Library Various locations, 04 394 7279, *dubaipubliclibrary.ae*
Hatta Public Library Hatta, 04 852 1022, *dubaipubliclibrary.ae*
Hor Al Anz Public Library Hor Al Anz, 04 266 1788, *dubaipubliclibrary.ae*
Juma Al Majid Center For Culture & Heritage Hor Al Anz, 04 607 4600, *almajidcenter.org*
The Old Library Al Barsha 1, 04 341 4777, *theoldlibrary.ae*
Reader's Paradise Various locations, 04 422 7495, *readersparadise-me.com*
Umm Suqeim Public Library Umm Suqeim 2, 04 348 2512, *dubaipubliclibrary.ae*

Special Needs & Learning Support

The UAE boasts an excellent private schooling system for expats, although children with special needs are often left sidelined when it comes to quality education.

If your child has physical or learning difficulties, there are several organisations that can help. In late 2009, it was announced by the Ministry of Education that private schools in the UAE would be required by law to provide adequate facilities for children with special needs. Recognising that less able children deserve the same quality of education as other children was a positive step, and one that was long overdue.

There are schools who have led the way in terms of opening doors to children with special needs. The American Community School in Sharjah boasts a state-of-the-art campus and actively addresses the needs of students with various different special needs. Certain other private schools in Dubai and Abu Dhabi offer places to children with mild dyslexia, Down Syndrome or who are 'slow' learners.

Angela Hollington, principal of Greenfield Community School (GCS) in Dubai, believes that as long as the school is able to meet the specific needs of a particular child in terms of facilities, curriculum and staff, then there is no reason to turn away a child with special needs.

She adds: "Each case is assessed individually and the school's main criteria is whether the child will benefit from being educated at GCS. In terms of special facilities and services, the school offers in-class and withdrawal support and a therapy room where visiting therapists can work with students with special needs. For some students, parents are requested to employ personal assistants to enable their child to remain focused in the classroom and access the curriculum."

Delice Scotto, principal at the Al-Mizhar American Academy for Girls, implements a similarly broad-minded approach. "All children who require learning support work in small groups and individually with learning support teachers according to Individualised Education Plans (IEPs)," she explains.

"With these support systems in place, learning support students at our school can be successfully integrated into mainstream school activities. Students are assessed at the admissions stage, and undergo a psycho-educational evaluation. Out of this assessment come recommendations that serve as a basis for that child's IEP, and as long as that child's needs are able to be met by our learning support department, they will be offered a study place."

There are currently three full-time learning support teachers at the Academy, all of whom have Master's degrees in special education from the United States, as well as extensive experience in dealing with students with a variety of special needs, from dyslexia and ADHD to emotional disabilities and the Autism spectrum. At Greenfield Community School, there is a similarly progressive approach to ensuring staff can meet the needs of all children.

Dubai Dyslexia Support Group, a non-profit support group that holds regular meetings for families affected by dyslexia, are also a great resource outside of the schooling system. The group is run by Anita Singhal, who is

well aware of the difficulties facing such families here: "not all schools offer support," she says. "The main problem is finding a school with a learning support unit or specialist help, and unfortunately, awareness is lacking in many schools."

However, it's not all bad news – according to Singhal, nearly all dyslexic children, bar those with severe dyslexia, can integrate fully into mainstream education with the correct support. And parents have a huge role to play in helping their children overcome learning challenges. "One of the key things a parent can do is to develop a dyslexic child's self-esteem," says Singhal. "Never compare them with other siblings or their peers, and encourage their strengths rather than focusing on weaknesses."

Unfortunately, the picture is not so bright for children with more severe learning difficulties or special needs. While in an ideal world it may be desirable for these children to attend 'normal' schools, the truth is that the majority of private schools in the UAE do not have sufficient facilities or support to cope with severe disabilities, or meet the special needs of some children. While this may result in, for example, a child with a physical disability not being able to attend a mainstream school despite not having any cognitive impairment, some parents feel that there is little point pushing the issue.

Children with Down Syndrome are among those who find inclusion in mainstream schools a challenge. Although more and more schools are opening their doors to children with Down Syndrome, there are still many schools and nurseries that refuse to allocate places to these children, according to Ingeborg Kroese, co-ordinator 0 to five years, All 4 Down Syndrome Support Group.

"Even those children with Down Syndrome who are in mainstream schools require part-time or full-time learning support assistants who help them access the curriculum," she says. "These learning support assistants are funded by the parents, and so financial constraints are a very real problem."

One of the key mandates of the All 4 Down Syndrome group is to encourage early intervention activities (physiotherapy, speech and language therapy and occupational therapy), which can stimulate development of children with Down Syndrome under the age of five. The group also holds regular talks with the Knowledge and Human Development Authority (KHDA) to discuss ways to increase inclusion of less able children in mainstream education organisations.

The kidsFIRST Medical Centre (kidsfirstmc.com) works hand-in-hand with teachers, administrators, and learning support staff at over 20 UAE schools to help improve education for children with special needs. It also runs the Triple P (Positive Parenting Program) and the Makaton Language Program, which teaches communication, language and literacy skills for children and adults with a broad range of communication and learning difficulties.

As well as providing educational consulting, kidsFIRST partners with educators and parents across Dubai to develop an Individual Education Plan (IEP) to suit a specific child's needs.

See the list of Special Needs schools and groups on p.175.

Health, Fitness & Well-Being

HEALTH

Both private and public healthcare services are available in the UAE. General standards are high, with English speaking staff and internationally trained medical staff in most facilities but, as in most countries, private healthcare is seen as preferable as you are likely to experience shorter waiting times and more comfortable inpatient facilities.

Under UAE labour law, an employer must provide access to healthcare for its employees. This can take two forms: either the employer pays for a private medical insurance policy, or it pays contributions towards government healthcare and covers the costs of obtaining a health card for each employee (p.181).

Government Healthcare

In Dubai, the Department of Health & Medical Services (dohms.gov.ae) runs the following hospitals: Dubai, Rashid and Latifa. Dubai Hospital is renowned as one of the best medical centres in the Middle East, while Latifa is a specialised maternity and paediatric hospital. DOHMS also operates a number of outpatient clinics. Al Baraha Hospital is run by the Ministry of Health. The Iranian Hospital, while not a government hospital, provides healthcare subsidised by the Iranian Red Crescent Society. With the exception of emergency care, you will need a health card to access government health services (see p.181). When you get your health card it will list a clinic or hospital to which you are assigned, although you're not obliged to use this one. In order to see a doctor, you will need to present your health card and a form of ID (Emirates ID, labour card, driving licence or passport) and will be charged a nominal fee for a consultation. Additional charges may apply for further tests, treatment and medication.

Private Healthcare

If you have private health insurance, you will have access to a network of private hospitals and clinics. Levels of cover vary depending on the policy, so check what you're entitled to. Dental care, maternity and screening tests aren't usually covered as standard, and you may need to have been on the policy for a year before you can receive maternity cover. Before making an appointment to see a healthcare professional, always check whether the clinic or hospital is part of your insurer's network to avoid being landed with the full costs yourself. Your insurer will also provide details about its payment policy; some companies offer direct billing, which means the insurer pays the hospital or clinic directly and you only pay a nominal fee each time you access medical services, while others require you to pay the cost of the consultation, treatment and medication up front and then file a claim to the insurer.

If your employer is paying for your medical insurance, your employment contract will state whether your spouse and dependants are included in the policy. If you plan to cover the cost of insuring your family yourself, you may need to purchase a separate policy for them as it's not always possible to extend existing policies.

For a list of companies providing healthcare insurance, see Insurance Companies, p.128.

Who You Gonna Call?

Need a doctor urgently? du customers have access to Mobile Doctors, a round-the-clock medical helpline. Licensed and experienced physicians from Dubai Healthcare City are standing by day and night to advise you over the phone and help you make an appointment with leading hospitals, clinics, pharmacies and other health services across the UAE. To subscribe, SMS 'MD' to 2470. For more information and to subscribe online, visit mobiledoctors24-7.com or call 800 63247; there is a daily fee of Dhs.29, and monthly subscriptions are also available.

Accidents & Emergencies

If you witness an accident or need an ambulance in an emergency situation, the number to call is 999.

Anyone can receive emergency treatment in government hospitals but charges apply to those without health cards. Some private hospitals have accident and emergency (A&E) departments but unless you have private medical insurance, you'll be landed with a large bill. Your best bet is to check with your insurer that you are covered for treatment in a particular hospital before heading there. Of the government hospitals, Rashid Hospital deals with most emergency cases as it has a well-equipped A&E department. This is the hospital that you're most likely to be taken to if you have an accident on the road. Dubai Hospital also has an emergency unit. Latifa Hospital offers emergency services to children under the age of 12 and women with maternity or gynaecological emergencies; it does not deal with trauma cases. The Iranian Hospital has a busy A&E.

While finding a place to get emergency treatment is easy, getting there is more problematic as Dubai's paramedic services are somewhat under-developed. Ambulance response times are below those in most western cities but the Dubai Health Authority, the Centre of Ambulance Services, and Dubai Police (who receive all 999 calls), have been making concerted efforts to improve upon these. In recent years, a large number of well-equipped response vehicles have been added and times have come down.

When you call 999, an ambulance will be dispatched to take the patient to the relevant hospital depending on the type of medical treatment needed.

Rashid Hospital receives all trauma patients; all other medical emergencies are transported to Dubai Hospital with the exception of cardiac, neurological and gastrointestinal patient, who are taken to Rashid or a specialty hospital.

General Medical Care

For general non-emergency medical care, there are a few different options available. Most hospitals have a walk-in clinic where you can simply turn up, present your health or insurance card, register and queue to see a general practitioner. It's commonplace to be seen by a triage nurse who will take down the details of your medical history and ailment before you see a doctor. These departments usually operate on a first come, first served basis. It's advisable to call the hospital prior to visiting to make sure that they operate a walk-in service and to check opening times. If you are on a private healthcare plan, make sure in advance that the hospital is on your insurer's network.

Many hospitals and smaller clinics offer family medicine, or general practice, as part of their outpatient services. You can usually call to make an appointment, but there's no guarantee that you'll get an appointment on the same day. If your usual family medicine department has no available appointments but you need immediate non-emergency medical care, they may admit you through the A&E department, but they will advise you of this when you call. American Hospital (p.182) offers a fast-track service through its A&E department for people needing immediate medical attention.

Finding A General Practitioner

While some people like the convenience of walk-in clinics, others prefer to register with a practice where they are familiar with the administrative procedures and can see the same doctor on return visits. There are countless clinics in Dubai which offer general practice and family medicine so, while standards are generally high, it's worth asking friends and colleagues for recommendations. Most areas of the city have a local medical centre, so if proximity to your home or place of work is important, you should be able to find something nearby.

General Practice Clinics

Al Diyafa Modern Medical Centre Al Bada'a, 04 345 4945
Al Mousa Medical Centre Jumeira 1, 04 345 2999, *almousamedical.com*
Al Noor Polyclinic Naif, 04 223 3324, *alnoorpolyclinic.ae*
Amber Clinics Al Rigga, 04 230 9100, *amber-clinics.com*
Aster Medical Centre Tecom, 04 453 4830, *astermedicalcentre.com*
Belgium Medical Services Umm Hurair 2, 04 362 4711
Belhoul European Hospital Al Bada'a, 04 345 4000, *belhouleuropean.com*
Canadian Specialist Hospital Hor Al Anz East, 04 707 2222, *csh.ae*
Crescent Medical Center Jumeira 1, 04 342 2288, *crescentmc.ae*
Dr Akel's General Medical Clinic (GMC) Jumeira 1, 04 349 4880, *gmcclinics.com*
Drs Nicolas & Asp Clinic Dubai Marina, 04 360 9977, *nicolasandasp.com*
Dubai London Clinic Umm Suqeim 2, 04 344 6663, *dubailondonclinic.com*
familyFIRST Medical Center >***p.196*** Umm Al Sheif, 04 380 5430, *familyfirst.ae*
General Medical Centre (GMC) Trade Centre 2, 04 331 3544, *gmcclinics.com*
General Medical Centre (GMC) Green Community, 04 885 3225, *gmcclinics.com*
Health Call Umm Hurair 2, 04 363 5343, *health-call.com*
Infinity Health Clinic Jumeira 3, 04 394 8994, *ihcdubai.com*
JTS Medical Centre >***p.201*** Jumeira 1, 04 379 9954, *jtsmedicalcentre.com*
kidsFIRST Medical Centre >***p.196*** Umm Suqeim 3, 04 348 5437, *kidsFIRSTmc.com*
Lifeline Medical Centre Dubai Marina Dubai Marina, 04 884 5905, *lifeline.ae*
Manchester Clinic Jumeira 1, 04 344 0300, *manchester-clinic.com*
Medcare Medical Centres Mirdif 04 284 0722 *medcarehospital.com*
Mediclinic Dubai Mall Downtown Dubai, 04 449 5111, *mediclinic.ae*
Mercato Family Clinic Jumeira 1, 04 344 8844
NMC Family Clinic Al Safa 1, 04 395 6660, *nmc.ae*
Symbiosis Medical Centre Dubai Silicon Oasis, 04 392 5577, *symbiosis-healthcare.com*

Medical History

It's worth requesting a copy of your medical history from your GP practice at home and giving it to your new clinic to ensure your medical background is taken into consideration when you seek medical advice. Most insurance policies don't cover holiday vaccinations so, if you plan to travel beyond the UAE, you can save yourself a lot of money and needles if you have a record of which jabs you've already had.

Health Cards

Employers in the UAE must pay for health cover for all of their employees. An employer can decide whether to provide health cards for its staff or pay for a private insurance policy. If your employer provides you with a health card, you are entitled to subsidised healthcare at government-run hospitals and clinics. The health card must be renewed each year, but you only need to take a new medical test when your visa is up for renewal. Your employer should start the process for you, by telling you which hospital to go to. Al Baraha (Kuwaiti) Hospital is the most common, although the tests can be carried out at a number of government health clinics as well. A health card costs Dhs.310.

Pharmacies & Medication

The UAE has a more relaxed policy on prescription drugs than many other countries and most can be bought over the counter. If you know what you need, it cuts out the hassle of having to see a doctor just to get a prescription. Pharmacists are willing to offer advice, but bear in mind that they don't know your medical history. Always tell the pharmacist if you have any pre-existing conditions and allergies or are taking other medication, and make sure that you understand the administration instructions in case these aren't available in English. You might find it frustrating that certain common medications from your home country are not available here (such as Gaviscon for infants and Pepto Bismol). You may find that there are similar products (such as Infacol instead of infant Gaviscon). There are pharmacies all over the city and a number are open 24 hours a day, such as Life Pharmacy on Al Wasl Road in Jumeira (04 344 1122). Supermarkets and petrol station convenience stores sell basic medications and first aid equipment.

Prohibited Medications

Certain medications do require a prescription, and there are some medications (such as codeine, diazepam and temazepam) that are actually banned here in the UAE, even though they are widely available on prescription in other countries. It is a crime to have these medicines in your possession or to take them, unless you can produce an official prescription from your doctor in your home country. The complete list of banned drugs can change regularly, so it is best to check with the Registration & Drug Control Department at the Ministry of Health (moh.gov.ae) before travelling with any medication.

Main Hospitals

In general, both private and government hospitals deliver high standards of care in Dubai. Most hospitals offer a comprehensive range of inpatient and outpatient facilities, so if you like a particular hospital but need to see a specific specialist, the chances are the hospital will be able to cater to your needs. Once you have registered with one hospital it is easier to return there for further treatment.

For very specialist treatment, you'll be referred to somewhere else in the city. Many of the services offered in hospitals are also offered in clinics and small practices, so if you have a hospital phobia, this might be a better option for non-emergency treatment. See Specialist Clinics & Practitioners, p.188.

It is worth having a look around the main hospitals to see which one suits you – especially if you are intending to have a baby in Dubai. For more information on Having a Baby in Dubai see p.139.

Al Baraha Hospital

Nr Naif Rd Al Baraha **04 271 0000**
albarahahospital.8m.com
Map **2 P4** Metro **Salah Al Din**
One of Dubai's older medical facilities, this government hospital is commonly referred to as the Kuwaiti Hospital and is situated on the Deira side of the Shindagha Tunnel. You're unlikely to use this hospital for treatment, but you might need to come here for your blood test when processing your residency or for a birth or death certificate.

Al Garhoud Private Hospital

Al Garhoud **04 454 5000**
gph.ae
Map **2 N7** Metro **GGICO**
Catering to almost all areas of medical service, this 52-bed multi-specialty private hospital offers general surgery, emergency care, and obstetrics and gynaecology; there is also an ENT department, plastic aesthetic surgery and physiotherapy.

Al Zahra Private Hospital

Nr Clock Tower R/A, Gulf Rd Sharjah **06 561 9999**
alzahra.com
Al Zahra Private Hospital is the one of the main hospitals in Sharjah. It is a private facility and operates a 24 hour GP clinic and emergency unit, with consultants on call around the clock. Its ENT department has a good reputation and the hospital's special cardiac care ambulance is equipped to respond to cardiac emergencies. Al Zahra Private Medical Centre (p.188), in Al Safa Tower on Sheikh Zayed Road in Dubai, offers a range of outpatient services with excellent care levels.

American Hospital Dubai *> p.183*

Nr Movenpick Hotel, Oud Metha Rd Oud Metha
04 377 3030
ahdubai.com
Map **2 L6** Metro **Oud Metha**
With excellent in and outpatient facilities and an A&E unit with a fast-track system, American Hospital is usually pretty busy. Recently expanded, it has top-of-the-range diagnostic equipment and a number of dedicated units including The Heart Centre and Cancer Care Centre. Its maternity unit is a popular choice among expectant mums, with packages for

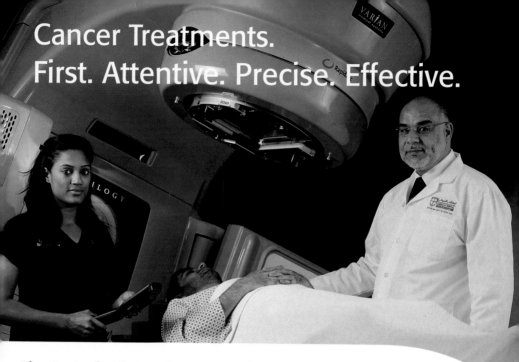

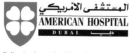

prenatal care and delivery, and private rooms on the labour ward. The medical staff hail from all corners of the globe. You can book appointments online.

Belhoul Speciality Hospital

2nd Street Al Baraha **04 273 3333**
belhoulspeciality.com
Map **2 P4** Metro **Palm Deira**
Belhoul Speciality Hospital's nephrology department offers state-of-the-art dialysis machines for kidney disorders. It also has advanced diagnostic technology and health check packages. It has an emergency room and a range of in and outpatient services. Services are efficient with good customer service.

Cedars Jebel Ali International Hospital

Off Exit 22, Shk Zayed Rd Jebel Ali **04 881 4000**
cedars-jaih.com
Map **1 D5** Metro **Danube**
Cedars Jebel Ali International Hospital is a private healthcare facility situated near to the Jebel Ali Free Zone. Services include a 24 hour emergency clinic and dedicated ambulance (04 881 4000 and 04 881 8816). It specialises in trauma and occupational medicine. A hospital extension is currently under construction.

Dubai Hospital

Nr Al Baraha Hospital Al Baraha **04 219 5000**
dha.gov.ae
Map **2 P4** Metro **Salah Al Din**
One of the best government hospitals, Dubai Hospital opened in 1983 but is clean and well maintained. It offers a full range of medical, dentistry and general surgical services. It is large and usually busy but has a very efficient emergency department.

Emirates Hospital

Jumeira Rd Jumeira 2 **04 349 6666**
emirateshospital.ae
Map **2 D4** Metro **Business Bay**
This small private hospital on Jumeira Road may not be the newest of Dubai's private medical facilities but it delivers a high standard of care. Primarily a surgical hospital, it also runs a number of outpatient clinics including a 24 hour walk-in clinic.

Iranian Hospital

Al Wasl Rd Al Bada'a **04 344 0250**
ihd.ae
Map **2 H4** Metro **Emirates Hospital**
The mosaic-fronted Iranian Hospital sits opposite the Iranian Mosque at the Satwa end of Al Wasl Road. The hospital is affiliated to the Red Crescent Society of Iran and therefore isn't strictly a UAE government hospital. It offers its own health card and the fee is reasonable. The card, which costs Dhs.300, offers 20% discount on in and outpatient services, but even without a card, the prices are very reasonable. In addition, some of the medicines which they prescribe are free. On the downside the hospital is rather busy, particularly at the walk-in clinic during peak hours.

Latifa Hospital

Oud Metha Rd Al Jaddaf **04 219 3000**
dha.gov.ae
Map **2 K7** Metro **Dubai Healthcare City**
The newly-renamed Latifa Hospital (was Al-Wasl) is a government facility specialising in obstetrics, gynaecology, paediatrics and paediatric surgery. It has an emergency department that provides 24 hour care, seven days a week, to children up to the age of 12 for medical, surgical and non-trauma cases, and women with serious problems relating to pregnancy and gynaecology. It is the only hospital which deals with emergency pregnancies and has a special baby care unit for premature and sick neonates. Expat residents admitted in an emergency without a valid health card are charged Dhs.100 a day plus the cost of any medication.

Medcare Hospital

Nr Safa Park Gate 1 Al Safa 1 **04 407 9100**
medcarehospital.com
Map **2 D5** Metro **Business Bay**
One of the most modern hospitals in Dubai, the 60 bed private Medcare Hospital offers advanced medical care and emergency services, with a particularly strong maternity department. Staff are qualified to international standards. A satellite clinic, Medcare Medical Centre, recently opened in Uptown Mirdif and takes walk-ins. There is also a multi-speciality clinic located on The Walk, Jumeirah Beach Residence.

GOOD HEALTH **Ken Petersen**, Dubai resident

I fell ill shortly after arriving in Dubai and before my company had arranged my private medical insurance. Because I didn't have a health card either my only choice was to go to the Iranian Hospital. I visited the General Medical Care department which had a walk-in clinic. I went to the hospital during the middle of the day, when it was pretty quiet, and I only had to wait about 15 minutes to see a triage nurse and doctor. I was sent for some investigations and asked to return two hours later for results. The doctor saw me straight away on my return and dispatched me to the pharmacy with a list of drugs, none of which I was charged for. All together I was charged under Dhs.200 and received excellent levels of care.

Serious Medical Conditions

Medical facilities for chronic medical conditions are continually improving in Dubai. Here's the lowdown on the most prevalent serious illnesses in the UAE and where to go to receive treatment for them.

If you suffer from a serious medical condition, you'll find a good range of services available in Dubai, and most clinics will help you seek treatment overseas or in your home country if services aren't available here.

Heart disease is the highest cause of death in the UAE with over 40% of UAE fatalities linked to heart problems, according to Ministry of Health figures. The MoH promotes heart disease awareness with regular campaigns to educate people about contributing factors such as smoking, obesity, stress, high blood pressure, diabetes and sedentary lifestyles, most of which have an above average prevalence in the UAE. Care for heart disease patients has improved dramatically in recent years with the opening of the German Heart Centre Bremen (p.189) and the Mayo Clinic (p.189) in Healthcare City and specialist heart units in hospitals such as American Hospital (p.182). Stroke is the third biggest killer in the UAE, after heart disease and accidents and, worldwide, is the most common cause of lifelong disability. Most major hospitals have a neurosciences department offering neurological screening, treatment and rehabilitation; the Neuro Spinal Hospital (p.186) has a dedicated stroke unit.

American Hospital has both an adult cancer care centre and a paediatric oncology unit. Tawam Hospital in Al Ain has a full oncology department, offering radiotherapy, chemotherapy, haematology, counselling and diagnostics. In the last few years, there has been a concerted breast cancer awareness campaign, much of it driven by the Safe & Sound programme based at BurJuman Shopping Centre, where many outreach initiatives take place. The campaign's website (safeandsound.ae) is packed with information on the disease, self examination and fundraising activities. Emirates Hospital (p.184), among others, has a dedicated breast cancer clinic.

With every chronic disease or serious illness it is imperative to seek medical attention as early as possible to improve the chances of survival and minimise any lasting effects. Some insurance policies do not cover pre-existing or chronic medical conditions, so check your paperwork carefully and consider taking out additional cover if you have a family history of disease or are particularly at risk through contributing factors.

Well woman, well man and well child packages are available at a number of hospitals and clinics throughout Dubai, including Welcare, American and Al Zahra Hospitals (see Main Hospitals, p.182). These packages are a good way to get an overall health check and assessment of any potential illness to which you may be particularly susceptible. A good package should involve a thorough medical examination, screenings for common diseases, routine tests (such as cervical smears for women) and offer wellbeing advice based on your lifestyle. You can even get your holiday vaccinations topped up as part of some packages.

Medcare Orthopaedics & Spine Hospital

Off Shk Zayed Rd Al Safa 1 **04 376 8400**
medcareorthopaedics.com
Map **2 C6** Metro **Business Bay**
MOSH exclusively caters to orthopaedic and spine patients, specialising in joint replacement, paediatric orthopaedic, foot and ankle, sports, and hand and spine. It boasts one of the largest and most comprehensive associations of private orthopaedic surgeons in the emirate.

Mediclinic City Hospital > *p.187*

Dubai Healthcare City Umm Hurair 2 **04 435 9999**
mediclinic.ae
Map **2 L7** Metro **Dubai Healthcare City**
Mediclinic City Hospital is a modern, multi-disciplinary hospital delivering world-class healthcare services. With the most advanced equipment available, the 226-bed premium facility offers specialised treatment in areas such as cardiology, neurology and neurosurgery, obstetrics and gynaecology, paediatrics, general surgery and radiology. Patient care units provide sophisticated diagnosis and treatment methods within fields as specialised as hand surgery, eye care, kidney stones and breast care. The maternity unit has a dedicated caesarean section theatre and a recently expanded neonatal intensive care unit, which is now one of the largest in the UAE.

Mediclinic Welcare Hospital

Nr Aviation Club Al Garhoud **04 282 7788**
mediclinic.ae
Map **2 N7** Metro **GGICO**
Welcare Hospital's special services include a contact lens clinic, diabetic clinic, holiday dialysis and home call consultations (specialist and GP). Its prenatal and delivery care is considered to be among the best in Dubai. Welcare does postnatal packages for parents and their new baby, which is a nice way to meet other new mums. Welcare also operates primary healthcare clinics in Mirdif (04 288 1302) and Al Qusais (04 258 6466) and an ambulatory care unit in Knowledge Village (04 366 1030) that comes highly recommended. Appointments can be booked online.

H1N1

Back in 2009 when there was a global outbreak, a number of cases of swine flu were reported in the UAE. Although a handful of swine flu cases resulted in death, figures were minimal compared to other affected countries. The Ministry of Health set up the Technical Health Committee for Combating H1N1 Virus to educate the population on the symptoms and work out a contingency plan should a mass outbreak occur. By the end of the year, the UAE had stockpiled the vaccine should another outbreak occur. Travellers arriving in the country must pass through thermal scanners at the airport and may be detained and tested for H1N1 if they show symptoms. Tamiflu, the main drug recommended for treating the virus, is available on prescription from pharmacies.

Al Maktoum Hospital

This hospital closed in 2010, with most medical services being transferred to the medical centre in Al Muhaisnah. The building of Al Maktoum Hospital will be preserved as a heritage centre.

Neuro Spinal Hospital > *p.viii-ix*

Nr Jumeira Beach Park, Jumeira Rd Jumeira 2
04 342 0000
nshdubai.com
Map **2 D4** Metro **Business Bay**
The Neuro Spinal Hospital has an emergency room that is open around the clock. The unit is prepared for all kinds of spinal, neurosurgical and neurological emergencies. The hospital has 40 beds and a multi-national team of specialists, doctors and nurses. As well as spinal treatment facilities, the hospital has a stroke centre for treatment of acute cerebro-vascular accidents and its own ambulance, which can be dispatched by calling 04 315 7777.

NMC Hospital

Salahuddin Rd Hor Al Anz **04 268 9800**
nmc.ae
Map **2 P6** Metro **Abu Hail**
NMC Private Hospital in Deira has a 24 hour walk-in general practice clinic so advance appointments are not necessary. The levels of service are high and the staff are generally efficient. The hospital has an emergency room and its own ambulance with attendant doctors. There is an NMC Specialty Hospital in Al Nahda (04 609 2222), with specialist clinics for allergies, reconstructive surgery, paediatrics and more.

Rashid Hospital

Nr Maktoum Bridge Umm Hurair 2 **04 219 2000**
alrashidhospital.org
Map **2 M6** Metro **Oud Metha**
The main government hospital for A&E, trauma, intensive care and paramedic services in Dubai. It's likely that you'll be brought here if you have an accident on Dubai's roads. It also offers diagnostics, surgery, maternity, paediatrics, physiotherapy and a social affairs unit. It delivers a good standard of care but because of its high demand you may be better off seeking non-emergency treatment in another government hospital.

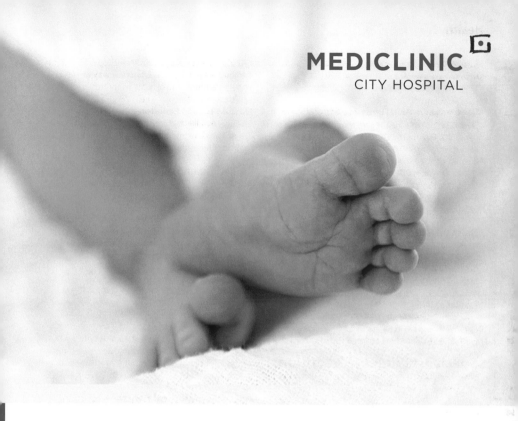

Saudi German Hospital > *p.178*
Nr American School of Dubai, Al Hessa Rd Al Barsha 3 **04 389 0000**
sghdubai.com
Map **1 P6** Metro **Dubai Internet City**
SGH has numerous healthcare establishments across the MENA region. The Dubai facility is an impressively state-of-the-art 300 bed specialty tertiary care hospital that is extremely convenient for many in New Dubai. It offers medical and surgical specialties and subspecialties including cardiac surgery, neurosurgery, oncology, maxillofacial surgery, orthopedics, and vascular surgery.

Zulekha Hospital
Nr Higher College of Technology Dubai Women's College Al Nahda 2 **04 267 8866**
zulekhahospitals.com
Map **2 T8** Metro **Al Nahda**
A multi-specialty hospital offering care from cardiology through to urology, as well as 24-hour emergency services. In 2012, Zulekha Hospital, which also has a hospital in Sharjah and a medical centre in Dubai, was awarded the coveted Dubai Quality Award.

Specialist Clinics & Practitioners
Whatever your ailment, the chances are you'll find at least one – and probably many more – relevant specialist in Dubai. You don't need a referral to be seen by a specialist, so you are free to seek whatever medical advice is relevant to your condition. If you are not sure what is wrong with you, or which kind of specialist you should consult, you can ask your doctor or ask advice from a hospital. Most places will advise you over the phone to save you the hassle of getting an appointment.

The majority of hospitals also offer a range of outpatient medical specialties (see Main Hospitals, p.182), although many people prefer the more personalised environment of smaller practices for long term medical care. In addition, many general practice clinics offer a range of medical services so it's worth checking at your local clinic before seeking specialist services elsewhere (see General Medical Care, p.181).

Al Borj Medical Centre
Mazaya Centre Al Wasl **04 321 2220**
Map **2 F6** Metro **Burj Khalifa/Dubai Mall**
Specialises in endocrinology, dermatology, plastic surgery, gynaecology, paediatrics and general surgery.

Al Shifa Al Khaleeji Medical Center
Al Shifa Bldg, Nr Clock Tower, Abu Baker Al Siddique Rd Al Rigga **04 294 0786**
Map **2 N6** Metro **Al Rigga**
This clinic offers paediatrics, gynaecology, dentistry, internal medicine and orthopaedic medical services.

Al Zahra Medical Centre > *p.xiii*
Al Safa Tower, Shk Zayed Rd Trade Centre 1 **04 331 5000**
alzahra.com
Map **2 H5** Metro **Emirates**
A large medical facility offering wellness packages, maternity care and diagnostics in addition to a full range of outpatient services.

Allied Diagnostics
Nr Satwa R/A, 2nd December St Al Satwa **04 332 8111**
allieddiagnostics.net
Map **2 J5** Metro **World Trade Centre**
Provides diagnostic services for clinics that do not have on-site facilities. You may be referred here for investigative procedures.

Amber Clinics
Rigga Business Centre, Al Rigga Rd Al Rigga **04 230 9100**
amber-clinics.com
Map **2 N6** Metro **Al Rigga**
One of a number of Amber establishments in Dubai, the Al Rigga clinic is a large, one-stop 'polyclinic' with numerous specialty departments and laboratories under one roof.

Atlas Star Medical Center
Khalid Bin Al Waleed Rd Al Raffa **04 359 6662**
asmc-uae.atlasera.com
Map **2 L4** Metro **Al Fahidi**
Offers general practice, general surgery, ENT, gynaecology and dental services.

British Medical Consulting Centre
Nr Mercato Jumeira 1 **04 344 2633**
bmccdubai.com
Map **2 F4** Metro **Financial Centre**
Western-trained medical staff specialising in cosmetic surgery, psychotherapy, psychology, dentistry, hair transplantation and marriage counselling.

The Diabetes & Endocrine Center
Dubai Healthcare City Umm Hurair 2 **04 375 2345**
dhcc.ae
Map **2 L7** Metro **Dubai Healthcare City**
Screening and treatment clinic for diabetes and thyroid problems.

Dr Al Rustom's Medical & Day Care Surgery Centre
Villa 41, Nr Jumeira Plaza Jumeira 1 **04 349 8800**
skin-and-laser.com
Map **2 H4** Metro **Emirates Towers**
A specialist dermatology clinic offering cancer services, laser surgery and cosmetic procedures.

Dr Mahaveer Mehta Skin Medical
Al Ghurair Centre Al Muraqqabat **04 221 9300**
skinlaserdubai.com
Map **2 N5** Metro **Union**
A laser surgery clinic offering treatment for dermatological conditions and cosmetic procedures.

Dr Mohamed Al Zubaidy Clinic
Burger King Bldg, Al Rigga St Al Rigga **04 227 7533**
Map **2 N4** Metro **Union**
Dr Al Zubaidy offers dermatology and venereology investigations and treatments.

Dr Ray's Medical Centre
Khalid Al Attar Bldg, Shk Khalifa Bin Zayed Rd Al Mankhool **04 397 3665**
Map **2 L5** Metro **BurJuman**
Offers obstetrics, gynaecology, homeopathy, dentistry and ophthalmology.

Dr Taher H Khalil Clinic
Zarouni Bldg, Al Rigga St Al Rigga **04 268 7655**
Map **2 N5** Metro **Al Rigga**
A general medical clinic specialising in hormone therapy including treatment for low fertility, diabetes and thyroid irregularities.

Doctor On Call

800 Doctor (800doctor.com, 800 362867), offers a doctor on call service 24 hours a day, seven days a week. Its team of certified doctors can visit your home, work or business, normally within an hour of your call. A house call will cost Dhs.500 plus prescriptions, injections etc – well worth the expense if you're feeling really unwell.

Dubai London Clinic
Jumeira Rd Umm Suqeim 2 **04 344 6663**
dubailondonclinic.com
Map **1 T4** Metro **First Gulf Bank**
A long-established clinic with brand new medical and surgical premises in Umm Suqeim. Another branch is located at Festival City (04 232 5751) and Dubai London Dental Centre is on Al Wasl Road (p.198). Dubai London Specialty Hospital is now open at the Umm Suqeim branch, offering round-the-clock emergency services, inpatient surgery, cosmetic surgery and comprehensive outpatient care.

Fetal Medicine & Genetic Center
Dubai Healthcare City Umm Hurair 2 **04 360 4040**
my-baby.net
Map **2 L7** Metro **Dubai Healthcare City**
Specialists in fetal care, offering first trimester screening tests, prenatal diagnostics, pregnancy assessment and patient care.

German Heart Centre Bremen
Dubai Healthcare City Umm Hurair 2 **04 362 4797**
german-heart-centre.com
Map **2 L7** Metro **Dubai Healthcare City**
Cardiac treatment, investigation and intervention services, and after treatment care from Germany's most renowned cardiology clinic.

German Medical Center
Dubai Healthcare City Umm Hurair 2 **04 362 2929**
gmcdhcc.com
Map **2 L7** Metro **Dubai Healthcare City**
Offering medical specialties including urology, andrology, infertility, gynaecology, obstetrics, internal medicine, general and orthopaedic surgeries and ENT.

Health Bay Clinic
Villa 977, Al Wasl Rd Umm Suqeim 2 **04 348 7140**
healthbayclinic.com
Map **1 U5** Metro **Noor Islamic Bank**
This family clinic is known for its strong paediatric, obstetric, gynaecologic and midwifery care, but it also offers internal medicine, gastroenterology, dermatology and allergology, and podiatry, with a team of western trained physicians.

Health Care Medical Centre
Jumeirah Centre Jumeira 1 **04 344 5550**
Map **2 H4** Metro **World Trade Centre**
A small practice offering ENT, dentistry and ophthalmology.

iCare Clinics
Oasis Centre Al Quoz 1 **04 384 7272**
icare-clinics.com
Map **2 L6** Metro **Noor Islamic Bank**
The first of 20 proposed iCARE Clinics is now open at the Oasis Centre on Sheikh Zayed Road. The clinics offer a wide range of medical services, including paediatrics, gynaecology, dental, radiology, pathology, family medicine, as well as general practitioner services.

Jebel Ali Hospital (Lifeline Hospital)
Nr Jebel Ali Primary School Jebel Ali **04 884 5666**
lifeline.ae
Map **1 F6** Metro **Ibn Battuta**
A boutique hospital offering luxury healthcare with chauffeur-driven transfers and private suites. It also has an excellent maternity wing.

Mayo Clinic
Dubai Healthcare City Umm Hurair 2 **04 362 2900**
mayoclinic.org
Map **2 L7** Metro **Dubai Healthcare City**
This clinic offers diagnostic and evaluative services, and surgical aftercare. Patients are referred to the Mayo Clinic in the US for treatment.

Medcare Medical Centre

Nr Umm Suqeim Municipality Bldg, Jumeira Rd Umm Suqeim 1 **04 395 3115**
medcarehospital.com
Map **2 A4** Metro **Noor Islamic Bank**
Offering primary, secondary and tertiary medical services including surgery, dentistry, family medicine, rheumatology, diagnostics, psychiatry, endocrinology, urology and paediatrics. There are also branches at Mirdif, Mirdif City Centre and The Walk at JBR.

Medic Polyclinic

Khalid Bin Al Waleed Rd Al Mankhool **04 355 4111**
Map **2 L5** Metro **BurJuman**
A medical clinic and a diagnostics centre.

Mediclinic Al Qusais

Dubai Residential Oasis Al Qusais Industrial 2 **04 258 6466**
mediclinic.ae
Map **2 S8** Metro **Al Qusais**
This Al Qusais clinic offers patients a wide range of services, including inpatient treatment at the renowned Welcare Hospital.

Mediclinic Al Sufouh

Block 10, Dubai Knowledge Village Al Sufouh 1 **04 366 1030**
mediclinic.ae
Map **1 N5** Metro **Dubai Internet City**
Has everything from onsite ambulance services to an operation theatre and 25 outpatient and specialty clinics that include daycare surgery, gastroenterology, paediatrics and urgent care. Open 08:00 to 22:30, Saturday to Thursday, 14:00 to 22:30 on Friday.

Mediclinic Arabian Ranches

Nr Arabian Ranches Community Centre Arabian Ranches **04 453 4020**
mediclinic.ae
Map **1 R13** Metro **Mall of the Emirates**
An 'ambulatory care centre' which almost serves as a mini-hospital, such is its array of facilities and services. General medicine and day surgery are provided along with specialties like dentistry, gynaecology, opthalmology and dermatology. Open 08:00 to 22:30 Saturday to Thursday and 14:00 to 22:30 on Friday.

Mediclinic Beach Road

Shk Hamdan Awards Complex, Jumeira Rd Al Mina **04 379 7711**
mediclinic.ae
Map **2 J4** Metro **Al Jafiliya**
Located in Sheikh Hamdan Complex in Jumeira, this newly-opened medical centre offers a range of specialist services, with facilities including an observation unit and its own in-house laboratory.

Mediclinic Dubai Mall

The Dubai Mall Downtown Dubai **04 449 5111**
mediclinic.ae
Map **2 F6** Metro **Burj Khalifa/Dubai Mall**
Offering the full range of general and specialty medicine, from cardiology to urology, this is the region's largest outpatient facility and has the latest facilities to boot.

Mediclinic Ibn Battuta

Ibn Battuta Mall The Gardens **04 440 9000**
mediclinic.ae
Map **1 G5** Metro **Ibn Battuta**
An ultra-modern, fully equipped multi-specialty clinic with its location in Ibn Battuta Mall, making it ideal for residents in the surrounding communities. Has support services like labs and x-rays.

Mediclinic Meadows

Nr Emirates International School, Meadows 2 Emirates Living **04 453 4040**
mediclinic.ae
Map **1 L6** Metro **Nakheel**
Combines advanced medical equipment, an onsite laboratory and diagnostic imaging centre, and a vast range of specialist medical services.

Mediclinic Mirdif

Uptown Mirdiff Mirdif **04 288 1302**
mediclinicl.ae
Map **2 Q13** Metro **Rashidiya**
Family healthcare clinic specialising in primary medical care, and a wide range of specialised services. Has a direct link to the Welcare Hospital and The Mediclinic City Hospital.

Men's Health Clinic

Al Muhaisnah Medical Fitness Centre Muhaisnah 2 **04 502 3939**
dha.gov.ae
Map **2 R11** Metro **Etisalat**
The region's first men-only clinic specialises in male-related diseases and health concerns such as heart disease, infertility and prostate cancer. The Ministry of Health is due to open more such clinics at its medical centres across the emirate.

Skin Sense

The strong sun in Dubai means you should be especially wary of any new moles or irregular marks that appear on your skin, or if existing moles change or grow in size. A number of clinics specialise in looking after your skin, including Mahaveer Mehta Skin Medical Centre (p.189) and Dr Al Rustom's clinic (p.188).

Dubai Healthcare City

To Your Health

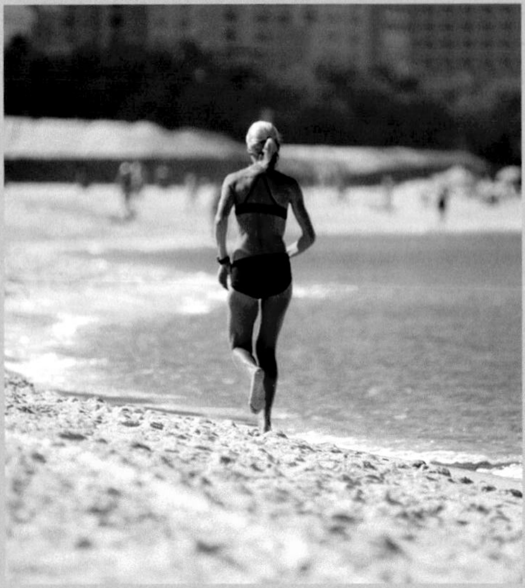

Putting On The Pounds

While many people in Dubai spend the greater portion of their time in outdoor pursuits during the winter months, the heat of the summer means that for four months of the year it's easy to fall into lazy ways. In general, people have a more sedentary lifestyle here, and the city's car culture, all-you-can-eat-and-drink brunches and fastfood outlets at every turn see many new expats gaining the infamous 'Dubai stone'. Fortunately, there are a number of weight loss groups and nutritionists on hand to help (p.208), as well as ample fitness centres and gyms (p.210) and opportunities to take part in sports (see Activity Finder, p.320) to keep you active and help shift the extra weight.

Diabetes

Obesity is a major factor contributing to the UAE's high incidence of diabetes. One in five people in the UAE is diabetic but nearly half don't know they have the disease; the majority of them have Type 2, a preventable form of diabetes which is strongly linked to lifestyle and eating habits. The government is aggressively promoting awareness campaigns headed up by organisations such as the Juvenile Diabetes Research Foundation (jdrf.org), to educate the population about preventative measures, healthy eating and the benefits of an active lifestyle.

The Landmark Group organises an annual Beat Diabetes Walkathon in Dubai to raise awareness. If you suffer from diabetes or think you may be at risk, you can speak to your doctor or contact a specialist diabetes clinic such as The Diabetes Endocrine Center (p.188) or the diabetes clinic at Welcare Hospital (p.186). There are also a number of nutritionists who can help you manage your condition through your diet (see Nutritionists & Slimming, p.208).

New Germs

The UAE is a transitory place and with so many people coming and going and bringing new germs with them, you may find that bugs and colds are more common. With the stresses involved in moving to a new place, you may find that your immune system is impaired for a while and you are not as resilient to germs as you normally are. Generally speaking, though, if you maintain an active lifestyle and a good diet, your immune system will fight off any unwanted bugs before you even know about it. It's worth keeping a closer eye on your kids and, if any strange symptoms appear, a trip to the doctor's is best, even if it's just to put your mind at rest.

While you're likely to enjoy a generous slice of the good life in Dubai, all-you-can-eat brunches and the party lifestyle will eventually take their toll. Living in hot, dry, dusty conditions can also have an effect on your well-being. Here are some of the common health complaints you should be aware of.

Sun Safety

It goes without saying that extra sun care needs to be taken when out and about in the UAE. The hot sun and high temperatures are recipes for sunburn and heat stroke if you are not prepared. Sun block is widely available in supermarkets and pharmacies. Sun hats, light, loose clothing that covers your limbs, sun glasses and seeking shade are recommended when out and about in the hotter parts of the day and during the summer months.

With high temperatures throughout the year, you should also ensure that you drink enough water to remain hydrated; this is particularly important when you exercise and during the summer months. It's wise to keep a couple of bottles of water in the car in case of emergencies. If you have a breakdown in busy traffic during the summer, you may be faced with an uncomfortable wait while the police or recovery truck come to the rescue.

You should also be aware of any changes to your skin, such as new moles or ones that change shape, colour or bleed. Contact your doctor or a dermatologist if you have any concerns.

Other Ailments

If you suffer from asthma, you may find that the dusty outdoor environment and the dry, conditioned air indoors aggravate your symptoms and you may need to rely on your inhaler more often than you would at home. A number of medical practices offer asthma clinics, including GMC (p.200). Sinusitis can also be triggered by the dust, although this is more common among people who have lived in the city for a number of years. Ear, nose and throat (ENT) specialists can advise on the best course of treatment and arrange surgery if necessary.

The average working week in the UAE is longer than in many other countries. Spending longer hours in the office can take its toll on your body, making you more susceptible to bugs and colds; it can also make you prone to suffering from stress injuries such as repetitive strain syndrome.

Mosquito Prevention

Finally, while the WHO declared the UAE malaria free in 2007, mosquitoes are common at the beginning and end of winter, particularly around the water, and the perfect al fresco evening can be ruined by bites from these tiny critters. Mild mosquito repellent sprays and lotions are usually effective enough to keep the mozzies at bay, so you shouldn't need to resort to DEET-based or tropical strength products.

If you prefer natural remedies, citronella oil is reportedly an effective mosquito repellent and is available in health food stores such as Nutrition Zone (see Health Food & Special Dietary Requirements, p.392) and Neal's Yard (Wafi, 04 324 5141). To save yourself from being bitten while you sleep, plug-in mosquito repellers are available from most supermarkets and pharmacies. Citronella candles are available from ACE (p.400) to keep the mozzies at bay in your garden.

Neuro Spinal Centre

Jumeira Rd Jumeira 2 **04 342 0000**
nshdubai.com
Map **2 D4** Metro **Business Bay**
A 40-bed neurosurgical, neurological, spinal and orthopaedic specialist facility offering superior diagnostic, rehabilitative and curative services. Located opposite Jumeirah Beach Park, the centre's facilities include emergency room, operating suite and radiology department.

NMC Specialty Hospital

Nr Higher College of Technology Dubai Women's College Al Nahda 2 **04 267 9999**
nmc.ae
Map **2 S6** Metro **Stadium**
Facilities including an excellent cardiac care and surgery department, a maternity ward, an allergy department and a sleep lab treating sleeping-related problems from snoring to narcolepsy.

Panacea Medical & Wellness Centre

Easa Saleh Al Gurg Bldg, Tariq Bin Ziyad Rd Umm Hurair 1 **04 358 2020**
panacea.ae
Map **2 M5** Metro **BurJuman**
A modern clinic that offers everything from the more traditional internal medicine, paediatrics, obstetrics, gynaecology, diagnostics and chiropractics to dietetics and homeopathy. Even has a dentistry department and an emergency department.

Prime Medical Center

Nr Jumeirah Plaza, Jumeira Rd Jumeira 1
04 349 4545
pmcdubai.com
Map **2 G4** Metro **Emirates Towers**
The Prime Healthcare Group actually runs six clinics throughout Dubai, offering a wide range of outpatient services, as well as a diagnostics centre in Deira (04 272 0720).

Wooridul Spine Centre

Sheikh Zayed Rd Al Safa 2 **04 304 6767**
wsc.ae
Map **1 A6** Metro **Noor Islamic Bank**
Provides patients with full spinal treatment programmes, from radiological and lab investigations to pain management, physiotherapy and complete surgical plans.

Obstetrics & Gynaecology

Most hospitals and general practice clinics in Dubai offer gynaecologic and obstetric medical services. In your home country you may be used to receiving reminders when you are due for a smear test or mammogram; in the UAE, you'll need to be more proactive, and while a gynaecologist can advise you on how frequently you should have check-ups, it will be up to you to remember when you're due and schedule an appointment. If you are looking for a long-term gynaecologist, it's worth checking out some of the specialist clinics listed below. Well woman check-ups can be done regularly (usually annually) and offer the chance to get all your checks done in one go, at the same time as a general health review.

Breastfeeding Support

Breastfeeding Q&A is a support group for mothers who do, or who want to, breastfeed. It provides encouragement and evidence-based information to members, predominantly online, but also during regular get-togethers. Visit facebook.com/groups/242418372502807.

Most contraceptives are available in Dubai (the morning after pill is not) and a gynaecologist can advise you on the most suitable form of contraception for you. If you take oral contraceptives, a variety of brands are available over the counter without prescription. Because of the risk of thrombosis, you should make a point of going to your doctor to have your blood pressure checked every six months, just to make sure everything is okay. Note that, while rarely enforced, the law is that you should be married in order to be prescribed or purchase contraceptives.

Maternity Care

If you are having a baby, the level of maternity care in Dubai is excellent. Among expats, the most popular maternity hospitals are Welcare, American and Latifa Hospitals (see Main Hospitals, p.182). Latifa Hospital may lack some of the private hospital frills but it has an excellent reputation for maternity care and paediatrics. Before you decide on a government hospital, check its policy regarding husbands and family members in the labour ward. Certain hospitals may not allow husbands in the labour ward (although they can be present at delivery and often, if you are persuasive and there are no local ladies admitted, they will allow access).

All government hospitals now charge expats for maternity services and delivery, and costs vary depending on the package you choose. Private hospitals will be more expensive, although if you shop around you may be surprised to find that in some cases the difference between government and private is not as great as you might think.

No matter which you choose, if you have medical insurance check that it covers maternity costs – some have a limitation clause (you normally need to have been with the insurer for at least 12 months before conception) and some may not cover any costs at all.

Private hospitals offer maternity packages that include prenatal care, delivery and postnatal care for you and the baby. But remember that the price you are quoted by the hospital is usually for the most basic 'best case scenario' delivery. Should you have additional requirements, such as an epidural (when the anaesthetist must be present) or an assisted delivery (when the paediatrician must be present), you will then be charged extra. If you give birth by Caesarean section, for example, the cost is usually significantly higher and the hospital stay is notably longer (five days, compared to just two days for a standard delivery).

If you go to an independent gynaecologist for your prenatal care, you will usually be offered a choice of hospitals and delivery packages, where your doctor can attend for the birth. For more information on the practicalities of having a baby in Dubai, see p.139.

Obstetrics & Gynaecology Clinics

Prenatal care and maternity services are offered at many main hospitals (p.182) and specialist clinics (p.188); the medical facilities and practitioners listed below are those which exclusively offer or specialise in obstetrics, gynaecology and pre and post-natal care. A number of gynaecology clinics offer fertility testing, but only a few clinics offer assisted reproductive technology and IVF treatment.

Bourn Hall Clinic

Shk Hamdan Centre Al Mina **04 705 5055**
bournhall-clinic.ae
Map **2 J4** Metro **Al Jafiliya**
A state-of-the-art IVF clinic equipped with the latest technology and staffed by expert physicians, nurses and scientists working in the field of Assisted Reproductive Technology.

Medcare Hospital

Dr Leila Soudah Clinic

Villa 467B, Jumeira Rd Jumeira 1 **04 395 5591**
Map **1 T4** Metro **Business Bay**
An independent gynaecology clinic offering pre and post-natal care. Dr Leila is affiliated with American Hospital, so most of her patients deliver there.

Dubai Gynaecology & Fertility Centre

Dubai Healthcare City Umm Hurair 2 **04 439 3800**
dgfc.ae
Map **2 L7** Metro **Dubai Healthcare City**
This clinic specialises in assisted reproductive technology. It is one of the few facilities in Dubai that offers IVF treatment. A range of gynaecological services are also available.

Fakih IVF

Villa 37, Nr 65b & 32b Streets, Al Wasl Rd Jumeira 1 **04 349 7600**
fakihivf.com
Map **2 D4** Metro **Burj Khalifa/Dubai Mall**
One of the leading fertility centres in the region, it specialises in IVF and assisted reproductive technology. Dr. Michael Fakih is a recognised leader in the field of assisted reproduction and is responsible for over 10,000 IVF deliveries. His clinic provides infertility treatments as well as PGD for gender selection, PGD for single gene disorders, preserving fertility in cancer patients, and more.

German Clinic

Dubai Healthcare City Umm Hurair 2 **04 429 8346**
germanclinic-dubai.com
Map **2 L7** Metro **Dubai Healthcare City**
A specialist gynaecology, obstetrics and paediatrics clinic designed to meet German standards of healthcare, based in Dubai Healthcare City. Wellness, fertility and antenatal packages are also available.

Mitera Clinic

Dubai Healthcare City Umm Hurair 2 **04 363 5464**
miteraclinic.com
Map **2 L7** Metro **Dubai Healthcare City**
Dr Rihab Awad has a number of long term patients who have followed her from American Hospital to her new clinic. She is progressive in terms of stem cell technology and also teaches breast examinations when you have a check-up. If you're looking for a long-term gynaecologist and obstetrician then it's worth getting on her patient list.

Primavera Medical Centre

Dubai Healthcare City Umm Hurair 2 **04 375 4669**
primaveraclinic.com
Map **2 L7** Metro **Dubai Healthcare City**
This clinic is run by highly recommended obstetrician, gynaecologist and fertility specialist Dr Rosalie Sant.

Paediatrics

Most public and private hospitals and medical centres in Dubai have full time paediatricians on staff, with a growing number having devoted paediatric departments. American Hospital and Mediclinic Welcare Hospital (both private) have teams of specialist paediatric doctors, while Latifa Hospital (government) has dedicated paediatric surgeons and neurodevelopment therapists who care for children with special needs and learning difficulties. Dr Anil Gupta at American Hospital, Dr Zuhair Mahmandar at Emirates Hospital and Dr Loubser at Infinity Clinic (04 394 8994) are popular paediatricians among expat parents. The GMC Clinic in Jumeira has friendly paediatricians who will take the trauma out of doctor's appointments for your child, and who specialise in allergies (04 3494 880). Health Call sends doctors for home visits 24 hours a day, seven days a week and is a handy service if your child is too sick to take to a surgery or hospital (04 363 5343, health-call.com). The clinics listed below specifically focus on paediatric care. For a full listing of clinics and hospitals that offer paediatric services, visit askexplorer.com.

Troubled Minds

If your child is having trouble adjusting to life in Dubai, finding it hard to fit in at a new school or missing friends and family back home, an outside perspective can sometimes help. The Dubai Community Health Centre (p.210) offers child counselling and psychology services, which are useful for children with emotional difficulties and those whose parents are going through divorce. The Counselling & Development Clinic (p.210) deals with psychiatric disorders in children and offers a range of therapies including counselling and family therapy. Rashid Hospital also has a mental health unit.

Cooper Health Clinic

Villa 1188, Al Reef Villas, Al Wasl Rd Umm Suqeim 2 **04 348 6344**
cooperhealthclinic.com
Map **1 T5** Metro **Noor Islamic Bank**
This family medicine clinic offers paediatric, obstetric and gynaecology specialties as well as antenatal classes and infant massage. Dr Khan at the clinic is a popular paediatrician.

Isis The French Clinic

Dubai Healthcare City Umm Hurair 2 **04 429 8450**
isisclinicdubai.com
Map **2 L7** Metro **Dubai Healthcare City**
Located close to the Alliance Francaise (p.175) and the Ecole George Pompidou (04 337 4161) this practice offers specialist paediatric pulmonary care in addition to asthma, allergies, paediatric general practice and neonatal clinics. Standards are monitored by Dubai Healthcare City and the Harvard Medical School.

Working Mums

Mums who have been in a private sector job for more than one year can claim up to 45 days' maternity leave on full pay. This can only be used directly before and after the birth. See Having a Baby p.139.

Keith Nicholl Medical Centre

Villa 610B, Jumeira Rd Umm Suqeim 1 **04 394 1000**
keithnicholl.com
Map **2 U4** Metro **Noor Islamic Bank**
A child-friendly practice staffed by a paediatrician, paediatric nurses and a parent counsellor and educator. In addition to standard paediatric services, it offers well baby check-ups, immunisations, development checks and first aid courses for parents, nannies and other caregivers.

kidsFIRST Medical Center >*p.197*

Al Wasl Rd Umm Al Sheif **04 348 5437**
kidsfirstmc.com
Map **1 S5** Metro **First Gulf Bank**
In addition to paediatric medicine, kidsFIRST offers occupational therapy, speech therapy and physiotherapy for kids. The kidsFIRST team serves children across a full range of special needs, such as autism, ADHD, cerebral palsy and dyslexia.

Dentists & Orthodontists

Dentistry in Dubai is, like most other medical services, of a high standard with prices to match. Standard health insurance packages don't generally cover dentistry, unless it's for emergency treatment brought about by an accident. You may be able to pay an additional premium to cover dentistry, but the insurer may first want proof that you've had regular, six-monthly check-ups for the previous two or three years.

PAEDIATRIC CARE **Dr. K. R. Menon,** Paediatrician, Panacea Medical & Wellness Centre

There are certainly conditions that are more prevalent in the UAE and parents should be aware of these. Atopic dermatitis, for example, is a common and chronic allergic condition in infants and children that is characterised by dry and itchy skin. Its incidence is high in the UAE. It is caused by a combination of genetic and environmental factors. The condition is usually self limiting and symptomatic treatment is adequate in most cases.

If you have a health card, you're entitled to dentistry at your assigned hospital, and if your hospital doesn't have a dental section, they'll refer you to another public hospital that does, such as Rashid Hospital. You will be charged Dhs.100 for the visit, as well as for any other services that are performed, such as cleaning and filling. Service is generally good, but the rates may not be any lower than at a private dental clinic.

For a standard filling you could be looking at paying anywhere between Dhs.100 and Dhs.1,000. If it is root canal treatment that you need, expect to part with anything from Dhs.600 to Dhs.3,000.

As well as routine and surgical dental treatment, cosmetic dentistry is also big business in Dubai, so if you're looking for a smile make-over, there is plenty of choice.

The clinics listed below are specialist dental clinics. Many primary healthcare clinics and hospitals also offer dental services. For a full listing of dental practices and surgeons in Dubai, visit askexplorer.com.

American Dental Clinic

Villa 54 JMR, Nr Dubai Zoo, Jumeira Rd Jumeira 1 **04 344 0668**
americandentalclinic.com
Map **2 G4** Metro **Financial Centre**
Among a wide range of dental services available, this surgery specialises in neuromuscular dentistry. It offers a special service for patients with disabilities and those who suffer from dental phobia and anxiety attacks when visiting the dentist.

British Dental Clinic

Nr Emirates Bank International, Al Wasl Rd Jumeira 1 **04 342 1318**
britishdentalclinic.com
Map **2 F4** Metro **Financial Centre**
This clinic delivers a wide range of dental services in comfortable surroundings. Evening appointments are only available on request.

Charly Polyclinic

Sana Fashions Bldg Al Karama **04 337 9191**
charlypolyclinic.com
Map **2 K5** Metro **Al Karama**
This practice offers a range in dental services including cosmetic, laser, implant and general dentistry, orthodontics and oral surgery. Also based at the Charly Polyclinic are an ophthalmologist, gynaecologist and two homeopaths.

The Dental Centre

Dubai Healthcare City Umm Hurair 2 **04 375 2175**
the-dental-center.com
Map **2 L7** Metro **Dubai Healthcare City**
This bright and modern clinic in Healthcare City offers cutting edge dentistry including virtual consultations with overseas specialists. Routine dentistry and cosmetic procedures, including dental make-overs, are available.

The Dental SPA

Jumeira Rd Jumeira 3 **04 395 2005**
thedentalspa.org
Map **2 B4** Metro **Noor Islamic Bank**
Bringing a pampering touch to dentistry, this clinic offers spa-like surroundings with calming mood music and aromatherapy pillows for your general or cosmetic dental treatment. You can also opt for foot and hand massages during your check-up.

Dr Michaels Dental Clinic

Villa 418, Al Wasl Rd Jumeira 2 **04 349 5900**
drmichaels.com
Map **2 F5** Metro **Financial Centre**
This clinic prides itself on its personalised service, high safety standards, state-of-the-art dental equipment and an international team of dentists who deliver a full range of dental services at its two branches in Jumeira and Umm Suqeim (04 394 9433).

Drs Nicolas & Asp Clinic

Villa 446, Nr Jumeirah Beach Park Jumeira 3 **04 394 7777**
nicolasandasp.com
Map **2 D4** Metro **Business Bay**
In addition to general practice (see p.181), Drs Nicolas & Asp offers comprehensive dental services with resident dentists and dental surgeons, plus a state-of-the-art dental lab for creating implants, veneers and crowns on site. Additionally, cosmetic dentistry, advanced brace fitting and oral maxillofacial surgery are available at its various dental clinics. The practice also runs a postgraduate dental college in Healthcare City.

Dubai London Clinic Dental Centre

440A, Al Wasl Rd Jumeira 2 **04 344 4359**
dubailondonclinic.com
Map **1 T4** Metro **Business Bay**
Dubai London Clinic runs a dedicated dental surgery for routine dental care and cosmetic treatment; there is also a periodontics specialist.

Dubai School Of Dental Medicine > *p.199*

Dubai Healthcare City Umm Hurair 2 **04 424 8703**
dsdm.ac.ae
Map **2 L7** Metro **Dubai Healthcare City**
A specialist clinic offering a complete range of dental services including fillings, crowns and bridges, cosmetic dentistry including tooth whitening procedures, orthodontics, root canal treatment, oral surgery and periodontal treatment. There is also a paediatric dentistry department.

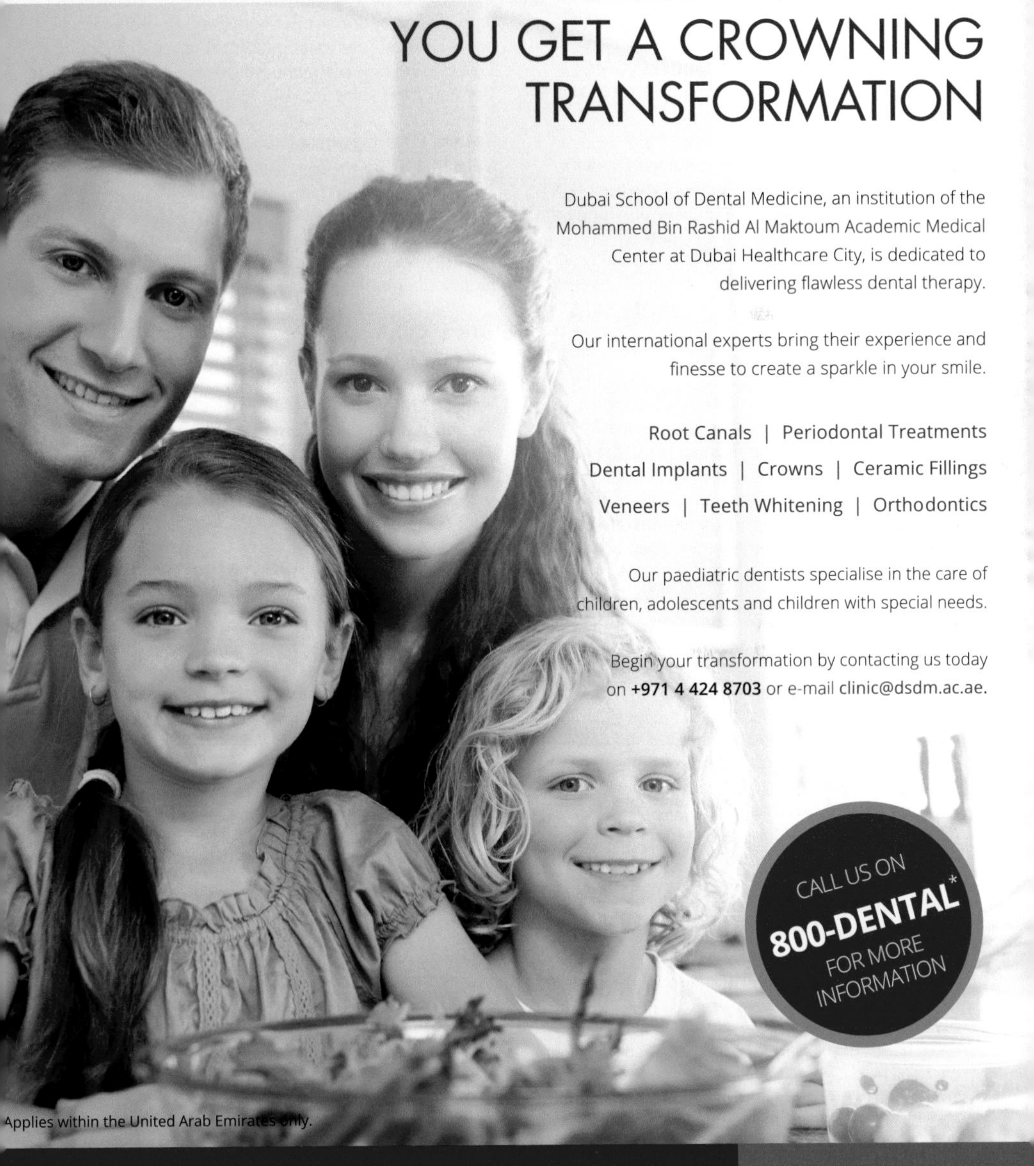
YOU GET A CROWNING
TRANSFORMATION
Dubai School of Dental Medicine, an institution of the Mohammed Bin Rashid Al Maktoum Academic Medical Center at Dubai Healthcare City, is dedicated to delivering flawless dental therapy.
Our international experts bring their experience and finesse to create a sparkle in your smile.
Root Canals | Periodontal Treatments
Dental Implants | Crowns | Ceramic Fillings
Veneers | Teeth Whitening | Orthodontics
Our paediatric dentists specialise in the care of children, adolescents and children with special needs.
Begin your transformation by contacting us today on +971 4 424 8703 or e-mail clinic@dsdm.ac.ae.
CALL US ON
800-DENTAL*
FOR MORE
INFORMATION
*Applies within the United Arab Emirates only.

Dubai Sky Clinic

BurJuman Business Tower, Shk Khalifa Bin Zayed St Al Mankhool **04 355 8808**
dubaiskyclinic.com
Map **2 L5** Metro **BurJuman**
Dubai Sky Clinic offers a full range of dental services from its high-tech clinic on the 21st floor of BurJuman Business Tower.

General Medical Centre Dental (GMC)

Magrudy's Mall, Jumeira Rd Jumeira 1 **04 344 9150**
gmcclinics.com
Map **2 H4** Metro **Financial Centre**
Using the latest laser dental technology, Dr Akel's promises painless treatment without the use of drills and anaesthetics, making it a good option for people with dental phobias.

Modern Dental Clinic

Dubai Knowledge Village Al Sufouh 1 **04 367 5091**
clinickv.com
Map **1 N5** Metro **Dubai Internet City**
A full range of routine, surgical and cosmetic dental procedures are available. In true Dubai bling-style, Modern Dental Clinic also offers dental jewellery. There is another branch at Uptown Mirdif (04 284 7888). Top Modern Dental Clinic in Dubai Marina (800 336 8478) has child-friendly rooms with cartoons painted on the walls, plus luxury treatment rooms with Marina views to soothe nervous dental patients.

Park Dental Centre

Al Mardoof Bldg, Nr BMW showroom, Shk Zayed Rd Al Safa 1 **04 346 6111**
parkdentalcenter.ae
Map **2 C6** Metro **Noor Islamic Bank**
Offers a comprehensive list of treatments including orthodontics, implantology, whitening and oral surgery, as well as general and cosmetic dentistry.

Seven Dental Centre

Nr HSBC, Jumeira Rd Jumeira 3 **04 395 2177**
sevendentalcentre.com
Map **2 C4** Metro **Business Bay**
A French dental practice with all French dental staff, offering a 'no pain' policy. Cosmetic, prosthetic and orthodontic procedures are available in addition to routine and children's dentistry.

Swedish Dental Clinic

Nasa Travel Bldg, Al Maktoum St Al Rigga **04 223 1297**
swedishdentalclinic.net
Map **2 N5** Metro **Union**
This experienced practice, established in Deira back in 1985, offers dental and orthodontic care for patients of all ages.

Swiss Dental Clinic

Crowne Plaza Dubai Trade Centre 1 **04 332 1444**
swissdentalclinic.com
Map **2 H5** Metro **Emirates Towers**
Dr Fedele at Swiss Dental Clinic offers a personable service and seeks to put patient's treatment anxieties to rest. General and aesthetic dentistry are available, as well as orthodontic treatments, and Dr Fedele will explain procedures to his patients thoroughly before undertaking any treatment. He speaks English, French, German, Italian and Spanish.

Talass Orthodontic & Dental Center

Villa 114, Nr Dubai Zoo, Jumeira Rd Jumeira 1 **04 349 2220**
Map **2 G4** Metro **Financial Centre**
Talass' dental surgeon specialises in cosmetic dentistry, including a number of crowns, veneers and teeth whitening procedures.

Tower Clinic

Dubai Healthcare City Umm Hurair 2 **04 362 2939**
towerclinic.com
Map **2 L7** Metro **Dubai Healthcare City**
This large, modern dental surgery offers general dentistry and orthodontics plus oral surgery and Zoom!, a one-hour, in-office tooth whitening treatment. Tooth replacements and inlays come with a six year guarantee.

Opticians & Ophthalmologists

You're never far from an optician in Dubai, with most malls and shopping centres having at least one outlet.

The dry, dusty environment in Dubai can cause problems for eyes, even if you've had no trouble in the past. Natural tear or refresher eye drops can increase eye comfort and are available in most opticians and pharmacies. Spending lengthy periods in air-conditioned environments can cause problems for contact lens wearers. Opticians can advise on the most suitable lenses. Sunglasses are an essential accessory in Dubai and prescription lenses are widely available.

For eye problems requiring specialist treatment, many hospitals and clinics, including Moorfields Eye Hospital (moorfields.ae) and The American Hospital Dubai (ahdubai.com), have well-equipped ophthalmology departments. If you want to ditch the glasses, a number of clinics and medical centres offer laser eye surgery. Prices start from around Dhs.4,000 per eye rising to around Dhs.7,500. All good laser surgery packages should include a complete year's follow-up care.

Even if you've never had an eye test in your life, you will need to undergo one in order to get a driving licence (see Driving Licence, p.55). This test can be carried out at most opticians for a minimal fee, sometimes free of charge.

Ophthalmologists & Vision Correction Clinics

The Atlanta Vision Clinic

Nr Jumeirah Beach Hotel, Jumeira Rd
Umm Suqeim 3 **04 348 6233**
dubailasik.com
Map **1 S5** Metro **First Gulf Bank**
This clinic specialises in Bausch & Lomb Z100 Zyoptix(TM) System vision correction, promising a more than 90% success rate for improved vision and in many cases to a 20/20 level. Patients can have a consultation to assess whether they are a candidate for LASIK.

Gulf Eye Centre

Fairmont Dubai Trade Centre 1 **04 329 1977**
gulfeyecenter.com
Map **2 J5** Metro **World Trade Centre**
Specialises in laser vision correction and surgery. Other ophthalmological services and eye-related cosmetic procedures are available.

Moorfields Eye Hospital > *p.203*

Dubai Healthcare City Umm Hurair 2 **04 429 7888**
moorfields.ae
Map **2 L7** Metro **Dubai Healthcare City**
The Dubai branch of this long-established and well-respected London eye hospital opened in 2006, providing high quality optometric, ophthalmic and orthoptic (relating to eye movement disorders) care. The services available range from simple eye tests to complex surgical procedures and ongoing non-surgical corrective treatment, with a special service for children's eyecare and assessment.

Sharif Eye Center

Dubai Healthcare City Umm Hurair 2 **04 423 3664**
sharifeyecenter.com
Map **2 L7** Metro **Dubai Healthcare City**
An eye surgery clinic specialising in vision correction.

Opticians

Al Jaber Optical Al Barsha 1, 04 341 1322, *aljabergallery.ae*
Barakat Optical Dubai Marina, 04 427 0565, *barakatoptical.com*
Dubai Opticals Dubai Marina, 04 435 5790, *dubaioptical.com*
Grand Optics Al Barsha 1, 04 341 0350, *grandoptics.com*
Lunettes Jumeira 1, 04 349 2270
Lutfi Opticals Centre Umm Hurair 2, 04 324 1865, *lutfioptical.com*
Magrabi Optical Al Barsha 1, 04 341 0445, *magrabioptical.com*
Optic Center Al Mizhar 1, 04 284 5550
OptiVision The Gardens, 04 368 5540, *dubaioptical.com*
Top Visions Optics 2nd December St, Al Satwa, 04 398 4888
Vision Express The Gardens, 04 368 5926, *alshaya.com*
Yateem Optician Al Mizhar 1, 04 284 5505, *yateemgroup.com*

Alternative Therapies

The UAE Ministry of Health grants licences to and administrates qualified practitioners of alternative medicine through its dedicated department for Traditional, Complementary & Alternative Medicine. Natural medicine can be very specialised, so when consulting with someone, do make sure that you ask questions and explain your needs and expectations. This will ensure that practitioners can indeed help with your situation. Prices vary greatly but are generally comparable to western medicine, however most insurance companies will not cover the costs of alternative therapies. As always, word of mouth is the best way of establishing who might offer the most appropriate treatment.

Yoga and Pilates are available at a number of studios and health clubs. Fitness-focused, clinical and classic, meditative forms of yoga are available (see Yoga & Pilates, p.352, 363). There is also a range of clinics that provide 'well-being' services, such as U Concept (p.209), which combines personal fitness, a balanced nutrition plan and numerous relaxation techniques, in order to help you achieve the healthy lifestyle you're looking for.

Al Karama Ayurvedic

Karama Centre Al Karama **04 335 5288**
Map **2 L5** Metro **Al Karama**
Operating for over 12 years, this centre is run by qualified professionals with expertise in the traditional systems of Ayurveda and herbal beauty care. They have all the necessary facilities to take care of healing, rejuvenation and beauty care. Separate areas are available for men and women.

The Art Of Living Foundation

Various locations **055 280 3815**
artofliving.org
Under the guidance of Sri Sri Ravi Shankar, this worldwide, non-profit NGO seeks social change through peaceful, individual empowerment. In Dubai, there are individual courses and corporate packages available, all of which teach the principles and practice of yoga, meditation and breathing techniques to bring inner peace and stress relief.

Check out the website for upcoming courses and timetable of all classes.

Beijing Tong Ren Tang Gulf

Dubai Healthcare City Umm Hurair 2 **04 435 6905**
trtgulf.com
Map **2 L7** Metro **Dubai Healthcare City**
A multi-specialty clinic that provides Chinese medicinal products and services including naturopathy, therapeutic massage, and traditional Chinese medicine to all nationalities.

Chaslu Dubai Well-being Centre

Villa 15, Street 7B, Jumeira Rd Umm Suqeim 1
04 395 5799
chasludubai.ae
Map **1 V5** Metro **Noor Islamic Bank**
A Chinese medical centre offering a wide range of traditional Chinese treatments, including acupuncture, massage and herbal remedies. Alternative treatments include flotation therapy, hot stone massage and cupping; a weight loss programme is also available, using natural herbal teas and remedies to help shed those excess pounds.

Detox Delight

Various locations **055 883 5072**
detox-delight.ae
A detox delivery service that brings well-being to your doorstep with daily deliveries of fresh-pressed juices, smoothies and vegetarian or raw food menus. Offerings include the comprehensive Juice and Dinner Delight menu and the entirely liquid, and vitamin-rich, Juice Delight menu.

Dubai Herbal & Treatment Centre

Nr Shk Hamdan's Palace Za'abeel 1 **04 335 1200**
dubaihtc.com
Map **2 J7** Metro **Dubai Healthcare City**
The Dubai Herbal & Treatment Centre offers a full range of Chinese, Indian and Arabic herbal medicines, while also offering nutrition advice and services as diverse as colonic hydrotherapy, homeopathy and allergy testing. The modern facility, which is unique in the GCC region, currently caters to outpatients only, but there are plans to expand the facility to offer in-patient services.

Feet First

Town Centre Jumeirah Jumeira 1
04 349 4334
feet1st.com
Map **2 F4** Metro **Financial Centre**
Alongside manicure and pedicure services, Feet First offers Oriental reflexology, deep tissue and shiatsu massage and acupressure facials in relaxing spa surroundings. A Chinese medicine slimming programme is also available. Branches are located around Dubai, with a men's studio at the Town Centre Jumeirah branch (04 349 4553).

GMCKS Pranic Energy Healing Centre

Ben Belisha Bldg, Shk Khalifa Bin Zayed Rd
Trade Centre 1 **04 336 0885**
pranichealingmea.com
Map **2 J5** Metro **World Trade Centre**
Intended as a complementary therapy to orthodox medicine, pranic healing is a method of rebalancing the body's energy field or aura and transferring life energy from the healer to the patient. As well as giving physical pain relief, it is said to help alleviate emotional, mental and spiritual problems.

The Healing Zone

Villa 71, Street 14A Umm Suqeim 3 **050 654 2998**
thehealingzone.net
Map **1 T5** Metro **Noor Islamic Bank**
This complementary therapy practice offers treatments including allergy testing, ear candling, and crystal therapy. Reiki training classes and other therapy workshops are held regularly.

Holistic Healing Medical Centre

Villa 101, Nr Police Academy, Al Wasl Rd
Umm Suqeim 3 **04 348 7172**
healthholistic.com
Map **1 T4** Metro **First Gulf Bank**
In addition to more common forms of alternative medicine such as Chinese medicine, Ayurveda and homeopathy, this centre offers iridology (medical diagnosis through the study of the iris), etiopathy (a form of diagnosis and painless manipulation of the joints and bones), non-linear health screening, colon hydrotherapy and yoga therapy.

King China Acupuncture Centre

Al Hana Centre, Al Mankhool Rd Al Jafiliya
04 398 5548
doctorzhengnan.com
Map **2 J5** Metro **Al Jafiliya**
At this small clinic Dr Zheng Nan specialises in acupuncture for conditions from chronic pain, fatigue and infertility to smoking cessation and weight loss. Cupping therapy, reflexology and meridian therapy are also available. The clinic may not be the most salubrious but it's good value and Dr Zheng is highly respected within the community.

Well-Being Medical Centre

Nr Choithrams, Al Wasl Rd Umm Suqeim 2
04 348 4406
well-beingmedicalcentre.com
Map **1 T5** Metro **Noor Islamic Bank**
Provides all manner of natural and alternative therapies, such as herbal medicine, homeopathy, therapeutic massage and acupuncture. Also offers useful packages to aid fertility and combat stress, allergies, pain and nutritional problems.

Sports Injuries

Many Dubai residents lead an active lifestyle, working hard and then playing harder. But accidents and injuries do happen, so whether you got roughed up playing rugby, pulled something in the gym or put your back out moving a wardrobe you'll be pleased to hear that the city has some excellent facilities with specialists from all around the world to help you on the road to recovery.

Chiropractic and osteopathic treatments are non-invasive and aim to improve the functioning of the nervous system or blood supply to the body through manipulation of the skeleton. Chiropractic therapy focuses on realigning the joints, especially those of the spinal column, while osteopathy combines skeletal manipulation with muscular massage.

Orthopaedics concerns the repair of damaged bones and joints, whether sustained through injury, disease or genetics. Pilates is said to be the safest form of neuromuscular reconditioning and back strengthening available. Classes are offered by a number of gyms as part of their group exercise schedules. For specialist Pilates studios, see p.352.

In addition to the clinics listed below, which specialise in various kinds of musculoskeletal assessment and treatment, Drs Nicolas & Asp (p.198) offers sports medicine and physiotherapy, as well as a range of other exercises that can help prevent future sports injuries.

California Chiropractic & Sports Medicine Center

Dubai Healthcare City Umm Hurair 2 **04 429 8292**
californiachiropracticcenter.com
Map **2 L7** Metro **Dubai Healthcare City**
Partnering a number of the UAE's major sports teams, groups and events, this clinic is a real sports specialist with experts who know their golf, running and cycling every bit as well as they know their bones, tendons and muscles.

Canadian Chiropractic & Natural Health Centre

Al Wasl Rd Jumeira 2 **04 342 0900**
Map **2 E5** Metro **Business Bay**
This clinic offers chiropractic treatments and acupuncture as well as reflexology. They also treat sports injuries and give advice for people with long term back problems.

Chiropractic Health & Medical Centre

Villa 967, Al Wasl Rd Al Manara **04 348 8262**
dubaichiropractor.net
Map **1 T5** Metro **First Gulf Bank**
This health clinic treats a range of health problems and sports injuries including ADHD, headaches, stress, scoliosis, neck pain, asthma and pain following accidents. A number of physiotherapists and a nutritionist are also based at the clinic.

Dubai Bone & Joint Center

Dubai Healthcare City Umm Hurair 2 **04 423 1400**
dbaj.ae
Map **2 L7** Metro **Dubai Healthcare City**
Focuses on research into and treatment of musculo-skeletal problems. Well-equipped with diagnostic technologies, the centre offers rehabilitative services including physiotherapy and sports medicine, and has a very high standard of facilities for joint replacements, orthopaedic, and back and neck surgeries.

Dubai Physiotherapy & Family Medicine Clinic > *p.205*

Town Centre Jumeirah Jumeira 1 **04 349 6333**
dubaiphysio.com
Map **2 F4** Metro **Financial Centre**
Open since 1992, this is one of Dubai's most established clinics. Specialising in physiotherapy for musculoskeletal disorders and sports injuries, it also offers family medicine, sports therapy, osteopathy, acupuncture, nutrition, speech therapy, orthotics, podiatry and psychology.

Emirates European Medical Centre

Villa 119, Al Thanya St Umm Suqeim 2 **04 348 1166**
chiropracticdubai.com
Map **1 T5** Metro **First Gulf Bank**
Located in the Emirates European Medical Centre is Chiropractic Dubai, which has a team of experienced chiropractors and physiotherapists who can diagnose all manner of injuries and create a treatment plan to fit the individual's needs.

OrthoSports Medical Center > *p.207*

Jumeira Rd Jumeira 1 **04 345 0601**
orthosp.com
Map **2 H4** Metro **World Trade Centre**
Specialises in orthopaedics and sports medicine, offering physiotherapy, hydrotherapy and orthopaedic surgery to international standards. Sports therapy for fitness and injury rehabilitation and hydrotherapy for a range of conditions including obesity, arthritis, back pain and joint replacements are also available.

Osteopathic Health Centre

Al Wasl Rd Umm Suqeim 2 **04 348 7366**
osteopathydubai.com
Map **1 T5** Metro **Noor Islamic Bank**
This practice has a number of therapists practising osteopathy in addition to physiotherapists, exercise therapists, a kinesiologist, and massage and orthotics specialists. The centre also offers antenatal classes, and hosts a number of support and discussion groups.

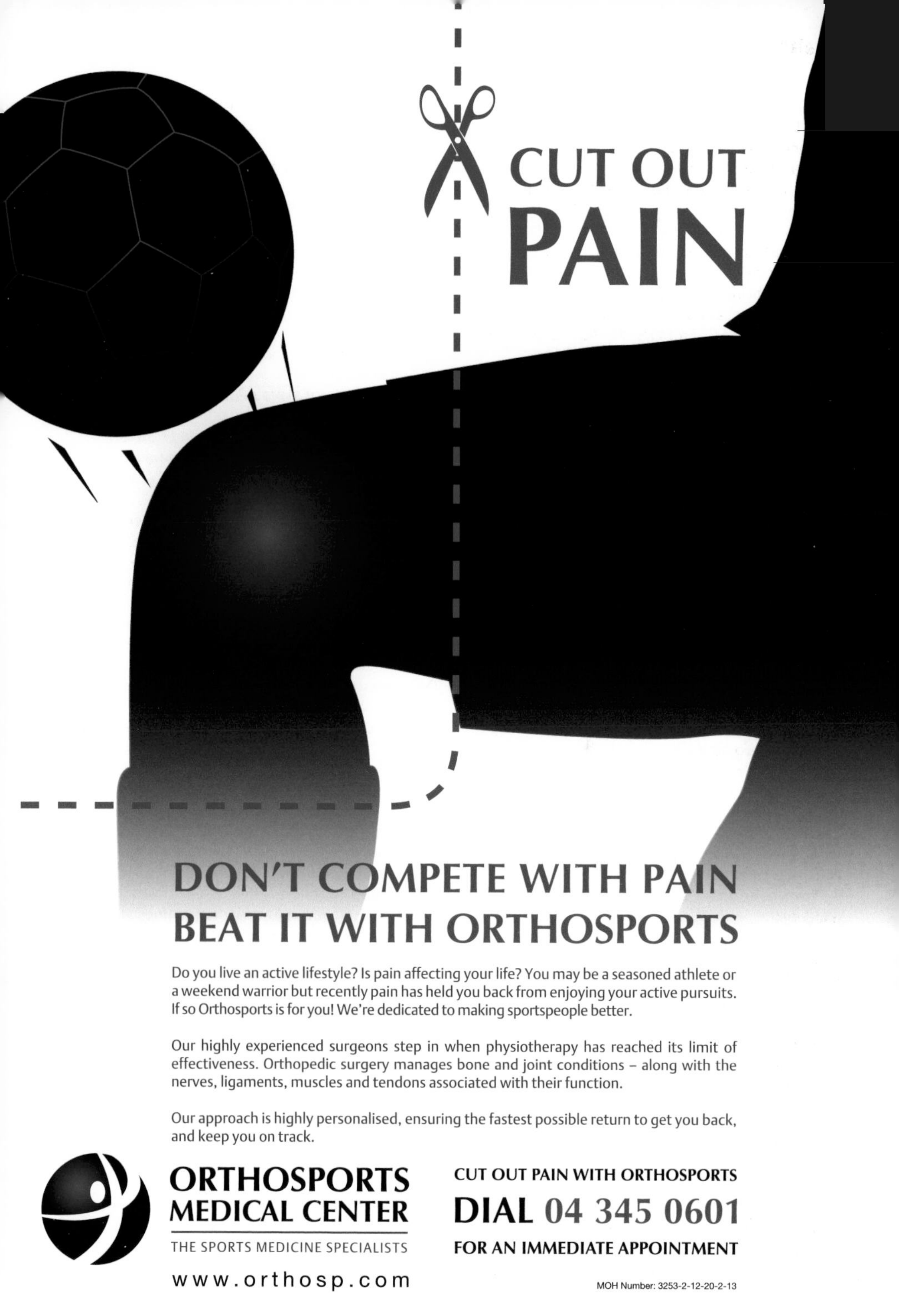
CUT OUT
PAIN
DON'T COMPETE WITH PAIN
BEAT IT WITH ORTHOSPORTS
Do you live an active lifestyle? Is pain affecting your life? You may be a seasoned athlete or a weekend warrior but recently pain has held you back from enjoying your active pursuits. If so Orthosports is for you! We're dedicated to making sportspeople better.
Our highly experienced surgeons step in when physiotherapy has reached its limit of effectiveness. Orthopedic surgery manages bone and joint conditions – along with the nerves, ligaments, muscles and tendons associated with their function.
Our approach is highly personalised, ensuring the fastest possible return to get you back, and keep you on track.
ORTHOSPORTS
MEDICAL CENTER
THE SPORTS MEDICINE SPECIALISTS
www.orthosp.com
CUT OUT PAIN WITH ORTHOSPORTS
DIAL 04 345 0601
FOR AN IMMEDIATE APPOINTMENT
MOH Number: 3253-2-12-20-2-13

Up & Running Integrated Sports Medical Center
Al Wasl Rd Al Manara **04 328 4600**
upandrunningdubai.com
Map **1 U5** Metro **Noor Islamic Bank**
Another sports medicine and rehabilitation centre that you'll find teaming up with major events and local teams, staff here are mainly UK and Australia-trained with extensive backgrounds in treating sports and occupational injuries. Also offers VO2 max testing, sports massage and sessions such as clinical pilates.

Nutritionists & Slimming
With such a variety of dining options in Dubai, and with the emphasis very much on lounging and relaxing, it's easy to let your diet suffer and pile on the pounds. Thankfully, a number of slimming clubs and nutritionists are on hand to help. In addition, plenty of clinics and hospitals offer nutritional advice weight loss surgeries. Dietary advice for diabetes, allergies, menopause, pregnancy and digestive disorders such as coeliacs is also available.

Of the hospitals, Mediclinic Welcare Hospital (p.186) provides a dietary counselling service, where a team of dieticians and nutritionists will educate and evaluate the patient's eating habits, and then point them in the right direction with a unique diet plan. The American Hospital (p.182) offers a food and nutrition service managed and provided by ADNH Compass. The hospital also runs a Diabetic Centre of Excellence. Emirates Hospital (p.184) has a weight reduction programme that uses liquid supplements and a very low calorie diet. The hospital has dietician and nutrition experts who specialise in medically supervised weight reduction programmes, obesity in children, obesity in diabetic patients and patients with high blood pressure or cholesterol. It also offers weight loss programmes through gastric band fitting.

For a more holistic approach to nutrition, the Osteopathic Health Centre offers a complete nutritionist service (p.206). Many small clinics and family practices have dieticians on staff including Cooper Health Clinic (p.196), Dubai London Clinic Medical & Surgical Centre (p.198) and Drs Nicolas & Asp (p.198). The Organic Foods and Cafe (p.417) sells fresh organic and biodynamic food and supplements, and a nutritionist is on hand at all its stores to give tailormade advice on supplements and vitamins, detox, weight loss and aromatherapy.

BiteRite
Lotus Marina & Spa Hotel Apartments Dubai Marina **04 292 8888**
biterite.ae
Map **1 J5** Metro **Jumeirah Lakes Towers**
Eat a nutritionally balanced meal in the cafe or use its tailormade healthy eating service. Low fat, low calorie, low sugar and low cholesterol meals are devised by dieticians and endocrinologists, freshly prepared and delivered direct to your door. The BiteRite Plan offers an online menu with over 100 varieties of meals.

Body Smart HYPOXI
Fitness First Health Club, Meadows Town Centre Emirates Living **04 363 8318**
bodysmart.ae
Map **2 N8** Metro **Nakheel**
Hypoxi combines cardiovascular exercise with applied pressure to increase the blood flow to fatty problem areas. Improvements can be noticed within four weeks and most results can be achieved within 12 weeks with three sessions a week. As a non-chemical, non-surgical therapy there are few side effects. Basically, you wear what feels like a wet suit and speed walk on a treadmill or cycle inside a vacuum pod. For most people, results are felt in reduced inches (and each session the trainer will measure your chest, waist and hips), although weight loss can also occur. There is also a Hypoxi studio at the Aviation Club (04 282 4122, aviationclub.ae).

Eternal MedSpa
Villa 397, Jumeira Rd Jumeira 2 **04 344 0008**
eternelmedspa.com
Map **2 D4** Metro **Business Bay**
Offers mesotherapy for cellulite treatment, botox, laser hair removal, slimming treatments as well as general wellness coaching.

Good Habits
Various locations **04 344 9692**
goodhabitsuae.com
Good Habits helps people lose weight through healthy eating. Meetings are held every week at various locations all over Dubai, and often include food tasting and cookery demos. Exercise classes are also organised and individual programmes are offered over six week periods. They have a cookery book available on the website with 90 recipes to keep you on the straight and narrow.

Health Factory
Warehouse 26 Al Quoz Industrial 3 **04 347 3808**
healthfactory.com
Map **1 T7** Metro **First Gulf Bank**
This nutrition company offers a variety of weight loss and weight management programmes. Contact Health Factory and first you'll do a consultation with one of their expert nutritionists, then you'll be sent three meals a day that'll help you to lose weight or get healthy according to your specific calorie and nutrient needs. Programmes also include a customised diet plan for mothers-to-be, a diabetic meal plan, and healthy eating for kids.

Lifestyle UAE

Cooper Health Clinic Umm Suqeim 2 **04 348 6344**
lifestyle-uae.com
Map **1 T5** Metro **Noor Islamic Bank**
Belinda Rennie is based at Cooper Health Clinic. She promotes a mind, body and spirit balance through healthy eating. Her nutritional advice focuses on meal planning based on lifestyle and finding the right balance of food, homeopathic mineral salts, and probiotic and wholefood supplements to achieve well being. Her approach is suitable for pregnancy, stress management, weight loss and a digestive disorders.

Live'ly

Al Manara **04 348 1008**
lively.ae
Map **1 T5** Metro **First Gulf Bank**
This new centre specialises in nutritional, educational and catering services to help people to manage their weight and live healthier. Clients are given personalised meal plans and support by a team of professional dieticians.

Perfect Figure

The Aviation Club Al Garhoud **800 497 694**
perfectfigure.ae
Map **2 N8** Metro **GGICO**
This studio creates personal weight loss and toning programmes, which combine exercise using Hypoxi and Vacunaut machines with nutritional advice.

Right Bite

Various locations **04 338 8763**
right-bite.com
Right Bite offers a tailormade healthy eating service. Tasty, low calorie, low fat and low cholesterol meals, devised by their own dieticians, are freshly prepared and delivered to your door.

Slim Spa

206 Al Attar Tower DIFC **056 745 3371**
slimspa.ae
Map **2 G6** Metro **Financial Centre**
There's a wide range of non-invasive treatments for weight and inch-loss, cellulite reduction, body sculpting, anti-ageing and rejuvenation. Slim Spa also offers personalised programmes, four and eight-week packages, massages and facial treatments.

U Concept

The Village Jumeira 1 **04 344 9060**
uconcept6.com
Map **2 H4** Metro **Emirates Towers**
U Concept offers a 'unique lifestyle service', combining personal training, nutritional advice and a range of relaxation treatments. A consultant will help you design a 12 week programme that allows you to meet your personal health and fitness goals, lose weight and cope with stress and advises on nutrition.

VLCC

Emarat Compound, Shk Zayed Rd Trade Centre 1 **800 8522**
vlccinternational.com
Map **2 F5** Metro **Financial Centre**
VLCC offers hair removal, beauty services and customised weight loss programmes which combine dietary advice, exercise and toning and detox therapies. There are women-only centres at Dubai Marina (04 447 1488) and Uptown Mirdif (04 288 4880); visit the website for a full list of locations.

Cosmetic Treatment & Surgery

Dubai is becoming established as a luxury healthcare destination. This is, in part, due to a concerted marketing effort by Dubai Government to attract the best renowned names in the medical industry to centres like Dubai Healthcare City. Cosmetic surgery is at the heart of this growing industry and the city now boasts a mass of clinics that specialise in reducing, reshaping, removing and enlarging various parts of your anatomy. The clinics listed below are exclusively cosmetic practices, but many of the private hospitals and independent clinics offer cosmetic services including aesthetic and reconstructive surgery. As with all medical facilities, standards are generally high, but it's worth checking out a few different clinics before you go under the knife. If you want a bit of sprucing and don't fancy slicing, a lot of the cosmetic clinics will do botox and other non-surgical treatments.

Cosmetic Treatment Clinics

Aesthetica Clinic Umm Hurair 2, 04 429 8533, *aestheticaclinic.com*
American Academy Of Cosmetic Surgery Hospital Umm Hurair 2, 04 423 7600, *aacsh.com*
Biolite Aesthetic Clinic Umm Hurair 2, 04 375 2122, *biolitedubai.com*
Cosmesurge Jumeira 2, 04 344 5915, *cosmesurge.com*
Dermalase Clinic Jumeira 2, 04 349 7880, *dermalase.ae*
Dubai Cosmetic Surgery Al Manara, 04 348 5575, *dubaicosmeticsurgery.com*
Dubai Medical Village Jumeira 3, 04 395 6200, *medicalvillage.ae*
EuroMed Clinic Jumeira 3, 04 394 5422, *euromedclinicdubai.com*
General Medical Centre (GMC) Trade Centre 2, 04 331 3544, *gmcclinics.com*
Gulf Specialty Hospital Al Muraqqabat, 04 269 9717, *gshdubai.net*
Imperial Healthcare Institute Umm Hurair 2, 04 439 3737, *imperialhealth.org*
Kaya Skin Clinic Mirdif, 04 283 9200, *kayaclinic.com*

London Centre For Aesthetic Surgery Umm Hurair 2, 04 375 2393, *dubaiplasticsurgery.ae*
Rebecca Treston Aesthetics At EuroMed Jumeira 3, 04 394 5422, *euromedclinicdubai.com*

Counselling & Therapy

Starting a new life in a different country can be a stressful process, and whether you are new to the city or not, sometimes it can help just to talk through whatever issues or anxieties you may be facing. Mental health services in the UAE are not as developed as in some other countries; Al Amal is Dubai's only psychiatric hospital, and Rashid Hospital (p.186) has a dedicated psychiatric ward, although levels of care here are generally high.

There are however a number of well-regarded therapy centres offering services including counselling, psychodynamic therapy, family and couples' therapy, paediatric psychiatry, treatment of mental health disorders and learning difficulties support. Dubai Community Health Centre offers a range of counselling and psychiatric services and provides space for support group meetings; it comes highly recommended, as does the Counselling & Development Clinic. In addition to the clinics and centres listed below, the British Medical Consulting Centre (p.188) and Drs Nicolas & Asp (p.198) are medical practices that have counsellors, family therapists and psychiatrists on staff. Dubai Herbal & Treatment Centre has a psychodynamic counsellor, a psychologist and a learning specialist, and is recommended for child counselling services (p.210).

Counselling & Development Clinic

Nr Jumeirah Beach Park Jumeira 3 **04 394 6122**
drmccarthypsychologyclinic.com
Map **2 D4** Metro **Business Bay**
This centre offers psychology services for adults and children. As well as assessing and treating psychological disorders, the clinic offers counselling, family therapy and couples' clinics. It is particularly well regarded for the treatment and management of bipolar disorder (manic depression), Asperger's syndrome and narcissism.

Dubai Community Health Centre

Jumeira Rd Jumeira 3 **04 395 3939**
dubaicommunityhealthcentre.org
Map **2 C4** Metro **Business Bay**
This private, non-profit facility provides mental health and developmental care services in a friendly and welcoming environment. In addition to counselling, psychology, family and marriage therapy, speech and language therapy, and parenting courses, it offers occupational therapy, dietetics, special needs education, homeopathy and yoga. Call to make an appointment.

Health Psychology UAE

Well Woman Clinic Al Satwa **04 332 7117**
healthpsychuae.com
Map **2 J5** Metro **World Trade Centre**
Dr Melanie C Schlatter is a health psychologist helping people to learn to manage the psychological impact of illnesses and medical conditions that they have. She also offers preventative health psychology in the form of stress management and coping with anxiety, phobias (particularly medical related such as the fear of injection needles), depression, grief and anger. Her website covers some of the main questions people have about receiving psychological help.

Human Relations Institute

Dubai Knowledge Village Al Sufouh 1 **04 331 4777**
hridubai.com
Map **2 L7** Metro **Dubai Internet City**
The HRI's services include clinical, forensic, organisational, educational and domestic psychology. It offers counselling, life coaching, psychotherapy and workshops for conditions including anxiety, phobias, addiction, behavioural and eating disorders, stress, low self-confidence and depression.

LifeWorks Counselling & Development

996 Al Wasl Rd Umm Suqeim 1 **04 394 2464**
counsellingdubai.com
Map **1 V5** Metro **Noor Islamic Bank**
This centre has counsellors with experience dealing with people from all walks of life; whether you need self-confidence, personal insight, CBT, marriage counselling, help with phobias or would like to join in one of the workshops call to make an appointment.

FITNESS

While the Dubai lifestyle can be conducive to inactivity and overindulgence, the great weather, open spaces and varied terrain beyond the city mean that it's a pretty active place too. So whether you need to shift that Dubai stone, or want to hit the beach bootcamp-style, you'll find plenty of reasons to get off your sofa. If you want to get involved with a new sport, check out the listings in Activities & Hobbies, p.320.

Gyms & Fitness Clubs

It's not uncommon to have access to fitness facilities in your accommodation, whether you live in an apartment block, community setting or independent villa. Some of the newer apartment towers have excellent facilities with pools, squash courts and gymnasiums available for residents' use. Other places have a pool and some have sports courts. See Housing (p.84) for an overview of accommodation facilities. There are a number of independent gyms and fitness centres. Most charge a monthly or yearly membership fee for access to facilities – look out in the local press for joining discounts and special offers. Most gyms offer a daily rate or visitor pass for around Dhs.100 to Dhs.250 and run aerobics classes, which may be included in the membership fees or paid for on a class-by-class basis.

Slimming Made Easy

If you can't stand the thought of going to the gym, try Hypoxi therapy. The training system is said to maximise cellulite and fat burn by combining exercise with vacuum suction. The method is non-invasive and painless and can be directed at those problem areas where you find it hard to lose weight. Visible results can be noticed after a couple of sessions and most results can be achieved in around 12 weeks. The treatment is gaining in popularity and you can try it at Techno Shape (050 255 9402), BodySmart (Meadows Town Centre, 04 363 8318), Perfect Figure Studio (800 497 694) and Active Plus Health Club & Spa (04 336 0001) in Oud Metha. Find out more at hypoxi.net.

In addition, many hotels offer memberships to their fitness facilities. Although usually more expensive, these gyms are often quieter and sometimes include access to spa facilities, so it's worth ringing around to compare quotes before you sign up. Some of the more popular ones are Le Meridien Mina Seyahi, the Grand Hyatt and Jebel Ali Golf Resort & Spa (see Dubai Hotels, p.234).

If losing weight is your goal, companies such as U Concept (p.209) and Time For Change (DHTC) (04 336 0455) can create a personal programme combining exercise and diet. If your motivation is your biggest exercise hurdle, there are options ranging from personal trainers to group fitness classes, and if you're serious about getting fit, military-style bootcamps, held in the early morning or evening on Dubai's beaches, are intensive training sessions aimed at increasing fitness levels in a short time frame. For more information on slimming and nutrition see p.208.

For the more sociable types, all kinds of sports are on offer in Dubai and for most of them you can find like-minded people to play with. See Activities p.320 for more details.

American Fitness Umm Suqeim 1, 050 198 0663, *americanfitness.me*
The Aviation Club Al Garhoud, 04 230 8560, *jumeirah.com*
Bodylines Health & Fitness Centre Trade Centre 1, 04 343 8000
Cleopatra's Spa & Wellness Umm Hurair 2, 04 324 7700, *wafi.com*
Core Studio Dubai Marina, 050 922 6247, *coredirection.com*
Crowne Fitness Trade Centre 1, 04 331 1111, *crowneplaza.com*
Dubai Ladies Club Jumeira 2, 04 349 9922, *dubailadiesclub.com*
Exhale Fitness Dubai Marina, 04 424 3777, *exhaledubai.com*
Fidelity Fitness Club Jumeirah Lakes Towers, 04 451 1133, *fidelityfitnessclub.com*
Fitness First Trade Centre 2, 04 363 7444, Emirates Living, 04 362 7785, *fitnessfirstme.com*
Fitness O2 Al Barsha 1, 04 374 5465, *fitness02.com*
Goal Attained Various locations, 056 693 9258, *goalattained.com*
The Health Club Trade Centre 2, 04 319 8888, *jumeirahemiratestowers.com*
In Shape Ladies Fitness Club Umm Suqeim 1, 04 395 5718, *inshapeme.com*
India Club Oud Metha, 04 337 1112, *indiaclubdubai.com*
Insportz Club Al Quoz Industrial 3, 04 347 5833, *insportzclub.com*
Motion Fitness Umm Suqeim 3, 04 328 2538, *motionfitnesscenter.com*
Original Fitness Co Trade Centre 2, 04 313 2081, *originalfitnessco.com*
The Pavilion Sports Club Umm Suqeim 3, 04 406 8800, *jumeirahbeachhotel.com*
The Quay Healthclub Al Sufouh 1, 04 366 6821, *jumeirah.com/quayhealthclub*
Sharjah Wanderers Sports Club Sharjah, 06 566 2105, *sharjahwanderers.com*
ShuiQi Fitness Centre Palm Jumeirah, 04 426 1020, *atlantisthepalm.com*
Sports Fit Al Mizhar 1, 04 236 2111
Spring Dubai Various locations, 050 378 7367, *springdubai.com*
Surf Fit Umm Suqeim 3, 050 504 3020, *surfingdubai.com*
Synergy Al Barsha 1, 04 454 1471
Talise Fitness Trade Centre 2, 04 319 8660, *jumeirah.com*
U Energy Dubai International Financial Centre (DIFC), Trade Centre 2, 04 422 8721, *uconcept6.com*

WELL-BEING

Whether it's shifting the Dubai stone, hitting the beach bootcamp-style, being pampered at a health spa, receiving meditation advice from a guru, or limbering up with a body massage: whatever your definition of well-being there's a good chance that someone, somewhere in Dubai will have the necessary facilities and skills to have you feeling better in no time.

Personal Grooming

Beauty is big business in Dubai. Salons are everywhere and with certain services such as manicures, pedicures and waxing costing less than in many other international cities, you may find that a trip to the beauticians becomes a more regular diary fixture than at home. Fridays are usually the busiest day so make sure you book ahead; on other days, many places accept walk-ins or bookings at short notice. In the lead up to big social events, such as Ladies' Day at the Dubai World Cup (p.26), appointments at the best salons are like gold dust, so make sure you book in plenty of time.

In hotels you'll find both male and female stylists working alongside each other, but in establishments located outside hotels, only female stylists are permitted to work in ladies' salons. These salons are very private and men are not permitted inside – even the windows are covered.

There are also numerous salons aimed primarily at Arabic ladies, which specialise in henna designs, so look out for a decorated hand poster in salon windows. The traditional practice of painting henna on the hands and feet, especially for weddings or special occasions, is still very popular with UAE Nationals. For tourists, a design on the hand, ankle or shoulder can make a great memento – it will cost about Dhs.40 and the intricate brown patterns fade after two to three weeks.

There are plenty of options for male grooming as well, with barbershops and salons to suit all budgets, and a growing number of specialist men's spas. So whether you're after a short back and sides, a traditional shave, a chest wax or a facial, there's something for all.

Many hair salons and nail bars offer a combination of services, but as the quality, prices and service vary greatly, trial and error and word of mouth are the best ways to find a dependable salon. The listings below are a good starting place if you're new to the city. For a full listing of hairdressers, beauty salons and nail bars, visit askexplorer.com.

Beauty Salons & Nail Bars

Beauty salons and nail bars are dotted all over Dubai, so whether you need plucking, waxing, polishing or buffing, there is plenty of choice. The Dubai Mall (p.426) houses a number of flagship stores for international beauty and cosmetics brands, many offering in-store makeovers and skin consultations. Spaces (04 515 4393) has special offers on Mondays, with the discounted treatment changing weekly. 'The Organic Glow Beauty Lounge is an environmentally minded beauty-haven, while Elche (p.216) offers skin consultations and treatments using 100% organic products.

With all-year round sunshine holding endless possibilities for strappy shoes, flip-flops, sandals and summery wedges, there's no excuse for having less than perfect pinkies. It's worth trying out a few different nail bars to find one that you really like because the chances are you'll be making regular appearances there. N.Bar, The Nail Spa and NStyle are all popular chains with numerous branches around Dubai.

Hello Kitty Spa (hellokittybeautyspa.com) offers a kitty-cure for girls, who can have their nails painted in pretty colours and decorated with stars and flowers – a great idea for some special mother and daughter time. Tips & Toes Nail Haven (tipsandtoes.com) offers slimming treatments in addition to a full range of nail, beauty and massage services. In addition to the salons below, many spas and hairdressers offer a side-line in beauty treatments.

Aroushi Beauty Salon Oud Metha, 04 336 2794, *aroushibeautysalon.com*
Chez Toi Various locations, 04 339 7117, *cheztoibeauty.com*
Clarins Boutique Downtown Dubai, 04 434 0522, *clarins.com*
Color Nail Beauty Lounge Al Quoz Industrial 1, 04 341 8848
Dermalogica Downtown Dubai, 04 339 8250, *dermalogica.com*
Elyazia Beauty Center International City, 04 422 6149, *elyaziabeautycenter.com*
Essentials Beauty Salon Al Safa 1, 04 395 5909, *essentialsdubai.com*
Hello Kitty Spa Jumeira 1, 04 344 9598, *hellokittybeautyspa.com*
N.Bar Jumeira 1, 04 346 1100, *thegroomingco.com*
Nail Moda Umm Hurair 2, 04 327 9088, *nailmoda.com*
The Nail Spa Al Garhoud, 04 282 1617
The Nail Spa Downtown Dubai, 04 339 9078, *thenailspa.com*
Nail Station Jumeira 1, 04 349 0123
Nail Zone Jumeira 2, 04 344 6969
Nails At Home Various locations, 04 298 0707, *nailsathome.ae*
Natalie Beauty Saloon JLT Jumeirah Lakes Towers, 04 435 8077, *nataliebeautysalon.com*
NStyle Nail Lounge Al Barsha 1, 04 341 3300, *nstyleintl.com*
The Organic Glow Beauty Lounge Jumeira 3, 04 380 4666, *organicglowuae.com*
Pastels Umm Suqeim 2, 04 388 3534, *pastels-salon.com*
Tilia & Finn Dubai Marina, 04 438 0636, *tiliaandfinn.ae*
Tips & Toes Dubai Marina, 04 429 3477, *tipsntoeshaven.com*
Version Francaise Dubai Marina, 04 360 5360, *version-francaise.com*

Hairdressers

If you're just looking for a trim and tidy-up, most malls have salons which take walk-ins. Usually, you'll need an appointment for a hairdresser, although you rarely need to book very far in advance. Salons normally charge separately for cutting and blow drying hair. Average prices for ladies are around Dhs.150 for a cut and Dhs.100 for a blow dry, and for men Dhs.70 for a wash and cut, although there's something for all budgets. There are a number of small barber shops and salons around Karama, Satwa, Bur Dubai and Deira. Gents can get a haircut (and relaxing head massage) for as little as Dhs.15, with the option of a shave with a cut-throat razor for a few extra dirhams. Ladies should be able to find salons where a basic haircut starts at around Dhs.60.

Straight To The Point

Say goodbye to wavy manes and hello to long-lasting straight tresses. Keratin hair straightening treatments are on offer at salons across Dubai, with prices starting from around Dhs.1,000 for short hair.

Many beauty salons and some spas offer hairdressing, so check the listings below for additional recommendations.

Alain & Milad Al Sufouh 1, 04 390 2815, *alainmilad.com*
Amaya Salon & Spa Oud Metha, 04 335 1101, *idm.ae*
Bare Gents Salon The Gardens, 04 368 5111, *baresalongroup.com*
Bilal Le Salon Jumeira 1, 04 346 1111
Camille Albane Dubai Festival City, 04 232 8550, *camillealbane.com*
Carla K Styling Al Wasl, 04 343 8544, *carla-k.com*
Code Men's Salon Jumeira 1, 04 386 9909, *codemenssalon.com*
The Edge Hair & Beauty Salon Umm Hurair 2, 04 324 0024
Elyazia Beauty Center International City, 04 422 6149, *elyaziabeautycenter.com*
Franck Provost Al Barsha 1, 04 341 3245, *franckprovostdubai.com*
The Gold Salon Trade Centre 2, 04 321 1425, *goldsalondubai.com*
The Hair Corridor Al Safa 1, 04 394 5622, *thehaircorridor.com*
The Hair Shop Trade Centre 2, 04 332 6616, *hairshop-uae.com*
Hair Station Mirdif, 04 288 6483
Hair@Pyramids Umm Hurair 2, 04 324 1490, *pyramidsrestaurantsatwafi.com*
Hairworks Al Safa 2, 04 394 0777
Hush Salon Downtown Dubai, 04 438 8165, *hush.ae*
Jen's Hair Studio Trade Centre 1, 800 5367, *jenshairstudio.com*
Juan Hair Salon Jumeirah Lakes Towers, 04 438 9570, *juansalon.com*
Maison de Joelle Al Barsha 1, 04 341 0000, *maisondejoelle.com*
Maria Dowling Al Hudaiba, 04 345 4225, *mariadowling.com*
Pace e Luce Downtown Dubai, 04 420 1165, *paceeluce.com*
Pastels Umm Suqeim 2, 04 388 3534, *pastels-salon.com*
Patsi Collins Hair Beauty Nails Al Garhoud, 04 286 9923, *dubaibeautysalon.com*
Reflection Hair & Beauty Centre Jumeira 1, 04 394 4595
Roots Salon Jumeira 2, 04 344 4040, *rootssalons.com*
Saks Hair Salon Downtown Dubai, 04 430 8572, *saks.co.uk*
ShuiQi Salon Palm Jumeirah, 04 426 1020, *atlantisthepalm.com*
Sisters Beauty Lounge Jumeira 1, 04 342 0787, *sistersbeautylounge.com*
SOS Beauty Salon Jumeira 1, 04 349 1144
Ted Morgan Hair Palm Jumeirah, 04 430 8190, *tedmorganhair.com*
Toni & Guy Trade Centre 2, 04 330 3345, *toniandguy.com*
Top Style Hair Salon Al Garhoud, 04 282 9663, *jumeirah.com*
Top Style Salon Al Garhoud, 04 282 9663, *topstylesalon.com*
VOG Color Your Life Jumeira 3, 04 380 8960, *vog.ae*
Youngsters Hair & Spa Jumeirah Lakes Towers, 04 434 3911, *youngsters.ae*
Zouari Hair Salon Al Sufouh 1, 04 399 9999, *oneandonlyresorts.com*

Health Spas & Massage

Soothing for the body, mind and soul, a massage could be a weekly treat, a gift to someone special, or a relaxing way to get you through a trying time at work. All sorts of unusual treatments are available in Dubai, such as a caviar body treatment at Assawan (p.215); a gold leaf body treatment at The Ritz-Carlton's spa (p.218); a chromatherapy massage at the Melia Hotel's YHI Spa (p.224); a grape-inspired body treatment at the Taj Palace Hotel (p.223); and a placenta facial at Biolite Aesthetic Clinic (p.209).

Numerous massage and relaxation techniques are available, but prices and standards vary, so it's worth doing your research into what's on offer. Spas range from those at opulent 'seven-star' hotels where every detail is customised for a blissful experience, to comfortable independent places which offer fewer facilities but better value for money if you just want someone to loosen your knots.

1847

Grosvenor House Dubai Marina **04 399 8989**
thegroomingco.com
Map **1 L5** Metro **Dubai Marina**
Men are the centre of attention at 1847, which was the first dedicated 'grooming lounge' for men to open in the Middle East. Skilled therapists offer traditional shaves, beard styling, facials, massages, manicures and pedicures, and simple haircuts, so whether you're looking for relaxation, invigoration or a regular spruce-up there's something on the menu for you. Other branches are located at The Walk at Jumeirah Beach Residences (04 437 0252) and Emirates Towers Boulevard (04 330 1847).

Ahasees Spa & Club

Grand Hyatt Dubai Umm Hurair 2 **04 317 2333**
dubai.grand.hyatt.com
Map **2 L8** Metro **Dubai Healthcare City**
Contrary to its name, this is a petite spa but it does win big praise for its atmosphere and attention to detail. The changing room and adjacent relaxation area have dark wooden floors and the walls are lit by rows of scented candles. The wet area is drizzled with rose petals and houses a Jacuzzi, plunge pool, sauna and steam room as well as spacious showers. The treatments on offer range from facials, all designed with preservation and attainment of youth in mind, to massages with specialist 'aromasoul' treatments using essential oils. Fusion packages allow you to combine a treatment, facial and an activity class for top-to-toe indulgence.

Akaru Spa

Jumeirah Creekside Hotel Al Garhoud **04 230 8565**
jumeirah.com
Map **2 M8** Metro **GGICO**
Offers a tranquil haven to escape the hustle and bustle. With friendly staff and comfortable surroundings, the wide range of massages are good value, or you can splurge on one of the deluxe Guinot Hydradermie facials, which are perfectly tailored by blending specific gels for your eyes, face and neck. Sky-treatments can be carried out on the secluded terraces, providing great views of the garden and an unusual spa experience. After being preened and pampered, you can relax by the tranquil water wall or head next door to The Nail Spa or Top Style Hair Salon to continue the indulgence.

Amara Spa Dubai

Park Hyatt Dubai Port Saeed **04 602 1234**
parkhyatt.com
Map **2 M7** Metro **GGICO**
Something of a breath of fresh air in Dubai's spa world which, while sublime, tends to follow the same formula. What sets Amara apart are the treatment rooms. After arriving, guests are escorted directly to the treatment room which acts as a personal spa. Here you have all the facilities of a changing room as well as a relaxation corner. After your treatment, or during if you are having a scrub or wrap, you can treat yourself to a shower under the sun in your very own private outdoor shower (very liberating) with a relaxation area for you to dry off under the warm rays.

Angsana Spa Arabian Ranches

Dubai Polo & Equestrian Club Dubai Studio City **04 361 8251**
angsanaspa.com
Map **1 N13** Metro **Mall of the Emirates**
The minimalist Asian surroundings feature rich, dark wood, while incense, exotic oils, low light and soft music set the tone for relaxation. The impeccably trained staff work wonders on stressed, aching bodies, turning tight muscles into putty and sending overworked minds to cloud nine. Unique massages, ranging from Balinese to Hawaiian to Thai, are at the higher end of the scale in terms of price, but the quality of treatment ensures value for money. Other locations include Dubai Marina (04 368 4356), Emirates Living (04 368 3222) and The Address Montgomerie Dubai (04 360 9322).

Armani/Spa

Armani Hotel Dubai Downtown Dubai **04 888 3888**
dubai.armanihotels.com
Map **2 F6** Metro **Burj Khalifa/Dubai Mall**
In keeping with the hotel and its Burj Khalifa location – modern, sleek and elegant – this space is unusual, with long corridors and multiple doors, which somehow add to the exclusivity. Changing rooms are functional and within the maze-like infrastructure there is a sauna, steam and shower room offering innovative experiences. There are three categories of treatment – Stillness (relaxing), Freedom (rejuvenating) and Fluidity (detoxifying), encompassing massages, facials and body wraps. The treatment rooms are pod-like and create a feeling of real disconnection to the outside world – perfect for floating off as you enjoy a relaxing massage.

Armonia Spa

Sheraton Jumeirah Beach Resort Dubai Marina **04 315 3450**
sheratonjumeirahbeach.com
Map **1 J4** Metro **Jumeirah Lakes Towers**
After a refreshing beverage, you'll begin with a welcome ritual involving a warm herbal aromatic foot massage in a wood-themed, candle-lit treatment room. Pampering options on offer include facials, full-body massages and luxurious body wraps for both men and women. The massage may be a little too gentle for some, so don't be afraid to tell your

therapist to increase the pressure if required. A sauna and steam room are available should you wish to arrive a little early. The spa is on the small side, and facilities not as comprehensive as some other spas in town, but this remains a good place to come for facials and massages.

Aroma Spa

Dubai Marine Beach Resort & Spa Jumeira 1
04 304 8081
dxbmarine.com
Map **2 H4** Metro **World Trade Centre**
A compact spa offering an excellent array of treatments with branded products from Guinot, Payot and Ionithermie. Particularly pleasurable is the hot stone massage that can be combined with a facial, manicure and pedicure. Also on offer are full and half-day packages and a limited range of treatments for men.

Assawan Spa & Health Club

Burj Al Arab Umm Suqeim 3 **04 301 7338**
jumeirah.com
Map **1 S4** Metro **Mall of the Emirates**
Situated on the 18th floor of the breathtaking Burj Al Arab, unsurprisingly, Assawan is an elaborate affair. There are female only and mixed environments, including a state of the art gym with studios for exercise classes, saunas, steam rooms, plunge pools and two wonderfully relaxing infinity pools decorated in mosaic and gold leaf tiles. You can literally swim to the edge of the pool, put your nose to the window, and enjoy the amazing views of the Palm and the World islands. For pure unadulterated indulgence, try the caviar body treatment. Also on offer is a 'men only' range including massage, facial, manicure, pedicure and more. If you want to feel like royalty then this seriously sublime spa is a dream come true.

B/Attitude Spa

Grosvenor House Dubai Marina **04 399 8888**
grosvenorhouse-dubai.com
Map **1 L5** Metro **Dubai Marina**
You'd be forgiven for thinking you've ventured into Buddha Bar as you step into the dimly-lit Asian-inspired lobby of B/Attitude. Dark colours set the mood and soothing tunes flow as you sink into the plush, velvety cushions in the relaxation area. Treatments range from Eastern massages to Ayurvedic facials and exotic body wraps; Swiss Bellefontaine treatments are also available but the overall vibe is decidedly Oriental chic – think Tibetan relaxation techniques, sacred stones and Ayurveda, all delivered in impressive treatment rooms that are named after the chakras. After a spot of Oriental pampering, pop over to the stunning communal areas which boast several Jacuzzis, saunas and steam rooms.

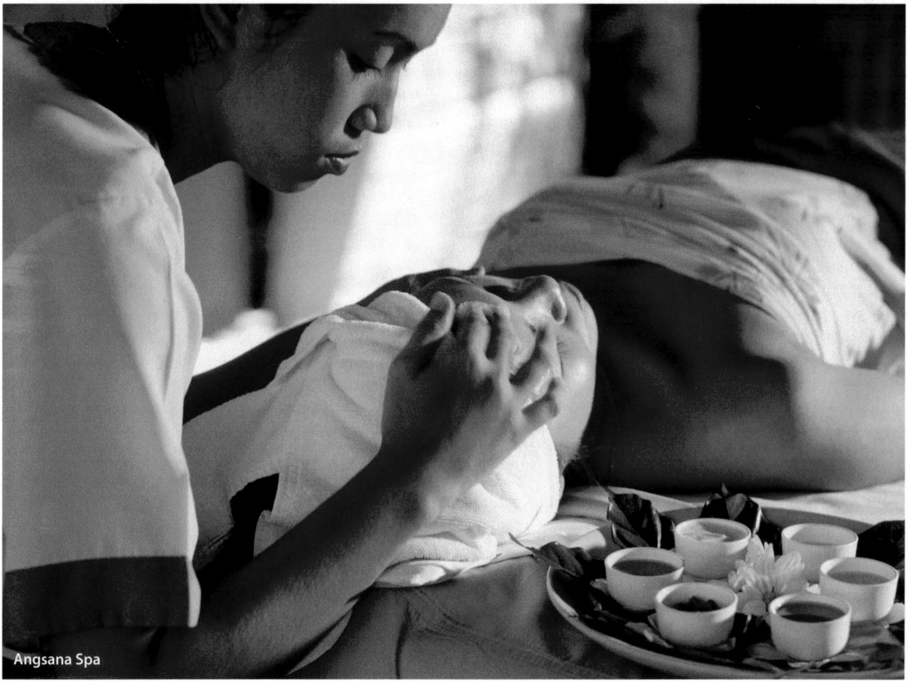

Angsana Spa

Balance Wellness Club

Oasis Centre Al Quoz 1 **04 384 7010**
balance-wellness-centre.com
Map **2 L6** Metro **Noor Islamic Bank**
This club has a 360 degree healing philosophy that encompasses all aspects of your life – exercise, diet, counselling, meditation, therapeutic massage and herbal therapies. Its holistic wellness programme includes a personal assessment, customised diet and therapies plans, yoga, pranayama and pilates. There are also regular yoga and pilates classes for all levels, body composition anaylsis and a variety of well-being therapies.

Calm Spa & Salon

Ocean View Hotel Jumeirah Beach Residence
04 814 5599
jaresortshotels.com
Map **1 K4** Metro **Jumeirah Lakes Towers**
From the cheerful welcome at the door to the luxurious treatment rooms, Calm is true to its word. Offering a menu of facials and massages to relax, rejuvenate, re-energise and re-balance your mind and body, this new spa is a perfect retreat. The Ocean View Signature Ritual begins with an exotic lime and ginger body scrub, followed by a massage and fruit active glow facial – over two hours of bliss. There are also men's treatments, 'on the go' massages for those in a hurry, and a menu of nail and hair services.

Cleopatra's Spa & Wellness

Wafi Umm Hurair 2 **04 324 7700**
wafi.com
Map **2 L7** Metro **Dubai Healthcare City**
Don't be put off by first impressions. The entrance and changing facilities may lack the opulence of some hotel spas, but what it lacks in ostentation it makes up for in occasion. The relaxation area is an ancient Egyptian affair with drapes, silk cushions and majlis-style seats. There is also a small plunge pool with Jacuzzi and sauna. The spa menu should satisfy all, with everything from massages (including pregnancy) and facials to body wraps and anti-ageing miracles.

Elche Natural Beauty Retreat

Villa 42, Nr Jumeira Plaza, Street 10C Jumeira 1
04 349 4942
elche.ae
Map **2 H4** Metro **Emirates Towers**
Elche uses 100% organic herbs, flowers, vegetables and fruit in its treatment products. Traditional know-how and contemporary scientific techniques combine to give Elche a unique advantage in Dubai's spa landscape. Warm tones decorate the interior of the villa, and are accented by sensuous music and a delicious aroma of fresh ingredients. The certified Hungarian beauty and massage therapists are specially trained in using Elche products, some of which have been specially developed to cope with Dubai's harsh climate. Your skin type will be assessed before a treatment is recommended. The two-hour cleansing facial with a unique paprika mask is fiercely popular.

Elixir Spa

Habtoor Grand Beach Resort & Spa Dubai Marina
04 399 5000
habtoorhotels.com
Map **1 L4** Metro **Dubai Marina**
Don't be fooled by the impression given by this spa's busy reception; the six large treatment rooms are the height of quiet relaxation and luxury. There is also a dry float room, rasul mud chamber, nail station, wet spa facilities and a recovery area stocked with herbal teas. Treatment offerings include Karin 02 Herzog skincare treatments from Switzerland, and the therapist will spend time explaining your treatment to ensure it results in you emerging feeling pampered and relaxed.

Emirates Grand Spa

Emirates Grand Hotel Trade Centre 2 **04 323 0000**
emiratesgrandhotel.com
Map **2 G6** Metro **Financial Centre**
Upon reaching the 8,000 sqft Roman-themed spa, way up on the 45th floor, prepare your body to experience tranquillity and revitalisation. The deep purples and dark woods of the spa create the perfect setting for relaxation. From Moroccan baths, to Swedish massages, to deep hydrotherapy and unusual scrubs, you will find some unique and affordable services at the Grand Spa. The private and couples' treatment rooms both have showers, Jacuzzis, Moroccan hammams, and sumptuous massage beds.

Eternal MedSpa

Villa 397, Jumeira Rd Jumeira 2 **04 344 0008**
eternelmedspa.com
Map **2 D4** Metro **Business Bay**
The fascinating medspa concept combines the pampering and decor of a spa with treatments performed by medical professionals. Eternal Medspa offers the same non-surgical treatments that are usually performed at cosmetic surgery and dermatology clinics. Several options are available, including fillers, thermage treatments and health coaching. The spa regularly has special offers, and patients can book treatment packages to suit their specific needs.

Heavenly Spa

The Westin Dubai Mina Seyahi Beach Resort & Marina Al Sufouh 1 **04 399 4141**
westinminaseyahi.com
Map **1 M4** Metro **Nakheel**
The Heavenly Spa leaves nothing to be desired: the therapists are neither neglectful nor intrusive,

making you feel instantly comfortable. The clean, contemporary decor manages to feel warm and inviting, helping to clear your mind for the gorgeous treatments that await. The spa's signature treatment is the Heavenly Massage, which uses four hands moving in synchronisation. The effect is unlike anything you're likely to experience again, unless you make this a regular occurrence.

Lime Spa

Desert Palm Dubai Warsan 2 **04 323 8888**
desertpalm.ae
Lime is more of a retreat than a spa, and with any treatment you get use of the facilities for the day, so you can linger in the relaxation rooms or lounge around the pool. The spa itself is one of the most beautiful in the city and has six treatment rooms, all naturally lit by large windows, overlooking the polo fields. The couples' treatment room has its own plunge pool and private relaxation area. The communal relaxation area is a sublime place to enjoy a cup of herbal tea after your treatment – the heated beds are heavenly. A range of massages and facials are available at the spa, all drawing on colour therapy to tailor each treatment to the needs of each individual. Highly recommended for a full-on, girly spa day out.

Man/Age

The Walk, Jumeirah Beach Residence Dubai Marina **04 435 5780**
managespa.com
Map **1 K5** Metro **Jumeirah Lakes Towers**
This luxury men's spa offers male grooming including haircuts and shaving, manicures, massages and facials. It also has a Moroccan bath. Both annual and six month memberships are available. A second branch is located in Media City (04 437 0868).

Mandara Spa

Mandara Spa

The H Hotel Dubai Trade Centre 1 **04 501 8888**
mandaraspa.com
Map **2 J5** Metro **World Trade Centre**
Although one of the newest additions to Dubai's luxury spa scene, Mandara Spa has an established feel. The spa's epicentre is a circular, cocoon-like chamber which contains a grand Jacuzzi pool, and from here you'll find your way to the communal changing room, sauna, steam room and atmospheric treatment rooms. Many of the body therapies on offer start with a foot washing ritual, and the spa's experience is evident, nowhere more so than in the four-hands massage which is executed with expert synchronicity.

Natural Elements Spa & Fitness

Le Meridien Dubai Al Garhoud **04 702 2550**
lemeridien-dubai.com
Map **2 N8** Metro **GGICO**
While the Natural Elements Spa is part of Le Meridien Dubai, the separate entrance allows the centre to feel more like a private club. Passing the dazzling fitness area, you enter the warmer, dimly lit spa quarters. It's still brighter than most spas around town though; pools of light shine into the large, pastel coloured relaxation room as you wait for your therapist. Most of the treatments use natural ingredients, and its signature treatment – the rainforest facial – takes elements directly from the rainforest, gently lathering in lotion after lotion of natural products that are said to reduce the signs of ageing. Gentle facial acupuncture unblocks the flow of energy along the facial lymphatic areas, ensuring you drift off into a deep sleep. Be warned though – organic treatments cost a pretty penny and a facial will set you back Dhs.850. Other treatments are decidedly cheaper, with a general focus on healthy options and plenty of slimming body wraps and sports massages for the over active. For a no-nonsense spa treatment to help revitalise oneself, it's a great hassle free option.

One&Only Private Spa

One&Only Royal Mirage Al Sufouh 1 **04 440 1010**
oneandonlyresorts.com
Map **1 M4** Metro **Nakheel**
Understated decor, neutral colours, natural light and soft music create a serene effect in the treatment rooms. While this spa offers a variety of facials and Swedish lymphatic drainage, slimming and sports massages, its speciality is the Canyon Love Stone Therapy – an energy-balancing massage using warm and cool stones. The volcanic stones have been specially selected, are 'charged' in the moonlight and cleansed with salt. The stones are placed on specific points around the body, and then used to massage the skin. For high-level pampering, opt for a peel, wrap or oil bath, exclusively with Espa products.

Oriental Hammam

One&Only Royal Mirage Al Sufouh 1 **04 315 2130**
oneandonlyresorts.com
Map **1 M4** Metro **Nakheel**
Welcomed by the attentive staff, you'll be put at ease as the Oriental Hammam Experience is explained. Like the Royal Mirage hotel itself, the spa surroundings are elegant but not overly opulent, with a warm traditional feel. The hammam and spa is an impressive area with mosaic arches and intricate carvings on the high domes. Hammam users also have access to the spa's Jacuzzi, plunge pools and the sensually sleep-inducing relaxation room.

Perfect Shape Up Beauty Centre

Villa 160A, Off Al Wasl Rd Jumeira 3 **04 342 7722**
perfectshapeup.com
Map **2 B5** Metro **Noor Islamic Bank**
Behind the doors of this unassuming villa lies a world of beauty services, from face and body treatments to tanning, waxing, nails and hair. Whether you get your toes polished or your hair highlighted in the dedicated areas, or opt for a facial or massage in one of the spacious treatment rooms upstairs, Perfect Shape Up bridges the gap between five-star spa and neighbourhood salon: you might not check in to spend the day lounging in a fluffy robe in between treatments, but compared to a standard salon the quality is just that little bit higher, the ambience just a little more peaceful. The knowledgeable and friendly beauty therapists take the time to explain your treatment and make recommendations based on your particular preferences. Many of the treatments have been imported from Brazil by owner Annalice – and with Perfect Shape Up she definitely proves there's a lot more to Brazilian beauty than below-the-belt grooming.

Raffles Spa

Raffles Dubai Umm Hurair 2 **04 324 8888**
raffles.com
Map **2 K7** Metro **Dubai Healthcare City**
As you might expect from Raffles Hotel, the Raffles Spa offers the height of decadent indulgence. Treatment rooms have private changing rooms, complete with power shower, fluffy towels and luxury toiletries. Atmospheric lighting, relaxing music a heated treatment bench with warmed towels await you, whichever treatment you chose. For the ultimate spa experience try Dubai Decadence – a full six hours of head-to-toe pampering including a steam bath, body scrub, hot stone massage, facial, manicure and pedicure. Male and female hair and beauty salons, a gym, pool, sauna, steam bath and whirlpool are also available, should you wish to delay your departure further. Couples' packages are also on offer. A true pampering experience.

The Ritz-Carlton Spa Dubai

The Ritz-Carlton, Dubai Dubai Marina **04 318 6132**
ritz-carlton.com
Map **1 L4** Metro **Dubai Marina**
Nestled inside the colonial style of the Ritz-Carlton is its alluring yet understated spa, offering a plethora of treatments and rituals. While the atmosphere might not immediately resemble the candle-lit warmth of many around town, the Ritz-Carlton Spa puts all its emphasis on the individual, inside each of the tastefully decorated treatment rooms. For a more unusual body massage, try the delightful Javanese Lular Body Ritual which promises total body and mind relaxation.

The Ritz-Carlton Spa, Dubai International Financial Centre

The Ritz-Carlton, Dubai International Financial Centre Trade Centre 2 **04 372 2777**
ritzcarlton.com
Map **2 G6** Metro **Financial Centre**
The total area may be cavernous and labyrinthine, but the service is tailored and personal at this excellent spa. No stone is left unturned, from the state-of-the-art beds to comforting warm packs placed on your tummy, as therapies, light music and expert hands take you to a world of relaxing bliss. Treatments combine the traditional with the cutting-edge and, although at the pricier end of the spectrum, this is unrefined luxury. The 'Express Lunch' (lunch and a facial in less than 90 minutes) is great value.

Rixos Royal Spa

Rixos The Palm Dubai Palm Jumeirah **04 457 5555**
rixos.com
Map **1 P3** Metro **Nakheel**
Styled from a palette of white and ice-blue, Rixos Royal Spa has a slightly futuristic feel. Treatments vary from facials to traditional massages, and the signature packages offer a complete head to toe experience for ultimate extravagance and pampering. The lymph drainage massage is strong yet wonderfully effective, and you'll leave feeling lighter and energised. The spa promises a relaxing experience from start to finish, with well-trained therapists who are friendly and attentive, and an indulgent fruit platter to enjoy after your treatment.

Royal Waters Health Spa

Al Mamzar Centre Hor Al Anz East **04 297 2053**
Map **2 R6** Metro **Al Qiyadah**
A warm welcome awaits from friendly, knowledgeable staff who will advise you on the vast range of treatments available here for health, relaxation and beauty. The spa has simple tiled decor with soft lighting and tranquil music. Walk through the well-equipped gym and head up to the roof,

Raffles Spa

Willow Stream Spa

Oriental Hammam

B/Attitude Spa

Talise Spa

and you'll find the swimming pool with views of the bustling area below. The spa offers treatments for cellulite and stretch marks, and they have a wonderful hydrotherapy circuit designed to leave you refreshed after a hard day. A sauna and steam room are also available.

Heavenly Henna

One of the region's first beauty treatments, henna is still popular today, particularly before weddings and celebrations. The intricate designs take around 30 minutes to paint and last for a couple of weeks before naturally fading away. Heritage For Henna has salons dotted around Dubai; visit heritageforhenna.com for locations.

Sanctuary Spa

Pullman Dubai Mall of the Emirates Al Barsha 1
04 377 2000
pullman-dubai.com
Map **1 R6** Metro **Mall of the Emirates**

This compact spa sits in an enviable position on the rooftop of the Pullman Dubai and, as all spa treatments come with complimentary access to the hotel's two rooftop pools, it's worth arriving early to take a dip in the delicious water as you survey a 360° panorama of Dubai. When you're suitably relaxed, head inside, where you can use the sauna, steam room and aquatherapy pool, before being collected for your treatment. The changing rooms are perhaps more functional and without the frills of some of the city's other luxury spas, but Sanctuary Spa more than makes up for this with its menu of soothing treatments, its calm ambience and its highly skilled therapists. After your treatment, enjoy a comforting cup of tea in the relaxation room or, if it's evening, head out to the pool terrace again, and soak up the city lights.

Saray Spa

Dubai Marriott Harbour Hotel & Suites
Dubai Marina **04 319 4630**
marriott.com
Map **1 L5** Metro **Dubai Marina**

Once inside this Asian-inspired spa, you can delve straight into your treatments or spend a few minutes using the sauna, steam room and Jacuzzi – your therapist will explain which will complement your treatments best. There are separate areas for men and women and each treatment room has soft lighting, ambient music, and a bed in the centre of the room. You'll find a comprehensive range of treatments here (sports massages, facials and even a massage used for Hawaiian royalty), which use products like Sodashi and Babor.

Satori Spa

Bab Al Shams Desert Resort & Spa Bawadi
04 809 6232
meydanhotels.com

The spa's location in the middle of the desert adds to the all natural feeling that you immediately get when you walk through the doors. Satori's treatments are worth every penny. Aromatherapy Associates is the oil of choice here, and a beguiling scent surrounds you as you are kneaded and massaged into a state of semi-conscious bliss. The treatment rooms feature a window with a wooden blind, which is quite unusual for spas in Dubai which are usually cosseted away in the deep innards of a hotel. Here, the sense of being close to the desert in its natural state seeps into the gently lit room, and the quiet tinkle of spa music empties your mind of everything but the rhythmic strokes of the therapist.

SensAsia Urban Spa

The Village Jumeira 1 **04 349 8850**
sensasiaspas.com
Map **2 H4** Metro **Emirates Towers**

SensAsia may not have all the trimmings of some five-star spas, but what it lacks in the way of plunge pools and Jacuzzis it makes up for in the 60+ minutes you spend in a heightened state of bliss. The hot stone massage is particularly sensational, with your choice of aroma, strength of massage and the temperature control of the stones. With treatments from Bali, Thailand and Japan, and prices that undercut the big spas, you'll want to make space in your diary every month. Plus, the relaxation areas, showers and treatment rooms are still of a very high standard. Also has branches at Emirates Gold Club (04 417 9820), Mall of the Emirates (04 354 9228) and The Palm Jumeirah (04 422 7115).

Senso Wellness Centre

Radisson Blu Hotel, Dubai Media City Al Sufouh 1
04 366 9111
radissonblu.com
Map **1 M5** Metro **Nakheel**

Senso is a delightful little sanctuary in the heart of Media City consisting of just five treatment rooms. It may be dainty, but the rooms themselves – each of which has a different Far Eastern theme – are fairly cavernous, more like small suites than traditional massage rooms, with luxurious bathroom, shower, baths and wardrobes keeping the treatment beds company. Following suit, the menu is manageable – there are nine massage styles on offer – but covers all bases, from the simple Swedish to hot stone and the signature Senso Synchronous. The service is pitched perfectly between friendly and professional, and, for a high end hotel spa, the prices are very reasonable – made even more so if you keep an eye out for the monthly special deals or opt for one of the spa packages, which usually include access to the pools and steam rooms.

ShuiQi Spa & Fitness

Atlantis The Palm Palm Jumeirah **04 426 1020**
atlantisthepalm.com
Map **1 N1** Metro **Nakheel**
You'll enter this spectacular spa with the highest of expectations and disappointment is definitely not on the menu here: from the minute you walk into the boutique area (where you can sample a wide range of products used in the spa, and load up on girly goodies) up until the end of your treatment, when you're sipping green tea in the relaxation lounge, it's a heavenly experience. Even though it has 27 treatment rooms, set over two floors, it doesn't feel like a big spa; perhaps because of the personal touch you will be treated to. Whether you choose a massage, a facial, a Bastien Gonzalez manicure or pedicure, or a four-hour Japanese ritual Shiseido spa journey, your therapist has one clear focus: you. For the ultimate in indulgence book yourself in for the whole day.

Slim Spa

Al Attar Tower DIFC **04 321 3485**
slimspa.ae
Map **2 G6** Metro **Emirates Towers**
More often than not, feeling great is synonymous with looking great. Slim Spa is there to make you look, and feel, great with a wide range of non-invasive treatments for weight and inch-loss, cellulite reduction, body sculpting, anti-ageing and rejuvenation – to help you get the figure and skin you've always dreamt of.

Softouch Spa

Kempinski Hotel Mall of the Emirates Al Barsha 1
04 409 5909
softouchspa.com
Map **1 R6** Metro **Mall of the Emirates**
Located within the busy Mall of the Emirates/ Kempinski Hotel Dubai complex, Softouch Spa is the perfect outlet for a post-shopping spree treatment. Tucked away on the first floor of the hotel, the Indian-inspired spa offers more than 60 treatments specialising in detoxification, rejuvenation and stress relief. With spacious and fully equipped treatment rooms – all oils and herbs are imported from various regions in India, while massage tables are made from Indian-sourced teak – Softouch Spa operates as a day spa for customers also interested in using the health club facilities, or a medical spa where treatments can be performed under the supervision of a doctor. Specialising in Ayurveda – a form of Indian alternative medicine that uses ingredients such as cardamom and cinnamon – Softouch's most requested treatments include the Siro Dhara (Dhs.750 for 75 minutes), a unique massage that originates from Kerala, followed by a stream of oil flowed onto the forehead.

The Spa At Fairmont Dubai

Fairmont Dubai Trade Centre 1 **04 332 5555**
fairmont.com
Map **2 J5** Metro **World Trade Centre**
In keeping with the eclectic decor of The Fairmont Dubai, the spa is decorated in a luxurious Greco-Roman style, with beautiful mosaics and sleek white pillars. Soft, white towels and subtle candlelight create a wonderful sense of calm. There is a comprehensive selection of top-to-toe spa and beauty treatments using Phytomer and Aromatherapy Associates product lines. Before or after your treatment you can use the steam room, sauna, Jacuzzi, fitness centre and the outdoor swimming pools, or simply relax with a herbal tea or fresh juice. It also has healing mineral pools and an excellent gym, and after you have worked out or spaced out you can enjoy a stroll around the lush gardens.

The Spa At Hilton Dubai Jumeirah Resort

Hilton Dubai Jumeirah Resort Dubai Marina
04 318 2406
hilton.com
Map **1 K4** Metro **Jumeirah Lakes Towers**
It takes a bit of navigating through Hilton Jumeirah's lobby and restaurant area to locate the hotel's no-fuss spa on the second floor; once there, you'll get to soak up the beach views from the relaxation area, a healthy drink in your hand, while waiting for the treatment to begin. Arrive early to take advantage of the steam room and sauna facilities before being guided to one of the small treatment rooms for a spot of pampering – be it a facial, slimming treatment or massage. Afterwards, you'll get to admire the view once more, with another soothing beverage and healthy snacks at your disposal.

The Spa At Jebel Ali Golf Resort

Jebel Ali Golf Resort Waterfront **04 814 5555**
jebelali-international.com
Metro **Danube**
An excellent level of service is offered for both men and women, in intimate and well-presented surroundings. The communal area has an invigorating shower, sauna, Jacuzzi and steam room. While the changing areas are a little small, they are equipped with Elemis goodies, and the tranquil after-treatment area overlooks the beach. Recommended is the 90 minute Royal Hammam Ritual which involves black soap, a henna mask, some exuberant exfoliating and a rasul mud mask before a darn good wash down. This style of pampering is literally from head to toe. Just leave any shyness at the marble door – but not your partner, if you're brave enough to try the couple's option.

The Spa At Shangri-La

Shangri-La Hotel Dubai Trade Centre 1 **04 405 2441**
shangri-la.com
Map **2 G5** Metro **Financial Centre**
Both the health club and spa have all of the facilities you would expect from a five-star location, as well as a salon and barber; a juice bar and a boutique complete the package. The surroundings are minimalist and the treatment rooms are a little on the clinical side, while the communal areas lean more towards fitness club than spa, with open spaces and not too much by way of privacy. That said, it's the ideal location for a healthy break for anyone working or living on the Sheikh Zayed Road strip.

Spa At The Address Downtown Dubai

The Address Downtown Dubai Downtown Dubai
04 436 8888
theaddress.com
Map **2 F7** Metro **Burj Khalifa/Dubai Mall**
Step into total relaxation from the moment you arrive at The Spa at The Address, thanks to muted decor, ambient music, and a cold towel and refreshing cucumber and mint drink handed to you. The Spa has male and female treatment rooms, a couple's room, and a range of treatments including facials, massages and wraps using ESPA products. Lie back and relax on heated beds while the therapist performs your treatment after a skin analysis, and then take some time to enjoy the beautiful views over the whole of the Downtown area.

Spa At The Address Dubai Marina

Spa At The Address Dubai Mall

The Address Dubai Mall Downtown Dubai
04 438 8888
theaddress.com
Map **2 F6** Metro **Burj Khalifa/Dubai Mall**
The spa reception, just along the corridor from the creche, feels very much part of the hotel's hustle and bustle, but once through the doors and into the heart of the spa, an aura of tranquillity descends. The shared changing rooms are ample, with monotone cream decor, but they lack the spa retreat touches of a Jacuzzi, steam room and sauna. The latter two are available to spa guests at the fitness centre and, if you decide to make the trek over there, you can also enjoy the hotel's divine infinity pool. Where this spa really excels is in its staff: if you're after a superb treatment at the end of a hard day (or want to snatch a peaceful hour while the kids are in the creche), and want a therapist who can knead your knots to soft butter, then this is just the ticket.

Spa At The Address Dubai Marina

The Address Dubai Marina Dubai Marina
04 436 7777
theaddress.com
Map **1 K5** Metro **Dubai Marina**
The Spa is perfectly appointed, with a dark, relaxing and comfortable vibe crafted from the moment you enter. Large, with separate men's and women's sections, the changing rooms are as luxurious as a five-star suite and, if the sights, sounds and smells are pitch-perfect, then it's the confident, friendly, expert hands here that make the spa something special… like being fine tuned by a master craftsman. Try the Arabian Oasis treatment, consisting of an exfoliating scrub, a Boreh wrap, an aromatherapy facial and, finally, a spiced oil massage. Originally an Eid special, it was so popular that it's now a regular fixture on the menu and is one of the star treatments in a city with plenty to offer.

The Spa At The Palace Downtown Dubai

The Palace Downtown Dubai Downtown Dubai
04 428 7805
theaddress.com
Map **2 F6** Metro **Burj Khalifa/Dubai Mall**
You couldn't find a more suitable address for the Spa at the Palace; a treatment here will leave you feeling like royalty. The facilities are wonderful and include two Oriental bath houses, monsoon showers and two Hydrospa bath tubs with therapy jets. Beautifully decorated with mosaic designs on the walls, it is a haven of tranquility. Sink in to a welcoming Hydrospa bath tub or unwind in the steam room until you are

called for your treatment – there is a huge range on offer, but for a unique regional experience, you really should try the hammam.

Spa Zen

Radisson Royal Hotel, Dubai Trade Centre 1
04 308 0000
radissonblu.com
Map **2 H5** Metro **World Trade Centre**

Not as opulent or over-the-top as many of Dubai's five-star spas, this is a fairly simple and modern affair but no less atmospheric or welcoming for it. It does exactly what it's supposed to, with excellent staff immediately putting you at ease and high quality therapists delivering the treatments. There are separate men's and women's areas, and the easy clean lines make it a good and welcoming choice for male clients, who also have their own range of reasonably-priced signature treatments, like the excellent Gentle Man Bliss facial, scrub and massage combo.

Spaces Spa & Salon

Oasis Centre Al Quoz 1 **04 515 4400**
Map **2 L6** Metro **Noor Islamic Bank**

The location of Spaces – on the top floor of the Oasis Centre, next to the plush 360 Wellness Centre – serves as a good metaphor for its services. This small salon is split into gents' and ladies' quarters and offers massages that are just as good as a premium spa's, but without the exorbitant five-star hotel prices. You won't find any trickling fountains or plush bathrobes here; this no-frills option instead creates total tranquility by giving really great rubdowns. Those looking to loosen up and attend to dehydrated skin should go for the relaxing body massage which costs Dhs.200 for one hour. Service is polite and exceptionally friendly. Offering a range of services from a deep tissue massage (Dhs.250) and facials that range from Dhs.200 to Dhs.325, to hair and nail treatments, Spaces is a nice, affordable option. And not breaking the bank makes it all the more relaxing.

Spadunya Colour Experience

The Walk, Jumeirah Beach Residence Dubai Marina
04 439 3669
spadunyaclub.com
Map **1 K4** Metro **Dubai Marina**

With a pioneering spa concept, Spadunya specialises in energy colour massages that harmonise the body's energy system. Signature treatments include face reflexology and a Body Harmonising Colour Treatment, which includes colour consultation, colour harmonising scrub, envelopment (wrap) and a heavenly massage. It's a completely, and rather refreshingly, different spa experience, that is perfectly complemented by the spa's treatment suites, hammam, hydrotherapy suite, studio, and steam, sauna and beauty rooms.

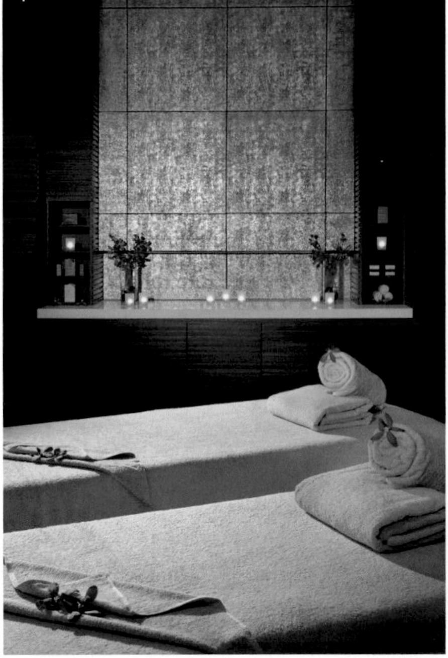

Spa At The Address Downtown Dubai

Taj Spa

Taj Palace Dubai Al Rigga **04 211 3101**
tajhotels.com
Map **2 N6** Metro **Al Rigga**

This tranquil spa has a mystical, romantic atmosphere, with scented candles, cleansing foot rituals and dreamy cups of ginger tea setting the mood. It offers modern Ayurvedic treatments as well as an extensive range of popular European, far eastern and natural therapies. Signature treatments include the Grape Vine treatment, an age-busting body scrub and massage that sends the mind and body into a rejuvenating spin. The changing rooms are welcoming and have a sauna and steam room, while the relaxation area is hard to tear yourself away from.

Talise Ottoman Spa

Jumeirah Zabeel Saray Palm Jumeirah **04 453 0456**
jumeirah.com
Map **1 L3** Metro **Nakheel**

Wandering through the Talise Ottoman Spa, you soon realise that the Zabeel Saray was actually built around the spa, rather than vice-versa, such is the central role the spa plays. With 50 treatment rooms, mineral pools, majlis areas, saunas, ice chambers, couples' suites, gyms and stunning hammams, the spa lays claim to being the biggest in the Middle East and one of the largest in the world. A perfect reconstruction of an opulent Ottoman palace, it's also one of the most luxurious. Male and female areas are apart, each with a full set of facilities and treatments on offer – from Thai massage in an outdoor cabana to a complete hydrotherapy journey. But it's the hammam, offering the most authentic Turkish experience in the UAE, that shouldn't be missed. Prices are at the higher end of the spectrum but the early bird offer (25% off between 09:00 and 11:00) and VIP/couples' suites (hired by the hour and including treatments) provide more economical options.

Talise Spa At Jumeirah Emirates Towers

Boulevard At Jumeirah Emirates Towers
Trade Centre 2 **04 319 8181**
jumeirah.com
Map **2 H6** Metro **Emirates Towers**
Located on the lower floor of Jumeirah Emirates Towers, this compact spa is a suitably suave affair for the prestigious address in one of Dubai's more established five-star hotels. Dark wood panelling, ambient lighting and flickering candles set the scene as you step into the little lap of luxury and spa indulgence and the tranquil atmosphere begins to iron out any stress before the treatment even begins. The menu features a handful of facials, but the real emphasis is on the body treatments. The massages range from Swedish to Hawaiian Lomi Lomi, and specialties like foot reflexology are also on offer. The real stars of the show, however, are Talise's signature rituals, many of which include floatation in the spa's fantastic salt water pool. A range of Aromatherapy Associates products is available to buy on your way out.

Talise Spa Madinat Jumeirah

Madinat Jumeirah Al Sufouh 1 **04 366 6818**
madinatjumeirah.com
Map0 **1 R4** Metro **Mall of the Emirates**
This regal spa is made up of luxurious lounges and treatment rooms connected by garden walkways. Rooms are exotic and well-appointed with warm shades and ambient music. The welcoming staff set this spot apart, advising on products and technique before your tailored treatment. The range of therapies is extensive but not overwhelming, with a focus on the use of natural oils. A true destination spa, take advantage of the steam room, sauna and plunge pools before or after your appointment, or read a magazine while sipping on ginger tea sweetened with honey in one of the chill out rooms. Yoga, including the popular classes held under the stars, is also available.

A Touch Of Arabia

For a typically Arabian pampering experience, opt for an Oriental Hammam. This treatment is traditional in the Middle East region and shares similarities with Turkish baths. The name refers to the bath (the room) in which the treatment takes place – typically an elaborate affair in Dubai's five-star spa scene. A hammam involves a variety of different experiences, including being bathed, scrubbed and massaged on a hot table. It's an absolute must-do while in Dubai, the hammams at The Spa at Jebel Ali Golf Resort & Spa (p.221) and Oriental Hammam (p.218) are highly recommended.

The Thai Elite Spa

Mercure Gold Hotel Al Mina **04 345 9992**
accorhotels.com
Map **1 J4** Metro **Al Jafiliya**
This quaint spa on the upper level of the Gold Swiss-Belhotel may lack the size, menu and facilities you'll find in some of the city's most pampered offerings, but its laid-back approach is refreshing and well judged. All the usual therapies are on offer, with the full-body scrub followed by a Thai oil massage a particularly relaxing and yet invigorating choice. Long opening hours and reasonable prices also make it an attractive option.

YHI Spa

Melia Dubai Al Raffa, Bur Dubai **04 386 8111**
melia-dubai.com
Map **2 K4** Metro **Al Fahidi**
Don't let the Bur Dubai location deter you; this is a sanctuary of relaxation where the oriental overtones, burnt orange and black decor, and serene layout make for a totally refreshing experience. The chromatherapy massage, where you can relax amidst a kaleidoscope of colours while unwinding on a warming, dry flotation bed, is a cut above the rest. There's a Moroccan bath, a ladies and gentlemen's separate sauna and Turkish bath, as well as a menu of massages, hammam treatments and body scrubs that invite you to be scrubbed, wrapped, hydrated and massaged to perfection.

Zen Asia Spa

W Cluster, Nr Tiffany Tower Jumeirah Lakes Towers
04 457 2374
Map **1 L5** Metro **Jumeirah Lakes Towers**
Catching uninterrupted sunshine from the newly created plaza it resides on, Zen Asia is a bright and friendly salon with staff to match. This international Thai inspired spa has something to suit every preference and budget, from the busy girl about town to those of us who have time to enjoy our days at a more leisurely pace. The salon boasts a vast array of treatments, from the classic mani-pedi to some truly cutting edge and unique treatments that will leave you feeling spoiled rotten. An ever popular treatment is the Dermalogica Customize-Me Facial. A trained therapist analyses zones and recommends products and techniques specific to your needs and skin type.

www.seawings.ae
Get a bird's eye view of Dubai as you soar across clear blue skies and glittering coastline onboard the Seawings™ seaplane.
Hold your breath as you witness present day wonders – Palm Jumeirah, The World Islands, Burj Al Arab, Burj Khalifa, the historic Dubai Creek, bustling Port Rashid and more. It's a view that will be remembered for a lifetime!
Follow 'Seawings Dubai' on TripAvisor, Viator, Google Reviews, Facebook and Twitter.
Call For Reservations
+971 4 8070708
or email reservations@seawings.ae
seawings
Seaplane Tours

Discover Dubai

DISCOVER DUBAI

Dubai has put itself well and truly on the global map over the past decade as one of the top places to visit. Its desire to build the biggest and best of everything has, as planned, caught much of the world's attention. Its ever-growing skyline, audacious man-made islands, mega malls, seven-star service and permanently sunny weather have combined with its position as a major airline hub to transform it into an international holiday destination, a regional shopping magnet, and the Middle East's most ostentatious, glamorous party capital.

All this is good news for the leisure time of expats lucky enough to have relocated to this headline-grabbing emirate – but there's more to Dubai than just the high-living holiday highlights. Scratch the surface and you'll discover plenty of cultural delights, multicultural attractions, traditional gems and even simple, sedate everyday leisure activities.

As an adopted Dubai local, there are plenty of ways to fill your spare time. Start by exploring the city. There's a definite divide between the old and the new parts of town. Head to the creek and its surrounding areas of Deira and Bur Dubai for a flavour of what Dubai used to be like before the economic boom turned it into a modern, international metropolis. Souks, narrow side streets, heritage sites, local restaurants and a bustling waterway make this a great part of town to investigate. In contrast, the mind-boggling modern developments that make up New Dubai – Downtown Dubai, Palm Jumeirah and Dubai Marina – accommodate spectacular buildings, first-class hotels, shopping delights, and more besides.

The city's art scene is starting to bubble up into something interesting too, with more and more modern galleries popping up in the industrial area of Al Quoz (see p.252), and there's a full calendar of international events to keep sports fans happy (p.272).

During the cooler months, there are some excellent outdoor options for get-togethers with family and friends; Dubai's green parks are superbly maintained, while the beaches draw crowds of sunbathers and swimmers at the weekends (p.258). There's family fun to be had too at the various waterparks, aquariums and amusement centres scattered around town (p.262).

You're not likely to tire of enjoying the urban attractions anytime soon, but even if you do, there's a huge adventure playground just beyond the city limits that's waiting to be explored. Head off-road to make the most of the awe-inspiring desert sands and wadi beds, hike in the mountain peaks, go camping or take to the sea for some excellent diving, snorkelling and sailing (p.353). And that's just Dubai – there are six other emirates to get to know too (see Out Of The City, p.284).

PLACES OF INTEREST

Deira & The Creek

Once the central residential hub of Dubai, Deira remains an incredibly atmospheric area. Narrow convoluted streets bustle with activity while gold, spices, perfumes and general goods are touted in its numerous souks. Likewise, Dubai Creek, beside which Deira sits, was the original centre of Dubai commerce, and it still buzzes today with boats plying their transport and cargo trades. Both sides of the creek are lined by corniches that come alive in the evenings as residents head out for a stroll and traders take stock. Take the time to meander along the Deira side, where men in traditional south Asian garb unload wooden dhows docked by the water's edge, tightly

Deira creekside

WATER TAXIS

In 2010, a fleet of James Bond-style water taxis launched to serve waterfront destinations from Al Mamzar and the Creek to Jebel Ali. The smart-looking taxis are available for private hire with fares starting from Dhs.50 and rising to Dhs.570 for the longest distance. They can also be hired on an hourly basis, starting at Dhs.400 per hour. Passengers can call the RTA on 800 9090 to be picked up from one of 23 taxi stops.

packed with everything from fruit and vegetables to televisions and maybe even a car or two, often traded with Iran, the UAE's neighbour across the Gulf.

No resident should miss the chance to experience a trip across the water on a commuter abra (p.53) for Dhs.1, or you can hire your own (plus driver) for an hour-long tour for around Dhs.100.

For a full creek experience, start at Bastakiya (p.229), wander through the Textile Souk (p.421) on the Bur Dubai side, before taking an abra towards Deira. Once on the Deira side, cross the corniche and head towards the souk district. First stop is the Spice Souk (p.421), where the aroma of saffron and cumin fills the air. Nearby, the streets in and around the Gold Souk (p.420) are crammed with shops shimmering with gold and platinum.

Take a wander around the area behind the souks to discover alleyways and narrow one-way streets with shops that deal in almost any kind of goods imaginable. Tiny cafeterias, old barbershops and odd knick-knack stores appear around almost every corner, and life in general seems to move at its own energetic pace.

Creek Tours

A cruise on Dubai Creek is a wonderful way to enjoy views of new and old parts of the city side by side. Many of the tours are in traditional wooden dhows, but even these often have air conditioning inside to avoid the summer heat and humidity. In the cooler months, the top deck is the place to be. Prices per adult range from about Dhs.45 for a daytime trip to Dhs.150 for a bargain dinner cruise and up to Dhs.325 for a top-class evening cruise with fine food. For more information see Boat Tours, p.275.

If it's rugs you want, then Deira Tower on Al Nasr Square is worth a visit. Around 40 shops offer a colourful profusion of carpets from Iran, Pakistan, Turkey and Afghanistan to suit most people's taste and pocket. For dinner with a view, head to the top of the Hyatt Regency where Al Dawaar (p.486) hosts an incredible buffet within its rotating dining room. Afterwards, you can burn off the buffet belly by strolling along the Gulf-side Deira corniche, which is where you'll find both the atmospheric Fish Market (p.420) and Mamzar Beach Park (p.257), a great spot for a day out by the sea.

Further up the creek, on the other side of the souks, are some fascinating buildings that seemed years ahead of their time when they were built. The large golf ball that sits atop the Etisalat building is testimony to the unique imagination of Dubai's modern architecture. The sparkling glass building housing the National Bank of Dubai (known fondly as the 'pregnant lady') is a sculptural vision, standing tall like a magnificent convex mirror that reflects the bustling activity of the creek.

Good As Gold

The Gold Souk is an Aladdin's cave of gold shopping. Bargaining is expected, and discounts depend on the season and the international gold rate. Dubai Shopping Festival and Dubai Summer Surprises are the main periods for low prices, when huge discounts attract gold lovers from around the world. Individual pieces can be made, or copies done to your own specifications, within a few days. Even if you aren't buying, an evening stroll through the Gold Souk, when it's glistening, is worth the experience.

It is also in this area that you can find three of Dubai's original five-star hotels: Hilton Dubai Creek, Sheraton Dubai Creek, and the Radisson Blu, Dubai Deira Creek (formerly the InterContinental). Nearby is the dhow wharfage area where more of the large wooden trading boats dock.

Inland is Deira City Centre (p.424), one of Dubai's first mega malls, while bordering the creek for about 1.5km between Maktoum and Garhoud bridges is an enticing stretch of carefully manicured greenery, home to the Dubai Creek Golf & Yacht Club (p.339). The impressive golf clubhouse is based on the shape of dhow sails (the image of this famous building is found on the Dhs.20 note), while the yacht club is aptly in the shape of a yacht. This is also the site of one of the city's top five-star hotels, the Park Hyatt Dubai (p.246), which features Mediterranean-style low buildings offering creek views and some great restaurants.

Bastakiya: Old Dubai

For a dose of tradition, step out of the modern world and into a pocket of the city that harks back to a bygone era. The Bastakiya area, which is in Bur Dubai by the creek, is one of the oldest heritage sites in Dubai and certainly the most atmospheric. The neighbourhood dates from the early 1900s when traders from the Bastak area of southern Iran were

Port & Leisure

To the south-west of Bur Dubai is Port Rashid, where you'll find the Dubai Ports Authority building, a large glass and chrome construction imaginatively designed like a paddle steamer; all the paraphernalia of a port can be glimpsed over the surrounding fence.

encouraged to settle there by tax concessions granted by Sheikh Maktoum bin Hashar, the ruler of Dubai at the time.

The area is characterised by traditional windtower houses, built around courtyards and clustered together along a winding maze of alleyways. The distinctive four-sided windtowers (barjeel), seen on top of the traditional flat-roofed buildings, were an early form of air conditioning. There are some excellent cultural establishments in and around Bastakiya, including Dubai Museum (p.249), XVA Gallery (p.256) and The Majlis Gallery (p.255), while a short stroll along the creek will bring you to the Textile Souk and abra station, from where you can cross the water to explore the souks on the Deira side (p.228).

You can make a single crossing on a communal abra for Dhs.1 (see p.53), or take a private tour up and down between Maktoum Bridge and Shindagha (the official RTA rate is Dhs.100 for an hour). Beyond the Textile Souk is Shindagha, another interesting old area where you'll find Sheikh Saeed Al Maktoum's House (see p.250) and the Heritage & Diving Villages (p.249).

BUR DUBAI

Up until only a few years ago, Bur Dubai, and Deira across the creek, were the business districts of the city. Today, the business hubs may have shifted to other, newer areas, but Bur Dubai remains an atmospheric, bustling part of the city. Here you'll find a multitude of nationalities living in squeezed-together multi-storey apartment blocks, busy shopping streets, seedy bars in older hotels, and some of the best historical and cultural attractions in Dubai. A walk along the corniche between Bastakiya and Shindagha (see above) will take you through crowds of people buying and selling fabrics from the Textile Souk, jostling to board an abra, or heading for prayers at one of the mosques or the atmospheric Hindu temple. From Bastakiya it is possible to follow the corniche up along the creekside where a number of luxury cruise boats moor (you can board one of these for a dinner cruise). The relaxed atmosphere of this stretch, with its grassy areas often full of people, makes it a great place to view the flashy buildings on the Deira side of the creek and watch the water traffic. Numerous embassies are located in this area, while further inland from the creek is the popular BurJuman shopping centre (p.423).

Take Your Time

While in the area, take time to linger and absorb the unique sights, sounds and smells of Bur Dubai over a meal at Kan Zaman (p.514) or Ravi's (p.531).

Jumeira

Jumeira might not have the exotic atmosphere or history of Deira, but its beaches, shopping centres and pleasant, wide streets make up for it. The area is traditionally one of the most desirable addresses for well-off expats, and the origin of the infamous 'Jumeira Jane' caricature – well-to-do expat women who fill their days shopping, spa-ing or lunching with fellow Janes in the establishments along Jumeira Road. The area is home to a range of stylish boutiques, Mercato Mall (p.432), and excellent cafes such as The Lime Tree Cafe & Kitchen (p.464) and THE One restaurant (p.528).

Just Outside Jumeira

Several places of interest surround the Jumeira area. To the south is Umm Suqeim, where the ultimate attraction has to be the iconic Burj Al Arab hotel (p.236) – be sure to visit its restaurants or spa at least once while you live here. If you prefer your leisure to be free of charge, there's plenty of public beach to enjoy – just turn up, pop your towel down and relax at Umm Suqeim beach (p.258), while for some more energetic aquatic fun there's Wild Wadi Water Park (p.260). Just behind Jumeira is the family-friendly Safa Park (p.257), which is one of the main highlights on the villa and shop lined Al Wasl Road – and one of the main open spaces in which Dubayans relax, play and hang out.

It's a great part of town for hitting the beach too. The popular Jumeira Open Beach has showers and lifeguards, but it unfortunately attracts a few voyeurs, so you may prefer to try the more private Jumeirah Beach Park opposite Chili's (p.502), where you can hire sunbeds and parasols.

That's not to say Jumeira is all sun, sea and shopping – there are some interesting cultural spots here too. Jumeirah Mosque (p.250) is one of the most recognisable places of worship in the city and welcomes visitors with tours and educational programmes, while a couple of galleries (p.250) will keep art enthusiasts happy.

Just outside Jumeira, on the border with Satwa, lies 2nd December Street. It offers a completely

Rising skyline

Bur Dubai

Dubai Marina

Bastakiya

Streetlife: Karama & Satwa

They may not offer too much in the way of spectacular modern developments or five-star luxury, but for a dose of interesting street life, plus a real flavour of the Indian subcontinent and the Philippines, Karama and Satwa are well worth a visit.

Karama mainly consists of low-rise apartment buildings, but is also home to a range of shops selling all kinds of cheap clothing and goods – some not always the genuine article. Dubai Central Post Office is also in the area, on Zaabeel Road.

Karama's merchants are a far cry from their mall counterparts, and you can expect to have to haggle to get your bargain. The other big draw for Karama is the range of excellent, low budget south Asian restaurants, serving fiery Indian, Sri Lankan and Pakistani fare. Highlights include Saravana Bhavan (p.535) and Karachi Darbar (p.514).

Satwa is a mix of villas and apartments, but the real character of the area shines through on its busy main thoroughfares, Al Diyafah Road (now officially called 2nd December Street) Plant Street and Satwa Road. Al Diyafah is the heartbeat of the area, where people go to eat, socialise and be seen. Satwa Road branches off Al Diyafah, and Plant Street runs parallel; here you'll find pots and plants, pet shops, fabric shops and hardware outlets, and a small area full of car repair shops. It's also a great spot to find a bargain tailor (see Tailoring & Bespoke Services, p.374). Head here on a Saturday evening to soak up the atmosphere, but women are advised to cover up to avoid being stared at.

different vibe to the sedate Jumeira suburbs; it's a hectic thoroughfare lined with shops and restaurants, and is the main destination for anyone needing to feed their post-club hunger, show off their expensive customised car, or watch the city pass by as they enjoy some street-side Lebanese fare. If you're out past midnight, don't miss having a bite at either Al Mallah (p.488) or the Dubai institution that is Ravi's (p.531).

Downtown Dubai

The newest place in town to explore, Downtown Dubai is a spectacular mix of shops, restaurants, entertainment and architecture, while nearby is a stretch of Dubai's stunning original skyscraper strip, which lines Sheikh Zayed Road and features some of the city's top hotels and building design.

At the heart of Downtown is the world's tallest tower, the shimmering Burj Khalifa, which points like a needle more than 800m skywards and contains exclusive apartments, the At The Top observatory (see box right), and the Armani Hotel Dubai (p.235), with more openings to come. By its base are The Dubai Mall and Old Town, while the centrepiece is the spectacular Dubai Fountain, which draws crowds to witness the regular evening shows where jets of water shoot 150m into the air along the length of Burj Lake to classical, modern and Arabic music. Take a seat at any of the restaurant terraces that line the lake for a perfect view. The Dubai Mall (p.426) is a huge shopping centre full of top-end retail brands, an array of excellent eateries and some fantastic entertainment options such as Dubai Aquarium (p.260), Dubai Ice Rink (p.343), Reel Cinemas (p.462) and SEGA Republic (p.264).

There are two Address hotels in the area (p.234, 235), with the views from the 63rd-floor Neos bar (p.561) at The Address Downtown well worth taking in. Old Town, which is home to the atmospheric Souk Al Bahar (p.421), takes strong influences from traditional Arabia, with windtowers, mosaics, courtyards, passageways and fortress-like finishes, all of which are beautifully lit at night. Other hotels in the Downtown area include The Palace and Al Manzil, which are home to Asado steakhouse (p.492) and upmarket sports bar Nezesaussi (p.561) respectively.

Just behind Downtown, the buzzing strip over on Sheikh Zayed Rd is known for the striking architecture of its high-rise residential buildings, office towers and top-class hotels including Jumeirah Emirates Towers (p.242) and the Shangri-La (p.248). From the Dubai World Trade Centre to Interchange One (known as Defence Roundabout), the wide, skyscraping 3.5km stretch is the subject of many a photo, as well as after-hours hook ups in the various happening hotspots. With so many residents, tourists and business people around, this area really comes to life at night, as the crowds flit from restaurants to bars to clubs.

The Dubai Fountain

The Dubai Fountain is the world's largest dancing fountain. Located in Burj Lake, it can be seen from throughout the area although the very best views are from either the restaurants on the Lower Ground Waterfront Promenade of The Dubai Mall, or those that line Souk Al Bahar. However, you can get an entirely different view if you head for drinks in Neos (p.561), The Cigar Lounge (p.554) or At.mosphere (p.492) or time your ascent of the Burj Khalifa to coincide with a performance. Set to Arabic, classical and world music, the fountain sends spray up to a height of 150m, with 22,000 gallons of water airborne at some points, all lit up by 1.5 million lumens of projected light. Performances are daily at 13:00 and 13:30, and then 18:00-23:00 at 30 minute intervals.

INSIDE BURJ KHALIFA

After growing like a beanstalk before the eyes of residents over the years, the Burj Khalifa finally reached its zenith in 2010, and at over 828m in height, is now officially the world's tallest building. Visitors can ride high-speed lifts all the way to the 124th floor to take in the staggering 360° views from the observation deck, At The Top (burjkhalifa.ae). While in record-breaking mood, try At.mosphere (p.492) which, found on the 122nd floor, is now officially the world's highest restaurant too. If you have cash to splash, you can enjoy dinner or a spa treatment at the Armani Hotel Dubai (p.235).

The Palm Jumeirah & Al Sufouh

This stretch of coastline, between Dubai Marina and Umm Suqeim, is home to some of the most prestigious and popular resorts in Dubai. From the exclusive, iconic Burj Al Arab and Jumeirah Beach Hotel at one end, along Jumeira Road past the One&Only Royal Mirage, The Westin and finally, at the other end, Le Meridien Mina Seyahi – with everyone's favourite beach party bar, Barasti (p.551) – this section of the Gulf contains more pricey hotels than a Monopoly set.

In the middle of all this, stretching several kilometres out to sea, is The Palm, Dubai's original mind-boggling man-made island, with its countless luxury villas and apartments, the Disney-esque Atlantis hotel and a raft of brand new deluxe hotels including One&Only The Palm (p.246) and Jumeirah Zabeel Saray (p.242). Aquaventure is Atlantis' thrilling waterpark (p.258), and you can get up close to the marine life at Dolphin Bay and the Lost Chambers aquarium (p.262). The Palm is also home to several top restaurants, including Nobu (p.327) and West 14th (p.546). You can drive the length of The Palm and around its perimeter for great views back to the shore, or you can take a ride on the monorail for an elevated view of the luxury-villa-lined fronds (p.54).

Within all of the resorts in Al Sufouh are dozens of excellent eating and drinking choices, open to all, while Souk Madinat Jumeirah (p.434) and, just back from the coast, Mall of the Emirates (p.431) are great spots for shopping, dining and entertainment.

Sun and water lovers are well catered for here too, with a great public beach (p.258) and another excellent waterpark, Wild Wadi (p.260).

Dubai Marina & JBR

Previously home to just a handful of waterfront hotels, the Marina is the epitome of new Dubai's rise to modern prominence. Apartment buildings (finished or still under construction) have sprouted up along every inch of the man-made waterway, while between the marina and the shore is the massive Jumeirah Beach Residence (JBR) development, which now dwarfs the five-star beach resorts such as the Hilton and Ritz-Carlton.

The pedestrianised walkways that run around the marina and parallel to the coast have evolved into lively strips of cafes and restaurants, which throng with people in the evenings when the lit-up skyscrapers are at their most impressive. Marina Walk boulevard provides continuous pedestrian access around the 11km perimeter of the water and is a popular circuit for morning joggers, skaters and cyclists. The popular area by Dubai Marina Towers was the first to be developed, and is home to several independent eateries, such as popular Lebanese restaurant and shisha spot Chandelier (p.500). It is a great place for a stroll any time but it really comes to life in the evenings and cooler months when you can sit and gaze out across the rows of gleaming yachts and flashing lights of high-rise hotels and apartments. Further along the walkway, on the same side of the water, is the Dubai Marina Mall (p.428).

Nearby, The Walk at JBR is an outdoor parade of shops, restaurants and hotels parallel to the beach that has become a huge leisure-time draw for Dubai residents. Walking from one end to the other of this 1.7km promenade will take you past a whole

Burj Al Arab

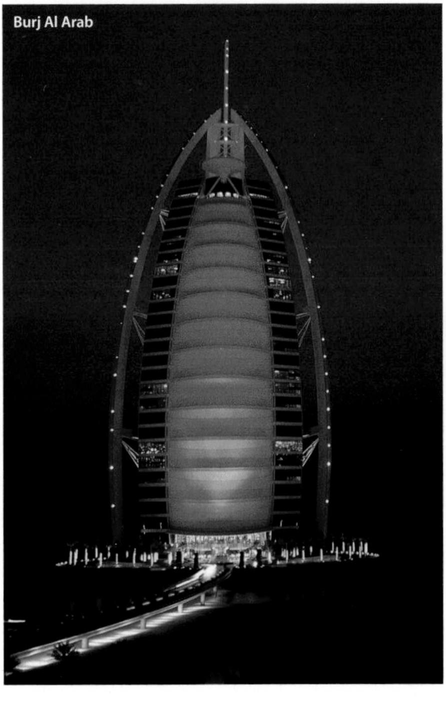

host of retail and eating options, with the scores of alfresco diners and Saturday strollers creating a lively atmosphere and providing some excellent people watching opportunities. From Wednesday to Saturday the outdoor Covent Garden Market by Rimal court is an added attraction, with street entertainers and craft stalls creating a colourful atmosphere (see p.419). There is also the recently-opened Meydan Beach Club next to the Ritz-Carlton along The Walk, with limited daily guest passes to the beach and pool (meydanbeach.com).

There's a good beach here, which is massively popular during the cooler months. The spaces in front of the hotels are reserved for guests, but there are plenty of areas in between that fill with crowds of families and groups of friends at weekends. The waters are fairly calm here and the shallow areas are scattered with bathers, while the hotels offer a variety of watersports such as parasailing and boat rides that anyone can sign up for. There is a big car park near the Rimal JBR block for beach goers, but access to this gets fairly congested at peak times.

DUBAI HOTELS

One thing you'll soon discover once you get to know Dubai is that much of the social scene revolves around the city's many hotels. Whereas in, say, Europe, where generally a city hotel's main purpose is to provide accommodation and host the odd corporate function, in Dubai hotels also act as places for residents to go for a drink, for dinner, to a nightclub, for a workout and to relax at the weekend.

There are dozens of the world's leading hotel brands to be found here, many of them housed in some of the city's most iconic buildings. Your first encounter with them may be when you come to Dubai on a reconnaissance mission before you make the decision to move permanently. You might also find yourself staying in one when you first move out, often hosted by your new company, while you find your feet and look for some accommodation of your own.

Once you're settled in, you'll soon become familiar with many of the places listed in this section. Whether you're going out for Friday brunch (p.548), after-work drinks or a romantic dinner, the UAE's licensing laws mean that it's likely to be in a hotel.

Dubai's popularity as a tourist destination means that you may soon find a continual stream of friends and family arriving and needing a place to stay. Putting your visitors up in a hotel (should lack of space dictate and budget allow) is something you may need to do. Fortunately, most hotels are excellently geared up for holidaymakers, with many located on the beach or near to some of the main attractions.

And, if you're a big fan of hotel life, you can always choose to live in one – serviced hotel apartments can be found throughout town, and prices have fallen enough recently for this to become a potential alternative to renting an apartment. See Hotel Apartments, p.68, for more details.

There is a vast array of hotels, ranging from one of the most superlative and opulent in the world, the Burj Al Arab (p.236), with a rack rate in the region of Dhs.11,000 for a night in a standard suite, right down to the cheapest digs in areas such as Deira costing under Dhs.200 a night. There are an increasing number of internationally branded budget hotels, plus a handful of B&Bs, and there's even a youth hostel (see Other Options, p.240). While the hotels at the higher end of the market offer superb surroundings and facilities, those at the cheaper end vary – and you certainly get what you pay for.

For people arriving in Dubai on a holiday package, hotels are normally five or four star, but if you are looking for cheaper accommodation, at the lower end of the market, make sure you check out the hotel and have a look at one of the rooms before checking in. Remember that, as with anywhere else in the world, you can usually get a discount on the rack rate or published price if you negotiate. Many hotels also offer seasonal discounts to GCC residents, particularly in the hot summer months when prices can be 50% lower than at peak times, providing a great opportunity for a bargain break.

The Dubai Department of Tourism & Commerce Marketing (DTCM) oversees a hotel classification system that gives an internationally recognised star rating to hotels and hotel apartments so visitors can judge more easily the standard of accommodation they will receive. This is being updated to include a budget hotel category, and Gold and Platinum Accolades for outstanding hotels and resorts.

The DTCM also operates a centralised internet reservation system for Dubai's hotels on its website (definitelydubai.com). This enables guests to reserve rooms online and allows them to take a virtual tour of the hotel before they book. Alternatively, the DTCM Welcome Bureau at Dubai International Airport provides an instant hotel reservations service, often at greatly discounted rates.

For restaurants and bars that operate in Dubai's hotels, refer to the index at the back of the book. Just look up the hotel name, and its outlets that are featured in the book will be listed underneath.

The Address Downtown Dubai > *p.IBC*

Emaar Blvd Downtown Dubai **04 436 8888**
theaddress.com
Map **2 F7** Metro **Burj Khalifa/Dubai Mall**

Even at over 300 metres in height, The Address is dwarfed by its neighbour, the Burj Khalifa – but breathtaking views, beautiful interiors and eight dining outlets (including Neos, the panoramic bar on the 63rd floor) make this one of the most popular spots in town. There are also two more The Address hotels, located at Dubai Mall and Dubai Marina, while The Address brand runs the small boutique hotel at The Montgomerie golf course and The Palace - The Old Town in Downtown Dubai.

The Address Dubai Mall

Financial Centre Rd Downtown Dubai **04 438 8888**
theaddress.com
Map **2 F6** Metro **Burj Khalifa/Dubai Mall**
With direct access to The Dubai Mall and all its kid-friendly attractions, this stylish hotel is a great base for families and shoppers. Its central location makes it ideal for business travellers too. Facilities include a fitness centre, spa and a sky-high infinity pool.

The Address Dubai Marina

Dubai Marina **04 436 7777**
theaddress.com
Map **1 K5** Metro **Dubai Marina**
This hotel dominates the Marina skyline, and is home to some impressive facilities. Its restaurants include a brasserie restaurant as well as a bar, Blends, overlooking the water. It's a handy spot for Marina residents to come to relax or put their visitors up for a short stay.

Al Bustan Rotana

Casablanca Rd Al Garhoud **04 282 0000**
rotana.com
Map **2 N7** Metro **GGICO**
A central location near the airport, Deira City Centre and the Dubai Creek makes this hotel accessible for tourists and business visitors. Renowned for its good restaurants, with Benihana (Japanese), Blue Elephant (Thai) and Rodeo Grill (steakhouse) standing out.

Al Manzil Hotel

Emaar Blvd, The Old Town Downtown Dubai
04 428 5888
almanzilhotel.ae
Map **2 F7** Metro **Burj Khalifa/Dubai Mall**
In the heart of Old Town, this beautiful four-star hotel is conveniently located for business and leisure trips. It also houses Nezesaussi, the popular Antipodean sports bar, and The Courtyard, a beautiful and atmospheric mezze and shisha cafe.

Al Murooj Rotana

Al Saffa St Trade Centre 2 **04 321 1111**
rotana.com
Map **2 G6** Metro **Financial Centre**
A luxurious resort hotel that is popular with both leisure tourists and business travellers, being ideally located right between Downtown and DIFC. It has a number of good bars and restaurants, including the popular and often raucous Double Decker bar.

Al Sahra Desert Resort

Dubailand **04 367 9500**
alsahra.com
Although it is located just 30 minutes out of Dubai, Al Sahra feels so distant that it could easily be in the heart of the Sahara – such is the feeling of deserted tranquillity. The stunning resort is a riff on Arabic architecture and there are plenty of traditional activities on hand, as well as plenty of areas to relax and unwind.

Amwaj Rotana

The Walk, Jumeirah Beach Residence Dubai Marina
04 428 2000
rotana.com
Map **1 K5** Metro **Dubai Marina**
Located on the bustling strip along new Dubai's seafront, this smart 200 room hotel features an outdoor pool, a fitness centre complete with steam room, sauna and Jacuzzi, and great dining venues including Italian bar Rosso and teppanyaki restaurant Benihana.

Armani Hotel Dubai

Burj Khalifa Downtown Dubai **04 888 3888**
dubai.armanihotels.com
Map **2 F6** Metro **Burj Khalifa/Dubai Mall**
Dubai's highest profile opening in recent years does not disappoint. This luxurious (and expensive) hotel, in the world's tallest tower, is remarkably without pretension, but its designer credentials are noticeable down to the nuts and bolts. As well as elegant suites kitted out with Armani/Casa goods, it is home to an Armani/Spa and a clutch of excellent dining venues.

Ascott Park Place Dubai > *p.101*

Shk Zayed Rd Trade Centre 1 **04 310 8503**
the-ascott.com
Map **3 K1** Metro **World Trade Centre**
This newly opened premises houses one, two and three-bedroom serviced residences, and two-storey loft apartments. Available for short and long-term lets, the fully furnished apartments are luxuriously kitted out. The property also features a 40-metre swimming pool, a well equipped gym, sauna, steam room and children's pool.

Asiana Hotel

Nr Reef Mall, Salahuddin Rd Al Muraqqabat
04 238 7777
asianahoteldubai.com
Map **2 N5** Metro **Union**
With a choice of four restaurants specialising in Chinese, Filipino, Japanese and Korean, this Deira-based five-star hotel is worth the trip. And if the quality, value and variety of food doesn't lure you in, then the trendy decor with Asian flair will do its very best to.

Atlantis The Palm > *p.259*

Crescent Rd Palm Jumeirah **04 426 0000**
atlantisthepalm.com
Map **1 N1** Metro **Nakheel**

With a staggering 1,539 rooms and suites, all with views of the sea or the Palm Jumeirah, Atlantis is certainly one of Dubai's grandest hotels. It has no less than four fancy restaurants featuring the cuisine of Michelin-starred chefs, including a branch of the world-famous chain Nobu. It is also home to Aquaventure and the Lost Chambers aquarium.

Bonnington Jumeirah Lakes Towers

Nr Almas Tower Jumeirah Lakes Towers **04 356 0000**
bonningtontower.com
Map **1 K5** Metro **Jumeirah Lakes Towers**

Containing both hotel suites and serviced apartments, as well as six restaurants and bars and a leisure deck with infinity pool, it has great connections to Dubai Marina via the nearby Metro.

Burj Al Arab

Jumeira Rd Umm Suqeim 3 **04 301 7777**
jumeirah.com
Map **1 S4** Metro **Mall of the Emirates**

Standing on its own man-made island, this dramatic Dubai icon's unique architecture is recognised around the world. Suites have two floors and are serviced by a team of butlers. To get into the hotel as a non-guest, you will need a restaurant reservation.

Crowne Plaza Dubai

Shk Zayed Rd Trade Centre 1 **04 331 1111**
ichotelsgroup.com
Map **2 H5** Metro **Emirates Towers**

One of Dubai's older five-star hotels, with an excellent collection of food and beverage outlets including Trader Vic's, Wagamama and Oscar's Vine Society. It's centrally located on Sheikh Zayed Road, so it's only a short drive to the beaches, malls and nightspots.

Crowne Plaza Dubai Deira

Nr Muraqaabat Police Station, Salahuddin Rd Muteena **04 262 5555**
ichotelsgroup.com
Map **2 P5** Metro **Abu Baker Al Siddique**

It may be slightly off the beaten track in the heart of Deira, but it pulls the crowds thanks to legendary buffet restaurant Spice Island; an all-you-can-eat-and-drink night here is a Dubai rite of passage.

Crowne Plaza Dubai Festival City

Al Rebat St Dubai Festival City **04 701 2222**
ichotelsgroup.com
Map **2 M9** Metro **Emirates**

On the banks of the Creek, this Crowne Plaza is excellently positioned within the Festival City complex. One of its highlights is the Belgian Beer Cafe, an atmospheric bar that serves a great selection of European beers and is extremely popular with Dubai residents and visitors alike.

Dubai Marine Beach Resort & Spa

Nr Jumeirah Mosque, Off Jumeira Rd Jumeira 1 **04 346 1111**
dxbmarine.com
Map **2 H4** Metro **World Trade Centre**

This beachside hotel has 195 villa-style rooms nestled among lush, green landscaped gardens, waterfalls and streams. The grounds offer three swimming pools, a spa, a health club and a small private beach. The restaurants and bars are perennially popular, especially the Ibiza-esque Sho Cho and beautiful hangout, Boudoir.

Dubai Marriott Harbour Hotel & Suites

Al Sufouh Rd Dubai Marina **04 319 4000**
dubaimarriottharbourhotel.com
Map **1 L5** Metro **Dubai Marina**

With 261 spacious suites, each with its own fitted kitchen, staying in The Harbour is like having your very own luxury apartment. The hotel is home to a range of dining options including The Observatory (offering great views from the 52nd floor) and 24 hour deli Counter Culture.

Dusit Thani Dubai

133 Shk Zayed Rd Trade Centre 2 **04 343 3333**
dusit.com
Map **2 G6** Metro **Financial Centre**

This member of the upmarket Thai hotel chain is situated in the 'clasped hands' (or 'pair of trousers') building on the main stretch of Sheikh Zayed Road. It features 321 rooms, and several food and beverage outlets including Benjarong, the 'royal Thai' restaurant and the Champagne Lounge.

NEW HOTELS

After a brief slowdown, tourism seems to be booming again in Dubai, and new hotels are still springing up across the city. Establishments that opened their doors in late 2012 included Jumeirah Creekside, Ocean View Hotel, Melia Dubai, Rixos The Palm Dubai, Fairmont The Palm and the JW Marriott Marquis, while as many as 30 more new hotels are set to open over the next three years. Highlights will include Anantara Dubai Palm Jumeirah Resort & Spa, Baccarat hotel, Sofitel Dubai Palm, Conrad Dubai, and the Palazzo Versace, while the next couple of years will see openings in areas until now unserved by hotels, such as Sports City and MotorCity.

The Address Downtown Dubai

Grosvenor House

The Palace – The Old Town

Atlantis The Palm

Fairmont Dubai

Nr Trade Centre R/A, Shk Zayed Rd Trade Centre 1
04 332 5555
fairmont.com/dubai
Map 2 J5 Metro World Trade Centre

Home to the legendary Spectrum on One restaurant, a beautiful rooftop pool and the renowned The Spa at Fairmont Dubai, this hotel is as notable for its modern interior as it is for its striking architecture, which is based on traditional Arabian windtowers and stands tall over the busy Sheikh Zayed Road strip.

Fairmont The Palm > *p.239*

Palm Jumeirah 04 457 3388
fairmont.com/palm
Map 1 M3 Metro Nakheel

Located on the trunk of the Palm Jumeirah, this is one of the island's most accessible venues. Relax and unwind at the Willow Stream Spa; enjoy the great outdoors at the hotel's private beach club with four swimming pools and outdoor leisure facilities; and take your pick from seven restaurants and lounges, serving Brazilian, pan-Chinese, Middle Eastern, Indian, Mediterranean and Asian cuisine. The Cigar Room features a walk-in humidor.

Grand Excelsior Hotel > *p.241*

Al Barsha 04 444 9999
grandexcelsior.ae
Map 1 R7 Metro Mall of the Emirates

With a striking cruise ship-style exterior, this 230-plus room hotel offers luxury amenities including a rooftop swimming pool and well-equipped gym. F&B outlets include an all-day dining restaurant, the Oak 'n' Barrel pub, a new Mediterranean venue, pool bar, and club.

Grand Hyatt Dubai

Nr Garhoud Bridge Umm Hurair 2 04 317 1234
dubai.grand.hyatt.com
Map 2 L8 Metro Dubai Healthcare City

The eye-catching design of this huge hotel near the Garhoud Bridge is not random: from the air the shape of the building spells out the word 'Dubai' in Arabic. It has excellent leisure facilities, a great selection of restaurants, and one of the most impressive lobbies in Dubai.

Grosvenor House

Al Sufouh Rd Dubai Marina 04 399 8888
grosvenorhouse-dubai.com
Map 1 L5 Metro Dubai Marina

This neon-blue skyscraper at the mouth of Dubai Marina is run by Le Meridien group, and features guest rooms, serviced apartments and some iconic nightlife venues: Buddha Bar, Gary Rhodes' Mezzanine and the crow's nest Bar 44 are all well worth a visit, with a second tower adding the likes of Toro Toro and Embassy. There's also a branch of luxury male-only spa 1847 here.

The H Hotel Dubai

Nr Trade Centre 1, Shk Zayed Rd Trade Centre 1
04 501 8888
h-hotel.com
Map 2 J5 Metro World Trade Centre

Previously The Monarch, the hotel may have changed names but its popular restaurants including Okku (p.526) and Ruth's Chris (p.534) stay the same. With 236 rooms and suites, including 53 serviced residential apartments, this hotel has one of the most desirable addresses in Dubai: One Sheikh Zayed Road.

Dubai Festival City

Habtoor Grand Beach Resort & Spa

Al Sufouh Rd Dubai Marina **04 408 4444**
habtoorhotels.com
Map **1 L4** Metro **Dubai Marina**

The twin-towered Habtoor Grand, on the beach at the northern end of Dubai Marina, offers 442 spacious rooms and suites with garden or sea views. Pools, restaurants and bars are set amid the hotel's tropical gardens bordering the Arabian Gulf, while The Underground bar draws in the expat football fan crowd for its multiple screens.

Hilton Dubai Creek

Baniyas Rd Al Rigga **04 227 1111**
hilton.com
Map **2 N5** Metro **Al Rigga**

With very flash yet understated elegance, this ultra-minimalist hotel features interiors of wood, glass and chrome. Centrally located and overlooking the Dubai Creek, with splendid views of the Arabian dhow trading posts, the hotel has two renowned restaurants: Glasshouse Brasserie and the Dubai gastronomic darling, Table 9 by Nick and Scott.

Hilton Dubai Jumeirah Resort

The Walk, Jumeirah Beach Residence Dubai Marina **04 399 1111**
hilton.com
Map **1 K4** Metro **Jumeirah Lakes Towers**

Situated between The Walk and the JBR beach, the Hilton Dubai Jumeirah features excellent restaurants, including the Italian BiCE and the Latin American Pachanga, as well as a sports bar, Studio One. There's a beach bar too – Wavebreaker – which is a great spot for sundowners. Dubai Marina is within walking distance.

Hyatt Regency Dubai

Nr Galleria Mall Corniche Deira **04 209 1234**
dubai.regency.hyatt.com
Map **2 N4** Metro **Palm Deira**

The restaurants alone in this hotel are well worth fighting the Deira traffic for – particularly Al Dawaar, Dubai's only revolving restaurant which boasts amazing views of the creek and coast. All 400 rooms have creek views too.

InterContinental Dubai Festival City

Al Rebat St Dubai Festival City **04 701 1111**
ichotelsgroup.com
Map **2 M9** Metro **Emirates**

Worth a visit if only to taste fine fare served up in Michelin-starred chef Pierre Gagnaire's excellent restaurant, or to enjoy the panoramic views from the Eclipse bar. The hotel also features an excellent spa, 498 rooms and suites, and access to the Festival Waterfront Centre.

Other Options

Aside from the headline hotels listed in this section, there are plenty of alternative options in which visitors can rest their heads. Radisson Blu (radissonblu.com), Rotana (rotana.com) and Holiday Inn (holidayinn.com) all have several outlets in Dubai. Al Barsha is home to a number of decent, less spectacular but well-priced hotels, while in Bur Dubai and Deira you'll find a number of places that offer good facilities and a central location, such as the Dhow Palace Hotel (dhowpalacedubai.com) and the newly opened Park Regis Kris Kin Hotel (parkregishotels.com).

Guest houses are also becoming more popular in Dubai. While smaller in size, B&Bs offer a homely feel and are ideal for guests who want to see more of the 'real Dubai'. Located in residential areas, they won't have access to private beaches, but there is no shortage of good public beaches to enjoy. Some will have their own pool and benefit from intimate surroundings, while owners will be only too happy to give personal recommendations on what to see and do.

Villa 47 (04 286 8239, villa47.com) has only two guest rooms, but is located close to the airport in Garhoud. Other establishment that receive good reviews are The Jumeirah Garden Guesthouse – a villa that features 10 rooms, peaceful gardens and a good restaurant – and the modern Fusion in Jumeira 3, both of which can be booked through the usual online portals.

Jumeirah Beach Hotel

Nr Wild Wadi, Jumeira Rd Umm Suqeim 3 **04 348 0000**
jumeirah.com
Map **1 S4** Metro **Mall of the Emirates**

Shaped like an ocean wave, with a fun and colourful interior, the hotel has 598 rooms and suites and 19 private villas, all with a sea view. It is also home to some excellent food and beverage outlets, including Uptown for happy hour cocktails and a great view of the Burj Al Arab.

Jumeirah Creekside Hotel > *p.527*

Nr Aviation Club Al Garhoud **04 230 8555**
jumeirah.com
Map **2 M8** Metro **GGICO**

A sleek yet eclectically designed hotel with an abundance of venues. Start your day at the lively Italian cafe, go light and healthy on lunch at Plumeria, choose either steak or seafood at Blue Flame or south Asian flavours at Nomad for dinner, and then finish off

the evening with mint and rum infused mojitos at the rooftop lounge Cu-ba. From the statement art, to the personalised service, to the new concept menus, this hotel breathes boutique and is sure to 'wow'.

Jumeirah Emirates Towers

Shk Zayed Rd Trade Centre 2 **04 330 0000**
jumeirah.com
Map **2 H6** Metro **Emirates Towers**

Sophisticated and elegant, this hotel forms one part of Dubai's original iconic twin skyscrapers. It has 400 rooms, some excellent restaurants and bars (including Harry Ghatto's for hilarious karaoke nights), as well as an exclusive shopping mall.

Jumeirah Zabeel Saray

Crescent Rd West Palm Jumeirah **04 453 0000**
jumeirahzabeelsaray.com
Map **1 L3** Metro **Nakheel**

So opulent, it was used for the lavish party scenes in Mission Impossible: Ghost Protocol, Zabeel Saray is an architectural wonder, drawing on Arabic and Turkish influences. There are several excellent outlets, although the real draw is the spa which is one of the world's biggest.

JW Marriott Hotel Dubai

Abu Baker Al Siddique Rd Deira **04 262 4444**
marriott.com
Map **2 P6** Metro **Abu Baker Al Siddique**

Set in the bustling heart of Deira, the Marriott is best known for its theme nights and legendary brunches in Bamboo Lagoon, the Market Place and Hofbrauhaus, three restaurants situated around a grand staircase that snakes up from the lobby.

JW Marriott Marquis Dubai

Shk Zayed Rd Business Bay **04 414 0000**
marriott.com
Map **2 E6** Metro **Business Bay**

A landmark in the making, this new five-star hotel rises above Business Bay at a staggering 355m, making it the world's tallest freestanding hotel. Spread across two iconic towers, there's a choice of leisure and business facilities, with the hyped restaurant Rang Mahal by Atul Kochhar tipped to open early 2013.

Kempinski Hotel Mall Of The Emirates

Mall of the Emirates Al Barsha 1 **04 341 0000**
kempinski.com
Map **1 R6** Metro **Mall of the Emirates**

With over 400 deluxe rooms this hotel features a spa, infinity pool, fitness centre, tennis court and the attached Ski Dubai (p.356). Check into one of the 15 exclusive ski chalets, remove your snow boots, put your feet up by the (fake) fire and tuck into an après-ski afternoon tea while enjoying the view of the piste.

Le Meridien Dubai

Airport Rd Al Garhoud **04 217 0000**
lemeridien-dubai.com
Map **2 N8** Metro **Airport Terminal 1**

Just a stone's throw from Dubai airport and the Aviation Club, guests and visitors can enjoy many excellent restaurants inside the hotel, many of which share a large alfresco terrace in the cooler months. With 383 rooms, the hotel is also home to trendy nightspot The Warehouse and Antipodean restaurant Yalumba, which offers a famous Friday brunch.

Le Meridien Mina Seyahi Beach Resort & Marina

Al Sufouh Rd Al Sufouh 1 **04 399 3333**
lemeridien-minaseyahi.com
Map **1 M4** Metro **Nakheel**

After a major refurbishment, the hotel recently reopened with a new club lounge, rooftop pool, extended ballroom and an extra 200 or so rooms, some with a personalised butler service. New restaurants include a Japanese eatery. The legendary beach bar, Barasti, remains and there's still a wide offering of watersports to enjoy along the hotel's long stretch of beach.

Le Royal Meridien Beach Resort & Spa

Al Sufouh Rd, Jumeirah Beach Dubai Marina
04 399 5555
leroyalmeridien-dubai.com
Map **1 L4** Metro **Dubai Marina**

Large-scale beach resort at Dubai Marina. Good leisure facilities and a big selection of bars and restaurants including Mexican Maya and seafood outlet Me Vida. A shuttle bus transfers guests through the Marina's construction and traffic hazards to allow access to the facilities of the nearby Grosvenor House.

Madinat Jumeirah

Nr Burj Al Arab, Jumeira Rd Al Sufouh 1 **04 366 8888**
jumeirah.com
Metro **1 R4 Mall of the Emirates**

This extravagant resort has two hotels, Al Qasr and Mina A'Salam, with no fewer than 940 luxurious rooms and suites, and the exclusive Dar Al Masyaf summer houses, all linked by man-made waterways navigated by wooden abra boats which whisk guests around the resort. Nestled between the two hotels is the Souk Madinat, with over 100 shops and 40 bars and restaurants. A third hotel is due to open in 2015.

Media One Hotel

Dubai Media City Al Sufouh 1 **04 427 1000**
mediaonehotel.com
Map **1 M5** Metro **Nakheel**

This fun, funky and functional hotel is great if you need to be in reach of Media City. The rooms are

geared towards the business traveller's needs, with workspaces, Wi-Fi and flat screen TVs, but they certainly don't lack style. CafeM and Z:ONE are popular post-work haunts, while The Med hosts a fun Friday brunch.

Melia Dubai

Kuwait St Al Raffa **04 386 8111** melia-dubai.com
Map **2 K4** Metro **Al Fahidi**

Contemporary and elegant, the Melia stands out in Bur Dubai for all the right reasons. Featuring two high-profile restaurants – Titanic (p.543) and Signature (p.537) – and a luxurious spa, this is a hidden gem worth discovering. The rooms are tastefully decorated, and the TVs disguised as mirrors add a stylish touch.

The Meydan Hotel *> p.245*

Meydan Racecourse, Al Meydan Rd Meydan
04 381 3231
meydanhotels.com
Map **2 E10** Metro **Business Bay**

There's no better place to watch the racing action at The Meydan horserace track than from the rooftop infinity pool of this decadent, five-star, landmark hotel, but the striking modern design, spa and excellent outlets including Prime and Shiba make this hotel a deluxe destination in itself. Guests can make use of free shuttle buses to destinations around Dubai.

Media Rotana *> p.461*

Nr Hessa Street Tecom **04 435 0000**
rotana.com/mediarotana
Map **1 P6** Metro **Dubai Internet City**

Ideally located close to Dubai Media City and Dubai Internet City, this city hotel boasts an outdoor pool and massage rooms. On the dining front, Prego's restaurant offers a cosy ambience with an open kitchen; Channels features live cooking; or you can try designer beers at Nelson's pub. Hugely popular is the alfresco brunch on The Terrace, held every Friday.

Mövenpick Hotel Deira

Nr Abu Backer Al Siddique Rd Muteena **04 444 0111**
moevenpick-hotels.com
Map **2 P6** Metro **Abu Baker Al Siddique**

Surprisingly elegant for a business hotel, this 216-room property offers all the mod cons for travelling executives. For a welcome respite from Deira's crowded streets, there is a rooftop pool, gym, and complimentary shuttle bus and access to a private beach club on The Palm Jumeirah.

Mövenpick Hotel Ibn Battuta Gate

Nr Ibn Battuta Mall The Gardens **04 444 0000**
moevenpick-hotels.com
Map **1 G5** Metro **Ibn Battuta**

Catering for travellers who want easy access to Dubai Marina and Jebel Ali, this five-star, strikingly designed hotel is themed on the territories to which the 14th century explorer Ibn Battuta travelled. The pool terrace offers stunning views over 'new Dubai' and its food outlets represent the cuisines of the world.

Mövenpick Hotel Jumeirah Beach

The Walk, Jumeirah Beach Residence Dubai Marina
04 449 8888
moevenpick-hotels.com
Map **1 K4** Metro **Dubai Marina**

Situated on The Walk at JBR this five-star, 300 room hotel has much to recommend it, not least its beachfront location and stunning sea-view pool bar, but also a couple of decent restaurants.

Oasis Beach Tower

The Walk, Jumeirah Beach Residence Dubai Marina
04 8145 700
jebelali-international.com
Map **1 K4** Metro **Dubai Marina**

Located in a prime spot in the middle of The Walk at JBR, this gleaming glass tower houses a range of two, three and four-bedroom hotel apartments for holiday or long-term use. At the foot of the twin tower complex are the popular eating and drinking spots Wagamama, Frankie's and Trader Vic's Mai Tai Lounge.

Ocean View Hotel *> p.243, 509, 557, 567*

The Walk, Jumeirah Beach Residence Dubai Marina
04 814 5599
jaresortshotels.com
Map **1 K4** Metro **Jumeirah Lakes Towers**

Thanks to its great location, right on the edge of The Walk and opposite the vast public beach, this hotel offers all the makings for a great holiday. All of the 340 plus rooms at 'Dubai's only four-star hotel on the beach' have sea views, and aqua-lovers can enjoy the swimming pool, the local beach or jump on a complimentary shuttle to the private beach at Jebel Ali Golf Resort. Dining highlights include Fogo Vivo, a Brazilian steakhouse with an open kitchen, and The Whistler, a cheese and wine bar. A popular choice for families, there is a shaded children's pool and kid's club for three to 11 year olds.

One&Only Royal Mirage *> p.485*

Al Sufouh Rd Al Sufouh 1 **04 399 9999**
oneandonlyresorts.com
Map **1 M4** Metro **Nakheel**

This stunningly beautiful resort is home to three different properties: The Palace, Arabian Court and Residence & Spa. The service and dining (opt for the Beach, Bar & Grill for a romantic evening out; try delectable Moroccan cuisine in the opulent Tagine; or enjoy cocktails with a view in The Rooftop and Sports Lounge) are renowned, and a luxury spa treatment here is the ultimate indulgence.

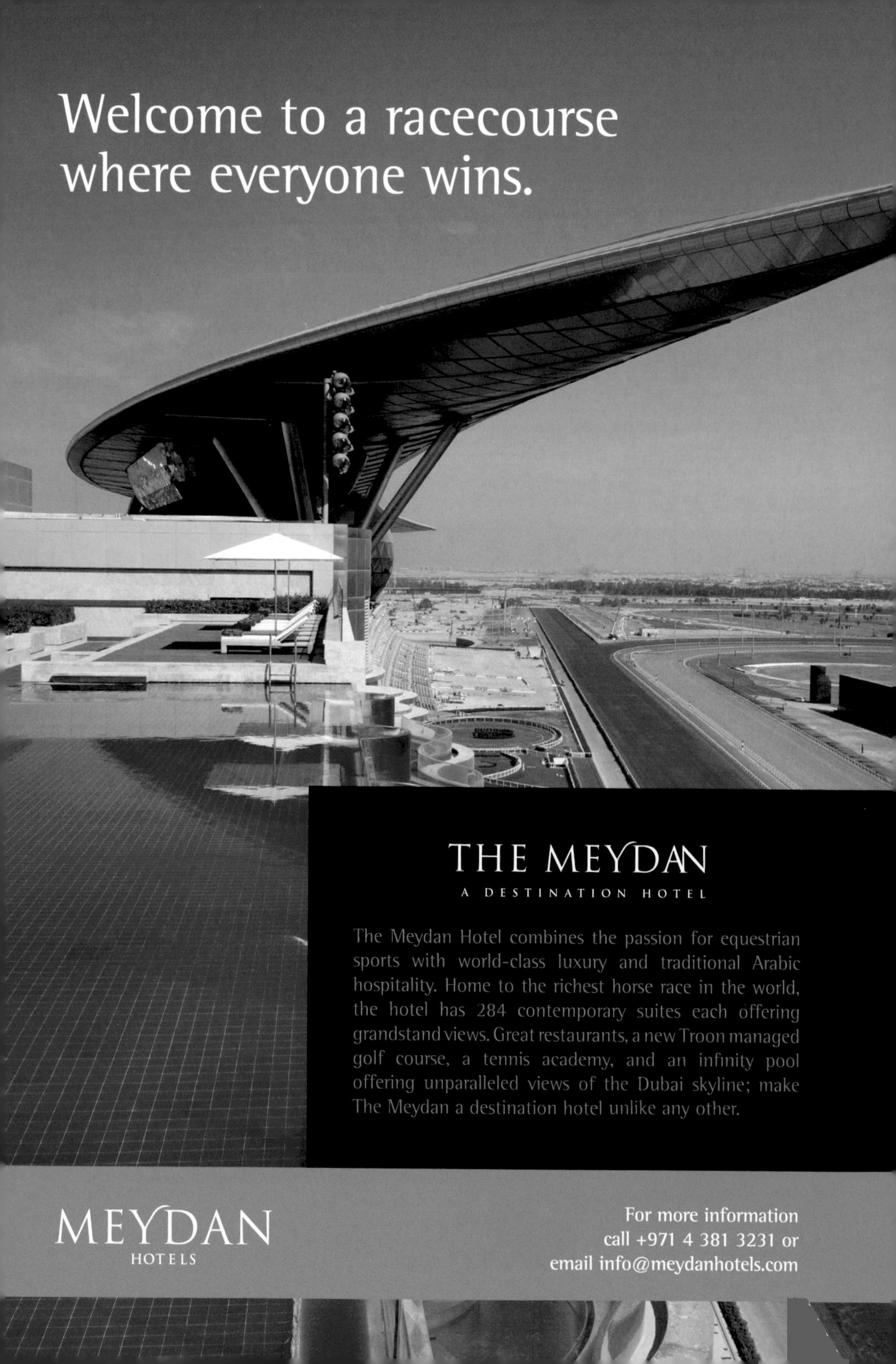
Welcome to a racecourse where everyone wins.
THE MEYDAN
A DESTINATION HOTEL
The Meydan Hotel combines the passion for equestrian sports with world-class luxury and traditional Arabic hospitality. Home to the richest horse race in the world, the hotel has 284 contemporary suites each offering grandstand views. Great restaurants, a new Troon managed golf course, a tennis academy, and an infinity pool offering unparalleled views of the Dubai skyline; make The Meydan a destination hotel unlike any other.
MEYDAN
HOTELS
For more information
call +971 4 381 3231 or
email info@meydanhotels.com

One&Only The Palm

Palm Island, The West Crescent Palm Jumeirah
04 440 1010
oneandonlyresorts.com
Map **1 L3** Metro **Nakheel**

A stunning boutique resort intended to create an intimate and indulgent setting. Designed in an Andalusian style, the 64 rooms, 26 suites and four beachfront villas feature free-standing bath tubs and rain showers, plus private terraces or balconies that take in the lights of Dubai Marina. Among the highlights is restaurant STAY by Yannick Alléno.

The Palace Downtown Dubai

Emaar Blvd Downtown Dubai **04 428 7888**
theaddress.com
Map **2 F6** Metro **Burj Khalifa/Dubai Mall**

Palatial indeed, The Palace looks out onto the mighty Burj Khalifa and the Dubai Fountain, and boasts 242 luxurious rooms and suites, a beautiful spa and some excellent restaurants, including Asado and Thiptara.

Park Hyatt Dubai

Nr Dubai Creek Golf & Yacht Club Port Saeed
04 602 1234
dubai.park.hyatt.com
Map **2 M7** Metro **Deira City Centre**

Enjoying a prime waterfront location within the grounds of Dubai Creek Golf & Yacht Club, the Park Hyatt is Mediterranean in style with low-rise buildings, natural colours and stylish decor. The hotel has 225 rooms and suites, all with beautiful views, as well as some great dining outlets and a luxurious spa, which features a luxury couple's massage option. Excellent restaurants inside the hotel include The Thai Kitchen and Traiteur.

Raffles Dubai

Pullman Deira City Centre Hotel

Nr Deira City Centre Port Saeed **04 294 1222**
pullmanhotels.com
Map **2 N7** Metro **Deira City Centre**

A good location adjoining Deira City Centre and views over the greens of Dubai Creek Golf & Yacht Club make this slightly tired hotel a great base for shoppers and golfers. The hotel also has a collection of serviced apartments.

Get Away

If you'd like to escape the city for a day or two, there are a number of excellent desert, beach and mountain resorts within Dubai emirate that are well worth checking out – see Desert Resorts & Getaways, p.266, for full details.

Pullman Dubai Mall Of The Emirates

Mall of the Emirates Al Barsha 1 **04 377 2000**
pullman-dubai.com
Map **1 R6** Metro **Mall of the Emirates**

This brand new luxury hotel retains the simple but elegant style of its French owners, with clean, unfussy design and comfortable rooms fitted with seamless technology touches. Excellent facilities including great restaurants, two divine rooftop pools, the Sanctuary Spa, a fitness centre and a shisha terrace – with one of Dubai's best panoramas – make staying here a pleasure whether you're in town for business or fun.

Radisson Blu Hotel, Dubai Deira Creek

Nr Dubai Municipality, Baniyas Rd Al Rigga
04 222 7171
radissonblu.com
Map **2 M5** Metro **Union**

Proving that sometimes the oldies are the goodies, this classic hotel on the banks of the creek features some popular restaurants and a great 'Old Dubai' location, particularly for business visitors.

Radisson Blu Hotel, Dubai Downtown

Nr Dubai Mall Downtown Dubai **04 450 2000**
radissonblu.com
Map **2 G7** Metro **Burj Khalifa/Dubai Mall**

With some rooms of its 242 rooms overlooking Burj Khalifa, the Radisson Blu is conveniently located just minutes from Dubai Mall. It's a comfortable and well-equipped hotel with a tasteful all-day dining restaurant and well-equipped, well-appointed business facilities; for pure relaxation there is a rooftop pool bar, as well as a fitness centre, outdoor pool, steam bath and sauna.

Radisson Blu Hotel, Dubai Media City
Dubai Media City Al Sufouh 1 **04 366 9111**
radissonblu.com
Map **1 M5** Metro **Nakheel**
A busy hotel in the heart of Media City. It is conveniently located for business travellers, and also popular with media types who make a beeline for Italian restaurant Certo and rooftop bar Tamanya Terrace after office hours.

Radisson Royal Hotel, Dubai
Shk Zayed Rd Trade Centre 1 **04 308 0000**
radissonblu.com
Map **2 H5** Metro **World Trade Centre**
Within walking distance of the World Trade Centre Metro Station, this city centre hotel is a popular choice with business travellers. But its appeal is far-reaching, thanks to its spa, Japanese restaurant Icho and, above all, trendy London nightclub Mo*Vida.

Raffles Dubai
Wafi Umm Hurair 2 **04 324 8888**
raffles.com
Map **2 L7** Metro **Dubai Healthcare City**
With 248 stunning suites, the renowned Raffles Spa and a unique Botanical Sky Garden, this is one of Dubai's most noteworthy city hotels. Eight food and beverage outlets offer a mix of international and far eastern cuisine.

The Ritz-Carlton, Dubai
Nr The Walk, Jumeirah Beach Residence
Dubai Marina **04 399 4000**
ritzcarlton.com
Map **1 L4** Metro **Dubai Marina**
Even though it is the only low-rise building amid the sea of Marina towers behind it, all 138 rooms have beautiful views of the Gulf – the Ritz-Carlton was, after all, here years before the rest of the marina was built. Afternoon tea in the Lobby Lounge is a must, and there are several other excellent restaurants and a very good spa onsite. The Ritz-Carlton has also added another property to its offerings, with a 341 room hotel in the DIFC area.

The Ritz-Carlton, Dubai International Financial Centre
Dubai International Financial Centre (DIFC)
Trade Centre 2 **04 372 2222**
ritzcarlton.com
Map **2 G6** Metro **Financial Centre**
Offering a mix of luxurious hotel accommodation and serviced apartments, this hotel is perfectly located for business guests, but the impressive range of high-end bars, restaurants, cafes and boutiques in DIFC means it's one of Dubai's latest leisure destinations in its own right.

Rixos The Palm Dubai
East Crescent Palm Jumeirah **04 457 5555**
rixos.com
Map **1 P3** Metro **Nakheel**
Located on the eastern crescent of the Palm Jumeirah, Rixos The Palm boasts incredible views in all directions – the Arabian Gulf, the Palm and the Dubai coastline – with many of the city's landmarks in sight, not least the Burj Al Arab, Burj Khalifa and Dubai Marina. It is a relaxing resort on a peaceful slice of beach, with a few dining options, great lounging areas and luxurious spa.

Shangri-La Hotel Dubai
Shk Zayed Rd Trade Centre 1 **04 343 8888**
shangri-la.com
Map **2 G5** Metro **Financial Centre**
Featuring great views of the coast and the city from Sheikh Zayed Road, this hotel has 301 guest rooms and suites, 126 serviced apartments, a health club and spa, two swimming pools and a variety of restaurants and bars including majestic Moroccan Marrakech and seafood specialist Amwaj.

Sheraton Dubai Creek Hotel & Towers
Nr National Bank of Dubai, Baniyas Rd Al Rigga
04 228 1111
sheratondubaicreek.com
Map **2 M5** Metro **Union**
This hotel's location on the Deira bank of the creek means that most of the 255 rooms have beautiful waterway views. There are some great eateries too; Ashiana is renowned as one of the best traditional Indian restaurants in Dubai, Creekside is a favoured Japanese diner and Vivaldi shines as a wonderful Italian venue with great views.

Sheraton Jumeirah Beach Resort
The Walk, Jumeirah Beach Residence Dubai Marina
04 399 5533
sheratonjumeirahbeach.com
Map **1 J4** Metro **Jumeirah Lakes Towers**
An older waterfront resort right at the southern end of JBR beach, this hotel has a secluded stretch of the golden sands to itself, plus green gardens and a couple of decent restaurants, including Peacock Chinese Restaurant and The Grill Room. It hosts a chill-out evening on Fridays, Ocean Club, which is popular with local residents.

Sofitel Dubai Jumeirah Beach
The Walk, Jumeirah Beach Residence Dubai Marina
04 448 4848
sofitel.com
Map **1 K4** Metro **Jumeirah Lakes Towers**
This chic, five-star, seafront property stands tall on Jumeirah Beach Residence's The Walk, and the hotel offers direct access to the beach as well as a host of

boutiques and cafes along the promenade. It features a Carita beauty salon, a pool bar with infinity pool, popular Irish sports bar The Hub, and signature French restaurant Rococo.

The Westin Dubai Mina Seyahi Beach Resort & Marina

Al Sufouh Rd Al Sufouh 1 **04 399 4141**
westinminaseyahi.com
Map **1 M4** Metro **Nakheel**

Set on 1,200 metres of private beach, The Westin has 294 spacious rooms and suites with all the luxury amenities you would expect of a five-star hotel, including the aptly named Heavenly Spa. There are plenty of dining venues, including perennially popular Italian Bussola, Senyar for cocktails and tapas, and wine and cheese bar Oeno.

ART & CULTURE

Heritage & Cultural Sites

Old Dubai features many fascinating places to visit, offering glimpses into a time when the city was nothing more than a small fishing and trading port. Many of the pre-oil heritage sites have been carefully restored, paying close attention to traditional design and using original building materials. Stroll through the Bastakiya area, with its many distinctive windtowers, and marvel at how people coped in Dubai before air-conditioning. Dubai Museum and Jumeirah Mosque both offer interesting insights into local culture.

Al Ahmadiya School & Heritage House

Nr Dubai Public Libraries, Al Khor St Al Ras
04 226 0286
definitelydubai.com
Map **2 M4** Metro **Al Ras**

Al Ahmadiya School was the earliest regular school in the city and a visit is an excellent opportunity to see the history of education in Dubai. Established in 1912 for Dubai's elite, this building was closed in 1963 when the school relocated to larger premises. Situated in what is becoming a small centre for heritage in Deira (Al Souk Al Kabeer), it sits just behind the Heritage House, an interesting example of a traditional Emirati family house and the former home of the school's founder, Mr Ahmadiya, dating back to 1890. Both buildings have been renovated and are great places for a glimpse of how life used to be. Admission to both is free. Open Saturday to Thursday 08:30 to 20:30 and 14:00 to 20:30 on Friday.

> **Ramadan Timings**
>
> During Ramadan, timings for many companies change significantly. Museums and heritage sites usually open slightly later in the morning than usual, and close earlier in the afternoon.

Dubai Museum

Al Fahidi Fort Al Souk Al Kabeer **04 353 1862**
definitelydubai.com
Map **2 M4** Metro **Al Fahidi**

Located in Al Fahidi Fort, this museum is creative, well thought-out and interesting for all the family. The fort was originally built in 1787 as the residence of the ruler of Dubai and for sea defence, and then renovated in 1970 to house the museum. All aspects of Dubai's past are represented. You can walk through a souk from the 1950s, stroll through an oasis, see into a traditional house, get up close to local wildlife, learn about the archaeological finds or go 'underwater' to discover the pearl diving and fishing industries. There are some entertaining mannequins to pose with too. Entry costs Dhs.3 for adults and Dhs.1 for children under 6 years old. Open daily 08:30 to 20:30 (14:30 to 20:30 on Fridays).

Falcon Museum & Heritage Sports Centre

Nr Nad Al Sheba Market, Meydan Rd Meydan
04 338 0201
Map **2 D9** Metro **Business Bay**

There's no better place to learn all about the national bird of prey than at the falconry centre, just outside Meydan. A hub for breeders and owners, this heritage landmark of Dubai offers a truly Arabian falconry experience. The centre has a souk for falcon traders and falcon breeders, as well as a small mosque, (a replica of the old Masjid Bin Suroor in Shindagha), a cafe and gift shop. Be dazzled by falconry displays in the outdoor courtyard and learn all about these fascinating birds at the museum, which showcases the history of falcons in three halls and a 3D light and sound show. The souk is open from 09:00 to 22:00 every day, except Friday, with some shops closing between 12:00 and 14:00.

Heritage & Diving Village

Nr Shk Saeed Al Maktoum House Al Shindagha
04 393 7139
definitelydubai.com
Map **2 M4** Metro **Al Ghubaiba**

Located near the mouth of Dubai Creek, the Heritage & Diving Village focuses on Dubai's maritime past, pearl diving traditions and architecture. Visitors can observe traditional potters and weavers practising their craft the way it has been done for centuries. Local women serve traditionally cooked snacks – one of the rare opportunities you'll have to sample genuine Emirati cuisine. It is particularly lively during the Dubai Shopping Festival and Eid celebrations, with performances including traditional sword dancing. Open daily 08:30 to 22:00 (Fridays 15:30-22:00). The village is very close to Sheikh Saeed Al Maktoum's House, the home of the much-loved former ruler of Dubai, which is a good example of a traditional home and houses a number of interesting photographic exhibits.

Jumeirah Mosque

Jumeira Rd Jumeira 1 **04 353 6666**
cultures.ae
Map **2 H4** Metro **World Trade Centre**

This is the most beautiful mosque in the city and perhaps the best known, as its image features on the Dhs.500 banknote. The Sheikh Mohammed Centre for Cultural Understanding (cultures.ae) organises mosque tours for non-Muslims on Saturday, Sunday, Tuesday and Thursday mornings at 10:00. Visitors are guided around the mosque and told all about the building, and then the hosts give a talk on Islam and prayer rituals. The tour offers a fascinating insight into the culture and beliefs of the local population, and is thoroughly recommended. You must dress conservatively – no shorts and no sleeveless tops. Women must also cover their hair with a head scarf or shawl, and all visitors will be asked to remove their shoes. Cameras are allowed, pre-booking is essential and there is a registration fee of Dhs.10 per person.

Majlis Ghorfat Um Al Sheif

Off Jumeira Rd Jumeira 3 **04 852 1374**
definitelydubai.com
Map **2 C4** Metro **Business Bay**

Constructed in 1955 from coral stone and gypsum, this simple building was used by the late Sheikh Rashid bin Saeed Al Maktoum as a summer residence. The ground floor is an open veranda (known as a leewan or rewaaq), while upstairs the majlis (the Arabic term for meeting place) is decorated with carpets, cushions, lanterns and rifles. The roof terrace was used for drying dates and even sleeping on and it originally offered an uninterrupted view of the sea, although all you can see now are villa rooftops. The site has a garden with a pond and traditional falaj irrigation system. In another corner there's a barasti shelter constructed from palm branches and leaves. The Majlis is located just inland from Jumeira Road on Street 17, beside Reem Al Bawardi Restaurant – look for the brown Municipality signs. Entry is Dhs.1 for adults and free for children under six years. Closed Friday mornings.

Naif Museum

Naif Fort Deira **04 226 0286**
definitelydubai.com
Map **2 N4** Metro **Baniyas Square**

Situated in the heart of Deira, Naif Fort gives a fascinating insight into the history and development of Dubai's police force, as well as the city's justice system. Built in 1939, almost entirely of clay, the fort is home to life-size models, interactive exhibits and museum displays. The fort, which has been extensively restored, was the former police headquarters and has also served as a prison. Open Saturday to Thursday 08:00-19:30, and Friday 14:30-19:30.

Sheikh Mohammed Centre For Cultural Understanding

Bastakiya Al Souk Al Kabeer **04 353 6666**
cultures.ae
Map **2 M4** Metro **Al Fahidi**

Located in the Bastakiya area of the city, this centre was established to help visitors and residents understand the customs and traditions of the UAE through various activities and programmes. These include cultural iftars during Ramadan, fascinating guided creekside tours and spoken Gulf Arabic classes. The building that houses the centre is also worth a look for the majlis-style rooms located around the courtyard and great views through the palm trees and windtowers. Open Sunday to Thursday 08:00 to 18:00, Saturday 09:00 to 13:00.

Sheikh Saeed Al Maktoum House

Nr Heritage & Diving Village Al Shindagha
04 393 7139
definitelydubai.com
Map **2 M4** Metro **Al Ghubaiba**

The modest home of Dubai's much-loved former ruler was once strategically located at the mouth of Dubai Creek but now lies close to the Bur Dubai entrance to Al Shindagha Tunnel. Dating from 1896, this carefully restored house-turned-museum is built in the traditional manner of the Gulf coast, using coral covered in lime and sand-coloured plaster. The interesting displays in many rooms show rare and wonderful photographs of all aspects of life in Dubai pre-oil. There is also an old currency and stamp collection and great views over the creek from the upper floor. Entry is Dhs.2 for adults, Dhs.1 for children and free for under six year olds.

Art Galleries

While there's nothing like the Tate or the Louvre in Dubai yet, there are a number of galleries that have interesting exhibitions of art and traditional Arabic artefacts, and more are springing up, particularly in the Al Quoz area. Most operate as a shop and a gallery, but some also provide studios for artists and are involved in the promotion of art within the emirates. The Majlis Gallery, The Courtyard and the XVA Gallery are all worth visiting for their architecture alone; they provide striking locations in which you can enjoy a wide range of art, both local and international, while at Opera Gallery you'll find the odd Renoir and Picasso. Many art shops also have galleries as well.

Visit askexplorer.com for up-to-date listings on new exhibitions throughout the year.

Art Couture

Al Badia Golf Club By InterContinental Dubai Festival City Dubai Festival City **04 601 0101**
artcoutureuae.com
Map **2 M10** Metro **Emirates**

With a number of regional and international solo and group exhibitions each year, this gallery also hosts the interesting Art & Coffee mornings that offer art fans a chance to chat to artists, watch live demonstrations and participate in discussions around a set theme.

Artsawa

Al Marabea Rd Al Quoz Industrial 1
04 340 8660
artsawa.com
Map **1 U7** Metro **Noor Islamic Bank**

Artsawa focuses on the promotion of contemporary Arab art in a variety of mediums including collage, etching, installation, painting, photography, sculpture and video. It also hosts performing arts performances, music recitals and educational workshops aimed at engaging the local and international communities.

Artspace

Dubai International Financial Centre (DIFC)
Trade Centre 2 **04 323 0820**
artspace-dubai.com
Map **2 G6** Metro **Financial Centre**

Previously located in Fairmont Dubai, the new DIFC gallery is one of Dubai's most sophisticated, specialising in showcasing contemporary art from Middle Eastern artists.

Ayyam Art Center Dubai

Alserkal Avenue, Street 8 Al Quoz Industrial 1
04 323 6242
ayyamgallery.com
Map **1 U6** Metro **Noor Islamic Bank**

The leading purveyor of Syrian art in Damascus has a branch in Al Quoz. As well as hosting a range of regional exhibitions, it also runs the Shabab Ayyam Project, a programme that encourages the development of new talent in the region.

Carbon 12 Dubai

Alserkal Avenue, Street 8 Al Quoz Industrial 1
04 340 6016
carbon12dubai.com
Map **1 U6** Metro **Noor Islamic Bank**

In the heart of Al Quoz, Carbon 12 hosts around 10 exhibitions a year, and states its mission as bringing together a colourful variety of international movements with one common point: contemporary at its best.

Creative Art Centre

Nr Mercato Mall, Jumeira Rd Jumeira 1
04 344 4394
Map **1 F4** Metro **Burj Khalifa/Dubai Mall**

This large gallery and shop has eight showrooms with a wide range of original art, framed maps, and Arabian antiques and gifts. The gallery specialises in the restoration of antiques and furniture, and also offers picture framing. To find it, take the turning inland between Choithrams supermarket and Town Centre shopping mall.

Cuadro Fine Art Gallery

Dubai International Financial Centre (DIFC)
Trade Centre 2 **04 425 0400**
cuadroart.com
Map **2 G6** Metro **Financial Centre**

Another DIFC gallery with a space every bit as beautiful as the art it displays. Exhibitions concentrate on contemporary pieces focusing on painting, paper, photography and sculpture. These are enhanced by the Cuadro Education Program, which organises lectures, workshops and panel discussions.

The Empty Quarter

Dubai International Financial Centre (DIFC)
Trade Centre 2 **04 323 1210**
theemptyquarter.com
Map **2 G6** Metro **Financial Centre**

This gallery deals exclusively in fine art photography, staging exhibitions from both emerging and established artists. Work displayed comes from across the globe and features works from abstract art to photo journalism. The gallery also features books, and audio and visual presentations on photographers.

The Farjam Collection

Dubai International Financial Centre (DIFC)
Trade Centre 2 **04 323 0303**
farjamcollection.org
Map **2 G6** Metro **Emirates Towers**

This gallery in DIFC features pieces from the private collection of a local arts patron. The rotating exhibitions include Quranic scripts, regional art and international masterpieces, and the gallery hosts guided tours and an art camp for kids in the summer.

Art Dubai

Art Dubai is an annual get-together of industry people from across the Middle East and Asian art world. Held in March at Madinat Jumeirah, one of the main events is the Global Art Forum, which attracts artists, curators, museum groups and international media representatives. Several exhibitions and events also run alongside the forum, drawing thousands of visitors.

Al Quoz – The Unlikely Art District

Meem Gallery

When it comes to exploring Dubai's neighbourhoods, Al Quoz is probably the last place you'd put on your 'must see' list. For the large part it's a dirty, dusty industrial zone, where polluting factories, box-kit warehouses and depressing-looking labour accommodation line the gridded network of roads. For the majority of tourists, and indeed most residents, it's a place to ignore. To do so though would be to miss out on what may be the country's most hopeful and expressive arts community. Tucked away in massive warehouses, often out of sight, are a collection of galleries and impressive interior design shops that are some of Dubai's best bets for truly joining the global arts landscape. Add to that an endless selection of cheap south Asian cafeterias, the Gold and Diamond Park, Times Square Centre and a few less-ambitious shopping centres, and Al Quoz quickly becomes a destination worth exploring.

Although less-publicised than massive state-sponsored cultural projects in Abu Dhabi or Doha, the Al Quoz art scene, and Al Serkal Avenue in particular, are the heart of the Arab art scene. It is here that lesser-known artists can find exhibition space, and the galleries are working to promote Arab art on the international scene. Find your way around this maze of art galleries with the aid of ArtMap (artinthecity.com).

At one end of the spectrum sit smaller Al Quoz galleries such as 4 Walls Art Gallery (4walls-dubai.com) and, at the other end, are the well-known, relatively long-established galleries that have experienced art collectors as their main clients. One of the best recognised is The Third Line (p.256). The gallery itself is impressive and the art it contains is some of the most innovative in the city. In addition to monthly exhibitions, the gallery hosts alternative programmes which include film screenings, debates and international multimedia forums, all with the intention of promoting interaction between regional artists and the public.

Equally impressive is Ayyam Art Centre Dubai (p.251), which had already established itself as a leading purveyor of Syrian art in Damascus before opening its warehouse gallery here. Ayyam is located in Al Serkal Avenue where the amazing and creative spaces are now almost back-to-back; look out for The Mojo Gallery (p.255), Green Art Gallery, Carbon12 and Gallery Isabelle Van Den Eynde (ivde.net), all of which tend to exhibit works from up and coming artists, both regional and international. A stone's throw away from Al Serkal is The Courtyard, home to the

Modern Art

Dubai is following in Abu Dhabi's footsteps with plans for a new cultural district in the emirate. The Dubai Modern Art Museum and Opera House District, which will be built in Downtown Dubai, will include an opera house and modern art museum, two 'art hotels' and several new galleries.

Some of Dubai's most significant culture is hidden away among the sand-covered warehouses, factories and labour camps of Al Quoz.

Total Arts Gallery (p.256), which has long showcased Middle Eastern art with an emphasis on Iranian artists. The Courtyard also stands out as being a little different as it frequently exhibits traditional handicrafts and antique furniture. Elsewhere in Al Quoz, you'll find great galleries like ArtSawa (p.251) and Traffic (p.256).

Along with the promotion and exhibition of regional art, Al Quoz has also become a centre for the creative process. The Jam Jar (p.254) offers an extensive schedule of workshops and open studio sessions geared towards amateur artists looking for a welcoming outlet. Workshops range from advanced painting skills to the basics of lomography. The Jam Jar also hosts several exhibitions each year in its gallery space.

Shelter (shelter.ae) promotes regional creatives with a host of entrepreneurial services including office space, business setup assistance and an environment to nurture contacts. Along with its office spaces and meeting rooms, Shelter includes a brasserie run by MORE Cafe and a boutique shop selling design-centric gifts and clothing produced by its members. And, at the top end of Al Quoz is The Fridge (04 347 7793) where the offering focuses more on performing arts.

Ayyam Gallery

The Flying House

House 18, 25 Street Al Quoz 1 04 265 3365
flyinghouse.net
Map 2 C6 Metro Business Bay

Al Quoz space dedicated to contemporary Emirati artists. The Flying House is a non-profit organisation that holds a collection of important Emirati works that have been assembled over a period of 30 years. Together with early works by some of the pioneers of contemporary art in the UAE, the gallery shows recent works by both established and young artists.

Abu Dhabi Art Scene

Establishing itself as a major centre for arts and culture is high on the agenda for Abu Dhabi, which promises to be great news for art lovers in the UAE. At the top of the bill of forthcoming attractions will be branches of the Louvre and the Guggenheim in the new Saadiyat Island Cultural District, which were scheduled to begin construction in 2013. Emirates Palace already regularly plays host to some excellent international exhibitions in association with some of the world's leading institutions, while the new gallery Manarat Al Saadiyat is already making waves (saadiyat.ae). There's also an increasingly important annual event on the calendar, the Abu Dhabi Art Fair (abudhabiartfair.ae), which is staged in November.

Gallery Etemad Dubai

Al Serkal Avenue, Street 8
Al Quoz Industrial 1
04 346 8649
galleryetemad.com
Map 1 U6 Metro Noor Islamic Bank

One of the largest galleries in Dubai, Etemad's large open space within a converted warehouse, along with its minimalist architecture, creates the perfect showcase for works by established and emerging international artists from America, Europe, Asia, and the Middle East.

Gallery Isabelle Van Den Eynde

Al Serkal Avenue, Street 8 Al Quoz Industrial 1
04 323 5052
ivde.net
Map 1 U6 Metro Noor Islamic Bank

Gallery Isabelle Van Den Eynde has become a significant player on the Dubai art scene. Credited with discovering and nurturing the talent of some of the most promising figures in the Middle East's contemporary art scene – including Rokni and Ramin Haerizadeh, Reza Aramesh, Khosrow Hassanzadeh and Lara Baladiwell – this gallery is one to watch for emerging artists from Iran and the Middle East.

Green Art Gallery

Al Serkal Avenue, Street 8 Al Quoz Industrial 1
04 346 9305
gagallery.com
Map 1 U6 Metro Noor Islamic Bank

Since it opened more than 15 years ago, this gallery has focused on art from the Arab world and has been a catalyst for a number of internationally recognised artists. With minimalist white walls and lots of floor space, Green Art makes a great stop-off if you fancy some peace and quiet and some incredible culture.

Hunar Gallery

Villa 6, Street 49A Al Rashidiya 04 286 2224
hunargallery.com
Map 2 P10 Metro Rashidiya

Exhibits international fine art. Beautifully decorated Japanese tiles, Belgian pewter and glass pieces fill the spaces between ever-changing, contemporary local and world art. Some artists receive more regular showings, but typically there is a diverse array of artists shown. Exhibitions last for around a month.

J+A Gallery

Warehouse 15, Street 4A Al Quoz Industrial 1
055 395 0495
ja-gallery.com
Map 1 V6 Metro Noor Islamic Bank

With a focus on rare industrial antiques and vintage items from the early 20th century, this gallery highlights the transition from traditional craft to industrial mass production after the First World War. There's also an impressive collection of contemporary German art.

The Jam Jar

RKM Properties, Nr Dubai Garden Centre, 17A Street Al Quoz Industrial 3 04 341 7303
thejamjardubai.com
Map 1 S6 Metro First Gulf Bank

A studio and workshop space for creatives, Jam Jar also hosts several exhibitions each year in its gallery, as well as hosting other arts events such as film screenings. Teambuilding days can be organised, and it's also a great place to introduce kids to the joys of art, with painting sessions and parties available.

Lawrie Shabibi

Al Serkal Avenue, Street 8 Al Quoz Industrial 1
04 346 9906
lawrieshabibi.com
Map 1 U6 Metro Noor Islamic Bank

A relative newcomer on the Dubai art scene, this is a contemporary gallery that focuses on modern art from the Middle East, North Africa, South and Central Asia. There are regular artist talks and screenings, both at the gallery and at other venues in the emirate, so there's often something new to check out.

The Majlis Gallery

Bastakiya Al Souk Al Kabeer **04 353 6233**
themajlisgallery.com
Map **2 M4** Metro **Al Fahidi**

The Majlis Gallery is a converted traditional Arabic house, complete with windtowers. Small whitewashed rooms lead off the central courtyard and host a variety of exhibitions by contemporary artists. There's also an extensive range of handmade glass, pottery, fabrics, frames, unusual pieces of furniture and other bits and bobs. The gallery hosts exhibitions throughout the year, but is worth visiting at any time. Closed Fridays.

Meem Gallery

Nr LuLu Hypermarket, Umm Suqeim Rd Al Quoz Industrial 3 **04 347 7883**
meemartgallery.com
Map **1 R6** Metro **First Gulf Bank**

Meem features work from modern and contemporary Middle Eastern artists. It's also home to The Noor Library of Islamic Art, which houses a comprehensive collection of books, journals and catalogues on regional and Islamic art. Open Saturday to Thursday.

Miraj Islamic Art Centre

582 Jumeira Rd Umm Suqeim 1 **04 394 1084**
mirajislamicartcentre.com
Map **2 B4** Metro **Noor Islamic Bank**

Miraj holds a fantastic collection of Islamic art objects from silver, metalware and marble, to intricate astrolabes, painstakingly crafted carpets and textiles, and displays of calligraphy and engraving. Just up the road is Saga World (04 395 9071), a souk-style, high-end department store, where you can buy a range of Middle Eastern and Indian handcraft products similar to those on display in the gallery.

The Mojo Gallery

Al Serkal Avenue, Street 8 Al Quoz Industrial 1
04 347 7388
themojogallery.com
Map **1 U6** Metro **Noor Islamic Bank**

Mojo is one of Dubai's newest galleries and among more traditional forms, focuses on conceptual art and new media forms, including digital media and video art. It also stages fine art workshops which are open to the public.

New Masters Art Gallery

Majestic Hotel Tower Al Mankhool **04 359 8888**
Map **2 L4** Metro **Al Fahidi**

Located in the heart of Bur Dubai, New Masters opened its doors to art lovers in 2011 with an offering of affordable European, Asian and American art. The gallery is doing its very best to stimulate new collectors by offering collectible art within a wide price range, combined with art advice and education.

Opera Gallery

Dubai International Financial Centre (DIFC)
Trade Centre 2 **04 323 0909**
operagallery.com
Map **2 G6** Metro **Financial Centre**

Part of an international chain, Opera Gallery opened in 2008 in Dubai International Financial Centre. It has a permanent collection of art on display and for sale, mainly European and Chinese, with visiting exhibitions changing throughout the year. The permanent collection also includes several masterpieces, so look out for the odd Dali or Picasso. A new branch is now open in The Dubai Mall (04 330 8262).

The Pavilion Downtown Dubai

Nr Burj Khalifa, Emaar Boulevard Downtown Dubai
04 447 7025
pavilion.ae
Map **2 F6** Metro **Burj Khalifa/Dubai Mall**

A non-profit contemporary art space that not only showcases new regional artists but provides a space for artists and aficionados to meet, with its restaurant, cinema, library, espresso cafe and lounge.

Rira Gallery

Dubai International Financial Centre (DIFC)
Trade Centre 2 **04 369 9339**
riragallery.com
Map **2 G6** Metro **Emirates Towers**

One of the newest galleries to open in Dubai, Rira Gallery hosts solo and group exhibitions featuring a strong selection of emerging and well-known artists from the Arab world. It hasn't disappointed so far, and its monthly exhibitions – along with a programme of alternative events – are making it a notable player in the Dubai art scene.

Tashkeel

Nr Nad Al Sheba Health Center Nad Al Sheba 1
04 336 3313
tashkeel.org
Map **2 F11** Metro **Creek**

A creative hub for artistic activity, Tashkeel is a vibrant workspace that makes the arts accessible for all. Members have access to studio facilities including photography studio and darkroom, MAC suite, jewellery and 3D studios, as well as fine art, printmaking and textile printing resources. There are also public creative workshops hosted by practicing artists.

The Art Bus

The ArtBus (p.274) runs regular art gallery tours and offers transport to the major exhibitions during the annual art fairs including Art Dubai (p.26), Bastakiya Art Fair (bastakiyaartfair.com) and Abu Dhabi Art Fair (p.28).

The Third Line

Nr Times Square Al Quoz Industrial 1 **04 341 1367**
thethirdline.com
Map **1 U6** Metro **Noor Islamic Bank**

One of the leading lights of the Dubai art scene, The Third Line gallery in Al Quoz hosts exhibitions by artists originating from or working in the Middle East. There are indoor and outdoor spaces for shows. Open Saturday to Thursday 10:00 to 19:00.

Total Arts

The Courtyard Al Quoz Industrial 1 **04 347 5050**
courtyard-uae.com
Map **1 U6** Metro **Noor Islamic Bank**

Dubai's biggest gallery occupies two floors of The Courtyard in Al Quoz. It exhibits works from a variety of cultures and continents, although there is a leaning towards regional talent (particularly Iranian). There are over 300 paintings on permanent display, and regular shows of traditional handicrafts and antique furniture. One of the main attractions is the beautiful cobbled courtyard itself, surrounded by different facades showcasing building styles from around the world.

Traffic

179 Umm Suqeim Rd Al Quoz Industrial 4
04 347 0209
viatraffic.org
Map **1 S7** Metro **First Gulf Bank**

A stylish multi-disciplinary art and design practice, which features a gallery, store and studio. Work is displayed from established designers as well as up and coming talents in the field, while the store sells a wide range of aesthetically pleasing items, from small items such as cutlery through to inspirational furniture.

XVA Gallery

Bastakiya Al Souk Al Kabeer **04 353 5383**
xvagallery.com
Map **2 M4** Metro **Al Fahidi**

Located in the centre of Bastakiya, this is one of Dubai's most interesting galleries. Originally a windtower house, it is now fully restored and worth a visit for its architecture and displays of local and international art. The gallery focuses on paintings and hosts many exhibitions throughout the year, as well as free film screenings. XVA can also lay claim to the title of Dubai's hippest hotel. A new branch has opened in Building 7, DIFC.

Read All About It

The Archive (thearchive.ae.) is a new library dedicated to Middle Eastern and North African art literature. Located near Gate 5 in Safa Park, it hosts various activities including public art initiatives. There is also a modern cafe and espresso bar.

PARKS, BEACHES & ATTRACTIONS

Parks

Dubai has a number of excellent parks, with lush green lawns and a variety of trees and shrubs creating the perfect escape from the concrete jungle of the city. In the winter months, the popular parks are very busy, especially at weekends. Most have a kiosk or cafe selling snacks and drinks, and some have barbecue pits (remember to take your own wood or charcoal).

Regulations at the parks vary, with some banning bikes and rollerblades, or limiting ball games to specific areas. Pets are not permitted and you should not take plant cuttings. Some parks have a ladies' day when entry is restricted to women, girls and young boys, and certain smaller ones actually ban anyone other than ladies through the week, while allowing families only at the weekends. Entrance to the smaller parks is generally free, while the larger ones charge up to Dhs.5 per person. The Al Mamzar and Jumeirah Beach Parks have the added bonus of sand and sea to accompany their green spaces. Opening hours of most parks change during Ramadan.

Al Barsha Pond Park

Nr Al Mawakeb School, 23 Street Al Barsha 3
Map **1 Q7** Metro **Sharaf DG**

A welcome focal point for the Al Barsha community, this incredibly well equipped new park has tennis and basketball courts and football pitches (book at the onsite office) as well as a cushioned 1.5km running track and additional cycling path. Scattered around a central lake are lots of green spaces to enjoy picnics on (as hundreds of families do at the weekend), and play areas to keep children amused.

Al Ittihad Park

Nr Shoreline Apartments & Golden Mile Developments Palm Jumeirah
Map **1 N4** Metro **Nakheel**

The recently opened Ittihad Park on the Palm Jumeirah boasts more than 60 species of indigenous trees and plants. Located behind the Golden Mile residential development, and running under the track for the Palm Jumeirah Monorail, the park covers around 10 hectares and is surrounded by a 3.2km jogging track. It's open 24 hours a day and features various play areas for children.

Creek Park

Nr Al Garhoud Bridge Umm Hurair 2 **04 336 7633**
dm.gov.ae
Map **2 L7** Metro **Dubai Healthcare City**

Situated in the heart of the city but blessed with acres of gardens, fishing piers, jogging tracks, barbecue sites, children's play areas, mini-golf, restaurants and kiosks, this is the ultimate in park life. There's also a mini falaj and a large amphitheatre. Running along the park's 2.5km stretch of creek frontage is a cable car system which allows visitors an unrestricted view from 30 metres in the air. From Gate 2, four-wheel cycles can be hired for Dhs.20 per hour (you can't use your own bike in the park). Rollerblading is permitted, and there are no ladies-only days. The park is also home to Dubai Dolphinarium and Children's City. Entrance fee: Dhs.5. Cable car: adults Dhs.25; children Dhs.15. Children's City: adults Dhs.15; children Dhs.10.

Jumeirah Beach Park

Nr Chili's, Jumeira Rd Jumeira 2
04 349 2555
dm.gov.ae
Map **2 D4** Metro **Business Bay**

You get the best of both worlds here with plenty of grassy areas and vast expanses of beach. The facilities include sunbed and parasol hire (Dhs.20 – get there early to ensure they haven't run out), lifeguards, toilets, showers, snack bar, play park and barbecue pits. Away from the beach there are plenty of grassy areas and landscaped gardens, children's play areas, and barbecue pits available for public use. Cycling is not allowed (except for small children) and neither is rollerblading. Entry is Dhs.5 per person or Dhs.20 per car, including all occupants. Mondays are for women and children only. Open daily from 07:30, closing at 22:00 Sunday to Wednesday, and at 23:00 Thursday to Saturday and public holidays.

Mamzar Beach Park

Al Khaleej Rd Al Mamzar **04 296 6201**
dm.gov.ae
Map **2 T4** Metro **Al Qiyadah**

With its four clean beaches, open spaces and plenty of greenery, Al Mamzar is a popular spot – although the previously clear sea views have become a little obstructed by the work on the Palm Deira. The well-maintained beaches have sheltered areas for swimming and changing rooms with showers. Air-conditioned chalets, with barbecues, can be rented, costing from Dhs.150 to Dhs.200. There are two pools with lifeguards on duty. Bike hire is also available. Entrance is Dhs.5 per person or Dhs.30 per car.

Mushrif Park

Al Khawaneej Rd Mushrif **04 288 3624**
dm.gov.ae
Metro **Rashidiya**

The grounds of Mushrif Park, close to Mirdif, are extensive, and although it is a 'desert park', there are many large stretches of beautiful green lawn. There are two large pools (one for men, one for women), and a smaller pool for young children. Numerous playgrounds are dotted around the park, and a central plaza features fairground rides and trampolines. You can get close to horses, camels, goats and even a turkey at the animal enclosure, while pony and camel rides are available from Dhs.5 for a short ride. There is also a mini-town, where you can wander around and into miniature houses themed on different building styles from around the world, while there's a train that tours the park in the afternoons (Dhs.2 per ride). Entry is Dhs.3 per person or Dhs.10 per car. Swimming pool entrance is Dhs.10 per adult and Dhs.5 per child. The path that flanks the park is also popular with joggers and cyclists.

Safa Park

Nr Al Wasl Rd & Al Hadiqa St Al Wasl
04 349 2111
dm.gov.ae
Map **2 D5** Metro **Business Bay**

This huge, artistically landscaped park is a great place to escape the commotion of nearby Sheikh Zayed Road. Its sports fields, barbecue sites and play areas make it one of the best parks in the city. There's a boating lake in the centre, a small maze, public tennis and basketball courts, and a flea market held on the first Saturday of every month. Various informal football and cricket games take place on the large areas of grass. The Archive arts library and cafe (thearchive.ae) makes for a welcome pit stop. Tuesday is ladies' day, and there is a permanent ladies' garden within the park. Bikes are available for hire. Entry costs Dhs.3 (free for children under three). There's a great running track around the park's perimeter.

Umm Suqeim Park

Nr Kangaroo Kids Nursery Umm Suqeim 2
04 348 4554
dm.gov.ae
Map **1 T4** Metro **First Gulf Bank**

This ladies' park is closed to men except for at weekends. It is fairly large and has three big, well-equipped sandy playgrounds. There are also plenty of shady, grassy areas so that mums can sit and rest while the kids let off steam. The park has become a popular venue to hold children's parties. Entrance is free.

Zabeel Park

Nr Trade Centre R/A, Shk Zayed Rd Al Kifaf
04 398 6888
dm.gov.ae
Map **2 J6** Metro **Al Jafiliya**

Zabeel Park is divided into three zones – alternative energy, communications and technology. There are recreational areas, a jogging track, a mini cricket pitch, a football field, boating lake and an amphitheatre, plus a number of restaurants and cafes. On Mondays, the park is open to ladies only. Entry costs Dhs.5. The park is open from 08:00 daily, closing at 23:00 Sunday to Wednesday, and at 23:30 Thursday to Saturday.

Beaches

Blessed with warm weather, calm ocean waters and long stretches of sand, Dubai offers its residents the choice of several beautiful beaches. There are three types of beach to choose from: public beaches (limited facilities but no entry fee), beach parks (good facilities and a nominal entrance fee), and private beaches (normally part of a hotel or resort).

Options for public beaches include the area around Al Mamzar Beach Park (p.257), which has a cordoned-off swimming area, chalets, jet skis for hire and free beaches along the lagoon to the south. South of Dubai Creek, you'll come to Jumeirah Open Beach, which is great for soaking up the sun, swimming and people watching. Moving down the coast past Jumeirah Beach Park (p.257) brings you to the small beaches between Dubai Offshore Sailing Club and Jumeirah Beach Hotel. One of these, Umm Suqeim beach, is close to the Burj Al Arab and is one of the busiest public beaches at the weekends. Another section of public beach, known unofficially as Palace Beach or 'secret beach', is on Al Sufouh in a gap amid the grand palaces between Madinat and The Palm, opposite the Barsha road.

Swim Safely

Although the waters off the coast generally look calm and unchallenging, very strong rip tides can carry the most confident swimmer away from the shore very quickly and drownings have occurred in the past. Take extra care when swimming off the public beaches where there are no lifeguards.

The long stretch of sand at JBR hosts some beach hotels, but it's also accessible to the public and is extremely popular with Marina residents in the cooler season. Just a little further from town, and great for kitesurfing, drive south of Jebel Ali and turn right at the first major junction, where the beaches are still quiet and, as yet, undeveloped.

Five beaches in Dubai have been awarded the internationally recognised Blue Flag award for cleanliness and safety: Jebel Ali Golf Resort, Jumeirah Open Beach, Al Mamzar Beach Park, Le Meridien Mina Seyahi and Le Meridien Al Aqah.

Regulations for public beaches are quite strict. Dogs are banned and so is driving. Officially, other off-limit activities include barbecues, camping without a permit and holding large parties. Contact the Public Parks & Recreation Section (04 221 5555) for clarification. It is fine to wear swimming costumes and bikinis on the beach, as long as you keep both parts on.

Beach Clubs

For those looking for that holiday beach experience, the many beachfront hotels in Dubai offer annual membership and day passes. From Dhs.13,000 (Single) for Dubai Marine Beach Resort to Dhs.22,000 (Single) for the Ritz-Carlton Beach Club, you can use the hotels' beach and pool facilities.

Day passes start from around Dhs.150. For a minimum spend of Dhs.150, you can lounge on the beach and use the facilities at Nasimi Beach at Atlantis The Palm. It also costs Dhs.150 to rent a lounger and use the facilities at RIVA at Shoreline, Palm Jumeirah. But, if you're looking to live the Dubai highlife, there's nothing else quite like Meydan Beach Club in Dubai Marina (meydanbeach.com); it's the ultimate beach club experience with an impressive Dhs.500 entrance fee. See askexplorer.com for more information.

Waterparks

Aquaplay

Mirdif City Centre Mirdif **04 231 6311**
playnationme.com
Map **2 P12** Metro **Rashidiya**

This is more of an indoor water-themed play centre than a traditional waterpark, but it goes down with the kids just as well. Designed for two to eight year olds, it features a variety of interactive games and water rides. Highlights include a leisurely boat ride and a more boisterous bumper boat attraction.

Aquaventure Waterpark, Atlantis The Palm > *p.259*

Atlantis The Palm Palm Jumeirah **04 426 0000**
atlantisthepalm.com
Map **1 N1** Metro **Nakheel**

The ultimate destination for thrill seekers. The Leap of Faith gets the adrenaline pumping with a 27 metre near-vertical drop that shoots you through a tunnel surrounded by shark-infested waters, while the Rapids take you on a tumultuous journey down a 2.3km river, complete with waterfalls and wave surges. For the little ones, there is Splashers, a fun water playground. Open daily from 10:00 until sunset. Entrance for those over 1.2m is Dhs.225, and Dhs.180 for those under that height. Children younger than two years old and Atlantis hotel guests get in for free, and there are reduced rates for UAE residents.

SplashLand

WonderLand Theme & Water Park Umm Hurair 2 **04 324 1222**
wonderlanduae.com
Map**2 L7** Metro **Dubai Healthcare City**

It may feel at times like a bit of a ghost town, but the waterpark within WonderLand offers fun for kids and adults with nine rides, including slides and twisters, a lazy river, an adults' pool and a children's activity pool with slides, bridges and water cannons. Alternatively, you can just relax by the pool and sunbathe. Lockers and changing rooms are available.

Water, Water Everywhere

When you've ridden the Tantrum Alley so many times that you've screamed yourself hoarse, and you've taken the Leap Of Faith so often you're on first-name terms with the sharks, it's time to head north for a new water challenge. Umm Al Quwain is home to Dreamland Aqua Park (p.304), a great family-friendly waterland with over 30 rides and attractions, as well as camping facilities, while the Ice Land Water Park (p.305) in Ras Al Khaimah is just 80km from Dubai and also features more than 30 slides, plus water football and a rain dance pool. Or, you can pop next door to Yas Island to the new Yas Waterworld Abu Dhabi, with the world's first 'rattling' waterslide complete with special effects.

Wild Wadi Water Park > p.261

Jumeira Rd Umm Suqeim 3 **04 348 4444**
wildwadi.com
Map **1 S4** Metro **Mall of the Emirates**

Spread over 12 acres beside Jumeirah Beach Hotel (p.240), this waterpark has a host of aquatic rides and attractions to suit all ages and bravery levels. Depending on how busy it is you may have to queue for some of the rides, but the wait is worth it. The highlights include Jumeirah Sceirah, the tallest and fastest freefall slide outside the United States; Wipeout (a permanently rolling wave that's perfect for showing off your body-boarding skills); and the four-seater Burj Surge. The park opens at 10:00; closing time varies throughout the year. Admission is Dhs.220 for adults and Dhs.175 for kids; family and season passes are available too.

Wildlife

Al Hurr Falconry Services

Falcon Heritage Centre, Nr Meydan Racecourse
Nad Al Sheba **04 323 4829**
alhurrfalconry.com
Map **2 D9** Metro **Business Bay**

Located in Nad Al Sheba, Al Hurr is where you can discover all you've ever wanted to know about falcons and falconry – one of the traditional symbols of Arabia. The trained handlers educate visitors about the majestic falcons and it's well worth making the trek up to Meydan to see the amazing shows these graceful creations put on.

Desert Ranch

Al Sahra Desert Resort Dubailand **04 427 4055**
alsahra.com

This eco-tourism concept is part of Jebel Ali International Hotels. The 2.4 sqkm desert ranch runs a wide variety of fun, desert-themed nature activities ranging from campfire Fridays, family picnics and educational field trips to horse riding (p.341), children's clubs, ranch tours, Bedouin farm tours and camel cuddling.

Dolphin Bay

Atlantis The Palm Palm Jumeirah **04 426 1030**
atlantisthepalm.com
Map **1 N1** Metro **Nakheel**

Playing with a bottlenose dolphin during the Shallow Water Interaction package at Dolphin Bay is an unforgettable experience. Touching, hugging, holding 'hands', playing ball and feeding are all encouraged, under the supervision of the marine specialists. A 90 minute session will set you back Dhs.790 per person (with discounts for hotel guests) and is open to all ages. Your family and friends can watch and take photos from the beach for Dhs.300, but this also grants them access to Aquaventure and the private beach. There's a deep water experience too, where visitors can swim and snorkel alongside the mammals with the aid of an underwater scooter.

Dubai Aquarium & Underwater Zoo

The Dubai Mall Downtown Dubai **04 448 5200**
thedubaiaquarium.com
Map **2 F6** Metro **Burj Khalifa/Dubai Mall**

Located, somewhat bizarrely, in the middle of The Dubai Mall, this aquarium displays over 33,000 tropical fish to passing shoppers free of charge. For a closer view of the main tank's inhabitants, however (which include fearsome looking but generally friendly

WILD TIMES ARE CALLING

While Dubai Zoo may not be the best facility in the world, there are several places beyond the city limits that are worth a visit for animal lovers. Al Ain Zoo (p.296) contains excellent facilities for an impressive range of animals from around the globe, including rare breeds like the white lion. Sharjah also has several places to get up close to birds, beasts and fish: it has its own aquarium (p.299); plus the Arabian Wildlife Centre and Children's Farm (both part of the Sharjah Desert Park, p.300); and the new Al Tamimi Stables (tamimistables.com), with pony rides, nature trails, a petting farm, equestrian and falconry shows. Closer to Dubai is Ras Al Khor Wildlife Sanctuary, a stopping off point for thousands of migrating birds each year, including about 1,500 flamingos. There are a number of hides from where to view the action: one beside Ras Al Khor Road, and two off Oud Metha Road (wildlife.ae, 04 606 6822/26).

sand tiger sharks) you can pay to walk through the 270° viewing tunnel. Also well worth a look is the Underwater Zoo, which includes residents such as penguins, piranhas and an octopus. If you're feeling really adventurous, you can even go for a scuba dive in the tank (call ahead to book), ride a glass-bottomed boat or feed the sharks.

Dubai Dolphinarium > *p.263*

Creek Park Umm Hurair 2 **04 336 9773**
dubaidolphinarium.ae
Map **2 L7** Metro **Dubai Healthcare City**

The Dolphinarium has proven to be a popular addition to Creek Park and the main attraction is the seal and dolphin show which runs twice a day during the week, and three times daily at weekends. During the show you will meet the resident black sea bottlenose dolphins and the four northern fur seals, and, afterwards, you can have your picture taken with them, or even get up close to them in the water. Prices start from Dhs.100 for an adult and Dhs.50 for a child, but a whole range of group and family discounts are available. There's an onsite restaurant and a gift shop too.

Dubai Zoo

Jumeira Rd Jumeira 1 **04 349 6444**
definitelydubai.com
Map **2 G4** Metro **Financial Centre**

This is an old-fashioned zoo, with lions, tigers, giraffes, monkeys, deer, snakes, bears, flamingos, giant tortoises and other animals housed in small cages. The curator and his staff do their best, with the woefully inadequate space and resources, to look after the animals, but it's not a place that animal lovers will enjoy. There are plans to replace this ageing zoo with a safari-style park in Al Warqa. Entry costs Dhs.2

Diving in Dubai Aquarium

per person, under twos go free. Closed on Tuesdays. Female visitors must cover shoulders and knees.

The Lost Chambers Aquarium, Atlantis The Palm

Atlantis The Palm Palm Jumeirah **04 426 0000**
atlantisthepalm.com
Map **1 N1** Metro **Nakheel**

The ruins of the mysterious lost city provide the theme for the aquarium at Atlantis. The maze of underwater halls and tunnels provides ample opportunity to get up close to the aquarium's 65,000 inhabitants, ranging from sharks and eels to rays and piranhas, as well as multitudes of exotic fish. The entrance fee is Dhs.100 for adults and Dhs.70 for three to 11 year olds. UAE residents can get discounted tickets and hotel guests get in for free; while you can see quite a lot from the windows in the hotel, it is worth splashing out for the views inside.

Amusement Centres

Children's City

Creek Park Umm Hurair 2 **04 334 0808**
childrencity.ae
Map **2 L7** Metro **Dubai Healthcare City**

Children's City is an educational project that offers kids their own learning zone and amusement facilities, by providing hands-on experiences relating to theory they have been taught at school. There's a planetarium focusing on the solar system and space exploration, a nature centre for information on land and sea environments, and the Discovery Space, which reveals the miracles and mysteries of the human body. It is aimed at five to 12 year olds, although there are items of interest included for toddlers and teenagers. The centre opens daily from 09:00 to 20:00, except on Fridays when it opens at 15:00. Entrance costs Dhs.10 for children under 16 and Dhs.15 for anyone over 16.

Encounter Zone

Wafi Umm Hurair 2 **04 324 7747**
wafi.com
Map **2 L7** Metro **Dubai Healthcare City**

With a range of activities for all ages, Encounter Zone is a great stop-off if you want to reward your kids for being good while you have shopped up a storm in Wafi's many boutiques. Galactica is for teenagers and adults and features an inline skating and skateboarding park. Lunarland is for kids aged one to eight, and is packed with activities designed especially for younger children, including a small soft-play area for little ones. Prices range from Dhs.3 to Dhs.27, or you can buy a five-hour pass for Dhs.45. Open from 10:00 to 22:00 Sunday to Wednesday and from 10:00 to midnight on Thursday and Friday.

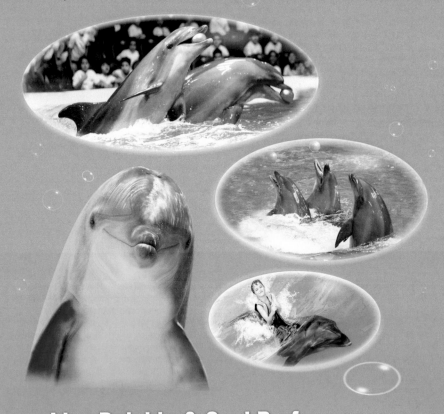

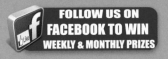

Extreme Fun
Nr Spinneys Dubai MotorCity **04 452 5543**
extremefunuae.com
Map **1 N12** Metro **Mall of the Emirates**
Big, bright and noisy, Extreme Fun is every child's dream. There are play areas, a birthday party room and kiddie rides, as well as arcade games and a Kidz Kutz salon. There's also plenty for youngsters to do with soft play and toddler areas, while parents can enjoy a relaxing coffee or snack in the cosy cafe. Extreme Fun recently opened an indoor play centre in the J3 Mall on Al Wasl Road, with an underwater adventure theme.

Fantasy Kingdom
Al Bustan Centre Al Qusais 1 **04 263 0000**
al-bustan.com
Map **2 R7** Metro **Al Nahda**
Themed as a medieval castle, Fantasy Kingdom offers adventure and excitement for the little ones. The centre has a 24,000 sqft indoor play area which is divided into sections for different age groups. Younger children can enjoy the merry-go-round, cars to ride and the soft-play area, while older kids can play interactive games, video games, bumper cars, pool and air hockey. There is also a children's cafe.

Fun City
BurJuman Al Mankhool **04 359 3336**
funcity.ae
Map **2 L5** Metro **BurJuman**
A combination of rides, games, sports and an indoor playground, Fun City caters to all younger family members and is especially popular for kids' parties, with a range of packages available from Dhs.55 per child. The daily (Sunday to Thursday) Mother's Club coffee mornings are also popular. There's a Kiddy Kutz salon here too. Other branches include Ibn Battuta, Mercato, Arabian Center, Reef Mall and Lamcy Plaza.

KidZania
The Dubai Mall Downtown Dubai **04 448 5222**
kidzania.ae
Map **2 F6** Metro **Burj Khalifa/Dubai Mall**
This new addition to The Dubai Mall offers kids the chance to become adults for the day. Billed as a 'real-life city' for children, youngsters can dress up and act out more than 75 different roles, from policeman to pilot and doctor to designer. The KidZania City even has its own currency, which children can earn and spend. It's intended to be both fun and educational.

Magic Planet > *p.265*
Deira City Centre Port Saeed **04 295 4333**
magicplanet.ae
Map **2 N7** Metro **Deira City Centre**
These blaring, boisterous play areas are located in Deira City Centre, Mall of the Emirates and Mirdif City Centre, and are hugely popular with kids accompanying their mums and dads on long shopping trips. There are various rides, including merry-go-rounds, a train, bumper cars and the latest video games. For tinier tots there is a large activity play gym and a small soft-play area. Entrance is free, and you use the facilities on a 'pay as you play' basis, or buy a Dhs.50 special pass for unlimited fun and entertainment.

Playnation
Mirdif City Centre Mirdif **800 386**
theplaymania.com
Map **2 P12** Metro **Rashidiya**
Playnation is Mirdif City Centre's dedicated leisure and entertainment destination. It offers a range of exciting activities (and not just for younger family members), integrating five 'experiences': indoor skydiving at iFLY Dubai (p.356), Soccer Circus Dubai (p.338), Little Explorers edutainment centre (p.144), Yalla! Bowling (p.323), and Magic Planet (p.264), which includes the nerve-wracking Sky Trail attraction. Each attraction has been designed to the latest health and safety standards with qualified supervisors and instructors on hand.

SEGA Republic
The Dubai Mall Downtown Dubai **04 448 8484**
segarepublic.com
Map **2 F6** Metro **Burj Khalifa/Dubai Mall**
This indoor theme park located in The Dubai Mall offers a range of thrills and spills, courtesy of the nine main attractions and the 150 arcade games. A Power Pass (Dhs.150) gets you all-day access to the big attractions, which include stomach-flipping rides like the Sonic Hopper, the SpinGear and the Halfpipe Canyon. Unlike many other shopping mall amusement centres, SEGA Republic is for all ages.

SEGA Republic

A REWARDING ADVENTURE
magic planet
Play the latest games and attractions in the region whilst winning tickets for you to redeem for a host of fantastic prizes and gifts.
www.magicplanet.ae
www.facebook.com/magicplanetdxb

Desert Resorts & Getaways

Out of the city limits but still within Dubai emirate there are several resorts that offer luxurious getaways and both day and night time activities for Dubai residents. You can make a short break or holiday of it by checking in for a few nights, or you can use most of the sports, leisure and dining facilities as a paying day visitor at many of the resorts.

The perfect desert break can be had at either Al Maha or Bab Al Shams. Al Maha is the more exclusive, with the resort's facilities, located in a desert conservation area, reserved for staying guests, while the upmarket Bab Al Shams, operated by Meydan Hotels, opens its stylish facilities and restaurants to day visitors. Hatta Fort Hotel (p.321) makes for a great day trip or break to the Hajar Mountains, Jebel Ali Resort offers beach, spa, golf and dining facilities, and Desert Palm provides respite just past the city limits.

Al Maha, A Luxury Collection Desert Resort & Spa

Dubai Desert Conservation Reserve, Dubai – Al Ain Rd 04 832 9900
al-maha.com

Set within the 225 sqkm Dubai Desert Conservation Reserve, with breathtaking views of picturesque dunes and rare wildlife, this luxury getaway was named as one of the best ecotourism models by National Geographic in 2008. Al Maha is designed to resemble a typical Bedouin camp, but conditions are anything but basic. Each suite is beautifully crafted and has its own private pool and butler service. Activities include horse riding, camel trekking and falconry. There is also a superb spa.

Bab Al Shams Desert Resort & Spa

Nr Endurance Village Bawadi **04 809 6100**
meydanhotels.com

Bab Al Shams ('The Gateway to the Sun') is a beautiful desert resort built in the style of a traditional Arabic Fort. Each of its 115 rooms is decorated with subtle yet stunning Arabian touches, and pristine desert dunes form the backdrop. The authentic, open-air, Arabic desert restaurant is highly recommended. There is a kids' club, a large swimming pool (complete with swim-up bar), lawn games and the luxurious Satori Spa.

Desert Palm Dubai

Al Awir Rd Warsan 2 **04 323 8888**
desertpalm.peraquum.com

Located just outside the city, Desert Palm is so tranquil you'll never want to leave. Overlooking polo fields, guests can choose from suites, or private villas with a pool. The extensive spa menu features massage and holistic therapies including reiki. Signature restaurant Rare (p.531) is a must for meat lovers, while Epicure is a lovely gourmet deli and a great breakfast venue.

Jebel Ali Golf Resort

Nr Palm Jebel Ali Waterfront **04 814 5555**
jaresortshotels.com
Metro **Danube**

Just far enough out of Dubai to escape the hustle and bustle, this resort offers 392 luxurious rooms in resplendent surroundings, with a peaceful atmosphere – the perfect place for a weekend break. The two distinct properties, the Jebel Ali Hotel and The Palm Tree Court & Spa, are set in 128 acres of lush, landscaped gardens, with an 800 metre private beach, a marina and a golf course. Guests can also enjoy horse riding, shooting and a variety of watersports. Although the trunk of Palm Jebel Ali (still under construction) is only 400 metres away, it doesn't detract from the tranquility.

OUT & ABOUT

The UAE has much more to offer than its headline-grabbing, metropolis-based attractions. Beyond the city limits, in all directions, is a varied and fascinating landscape that has great potential for exploring and leisure-time activities.

Getting out into the deserts and wadis by four wheel drive is a must-do while you're a Dubai resident, and once you're out there, there are some super hiking and camping spots to take advantage of too. The sea that surrounds the country is also a great adventure playground, and the warm Gulf waters provide a wonderful opportunity to try snorkelling, diving and sailing.

Off-Roading

With the vast areas of virtually untouched wilderness in the UAE, wadi and dune bashing are very popular pastimes. Every other vehicle on the road in Dubai seems to be a four wheel drive, but unlike in many countries, in the UAE there's ample opportunity to truly put them to the test in an off-road environment.

Dune bashing, or desert driving, is one of the toughest challenges for both car and driver, but once you have mastered it, it's also the most fun. Driving in the wadis is a bit more straightforward. Wadis are (usually) dry gullies, carved through the rock by rushing floodwaters, following the course of seasonal rivers. See p.268 for an introduction to desert driving.

Weekend Breaks

If you want more ideas on the best places to head for a city escape, get hold of *Weekend Breaks Oman & UAE*. The book features detailed reviews of some of the region's top hotels, as well as sightseeing highlights. See askexplorer.com.

Some of the UAE's regional highlights include:

Northern Emirates: For a full day out, with some of the best driving in the emirates, combine the mountains around Wadi Bih, near Ras Al Khaimah, with one of the interesting wadi routes on the east coast.

East Coast: From Dubai, the east coast can be reached in about two hours. The mountains and beaches are fantastic spots for camping, barbecues and weekend breaks, as well as various other activities. There are some great wadi and mountain routes here, and the area is also renowned for its diving and snorkelling opportunities, particularly around Snoopy Island.

Hatta: The Hatta region is home to the popular Big Red sand dune, a huge draw and a must-do challenge for off-roaders and quad bikers, as well as the Hatta Pools, a great swimming spot in the Hajar Mountains.

Al Ain: The oasis town of Al Ain is worthy of a visit in its own right, while nearby are the imposing Jebel Hafeet and Hanging Gardens, a great trekking spot.

Liwa: A trip to Liwa is one you'll never forget – it's one of the few remaining chances to experience unspoiled dunes. The drive from Abu Dhabi or Dubai is long, more suitable for a two or three day camping trip, but the journey is worth it. Prepare for the most adventurous off-road driving the UAE has to offer, and some of its most incredible scenery.

For further information and tips on driving off-road check out both the *UAE Off-Road Explorer* and *Oman Off-Road Explorer*. These books feature a multitude of detailed routes and give advice on how to stay safe, where to camp and things to do along the way.

If you want a wilderness adventure but don't know where to start, contact any of the major tour companies (see Tour Operators, p.279). All offer a range of desert and mountain safaris.

If you're really keen to learn in a controlled environment, then OffRoad-Zone (p.332) runs a driving centre at the Jebel Ali Shooting Club where you can practise tackling all manner of obstacles that you might find while off-roading, including deep water, loose rocks and steep descents. Tutors are on hand to show you the proper technique too.

ADRENALINE SPORTS

Thrill-seekers don't need to head out to sea or to distant shores to get a taste of extreme adventure; you can spend the morning diving with sharks, the afternoon driving like an F1 racer, and the evening catching air on a snowboard, all without leaving the city limits.

Dubai Aquarium (p.260) offers the chance to climb inside its 10 million litre tank and get up close to some of the 33,000 aquatic inhabitants. Whether you're an experienced diver or have never strapped on a tank before, the highly qualified instructors from Al Boom Diving can guide you through the waters, allowing you to mingle with some of the exotic residents, including sand tiger sharks, stingrays and giant groupers, and be part of the attraction yourself.

At Dubai Autodrome (p.346) speed junkies can climb inside a racing car and tear up the track as part of the F1 Style Single Seater Experience package. You'll be fully briefed and supervised as you roar out of the pits and follow a leader car around the hair-pins and straights. If you get the bug, come back for more to crank it up a notch and be a bit more adventurous with your driving.

Finally, if you've moved to Dubai from cooler climes and are missing your fix of powder and mountains, head to Ski Dubai (p.356) – the indoor piste in the heart of the city, complete with its very own 'black run'. Lessons for beginners are available, while experienced downhillers can go on Freestyle Night to get some serious air on the jumps, kickers and rails.

Camping

Constant sunshine and an awe-inspiring array of locations make camping a much-loved activity in Dubai and the UAE. In general, warm temperatures and next to no rain means you can camp with much less equipment and preparation than in other countries, and many first-timers or families with children find that camping becomes their favourite weekend break. For most, the best time to go is between October and April, as in the summer it can get unbearably hot sleeping outside.

Choose between the peace and tranquility of the desert, or camp among the wadis and mountains next to trickling streams in picturesque oases. Many good campsites are easily accessible from tarmac roads so a 4WD is not always required. You can camp just about anywhere, but there are some stand-out spots that are super places to pitch up. Jebel Yibir is the UAE's highest peak and, as such, camping out on the mountain (there's a road up to the summit) is a good option for the warmer months as the temperatures up there are much cooler than down below. The Wadi Sidr off-road route leads to a plateau that offers some good places to camp, with great views, while both Fossil Rock and the drive from Madam to Madah provide terrific, accessible dune driving and camping spots. The ultimate camping experience however is to be had in the sea of dunes at Liwa, where you can go to sleep beneath a perfect starry sky and then wake up completely surrounded by one of the world's most mesmerising dunescapes (see Out Of The City, p.286). For more information on off-road adventuring and places to camp, refer to the *UAE Off-Road Explorer*.

Beginners' Guide To Desert Driving

Off-road driving is exciting and adventurous, but it shouldn't be undertaken lightly; it requires skill, the correct equipment, and a little planning before venturing out for the first time.

The key to driving on sand is maintaining controlled momentum and always looking ahead so you can plan for obstacles before you reach them. Most of the tracks on routes such as Fossil Rock (see the feature in Out Of The City, p.311) shouldn't present any problems, but they will get you used to how your car handles on sand and the different style needed to driving on hard surfaces.

Before you start driving, deflate your tyres to 15-18psi. This increases the surface area of the tyre in contact with the sand, providing added traction for the soft conditions and saving your engine from being overworked.

Make sure you are in 4WD (high range), and use the lower gears at higher than normal revs. You will find you use first and second a lot, but on more open and flatter tracks, you will get into third and even fourth, and at times it will feel very similar to driving on the road.

When the track becomes undulating or you head into the dunes, slow down, keep a steady pace and stay alert for obstacles. You should try to use the accelerator more than anything else, barely touching the brakes or clutch. If you do brake, do so lightly and smoothly to avoid sinking into the sand.

At first even small dunes can seem quite extreme, so take things cautiously. Plan your ascents to take the smoothest route and try to reduce your speed so that you coast over the top of a rise or a dune at close to walking pace so you will be in control for the descent. Go easy on the gas – it is far better to fail to make a climb because you were going too slow than to end up jumping over the top of a dune.

When you get over the top, brake gently and stop just on the downward slope. This will allow you to start going again easily. You will often not know what the slope is like until you are right on it; point your car straight down the dune and let your engine do most of the controlling of your speed.

Drivers of automatic cars can do the same using the accelerator; pressing down hard will change down gears, but you may need to use the gear stick to ensure the car doesn't change back up before you want it to, robbing you of the momentum and power you need to climb dunes. Descending, you will need to change into first or second so the car doesn't race away from you.

Don't worry too much about getting stuck, it happens to everyone. If you do, don't keep revving the engine – chances are it will just dig you in further. Get out of your car to assess the situation, and try to work out how it happened so you can learn for next time. Clearing a little sand from around the wheels and getting a few people to push will get most cars out of minor problems. If you are in deeper, you may need to dig the car free, lower the tyre pressures more or get someone to tow you out.

"Don't worry too much about getting stuck – it happens to everyone. Clearing a little sand from around the wheels and a few people pushing will get most cars out of minor problems."

Essential Equipment

There are some basic technical requirements for anyone driving in the desert. A well-maintained and fully serviced vehicle, a spare tyre in good condition, a jack, a tool kit including everything to change a tyre, a sturdy plank or block of wood in case you need to change wheels in sand, a tow rope and shackles, a pressure gauge and a shovel are all essential. And as with any other time you venture out into the desert, you should always have at least one other car with you – even on the simplest routes you might get stuck deep enough to need towing out. Remember to make sure you have plenty of fuel in the tank too.

Other things that can help get you out of sticky situations include sand mats or trays (or your floor mats if you are not too attached to them), a compressor to re-inflate tyres, heavy duty gloves, jump leads, a fully charged mobile phone, and a GPS, which can help take the guesswork out of navigation. Also make sure everyone in your car has plenty of water, sun cream and a hat, and shoes rather than sandals, as the sand can still get very hot.

Hiking

Despite Dubai's flat terrain, spectacular hiking locations can be found just an hour outside the city limits. To the north, the Ru'us Al Jibal Mountains contain the highest peaks in the area and stand proud at over 2,000 metres. To the east, the impressive Hajar Mountains form the border between the UAE and Oman, stretching from Musandam to the Empty Quarter desert, hundreds of kilometres to the south.

Most of the terrain is heavily eroded due to the harsh climate, but there are still places where you can walk through shady palm plantations and lush oases. Routes range from short, easy walks leading to spectacular viewpoints, to all-day treks over difficult terrain, and can include major mountaineering. Some hikes follow centuries old Bedouin and Shihuh mountain paths, a few of which are still being used.

One of the nearest and easiest places to reach is the foothills of the Hajar Mountains on the Hatta Road, near the Oman border. After passing through the desert, the flat stark, rugged outcrops transform the landscape. Explore any turning you like, or take the road to Madah, along which you'll find several options.

Other great areas for hiking and exploring include Al Ain and its surroundings, many places in the mountains in and around Musandam, and the mountains near the east coast. The mountains in the UAE don't generally disappoint, and the further off the beaten track you get, the more likely you are to find interesting villages where residents live much the same way as they did centuries ago. You can find details of local hikes in the *UAE Off-Road Explorer*; and for for somewhere a bit further afield see *Oman Trekking*, a guidebook from Explorer with pull-out maps covering major signed routes in Oman. Visit askexplorer.com to order copies.

As with any trip into the UAE 'outback', take sensible precautions. Tell someone where you are going and when you should be back and don't forget to take a map, compass, GPS equipment and robust hiking boots. Don't underestimate the strength of the sun – take sunscreen and, most importantly, loads of water.

For most people, the cooler and less humid winter months are the best season for serious mountain hiking. Be particularly careful in wadis (dry riverbeds) during the wet season as flash floods can immerse a wadi in seconds. Also note that there are no mountain rescue services in the UAE, so anyone venturing out should be reasonably experienced or accompanied by someone who knows the area.

See Hiking, p.341, for companies that offer organised hikes, and Climbing, p.326, for details of local rock climbing groups.

DRIVE WITH CARE

To protect the environment from damage, you should try to stick to existing tracks rather than create new tracks across virgin countryside. While it may be hard to deviate from the track when wadi bashing, dunes are ever changing so obvious paths are less common. Although the sandy dunes may look devoid of life, there is a surprising variety of flora and fauna that exists.

The main safety precaution to take when wadi bashing is to keep your eyes open for developing rare, but not impossible, thunderstorms – the wadis can fill up quickly and you will need to make your way to higher ground pretty quickly to avoid flash floods.

Diving

The UAE offers diving that's really very special; the lower Arabian Gulf and the Gulf of Oman will satisfy all tastes and levels of experience for divers and snorkellers alike. You can choose from over 30 wrecks in relatively shallow water, tropical coral reefs and dramatic coastlines that are virtually undived. And these are bathed in warm water all year round.

Water temperatures range from a cooler 20°C in January to a warmer 35°C in July and August. Although the land temperatures can be in the high 40s in the summer months, it is rarely too hot when out at sea or dipping into the water.

The UAE's coastal waters are home to a variety of marine species, coral life and even shipwrecks. You'll see some exotic fish, like clownfish and seahorses, and possibly even spotted eagle rays, moray eels, small sharks, barracuda, sea snakes and stingrays. Most of the wrecks are on the west coast, while the beautiful flora and fauna of coral reefs can be seen on the east coast.

There are many dive sites on the west coast that are easily accessible from Dubai. Cement Barge, Mariam Express and the MV Dara wrecks are some of the more popular dive sites. Off the east coast, a well-known dive site is Martini Rock, a small, underwater mountain covered with colourful soft coral, with a depth range of three to 19 metres. North of Khor Fakkan is the Car Cemetery, a reef that has thrived around a number of cars placed 16 metres below water. Visibility off both coasts ranges from five to 20 metres.

Another option for diving enthusiasts is to take a trip to Musandam (p.314). This area, which is part of the Sultanate of Oman, is often described as the 'Norway of the Middle East' due to the many inlets and the way the sheer cliffs plunge directly into the sea. It offers some spectacular dive sites. Sheer wall dives with strong currents and clear waters are more suitable for advanced divers, while the huge bays, with their calm waters and shallow reefs, are ideal for the less experienced. Visibility here is between 10 and 35 metres.

Carry When Camping

Although the UAE has low rainfall, care should be taken in and near wadis as flash floods can and do occur (remember, it may be raining in the mountains miles from where you are). You should consider taking the following equipment with you:

- Tent
- Lightweight sleeping bag (or light blankets and sheets)
- Thin mattress (or air bed)
- Torches and spare batteries
- Cool box for food
- Water (always take too much)
- Camping stove, or BBQ and charcoal if preferred
- Firewood and matches
- Insect repellent and antihistamine cream
- First aid kit (including any personal medication)
- Sun protection (hats, sunglasses, sunscreen)
- Jumper/warm clothing for cooler evenings
- Spade
- Toilet rolls
- Rubbish bags (ensure you leave nothing behind)
- Navigation equipment (maps, compass, Global Positioning System)
- Mobile phone (fully charged)

If you plan to travel to Khasab, the capital of the Musandam region, you may not be able to take your own air tanks across the border and will have to rent from one of the dive centres there. You may also require an Omani visa. Alternatively, from Dibba on the UAE east coast, you can hire a fast dive boat to take you anywhere from five to 75 kilometres up the coast. The cost ranges between Dhs.150 and Dhs.500, for what is usually a two-dive trip.

There are plenty of dive companies in the UAE where you can try diving for the first time, or improve on your existing diving skills (see Activities, p.333). Most companies offer both tuition and straightforward dive outings, with equipment hire; online PADI e-Learning courses are available through Al Boom Diving (alboomdiving.com).

Snorkelling

Snorkelling is a great hobby and with the conditions in the UAE consisting of relatively calm waters for most of the year, this is the perfect place to get into it. Whatever your age or fitness levels, snorkelling will get you into the sea and, the minute you get your first glimpse of bright reef life, you'll be hooked.

Snorkelling offers a different experience to diving, with many interesting creatures such as turtles, rays and even sharks all frequently seen near the surface. It's a great way for the family to enjoy an activity together, and all you need is some basic equipment and you're ready to go. You can pretty much snorkel anywhere off a boat – all you need is a mask and fins, and you'll likely see something swimming around – but there are certain areas where you're guaranteed to enjoy great marine action.

The east coast is a great area for snorkelling and has the most diverse marine life. Most dive centres take snorkellers out on their boats (along with divers, and the trip lasts for about two hours in total). Some centres can make arrangements to take you to Shark Island (also called Khor Fakkan Island) where you can spend the day. They'll come and collect you at the time you agree on. If that's what you'd like to do, it's best to arrange this with your dive centre in advance. Depending on your swimming ability and the water conditions, you can go to Sandy Beach Hotel and spend the day on the beach and swim out to Snoopy Island, just a short distance from shore. In winter time the water recedes a long way and the distance you have to swim is even less – but the water temperature will be considerably cooler too.

The west coast is not so great, with the best places for seeing fish mainly the waters by harbour walls, but take care: on the outside of harbour walls, the waves tend to bash against the rocks and you may get caught off guard by a rogue wave (created by boats in the construction areas). You can snorkel on the inside of the harbour walls, but the water is rather still and tends to silt up. The fish also prefer the outside walls.

Musandam offers good snorkelling too, but the waters can have strong currents so it's a good idea to go with a tour company and have a guide to point out the best sites. The best fish life is to be found between the surface and 10 metres below, so try to snorkel along the side of rocks and islands. There are a number of tour companies that offer dhow trips for dolphin watching and snorkelling, and the boats usually moor in areas that are safe for snorkelling in (see p.271).

Check out the *UAE Underwater Explorer* for further information on where to go snorkelling. Go to askexplorer.com to purchase a copy.

Boating

With calm waters and year-round sunshine, the UAE offers ideal conditions for those wishing to sample life on the ocean waves. A number of companies provide boat charters, offering everything from sundowner cruises of a couple of hours and overnight trips with snorkelling stopovers, to scuba diving excursions to remote destinations such as Musandam. Large sailing yachts, speedboats and other motorboats can be hired for private charter and corporate events; other companies offer outings on dhows and also cater for weddings and birthday parties. Fishing trips and watersports packages are also available. If you're on the east coast and fancy a traditional boating experience, large independent groups can charter a dhow from the fishermen at Dibba. If you haggle you can usually knock the price down substantially. Respected UAE charter companies include ART Marine (artmarine.net), Bristol Middle East Yacht Solution (bristol-middleeast.com), Leisure Marine – Middle East (leisuremarine-me.com), Marine Concept (marine-charter-concept.com) and Ocean Active (oceanactive.com). See Activities, p.320, for more details.

Water Choice

As well as boating, diving and snorkelling, there are plenty of other waterborne activities you can fill your leisure time with. Kitesurfing (p.344) is a growing pastime worldwide, and there are a couple of good spots in town. Regular surfing is possible in Dubai, although the waves are more Clacton than California. Nonetheless there is a local group, Surf Dubai, that is open to beginners and die-hards alike (p.358). Windsurfing, jetskiing and waterskiing are all available from various beachfront hotels and sports clubs (p.362), while canoeists and kayakers can take advantage of the mangroves and lagoons on both of the UAE's coastlines for some first-class exploring (see p.324).

UAE Yachting & Boating has advice on buying and mooring a boat, details of local marinas, local rules and regulations, handy maps, suggested cruising areas and a comprehensive contacts directory. With so much invaluable information, this is the ultimate resource for boaters old and new.

SPECTATOR SPORTS

For eight months of the year, Dubai residents can enjoy a packed calendar of sporting events. The UAE's sunny winter climate, its location within easy reach of Europe and Asia, and its development of some excellent sporting facilities means the country is growing ever more attractive as a venue for international sporting associations to include on their schedules. All of this is great news for sports fans; from big headline events such as the Abu Dhabi Grand Prix and Race To Dubai finale, to regular tennis and golf tournaments and even local horse and camel racing meets, there's an awful lot going on.

Camel Racing

This is a chance to see a truly traditional local sport up close. Apart from great photo opportunities and the excitement of the races, you can also have a browse around the stalls; most race tracks have camel markets alongside (they are dark and dusty but should not be missed). The best buys are the large cotton blankets (used as camel blankets), which make excellent bedspreads, throws and picnic blankets, and only cost around Dhs.40. It is also interesting to see the old traders sitting on the floor of their shop, hand weaving camel halters and lead-ropes.

Races take place during the winter months, usually on Thursday and Friday mornings, at tracks in Dubai, Ras Al Khaimah, Umm Al Quwain, Al Ain and Abu Dhabi. Often, additional races are held on National Day and certain other public holidays. Races start early (about 07:30) and are usually over by 08:30. Admission is free.

Ras Al Khaimah has one of the best race tracks in the country at Digdagga, situated on a plain between the dunes and the mountains, about 10km south of the town.

Robotic Jockeys

Racing camels used to be ridden by children, but this practice has been outlawed – and robotic jockeys have taken over. The operators follow the race in 4WDs while directing the jockeys by remote control – quite a bizarre sight.

The camel race track in Dubai used to be near Nad Al Sheba, but it has now been moved to make way for the Meydan development. To find the new location (it's always a good place to take visitors), head up the Al Ain Road, past the Dubai Outlet Mall, until you reach the Al Lisali exit. Turn right off this exit and you will see the big track on your right. Races are usually early on a Friday morning, but you should see plenty of camels being exercised throughout the day in the cooler months.

Cricket

Dubai has a large population from the Indian subcontinent, so, naturally, cricket is a favourite sport of many residents. Although there isn't much on offer in the way of professional domestic leagues, Dubai now boasts a world-class cricket venue: the 25,000 seat Dubai Sports City's Cricket Stadium (dubaisportscity.ae).

The opening of this arena, coupled with the fact that the International Cricket Council has its headquarters in the city, and runs a cricket academy at the stadium, looks set to ensure that Dubai hosts its fair share of major international matches in the future. The likes of Pakistan, England, Australia, New Zealand, South Africa and Sri Lanka have all played here. Keep an eye on local media and dubaisportscity.ae for news of upcoming fixtures.

Football

Football is as popular in the UAE as it is the world over, and in recent years there has been plenty of action for fans of the game to watch. Abu Dhabi was awarded the honour of hosting the Fifa World Club Cup in 2009 and 2010, a tournament that saw the champion clubs of each continent competing in a one-off knock-out competition and which was won by Barcelona on both occasions. In 2009, Dubai hosted the Fifa Beach Soccer World Cup, and the city regularly plays host to winter friendly matches between big European teams, with even more teams heading over for winter training camps during international breaks.

The news that nearby Qatar is to host the Fifa World Cup in 2022 has been much welcomed in the UAE and, as plans in Doha progress towards the distant deadline, the UAE will undoubtedly benefit from the increased attention on the sport in the region and love of the beautiful game will continue to flourish.

There's also a strong domestic competition, the UAE Pro League (proleague.ae), and attending one of these games makes for a really colourful experience – Emirati supporters are fanatical about their teams, and there are some strong local rivalries. There are also some great characters in the game with football legends Diego Maradona and Fabio Cannavaro having plied their trade in the league as manager and player respectively.

Making A Splash

In 2012, the UAE hosted three major international swimming events at Dubai's Hamdan bin Mohammed bin Rashid Sports Complex – the FINA/ARENA Swimming World Cup, the first International Water Polo and Synchronised Swimming Championships, and the 9th Asian Swimming Championships.

Abu Dhabi's Al Wahda, Al Ahli, Al Ain and Al Wasl are the traditionally strong teams. There are also several opportunities to see the UAE national team play in qualifying matches for the major international tournaments. See uefa.ae for fixture details.

Golf

Dubai has become a major destination on the world golf circuit. Its first-class courses are a magnet not only for keen amateurs, but also for some of the game's top professional players.

Each February, the Dubai Desert Classic is staged at Emirates Golf Club. Part of the European PGA Tour, previous winners include Tiger Woods, Miguel Angel Jiménez and Rory McIlroy. The competition lasts for four days, and is a popular event with spectators who can follow their favourite players round the course, or take a seat in one of the grandstands and watch the whole cast of golfers play past. See dubaidesertclassic.com for dates ticket details. The DP World Tour Championship (p.28), staged annually at the Jumeirah Golf Estates, is the culmination of the European Tour's Race To Dubai. Golf fans also have another major international tournament to look forward to: the Abu Dhabi HSBC Golf Championship (p.25), staged at Abu Dhabi Golf Course each January.

Horse Racing

A trip to the races is an essential experience for anyone living in Dubai. Previously, the main Nad Al Sheba course held exciting race nights and the world's richest horse race, the Dubai World Cup (see p.26). It was one of the top international racing facilities, with top jockeys from Australia, Europe and the USA regularly competing throughout the season (October-April), as well as home to the incredibly successful Godolphin racing stables. It closed for good, however, in 2009, to make way for a brand new development, Meydan, which opened for the 2009-10 season and took over the hosting of both the race nights and Dubai World Cup. This state-of-the-art facility incorporates the futuristic trackside The Meydan Hotel, and offers special racing packages and stable tours throughout the season.

Race nights under the floodlights are an atmospheric affair. There is officially no gambling, in line with the country's rules, but everyone can take part in various free competitions to select the winning horses, with the ultimate aim of taking home prizes or cash. You can also catch a slightly more raw form of horse racing at Jebel Ali racecourse, near the Greens, every other Friday afternoon during the season. See dubairacingclub.com for the season's full schedule.

For horse excitement of a different kind, the Dubai Polo & Equestrian Club (p.342) stages Friday chukka events during the polo season. For Dhs.50 you can drive pitchside and set up your picnic chairs, blanket and cool box full of Spinneys' finest. For a more extravagant option, order a bespoke Polo Picnic Box from the Clubhouse and then mingle with the players for the polo after-party from 18:00 to midnight. Polo matches start around 15:00 but arrive from 13:30 to get the pick of the parking spots.

Motorsports

The Abu Dhabi Grand Prix is the UAE's headline motor racing event, and is a roaring success, held at the Yas Marina Circuit. The season closing race for its first two years, it no longer holds that position in the calendar but is still held towards the end of the season in November. But motorsports fans don't need to wait all year to get their fix. Yas Marina Circuit holds races and rallies throughout the year including supercar, drag racing, GP2 and FIA GT1 events. Closer to home, Dubai Autodrome hosts events of various categories year round, from GT to saloon to endurance races, plus events at the indoor and outdoor kartdromes which are part of the Autodrome complex. Race days at the Autodrome are open to the public and free of charge, and offer car enthusiasts the chance to chat to the drivers and get up close to the machines they drive. See dubaiautodrome.com for a full calendar of meetings. Both race tracks also offer a range of track days if you want to get behind the wheel yourself. The annual Abu Dhabi Desert Challenge (p.26), held in March, is a great spectator event for rally fans.

Rugby

Although amateur club matches take place in Dubai, Sharjah, Abu Dhabi and Al Ain throughout the year, the big rugby event takes place every December, when fans of the oval ball from around the country and beyond head to the The Sevens stadium on the Al Ain Road for the Emirates Airline Dubai Rugby Sevens (dubairugby7s.com) – three days of rugby and revelry. This 'light' version of the sport is fast paced and competitive, with young, up-and-coming international stars taking centre stage. As much about the atmosphere as the sport, it's a great day out for groups of friends.

Tennis & Squash

One of the highlights of Dubai's sporting calendar is the Dubai Duty Free Tennis Championships, which is held at The Aviation Club every February. It is a great opportunity to catch some of the top players in the game at close quarters, and features both men's and ladies' tournaments. Tickets for the later stages sell out in advance so keep an eye out for sale details, although entrance to some of the earlier rounds can be bought on the day. See dubaidutyfreetennischampionships.com. A newer fixture on the UAE's annual sporting calendar is the Mubadala World Tennis Championship (p.29), held at Abu Dhabi International Tennis Complex in Zayed Sports City, which usually falls around the New Year's Day public holiday.

Watersports

Sailing is an important part of Dubai's heritage, and this is reflected in the number of water-based sporting events that take place. The emirate's waters are a major venue on the Class 1 World Power Boating Championship (class-1.com). These stylish heavyweights of the powerboating world race around a grand prix circuit through Mina Seyahi lagoon at speeds of up to 160mph, just metres from the beach. Held at the end of November and beginning of December, the twin Dubai competitions represent the finale of the European circuit, which has seen Dubai's Victory Team win the series an impressive eight times. Up the road in Sharjah, the UIM F1 H2O World Championship takes place each December as part of Sharjah Water Festival (p.29). For a quieter but still vigorous display of boating prowess, look out for the various dragon boat events held throughout the year (dubaidragonboat.com), and keep an eye open for the many sailing and dhow racing events that take place off Dubai's shoreline, including the 10-day Maktoum Sailing Trophy, which takes place every February (dimc.ae).

TOURS & SIGHTSEEING

As befits a leading international tourist destination, Dubai is well geared up for taking people on tours of its attractions and highlights. While many of these are primarily aimed at visitors, there's nothing to stop residents getting to know – and simply enjoying – the various leisure pursuits on offer to holidaymakers.

Some tours are offered by most operators, particularly desert experiences and dhow cruises; both of these are great options for when you have guests in town. Other companies run memorable, specialised tours, such as diving trips, aerial sightseeing and trekking, while almost all the firms listed here will tailor programmes to suit individual needs.

The classic option is the desert safari. Expert drivers blast four wheel drives up, down and around massive dunes while passing old Bedouin villages and pointing out incredible natural attractions. Mountain safaris lead passengers through the narrow wadis and steep passes of the Hajar Mountains. Most driving safaris include pickup from your place of residence and lunch. Some end the day of daredevil driving at a replica Bedouin camp where passengers can watch a belly dancer, eat Arabic delicacies and smoke shisha. Some operators even run overnight safaris that combine half-day treks with some sort of driving adventure. When booking your tour, it is useful to reserve a place three or four days in advance, especially at weekends.

Bus Tours

If you've got visitors here on a short visit or on a whirlwind stopover in Dubai before they jet off elsewhere, a bus tour of the city is a great way to take in all the highlights in one go. It's also a good way to get acquainted with what's where when you first move to Dubai.

ArtBus

Various locations **04 341 7305**
artinthecity.com

Bus service that runs from The Jam Jar to galleries across town during major art festivals and exhibitions. A service to and around the capital operates during Abu Dhabi Art Fair (p.28).

Big Bus Tours

Various locations **04 340 7709**
bigbustours.com

A fleet of double-decker buses that provide a hop-on hop-off service, with audio commentary, to major attractions across town. Tickets are valid for either 24 or 48 hours.

Easy Tour Dubai

Various locations **04 331 1399**
easytour.ae

Offers day and night guided bus tours around Dubai at 09:00, 14:30 and 22:00. The four and two-hour round trips include free entrance to Dubai Museum and a walking tour in The Dubai Mall.

Trolley Bus

The Dubai Mall Downtown Dubai **800 38224 6255**
dubaimall.com
Map **2 F6** Metro **Burj Khalifa/Dubai Mall**

Whisks you around Downtown and, with a day ticket, you can hop on and off at any of the four stops. Runs 10:00-22:00 during the week and 10:00-00:00 at weekends.

Wonder Bus Tours

BurJuman Al Mankhool **04 359 5656**
wonderbustours.net
Map **2 L5** Metro **BurJuman**

Book a two-hour mini tour which travels along, and on, Dubai Creek in an amphibious bus. The tour covers Creek Park and Dubai Creek Golf & Yacht Club, and heads under Maktoum Bridge towards Garhoud Bridge, then returns to BurJuman.

Desert & Mountain Tours

Desert safaris are by far the most popular tour available, perhaps because a good safari offers many activities in one day. Starting with an exciting ride up and down some of the desert's biggest dunes, you can try sand skiing before watching the sun set over the desert. After driving a short distance further to a permanent Bedouin-style camp, you are treated to a sumptuous barbecue, followed by shisha, belly dancing, camel rides and henna painting.

You can vary the length of your safari, choosing to stay overnight or combine it with a trip into the mountains, if desired. However, a safari to the mountains is highly recommended, if only to see how the landscape changes from orange sand dunes to craggy mountains within the space of just a few short kilometres.

The approximate cost for a desert safari is Dhs.150-Dhs.300 (overnight up to Dhs.500). Many companies offer these types of tour (see Main Tour Operators, p.279); below is a selection of typical itineraries from which you can choose.

Dune Dinners

Enjoy some thrilling off-road desert driving before settling down to watch the sun set behind the dunes. Starting around 16:00, tours typically pass camel farms and fascinating scenery that provide great photo opportunities. At an Arabian campsite, enjoy a delicious dinner and the calm of a starlit desert night, returning around 22:00.

Full-Day Safari

This day-long tour usually passes through traditional Bedouin villages and camel farms in the desert, with a drive through sand dunes of varying colours and heights. Tours often visit either Fossil Rock or the Hajar Mountains. A cold buffet lunch may be provided in the mountains before the drive home.

Hatta Pools Safari

Hatta is a quiet, old-fashioned town nestled in the foothills of the Hajar Mountains, famed for its fresh water rock pools that you can swim in. The full-day trip usually includes a stop at the Hatta Fort Hotel, where you can enjoy the pool, landscaped gardens, archery, and nine-hole golf course. Lunch is served either in the hotel, or alfresco in the mountains. The trip costs Dhs.260-Dhs.350.

Mountain Safari

Normally a full-day tour takes you to the east coast, heading inland at Dibba and entering the spectacular Hajar Mountains. You will travel through rugged canyons onto steep winding tracks, past terraced mountainsides and old stone houses. It returns via Dibba, where the journey homewards stops off at Masafi Market on the way.

Overnight Safari

This 24 hour tour starts at about 15:00 with a drive through the dunes to a Bedouin-style campsite. Dine under the stars, sleep in the fresh air and wake to the smell of freshly brewed coffee, before heading for the mountains. The drive takes you through spectacular rugged scenery, past dunes and along wadis, before stopping for a buffet lunch and returning to Dubai.

Boat Tours

An evening aboard a dhow, either on Dubai Creek or sailing along the coast, is a wonderfully atmospheric and memorable experience. Some companies run regular, scheduled trips, while others will charter out boats to private parties. Many boats also offer dinner cruises from the Bur Dubai side of the creek. Charters of luxury yachts, catamarans and fishing boats are available from several operators, and many firms will consider letting out their tour boats for the right price. If you want to go further afield, a dhow cruise in Musandam (p.314) is a must and some dhow cruise companies offer transfers from Dubai. Alternatively, a number of dive companies, such as Al Boom Diving, offer sightseeing cruises – either as part of a dive trip or as a separate offering (see Diving, p.270 and Snorkelling, p.271).

4Yacht Arabia

JAFZA View 18, Jebel Ali Free Zone Jebel Ali 04 886 5755
4yachtarabia.ae
Map 1 B7 Metro Jebel Ali

A luxury yacht charter and sales company with five Dubai-based yachts for charter, plus water taxis, and three vessels moored in Greece, if you fancy a cruising holiday.

Al Boom Tourist Village

Nr Wonderland Amusement Park, Shk Rashid Rd Umm Hurair 2 04 324 3000
alboom.ae
Map 2 L7 Metro Dubai Healthcare City

Operates several dhows on the creek, with capacities ranging from 20 to 350 passengers. Various packages are available.

Al Marsa Travel & Tourism

Nr Al Shola Private School, University City Rd Sharjah 06 544 1232
almarsamusandam.com

Runs dhow voyages off Musandam for divers, snorkellers and sightseers, lasting from half a day to a whole week.

Al Wasl Cruising & Fishing

Al Owais Bldg, Nr Nissan Showroom Port Saeed 04 295 9477
cruiseindubai.com
Map 2 N6 Metro Deira City Centre

Specialises in a variety of deep sea fishing trips and yacht charters with a fleet of modern vessels.

ART Marine

3rd Interchange, Shk Zayed Rd Al Quoz Industrial 1 04 338 8955
artmarine.net
Map 1 U6 Metro Noor Islamic Bank

Offers chartered yacht experiences from locations around the region, including Jumeirah Beach Hotel in Dubai, Emirates Palace and Yas Marina in Abu Dhabi, and the stunning Zighy Marina in Oman.

Athena Charter Yacht

Dubai Marina Yacht Club Dubai Marina 04 362 7900
dubaimarinayachtclub.com
Map 1 K5 Metro Jumeirah Lakes Towers

A 50 foot yacht available for cruises around Dubai Marina, The Palm Jumeirah and along the Jumeira coastline, for up to 12 people at a time. On-board dining is also available.

Bateaux Dubai

Nr British Embassy Al Hamriya 04 399 4994
bateauxdubai.com
Map 2 M5 Metro BurJuman

This sleek sightseeing vessel offers daily tours but it's the dinner cruises that offer the best and most unique experience. The boat can also be privately chartered to cater for parties of up to 300 people.

Bristol Middle East Yacht Solution

Marina Walk Dubai Marina 04 366 3538
bristol-middleeast.com
Map 1 K5 Metro Dubai Marina

Marina-based company that offers charters and packages on boats of all shapes and sizes, from luxury yachts to its old wooden dhow, Captain Jack, which regularly takes one-hour pleasure cruises along the coast from Dubai Marina. The firm puts together land and air tours too.

DHOW & OUT

An option for large independent groups is to charter a dhow from the fishermen at Dibba on the east coast to travel up the coast to Musandam (p.314). If you're prepared to haggle you can usually knock the price down substantially, especially if you know a bit of Arabic. Expect to pay around Dhs.2,500 per day for a dhow large enough to take 20-25 people, or Dhs.100 per hour for a smaller one. You'll need to take your own food and water, as nothing is supplied onboard except ice lockers suitable for storing supplies. Conditions are basic, but you'll have the freedom to plan your own route and to see the beautiful fjord-like scenery of Musandam from a traditional wooden dhow.

The waters in the area are beautifully clear and turtles and dolphins can often be seen from the boat, although sometimes unfavourable weather conditions can seriously reduce visibility for divers. If you leave from Dibba (or Daba), Omani visas are not required, even though you enter Omani waters.

It is also possible to arrange stops along the coast and it's worth taking camping equipment for the night, although you can sleep on board. This kind of trip is ideal for diving but you should hire any equipment you may need before you get to Dibba (see Diving, p.270). If diving is not your thing, you can just spend the day swimming, snorkelling and soaking up the sun.

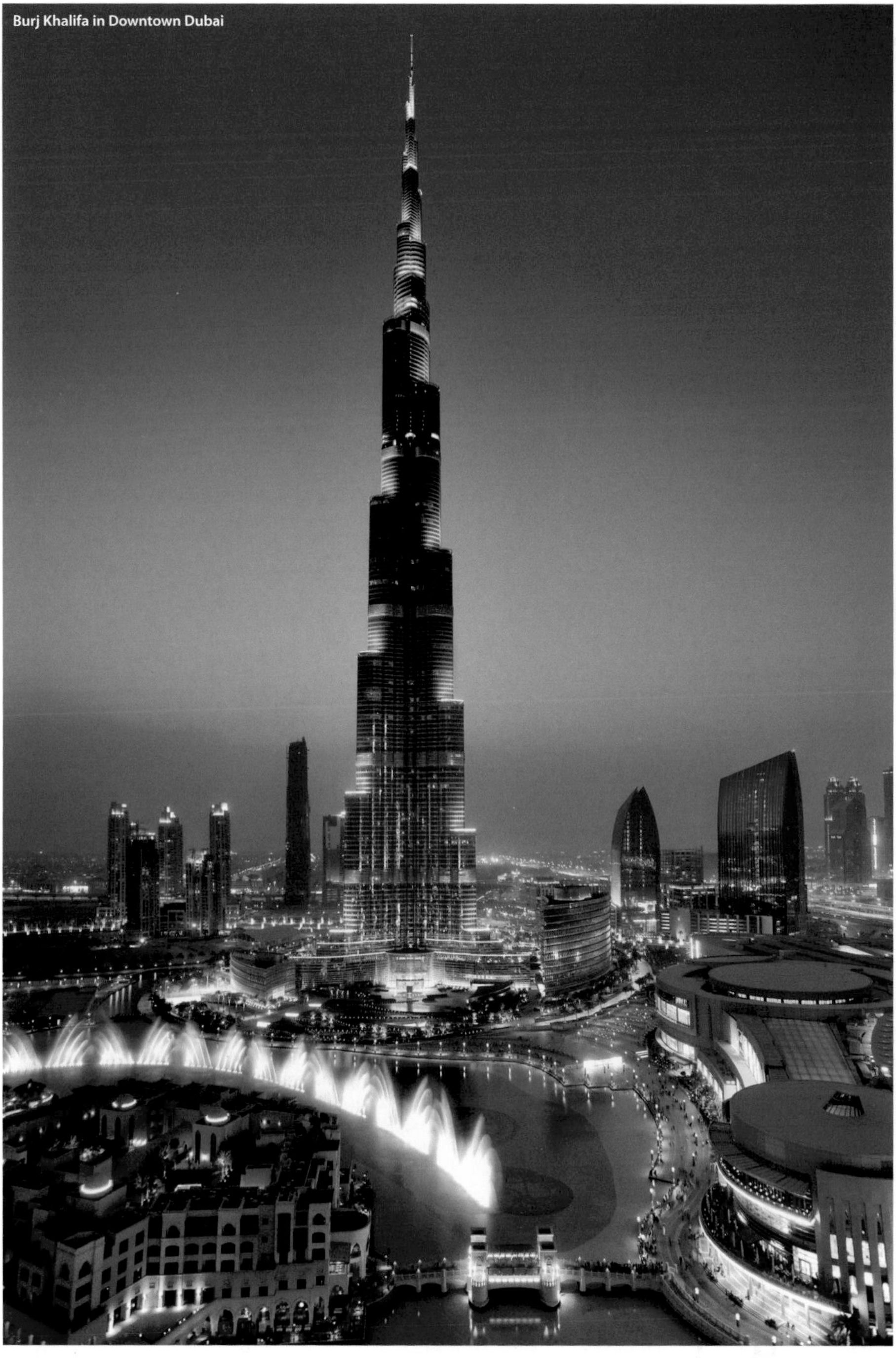

Burj Khalifa in Downtown Dubai

Cruise With Nakheel

Various locations **04 390 3333**
nakheel.com

Experience striking views of the Palm Jumeirah from the deck of a double-decker houseboat or smaller vessel. The 'Cruise with Nakheel' service runs trips for groups of up to 12, 15 and 30 people around the landmark island, with prices starting from around Dhs.1,000 per boat.

Divaz

Jebel Ali Golf Resort Waterfront **04 814 5604**
funkyhipvenues.com
Metro **Danube**

More floating party than traditional boat trip, Divaz offers chilled dining experiences, wedding parties, raucous brunches or elegant night-time gatherings... all on the open waves.

El Mundo

Dubai International Marine Club Dubai Marina **050 551 7406**
elmundodubai.com
Map **1 M4** Metro **Dubai Marina**

El Mundo is a 60 foot catamaran that offers four-hour cruises on Thursdays and Fridays, and can be privately chartered for all manner of occasions.

Jebel Ali Golf Resort

Nr Palm Jebel Ali Waterfront **04 814 5555**
jaresortshotels.com
Metro **Danube**

One or two-hour long leisure boat trips for up to seven people on board Club Joumana's 36ft fishing boat.

Khasab Travel & Tours

Warba Centre Al Muraqqabat **04 266 9950**
khasabtours.com
Map **2 P6** Metro **Abu Baker Al Siddique**

Runs a dhow cruise from Khasab in Musandam that includes lunch, refreshments, snorkelling and a spot of fishing. Can also organise pickups from Dubai.

Ocean Group

Wafi Residences Umm Hurair 2 **04 324 3327**
oceanindependence.com
Map **2 L7** Metro **Dubai Healthcare City**

Provides a range of luxury yacht charters from short trips to overnight stays and holidays on the water. Also sells vessels and runs charters internationally.

Sheesa Beach Dive Center

Musandam Dibba **968 26836551**
sheesabeach.com

Day and overnight dhow cruises in Musandam, with transfers from Dubai available. Diving trips, PADI training and camping are also offered.

Tour Dubai

Nr British Embassy Al Hamriya **04 336 8407**
tour-dubai.com
Map **2 L6** Metro **BurJuman**

Offers a variety of creek dhow tours and charter packages that range from romantic dinners for two to corporate hospitality for up to 200 guests.

Ultimate Charter

Fairmont Dubai Trade Centre 1 **04 346 4194**
dubaiultimatecharter.com
Map **2 J5** Metro **World Trade Centre**

As well as two-hour dhow dinner cruises along Dubai Marina and the Palm Jumeirah, there are catamaran party cruises, luxury motor yachts, super yachts and mega yachts available for charter, and fishing boats offering a guaranteed catch.

Shopping Tours

Dubai's reputation as the shopping capital of the Middle East is well-deserved. From designer clothes, shoes and jewellery in the malls, to electronics, spices and gold in the souks, everything is available. A half-day shopping tour takes you round some of the best shopping spots. Whether or not you bag some bargains depends on your haggling skills.

Waterworld Yacht Rental

Dubai Marina Yacht Club Dubai Marina **04 422 8729**
Map **1 K5** Metro **Jumeirah Lakes Towers**

As well as yacht rentals from Dhs.699 per hour, this company offers deep sea fishing trips, BBQ cruises and dhow dinner cruises.

Xclusive Yachts Sport Fishing & Yacht Charter

Dubai Marina Yacht Club Dubai Marina **04 432 7233**
xclusiveyachts.com
Map**1 K5** Metro **Jumeirah Lakes Towers**

Offering everything from 22ft to 90ft boats, Xclusive can organise sightseeing or fishing trips for groups of family or friends, or you can simply charter a boat and follow your own itinerary. Watersports including banana boating and parasailing can be included.

Aerial Tours

With its soaring skyscrapers, rolling sand dunes and spectacular man-made islands, Dubai from the air is an impressive and truly unique sight. Swoop over the cityscape in a helicopter, fly along the coast in a seaplane, or take in the serenity of the desert from a graceful hot air balloon flight – any one of these experiences will live long in the memory. As with boat tours, most aerial tour companies offer a seat on a set tour as well as charter options.

Aerogulf Services Company
Dubai International Airport Al Garhoud 04 220 0331
aerogulfservices.com
Map 2 P8 Metro Airport Terminal 1
Provides helicopter tours over the city and its main landmarks. A half-hour tour for four people costs Dhs.3,200, or you can opt to charter a chopper by the hour and choose your route.

Amigos Balloons
Various locations 04 289 9295
amigos-balloons.com
Take a dawn hot air balloon flight over the desert out near Fossil Rock and watch the changing colour of the sands as the sun rises. Flights operate from September to June and cost Dhs.950 per person.

Balloon Adventures Emirates > *p.359*
Nr Bin Sougat Centre Al Rashidiya 04 285 4949
ballooning.ae
Map 2 P10 Metro Rashidiya
Tours for individuals and groups in four large, advanced balloons. Flights depart before sunrise between October and May, and are followed by dune driving.

Fujairah Aviation Academy
Fujairah International Airport Fujairah 09 222 4747
fujaa.ae
An enthralling bird's-eye view of Fujairah's coastline, rugged mountains, villages and date plantations. Flights can accommodate one to three people.

Seawings > *p.226*
Jebel Ali Golf Resort Waterfront 04 807 0708
seawings.ae
Metro Danube
Take off from the water in a seaplane from Jebel Ali or Dubai Creek for spectacular flights over the Gulf and city. Various package options are available.

Main Tour Operators
Most operators offer variations on the main types of excursions: city tours, desert safaris and mountain safaris. Some offer more unique activities, such as fishing or diving trips, expeditions to the Empty Quarter, helicopter tours and desert driving courses. The main tour companies, and those that offer something a little bit different, are listed in this section – contact them directly for information on their full programmes and tours.

Alpha Tours
Al Owais Bldg, Al Ittihad Rd Port Saeed 04 294 9888
alphatoursdubai.com
Map 2 N6 Metro Deira City Centre
Provides a full range of tours including shopping trips, desert safaris, flights and cruises.

Arabia Outdoors
Various locations 055 955 6209
arabiaoutdoors.com
An outdoor adventure company which specialises in guided hikes, rock climbing, kayaking and camping.

Arabian Adventures
Emirates Holiday Bldg, Shk Zayed Rd Business Bay
04 303 4888
arabian-adventures.com
Map 2 E6 Metro Business Bay
Offers a range of tours and itineraries including desert safaris, city tours, sand skiing, dhow cruises, camel riding, and wadi and dune bashing.

Arabian Nights Tours
Nr Villa Rotana, Shk Zayed Rd Al Wasl 04 321 6565
arabiannightstours.com
Map 2 E6 Metro Business Bay
Reputable operator that covers all bases, from dinner dhow cruises to safaris, Musandam and city tours.

Asia Pacific Travels & Tourism
Al Owais Bldg, Al Ittihad Rd Port Saeed 04 239 4764
apttdubai.com
Map 2 R7 Metro Stadium
Offers all manner of tours and activities that focus firmly on the traditional Arabian offerings that Dubai has become famous for.

Dadabhai Travel
Sama Bldg, Al Ittihad Rd Al Qusais 1 04 220 9393
dadabhaitravel.ae
Map 2 R7 Metro Stadium
One of the operators with the most extensive ranges of tours, covering everything from shopping and culture to overnight camps, it has a great Bedouin camp out near Al Aweer and offers a dune bashing tour that combines dunes and adrenaline.

Desert Adventures
Qatar Airways Bldg, Al Maktoum Rd Al Rigga
800 4230
desertadventures.com
Map 2 N6 Metro Al Rigga
Offers a full range of city and desert tours throughout the Emirate with some particularly interesting and creative city tours.

Desert Rangers
Nr American Hospital, 18 Street Oud Metha
04 357 2200
desertrangers.com
Map 2 T6 Metro Oud Metha
Runs a wide variety of standard and specialist desert and mountain tours, including activities such as rock climbing, helicopter tours and kayaking.

Desert Rose Tourism
Platinum Business Center Al Nahda 2 050 778 5707
desertrose-tourism.com
Map 2 T7 Metro Al Nahda
Offers city discovery tours with a guide, plus various trips around the UAE and Oman, including desert and camel safaris and dhow dinner cruises.

Desert Safari Abu Dhabi & Dubai
Various locations 04 361 7530
desertsafariabudhabi.ae
Specialising in desert safaris, dune bashing and dune buggying, this company also offers city tours and water-based excursions.

Dream Explorer
Al Musalla Bldg, Meena Bazar Al Souk Al Kabeer
04 354 4481
dreamexplorerdubai.com
Map 2 H5 Metro Al Fahidi
Desert and mountain tours, dune buggying, plus white-knuckle jet boat rides. A luxury option combines dune driving with a visit to the Bab Al Shams Desert Resort.

Dubai Travel & Tourist Services
Al Abbar Bldg, Nr Ramee Royal Hotel Al Karama
04 336 7727
dubai-travel.ae
Map 2 L6 Metro Oud Metha
City shopping tours, creek dinner cruises, cultural tours to Sharjah and Ajman, plus desert, mountain and East Coast excursions.

Gulf Ventures > p.281
dnata Travel Centre Business Bay 04 404 5880
gulfventures.ae
Map 2 D6 Metro Business Bay
There's a wide range of activities including Bedouin camps, creek cruises and east coast tours on land and sea, plus fishing, polo and ballooning. More unusually, camel polo is a fun-packed day out, with the rare opportunity to learn the basics of polo.

Lama Tours
Oud Metha Rd Oud Metha 04 334 4330
lamadubai.com
Map 2 K6 Metro Oud Metha
Tours include an excellent desert safari experience, dhow cruises, city excursions and fishing tours.

Net Tours
Al Masaood Tower, Al Maktoum Rd Port Saeed
04 602 8888
nettours-uae.com
Map 2 N6 Metro Deira City Centre
Offers mountain tours and treks, theme park excursions, helicopter and balloon flights, dhow dinner cruises and desert safaris, plus of course the usual Bedouin desert campsite experience.

Oasis Palm Tourism
Royal Plaza Bldg, Al Rigga Rd Al Rigga
04 262 8889
opdubai.com
Map 2 N6 Metro Al Rigga
One of the biggest and best known tour operators, Oasis Palm offers desert safaris, dhow dinner cruises and wadi trips, plus east coast tours, diving and deep sea fishing trips.

Omeir Travel Agency
Nr Lamcy Plaza Oud Metha 04 337 7727
omeir.com
Map 2 K6 Metro Oud Metha
A full-blown travel agency that also organises a wide range of water, land and air based tours, focusing on corporate excursions.

Orient Tours
Nr Le Meridien Fairway Al Garhoud 04 282 8238
orienttours.ae
Map 2 N7 Metro GGICO
City tours, including trips to the horse and camel races, desert safaris, sea safaris around Musandam, off-road trips to Hatta and day tours of the Empty Quarter in Liwa.

Planet Travel & Tours
Abulhoul Bldg, Airport Rd Al Garhoud
04 282 2199
planettours.co
Map 2 N7 Metro GGICO
A large travel company with plenty of resources to call on, Planet Travel Tours offers coach, heritage and shopping tours within Dubai, plus safari and desert tours.

Sunflower Tours
Zomorrodah Bldg, Zabeel Rd Al Karama
04 334 5554
sunflowerdubai.com
Map 2 L6 Metro Oud Metha
Desert and city tours, as well as camel safaris, crab hunting, diving, fishing and helicopter tours, plus chauffeur and limousine services.

Tour Tips
If you are booking a tour, make sure you ring around to get the best price. Dubai is dedicated to discounts and you can often get a better rate as a resident. Just remember it is all about putting on the charm – not being a cheeky customer.

Out Of The City

OUT OF THE CITY

Dubai may have everything from ski slopes and souks to boutiques and beaches, but there are a number of interesting and varied areas outside the city and country that deserve a place in your weekend plans. There are six other emirates in the UAE and five other countries in the GCC, all of which warrant exploration.

All six of the other emirates in the UAE – Abu Dhabi, Sharjah, Ras Al Khaimah, Umm Al Quwain, Ajman and Fujairah – are within a two-hour drive of the centre of Dubai. From the sleepy streets of Umm Al Quwain and the rugged mountains of Ras Al Khaimah to the cultural grandiose of Sharjah, each emirate has something different to offer, and each can be explored, at least in part, over a weekend. The country's vast deserts and harsh-looking mountains are equally accessible, with a copy of the *UAE Off-Road Explorer*, and can be reached within a 45 minute drive of Dubai, if you need to avoid civilisation for a while.

Book It Online!

Don't waste hours scouring the internet... Whether you want to book an extravagant honeymoon trip to the Seychelles or a shoestring weekend break to Europe, dnata (dnatatravel.com) is a one-stop shop for hotels, flights and holiday packages. Book online or call 04 316 6666 – and sign up on the website for all the latest travel deals.

Dubai's status as an international hub means it's easy to find quick, cheap flights to the neighbouring GCC countries of Oman, Saudi Arabia, Qatar, Bahrain and Kuwait, none of which are more than 90 minutes' flight away. Oman is considered by many to be one of the most beautiful and culturally interesting countries in the region and it can easily be reached and explored by car – Muscat is only a four-hour drive from Dubai.

Like the UAE, the countries in the GCC are growing at a phenomenal rate and are trying to attract more tourism. Many hotels in the GCC, including in the UAE, regularly offer discounted room rates, especially in the summer months. It's a good idea to sign up to the mailing lists of regional travel agencies, such as dnata (dnatatravel.com), to find out about any weekend getaway packages they offer.

UAE – THE OTHER EMIRATES

Abu Dhabi

Dubai may be the UAE's brashest member, but Abu Dhabi remains both the nation's capital and the richest of all the emirates, with a blossoming, burgeoning city to prove it. Recently, there has been a greater commitment to tourism, and projects such as Yas Island with its Grand Prix racetrack (p.28), Yas Waterworld, and Ferrari World theme park (p.286), and the development of the Desert Islands, are proof of that. While there isn't much you can get in Abu Dhabi that you can't find in Dubai, its slightly slower pace makes for a refreshing change. The city lies on an island and is connected to the mainland by bridges. It is home to numerous internationally renowned hotels, a few shiny shopping malls, and of heritage sites and souks. Abu Dhabi is marketed as the cultural capital of the UAE and is home to an annual jazz festival, a film festival, and a music and arts festival; it also hosts numerous exhibitions throughout the year. Once complete, Saadiyat Island will become the focus for much of the cultural activity. Find out more from the Abu Dhabi Tourism and Culture Authority (adach.ae).

In the cooler months, the extended Corniche is a lovely spot for a stroll, and on weekend evenings the area comes alive with families meeting up to enjoy a barbecue and shisha.

The many islands to the west of the city are popular with boating and watersports enthusiasts, and driving west past the city reveals kilometre upon kilometre of gorgeous, untouched sea and a few open beaches. The coast between Dubai and Abu Dhabi is also home to a few beaches that are popular with watersports enthusiasts, jetskiers in particular, and provide a good, quick getaway from Dubai.

Bird Watchers

The Abu Dhabi Falcon Hospital (02 575 5155, falconhospital.com) specialises in treating the region's falcons and various other species of birds. The hospital offers two-hour guided tours on weekdays that must be booked in advance.

The emirate is also home to a large part of the Empty Quarter (Rub Al Khali), the largest sand desert in the world. The large Liwa Oasis crescent acts as a gateway to the endless dunes and is a popular weekend destination for adventure-hungry residents from Dubai.

For further information, check out the *Abu Dhabi Mini Visitors' Guide, Al Gharbia Visitors' Guide or the Abu Dhabi Residents' Guide* – see askexplorer.com.

Abu Dhabi Attractions

Al Bateen

Nr Khaleej al Arabi and Sultan bin Zayed St
Abu Dhabi

This is one of Abu Dhabi's oldest districts and home to a dhow building yard, the Al Bateen Marina, a few historically accurate buildings and the future Al Bateen Wharf. It's a nice area to walk around, with plenty of open green spaces.

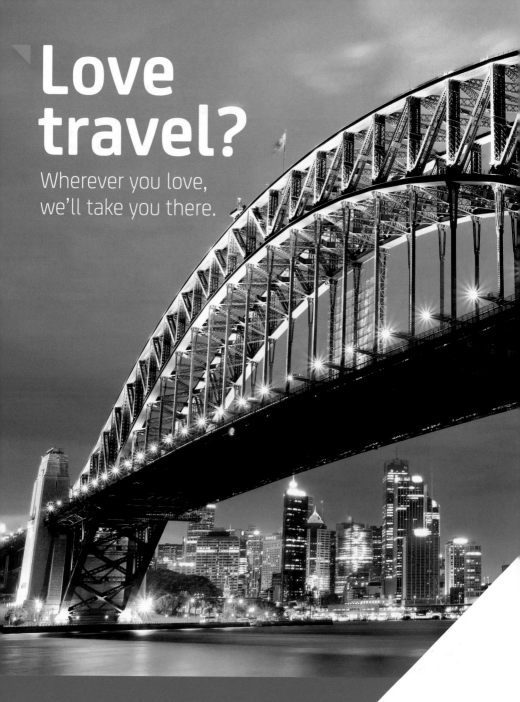

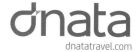

Liwa Oasis & Al Gharbia

Located way west of Abu Dhabi, further than most people usually venture, the Gharbia region makes up over two thirds of the UAE. Its 100km of coastline is home to stunning beaches, as well as a number of islands that are being developed and promoted to visitors. But the main reason to make the drive is Liwa – a destination that will blow you away with massive expanses of awesome desert and the biggest dunes this side of the Sahara.

The Liwa Oasis sits at the entrance to the Rub Al Khali, the largest sand desert in the world. Most of the Rub Al Khali (Empty Quarter) is uninhabitable, and Bedouin tribes occupy only the outer fringes. The Liwa Oasis is a fertile crescent, dotted with small villages, that stretches over 150km. A five-hour drive from Dubai, a weekend of camping and sensational dune-bashing is a must for any Dubai resident. There are a few hotels, including the luxurious Qasr Al Sarab (p.290), Tilal Liwa (02 894 6111) and the Liwa Hotel (p.290).

Abu Dhabi's coast stretches far beyond the city, nearly all the way to Qatar. Just offshore lie the Desert Islands, including Sir Bani Yas Island (p.288). One of the more impressive is Delma, which has been populated for over 7,000 years. Once the centre of the region's pearl-diving trade, it can be accessed by ferry. Also worth a trip is Al Mirfa Public Beach,120km from Abu Dhabi; it's almost always empty and the best place to enjoy a weekend of beachside camping.

Pick up a copy of the *Al Gharbia Visitors' Guide* or the *UAE Off-Road Explorer* to better understand the entire Al Gharbia region.

The Corniche

Off Corniche Rd Abu Dhabi

Corniche Road boasts six kilometres of parks that include children's play areas, separate cycle and pedestrian paths, cafes and restaurants, and a lifeguarded beach park. There is plenty of parking on the city side of Corniche Road, and underpasses at all the major intersections connect to the waterfront side. Bikes can also be rented from outside the Hiltonia Beach Club for Dhs.20 per day.

Ferrari World Abu Dhabi > *p.287*

Yas Island Abu Dhabi **02 496 8001**

ferrariworldabudhabi.com

Billed as the world's largest indoor theme park, Ferrari World is part F1 amusement park and part museum dedicated to the Italian supercar marque. There's plenty to keep little ones entertained and high adrenaline rides (including the world's fastest rollercoaster) for teens and adults. The whole park sits under a giant, sweeping roof and the comfort of air conditioning makes it great for a family day out during those stifling summer months. General admission: Dhs.225 for adults and Dhs.185 for kids (under 1.3m).

Heritage Village

Nr Marina Mall Abu Dhabi **02 681 4455**

torath.ae

Located near Marina Mall, this educational village offers a glimpse into the country's past. Traditional aspects of Bedouin life are explained and craftsmen demonstrate traditional skills.

Manarat Al Saadiyat

Saadiyat Cultural District Abu Dhabi **02 406 1400**

saadiyat.ae

This visitors' centre is a taster of the cultural offerings to come on Saadiyat. Along with a presentation on the island's future development, there are exhibition spaces that have welcomed some impressive displays.

Emirates Palace Attractions

More than just a grand hotel, Emirates Palace (p.290) is also one of Abu Dhabi's top cultural and entertainment centres. It stages several international music concerts each year, ranging from the annual Abu Dhabi Classics season (abudhabiclassics.com) to world-renowned pop artists like Coldplay, The Killers and Elton John. Emirates Palace also hosts major art exhibitions, which have featured pieces from the likes of Pablo Picasso, as well as the yearly Abu Dhabi Art Fair (abudhabiartfair.ae). Keep an eye on the Abu Dhabi Tourism website (abudhabitourism.ae) for details of upcoming events.

Qasr Al Hosn

Shk Zayed First St Abu Dhabi **02 657 6171**
adach.ae
Also known as the Old or White Fort, this is the oldest building in Abu Dhabi and dates back to 1793. Located in central Abu Dhabi, the fort has undergone a series of renovations over the years and, at the time of writing, it was closed for a major renovation.

Saadiyat Island

500m north of Abu Dhabi 800 8342
saaadiyat.ae
A leisure and tourism hub that's home to the Monte-Carlo Beach Club (montecarlobeachclub.ae), Saadiyat Beach Golf Club and two hotels. Branches of the Louvre and Guggenheim are due to open in 2015.

Sheikh Zayed Grand Mosque

Shk Rashid Bin Saeed Al Maktoum St Abu Dhabi **02 441 6444**
szgmc.ae
One of the largest mosques in the world, this architectural masterpiece can accommodate 40,000 worshippers. It features 82 domes and the world's largest hand-woven Persian carpet. It is open to non-Muslims every day except Friday mornings, from 10:00 to 20:00, Sunday to Thursday.

Sir Bani Yas Island

Abu Dhabi **02 406 1400**
desertislands.com
Half nature reserve, half luxury resort and spa, this is the centrepiece of Abu Dhabi's Desert Islands development. Home to the Arabian Wildlife Park, and Desert Islands Resort and Spa by Anantara, the island has thousands of free-roaming animals. Hiking, mountain biking and 4WD safaris, as well as snorkelling and kayaking trips, are available and you can reach the island by a private seaplane.

The Souk At Qaryat Al Beri

Qaryat Al Beri Complex Abu Dhabi **02 558 1670**
soukqaryatalberi.com
A recreation of a traditional Arabian souk, with small canals that weave their way between boutiques, cafes, restaurants and bars, many of which have spectacular views over the creek. The Shangri-La and Traders hotels make up part of the complex.

World Trade Centre Souk

Shk Hamdan Bin Mohammed St Abu Dhabi
wtcad.ae
The capital's latest shopping offering is rapidly becoming one of the city's major hubs, offering a mix of high fashion, traditional goods and great eating and drinking options. The Marriott Renaissance and Marriott Courtyard onsite offer further F&B options.

Yas Island

North-east of Abu Dhabi Abu Dhabi
yasisland.ae
Abu Dhabi's latest tourism hotspot is Yas Island; in addition to hosting the annual Formula 1 Grand Prix at Yas Marina Circuit, the island boasts several resorts with luxurious hotels, spas, and restaurants, a world-class golf course, Yas Waterworld, and Ferrari World, which houses the world's fastest rollercoaster. du Arena and Flash Forum stadiums stage regular concerts by internationally acclaimed musicians; the largest IKEA in the UAE opened its doors in 2011; and there's the iconic Yas Viceroy Hotel. Yas Mall and more hotels are set to open from 2013.

Yas Waterworld Abu Dhabi > *p.289*

Nr Ferrari World, Yas Island Abu Dhabi **02 414 2000**
yaswaterworld.com
With 43 rides and four world-firsts, Yas Waterworld is a must-do in the region. Visitors can slither down the world's first 'rattling' waterslide, or defy gravity on the Liwa Loop: the first looping waterslide in the Middle East. The Water Bomber rollercoaster reaches speeds of up to 55km/h, and the Aqualoop spins rider 360 degrees. Only the most daring will queue up to try Dawwama, a six-seater tornado waterslide complete with the world's longest funnel run-in at 238m.

Abu Dhabi Hotels

Al Raha Beach Hotel

Nr Al Raha Mall Abu Dhabi **02 508 0555**
danathotels.com
Excellent service, a gorgeous spa and unsurpassed comfort in an idyllic boutique beach setting just outside Abu Dhabi city.

Aloft Abu Dhabi

Abu Dhabi National Exhibition Centre (ADNEC) Abu Dhabi **02 654 5000**
aloftabudhabi.com
A real designer offering at the National Exhibition Centre, Aloft is a modern, trendy 408 bedroom affair.

Beach Rotana Abu Dhabi

Nr Abu Dhabi Mall, Tourist Club St Abu Dhabi **02 697 9000**
rotana.com
Offering loads of popular dining options, as well as a private beach, sports courts and the Zen spa.

Crowne Plaza Abu Dhabi Yas Island

Golf Plaza Abu Dhabi **02 656 3000**
ichotelsgroup.com
Sitting right next to Yas Links, this well-equipped hotel is just five minutes from Yas Marina and Ferrari World.

Danat Jebel Dhanna Resort
Jebel Dhanna **02 801 2222**
danathotels.com
Located 240km west of Abu Dhabi city, close to Sir Bani Yas Island, this resort features plenty of watersports, a private beach stretching for 800m, and a health and spa centre.

Emirates Palace
West Corniche Rd Abu Dhabi **02 690 9000**
kempinski.com
Emirates Palace is the ultimate in ostentatious luxury, with 14 bars and restaurants, 394 rooms and suites with butler service, an amazing collection of pools and a private beach. You can explore the hotel, and then call into Al Majlis coffee lounge or the Viennese-style cafe for afternoon tea. Large, open-air concerts are held in the 200-acre palace gardens in the cooler months. Check the website for details of what's on.

Fairmont Bab Al Bahr
Nr Al Maqta & Mussafa Bridges Abu Dhabi **02 654 3333**
fairmont.com
This luxury hotel overlooks the creek between the mainland and the city's island, next door to the Qaryat Al Beri complex. It is also home to some of the city's best new restaurants and bars.

Golden Tulip Al Jazira Hotel & Resort
Nr Racing & Polo Club, Dubai – Abu Dhabi Rd Abu Dhabi **02 562 9100**
goldentulipaljazira.com
Less than an hour's drive from Dubai, this hotel in Abu Dhabi emirate offers luxury beach bungalows, which are great for a weekend getaway.

Hilton Abu Dhabi
West Corniche Rd Abu Dhabi **02 681 1900**
hilton.com
This 10 storey luxury hotel on Corniche Road has three swimming pools and a private beach, plus a wide range of watersports. Each room boasts enviable views, and the hotel houses some of the best restaurants in the city, including Bocca.

InterContinental Abu Dhabi
Bainouna St Abu Dhabi **02 666 6888**
ichotelsgroup.com
Adjacent to the marina, the hotel is surrounded by lush parks and gardens. With five restaurants, four bars and 330 deluxe rooms offering views of the city and the Arabian Gulf, the hotel is popular with business travellers. Following the hotel's recent renovation, many of the restaurants and bars are worth a visit.

Le Meridien Abu Dhabi
Nr Old Abu Dhabi Co-Op Society Abu Dhabi **02 644 6666**
lemeridienabudhabi.com
Famous for its health club and spa, private beach, and Culinary Village, there is a children's swimming pool and activities including tennis, squash and volleyball.

Liwa Hotel > *p.291*
Mezaira Abu Dhabi **02 882 2000**
liwahotel.net
The majestic Liwa Hotel overlooks the Rub Al Khali desert, one of the most stunning panoramas in the world. Facilities include a beautiful pool, a sauna, Jacuzzi and steam room, tennis and volleyball courts.

Mirfa Hotel > *p.291*
Dubai – Sila Highway, Mirfa Abu Dhabi **02 883 3030**
mirfahotel.com
Escape the hustle and bustle of city life at the four-star hotel set within a stunning landscape and overlooking the magnificent coastline of Mirfa. Perfectly located between Abu Dhabi and the city of Doha, this coastal retreat has a glorious seafood restaurant, swimming pools and tennis courts, and a choice of watersports on offer too.

One To One Hotel – The Village
Al Salam St Abu Dhabi **02 495 2000**
onetoonehotels.com
Resembling a boutique European hotel, this resort offers a personal experience with stylish rooms and some impressive F&B outlets.

Qasr Al Sarab Desert Resort By Anantara
1 Qasr Al Sarab Rd Abu Dhabi **02 886 2088**
anantara.com
This hotel has a stunning location amid the giant dunes outside Liwa. Designed as an Arabic fort, guests can enjoy a wide range of desert activities before relaxing in oversized bathtubs, dining on gourmet dishes and being pampered in the spa. You can also book the 25 minute Rotana Jet service from Abu Dhabi to Sir Bani Yas island for the ultimate city break.

Shangri-La Hotel, Qaryat Al Beri
Nr Bridges, Qaryat Al Beri Complex Abu Dhabi **02 509 8888**
shangri-la.com
Overlooking the creek that separates Abu Dhabi island from the mainland, the 214 rooms and suites all have private terraces. The adjoining Souk Qaryat Al Beri houses a variety of shops and restaurants connected by waterways. Leave time for an indulgent massage at the CHI spa.

فندق المرفا
MIRFA HOTEL
he Coastal Retreat
WATER SPORTS ACTIVITIES
• Jet Skiing
• Kayaking
• Wake Boarding
HOTEL FEATURES
• Newly renovated 114 rooms and suites
• Beach front
• Restaurant & Bars
For information and reservation
Tel : +971 2 8833030
Fax : +971 2 8836400
Email: rsvn@mirfahotel.com
Web : www.mirfahotel.com
An Oasis of Tranquility
LIWA
HOTEL
LEISURE ACTIVITIES
• Camel Riding
• Quad Bike
HOTEL FEATURES:
• Ayurvedic Massage and Yoga
• 3 Bedrooms Private Villas
• Newly renovated rooms
• Restaurant and Bars
For information and reservation
T: +971 2 8822000
F: +971 2 8822830
E: rsvn@liwahotel.net
W: www.liwahotel.net

LONG-WEEKEND TRIPS

There are plenty of regional outings that won't eat up your annual holiday allowance or your bank account.

Dubai's central location makes it an ideal base for exploring the region beyond. If you can't find a cheap flight from Dubai International Airport, don't hesitate to look for better deals departing from either Abu Dhabi or Sharjah. The country now has two low-cost carriers, Air Arabia at Sharjah Airport and flydubai at Dubai Airport. If you'd rather fly in style, both Emirates and Etihad fly to enough locations to keep you planning for years to come. If you need help planning and booking your trip, head to dnata Travel (dnatatravel.com), a one-stop shop for hotels, flights and holiday packages.

AQABA

Aqaba's centuries-old monuments and picturesque mountains are a must visit for any avid sightseer. However, it's the reefs of the Red Sea – home to hundreds of types of corals and sponges with a wealth of brilliantly coloured fish – that is the highlight of this Jordanian coastal city. Whether you're a beginner or seasoned pro, the Ahlan Aqaba Scuba Diving Centre (diveinaqaba.com) receives rave reviews as one of the best diving operators in the city. Dedicate some time to also visiting Wadi Rum and the Nabatean city of Petra, which are a short drive away. Your hotel should be able to help you choose and book a tour.

Fly: Royal Jordanian from Dubai via Amman

GOA

With its pristine beaches, beautiful scenery and charming residents, it is not surprising that Goa attracts 2.5 million visitors every year and is a favourite with GCC travellers. On the west coast of India, Goa offers the perfect mix of east-meets-west thanks to the influence of the Portuguese rule that isolated it from the rest of India for 451 years. Goans firmly believe in the mantra: 'Work for today, plan for tomorrow, party tonight,' so it is perfectly normal to eat, drink and dance your heart out at one of the many clubs following a day of meditation on the beach. Summer is very hot with monsoon season June to September, so winter is the perfect time to visit.

Fly: Air India from Dubai

ISTANBUL

This city has been the capital of more than one dynasty and each era has left its mark in lavish Ottoman palaces, ancient Christian churches and some of the most impressive mosques ever built. But The Bull (as it's called by locals) is not just for history fans. The bustling streets are dotted with galleries full of sleek modern art that rival those anywhere in the world. You'll also find a vibrant nightlife scene, busy street markets and a fantastic culinary landscape that takes influences from Turkey's fascinating location between Europe and Asia.

Fly: Emirates, Etihad, flydubai and Turkish Airlines

LEBANON

The mountains are home to a handful of small but vibrant ski stations in winter and Mzaar-Kfardebian is Lebanon's biggest resort. An hour's drive from Beirut, it's a popular weekend destination among locals, with a lively après-ski scene. Other destinations include The Cedars, Laklouk and Faqra Club – see skileb.com for information on all four. The first snow falls in December. Conditions remain far cooler all year round in Lebanon, making it the ideal place for an escape during those hotter months too. Travel warnings were issued by the UAE in 2012, and you're advised to check with your embassy before travelling.

Fly: Emirates, Etihad, flydubai and Middle Eastern Airlines from Dubai and Abu Dhabi

MUMBAI

Noisy, chaotic and crowded, Mumbai divides opinions – a vibrant metropolis or an urban nightmare? Decide for yourself: November to March sees cooler breezes and clear skies, making winter the best time to experience the city. Flights from the UAE take just a couple of hours – which makes Mumbai close enough for a weekend getaway. Book a city tour with Sam-San Travels (samsantravels.com) and sample colourful saris, fiery curries and bazaar bustle. Throw in the speeding tuctucs, endless crowds and the occasional cow, and you've got a street scene unlike any other. Under its chaotic cover, Mumbai boasts historic relics and colonial charms. Elsewhere, gleaming towers, luxury condos and trendy clubs showcase the city's wealth. Turn a corner and you're rubbing shoulders with would-be movie stars in Bollywood.

Fly: Air India, Emirates, Etihad, flydubai and Kingfisher from Dubai and Abu Dhabi

SALALAH

For a quick break close to home, just think Oman. Salalah – the capital of Dhofar, the southernmost region of Oman – is popular with visitors who flock to enjoy the lush greenery and cool weather. Dhofar frankincense is regarded as the finest in the world; the Frankincense Trail reveals the impressive grouping of trees in Wadi Qahsan that runs through the mountainous backdrop of the Mughsayl-Sarfait road. This is where frankincense trees grow. Nabi Ayoub's Tomb is also a popular sightseeing spot. The shrine of Nabi Ayoub – also known as Prophet Job – is perched high up on the Jebel Atteen range.

Fly: Oman Air from Dubai and Abu Dhabi via Muscat

SHARM EL SHEIKH

Being so popular with scuba divers, it is easy to forget that Sharm El Sheikh also offers plenty of activities for adventure junkies, such as extreme water sports and desert off-roading. Kite Junkies Sharm El Sheikh (kitejunkies.com) is the only IKO-affiliated kite-surfing centre in the city, offering courses and rental packages. For land-based fun, the quad safari by Sinai Safari Adventures (sinaisafariadventures.com) involves a trip across the Sinai desert and into the mountains on quad bikes, passing by Bedouin villages.

Fly: Egypt Air from Dubai and Abu Dhabi via Cairo

THE MALDIVES

The four hour flight to the Maldives makes the tropical island nation a perfect beach escape for sheer relaxation. Thanks to its nearly 2,000 islands, you can be sure to find your own tropical paradise; stilted bungalows are popular and most resorts boast polished five-star luxury and lavish facilities, from top-end spas to amazing wine cellars.

Also a scuba paradise, the Maldives offers great snorkelling and diving. Many resorts have their own dive centres, but it's also possible to book a liveaboard tour (maldivesliveaboards.com), where you stay on a scuba boat and visit remote islands and atolls.

Fly: Emirates and Etihad from Dubai and Abu Dhabi direct to Male

DIRECTORY:

Air India – airindia.in
Egypt Air – egyptair.com
Emirates – emirates.com
Etihad – etihadairways.com
flydubai – flydubai.com
Kingfisher – flykingfisher.com
Middle Eastern Airlines – mea.com
Oman Air – omanair.com
Royal Jordanian – rj.com
Turkish Airlines – turkishairlines.com

Turkey

Yas Island Rotana

Golf Plaza Abu Dhabi **02 656 4000**
rotana.com
Another superb Yas hotel, with sports, fitness and spa facilities that are modern and top notch in terms of quality, as are the rooms and restaurants.

Yas Viceroy Abu Dhabi

Nr Yas Marina Yas Island **02 656 0000**
viceroyhotelsandresorts.com
Another of the UAE's iconic hotels, this architectural wonder straddles the F1 circuit with a bridge that offers the best views come race day. The hotel has 499 space-age rooms and some of the capital's best restaurants.

Al Ain

Al Ain is Abu Dhabi emirate's second city and of great historical significance in the UAE. Its location, on ancient trading routes between Oman and the Arabian Gulf, rendered the oasis strategically important.

Commonly known as 'The Garden City', Al Ain features many oases and lovely patches of greenery for the public to enjoy. After a greening programme instigated by the late Sheikh Zayed, the seven natural oases are now set amid tree-lined streets and beautiful urban parks. Its unique history means that Al Ain is home to interesting sights and attractions, including the Hili Archaeological Garden, Hili Fun City, and the Al Ain Museum.

Just outside the city sits one of the largest mountains in the UAE, Jebel Hafeet. The rolling, grass-covered hills of Green Mubazzarah Park at the bottom of the mountain are great for picnics and mid afternoon naps. Al Ain's archaeological and historical legacy is of such significance that the city was recently placed on the list of World Heritage Sites by UNESCO.

Al Ain Attractions

Al Ain Camel & Livestock Souk

Nr Bawadi Mall, Zayed Bin Sultan St Al Ain
adach.ae
Conditions at the souk have improved dramatically with spacious pens for the animals and ample parking for visitors. A visit to the market is a fantastic way to mingle with locals and witness camel and goat trading as it's taken place for centuries. Arrive early, preferably before 09:00, to soak up the atmosphere.

Al Ain National Museum

Nr Sultan Fort, Zayed Bin Sultan St Al Ain
03 764 1595
adach.ae
Divided into three main sections – archaeology, ethnography and gifts – the presentations include photographs, Bedouin jewellery, musical instruments, weapons and a traditional majlis.

Hats Off To Hatta

Out of the city, but not strictly out of Dubai, is the mountain town of Hatta. It lies within Dubai emirate, about an hour's drive south-east of the city, but makes for a great overnight out-of-town trip.

The Hatta Fort Hotel (04 809 9333, jaresortshotels.com) is a perfectly secluded mountain retreat in tranquil gardens. The hotel is fully equipped with numerous facilities and activities, including two swimming pools, a children's pool, a bar and restaurant, the Senses Beauty Salon, a driving range and chipping green, floodlit tennis courts and archery. The 50 spacious chalet-style rooms and suites all come with patios overlooking the impressive Hajars.

There are several good off-road options for those who want to do some 4WD exploring, including the nearby Hatta Pools, in which you can swim. They're fairly accessible from the town along an unpaved road, and there are signs to guide you there. Pick up a copy of *UAE Off-Road Explorer* for other great routes in the area.

Back in town is the Hatta Heritage Village (definitelydubai.com). It is constructed around an old settlement and was restored in the style of a traditional mountain village. Explore the tranquil oasis, and the narrow alleyways, and discover the traditional way of life in the mud and barasti houses. Hatta's history goes back over 3,000 years and the area includes a 200 year-old mosque and the fortress built by Sheikh Maktoum bin Hasher Al Maktoum in 1896, which is now used as a weaponry museum. Entry is free.

Sheikh Zayed Grand Mosque, Abu Dhabi

Abu Dhabi Corniche

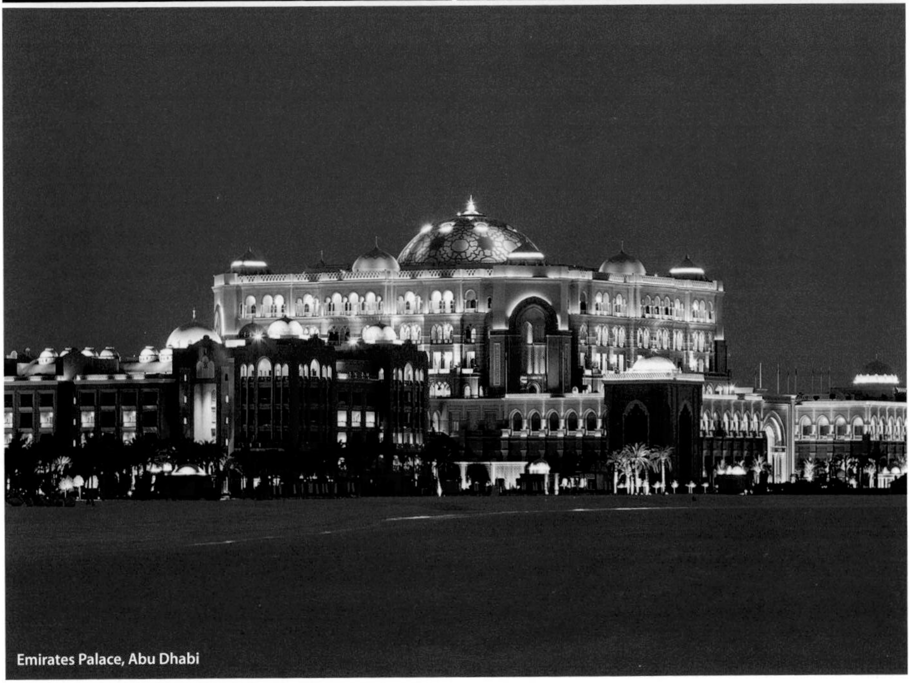
Emirates Palace, Abu Dhabi

Al Ain Oasis

Nr Al Ain National Museum Al Ain

This impressive oasis in the heart of the city is filled with palm plantations, many of which are still working farms. The cool, shady walkways transport you from the heat and noise of the city to an otherworldly, tranquil haven. You are welcome to wander through the plantations, but it's best to stick to the paved areas. The farms have plenty of working examples of falaj, the traditional irrigation system which has been used for centuries to tap into underground wells. There are eight different entrances, some of which have arched gates, and there is no entry fee.

Al Ain Zoo > *p.ii-iii*

Public Institution Zoo & Aquarium Nhayyan Al Awwal St Al Ain **800 555**

alainzoo.ae

Stretching over 900 hectares, this is one of the largest and best zoos in the Gulf region. With ample greenery, a casual stroll through the paths that criss-cross the park makes for a wonderful family day out. As well as seeing large mammals, reptiles and big cats, you can get up close to some rare and common local species such as the Arabian Oryx and sand gazelle, or pay a visit to the fantastic birdhouse. Since its founding, the zoo has been a centre for endangered species' conservation and visitors can look forward to spotting true rarities. Nearly 30% of the 180 species are endangered and the park is even home to a stunning pair of white tigers and white lions. Family nights with activities from sports games to cartoon screenings take place on Wednesdays. A park train regularly departs from the central concourse, providing a whirlwind tour of the zoo. The park is open daily from 09:00 to 20:00 in winter and from 16:00 to 22:00 during summer. Entrance is Dhs.15 for adults, Dhs.5 for children and it's free for under twos.

Al Jahili Fort & Park

Nr Central Public Gardens Al Ain

adach.ae

Celebrated as the birthplace of the late Sheikh Zayed bin Sultan Al Nahyan, the picturesque fort was erected in 1891 to defend Al Ain's precious palm groves. It is set in beautifully landscaped gardens and visitors are encouraged to explore the exterior. It's also the stunning venue for a number of concerts in the Abu Dhabi Classics series.

Hili Archaeological Park

Mohd Ibn Khalifa St Al Ain

adach.ae

Located 10 kilometres outside Al Ain on the Dubai-Al Ain highway, the landscaped gardens are home to a Bronze Age settlement (2,500 – 2,000BC), which was excavated and restored in 1995. Many of the artefacts found during the excavation are displayed in the Al Ain National Museum (p.294). Other remains, including tombs and an Iron Age falaj, are largely located in a protected area outside the park. Entry is Dhs.1.

Hili Fun City > *p.297*

Off Emirates St Al Ain **03 784 5542**

hilifuncity.ae

This 22 hectare spacious, leafy park is perfect for family outings. There are plenty of beautifully landscaped spaces for picnics and barbecues, with arcade games and refreshment stands nearby. The park is being gradually updated and there are now more than 30 attractions – ranging from gentle toddler rides to white-knuckle thrillers for teens and adults – with more rides on the way. The park has an amphitheatre where various singing, dancing and circus shows are put on throughout the day. The park is open 16:00 to 22:00 (Monday to Thursday), 12:00

Al Ain Palace Museum

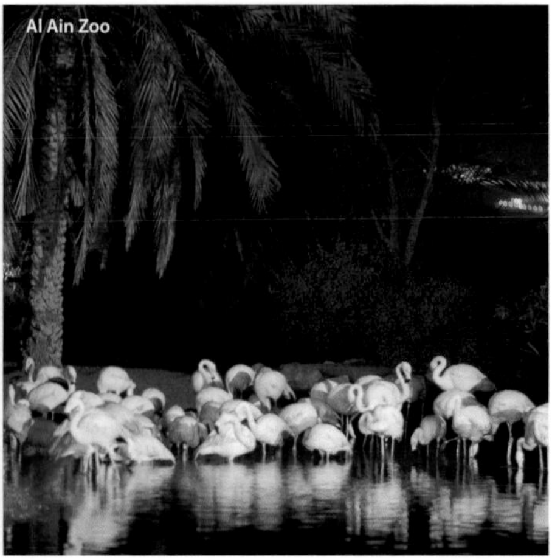

Al Ain Zoo

HILI FUN CITY
UNLIMITED FAMILY FUN
IN AL AIN
ONLY 50 DHS

to 22:00 (Friday and Saturday), with Wednesdays reserved for ladies and children only.

The park is closed on Sundays and for Ramadan (when annual maintenance takes place). Special opening hours apply for the June-September period. Entrance costs Dhs.50 (Dhs.45 on Mondays and Tuesdays); admission is free for kids up to 89cm tall. Located on the eastern side of the park is an ice rink.

Wadi Adventure > *p.325*

Nr Green Mubazzarah, Off Al Ain Fayda Rd Al Ain **03 781 8422**

wadiadventure.ae

Located at the bottom of Jebel Hafeet and beside Green Mubazzarah, Wadi Adventure is a man-made water adventure park. The three whitewater rafting and kayaking runs – with a combined length of more than 1.1km – are among the major draws, but you'll also find a gigantic surf pool complete with a man-made beach and three-metre waves. The other facilities include regular swimming pools for adults and kids, a rope course, zip line and climbing wall, as well as several food and beverage outlets.

Al Ain Hotels

Al Ain Rotana

Shk Zayed Rd Al Ain **03 754 5111**

rotana.com

Located in the centre of the city, the hotel's rooms, suites and chalets are extremely spacious and modern. The other facilities include a beautiful garden pool and good fitness facilities. In addition, the hotel is also a nightlife hub with six dining venues, including the ever-popular Trader Vic's and a highly recommended Lebanese restaurant.

Al Massa Hotel

Nr Hamdan Bin Mohd & Al Baladiah Sts Al Ain **03 763 9003**

almasahotels.com

This city centre establishment has 50 rooms and 12 suites, along with a cafe and Lebanese-style restaurant. It is a little dated but clean and welcoming if you're simply looking for a place to stay in the centre of town.

Asfar Resort

Nr Safeer Mall, Al Masoody Rd Al Ain **03 762 8882**

asfarhotels.com

Located near Safeer Mall, around 4km from the Omani border, this relaxed resort offers 53 well-equipped rooms ranging from studios to two-bedroom suites. In addition to a sunny swimming pool and a palm tree lined lounging area, the facilities include a gym, while the resort's onsite restaurant, Rendezvous, serves up a wide range of international dishes.

Ayla Hotel

Khalifa Bin Zayed Al Awwal St Al Ain **03 761 0111**

aylahotels.com

The rooms are practical and tasteful, while there's a modern gym, indoor pool, sauna, Jacuzzi and basic spa offerings. Dining options are simple but adequate, but Ayla is aimed mainly at an Arabic market and outlets are not licensed. Western tourists shouldn't be put off – the hotel has a welcoming atmosphere.

Camel Safaris

Al Ain Golden Sands Camel Safaris offers a selection of tours that include a camel ride over the dunes of Bida Bint Saud. The rides usually last one to two and a half hours, and all tours include transfers, Arabic coffee and dates, and soft drinks. Call 03 768 8006 for more information.

City Seasons Hotel Al Ain

Khalifa Bin Zayed St Al Ain **03 755 0220**

cityseasonsgroup.com

This hotel has 89 lovely rooms and suites with excellent facilities. Executive suites have a separate living room and kitchen facilities. The hotel has a fitness centre, swimming pool and sun deck.

Danat Al Ain Resort

Nr Khalid Bin Sultan & Al Salam Sts Al Ain **03 704 6000**

danathotels.com

One of the most enjoyable inland resorts in the UAE, this hotel has landscaped gardens, swimming pools, luxurious guestrooms, deluxe villas and a Royal Villa with a private Jacuzzi. It also has great facilities for families and a delightful spa.

Hilton Al Ain

Nr Khalid Bin Sultan & Zayed Bin Sultan Sts Al Ain **03 768 6666**

hilton.com

Located near the heart of Al Ain, this ageing hotel is a key landmark and sits in lush, landscaped gardens that contain a nine hole golf course, tennis and squash courts, a health club and a nice pool area. It is particularly convenient for visiting Al Ain Zoo. The Hiltonia Sports Bar and Paco's Bar are popular haunts.

Mercure Grand Jebel Hafeet Al Ain

Al Ain **03 783 8888**

mercure.com

Situated in a spectacular location near the top of Jebel Hafeet, the Mercure offers incredible views of Al Ain from all of its simply decorated rooms and terraced restaurants. There are also three swimming pools, and a water slide. There is a pub, buffet restaurant and poolside cafe serving excellent evening barbecues.

Sharjah

Despite being eclipsed by Dubai in the international spotlight, Sharjah has substantially more culture and heritage to offer. So much so, that it was named the cultural capital of the Arab world by UNESCO in 1998, thanks to its eclectic mix of museums, heritage sites and traditional souks. The border between Dubai and Sharjah cities is barely noticeable when driving from one to the other. This means it's easy to explore Sharjah without having to check into a hotel.

Sharjah is built around Khalid Lagoon, also known as the creek, and the surrounding Buheirah Corniche is a popular spot for an evening stroll. From various points around the lagoon, small dhows can be hired to take you out on the water to see the city lights. Joining Khalid Lagoon to Al Khan Lagoon, Al Qasba (opposite) is home to a variety of cultural events, exhibitions, theatre and music – all held on the canal-side walkways or at dedicated venues. The city's main cultural centres, The Heritage Area (p.302) and The Arts Area, are two of the most impressive collections of museums and heritage sites in the region. The ruling Al Qassimi family are renowned collectors of historical artefacts and art and, in an emirate known for its conservatism, many of the works held within the Arts Area are surprising in their modernity. Sharjah's cultural worth is so great that visitors should avoid trying to absorb it all in one trip.

Shoppers will have a blast too, searching for gifts in Sharjah's souks. Souk Al Arsah (p.422) is the oldest souk in the emirate, while the Central Souk is known for its well-respected carpet shops. There's also high-street shopping at Sharjah Mega Mall (megamall.ae).

For further information on Sharjah, check out the *Sharjah Mini Visitors' Guide*, available in bookstores and at askexplorer.com.

Sharjah Museum of Islamic Civilisation

Sharjah Attractions

Al Mahatta Museum

King Abdul Aziz St Sharjah **06 573 3079**
sharjahmuseums.ae

Home to the first airfield in the Gulf, opened in 1932, Sharjah played an important role as a primary stop-off point for the first commercial flights from Britain to India, and the museum looks at the impact this had on the traditional way of life in Sharjah and beyond. Four of the original propeller planes have been fully restored and are on display. Located behind Al Estiqlal Street, entry is Dhs.5 for adults and Dhs.10 for families.

Al Qasba

Nr Al Khan Lagoon Sharjah **06 556 0777**
alqasba.ae

With an ever-changing events calendar that includes Arabic poetry readings, film viewings and musical events, the emphasis at Al Qasba is clearly on culture, but there's more on offer. The complex's shops, event spaces and restaurants are laid out between Sharjah's two lagoons and are packed on cooler evenings with window shoppers, diners and families. Motorised abras provide tours up and down the canal, but the biggest and most visible draw is the Eye of the Emirates – a 60 metre high observation wheel offering amazing views over Sharjah and across to Dubai.

Al Tamimi Stables

Exit 81 off E311 Sharjah **06 743 1122**
tamimistables.com

This private but friendly farm offers kids the chance to get up close to their favourite animals, from little mice to fluffy rabbits and even a friendly parrot. There's also pony rides, falcon shows, horse displays and guided nature trails, making for the perfect family day out.

City Sightseeing Sharjah

Various locations Sharjah **06 525 5200**
city-sightseeing.com

This hop on, hop off sightseeing bus gives you the freedom to explore the city aboard a double-decker; bus; take a seat in the lower deck or the open top deck. Landmarks and hotspots en route include the Central Souq, Al Qasba, Sharjah Aquarium and Maritime Museum, the Fish Market, Marbella Beach Resort, and the Radisson Blu hotel. Tours are given in English, Arabic, German and Russian. Tickets, valid for 24 hours, cost Dhs.85 for adults, Dhs.45 for children aged five to 12.

Sharjah Aquarium

Nr Sharjah Maritime Museum Sharjah **06 528 5288**
sharjahaquarium.ae

Sharjah Aquarium draws big crowds, especially at the weekends. Situated next door to Sharjah Maritime

Museum at the mouth of Al Khan Lagoon, its location allows visitors to view the Gulf's natural underwater life. There are over 250 species in the aquarium, as well as many interactive displays. Open 08:00 to 20:00 Monday to Thursday, 16:00 to 21:00 on Fridays and 08:00 to 21:00 on Saturdays. Admission is Dhs.20 for adults, Dhs.10 for children, and Dhs.50 for families.

Sharjah Archaeology Museum

Shk Rashid Bin Saqr Al Qasimi Rd Sharjah
06 566 5466
archaeologymuseum.ae

This hi-tech museum offers an interesting display of antiquities from the region. Using well-designed displays and documentary film, the museum traces man's first steps and progress across the Arabian Peninsula through the ages, and one area features the latest discoveries from excavation sites in the UAE.

Sharjah Art Museum

Sharjah Arts Area Sharjah **06 568 8222**
sharjahmuseums.ae

The Arts Area centrepiece, the Art Museum was originally built to house the personal collection of over 300 paintings and maps belonging to the ruler, HH Dr Sheikh Sultan bin Mohammed Al Qassimi. Permanent displays include the work of 18th century artists, with oil paintings and watercolours depicting life in the Arab world, while other exhibits change frequently. There's an art reference library, bookshop and coffee shop, and the museum hosts various cultural activities.

Sharjah Classic Car Museum

Nr Sharjah International Airport Sharjah
06 558 0058

Recently renovated, this collection of classic cars includes a Ford Model T, a Mercedes-Benz Pullman limousine, Ford Mustang and MG Midget. There's also an interactive play area for kids. Tickets costs Dhs.5 for adults, Dhs.10 for a family.

Sharjah Desert Park

Interchange 9, Al Dhaid Rd, Al Sajaá Sharjah
06 531 1501
epaa-shj.gov.ae

Located 25 kilometres outside the city, the Sharjah Desert Park complex comprises the Natural History Museum, the Arabian Wildlife Centre, the Children's Farm and the recently opened Sharjah Botanical Museum. The Natural History and Botanical Museums feature interactive displays on the relationships between man and the natural world in the UAE and beyond, while at the Arabian Wildlife Centre you get the chance to see many reptiles, birds and mammals, including the rare Arabian leopard. The facilities are excellent and the animals are treated well. There is also a Children's Farm with animals that can be fed and petted. Picnic areas are available, plus cafes and shops. Closed on Tuesdays, entry costs Dhs.5 for children, Dhs.15 for adults.

Sharjah Discovery Centre

Nr Sharjah International Airport, Al Dhaid Rd Sharjah **06 558 6577**
discoverycentre.ae

The Discovery Centre is a great family day out and children of all ages, including toddlers, can explore the many themed areas and interact with the exhibits. Explore the dynamics of water, the five senses and the mechanisms of building, or become a star on TV, climb a wall, and 'shop till you drop' in the children's supermarket. The aim is to teach youngsters in a practical, fun and interesting, way. There is good pushchair access, an in-house cafe, and ample parking.

Sharjah Corniche (image courtesy SCTDA)

Entrance is Dhs.5 for children and Dhs.10 for adults. The centre is open from 08:00 to 14:00 Sunday to Thursday, and 16:00 to 20:00 Friday and Saturday.

Sharjah Heritage Area

Nr Sharjah Arts Area, Al Merraija Sharjah
sharjahtourism.ae

The beautifully restored heritage area is a cultural treasure trove that includes a number of old buildings, such as Al Hisn Fort (Sharjah Fort), Sharjah Islamic Museum, Sharjah Heritage Museum (Bait Al Naboodah), the Maritime Museum, the Majlis of Ibrahim Mohammed Al Midfa and the Old Souk (Souk Al Arsah). Traditional local architecture and life from the past 150 years is described, depicted and displayed throughout this extensive area. When the time comes for a rest, there's an Arabic coffee shop in the shaded courtyard of Souk Al Arsah.

Sharjah Heritage Museum > *p.301*

Sharjah **06 568 0006**
sharjahmuseums.ae

Step back into Sharjah's past with a visit to the museum's five galleries, which focus on landscape, lifestyle, the UAE's heritage, domestic trade and folk medicine. There is also an interactive gallery that displays the UAE's heritage in proverbs, popular riddles and children's stories. Having recently opened in a renovated historic house, this museum has become a new landmark in the heart of Sharjah.

Sharjah Maritime Museum

Nr Sharjah Aquarium Sharjah **06 522 2002**
sharjahmuseums.ae

With the goal of documenting the development of seafaring in the Middle East, the museum's displays feature fishing, trading, pearl diving and boat construction methods native to the UAE. Each room in the museum informs visitors about a different aspect of the marine industry. The museum also houses several real examples of traditional seafaring boats. Open 08:00 to 20:00, Saturday to Thursday, and 16:00 to 20:00 Fridays.

Sharjah Museum Of Islamic Civilization

Nr Sharjah Creek, Corniche St Sharjah **06 565 5455**
islamicmuseum.ae

With vaulted rooms, and impressive galleries and halls, the architecture of this recently-opened museum alone makes a visit worthwhile, but with over 5,000 Islamic artefacts, this is one of the best places to learn about Islam and Islamic culture. The museum is organised according to five themes: the Islamic religion, Islamic art, artefacts, craftsmen and weaponry, each in its own gallery. The Temporary Exhibition Gallery hosts a programme of visiting exhibitions. Entry for adults is Dhs.5; children are free.

Sharjah Science Museum

Nr Cultural Square Sharjah **06 551 4777**
sdci.gov.ae

The interactive museum's exhibits and demonstrations cover subjects such as aerodynamics, cryogenics, electricity and colour. There's also a planetarium and children's area where the under fives and their parents can learn together. The Learning Centre offers more in-depth programmes on many of the subjects covered in the museum. Entry costs Dhs.5 for children aged three to 17 years and Dhs.10 for adults.

Sharjah Hotels

Corniche Al Buhaira Hotel

Buhaira Corniche Rd Sharjah **06 519 2222**
cornichealbuhairahotel.com

A beautiful new resort which is located right on the Corniche and boasts some of the best facilities in the emirate. Enjoy succulent kebabs at the authentic Shiraz restaurant or indulge in a chilled mocktail on the pool terrace.

Lou' Lou'a Beach Resort

Shk Sultan Al Awal Rd Sharjah **06 528 5000**
loulouabeach.com

A beach resort situated on the Sharjah coast, offering watersports and spa facilities.

Radisson Blu Resort, Sharjah

Corniche Rd Sharjah **06 565 7777**
radissonblu.com

Located on the Sharjah Corniche, close to the city's main cultural attractions, the hotel has its own beach.

Sharjah Rotana

Al Arouba St Sharjah **06 563 7777**
rotana.com

Well-located in the centre of the city, the Rotana caters mostly to business travellers.

Ajman

The smallest of the emirates, Ajman's centre is just 10 kilometres from Sharjah city centre, and the two cities pretty much merge along the coast. Ajman has a nice stretch of beach and a pleasant corniche to walk along, while the Ajman Kempinksi Hotel and Resort is a grand offering for those wanting a luxurious stay. If you're on a tighter budget, there are several cheaper options along the beach.

Ajman Museum (p.304) houses a variety of interesting displays in a restored fort that is well worth visiting, as much for the building as for its contents. There are plans to develop a heritage city between the museum and the corniche to include a roofed market and cultural quarter; the museum square, gold market quarter and craft workshops will also be restored.

The tiny emirate is known for being one of the largest boat building centres in the region. While mainly modern boats emerge from the yards these days, you may still catch a glimpse of a traditionally built wooden dhow sailing out to sea. The emirate's main souk is a reminder of a slower pace of life and of days gone by, while the modern Ajman City Centre is home to shops, foodcourts and a cinema.

Ajman Attractions

Ajman Museum

Nr Clock Tower R/A, Al Bustan Ajman **06 742 3824**
acm.gov.ae

Ajman Museum's interesting and well arranged displays have descriptions in both English and Arabic. The museum has a variety of exhibits, including a collection of Ajman-issued passports and dioramas of ancient life, but it's the building itself that will most impress visitors. Housed in a fortress dating back to around 1775, the museum is a fascinating example of traditional architecture, with imposing watchtowers and traditional windtowers. Entry is Dhs.5 for adults. Morning opening times are 09:00 to 13:00 then 16:00 to 19:00 in the evening. Closed on Fridays.

Ajman Hotels

Kempinski Hotel Ajman

Shk Humaid Bin Rashid Al Nuaimi St Ajman
06 714 5555
kempinski.com

Visitors to Ajman can relax on half a kilometre of the Kempinski's private beach or around its superb pool facilities. The hotel has 185 seaview rooms and a diverse range of international restaurants, cafes and bars, as well as a grand ballroom. The Laguna Spa offers a comprehensive spa menu, including an outdoor Balinese massage.

Ramada Hotel & Suites Ajman

Shk Khalifa Bin Zayed St Ajman **06 703 1111**
ramadaajman.com

A decent hotel ideally placed near Ajman Beach Road and the city's major shopping and commercial areas, with all the usual offerings for leisure and business travellers.

Umm Al Quwain

Nestled between Ajman and Ras Al Khaimah, not much has changed in Umm Al Quwain over the years. The main industries are still fishing and date cultivation. The emirate has six forts, and a few old watchtowers surround the town. With plenty of mangroves and birdlife, the emirate's lagoon is a popular weekend spot for boat trips, windsurfing and other watersports. Another popular family activity is crab hunting at Flamingo Beach Resort. At nightfall, groups of hunters set off into the shallow mangrove waters with a guide, where they spear crabs which are barbecued and served on return to the resort.

The area north of the lagoon is a regional activity centre. Emirates Motorplex (motorplex.ae) hosts motorsport events, including the Emirates Motocross Championship, and Dreamland Aqua Park is one of the emirate's most popular attractions. Barracuda Beach Resort is a favoured destination for Dubai residents thanks to its well-stocked duty-free liquor store.

The emirate has not escaped the attention of the developers and a project currently underway will see over 9,000 homes and a marina emerge on the shore of the Khor Al Beidah wildlife area.

Umm Al Quwain Attractions

Dreamland Aqua Park > *p.xv*

Ras Al Khaimah Highway Umm Al Quwain
06 768 1888
dreamlanduae.com

With over 25 water rides, including four 'twisting dragons', Dreamland Aqua Park is massive. If extreme slides aren't your thing, there's the lazy river, a wave pool, an aqua play area, and a high-salinity floating pool. Overnight accommodation in tents or wooden cabins is also available, with BBQ packages as well. Admission is Dhs.135 for adults and Dhs.85 for children under 1.2m, while children under two go free. The park is open all-year-round; Fridays, Saturdays and holidays are for families only.

Umm Al Quwain Hotels

Barracuda Beach Resort

Nr Dreamland Aqua Park, Khor Al Beidah
Umm Al Quwain **06 768 1555**
barracuda.ae

Known throughout the UAE for its popular tax-free booze emporium, Barracuda is also a pleasant resort for quick weekend getaways. Aside from the main hotel, the resort offers several lagoon-side one-bedroom chalets that can each accommodate up to five people. The chalets come with kitchenettes and barbecues – perfect for private overnight parties. There's also a large pool and Jacuzzi.

Flamingo Beach Resort

Nr Horsehead R/A Umm Al Quwain **06 765 0000**
flamingoresort.ae

Cheap and cheerful, this resort is surrounded by a shallow lagoon interspersed with green islands that attract birdlife including migrating flamingos. Evening crab hunts are available for non-guests, as well as a flamingo tour by boat and deep sea fishing trips. There's a beach bar, cafe and dhow restaurant too.

Ras Al Khaimah

With the Hajar Mountains rising just behind the city, the Arabian Gulf stretching out from the shore and the desert starting in the south near the farms and ghaf forests of Digdagga, Ras Al Khaimah (RAK) has possibly the best scenery of any emirate. The most northerly emirate, a creek divides the main city into the old town and the newer Al Nakheel district.

The past couple of years have witnessed RAK's transformation into a prominent weekend destination, and several new resorts have opened for the overworked residents of Dubai and Abu Dhabi. The Tower Links Golf Course (07 227 9939, towerlinks.com) is laid out among the mangroves around the creek and is popular at weekends, as is the Al Hamra Village Golf And Beach Resort (casahotels.com).

Stellar Cellar

Al Hamra Cellar, although owned by MMI (mmidubai.com), is a tax-free liquor store that is well worth the trip. You won't find dodgy booze past its sell-by date; instead, you can browse a wide range of fine wines, spirits and beers in a pleasant environment at tax-free (and very competitive) prices. Its loyalty programme means the more you buy the better deal you'll get on your next visit. Call 07 244 7403 for more info.

Ras Al Khaimah contains several archaeological sites, some dating back all the way to 3,000BC. Take the Al Ram road out of the Al Nakheel district and towards the Hajar Mountains to discover some of the area's history, including the Dhayah Fort, Shimal Archaeological Site and Sheba's Palace. The bare ruins of the Dhayah Fort can be spotted from the road, but you might need a 4WD to access them. Further inland are the Shimal archaeological site and Sheba's Palace. Both are a little obscure, but worth the difficulty of finding them. Shimal includes a tomb from the Umm An Nar period, roughly 5,000 years ago. Built as a communal burial place, the remains of more than 400 bodies have now been found there. Further down the same road is another tomb dating back to the Wadi Suq period (2,000BC). Many of the artefacts discovered in these locations are at the National Museum, while the Pearl Excursion and Pearl Museum (rakpearls.com) showcase more recent heritage and trade.

At the other end of the spectrum, Manar Mall (manarmall.com) is a large shopping and leisure facility, housing a cinema complex, family entertainment centre and dining options overlooking the creek and mangroves; Al Hamra Mall (alhamramall.com) and Safeer Mall (mysafeer.com) are also popular.

The town is quiet, relaxing and a good starting point for exploring the surrounding mountains, visiting the ancient sites of Ghalilah and Shimal, the hot springs at Khatt and the camel race track at Digdagga. There are also several chances to get into the mountains north of the city, as well as south of RAK in places like Jebel Yibir – the tallest mountain in the country, where a new track takes you close to the top for spectacular views.

Ras Al Khaimah Attractions

Bassata Desert Camp

Bassata Desert Village Ras Al Khaimah
07 204 9555

This ultimate desert experience is run by Sun and Fun, with activities including Bedouin shows, a belly dancer, BBQ dinner and dune-bashing.

Ice Land Water Park

Al Jazeera, Al Hamra Ras Al Khaimah **07 206 7888**
icelandwaterpark.com

This impressive waterpark is the first major attraction to open in the giant WOW RAK tourist destination. The polar-themed Ice Land has more than 50 rides and attractions, including Penguin Falls, Snow River and Mount Cyclone. Open from 10:00 every day. Entry is Dhs.150 for adults, Dhs.100 for children under 1.2m.

Jazirah Aviation Club

Ras Al Khaimah **07 244 6416**
jac-uae.net

Enjoy scenic views of the desert, sandy beaches, the sea and RAK mountains while flying in micro-flight aircrafts or powered parachutes.

Prince Of The Sea

07 205 9555 rasalkhaimahtourism.com

This luxurious two-mast sailing motor yacht is available for sunset cruises, as well as lunch and dinner cruises for up to 75 people, with live entertainment.

Ras Al Khaimah Hotels

Al Hamra Fort Hotel & Beach Resort

Al Jazeerah St Ras Al Khaimah **07 244 6666**
alhamrafort.com

With traditional Arabic architecture set among acres of lush gardens and along a strip of sandy beach, this hotel offers a peaceful getaway. A range of watersports and activities, including two floodlit golf courses and an onsite dive centre, will keep you entertained, and the eight themed eateries offer a wide variety of international cuisines and atmosphere.

Al Hamra Palace Beach Resort

Al Hamra Village Ras Al Khaimah **07 206 7222**
casahotels.com

Located on a private beach in the Arabian Gulf, this five-star resort offers luxurious suites with fully equipped kitchenettes. The Sea Breeze restaurant serves traditional Arabic food, while guests can have a refreshing swim in the outdoor pool or enjoy the tennis court and fitness centre. The resort is just a five minute drive from Al Hamra Golf Club.

Banyan Tree Al Wadi

Al Mazraa Ras Al Khaimah **07 206 7777**
banyantree.com

Banyan Tree Al Wadi combines superior luxury with exclusive spa facilities, desert activities and a wildlife conservation area. Set within Wadi Khadeja, the villas are designed for optimum relaxation with private pools and views of the desert.

Banyan Tree Ras Al Khaimah Beach

Al Jazirah Al Hamra Ras Al Khaimah **07 206 7777**
banyantree.com

This opulent resort set amidst the impressive desert landscape of Wadi Khadeja, just 20 minutes away from Ras Al Khaimah, is an oasis of calm. All of the 101 villas have a pool and a sun deck; there are two restaurants and two bars including the signature venue Saffron, which serves excellent Thai and South Asian delicacies.

Bin Majid Beach Hotel

Al Faisal Street, Beachfront Ras Al Khaimah
07 235 2233
hotel.binmajid.com

Guests can relax and unwind along an 800m sandy beach at this hotel. As well as plenty of sports facilities for the active, including jet-skiing and parasailing, there is a great selection of licensed bars and restaurants serving Indian and international dishes.

The Cove Rotana Resort

Off Shk Mohd Bin Salem Rd Ras Al Khaimah
07 206 6000
rotana.com

Built into the hills overlooking the Arabian Gulf, The Cove's sprawling layout of 204 rooms, 72 private villas and winding pathways is reminiscent of an old Mediterranean hill town. The resort revolves around an immaculate lagoon, protected from the sea by 600 metres of pristine beach. A Bodylines spa and several impressive restaurants round out the package.

Golden Tulip Khatt Springs Resort & Spa

Nr Hajar Mountains, Khatt Ras Al Khaimah
07 244 8777
goldentulipkhattsprings.com

Simple and subdued, Golden Tulip Khatt Springs Resort & Spa relies on mountain views, uninterrupted tranquillity and incredible spa packages to attract weekend visitors. Next to the hotel, you can take a dip in the public Khatt Hot Springs – piping hot water which, it is claimed, has curative powers. Men and women have separate pools and a variety of massages is also available. It's a good idea to visit the hot springs in the morning and avoid Fridays as it can get very busy with families.

Hilton Ras Al Khaimah Resort & Spa

Al Maareedh St, Al Mairid Ras Al Khaimah
07 228 8844
hilton.com

Tucked away on an exclusive bay, out of sight of the city, the resort's many guest rooms and villas are perfect for a beach break. The pool bar, spa and laid-back dining options make this one of the most relaxing destinations in the region. Guests of the older Hilton Ras Al Khaimah (07 228 8888, hilton.com), located in the city, can use the facilities.

Fujairah

A trip to the east coast is a must – made up of the emirate of Fujairah and several enclaves belonging to Sharjah, the villages along the east coast sit between the rugged Hajar Mountains and the gorgeous Gulf of Oman. Fujairah city has seen little development compared to cities on the west coast, but the real draw here is the landscape. The mountains and wadis that stretch west of the coast contain some of the country's best and most accessible camping spots and the beaches, reefs and villages that line the coast attract visitors from Dubai throughout the year.

Previously, the journey to the east coast involved a two-hour drive that took in some of the country's most scenic mountain passes. If you're happy to sacrifice some of those views for time, however, the new Sheikh Khalifa Highway cuts the journey time between Dubai and Fujairah to just 30 minutes.

East Coast Made Easy

To reach the UAE's east coast from Dubai takes anything from 30-90 minutes. One popular route is the E88 from Sharjah to Masafi, and then turn left to Dibba or right to Fujairah. If you're heading to Dibba outside of rush hour, it's usually quicker to head north on Sheikh Mohammed bin Zayed Rd and take the truck road (at exit 119) across the country to the E87, which brings you to Dibba. A quieter alternative is the S116, which heads south-east out of Sharjah, past Fossil Rock and through the Hajar Mountains, hitting the coast at Kalba. For speed alone, hit the new Sheikh Khalifa Highway.

Bidiyah

The site of the oldest mosque in the UAE, Bidiyah is one of the oldest settlements on the east coast and is believed to have been inhabited since 3,000BC. The mosque is made from gypsum, stone and mud

Find paradise in Ras Al Khaimah
Located just 45 minutes from Dubai International Airport, Ras Al Khaimah offers a variety of entertainment and relaxation facilities including exclusive Hotels & Resorts, international cuisines and world-class spas, all at a great value for money. with a wide range of adventure and sports activities covering desert camps, golf courses, watersports and micro light aviation, the emirate of Ras Al Khaimah offers the ultimate outdoor experience.
www.rasalkhaimahtourism.com
Ras Al Khaimah
A RISING EMIRATE

bricks finished off with plaster, and its original design of four domes supported by a central pillar was considered unique, but the shape was changed to stepped domes during renovations. It is believed to date back to the middle of the 15th century. The mosque is still used for daily prayer, so non-Muslim visitors can't enter. Built next to a low hillside with several watchtowers on the ridge behind, the area is now colourfully lit up at night.

Dibba

Located at the northern-most point of the east coast, on the border with Musandam (p.314), Dibba is made up of three fishing villages. Unusually, each part comes under a different jurisdiction: Dibba Al Hisn is part of Sharjah, Dibba Muhallab is Fujairah and Dibba Bayah is Oman. The three Dibbas share an attractive bay, fishing communities, and excellent diving locations – from here you can arrange dhow trips to take you to unspoilt dive locations in Musandam (see Tour Operators, p.279).

The Hajar Mountains, which run parallel to the east coast, provide a wonderful backdrop, rising in places to over 1,800 metres. There are some good public beaches too, where your only company will be crabs and seagulls, and where seashell collectors may find a few treasures.

Fujairah

Fujairah town is a mix of old and new. Its hillsides are dotted with ancient forts and watchtowers, which add an air of mystery and charm; most are undergoing restoration work. Fujairah is also a busy trading centre, with its modern container port and a thriving free zone attracting major companies from around the world.

> **Bull Butting**
>
> On Fridays during winter, crowds gather between the Hilton Hotel and the Khor Kalba area to watch 'bull butting'. This ancient Portuguese sport consists of two huge bulls going head to head for several rounds, until after a few nudges and a bit of hoof bashing, a winner is determined. It's not as cruel or barbaric as other forms of bullfighting, but animal lovers may still want to avoid it.

Off the coast, the seas and coral reefs are great for fishing, diving and watersports. It is a good place for birdwatching during the spring and autumn migrations as it is on the route from Africa to Central Asia. Since Fujairah is close to the mountains and many areas of natural beauty, it makes an excellent base from which to explore the countryside and discover stunning wadis, forts, waterfalls and even natural hot springs.

Kalba

Just to the south of Fujairah you'll find Kalba, which is renowned for its mangrove forest and golden beaches. It's a pretty fishing village that still manages to retain much of its historical charm. The road through the mountains linking Kalba to Hatta makes for an interesting alternative for returning to Dubai.

Khor Kalba

Set in a beautiful tidal estuary (khor is the Arabic word for creek), Khor Kalba is one of the oldest mangrove forests in Arabia and is home to a variety of plant, marine and birdlife not found anywhere else in the UAE. The mangroves in the estuary flourish thanks to a mix of seawater and freshwater from the mountains, but they are now receding due to the excessive use of water from inland wells.

For birdwatchers, the area is especially good during the spring and autumn migrations when special species of bird include Sykes's warbler. It is also home to a rare subspecies of white collared kingfisher, which breeds here and in Oman, and nowhere else in the world. A canoe tour by Desert Rangers (p.279) is ideal for reaching the heart of the reserve. There is also the distinct possibility that you'll catch a glimpse of the region's endangered turtles.

Al Hisn Kalba

Nr Bait Shk Saeed Bin Hamed Al Qasimi Kalba
09 512 3333
sdci.gov.ae

This complex consists of the restored residence of Sheikh Sayed Al Qassimi and Al Hisn Fort. It houses the town's museum and contains a limited display of weapons. It doesn't take long to get round but there's also a collection of rides for children. Entrance is Dhs.3 for individuals and Dhs.6 for families.

Fujairah Attractions

Dibba Castle

Dibba

Hidden away in the Omani part of Dibba (aka Daba), next to vast farms and plantations, Dibba Castle is an interesting place to have a walk around. Built over 180 years ago, it has been restored and, while there aren't a lot of artefacts on show, you can access all the rooms and climb up the towers, where you'll get views over the castle and its surroundings. It is signposted off the road past the UAE border check post.

Fujairah City Centre

Nr Fujairah Police Station Fujairah **09 201 2310**
fujairahcitycenter.com

The largest retail, leisure and entertainment destination in the emirate, Fujairah City Centre opened in April 2012, with shops including New

Look, Nine West, Paris Gallery, Splash, and a Carrefour hypermarket. There is also a Magic Planet and plans for an 11-screen VOX Cinemas multiplex.

Fujairah Fort

Nr Fujairah Heritage Village, Al Sharia Fujairah

Part of the east coast's rich heritage, Fujairah Fort has recently undergone a major renovation programme. Although you cannot enter the fort itself, the surrounding heritage buildings are open for viewing. Carbon dating estimates the main part of the fort to be over 500 years old.

Fujairah Heritage Village

Nr Fujairah Fort, Al Sharia Fujairah **09 222 7000**
fujmun.gov.ae/En/Fujairah/HeritageVillage.aspx

Situated just outside Fujairah city, this collection of fishing boats, simple dhows and tools depicts life in the UAE before oil was discovered. There are two spring-fed swimming pools for men and women and chalets can be hired by the day.

Fujairah Museum

Nr Fujairah Heritage Village, Al Sharia Fujairah **09 222 9085**

This interesting museum offers permanent exhibitions on traditional ways of life including the not-so-distant nomadic Bedouin culture. There are also several artefacts on display that were found during archaeological excavations throughout the emirate. Some of the items include weapons from the bronze and iron ages, finely painted pottery, carved soapstone vessels and silver coins. The museum is open from 07:30 to 18:00 from Saturday to Thursday and from 14:00 to 18:00 on Friday. Entry fee is Dhs.5.

Fujairah Hotels

Fujairah Rotana Resort & Spa – Al Aqah Beach

Al Aqah Beach Fujairah **09 244 9888**
rotana.com

Each of the 250 guest rooms and suites has its own balcony and view over the sea. The hotel offers some of the best dining options on the east coast, as well as an indulgent spa, a private beach and a huge pool with pool bar. Massages with a fantastic view of the sea are available in huts on the beach.

Golden Tulip Resort Dibba

Mina Rd Dibba **+968 26 836 654**
goldentulipdibba.com

Simple, clean rooms and a great stretch of beach make this a good option for an affordable getaway. From the nearby Dibba Port you can take a dhow cruise, and the hotel is also in a great location for some impressive snorkelling.

Hilton Fujairah Resort

Al Ghourfa Rd Fujairah **09 222 2411**
hilton.com

Set at the north end of Fujairah's corniche, just a stone's throw from the foothills of the Hajars, this relaxing resort has all facilities needed for a wonderful weekend away. If you get tired of lounging by the swimming pool, or activities like tennis, snooker, basketball or even watersports on the private beach, you could always explore the rugged splendour of the surrounding mountains. The hotel is great for families, and there is a safe play area for children.

Iberotel Miramar Al Aqah Beach Resort

Dibba Road Fujairah **09 244 9994**
iberotel.com

A lovely low-rise Moroccan style resort with luxurious rooms spread around a huge pool area, the hotel has onsite shops, a spa, a gym and several good restaurants. Also boasts a watersports centre.

Le Meridien Al Aqah Beach Resort > *p.309*

Dibba – Khor Fakkan Rd Fujairah **09 244 9000**
lemeridien-alaqah.com

All of the rooms at Le Meridien Al Aqah have views over the Indian Ocean, and the grounds are covered by lush foliage. It is particularly geared up for families, with a kids' pool and outdoor and indoor play areas. There's an extensive spa, a dive centre, and entertainment options include a cinema, bars and restaurants serving a range of Thai, Indian and European cuisine.

Radisson Blu Resort, Fujairah

Al Faqeet, Dibba Fujairah **09 244 9700**
radissonblu.com

Its pastel exterior might be an acquired taste, but the modern, business-like interior and wonderful restaurants that lie within make this hotel a bit of a treat for the senses. The whole place is reminiscent of a spa, with clean lines and wholesome colours. There is, in fact, a wonderful Japanese spa and plenty of private beach.

Sandy Beach Hotel & Resort

Dibba – Khor Fakkan Rd Fujairah **09 244 5555**
sandybm.com

Snoopy Island, one of the best diving spots in the country, is right off the coast from the Sandy Beach Hotel, making it a firm favourite with UAE residents. Day trippers can purchase a day-pass to access the temperature-controlled pool, watersports and beach bar services. There is also a five-star PADI Dive Centre within the hotel that rents diving and snorkelling gear for exploring the reefs around Snoopy Island. Open for all-day dining, there's a basic but reasonable restaurant.

Exploring Fossil Rock

A brief guide to the perfect route for first-time off-roaders.

Fossil Rock is the UAE's easiest desert route to access, and to drive, with some superb and varied scenery along the way. Starting at Al Awir, off the E44 Hatta road only 20 minutes outside Dubai, it is the perfect drive for absolute beginners and novices to cut their teeth on in the desert and gain some valuable lessons, but as with anywhere, it's definitely better to accompany an experienced driver the first couple of times you head out.

The route is pretty easy to navigate – the driving starts along a sandy track then graduates to rolling through some easy medium-sized dunes later on.

Making its way to the starting point in the fertile oasis town of Al Awir, the road weaves through a surprising amount of greenery, trees and farms, and many palaces and stately homes. Keep a look out for the estate that's home to herds of gazelle and deer, race horses that can often be spotted training, and the long wall of the summer palace belonging to the Al Maktoum family.

Existing tracks normally define the best path to take, especially on this route. They offer the easiest route, with only gentle inclines and descents, and limit damage to flora and fauna. However, when you start to get the hang of it, there are some places where you can climb up to the top of the dunes beside the track to weave your way along the ridges.

Off-Road Expert

For more information on everything to do with driving off-road and exploring all corners of the country, pick up a copy of the *UAE Off-Road Explorer*. Fossil Rock is one of 26 routes featured in full detail, with annotated satellite images and detailed descriptions of the route along with attractions and activities along the way.

The first half of the route finishes in sight of a main road, where it turns and follows the sandy river bed of Wadi Fayah along the bottom of the dunes. This fast and fun track weaves through bushes, trees, dunes and some rocky outcrops to a short gravely climb out onto the road.

After crossing the road, sticking with the main undulating sandy track heading up into the dunes will take you quite smoothly and easily towards Fossil Rock, clearly visible ahead. If you are feeling confident with your new skills, there is plenty of adventurous terrain just off the main track to test your driving among the dunes and bowls on either side, including in the area around the rock known as Camel Rock. The striking Fossil Rock is always there as a landmark to help you avoid getting lost, and whenever you have had enough, just pick up the track again and head towards the rock.

When you reach the hard track under the pylons, with Fossil Rock directly in front of you, the quickest and easiest exit route is to turn right and head back past the village of Maleihah and the main road. It is possible to head straight on for even more challenging driving and the climb up to Fossil Rock (or Jebel Maleihah as it is officially called) itself, but this is more one for expert drivers.

If you do make it up to the top, whether on foot or behind the wheel, it is a fun place for a scramble, and for the views and a poke around to see if you can spot a fossil or two.

After leaving the desert, don't forget to re-inflate your tyres as soon as possible, as driving on tarmac with soft tyres can cause blowouts. To get to the nearest petrol station, when you meet the tarmac road turn left and it is roughly two kilometres along the road on the right. If you carry on a little further, you will reach the S116 – the fastest way back to civilisation.

MUSCAT

Sandwiched between spectacular rocky mountains and beautiful beaches, Muscat is one of the Middle East's most striking cities.

One of the most attractive and charismatic cities in the Middle East, once you've visited, you'll understand why many count Muscat as their favourite regional city. It is visually striking, perhaps because it looks so little like a normal city; rather than a bustling CBD characterised by countless skyscrapers, gridlocked traffic and dirty smog, Muscat has many separate areas nestling between the low craggy mountains and the Indian Ocean. There is no one area that defines Muscat on its own – each part has its own distinctive character and charm.

Great care has been taken to ensure that, while it is definitely a modern city, it retains a cohesive and traditional Arabic element. Visit the old town of Muscat or the Mutrah Souk for an idea of what life has been like for decades for the people that still live in the area.

Muscat is clean and features a lot more greenery than you may be used to in Dubai. With beautiful beaches, bustling souks, a collection of great restaurants and cafes, and some fascinating museums, you'll need at least a few days to fully discover this friendly city. The main areas worth exploring are around the old town and the fishing port of Mutrah, although taking long walks along the beach in Qurm or exploring the natural lagoons in Qantab are also worthwhile activities.

The Old Town

Located on the coast at the eastern end of the greater Muscat area between Mutrah and Sidab, the old town is quiet and atmospheric, based around a sheltered port that was historically important for trade. The area is home to some very interesting museums. Muscat Gate Museum is located in one of the fortified gates of the old city walls, and illustrates the history of Muscat and Oman from ancient times right up to the present day. The view from the roof is worth the visit alone. Bait Al Zubair is in a beautifully-restored house and features major displays of men's traditional jewellery, including the khanjar, women's jewellery and attire, household items, and swords and firearms. The Omani French Museum celebrates the close ties between these two countries, and is on the site of the first French Embassy. Other highlights include the striking Alam Palace, home of Sultan Qaboos, and Jalali Fort and Mirani Fort overlooking the harbour.

Mutrah

Mutrah rests between the sea and a protective circle of hills, and has grown around its port, which today is far more vibrant than the port in Muscat's old town. Mutrah Corniche is lined with pristine gardens, parks, waterfalls and statues. Further east you'll find Riyam Park, where a huge incense burner sits on a rocky outcrop, while nearby is an ancient watchtower overlooking Mutrah – the view at the top is lovely and well worth the steep climb. One of Muscat's most famous shopping experiences lies in this area: the Mutrah Souk. Always buzzing with activity, it is renowned as one of the best souks in the region.

Other Areas

Although primarily a residential area, Qurm has some great shopping, good quality restaurants and cafes, the city's largest park (Qurm National Park) and arguably the best beach in Muscat. It is also home to some of the top hotels.

The villages of Al Bustan and Sidab provide an interesting diversion from the main Muscat areas. Head south along Al Bustan Street out of Ruwi on the spectacular mountain road to get to the village of Al Bustan and the Al Bustan Palace Hotel, one of the most famous hotels in the region.

Sultan Qaboos Mosque

Mutrah Fort

Get the lowdown on the best weekend breaks in Oman and the UAE.

Further down the coast, the mountains increase in height and the landscape gets more rugged. However, this undulating rocky coastline hides a number of beautiful secluded coves. These bays, mostly reachable by roads winding over the mountains, are home to the beaches of Qantab and Jissah, the Oman Dive Center – one of the top dive centres in the world – and the Shangri-La Barr Al Jissah Resort. Many of the bays in this area have stretches of sandy beach sheltered by the rocky cliffs, and crystal clear waters that are perfect for snorkelling, diving and fishing.

The Wave, Muscat is Oman's answer to The Palm Jumeirah or Yas Island, a sculpted residential and lifestyle destination that has now become an integrated area of the city. The lush parks and six kilometres of beaches are tourist draws in their own right, but The Wave also offers visitors that little extra touch of luxury in the form of the 18-hole Greg Norman designed Almouj golf course and a 400 berth marina flanked by bars, restaurants, cafes and stores.

Outside Muscat

Not much further out of Muscat than the Shangri-La Barr Al Jissah Resort is Yiti Beach. While once a popular daytrip from Muscat, it is now sadly becoming off limits due to the construction of a huge development called Salam Yiti. The As Sifah beach, a little further down the coast, is popular. The well-travelled path past the last of the houses in As Sifah leads to a beach which slopes gently towards the ocean at low tide. If you're keen to snorkel, head towards the northern edge of the beach. If you enjoy hiking, you can explore the headlands on foot (and maybe even find a secluded beach or two further along). There are some excellent off-road routes you can do from Muscat within a day, or on an overnight camping trip. For more information on off-roading in Oman, get a copy of the *Oman Off-Road Explorer*.

GCC

Over the past decade, the countries that make up the Gulf Cooperation Council (Kuwait, Bahrain, Qatar, Oman, UAE, and Saudi Arabia) have been building tourism industries in an effort to diversify their oil-based economies. Several international brands have opened hotels and governments have made a real effort to promote heritage and culture. To learn more about the region's history, see p.2.

Oman

The most accessible country in the GCC for Dubai residents, Oman is a peaceful and breathtaking place, with history, culture and spectacular scenery to spare. The capital, Muscat, has enough attractions to keep you busy for a long weekend, with beautiful beaches, great restaurants and cafes, the mesmerising old souk at Mutrah, and the Sultan Qaboos Mosque. Outside the capital are many historic old towns and forts. You'll also discover some of the most stunning mountain and wadi scenery in the Middle East. Salalah in the south has the added bonus of being cool and wet in the summer. A flight from Dubai to Muscat takes just 45 minutes but, when you factor in the rigmarole of check-in times and clearing customs, it's actually not much quicker than driving – and you miss out on some stunning views en route. There are daily flights from Dubai with Emirates and Oman Air, while Air Arabia flies from Sharjah. Regular flights direct to Salalah from Dubai are also available. There is a bus service from Dubai to both Muscat and Salalah, taking six and 16 hours respectively, and costing from Dhs.50 for Dubai to Muscat (ontcoman.com).

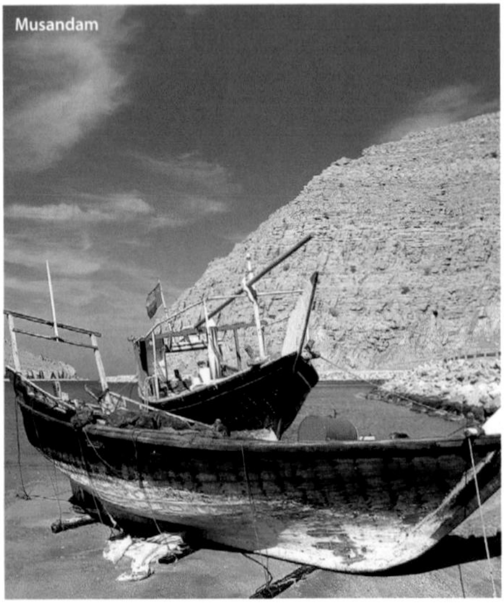

Musandam

For further information on Oman, check out the *Oman Residents' & Visitors' Guide*, *Oman Off-Road* and *Oman Trekking*, all of which are available in bookstores and at askexplorer.com.

Musandam

The UAE's northern neighbour, Musandam is an isolated enclave belonging to Oman. The region is dominated by the same Hajar Mountains that run through the eastern UAE. As the peninsula juts into the Strait of Hormuz, it splits into a myriad of jagged, picturesque fjords. Spending a day exploring the fjords on a wooden dhow is a must for any Dubai resident. Most trips originate from the region's capital, Khasab. Alternatively, you can access the famous Wadi Bih off-road route from Dibba and spend a weekend camping atop some of the region's most magnificent mountains. See the *UAE Off-Road Explorer* for information about the route.

Nizwa

After driving deep into the Hajar Mountains, you'll find Nizwa, the largest city in Oman's interior. This oasis city offers fascinating sights and heritage, including the 17th century Nizwa Fort and the Jabrin Fort, notable for its secret passageways.

Salalah

Home to several museums and souks, Salalah is best known for its lush landscape. The scenery is especially attractive during summer, when it catches the Indian monsoon. Salalah is a major frankincense producer and you can visit farms along the Yemen border to witness how it is extracted. A 16 hour drive from Dubai, spend a few days here to make the most of it.

Oman Hotels

The Chedi Muscat

18th November St Muscat **+968 24 524 400**
chedimuscat.com

This beautiful boutique hotel on the shore is famed for its clean lines, luxury and an impressive sense of calm. The stunning spa and outstanding restaurant don't hurt either. With an infinity pool, private beach and library, this is a destination for a break from bustle and perhaps isn't an ideal choice for families.

Crowne Plaza Muscat

Off Al Qurm St Muscat **+968 24 660 660**
ichotelsgroup.com

This hotel boasts cliff top views over Al Qurum and the beach below. Many of the 200 guest rooms benefit from the striking vistas and several of the restaurants also boast outdoor terraces. There's a large swimming pool, gym, spa and dolphin watching trips available. It's a great choice for those looking for relaxation and for visitors who want an action packed break.

InterContinental Muscat

Al Kharjiya St Muscat **+968 24 680 000**
intercontinental.com
An older hotel that has undergone a major facelift, the InterContinental continues to be popular for its outdoor facilities, international restaurants and regular entertainment in the form of dinner theatres and visiting bands. Alfresco restaurant, Tomato, is a must-try. Trader Vic's, with its legendary cocktails, is perennially popular. All of the rooms have views of Qurum Beach, landscaped gardens or the mountains.

Oman Dive Center

Nr Qantab & Barr Al Jissah Resort Muscat
+968 24 824 240
extradivers-worldwide.com
Just south of Muscat, a stay here is an amazing and sociable experience; and one that is highly enjoyable whether you're a diver or not. You can book a barasti hut (they are actually made of stone, with barasti covering) for an average of RO.66 for two people (depending on season). The room price includes breakfast and dinner in the centre's licensed restaurant. For keen divers, the centre offers dive training and excursions, as well as boat tours in the surrounding area.

Al Hoota Cave

Now open to the public, this cave has a large chamber with some amazing rock formations, an underground lake and a fascinating ecosystem. Facilities include a train that transports you into the cave, knowledgeable Omani guides, a restaurant and a natural history museum. Photography is not allowed. All visitors need to book at least 24 hours in advance, as only a limited number of people are allowed into the cave at any time (+968 24 490 060, alhootacave.com).

Shangri-La Barr Al Jissah Resort & Spa

Off Al Jissah St Muscat **+968 24 776 666**
shangri-la.com
With three hotels catering for families, business travellers and luxury seekers, the Shangri-La is one of the most gorgeous resorts in the region. The hotels have several swimming pools and enough play areas to keep children occupied for days. The exclusive, six-star Al Husn is incredibly luxurious and perfect for a weekend of out-of-town pampering.

Six Senses Zighy Bay > *p.282*

Zighy Bay, Musandam Daba **+968 26 735 555**
sixsenses.com
Located in a secluded cove in Musandam, the resort has been designed in true rustic style and is made up of individual pool villas. Like all Six Senses resorts, the focus here is on relaxation. The spa treatments available are of the highest quality and expertly prepared dinners can be enjoyed from the comfort of your own villa, or from the mountainside restaurant with breathtaking views of the bay.

Bahrain

Just a 45 minute flight away, near neighbour Bahrain is small enough to be explored in a weekend. With traditional architecture, miles of souks, excellent shopping and some truly outstanding bars and restaurants, you can choose from a cultural escape or fun-packed break. Formula 1 fans won't want to miss the Grand Prix that usually takes place in April.

Bahrain Attractions

Bahrain Fort

Nr Karbabad Village, Karbabad Manama
bahraintourism.com
This impressive 16th century Portuguese fort is built on the remains of several previous settlements, going back to the Dilmun era around 2,800BC. There are several large, informative notices dotted around the area, and some information booklets are available in English. Entry is free and the fort is open from 08:00 to 20:00 every day including Friday. The village at the entrance to the fort is worth a visit on its own. Nearly every square inch of the place, from walls to satellite dishes, is covered in brightly coloured murals.

Bahrain National Museum

Nr Al Fatih Highway Manama **+973 17 298 718**
bahraintourism.com
Situated on the corniche, this museum documents Bahraini life before the introduction of oil. Children will love the Hall of Graves and the museum often hosts impressive international exhibits.

Beit Al Qur'an

Nr Diplomat Radisson Blu Hotel Manama
+973 17 290 101
bahraintourism.com
The building may not look like much from afar, but a closer inspection reveals walls covered in beautiful Arabic calligraphy. The museum displays examples of historical calligraphy and Islamic manuscripts. Entrance is free, but donations are welcome.

The Burial Mounds

South of Saar Village & West of A'ali Village
Hamad Town
bahraintourism.com
One of the most remarkable sights in Bahrain is the vast area of burial mounds at Saar, near A'ali Village, at Hamad Town and at Sakhir. The mounds were built during the Dilmun, Tylos and Helenistic periods and

are anything from 2,000 to 4,000 years old. The largest burial mounds, which are known as the Royal Tombs, are found in and around A'ali Village.

La Fontaine Centre Of Contemporary Art

92 Hoora Avenue Manama **+973 17 230 123**
lafontaineartcentre.net

This place is a true architectural gem. There are wind towers, cool corridors, a Pilates studio that has to be seen to be believed, a world-class restaurant, an extensive spa, regular film screenings and art exhibitions. These make La Fontaine a unique jewel in Bahrain's crown. The enormous fountain in the courtyard is worth a visit.

Bahrain Hotels

Al Bander Hotel & Resort

Nr Bahrain Yacht Club, Maámeer Sitra
+973 17 701 201
albander.com

Located at the southern end of Sitra, this resort has a wide range of facilities including swimming pools and watersports at their private beach. Rooms are either cabana style or in chalets, and there are activities for kids and a variety of food and dining options.

Novotel Al Dana Resort Bahrain

121 Shk Hamad Causeway, Al Muharraq Manama
+973 17 298 008
novotel.com

Conveniently located on the causeway just minutes from the airport and close to the city, yet with its own beach, this hotel is a great choice for families. There's also a large pool, an indoor and outdoor play area, as well as good watersports facilities.

The Ritz-Carlton, Bahrain Hotel & Spa

Off King Abdulla The Second Ave Manama
+973 17 580 000
ritzcarlton.com

The hotel has one of the best beaches in Bahrain, in a man-made lagoon surrounded by lush gardens. The 600 metre private beach sweeps round the lagoon with its own island and private marina. Along with the nine quality dining venues and comprehensive business facilities, hotel residents have access to all of the club facilities, including the racquet sport courts, the luxurious spa and watersports activities.

Kuwait

Kuwait may be one of the world's smallest countries but its 500 kilometre coastline has endless golden beaches that remain refreshingly tranquil. From the Grand Mosque to the Kuwait Towers there are many architectural splendours to explore, while Al Qurain House, which still shows the scars of war with its immortal bullet holes, gives you a fascinating insight into the troubled times of the Iraqi invasion. There is also Green Island, an artificial island home to restaurants, a children's play area and a great alternative view of Kuwait's shoreline. For accommodation options, try the Four Points by Sheraton (+965 2242 2055, fourpointskuwait.com), Courtyard Kuwait City (+965 2299 7000, marriott.com) or the Radisson Blu Hotel (+965 2567 3000, radissonblu.com).

Qatar

Qatar once had a sleepy reputation, but things are changing fast. Development and investment in the country means it is becoming increasingly popular with visitors – and even more money is set to pour in following the announcement that Qatar will host the 2022 World Cup, the first major global sporting event to be held in the Middle East. With an attractive corniche, world-class museums (the architecturally-stunning Arab Museum of Modern Art opened to much fanfare in 2011) and cultural centres, and plenty of hotels with leisure and entertainment facilities, the capital Doha makes a perfect weekend retreat. Away from the city, the inland sea (Khor Al Udaid) in the south of the country makes a great day trip. The *Qatar Mini Visitors' Guide* has details of all these activities and includes a pull-out map.

Qatar Attractions

Education City

Al Luqta St Doha **+974 44 540 400**
myeducationcity.com

This massive complex contains some of the most tasteful contemporary architecture in the Middle East. Education City is home to a number of the world's best universities and is a clear example of Qatar's plans for the future. A drive through the campuses will no doubt impress any architecture buffs.

Katara Cultural Village

Off Lusail St Doha **+974 44 080 000**
katara.net

Designed as a recreation of a large Qatari village, this is a unique space where musicians, dancers, actors, photographers and artists can meet to collaborate on projects. Open to the public too, there are two concert halls for opera, ballet and theatrical productions, an outdoor amphitheatre, galleries, workshops, cafes, restaurants and souks.

Mathaf – Arab Museum Of Modern Art

Education City Doha **+974 44 028 855**
mathaf.org.qa

Housed in a former school, redesigned by the French architect Jean-François Bodin, Mathaf holds its own impressive permanent collection and regularly welcomes other exhibitions. Education is central to the museum, and there's a great library full of resources, as well as a museum shop and relaxed, contemporary cafe space.

Museum Of Islamic Art

The Corniche Doha **+974 4422 4444**
mia.org.qa
Architect IM Pei has created an elegant home for this impressive collection. The building is beautifully subtle, with details drawn from a wide range of Islamic influences. The collection is showcased as a journey through time, countries and cultures, and the oldest pieces date from the ninth century.

Souk Waqif

Off Grand Hamad St Doha
qatartourism.gov.qa
The city's oldest market, Souk Waqif, was renovated in 2004 using traditional building methods and materials. The resulting complex is now one of the most beautiful and authentic modern souks in the Gulf. The most refreshing aspect of the souk area is its dual purpose – tourists can easily stroll the narrow alleys in search of souvenirs while locals can purchase everything from fishing nets to pots and pans. Aside from the many shops and restaurants, there is the Waqif Art Centre, which houses several small galleries and craft shops.

Qatar Hotels

Four Seasons Hotel

Al Corniche St Doha **+974 44 948 888**
fourseasons.com
One of the finest hotels in the city, the Four Seasons has an exclusive beach and marina, first-class service and excellent restaurants, including the classy Italian eatery Il Teatro.

La Cigale Hotel

60 Suhaim Bin Hamad St Doha **+974 44 288 888**
lacigalehotel.com
A short drive from the airport, La Cigale has a reputation for first-class hospitality and is an exclusive nightlife destination. It has five restaurants.

Movenpick Hotel Doha

Corniche Rd, Al Salata Doha **+974 44 291 111**
moevenpick-hotels.com
This modern hotel boasts breathtaking views of the corniche, where guests can enjoy a morning jog or afternoon stroll. Popular with business travellers, this boutique-style hotel also attracts tourists with its excellent restaurants and leisure facilities which include a swimming pool, whirlpool and steam bath.

Radisson Blu Hotel, Doha

Nr C Ring Rd & Salwa Rd, Al Muntazah Doha
+974 44 281 428
radissonblu.com
With plenty of restaurants, bars and lounges to enjoy, this is a staple of Doha's nightlife. Renovated in 2012, the hotel's draws include a large swimming pool and a wide variety of fitness facilities. There is a champagne bar, and an excellent seafood restaurant, Pier 12.

The Ritz-Carlton, Doha

West Bay Lagoon Doha **+974 44 848 000**
ritzcarlton.com
The opulent Ritz-Carlton is a perfect stop-off if you're sailing in the region, with its 235 berth marina and clubhouse. You can expect five-star touches as standard at this resort. All of the 374 rooms and suites have breathtaking views over the sea or marina. The beach club has a great selection of watersports and there's a lavish spa. You'll be spoilt for choice with nine international and local restaurants, and can finish the night with either a cigar at Habanos or a cocktail at the Admiral Club.

Sharq Village & Spa

Ras Abu Abboud St Doha **+974 44 256 666**
sharqvillage.com
Reminiscent of a traditional Qatari town, Sharq Village & Spa is another example of Qatar's insistence on spectacular architecture. The Six Senses Spa was constructed using traditional building techniques and the resort's restaurants are some of the finest in Doha.

W Doha Hotel & Residences

Off Diplomatic St Doha **+974 44 535 000**
whoteldoha.com
Adding a touch of fun to Doha's rather conservative luxury hotel scene, the W Hotel chain is known for its funky design and fabulous level and quality of individualised service. Every inch of the hotel is an exercise in architectural minimalism, and its central location makes exploring Doha easy.

Saudi Arabia

The Kingdom of Saudi Arabia has some incredible scenery, fascinating heritage sites, and diving locations that are among the best in the world. Sadly, due to the difficulty in obtaining tourist visas, few expats are likely to experience this diverse and intriguing country. Limited transit visas, available through agents, allow visitors a three-day stay in the Kingdom en route to another country, such as the UAE or Bahrain. It has been suggested that the Kingdom will issue more tourist visas in order to boost tourism, and give better access to business travellers now that it is part of the WTO. Until then, take a look at sauditourism.com.sa/en to see what you're missing.

Activities & Hobbies

ACTIVITIES & HOBBIES

With so many different cultures converging in Dubai, it's little surprise that there is such a diverse range of activities available to fill your free time with. Everything from jumping out of an airplane to scrapbooking is covered in this section and, for every traditional pursuit such as tennis, running or football, there is the opportunity to try something completely different that you never even dreamed of doing back home, such as kitesurfing, yogilates or even caving.

For the adventurous, the UAE's diverse topography lends itself perfectly to a range of outdoor pursuits including rock climbing, mountain biking, dune bashing, wadi driving and skydiving. Thanks to the miles of coastline, watersports are particularly popular as well, with scuba diving, snorkelling, sailing, surfing and water-skiing all firm favourites.

Of course, not all activities require a dose of adrenaline or a slice of the great outdoors to get involved; there are an increasing number of groups that meet indoors for everything from Scrabble to amateur dramatics. Whatever your hobby or interest, the chances are there are like-minded people in Dubai who would love to enjoy it with you. If you don't find what you're looking for, why not set up a club yourself? Social networking sites, like Facebook, are a great way to reach people with similar interests to you. For more information on fitness and well-being see p.210, p.211.

American Football

The Emirates American Football League offers full-contact American football in the UAE for players of all skill levels, from beginner to experienced. There are both adult and youth teams, as well as recreational flag league teams. Contact info@eafl.ae for info.
To find out how to join the Duplays Mighty Eagle I flag football league, as an individual or a team, visit duplays.com.

Archery

Dubai Archers

Nr Sharjah National Park Sharjah **050 454 3099**
dubaiarchers.com

Dubai Archers meet at their new location near Sharjah International Airport and just past Sharjah National Park every Friday. Timings change according to the season, but are usually around 09:00-12:00 and

Activity Finder

cost Dhs.70 for two hours including equipment and instruction for those who require it.

Hatta Fort Hotel

Dubai – Hatta Rd Hatta **04 809 9333**
jaresortshotels.com
The 25 metre range has eight targets and the hotel hosts an eagerly-anticipated annual archery competition. Dubai Archers (above) also holds its annual tournament at the Hatta Fort Hotel. A 30 minute target practice costs Dhs.50 with all equipment included.

Sharjah Golf & Shooting Club

Nr Tasjeel Auto Village Sharjah
06 548 7777
golfandshootingshj.com
The shooting club's indoor range offers target practice at Dhs.60 for 20 arrows for members and Dhs.70 for non-members. You can also try your hand at pistol and rifle shooting.

Arts & Crafts

Art Labs

Various locations **04 374 6208**
artlabs.me
Holds courses at Dubai Ladies Club and The Pavillion Downtown on everything from sospeso trasparente and sugar wires to jewellery making and decorating techniques. Also has an online store through which you can buy supplies.

Cafe Ceramique

Town Centre Jumeirah Jumeira 1 **04 344 7331**
cafeceramique.ae
Map **2 F4** Metro **Burj Khalifa/Dubai Mall**
Indulge your creative streak with a choice of blank pottery which the cafe will glaze and fire once decorated. Events include Art4fun Workshops and the Kidz4art Summer Camp. Also has a cafe in Festival Centre (04 232 8616).

Craft Land

Town Centre Jumeirah Jumeira 1 **04 342 2237**
mycraftland.com
Map **2 F4** Metro **Burj Khalifa/Dubai Mall**
Runs all manner of needlecraft workshops, courses, clubs and clinics, such as machine sewing, quilting, hand embroidery, knitting and crocheting. Some classes are aimed at beginners, with others for the more experienced, with most sessions lasting around 90 minutes. Some are charged by the class (roughly Dhs.40) while others require signing up and paying for a full course (prices vary). Club meetings take place on Tuesday mornings and Saturday afternoons and membership is Dhs.50 per session.

Creative Hands

Mayfair Bldg, Nr Green Community Market
Green Community **04 884 9343**
creativehandsdubai.com
Map **1 G10** Metro **Ibn Battuta**
Creative Hands has a store in The Green Community, as well as an online store. The company also offers workshops and sessions in crafts such as scrapbooking and card making at various other locations across the whole city.

Dubai Community Theatre & Arts Centre (DUCTAC)

Mall of the Emirates Al Barsha 1 **04 341 4777**
ductac.org
Map **1 R6** Metro **Mall of the Emirates**
A cultural hub offering art classes for all ages. Decorative arts, drawing, painting, photography, sculpture and paper craft are just some of the wide variety of activities offered to help budding artists hone their creative talents. A variety of artist-led classes are held at the centre, and details are listed online and updated regularly. DUCTAC also has art galleries and studios for performance, comedy and dance. There's a cafe, art supplies shop and lending library. Open daily 09:00 to 22:00 and 14:00 to 22:00 on Fridays.

Dubai International Art Centre

Villa 27, Street 75B, Off Jumeira Rd Jumeira 1
04 344 4398
artdubai.com
Map **2 F4** Metro **Business Bay**
Villa-based art centre offering six to eight week courses in over 70 subjects, including painting, drawing, dressmaking, etching, pottery and photography. Annual membership starts from Dhs.350 for adults, Dhs.450 for families and Dhs.120 for under 18s.

Ikebana Sogetsu Group

Villa 13, 132 Street 15 Al Wuheida **04 262 0282**
Map **2 Q5** Metro **Al Qiyadah**
Ikebana is the intricate and beautiful Japanese art of flower arranging. This Dubai-based group attempts to deepen cultural understanding among the city's multinational society through exhibitions, demonstrations and workshops. Classes are taught by a qualified teacher from Japan.

The Jam Jar

RKM Properties, Nr Dubai Garden Centre, 17A Street Al Quoz Industrial 3 **04 341 7303**
thejamjardubai.com
Map **1 S6** Metro **First Gulf Bank**
A canvas, paints and the obligatory jam jar are yours starting at Dhs.195 for four hours of self-inspired creativity; all you need to bring is your inspiration. The 'Jam-To-Go' service brings the experience to you

– a novel idea for a garden party or corporate event. Open weekdays from 10:00 to 20:00; Fridays 14:00 to 20:00; closed on Sundays.

Paper Lane

Town Centre Jumeirah Jumeira 1 **04 344 3633**
dubaiscrapbookstore.com
Map **2 F4** Metro **Financial Centre**
One of the city's biggest scrapbooking shops, Paper Lane carries all the materials you'll need to create a memorable album, and hosts classes for all ages and levels, with families welcome.

Paper@ARTE

Times Square Al Qusais Industrial 1 **04 341 8020**
arte.ae
Map **1 T6** Metro **First Gulf Bank**
Paper@ARTE is part of Arte Souk, held at the Times Square Centre or Festival Centre most Fridays. All scrapbookers can join the workshops and Creative Hands (above) bring supplies to buy and use.

Baseball

Dubai Little League

Nr Al Quoz Pond Park, Off Al Khail Rd Al Quoz 2
050 293 3855
eteamz.com/DubaiLittleLeague
Map **2 D7** Metro **Business Bay**
Parent volunteers field over 20 baseball teams for boys and girls aged five to 16. Beginners are welcome. Dhs.850 registration includes season fees, team picture, uniform and year-end trophy.

Basketball

Dubai has a number of public basketball courts but getting a game on them can be tricky during the evenings as they are very popular with regular teams. There are courts near the Canadian University of Dubai, at Hamriya Park in Abu Hail and on Al Diyafah Road in Satwa, next to Chelsea Plaza Hotel. You can also go to Safa Park (p.257) and Al Barsha Pond Park (p.256) and get regular pick up games on Wednesday, Thursday and Sunday evenings. Air-conditioned indoor courts can be hired for Dhs.35 per person per hour at Chevrolet Insportz (insportzclub.com), behind Dubai Garden Centre in Al Quoz 3. Duplays organises men's and women's recreational and competitive leagues (duplays.com).

Basketball Academy Of Dubai

Raffles International School Umm Suqeim 3
050 731 6745
badubai.com
Map **1 S5** Metro **First Gulf Bank**
A children's academy offering everything from slam dunking for beginners to clinics, camps, leagues and

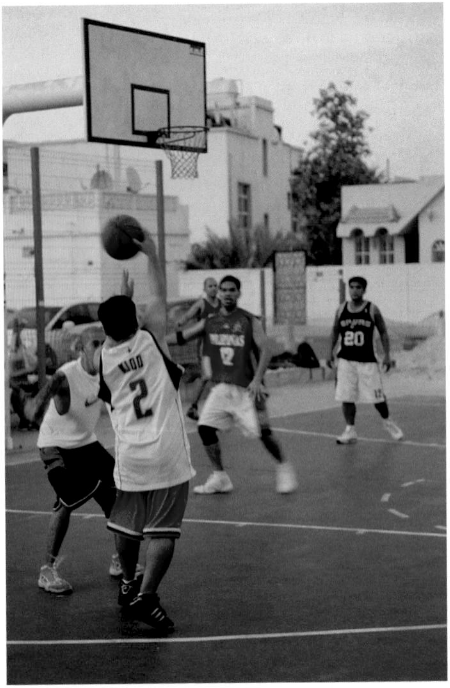

pickup sessions. All of the highly qualified staff are properly trained in instructing children. Call Academy Director, Marc Roberts, on 056 683 0665 for more info.

Belly Dancing

The ancient art of belly dancing is a great way to keep fit. The Ballet Centre (04 344 9776) holds lessons for Dhs.40 on Tuesdays and Saturdays. Milla Tenorio teaches at the Rotana Towers on Sundays and Tuesdays at 18:00; classes cost from Dhs.50 (050 395 5983). Nora Dance Group also offers belly dancing classes (p.332) and Exhale Fitness offers belly dance fitness classes (exhaledubai.com).

Birdwatching

Emirates Bird Records Committee

Various locations
uaebirding.com
Collates information on birds in the UAE and requests local and visiting birders to submit details of sightings. A weekly roundup of bird sightings and a monthly report are available via email upon request from Tommy Pedersen at 777sandman@gmail.com.

Bowling

There are a number of places that you can go bowling – be they independent centres where the lanes are cheap and you can have an alcoholic drink while you play, or as a fun diversion to a long shopping trip. If you want to join a bowling league, contact Dubai International Bowling Centre and they will put you in touch with Dubai's leagues.

Al Nasr Leisureland

Nr American Hospital Oud Metha **04 337 1234**
alnasrll.com
Map **2 L6** Metro **Oud Metha**
Eight lanes surrounded by fast food outlets and a bar where you can buy alcohol. Booking is recommended. The first game costs Dhs.15, including shoe rental.

Bowling City

Festival Centre Dubai Festival City **04 232 8600**
bowling-city.com
Map **2 M9** Metro **Emirates**
Bowling City, located on the balcony level of Festival Centre, has 12 bowling lanes, as well as nine billiard tables and a 24 station PC gaming network. After you've celebrated making a few strikes, you can take your adrenalin into a karaoke cabin and belt out We Are The Champions.

Dubai Bowling Centre

Meydan Rd Al Quoz 1 **04 339 1010**
bowlingdubai.com
Map **2 D6** Metro **Business Bay**
With 24 professional series lanes for recreational and professional bowling and a gaming area for kids, the bowling centre has leagues for serious players as well as those who bowl for fun. It caters for professional tournaments, corporate events and kids' parties. Prices are from Dhs.15 per game or Dhs.130 per hour for a lane.

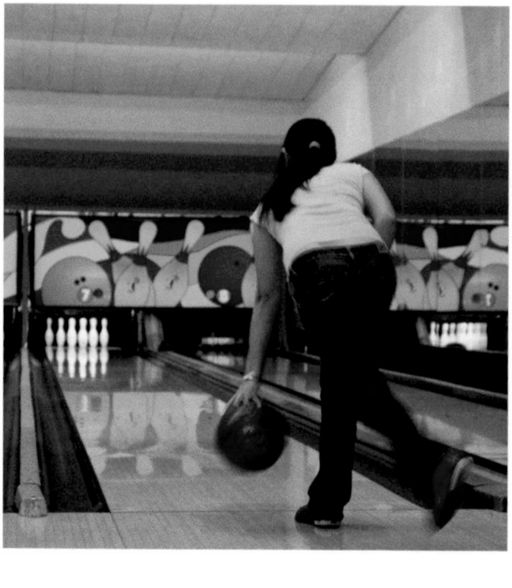

Dubai International Bowling Centre

Nr Al Shabab Club & Century Mall Hor Al Anz East **04 296 9222**
dubaibowlingcentre.com
Map **2 R6** Metro **Al Qiyadah**
Dubai's biggest bowling centre boasts 36 state-of-the-art computerised lanes as well as amusement games, snooker, billiards and food outlets. Several of Dubai's clubs and leagues are based here and the centre hosts regular competitions.

Funky Lanes Bowling Centre

Arabian Centre Al Mizhar 1 **04 239 3636**
Map **2 S13** Metro **Rashidiya**
A new 10-lane bowling centre, with billiards lounge, arcade games zone and a private party room.

Magic Planet

Mall of the Emirates Al Barsha 1 **04 341 4444**
magicplanet.ae
Map **1 R6** Metro **Mall of the Emirates**
This branch of Magic Planet has a number of bowling lanes in its games arcade. Prices per player per game start at Dhs.20 on weekdays and Dhs.25 on weekends.

Switch Bowling Dubai

Ibn Battuta Mall The Gardens **04 440 5961**
switchbowlingdubai.com
Map **1 G5** Metro **Ibn Battuta**
Enjoy the ultimate bowling experience with state-of-the-art lighting and sound effects at this 12-lane bowling centre set within the Indian Court. There's fun for all the family with billiard tables, an internet cyber room, karaoke and PlayStation rooms, a cafe and lounge area. From Dhs.25 per game.

Yalla! Bowling Lanes & Lounge

Mirdif City Centre Mirdif **800 534 7873**
playnationme.com
Map **2 P12** Metro **Rashidiya**
Yalla! is Dubai's latest bowling centre, set within Mirdif City Centre's Playnation. It features 12 illuminated lanes of dayglo bowling, along with the usual glut of video simulators, video games and pool tables. Open daily 10:00-00:00.

Boxing

Al Nasr Leisureland

Nr American Hospital Oud Metha **04 337 1234**
alnasrll.com
Map **2 L6** Metro **Oud Metha**
Boxing classes are held every Saturday, Monday and Wednesday from 20:30 to 22:30. A 12 lesson package costs Dhs.550. For more information on the different weight classes, contact the resident coach, Mr Iraj Dortolouee, on the above number.

Colosseum Muay Thai Health & Fitness Club
Montana Centre Bldg, Zaabeel Rd Al Karama
04 337 2755
colosseumuae.com
Map **2 L6** Metro **Oud Metha**
Gym specialising in boxing, Muay Thai (Thai boxing), kickboxing and street fighting. Group classes meet daily between 20:30 and 22:00 and cost Dhs.75 per session.

Dubai Fight Academy
Nr Ace Hardware, Shk Zayed Rd Al Quoz Industrial 1
050 712 9333
fightacademy.ae
Map **1 U6** Metro **Noor Islamic Bank**
The academy offers Thai boxing lessons and holds tournaments. Membership is Dhs.1,500 for six months including use of gym and pool. Another branch is located in Jumeira (050 650 1184).

Bridge

Dubai Ladies Bridge Club
Dubai International Women's Club Jumeira 1
050 659 1300
Map **2 F4** Metro **Business Bay**
Ladies-only bridge mornings are held at 09:00 on Sundays and Wednesdays. Contact Marzie Polad on the number above or Jan Irvine on 050 645 4395.

Canoeing & Kayaking
Canoeing and kayaking are great ways to get close to the varied marine and birdlife of the UAE. Khor Kalba (p.308) on the East Coast is a popular canoeing spot, as are the mangrove-covered islands north of Abu Dhabi (p.284). Sea canoes can be used in the Musandam (p.314) to visit secluded bays and spectacular rocky coastlines where many species of turtles can often be found soaking up the sun. There are a number of specialist tour companies who offer canoeing and kayaking trips to all of these areas, including Desert Rangers and Noukhada. For more details, see Main Tour Operators p.279. Alternatively, you can test your skills at the new, artificial whitewater rafting venue at Wadi Adventure.

Dubai Paddling School
Kite Beach, Umm Suqeim
050 640 6087
Map **1 U4** Metro **Noor Islamic Bank**
The school offers private and group lessons in surfskiing, using long, open-top kayaks. There are squad training sessions throughout the week, which is the ideal way to train for the Shamaal International Surfski Race, which is held each National Day (2 December). Email dubaipaddlingschool@gmail.com.

Dubai Surfski & Kayak Club
Nr Saga World Umm Suqeim 1 **050 640 6087**
dskc.hu
Map **1 V4** Metro **Noor Islamic Bank**
Holds the annual Shamaal International Surfski Race and organises a range of kayaking trips. Dhs.1,200 for membership with berth, Dhs.250 without.

Explorer Tours
Nr Nadd Shamma Park Umm Ramoul **04 286 1991**
explorertours.ae
Map **2 P11** Metro **Emirates**
Offers canoe and kayak trips in Khor Kalba from Dhs.300 per person with transportation, or Dhs.200 per person without. Explore the tranquil mangroves of the east coast, famous for its wide variety of birds and marine life.

Sandy Beach Hotel & Resort
Dibba – Khorfakkan Rd Fujairah **09 244 5555**
sandybm.com
This chalet resort on the east coast has equipment to rent or buy. Single kayaks are available for hire at Dhs.40 for 45 minutes, or you could go for a two-seater for Dhs.70 to explore the neighbouring Snoopy Island.

Sky & Sea Adventures
Sheraton Jumeirah Beach Resort Dubai Marina
04 399 9005
watersportsdubai.com
Map **1 J4** Metro **Jumeirah Lakes Towers**
Leisure kayaks are available for hire by the hour. Hourly prices are Dhs.100 for a single kayak and Dhs.150 for a double.

Wadi Adventure > *p.325*
Nr Green Mubazzarah, Off Al Ain Fayda Rd Al Ain
03 781 8422
wadiadventure.ae
Wadi Adventure offers man-made whitewater kayaking in a brand new facility at the foot of Jebel Hafeet. Park entry costs Dhs.100 per adult (Dhs.50 per child) and kayaking costs an extra Dhs.100 for an all-day pass, including equipment.

Caving
The cave network in the Hajar Mountains is extensive and much of it has yet to be explored. Some of the best caves are located near Al Ain, the Jebel Hafeet area and just past Buraimi near the Oman border. Many of the underground passages and caves have spectacular displays of curtains, stalagmites and stalactites, as well as gypsum flowers.

In Oman, the range includes what is still believed to be the second largest cave system in the world, as well as the Majlis Al Jinn Cave – the second largest chamber in the world.

Wadi Adventure
explore your limits

Wadi Adventure is the Middle East's first man made surfing, whitewater rafting, and kayaking destination and it is located right here in Al Ain! We also have an airpark, climbing wall and zip line just in case your adventure fix needs topping up!

With our world class activities and facilities, excellent service and a backdrop like no other, your day with us can be as exhilarating or relaxed as you want it to be. You will also find a family swimming pool and splash pad for our younger adventurers, as well as a number of food outlets to satisfy a variety of tastes.

If you are thinking of bringing a group of friends or your colleagues from work for some team building fun, then Wadi Adventure can cater for that too. With event space to seat upto 160 indoors (overlooking the surf pool) and a further 80 outside, its the perfect venue for your party, meeting or just about any function.

For further information, get in touch with the team at Wadi Adventure.

Explore your limits!

WADI ADVENTURE
RAFT • KAYAK • SURF

For enquiries please call us on +971 (0)3 781 8422
email: info@wadiadventure.ae
www.wadiadventure.ae

To arrange caving trips in Oman, contact a local tour operator such as Gulf Leisure (+968 99 013 424, gulfleisure.com) or Muscat Diving & Adventure Centre (holiday-in-oman.com). Within the region, caving ranges from fairly safe to extremely dangerous and, as no mountain rescue services exist, anyone venturing out into the mountains should always be well-equipped and accompanied by an experienced leader.

Mountain High Middle East

Dubai Media City Al Sufouh 1 **050 659 5536**
mountainhighme.com
Map **1 M5** Metro **Nakheel**
Offers guided tours in and around the caves of Al Ain, plus canyoning and other adventures from Dhs.500 per person per day.

Chess

Dubai Chess & Culture Club

Nr Century Mall Hor Al Anz East **04 296 6664**
dubaichess.ae
Map **2 R6** Metro **Al Qiyadah**
Home of the UAE's national chess team, this club is involved in all aspects of chess from grassroots up. Members can play at the club seven nights a week, and competitions are organised on a regular basis. The club also promotes international competitions, including the Dubai International Open, Emirates Open and Dubai Junior Open. Membership costs Dhs.100 a year.

Climbing

For those who feel at home on a vertical or overhanging plane, excellent climbing can be found in various locations around the UAE, including Ras Al Khaimah, Dibba, Hatta and the Al Ain/Buraimi region; in fact, more than 600 routes have been recorded since the 1970s. These vary from short outcrop routes to difficult mountain routes of alpine proportions. Most range from Very Severe up to Extreme. However, there are some easier routes for newer climbers, especially in Wadi Bih and Wadi Khab Al Shamis.

To meet like-minded people, head to Wadi Bih where you're sure to find climbers nearly every weekend, or go to one of the climbing walls listed below. For more information, contact John Gregory on 050 647 7120 or email arabex@eim.ae. Other excellent resources are uaeclimbing.com and the book UAE Rock Climbing by Toby Foord-Kelcey.

Adventure HQ

Times Square Al Qusais Industrial 1 **04 346 6824**
adventurehq.ae
Map **1 T6** Metro **First Gulf Bank**
As well as being arguably the best place in the UAE to pick up climbing gear, Adventure HQ has a state-of-the-art climbing wall and cable obstacle course that can be tackled, with climbing rates starting from Dhs.50 per person. Test your climbing gear for cold conditions in the Chill Chamber.

Cleopatra's Spa & Wellness

Wafi Umm Hurair 2 **04 324 7700**
cleopatrasspaandwellness.com
Map **2 L7** Metro **Dubai Healthcare City**
The indoor climbing wall at Cleopatra's Spa and Wellness in Wafi offers a range of courses for all abilities, including beginners' classes as well as public sessions for experienced climbers. The wall has climbing routes of varying difficulty and crash mats are provided for bouldering. Lessons cost Dhs.62 per hour and are limited to six people per instructor.

Climbing Dubai

Dubai Trade Centre Hotel Apartments
Trade Centre 2 **04 306 5061**
dorellsports.com
Map **2 J5** Metro **World Trade Centre**
The Middle East's tallest outdoor climbing wall can be found at Dubai World Trade Centre Hotel Apartments. Learn to scale its 16 metres with an introductory lesson for Dhs.85. Courses for adults (Dhs.350 for five classes) and kids (Dhs.250 for five classes) are available. A day pass costs Dhs.60. Climbing Dubai also has an eight metre climbing tower at Horizon School Dubai, next to Safa Park Gate 4 (050 659 8500).

E-Sports

The Aviation Club Al Garhoud **04 282 4540**
esportsuae.com
Map **2 N8** Metro **GGICO**
E-Sports offers climbing lessons for children and adults at GEMS World Academy, Jumeirah Primary School and GEMS Wellington International School. Advanced outdoor classes are offered too, so you can classify a climb, examine ropes and equipment for faults, evaluate the safety of a climb and know exactly what to do in an emergency situation. E-Sports also organises climbing and hiking holidays to destinations such as the French Alps.

Wadi Adventure > *p.325*

Nr Green Mubazzarah, Off Al Ain Fayda Rd Al Ain
03 781 8422
wadiadventure.ae
The latest climbing wall to open in the UAE, park entry costs Dhs.100 (adult) or Dhs.50 (children) with 20 minutes of climbing, including instruction and equipment, costing an extra Dhs.40. There's also an air park and zip line to try.

Cookery Classes

Eating out is a national pastime in Dubai and gastronomes can also learn how to cook a range of global cuisines. Many hotels provide this service, either by special request if you particularly like one of their dishes, or as an advertised activity. There are also wine tasting classes and courses for budding oenophiles or those just wanting to up their dinner party game.

You can learn the art of sushi making at Nobu (04 426 0760) every first Saturday of the month; classes are priced at Dhs.1,250 per person including lunch. Al Bustan Rotana has classes at the Blue Elephant's Thai cookery course on the first Saturday of the month costs Dhs.199 (04 282 0000). Further afield there's the Six Senses Resort in Dibba (p.308), which holds Arabic cooking classes for guests.

There are also several places offering cooking classes for children; try Sway 2the Heart (sway2the heart.net, Dhs.80 per class) or Le Meridien Dubai's Little Pastry Chef sessions at L'atelier des Chefs (atelierdeschefsdubai.com, Dhs.150 – also does adult cookery lessons).

Armani Hotel Dubai

Burj Khalifa Downtown Dubai **04 888 3888**
dubai.armanihotels.com
Map **2 F6** Metro **Burj Khalifa/Dubai Mall**
The teams of chefs at several of the Armani Hotel's most popular restaurants teach willing students how to make some of their specialities at home. Between Saturdays and Wednesdays, 16:30 to 18:00, you can learn to prepare a classic three-course Italian meal, master Indian cuisine or perfect the intricacies of Japanese fare. Classes range in price from Dhs.1,100 to Dhs.1,300.

The Balance Cafe Cookery School

Oasis Centre Al Quoz 1 **04 384 7010**
balance-wellness-centre.com
Map **2 L6** Metro **Noor Islamic Bank**
Award-winning chefs from restaurants across Dubai, including Carluccio's, Ushna and Mango Tree offer hands-on training in a variety of cuisines such as Thai, Italian, sushi and Indian, all with a focus on healthy eating. The Balance Cafe cookery courses are designed for everyone from amateurs to professionals, with prices starting at Dhs.250 per class and Dhs.800 for any four classes.

Blue Flame

Jumeirah Creekside Hotel Al Garhoud **04 230 8580**
jumeirah.com
Map **2 M8** Metro **GGICO**
Learn the secrets of preparing gourmet dishes such as brick baby chicken and seafood papillote at the Blue Flame cookery school. Classes are held every day at 7pm in a state of the art cooking pod. Prices start at Dhs.300, which includes a signed copy of the menu and Blue Flame apron.

Cooking At Home

056 244 5082
Learn how to prepare traditional Italian family recipes, with two-hour weekly classes for Dhs.150 or weekend courses for Dhs.180. Private classes are also available.

De Dietrich Cuisine Academy

Dubai Ladies Club Jumeira 2 **050 550 1612**
de-dietrich-academy.ae
Map **2 E4** Metro **Business Bay**
Brush up on your culinary skills with courses in French, Italian, Asian, sushi and special pastries. Learn how to make the perfect seasonal menu, prepare mocktails, cook fresh and healthy cuisine, or make special meals for kids. Classes cost from Dhs.130 to Dhs.350, and special packages for birthdays, baby showers and bridal parties are also available.

International Centre For Culinary Arts Dubai

Al Hana Centre Al Jafiliya **04 398 9745**
iccadubai.ae
Map **2 J5** Metro **Al Jafiliya**
There's a wide range of cookery classes available, from industry training for professionals to cooking for fun courses for amateurs. This culinary training centre is accredited by City & Guilds London.

Jones The Grocer

Indigo Central 8, Nr Times Square, Shk Zayed Rd
Al Manara **04 346 6886**
jonesthegrocer.com
Map **1 T6** Metro **Noor Islamic Bank**
Australia's gourmet deli and cafe hosts weekly cooking classes where you can master the art of pastries and breads, learn how to make pasta, or create your own soups – and then enjoy what you've cooked with selected beverages and desserts. A chocolate masterclass is also held once a month. Classes start at 6pm and cost Dhs.375, and prior booking is necessary.

L'atelier des Chefs

Le Meridien Dubai Al Garhoud **056 690 0480**
atelierdeschefsdubai.com
Map **2 N8** Metro **GGICO**
This French cooking school offers a wide range of classes including Arabic, Indian and French cuisine, plus sushi, seafood and pastry making. Classes cost from Dhs.120 for half an hour to Dhs.350 for two hours, depending on the type of class.

Nobu

Atlantis The Palm Palm Jumeirah **04 426 2626**
atlantisthepalm.com
Map **1 N1** Metro **Nakheel**
Learn how to cook like the master chef Nobu Matsuhisa at Nobu's three-hour class on the first

Saturday of every month. Costs Dhs.1,250 per person with lunch.

Prego's
Media Rotana Tecom **04 435 0000**
rotana.com
Map **1 P6** Metro **Dubai Internet City**
Cooking has been in Chef Mauro's family for generations, and he makes for a charismatic and easy guide through some of his kitchen's most famous Italian dishes.

Rococo
Sofitel Dubai Jumeirah Beach Dubai Marina
04 448 4848
sofitel.com
Map **1 K4** Metro **Jumeirah Lakes Towers**
These two-and-a-half hour Italian cookery classes can be privately organised for groups of eight or more and offer great value at Dhs.250 per person, including dinner.

Spice & Aroma
Al Wasl Plaza, Al Wasl Rd Al Wasl **04 349 2577**
spiceandaroma.com
Map **2 E5** Metro **Business Bay**
Learn the art of spice-friendly cooking at this master class in Indian and oriental cuisine. Costs Dhs.150-Dhs.200 (inclusive of meal).

Table 9 By Nick & Scott
Hilton Dubai Creek Al Rigga **04 212 7551**
table9dubai.com
Map **2 N5** Metro **Al Rigga**
Gordon Ramsay proteges and Table 9 head chefs Nick Alvis and Scott Price share their Michelin secrets with weekly masterclasses ranging from breadmaking to the perfect hot chocolate fondant. Costs Dhs.495 per person, and you'll leave with a Table 9 apron and a set of recipes.

Tavola
Century Plaza Jumeira 1 **04 344 5624**
tavola.ae
Map **2 H4** Metro **Emirates Towers**
Cake decoration, with an authorised Wilton method instructor. A course consists of four three-hour sessions and costs Dhs.750.

Thiptara
The Palace Downtown Dubai Downtown Dubai
04 888 3444
theaddress.com
Map **2 F6** Metro **Burj Khalifa/Dubai Mall**
Culinary classes with Chef Mac cost Dhs.295, including the two-hour demonstration, some hands-on practice, lunch and a diploma in Thai cuisine.

Zuma
Dubai International Financial Centre (DIFC)
Trade Centre 2 **04 425 5660**
zumarestaurant.com
Map **2 G6** Metro **Emirates Towers**
As the man behind arguably the city's best sushi counter, Zuma's Masaharu Kondo is the perfect host for these two-hour sushi masterclasses which cost Dhs.500 and allow for plenty of delicious sampling.

Cricket
At the weekend, you'll see informal cricket games springing up on scratchy patches of open space on the outskirts of the city. But, if you prefer a little more green for your stumps, Zabeel and Safa parks are favourite spots. There are also several small-scale training centres, such as the Emirates Cricket Training Centre (050 497 3461). International matches are regularly hosted in the United Arab Emirates, particularly at the state-of-the-art cricket ground in Dubai Sports City (dubaisportscity.ae) where it's possible to see some of the world's best teams in action.

ICC Global Cricket Academy > *p.318*
Nr Autodrome Dubai Sports City **04 448 1355**
iccgca.com
Map **1 L11** Metro **Dubai Internet City**
The ICC cricket academy opened in Dubai Sports City in early 2010, offering cricket coaching for all ages with ICC-affiliated coaches and some of the most state-of-the-art facilities in the cricketing world.

Insportz Club
Nr Dubai Garden Centre, 17A Street
Al Quoz Industrial 3 **04 347 5833**
insportzclub.com
Map **1 S6** Metro **First Gulf Bank**
Insportz has three main net courts with a scoreboard and one side court, available for playing a social game as part of a league, or just to practise on.

Last Man Stands
Zabeel Park Al Kifaf
lastmanstands.com
Map **2 J6** Metro **Al Jafiliya**
Amateur T20 cricket league with several Dubai teams taking part. Registration fees are Dhs.640 per year. Matches are played at Zabeel Park.

Cycling
Dubai is not a particularly bicycle-friendly city, but there are pleasant areas where you can ride, such as along both sides of the creek and Jumeira Road, and on the cycle tracks at Mamzar Park and Jumeira Open Beach. Also, try out the Meydan Cycle Park, a converted camel racing track with varying distances (4km, 6km and 8km), and the Dubai Autodrome.

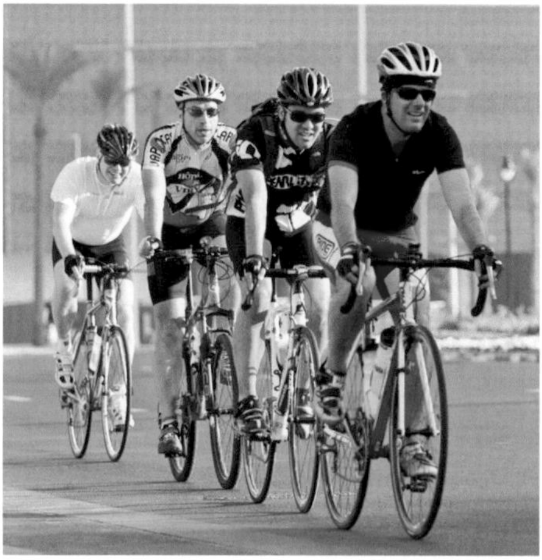

Jebel Hafeet, Hatta and the central area in the mountains near Masafi down to Fujairah and Dibba offer interesting paved roads with better views, but much care is required and they are best tackled in a large group. The new road from Hatta through the mountains to Kalba on the east coast is one of the most scenic routes in the country.

Both Dubai Autodrome and Yas Marina Circuit host weekly track cycling sessions, which you can keep up to date on by joining the CycleSafeDubai Facebook page. Check the discussion threads for the next event. Wolfi's Bike Shop (p.379) and Probike (p.379) can both offer equipment, advice on improving technique and recommend some weekly riding groups you may want to get involved with.

For more on cycling as a mode of transport in Dubai, see Getting Around, p.51.

Cycle Safe Dubai

Various locations
cyclechallenge.ae

Organises several races, including the Spinneys Dubai 92 Cycle Challenge. Cycle Safe also arranges regular Friday morning rides over varying distances (from 35 to 100km) and the Saturday morning Bab Al Shams coffee ride. It is the brains behind the Wednesday cycle nights at the Dubai Autodrome, where expert cyclists are also on hand to teach beginners the basics. For Dhs.500 a year, you can join Team CSD and get a range of services and discounts (as well as a team jersey) but membership is not mandatory to join in the rides.

Dubai Roadsters

Various locations **04 339 4453**
dubairoadsters.com

Possibly the more serious of the organised groups and rides, the Friday ride offers options of 80km, 120km and, occasionally, 140km, with weekday rides ranging from 30km to 50km. There are also a number of special events, from the epic twice-yearly 240km coast-to-coast ride, to group training rides in the Hatta hills. A number of socials are held throughout the year, making the group a great place to meet like-minded people.

Dance Classes

Whether your feet tap to classical or contemporary rhythms, all dancing tastes are catered for in Dubai. In addition to established dancing institutions, a number of health clubs, restaurants and bars hold weekly sessions in flamenco, salsa, samba, jazz dance, ballroom and more (see Salsa Dancing, p.354).

Arthur Murray Dance Centre

201 Reef Tower Jumeirah Lakes Towers **04 448 6458**
arthurmurraydubai.com
Map **1 K5** Metro **Jumeirah Lakes Towers**

Teaches rhythm and Latin, smooth and standard, country western and speciality dances, all according to the 'Arthur Murray method' which has been successfully exported all over the globe. There's a second branch at Souk Al Bahar (04 450 8648).

The Ballet Centre

Nr Jumeira Plaza, Jumeira Rd Jumeira 1 **04 344 9776**
balletcentre.com
Map **2 H4** Metro **Emirates Towers**

Classes on offer include ballet, tap, modern, salsa, Irish, jazz and belly dancing. Adult and children's classes are available, with youngsters aged three years and above accepted for enrolments. Training for the Imperial Society for Teachers of Dancing (ISTD) and the Royal Academy of Dance examinations is encouraged.

Cello Music & Ballet Centre

Fitness First, Town Centre, The Springs
Emirates Living **04 422 2452**
cellodubai.com
Map **1 K8** Metro **Nakheel**

Offering dance and music classes to children and adults of all ages at eight locations across Dubai: Springs, Lakes, Arabian Ranches, JBR, Umm Suqeim, Dubai Marina, Palm Jumeirah and Al Quoz Sheikh Zayed. Other classes include belly dance, jazz, modern, tap dance, Irish dance, hip hop and martial arts.

Ceroc Arabia

Various locations
cerocarabia.com

Easy to learn and similar to salsa (without the fancy footwork), this modern jive can be danced to all kinds of different music, including club and chart hits, classics, swing, Latin and rock 'n' roll. Classes, socials and private tuition are available.

Dance Horizons

Various locations **050 644 2972**
horizonschooldubai.com
A specialist ballet school that offers the Royal Academy of Dance Examination syllabus for beginners and advanced dancers, and a specialised music and movement programme for age three and older. Classes are held at Horizon School near Safa Park and Safa School on Meydan Road in fully equipped ballet studios with sprung floors, barres and mirrors, and are led by highly qualified, RAD registered, teaching staff.

Disco Dance Dubai

Kings' Dubai Umm Suqeim 3 **050 289 6735**
Map **1 S5** Metro **First Gulf Bank**
Dance routines to Hannah Montana, Mamma Mia and songs from High School Musical are taught by RAD and IDTA trained director, Becky Kerrigan. Contact Becky for times and prices.

Dubai Liners

Safa Kindergarten Nursery Trade Centre 1
050 654 5960
Map **2 F6** Metro **Burj Khalifa/Dubai Mall**
Not all country and western; here, you can line dance to disco, rock 'n' roll, salsa, jazz, R&B, waltzes and ballads. Beginner classes are held on Saturdays from 09:30 to 11:30, and intermediates dance from 11:00 to 13:00, with another class on Wednesdays from 19:00 to 20:30.

El Firulete BNF Dance Company Dubai

Dubai Knowledge Village Al Sufouh 1 **04 364 4882**
elfiruletebnf.com
Map **1 N5** Metro **Dubai Internet City**
The BNF is a celebrated Columbian dance school and the Dubai branch offers private and group instruction in tango, salsa and belly dancing, among other styles. In the past, students have showcased their talent at public performances including the Middle East Latin Competition and Tango Seduction 2012.

First International Dance Studio

Dubai Shopping Centre 04 294 0049
firstids.com
Map **2 N7** Metro **Deira City Centre**
Hip hop and breakdance are the main dance disciplines offered at this school, but other modern and classical styles are also available. Dhs.800 per month for three group classes a week; get a taster with a free introductory lesson. Classes are available for kids, teenagers and adults

Highland Dance Dubai

Greenfield Community School Green Community
050 765 8007
highlanddancedubai.com
Map **1 F12** Metro **Ibn Battuta**
Certified instructor, Clarissa Crowley, teaches male and female students of all ages and abilities about the technique and form of traditional Scottish dancing. The first class is free, with further classes costing Dhs.35-50 per hour, depending on your level. Visit the website for timings and more information.

James & Alex Dance Studios

Dubai Media City Al Sufouh 1 **04 447 0773**
jamesandalex.com
Map **1 J5** Metro **Nakheel**
Set up by salsa dancing partners James and Alex, this three-studio venue offers a variety of classes for adults and children, from ballet and jazz to belly dance and salsa. There's also new pole fitness classes for beginners and intermediates.

Nora Dance Group
Various locations **050 875 0111**
noradancegroup.com
Offers instruction in an array of styles including hip-hop, ballet, jazz, tango and modern freestyle, as well as belly dancing and Bollywood. Classes are held at Knowledge Village, DUCTAC and Dubai Marina Mall. Available for adults and children, group lessons or private instruction.

Prima Performing Arts
Various locations **055 771 4526**
primauae.com
Prima Performing Arts offers a fun way for children to learn to dance and get fit. There's classes for all ages, with Dinky Dances for 18 month olds, movement classes for mums and toddler using fun props and pop music, and ballet classes for three to 18 year-olds. The dance academy also holds annual dance exams and performances in hip hop, contemporary, dance/gymnastics, musical theatre, jazz and tap.

Solid Rock
Pinnacle Bldg, Nr Caesar Confectionery, Shk Zayed Rd Al Barsha 1 **04 395 7808**
solidrockdubai.com
Map **1 Q6** Metro **Sharaf DG**
A complete performing arts studio, covering both music and dance, with hip hop, salsa and jazz on the menu for those who love to boogie. Offers the first group lesson for free, so you can see if you like it before signing up for more. Classes are available from beginners through to advanced.

Swing Arabia
Various locations **04 367 2217**
cerocarabia.com/lindyswing
Fans of popular TV shows Strictly Come Dancing and Dancing With The Stars will be familiar with swing dancing or lindy hop. This energetic form of dance involves intricate footwork and jazz steps from dances like the Charleston through to music from jazz greats like Count Basie and Duke Ellington. Call Des for further information.

Tango Dubai
Dubai Community Theatre & Arts Centre (DUCTAC) Al Barsha 1 **050 451 6281**
tangodubai.com
Map **1 R6** Metro **Mall of the Emirates**
Tuesday classes are held for beginners and advanced dancers at Evory Bar, Kempinski Hotel and at DUCTAC, Mall of the Emirates respectively. Call Eleanor on 050 451 6281 or Maya on 050 622 3679 for more info. Lessons cost Dhs.200 for four beginner's classes and Dhs.240 for advanced. Tango Dubai also runs dance nights at Sezzam and Pachanga.

Turning Pointe
Russia International City **04 422 1592**
turningpointe.ae
Metro **Rashidiya**
Turning Pointe has over 35 studios throughout the UAE, offering everything from ballet for three years up (with Royal Academy of Dance Syllabus and Examinations) to Hip Hop, Street Jazz and Jazz2Pop, plus there's the popular TP Glee Club! All teachers are recruited from the UK and fully qualified dance teachers who encourage a love of dance.

Desert Driving Courses
Don't just settle for doing the school run – while in Dubai, you should make the most of your 4WD and take a crash course in desert driving. With several organisations offering instruction from professional drivers, you'll quickly master the art of driving in the sand without getting stuck and learn how to get yourself out when you do. In addition, if you intend to go out camping anytime, it is a really good idea to have some experience in desert driving.

Al Futtaim Training Centre
Nr Dubai Duty Free, Marrakech St Umm Ramoul **04 292 0555**
traininguae.com
Map **2 N9** Metro **Emirates**
Classroom and practical tuition for off-road driving enthusiasts to venture safely into the desert.

Desert Rangers
Nr American Hospital, 18th Street Oud Metha **04 357 2200**
desertrangers.com
Map **2 L6** Metro **Oud Metha**
Experience a four-hour desert driving safari with the chance to spend one hour behind the wheel. The costs are Dhs.1,000 with own vehicle, or Dhs.1,800 without.

Emirates Driving Institute
Off Doha Rd Al Qusais 1 **04 263 1100**
edi-uae.com
Map **2 R8** Metro **Al Nahda**
Offers an eight-hour desert driving course from Dhs.500 or Dhs.550 on Fridays.

OffRoad-Zone
Street 8 Al Quoz Industrial 1 **04 339 2449**
offroad-zone.com
Map **2 U5** Metro **Noor Islamic Bank**
Drivers are taught how to handle a 4WD in a controlled environment, on a training course in Jebel Ali with simulated obstacles. From deep water crossings to sandy descents, all terrains are covered. Bring your own 4WD or rent one from OffRoad-Zone; Dhs.850 per person for three hours.

Diving

There are plenty of dive companies in the UAE where you can improve your diving skills. Courses are offered under the usual international training organisations. For more information on diving in the UAE, see p.270.

7 Seas Divers

Nr Safeer Centre, Al Mudifi Khor Fakkan **09 238 7400**
7seasdivers.com
This PADI dive centre offers day and night diving trips to sites around Khor Fakkan, Musandam and Lima Rock. Training is provided from beginner to instructor level, in a variety of languages.

Al Boom Diving

Nr Iranian Hospital, Al Wasl Rd Jumeira 1
04 342 2993
alboomdiving.com
Map **2 H4** Metro **World Trade Centre**
Al Boom's Aqua Centre on Al Wasl Road (there are centres in Fujairah, Dibba and Jebel Ali too) is a purpose-built school with a diving shop. There are diving trips daily. PADI certification starts from Dhs.1,750 for Scuba Diver; novices can try a dive experience for Dhs.150. Al Boom also runs the Diving With Sharks experience in Dubai Aquarium at The Dubai Mall. For more details, see thedubaiaquarium.com.

Arabian Diver

Hilton Ras Al Khaimah Resort & Spa Ras Al Khaimah
07 243 3800
arabiandiver.com
This dive centre has a complete range of diving courses and adventure packages, all based in the waters surrounding the Musandam Peninsula. Guests can enjoy a fusion of Caribbean and Arabian seafood onboard, as well as activities such as environmental education classes.

Atlantis Dive Centre

Atlantis The Palm Palm Jumeirah **04 426 3000**
atlantisdivecentre.com
Map **1 N1** Metro **Nakheel**
This top level, accredited PADI facility is one of the best equipped in the country with indoor saltwater pools, classrooms, equipment and boat rental. All major courses are available, as well as a variety of trips and tours. The Family Fun Days provide a free introduction to diving for the whole family.

BSAC 406 Wanderers Dive Club

Sharjah Wanderers Sports Club Sharjah **06 566 2105**
bsac406.com
This club is a member of the British Sub Aqua Club and follows its training, certification and diving practices. Clubhouse facilities include a training room, social area, equipment room, compressors, dive gear and two dive boats. The club dives mainly shipwrecks in the Arabian Gulf, and launches boats from both Sharjah and Dubai, depending on the dive site.

Desert Sport Diving Club

Off Shk Zayed Rd Al Quoz 1 **050 454 1960**
desertsportsdivingclub.net
Map **2 C7** Metro **Noor Islamic Bank**
Dubai's only independent diving group meets on Mondays and Wednesdays at the clubhouse near Sheikh Zayed Road to plan dives. The group has two boats in Dubai and one on the east coast. A Dhs.1,650 fee entitles members to unlimited free dives on club boats. Guests pay Dhs.75 per dive.

Divers Down UAE

Iberotel Miramar Al Aqah Beach Resort Fujairah
09 237 0299
diversdown-uae.com
Offers PADI courses for all abilities, and organises a variety of diving adventures including wreck dives, wall dives, deep dives and night dives, as well as dives in the Gulf of Oman. It runs two boats, operates three dives per day, and is open seven days a week; transport can be provided. Check the website for rates and diving information.

Emirates Diving Association

Heritage & Diving Village Al Shindagha **04 393 9390**
emiratesdiving.com
Map **2 M4** Metro **Al Ghubaiba**
A non-profit organisation that seeks to protect the UAE's marine resources. It runs a coral monitoring project and annual Clean-Up Arabia campaigns. Divers are encouraged to join for Dhs.100 per year.

Freediving UAE

Abu Dhabi
freedivinguae.com
This Abu Dhabi based company teaches you how to dive deep without the aid of scuba equipment. Allowing divers to enjoy a whole new sense of freedom, freediving is rapidly gaining in popularity. Freediving UAE offers all levels of training courses.

Freestyle Divers

Royal Beach Al Faqeet Hotel & Resort Fujairah **09 244 5756**
freestyledivers.com
A quality dive centre with learning premises on Al Wasl Road as well as a dive centre at the Royal Beach Hotel in Dibba. Offers courses and certification from beginner to advanced divers and organises regular trips. The full PADI Open Water Diver course costs Dhs.2,100.

Nomad Ocean Adventures

Nr The Harbour, Al Biah Dibba **+968 26 836 069**
discovernomad.com
Dive, dhow and overnight camping trips can be tailored for individual parties. A two-dive trip with equipment starts at Dhs.450, a beginner's trial dive costs Dhs.500 and the open water course (including nine dives and certification) costs Dhs.1,800. Call Christophe on the number above or +968 98 155 906.

The Pavilion Dive Centre

Jumeirah Beach Hotel Umm Suqeim 3 **04 406 8828**
jumeirah.com
Map **1 S4** Metro **Mall of the Emirates**
This PADI Gold Palm IDC Centre is run by PADI course directors. Daily dive charters for certified divers are available in Dubai; charters to Musandam can be organised upon request from Dhs.650 with equipment. Open Water certification is Dhs.1,850.

Sandy Beach Hotel & Resort

Dibba – Khorfakkan Rd Fujairah **09 244 5555**
sandybm.com
Located in a chalet beach resort, the centre, which sells dive equipment, is open year-round. Nearby Snoopy Island, alive with hard coral and marine life, is an excellent spot for snorkelling and diving.

Scuba 2000

Al Bidiya Beach, Al Bidiyah Fujairah **09 238 8477**
scuba-2000.com
This east coast dive centre provides daily trips to Dibba and Khor Fakkan, as well as a range of courses starting at Dhs.400 for Discover Scuba and rising to Dhs.2,200 for Open Water certification.

Scubatec

Sana Bldg Al Karama **04 334 8988**
scubatecdiving.com
Metro **2 K5** Metro **Al Karama**
A five-star IDC operator, licensed by PADI and TDI, offering courses from beginner to instructor level. Dives are available in Dubai and on the east coast.

Sheesa Beach Dive Centre

Musandam Dibba **+968 26 836551**
sheesabeach.com
The perfect dive centre for those wanting to explore the amazing dive sites of Musandam – said to be amongst the world's very best. As well as its resort in Dibba, Sheesa offers all manner of diving, from kids' courses and speciality diving to PADI certification. It also offers trips on speedboats and dhows, from a few hours' duration to several days.

Dodgeball

Duplays

Indigo Icon Tower Jumeirah Lakes Towers **04 447 2394**
duplays.com
Map **1 K5** Metro **Jumeirah Lakes Towers**
Register a team for Dhs.2,700 or join as an individual for Dhs.300 and you'll be allocated to a team. The Duplays mixed recreational league welcomes experienced players as well as beginners and, if you've never played before, you'll soon learn to dip, duck, dive and dodge the soft balls thrown by other contestants.

Dragon Boat Racing

Training sessions in the ancient eastern sport of dragon boat racing are held most mornings and evenings at either Dubai Festival City or Le Meridien Mina Seyahi. It is an increasingly popular sport and there are several teams based in Dubai who regularly compete against each other as well as teams from Abu Dhabi. Most are more than happy to accept new members with little or no experience. The UAE Dragon Boat Association lists all of the country's teams: for training times and joining details, visit dubaidragonboat.com.

Dubai Dawn Patrol

The Westin Dubai Mina Seyahi Beach Resort & Marina Al Sufouh 1 **050 879 5645**
dubaidawnpatrol.org
Map **1 M4** Metro **Nakheel**
Set up in 2008, Dawn Patrol combines some serious sporting dedication with a fun, light-hearted environment and general love of the water and the outdoors. The team is both diverse and multinational. Training takes place on Tuesday and Thursday mornings (05:45 to 07:00) and Saturday evenings (16:30 to 18:00) in the Dubai Marina area; the first three sessions are free and then there's an annual membership fee of Dhs.1,000.

Dubai Diggers

Jumeirah Beach Hotel Umm Suqeim 3 **050 718 5104**
dubai-diggers.com
Map **1 S4** Metro **Mall of the Emirates**
Hailing from a wide range of nationalities and backgrounds, the Dubai Diggers is coached by Nick Hando, the founder of Australia's Bondi Diggers team. The Dubai Diggers train three times a week, and beginners can attend any session, although the sessions held from 07:30 to 09:30 on Friday mornings at Jumeirah Beach Hotel (which include some circuit training) are recommended for a first taste of the sport. Other sessions are held on Mondays and Wednesdays between 06:00 and 07:00.

Dubai Flying Dragons

Le Meridien Mina Seyahi Beach Resort & Marina Al Sufouh 1 **050 640 9017**
dubaidragonboat.com
Map **1 M4** Metro **Nakheel**
Holds training sessions at Le Meridien Mina Seyahi. Email info@dubaidragons.com for more information. Serious paddlers can try out for international dragon boat competitions.

Move One Dubai Sea Dragons

Le Meridien Mina Seyahi Beach Resort & Marina Al Sufouh 1 **050 354 9193**
dubaiseadragons.net
Map **1 M4** Metro **Nakheel**
An independent dragon boating club, affiliated with the International Dragon Boat Federation and DBA Federation. The Sea Dragons participate regularly in local and international competitions and newcomers are welcome at sessions. The one-hour training sessions take place Mondays and Wednesdays (at both 08:00 and 17:00), and Saturday mornings at 08:00, all on the beach at Mina Seyahi and costing Dhs.50 per session.

Drama Groups

Drama Dubai

Dubai Community Theatre & Arts Centre (DUCTAC) Al Barsha 1 **050 986 1761**
dramaworkshopsdubai.com
Map **1 R6** Metro **Mall of the Emirates**
This extremely active drama school runs classes for both children and adults, with a focus on the different elements and techniques of acting. School workshops in circus fighting, comedy and Shakespeare (among others) are also offered. Private tuition and corporate training can be arranged.

Dubai Drama Group

Dubai Community Theatre & Arts Centre (DUCTAC) Al Barsha 1
dubaidramagroup.com
Map **1 R6** Metro **Mall of the Emirates**
Members of this group include actors, directors, singers, dancers, and behind the scenes personnel. Four productions are staged each year, and there are workshops, socials and an internet forum. Annual membership is Dhs.100.

Manhattan Film Academy

Dubai Knowledge Village Al Sufouh 1
mfacademy.com
Map **1 N5** Metro **Dubai Internet City**
The Dubai branch of this world-famous New York film school offers workshops in screenwriting, directing and acting.

Scenez Group Productions

Dubai Media City Al Sufouh 1 **04 391 5290**
scenezgroup.com
Map **1 M5** Metro **Nakheel**
Budding acting talent between six and 16 can get involved with all kinds of theatre and backstage productions through its workshops and events, including courses on scriptwriting, costume design, acting and mime.

Environmental Groups

In recent years, the determined clamour of environmentally conscious campaigners and groups has begun to make an impact in a country where concepts like carbon-offsetting, recycling and re-using are still nascent.

In 1998, HH Sheikh Mohammed Bin Rashid Al Maktoum, Crown Prince of Dubai, established an environmental award which recognises an individual or organisation for work carried out on behalf of the environment. At an everyday level, there are increasing numbers of glass, plastic and paper recycling points around the city, mainly around shopping centres (see Going Green, p.12). However, overall, little seems to be done to persuade the average citizen to be more environmentally active, for instance by encouraging the reduction of littering.

If you want to take action, there are a couple of groups, such as Emirates Environmental Group (p.333), who always need volunteers and funds.

Dubai Natural History Group

The Emirates Academy Of Hospitality Management Umm Suqeim 3 **04 282 3952**
dnhg.org
Map **1 S5** Metro **First Gulf Bank**

Monthly meetings feature expert lectures about flora, fauna, geology, archaeology and the natural environment of the UAE. Regular trips are organised and the group maintains a library of natural history publications for members to borrow. Annual membership is Dhs.100 for couples and Dhs.50 for individuals. Contact chairman Gary Feulner (04 306 5570; grfeulner@gmail.com).

Emirates Environmental Group

Nr Dubai Zoo & Beach Centre Jumeira 1 **04 344 8622**
eeg-uae.org
Map **2 G4** Metro **Financial Centre**

A voluntary organisation devoted to the protection of the environment through education, action programmes and community involvement. Activities include evening lectures from experts and special events such as recycling collections and clean-up campaigns. Annual membership costs Dhs.200 for adults and Dhs.50 for college students.

Fencing

MK Fencing Academy

Raffles International School Umm Suqeim 3
050 794 4190
mkfencingacademy.com
Map **1 S5** Metro **First Gulf Bank**

Offers individual (Dhs.200) and group (Dhs.55) training in epée and foil for all levels. Fencers receive masks, gloves and weapons, with three fencing paths. Electrical scoring and weapons are available for advanced levels.

UAE Fencing Federation

Nr Ramada Hotel Al Mankhool **04 269 9866**
Map **2 L5** Metro **Al Fahidi**

This body organises and supervises fencing in the UAE and has affiliations with local competition organisers and the UAE national team.

Fishing

The Dubai government has introduced regulations to protect fish stocks, however you can still fish, as long as you have the right permit or you charter a licensed tour guide. The best fishing is from September to April, although it is still possible to catch sailfish and queen fish in the summer. Fish commonly caught in the region include king mackerel, tuna, trevally, bonito, kingfish, cobia and dorado. Beach or surf fishing is popular along the coast and, in season, you can even catch barracuda from the shore; the creek front in Creekside Park is a popular spot.

Alternatively, on a Friday, you can hire an abra for the morning at the Bur Dubai or Deira landing steps and ask your driver to take you to the mouth of the creek. You could also consider a deep-sea fishing trip with one of the charter companies listed. For more competitive anglers, the UAQ Marine Club (uaqmarineclub.com) sponsors a fishing competition twice a year, in April and October. Call 06 766 6644 for more details.

A good selection of fishing rods, tackle and equipment is available at Barracuda Dubai (barracudadubai.com). You can even post your catch of the day on their website.

Licence To Krill

Unless you set off with a registered fishing charter, you'll need to obtain a fishing licence from the Dubai government. There are different permits for leisure boats and offshore fishing, but both are free and can be applied for through the government portal, dm.gov.ae.

Club Joumana

Jebel Ali Golf Resort Waterfront
04 814 5555
jaresortshotels.com
Metro **Danube**

For budding fishermen, fully-equipped fishing boats carrying experienced crew and refreshments are available for charter; serious contenders can fish under IGFA rules.

Dubai Creek Golf & Yacht Club

Nr Deira City Centre, Baniyas Rd Port Saeed
04 295 6000
dubaigolf.com
Map **2 M7** Metro **Deira City Centre**

Charter the club's yacht, Sneakaway, and disappear into the Arabian Gulf to experience big game sport fishing. The 32 foot Hatteras carries up to six passengers and a Dhs.3,500 hire fee includes four hours at sea (or Dhs.4,500 for eight hours) plus tackle, bait, ice, fuel and a friendly crew.

Ocean Active
Dubai Garden Centre Al Quoz Industrial 3
050 502 2924
oceanactive.com
Map 1 S6 Metro First Gulf Bank
This experienced boat charter company offers live-aboard and daily fishing trips to various locations in the UAE and Oman; fishing charters across the Middle East are also available.

The Oceanic Hotel & Resort
Beach Rd Khor Fakkan 09 238 5111
oceanichotel.com
A fishing boat for up to five people costs Dhs.600 per hour. Hotel guests' catch of the day can be cooked by the hotel chef for a nominal fee. Non-guests take their catch home.

Soolyman Sport Fishing
Fishermen Port 2, Jumeira Beach Umm Suqeim 2
050 886 6227
soolymansportfishing.com
Map 1 T4 Metro First Gulf Bank
Operates a fleet of fishing boats captained by an experienced South African crew. Costs Dhs.2,300 for four hours, Dhs.2,800 for six hours or Dhs.3,300 for eight hours.

Xclusive Yachts Sport Fishing & Yacht Charter
Dubai Marina Yacht Club Dubai Marina 04 432 7233
xclusiveyachts.com
Map1 K5 Metro Jumeirah Lakes Towers
Two hour cruises and four hour fishing trips are available. A new 37 foot sport fishing boat operates out of the Dubai Marina Yacht Club.

Flying

Emirates Flying School
Dubai International Airport Al Garhoud
04 299 5155
emiratesaviationservices.com
Map 2 Q7 Metro Airport Terminal 1
The only approved flight training institution in Dubai offers private and commercial licences, and will convert international licences to UAE. A Private Pilot Licence course costs upwards of Dhs.48,720.

Fujairah Aviation Academy
Fujairah International Airport Fujairah 09 222 4747
fujaa.ae
Facilities include single and twin-engine aircraft, an instrument flight simulator and a repair workshop. Training is offered for private and commercial licences, instrument rating and multi-engine rating. New courses include aviation engineering and ELP test.

Jazirah Aviation Club
Dubai – Ras Al Khaimah Highway, Jazirat Al Hamra
Ras Al Khaimah 07 244 6416
jac-uae.net
Dedicated solely to microlight/ultralight flying and also offers training and pleasure flights. A Microlight Pilot's Licence course, with around 25 hours flying time, costs Dhs.500 per hour.

Micro Aviation Club
Nr Bab Al Shams, off Shk Mohammed bin Zayed Rd
Umm Al Quwain 055 212 0155
microaviation.org
Micro Aviation Club offers training courses in microlight flying, paragliding and paramotoring. Courses start from Dhs.3,500, with an annual registration fee of Dhs.250.

Football
Football (or soccer) is much-loved here in the UAE, with both impromptu kickabouts in parks and more organised team practice and matches taking place regularly. InSportz (insportzclub.com) in Al Quoz has five indoor five-a-side pitches, and some universities and schools will rent out their outdoor and five-a-side pitches. See Gyms & Fitness Clubs, p.210, for more details. If you'd rather watch than play, the UAE league has regular fixtures in Dubai. See Spectator Sports, p.272. Gaelic Football fans should contact Dubai Celts GAA – details can be found in Gaelic Games on p.338. For American Football, see p.320.

Dubai Amateur Football League
Various locations
dubaifootball.com
The 'Expat League' hosts two divisions of 12 teams. It runs an 11-a-side league and cup games between September and April at various locations, and seven-a-side games during the summer.

Dubai Football Academy
Various locations 04 282 4540
esportsdubai.com
Provides comprehensive football training to youngsters at various locations. Players are encouraged to join one of the teams competing in the Dubai Junior Football League. A 15 week course costs Dhs.1,400 for one session a week or Dhs.2,500 for two sessions a week.

Dubai Irish Football Club
Various locations 050 465 1087
dubaiirish.leaguerepublic.com
Dubai Irish consists of players of all nationalities and participates in the Dubai Amateur Football League. Despite competing in the more competitive division one, the team welcomes players of all skill levels.

Dubai Schools Football League

Various locations **04 296 6804**
dubaischoolsleague.com
This is the umbrella organisation that oversees league football – for both girls and boys – in Dubai. Children wishing to participate in school league football should do so through their schools themselves, but questions about league set-up, results and fixtures can usually be answered here.

Dubai Women's Football Association

Jebel Ali International Shooting Club & Centre Of Excellence Waterfront **050 659 8767**
dubaiwfa.com
Metro **Danube**
Features 15 women's teams that compete across two divisions. Players train once a week, and then play weekly matches.

Duplays

Indigo Icon Tower Jumeirah Lakes Towers
04 447 2394
duplays.com
Map **1 K5** Metro **Jumeirah Lakes Towers**
Duplays runs competitive and recreational five-a-side indoor and seven-a-side outdoor leagues, and has recently added a women's five-a-side league as well as the Mighty Eagles, an outdoor flag football league.

International Football Academy

IFA Sport, Shk Noora Bldg Tecom **04 454 1683**
ifasport.com
Map **1 N6** Metro **Dubai Internet City**
Offers training for four to 16 year olds from internationally qualified coaches. Provides tailored coaching to schools, as well as existing teams.

Socatots > *p.318*

Bradenton Preparatory Academy Dubai Sports City
04 425 1111
footballacademydubai.com
Map **2 M12** Metro **Jebel Ali**
This is a fun, musical, soccer-specific play programme for toddlers from walking age to five years. It covers various aspects of physical, mental and social development, and involves active parent participation. Sessions, held from Thursdays to Saturdays, also take place at Emirates International School.

Soccer Circus Dubai

Mirdif City Centre Mirdif **800 586**
soccercircusme.com
Map **2 P12** Metro **Rashidiya**
Interactive football attraction in Playnation Mirdif City Centre, which offers visitors a series of challenges aimed at improving skills. A big hit with families and groups of youths, it's a great choice for a boys' birthday party. If the Training Academy and Powerplay simulated stadium experience whet the appetite, there's a huge indoor multisports pitch that can be hired for matches.

UAE English Soccer School Of Excellence

Various locations **050 476 4877**
soccerkidsdubai.com
Soccer Kids Dubai offers soccer training in a number of locations across Dubai for ages three to 16 years. Soccer camps during the school holidays and kids' parties are also available. Call James on 050 476 4877.

Gaelic Games

Dubai Celts GAA

Various locations **055 660 8357**
dubaicelts.com
Dubai Celts GAA holds games and organises training in men's and ladies' Gaelic football, hurling and camogie. In addition to the monthly matches played within the UAE, international tournaments are held in Bahrain (November) and Dubai (March) each year. Training sessions are held every Monday and Wednesday at 19:00.

Gardening

Dubai Gardening Group

Villa 97, Street 16D Jumeira 1 **04 344 5999**
Map **2 D5** Metro **World Trade Centre**
This group shares its communal gardening know-how in a friendly and informal atmosphere, with seminars and practical demonstrations from experts, trips to garden nurseries and members' gardens also arranged. If you want advice on how to improve your gardening skills, or just want to mingle with other green fingered Dubaians and chat plants, then this group is for you. For more information on Gardening, see p.108.

Golf

With stars like Nick Faldo, Colin Montgomerie, Ernie Els and Ian Baker-Finch all lending their star-power to Dubai's greens through their successful design collaborations, it is little surprise that the popularity of the city as a world-class golf destination has now been cemented. The arrival of several of the game's biggest events hasn't hurt either though. Emirates Golf Club hosts the annual Dubai Desert Classic tournament, and the DP World Tour Championship is hosted by Jumeirah Golf Estates. For amateur enthusiasts, there are local monthly tournaments and annual competitions open to all, such as the Emirates Mixed Amateur Open, the Emirates Ladies' Amateur Open (handicap of 21 or less), and the Emirates Men's Amateur Open (handicap of five or less).

To get your official handicap in the UAE, you will need to register with the Emirates Golf Federation and submit three score cards. You will then be issued with a member card and handicap card enabling you to enter competitions.

Dubai Golf operates a central reservation system for those wishing to book a round of golf on any of the major courses in the emirate. For further information visit dubaigolf.com or email golfbooking@dubaigolf.com. Don't leave it until the actual day you want to play or you may struggle to get a tee time.

If you don't want to join a golf club – the fees are pretty steep – it might be an idea to join an amateur golf society (like the Kegs who play at the Emirates Golf Club every Tuesday evening; dubaigolf.com), or start one yourself with fellow players, as large groups can often get concessionary rates.

Al Badia Golf Club By InterContinental Dubai Festival City

Dubai Festival City **04 601 0111**
albadiagolfclub.ae
Map **2 M10** Metro **Emirates**

This Robert Trent Jones-designed course features a plush club house, 11 lakes and eco-friendly salt-tolerant grass, meaning the 7,303 yard, par 72 championship course can be irrigated with sea water.

Al Hamra Golf Club

Al Hamra Village Ras Al Khaimah **07 244 7474**
alhamragolf.com

Although it's a bit of a drive, Al Hamra Golf Club offers a break from the city courses and their higher prices. Its 7,325 yard, par 72 links course surrounds a huge lagoon and features several interconnected lakes.

Arabian Ranches Golf Club

Arabian Ranches Golf Club Arabian Ranches
04 366 3000
arabianranchesgolfdubai.com
Map **1 Q13**

Designed by Ian Baker-Finch and Nicklaus Design, this par 72 grass course incorporates natural desert terrain and features indigenous plants. Facilities include an academy with a floodlit range, an extensive short game practice area, GPS on golf carts and a pleasant clubhouse housing the Ranches restaurant (p.529).

Dubai Creek Golf & Yacht Club

Nr Deira City Centre, Baniyas Rd Port Saeed
04 295 6000
dubaigolf.com
Map **2 M7** Metro **Deira City Centre**

Dubai Creek Golf & Yacht Club offers one of the most scenic 18 hole championship courses in Dubai, located in the heart of the city to boot. Peak winter rates are Dhs.795 for an 18 hole round, but nine hole rounds and off-peak rates are also available and there's also a par 3 (Adults: Dhs.80; members and juniors: AED 60). For bookings, call 04 380 1234 or email golfbooking@dubaigolf.com.

The Els Club > *p.318*

Shk Mohammed bin Zayed Rd Dubai Sports City
04 425 1010 elsclubdubai.com
Map **1 L11**

The 7,538 yard, par 72 signature course was designed by Ernie Els and includes a Butch Harmon School of Golf for players of all ages and skills, and a Mediterranean club house, managed by Troon Golf.

Emirates Golf Club

Off Shk Zayed Rd Emirates Living **04 380 1919**
dubaigolf.com
Map **1 M5** Metro **Nakheel**

Host of the European Tour Omega Dubai Desert Classic and Omega Dubai Ladies Masters, this was the first all-grass championship golf course in the Middle East when it opened in 1988. The club still has two of the city's best courses. Peak winter rates – including green fees, cart hire and range balls – are Dhs.995 for a round on the Majlis course and Dhs.695 on the Faldo course; look-out for off-peak or night golf reductions. For bookings, call 04 380 1234 or email golfbooking@dubaigolf.com.

Emirates Golf Federation

Dubai Creek Golf & Yacht Club Port Saeed **04 295 2277**
ugagolf.com
Map **2 M7** Metro **Deira City Centre**

Affiliated to R&A (golf's rulemaking body) and the International Golf Federation, this non-profit organisation is the governing body for amateur golf in the UAE. It supports junior players, develops the national team and issues official handicap cards. It also has a hole-in-one club where golfers can record their glorious moments. The affiliate membership rate is Dhs.200 for a quarter. The EGF office is open between 09:00 and 17:00 on Sunday through to Thursday. It is closed on Fridays, Saturdays and public holidays.

Jebel Ali Golf Resort
Nr Palm Jebel Ali Waterfront **04 814 5555**
jaresortshotels.com
Metro **Danube**

This nine hole, par 36 course has peacocks to keep golfers company and Gulf views to distract them. It hosts the Jebel Ali Golf Resort & Spa Challenge, the curtain raiser to the Omega Dubai Desert Classic (p.25) and, for family members who take their golf a little less seriously, there's now a mini golf course (p.346).

Jumeirah Golf Estates
Off Shk Mohammed bin Zayed Rd Dubai
04 375 9999 jumeirahgolfestates.com
Map **1 J11** Metro **Nakheel**

Dubai's newest golf course and home to the DP World Tour Championship (p.28). The golf club has four themed courses, Earth, Fire, Wind and Water, although only Fire and Earth are currently open for play. Both designed by Greg Norman, the Fire course features desert terrain and greens, with red sand bunkers; Earth is reminiscent of European parklands. Annual membership packages offer access to both courses.

Montgomerie Golf Club
The Address Montgomerie Dubai Emirates Living
04 390 5600
themontgomerie.com
Map **1 L7** Metro **Nakheel**

Set on 265 acres of land, the 18 hole, par 72 course has some unique characteristics, including the mammoth 656 yard 18th hole. Facilities include a driving range, putting greens and a swing analysis studio, while the clubhouse is managed by The Address and boasts guest rooms, an Angsana spa (04 390 5600), and various F&B outlets including Nineteen (p.524).

Sharjah Golf & Shooting Club
Nr Tasjeel Auto Village Sharjah
06 548 7777
golfandshootingshj.com

The club sponsors a junior development programme for youngsters interested in improving their game, and floodlights have been added for night play. Members pay Dhs.175 for 18 holes including kart at off peak times, Dhs.125 for nine holes. This is a popular option for Dubai residents who are not club members and want a more affordable 18 holes. Competitions are also held here.

The Track Meydan Golf
Meydan **04 381 3733**
meydangolf.com
Map **2 E10**

Located at the world famous Dubai racecourse, this 'pay-and-play' golf course can be played as nine or 18 holes. Designed by Peter Harradine the course works its way between a series of natural lakes, and will challenge golfers of all skill levels. Great for the casual golfer, there's no membership fee and you simply book a tee time to play. Tuition packages and one-off lessons are also available.

Gymnastics

Whether you're looking for professional coaching, something to keep the kids active or to just try out a new activity, there are gymnast facilities and training for all. For baby and toddler gymnastics, see Activities for Kids p.141.

Dubai Olympic Gymnastics Club
Nr Jumeira Post Office, Off Al Wasl Rd Al Wasl
050 765 1515
Map **2 E5** Metro **Business Bay**

Run by UK gymnastics champion Dean Johnstone, the club offers courses for gymnasts of all levels. Geared specifically towards children, classes correspond with school terms.

DuGym Gymnastics Club
Various locations **050 553 6283**
dugym.com

Gymnastics and trampoline coaching for children of all abilities. DuGym runs gym tots lessons, as well as club competitions throughout the year. Operates at locations including the GEMS World Academy, Jumeirah English Speaking School and Emirates International School. Classes held from Sunday to Thursday. Contact Suzanne for more info.

GymnastEx
Prism Tower Business Bay **04 445 8244**
gymnast-ex.com
Map **2 E6** Metro **Business Bay**

Budding gymnasts can sign up for something different with the GymnastEx combo classes, which combine three different disciplines in one session: rhythmic, arobatics and sports aerobics. Coaching in martial arts for boys and yoga for parents, is also available, as well as classes in baby and educational gymnastics.

Hashing

Billed as 'drinking clubs with a running problem', Hash House Harriers is a global network of clubs with an emphasis on taking part and socialising afterwards, rather than serious running. A fun way to get fit and meet people.

Creek Hash House Harriers
Various locations **050 451 5847**
creekhash.net
This group meets every Tuesday, and runs last for around 45 minutes.

Desert Hash House Harriers
Various locations **050 398 1584**
deserthash.org
This group runs every Sunday, meeting an hour before sunset. The fee is Dhs.50 including refreshments.

Hiking
If you've always wanted to get into hiking but are a little daunted by the prospect of setting out into the wild on your own, then going on an organised hike is the best way to introduce yourself to the UAE's great outdoors. It can be easy to live in Dubai and rarely walk anywhere so even the most gentle of hikes can be good for the heart. For more information on hiking see p.270.

Absolute Adventure
Al Diyafah Centre Al Bada'a **04 345 9900**
adventure.ae
Map **2 J3** Metro **World Trade Centre**
This adventure tour operator offers a range of treks, varying in difficulty, including extreme trekking at Jebel Qihwi and an eight-hour coastal village trek.

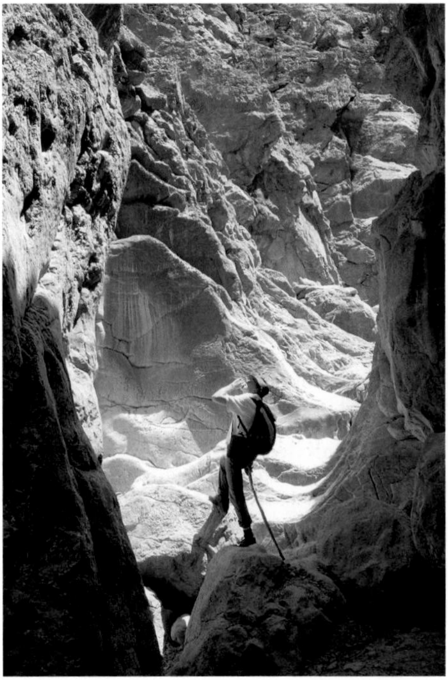

The activity centre, located directly on Dibba's beach, can accommodate 14 people for group stays with a barbecue on the beach. Also organises treks for serious hikers to far flung places like Nepal. Check the website for details of upcoming trips.

Arabia Outdoors
Various locations **055 955 6209**
arabiaoutdoors.com
Organises individual, group and corporate hikes along routes such as Jebel Qihwi, Jebel Hafeet and Stairway To Heaven. Also offers camping, climbing and kayaking, and runs team building camps and events.

Desert Rangers
Nr American Hospital, 18th Street Oud Metha
04 357 2200
desertrangers.com
Map **2 L6** Metro **Oud Metha**
Offers hikes for individuals and groups of up to 100 people by dividing them into smaller teams and taking different trails to the summit. A variety of routes are offered according to age and fitness. Locations include Fujairah, Dibba, Masafi, Ras Al Khaimah and Al Ain, with prices starting at Dhs.275 per person.

Hockey

Dubai Hockey Club
Nr Cricket Stadium & ICC HQ
Dubai Sports City **055 917 0622**
dubaihockeyclub.com
Map **1 L10** Metro **Dubai Internet City**
Club training sessions take place every Sunday and Wednesday evening. All abilities are welcome and both men and women can join. The club plays in local tournaments on grass and takes part in friendly games. International tours to locations such as Singapore, Hong Kong and the UK are organised fairly regularly.

Sharjah Wanderers Racket & Hockey Club
Sharjah Wanderers Sports Club Sharjah
06 566 2105
sharjahwanderers.com
The club's hockey section was the first mixed team in the Gulf. The approach at the club is to play sport within a friendly, but competitive, environment.

Horse Riding
Horse riding is a national sport in the UAE and there are a number of excellent stables and equestrian clubs in Dubai. While keeping your own horse comes at huge expense, you may find that horse riding lessons cost less here than in your home country. That said, many of the equestrian clubs are so in demand that they have waiting lists for lessons. There are a few

places, such as The Desert Palm Riding School where you can take your kids for a horse ride – they will be trotted around the track for 10 minutes or so.

If you are a dressage rider and would like to get involved in shows in the UAE you can contact some of the stables, such as Godolphin (godolphin.com), the Abu Dhabi Equestrian Club (emiratesracing.com), or Al Zobair Stud Farm in Sharjah (alzobairstud.com).

Horse racing in Dubai is extremely popular, with most races, including the Dubai World Cup (p.26, the richest horse race in the world, taking place at the impressive Meydan racetrack.

Al Ahli Horse Riding Club

Nr Al Mulla Plaza & Lulu Hypermarket Al Qusais 1
04 298 8408
alahliclub.info
Map **2 R7** Metro **Stadium**

A well-established club offering a wide selection of horse associated activities throughout the year, including bare back lessons, dressage and jumping. There's also special pony clubs and horseman ship clubs for younger riders aged 4 and up, as well as arts and craft groups and mother and baby groups.

Al Jiyad Stables

Nr Bab Al Shams Desert Resort & Spa Bawadi
050 599 5866

Offers lessons for riders of all levels of experience, as well as organising individual or group desert hacks. The excellent stables are home to more than 60 different horses.

Al Sahra Desert Resort Equestrian Centre

Al Sahra Desert Resort Dubailand **056 177 2856**
jebelali-international.com

Ideally set in the Dubai desert, this eco-tourism resort offers horse riding, individual and group horse riding lessons, as well as private livery for a limited number of horses.

The Desert Equestrian Club

Various locations **050 309 9770**

If you've got your own horse, the Desert Equestrian Club offers livery services for Dhs.1,500 a month, while accomplished riders can pay Dhs.100 to use one of the stable's horses. Private lessons are Dhs.80 for adults and Dhs.50 for children under 16.

The Desert Palm Riding School

Desert Palm Dubai Warsan 2 **050 451 7773**
desertpalm.ae

This state-of-the-art riding school offers classes for all ages, in group, semi-private or one-to-one sessions. Prices are Dhs.95 per 30 minutes for child beginners and Dhs.175 per hour for adults, including all equipment.

Dubai Polo & Equestrian Club

Nr Arabian Ranches, Al Qudra Rd Dubai Studio City
04 361 8111
poloclubdubai.com
Map **1 N13** Metro **Dubai Internet City**

This top-notch facility features a sandplast arena (sandplast is one of the best surfaces to ride on), a riding school and a polo club. Horse riding lessons are available for all abilities; beginners' courses start at Dhs.1,400 for 10 lessons. If you don't fancy taking lessons, you can always enjoy a picnic pitchside during chukkas, held every weekend during the winter. You can pack your own sandwiches or order bespoke picnics through the website.

Emirates Equestrian Centre

Nr Bab Al Shams Desert Resort & Spa Bawadi
050 553 7986
emiratesequestriancentre.com

This centre is home to more than 80 horses and facilities include an international size floodlit arena, a riding school, and dressage and lunging rings. It can cater for very small children and hosts regular competitions, gymkhanas and shows. The centre also has regular clinics and stable management courses.

Hoofbeatz

Dubai Polo & Equestrian Club Dubai Studio City
050 181 0401
hoofbeatz.com
Map **1 N13** Metro **Dubai Internet City**

The Hoofbeatz Horsemanship Club runs every Friday and Saturday afternoon, from 4pm-6pm, for beginner and novice horse lovers aged five to 18 years. The centre also runs an all-round horsemanship course covering stable management and horse care skills.

Jebel Ali Equestrian Club

Nr Jebel Ali Hospital & Ibn Battuta Mall Jebel Ali Village **04 884 5101**
Map **1 F5** Metro **Ibn Battuta**

Qualified instructors teach all levels of dressage, jumping, gymkhana games and hacking. Newcomers can try a one-day lesson, after which a 10 lesson package costs Dhs.800 for children and Dhs.1,000 for adults, plus a Dhs.120 annual registration fee.

Jebel Ali Golf Resort

Nr Palm Jebel Ali Waterfront **04 814 5555**
jaresortshotels.com
Metro **Danube**

The riding centre has nine horses and air-conditioned stables. Instructors give private lessons from Tuesday to Sunday, while experienced riders can tackle one-hour desert rides. 30 minute lessons cost Dhs.200 (private) and Dhs.150 (semi-private).

Riding For The Disabled Association Of Dubai

Desert Palm Dubai Warsan 2
rdad.ae
A charity that uses horse riding and hippotherapy (physical and speech therapy using the movement of a horse) to attain a variety of therapeutic goals for those suffering from autism, cerebral palsy, Down Syndrome, spina bifida and learning disabilities. The aim is to improve poise, posture, strength and flexibility while boosting confidence. Classes usually last around 45 minutes.

Sharjah Equestrian & Racing Club

Interchange 6, Al Dhaid Rd, Al Atain Sharjah **06 531 1188**
serc.ae
Facilities at this equine training centre include a floodlit sand arena and paddock, a grass show jumping arena, hacking trails into the desert and a training centre. During the hot summer all riders can train inside the big indoor air conditioned arena. Group lessons start at Dhs.120 for 50 minutes, with five classes costing Dhs.400.

Ice Hockey

Ice hockey has been a fixture on the local sports scene ever since Al Nasr Leisureland opened in 1979. With the opening of Dubai Ice Rink, teams now have two venues in Dubai to play at. The Skate Shop next to the ice rink at The Dubai Mall stocks hockey kit including skates, sticks, body armour, jerseys and helmets in both children's and adult sizes. Call Dubai Ice Rink for stock details (04 448 5111).

Dubai Mighty Camels Ice Hockey Club

Al Nasr Leisureland Oud Metha **04 337 1234**
dubaimightycamels.com
Map **2 L6** Metro **Oud Metha**
This amateur ice hockey league has more than 120 adult members and participates in the Emirates Hockey League (EHL). It organises regular social get-togethers run from September to May. The club also hosts an annual tournament in April, which attracts up to 20 teams from the Gulf, Europe and the Far East.

Dubai Sandstorms Ice Hockey Club

Al Nasr Leisureland Oud Metha **050 775 8713**
eteamz.com/dubaisandstorm
Map **2 L6** Metro **Oud Metha**
Practice sessions are held twice a week for youngsters aged four to 18. The emphasis is on teamwork and sportsmanship. Matches are played against teams from Dubai, Abu Dhabi, Al Ain Oman and Qatar. The Sandstorms website has a noticeboard for buying and selling ice hockey equipment.

Ice Skating

Al Nasr Leisureland

Nr American Hospital Oud Metha **04 337 1234**
alnasrll.com
Map **2 L6** Metro **Oud Metha**
This Olympic-size rink is part of a large leisure complex that also includes a bowling alley, squash and tennis courts, arcade games and shops. Entry is Dhs.10 for adults and Dhs.5 for children under 10, with skate hire at Dhs.20 per two hours. There is an ice skating school, teaching all ages, and ice shows are regularly performed for the public. Call in advance to check the session times, as the rink is sometimes closed for practice sessions.

Dubai Ice Rink

The Dubai Mall Downtown Dubai **04 448 5111**
dubaiicerink.com
Map **2 F6** Metro **Burj Khalifa/Dubai Mall**
The largest and newest rink in the UAE, this Olympic-size arena has daily public skating sessions, disco nights and special events. There are also daily group and private lessons.

Galleria Ice Rink

The Galleria Residence Corniche, Deira **04 209 6000**
dubai.regency.hyatt.com
Map **2 N4** Metro **Palm Deira**
Public skating costs Dhs.35 per person (including skate hire). Membership rates start at Dhs.400 per month, or Dhs.2,075 per year, with unlimited skating. Lessons are available and start at Dhs.200 for members and Dhs.300 for non-members for five 15 minute classes.Other packages include professional figure skating coaching, birthday celebrations,and disco nights.

Hili Fun City > *p.297*

Off Emirates St Al Ain **03 784 5542**
hilifuncity.ae
One of Al Ain's most popular leisure attractions, the large ice rink makes up part of Hili Fun City and, like much of the theme park, it is currently being redeveloped by TDIC. However, it remains open to the public for skating, while it is also the venue for Vipers and Thebes ice hockey matches.

Queen Of Ice World

Plaza Bldg, Nr Al Nasr Leisureland Oud Metha **04 358 4778**
queenoficeworld.org
Map **2 L6** Metro **Oud Metha**
The biggest supplier of skating equipment and clothing in the Middle East, Queen Of Ice World also runs a school out of the rinks at Al Nasr Leisureland and The Dubai Mall, teaching everyone from toddlers

getting on the ice for the first time to experienced skaters looking to jump, spiral and dance. Also organises a popular summer skate programme.

Jetskiing

Due to complaints of noise pollution and safety issues concerning swimmers, the Dubai Maritime City Authority has introduced licences and regulations for jetskiing. You must now obtain a licence through DMCA (dmca.ae) and are only allowed to jetski within restricted areas between sunrise and sunset. If you do go jetskiing, it may be worth checking that your medical insurance covers you. You may also want to consider whether you have any personal liability insurance in case you injure a third party.

Karting

Dubai Autodrome > *p.347*

Shk Mohammed bin Zayed Rd Dubai MotorCity
04 367 8700
dubaiautodrome.com
Map **1 N11**

The autodrome has a 500 metre indoor circuit as well as a 1.2km outdoor track which has a challenging 17 corners. After a safety briefing. you take to your 390cc kart (there are 120cc karts for kids over seven years) and hit the tarmac. There are timed races for the International Leisure Ranking, plus the Dubai Autodrome Championship for more serious racers. Races are Dhs.100 (indoor track) or Dhs.110 (outdoor track), including kart and clothing, and they last 15 minutes. Those with their own karts can use the track at certain times.

Blokarting

Get involved with the latest extreme sports craze in Dubai. Blokarting, or landsailing, takes the principles of windsurfing and applies them on land – or to a buggy on land, to be specific. A Blokarting experience for two costs Dhs.550 through Dreamdays (dreamdays.ae) and once you've got the bug, join Duplays' blokart racing league at Jumeirah Beach Park. Find out more at duplays.com.

Emirates Kart Centre

Nr Jebel Ali Golf Resort & Spa Waterfront
04 282 7111
emsf.ae
Metro **Danube**

Operated by Emirates Motor Sports Federation, the floodlit track has straights, hairpins and chicanes. Professional and junior karts are available for Dhs.100 per half hour and the centre is open 15:00-22:00 daily.

Kitesurfing

Kitesurfing is an extreme sport that fuses elements of windsurfing, wakeboarding and kite flying. You may see kitesurfers showing off along several of Dubai's beaches, but the Kite Beach in Umm Suqeim (behind Sunset Mall, between the Dubai Offshore Sailing Club and Jumeirah Beach Park) is the only place where kiting is officially permitted; Dubai Municipality has eased up restrictions, dropping the requirement for kiters to hold a licence.

Dubai Kite Forum (dubaikiteforum.com) is a good place to find out the latest on regulations. Kite People (kitepeople.ae) and Kitesurfing in Dubai (dubaikiters.com) are good online resources for buying equipment and locating IKO instructors.

Dubai Kitefly Club

Kite Beach, Off Jumeira Rd Umm Suqeim 1
050 254 7440
kitesurf.ae
Map **1 T4** Metro **Noor Islamic Bank**

The Kitefly Club offers lessons in kitesurfing to groups, starting at Dhs.190 per person, while private tuition is also available from Dhs.300 per hour. Both include all the equipment.

Dubai Kitesurf School

Kite Beach Umm Suqeim 1 **050 496 5107**
dubaikitesurfschool.com
Map **1 T4** Metro **Noor Islamic Bank**

Adventure sports enthusiasts can master how to handle the power of the kite with hands-on training from qualified IKO instructors. Complete the kite school course to receive an IKO-kiteboarding pass, which allows you to rent equipment in the UAE and abroad. Private lessons cost Dhs.300 per hour, and you can rent equipment from Dhs.350 per hour.

Duco Maritime
Various locations **050 870 3427**
ducomaritime.com
Classes are available every day by request on beaches in Dubai, RAK and Abu Dhabi. Two-hour lessons by IKO qualified instructors are available for beginners, charged at Dhs.300 per hour including equipment. Stand up paddleboarding lessons also available.

Kitesurfinguae.com
Various locations **050 456 5951**
kitesurfinguae.com
A number of private International Kiteboarding Organisation certified instructors are available for kiteboarding lessons. An hour's instruction including equipment costs Dhs.300.

Martial Arts
Aspiring Bruce Lees and Jacky Chans are well catered for with many centres offering courses in judo, aikido, karate, kickboxing and other martial arts. In addition, many fitness clubs and gyms offer Thai boxing, kung fu, self-defence and other martial arts alongside their group exercise programmes. For kids, the Active Sports Academy (p.142) has an excellent range of disciplines for all ages and runs after-school classes as well as holiday camps.

Colosseum Muay Thai Health & Fitness Club
Montana Centre Bldg, Zaabeel Rd Al Karama **04 337 2755**
colosseumuae.com
Map **2 L6** Metro **Oud Metha**
Classes are held daily from 20:30 to 22:00, except for Fridays (Dhs.50). Personal training is available for those over eight years old. Colosseum organises competitions between clubs in the area.

Dubai Karate Centre
Al Raizi Boys School Training Hall Al Safa 1 **04 344 7797**
dubaikarate.com
Map **2 C5** Metro **Business Bay**
This club is a member of the Japanese Karate Association (JKA) and has a team of black belt, JKA qualified instructors who teach a range of martial arts that include shotokan karate, taekwondo, aikido, Muay Thai, judo, kudo, iado, laido and wingtzun. This centre also runs regular courses in self defence. Registration is Dhs.100 with monthly membership from Dhs.380.

Dubai Kendo Club
Various locations **04 348 9804**
dubaikendo.com
The focus here is on a martial art based on the ancient Japanese swordsmanship traditions. The club meets on Wednesdays at 19:45 and on Saturdays at 16:00 at Emirates International School Jumeirah. The two-hour classes cost Dhs.50 for adults, Dhs.30 for children.

EBMAS School Of Self Defence
Dubai Community Theatre & Arts Centre (DUCTAC) Al Barsha 1 **055 605 8128**
ebmas-selfdefense.com
Map **1 R6** Metro **Mall of the Emirates**
Emin Boztepe Martial Arts System (EBMAS) is a popular form of self-defence which is now taught in more than 40 countries around the world; this school teaches both armed and unarmed forms of EBMAS. Classes are held on Sundays and Wednesdays from 20:30 to 21:45.

Golden Falcon Karate Centre
Nr Choithrams Al Karama **04 336 0243**
goldenfalconkarate.com
Map **2 K6** Metro **Al Karama**
Established in 1990, the centre is affiliated with the International Karate Budokan and the UAE Judo, Taekwondo & Karate Federation. The centre is open throughout the week and students can choose class times to suit their schedules. Training costs Dhs.150 for two classes per week, and sessions are held at other locations across Dubai including Jebel Ali, Meadows, Oud Metha and JLT.

Golden Fist Karate Club
Al Riffa Plaza, Nr Ramada R/A Al Raffa **04 355 1029**
goldenfistkarate.net
Map **2 L5** Metro **Al Fahidi**
This club is popular for the flexible times it provides for training in martial arts including karate and kung fu. If you're in a hurry, a nine-month black belt crash course is available too. Two and six classes a week, from Dhs.150 to Dhs.320 per month (plus a Dhs.50 admission fee). Yoga, swimming and aerobics classes are also offered.

Raifet N Shawe
The Boulevard At Jumeirah Emirates Towers Trade Centre 2 **050 495 4446**
Map **2 H6** Metro **Emirates Towers**
A black belt teacher in karate, kickboxing, judo and Muay Thai who holds classes at Emirates Towers (04 319 8660) on Mondays, Wednesdays and Saturdays from 17:30 to 18:30.

Taekwondo
The Ballet Centre Jumeira 1 **04 344 9776**
balletcentre.com
Map **2 H4** Metro **Emirates Towers**
This martial art teaches mental strength and self-control. Adult classes are held on Tuesdays at 19:00 and cost Dhs.40.

Zanshinkan Aikido Club Dubai

Al Raizi Boys School, Nr Al Safa Park Al Safa 1
050 795 2716
aikido.ae
Map **2 C5** Metro **Business Bay**
Classes for both children and adults are held throughout the week at the Dubai Karate Centre. Lifetime registration costs Dhs.100; kids' classes are Dhs.350 for eight classes a month and adult training costs Dhs.500 for 12 sessions a month.

Mini Golf

Hyatt Regency Dubai Golf Park

Hyatt Regency Dubai Corniche Deira **04 209 6747**
dubai.regency.hyatt.com
Map **2 N4** Metro **Palm Deira**
Bring your own clubs and golf balls for the nine-hole pitch and putt grass course (Dhs.30 for one round) or rent it all at the 18 hole crazy golf course (Dhs.15 per person). No membership required.

Jebel Ali Golf Resort

Nr Palm Jebel Ali Waterfront **04 814 5555**
jaresortshotels.com
Metro **Danube**
The latest mini golf course on the scene is at Jebel Ali Golf Resort. The 18 holer features plenty of tricks and traps, including one particularly challenging loop the loop hole. Dhs.20 per person.

Motocross

Dubai Motocross Club (DMX)

Nr Jebel Ali Go Kart Track Waterfront **050 452 6489**
dubaimotocross.com
Metro **Danube**
Dubai Motocross (DMX) runs classes for cadets, juniors, 65cc, 85cc, 125cc and adults. The facility features two tracks, one for juniors and one for seniors, and organises eight championship events per year. The entry fee is Dhs.150 for members and starts at Dhs.250 for non-members.

Motorcycling

Automobile & Touring Club Of The UAE

Nr Century Mall, Al Wuheida St Hor Al Anz East
04 296 1122
atcuae.ae
Map **2 R5** Metro **Al Qiyadah**
The club is the UAE's FIM representative. Regular motocross and off-road enduros are held between September and April, and activity centres at the DMX Club and in Umm Al Quwain host quad and drag races. It organises the Abu Dhabi Desert Challenge, and the opening round of the FIA Cross Country Rally.

Harley Owners Group (HOG) Dubai

Various locations **04 339 1909**
hoguae.com
Meet at various locations for rides across the region, including the Middle East HOG Rally in Fujairah.

Royal Enfield Dubai

Warehouse 4, Dubai Islamic Bank Bldg, Nr Times Square Al Quoz Industrial 1 **04 340 1855**
royalenfieldduae.com
Map **1 U6** Metro **Noor Islamic Bank**
The social club organises city rides, long-distance trips and informal gatherings, as well as an annual gala. Although the club is named Royal Enfield Dubai, riders of any bikes are welcome.

Motorsports

Dubai Autodrome > *p.347*

Shk Mohd bin Zayed Rd Dubai MotorCity
04 367 8700
dubaiautodrome.com
Map **1 N11**
Dubai's motorsport home has six different track configurations, including a 5.39km FIA-sanctioned GP circuit, state-of-the-art pit facilities and a 7,000 seat grandstand. The venue hosts events including rounds of the FIA GT Championship.

Emirates Motor Sports Federation

Villa 1, Nr Aviation Club, Casablanca Rd Al Garhoud
04 282 7111
emsf.ae
Map **2 M8** Metro **GGICO**
Emirates Motor Sports Federation organises events throughout the year, such as the 4WD 1000 Dunes Rally, the Champions Rally for saloon cars, road safety campaigns and classic car exhibitions. Membership including competition licence is Dhs.500 per year; non-members can race for a fee.

Yas Marina Circuit

Abu Dhabi **02 659 9800**
yasmarinacircuit.com
While most famous as the home of the annual F1 event (p.28), Yas Marina Circuit is a year-round venue for petrolheads. The possibilities include karting and drag racing, as well as a whole host of other options from supercar driving to passenger experiences.

Mountain Biking

Away from the cities, the UAE has a lot to offer outdoor enthusiasts, especially mountain bikers. On a mountain bike it's possible to see the most remote and untouched places that are not even accessible in 4WDs. For hardcore, experienced bikers there is some good terrain, from super-technical rocky trails

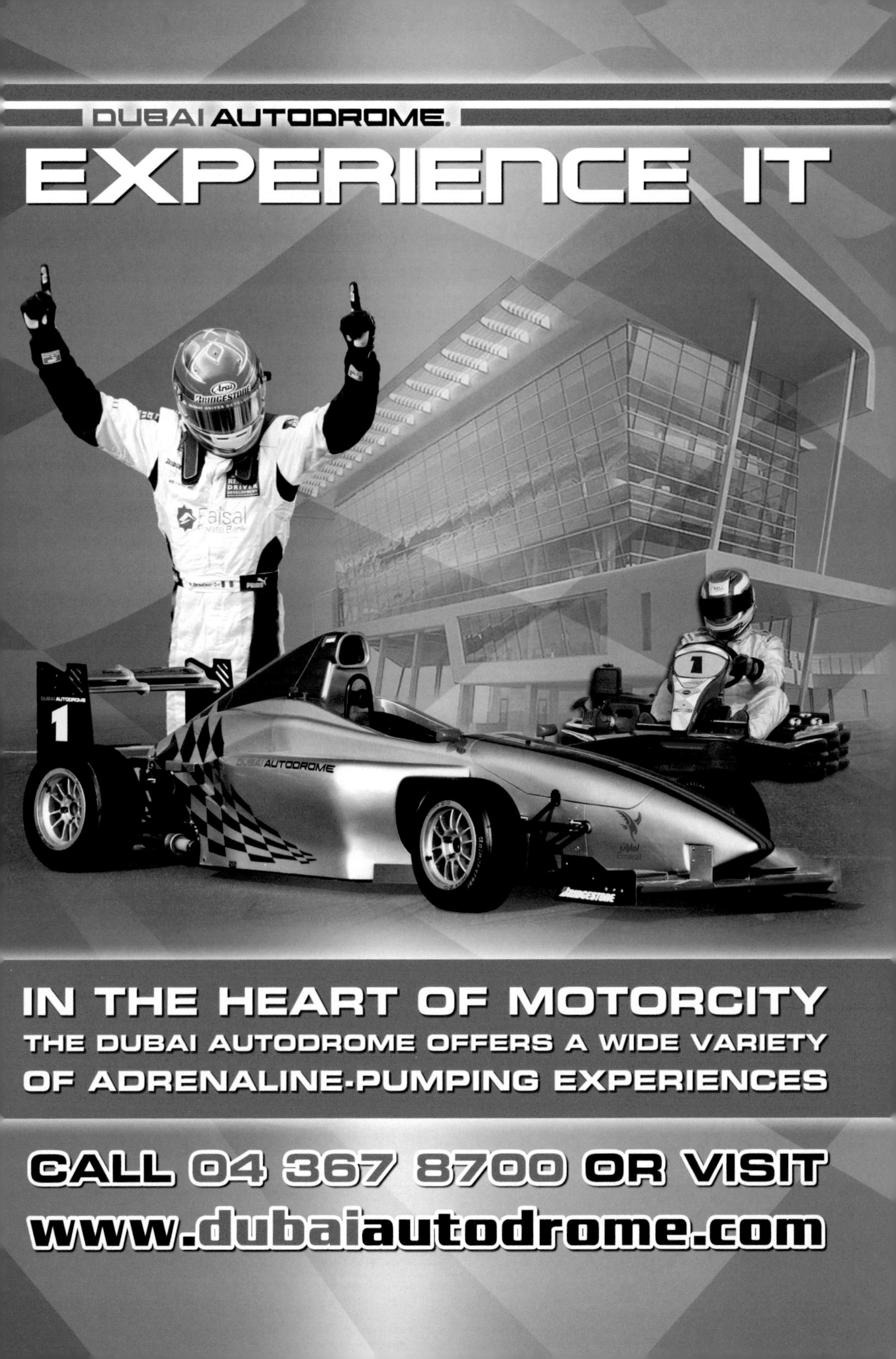
DUBAI AUTODROME
EXPERIENCE IT
IN THE HEART OF MOTORCITY
THE DUBAI AUTODROME OFFERS A WIDE VARIETY
OF ADRENALINE-PUMPING EXPERIENCES
CALL 04 367 8700 OR VISIT
www.dubaiautodrome.com

in areas like Fili and Siji, to mountain routes like Wadi Bih, which climb to over 1000m and can be descended in minutes. The riding is mainly rocky, technical and challenging. Even if you are experienced, always be sensible and go prepared – the sun is strong, you will need far more water than you think, and it's easy to get lost. Wide, knobbly tires work much better on the loose, sharp rocks. For further information on mountain biking in the UAE, including details of possible routes, refer to the *UAE Off-Road Explorer.*

Hot-Cog Mountain Bike Club
Various locations **056 170 8087**
hot-cog.com
An active group of enthusiasts who organise weekend trips all over the country and midweek off-road night rides. They also camp, hike and barbecue, and new riders are always welcome.

Music Lessons
There are a number of music schools in Dubai where you and your kids can have music lessons. In addition, you may find that some schools offer extra-curricular music programmes (for a fee) for students.

Centre For Musical Arts
Gold & Diamond Park Al Quoz Industrial 3
04 341 8872
cmadubai.com
Map **1 S6** Metro **First Gulf Bank**
Offers instruction in string, woodwind and brass instruments, as well as piano. Group lessons start at Dhs.975 and individual lessons from Dhs.1,625 per term.

Dubai Music School
Stalco Bldg, Nr General Post Office, Zabeel Rd
Al Karama **04 396 4834**
dubaimusicschool.com
Map **2 L6** Metro **Al Karama**
One-hour lessons in guitar, piano, organ, violin, brass, drums, singing and composing, leading to Trinity College of Music examinations.

Juli Music Centre
Nr Mazaya Shopping Centre, Shk Zayed Rd Al Wasl
04 321 2588
imi-jmc.net
Map **2 E6** Metro **Burj Khalifa/Dubai Mall**
In addition to selling a variety of musical instruments including new and used pianos, brass, woodwind, strings, and percussion, Juli Music Centre also offers lessons in various instruments from Dhs.180 per hour.

Jumeirah Music Centre
Jumeirah Plaza Jumeira 1 **04 349 2662**
jumeirah-music.com
Map **2 H4** Metro **Emirates Towers**
Lessons in piano, guitar, flute, violin, drums and voice for all ages at Dhs.90 per half hour. All children are welcome to audition for the choir, which puts on a concert every year.

Little Musicians
Various locations **055 364 9421**
littlemusiciansdubai.com
Holds classes all over Dubai (Arabian Ranches, Jumeirah Ballet Centre, Dubai Marina Yacht Club, Dubai Marina Mall and Indigo Icon Office Tower JLT) in all manner of fun and brightly-coloured instruments. The emphasis is very much on making music enjoyable and achievable, rather than more rigid theory.

The Music Chamber
Times Square Al Qusais Industrial 1 **04 346 8056**
musicchamber.net
Map **1 T6** Metro **First Gulf Bank**
Boasting a large variety of instruments, accessories and books, The Music Chamber gives lessons in all instruments, from electric and classical guitar to cello, piano and percussions, as well as teaching music theory and vocal training. Recognised by the Associated Board of Royal Schools of Music in London.

The Music Institute
The Walk, Jumeirah Beach Residence Dubai Marina
04 424 3818
themusic-uae.com
Map **1 K5** Metro **Dubai Marina**
Piano, violin, guitar and drum lessons with musical theory for all ages, plus group guitar and violin

SkyDive Dubai

Life on the open water

Dreamland Aqua Park

Ski Dubai

lessons. Practice rooms available to hire and show recitals are also held.

Popular Music Institute
Wafi Umm Hurair 2 **04 324 2626**
thomsunpuremusic.com
Map **2 L7** Metro **Dubai Healthcare City**
From its location in Wafi, Thomsun Pure Music runs the Popular Music Institute and the Sing & Swing Training Centre, which teach both instruments, musicianship, theory and performance, as well as preparing students for music exams.

Solid Rock
Pinnacle Bldg, Nr Caesar Confectionery, Shk Zayed Rd Al Barsha 1 **04 395 7808**
solidrockdubai.com
Map **1 Q6** Metro **Sharaf DG**
Teaches both modern music and dance at its Al Barsha studios, with particular focus on piano, guitar and drums – the staples of rock music. Both private and group classes are available, and the school offers the first group session for free, so you can check that it's a good fit before you sign up.

Netball

Dubai Netball League
The Sevens Dubailand
dubainetballleague.com
Four divisions compete between September and May. Training is on Sundays or Mondays and league nights fall on Wednesdays. Players also have the chance to be selected for the annual inter-Gulf championship. New players of all levels are welcome.

Duplays
Indigo Icon Tower Jumeirah Lakes Towers
04 447 2394
duplays.com
Map **1 K5** Metro **Jumeirah Lakes Towers**
Duplays' competitive women's league is contested on Sunday evenings, and games in the recreational league take place on Monday evenings. Players can either sign up as individuals and be allocated to a team for Dhs.450, or enter a full team for Dhs.3,900 per season.

Orchestras & Bands

Centre For Musical Arts
Gold & Diamond Park Al Quoz Industrial 3
04 341 8872
cmadubai.com
Map **1 S6** Metro **First Gulf Bank**
The centre is home to a number of adult and children's musical groups, including ensembles for string, flute, saxophone and guitar players. It also offers instrumental and choral tuition and has an instrument hire and repair service.

Dubai Chamber Orchestra
Safa School, Meydan Road Jumeira **04 349 0423**
Map **1 S5** Metro **Noor Islamic Bank**
Founded by an international group of musicians now residing in the UAE, the chamber orchestra practises every Wednesday evening and gives three public performances a year. There are currently over 40 members hailing from more than 15 countries and other musicians are always welcome. Its varied programme features both chamber and modern orchestral pieces.

Dubai Classical Guitar Orchestra
Dubai Community Theatre & Arts Centre (DUCTAC) Al Barsha 1 **04 341 4666**
dcgo.ae
Map **1 R6** Metro **Mall of the Emirates**
This classical guitar ensemble rehearses at DUCTAC every Tuesday from 18:00 to 20:00. People of all ages and levels of skill are welcome to join or learn. Look out for the regular performances too.

Dubai Drums
Dubai Media City Al Sufouh 1 **04 347 4790**
dubaidrums.com
Map **1 M5** Metro **Nakheel**
Dubai Drums runs African Djembe drumming circles every Monday. A leader guides the group from simple rhythms right through to more complex performances. Classes cost Dhs.50 with drums provided. On Saturdays, Kidz Drum Club is held at DUCTAC, from 10:15-11:15 and also costs Dhs.50. Dubai Drums organises other events throughout the year, such as Full Moon and Desert Drumming.

UAE Philharmonic Orchestra
Abu Dhabi
uaephilharmonic.com
The only full orchestra in the UAE consists of musicians from more than 20 countries who perform in public regularly, as well as for private events. Musicians are welcome to audition, as long as they're committed to the regular rehearsals.

Paintballing & Laser Games

Laserdrome Dubai
Dubai Autodrome Dubai MotorCity **04 436 1422**
dubaiautodrome.com
Map **1 N11**
Players wear special vests that detect their enemies' lasers. At the end of each round, contestants can see how many times they got shot and who shot them. The charges are Dhs.80 per person for 15 minutes.

Pursuit Games
WonderLand Theme & Water Park Umm Hurair 2
04 324 4755
paintballdubai.com
Map **2 L8** Metro **Dubai Healthcare City**
The Pursuit Games version of paintball is a combination of speedball and paintball and the arena capitalises on the desert terrain. Sessions start at Dhs.90 for two hours, including 100 paintballs and gear.

Sharjah Paintball Park
Sharjah Golf & Shooting Club Sharjah **06 548 7777**
paintballuae.com
This paintball park has two arenas. The first is a woodland area strewn with army jeeps and plane carcasses; with sniper towers and plenty of obstacles to hide behind, it calls for a strategic battle plan. The second is smaller and more open, meaning that the paintball battles are more frantic. A variety of different packages are available ranging from Dhs.85 for 100 paintballs and basic equipment to Dhs.500 for 800 balls plus extra body armour and equipment.

Photography & Film
Photography and film are increasingly popular in the region. Although three film festivals, DIFF, ADFF and Gulf Film Festival (see UAE Calendar, p.25) shine an encouraging spotlight on the region's film making, there is still a dearth of serious funding. However, for amateur film fans, there are several groups that bring the filmmaking community together for screenings, workshops and presentations.

Shelter (shelter.ae) has a small screening room and holds regular film nights which are open to non-members. The Alliance Francaise (p.175) has its own francophonic cine club, and award-winning filmmaker, Mahmood Kabour, holds a film series at the Jam Jar; details are available on the Mahmovies! group Facebook page. The Picturehouse at Reel Cinemas in Dubai Mall screens arthouse films and documentaries that don't make it onto the main screens.

For photographers, Soura of the Middleeast (http://soura.me/forum) is a web-based community where local photography enthusiasts can exchange tips and ideas, post their pictures, and buy and sell equipment.

Gulf Photo Plus
Alserkal Avenue, 8th Street Al Quoz Industrial 1
04 380 8545
gulfphotoplus.com
Map **1 U6** Metro **Noor Islamic Bank**
Gulf Photo Plus offers a range of digital photography classes for beginner and intermediate photographers, and organises workshops and events with master photographers. Introductory classes to Photoshop are also available if you want to learn how to touch up your shots. There is also a well-stocked store selling lenses, lights, literature and other photography kit.

Lightform
Various locations
lightform.ae
An International Filipino Photographer's Guild photographic society, it organises regular workshops, field trips and events for members. Members must complete a basic class to join.

SAE Institute Dubai
Dubai Knowledge Village Al Sufouh 1 **04 361 6173**
sae.edu
Map **1 N5** Metro **Dubai Internet City**
The world's largest private college for film and audio production, animation and multimedia offers a degree in filmmaking, as well as photography bootcamps.

The Scene Club
Dubai Media City Al Sufouh 1 **04 391 0051**
thesceneclub.com
Map **1 M5** Metro **Nakheel**
Dubai's first official film club for true buffs offers workshops as well as screenings of films and documentaries that may not make the box office but are felt to be culturally significant.

Pilates

Club Stretch
Nr Mercure Hotel, Al Mina Rd Al Hudaiba **04 345 2131**
clubstretch.ae
Map **2 J4** Metro **Al Jafiliya**
Club Stretch offers reformer pilates classes taught by highly qualified instructors who also teach Bikram yoga at the studio (p.363).

Exhale Fitness
Jumeirah Beach Residence Dubai Marina
04 424 3777
exhaledubai.com
Map **1 K4** Metro **Dubai Marina**
This ladies-only centre specialises in pilates and yoga. Prices start at Dhs.80 for a single pilates reformer class; a set of ten Exhale classes costs Dhs.750 and is valid for two months. Exhale has another studio in Dubai MotorCity (04 447 4220).

The Hundred Pilates Studio
Dubai Healthcare City Umm Hurair 2 **04 429 8433**
thehundred.ae
Map **2 L7** Metro **Dubai Healthcare City**
Personalised pilates sessions are available, as well as small group classes with a maximum four participants. Prices start at Dhs.90 for a single class.

Real Pilates
Palm Strip, Jumeira Road, Jumeira 1 **04 345 3228**
real-pilates.com
Map **2 H4** Metro **World Trade Centre**
At its bright studio, Real Pilates focuses on STOTT pilates and has high quality equipment and well qualified instructors. Single sessions start at Dhs.65 with block booking offers available. A full list of sessions and timetables can be found online.

Zen Yoga
Town Centre, Emirates Hills Emirates Living
04 422 4643
yoga.ae
Map **1 K8** Metro **Nakheel**
Mat and reformer pilates (using a machine to increase intensity) are available, with Yogilates also offered; expectant mums can join prenatal pilates classes. A trial lesson costs Dhs.90, with five classes for Dhs.450. Emirates Living (04 422 4643), Dubai Media City (04 367 0435), Town Centre Jumeirah (04 349 2933).

Polo

Dubai Polo & Equestrian Club
Nr Arabian Ranches, Al Qudra Rd Dubai Studio City
04 361 8111
poloclubdubai.com
Map **1 N13** Metro **Dubai Internet City**
With its two full-size pitches, this is a regular venue for both local and international polo competitions that attract the very best players in the world. To get involved yourself, coaching is offered for all levels, from 40 minute lessons to six-day courses. An introductory 1.5 hour lesson is Dhs.800.

Camel Polo
For a fun twist on the game, head to the Dubai Polo & Equestrian Club for a spot of camel polo. It's not as fast-paced as the real thing, but you'll come away with plenty of stories. Any group of eight or more people is welcome to book a session. Call 04 404 5880 for reservations or, for more info email camelpolo@gulfventures.com.

Ghantoot Racing & Polo Club
Abu Dhabi **02 562 9050**
grpc.ae
The club's extensive facilities include seven international standard polo fields (three of which are floodlit), two stick and ball fields, three tennis courts, a pool, gym, sauna and restaurant. One of the world's foremost polo facilities, it has 200 polo ponies which are supported by six fully equipped stables, five paddocks and an outdoor training ring.

Rugby

Dubai Exiles Rugby Football Club

Various locations **050 459 8603**
dubaiexiles.com
The Exiles is Dubai's most serious rugby club and has a 1st and 2nd XV that competes in the AGRFU leagues, as well as veterans, U19s, ladies', girls' U17s and a minis and youth section. The Exiles club also hosts a tournament alongside the annual Dubai IRB Sevens Tournament.

Dubai Hurricanes Rugby Football Club

The Sevens Dubailand **050 288 1491**
dubaihurricanes.com
Having started as a social outfit, the Hurricanes now compete in the Dubai Sevens. The club also has a ladies' team and players of all ages and abilities are welcome. Training is on Mondays and Wednesdays at 18:30.

Running

For over half the year, Dubai's weather is perfect for running and many groups and clubs meet up for runs on a regular basis. There are several running events, such as the excellent Creek Striders Half Marathon (dubaicreekstriders@gmail.com), the Dubai Marathon (dubaimarathon.org), and the Wadi Bih Race (wadibih.com). For suggestions of places to run, see Walk This Way, p.364.

Dubai Creek Striders

Various locations
dubaicreekstriders.org
Established in 1995, the Striders meet every Friday morning (on the road opposite the Novotel next to the Trade Centre) for a long-distance run, with training geared at members taking part in the 42.2km Dubai Marathon in January. For more info you can email them on dubai.creek.striders@gmail.com.

Dubai Road Runners

Safa Park Al Wasl **050 624 3213**
dubai-road-runners.com
Map **2 D5** Metro **Business Bay**
This running club meets on Saturdays at 18:30 by gate four of Safa Park to run 3.4km to 7km (the park charges Dhs.5 entrance fee). For fun, runners predict their times, with a prize for the winner.

Mirdif Milers

Various locations
050 652 4149
mirdifmilers.com
This friendly group meets for runs every Monday at 19:00 outside Mushrif Park. It also organises longer runs leading up to marathons and half marathons.

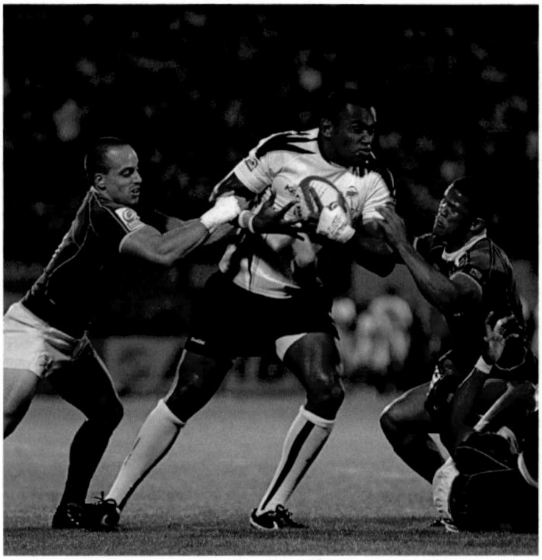

Nike+ Run Club

Various locations
facebook.com/NikeRunningMiddleEast
Particularly suited to beginners or intermediates, these sessions take place at Festival City (Tuesday evenings) and Downtown (Friday mornings) and are expertly coached, not to mention free.

Reebok Running Club

Dubai Marina Mall Dubai Marina **055 369 5664**
urbanenergyfitness.com
Map **1 K5** Metro **Jumeirah Lakes Towers**
Located at Dubai Marina Mall and organised in partnership with fitness experts Urban Energy, this new running club will help people of all abilities and fitness levels to ignite their passion for running by coming together twice a week to run in a fun, motivating atmosphere and share advice on training, nutrition and general health tips.

Stride For Life

Various locations **050 657 7057**
strideforlife.com
Stride for Life offers aerobic walking and running for all abilities. Following a fitness assessment, a thrice-weekly programme is recommended. Stride for Life also does Nordic and mall walking, and 'training journeys' for novices preparing for long distance events. Fees are Dhs.1,600 for a one-year membership.

Sailing

Temperatures in winter are perfect for sailing and taking to the sea in summer serves as an escape from the heat. Membership at one of Dubai's sailing clubs allows you to participate in club activities and to rent sailing and watersports equipment. You can also use leisure facilities and the club's beach, and moor your boat at an additional cost. If you've not found your sea legs but would like to, there are a few places that will teach you to be your own captain. Long distance races such as the annual Dubai to Muscat race, held in March. The traditional dhow races (p.25) are an exciting spectacle as is the Powerboat Formula One Grand Prix (p.29), while Abu Dhabi recently made a splash not only as the first Middle East venue to serve as a host port for the Volvo Ocean Race, but because the emirate also entered its own boat. For further information on sailing in the region, check out Explorer's *UAE Boating & Yachting*, available at askexplorer.com and in bookstores.

Dubai International Marine Club
Mina Seyahi, Off Al Sufouh Rd Dubai Marina
04 399 5777
dimc.ae
Map **1 M4** Metro **Dubai Marina**
Offers sailing lessons for children. A 12 hour course sets members back Dhs.1,500. See the website for more details on lessons and membership.

Dubai Offshore Sailing Club
Jumeira Rd Umm Suqeim 1 **04 394 1669**
dosc.ae
Map **2 B4** Metro **Noor Islamic Bank**
This Royal Yachting Association Training Centre offers dinghy and keelboat courses throughout the year.

Salsa Dancing
If you fancy a bit of salsa there are a number of places you can get serious at or just have a bit of fun. Check out dubaisalsa.com for more information.

The Address Dubai Marina
Shk Mohd Rashid Blvd Dubai Marina **04 436 7777**
theaddress.com
Map **1 K5** Metro **Dubai Marina**
Every Wednesday is Havana Night at Blends with salsa instructor Aloy Junco, Cuban-Latino sounds and complimentary Cuban salsa classes and beverages for the ladies, from 19:00 till midnight.

El Malecon
Dubai Marine Beach Resort & Spa Jumeira 1
04 346 1111
dxbmarine.com
Map **2 H4** Metro **World Trade Centre**
Salsa dancing every Saturday night from 22:00 onwards for Dhs.40. If you order food, the dancing is free.

Familia De La Salsa
Various locations **050 277 7475**
familiadelasalsa.com
Salsa dancing lessons for beginners and enthusiastic salseros/salseras in a friendly and relaxed atmosphere at locations across Dubai. There are also children's dancing classes held at the Dubai Ballet Centre every Saturday. Classes start from Dhs.40.

Ritmo De Havana
Dubai Community Theatre & Arts Centre (DUCTAC)
Al Barsha 1 **050 696 3520**
ritmo-de-havana.com
Map **1 R6** Metro **Mall of the Emirates**
Del Piero is a certified instructor; his courses start from Dhs.600 per person and run in batches so check the website for the most up-to-date timings.

Salsa Dubai
Wafi Umm Hurair 2 **050 565 6420**
Map **2 L7** Metro **Dubai Healthcare City**
Instructor Phil has 13 years' experience in Cuban, New York and Spanish dance styles. Classes are tailored to the individual, and members can learn the famous La Rueda Cuban dance. Find schedules on 'The Original Salsa Dubai' Facebook page.

Savage Garden
Capitol Hotel Al Mina **04 346 0111**
Map **2 J4** Metro **Al Jafiliya**
On Monday, Tuesday, Thursday and Friday nights, this unique Latin American restaurant and nightclub serves up Latino food with a side order of salsa and merengue classes. Beginners' lessons are from 20:00 to 21:00 and intermediate and advanced dancers take to the floor from 21:00 to 22:00. Classes cost Dhs.40 a pop. Contact George or Tatiana on 050 597 5058 for more details.

Sandboarding & Sandskiing
Sandboarding or sandskiing (also known as sand surfing) down a big sand dune is not as fast or smooth as snowboarding, but it can be a lot of fun. Standard snowboards and skis are pretty similar to sandboards and skis. Alternatively, you can use a plastic sled. However, the terrain does make a big difference so don't expect a couple of lessons at SkiDubai to have you set for the dunes. You'll have to walk to the top of the dune after every run or hitch a ride with a dune buggy, but on the up-side sand dunes are usually available all year round. All major tour companies (p.279) offer sandboarding and skiing experiences.

Scouts & Guides
The majority of Scout and Guide groups in Dubai are held at schools, so check with your kids' school if you would like to enrol them. With each new group also comes a need for adult volunteers. If you have experience with Scout or Guide groups, or your child that was once a member, contact Mary Dunn (ja.mc.dunn@gmail.com) or Dawn Tate (050 654 2180) to get involved.

British Guides In Foreign Countries
Various locations
bgifc.org.uk
Various groups for girls of different age ranges include Rainbows (five to seven), Brownies (seven to 10), Guides (10 to 14), and Young Leaders and Rangers (14 to 26) with groups in Jumeira, Jebel Ali, Emirates Living and Arabian Ranches. For more information call Jane Henderson (04 340 8441), Patsy (04 348 9767), or Caroline Kellett (050 640 4133).

Scouts Association (British Groups Abroad)
Various locations
scouts.org.uk
The Scout Association encourages the development of youngsters through weekly activities and outings for ages six to 18 and 18-25. Contact andy@the-bairds.net for more information on Dubai Scout groups.

Scrabble

Dubai Scrabble League
Various locations **050 653 7992**
Meets once a month for friendly games between players of all levels. Regular competitions are held, and players also attend competitions overseas. The UAE Open is the qualifier for the Gulf Open in Bahrain. For more information, contact Selwyn Lobo.

Shooting

Jebel Ali International Shooting Club & Centre Of Excellence
Nr Jebel Ali Golf Resort & Spa Waterfront
04 883 6555
jebelali-international.com
Metro **Danube**
Five floodlit clay shooting ranges consisting of skeet, trap and sporting. Instructors give detailed lessons and experienced shooters can also try clay shooting. Members and non-members welcome.

Ras Al Khaimah Shooting Club
Nr RAK Airport Ras Al Khaimah **07 236 3622**
RAK Shooting Club offers lessons in firing shotguns and long rifles, as well as recreational visits for people wishing to try their hand at shooting. The club boasts a 50m indoor range and 200m outdoor rifle range. You can make group bookings by calling in advance.

Sharjah Golf & Shooting Club
Nr Tasjeel Auto Village, Shk Mohammed bin Zayed Rd Sharjah **06 548 7777**
golfandshootingshj.com
The shooting range features indoor pistols, rifles and revolvers, as well as 25m and 50m ranges. A fully trained safety instructor is on hand at all times. Thirty minute beginner lessons with .22 calibre weapons cost Dhs.170 for non-members and Dhs.130 for members. 25 shots with standard weapons are charged at Dhs.90 for non-members and Dhs.70 for members.

Singing

Dubai Chamber Choir
Various locations
dubaichamberchoir.com
Provides choral education and training, as well as performing concerts throughout the year, with the Christmas series a seasonal highlight. Contact the choir if you're interested in joining up.

Dubai Harmony
GEMS Jumeirah Primary School Al Safa 1
056 690 7052
dubai-harmony.com
Map **2 C5** Metro **Business Bay**
A barbershop-style group with an all-female ensemble. New members are always welcome and musical training is not required.

Dubai Singers
Kindermusik, 15B Street Umm Suqeim 3
04 344 8883
dubaisingers.info
Map **1 S5** Metro **Mall of the Emirates**
This is a group of amateur singers who meet regularly to create music in a variety of styles, including requiems, choral works, Christmas carols, musicals and variety shows. Membership is open to everyone; sheet music is provided.

Skateboarding & Rollerblading
Dubai's many parks provide some excellent locations for rollerblading. The likes of Creek Park (p.256) and Safa Park (p.257) have plenty of wide pathways, relatively few people and enough slopes and turns to make it interesting. Alternatively, check out both sides of Dubai Creek, the seafront near the Hyatt Regency Hotel or the promenades at the Jumeira Beach corniche and in Deira along towards Al Mamzar Beach Park (p.257), where the views are an added bonus. Burj Boulevard, running through the Downtown area, The Walk at Jumeirah Beach Residence, and the promenade running around Dubai Marina also have wide promenades which are great for skating.

Rage Bowl
The Dubai Mall Downtown Dubai **04 434 1549**
rage-shop.com
Map **2 F6** Metro **Burj Khalifa/Dubai Mall**
This indoor skateboarding bowl is open Sunday to Wednesday, 10:00 to 22:00, and 10:00 until midnight

at the weekends. Kids can use the area in two-hour sessions for Dhs.25; helmets can also be hired for Dhs.10. Lessons are available at Dhs.85 per hour on weekdays and Dhs.125 on weekends, and no previous experience is required. Check the website for happy hour timings when skating is free. You can also sign up for newsletters, watch skills videos and meet other skaters on the forum.

Skiing & Snowboarding

Dubai Ski Club

Ski Dubai Al Barsha 1
dubaiskiclub.com
Map **1 R6** Metro **Mall of the Emirates**
The club has over 1,400 members and meets at 18:00 on the last Saturday of every month, next to Ski Dubai's ticket counter, for social skiing or snowboarding, race training and races, followed by apres ski. Membership benefits include a reduced fee for the slope pass and use of the 'advance booking' lane when purchasing tickets, plus special offers on equipment, clothing, accessories and holidays. Membership is Dhs.300.

Ski Dubai > *p.357*

Mall of the Emirates Al Barsha 1 **800 386**
skidxb.com
Map **1 R6** Metro **Mall of the Emirates**
Ski Dubai is the Middle East's first indoor ski resort, with more than 22,500 square metres of real snow. The temperature hovers around -3°C even when it's closer to 50°C outside, making for a cool escape from the summer heat. Competent skiers and boarders can choose between five runs and a freestyle area; skiing and snowboarding lessons are available for beginners; and there is a huge snowpark for the little ones. You can roll down the Giant Ball run, turn down the tube slides, sightsee in the chairlift, or enjoy a mug of hot chocolate at -4°C. You can even get up close with a colony of snow penguins. Slope pass and lesson prices include the hire charge for jackets, trousers, boots, socks, helmets – and either skis and poles or a snowboard – but it's worth bringing your own gloves as these are charged extra. Freestyle nights are held every other week on Mondays from 20:00 to 23:00.

Skydiving

iFLY Dubai

Mirdif City Centre Mirdif
04 231 6292
theplaymania.com
Map **2 P12** Metro **Rashidiya**
The ideal place to practise before making the big jump for real, iFLY is an indoor skydiving centre located in Playnation Mirdif City Centre. Giant vertical wind tunnels simulate the sensation of jumping from a plane but at a fraction of the cost and with an instructor on hand. A fun experience for kids and adults, it's so realistic that actual skydivers head to iFLY for the longer 'freefall' time.

SkyDive Dubai

Various locations **050 153 3222**
skydivedubai.ae
Offers stunning skydives over The Palm Jumeirah and Dubai Marina. A first-time tandem jump costs Dhs.1,750 (with digital stills and DVD). Also offers a skydive school to become a licensed jumper, as well as jumps and gear rental for licensed skydivers.

Snooker

Dubai Snooker Club

Nr Karama Post Office Al Karama **04 337 5338**
dubaisnooker.com
Map **2 L6** Metro **Al Karama**
The club's facilities include 12 tournament-class snooker tables, 13 pool tables, two private snooker rooms and a private pool room. Table charges are Dhs.20 per hour, and food is available. Membership isn't required to play.

Take Your Shot

Knight Shot (04 343 5678), near the Mazaya Centre, sells all manner of pool and billiards equipment and, as one of the main sponsors of the games in the region, it's a good place to chat to staff and find out about local tournaments.

Softball

Dubai Softball League

Nr Dnata Travel Centre, Shk Zayed Rd Business Bay
050 651 4970
dubaisoftball.com
Map **2 D6** Metro **Business Bay**
Over 16s can join one of over 20 teams in three leagues (two men's, one mixed) and take part in the Middle East Softball Championships in April. The season runs from September to December and from January to May.

Duplays

Indigo Icon Tower Jumeirah Lakes Towers
04 447 2394
duplays.com
Map **1 K5** Metro **Jumeirah Lakes Towers**
Duplays runs a mixed recreational softball league on Wednesdays. Matches are held at the sports field near Business Bay on Sheikh Zayed Road.

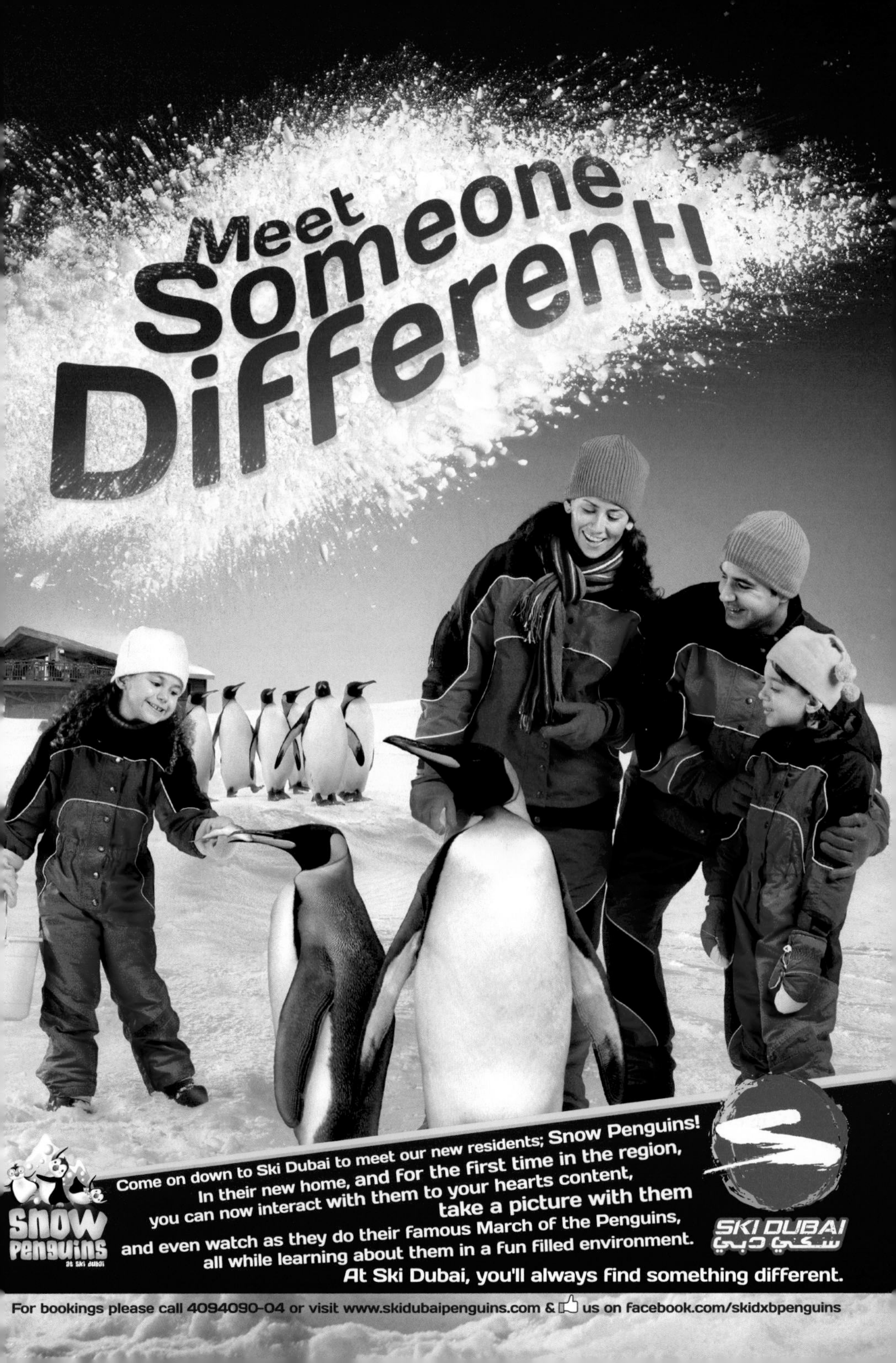

Meet Someone Different!
Come on down to Ski Dubai to meet our new residents; Snow Penguins!
In their new home, and for the first time in the region,
you can now interact with them to your hearts content,
take a picture with them
and even watch as they do their famous March of the Penguins,
all while learning about them in a fun filled environment.
At Ski Dubai, you'll always find something different.
Snow Penguins at Ski Dubai
SKI DUBAI
سكي دبي
For bookings please call 4094090-04 or visit www.skidubaipenguins.com & us on facebook.com/skidxbpenguins

Squash

Dubai Squash

Emirates Golf Club Emirates Living
Map **1 M5** Metro **Nakheel**
The league has been active in Dubai and Sharjah since the 1970s and is run by the UAE Squash Rackets Association. Around 250 competitors in 25 teams play three 10 week seasons. Teams meet on Mondays at 19:30 and each team fields four players.

Surfing

Dubai isn't well-known as a surfing destination but if you're looking to catch some waves, you'll find an enthusiastic community of surfers who are out whenever there's a swell. You can sign up for Swell Alerts through Surfing Dubai. Dubai Municipality has periodically cracked down on surfing at public beaches in the past – check with Surfing Dubai for the latest before paddling out. Sunset Beach (Umm Suqeim open beach) has smallish but decent waves as does the Sheraton Beach between the Hilton and Sheraton in Dubai Marina.

Surfing season in Dubai is between October and April, with the peak months being December to February; surfers also head to the south of Oman for the bigger waves between May and August. The largest wave recorded in Dubai is 3.5m and the average surf is between 0.5 and 1m in peak season. Manageable waves and year-round warm water makes Dubai a perfect location for beginners.

Boards and other equipment can be bought at Surf Shop Arabia (04 379 1998).

Surf Dubai

Villa 12A, 3A Street Umm Suqeim 3 **050 504 3020**
surfingdubai.com
Map **1 T4** Metro **First Gulf Bank**
Dubai's original surf school offers group lessons for beginner and intermediate surfers from Dhs.200, with board rental from Dhs.75 per hour. It also organises surfing package holidays to Sri Lanka, Bali, Japan, Morocco and the Philippines. The school's website is a useful resource – the weekly surf timetable shows when swells are predicted for Dubai's unreliable surf so that you can be sure you're there when the good waves come. If they don't, try your hand at a bit of stand up paddleboarding here instead.

Surf School UAE

Sunset Beach Umm Suqeim 3 **055 601 0997**
surfschooluae.com
Map **1 T4** Metro **First Gulf Bank**
Owned and managed by keen and experienced surfers, and certified by the International Surf Association. Lessons are available in a range of languages to wannabe surfers of any age, in both Dubai and Abu Dhabi. Lessons are available throughout the week and cost Dhs.125 per 90 minutes, or Dhs.500 for four.

Wadi Adventure > *p.325*

Nr Green Mubazzarah, Off Al Ain Fayda Rd Al Ain **03 781 8422**
wadiadventure.ae
The waves aren't always reliable in Dubai, unless you head for the hills that is. Located near Jebel Hafeet in Al Ain, entry to Wadi Adventure costs Dhs.50 to Dhs.100, with an hour in the surf pool (where waves reach three metres) costing Dhs.100 further, including equipment.

Swimming

Dubai has some great swimming spots, whether it's at the public beaches, in the private pools, in a beach club or one of the beach parks. The water temperature rarely dips below 20°C in winter, although during the summer it can feel like stepping into a bath. As with sea swimming elsewhere, rip tides and undertows can catch out even the strongest swimmer, so never ignore flags or signs ordering you not to swim. You might also run into quite a lot of jellyfish towards the end of the summer.

Around the UAE there are occasional outbreaks of red tide, a naturally occurring algal bloom which turns the water red and gives it an unpleasant smell – but these generally affect the east coast and are relatively uncommon in Dubai.

Many hotels, beach clubs and health clubs have swimming pools that are open for public use for a day entrance fee. Lessons are widely available from health and beach clubs too. For children's lessons, check with your school whether they offer any extra-curricular swimming coaching.

Balloon Adventures
into the Heart of the Desert
Leave the glitz and the glamour of the city behind and join our balloon adventure deep into the desert!
Enjoy a magic carpet ride over giant red sand dunes, emerald green oases, wild gazelles and wandering camels. Be welcomed by the warmth of the desert people we chance to meet on landing.
Price: AED 995.00 per person
Memories of a lifetime included!
FLY WITH THE WORLD'S MOST EXPERIENCED BALLOON COMPANY!
Balloon Adventures Emirates
FOR BOOKINGS
call: 04 2854949
or visit
www.ballooning.ae

Keen swimmers can sign up for the annual Wild Wadi Swim Around The Burj challenge, held each year in aid of Medecins Sans Frontieres (swim.msf-me.org). Over 500 participants tackle the 1km distance and all swimmers are given plenty of encouragement from beach spectators.

Active Sports Academy

Corner City, Nr Coca Cola Office Dubai Festival City **050 559 7055**
activeuae.com
Map **2 M9** Metro **Emirates**
Classes, held in various locations around Dubai, include water babies, parent and toddlers, and lessons for beginner to advanced swimmers.

Aqua Sports Academy

Kings' Dubai Umm Suqeim 3 **050 574 7942**
aquaswim.ae
Map **1 S5** Metro **First Gulf Bank**
Operating mainly out of the 25m pool at Kings' School in Umm Suqeim, Aqua Sports runs everything from parent and baby sessions, kids' swim lessons and one to one clinics, to competitive squads and holiday camps. It also runs the city's most popular masters' swim programme for swimmers aged 16 and up, which caters to casual keep-fit swimmers as well as competitive age group swimmers and triathletes. See the website for session times and special events.

Australian International Swim Schools (AISS)

The Fairmont Dubai, Shk Zayed Rd Trade Centre 1 **04 386 5718**
aiswimschools.com
Map **2 J5** Metro **World Trade Centre**
Austswim certified instructors provide swimming lessons at a number of pools throughout Dubai. This company also runs many of the schools' swimming programmes. Swimming training is provided at all levels, from parent and baby classes to adult triathlon swimming squads.

Desert Sport Services

Various locations **04 326 2822**
desertsportservices.com
The swim programme runs from parent & baby/toddler through to learn to swim, stroke development, and competitive training sessions; there is also a full adult swim program.

Excel Sports

Various locations **050 794 3656**
excelsportsuae.com
Excel Sports offers coaching in swimming, cricket, soccer and gymnastics. The emphasis is firmly on having fun and being confident in the water, and the company also runs holiday camps that include swimming in the programme.

Speedo Swim Squads

Various locations **04 354 9525**
speedodubai.net
This private club offers tuition for all ages and abilities, from duckling to squad training. It also offers ASA teacher training and water polo classes. Lessons take place at a number of locations including Horizon School, Uptown High School, Dubai International Academy and Emirates International School.

Table Tennis

Table tennis can be played for Dhs.20 per hour, including equipment, at Insportz just behind Dubai Garden Centre on Sheikh Zayed Road; booking is required. Several of the older leisure clubs provide table tennis, although the equipment is usually a bit rusty. The UAE Table Tennis Association is based in Dubai (04 254 7111), and can provide some information on how to get into leagues and high level competitions, but unfortunately most of the local clubs only accept UAE Nationals.

Tennis

Dubai is firmly established on the international tennis circuit, with the annual Dubai Duty Free Tennis Championships attracting the best players in the world (p.26). There are plenty of venues to enjoy a game. Outdoor courts are available at most health and beach clubs, many of which are floodlit. There are indoor courts for hire at InSportz (04 347 5833).

Ace Sports Academy

Emirates Grand Hotel Trade Centre 2 **055 452 2066**
acesportsacademy.com
Map **2 G6** Metro **Financial Centre**
This tennis school offers everything from tots' tennis and junior development to ladies' mornings, adult lessons and tournaments. Private, semi-private and family lessons are available, and ball machines can be hired for those wishing to practise alone. Membership and lesson costs differ according to the programmes – check the website for details. Also located at Mirdif Tennis Courts, near Mirdif City Centre.

The Atlantis Tennis Academy

Atlantis The Palm Palm Jumeirah **04 426 1433**
atlantisthepalm.com
Map **1 N1** Metro **Nakheel**
Provides world-class coaching for players of all ages and levels. The state-of-the-art facilities include the latest court surfaces plus video technology for technique analysis. The academy also organises regular social events and tournament afternoons for its members.

Clark Francis Tennis Academy

Various locations **04 282 4540**
clarkfrancistennis.com
This tennis school offers group and individual tennis coaching for children and adults. A ladies' morning is held at the Grand Hyatt on Mondays from 08:15. Cardio Tennis classes (a cross between tennis and circuit training) are held every Tuesday from 18:45 at the Aviation Club. It also organises competitive leagues in a variety of categories including juniors. Ball kid training (for the Dubai Tennis Championships) is available, and the service centre can have your racket restrung and returned to you within 12 hours.

Dubai Tennis Academy

American University In Dubai Al Sufouh 1
050 286 8025
dubaitennisacademy.com
Map **1 M5** Metro **Nakheel**
Provides training for all levels, with internationally qualified coaches, at American University Dubai, Dubai Men's College and Atlantis. Programmes include private lessons, group clinics, competitions, ladies' tennis mornings and school holiday camps.

Duet Sports Club

Dubai Men's College Dubai International Academic City **055 881 1974**
dubaiunitedexpattennis.com
With more than 1,200 registered members, you are sure to find your hitting partner, tennis coach or tennis buddy at DUET. This active social tennis group has an informative website about the sport in the region, and can provide players with partners, organise tennis events, and offer professional coaching to all ages and levels. It has expanded into other sports to run soccer leagues, and basketball and swimming lessons.

Emirates Golf Club

Off Shk Zayed Rd Emirates Living **04 380 1919**
dubaigolf.com
Map **1 M5** Metro **Nakheel**
Open to non-members of all levels for coaching by qualified USPTR professionals. The centre has four courts. Two teams play in the ladies' Spinneys League and one in the men's Prince League.

Triathlon

Emirates Triathlete

Golden Tulip Al Jazira Hotel & Resort Abu Dhabi
emiratestriathlete.com
During the winter season, Emirates Triathlete organises monthly sprint races at the Golden Tulip Al Jazira, Ghantoot. Emirates Triathlete is also linked to the Tri2Aspire team, which provides coaching programmes and training to triathletes of all levels.

Ultimate Frisbee

Duplays (duplays.com) organises a friendly league which you can enter as a team or individual and be placed in a team. Games are played on Monday nights on the field near Business Bay. Pickup games are held in Safa Park on Saturday afternoons.

Volleyball

EK Volleyball Club

Various locations **050 358 1603**
ekvolleyballclub.com
Organises various events around Dubai including pickup nights, indoor and beach volleyball. Prices vary but a two-hour community game starts from Dhs.25. Many players play at Kite Beach/ Beach Volleyball Park on Fridays and Saturdays after 10am.

Watersports

Most beach hotels offer watersports. Activities are often discounted to guests and beach club members but day visitors can pay an extra fee to access the beach. Waterskiing, windsurfing, jet skiing, laser sailing, kayaking and wakeboarding are all available.; contact the hotels directly for details (see Dubai Hotels, p.234). For more info on canoeing and kayaking, see p.324; for surfing, see p.358; for diving, see p.333 and for kitesurfing, see p.344.

Go West

Al Gharbia Watersports Festival is held on Mirfa Beach in Abu Dhabi's western region. A calendar highlight for watersports fans, previous events have included competitive kite board, surfski kayak and wakeboard events, as well as a sports photography competition. For more details, see algharbiafestivals.com/watersports.

Bristol Middle East Yacht Solution

Marina Walk Dubai Marina **04 366 3538**
bristol-middleeast.com
Map **1 K5** Metro **Dubai Marina**

Has a watersports division that covers water skiing, wakeboarding, surf skiing, kneeboarding, banana boating, donut rides and speed boat trips. Banana boating costs Dhs.40 per person, with most other activities costing Dhs.150 (all for 15 minutes).

Club Joumana

Jebel Ali Golf Resort Waterfront **04 814 5555**
jaresortshotels.com
Metro **Danube**

Windsurfing, waterskiing, kayaking, catamaran, Laser sailing and banana boat rides are available. Non-residents are charged an additional fee for day access to the beach and pools.

Dubai International Marine Club

Mina Seyahi, Off Al Sufouh Rd Dubai Marina
04 399 5777
dimc.ae
Map **1 M4** Metro **Dubai Marina**

DIMC is the home of Mina Seyahi Watersports Club. Kayaks, surfskis, lasers, catamarans, wakeboards, jetskis and kneeboards are available to hire.

Dubai Surfski & Kayak Club

Nr Saga World Umm Suqeim 1 **050 640 6087**
dskc.hu
Map **1 V4** Metro **Noor Islamic Bank**

This club has a paddling school offering training for surfski or kayak beginners, and coaching for advanced paddlers. Activities include the 10km DSKC Squall on the last Friday of every month at Mina Seyahi.

The Flow Club

Wild Wadi Water Park Umm Suqeim 3 **04 348 4444**
wildwadi.com
Map **1 S4** Metro **Mall of the Emirates**

Similar to body boarding and surfing, flowriding is an exciting sport that all ages can enjoy. The Flow Club at Wild Wadi holds different sessions for all levels, with experts on hand to provide pointers.

Sky & Sea Adventures

Sheraton Jumeirah Beach Resort Dubai Marina
04 399 9005
watersportsdubai.com
Map **1 J4** Metro **Jumeirah Lakes Towers**

Offers body boarding, kayaking, waterskiing, snorkelling, parasailing, windsurfing and

wakeboarding. Also runs courses in waterskiing, sailing and windsurfing.

Watercooled
Jebel Ali Golf Resort Waterfront **04 887 6771**
watercooleddubai.com
Metro **Danube**
Offers a good range of watersports – from sailing to power boating, kitesurfing to windsurfing – as well a variety of RYA courses.

Yoga
A low-impact (but deceptively challenging) form of holistic exercise, yoga involves holding sequences of poses or 'asanas' that, combined with breathing exercises, gently but powerfully help your body become stronger and more flexible. Many health and fitness clubs offer yoga as part of their weekly schedule, (see Gyms & Fitness Clubs, p.210) as do some alternative therapy centres (p.202).

Bharat Thakur's Artistic Yoga
Various locations **800 9642**
artisticyoga.com
The latest twist in this flexible form of inner and outer exercise combines ancient yogic techniques with modern cardio training. Morning and evening classes, from Dhs.65, are held at Angsana Spa, Body & Soul Spa Al Ghusais and Al Hana Centre.

Club Stretch
Nr Mercure Hotel, Al Mina Rd Al Hudaiba
04 345 2131
clubstretch.ae
Map **2 J4** Metro **Al Jafiliya**
The only studio in Dubai that offers Bikram yoga, practised in a hot room to aid muscle warming and stretching. Pilates is also offered. An unlimited 10-day introduction pass costs Dhs.120.

Exhale Fitness
Jumeirah Beach Residence Dubai Marina **04 424 3777**
exhaledubai.com
Map **1 K4** Metro **Dubai Marina**
This ladies-only fitness centre offers classes in vinyasa, ashtanga and power yoga, as well as yoga for pregnant women and those wanting to slim down. The cost per session is Dhs.60, with packages of 10 costing Dhs.650 and valid for two months.

Fitness First
Nr Al Manzil Hotel Downtown Dubai **04 367 3282**
fitnessfirstme.com
Map **2 F7** Metro **Burj Khalifa/Dubai Mall**
Great for yoga newbies, hatha classes are held most days of the week, with a couple of power yoga sessions in there too. Prices start at Dhs.45 for non members and the timetable varies a little month to month. Other studios at The Meadows and Lakes.

Gems Of Yoga
White Crown Bldg, Shk Zayed Rd Trade Centre 1
04 331 5161
gemsofyogadubai.com
Map **2 H5** Metro **World Trade Centre**
Classes in hatha, ashtanga and power yoga are offered as well as classes just for ladies, children and elderly adults. Expect to pay around Dhs.650 for 10 classes. There are also intensive half-day classes on Fridays (10:00-13:30 and 15:00-20:00) for Dhs.650 per person.

Yogalates Bliss
Fraser Suites Dubai Al Sufouh 1 **050 328 9642**
yogalatesblissindubai.com
Map **1 P5** Metro **Dubai Internet City**
Take a breath of fresh air as you exercise with this offering of Yogalates classes, a fusion of yoga and pilates that's designed to melt away muscular tension, improve core and pelvic floor strength while balancing the body and mind. Classes are held on the seventh-floor outdoor terrace. There's also Funky Fireflies kids yoga, as well as yoga teacher training workshops.

Zen Yoga
Dubai Media City Al Sufouh 1 **04 367 0435**
yoga.ae
Map **1 M5** Metro **Nakheel**
A yoga and pilates specialist, Zen Yoga has three modern centres featuring mirrored walls to help you check your posture. A one month unlimited yoga trial costs Dhs.700 and regular classes are Dhs.75. The studios are located in Emirates Hills (04 422 4643), Dubai Media City (04 367 0435), and Town Centre Jumeirah (04 349 2933).

Walk This Way

There are plenty of great places in Dubai to stretch your legs if you're feeling cooped up indoors.

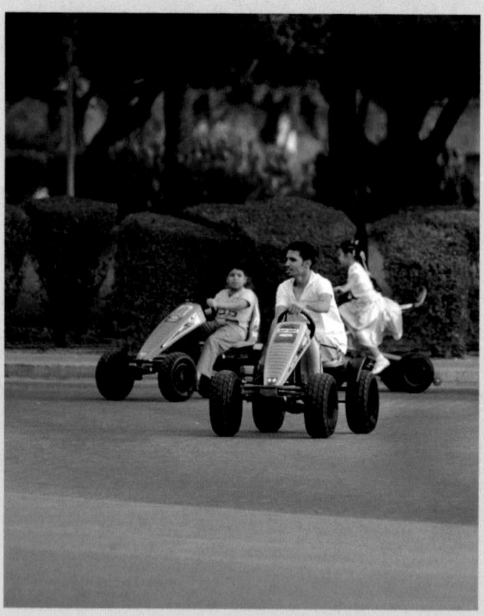

Jumeirah Beach Residence

Boasting big name shops like Boutique 1 and Gallery One, an evening stroll could quickly turn into a shopping spree. The shorefront development covers 1.7km and there are fountains, grassy areas and benches should you need a rest. See p.413.

Down By The Creek

From the embassy area, stroll along the creek, taking photos of the much-loved NBD building opposite. Explore Bastakiya, the historic district of Dubai, where hidden alleyways, secret shops and tiny cafes abound. From here, walk towards the Majlis Gallery (p.255), stopping for a much needed juice at XVA Gallery (p.256). Continue past the Dubai Museum (p.249), through the textile souk (p.421) and down towards the creek. Take an abra across the creek and you will find yourself at the entrance to the spice souk (p.421). You can then wander through the packed streets of Deira towards the gold souk (p.420). Fridays are the quietest, as are the early afternoons when stores often close for a break.

Safa Park

This huge park is a great place to exercise and escape the hustle, or simply to enjoy the boating lake, multitude of play areas, maze or new library-cafe, Archive. Entry costs Dhs.3 (free for children under three years old). There's a great 3km spongy running track around the park's perimeter, not to mention the countless paths that criss-cross the grassy space. Tuesday is ladies' day, and there is also a permanent ladies' garden within the park. See p.257.

Ernie Els Club

If you're going to ruin a good walk, do it in style at the Ernie Els golf course (p.339). Located in Sports City, it is difficult with challenging putting surfaces, but visually sumptuous and full of mystery. Stretching over 7,538 yards, it features natural dunes and plants native to the UAE. Nearby, paths wind through the Arabian Ranches golf course (p.339) and an excellent pedestrian path runs 10km around the exterior of the development too.

Creekside Park

It may be in the heart of the city but Creek Park (p.256) is a welcome slice of green with expansive gardens, fishing piers, jogging tracks, barbecue sites, children's play areas, restaurants and kiosks. Rest your legs and take the cable car that runs the 2.3km length of the park. Alternatively, four-wheel cycles can be hired from Gate Two for Dhs.20 per hour. Admission costs Dhs.5.

Downtown Dubai

Wander along wide promenades, linger by the lake or get lost in the narrow passageways of Old Town; one of Dubai's trendiest residential communities, this area was designed for getting around on foot. With cafes, restaurants and coffee shops at every turn, there are plenty of pit-stop possibilities. See p.232.

Mirdif

As a residential area, Mirdif is good for walking and is also home to two community parks. Both have sprung walking tracks around their perimeter – perfect for wannabe yummy mummies; provided your kids are old enough to tackle the climbing frames on their own, you can walk a few laps, keeping them in sight the whole time. Uptown Mirdif shopping centre also makes for a nice outdoor stroll – although you might spend more time shopping and eating than walking. See uptownmirdiff.ae.

Jumeira Open Beach Running Track

An early morning walk on the beach got easier (and less sandy) when the 1.5km track on Jumeira Open Beach opened. With running and cycling lanes, distance markers and regular maintenance, it offers a fun and free way to get active while enjoying some people watching and sunshine. The track starts near Dubai Marine Resort and is open 24 hours.

Mall Walkers

Indulge in (speedy) window shopping at Mall of the Emirates (before the crowds descend) with Mall Walkers. Register at the customer service desk on the ground floor near parking area A and turn up at car park entrance A-F, on the first floor, at 08:30 on Saturday, Monday or Wednesday mornings wearing running or walking shoes. There's another club at Oasis Centre Mall which meets outside Fitness First at 08:00 on Tuesdays and Saturdays.

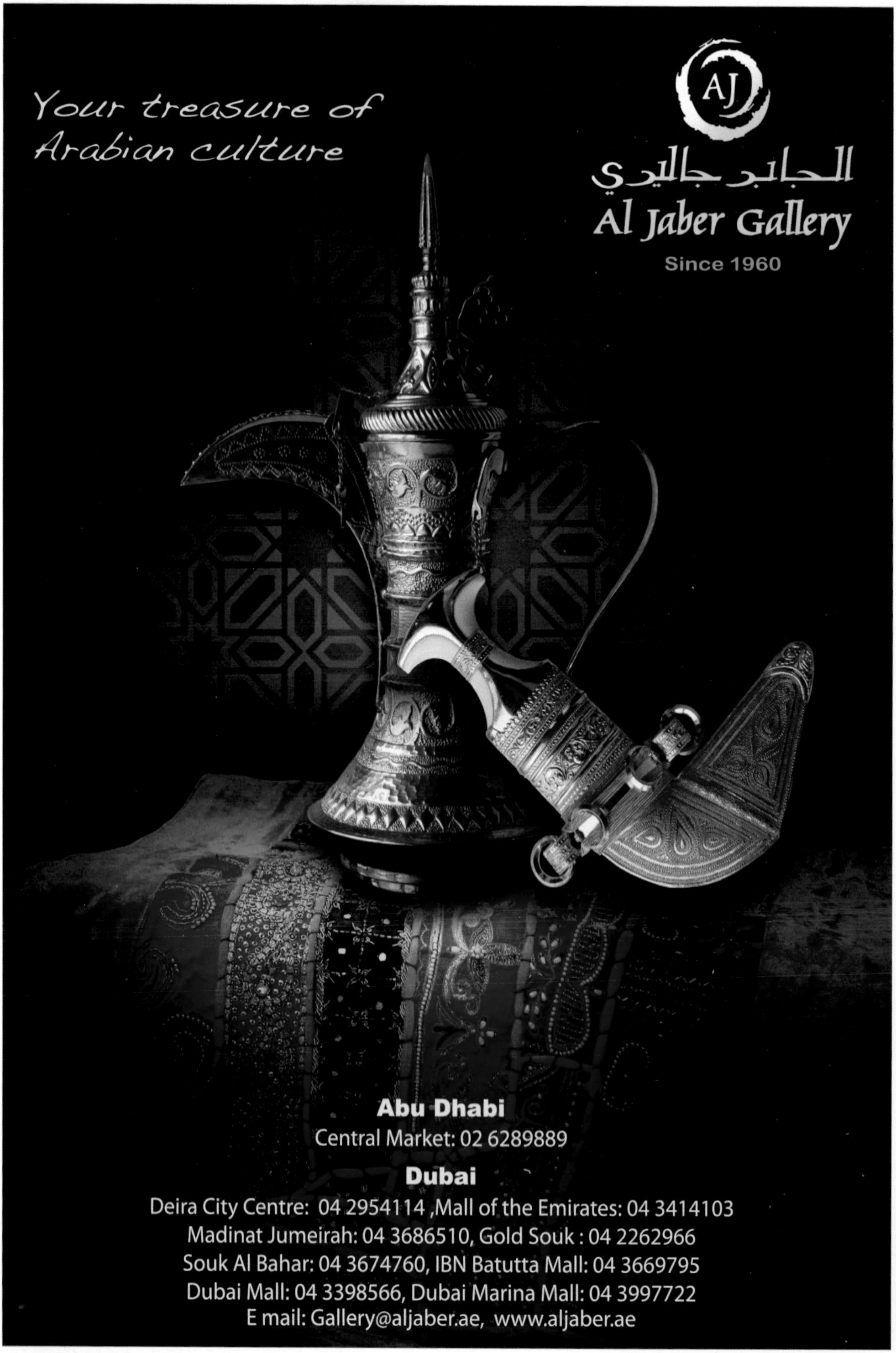
Your treasure of
Arabian culture
AJ
الجابر جاليري
Al Jaber Gallery
Since 1960
Abu Dhabi
Central Market: 02 6289889
Dubai
Deira City Centre: 04 2954114 ,Mall of the Emirates: 04 3414103
Madinat Jumeirah: 04 3686510, Gold Souk : 04 2262966
Souk Al Bahar: 04 3674760, IBN Batutta Mall: 04 3669795
Dubai Mall: 04 3398566, Dubai Marina Mall: 04 3997722
E mail: Gallery@aljaber.ae, www.aljaber.ae

Shopping

SHOPPING

The variety of shops on offer in Dubai is impressive and the contribution retail makes to the emirate's economy is not to be underestimated. The Dubai Shopping Festival, a month dedicated to consumerism, takes place annually with sweeping discounts, entertainment and promotions (although sales seem to happen all year round). Dubai's development is inextricably linked to shopping, and with each new development comes a new mall.

The city's shopping highlights include markets, boutiques, a few thrift shops and a plethora of designer names. Shopping revolves around the malls, both big and small (see p.422), but the expanding numbers of independent stores (see p.417), though harder to find, are invariably more original than anything the malls have to offer.

While shopping is definitely part of the tourism strategy in Dubai, you'll find that the focus is on offering a fantastic range of products rather than offering surprisingly low prices. There are bargains to be had, particularly if you hold out for the sales, but fashion items are often more expensive than they are in other countries.

Practicality plays a large part in the mall culture; during the hotter months, malls are oases of cool in the sweltering city – somewhere to walk, shop, eat and be entertained. From the smaller community malls, to the mega malls that have changed the skyline, shopping opportunities abound and most shops are open until 22:00 every night and even later at the weekends. The malls are particularly busy at the weekends, especially on Friday evenings. The various shopping areas, the closest that Dubai has to high streets, are great for their eclectic mix of shops.

Like in many countries, the cost of living is increasing and while some of what is available is still cheaper than elsewhere, groceries seem to be more expensive every week. While average prices for most items are comparable, there are not many places that can beat Dubai's range and frequency of the sales. Cars are, on the whole, a good buy and petrol, though prices are rising, is still cheap enough to make large 4WDs practical for the school run. Electronics can be cheaper, but it depends what you are used to; and Dubai is the world's leading re-exporter of gold.

The variety of goods on sale in the city means there is very little that is not available. For most items there is enough choice to fit any budget, from the streets of Karama with its fake designer goods, to the shops in the malls that sell the real thing.

One of the few retail sectors where Dubai is lacking is second-hand shops (see Second-Hand Items on p.405), although there are a few linked to various charities. With the population still being largely transitory, there is no shortage of second-hand goods, with many being advertised on the noticeboards in supermarkets, in the classified section of newspapers, and on websites (such as dubizzle.com).

Further afield, Sharjah's modern malls offer a similar selection of brands and they are convenient for those living on that side of the city. Sharjah's souks, Al Arsah Souk in particular, are more traditional than those in Dubai and are great for unique gifts. Sharjah is also renowned for its furniture warehouses, especially those selling Indian pieces, such as Lucky's, Pinky's and Khan's. Ajman is developing as the population grows, and has its own City Centre mall and an area with garment factories and their outlet shops. The traffic to both emirates can be heavy and they are more traditional, with many companies still working split shifts (closing between 13:00 and 16:00).

Online Shopping

The range of products you can find online, and perhaps the discounted prices, make online shopping more appealing, particularly for items you can't find locally. However, not all companies will ship to the UAE and if they do, the shipping charges can be prohibitive.

Quick Reference

The use of PayPal can often cause problems as the facility is only available to those with a US or UK credit card, but vendors on sites like eBay may be flexible if you explain the situation. Many sites will accept other forms of payment. Sites like Amazon should provide little difficulty, although its branded packaging may be opened at customs. Companies without representation in the region will sometimes agree to sell directly to individual customers if requested.

Online shopping in Dubai is still in its infancy, but you can get a range of items delivered to your door. A select range of non-perishable food and household items can be ordered locally through bebida.ae, and you can buy non-food items from Carrefour's website, (ic4uae.com), and groceries from SuperMart (supermart.ae).

Hellwafashion (hellwafashion.com) is an online resource providing information on the clothes on offer in Dubai's independent stores (p.417) and designer boutiques. Vivre is an upmarket online fashion and accessories store (vivre.com), while Fashionation.me is a 'members-only' luxury retailer of designer and lifestyle brands.

Emirates' range of in-flight merchandise is available to buy online (emirateshighstreet.com), while nahel.com sells a range of lifestyle goods, with the aim of being cheap and able to source any item you can't find. Jacky's Electronics (jackys.com) has a fairly comprehensive site with good deals; Magrudy's website (magrudy.com) allows for both buying and reserving books; visit askexplorer.com for residents' guides, maps, off-road routes and visitors' guides to the region; and martarabia.com sells fashion, shoes and cosmetics. There are also sites based in the UAE that will arrange for gifts to be delivered both here and internationally, such as quickdubai.com and papagiftexpress.com, which delivers to India, Sri Lanka, Qatar, Oman and the UAE.

Second-hand items can be bought through sites such as dubizzle.com, expatwoman.com, souk.ae, souq.com and websouq.com.

Aramex (see also Shipping, p.370) provides a 'Shop & Ship' service which sets up a mailbox in both the UK and US, great for dealing with sites which do not offer international shipping. Borderlinx (borderlinx.com) provides a similar service for stores that will only ship to the USA. Aramex also offers a Web Surfer card, a prepaid MasterCard for use online.

Refunds, Exchanges & Consumer Rights

The policies on refunds and exchanges vary from shop to shop. There is more chance of success with faulty goods rather than if you have simply changed your mind, and it is more common to be offered an exchange or credit note rather than a refund. Even with tags attached, many stores will not even consider an exchange unless you have the receipt. For some items, such as those in sealed packages, shops insist that the packaging should be intact so that the item can be resold – a fairly illogical stance if the item proves to be faulty.

If you are having no success with customer services, ask to speak to the manager, as the person on the shop floor is often not authorised to deviate from standard policy whereas managers may be more flexible.

Store Finder

The following pages detail key information about shopping in Dubai's shopping areas (p.410), malls (p.422) and souks (p.419). Use the Store Finder on p.410 to locate various stores; for the lowdown on Dubai's most popular malls, including listings of their various outlets, see p.422.

The Consumer Protection Department of the UAE Ministry of Economy has been established to safeguard the interests of shoppers. The department tracks and regulates retail prices and has rejected planned price increases for staple goods. It has also mandated that all retail outlets display a notice of their consumer rights policy in the store. Consumers wishing to complain about a retailer can complete a form on the website economy.gov.ae, send an email to consumer@economy.ae, or call the freephone hotline on 600 522 225. The hotline is manned by non-English speakers so it may be best to stick to the other methods. In Dubai, the Consumer Rights Unit within the Dubai Economic Department (600 545555, dubaided.gov.ae) primarily deals with unfit food, but can be contacted to report faulty goods or to complain if a guarantee is not honoured.

Shipping & Couriers

Due to the number of international and local shipping and courier agencies, it is possible to transport just about anything. Both air freight and sea freight are available; air freight is faster and you can track the items, but it's more expensive and not really suitable for large or heavy objects. Sea freight takes several weeks to arrive but it is cheaper and you can rent containers for larger items. It is worth getting a few quotes and finding out what will happen when the goods arrive; some offer no services at the destination while others, usually the bigger ones, will clear customs and deliver right to the door. Check for discounts during the Dubai Shopping Festival (p.25) or Dubai Summer Surprises (p.27). Empost (600 565 555), the Emirates Postal Service, offers both local and international courier and air freight services – its prices are competitive and packages can be tracked.

Several courier companies can arrange for items to be delivered to Dubai, and Aramex (600 544 000) offers a great service called 'Shop & Ship' for those wishing to buy online. For a one-off payment of $45, Aramex will set up a mailbox for you in both the UK and the US. The company will then arrange deliveries up to three times a week; packages can be tracked.

How To Pay

You'll have few problems parting with your money. Credit cards (American Express, Diners Club, MasterCard and Visa) and debit cards (Visa Electron) are accepted in shopping malls, supermarkets and many independent shops. All cards now use the chip-and-pin system. However, you can only pay with cash at petrol stations for fuel. You are never too far from an ATM in the city and it is preferable to pay with cash in souks and smaller shops – try to have a variety of denominations, because it is better to hand over close to the exact amount. US dollars and other foreign currencies are accepted in some larger shops (and in airport duty free).

Bargaining

Bargaining is still common practice in the souks and shopping areas of the UAE; you'll need to give it a go to get the best prices. Before you take the plunge, try to get an idea of prices from a few shops, as there can often be a significant difference. Once you've decided how much to spend, offer an initial bid that is roughly around half that price. Stay laidback and vaguely uninterested. When your initial offer is rejected (and it will be), keep going until you reach an agreement or until you have reached your limit. If the price isn't right, say so and walk out – the vendor will often follow and suggest a compromise price. The more you buy, the better the discount. When the price is agreed, it is considered bad form to back out of the sale.

Bargaining isn't commonly accepted in malls and independent shops. However, some shops such as jewellery stores, smaller electronics stores and eyewear optical centres do operate a set discount system so you never know: ask whether there is a discount on the marked price and you may bag a bargain.

Buyer Beware!

Traps for the unwary shopper do exist in Dubai. Some of the international stores sell items at prices that are far more expensive than in their country of origin (you can even still see the original price tags). This can be as much as 30% higher – so beware.

Sending Gifts Home

Sending gifts to your friends and family back home shouldn't be too taxing as there are several online stores that offer international delivery services. For cards and flowers, moonpig.com is a great online store where you can customise your own cards by uploading photos, and have them sent to a variety of locations. Interflora (fleurop.com) also delivers a selection of gifts internationally and can often accommodate same day or next day delivery.

Shoes & Clothing Sizes

Figuring out your size isn't rocket science, just a bit of a pain. Firstly, check the label – international sizes are often printed on them. Secondly, check the store – they will usually have a conversion chart on display. Otherwise, a UK size is always two higher than a US size (so a UK 10 is a US 6). To convert European sizes into US sizes, subtract 32 (so a European 38 is a actually a US 6 or a UK 10).

To convert European sizes into UK sizes, a 38 is roughly a 10. As for shoes, a woman's UK 6 is a European 39 or a US 8.5, and a men's UK 10 is a European 44 or a US 10.5. If in any doubt, just ask a store assistant for help.

Specialist Sizes

Clothing sizes in Dubai's stores usually range from a UK 8 to 16. However, petite ranges are available in many stores, including Debenhams, Splash and Marks & Spencer, while H&M, New Look, Wallis, Bhs, Liz Claiborne and Woolworths all carry plus-size collections (also look out for Evans in Debenhams and Scarlett's in Splash).

For more exclusive lines for the fuller figure, try Irene Sieber, Oui Plus and Samoon (all in Wafi), Charisma in the Beach Centre in Jumeira, or the excellent Ulla Popken, which has stores in Marina Mall, Barsha Mall, The Dubai Mall and Mirdif City Centre.

Men looking for larger sizes should head to Big & Tall (04 397 3873) on Bank Street. It caters for waist sizes from 40 plus and shirts up to 6XL.

Harvey Nichols

S*uce

Dubai Outlet Mall

Mirdif City Centre

Top 10 Things That Are Cheaper In Dubai

Eating Out

Enjoying a three-course dinner and a few rounds of drinks in a fine-dining restaurant will probably cost more-or-less the same as in other cities, but cheap, street-side dining is one of Dubai's great bargains. Whether you snack on a Dhs.6 chicken shawarma at Al Mallah in Satwa, or feast on a Dhs.17 Thali lunch (refillable pots of yummy vegetarian curry) from Karama's Saravanna Bhavan, it's hard to find such delicious, authentic food at a cheaper price.

Home Help

Having a cleaner come in a few times a week to hoover and dust would be an unaffordable luxury for most people living in their home countries, but here in Dubai it is as normal as eating breakfast in the morning. For as little as Dhs.35 per hour, you can organise a maid service to do all the stuff you're too busy – or too lazy – to do. Frazzled parents can also rejoice at the bargain babysitters' rates available in Dubai. Call Molly Maid (04 339 7799) or Ready Maids (04 396 6779) for more info (also see p.107).

Personal Grooming

Having pretty hands and feet comes cheap in Dubai, where there is seemingly a nail salon on every street corner, and you'll pay as little as Dhs.70 for a manicure and pedicure. Even the boys aren't left out: gents can enjoy a shampoo, a hot oil treatment, a haircut, a shave and a head massage, all for around Dhs.40 at your typical Karama-based men's salon.

Cigarettes

That Dhs.9 pack of Marlboro Lights would set you back the equivalent of over Dhs.35 in the UK, Dhs.15 in the US, and Dhs.25 in Australia. It's good news for visiting relatives, who always want to take back a few sneaky cartons, and bad news for smokers, who have little financial incentive to quit here; but at least you don't have to charge your friends 50p every time they cadge a smoke off you.

Taxis

In many of our home countries, a night on the tiles would involve an elaborate plan to recruit a designated driver, or a lengthy wait in a queue for a taxi. Here in Dubai, walking out of a restaurant or club to find a line of cabs ready and waiting to take you home, at a very reasonable price, is the norm. However, since January 2013, passengers now have to pay the Dhs.4 fee every time the taxi passes through a Salik toll gate.

Soft Drinks

Seemingly, since the beginning of time, a can of Coke or Pepsi used to cost just one little dirham when bought from a cornershop, a petrol station or a supermarket. Although the price was increased to Dhs.1.5 in 2011, it's still quite a bargain. Unfortunately, the attractive price doesn't always survive the transition to restaurant menus, where that Dhs.1.5 can of pop can set you back a shocking Dhs.15 or more. That's quite a mark-up.

Petrol

Filling up your car here is cheaper than in many other countries, and often significantly so. For a litre of petrol you'll pay around Dhs.1.72 at a Dubai pump. As a rule of thumb, it costs roughly a quarter of what you'd pay in parts of Europe, a third of that in Australia or India, and about half the price of petrol in America.

Cinema Tickets

You'll pay between Dhs.35 for a cinema ticket in Dubai (or Dhs.130 for VIP luxury seating). A ticket will set you back around Dhs.50 in London, Dhs.45 in New York, Dhs.45 in Dublin and Dhs.67 in Tokyo. The downside is that here in Dubai, there are no concessions if you are a child, a student or a pensioner, and the ticket price is the same, no matter what time of day it is (whereas in other cities, morning and matinee shows are cheaper).

Tailoring

Having a tailor whip up a made-to-measure piece of clothing is prohibitively expensive in many cities, where a simple shift dress could cost you as much as Dhs.1,000 and you'll need at least Dhs.5,000 for a bespoke suit. In Dubai, however, there are tailors who can create a long dress for around Dhs.100, a blouse for Dhs.50, and a suit starting from as little as Dhs.1,600.

Trips To Oman

It's fast becoming one of the most popular Middle Eastern destinations for tourists from Europe, and it's not hard to understand why: Oman is a breathtaking country combining scenery, culture and luxury hotels. And it's just a four-hour drive to Muscat from Dubai, so you can visit without forking out high prices for a plane ticket. Regional visitors often get good rates on hotels too. For more information see Out Of The City, p.314.

Laundry & Dry Cleaning

There are no self-service launderettes, but laundries are everywhere in the city. As well as dry cleaning and laundry, they also offer an ironing service. The service is usually exceptional and you can opt to pick up your clothes or have them delivered. Compensation polices for lost or damaged items vary, but losses are rare. Large chains normally have a free delivery service. The prices for laundry are reasonable. Expect to pay Dhs.8 for a shirt, Dhs.25 for a suit and Dhs.35 for a quilt.

Repairs & Cobbling

Dubai's multitude of tailors will repair or alter garments for a reasonable price (see below), but there are fewer companies who mend shoes. Locksmiths in the city often offer the service and you'll find stores in Satwa and Kuwait Street in Karama. Minutes (p.448) offers shoe repairs in addition to its key cutting service and it has outlets located in many of the main malls. 60 Second Lock & Shoe Repair (04 355 2600) is located near Spinneys (p.417) in Bur Dubai and Al Fareed Shoes (04 359 2862) is located on Musalla Road. NDust Shoe Repairs offers a handy collection and delivery service (ndustshoes.com).

Tailoring & Bespoke Services

Tailors can be found in most areas, but there is a concentration of stores in Meena Bazaar, near to Dubai Museum in Bur Dubai, and on the main street in Satwa. If you need simple alterations, such as hemming, then head to one of these areas and take your pick – for simple work, the general standard is fine. For anything more complex, the best way to select a tailor is by recommendation. A good tailor can make a garment from scratch, either from a photo or by copying an existing garment. It may take a few fitting sessions and alterations to get it just right, but it's worth the effort, and with tailoring services so cheap compared to other international cities, it's well worth getting some custom-made clothes while living in Dubai.

In Satwa, Deepa's (04 349 9733), Deepak's (04 344 8836) and Dream Girl Tailors (04 337 7287, another branch in Meena Bazaar) are popular and will take on all tailoring jobs from taking up trousers to making ball gowns. Skirts cost upwards of Dhs.70 and dresses from around Dhs.120. Khamis Abdullah Trading & Embroidery (04 225 5940) in Rashidiya is one of the least expensive in town.

Dream Boy (04 352 1840), near Dubai Museum, is good for shirts and suits, as are Kachins (04 352 1386) and Whistle & Flute (04 342 9229); shirts usually start from Dhs.30 and suits from Dhs.500. Stitches has stores in The Village Mall (04 342 1476) and Jumeira (04 348 6110). Lobo in Meena Bazaar is also good for suits, which range from Dhs.1,500-2,500 (04 352 3760) including fabric and stitching.

WHAT & WHERE TO BUY

With so much choice there should be little problem finding what you need. From antiques to the latest technology, and from tools to toys, the aim of this section is to let you know what's out there and the best places to buy.

Alcohol

It is legal for anyone over the age of 21 to buy alcohol in Dubai's restaurants and licensed bars, and some clubs, for consumption on the premises. If you wish to drink at home you will need a liquor licence (see p.40); how much you are permitted to buy is dependent on your monthly salary.

Two companies operate liquor stores in Dubai: African + Eastern (A+E) and Maritime & Mercantile International (MMI). Both have branches in several locations around the city, the most handy being the ones near supermarkets. The selection is decent, and prices are not so bad: wine costs from around Dhs.35 and upwards; vodka from Dhs.60; whisky from Dhs.80; and beer from Dhs.4 to Dhs.8 per can or Dhs.100 to Dhs.135 per case. Alcohol is, however, subject to 30% tax on the marked prices.

There is a good selection of alcohol (and several other products including perfume, confectionEry and cosmetics) available at the airport Duty Free. The alcohol available at the airport is similar in price to the shops in town, but you don't pay the tax.

There are a number of 'hole in the wall' stores close to Dubai that sell duty-free alcohol to members of the public, even if you don't have a licence. Prices are reasonable and there is no tax. You can pick up a cheap bottle of wine from around Dhs.30, and most international brands of beer, wine and spirits are available. Certain brands are offered exclusively in certain stores, so it is worth comparing what's on offer if you are looking for something different.

You don't need to worry about being busted buying booze illegally, but you should be careful when driving home; it is the transporting of alcohol that could get you into trouble, especially if you are stopped within the borders of Sharjah, which is a 'dry' emirate. There have been reports of random police checks on vehicles driving from Ajman into Sharjah. Also, if you have an accident and you're found to have a boot full of liquor, your day could take a sudden turn for the worse.

African + Eastern > p.43, 375

Spinneys Centre Al Safa 2 **800 243 377**
africaneastern.com
Map **2 B5** Metro **Noor Islamic Bank**

Conveniently located in shopping areas and stocking a wide variety of products, A&E outlets remain a good place to purchase wine, spirits and beer. Its stores sell

AND HERE
AND HERE
AND HERE
AND HERE
AND HERE
YOU ARE HERE
WE ARE HERE

the typical brands and a few imports of Japanese and German beer. It is also worth checking out its regular promotions as a particular brand of beer or wine is selected each month for a tax-free promotion. For other locations see the Store Finder p.440.

Al Hamra Cellar

Nr RAK Ceramics, Al Hamra Village Development
Ras Al Khaimah **07 424 5000**
mmidubai.com

MMI-owned Al Hamra Cellar is around an hour's drive from Dubai along Sheikh Mohammed Bin Zayed Rd. The store stocks an amazing selection of beers, spirits and award-winning wines from around the world – it also has properly chilled storage facilities and wine specially selected by guru Oz Clarke.

Barracuda Beach Resort

Nr Dreamland Aqua Park, Khor Al Baida
Umm Al Quwain **06 768 1555**
barracuda.ae

A tax-free, licence-free outlet that is popular with Dubai's residents. The store has recently undergone some renovation and the new building houses a bigger variety of stock. There is a superb selection, including the regular brands of beer, wine and spirits.

Centaurus International RAK

Ras Al Selaab Ras Al Khaimah **07 244 5866**
centaurusint.info

This is another 'hole in the wall' outlet which offers a good range of products. You can view its range of wine, beer and spirits on its online shop, and it also offers a delivery service.

MMI

Nr Spinneys Centre, Shk Khalifa Bin Zayed St
Al Mankhool **04 352 3091**
mmidubai.com
Map **2 L5** Metro **BurJuman**

Similar to A&E, this store offers a broad selection of international brands and lesser known names. To get the best value for money, choose from its bin end discounts on wine which select new or lesser known brands for promotion. Its more exclusive store Le Clos in Emirates Terminal 3 offers a premium selection of alcohol that can only be pre-ordered on departure and collected on arrival at the terminal. See the website (leclos.net) for more details, or call (04 220 3633). For other locations see the Store Finder, p.448.

Art

The art scene in Dubai, quiet for so long, is now enjoying rapid growth. Several of the galleries (p.250) in Dubai display traditional and contemporary art by Arabic and international artists which is also for sale.

Art Dubai (artdubai.ae) is a commercial art fair that draws together artwork from many of Dubai's galleries. The event will run from 20-23 March in 2013 and is a great opportunity to check out the variety of art on offer in the city.

The Majlis Gallery in Bastakiya is a great venue for fine art, handmade glass, pottery and other unusual pieces. For cutting edge art, check out the XVA Gallery (xvagallery.com) and Boutique 1 Gallery (boutique1.com). The Art Source in Deira stocks a range of original artwork – it also offers a framing service. For funky, but inexpensive, you'll find a limited selection in furniture stores like IKEA (p.386) and THE One (p.386).

ARTE Souk

Artisans of the Emirates (ARTE) occasionally sets up markets selling arts and crafts in Times Square Centre (p.439) and Festival Centre (p.429). These stalls sell a range of items including photographs, jewellery and a variety of art. For more information on the stalls and market dates, visit arte.ae.

Gallery One (g-1.com) sells a selection of stylish photographs and canvas prints and is particularly good if you want images of the region.

If your knowledge of art isn't up to speed, Police Pigalle (policepigalle.com) offers art consultations and will help source artwork from within the UAE or abroad. You can also find information on art auctions, art fairs and gallery openings at artinthecity.com. Souk Madinat Jumeirah has a large concentration of boutiques selling art, glass and photographs, both originals and reproductions. The style and subjects are diverse, from traditional to modern, Arabic to international. And Dubai's up-and-coming art district in Al Quoz (p.252) is home to a variety of art galleries.

XVA Gallery

Many of the galleries and showrooms in Dubai have a framing service or can recommend one. There are some excellent framing shops on Plant Street in Satwa (p.411) and in Karama (p.411) – they can frame anything from prints to sports jerseys. You can also create your own art by transferring your photos onto canvas. There are a few stores that offer the service including Riot Studio (04 445 8488, riotstudio.com), as well as Portfolio (portfolio-uae.com) in Festival Centre and Mercato Mall. If you want to have a piece of art commissioned, London-based Dubai Art (dubaiart.org) specialises in bespoke art, from personal portraits to commercial paintings.

New Art Dimensions

For a unique touch to your home, MacKenzie Art will hand paint original or existing designs onto canvas or entire walls or ceilings. From children's bedrooms and dining rooms to five-star hotel suites, rooms can be livened up and 'dramatically enhanced' or 'subtly subdued,' depending on your personal taste and the artist's recommendation. Visit mackenzieart.com for inspiration or call 04 341 9803 for a consultation.

Art & Craft Supplies

A number of shops sell a good range of art and craft supplies, with everything from paints and crayons for children to top-quality oils available. Particularly good places to find materials are Bin Sougat Mall in Rashidiya (p.436), and the Holiday Centre on Sheikh Zayed Road. Emirates Trading (04 334 4900) stocks everything from children's crayons to industrial spray booths and it is a supplier of Windsor & Newton and Daler-Rowney products. Craft Land (mycraftland.com) supplies materials, machines, tools and gadgets for a host of needle crafts, including knitting, sewing, embroidery, quilting and crochet, and also offers classes, clinics and clubs for keen crafters.

Wasco White Star (04 342 2179) stocks craft supplies that are suitable for children's projects and difficult to find elsewhere. Prices can be expensive for some speciality items, such as mosaic tiles, but art materials are reasonably priced. For DIY picture framing, Rafi Frame Store (04 337 6989), aka Al Warda Gallery, in Karama is the place to find the necessary equipment, including mountboards.

Baby Items

The basic baby items are all available in Dubai and, while there may not be the full range from your home country, you should find nursery essentials like bottles, buggies, car seats, changing bags, cots, prams, rocking chairs and travel cots.

Supermarkets stock formula, nappies and wipes and many sell a good range of bottles and feeding equipment. Choithrams (p.416) has the best selection of formulas, stocking popular UK brands SMA and Cow & Gate. If you can't find an item, check with the store because some are kept behind the counter. A good range of jars of baby food are available but prices are slightly higher than what you'd pay at home. Pharmacies sell baby essentials and some have breast pumps.

Organic Foods & Cafe (p.417) at The Greens – and opening soon on Sheikh Zayed Rd and at The Village Mall – sells a wide selection of natural and ecofriendly baby items, including biodegradable and terry cloth nappies, wooden toys, organic baby food and children's mattresses made from organic fibres. Visit mumzworld.com for all those baby essentials, from walkers and playpens to clothing and skincare.

Toys R Us has large baby departments (Babies R Us) at its Deira, Dubai Festival City and Times Square Centre stores, which stock a wide range of products, from pushchairs to baby bottles, cots to travel accessories. The quality of the items is good and most conform to international safety standards. Safety 1st and Maxi Cosi car seats are widely available and should fit most cars; all shops will offer to help fit car seats but the staff aren't always knowledgeable about what is most suitable. You can also rent car seats, buggies, strollers and other equipment from Rentacrib (rentacrib.ae) – if you hire a car seat its staff will fit it for you free of charge.

The range of slings on sale is pretty limited and backpacks to put your baby in are hard to find, so you may need to order these items from overseas or look online at Bubs Boutique (bubsboutique.com) or Baby Souk (babysouk.com).

For clothing, there are several stores to choose from. The Dubai Mall (p.426) has a very good selection of well-known stores and a range of high-end brands like Cacharel Paris, Burberry Children, Jacadi and Armani Junior. Online store DubaiBabies (dubaibabies.com) also stocks a fabulous range of products for babies and parents. IKEA (p.386) has a small range of nursery furniture such as cots, changing tables and bathtubs; it also makes a selection of cot sheets and blankets and some baby-safe toys. Worth waiting for are Babyshop's sales, held several times a year.

Babyshop

Mall of the Emirates Al Barsha 1 **04 341 0604**
babyshopstores.com
Map **1 R6** Metro **Mall of the Emirates**

Babyshop sells low-cost baby clothing and essentials such as feeding items, clothing, toys and even baby monitors. It also stocks feeding pillows, safety rails and sterilisers. Its affordable newborn items come in value packs, perfect for the temporary items you can't live without, but know you won't keep. For other locations see Store Finder, p.441.

DubaiBabies

050 600 3199
dubaibabies.com

Shop at your leisure at this online boutique selling blankets, feeding essentials, slings and skincare products, among other items. The store also offers a good selection of gifts that are perfect for baby showers, such as cupcakes, gift baskets, balloons and books for new parents. It has a small kiosk in Mercato Mall (p.432) and offers free delivery within Dubai.

Goodbaby

Nr Spinneys, Shk Khalifa Bin Zayed Rd Al Karama
04 397 5653
goodbabydubai.com
Map **2 L5** Metro **BurJuman**

A great store for key items like car seats and changing mats. You'll find a large selection of buggies too from Maclaren, Quinny and Phil & Teds. The store also stocks stairguards, walkers, cots and engaging toys for kids.

Just Kidding

Gold & Diamond Park Al Quoz Industrial 3
04 341 3922
justkidding-uae.com
Map **1 S6** Metro **First Gulf Bank**

Not for the budget conscious, Just Kidding sells baby items, furniture and clothes from Europe, including Bugaboo buggies, Little Company bags and Stokke high chairs. You'll find interesting toys for playtime and a catalogue of items that includes maternity wear, gift sets and slings. The store offers free delivery to Dubai and a gift registry service for baby showers.

Kidz Inc Dubai

Nr ACE Hardware, Off Shk Zayed Rd Al Quoz Industrial 1 **04 328 5775**
kidzincdubai.com
Map **1 U6** Metro **Noor Islamic Bank**

For some really interesting and unique furniture, toys and accessories, pop into Kidzinc's Al Quoz showroom. It stocks more than 20 quality European children's brands that you'll not find anywhere else in the country.

Mamas & Papas

Mercato Jumeira 1 **04 344 0981**
mamasandpapas.com
Map **2 F4** Metro **Financial Centre**

A household name for well-designed, stylish products for babies and mums-to-be, this shop has several dedicated locations across Dubai (see Store Finder, p.448) and a small concessions store in Harvey Nichols (p.414). The store stocks all you need from toys, car seats, pushchairs, cribs, nursery items and decorations, to maternity clothes and feeding items. Although this is one of the more costly options, it remains a popular spot for gifts and newborn essentials.

Mothercare

The Dubai Mall Downtown Dubai **04 339 9812**
mothercare.com
Map **2 F6** Metro **Burj Khalifa/Dubai Mall**

Mothercare is a long-established store which remains a reliable place to shop for baby essentials. It has a particularly good selection of clothes and many of its larger stores stock cots, prams and car seats. You can order mattresses in specific sizes and items you've seen online or in a UK catalogue can also be ordered, but the delivery time is a minimum of four weeks. The largest branch, in The Dubai Mall, has a fantastic parents' area with changing mats and bottle warmers. See the Store Finder on p.449.

Second-Hand Stuff

Second-hand baby items are widely available in Dubai – you just need to know where to look. There are classifieds listings on dubizzle.com and expatwoman.com, and then of course there's always the supermarket noticeboards.

Bicycles

Dubai may not be the most bicycle-friendly city, but there is an active cycling scene. Road and mountain biking are popular and you can find an adequate (although sometimes expensive) range of equipment for both.

For serious cyclists, an increasing number of shops, and brands, in town offer a good selection of bikes, safety equipment and any accessories you may need. The shops will also repair and service bikes. Kona has a store near Lamcy Plaza, and Ride Bike Shop has in-store workshops on Sheikh Zayed Road and at Mirdif City Centre. Located on Sheikh Zayed Road near the Oasis Centre (p.438), the Specialized Dubai Showroom (050 3469915) stocks a wide range of bikes, clothing and accessories. Wolfi's (see opposite) stocks brands such as Scott, Felt, Merida and Storck.

For the casual cyclist, Toys R Us (p.395) and larger sports shops such as Decathlon at Mirdif City Centre sell more basic models at reasonable prices. Go Sport (p.407) has a large bike section and a workshop in its Mall of the Emirates store. The 'sit-up-and-beg' models – popular with gardeners and delivery cyclists – can be found in the smaller bike shops all over the city (check out Karama and Satwa). Supermarket noticeboards and dubizzle.com are good places for second-hand bikes.

Children's bicycles are widely available in bike and sports shops, and shops like Babyshop (p.377), Toys R Us (p.395) and Goodbaby (p.378) have a range for tiny Bradley Wiggins'. If you want to make cycling a family activity, Wolfi's and Go Sport (p.407) have a selection of children's seats, priced from Dhs.150 to Dhs.300, which its staff will fit for you. Both adults' and children's helmets are available at the main retailers.

Adventure HQ

Times Square Centre Al Qusais1 **04 346 6824**
adventurehq.ae
Map **1 T6** Metro **First Gulf Bank**
Has a good range of Merida and BMC bikes, covering everything from mountain bikes to hybrids and high-end road racers. Also stocks a variety of apparel and accessories and offers servicing, as well as renting out bikes.

Probike

Shk Juma Bin Ahmed Al Maktoum Bldg Al Barsha 1 **04 325 5705**
probike.ae
Map **1 R6** Metro **Mall of the Emirates**
Probike stocks mountain, road and triathlon bikes for all levels, as well as shoes, helmets, apparel and components. Probike is the UAE dealer for Planet X bikes, which are renowned for their value for money. Both bike servicing and a professional fitting service are available and good road bikes can be rented by the day.

Ride Bike Shop

Mirdif City Centre Mirdif **04 284 0038**
ridebikeshop.com
Map **2 P12** Metro **Rashidiya**
Ride has a good range of stock for both serious cyclists and those who just need something for recreational use, and staff will advise on the most suitable bike for your needs. The in-store workshop offers a high standard of maintenance to ensure that you are constantly kept on your saddle! There is a second branch on Sheikh Zayed Road (see Store Finder, p.451).

Wolfi's Bike Shop

Nr Oasis Centre, Shk Zayed Rd Al Quoz 3 **04 339 4453**
wbs.ae
Map **2 B6** Metro **Noor Islamic Bank**
For the cycling community, Wolfi's is more of an institution than simply a shop, although it is also the UAE's biggest dedicated cycle store, where you'll find everything from kids' and leisure bikes to hardcore carbon time trial machines, and plenty in between. The store specialises in top-end brands like Scott, Felt, Storck, Profile Design and Zipp, and staff are all passionate cyclists who are happy to assist. Bike fitting, servicing and bike hire are also available in-store.

Books

You'll find both international bookstores and good local stores in Dubai. Virgin Megastore (p.398) also carries an interesting selection of books related to music and popular culture, and a small selection of books sell in hypermarkets like Carrefour (p.416) and Géant (p.416). All malls feature at least one book store, and if you cannot find a publication, the larger stores often have customer service sections where you can search for titles, place an order or enquire whether it is available in another branch.

The popular online store Amazon also delivers to the UAE – it's usually better to order from the UK site (amazon.co.uk) than the US site (amazon.com), so that you can take advantage of the cheaper delivery rates. Unless you choose the super-expensive express delivery it will take around two weeks to receive your order and your package may be inspected by UAE customs.

Dubai's transitory residents furnish the second-hand book shops – you'll find a wide range of books, particularly fiction, many of which have only been read once. Both House of Prose (p.380) and Book World (below), buy and sell, and they'll also give you back 50% of what you paid on books you've bought from them.

There are regular charity book sales, the most notable being the ones organised by Medecins Sans Frontieres (msf-me.org). They are held several times throughout the year, usually in the Dune Centre in Satwa. You can also buy books by Explorer in the below bookstores or online at askexplorer.com.

Book N Bean

ACE Dubai Festival City **04 232 6992**
Map **2 M9** Metro **Emirates**
Tucked away inside ACE, this second-hand bookshop (a spin-off of House of Prose) sells used books from Dhs.25. Once read, return your books and you'll receive half your money back to put towards the next book you buy. Choose from a good range of recent titles by best-selling authors, all in good condition.

Book World

Nr Satwa Flower Shop Al Satwa **04 349 1914**
Map **2 H5** Metro **World Trade Centre**
Step inside this second-hand bookshop and browse an assortment of pre-loved titles and new books, as well as a fascinating collection of comics. A literary paradise for all bookworms.

Book World By Kinokuniya > *p.427*

The Dubai Mall Downtown Dubai **04 434 0111**
kinokuniya.com
Map **2 F6** Metro **Burj Khalifa/Dubai Mall**
At over 65,000 square feet, Kinokuniya is the biggest bookshop in Dubai. The Japanese chain is a household name in many Asian countries but its store in The Dubai Mall is its first in the Middle East. You will find a variety of international titles, including a particularly good selection of Japanese books, which rivals many of the city's current big players, and a great selection of comics. The store also has a large stationery section, a fantastic range of childrens' books, and an extensive selection of magazines and journals.

Booksplus

Festival Centre Dubai Festival City **04 232 5563**
Map **2 M9** Metro **Emirates**
A fairly comprehensive range of titles and international magazines are stocked at this small bookstore. This is a perfect place to pick up light reads and popular titles. For other locations see Store Finder, p.442.

Bookworm

Nr Park n Shop Al Safa 1 **04 394 5770**
Map **2 C5** Metro **Business Bay**
A great store for inspiring kids to read, Bookworm has an extensive range of titles that covers everything from read-to books for very young kids up to young adults. In addition to its assortment of educational books, it also a stocks a fun selection of toys and gifts. For other locations see Store Finder, p.442.

Borders

Mall of the Emirates Al Barsha 1 **04 341 5758**
almayagroup.com
Map **1 R6** Metro **Mall of the Emirates**
This US chain has stores in Mall of the Emirates, Deira and Mirdif City Centres, Dubai Marina Mall, Ibn Battuta and DIFC. The variety of books on sale is vast and its larger stores have a fantastic selection of the latest international magazines. Several branches also contain a Starbucks where you can peruse your purchases over a coffee. Borders stocks a good range of Paperchase stationery items, a small gift range, and one of the better selections of diaries and calendars. See Store Finder, p.442.

Culture & Co

Al Nasr Plaza, Umm Hurair St Oud Metha
04 357 3603
culturecodubai.net
Map **2 L6** Metro **Oud Metha**
A great option for French speakers and readers, or students of the language, this bookshop in Oud Metha sells a good selection of French novels, guidebooks, magazines and papers.

House Of Prose

Dubai Garden Centre Al Quoz Industrial 3
04 340 0006
Map **1 S6** Metro **First Gulf Bank**
If your reading habit is breaking the bank, head for House of Prose and spend an hour browsing through a huge collection of second-hand books; there's a great choice of English fiction for children and adults alike. Most of the stock is in excellent condition, and you may be able to pick up a new release that has only been read once, for around half the price it would cost if you bought it new. For other locations see Store Finder, p.446.

Jashanmal Bookstore

Mall of the Emirates Al Barsha 1 **04 340 6789**
jashanmalbooks.com
Map **1 R6** Metro **Mall of the Emirates**
Jashanmal's selection is wide-ranging, with international books and magazines. Head here during the sales and you can grab some really good bargains. For other locations see Store Finder p.446.

Magrudy's

Magrudy's Mall Jumeira 1 **04 344 4193**
magrudy.com
Map **2 H4** Metro **Emirates Towers**
This local chain has a wide selection covering new releases, reference, travel, fiction, children's books and much more. It now has seven retail outlets in Dubai, as well as a dedicated educational resource centre. The store also holds an annual warehouse sale where you can pick up discounted books, toys and gifts. For other locations see Store Finder, p.448.

The Old Library

Dubai Community Theatre & Arts Centre (DUCTAC)
Al Barsha 1 **04 341 4777**
theoldlibrary.ae
Map **1 R6** Metro **Mall of the Emirates**
Established in 1969, this is the oldest English language library serving Dubai's expat community. Nestled within DUCTAC in the Mall of the Emirates, the library has a collection of over 19,000 adult fiction and general reference books, as well as children and teenagers, science fiction, fantasy fiction, romance and the Middle East. There's also a selection of second-hand books for sale.

Camera Equipment

From single-use cameras to darkroom equipment, photographers can usually find most things in Dubai. Like the rest of the world, digital models dominate the shelves and can be bought in the city's electronics shops, hypermarkets, and photo processing outlets; all the major brands are represented.

The jury's still out on whether cameras here are cheaper than elsewhere; it really depends on where else you are looking. Camera and equipment prices in Asia, for example, are often lower than in Dubai, while in most of Europe they will be higher. Within Dubai, prices will vary between the larger outlets, where prices are fixed, and the electronics shops of Bur Dubai (p.410). However, while you might be able to bag a bargain from the independent retailers using your superior powers of negotiation, you will ultimately get more protection buying from the larger outlets. The most important consideration, if you are buying the camera to take abroad, is to ensure your warranty is international; and don't just take the retailer's word for it, ask to read the warranty to make sure.

For specialist equipment and a good range of film cameras, the main outlets are Grand Stores and Salam Studio. Grand Stores sells Fuji, Nikon, Canon and Mamiya; Salam Studio carries Bronica, Leica, Minolta and Pentax; they both sell a selection of filters, tripods and studio equipment as well as the usual spares, cables and cases. The alternative to buying locally is to use an online retailer. B&H Photo (bhphotovideo.com) and Adorama (adorama.com) are extremely popular.

For second-hand equipment, gulfphotoplus.com (an essential site for all photography enthusiasts) has an equipment noticeboard, as well as being a great source of information, a good networking site and having details of upcoming courses.

Grand Stores offers a repair service and HN Camera Repairs (04 349 0971) offers in-house repairs for all makes of camera.

Grand Stores Digital

The Dubai Mall Downtown Dubai **04 339 8614**
grandstores.com
Map **2 F6** Metro **Burj Khalifa/Dubai Mall**

This is the main retailer for Nikon cameras in Dubai; the store also stocks Fuji, Canon and Mamiya. You can have your camera cleaned and repaired in its stores, which can be found in several locations across Dubai (for other locations, see Store Finder, p.446).

MK Trading Co.

Nr Twin Towers, Baniyas Rd Al Rigga **04 222 5745**
mktradingco.com
Map **2 N5** Metro **Union**

This store is the place to purchase Sigma cameras and lenses, as well as other leading brands; it also stocks a particularly good selection of filters. The store offers a repair facility.

National Store

Khansaheb Bldg, Al Fahidi St Al Souk Al Kabeer **04 353 6074**
Map **2 L4** Metro **Al Ghubaiba**

This store is a distributor of Canon products and you'll find a good selection of cameras, printers and camera accessories from the well-known brand. There are several branches of this store in Dubai (see Store Finder, p.449).

Salam

Wafi Mall Umm Hurair 2 **04 704 8484**
salams.com
Map **2 L7** Metro **Dubai Healthcare City**

Stocking a complete range of professional-grade camera and studio equipment, this department store is considered by many to be the most comprehensive photography store in the city. It carries Bronica, Leica, Minolta and Pentax – there is also a good selection of filters, tripods and studio equipment.

Car Accessories

Cars and their accessories are big business in Dubai, so you won't struggle to find the accessories you need. ACE (p.400) and Carrefour (p.416) have large departments selling everything from steering wheel covers to fridges which run off the car battery, and there is a wide selection of tools in larger stores and in the smaller shops in Satwa. You'll find a fantastic selection of products in Yellow Hat in Times Square (p.439), or head further out to Sharjah industrial area for slightly cheaper outlets than you'll find in Dubai.

GPS systems are available from Picnico (04 395 1113) and Abdulla Mohammed Ibrahim Trading (04 229 1195) who recommend the Garmin brand, and even from more mainstream shops like Plug-Ins (p.392), Carrefour (p.416) and Sharaf DG (p.392). The AAA (aaadubai.com) sells specialist sand tracks and heavy duty jacks and winches – if your car is fitted with a GPS system the company can rescue you from the most remote dune or wadi. Car stereos are widely available, and are sold by most electronics shops, with some of the car dealerships stocking alternative models for their cars. To have them fitted, head either to the workshops of Rashidiya or Satwa, or AAA and the dealers – it should cost around Dhs.500 if you are providing all the parts.

Many car owners try to beat the heat by having their car windows tinted. The legal limit is 30% tint; if you get your windows tinted any darker you could be fined, and your car won't pass its annual inspection. Be aware though that company-owned cars are not allowed tinted windows.The options range from the Dhs.75 plastic film from the workshops in Satwa, to Dhs.1,300 to Dhs.1,500 at After Dark (covered by a 10-year warranty), and up to Dhs.5,000 at V-Kool (04 330 6866), which is also covered by warranty, and its clear film is more heat resistant than the tinted one.

If you are just looking for some memorabilia, or if you simply love fast cars, the Ferrari Stores in Festival Centre (p.429) and The Dubai Mall (p.426) have showrooms where they sell memorabilia and accessories. Head to Al Quoz and Rashidiya to customise your car by increasing its performance – West Coast Customs (as featured on the MTV series Pimp My Ride) now has a showroom and workshop in Al Quoz.

Yellow Hat

Times Square Centre Al Quoz Industrial 1 **04 341 8592**
yellowhat.ae
Map **1 T6** Metro **First Gulf Bank**

Yellow Hat is a one-stop shop for car accessories, supplying everything from tyres and sound systems to engine tuning. Head here to pick up breakdown kits, steering wheels, air filters or alloy wheels. The store also offers car cleaning and servicing.

Carpets & Rugs

Carpets are one of the region's signature items. The ones on sale here tend to be imported from Iran, Turkey, Pakistan and Central Asia. A carpet will vary in price depending on a number of factors such as its origin, the material used, the number of knots, and whether or not it is handmade. The most expensive carpets are usually those hand-made with silk, in Iran.

Inspect carpets by turning them over – if the pattern is clearly depicted on the back and the knots are all neat, the carpet is of higher quality than those that are indistinct. Try to do some research so that you have a basic idea of what you are looking for before you go, just in case you happen to meet an unscrupulous carpet dealer who could take advantage of your naivety.

Fortunately, carpet conmen are rare, and most will happily explain the differences between the rugs and share their extensive knowledge with you. If you ask the dealer, you can often garner some interesting information about the carpets and where they were made – for example, some carpets have family names sewn into the designs.

National Iranian Carpets has a section on its website (niccarpets.com) about the history and development of carpets from the various regions.

Ask to see a variety of carpets so that you can get a feel for the differences between hand-made or machine-made, silk, wool or blend carpets. Of course, asking may not be necessary, since carpet vendors will undoubtedly start unrolling carpets before you at a furious pace.

Carpets range in price from a few hundred dirhams to tens of thousands. It is always worth bargaining; make sure the seller knows you are not a tourist, and remain polite at all times to maximise the success of your haggling.

Deira Tower on Al Nasr Square has a huge number of carpet outlets under one roof, and the Blue Souk in Sharjah also has a great range. If you happen to venture further out, the road to Hatta (p.294) is lined with stalls selling carpets and the Friday Market in Fujairah is also a good place to pick them up.

Mall of the Emirates and The Dubai Mall have a selection of shops selling traditional carpets, as does Souk Al Bahar, but just bear in mind that prices may be steeper here.

Occasionally, you might get a travelling carpet seller ringing your doorbell – they usually drive around an area in a truck that is packed to the roof with carpets. The quality isn't great, and if you show the slightest bit of interest they'll keep coming back.

Carpetland is a one-stop-shop for carpets, whether you're after a Persian antique or a shagpile. For something practical rather than decorative, head to Fabindia (p.418), Home Centre (p.385), IKEA (p.286) Carrefour (p.416) or THE One (p.286).

Al Orooba Oriental Carpets BurJuman, Al Mankhool, 04 351 0919
Carpetland Pyramid Centre, Umm Hurair Rd, Oud Metha, 04 337 7677, *aaf-me.com*
National Iranian Carpets Souk Al Bahar, Downtown Dubai, 04 420 0264, *niccarpets.com* (see also Store Finder, p.449)
The Orientalist Woven Art 829 Al Wasl Rd, Al Safa 2, 04 394 6989, *theorientalist.com*
Pride Of Kashmir Mall of the Emirates, Al Barsha 1, 04 341 4477, *prideofkashmir.com*
Qum Persian Carpets & Novelties Sheraton Dubai Creek Hotel & Towers, Al Rigga, 04 228 1848, *qumcarpets.com*

Computers

The latest computer equipment and technology is easy to find in the city and there's even a mall dedicated to it: Al Ain Mall in Bur Dubai. Every year, Dubai hosts GITEX (the Gulf Information Technology Exhibition), the largest IT exhibition in the region. The phenomenally popular GITEX Computer Shopper is also a great place to bag the latest technology at lower prices (gitex.com).

Computer equipment is on sale in a surprising number of outlets, from Carrefour (p.416) to Plug-Ins (p.392), and all the main manufacturers are represented. You'll also find a row of stores on the way to the Metro station inside Mall of the Emirates. CompuMe has a great website where you can order products online (compume.com).

The market is dominated by PCs, but Macs are available from a growing number of stores including CompuMe, PACC, Virgin Megastore, the Mac Store in Ibn Battuta and iStyle (istyle.ae) in Dubai Festival Centre and The Dubai Mall.

The government has been cracking down on the sale of pirated software, and consequently the software and hardware that is available is genuine and should be of good quality.

If you have a poorly PC, contact St George Computers who do repairs and upgrades. For more information call 050 456 2821. WildIT also provides repairs, upgrades, new systems and home networking. Its experienced, British-qualified technicians offer fast, competitive and secure services from the smallest virus removal to creating a state-of-the-art gaming powerhouse. Email info@wildit.co.uk or call Andy on 050 871 0463.

Fashion

Clothes dominate Dubai's shopping scene; not only is the selection amazing, but its sweeping sales several times a year mean you can also bag great discounts on designer goods. The malls have their fair share of exclusive brands, but they also offer more affordable fashion. You'll find that areas of the larger malls are home to the likes of H&M (p.446), Forever 21 (p.445) and Topshop (p.453) and others feature premium designers like Donna Karan (04 325 3800), Ralph Lauren (p.451), Hermes (p.446) and Matthew Williamson.

For those events when only the very best will do, Fashion Avenue in The Dubai Mall (p.426) is dedicated to high-end fashion. Then again, Saks Fifth Avenue in BurJuman, Boutique 1 (p.418) at The Walk, Jumeirah Beach Residence and Harvey Nichols in Mall of the Emirates, hold their fair share of cutting-edge couture.

Mall of the Emirates and The Dubai Mall are the big rollers, offering an astounding number of stores, boutiques and department stores. However, The Dubai Mall pips the post with its large branches of department stores Galeries Lafayette (p.413), Debenhams (p.413), Marks & Spencer (p.414), Paris Gallery (p.404) and Bloomingdale's (p.413).

If you are looking for fashion that's less mainstream, head to stores like Kitsch, S*uce and Five Green for their eclectic mix of funky fashion (see Boutiques & Independent Stores p.417). Eve Michelle in Magrudy's Mall (p.448) has a loyal following for its range of exclusive European creations for ladies. Stores like Etoile La Boutique (p.445), Rodeo Drive (p.451), and Ginger & Lace (p.445) combine a chic selection of high-end designer brands and are great if you like to splurge on labels. If you love designers but not the price tags, browse the selection online at mapochette.com. The online store stocks designer bags from Miu Miu, Versace and Prada and offers a rental service and will deliver one of its designer bags straight to your door.

For something a little different, you can get beautiful hand-crafted fabrics and traditional Indian clothing at Fabindia (see also p.418) on Al Mankhool Road, or Melangè (04 344 4721) in Jumeirah Plaza.

Men should head to Maktoum Road (between the Clock Tower Roundabout and Al Khaleej Palace Hotel) which is lined with stores selling men's designer clothing, and there are also plenty of options inside the Twin Towers Mall in Deira. There are a couple of suit shops along 2nd December Street in Satwa too. Of course, most of the shops loved by women also have excellent men's sections, such as Debenhams, Marks & Spencer, Next, Zara and Massimo Dutti.

Men can pick up funky T-shirts in H&M (p.446), Topman (p.453), Desigual (04 339 9408) and Zadig and Voltaire in JBR. Soboho in Dubai Marina Mall has a great range of T-shirts with quirky graphics.

Bargain hunters have lots to choose from. The Dubai Outlet Mall (p.437) houses a number of well-known brands selling end-of-line stock at reduced prices. Try Sana Fashions (p.452), Carrefour (p.416) and Géant (p.416) for really good bargains – they receive regular deliveries of factory seconds and retailer overruns, and there are plenty of well-known brands available if you get there early, such as Gap, George and Cherokee. Lamcy Plaza (p.438) is a real bargain-hunter's mall – Mexx for Less, Peacocks and Factory Fashions (stocking overruns from Adams and Pumpkin Patch) are all excellent, as are Jennyfer and Mr Price.

The Karama Complex (p.411) is perhaps the main contender for bargain shopping in Dubai. The area features rows of shops selling designer labels, both the genuine article and some quite convincing knock-offs.

Footwear

When it comes to shoes, the choice is enormous. Shoe District at The Dubai Mall is the largest shoe store in the world, and home to over 250 brands from Dior to Puma. Designer labels mingle with middle-of-the-range creations from Bally (p.441), Milano (p.448), Faith (p.445), and Nine West (p.449), with cheap-as-chips flip-flops and sandals available in the big hypermarkets. For stylish shoes on a budget, Shoe Mart (p.452), Brantano Shoe City and Avenue carry fashionable and practical shoes, as do the many shoe shops in Karama Market. Morgan Miller at Dubai Marina Mall will design a pair of shoes to your requirements (04 434 2700). You'll probably find that sports shoes are cheaper than in your home country, but you might not be able to get the latest styles. Stadium (p.407) is good for active-wear shoes and sandals. Because of the weather, children spend a lot of time in sandals and Crocs, which are widely available. If you are planning a trip to colder climes, it can be hard to find good winter shoes – if you see a pair, grab them.

Furniture

This is one of Dubai's most buoyant retail sectors, perhaps because of the unlimited supply of new villas and apartments that keep popping up, all in need of furnishing. Most tastes are catered for, from ethnic pieces to the latest designer concepts and specialist children's furniture stores.

The industrial area between interchanges three and four of Sheikh Zayed Road is home to a number of furniture warehouses, many of which sell pieces crafted from Indonesian teak. Their hot, dusty warehouses are not the most chic of all options, but prices are excellent and after a good polish the furniture looks fabulous. Genuine antiques are available but very rare (and therefore very expensive); many antique pieces come from Oman and Yemen.

The Walk, Jumeirah Beach Residence has a few independent homeware stores, and there is a good selection of stores in Mall of the Emirates and The Dubai Mall. You'll also find plenty of shops selling accessories to add the finishing touches to your home like @Home (p.440) and Fabindia (p.418).

Real investment pieces, that you'll want to keep and take back home, can be bought at Natuzzi (04 338 0777) in Al Quoz. For exotic designs, try Safita Trading Est (04 339 3230, Al Quoz) which stocks a range of items from India and the Far East. For unusual designer items, head to THE One Fusion in Al Quoz.

House of the World provides advice on interior design and sells a range of art and photography, and Panache Interiors (050 351 7100) offers design services and ready-made home accessories. Zara Home's (p.388) fresh, European designs are available in a number of malls, or try the stylish range of furniture at Crate & Barrel (opposite), BoConcept (opposite) and Traffic (04 347 0209).

Bloomingdale's has opened a dedicated homestore in The Dubai Mall and other American home stores now open in Dubai include Pottery Barn and Ethan Allen. Debenhams (p.413) is good for homeware, bedding and kitchenware – this is where you can buy Jamie Oliver branded cookware – and Kitchenalia junkies will love Tavola (p.328) and Harvest Home's (04 342 0225) mix of quirky items

If your needs are more specific, then you're bound to find a store to suit. BAFCO, for example, is the place to hit if you're looking for office furniture, while you can try Bellini or Just Kidding if you're looking specifically for kids' furniture.

For curtains, Dubai Blinds has a good range; see p.102 for more options, as well as interior design companies who can help you shop for furniture.

For children's rooms, Kidz Inc in Al Quoz is the sole agent for Haba – its German, hand-made, wooden furniture doesn't come cheap but all pieces meet European and American safety standards and come with a warranty. Especially good is the range of themed beds (think pirate ships and flowery glades), with matching furniture and accessories. Indigo Living (04 339 7705, indigo-living.com) has a new range of children's furniture, branded as Noah. Laura Ashley at Mercato Mall and The Dubai Mall stocks a stylish range of bedroom accessories for boys and girls, including lighting, wallpaper, bedding, wall art and rugs. Pottery Barn Kids (p.450) also has a range of quality kids furniture, including personalised toddler chairs.

For an artistic touch, MacKenzie Art can hand paint gold, antique or modern flowers or cartoon characters onto your furniture. Commissioned canvases, murals and sculptures can also be created with your specific colour scheme in mind. Visit mackenzieart.com or call 04 341 9803 for further information.

The transient nature of some of Dubai's population results in an active second-hand furniture market. Items are advertised in the classified sections of the local newspapers and on websites like dubizzle.com, but the supermarket noticeboards are the best source; this is also the place to find garage sales.

General Furniture

BoConcept

Mall of the Emirates Al Barsha 1 **04 341 4144**
boconcept.ae
Map **1 R6** Metro **Mall of the Emirates**

A varied selection of sofas, tables, chairs, beds and accessories all created for the design conscious, but without a price tag to match. Designed and manufactured in Denmark, most of the furniture is urban and contemporary. The store, which is due to open a second Dubai branch on Sheikh Zayed Road, also offers an interior decoration service.

Crate & Barrel

Mall of the Emirates, Sheikh Zayed Rd
Al Barsha 1 **04 399 0125**
crateandbarrel.com
Map **1 R6** Metro **Mall of the Emirates**

Contemporary, stylish and functional sums up the modern designs of this American home store. Whether you're shopping for bedrooms, dining rooms or living rooms, classic or hip and trendy styles, furniture, home decor, gifts, or housewares – there is something for all tastes. Its clean-cut furniture particularly appeals to those who enjoy entertaining at home. There's a second store at Mirdif City Centre (04 284 3151).

Home Centre

Mall of the Emirates Al Barsha 1 **04 341 4441**
homecentrestores.com
Map **1 R6** Metro **Mall of the Emirates**

Step into one of Home Centre's growing number of stores and you won't know which way to turn. The large and inspiring stores are filled by a huge assortment of items and ideas. There are large ranges of bath towels, kitchenware and accessories before you arrive at the wooden tables, sofas and bedroom furniture – both traditional and modern. For other locations, see Store Finder, p.446.

Homes r Us

Mazaya Centre Sheikh Zayed Road **04 321 3444**
homesrusgroup.com
Map **2 F6** Metro **Burj Khalifa/Dubai Mall**
A one-stop store for stylish home concepts, Homes r Us is a complete lifestyle destination showcasing a wide range of home furniture, furnishings and accessories. There are also stores at Ibn Batutta Mall (04 4469820) and Arabian Centre, Mirdif (04 284 5736).

ID Design > *p.387*

Mall of the Emirates Al Barsha 1 **04 341 3434**
iddesignuae.com
Map **1 R6** Metro **Mall of the Emirates**
ID Design sells a selection of modern furniture for the home or office, and it also stocks a decent range of outdoor furniture. Both of its stores offer an interior design service and will reupholster furniture and custom-make curtains, pillows and other accessories. The store offers a gift registry and delivery service too. For other locations see Store Finder, p.446.

IKEA

Festival Centre Dubai Festival City **04 203 7555**
ikea.com
Map **2 M9** Metro **Emirates**
This enormous showroom in Festival Centre sells a great range of good value furniture. Its selection is suitable for most budgets, and it stocks everything from Dhs.1 tealight holders to Dhs.20,000 kitchens. The store also has a selection of reasonably priced kids' furniture.

THE One

Various locations **04 395 5889**
theone.com
A favourite among the expat crowd because of its funky, modern style (that is highly decorative, but not gaudy) and good selection of home accessories that can add a much-needed flourish to impersonal apartments or villas. It's eclectic showroom now also features THE One Junior collection for kids, and its partner store THE One Fusion on Sheikh Zayed Road stocks an imaginative range of quirky collectables, oversized originals and cool one-offs.

Pan Emirates

Nr Mall of the Emirates, Umm Suqeim Rd
Al Barsha 1 **04 383 0800**
panemirates.com
Map **1 R6** Metro **Mall of the Emirates**
Kit out your home with a stylish range of modern furniture at this store – If your tastes are more traditional, its selection of wooden beds and furniture will also appeal. The store also sells home accessories, rugs, mattresses and a small range of garden furniture. For other locations see Store Finder, p.450.

Pottery Barn

Mirdif City Centre Mirdif **04 606 2610**
potterybarn.me
Map **2 P12** Metro **Rashidiya**
The American giant made its long-mooted debut in Dubai at Mirdif City Centre mall and it has since opened another store in The Dubai Mall. It sells a good range of quality household furniture and accessories, and also has an in-store design studio where customers can get advice on their home furnishing needs and ideas. There are separate Pottery Barn Kids outlets in the same malls, which stock cute lines of children's furniture.

United Furniture > *p.xvii*

Nr College of Islamic and Arabic Studies, Zabeel Rd
Al Karama **04 337 0131**
unitedfurnitureco.com
Map **2 L5** Metro **Al Karama**
United Furniture is home to a wide-ranging collection of home and office furniture and accessories. There's styles to suit international tastes, from the contemporary to the classic, and all at affordable pocket-friendly prices. The showroom features a variety of kids bedroom interiors, as well as dining tables, sofas, lighting and coffee tables.

Contemporary Designer Furniture

Aati Zabeel Rd, Al Karama, 04 337 7825, *altayer.com*
Armani/Casa The Dubai Mall, Downtown Dubai, 04 448 5100, *armanicasa.com*
B&B Italia Mall of the Emirates, Al Barsha 1, 04 340 5797, *baituti.com*
B5 The Art Of Living Sidra Tower, Shk Zayed Rd, Al Sufouh 1, 04 447 3973, *b5living.com*
Ethan Allen The Dubai Mall, Downtown Dubai, 04 330 8871, *ethanallen.com*
Filini Nr Times Square, Al Quoz Industrial 1, 04 323 3636, *filini.com*
Hastens Sunset Mall, Jumeira 3, 04 380 9565, *hastensdubai.com*
Irony Home The Dubai Mall, Downtown Dubai, 04 434 0166, *ironyhomelifestyle.com*
Kartell Villa 746, Jumeira Rd, Umm Suqeim 2, 04 348 8169, *kartdesign.net*
Muri Lunghi Italian Furniture Al Reem Residence, Umm Hurair Rd, Al Karama, 04 358 2341, *murilunghi.com*
Natuzzi Nr InterChange 2 & 3, Shk Zayed Rd, Al Quoz 3, 04 338 0777, *int.natuzzi.com*
Objekts Of Design (OD) Al Kuthban Bldg, Shk Zayed Rd, Al Quoz Industrial 1, 04 328 4300, *od.ae*
Roche Bobois Shk Zayed Rd, Al Barsha 1, 04 399 0393, *roche-bobois.com*
Singways/Maison Decor Mall of the Emirates, Al Barsha 1, 04 340 9116, *singways.com*

Go home with a new home
Find everything from accessories for your living room to wardrobes for your bedroom, table linen, sheets, wallpaper, dining tables, couches and more. And if you're spoilt for choice, let our interior design consultants help you decide.
IDdesign
More Living, More Styles, More Trends.
Mall of the Emirates: 04 3413434 • Dubai - Sharjah Road - Outlet store: 04 2666751 • Mirdif City Centre: 04 2839943 • Al Wahda Mall, Abu Dhabi: 02 4437557 • e-mail: iddesign@emirates.net.ae • Website: www.iddesignuae.com

Traffic 179 Umm Suqeim Rd, Al Quoz Industrial 4, 04 347 0209, *viatraffic.org*
Zen Interiors Nr United Bank Limited & Essa Lutfi Bldgs, Al Barsha 1, 04 340 5050, *zeninteriors.net*

Modern Furniture & Home Decor

Artikel Mall of the Emirates, Al Barsha 1, 04 341 0661
Bayti Times Square, Al Quoz Industrial 1, 04 341 8040
Crate & Barrel Mall of the Emirates, Al Barsha 1, 04 399 0125, *crateandbarrel.com*
Dogtas > *p.x-xi* Sheikh Zayed Rd, 04 388 1131 *dogtasuae.com*
Dwell Festival Centre Dubai, Festival City, 04 232 5435, *liwastores.com* (see also Store Finder, p.444)
Heritage Touch Springs Village, Emirates Living, 04 2265 086, *heritagetouch-me.com*
Homes r Us Ibn Battuta Mall, The Gardens, 04 446 9820, *homesrusgroup.com* (see also Store Finder, p.446)
House Of Zunn Villa 11, Jumeira Rd, Umm Suqeim 2, 04 346 7366, *zunndesigns.com*
Index Living Mall The Dubai Mall, Downtown Dubai, 04 330 8132, *indexlivingmall.ae*
Indigo Living Oasis Centre, Al Quoz 1, 04 339 7705, *indigo-living.com*
iwannagohome! The Dubai Mall, Downtown Dubai, 04 339 8952, *iwannagohome.com.sg*
THE One Jumeira Theatre & Deli, Jumeira Rd, Jumeira 1, 04 345 6687, *theone.com*
Pier Import Mazaya Centre, Al Wasl, 04 343 2002, *pierimport-me.com*
Rono Interiors Sheikh Zayed Rd, Al Quoz 3, 04 338 8540, *ronointeriors.com*
Zara Home Mall of the Emirates, Al Barsha 1, 04 341 4184 *zarahome.com* (see Store Finder, p.454)

Outdoor Furniture

ACE > *p.401* Nr Times Square, Shk Zayed Rd, 1 04 341 1906, *aceuae.com* (see also Store Finder, p.440)
Ambar Garden Furniture Umm Suqeim Rd, Al Quoz Industrial 3, 04 323 2405, *ambargardenfurniture.com*
B&B Italia Mall of the Emirates, Al Barsha 1, 04 340 5797, *baituti.com*
Desert River Nr Times Square, Al Quoz Industrial 1, 04 323 3636, *desertriver.com*
Finasi Al Ittihad Rd, Al Khabaisi, 04 297 1777, *finasi.ae*
Haif Hospitality Furnishings Al Nasr Plaza, Oud Metha, 04 357 3221, *hhfuae.ae*
Nakkash Gallery Nr Indian Palace Restaurant, Shk Rashid Rd, Al Garhoud, 04 282 6767, *nakkashgallery.com*
Parasol Garden Furniture Umm Suqeim Rd, Al Quoz Industrial 4, 04 347 9003, *parasoldubai.com*
Rainbow Play Systems Shed # 3, Al Jowass Building, St 27C, Al Quoz Industrial 3, 050 450 7610, *rainbowplayuae.com*
Royal Gardenscape Nr Enoc Station & National Paints, Al Quoz Industrial 4, 04 340 0648, *royalgardenscape.com*
Soubra Tents & Awnings Nr Mall of the Emirates, Al Barsha 1, 04 340 9594, *soubra-uae.ae*
Sultan Garden Centre Nr Dubai Zoo, Jumeira Rd, Jumeira 1, 04 344 5544, *sultangardencenter.com*

Wooden Furniture

Falaknaz – The Warehouse > *p.389*

Sheikh Zayed Road, Al Quoz 1
04 328 5859
falaknazthewarehouse.com
Map **1 T6** Metro **First Gulf Bank**

A big depot in the depths of Al Quoz, full to the brim with colonial-style teak home furniture and a good range of outdoor garden items. The firm can also have furniture custom-made by its factory in Indonesia.

Lucky's

Industrial Area 11 Sharjah **06 534 1937**
luckyfurnitureuae.com

This store is in Sharjah is popular with expats seeking well-priced furniture. The range is vast, but the staff will happily explain the origin and design of the pieces, and can paint, varnish or make alterations.

Marina Exotic Home Interiors > *p.iv-v*

Mall of the Emirates Al Barsha 1 **800 4360**
marinagulf.com
Map **1 R6** Metro **Mall of the Emirates**

Pick up key pieces that reflect the region at this popular store – the items here will add an exotic touch to your home and are generally more individual than you'll find at the usual furniture stores. You can pick up large wardrobes, tables, ornate chests and various other types of wooden furniture. There is also a selection of garden furniture. For other locations see the Store Finder on p.448.

Pinky Furniture & Novelties

Al Samrya Bldg, Nr Dubai American Academy
Al Barsha 1 **04 422 1720**
pinkyfurnitureuae.com
Map **1 R7** Metro **Mall of the Emirates**

Much like Lucky's, Pinky has long been an expat favourite for traditional, handmade Indian furniture. The new Barsha showroom saves customers the trip into Sharjah.

Gold & Diamonds

Dubai is the world's leading re-exporter of gold and you'll find at least one jewellery shop in even the smallest malls, and large areas dedicated to shops selling it in larger malls. Gold is sold according to the international daily gold rate, so wherever you

buy it there will be very little difference in the price of the actual metal. Where the price varies is in the workmanship that has gone into a particular piece.

While gold jewellery may be the most prevalent, silver, platinum, precious stones, gems and pearls are all sold, either separately or crafted into jewellery. Most outlets can make up a piece for you, working from a diagram or photograph. Just ensure that you are not obliged to buy it if it doesn't turn out quite how you had imagined. A pendant with your name spelled out in Arabic, or some jewellery crafted with black pearls, are traditional gifts. The Gold Souk (p.420) is the best place to start in terms of choice, but some of the air-conditioned alternatives may be preferable in the summer.

All That Glitters

The Gold & Diamond Park (at junction four on Sheikh Zayed Road) has branches of many of the same shops as the Gold Souk (p.420) but in a calmer, air-conditioned atmosphere. You can still barter, and there is the added bonus of cafes to wait in while the jeweller makes any alterations. This is also a good spot to head for if you are looking for engagement or wedding rings and, like at the outlets in the souk, you are able to commission pieces. (goldanddiamondpark.com)

Many of the world's finest jewellers are represented in Saks Fifth Avenue's jewellery department, such as Cartier, Tiffany & Co, Graff and De Beers. For watches, whether it's a Rolex, Breitling, Tag Heuer, Swatch, Casio or Timex, you'll find most models here. Costume jewellery and watches can be found in most department stores as well as at Eve Michelle; there's a beautiful Swarovski range at Tanagra (04 324 2340), in Wafi. Several fashion stores also stock a small range of jewellery, and branches of Accessorize and Claire's Accessories can be found in many of the malls; For Love 21 in Deira City Centre has a great range.

Al Fardan Jewels & Precious Stones Deira City Centre, Port Saeed, 04 295 3780, *alfardangroup.com* (see also Store Finder, p.440)
Al Futtaim Jewellery Deira City Centre, Port Saeed, 04 295 2906, *watchesuae.com* (see Store Finder, p.440)
Damas BurJuman, Al Mankhool, 04 352 5566, *damasjewel.com* (see also Store Finder, p.444)
Golden Ring Deira City Centre, Port Saeed, 04 295 0373 (see also Store Finder, p.446)
Liali Jewellery Mercato, Jumeira 1, 04 344 5055, *lialijewellery.com* (see also Store Finder, p.447)
Mansoor Jewellers Mall of the Emirates, Al Barsha 1, 04 341 1661
Paris Gallery Deira City Centre, Port Saeed, 04 295 5550, *parisgallery.com* (see Store Finder, p.450)
Prima Gold BurJuman, Al Mankhool, 04 355 1988, *primagold.net* (see also Store Finder, p.450)
Pure Gold Mercato, Jumeira 1, 04 349 2400, *pugold.com* (see also Store Finder, p.451)
Raymond Weil Deira City Centre, Port Saeed, 04 295 2906, *raymond-weil.com* (see also Store Finder, p.451)
Saks Fifth Avenue BurJuman, Al Mankhool, 04 351 5551
Tanagra Wafi, Umm Hurair 2, 04 324 2340, *chalhoub-group.com* (see also Store Finder, p.453)
Vhernier Jumeirah Emirates Towers, Trade Centre 2, 04 354 4017, *vhernier.com*

Home Appliances

Whether you are setting up home in Dubai, or are moving house, you'll have to spend some time looking for white goods. While you may be used to essential items like a cooker, washing machine or fridge, coming as part and parcel of a lease, in Dubai, unfurnished really means unfurnished and you'll have to fork out for the most standard items like curtain rails for your windows.

Unsurprisingly, there are plenty of places where you can buy goods and several large international brands are sold here, like LG, Samsung and Siemens. The Dubai Mall (p.426) and Mall of the Emirates (p.431) have a large selection of shops. You'll also find some high end brands like Gaggenau (04 394 4049) on Jumeira Road and Miele (04 341 8444) at Dubai World Trade Centre roundabout.

A Greener Future

The Change Initiative (thechangeinitiative.com) is an exciting one-stop eco-store, offering environmentally-friendly and sustainable products. There's a range of household goods, appliances and building solutions that combine technology and good design, from ideas to improve insulation and lessen energy use, to eco-friendly furniture, paints and fashion accessories. Shop online or visit the store in Al Barsha 1, near the Ibis on Sheikh Zayed Rd.

Many of the hypermarkets, like Carrefour (p.416), Géant (p.416) and HyperPanda (p.416), stock a superb range of goods from well-known brands (and some lesser known ones that also do the job) and usually offer a delivery and installation service. Sharaf DG (p.392), Jacky's Electronics (p.392), Jumbo Electronics (p.392) and Better Life (p.442) also stock a selection of home appliances.

For stylish kitchen appliances, head to Tavola (p.328), Bloomingdale's (p.413) and Galeries Lafayette (p.413) – all The Dubai Mall.

You can buy water coolers and water dispensers in all the larger supermarkets, or you can get them directly from the companies that deliver bottled water (see p.104).

Competition is high, so prices are reasonable and most dealers will offer warranties – some will offer a warranty extension for an extra year or two. Check that the warranty is valid internationally if you wish to take items back to your home country. Also check that the item will work in all areas of the world and whether you will have to pay any import duty if you return back home. Find out who will service the items if there are problems. For second-hand items, check the adverts placed on supermarket noticeboards and online classifieds, like dubizzle.com.

Home Audio & Visual

When it comes to home entertainment, the stores in Dubai don't scrimp on size, quality or range. There are several stores dedicated to electronics in each of the larger malls and you'll find large sections in the supermarkets which stock top-of-the-range high-definition televisions, plasma screens, DVD players, games consoles and stereos. Whether goods here are cheaper than those sold in other countries depends on where you compare them, but it's worth waiting for the sales as there can be a noticeable drop in prices.

Many of the stores display operational products so you can see or hear the quality, and staff are often happy to explain the differences and benefits between models and brands. Bang & Olufsen (p.441) and Bose (p.442) offer a pricey, but undeniably stylish, range of goods for the home, but you'll find a similar range of products in all of the electronic stores. Many stores also offer delivery and installation services, which take the hassle out of mounting a plasma screen or setting up your surround sound system.

Dubai Audio

Nr Safestway, Shk Zayed Rd Al Wasl **04 343 1441**
dubaiaudio.com
Map **2 E6** Metro **Business Bay**

Head to this store for a super stylish range of designer electronics from premium brands including Lexicon, Conrad Johnson and Linn. The range of stock on offer includes luxury home cinema and audio equipment and multi-room audio systems.

Jacky's Electronics

The Dubai Mall Downtown Dubai **04 434 0222**
jackys.com
Map **2 F6** Metro **Burj Khalifa/Dubai Mall**

A wide range of electronics are stocked here including well-known brands – particularly Sony products. The store offers home delivery and installation for some of its products as well as warranties and protection plans. For other locations see Store Finder, p.446.

Jumbo Electronics

BurJuman Al Mankhool **800 58626**
jumbocorp.com
Map **2 L5** Metro **BurJuman**

The selection on offer at this store is vast; head here for its popular brands, good deals and helpful staff. This is also a good place to head to if you are looking for Sony LCD televisions and home theatre systems. For other locations see the Store Finder on p.447.

Plug-Ins

Festival Centre Dubai Festival City **800 758 4467**
pluginselectronix.com
Map **2 M9** Metro **Emirates**

A comprehensive range of electronics is offered at this store, where you'll find the latest products from Panasonic, Bose, Sony and LG. For other locations see Store Finder, p.450.

Sharaf DG

Times Square Al Quoz 1 **04 341 8060**
sharafdg.com
Map **1 T6** Metro **First Gulf Bank**

This is many residents' first port of call because of its range of gadgets and good service. Its stores carry everything from plasma televisions and laptop computers to mobile phones and irons. For other locations see the Store Finder p.452.

Hardware & DIY

With a number of companies offering handyman services (see Domestic Help on p.107), it may be easier and cheaper to find a 'man who can' rather than invest in the tools and materials you need for DIY jobs. However, ACE (p.400) and Speedex (04 339 1929) on Sheikh Zayed Road stock comprehensive ranges of tools, along with all the nails, nuts, bolts and screws you may need. Carrefour (p.416) has a DIY section and there are numerous independent shops selling a broad range of items in Satwa. Dragon Mart (p.437) in International City, has a section for builder's merchants and here you can find tiles, power tools and other hardware items.

Health Food & Special Dietary Requirements

The range of health and speciality food is improving, and although prices are generally high it is worth shopping around as costs vary from shop to shop. Shops selling sports supplements, energy bars and protein powders are often classified as health food shops and some are now diversifying into selling speciality foodstuffs.

Nutrition Zone specialises in vitamins, health supplements and detoxifying products from Holland & Barrett. It also carries a range of health food, grains, gluten and wheat-free products, as well as Green &

Blacks chocolate and some ecological household products. Its prices are reasonable and below those of the supermarkets for many items.

The main supermarkets stock increasing varieties of speciality foods and they all now carry products for diabetics; Choithrams (p.416) has possibly the widest range – it also stocks dairy-free, gluten-free and wheat-free products that range from bread to ice cream. A wide selection of organic groceries can be bought at the Organic Foods & Cafe (p.393), while the excellent Ripe farmers' market is held at the Courtyard, Al Quoz every Saturday morning. Spinneys (p.417) carries a limited selection of organic fruit and veg and, through its partnership with Waitrose, an organic range that includes beans, pulses, biscuits and fruit juice. Local Harvest, a new line of locally grown produce, is now available at Spinneys, Carrefour, Géant and LuLu.

Waitrose stocks the Perfectly Balanced range and some Weight Watchers products. Park n Shop's (p.417) health food range includes breads made from spelt or rye flour; it even makes spelt hot cross buns and mince pies. Carrefour's (p.416) range is increasing and features some own-brand organic products.

Dubai hosts the annual Middle East Natural & Organic Products Expo, which sees over 300 companies from 35 countries exhibiting a range of natural products and treatments. See naturalproductme.com for details.

Kids' Items

There is a high concentration of shops selling toys and clothes for children and you'll find a good selection of well-known stores and smaller outlets. Magrudy's (p.380) sells toys for younger children and Park n Shop (p.417) has a great toy department with some good 'pocket money' toys, as does Book Worm (p.380). IKEA (p.386) and Kidz Inc in Al Quoz (04 328 5775) carry good quality toys that are built to last.

School Uniforms

Most schools will suggest a preferred supplier for its school uniforms, and Dar Al Tasmim Uniforms (04 394 1477), Magrudy's (p.380) and Zaks (04 342 9828) produce uniforms for many of the schools in Dubai. You can also buy generic uniform from Marks & Spencer (p.414).

Most electronics stores stock a wide range of games for the various platforms. Try Geekay (p.445) and Carrefour (p.416) which have a good selection. For inexpensive birthday presents and stocking fillers, Carrefour (p.416) and Géant (p.416) both have toy departments, and the little shops around Karama and Satwa are excellent for cheap toys (just don't expect them to last a long time). Remember that not all toys conform to international safety standards and therefore should only be used under supervision.

When it comes to clothing, there is plenty of choice, whether it is high-end designer fashion like Christian Lacroix (04 351 7133) and Armani (p.441) or factory seconds from Sana (p.452). Many of the department stores (p.413) have children's departments and, for real indulgence, The Dubai Mall (p.426) has a section dedicated to premium brands such as Armani Junior (p.441), Diesel Kids (04 339 9163) and Cacharel (04 339 8661). You'll also find Lola et Moi stocked in the Galeries Lafayette store there.

For babies and younger children, Babyshop (p.377), Mamas and Papas (p.378), Mothercare (p.378), Woolworths (p.454) and Next (p.415) carry the essentials and have great outfits at reasonable prices. Okaidi (p.449) and Pumpkin Patch (p.451) sell bright, colourful and practical clothes. Monsoon (p.449) has a good range of party clothes, particularly for girls.

The majority of clothes shops stock shoes and there are some specialist stores. Pablosky (p.450) has a range of colourful shoes for babies and children, and Shoe Mart (p.452) and Debenhams have children's sections. Adams (p.440), The Athlete's Foot (p.441) and Ecco (p.444) carry good ranges.

For party costumes at any time of the year, check out the Early Learning Centre (p.394), Toys R Us (p.395), Hamleys, The Toy Store and Mr Ben's Costume Closet (04 346 3494). Supermarkets (p.415) stock some items in the run up to events like Halloween and Christmas.

Early Learning Centre

Wafi Umm Hurair 2 **04 324 2730**
elc.com
Map **2 L7** Metro **Dubai Healthcare City**

Early Learning Centre stocks a good range of educational products and toys that stimulate play and imagination. On the whole, it has a good reputation for the quality of its products. There are several outlets in Dubai, but they are often rather small and quite cluttered. There are still some good buys to be had, including wooden toys, and you'll find items like inflatable pools, along with swimming jackets and arm bands for safety. For other locations, including a large branch in Deira City Centre, see Store Finder, p.444.

Hamleys

The Dubai Mall Downtown Dubai **04 339 8889**
hamleys.com
Map **2 F6** Metro **Burj Khalifa/Dubai Mall**

Hold on to your kids, this store is well known for offering the best, and the biggest, variety of toys. Hamleys' store, in The Dubai Mall, lives up to expectations with its vibrant staff (who tantalise kids from the doorway) and plethora of toys for preschoolers through to early teens. There's a second branch in Mirdif City Centre (04 284 3336).

Can't Find What You Need?

If you've scoured the city for a particular item and still not found it, log on to askexplorer.com and ask advice from your fellow expats. If we've missed your favourite store, log on and let us know why you love it.

The Toy Store

Mall of the Emirates Al Barsha 1 **04 341 2473**
the-toystore.com/info/
Map **1 R6** Metro **Mall of the Emirates**
Recognisable by the large toy animals peering out of its open store front, The Toy Store is a great place to amaze kids. The store in Mall of the Emirates is set over two floors and is filled with a broad variety of toys. For other locations see the Store Finder p.453.

Toys R Us

Festival Centre Dubai Festival City **04 206 6552**
toysrusuae.com
Map **2 M9** Metro **Emirates**
This well-known toy emporium offers a good selection of products, guaranteed to get your little ones excited. The range is comprehensive and, whether you are looking for small toys or games to amuse kids, or larger gifts like bikes, electronic games and play sets, you'll probably be in luck here. Its stores also have Ladybird concessions. For other locations, see Store Finder (p.453).

ZaZeeZou

Jumeirah Centre Jumeira 1 **04 344 0204**
harvesthomegroup.com/zaazeezou/
Map **2 H4** Metro **Emirates Towers**
For anyone looking for those 'not on the high street' brands, ZaZeeZou is a treasure trove of toys, nursery products and children's clothes. Sticking a select range of small, independent brands that are hard to find in the UAE, including Emma Bridgewater's children's crockery to beautiful traditional wooden toys by the French brand Moulin Roty. There's also clothes by funky London label No Added Sugar, Kidorable and Rock Abye Baby, as well as locally made products, such as Sandu Star's Sock Monkey toys.

Maternity Items

Many retailers have jumped on the maternity fashion bandwagon and now offer fashionable outfits for mums-in-training. Dorothy Perkins (p.444), New Look (p.449), H&M (p.446) and Topshop (p.453) are great for fun, fashionable items, and Debenhams (p.413), Mothercare (p.378), Mamas and Papas (p.378) and Woolworths (p.454) also stock good selections of maternity clothes.

Jenny Rose carries the latest styles, and is a good place to find speciality items such as swimwear, underwear and evening wear. As well as buggies and nursery furniture, Just Kidding (justkidding-me.com) carries Noppies maternity wear from Holland. And you can shop online at blushandbloom.com and luxelittle.com for fashionable maternity lingerie, nightwear, dresses and 'mama and baby' twinsets.

For other maternity items, like cool packs, creams and bras, you'll have to shop around in Mothercare (p.378), Babyshop (p.377), Debenhams (p.413), Marks & Spencer (p.414) or Jenny Rose (p.395) – ranges vary and may be limited.

Babyshop and Mothercare also stock a range of breast pumps, or you could try one of the larger pharmacies if you want a really heavy duty one (you can also rent one; try Susi on 050 658 8905).

Storage bags for breast milk are widely available (Playtex, Medela and Avent brands). Boppy breastfeeding pillows are available in Toys R Us, and Arabian Home Health Care (arabianhomecare.com), opposite Rashid Hospital, also stocks pillows for breastfeeding – you need to ask for them when you go in.

Other essential accessories for pregnancy are available here – one example is a 'Bump Belt', a device that redirects your car seatbelt under your bump for protection, and which can be found in Mothercare and some Spinneys (p.417). For more information on having a baby see p.139.

Blossom Mother & Child

The Dubai Mall Downtown Dubai **04 434 0103**
blossommotherandchild.com
Map **2 F6** Metro **Dubai Mall**
A premium range of maternity items is sold at this store, all from well-known designers. The store also has a denim bar which features popular brands like J Brand Jeans and 7 For All Mankind, customised with the Blossom Band.

Jenny Rose

Mall of the Emirates Al Barsha 1 **04 341 0577**
jennyrose.net
Map **1 R6** Metro **Mall of the Emirates**
Fashionable mums should head to this store for classy clothes for the day or night. Its collection is particularly suitable for Dubai's warm climate and you'll find a good assortment of dresses, sleeveless tops and comfortable trousers. There is also a small selection of sportswear and lingerie.

Pregmamma

J3 Mall Al Wasl Rd, Umm Suqeim **04 388 3993**
pregmamma.com
Map **1 U5** Metro **Noor Islamic Bank**
A complete maternity range for mums to be, all with a comfortable and fashionable touch. Shop in-store or online at pregmamma.com.

Places To Shop For Kids

Dubai is home to all manner of kids' items – from novelty T-shirts to toys galore. Get ready to spoil them!

Whether you need to get a gift, re-stock a wardrobe or fulfil a curriculum requirement, shopping for your (or your friends') kids can be an expensive and exhausting task. But with a little bit of planning and a lot of imagination you can have the best-dressed, most-educated and well-occupied child in Dubai…

Kids' Fashion

The good news is that Dubai has a wide variety of international brands (see Kids' Items, p.394) and many adult fashion stores have kids' ranges. H&M has a great range of on-trend kids clothes and shoes, while Marks & Spencer (p.414) and Next (p.415) have good quality ranges. Check out Women's Secrets for unique baby and toddler wear, and Beyond the Beach for some super cool surf gear. For novelty T-shirts and babygros (My Dad's Cooler Than Yours, etc.) check out concession stalls found in most malls.

Kids' Sportsgear

For swimming suits with built in floats check out Mothercare (p.378), Early Learning Centre (p.394) and most sports shops (p.406). Sun and Sand Sports (p.408) has a great range of sporting items for kids including roller blades, trampolines (also try Intersport, p.407 and Toys R Us, p.395), bikes (see also p.378), miniature pool tables, tennis rackets and golf clubs. For specialist sportswear, like martial arts outfits and ballet outfits, you will probably have to buy from one of the academies (see Activities For Kids, p.141), although Marks & Spencer (p.414) sometimes carries ballet outfits.

Musical Instruments

There are a number of specialists shops (see p.398) but you can also find basic drum kits and keyboards in Toys R Us, and Sharaf DG (p.392) has an excellent range of keyboards, as well as digital music games. You might also be able to pick up a second-hand guitar or piano – check out dubizzle.com – or put a notice on expatwoman.com. If you're looking for sheet music (often teachers will request parents to buy the required sheet music) Magrudy's has a large range, including exam papers, and can generally order specific books for you.

Bedroom Design

If you want to decorate your kid's room but don't want to paint it you can get family photos printed on canvas, recreate a night time scene (with stars and a moon) or garden setting (with flowers and a ladybird) in wall lighting from IKEA (p.386). Alternatively go for wall stickers – Just Kidding stocks wall stickers for children from funky and friendly animal stickers for nurseries to flowers and rockets for young children's rooms. Order online at justkidding-me.com or pop into the store in Al Quoz (800 5878).

Bags & Stationery

While a lot of schools have book bags as part of their uniform, many kids also take their own school bag in order to fit in their gym kit and packed lunch. Pull-along wheeled bags are popular and can be found in Toys R Us in all manner of characters. If you're looking for pencil cases and the like, Magrudy's and Early Learning Centre (p.394) stock good ranges, whilst Dubai Library Distributors in Bin Sougat Centre and various other locations (p.444) has a huge range of stationery items, pens, pads, arts and crafts, etc.

Affordable Gifts

Once your kids get to school age you will find that they will be invited to a birthday party nearly every month. So buying birthday gifts can get expensive – try Dragon Mart (p.437) for electronic cars, Candylicious in The Dubai Mall (04 330 8700) for party bag ingredients, Daiso (p.444) for all sorts of fun items like glow sticks and tattoos – and the hypermarkets (p.415) are always a good bet.

Music & Movies

Unless you have particularly eclectic taste, you should find a satisfying collection of music in the city's supermarkets and record stores. The advantage of Dubai's multicultural society is that you can open yourself up to new genres – Arabic dance music for example, is very popular. Everything has to go through the censor, so any music or DVDs deemed offensive will not be sold here, unless it can be edited to make it more acceptable.

Hollywood blockbusters and mainstream titles can be picked up in many supermarkets. Music and DVDs are generally more expensive than they are in other countries. Disco 2000 (04 394 0139) stocks a good range of items, particularly BBC and children's titles – it also has a rental section. Carrefour has good value bargain bins and although they are usually filled with Hollywood titles, there are occasional gems and the odd BBC children's title. Bollywood films are extremely popular and available in most shops. In common with the rest of the world, video is being phased out, and the DVD is now prevalent.

Movie Rentals

There are a few places where you can rent DVDs in the city; Spinneys stores often have rental sections where you can sign up. Some supermarkets have a self service DVD dispenser from Moviebank or Davina Box, where you pay to join and you are charged by the day – you simply return the DVD to the dispenser when you are finished. If DVDs are too old school for you, OSN's On Demand service allows subscribers to rent movies and series through their cable or satellite receiver. See TV, p.24 for more info.

Retailers will order titles that are on the approved list for the UAE. Online shopping is an alternative if you can't find an item and you'll find more variety on sites like Amazon (amazon.com and amazon.co.uk). Amazon's postal charges are usually fairly high and its branded packages are occasionally inspected at the post office (see online shopping p.368). The UAE iTunes store currently only sells apps, so if you want to download music, TV shows, movies and iBooks from the extensive iTunes collection, you'll need to log in to the UK or US sites – but you need a UK or US registered credit card for these.

Ohm Records

Nr BurJuman Centre Al Mankhool **04 397 3728**
ohmrecords.com
Map **2 L5** Metro **BurJuman**
Vinyl fans and those into electronic mixing should head to this speciality shop – a selection of its music comes from independent labels. The store also holds a range of very mainstream DVDs and videos and a few independent films. You can buy processors and turntables, as well as record bags, accessories and a select line of streetwear.

Virgin Megastore

Mall of the Emirates Al Barsha 1 **04 341 4353**
virginmegastore.me
Map **1 R6** Metro **Mall of the Emirates**
The widest selection of mainstream music is stocked at this store. Its sizeable range is well organised by genre and it holds an excellent range of DVD boxsets.

Musical Instruments

Things are looking up for the Dubai's music scene; several new stores have opened and you should find a decent selection of products.

Juli Music, on Sheikh Zayed Road, stocks a good range of instruments and can also arrange lessons (see Music Lessons, p.348). Particularly useful is its 'hire before you buy' policy. Sowira Pianos offers rental and sales on a range of new and used pianos. The Music Room (04 359 8888) is run by an experienced music teacher, and has the widest range of sheet music in Dubai. Here you'll find a range of instruments including clarinets, flutes, violins, trumpets and guitars, and their associated accessories. The store is an agent for Steinway & Sons pianos, but if you don't have the space it also stocks Kawai grand, upright and digital pianos. Prices for pianos are considerably lower than elsewhere in the world. Thomsun Music House at Wafi has a wide range of mainly Yamaha instruments, from pianos to drum kits and guitars, and also sells mixing desks and equipment for digital music-making (there are also Thomsun Pure Music branches across Dubai, see p.453). Sharaf DG, Carrefour, Géant and other large supermarkets stock basic keyboards and guitars, which are fine for beginners.

The Music Chamber

Times Square Al Quoz Industrial 1 **04 346 8056**
musicchamber.net
Map **1 T6** Metro **First Gulf Bank**
Sells instruments, such as guitars, pianos and ouds, as well as sheet music, strings, tuners and many other accessories you may not be able to find elsewhere. Brands stocked include Godin, Seagull, Ritmuller, D'Addario, Jinbao and Oud Sekar.

The Music Institute

The Walk, Jumeirah Beach Residence Dubai Marina
04 424 3818
themusic-uae.com
Map **1 K5** Metro **Dubai Marina**
A small range of items are stocked here such as digital pianos, guitars, violins and guitar accessories, but the range is primarily to support its students.

Sadek Music

Souk Madinat Jumeirah Al Sufouh 1 04 368 6570
sadek-music.com
Map 1 R4 Metro Mall of the Emirates

Sadek Music stocks an assortment of eastern and western instruments. The store offers a repair service and music lessons, and you can also rent a selection of its instruments. Its branch in The Dubai Mall carries a good selection of guitars. For other locations see the Store Finder on p.452.

Thomsun Pure Music *> p.399*

Ibn Battuta Mall The Gardens 04 366 9385
thomsunmusiconline.com
Map 1 G5 Metro Ibn Battuta

One of the largest distributors in the Middle East for Yamaha musical instruments, Thomsun offers a huge selection of grand pianos, keyboards, guitars, violins, percussion and wind instruments. This is also a one-stop shop for musical instruments and accessories, home audio systems and professional audio solutions by brands including Fender, Bose, Polk Audio, and many more. See Store Finder (p.453) for other branches. Thomsun Musical Institutes offer music lessons at Wafi, Ibn Battuta and Dubai Festival Centre.

Turning Pointe Music

Bldg V23, Russia Cluster International City
04 422 1592
turningpointe.ae
Metro Rashidiya

Sells everything ranging from guitars and string instruments, through to keyboards and brass instruments, in addition to stands, cases, strings, picks and oils. Also leases instruments to students.

Zak Electronics & Musical Instruments

BurJuman Al Mankhool 04 336 8857
zakelectronics.com
Map 2 L5 Metro BurJuman

This store carries grand pianos, keyboards, amplifiers and guitar accessories. You'll also find a good range of brands including Roland, Kawai and Fender.

Outdoor Goods

Exploring the great outdoors is a popular pastime in the UAE, especially when the weather cools. The largest specialist camping shop is Adventure HQ at Times Square, but basic gear is also readily available in Carrefour (p.416), Go Sport (p.407), Géant (p.416), ACE (opposite) and Intersport (p.407). Items are suitable for weekend campers, but would not withstand extremes, so if you are intending to do anything more strenuous you should consider ordering kit online.

Go Sport produces its range of camping equipment as well as importing ranges from other suppliers. Caveman Make Fire (cavemanmakefire.com) produces a range of barbecues and heaters which you can pick up at Géant (p.416) or Spinneys (p.417) and HyperPanda (p.416), or you can have them delivered free of charge. GPS equipment can be found in Sharaf DG – the Times Square branch has the biggest selection – and at Picnico. For outdoor sports enthusiasts there are a number of options (see Sports Goods on p.406). Fishing equipment is available from Al Hamur Marine, Picnico (below) and Go Sport (p.407).

Serious climbers and hikers should consider getting their boots and equipment from overseas, as a very limited range of boots are available and are often aimed more towards the fashion market. You can order a good range of items from REI (rei.com) and Mountain Equipment Co-op (mec.ca). You can also buy boots from Timberland (p.408) and some of the stores in Karama (p.411). While hydration packs (backpacks that you can fill with water, complete with a long tube and mouthpiece) are becoming more widely available in sports shops, anything larger than a day pack should be bought overseas.

Hiking accessories for parents who want to take their small children with them, such as backpack carriers, are not widely available here and should be bought online or from overseas.

ACE *> p.401*

Nr Times Square, Shk Zayed Rd Al Quoz Industrial 1
04 341 1906
aceuae.com
Map 1 T6 Metro Noor Islamic Bank

You can buy all the basic equipment you need for your jaunt in the desert at this store, including tents, sleeping bags and cool boxes. The store also stocks a good range of hardware and accessories.

Adventure HQ

Times Square Al Qusais Industrial 1 04 346 6824
adventurehq.ae
Map 1 T6 Metro First Gulf Bank

An outdoor sport and camping specialist, you'll find everything here from tents, sleeping bags, base layers and hiking boots, to full climbing gear, kayaks, rucksacks, base layers and camping accessories.

Picnico General Trading

Al Faraidooni Bldg, Shk Zayed Rd Al Barsha 1
04 395 1113
picnico.ae
Map 1 R6 Metro Sharaf DG

Picnico are outdoor specialists, stocking a good range of Coleman and Campingaz equipment like cooler bags, tents and accessories. The store also stocks GPS systems and rock climbing gear and footwear. It has one of the largest ranges of hydration packs and it carries Dakine (kitesurfing kit), sea kayaks, diving gear and angling equipment.

Party Accessories

Party accessories are available, on a small scale, in most supermarkets and toy shops but there are several specialist stores that stock everything for children's or adults' parties. If you want a party at home but without the bother, there are a number of companies who will do it for you (see Parties at Home, p.463). You can always go the easier route and have a party at one of the various play centres around town. Tickles & Giggles is a party zone for kids which also has a well-stocked party store. Partyzone (04 344 8464) in Jumeirah Town Centre, covers the basics; Carrefour (p.416), Park n Shop (p.417) and Toys R Us (p.395) all sell themed party essentials, such as paper cups, gift bags, balloons and plates. The range isn't huge and tends to be either Winnie the Pooh, Barbie or Mickey Mouse, so if your child has a preference you may have to order online.

For certain occasions, like Halloween and Easter, specialist shops and even supermarkets (Park n Shop, Carrefour and Spinneys) really get into the spirit of things, selling a range of costumes, sweets and accessories. Costume ranges tend to be a bit limited. Mr Ben's Costume Closet (04 346 3494), in Al Ghazal Mall, is dedicated to fancy dress, with costumes for children and adults available for purchase and hire.

Fabric is inexpensive and it doesn't cost much to hire the services of a tailor, so you can easily have a costume made (see Tailors, p.374).

For cakes, try Coco's (04 332 6333), Boulevard Gourmet (04 222 7171) or the French Bakery (frenchbakery.ae). House of Cakes has an incredible range of inventive cakes for all occasions; visit the website for inspiration (houseofcakesdubai.com) You can get a customised cake made at Park n Shop (p.417); choose one of its designs or take your own picture in and the staff will scan it onto edible paper and place it on top of your cake. Hey Sugar's bakery (p.511) and Sweet Stuff (04 346 3700) can create customised cupcakes. Baskin Robbins (04 285 7885) makes a range of ice cream party cakes and Caesars (04 335 3700) does some elaborately iced creations.

For party entertainment (Flying Elephant (04 347 9170) can provide bouncy castles, soft-play areas and more. Tumble Time (tumbletimedubai.com) are bouncy castle specialists, and Harlequin (harlequinmarquees.com) provide marquees and even outdoor cooling units. Planet Hollywood (p.530), Café Céramique (p.498) and The Jam Jar (p.254) all cater for children's parties, as do many hotel clubs. Whether it's a Hello Kitty themed party or a Barney and Friends adventure, Crash in Castles (crashincastles.ae) can tailor parties to suit your wishes. For entertainment at an adult's party, try Andy Stuart (050 840 1770, andystuartentertainments.com), whose acts range from the amazing (magic tricks and fire eating) to the bizarre (encasing his whole body in a big balloon).

Balloon Lady

Jumeira Plaza Jumeira 1 **04 344 1062**
balloonladyme.com
Map **2 H4** Metro **Emirates Towers**

This store is the place to buy balloons and seasonal items; you can also hire bouncy castles and purchase costumes for special events. The store offers a balloon decoration service and can also customise balloons.

Mr Ben's Costume Closet

Al Ghazal Complex & Shopping Mall Al Bada'a
04 346 3494
mrbenscostumecloset.com
Map **2 J4** Metro **World Trade Centre**

This is the ultimate store for fancy dress outfits and accessories – available for adults and children to buy or to rent. From character outfits to historical garbs, wigs to masks, there is a an overwhelming choice of costumes to suit each and every occasion, including a huge choice for Halloween.

The Party Centre > *p.403*

Nr Welcare Hospital Al Garhoud **04 283 1353**
mypartycentre.com
Map **2 N7** Metro **GGICO**

The Party Centre is enormous and stocks pretty much everything you will need, no matter what the occasion. This is a one-stop shop for decorations and party accessories, and it even sells children's fancy dress outfits.

Perfumes & Cosmetics

Perfumes and cosmetics are big business here, from local scents like frankincense and oud, to the latest designer offerings. These tend to be strong and spicy – you can often locate the stores by the smell of the incense they burn in their doorways. The department stores (Harvey Nichols, Saks Fifth Avenue and Debenhams) and local chains (such as Areej and Paris Gallery) stock the most comprehensive ranges of international brand perfumes and cosmetics.

The Body Shop (p.442), MAC (p.448), Bobbi Brown (p.442) and Red Earth (p.451) are found in many of the city's malls, while Boots (p.442) now has several branches. Sephora (p.452) has a wide selection of brands and its staff will also offer tips on application. L'Occitaine is also worth seeking out for its natural skincare products. Larger supermarkets and pharmacies stock skincare products and some make-up. Anti-allergenic ranges are available at some of the larger pharmacies. Most needs are covered but if yours aren't, specialist retailers often have online shopping facilities.

Ajmal and Arabian Oud outlets are found in most malls, but they largely cater to the Arab population and don't always have English-speaking shop assistants on duty.

Prices for perfumes and cosmetics are similar to those in some other countries, although certain nationalities might find perfume is cheaper here than in their home country. There are no sales taxes, so there is rarely a difference between duty free and shopping mall prices.

Amouage

Deira City Centre Port Saeed **04 295 5550**
amouage.com
Map **2 N7** Metro **Deira City Centre**
Amouage, 'the world's most valuable perfume,' is made in Oman. The luxurious brand is sold exclusively in Paris Gallery stores (p.404) and Dubai and Abu Dhabi Duty Free. A standalone store has also opened in The Dubai Mall (p.426).

Bath & Body Works

Mirdif City Centre Mirdif **04 231 6751**
bathandbodyworks.com
Map **2 P12** Metro **Rashidiya**
A one-stop shop for all things scented, this US-based chain has made its first foray into the UAE at Mirdif City Centre, and has opened further stores in Dubai at Mall of the Emirates and The Dubai Mall. All kinds of fragrant bath and beauty products are available here, including a men's range, and customers are welcome to try out the scents as they browse; the company's attitude is one of 'spray before you pay'.

Faces

BurJuman Al Mankhool **04 352 1441**
faces-me.com
Map **2 L5** Metro **BurJuman**
All manner of lotions and potions are sold in this store. Get all of your monthly makeup, perfume and skincare buys here, from brands like Clarins, Lancome, Givenchy and Clinique. There are several locations in Dubai (see Store Finder, p.445).

Paris Gallery

Ibn Battuta Mall The Gardens **04 368 5500**
parisgallery.com
Map **1 G5** Metro **Ibn Battuta**
Although it stocks a wide selection of perfumes and cosmetics (and a good range of shoes, eyewear and jewellery), its stores never feel too busy, which allows plenty of freedom to browse. For other locations see Store Finder, p.450.

Pets

Most supermarkets carry basic ranges of cat, dog, bird and fish food, although the choice is limited. If your pet has specific dietary requirements, many of the veterinary clinics (p.150) carry specialist foods. If your pooch has a taste for the finer things in life, you'll find a range of couture pet beds and exclusive accessories and fashion at the Pampered Pets boutique in Dubai Marina.

Some pet shops are a bit on the dismal side here – standards are low and animals are usually in tiny cages without water for long periods. The pet shops along Plant Street in Satwa are notoriously the worst offenders and animals purchased there are often malnourished and diseased. Dubai Municipality has laid down regulations but if they are contravened the shop will often be closed down for just one day. Even the pet shops that most animal lovers can bear to go into have a long way to go before standards are acceptable. Petland (04 338 4040) in Al Quoz, Paws and Claws in Uptown Mirdif, Petzone (04 321 1424) on Sheikh Zayed Road, and Animal World (04 344 4422) on Jumeira Road, are the most acceptable. All sell a range of pet accessories, food, animals, birds and fish.

If you are looking for a family pet, consider contacting Feline Friends or K9 Friends (see p.123) who have hundreds of cats and dogs looking for homes. See the Pets section in the Family chapter for more details (p.148).

Glam Paws UAE 050 344 1984
Pampered Pets Dreams Tower 2, Nr Emaar Yacht Club, Dubai Marina, 04 447 5330, *pamperedpets.ae*
Pet's Delight Arabian Ranches Centre, Arabian Ranches, 04 361 8184, *pets-delight.com*
Petzone Nr Times Square Centre, Al Quoz Industrial 1, 04 321 1424, *petzoneonline.com*
World Of Pets Jumeira Rd, Jumeira 3, 04 395 5701, *worldofpetsme.com*

Second-Hand Items

There is an active second-hand market in Dubai, as people are always leaving, redecorating or downsizing, and need to get rid of their stuff. Supermarket noticeboards are a great place to start, as many people post 'for sale' notices with pictures of all the items. Garage sales are also popular on Fridays and you'll notice signs going up in your neighbourhood from time to time.

For the Dhs.3 entry fee into Safa Park you can peruse the flea market which has stalls filled with furniture, books, clothing and a broad range of unwanted items and homemade crafts. The flea market is set up on the first Saturday of every month near Gate 5 (for more information see dubai-fleamarket.com). A car boot sale is held every Friday in the cooler winter months at the Autodrome (p.346); it's free for shoppers and Dhs.150 per car for those wishing to sell. There are also a number of websites with classifieds sections. Try expatwoman.com, dubizzle.com, souq.com, and websouq.com.

There are a number of second-hand shops, often linked to churches and special needs schools, but the opening hours can be somewhat eccentric. The Holy Trinity Thrift Centre (04 337 8192) gives you back 50% of what your items sell for, so you can even make money out of being charitable. It is good for high-quality items and books in particular, and proceeds go towards a number of orphanages supported by the church. The Al Noor shop raises funds for the Al Noor School for Special Needs, and always welcomes donations of second-hand clothing in good condition.

The Dubai Charity Centre (04 337 8246), behind Choithram in Karama, is the biggest of the charity shops. This store supports the students who attend The Dubai Centre for Special Needs, and finances a number of places for those who are unable to afford them. It stocks a good range of clothes, books and toys. The Rashid Paediatric Therapy Centre (rashidc.ae), behind Dubai American Academic in Al Barsha, has a decent range of items and raises money for projects at the centre.

If you are looking to clear some space on your bookshelves, Book World in Karama and Satwa, House of Prose (which has branches in Jumeirah Plaza and Dubai Garden Centre) and Book & Bean at ACE in Festival City all buy books in good condition that they will be able to sell. Any books bought from them will be worth 50% of the purchase price if returned in good condition.

Souvenirs

From typical holiday trinkets to tasteful keepsakes, there is a good range of souvenirs in Dubai. Many of the items are regional rather than local, and several are mass produced in India, Pakistan and Oman. You will find a good selection of traditional gifts like antique wooden wedding chests or pashminas, and the typical holiday buys like fridge magnets, T-shirts and soft toys.

Tourist hotspots, like Souk Madinat Jumeirah (p.434) and Mall of the Emirates (p.431), all sell a good selection of souvenirs, but warehouse stores like the Antique Museum (p.406) and Pinky's (p.388) stock a wide range of goodies too. You'll also find a selection of stores in Trade Routes in Festival Centre (p.429) and Khan Murjan (p.421). If you make it clear you are a resident and you'll be back for more if the prices are good, you should get a better price (see Bargaining, p.370).

You'll find that camels feature heavily in souvenir shops; wooden carvings, camel pot stands and even carvings made from camel bones are all widely available and are great as novelty presents. Perhaps the tackiest souvenirs are plastic alarm clocks in the shape of a mosque – they only cost Dhs.10 and they wake you up with a loud call to prayer.

Coffee pots are symbols of Arabic hospitality and another popular souvenir item. Prices vary enormously from Dhs.100 for a brand new, shiny one, to several thousand dirhams for a genuine antique. Traditional silver items, such as the Arabic dagger (khanjar) and silver wedding jewellery, are excellent souvenirs, and are available both framed and unframed.

Wooden items are popular and representative of the region; trinket boxes (often with elaborate carvings or brass inlays) start from around Dhs.10. Elaborate Arabic doors and wedding chests, costing thousands, are also popular. The doors can be hung as art, or converted into tables or headboards.

While carpets are a good buy, it is worth doing some research before investing (see p.383 for more information). For a smaller, cheaper option, many shops sell woven coasters and camel bags, or you can buy a Persian carpet mouse pad.

You can hardly walk through a mall or shopping area without being offered a pashmina – they are available in an abundant range of colours and styles. Most are a cotton or silk mix and the ratio dictates the price. It is a good idea to check out a few shops before buying as prices vary and, as with most items, the more you buy the cheaper they are. For a decent quality pashmina, prices start from around Dhs.50. Shisha pipes make fun souvenirs and can be bought with various flavours of tobacco, such as apple or strawberry. Both functional and ornamental examples are on sale, prices start from around Dhs.75 in Carrefour.

Local scents, like oud and frankincense, make good gifts and are widely available in outlets including Arabian Oud. These perfumes and scents tend to be strong and spicy – you can often locate these stores by the smell of the incense they burn in their doorways. Amouage produces some of the world's most valuable perfumes, made with rare ingredients. Its products can be found in airports and branches of Paris Gallery (p.404). Ajmal and Arabian Oud outlets are found in most malls, but they cater to the Arab population and don't always have English-speaking shop assistants on duty.

For book lovers, there are a number of great coffee table books with stunning photos depicting the diversity of this vibrant city. Grab a copy of *Dubai: Tomorrow's City Today, Impressions Dubai*, or *Images of Dubai and the UAE*. *Dubai Discovered* is a concise pictorial souvenir of Dubai and is available in five languages (English, Japanese, French, German as well as Russian). Visit askexplorer.com to order copies.

If you've scoured the souvenir shops of Dubai and still can't find what you're looking for, head for Souk Al Arsah in Sharjah, where you can shop for traditional items in a traditional setting.

Al Jaber Gallery > *p.366*

The Dubai Mall Downtown Dubai **04 339 8566**
aljabergallery.ae
Map **2 F6** Metro **Burj Khalifa/Dubai Mall**

Colourful accessories, souvenirs and carpets are sold at this eclectic store. The range of items on sale is quite remarkable, making a good store to browse if you're short on inspiration for a gift. Rummage through the tackier items (think plastic replicas of the Burj and 'I love Dubai' fridge magnets) and you'll find colourfully painted mezze bowls, replica 'traditional' necklaces, embroidered pashminas and a whole pile of gifts that you'd actually be proud to present to someone. It's the perfect spot to take out of town visitors, or if you need a few traditional items to spice up your home. For other locations see the Store Finder p.440.

Antique Museum

Nr Kanoo Int Paints Al Quoz Industrial 1 **04 347 9935**
fakihcollections.com
Map **1 U6** Metro **Noor Islamic Bank**

Upon entering this store's gilded doors, you'll be met by an eclectic mix of wooden furniture, soft furnishings and accessories and an impressive selection of decorative wooden statues. It has a large section devoted to teak Indian furniture and silver chests. The store also has a fantastic selection of token holiday tat – cheaper than you'll find in tourist havens like the Souk Madinat Jumeirah (p.434), but you can also pick up pashminas, Omani silver boxes, Arabian lanterns and other traditional souvenirs. A guide will lead you through the store's maze of products, buried doorways and secret rooms – it's hard to shop alone as there are no prices.

The Sultani Lifestyle Gallerie

Souk Al Bahar Downtown Dubai **04 420 3676**
Map **2 F6** Metro **Burj Khalifa/Dubai Mall**

Head here for traditional souvenirs, carpets and exotic items from the region. The store also carries a good selection of postcards and elaborate home furnishings. For other locations see the Store Finder on p.453.

Sports Goods

Sport is already big business in Dubai, but the development of Sports City (part of Dubailand) should heighten this interest. Sports stores are found in most malls and sell basic equipment, clothing and footwear, as well as equipment for 'core sports' like running, basketball, cricket, football, swimming, badminton, squash and tennis. The usual sports brands are sold in the larger sportswear stores and The Dubai Mall has a whole strip of stores featuring well-known brands such as Adidas (p.440), Nike (p.449), Puma (p.450) and Element (04 434 0638) for skateboarding gear. Stadium (p.407) stocks New Balance footwear and has a large Speedo and Reebok collection.

Stylish boarding brands, Billabong (p.442) and Rip Curl (04 341 0794) all have stores in Dubai and you'll also find branches of Columbia (p.443) and Timberland (p.408). The top Australian fitness wear brand Lorna Jane can now be bought at the J3 Mall on Al Wasl Road.

Several stores in Karama Complex (p.411) have decent ranges that are often cheaper than the bigger stores – just remember, if the item you are buying is much cheaper than normal, it could be a fake.

Golf is extremely popular and clubs, balls and bags are available in most sports shops. Golf House (04 434 0655) and the pro shops are the best places for decent kit. Knight Shot Inc (04 343 5678), in Trade Centre 1, specialise in pool and snooker tables and equipment.

Clubs that organise specialist sports, such as Dubai Surfski Kayak Club (dskc.hu), can often be approached for equipment. Kitesurfing equipment is stocked in several shops; Al Boom Diving stocks North Kites at the Jumeira Road showroom, and Picnico (p.400), next door, stocks Dakine.

Al Boom also stocks equipment for other watersports, including waterskiing and diving. Magic Swell (magicswell.com) is an online shop that sells a wide range of watersports accessories such as wetsuits, harnesses and helmets.

Al Boom Diving

Nr Iranian Hospital, Al Wasl Rd Jumeira 1 **04 342 2993**
alboomdiving.com
Map **2 H4** Metro **World Trade Centre**

The main outlet of the region's major diving company sells a good range of sub-aqua and watersports gear. All the main brands of technical scuba equipment can be found, including Technisub and GoPro, as well as snorkelling gear and beachwear.

Decathlon Dubai

Mirdif City Centre Mirdif **04 283 9392**
Map **2 P12** Metro **Rashidiya**

The French sporting giant has opened a cavernous Mirdif City Centre store. Covering everything from tracksuits and trainers to camping, climbing and equestrian gear, Decathlon has several of its own brands (Btwin, Quechua, Kalenji) which offer exceptional value alternatives to the big name brands the store also stocks.

Go Sport

Ibn Battuta Mall The Gardens **04 368 5344**
go-sport.com
Map **1 G5** Metro **Ibn Battuta**

Go Sport has the most comprehensive collection of sports goods. Its large stores in Ibn Battuta shopping mall and Mall of the Emirates sell equipment for popular sports like running, basketball and tennis, and it also stocks cycling, camping and golfing gear. The range of products and brands on offer is very good but specialist advice is harder to come by – know exactly what you need before you head here. For other locations see Store Finder, p.446.

Intersport

Times Square Al Quoz 1 **04 341 8214**
intersport.ae
Map **1 T6** Metro **First Gulf Bank**

The world's largest sports retailer, its superstores are laid out according to sports rather than brands, and cover football, rugby, basketball, running, triathlon, fitness, racket sports, cycling, camping, swimming, watersports and games. You'll find all the major international labels, as well as services including footscan technology, racket stringing, jersey printing and bike maintenance/fitting. The concept store in Festival City has an outdoor activity and demo area.

JetPad

Nr Ibis Hotel Al Barsha 1 **04 399 6199**
jet-pad.com
Map **1 P6** Metro **Sharaf DG**

JetPads are available to buy from approximately Dhs.60,000 each. There's no actual store so just call them to find out more about this environmentally friendly (electric) watercraft – or to request a demo.

Knight Shot

Nr Mazaya Centre, Shk Zayed Rd Al Wasl **04 343 5678**
knightshot.com
Map **2 F6** Metro **Burj Khalifa/Dubai Mall**

For fans of table sports, Knight Shot is the must-know store in the UAE, selling everything from snooker, pool and table tennis tables (plus dartboards, table football and air hockey tables) to cues, bridges, chalk and apparel. Its experts can also retip your cues or service, clean and refelt tables.

Stadium

Deira City Centre Port Saeed **04 295 0261**
shopstadiumsports.com
Map **2 N7** Metro **Deira City Centre**

Stadium (as well as sister store Studio R) sells brands that cater to those with an active lifestyle. With a range of well-known clothing labels (Quiksilver, Rockport and Union Bay), and sports brands (Adidas, New Balance, Reebok and Speedo), Stadium has created its own niche. It also stocks Teva, which make a range of practical sandals. The store has sales throughout the year when prices are heavily discounted. For other locations see the Store Finder on p.453.

Sun & Sand Sports

Ibn Battuta Mall The Gardens **04 366 9777**
sunandsandsports.com
Map **1 G5** Metro **Ibn Battuta**

This is one of the larger sports stores in the city. You'll find a good range of home gym equipment, from treadmills to rowing machines, as well as a limited range of pool and snooker tables. Larger branches have Nike, Columbia and Timberland departments. Has branches in The Dubai Mall, Ibn Battuta and Mirdif City Centre, and there's a good outlet store in Al Quoz 3 behind the Gold & Diamond Park; for all locations see the Store Finder on p.453.

Surf Shop Arabia

Nr Times Square Al Quoz Industrial 1 **04 399 0989**
surfshopdubai.com
Map **1 U6** Metro **Noor Islamic Bank**

Surf Shop Dubai has a range of new and used surfboards, as well as surfing products, stand up paddleboard (SUP) boards, kitesurfing gear and surf ski accessories.

Timberland

The Dubai Mall Downtown Dubai **04 434 1291**
timberland.com
Map **2 F6** Metro **Burj Khalifa/Dubai Mall**

Get dressed for the great outdoors with Timberland and its timeless collection of hiking boots, outdoor clothing and sporting products for men, women and children. Also has branches at Mall of the Emirates, Ibn Battuta Mall, Arabian Centre and Dubai Outlet Mall.

Textiles & Haberdashery

You have three options if you are looking for fabric: the Textile Souk, also known as Meena Bazaar (near Al Fahidi Street), Satwa, or the shopping malls (most of which have at least one fabric outlet). Prices start from a few dirhams for a metre of basic cotton. The Textile Souk can get busy and parking is difficult, but the sheer range of fabrics makes it worthwhile. There are several haberdashery shops in the same area should you wish to buy matching buttons, bows or cotton. Satwa Road has a good collection of general fabric stores and a few good haberdashers.

Al Masroor Textiles (04 225 5343) in Deira has a good selection of fabric; Plant Street in Satwa is the place to go for upholstery fabrics. IKEA (p.386) and Fabindia (p.418) also stock a range of vibrant fabrics that can be used for cushions, curtains or bedding.

Deepak's

Nr Satwa Clinic Al Bada'a **04 344 8836**
deepakstextiles.com
Map **2 J4** Metro **World Trade Centre**

Deepak's is well-stocked with a fantastic range of fabrics – pick up anything from casual denim to more glamorous silks, chiffons and pure linen at its stores. For other locations see Store Finder, p.444.

Regal Textiles

Nr Satwa Parking Al Bada'a **04 344 9092**
regaldubai.com
Map **2 H5** Metro **World Trade Centre**

This store stocks a good selection of fabrics including French chiffon, printed silks, Swiss cotton and French lace. Its range of textiles are perfect for casual designs, cocktail dresses, wedding gowns, or African and Asian fashion. For other locations see the Store Finder on p.451.

Rivoli Textiles

Zabeel Rd Al Karama **04 335 0075**
rivoligroup.com
Map **2 L6** Metro **Al Karama**
This classy textile store has a broad range of fabrics and a personalised tailoring service. Its store in Satwa (04 344 6602) caters to women and stocks a good range of fabrics. If you need a custom-made suit, men or women can head to its Dubai Marina branch (04 422 1542). For other locations see the Store Finder on p.451.

Wedding Items

Many people choose to hold their wedding in Dubai, so it shouldn't be too difficult to find the key items for your big day. You can begin your wedding research by looking up wedding etiquette, traditions and fashion at Magrudy's (p.380), Book World by Kinokuniya (p.379) and Marks & Spencer (p.414) which have a limited range of books and magazines.

For dresses, head to Jumeira Road where you'll find several bridal stores including The Bridal Room (04 344 6076) and Frost. For designer gowns head to Saks Fifth Avenue's (p.415) bridal department, which stocks the latest off-the-peg designer wedding gowns by Vera Wang and Reem Acra. The store keeps some gowns in stock, but others can be ordered (allow around four months for delivery). The bride will need to attend a number of fittings, but alterations are done in-house and they are up to couture standards. Cocoon (04 295 4133) in Deira City Centre (p.424) has a good, but unusual, selection of designs.

There are several specialist bridal designers with workshops in Dubai, but Arushi (04 344 4103) is renowned as one of the best. You can select the fabric yourself or it can be selected during the first meeting with the designer. Gowns take around one month to make, but as Arushi is so popular, there is often a waiting list. Some of the city's tailors are also able to work from pictures to create your ideal dress. While you can have a simple white dress tailored from Dhs.150 upwards, a traditional wedding dress will cost upwards of Dhs.2,000 (including tailoring and fabric), reaching in excess of Dhs.10,000 for a complex design and expensive fabric. Bridal accessories and shoes are available at Saks Fifth Avenue (p.415).

For the groom, there are several shops where formal wear can be hired, including The Wedding Shop, Elegance, and Formal Wear on 2nd December Street. Girls' bridesmaids dresses are sold in the children's department of Saks Fifth Avenue. Debenhams (p.413) and Monsoon (p.449) both sell suitable ranges; if the style or shade you are looking for aren't available, you can also have them made up by a tailor (p.374). Mothers of the bride and groom, and guests, are well catered for at Coast, Debenhams and Monsoon among many others.

Amal & Amal in the Jumeirah Centre makes bespoke wedding stationery and Cadorim, located in the Village Mall, does tailormade favours and ring boxes. A Little Bit Of Sol will consult with you on your wedding theme and then go away and design all of your stationery from scratch (studiosol.me). Magrudy's (p.380) and Susan Walpole (p.453) stock invitations, guest books and photo albums, while The Paper Room in The Dubai Mall has a particularly good range of stationery. Debenhams and THE One both offer wedding list services. For any items that you can't find here, confetti.co.uk accepts international orders. For more information and ideas, see Getting Married on p.138.

As well as offering wedding planning services, several of the hotels can be commissioned to make the wedding cake; see also Party Accessories, p.402. Most of the city's florists can turn their hands to wedding bouquets and arrangements, with certain florists like Mamosa Flowers (mamoso.com) specialising in weddings. Discuss your requirements with them to find out what will be available.

For rings, check out Gold & Diamonds, p.388.

The Bridal Showroom

Jumeirah Business Centre 2 (JBC 2)
Jumeirah Lakes Towers **04 457 9400**
dubaibridalshowroom.com
Map **1 K5** Metro **Jumeirah Lakes Towers**
The helpful consultants at The Bridal Showroom will help you find the perfect dress for your big day. Book an appointment to try a range of dresses from designers including James Clifford, Kitty Chen, Allure Bridals and Sophia Tolli. There's also a stunning collection of bridal accessories, flower girl outfits and evening gowns.

Frost

Palm Strip Jumeira 1 **04 345 5690**
frostdubai.com
Map **2 H4** Metro **Emirates Towers**
Head here if you want contemporary wedding dresses from top US and European designers. The store has a great set-up for trying dresses on and the exceptionally friendly staff are on hand to help. There's also a decent selection of evening gowns and bridesmaid dresses. There's also a branch in Galeries Lafayette, The Dubai Mall (04 339 9933).

The Wedding Shop

Jumeirah Centre Jumeira 1 **04 344 1618**
theweddingshop.ae
Map **2 H4** Metro **Emirates Towers**
You'll find everything but the cake here, and it is a great place to get your confetti, guest books and photo albums, not to mention a healthy dollop of inspiration. However, some of the designers may be slightly dated or a little flamboyant for some brides' tastes.

PLACES TO SHOP

Shopping By Area

Al Fahidi Street

Nr Astoria Hotel Bur Dubai
Map **2 L4** Metro **Al Fahidi**

Al Fahidi Street is part of the commercial area that runs from the Bastakiya area all the way to Shindagha and takes in Dubai Museum, the Electronics Souk and the Textile Souk. A great place to wander round in the cooler evenings, it's perfect for a bit of local colour and some great shopping. There is a good range of inexpensive places to eat, including some fantastic vegetarian restaurants near the museum, and the outlets in the Astoria (04 353 4300) and Ambassador hotels (04 393 9444). This area is always busy but it really comes to life at night – if you're not sure you're in the right place, just head for the neon lights. The Electronics Souk has several shops selling top global brands such as Canon, JVC, LG, Panasonic, Philips and Sony. Prices are negotiable and competitive but the vendors know the value of what they're selling. To get the best deal, don't make your purchases at the first store you come to; instead, compare product ranges and prices between a few stores before you buy. Although goods are often cheaper here, if you are making a big purchase it may be worth paying a little bit extra at a major retailer, so that you have more security if something goes wrong.

Al Wasl

Al Wasl Rd Jumeira and Umm Suqeim
Map **2 D5** Metro **Business Bay**

Al Wasl is a residential area in west Dubai situated between Jumeira, Al Safa, and Business Bay, with a wealth of shops and small malls to explore. As well as a variety of art galleries, garden stores, hair salons, dentists and vets – all accessed by service roads – there is the ever-popular Spinneys Centre with supermarket, Starbucks, Mothercare and much more. The Al Safa Centre, a community shopping centre that's home to Park n Shop and Pizza Express, is another expat favourite. And, at the Satwa end of Al Wasl Road is the Al-Ghazal Complex, perhaps most well-known by partygoers for Mr Ben's Costume Closet. There's also a huge choice of supermarkets including Choitrams, the Union Co-operative Society, and a Carrefour Express. The jewel of Jumeira is quite possible the new open-air Al Wasl Square. There's already a Japanese cafe, Tim Horton's, Subway, gourmet butcher, sushi restaurant, and a musical instruments store, as well as the gourmet dine-in and takeaway venue, The Pantry Cafe. Female shoppers will love the S*uce Gift store and the Mary Foot Spa, while there's a barbershop for the men. A Japanese bakery and Swiss supermarket are due to open their doors very soon. And, further along the road is the new J3 Mall, with a cafe, soft play centre, boutique shops and express Choitrams.

Downtown Dubai & The Dubai Mall

Downtown Dubai **04 362 7500**
thedubaimall.com
Map **2 F6** Metro **Burj Khalifa/Dubai Mall**

This area has dusted off the sand and grown into a key place to meet, eat and shop. The Dubai Mall (p.426) now has around 1,200 shops, and those keen to spend won't be disappointed with the extensive store listing. Those looking for high-street fashion will be happy with its range of favourites like Topshop, Gap, S*uce (p.419), and a superb branch of Forever 21. It also has large department stores: Galeries Lafayette (p.413), Debenhams (p.413), Marks & Spencer (p.414), Paris Gallery (p.404), and the headline-grabber Bloomingdale's (p.413), the famous American department store. The high-end market is also catered for with a range of designer stores such as Tiffany & Co., Chanel, Dior, and Jimmy Choo, and there are dozens of eating and entertainment options.

For a more laidback atmosphere, Souk Al Bahar's passageways, resembling a traditional souk, hold shops selling Arabian wares such as carpets, ornaments, paintings, jewellery, clothes and perfumes. You'll find that there are a number of useful outlets catering for residents such as banks, a branch of Jacky's electronics, Waitrose and Spinneys. Many of the shops cater to tourists, but you will find a few international brands and the odd funky boutique. The souks never feel too busy and most folk seem to head here for the views of the Burj Khalifa and the range of eateries. To round off a day's shopping, try the Rivington Grill for British dining and great Burj views, New York's gourmet cafe Dean & DeLuca (04 420 0336), The Meat Co. (p.522) for great South African steaks, or the Mezza House (p.523) for Arabic cuisine with an international flavour.

Jumeira Road (Beach Road)

Nr Umm Suqeim & Jumeira Jumeira 1
Map **2 J4** Metro **World Trade Centre**

The community feel of this area is a pleasant contrast to the large malls that shoppers are used to in Dubai. While you may not be able to walk the whole strip (Jumeira Road stretches from Souk Madinat Jumeirah up to 2nd December Street), head to the cluster of stores at the Beach Centre (p.436) and Jumeira Plaza (p.438). There is a particularly good branch of THE One (p.386), which also includes THE One Restaurant (p.528), near Jumeira Mosque, and a branch of Magrudy's (p.380) nearby. As you head down the road, you'll notice several businesses located in villas; these are mostly spas, dentists, hairdressers, and cosmetic surgery clinics. As well as the range of outlets in the malls, you'll find a few independent stores selling

Middle Eastern and Asian clothing along the strip and several bridal stores like Frost (p.409) and The Wedding Shop (p.409). There is a collection of smaller community malls, including Palm Strip (p.438), which has high-end boutiques, the new Sunset Mall (p.439), The Village (p.439) and Jumeirah Centre (p.438). At the far end of the strip is Mercato (p.432) which has a number of popular high-street shops. When you are done perusing the shops, pitch up at one of the cafes – Lime Tree Cafe (p.519) is perennially popular and Arz Lebanon is particularly good for people watching.

Karama

Nr Shk Rashid Rd & Zabeel Rd Al Karama
04 336 7721
Map **2 K6** Metro **Al Karama**

Karama is one of the older residential districts in Dubai, and it has a big shopping area that is one of the best places to find a bargain. The best spot is the Karama Complex, a long street running through the middle of the district that is lined by shops on both sides. The area is best known for bargain clothing, sports goods, gifts and souvenirs, and it is notorious for being the hotbed of counterfeit items in Dubai. As you wander round you will be offered 'copy watches, copy bags' with every step, and if you show any interest you will be whisked into a back room to view the goods. If you're not interested, a simple 'no thank you' will suffice, or even just ignore the vendor completely – it may seem rude, but sometimes it's the only way to cope with the incessant invitations to view counterfeit items. Two of the most popular shops are Blue Marine (04 337 6806) and Green Eye (04 337 7721, while Asda is around the corner, and offers high quality handbags and accessories crammed into two floors. It's pretty claustrophobic but the range is excellent.

Karama

There's a huge range of T-shirts, shoes, shorts and sunglasses at very reasonable prices in Karama. There are several shops selling gifts and souvenirs, from toy camels to mosque alarm clocks and stuffed scorpions to pashminas. Gifts Tent (04 335 4416) is one of the larger outlets and has a wide range, including every colour of pashmina imaginable. With loads of small, inexpensive restaurants, you won't go hungry while pounding the streets of Karama. Try Chef Lanka (p.500), Aryaas (p.492) or Saravana Bhavan (p.535), or head for the large fish, fruit and vegetable market.

Mirdif

Tripoli Street Mirdif
Map **2 Q13** Metro **Rashidiya**

The family suburb of Mirdif is well served by a huge shopping mall, as well as neighbourhood shops. Mirdif houses various 'collections' of small cornershops and supermarkets, usually centred around a mosque; these include Mirdif Golden Gate and the Pink Mall. Not a key shopping destination, but the open-air Uptown Mirdif does have a sense of community that attracts plenty of families living in the area. Uptown Mirdiff Mall (uptownmirdiff.ae) has all the essentials: a Spinneys, an A&E liquor store, banks, pharmacy, gym, cafes and restaurants. But Mirdif City Centre is the key shopping destination here. Ideally located on Sheikh Mohammad Bin Zayed Road and Tripoli Street, it has over 430 stores, leisure and entertainment attractions, and a host of tasty food outlets.

Satwa

Nr World Trade Centre & Al Badaa Al Satwa
Map **2 G5** Metro **World Trade Centre**

Satwa, one of Dubai's original retail areas, has something of a village feel about it. Primarily arranged over four roads, the area is best known for its fabric shops and tailors, but it holds a real mix of stores. Although parts of Satwa have been demolished, many of the retail outlets still remain and the area tends to cater to the lower end of the market and is great fun to look around. Popular reasons to visit Satwa include buying traditional majlis seating and getting your car windows tinted. The pick of the fabric shops is Deepak's (p.408), with an amazing range, reasonable prices and helpful staff.

Shop around, because whatever you are looking for there's bound to be more than one outlet selling it and prices vary. There are a number of shops on 'Plant Street' with good indoor and outdoor plants. This is also the street for upholstery and paint, with Dulux, Jotun and National Paints' outlets and several upholstery shops. Animal lovers should probably avoid the pet shops – conditions are awful, despite regulations, and the animals are often in a sorry state.

2nd December Street (still often called by its former name, Al Diyafah Road) is a great place for a lively evening stroll. There's an eclectic mix of shops and fastfood outlets but, for some reason, there is a fairly high shop turnover so don't count on finding the same outlets if you visit twice.

Al Mallah (p.488), the popular Lebanese restaurant, recognisable by its green umbrellas and neon lighting, is highly recommended for delicious and authentic local food (arguably the best falafel in Dubai). Along 2nd December Street you'll also find an off-road motorbike gear shop and a shop hiring formal evening wear, both men's and women's.

Satwa is renowned for its fastfood outlets and reasonably priced restaurants. Ravi's (p.531) is an institution in Dubai, serving good Pakistani food at incredible prices; Mini Chinese (04 345 9976) has been going for years and serves great Chinese food. Rydges Plaza Hotel (04 398 2222) has a number of popular, licensed bars and restaurants.

Satwa is also home to some great salons, where you can get various treatments at low prices. They might not be as smooth as the upper-end salons, but they are great for a quick treatment. Try Pretty Lady (04 398 5255) or Honeymoon (04 398 3799).

Sheikh Zayed Road

Nr World Trade Centre & Jebel Ali Trade Centre 1
Map **2 J6** Metro **World Trade Centre**

More than just the highway connecting Abu Dhabi and Dubai, Sheikh Zayed Road, between the Trade Centre and Jebel Ali, is the main artery along which many of Dubai's main shopping districts lie. The area that runs alongside the road is surrounded by a mixture of industrial units (some of which contain giant furniture outlets) and retail units which house some of the city's larger independent stores.

Beginning at the Trade Centre end, this portion of the highway is flanked by some of Dubai's tallest buildings – it is worth checking out the stores at ground level. On the left are Emirates Towers (home to Boulevard at Jumeriah Emirates Towers – see p.437), and a number of sports shops; while on the right are the Holiday Centre, Lifco supermarket, and a number of cafes and fastfood outlets.

The left-hand side of the stretch between Junction One (Defence Roundabout) and Junction Two (Safa Park) is home to Emaar's Downtown district, Burj Khalifa (p.233) and The Dubai Mall (p.426). On the right-hand side are Safestway supermarket, the Mazaya Centre (p. 04 343 8333) and a number of used-car dealers. After Junction Two, the right-hand side of the road is almost entirely residential while, on the left-hand side, there are a number of retail outlets and car dealerships, plus Oasis Centre (p.438) and Wolfi's Bike Shop (p.379). Behind the Pepsi factory is Safita, which sells well-priced wooden Indian furniture. For those looking to make home improvements, ACE (p.400) and Speedex (04 339 1929) will have the equipment to do the job.

The area between Junctions Three and Four has some real gems to be discovered. Kidz Inc (04 340 5059) sells furniture, puzzles and toys for children. Just Kidding (p.378) has all the latest baby equipment, furniture and fashion from Europe, as well as maternity wear. The Courtyard (04 347 5050), near the Spinneys warehouse, is home to a collection of interesting shops and galleries; there's even a coffee shop here. Speaking of which, the nearby branch of Lime Tree Cafe has some lovely edible and kitchen goodies that make lovely gifts. This is also the area to head for if you have green fingers or enjoy the alfresco lifestyle; Dubai Garden Centre (04 340 0006) has everything for the garden pretty much covered. The Gold & Diamond Park (04 347 7788), right by junction four, has almost as much to offer as the Gold Souk (p.420), but you can browse in air-conditioned comfort.

Boulevard at Jumeriah Emirates Towers

Mall of the Emirates (MOE, p.431) is the place to enjoy shopping and skiing. After MOE, there is little else other than high-rise buildings but there are a few shops around the Greens area, including a branch of Organic Foods & Café (p.417). The Walk, a new outdoor shopping area beneath the Jumeirah Beach Residence, is where you'll find the Covent Garden Market (p.419) and a number of shops and eateries; Dubai Marina Mall (p.428) is also nearby. It's then not far to Ibn Battuta Mall (p.430). After that you'll be hard pressed to part with your cash until you reach Abu Dhabi; be sure to have a copy of the *Abu Dhabi Residents' Guide* on hand when you arrive.

The Walk, Jumeirah Beach Residence

Jumeirah Beach Residence Dubai Marina **04 390 0091**
dubaipropertiesgroup.ae/en/properties/Jumeirah-Beach-Residence
Map **1 K4** Metro **Dubai Marina**

A solution to the age old gripe – there aren't enough places to walk in Dubai – The Walk, Jumeirah Beach Residence moves away from glitzy mall interiors to street-side shops and cafes. The fully pedestrianised area stretches 1.7 kilometres along the beachfront attracting beach strollers, wandering window shoppers and guests from the nearby hotels. Outlets are located either on the ground level or on the plaza level of six clusters of towers called Murjan, Sadaf, Bahar, Rimal, Amwaj and Shams. There is a concentration of stores on the ground levels of Murjan and Sadaf, but other stores are dotted further along The Walk. The plaza level of each cluster can be accessed from large staircases, or by the lifts at ground level and in the carpark.

Fashion forward shoppers will be pleased with stores like Boutique 1 (p.418), Saks Fifth Avenue (p.415) – which mainly carries men's fashion, although a small women's section has emerged – and Zadig Voltaire. There is also a branch of ACT Marine, which sells a good range of equipment for watersports, and a few convenient stores for nearby residents such as Al Maya Supermarket (p.415). There's also the Covent Garden Market Dubai along The Walk every Wednesday, Thursday, Friday and Saturday from October until the end of May – a great place to browse art and craft stalls (coventgardenmarket.ae).

In the afternoons, people congregate in the cafes along The Walk (particularly popular are Le Pain Quotidien (04 437 0141) and Starbucks (04 367 5468), and there are plenty of restaurants to dine in come the evening. There's a big carpark next to the Hilton, or you can also park in designated areas of the Murjan carpark. Most shops open at 10:00 and close at 22:00. The recently opened Ocean View Hotel near The Walk adds to the long list of eateries with a licensed pub, Girders, and a Brazilian restaurant, Fogo Vivo.

Department Stores

Department stores anchor some of Dubai's biggest malls and you'll find anything from the epitome of chic, Saks Fifth Avenue, to stalwarts like Marks & Spencer that provide the essentials. Renowned department store Bloomingdale's became one of the biggest names to join the roster when it opened a few years ago at The Dubai Mall.

Bloomingdale's

The Dubai Mall Downtown Dubai **04 350 5333**
bloomingdales.com
Map **2 F6** Metro **Burj Khalifa/Dubai Mall**

The first Bloomingdale's to open outside the USA took up residency in The Dubai Mall in 2010, bringing with it its exclusivity that has attracted well-heeled New Yorkers for many a decade. The main store features three storeys of high-end lines of fashion, jewellery and accessories, while a separate home department focuses on furnishings and a gift registry. The homestore (located on the lower ground floor) sells high-end homewares from designer bed sheets to funky home accessories. As well as the goods on sale, and some classic touches like the store's famous 'big brown bags' and black-and-white floor in the beauty department, Bloomingdale's customers can enjoy a taste of Manhattan in Magnolia's Bakery.

Debenhams

Deira City Centre Port Saeed **04 294 0011**
debenhams.com
Map **2 N7** Metro **Deira City Centre**

A stalwart of the British high street, Debenhams has five stores in Dubai: Deira City Centre, Ibn Battuta, Mall of the Emirates, Mirdif City Centre and The Dubai Mall. All stores stock perfumes, cosmetics, and clothing for men, women and children. You'll also find a good selection of homewares, including Jamie Oliver's cookware.There are several concessions including Evans, for plus-size clothing, Motivi, Warehouse, Oasis, Coast, Miss Selfridge and Dorothy Perkins. And, for quality items at reasonable prices, browse the Designers at Debenhams ranges by John Rocha, Jasper Conran and Pearce Fionda.

Galeries Lafayette

The Dubai Mall Downtown Dubai **04 339 9933**
galerieslafayette.com
Map **2 F6** Metro **Burj Khalifa/Dubai Mall**

Galeries Lafayette adds more designer brands to The Dubai Mall's extensive store list. Whether you are after a glamorous frock or stylish shoes, this French department store has it all including cosmetics, children's wear, lingerie and a homeware section. The Lafayette Gourmet food store stocks a range of original and innovative edible treats, and there's the option to dine in too.

Harvey Nichols

Mall of the Emirates Al Barsha 1
04 409 8888
harveynichols.com/stores-abroad
Map **1 R6** Metro **Mall of the Emirates**

The epitome of chic shopping, Harvey Nics (as it is affectionately called) offers a large selection of high-rolling fashion (for men, women and kids), beauty and homeware brands. Here's where you'll find Jimmy Choo, Diane Von Furstenberg, Juicy Couture, Hermes and Sergio Rossi, rubbing shoulders with other swish brands. Take note of its animated (and very realistic) mannequins, good range of designer denim and its extensive collection of designer shoes and handbags. There is a lingerie section hidden at the back of the ladies' department, which also sells a great range of swimwear. There is a small range of gourmet products in the Foodmarket on the first floor next to swish restaurant Almaz by Momo (p.489); a great mid-shop pit stop.

ICONIC

Deira City Centre Port Saeed
04 294 3444
Map **2 N7** Metro **Deira City Centre**

This funky store in Deira City Centre stocks over 130 brands of cutting edge and cult fashion, gadgets and accessories. Aimed at a youthful market, fashion labels featured include Elen Paris, Hard Soda, Friday Kinyobi, Reiss, Nexus and Zync. There's a big range of electronic items, and a Spaces beauty treatment centre for both sexes. You round off the experience by tucking into some designer eastern fare at the store's Wild Ginger, or by picking up some funky cupcakes to go at Hey Sugar (p.511).There are other branches at Dubai Marina Mall and The Dubai Mall.

Jashanmal

The Dubai Mall Downtown Dubai **04 417 4800**
jashanmalgroup.com
Map **2 F6** Metro **Burj Khalifa/Dubai Mall**

The largest Jashanmal department store is now open in The Dubai Mall, the go-to shopping destination for dinnerware, cookware, bed and bath accessories, home appliances as well as luggage. You'll find brands such as Lenox, Dankotuwa, Rimowa, Victorinox, Berghoff and Bugatti here, as well as luxury fashion labels and high street names including Salvatore Ferragamo, Bally, Porsche Design, Kate Spade New York, L.K.Bennett, Calvin Klein and Clarks.

Marks & Spencer

Festival Centre Dubai Festival City **04 206 6466**
markspencerme.com
Map **2 M9** Metro **Emirates**

M&S, as it is known to Brits, is a renowned UK brand which sells clothes and shoes for men, women and children, along with a small, but cultishly popular, selection of food and sweets. It's usually a good bet if you're looking for seasonal items that are hard to find elsewhere (such as Christmas cards, chocolate Easter bunnies, advent calendars and so on). The Dubai stores all carry selected ranges of its chic Per Una brand, as well as its more classic lines and its revered lingerie line. For other locations see the Store Finder on p.448.

Matalan

Lamcy Plaza Oud Metha **04 335 5051**
matalan-me.com/
Map **2 K6** Metro **Oud Metha**

Matalan is a popular department store chain in the UK, with more than 200 outlets around Britain. The Lamcy Plaza Matalan is the company's third branch in Dubai (other stores are at the Arabian Centre in Mirdif and Mirdif City Centre). As well as its broad selection of clothing, Matalan's primary attraction is its homeware range, which includes soft furnishings, bedding, bathroom accessories and kitchenware at particularly attractive prices.

Mudo City

The Dubai Mall Downtown Dubai
04 325 3246
Map **2 F6** Metro **Burj Khalifa/Dubai Mall**

One of the most famous brands in Turkey, Mudo City brings its lifestyle store with its collection of furniture, home furnishings, kitchen, bathroom and personal accessories, home textiles and lighting to Dubai. This is a store where you can pick up an affordable T-shirt for Dhs.70 or a quirky, designer table for more than Dhs.10,000. It's an eclectic mix of fashion and home decor, all with a modern-classic style.

Next

Deira City Centre Port Saeed 04 295 5025
next.co.uk
Map 2 N7 Metro Deira City Centre

This popular British chain has several stores in the UAE. On sale are clothes for men, women and children, as well as shoes, underwear, accessories and homeware. It's a great place to go clothes shopping for all occasions – whether you need a smart, professional look for the office, glittery party wear for hitting Dubai's nightspots or something cosy for snuggling up on the couch. The kids' clothing section has a great selection for all ages. For other locations see Store Finder, p.449.

Redtag

Ibn Battuta Mall The Gardens 04 445 6966
redtag.ae
Map 1 G5 Metro Ibn Battuta

A big name in fashion in Saudi Arabia, with more than 40 stores across the Kingdom, this branch in Ibn Battuta's India Court was the first Dubai location for the brand when it opened back in 2010. With a strategy of offering value ranges of men's, women's and children's clothing, Redtag is a popular regional choice; other outlets include Arabian Centre in Mirdif and Lamcy Plaza.

Saks Fifth Avenue

BurJuman Al Mankhool 04 351 5551
saksincorporated.com
Map 2 L5 Metro BurJuman

Anchoring the extension to BurJuman is the second-largest Saks Fifth Avenue outside the US. Even in Dubai's cultured retail sector, this store has an air of sophistication. The first level is all about pampering, with cosmetics and perfumes, designer sunglasses

and the Saks Nail Studio; it also houses the D&G Boutique, the children's department (with designer clothes for little ones), the men's store, and a chocolate bar and cafe. The second level holds designer boutiques including Christian Dior, Jean Paul Gaultier and Prada. This is where to head for accessories, jewellery and an exclusive bridal salon that stocks Vera Wang gowns. There is also a branch of lingerie store Agent Provocateur. The Fifth Avenue Club is a personalised shopping service, where members can browse the store with the helpful guidance of a specialist consultant.

Salam

Wafi Umm Hurair 2 04 704 8484
salams.com
Map 2 L7 Metro Dubai Healthcare City

This local department store has a swanky decor and a good mix of brands. While its spacious store in Wafi seldom sees customers arriving in their droves, it does stock a good selection of homeware, jewellery and clothing and you'll have ample opportunity to browse. The store also has a particularly good selection of photography accessories from well-known brands. Designer names on offer include Betsey Johnson, Roberto Cavalli, Prada and Missoni. The store also sells a range of clothes from LA brand Gypsy 05 – great for maxi dresses and summer essentials.

Supermarkets & Hypermarkets

1004 Mart

Coral Al Khoory Hotel Apartments Al Barsha 1
04 323 4536
my1004mart.com
Map 1 R6 Metro Sharaf DG

If you're looking for Asian ingredients for that special dish, then this is the place to go to. Stocks Chinese, Korean, Japanese and Thai food, with more than 3,000 Asian ingredients and seasonal fruits and vegetables available. Also supplies to the likes of Nobu (p.526) and Zuma (p.550).

Al Maya Supermarket > *p.xxiii*

The Walk, Jumeirah Beach Residence Dubai Marina
04 437 0166
almayagroup.com
Map 1 K4 Metro Dubai Marina

This city-wide chain has several stores at JBR, including ones at Bahar and Sadaf, as well as at locations in Dubai Marina, Bur Dubai and Satwa. Its stores carry a good range of items, a bakery and fresh meat and fish. It also has a pork section selling a wide range of goods. Many of its branches are open 24 hours and offer free home delivery for a minimum order of Dhs.50. For other locations see Store Finder on p.440.

Carrefour

Deira City Centre Port Saeed **800 73232**
carrefouruae.com
Map **2 N7** Metro **Deira City Centre**
Branches of this French hypermarket chain can be found throughout the city. As well as food, each large store carries fairly comprehensive ranges of electronics, household goods, luggage, mobile phones, and white goods. Camping gear and car accessories are also on sale here, in addition to clothes and shoes for men, women and children, garden furniture, hardware, music and DVDs, toys and stationery. The store offers a good range of French products (it's the best place to get crusty, freshly baked French sticks) and it has a small health food section and pharmacy. Carrefour is renowned for its competitive pricing and special offers. There is also a new option to purchase non-food items online (see ic4uae.com). For other locations see p.443.

Choithrams

Nr Ramada Hotel, Al Mankhool Rd Al Mankhool
04 352 6946
choithram.com
Map **2 L4** Metro **Al Fahidi**
With 17 branches across the city, Choithram is technically Dubai's largest supermarket chain (the 'mothership' is on Al Wasl Road next to Union Coop). Its stores are renowned for stocking British, American and Asian products that can't be found elsewhere (such as the Quorn range), but they are also known for being fairly expensive. Its stores also have pork sections, excellent frozen sections and a great range of baby products – particularly food and formula. For other locations see the Store Finder on p.443.

Emirates Gourmet General Trading

Jumeira Plaza Jumeira 1 **04 349 3181**
emiratesgourmetdubai.com
Map **2 H4** Metro **Emirates Towers**
High-end delicatessens are on the rise in Dubai, and Emirates Gourmet General Trading is a favourite on the scene. Shelves are stacked with a fine collection of speciality gourmet foods from France, Italy, Spain, Germany, Belgium, USA and Lebanon. There's condiments and olives, chocolates and chutnies. Brands include Stonewall Kitchen and there is also an enticing collection of seasonal goods for the Christmas, Thanksgiving or Easter shopping trip.

Géant Hypermarket

Ibn Battuta Mall The Gardens **04 368 5880**
geant-uae.com
Map **1 G5** Metro **Ibn Battuta**
Géant stocks a massive selection of produce that is similar to that of Carrefour. It is well worth a visit for the cheap fruit and vegetables and the huge selection of nuts (great almonds). You'll also find a massive selection of very reasonably priced towels and bedding, a good selection of electronics, a car accessories section and it's also a good destination for DVD boxsets. The store is particularly handy for the residents of Jebel Ali and Dubai Marina.

HyperPanda

Festival Centre Dubai Festival City **04 232 5997**
panda.com.sa/dubai
Map **2 M9** Metro **Emirates**
HyperPanda is enormous; however it is a lot quieter than similar stores, so it's a good choice when you need hypermarket shopping without the hyperactive crowds. The store's selection of produce isn't as extensive as some of the other hypermarkets, but it does have a healthcare department, a good electronics department and more than the basic range of goods. The parking is good and it allows easy access to other outlets.

Jones The Grocer

Indigo Central 8, Shk Zayed Rd
Al Manara **04 346 6886**
jonesthegrocer.com
Map **1 T6** Metro **Noor Islamic Bank**
The Australian gourmet foodstore brings its artisan products to Dubai, with an extensive selection of deli items and fresh produce. It has an on-site bakery and cafe, and also offers a catering service. This is the perfect food emporium for connoisseurs looking to shop for a picnic basket or alfresco dining at home.

Lifco Supermarket

Nr Al Moosa Tower, Shk Zayed Rd Trade Centre 1
04 332 7899
lifco.com
Map **2 H5** Metro **Emirates Towers**
Although not the largest of the city's supermarkets, Lifco stocks a great range of items in terms of convenience. It is a good place to go for fresh olives. The store has regular special offers where you can buy two or three items banded together for a discount. For other locations see the Store Finder on p.447.

LuLu Hypermarket

Nr Dubai Municipality Al Karama **04 336 7070**
luluhypermarket.com
Map **1 K6** Metro **Al Karama**
The store is great for those on a budget; its hot food counters, salad bars and fishmongers are particularly good value. Stores have an Aladdin's cave quality about them and there's not much that they don't sell – from luggage and electronics to food and clothing. The grocery selection is very good and while you may not find all of your favourite Western brands, it stocks a good range of ethnic food. Each store has a good range

of home appliances and an area selling colourful saris. For other locations see the Store Finder on p.448.

Milk & Honey

Shoreline Bldg # 10 Palm Jumeirah **04 432 8686**
milkandhoney.ae
Map **1 N3** Metro **Nakheel**

This boutique supermarket has a range of organic products and everyday household essentials, with a focus on high-end brands and gourmet living. Shelves are stocked with Hey Sugar's cupcakes and Eric Kayser's fresh breads and pastries, as well as Australian brands like Preshafood, Naturally Good and Select Harvests. There is a second outlet at Meadows Town Centre (04 435 6363).

Organic Foods & Cafe *> p.393*

Emaar Business Park 2 The Greens **04 361 7974**
organicfoodsandcafe.com
Map **1 N5** Metro **Dubai Internet City**

Do something good for the environment and for your body by shopping at the only certified organic supermarket in Dubai. It's easy to stock up on fresh organic fruit, veg, meat, fish and bread every week. If you think organic food is too pricey think again; they offer weekly specials, and 20% off products every third Saturday of the month. The adjoining cafe serves food prepared with organic ingredients and is a popular spot. New outlets are due to open early 2013 at The Village Mall, Jumeira and on Sheikh Zayed Rd, next to the Oasis Centre.

Park n Shop

Al Wasl Rd Al Safa 1 **04 394 5671**
Map **2 C5** Metro **Noor Islamic Bank**

Although it is small, Park n Shop is worth a trip simply because it has the best bakery and butchery in the city. The bakery sells a range of wheat-free breads (made with alternatives such as spelt), as well as a range of delicious and incredibly fresh goodies, including reputedly the best jam doughnuts in Dubai. Famous for its birthday cakes, come Christmas time this is where you'll get your mince pies and, come Easter, your hot cross buns. The butchery sells a range of marinated cuts ideal for the barbecue, and it also has a Christmas ordering service for your turkey and ham. See Store Finder (p.450) for other locations, including the new 100,000 sq ft Cash n Carry store at Dubai Investment Park.

Spinneys

Nr Centrepoint Al Mankhool **04 351 1777**
spinneys-dubai.com
Map **2 L5** Metro **Al Karama**

With branches across Dubai, from Mirdif to the Marina, you're never far from this well-known supermarket. Products are competitively priced (and there are promotions on fresh fruits, meat products and bakery items every Monday). It has a great range of South African and Australian, as well as British and American items. Spinneys stocks a selection of Waitrose products (a supermarket renowned in the UK for its quality), and the freezer section and vegetarian options are both good. Also worth a try are items from the deli counter which are great for picnics, along with the ever popular roasted chickens – if you stay in town for Christmas you can order your seasonal goodies from here. For other locations see the Store Finder on p.452.

Union Co-operative Society

Nr Rashidiya Police Station Al Rashidiya **04 286 2434**
ucs.ae
Map **1 P11** Metro **Rashidiya**

It may lack the shine of other hypermarkets, but this is an essential place to shop if you're trying to shave a few dirhams off your grocery bill. The huge fruit and veg section is packed with farm-fresh produce at great prices, and because it is very popular with locals, it has a super selection of Arabic cheeses, olives, and family size bargain packs. There are several branches, but the one on Al Wasl Road is open 24 hours a day. For other locations see the Store Finder on p.454.

Waitrose

The Dubai Mall Downtown Dubai **04 434 0700**
waitrose.com
Map **2 F6** Metro **Burj Khalifa/Dubai Mall**

UK supermarket Waitrose is well known for its premium range of British produce and gourmet goods. Its stores offer a good range of items, including basic household goods, glassware, flowers and a good selection of books and DVDs. It has a well-stocked deli filled with hot and cold selections of pre-made dishes, perfect for picnics, and its selection of baked goods, meat and cheese are some of the best in Dubai. For other locations see Store Finder, p.454.

Boutiques & Independent Shops

Independent stores and boutiques are opening, predominantly in converted villas, all over the city. A few stores have opened in some of the larger malls and shopping areas, but the biggest cluster of stores is along Jumeira Road. Modern souks like Khan Murjan (p.421), Souk Al Bahar (p.42) and Souk Madinat Jumeirah (p.434) also hold a few independent outlets.

Ayesha Depala Boutique

The Village Jumeira 1 **04 344 5378**
Map **2 H4** Metro **Emirates Towers**

Ayesha studied at London's prestigious St Martins College of Art & Design and is now based in Dubai. Her boutique holds all her own creations. Pick up couture frocks, shimmering fabrics and feminine accessories. As well as items fit for the catwalk, the store offers a bridal service, ready-to-wear and vintage pieces.

Bambah

Nr Dubai Zoo, 142 Jumeira Rd Jumeira 1
050 674 1754
bambah.com
Map **2 G4** Metro **Financial Centre**

Bambah is all about vintage. This boutique offers an exquisite collection of fashion from the 1930s to the 1980s, with a mixture of everyday classics and designer pieces such as Yves Saint Laurent, Lanvin, Dior, and Nina Ricci. Perfect for fashionistas of Dubai who want to stand out in the crowd, this is a haven for unique items and individual pieces.

Boutique 1

The Walk, Jumeirah Beach Residence Dubai Marina
04 425 7888
boutique1.com
Map **1 K5** Metro **Dubai Marina**

A regular haunt for fashion foragers, the Dubai flagship store holds sought-after designer brands, elegant evening wear, cosmetics and clothing for men and women. It also has a gallery on the first floor, a small cosmetics section, a chic range of furniture, a small cafe and a spa. Not an option for the budget conscious – products are high-end and high-priced!

Fabindia

Nashwan Bldg, Al Mankhool Rd Al Mankhool
04 398 9633
fabindia.com
Map **2 K4** Metro **Al Fahidi**

Ranges for men, women and children combine Indian and western styles – from capri pants to kurtas, the cotton-based designs are guaranteed to add a splash of colour to any wardrobe. You can also pick up soft furnishings and a beautiful range of rugs and hard-wearing dhurries to liven up dreary white floor tiles. Its products are handcrafted in villages, creating a livelihood for many and supporting rural communities. Considering this, its prices are very reasonable – shirts start from around Dhs.40, large tablecloths from Dhs.120 and quilts from Dhs.300.

Garderobe

Nr Miraj Islamic Art Centre, Jumeira Rd
Umm Suqeim 1 **04 394 2753**
garderobevintage.com
Map **2 B4** Metro **Noor Islamic Bank**

Garderobe will appeal to 'bargain hunters' with its collection of pre-loved designer wear. Clothing, shoes, bags and accessories from world-known designers such as Chanel, Hermes and Balenciaga or up-coming designers such as Alexander Wang, are available at fantastic prices. You can also pop by the store with designer wares, and if suitable they will display them and split the profit 50/50 when and if the items sell.

Momentum Dubai

Dubai International Financial Centre (DIFC)
Trade Centre 2 **04 4327 4320**
momentum-dubai.com
Map **2 G6** Metro **Financial Centre**

A fairly new Dubai boutique focused on vintage and classic watches. There are unique ranges available, vintage straps and quality repair services provided by the master watchmaker.

Fashion For Less

If you need to save the pennies, but don't want to scrimp on fashion, head to Karama (p.411) for its range of fake designer goods; Dubai Outlet Mall (p.437) has outlet stores for well-known brands, and Matalan (p.414) for its well-priced essentials. Avenue (04 397 9983) stocks the basics and Sana Fashions (04 337 7726) offers a superb range of low-cost branded clothing. The Sun & Sands Sports outlet in Al Quoz is great for cut-price sports kit including training gear, trainers, swimwear and casual wear, plus sports equipment.

O Concept

Beach Residents Bldg, Nr Saladicious & The ONE
Jumeira 1 **04 345 5557**
Map **2 H4** Metro **World Trade Centre**

O Concept is a jack of all trades boutique: part clothes emporium, part home design, part art gallery – and a cafe too! As well as its exclusive selection of fashion and glamorous coffee tables, you'll find eastern-made art pieces alongside art students' creations and one-of-a-kind designer shoes. It's the perfect mix of all things fashionable and unique, boasting some of the region's most exciting designers such as Khaleda Rajab, Poca & Poca, ByKAL by Khalid Sharan, and Toby as well as international brands such as Dalaleo, Haikure and My Gemma Swimwear to name but a few.

O'de Rose

Villa 999, Al Wasl Rd Umm Suqeim 2 **04 348 7990**
o-derose.com
Map **1 T5** Metro **First Gulf Bank**

O'de Rose arrived on the city's shopping scene with a feminine flounce. The gorgeous boutique, in a spacious villa, is devoted to clothing, art and furniture, with embellished kaftans, clutch bags and homeware at every turn. Minimal it is not. With pieces from all over the world, a trip to O'de Rose is as good as a mini-break – with better souvenirs. Now also at Galeries Lafayette, The Dubai Mall.

Reem's Closet

Mazaya Centre Al Wasl **04 343 9553**
reemscloset.com
Map **2 F6** Metro **Burj Khalifa/Dubai Mall**
Tucked away in the decidedly non-flashy Mazaya Centre off Sheikh Zayed Road, is a second-hand clothing haven, packed to the rafters with quality designer clobber at astonishing prices. Bring in the 'it bag' you've tired of, pick up some vintage pieces or discover an unwanted item from last season. The store accepts designer pieces or items off the high street; what is essential is that they offer the same attractive quirky high-fashion as the store's stock. What you won't find are Karama's finest genuine fakes – quality control is uncompromised so fashionistas can buy with confidence.

S*uce

The Village Jumeira 1 **04 344 7270**
shopatsauce.com
Map **2 H4** Metro **Emirates Towers**
The items at S*uce are anything but basic, and it's the place to come to peruse the funky accessories, quirky high-fashion and individual pieces at this eclectic boutique. Fashionistas head here for token buys that are less likely to be seen on anyone else. You'll find clothes by international designers such as Chloè. The store also offers a loyalty card, and a personal shopper for those needing advice on the season's key buys. For other locations see Store Finder, p.452.

Sconto

Dubai Marina Mall Dubai Marina **04 399 7899**
Map **1 K5** Metro **Jumeirah Lakes Towers**
Bargain hunters will love this Italian boutique, a haven for runway designs at pocket-friendly (ish) prices. This is the place to find designer labels by Balmain, See by Chloe, Poika, Gianmarco Lorenzi, Fisico and D Squared shoes with 70% off.

Markets & Souks

There are a number of souks and markets in Dubai. The souks are the traditional trading areas, some more formally demarcated than others. In keeping with tradition, bargaining is expected and cash gives the best leverage.

The Gold, Spice and Textile Souks line either side of the creek, but parking is limited, so if possible it is better to go to these areas by taxi or, if you are visiting all three, park on one side of the creek and take an abra (p.53) to the other side.

Western-style markets are becoming more popular: they are usually based around crafts and are often seasonal. For example, the Covent Garden Market (opposite) is set up along The Walk, Jumeirah Beach Residence, during the cooler months, with artists, jewellers and other crafty types displaying their wares.

Artisans Of The Emirates (ARTE)

Times Square Al Quoz Industrial 1
04 341 8020
arte.ae
Map **1 T6** Metro **First Gulf Bank**
Taking place most weeks (alternating between its Festival Centre and Times Square venues), this is where you'll find all manner of individual and quirky products unlike anything you'll find in any of the bigger markets, from hand-printed cards or personalised artwork to bags, cushions and jewellery created by talented local designers.

Covent Garden Market Dubai

The Walk, Jumeirah Beach Residence Dubai Marina
04 325 5123
coventgardenmarket.ae
Map **1 K5** Metro **Dubai Marina**
The vibrancy of this street market comes from its street entertainers, open stalls and all-day strollers along Jumeirah Beach Residence's cobbled beachfront promenade. You can pick up canvas or watercolour paintings from emerging artists for a rock bottom price. You will also find stalls selling fashion items, handmade jewellery, confectionary and kids' toys. The market is located in the Rimal sector of JBR on Wednesdays and Thursdays 17:00 till midnight, and on Fridays and Saturdays 10:00 to 21:00.

Cultural Night Market

Safa Park Al Wasl, Jumeira **050 461 8888**
coventgardenmarket.ae
Map **2 D5** Metro **Business Bay**
Providing an urban public space for local and international artists to develop and showcase their art, the Cultural Night Market offers music, paintings, sculptures, dance and theatre, as well as a world food market. There's a kids' corner, artistic market, books area and life performances in the park amphitheatre. Held every last Friday and Saturday of the month, 15:00 to 23:00, from September through to April. Admission costs Dhs.15 per person; free for children under 10.

Dubai Designer Market

The Beach Centre Jumeira 1 **055 452 6030**
dubaidesignermarket.com
Map **2 G4** Metro **Emirates Towers**
Thrifty fashionistas should head to the Dubai Designer Market for chic and boutique designer goods at affordable prices. Think rails of high-end brands like GUCCI, Prada, and Chanel, as well as vintage items and collections by young, up and coming designers. The Market has a strict original brands and high-end goods only policy, so no fakes allowed! Held every second Saturday of each month at The Beach Centre, Jumeira.

Dubai Flea Market

Safa Park Al Wasl, Jumeira **04 452 6030**
dubai-fleamarket.com
Map **2 D5** Metro **Business Bay**

This flea market is a great place to take advantage of Dubai's transient population. As people pack up and move on, one escapee's excess baggage could become a bargain hunter's treasure. For the Dhs.3 entry fee into Safa Park, you can peruse the stalls covered with furniture, books, clothing and a broad range of unwanted items and homemade crafts. The flea market is set up on the first Saturday of every month at Safa Park from October through to May. It's proved to be so popular that a second site has been set up, held every second Friday of the month at Uptown Mirdif. There's also a spin-off Designer Market held monthly in Jumeira (dubaidesignermarket.com). Opens from 8am; arrive early to grab the bargains!

The Farmers' Market

Souk Al Bahar Downtown Dubai
Map **2 F6** Metro **Burj Khalifa/Dubai Mall**

The Farmers' Market On The Terrace takes place every Friday from 09:00 to 13:00 throughout the cooler months, selling local produce grown on UAE farms and fresh bread and cakes baked by Baker & Spice and Sweet Connections Gluten Free Baking. Rediscover the joy of buying freshly picked produce such as locally grown tomatoes, cucumbers, capsicum, chillies, rocket, lettuce and herbs, as well as organic eggs, chicken, turkey and a few more surprises. What's more, the farmers will be on hand to answer any questions. A second market is held every Saturday during the winter from 09:00 to 13:00 outside Baker & Spice on Dubai Marina Promenade.

Fish Market

Nr Shindagha Tunnel Deira
Map **2 N4** Metro **Palm Deira**

The Fish Market in Deira is hard to ignore if you're in the area, especially during the hotter months – maybe not the best place to visit if you don't like the smell of fish. To get the freshest fish for your evening meal, and to experience the vibrancy of this working market, head down early in the morning or late at night as the catch is coming in. There is an incredible range of seafood on display. The emphasis is on wholesale but the traders are usually more than happy to sell to individuals and, for those of a squeamish disposition, the fish can be cleaned and gutted for you.

Fruit & Vegetable Market

Nr Used Car Market, Dubai – Hatta Rd Ras Al Khor Industrial 3
Map **2 K13** Metro **Rashidiya**

There are a number of small fruit and vegetable markets around the city, like the one in Karama. The main market is now located off Sheikh Mohammed Bin Zayed Rd (Emirates Rd) in Al Awir. It is a wholesale market but, like the Fish Market (p.420), the traders are usually happy to sell by the kilo rather than the box. There is a huge variety of produce on offer and it is usually fresher than in the supermarkets. Be sure to haggle; you can often tell if you have paid more than the trader thinks the goods are worth if they give you freebies. The location is not convenient for most people but take a look if you are out that way. It is well signposted as you drive along the Dubai-Hatta Road. Mornings are the best time to visit.

Global Village

Nr Arabian Ranches Dubailand
04 362 4114
globalvillage.ae
Map **1 S 13**

Aptly described as a little window on the world, Global Village is a multi-cultural shopping destination, featuring a market with more than 40 country-themed pavilions. Stalls from India to Australia, the United States to Thailand sell all manner of trinkets, foodstuffs and handicrafts; traders give live demonstrations of their crafts too. It is a good spot to pick up everything from Chinese lanterns to honey from Yemen. You can spend hours exploring the wares before enjoying a unique range of dishes in the international foodcourt. Just don't overdo dinner before getting on the rides. Global Village is open from 16:00 to midnight, Saturday to Wednesday, and until 01:00 on Thursday and Friday. Entrance is Dhs.5, free for under twos. The annual festival runs from November through to March.

Gold Souk

Baniyas Rd Al Ras
goldsouks.com
Map **2 M4** Metro **Al Ras**

This is Dubai's best-known souk and a must-do for every visitor. It's a good place to buy customised jewellery for unique souvenirs and gifts at a reasonable price. On the Deira side of the creek, the meandering lanes are lined with shops selling gold, silver, pearls and precious stones. These can be bought as they are or in a variety of settings so this is definitely a place to try your bargaining skills – but don't expect a massive discount. Gold is sold by weight according to the daily international price and so will be much the same as in the shops in malls – the price of the workmanship is where you will have more bargaining power. Most of the outlets operate split shifts, so try not to visit between 13:00 and 16:00 as many will be closed. The Gold Souk is always busy, and it is shaded. If you are more interested in buying than enjoying the souk experience, visit the Gold & Diamond Park (04 362 7777, goldanddiamondpark.com), by interchange four on Sheikh Zayed Road.

Khan Murjan

Wafi Umm Hurair 2 **04 324 4555**
wafi.com
Map **2 L7** Metro **Dubai Healthcare City**
For something a little different, head to Wafi's underground souk. Khan Murjan's magnificent stained glass ceiling (which stretches 64 metres) and long curved arches help make this an atmospheric place to shop. The souk features over 150 stalls selling jewellery, antiques, Arabic perfume and souvenirs. It is particularly good if you wish to spice up your home with traditional arts and crafts; there are workshops where artisans can create various bits of arts and crafts on site. In the centre of the souk, you'll find an open air marble courtyard which houses the highly recommended Khan Murjan Arabic restaurant (04 327 9795).

Naif Souk

Nr Naif Police Station Naif
Map **2 N4** Metro **Baniyas Square**
This souk in the heart of Deira reopened in 2010, two years after the original burned down in a fire that destroyed most of the buildings. There are more than 200 retailers selling their wares over two floors (the original was a single-storey building). Before the inferno, this souk was a big draw for visitors and locals alike, and the new facilities – more modern, less rustic than the Naif of old – still bring crowds of shoppers and tourists back to look for bargains from the range of goods on sale.

RIPE

The Courtyard, Al Quoz **04 380 7602**
ripeme.com
Looking to stock up on fresh fruit and veg? RIPE hosts a farmers' market every Saturday at The Courtyard, Al Quoz, selling cardboard boxes packed with fresh local produce. Produce varies according to the season and can include anything from leafy, fragrant basil and irregular-sized courgettes to potatoes with the dirt still clinging to them. There are also stalls selling tasty treats such as locally made cheeses and chunky chutneys, as well as designer gifts and kitsch crafts.

Souk Al Bahar

Nr The Dubai Mall, Shk Zayed Rd Downtown Dubai **04 362 7011**
soukalbahar.ae
Map **2 F6** Metro **Burj Khalifa/Dubai Mall**
While this isn't a souk in conventional terms, Souk Al Bahar in Downtown Dubai is an Arabian-style mall similar to the souk at Madinat Jumeirah (p.242). Although many of the outlets serve the tourist market, Souk Al Bahar also has shops for the more discerning shopper. Marina Interiors (04 420 0191) and Sia (04 423 0914) sell contemporary home furnishings and interior design, or try Pride of Kashmir (04 420 3606), Fortix (04 420 3680) or Emad Carpets (04 368 9576) for a more Arabian look. There are also several food outlets; you can grab light bites at Dean & Deluca and Shakespeare & Co or something heartier at Margaux (p.521) and the Rivington Grill (p.532). Karma Kafe (p.559) and Left Bank (p.559) are perfect bars for a post-shop chill out. On Friday mornings, from 09:00, Souk Al Bahar hosts a superb farmers' market, with local producers pitching up to sell their fresh produce. For other shopping possibilities in Downtown Dubai, see p.410.

> **Mobile Phones**
>
> Mobiles are big business and you won't need to go too far to find one. Most of the larger supermarkets have areas dedicated to the popular brands. Handsets can be purchased directly from du or Etisalat (etisalat.ae); it is often cheaper to purchase a phone from them as part of a package.

Spice Souk

Nr Gold Souk Al Ras
Map **2 M4** Metro **Al Ras**
The Spice Souk's narrow streets and exotic aromas are a great way to get a feel for the way the city used to be. The number of spice shops is diminishing, due in part to hypermarkets like Carrefour having areas dedicated to spices and supermarkets selling a wider range. Most of the stalls sell the same range and the vendors are usually happy to give advice on the types of spices and their uses. You are unlikely to shop here on a regular basis, but the experience of buying from the Spice Souk is more memorable than picking a packet off a shelf. You may even be able to pick up some saffron at a bargain price. The shops operate split shifts but, whether you visit in the morning or the evening, this is a bustling area of the city.

Textile Souk

Nr Abra Station Al Souk Al Kabeer
Map **2 M4** Metro **Al Ghubaiba**
The Textile Souk in Bur Dubai is stocked with every fabric and colour imaginable. The textiles are imported from all over the world, with many of the more elaborate designs coming from the subcontinent and the Far East. There are silks and satins in an amazing array of colours and patterns, velvets and intricately embroidered fabrics. Basic cottons can sometimes be harder to find but you can always try Satwa (p.411). Prices here are somewhat negotiable and there are often sales, particularly around Eid and Diwali, and the shopping festivals. It is worth having a look in a few shops before parting with your cash as they may have different stock and at better prices. The mornings tend to be a more relaxed time to browse.

Meena Bazaar (04 353 9304) is the shop that most taxi drivers head for if you ask for the Textile Souk. It has an impressive selection of fabrics but prepare to haggle. Rivoli (04 335 0075) has a range of textiles for men on the ground floor and for women upstairs. The assistants are keen to offer the 'best discount', but it is always worth bartering to see if the price will drop further.

A number of tailors are located around the Textile Souk. See p.374 for more information on tailoring.

SHOPPING MALLS

Shopping malls are not just places to shop; a huge mall culture exists here, and they are places to meet, eat and mingle. Many malls provide entertainment for people of all ages. Recent changes to the law have resulted in a smoking ban in all of Dubai's malls (and some of the bars attached to them), which has been largely welcomed.

With so much choice out there, malls make sure they can offer something unique to shoppers to draw the crowds. In terms of architecture, Ibn Battuta is remarkable – six distinct architectural styles reflecting the sights of Egypt, China, India, Persia, Tunisia and Andalusia. Mall of the Emirates has got its unique selling point covered – a community theatre and a huge ski slope has made this one of the busier malls.

Mall Parking

Whereas all mall parking used to be free, since the opening of the Metro, both Mall of the Emirates and Deira City Centre introduced parking charges to discourage commuters from leaving their cars at the mall for extended periods. Parking in both malls is free for the first four hours and charged at Dhs.20 per hour thereafter. Parking is also free on Fridays, Saturdays and public holidays.

The Dubai Mall is spectacular because of its size and its selection of shops (covering both the high-end and the high-street markets), entertainment and eateries. Deira City Centre is the old kid on the block and yet is still consistently popular because of its excellent range of shops, its huge cinema multiplex and wide range of food outlets. Wafi and BurJuman, meanwhile, have cornered the market for exclusive boutiques and designer labels.

Special events are held during Dubai Shopping Festival, Dubai Summer Surprises and Ramadan, with entertainment for children and some special offers in the shops. These are peak shopping times and an evening in the larger malls at this time is not for the feint-hearted. Most of the malls have plenty of parking – often stretched to the limits at the weekends; all have taxi ranks and many are handy for bus routes.

Shop In Sharjah

Sharjah Central Souk (Blue Souk)

Nr Corniche Sharjah
sharjah-welcome.com

Situated beside the lagoon, the Sharjah Central Market, or Blue Souk, is an unmissable sight. Consisting of two long, low buildings running parallel to each other and connected by footbridges, the souk is intricately decorated and imaginatively built according to Islamic design. Each building is covered and air-conditioned to protect shoppers from the hot sun, with one side selling a range of gifts, knick-knacks, furniture, carved wood and souvenirs, and the other given over almost entirely to jewellery stores. There are over 600 individual shops, and the upper floors have a traditional souk feel with narrow passages and staircases. The souk also has shops selling a fabulous range of carpets from all over the world. For visitors and residents, a half-hour trip into the Blue Souk can easily turn into half a day.

Souk Al Arsah (Courtyard Souk)

Nr Bank St Sharjah

This is probably the oldest souk in Sharjah. It has been renovated in recent years, so although the style is reminiscent of an old market, the souk is covered (to provide shade from the sun) and air-conditioned. Around 100 tiny shops line a labyrinth of peaceful alleyways, selling silver jewellery, perfumes, spices, coffee pots and wedding chests. There is a small coffee shop where you can get Arabic coffee and sweets. Shop closing times do vary, with some closing by 20:30 and others staying open until 22:00.

Souk Al Arsah

BurJuman

Shk Khalifa Bin Zayed Rd Al Mankhool **04 352 0222**
burjuman.com
Map **2 L5** Metro **BurJuman**

BurJuman is renowned for its blend of designer and high-street brands attracting many a well-heeled shopper. The mall houses many famous brands such as Versace, Ralph Lauren, Hermes and Christian Dior, as well as some interesting smaller shops and New York department store Saks Fifth Avenue. For everyday fashion, Massimo Dutti, Gap and Zara lead the way. If you are into music or DVDs, the independent music shops sell a good range and there's a branch of Virgin Megastore where you can buy tickets for local events. Home stores include THE One. There is a Fitness First gym with a pool and spa on site too.

There are a few shops on the ground level that are often overlooked, including a bank and a pharmacy. There's also branches of Yo! Sushi, and Dôme on the same level.

BurJuman is part of the Dubai Shopping Festival and Dubai Summer Surprises and is heavily involved with the Safe & Sound breast cancer awareness programme; during October (breast cancer awareness month) it gets decked out in pink ribbon and organises a walkathon.

There are two foodcourts and numerous cafes, well arranged for people watching, including the popular Pavillion Gardens on the third floor, and Paul on the ground floor. Restaurants cater to all tastes, from Noodle House to Masala House. The mall has direct access to the Dubai Metro, and there is plenty of underground parking and a taxi rank just outside the mall; this does get very busy at peak times.

There are plans to extend the mall in 2013 with a 14-screen VOX Cinemas and Carrefour hypermarket.

BurJuman Stores

Department Store
Saks Fifth Avenue

Electronics & Computers
Bang & Olufsen
Digital (Grand Stores)
Jumbo Electronics
Vertu
Virgin Megastore

Fashion
Bebe
Bhs
Bugatti
Chanel
Diesel
Dior
DKNY
Dolce & Gabbana
Escada
Esprit
Etoile
Fendi
Fred Perry
G 2000
Gap
Gianfranco Ferre
Giordano
Guess
Hangten
Hermes
Hugo Boss
Just Cavalli
Kenneth Cole
Lacoste
La Perla
La Senza
Lacoste
Laurel
Levi`s
Mango
Marina Rinaldi
Massimo Dutti
Miu Miu
Mumbai Se
Paul & Shark
Paul Smith
Pierre Cardin
Prada
Promod
Quiksilver
Ralph Lauren
Riva
Rodeo Drive
Salsa
Ted Baker
Ted Lapidus
Valentino
Versace
Victoria's Secret
Zara

Footwear
Adidas
Aldo
Baldinini
Chanel
Charles & Keith
D & G
Dune
Fendi
Gianfranco Ferre
Nine West
Saks Fifth Avenue
Tod's
Versace
Vincci

Furniture & Homewares
Bhs
Descamps
Grand Stores
Hermes
Jadhafs
Reshi Arts & Crafts
Sharief
THE One
Valentino
Villeroy & Boch

Jewellery
Cartier
Damas Jewellery
Shenoy Jewellery

Perfume & Cosmetics
Ajmal Perfumes
The Body Shop
Faces
Inglot
MAC
Paris Gallery
Rasasi Perfumes

Deira City Centre

Al Ittihad Rd Port Saeed 04 295 1010
deiracitycentre.com
Map 2 N7 Metro Deira City Centre

A stalwart of Dubai's mall scene, this centre attracts the most cosmopolitan crowd. Deira City Centre is popular with residents and visitors alike, particularly at the weekends.

The three floors offer a diverse range of shops where you can find anything from a postcard to a Persian carpet. There's an 11-screen cinema, a children's entertainment centre, an eight-lane cosmic bowling arena, a jewellery court, a textiles court and an area dedicated to local furniture, gifts and souvenirs. It is all anchored by a huge Carrefour hypermarket, a Debenhams department store and Paris Gallery. Most of the high-street brands are represented, including Gap, Forever 21, New Look, River Island and H&M.

A number of designer boutiques can be found, mostly on the top floor. The City Gate section (on the same level as car parks P2 and P3) is dominated by electronics retailers, although there is also a pharmacy and information desk.

The mall has two foodcourts: one on the first floor, next to Magic Planet, serving mainly fastfood, and one on the second floor, featuring several good sit-down restaurants such as Noodle House and Japengo.

The opening of the Deira City Centre Metro station means that it is even easier to get to and from the mall, which is great because the taxi queues can get very long, especially during weekends and in the evenings. Another City Centre mall has also opened in Mirdif (see p.433).

Deira City Centre Stores

Books & Stationery
Borders
Gulf Greetings

Department Stores
Carrefour
Debenhams
Paris Gallery
Stadium
Woolworths

Electronics & Computers
Axiom
Eros Digital Home
Grand Stores Digital
Harman House
Jacky's Electronics
Jumbo Electronics
Sharaf DG

Fashion
American Eagle Outfitters
Armani Exchange
Balmain
Bebe
Bershka
Bossini
Burberry
Calvin Klein Underwear
Cocoon
Diesel
DKNY Jeans
Dockers
Esprit
Forever 21
French Connection UK
Gant
Gap
Giordano
Guess
H&M
Hangten
Jane Norman
Jennyfer
Juicy Couture
Karen Millen
La Senza
Lacoste
Levi's
Man & Moda
Mango
Massimo Dutti
Monsoon
Morgan
Nautica
New Look
Next
Pierre Cardin
Promod
Pull & Bear
Rectangle Jaune
Replay
Riva
River Island
Sacoor Brothers
Salsa
Splash
Springfield
Stradivarius
Ted Baker
Ted Lapidus
Tommy Hilfiger
Verri
Wrangler
Zara

Footwear
Aldo
Birkenstock
Clarks
Ecco
Geox
Havaianas
Nine West
Pretty Fit
Shoe Mart
Valencia
Vincci

Furniture & Homewares
Villeroy & Boch
Zara Home

Kids' Items
Adams
Babies R Us
Bhs
Carter's
Early Learning Centre
Gap
Geekay Toys & Games
H&M
Mothercare
Okaidi
Osh Kosh B'Gosh
Tommy Hilfiger Kids

The Dubai Mall

Financial Centre Rd Downtown Dubai **04 362 7500**
thedubaimall.com
Map **2 F6** Metro **Burj Khalifa/Dubai Mall**

Anyone who thinks some of Dubai's other malls are big will be stunned by this colossus shopping centre. The Dubai Mall holds more than 1,200 retail outlets and over 160 eateries. The complex also houses an Olympic size ice rink, a catwalk for fashion shows, an enormous aquarium and underwater zoo, a 22-screen cinema, an indoor theme park called SEGA Republic (p.264), a luxury hotel, and children's 'edutainment' centre, Kidzania (p.264).

The shopping highlights are manifold, but unique to Dubai Mall are the regional flagship stores for New York department store Bloomingdale's, French department store Galeries Lafayette (p.413), and the world-renowned toy shop Hamleys (p.394). You'll find all of the haute couture designer brands along Fashion Avenue, several high street favourites like Topshop, New Look, Express and Forever 21, and a sprawling gold souk with over 60 gold and jewellery outlets. There's Dubai's largest bookstore, Kinokuniya, and a huge Waitrose. When you need to check your funds, you'll also find branches of the major banks on the ground floor. For refreshment, there is a huge variety of fastfood outlets, cafes and restaurants.

If you are there for some late night shopping, don't miss the fountain show beside the Burj Khalifa that starts at 18:00 and runs every half hour; there are also afternoon performances at 13.00 and 13.30.

For a complete contrast, cross the wooden bridge over the Burj Lake to Souk Al Bahar (p.421), offering a more relaxing stop after the onslaught of the mall.

The Dubai Mall Stores

Books & Stationery
Hallmark
Kinokuniya (Book World)
WH Smith

Department Stores
Bloomingdale's
Debenhams
Galeries Lafayette
Marks & Spencer
Paris Gallery

Electronics & Computers
Grand Stores Digital
iStyle
Jacky's Electronics
Jumbo Electronics
LG Lifestyle
Plug-Ins Electronix
Sharaf DG
Virgin Megastores

Fashion
Alexander McQueen
Armani Exchange
Banana Republic
Bhs
Burberry
Calvin Klein
Chanel
Christian Audigier
Cotton On
Desigual
Diesel
Dior
DKNY Jeans
Dolce & Gabbana
Esprit
Express
Fendi
Forever 21
Fred Perry
French Connection
Gap
Giordano
Guess
H&M
Hugo Boss
Jean Paul Gaultier
Joseph
Just Cavalli
Karen Millen
Kate Spade
Kenzo
Lacoste
Levi's
Mango
M Missoni
M&Co
Marc By Marc Jacobs
Massimo Dutti
Matthew Williamson
Monsoon
Moschino
Nautica
New Look
Next
Oasis
Oscar de la Renta
Paul Smith
Pull & Bear
Ralph Lauren
Reiss
River Island
Roberto Cavalli
S*uce
Sacoor Brothers
Salvatore Ferragamo
Stella McCartney
Ted Baker
Temperley
Thomas Pink
Tommy Hilfiger
United Colors Of Benetton
Versace
Wrangler
Zadig & Voltaire
Zara

Furniture & Homewares
@ Home
Crate & Barrel
Ethan Allen
Jashanmal
Marina
Pottery Barn
Villeroy & Boch
The White Company
Zara Home

Kids' Items
Adams
Armani Junior
Baby Shop
Bubbles & Giggles
Burberry Children
Cacharel Paris
Diesel Kids
Dior Kids
Geekay Games
Guess Kids
Hamleys

Dubai Marina Mall

Off Shk Zayed Rd Dubai Marina **04 436 1020**
dubaimarinamall.com
Map **1 K5** Metro **Jumeirah Lakes Towers**

Located in Dubai Marina's thriving community, and within walking distance of The Walk, Jumeirah Beach Residence (p.413), this relatively new, compact mall's 130 outlets offer a mix of plush designer goods and high-street regulars.

Virtually all of the stores are now open, and it offers Marina residents some good local, reasonably priced fashion outlets without having to venture far. Options include shops like New Look, Reiss and Accessorize.

Shoppers can pick up kids' clothes at Mamas & Papas, Mothercare and Okaidi, and there's a small Early Learning Centre for toys. There are banks, an exchange centre, opticians, a travel agency, a tailor and dry cleaner on site – all handy local amenities for local residents. The Waitrose supermarket is a huge draw for expats.

A number of dining options are available. There is a large foodcourt with many of the usual suspects, and several restaurants, including Carluccio's, Gourmet Burger Kitchen and Yo! Sushi. Gourmet dates are available at Bateel.

The Favourite Things Mother and Child play area provides plenty of entertainment for kids, and you can leave your little ones there so they can enjoy supervised play while you shop. A carousel on the promenade is popular, as are the regular train rides around the mall.

For grown-up entertainment there's a six-screen Reel Cinemas (p.462), and an adjacent Gourmet Tower, which will offer world-class cuisine with waterfront views when open. There's also an Address hotel (p.235) connected to the mall, with restaurants and bars.

Dubai Marina Mall Stores

Books & Stationery
Borders Express
Gulf Greetings

Electronics & Computers
Axiom Telecom
Grand Stores Digital

Eyewear
Al Jaber Optical
Magrabi Opticals
Vision Express

Fashion
Accessorize
Aldo
Balmain
Bebe
Billabong
Coast
Cube
Desigual
Diesel
Ecco
Folli Follie
Galvani
Giordano
Giovanni Calli
Guess by Marciano
H&M
Juicy Couture
Just Accessories
Karen Millen
Koton
Kurt Geiger
La Senza
Levi's
List
Mango
Monsoon
NaraCamicie
Nautica
New Look
Novo
Patrizia Pepe
Paul & Shark
Promod
Reiss
Rocco Barocco
Rockport
Roxy
Sacoor Brothers
Suite Blanco
Springfield
Ted Baker
Tommy Hilfiger
Ulla Popken
Yamamay

Homewares
@ Home
Al Jaber Gallery
Q Home Decor

Health & Beauty
Areej
Bobbi Brown
Boots Pharmacy
L'Occitane
MAC
N. Style Nail Lounge
Pace E Luce Hair & Beauty Salon
Sephora
The Body Shop

Jewellery & Watches
Ahmed Seddiqi & Sons
Damas Les Exclusives
Mahallati Jewellery
Rivoli

Kids' Items
Build-A-Bear Workshop
Early Learning Centre
Gymboree
M&Co
Mamas & Papas
Mothercare
Okaidi
Smitten Boutique
Toy Store

Sports & Outdoor Goods
Adidas
Billabong
Nike
Quiksilver
Reebok
Stadium Sports

Supermarket
Waitrose

Festival Centre

Crescent Drive Dubai Festival City **04 8003 3232**
festivalcentre.com
Map **2 M9** Metro **Emirates**

Located at the heart of Dubai Festival City, this waterfront destination features around 600 retail outlets (including 25 flagship stores) and 100 restaurants, including 40 alfresco dining options.

The need for retail therapy can be sated by the broad range of fashion, electronics and homeware outlets spread over 2.8 million square feet of retail space. Some of the biggest names in homeware, such as The White Company and the largest IKEA in the UAE are featured, and it is home to HyperPanda (p.416) and a large Plug-Ins. There is also a 25,000 square foot modern gold souk where you can peruse gold from all over the world. Dubai Festival City is home to the largest ACE store outside of North America.

The mall also features Brit favourite Marks & Spencer, high-street brands Ted Baker and Reiss and designer stores like Marc By Marc Jacobs. You'll find a branch of the Dubai London Clinic here too, a pharmacy, banks and dry cleaners.

There's plenty for kids too, from Toys R Us to the Cool Times soft play area with an Art Zone.

It's not just shopping though; The Festival Waterfront Centre has dramatic water features and performance spaces, there is a Grand Cinemas

(p.462) and a 10-lane bowling alley on site. You can happily spend an entire day here, dining at Romano's Macaroni Grill, before relaxing in the Belgian Beer Cafe (p.551). The latest dining venues here are celeb chef Jamie Oliver's venture Jamie's Italian and the hugely popular Hard Rock Cafe and Trader Vic's.

Events include the monthly community art market and the Whatever Floats Your Boat challenge.

Festival Centre Stores

Books & Stationery
Book Plus
Gulf Greetings
News Centre
Paperchase

Department Stores
HyperPanda
Marks & Spencer
Jashanmal

Electronics & Computers
Aftron
Axiom
Eros
Grand Stores Digital
iStyle
LG
Panasonic
Plug-Ins
Sony
Toshiba

Fashion
Aeropostale
Balmain
Bebe
Bench
Bhs
Bossini
Camaieu
Carolina Herrera
Diesel
DKNY
Dunhill
Esprit
Ferrari
Forever 21
Fred Perry
G 2000
Gant
Gas
Giordano
Guess
Hobbs
Hugo Boss
Karen Millen
Koton
Lacoste
Laura Ashley
Levis
Mango
Marc By Marc Jacobs
Marco Azzali
Massimo Dutti
Monsoon
Mumbai Se
Nautica
New Yorker
Part Two
Paul Smith
Pierre Cardin
Reiss
River Woods
Rodeo Drive
Sacoor Borthers
Salsa
Samuel & Kevin
Springfield
Stradivarius
Ted Baker
Ted Lapidus
Tommy Hilfiger
Vero Moda
Yours

Footwear
Aldo
Anne Klein
Charles & Keith
Chic Shoes
Clarks
Dune
Ecco
Geox
Hush Puppies
Kickers
Naturalizer
Nine West
Spring

Furniture & Homewares
Bayti
Dwell
IKEA
Kas Australia
The White Company

Kids' Items
Build A Bear
Diesel Kids
Early Learning Centre
Geekay Games
Okaidi
Sanrio Hello Kity
Toys R Us

Ibn Battuta Mall

Off Shk Zayed Rd The Gardens **04 368 5543**
ibnbattutamall.com
Map **1 G5** Metro **Ibn Battuta**

This mall is divided into six zones, each based on a region that explorer Ibn Battuta visited in the 14th century (China, India, Egypt, Tunisia, Andalusia and Persia). Guided tours that illuminate the mall's unusual features, such as the full-size replica of a Chinese Junk and Al Jazari's Elephant Clock, are available.

There is a good range of mostly international stores and several anchor stores such as Debenhams and Géant hypermarket. Shops are loosely grouped: China Court is dedicated to entertainment, with several restaurants, a Fitness First gym and a 21-screen cinema; the IMAX screens regular films as well as blockbusters. The fashion conscious should head to Persia and India Courts for H&M, Forever 21, Oasis, Topshop and Splash. Persia Court is styled as the lifestyle area, anchored by Debenhams – when you get to Starbucks, look up to see the ceiling detail. Egypt Court is for sporty types; Géant is the hub of Tunisia Court and the place to head for your weekly shop. Andalusia Court covers life's necessities such as banking, dry cleaning, key cutting, and DVD and video rental.

Foodcourts are located at either end of the mall. There are several restaurants in China Court (including the excellent Finz) and a group of fastfood outlets in Tunisia Court. Several restaurants and coffee shops are also dotted around other areas of the mall. To reward the kids for trailing round after you, there's a Fun City in Tunisia Court. It is an enjoyable mall to wander around, but it can be a long way back if there's something you've missed. There are 10 car parks (the numerical order is a little eccentric), so remember which zone you came in through – and that taxi ranks are at either end of the mall.

Ibn Battuta Mall Stores

Books & Stationery
Books Plus
Gulf Greetings
House of Prose

Department Stores
Bhs
Debenhams
Fitz & Simons
Grand Stores
Lifestyle
Paris Gallery
Woolworths

Electronics & Computers
Axiom Telecom
Cell-U-Com
Digicom
iStyle
Jacky's Electronics
Jumbo Electronics
LG
Sharaf DG
Sharaf Digital

Fashion
Arrow
B C Bulgari
Bauhaus
Bench
Betsey Johnson
Daniel Hechter
Element
Elle
Evisu
Forever 21
Ginger & Lace
Guy Laroche
Giordano
H&M
Joe Bloggs
Lacoste
Le Chateau
Levi's
Max
Nayomi
Nautica
Next
Oasis
Peacocks
Pierre Cardin
Plus It
River Island
Splash
Ted Lapidus
Topshop/Topman
Verri
Wallis
Wrangler

Footwear
Aldo
Charles & Keith
El Dantes
Faith
Geox
Milano
Naturalizer
Nicoli
Nine West
Prince Shoes
Rodo
Shoe Mart
Skechers
Tosca Blu
Zu

Supermarket
Geant

Furniture & Homewares
@home
Bayti
Homes r Us
Howards Storage World

Kids' Items
Giordano Junior
H&M
La Senza Girl
Max
Mini Me
Mothercare
Nautica
Next
Pablosky
Sanrio
Tammy
The Toy Store
Tuc Tuc
Wizz

Mall of the Emirates

Shk Zayed Rd Al Barsha 1 **04 409 9000**
mallofttheemirates.com
Map **1 R6** Metro **Mall of the Emirates**

This is more than a mall, it's a lifestyle destination. Mall of the Emirates houses an indoor ski slope (Ski Dubai, see p.356), the Kempinski Mall of the Emirates Hotel (p.242) and the Dubai Community Theatre & Arts Centre (p.321). There are over 500 outlets selling everything from forks to high fashion here. Label devotees should head for Via Rodeo for designer labels like Burberry, Dolce & Gabanna, Salvatore Ferragamo, Tod's and Versace. There's also a new Fashion Dome extension to the mall, which features 40 stores including Boutique 1, Dior, Giorgio Armani and Louis Vuitton, as well as eating options like MORE Cafe. If you're more into street chic, there are two H&M stores, Fat Face, Phat Farm and Forever 21, while Rampage and Staff stock cool styles for the ski slopes.

The mall is anchored by Carrefour hypermarket, Dubai's largest branch of Debenhams, trendy department store Harvey Nichols, and Centrepoint, which is home to Baby Shop, Home Centre, Lifestyle, Shoemart and Splash. There is also a VOX cinema which offers Gold Class film showings, while the entertainment centre Magic Planet includes a bowling alley and a myriad of games and rides. When it comes to homeware, Home Centre, Marina Gulf, BoConcept, B&B Italia, THE One, and Zara Home are just a few of the stores on offer, while Jacky's and Jumbo Electronics offer an extensive range of electronics.

The mall is open from Sunday to Wednesday 10:00 to 22:00, Thursday to Saturday 10:00 to midnight and Carrefour opens from 09:00 to midnight every day. There is a wide range of dining options from the Swiss chalet feel of Après (p.490) to popular American eatery The Cheesecake Factory and modern Indian Asha's, as well as three separate foodcourts.

Mall of the Emirates Stores

Books & Stationery
Borders
Carlton Cards (Jashanmal)
Gulf Greetings/Hallmark

Department Stores
Carrefour
Centrepoint
Debenhams
Harvey Nichols
Jashanmal
Lifestyle
Marks & Spencer

Electronics & Computers
Axiom Telecom
CompuMe
Grand Stores Digital
Jacky's Electronics
Jashanmal
Jumbo Electronics
Virgin Megastore

Fashion
BCBG Max Azria
Bershka
Betty Barclay
Boutique 1
Carolina Herrera
Celine
Cocoon
Diane Von Furstenberg
Diesel
Dior
DKNY
Dolce & Gabbana
Emporio Armani
Esprit
Etoile
Forever 21
French Connection
Giorgio Armani
Gucci
Guess
H&M
Hugo Boss
Kenneth Cole
Lipsy
Levi's
Louis Vuitton
M Missoni
Mango
Marc Jacobs
Massimo Dutti
Mexx
Miss Sixty
Missoni
Monsoon
Nautica
Next
Paul & Smith
Phat Farm
Pimkie
Prada
Pull & Bear
Ralph Lauren
Reiss
River Island
Roberto Cavalli
Rodeo Drive
Tommy Hilfiger
United Colors of Benetton
Versace
Whistles
Zara

Footwear
Aldo
Berluti
Birkenstock
Charles & Keith
Clarks
Dune
Ecco
Fabi
Geox
Kurt Geiger
Naturalizer
Nine West
PrettyFIT

Furniture & Homewares
@ Home
Artikel
Better Life
Flamant Home Interiors
Grand Stores Home
Home Design
ID Design
Lakeland
Marina Exotic Home
Interiors
Singways
Tavola
THE One
The White Company
Zara Home

Mercato

Jumeira Rd Jumeira 1 **04 344 4161**
mercatoshoppingmall.com
Map **2 F4** Metro **Financial Centre**

The largest mall in Jumeira, with over 120 shops, restaurants, cafes and a cinema. The Renaissance-style architecture really makes this mall stand out and, once inside, the huge glass roof provides a lot of natural light, enhancing its Mediterranean feel. The layout is more interesting than many of the malls and it's worth investigating the 'lanes' so you don't miss anything.

The mall is anchored by Spinneys which has a dry cleaners, photo lab and music shop; a large Virgin Megastore (that has a decent book department); Laura Ashley Home, and Gap. There are also a few good options for kids such as Early Learning Centre, Toy Store Express and Armani Junior. The mix of designer boutiques and high-street brands mean you can peruse the reasonably priced Pull & Bear then find a more exclusive range at Hugo Boss. Shoes and accessories are covered by favourites like Aldo and Nine West, while cosmetics can be picked up at MAC.

There is a foodcourt and a number of cafes and restaurants, including Paul, a French cafe renowned for its patisserie, and Bella Donna, an Italian restaurant where you can dine alfresco. VOX Cinemas (due to open early 2013) and a large Fun City play area near the food court should keep most of the family occupied. There is also a nail salon, hair salon and mother and baby room on the upper floor, in addition to ATMs, a money exchange, and a branch of HSBC (it doesn't handle money but can offer advice and do the paperwork) and a key cutting and shoe repair shop.

Mercato Stores

Books & Stationery
Gulf Greetings (Hallmark)

Electronics & Computers
Axiom Telecom
Sharaf Digital
Virgin Megastore

Fashion
Armani Jeans
Aeropostale
Bershka
Beyond the Beach
Diesel
Fleurt
Gant
Gap
Genevieve Lethu
GF Ferre
Hugo Boss Men & Women
IVY
Jack Wills
La Senza Lingerie
Laura Ashley
List
Mamas & Papas
Mango
Massimo Dutti
Nayomi
Nautica
Nike
Promod
Pull & Bear
River Woods
Sacoor Brothers
TopShop
Triumph
Zin Zin

Footwear
Aldo
Crocs
Hobbs
Milano
Nine West
PrettyFIT
Rossini Shoes

Furniture & Homewares
@ home
KAS Australia
Laura Ashley Home
Tavola Trading

Jewellery & Accessories
Aldo Accessories
Al Liali Jewellery
Claire's
KC Jewels
Damas
Pandora
Pure Gold Jewellers

Kids' Items
Armani Junior
Db Babies
Early Learning Centre
GAP
MAK Toys
Mamms & Papas
Monsoon Children
River Woods
Sanrio
Sparkles
The Toy Store Express

Perfume & Cosmetics
Areej
The Body Shop
L'occitane
MAC

Supermarkets
Spinneys

Mirdif City Centre

Nr Tripoli St Mirdif **04 800 6422**
mirdifcitycentre.com
Map **2 P12** Metro **Rashidiya**

This is one of the newest malls in town and Mirdif's very own slice of upmarket retail action. Mirdif City Centre opened in 2010, and, like sister mall Deira City Centre, it offers a (relatively) compact yet comprehensive shopping facility housing everything from fashion and furniture, right through to food shops and food courts, all on the doorstep of Dubai's favourite family suburb.

There are more than 400 stores, with key 'anchor' outlets including Debenhams, Emax, Centrepoint, Home Centre and Fitness First. There are some great home stores here too, including the Dubai debut of Pottery Barn, plus household favourites Marina, Crate & Barrel, Lakeland and ID Design.

Mirdif mums are well catered for, with dozens of fashion outlets including Miss Selfridge, H&M, Forever 21 and Dorothy Perkins, as well as Nine West and Aldo for shoe shopping. Kids won't mind being dragged shopping here too; the VOX cinema houses 10 screens, and the Playnation centre (p.264) has a number of attractions including a water play area called Aquaplay (p.258), the footy-based Soccer Circus, video arcades, a bowling alley, a children's activity centre and even an indoor sky diving facility, iFLY Dubai.

There's a huge food court, serving up the typical mall-based fare, and numerous coffee shops and more upscale eateries such as MORE Cafe (04 323 4350), Mango Tree Bistro (p.521), Butcher Shop & Grill (p.498) and Carluccio's (p.499). And of course, when in suburbia, a large supermarket is a necessity – and Mirdif City Centre's Carrefour certainly fits the bill.

If you're coming from further afield, the nearest Metro stop is Rashidiya, from where a feeder bus connects to the mall. There's also plenty of parking.

Mirdif City Centre Stores

Books & Stationery
Borders
Gulf Greetings
Paperchase

Department Stores
Centrepoint
Debenhams

Electronics & Computers
Bose
Emax
Eros Electricals
Grand Stores Digital
Jacky's
Jumbo Electronics
LG
Sharaf DG 4U
Virgin Megastore

Fashion
Balmain
Bhs
Boutique 1
Coast
Columbia
Dorothy Perkins
Esprit
Evans
French Connection
Forever 21
Gap
Garage
Giordano
H&M
Lacoste
Levi's
Lindex
Mango
Massimo Dutti
Miss Selfridge
Monsoon
New Look
Next
Pal Zileri
Stradivarius
Tchibo
Ted Lapidus
Ulla Popken
Un1, Deux2, Trois3

Footwear
Aldo Shoes
Antonio Trading
Bally
Charles & Keith
Chic Shoes
Clarks
Dumond
Dune
Ecco
Foot Solutions
Naturalizer
Nine West
Payless Shoes
Shoe Citi
Shoe Express
Steve Madden
Via Uno
Vincci

Furniture & Homewares
Cottage Chic
Crate & Barrel
Dwell
Home Centre
ID Design
Kas Australia
Lakeland
Marina Gulf
Pottery Barn
Q Hom Decor
Shatex

Kids' Items
Adams Kids
Bhs Kids
Carter's
Diesel Kids
Early Learning Centre
Ecco Kids
Gymboree
Hamleys
Mamas and Papas
Monsoon Kids
Mothercare
Okaidi and Obaidi
Pottery Barn Kids
Pumpkin Patch
Salam Kido
Tape a L'Oeil

Souk Madinat Jumeirah

Jumeira Rd Al Sufouh 1 **04 366 8888**
jumeirah.com
Map **1 R4** Metro **Mall of the Emirates**

Souk Madinat Jumeirah is a recreation of a traditional souk, complete with narrow alleyways, authentic architecture and motorised abras. The blend of outlets is unlike anywhere else in Dubai, with boutique shops, galleries, cafes, restaurants and bars. The souk is best appreciated if you have time to walk around and enjoy the experience. During the cooler months the doors and glass walls are opened to add an alfresco element and there is shisha on offer in the courtyard.

The layout can be a little confusing, but that's part of the souk's quest for authenticity; there are location maps throughout and the main features are signposted. If you're really lost, a member of staff will be able to point you in the right direction.
With an emphasis on unique brands, there are a large number of speciality outlets that aren't found anywhere else in Dubai.

The souk is home to a concentration of art boutiques, including Gallery One (g-1.com) which sells photos with a local flavour and Mirage Glass (04 880 4360). The stalls in the outside areas sell souvenirs, some tasteful and some tacky. Eye-catching, but expensive, swimming gear can be found at Vilebrequin (04 368 6531); Rodeo Drive (04 368 6568) is good for label hunters; or head over

to Tommy Bahama (04 368 6031) for some tropical flavour. There are more than 20 waterfront cafes, bars and restaurants to choose from, including some of Dubai's hottest night spots, and you'll find Left Bank (p.559), Trader Vic's (04 366 5646), Jambase (p.559) and BarZar (p.551) to name a few. There's also the impressive Madinat Theatre (madinattheatre.com) which sees international and regional artists perform everything from ballet to comedy.

Souk Madinat Jumeirah Stores

Art & Photography
Gallery One
Sadek Music
Spirit of Art Gallery

Arts & Crafts Supplies
Indian Emporium
Kashmir Cottage Arts
Lata's
Modern Antiques
Orient Spirit
Scarabee
Wood & Copper

Beachwear
Grain De Sable
Havaianas
Leto
Rodeo Drive
Sun & Sands Sports
Vilebrequin

Carpets
National Iranian Carpets
Persian Carpet House

Eyewear & Opticians
Al Jaber Optical Centre
Yateem Optician

Fashion (Men)
The Emperor 1688
Paris Moda
Tie Shop

Fashion (Unisex)
Braschi
Carlotta
Converse
Kuna by Alpaca 111
Louise Harrison Couture
Via Rodeo
Sun & Sands Sports
Tommy Bahamas
Vilebrequin

Fashion (Women)
Cotton Club

Footwear
Havaianas

Furniture & Homewares
Kashmir Cottage Arts
Marina Home Interiors
Miri
Pride of Kashmir
Sinbad
Toshkhana

Jewellery & Accessories
Al Liali Jewellery
Damas
Ferini Jewels
GB Gems
Le Brilliante Jewellery
La Marquise Diamond & Watches
Le Paris Diamond
Mademoiselle Accessories
Pure Gold
Rivoli
Tejori
Three Star Jewellery
Zayoon

Kids' Items
Early Learning Centre

Perfume & Cosmetics
Al Quraishi
Caravella
Henna Heritage

Services & Utilities
Al Ansari Exchange
Emirates NBD

Souvenirs & Gifts
Al Dukan
Modern Antiques
The Camel Company
Royal Fashions
Smokers Centre

Textiles, Haberdashery & Tailoring
Indian Emporium

Wafi

Nr Oud Metha Rd & Shk Rashid Rd Umm Hurair 2
04 324 4555
wafi.com
Map **2 L7** Metro **Dubai Healthcare City**

Wafi's Egyptian theme, designer stores and layout make this one of the more interesting malls to wander around, and it rarely feels busy. The distinctive building has three pyramids forming part of the roof and a large stained glass window. Two of the pyramids are decorated with stained glass, depicting Egyptian scenes – best viewed during daylight.

Its store directory reads like a who's who in design, be it jewellery or couture, and the likes of Versace, Escada, Calvin Klein and Roberto Cavalli mix with well-known high-street shops like Oasis and a large branch of UK stalwart Marks & Spencer. THE One, a popular Dubai furniture store, has a branch here, as does Villeroy & Boch and Tanagra.

For something different head to Khan Murjan, the mall's impressive underground souk. Its magnificent stained glass ceiling and atmospheric archways house over 150 stalls selling an eclectic mix of items, including jewellery, antiques, perfume and souvenirs. The area is particularly good for spicing up your home with traditional arts and crafts – there are workshops where artisans can create pieces on site.

There are also a number of cafes and restaurants, including Biella and the highly recommended Khan Murjan Arabic restaurant, where you can enjoy

your meal in an alfresco dining area. The children's entertainment area, Encounter Zone, is very popular and has age-specific attractions. Events include the Return of the Pharaohs light show and Movies Under the Stars screenings on the rooftop.

Wafi is home to the exclusive Raffles Dubai (p.248) hotel, with its Raffles Spa and Fire And Ice restaurant. If you feel the need for pampering, or an evening out, head to the Pyramids where there are some excellent bars, restaurants, a club and a renowned spa.

Wafi Stores

Books & Stationery
Gulf Greetings
Montblanc
Montegrappa
Rivoli

Department Stores
Jashanmal
Marks & Spencer
Paris Gallery
Philipp Plein
Salam

Electronics & Computers
Axiom Telecom
Digi-Com/Nokia
Jumbo Electronics
Vertu

Fashion
Baby Phat
Betty Barclay
Bugatti B More
Burberry
By Malene Birger
Calvin Klein
Canali
Caresse
Chanel
Daniela Hechter
Desert Rose
Dunhill
Designer's Club
Ed Hardy
Escada
Esmod Fashion Store
Etoile La Boutique
Ferre
Ferre Milano – Men
Gant
Gelco
Gerizim
Ginger & Lace
Jaeger
Josef Seibel
Kennth Cole
Laurèl
Majestic Angels
Mary May Fashion
Miss Sixty
Oasis Fashion
Oui
Pantera
Pal Sileri
Paramour
Pierre Cardin
Roberto Cavalli
Ted Lapidus
Topshop/Topman
Tru Trussardi
Versace JC
Zilli

Footwear
Alberto Guardiani
Baldinini
Comfort Shoes
Opera Shoes
Organdy
Pointure
Rossini
Ruco Line
Umberto Bilancioni
Via Rossi
Walter Steiger

Furniture & Homewares
Bombay
Crystalline
Edra
Eternal by Ajmal
Frette
La Murrina
Memoires
Petals
Rudolf Kampf
Tanagra
THE One
The White Company
Villeroy & Boch

Kids' Items
Angels
Calvin Klein
Early Learning Centre
Little Castle
Marks and Spencer
Primigi
Pynkiss Milano

Al Barsha Mall

Nr Al Barsha Pond Park, 24th Street Al Barsha 1
04 455 7150
Map **1 Q7** Metro **Mall of the Emirates**

A new mall serving the large and popular Barsha residential area. The large Union Cooperative Society supermarket is arguably the main draw, although there are also a range of services available, a few fashion brands, Mothercare, Boots, Sharaf DG, a Man/Age spa and a Gold's Gym.

Al Ghurair City

Al Rigga Rd Al Muraqqabat **04 222 5222**
alghuraircentre.com
Map **2 N5** Metro **Union**

Far from obsolete, Al Ghurair City houses an eight-screen cinema, a Spinneys, and a good range of shops. The layout of the two-storey mall, Dubai's oldest, owes something to the maze-like quality of a souk. There are a number of international brands, including Bhs, Book Corner and Mothercare, along with smaller boutiques.

Al Wasl Square

Nr Al Wasl Rd & Hadiqa St Al Safa 1 **800 9275**
waslsquare.wasl.ae.
Map **2 D5** Metro **Business Bay**

A new retail hotspot right next to Safa Park, this open-air shopping development has a number of interesting stores and restaurants, with many more opening throughout 2013.

Arabian Centre

Al Khawaneej Rd Al Mizhar 1 **04 284 5555**
arabiancenter.ae
Map **2 S13** Metro **Rashidiya**

This mall may be smaller than the majority of its counterparts but it still manages to tick all the boxes. There is a selection of more than 200 stores where you can pick up home appliances or creature comforts (at Homes r Us, Sharaf DG and Eros Digital) and reasonably priced fashion at New Look, Splash, Topshop, Mango and H&M. The mall features a good selection of sports stores including Sport's Market, Adidas and Footlocker. Also at the mall is a cinema, hypermarket, Fun City play area for kids and Spaces Ladies Salon & Spa.

The Beach Centre

Nr Dubai Zoo, Jumeira Rd Jumeira 1 **04 344 7077**
Map **2 G4** Metro **Emirates Towers**

This unassuming mall has a number of interesting independent shops selling everything from books to furniture and jewellery. Notably, the mall includes two branches of White Star Bookshop; one stocks craft materials and the other specialises in teachers' supplies. It also houses Charisma, an independent plus-size women's clothes shop, and the Music Room, which has the largest supply of sheet music in Dubai and a selection of instruments. With Kuts 4 Kids, a children's hairdressers, and an opticians, pharmacy and Cyber Café, this is a good community mall.

Bin Sougat Centre

Airport Rd Al Rashidiya **04 286 3000**
binsougatcenter.com
Map **2 P10** Metro **Rashidiya**

Anchored by a comprehensive branch of Spinneys (p.452), this mall is particularly convenient for Mirdif dwellers. There is an interesting mix of stores including Emirates Trading, which sells professional art supplies and equipment, and Dubai Library Distributors, which is excellent for stationery. Head to the basement for Orient Curios Furniture. There is also a Secrets Boutique which sells a limited range of lingerie in

Al Ghurair City

larger sizes. There are several food outlets in the mall and ample parking, except on Fridays when the mosque next door is busy. Other outlets include: Al Ansari Money Exchange, Damas Jewellers, London Café, Kuts 4 Kids, San Marco and Union National Bank.

The Boulevard At Jumeirah Emirates Towers

Jumeirah Emirates Towers Trade Centre 2
04 319 8999
boulevarddubai.com
Map **2 H6** Metro **Emirates Towers**

Houses some of Dubai's most exclusive boutiques, popular restaurants and bars. The area links the Emirates Towers Hotel and Emirates Towers Offices, and is accessible from both. Boutiques include Cartier, Gucci, Yves Saint Laurent and Jimmy Choo. If you're into more than shopping, there's a health club and a men-only spa. There are cafes (some with Wi-Fi access), licensed restaurants (Scarlett's and Noodle House), and the ever-popular early evening hangout, The Agency. Head here for high fashion at high prices – the steep parking charge (first hour is free, thereafter it is Dhs.20 per hour) says it all.

Centrepoint

Shk Khalifa Bin Zayed Rd Al Mankhool **04 359 9335**
centrepointstores.com
Map **2 L5** Metro **BurJuman**

Shopaholics will love this store, a one-stop shopping destination that houses Babyshop, Splash, Lifestyle, Shoe Mart and Beautybay all under one roof. You can dress you and your family head to toe in one easy shopping trip – and all without breaking the bank! Branches include Mall of the Emirates (04 341 1988) and Mirdif City Centre (04 284 3343).

Century Mall

Nr Al Shabab Club, Al Wuheida Rd Hor Al Anz East
04 296 7450
mysafeer.com
Map **2 R6** Metro **Al Qiyadah**

Shopping meets entertainment at the Century Mall, with 75 specialty stores selling the latest in electronics, mobiles, fashion, lifestyle, gift ideas, home furnishings, jewellery, health and beauty. Brands including Shoes4Us, Smart Baby and Eternity Style, as well as Carrefour, a foodcourt and Jungle Bungle, an indoor themed amusement centre.

Dragon Mart

Al Awir Rd Warsan 1 **04 453 4184**
dragonmart.ae

Reportedly has the largest concentration of Chinese traders outside China. Over one kilometre in length, it takes about three hours to have a good look round. The mall is divided into zones by commodity, but these demarcations have been blurred. From building materials to toys, household items to quad bikes, everything is available – and cheaper than elsewhere in the city. There's an incredible amount of tat, but items worth looking out for include garden furniture, fancy dress costumes and props, and cheap and cheerful luggage. If you can dedicate a couple of hours to tracking down different retailers and comparing prices, you should be able to get yourself a good deal. Open from 10:00 to 22:00 or 23:00, but many of the shops don't open till 17:00. The quality isn't great, but if you're looking for something cheap and for the short haul, you can't go wrong. There are plans to extend the mall, bringing the total size of Dragon Mart to 335,000 sqm – equivalent to 47 international football pitches!

Dubai Outlet Mall

Dubai Al-Ain Rd Dubailand **04 423 4666**
dubaioutletmall.com
Map **2 F13**

In a city where the emphasis in on excess, it is refreshing (not only for the wallet) to find a mall dedicated to saving money. Dubai's first 'outlet' concept mall may be a way out of town (20 minutes down the Al Ain road) but it's worth the drive. Big discounts on major retailers and labels are available; think T-shirts for under Dhs.30 and Karama-esque prices for Marc Jacobs handbags. High street shops including Massimo Dutti and Dune sit alongside designer names such as Tommy Hilfiger and DKNY, with city style and sports casual equally catered for.

Pick up trainers from Adidas, Nike and Puma, reduced eyewear from Al Jaber or Magrabi, jewellery from Damas, cosmetics from Paris Gallery and a range of electronics and homewares from more than 10 different outlets. There are several pharmacies, a barber, Starbucks, Stone Fire Pizza Kitchen and Automatic as well as the usual foodcourt suspects. And to keep the little ones engaged there's Chuck E Cheese – a US institution serving up food and entertainment. Other outlets include Adams, Diesel, Gap, Monsoon, Nine West, Pumpkin Patch, Replay, Samsonite, Sports Direct Outlet and Timberland.

Etihad Mall

Al Khawaneej Rd Muhaisnah 1 **04 284 3663**
etihadmall.ae
Map **2 R12** Metro **Rashidiya**

Another recently opened shopping centre, aimed more at the local community than as a 'destination mall' like The Dubai Mall or Mall of the Emirates, Etihad Mall has numerous fashion brands – including several aimed squarely at the Arab market – as well as services like opticians, banks and pharmacies. There's an indoor amusement centre for kids, while the foodcourt has more than 15 outlets.

J3 Mall

Al Wasl Rd Al Manara **04 388 4433**
j3mall.com
Map **1 U5** Metro **Noor Islamic Bank**
Set in the heart of Umm Suqeim, this new, stylish shopping mall on Al Wasl Road is packed with outlets for all the family. From Choitrams and Tim Horton's to the SPERA fashion boutique and the Extreme Fun indoor play centre for kids, there is a wide range of outlets jammed into a compact shopping plaza.

Jumeira Plaza

Jumeira Rd Jumeira 1 **04 349 7111**
Map **2 H4** Metro **Emirates Towers**
The 'pink mall' has an interesting range of independent shops. The ground floor is dominated by a play area for kids and the Dôme Cafe. Downstairs, there are outlets selling everything from furniture to greeting cards. House of Prose is a popular second-hand book shop; there are also a number of home decor, trinket and card shops, and a small branch of the Dubai Police – great for paying fines without having to queue. Upstairs, Melangé has an interesting selection of clothing, jewellery and soft furnishings from India. This is a busy area and parking spaces can be hard to find; there is parking under the mall but the entrance is a squeeze – especially for larger cars or 4WDs. Other outlets include: Art Stop, Balloon Lady, Blue White, Girls' Talk Beauty Centre, Kashmir Craft, KKids, Susan Walpole and Safeplay.

Jumeirah Centre

Jumeira Rd Jumeira 1 **04 349 9702**
jumeirahcentre.net
Map **2 H4** Metro **Emirates Towers**
Packs a lot into a small space. There are branches of several established chains including Benetton and Nike; and a number of independents. Kazim has a good range of stationery and art supplies. Upstairs, independent shops abound and include Elves & Fairies (a crafts and hobbies shop), Panache (for accessories made only from natural materials), and the Wedding Shop. There are also some interesting clothes shops, and a gallery here. Harvest Home has two shops selling gifts and kitchenalia. For refreshment, head to Coffee Bean & Tea Leaf or Costa Coffee. Other outlets include: Blue Cactus, Caviar Classic, Cut Above, Kazim Gulf Traders, Lunnettes, Nutrition Centre, Photo Magic, Rivoli, The Barber Shop and Thomas Cook.

Lamcy Plaza

Shk Rashid Rd Oud Metha **04 335 9999**
lamcyplaza.com
Map **2 K6** Metro **Oud Metha**
With five floors of shopping, and open at 10:00 seven days a week, Lamcy is consistently popular. There's a great variety of shops in close quarters; entertainment dominates the ground floor, with a huge foodcourt and play area. There is a pharmacy, a money exchange, a florist and a post office counter, as well as a fascinating feng shui shop that is crammed with interesting knick-knacks. Also on the ground floor is a photo developing outlet, a key cutting service and a branch of Belhasa Driving Centre. The first floor is for women's fashion and shoes (Dorothy Perkins, Guess, Monsoon and Hush Puppies). The second floor is great for parents, with Mothercare, Pumpkin Patch and Adams. Mexx for Less sells discounted clothing; Peacocks and Matalan sell reasonably priced fashion. Factory Fashions carries Adams and Pumpkin Patch overstocks. Men's clothing and sports shops are located on the third floor. This is the destination for bargain hunters too; Daiso is a Japanese store where almost everything costs Dhs.6. The top floor is dedicated to the hypermarket. Other outlets include: Aldo, Athlete's Foot, Books Plus, Bhs, Bossini, Giordano, Golf House, Hang Ten, Hush Puppies, La Senza, Nine West, Shoe Mart and Watch House.

Madina Mall

Beirut St Muhaisnah 4 **04 264 1944**
Map **2 T9** Metro **Al Qusais**
This two-floor shopping mall with around 120 shops, food court, family entertainment area, and hypermarket (Carrefour), is a shopper's paradise. Packed with outlets selling everything from homewares to fashion, this strikingly designed mall has become most well-known perhaps for being home to the Middle East's first Poundstretcher, a popular bargain basement brand from the UK.

Oasis Centre

Shk Zayed Rd Al Quoz 1 **04 515 4000**
oasiscentremall.com
Map **2 L6** Metro **Noor Islamic Bank**
It may not have the size or glamour of some of Dubai's other mega malls, but Oasis Centre offers a good selection of outlets including a Home Centre, New Look, Carrefour Express, Fitness First and Centrepoint. There is a small foodcourt which offers the usual fastfood outlets, but for something different, head to Le Pain de France which sells a good range of cooked food and sandwiches. Other outlets include: Adidas, Bossini, Claires, Damas, Game King, Joyallukas, Koton, Lifestyle, Max, Mothercare, Nike, Q Home Decor, Rage Bike Shop, Sun & Sands Sports, Splash, Springfield.

Palm Strip

Jumeira Rd Jumeira 1 **04 346 1462**
Map **2 H4** Metro **World Trade Centre**
Palm Strip is across the road from Jumeirah Mosque, and is more of an arcade than a mall. Upmarket boutiques dominate; there are also speciality shops for Arabic perfumes (Rusasi), maternity wear (Great

Expectations), and chocolate (Jeff de Bruges). There are two beauty salons and a walk-in branch of N-Bar. Palm Strip is often quiet during the day, getting a little livelier in the evenings with the popular Japengo Café. If the shaded parking at the front is full, there's an underground carpark, with access from the side. Zara Home has an outlet selling bright and stylish accessories. Other outlets include: Beyond the Beach, Elite Fashion, Gulf Pharmacy, Hagen-Dazs, Oceano, Starbucks and Zara Home.

Reef Mall

Salahuddin Rd Al Muraqqabat **04 352 0222**
reefmall.com
Map **2 N5** Metro **Salah Al Din**

This surprisingly large mall is anchored by Home Centre, Lifestyle, Splash and Babyshop. Among many other outlets are branches of Emax and Daiso. There's a huge Fun City here, a great place where kids (toddlers to teens) can burn off a bit of energy. There's a small foodcourt, several cafes and a supermarket. Other outlets include: Aldo Accessories, Babyshop, Bench, Bossini, Charles & Keith, Comtel, Damas, Grand Optics, Karisma, McDonald's, Nayomi, Nine West, and Dome Café.

Spinneys Centre

Nr Umm Al Sheif Rd & Al Wasl Rd Al Safa 2
04 394 1657
spinneys-dubai.com
Map **2 B5** Metro **Noor Islamic Bank**

This small mall, just off Al Wasl Road, centres around a large Spinneys supermarket. There are a small number of other shops including Early Learning Centre and Mothercare, Tavola (for kitchenalia), and Disco 2000, which is one of Dubai's better music and DVD shops. There are branches of both MMI and A&E, along with cafes and a large Fun Corner play area for children. It gets quite busy at weekends and the small carpark is nearly always full. Other outlets include: Arabella Pharmacy, Areej, Axiom Telecom, Baskin Robbins, Beyond the Beach, Books Plus, Café Havana, Champion Cleaners, Damas, Emirates Bank, Gulf Greetings, Hair Works, The Healing Zone, Marina, Starbucks and Uniform Shop.

Sunset Mall

Jumeira Rd Jumeira 3 **04 330 7333**
sunsetmall.ae
Map **2 C4** Metro **Noor Islamic Bank**

With a sleek glass and steel exterior this boutique mall – and its sea-facing apartments – is home to luxury brands including Pasaya (Thai bed linens), Hästens (Swedish beds), and other niche venues like Milk & Honey Gourmet and Vallkeydez, Rivaage Boutique and Tropicana Flowers. A chic and stylish shopping destination.

Times Square

Shk Zayed Rd Al Quoz Industrial 1 **04 341 8020**
timessquarecenter.ae
Map **1 T6** Metro **Noor Islamic Bank**

The huge outdoor and adventure sport megastore Adventure HQ, which has a climbing wall and aerial obstacle course, is the biggest draw for this small but modern mall. You'll find large branches of Sharaf DG, Intersport, Toys R Us and Yellow Hat (for car accessories). Head to the Chillout ice lounge (unlicensed), if only for the novelty, for a sub-zero mocktail. In addition to the large foodcourt, there is Caribou Coffee and Biella. There's also a pharmacy, an opticians and a few children's clothes stores; a hypermarket is due to open in 2013. Other outlets include: Bayti, InWear, Ladybird, Sanrio (Hello Kitty) and Watch Square. The mall is well worth visiting on the weekends when the ARTE craft market takes over the ground floor.

Town Centre Jumeirah

Jumeira Rd Jumeira 1 **04 344 0111**
towncentrejumeirah.com
Map **2 F4** Metro **Financial Centre**

Town Centre is a community mall on Jumeira Road, next to Mercato. There is an interesting blend of outlets and several cafes, including Cafe Céramique where you can customise a piece of pottery while you dine. For pampering, there's Feet First (reflexology and massage for men and women), Kaya Beauty Centre, Nail Station and SOS Salon. There are also clothing shops including Heat Waves (for beachwear) and Anne Klein (fashion accessories) a large branch of Paris Gallery, an Empost counter and an Etisalat machine. Other outlets include: Al Jaber Optical, Bateel, Bayti, Hello Kitty Spa, Marie Claire, Nutrition Zone, Papermoon, Paris Gallery, Zen Yoga and Little Luxurious.

The Village

Nr Jumeirah Plaza, Jumeira Rd Jumeira 1
04 344 9514
thevillagedubai.com
Map **2 H4** Metro **Emirates Towers**

The Village Mall, with its Mediterranean theme, has more of a community feel than many of the malls in Dubai. The niche boutiques are great if you're looking for something different, whether it's clothing or something for the home, and there are some audaciously feminine outlets like S*uce, Ayesha Depala and Shakespeare & Co (a cafe that embraces chintz). Peekaboo, the children's play area, is bright and fun for younger children – it also runs activities. There are a number of places to eat, including Thai Time and Shakespeare & Co. Other outlets include: Books Gallery, Boots, Irony Home, Julian Hairdressing for Men, Offshore Legends, Hey Sugar, Sisters Beauty Lounge and Sensasia Urban Spa.

STORE FINDER

@Home Dubai Marina Mall, Ibn Battuta Mall, Mercato, The Dubai Mall

Accessorize Arabian Centre, BurJuman, Deira City Centre, Dubai Marina Mall, Festival Centre, Lamcy Plaza, Mall of the Emirates, Mirdif City Centre, The Dubai Mall, Uptown Mirdif, Wafi

ACE Festival Centre, Sharjah (Nr King Faisal & Al Wahda Sts), Al Quoz Industrial 1 (Nr Times Square, Shk Zayed Rd)

Adams Al Ghurair Centre, Arabian Centre, BurJuman, Deira City Centre, Festival Centre, Lamcy Plaza, Mirdif City Centre, The Dubai Mall, Uptown Mirdif

Adidas Al Ghazal Complex & Shopping Mall, Al Ghurair Centre, Arabian Centre, BurJuman, Deira City Centre, Dubai Outlet Mall, Festival Centre, Ibn Battuta Mall, Mall of the Emirates, Oasis Centre, Uptown Mirdif

Aeropostale Arabian Centre, BurJuman, Ibn Battuta Mall, Mercato, Mirdif City Centre, Oasis Centre, The Dubai Mall

African + Eastern Al Karama (Nr Karama Market, 20B Street), Al Mankhool (Nr Spinneys, Al Mankhool Rd), Arabian Ranches (Arabian Ranches Community Center), Deira (Nr Mayfair Hotel, Al Maktoum Rd), Dubai Marina (Marina Walk), Green Community (Nr Choithrams), Grosvenor Business Tower, Le Meridien Dubai, Jumeira 1 (Nr Spinneys, Jumeira Rd), Mirdif (Nr Spinneys, Uptown Mirdif), Spinneys Centre (Nr Umm Al Sheif Rd & Al Wasl Rd)

Aftershock ICONIC, Mall of the Emirates, Mirdif City Centre, The Dubai Mall

Aigner Deira City Centre, Mall of the Emirates, The Dubai Mall

Ajmal Eternal Al Muraqqabat (Hamarain centre)

Ajmal Perfumes Al Ghurair Centre, Al Mizhar 2 (Emirates Co-operative), Al Satwa (Nr Emirates NBD), Bin Sougat Centre, BurJuman, Deira City Centre, Deira (Murshid Bazaar), Deira (Nr Kuwaiti Mosque), Gold Souk, Jumeirah Emirates Towers, Mall of the Emirates, Mirdif City Centre, Union Co-operative Society

AK Anne Klein BurJuman, Festival Centre, Town Centre Jumeirah

Al Boom Marine Jumeira 3 (Jumeira Rd), Ras Al Khor (Nadd al Hamar Rd)

Al Fahidi Stationery DeiraBur Dubai (Al Fahidi St), Deira (Nr Al Khaleej Hotel, Nasser Square), Al Ras (Nr Gold Souk)

Al Fardan Jewels & Precious Stones Deira City Centre, Hamarain Centre, InterContinental Dubai Festival City, Mall of the Emirates

Al Fardan Jewels & Precious Stones The Dubai Mall

Al Futtaim Jewellery BurJuman, Deira City Centre, Festival Centre, Lamcy Plaza, Mall of the Emirates, The Dubai Mall

Al Hamra Cellar Ras Al Khaimah (Nr RAK Ceramics, Al Hamra Village Development)

Al Jaber Gallery Deira City Centre, Dubai Marina Mall, Gold Souk, Mall of the Emirates, Souk Madinat Jumeirah, The Dubai Mall

Al Jaber Optical Al Ghurair Centre, Arabian Centre, Bin Sougat Centre, Deira City Centre, Dubai Marina Mall, Dubai Outlet Mall, Emirates Living (Emaar Town Centre), Festival Centre, Ibn Battuta Mall, Lamcy Plaza, Mall of the Emirates, Trade Centre 1 (Nr Coco's Restaurant, Shk Zayed Rd), Al Souk Al Kabeer (Nr Cosmos), Souk Al Bahar, Souk Madinat Jumeirah, The Dubai Mall, Town Centre Jumeirah, Wafi

Al Kamda Al Wasl (Nr Mazaya Centre), Deira (Salahudhin Rd)

Al Maya Supermarket Al Bada'a (2nd December St), Al Ittihad Rd (Hor Al Anz East), Al Satwa (Nr Satwa Bus Station), Bur Dubai (Nr Souk Al Kabeer), Deira (Al Rigga Rd), Downtown Dubai (Boulevard 8), Downtown Dubai (Nr Al Murooj Rotana Hotel), Dubai Marina (Dream Tower), Dubai Marina (Dubai Marina Promenade), Hor Al Anz East (Al Mamzar Business Centre, Jumeirah Beach Residence, The Walk at Jumeirah Beach Residence

ALDO Al Ghurair Centre, Arabian Centre, BurJuman, Deira City Centre, Dubai Marina Mall, Dubai Outlet Mall, Festival Centre, Ibn Battuta Mall, Lamcy Plaza, Mall of the Emirates, Mercato, The Dubai Mall, Uptown Mirdif

Aldo Accessories Al Ghurair Centre, Arabian Centre, BurJuman, Deira City Centre, Dukkan Al Manzil Souk, Festival Centre, Ibn Battuta Mall, Lamcy Plaza, Mall of the Emirates, Mercato, Mirdif City Centre, Reef Mall, The Dubai Mall, Uptown Mirdif

Amouage Al Bustan Centre & Residence, Al Ghurair Centre, Arabian Centre, Burj Al Arab, BurJuman, Deira City Centre, Festival Centre, Hamarain Centre, Ibn Battuta Mall, Lamcy Plaza, The Dubai Mall, Town Centre Jumeirah, Uptown Mirdif, Wafi Mall

And So To Bed Bur Dubai (Business Center Bldg, Nr BurJuman, Khalid Bin Al Waleed Rd), Jumeira 3 (Villa 4, Street 325-25B, Jumeira Rd)

Angels Wafi

Aptec Mobiles Al Ghurair Centre, Arabian Ranches (Community Centre), Deira (Danat Al Khaleej Bldg), Lamcy Plaza, The Dubai Mall

Arabian Oud Al Bustan Centre & Residence, Al Ghurair Centre, Naif (Al Manal Centre 1), Naif (Al Manal Centre 2), Deira City Centre, Dubai Outlet Mall, Emirates Concorde Hotel & Suites, Gold Souk, Hamarain Centre, Ibn Battuta Mall, The Dubai Mall, Wafi

Areej Dubai Marina Mall, Ibn Battuta Mall, Jumeirah Emirates Towers, Mall of the Emirates, Mercato, Mirdif City Centre, The Dubai Mall

Armani Deira City Centre, Mercato, The Boulevard At Jumeirah Emirates Towers, The Dubai Mall

Armani Exchange Deira City Centre, The Dubai Mall

Armani Junior BurJuman, Mall of the Emirates, Mercato, The Dubai Mall

Artikel Mall of the Emirates

The Athlete's Foot Dubai Outlet Mall, Emirates Living (Greens Community Centre, The Greens), Festival Centre, Ibn Battuta Mall, Mall of the Emirates, Emirates Living (Meadows Community Centre, The Meadows), Reef Mall, Uptown Mirdif

Audemars Piguet Mall of the Emirates

Axiom Telecom Al Ghurair Centre, Arabian Centre, Bin Sougat Centre, Bur Dubai (Nr Ramada), Century Mall, Deira City Centre, Dubai International Financial Centre (DIFC), Dubai Internet City, Dubai Marina Mall, Dubai World Trade Centre, Emirates Living (Nr Emirates Golf Club, Shk Zayed Rd), Festival Centre, Grand Cineplex, Hyatt Regency Dubai, Ibn Battuta Mall, Mall of the Emirates, Mercato, Mirdif City Centre, Trade Centre 2 (Nr Dusit Dubai, Shk Zayed Rd), Souk Al Bahar, Spinneys Centre ((Nr Umm Al Sheif Rd & Al Wasl Rd), The Dubai Mall, Town Centre Jumeirah, Wafi

Babyshop Abu Hail Center, Al Ghurair Centre, Centrepoint, Ibn Battuta Mall, Madina Mall, Mall of the Emirates, Mirdif City Centre, Oasis Centre, Reef Mall, The Dubai Mall, Al Karama (Zaabel Rd)

Baituti Al Karama (Baituti Bldg, Za'abeel Rd), Mall of the Emirates

Baldinini BurJuman, Dubai Outlet Mall, Festival Centre, The Dubai Mall

Balloon Lady Jumeira Plaza

Bally Mirdif City Centre, The Dubai Mall

Balmain Deira City Centre, Dubai Marina Mall, Festival Centre

Banana Republic Deira City Centre, The Dubai Mall

Bang & Olufsen BurJuman, The Dubai Mall, Town Centre Jumeirah

Barakat Optical Dubai Outlet Mall, Festival Centre, Jumeira Plaza, The Dubai Mall, The Walk at Jumeirah Beach Residence, Umm Suqeim 1 (Jumeira Rd), Uptown Mirdif

Bareeze Bur Dubai, Al Satwa (2nd December St)

Basler BurJuman, Deira City Centre, Ibn Battuta Mall, Mall of the Emirates

Bata Deira City Centre, Mall of the Emirates, The Dubai Mall

Bath & Body Works Deira City Centre, Ibn Battuta Mall, Mall of the Emirates, Mirdif City Centre, The Dubai Mall

Bauhaus Dubai Outlet Mall, Ibn Battuta Mall

Bayti Deira City Centre, Festival Centre, Times Square, Town Centre Jumeirah

BCBGMAXAZRIA BurJuman, Mall of the Emirates, The Dubai Mall

Beach Bunny Swimwear Atlantis The Palm, Burj Al Arab, BurJuman, Grosvenor House, Jumeirah Beach Hotel, Souk Madinat Jumeirah

Bebe BurJuman, Deira City Centre, Dubai Marina Mall, Festival Centre, Mall of the Emirates, The Dubai Mall

Bendon Arabian Centre, Dubai Outlet Mall, Festival Centre, Mall of the Emirates, The Dubai Mall

Bershka Deira City Centre, Mall of the Emirates, Mercato, The Dubai Mall

Better Life Deira (Al Ittihad Rd), Mall of the Emirates

Beyond The Beach Arabian Court At One&Only Royal Mirage, Emirates Living (Emaar Town Centre, The Springs), Green Community Market, Grosvenor House, Mercato, Dubai MotorCity (MotorCity), One&Only Royal Mirage, Uptown Mirdif

Bhs Al Ghurair Centre, BurJuman, Deira City Centre, Dubai Outlet Mall, Festival Centre, Ibn Battuta Mall, Lamcy Plaza, Mirdif City Centre

Bhs Kids Mall of the Emirates

The Bike Shop The Gardens (Nr Ibn Battuta Mall), Al Quoz (Nr to BMW showroom)

Billabong Dubai Marina Mall, Festival Centre, Mirdif City Centre, The Dubai Mall

BinHendi Jewellery Burj Al Arab, BurJuman, Dubai International Financial Centre (DIFC), Festival Centre, The Dubai Mall

Blush Al Ghurair Centre, Festival Centre

Bobbi Brown BurJuman, Deira City Centre, Dubai Marina Mall, Festival Centre, Mall of the Emirates

Boboli BurJuman, Dubai Outlet Mall, Festival Centre, The Dubai Mall

The Body Shop Al Ghurair Centre, Arabian Centre, BurJuman, Deira City Centre, Dubai Marina Mall, Festival Centre, Ibn Battuta Mall, Jumeirah Centre, Lamcy Plaza, Mall of the Emirates, Mercato, Mirdif City Centre, The Dubai Mall, Wafi

Bombay & Zone Mall of the Emirates

Book World Al Karama (Nr Bikanervala), Al Satwa (Nr Satwa Flower Shop)

Booksplus Arabian Ranches Centre, Festival Centre, Emirates Living (Spring Community Centre, The Springs), Green Community Market, Spinneys Centre (Nr Umm Al Sheif Rd & Al Wasl Rd), The Greens Village

Bookworm Al Safa 1 (Al Safa Centre, Al Wasl Rd), Emirates Living (The Meadows)

Boots Al Safa 1 (Nr Al Safa Park), Arabian Centre, Deira City Centre, Downtown Dubai (Residence Tower 1), Dubai International Financial Centre (DIFC), Dubai Marina Mall, Ibn Battuta Mall, Jumeirah Beach Residence, Lamcy Plaza, Latifa Hospital, Mall of the Emirates, Satwa, Trade Centre 1 (Al Ghadeer Tower, Shk Zayed Rd), The Boulevard At Jumeirah Emirates Towers, The Dubai Mall, The Village, Wafi

Borders Deira City Centre, Dubai Marina Mall, Ibn Battuta Mall, Mall of the Emirates, Mirdif City Centre

Bose The Dubai Mall

Bossini Al Ghurair Centre, Al Manal Centre, Arabian Centre, BurJuman, Festival Centre, Mall of the Emirates, Bur Dubai (Meena Bazaar, Cosmos Lane), Oasis Centre, The Beach Centre, The Dubai Mall

Braccialini Festival Centre, Holiday Centre Mall, Mall of the Emirates, The Dubai Mall

Brands For Less Al Bada'a (Nr Iranian Hospital), Al Ghazal Complex & Shopping Mall, Al Mankhool (Nr BurJuman, Umm Hurair First St), Al Muraqqabat (Al Bakhit Center), Al Muraqqabat (Al Muraqqabat St), Lamcy Plaza,

Breitling Deira City Centre, Dubai International Airport, Dubai International Airport, Festival Centre, Mall of the Emirates, Sheraton Dubai Creek Hotel & Towers, The Ritz-Carlton, Dubai, The Westin Dubai Mina Seyahi Beach Resort & Marina, Wafi

Burberry BurJuman, Deira City Centre, Dubai Outlet Mall, Mall of the Emirates, The Dubai Mall

Bvlgari Dubai International Airport, Mall of the Emirates, The Boulevard At Jumeirah Emirates Towers, The Dubai Mall

Cafe Cotton Dubai Outlet Mall, Festival Centre, Mall of the Emirates, The Dubai Mall

Calvin Klein Al Ghurair Centre, Wafi

Calvin Klein Underwear Deira City Centre, Festival Centre, Mall of the Emirates, Wafi

Camaieu Arabian Centre, Festival Centre, Lamcy Plaza, Mall of the Emirates, The Dubai Mall

Canali BurJuman, The Dubai Mall, Wafi

Carl F. Bucherer Burj Al Arab, BurJuman, Deira City Centre, Dubai Marina Mall, Festival Centre, Mall of the Emirates, Mercato, Souk Madinat Jumeirah, The Dubai Mall, Wafi

Carlton Cards Deira City Centre, Lamcy Plaza, Mall of the Emirates

Carolina Herrera Festival Centre, Mall of the Emirates, The Dubai Mall

Carpetland Oud Metha (Pyramid Centre, Umm Hurair Rd), The Village

Carrefour Al Shindagha (Al Ghubaiba Rd), Century Mall, Deira City Centre, Madina Mall, Mall of the Emirates

Carrefour Market Al Ghazal Complex & Shopping Mall, Al Hudaiba (Al Mankhool Rd), Al Qusais 2 (Al Ghurair Bldg, Al Nahda Rd), Dubai Marina (Marina Crown Bldg), Dubai Marina (Marina Silverine, Nr Dubai International Marine Club), Hamarain Centre, Jumeirah Lakes Towers, Mazaya Centre, Muteena (ETA Star Bldg), Oasis Centre, Tecom (Tecom Bldg), Warsan 1 (Nr Dragon Mart), Wafi

Cartier Al Ghurair Centre, Atlantis The Palm, Burj Al Arab, BurJuman, Deira City Centre, Dubai International Airport, Festival Centre, Gold & Diamond Park, Gold Souk, Ibn Battuta Mall, The Boulevard At Jumeirah Emirates Towers, The Dubai Mall, Uptown Mirdif

Casadei The Dubai Mall

Cellar Saver Bur Dubai Bur Dubai (Nr Sea Shell Hotel, Computer St)

Cellar Saver Karama Al Karama (Al Maskan Bldg. Nr Karama Emarat station)

Centrepoint Al Mankhool (Shk Khalifa Bin Zayed Rd), Mall of the Emirates, Mirdif City Centre, Oasis Centre

Cerruti BurJuman, Wafi

Cerruti Jeans Mall of the Emirates

Cesare Paciotti BurJuman, Dubai Outlet Mall, The Dubai Mall, Wafi

Chanel BurJuman, The Dubai Mall, Wafi

Charles & Keith Al Ghurair Centre, Arabian Centre, BurJuman, Festival Centre, Ibn Battuta Mall, Mall of the Emirates, Mirdif City Centre, Reef Mall, The Dubai Mall, Uptown Mirdif

Chevignon Festival Centre, Mall of the Emirates

Choithrams Al Garhoud (Casablanca Rd), Al Karama (Nr Iranian School), Al Mankhool (Nr Ramada Hotel, Al Mankhool Rd), Al Raffa (Al Fahidi St), Deira (Al Nasser Square), Dubai Marina (Amwaj, Jumeirah Beach Residence), Dubai Marina (DEC Towers), Dubai Silicon Oasis (Nr GEMS Wellington School), Emirates Living (The Lakes), Emirates Living (The Springs), Green Community Market, Hyatt Regency Dubai, Jumeira (Al Wasl Rd), Jumeira 3 (Nr Al Safa Park, Al Wasl Rd), Layan Community, The Greens Village, Umm Suqeim 2 (Al Wasl Rd)

Chopard Atlantis The Palm**,** BurJuman, Deira City Centre, Al Rigga (Deira Tower), Festival Centre, Grand Hyatt Dubai, Grosvenor House**,** Jumeirah Beach Hotel, Jumeirah Emirates Towers**,** Le Royal Meridien Beach Resort & Spa, Mall of the Emirates, Deira (Murshid Bazaar), Souk Madinat Jumeirah, The Dubai Mall, Wafi

Christian Lacroix BurJuman, Wafi

Christian Louboutin Mall of the Emirates, The Dubai Mall

Calvin Klein BurJuman, The Dubai Mall

CK Jeans Deira City Centre, Mall of the Emirates

Claire's Al Ghazal Complex & Shopping Mall, Al Ghurair Centre, Arabian Centre, Deira City Centre, Emirates Living (Emaar Town Center), Festival Centre, bn Battuta Mall, Lamcy Plaza, Mall of the Emirates, Mercato, The Dubai Mall, Uptown Mirdif

Clarks Al Ghurair Centre, Deira City Centre, Festival Centre, Lamcy Plaza, Mall of the Emirates, Mirdif City Centre, The Dubai Mall

Club Monaco Deira City Centre

Coach Mall of the Emirates, The Boulevard At Jumeirah Emirates Towers, The Dubai Mall

Coast Deira City Centre, Dubai Marina Mall, Ibn Battuta Mall, Mall of the Emirates, Mirdif City Centre, The Dubai Mall

Columbia Deira City Centre, Festival Centre, Ibn Battuta Mall, The Dubai Mall

Columbia Sportswear Company Mall of the Emirates

Cortefiel Festival Centre, Ibn Battuta Mall, The Dubai Mall

Cotton On Ibn Battuta Mall, Mirdif City Centre, The Dubai Mall

Daiso Al Barsha Mall, Arabian Centre, Ibn Battuta Mall, Lamcy Plaza, Mirdif City Centre, Al Souk Al Kabeer (Nr Choithrams, Al Fahidi St), Oasis Centre, Reef Mall, Union Co-operative Society

Damas Al Awir (Union Co-Operative), Al Awir (Awir Co-operative), Al Bustan Centre & Residence, Al Ghurair Centre, Al Karama (Lulu Centre), Al Barsha 1 (Lulu Hypermarket), Al Twar 3 (Emirates Co-Operative), Al Twar 1 (Union Co-Operative Society, Al Nahda Rd), , Al Rashidiya (Union Co-operative), Arabian Centre, Bin Sougat Centre, BurJuman, Century Mall, Deira City Centre, Dubai Deira Creek, Dubai Outlet Mall, Festival Centre, Gold & Diamond Park, Gold Souk, Grand Hyatt Dubai, Green Community Market, Hamarain Centre, Holiday Centre Mall, Jebel Ali Beach Hotel, Jumeira 1, Jumeirah Beach Hotel, Jumeira 3, Le Royal Meridien Beach Resort & Spa, Oud Al Muteena 1 (Emirates Co-operative), LuLu Hypermarket, Magrudy's Mall, Mercato, Oasis Centre, One&Only Royal Mirage, Radisson Blu Hotel, Reef Mall, The Dubai Mall, The Walk, Jumeirah Beach Residence, Town Centre Jumeirah, Umm Suqeim (Spinney's Centre)

Damas 18K Festival Centre, Ibn Battuta Mall, Mercato, The Dubai Mall, Uptown Mirdif

Damas 21K Festival Centre, Uptown Mirdif

Damas 22K Al Karama (Karama Gold), Al Qusais 1 (Shk Rashid Colony), Al Shindagha (Carrefour), Al Satwa (Nr Satwa bus station), Bur Dubai (Al Baker Bldg), Bur Dubai (Al Fahidi St), Festival Centre, Karama Centre, Lamcy Plaza,

Damas Les Exclusives Burj Al Arab, BurJuman, Dubai International Financial Centre (DIFC), Dubai Marina Mall, Mall of the Emirates, Mina A'Salam, The Boulevard At Jumeirah Emirates Towers, The Dubai Mall, Wafi

Danier Festival Centre, The Dubai Mall

Dar Al Tasmim Uniforms Spinneys Centre

De Beers Mall of the Emirates

Debenhams Deira City Centre, Ibn Battuta Mall, Mall of the Emirates, Mirdif City Centre, The Dubai Mall

Deepak's Al Satwa (Nr Emarat Gas Station), Al Bada'a (Nr Satwa Clinic), Dubai Outlet Mall, Oasis Centre

Desigual Dubai Marina Mall, The Dubai Mall

Diesel BurJuman, Deira City Centre, Dubai Marina Mall, Dubai Outlet Mall, Festival Centre, Mall of the Emirates, Mercato, The Dubai Mall

Dior BurJuman, Mall of the Emirates, The Dubai Mall

DKNY BurJuman, Deira City Centre, Festival Centre, Mall of the Emirates

Dockers Deira City Centre, Festival Centre, The Dubai Mall

Dogtas Exclusive Al Quoz Industrial 1 (Ain Tasneem Furniture Trading, Al Joud Bldg, 15A St, Shk Zayed Rd)

Dolce & Gabbana BurJuman, Mall of the Emirates, The Dubai Mall

Domino Al Ghurair Centre

Dorothy Perkins Ibn Battuta Mall, Lamcy Plaza, Mall of the Emirates

Dream Girl Tailors Meena Bazaar Fashions, Al Karama (Nr LuLu hypermarket), Al Satwa (Nr New Emirates Bank)

Dubai Library Distributors Al Satwa (Nr Post Office, Satwa Rd), Al Quoz (Shk Zayed Rd), Al Qusais (Nasser Lootah Old Bldg), Bin Sougat Centre, Hor Al Anz (Al Yasmeen Bldg, Salahudhin Rd), Hor Al Anz (Yasmeen Bldg, Salahuddin Rd), Naif (Nr Naif Police Station, Naif Rd), Al Rashidiya (Nr Police Station)

Dune Arabian Centre, BurJuman, Dubai Marina Mall, Dubai Outlet Mall, Festival Centre, Mall of the Emirates, Mirdif City Centre, The Dubai Mall

Dwell Festival Centre, The Dubai Mall

Early Learning Centre Al Ghurair Centre, Arabian Centre, BurJuman, Deira City Centre, Dubai Marina Mall, Dukkan Al Manzil Souk, Festival Centre, Mall of the Emirates, Mercato, Souk Madinat Jumeirah, Spinneys Centre, The Dubai Mall, Uptown Mirdif, Wafi

Ecco Al Ghurair Centre, Deira City Centre, Dubai Marina Mall, Dubai Outlet Mall, Festival Centre, Mall of the Emirates, Reef Mall, The Dubai Mall

Ed Hardy Dubai Marina Mall, Festival Centre, The Dubai Mall, Wafi

Elle Deira City Centre, Ibn Battuta Mall, Reef Mall

Emax Centrepoint, Mall of the Emirates, Mirdif City Centre, Oasis Centre, Reef Mall, The Dubai Mall

Emirates Trading Est. Bin Sougat Centre, Dubai Community Theatre & Arts Centre (DUCTAC), Jumeira 1 (Villa 27, Nr Mercato, Street 75B)

Emporio Armani Mall of the Emirates

Eros Digital Home Mall of the Emirates

Eros Electricals Al Karama (Abdul Aziz Mirza Bldg), Deira (Baniyas Rd), Deira City Centre

Escada BurJuman, Mall of the Emirates, The Dubai Mall, Wafi

Esprit Al Ghurair Centre, BurJuman, Deira City Centre, Dubai Outlet Mall, Festival Centre, Mall of the Emirates, The Dubai Mall

Etoile La Boutique BurJuman, Mall of the Emirates, Wafi

Etro BurJuman, Mall of the Emirates, The Dubai Mall

Evans Al Ghurair Centre, Deira City Centre, Ibn Battuta Mall, Mall of the Emirates

Evita Peroni BurJuman, Deira City Centre, Dubai Marina Mall, Jumeirah Beach Hotel, The Dubai Mall

Fabi Festival Centre, Mall of the Emirates, The Dubai Mall

Faces Atlantis The Palm, BurJuman, Festival Centre, Ibn Battuta Mall, Mall of the Emirates, The Dubai Mall, Uptown Mirdif

Faith Deira City Centre, Ibn Battuta Mall, Mall of the Emirates, The Dubai Mall

Falaknaz – The Warehouse Al Quoz Industrial 3 (Nr Dubai Garden Centre), Al Quoz 3 (Shk Zayed Rd)

FCUK Al Ghurair Centre, Deira City Centre, Festival Centre

Feshwari Al Quoz 3 (Shk Zayed Rd)

Fila Deira City Centre, Ibn Battuta Mall, Mall of the Emirates, The Dubai Mall

Folli Follie BurJuman, Dubai Marina Mall, Festival Centre, Mall of the Emirates, The Dubai Mall

Fono Arabian Centre, Deira City Centre, Festival Centre, Mall of the Emirates, The Dubai Mall, Trade Centre 2 (Al Murooj Rotana Complex), Uptown Mirdif

Forever 21 Deira City Centre, Festival Centre, Ibn Battuta Mall, Mall of the Emirates, Mirdif City Centre, The Dubai Mall

Fossil BurJuman, Festival Centre, Lamcy Plaza, Mall of the Emirates, Nasr Square (The Watch House, Al-Futtaim Tower), The Dubai Mall

French Connection (FCUK) Mall of the Emirates

Frost Palm Strip, The Dubai Mall

Furla BurJuman, Mall of the Emirates, The Dubai Mall

G2000 Al Ghurair Centre, BurJuman, Festival Centre, Lamcy Plaza, Mall of the Emirates, Reef Mall, The Dubai Mall

Gallery One Mall of the Emirates, Souk Al Bahar, Souk Madinat Jumeirah, The Dubai Mall, The Walk, JBR

Galliano Mall of the Emirates

Gant Deira City Centre, Festival Centre, Mall of the Emirates, Mirdif City Centre, The Dubai Mall

Gap Arabian Centre, BurJuman, Deira City Centre, Ibn Battuta Mall, Mall of the Emirates, Mercato, Mirdif City Centre, The Dubai Mall

Geant Easy Tecom (Dubai Gate 1, Jumeirah Lake Towers, Shk Zyed Rd), International City (France Cluster), Al Raffa (Nr York Hotel)

Geekay Games Deira City Centre, Festival Centre, Mall of the Emirates, Mirdif City Centre, The Dubai Mall

Genevieve Lethu Mercato

GEOX Deira City Centre, Festival Centre, Ibn Battuta Mall, Mall of the Emirates, The Dubai Mall

Gianfranco Ferre BurJuman, The Dubai Mall

Ginger & Lace Ibn Battuta Mall, Wafi

Giordano Al Fahidi St, Al Ghurair Centre, Al Manal Centre, Al Nasr Square, Al Satwa (Nr Ravi) Al Sabkha Corner, BurJuman, Century Mall, Deira City Centre, Dubai Marina Mall, Dubai Outlet Mall, Festival Centre, Ibn Battuta Mall, Karama Complex, Lamcy Plaza, Mall of the Emirates, Mirdif City Centre, Reef Mall, The Dubai Mall

Go Sport Ibn Battuta Mall, Mall of the Emirates, Mirdif City Centre, The Dubai Mall

Gocco Festival Centre

Golden Ring Jewellery Deira City Centre, The Dubai Mall

Golf House Deira City Centre, Ibn Battuta Mall, Mall of the Emirates, The Dubai Mall

Graff Atlantis The Palm, Burj Al Arab, The Dubai Mall

Grand Optics Arabian Ranches Centre, Carrefour, Deira City Centre, Emirates Living (Meadows Community), Festival Centre, Jumeirah Beach Residence, Mall of the Emirates, Reef Mall, The Dubai Mall

Grand Stores Al Garhoud (Saleh Bin Lahej Bldg), Al Rigga (Al Maktoum Rd), BurJuman, Deira City Centre, Dubai Marina Mall, Dubai Outlet Mall, Festival Centre, Ibn Battuta Mall, Mall of the Emirates, The Dubai Mall

Gucci Bloomingdale's, Harvey Nichols, Mall of the Emirates, The Dubai Mall

Gulf Greetings Dubai Silicon Oasis (Community Centre), Deira City Centre, Dubai Marina Mall, Festival Centre, Green Community Market, Ibn Battuta Mall, LuLu Hypermarket, Mall of the Emirates, Mercato, Mirdif City Centre, Spinneys Centre, Spinneys (Trade Centre Rd), The Dubai Mall, (The Meadows), Uptown Mirdif, Wafi

H&M Arabian Centre, Deira City Centre, Dubai Marina Mall, Ibn Battuta Mall, Mirdif City Centre, The Dubai Mall

Hamac Atlantis The Palm, Dubai Marine Beach Resort & Spa, Festival Centre, Jumeirah Beach Hotel, The Dubai Mall

Hang Ten Al Ghurair Centre, Al Khaleej Centre, BurJuman, Century Mall, Deira City Centre, Dubai Outlet Mall, Festival Centre, Ibn Battuta Mall, Lamcy Plaza, Mall of the Emirates, The Dubai Mall

Harman House Deira City Centre, Festival Centre, Mall of the Emirates, Mirdif City Centre, Naif (Al Nassr Square), The Dubai Mall, Trade Centre 1 (Al Hawai Tower, Shk Zayed Rd)

Harman Middle East Jebel Ali

Havaianas Deira City Centre, Souk Al Bahar, Souk Madinat Jumeirah

Heritage Touch Al Quoz Industrial 3, Emirates Living (Springs Village)

Hermes BurJuman, The Dubai Mall

Hobbs Festival Centre, Mercato

Home Centre Mall of the Emirates, Mirdif City Centre, Oasis Centre, Reef Mall

Homes R Us Arabian Centre, Hor Al Anz East (Hamriya Shopping Center), Ibn Battuta Mall, Mazaya Centre

Hour Choice Al Ghurair Centre, Arabian Centre, BurJuman, Deira City Centre, Dubai Marina Mall, Festival Centre, Ibn Battuta Mall, Lamcy Plaza, Mall of the Emirates, Mercato, Mirdif City Centre, Oasis Centre, Reef Mall, The Dubai Mall, Wafi

House Of Prose Dubai Garden Centre, Jumeira Plaza

Hugo Boss Festival Centre, Mall of the Emirates, Mercato, Mirdif City Centre, The Dubai Mall

ID Design Mall of the Emirates, Mirdif City Centre, Al Khabaisi (Nr Galadari Signal)

Indigo Living Mall of the Emirates, Al Safa 1 (Nr Al Safa Park), Oasis Centre

Intersport Festival Centre, Times Square

iStyle Festival Centre, Ibn Battuta Mall, Mercato, Mirdif City Centre, The Dubai Mall

Jack & Jones Festival Centre, Mall of the Emirates, The Dubai Mall

Jacky's Electronics Al Garhoud (Airport Rd), Deira City Centre, Ibn Battuta Mall, JAFZA South, Mall of the Emirates, Mirdif City Centre**,** Naif (Al Nasser Square)

Jacky's Express Century Mall, The Dubai Mall

Jafferjees BurJuman, Sunset Mall

Jashanmal Al Ghurair Centre, Festival Centre, Mirdif City Centre

Jashanmal Bookstores Al Ghurair Centre, Mall of the Emirates

Jeanswest Al Ghurair Centre, Arabian Centre, BurJuman, Festival Centre, Mall of the Emirates, The Dubai Mall

Juicy Couture Dubai Marina Mall, Mall of the Emirates, Mirdif City Centre, The Boulevard At Jumeirah Emirates Towers, The Dubai Mall

Jumbo Electronics Bur Dubai (Nr Al Ain Center and Khaleej Center), BurJuman, Deira City Centre, Festival Centre, Ibn Battuta Mall, Mall of the Emirates, Mirdif City Centre, Naif (Al Nasr Square, Nr HSBC), The Dubai Mall

Just Cavalli BurJuman, Mall of the Emirates, The Dubai Mall

Just Optics BurJuman, Ibn Battuta Mall

K-Lynn Deira City Centre, Festival Centre, Mall of the Emirates, Mirdif City Centre

K.M. Retail Al Rigga (Al Dana Centre, Al Maktoum Rd), Hor Al Anz East (Nr Canadian Hospital, Abu Hail Rd)

Karen Millen Deira City Centre, Dubai Marina Mall, Festival Centre, The Dubai Mall

Kenneth Cole BurJuman, Festival Centre, Mall of the Emirates

Kenzo The Dubai Mall

Kingsley Heath Deira City Centre, Dubai Marina Mall, The Dubai Mall

Kipling Al Ghurair Centre, Deira City Centre, Festival Centre, Mall of the Emirates, The Dubai Mall

Koton Festival Centre, Ibn Battuta Mall, Mall of the Emirates, Marina Mall, Oasis Centre, The Dubai Mall

Kurt Geiger Mall of the Emirates, The Dubai Mall

L'Occitane Dubai Marina Mall, Festival Centre, Ibn Battuta Mall, Mall of the Emirates, Mercato, Mirdif City Centre, The Dubai Mall

La Marquise Deira City Centre, Festival Centre, Mall of the Emirates, Mirdif City Centre, Souk Madinat Jumeirah, The Dubai Mall

La Perla Mall of the Emirates, The Dubai Mall

La Senza Al Ghurair Centre, Arabian Centre, Deira City Centre, Dubai Marina Mall, Festival Centre, Ibn Battuta Mall, Lamcy Plaza, Mall of the Emirates, Mercato, Mirdif City Centre, Oasis Centre, The Dubai Mall, Wafi

La Senza Girl Al Ghurair Centre, Arabian Centre, Festival Centre, Ibn Battuta Mall, The Dubai Mall

Lacoste Atlantis The Palm, BurJuman, Deira City Centre, Festival Centre, Ibn Battuta Mall, Mall of the Emirates, Mirdif City Centre, The Dubai Mall

Lancel The Dubai Mall

Laura Ashley Festival Centre, Mercato

Le Chateau Ibn Battuta Mall

Le Clos Dubai International Airport (Nr Gate 214)

Leather Palace Al Ghurair Centre, Al Manal Centre, BurJuman, Mall of the Emirates

Levi's Al Ghurair Centre, Al Khaleej Centre, Arabian Centre, BurJuman, Deira City Centre, Dubai Marina Mall, Dubai Outlet Mall, Ibn Battuta Mall, Lamcy Plaza, Mall of the Emirates, Mirdif City Centre, The Dubai Mall

LG Festival Centre, Ibn Battuta Mall, Mirdif City Centre, The Dubai Mall

LG Lifestyle Gallery The Dubai Mall

Liali Jewellery BurJuman, Ibn Battuta Mall, Jebel Ali Golf Resort, Madinat Jumeirah, Mall of the Emirates, (Meadows Town Centre, Nr Spinney's), Al Souk Al Kabeer (Meena Bazaar), Mercato, Mirdif City Centre, Spinneys Centre, The Dubai Mall

Lifco Supermarket Al Barsha 1 (Nr Starbucks), Al Garhoud, Al Nahda 1 (Al Kamda Bldg, Nr NMC Hospital, Al Nahda Rd), Mirdif (Nr Uptown R/A, Street 37), Trade Centre 1 (Shk Zayed Rd)

Life Style Fine Jewellery Al Ghurair Centre, Arabian Centre, Dubai Outlet Mall, Gold & Diamond Park, Gold Centre, Ibn Battuta Mall, Lamcy Plaza, The Dubai Mall

Lifestyle Al MankhoolIbn Battuta Mall, Mall of the Emirates, Mirdif City Centre, Oasis Centre, Reef Mall, The Dubai Mall

Lifestyle Nutrition Al Mulla Plaza, BurJuman, Deira City Centre, Downtown Dubai (Dubai Mall Metro Link), Dubai Marina Mall, Dubai Marina (Dubai Marina Walk), Festival Centre, J3 Mall, Mall of the Emirates, Mirdif City Centre, The Dubai Mall, Emirates Living (The Meadows)

Lipsy Mall of the Emirates, Mirdif City Centre, The Dubai Mall

Liu Jo Mirdif City Centre, The Dubai Mall

The Living Zone Mall of the Emirates, Mercato, Wafi

Loewe The Dubai Mall

Louis Vuitton BurJuman, The Dubai Mall

LuLu Centre Al Karama (Nr Karama Shopping Centre, Shk Rashid Rd), Muteena (Nr Sheraton, Al Muteena St)

LuLu Express International City (France Q3)

LuLu Hypermarket Al Barsha 1 (Nr Mall of the Emirates), Al Karama (Nr Zabeel Park), Arabian Centre, Al Qusais 1 (Nr Al Ahli Club, Al Nadhda Rd), Muteena (Nr Sheraton, Al Muteena St)

LuLu Supermarket Al Karama (Nr Dubai Municipality)

LuLu Village Deira (Al Muhaisnah 4, Nr Dubai Taxi Stand)

Lutfi Optical Centre Deira, Reef Mall, Wafi

M&Co Dubai Marina Mall, The Dubai Mall

M.A.C Arabian Centre, BurJuman, Deira City Centre, Ibn Battuta Mall, Mall of the Emirates, Mercato, Wafi

Magrudy's Magrudy's Mall, Ittihad Rd

Mahallati Jewellery Gold Souk, Mall of the Emirates, The Dubai Mall, Wafi

Make Up For Ever Arabian Centre, BurJuman, Deira City Centre, Festival Centre, Ibn Battuta Mall, Mall of the Emirates, Mirdif City Centre, Town Centre Jumeirah

Mamas & Papas Dubai Marina Mall, Dubai Outlet Mall, Mall of the Emirates, Mercato, Mirdif City Centre, The Dubai Mall

Man & Moda Deira City Centre, Mall of the Emirates

Mango Deira City Centre, Mercato, Mall of the Emirates, Mirdif City Centre, The Dubai Mall

Mansoor Jewellers Mall of the Emirates

Marc By Marc Jacobs Mall of the Emirates

Marc Jacobs Festival Centre, Mall of the Emirates, The Dubai Mall

Marina Exotic Home Interiors Al Quoz Industrial 4 (Nr ENOC Petrol Station), Mall of the Emirates, Mirdif City Centre, Souk Al Bahar, Souk Madinat Jumeirah, Spinneys, The Dubai Mall, The Walk at Jumeirah Beach Residence

Marks & Spencer Deira City Centre, Festival Centre, The Dubai Mall, Wafi

Massimo Dutti BurJuman, Deira City Centre, Dubai Festival City, Mall of the Emirates, The Dubai Mall

Matalan Arabian Centre, Lamcy Plaza

Max Al Ghurair Centre, Al Mankhool (Khalid Al Attar Bldg, Khalid Bin Al Waleed Rd), Mirdif City Centre, Hor Al Anz (Nr Abu Hail Center, Abu Hail Rd), Ibn Battuta Mall, Oasis Centre

Merle Norman Cosmetics Festival Centre, Jumeira 2 (Nr Mercato, Villa 164-B, Jumeira Rd), Mirdif City Centre

Mexx Mall of the Emirates

Mikyajy Deira City Centre, Mall of the Emirates, The Dubai Mall

Milano Al Ghurair Centre, Arabian Centre, Deira City Centre, Ibn Battuta Mall, Mall of the Emirates, Mercato, Uptown Mirdif

Minutes Deira City Centre, Ibn Battuta Mall, Mall of the Emirates, The Dubai Mall

Minutes Cobbler Shop Mercato

Miri Mall of the Emirates, Souk Madinat Jumeirah

Miss Selfridge The Dubai Mall

Miss Sixty Mall of the Emirates, The Dubai Mall

MMI Al Mankhool (Nr Spinneys), Al Rigga (Nr Clock Tower, Emirates Group HQ), Dubai MotorCity (Nr Spinneys), Dubai Silicon Oasis (Semmer Villas Community Centre), Festival Centre, Green Community (Nr Choithrams, Dubai Investment Park), Ibn Battuta Mall, Mall of the Emirates, Trade Centre 1 (Saeed Tower 2), Spinneys Centre

Monet & Co Mall of the Emirates

Monsoon Arabian Centre, BurJuman, Deira City Centre, Dubai Marina Mall, Dubai Outlet Mall, Festival Centre, Mall of the Emirates, Mercato, Mirdif City Centre, The Dubai Mall

Montblanc BurJuman, Deira City Centre, Festival Centre, Grand Hyatt Dubai, Ibn Battuta Mall, Jumeirah Beach Residence, Mall of the Emirates, Mirdif City Centre, Oasis Centre, The Dubai Mall, Wafi

Moreschi The Dubai Mall

Mothercare Al Ghurair Centre, Arabian Centre, BurJuman, Deira City Centre, Dubai Marina Mall, Ibn Battuta Mall, Jumeirah Beach Residence, Jumeirah Centre, Lamcy Plaza, Mall of the Emirates, Mirdif City Centre, Oasis Centre, Spinneys Centre, The Dubai Mall, Uptown Mirdif

Mulberry Mall of the Emirates, The Dubai Mall

Mumbai Se BurJuman, Dubai Marina Mall, Festival Centre, The Dubai Mall

The Music Institute Uptown Mirdif

National Iranian Carpets Mall of the Emirates, Souk Al Bahar, Souk Madinat Jumeirah

National Store Al Souk Al Kabeer (Al Fahidi St), Ibn Battuta Mall, Mirdif City Centre, The Dubai Mall

Naturalizer Al Ghurair Centre, Arabian Centre, Dubai Outlet Mall, Festival Centre, Ibn Battuta Mall, Mall of the Emirates, Mirdif City Centre, The Dubai Mall, Town Centre Jumeirah

Nautica Deira City Centre, Dubai Marina Mall, Festival Centre, Ibn Battuta Mall, Mall of the Emirates, Mirdif City Centre, The Dubai Mall

Nayomi Al Ghurair Centre, Arabian Centre, Bin Sougat Centre, Century Mall, Dubai Outlet Mall, Festival Centre, Ibn Battuta Mall, Lamcy Plaza, Mall of the Emirates, Mercato, Reef Mall, The Dubai Mall, Uptown Mirdif

New Look Arabian Centre, BurJuman, Deira City Centre, Dubai Marina Mall, Ibn Battuta Mall, Mirdif City Centre, Oasis Centre, The Dubai Mall

New Yorker Festival Centre, The Dubai Mall

Next Arabian Centre, BurJuman, Deira City Centre, Ibn Battuta Mall, Lamcy Plaza, Mall of the Emirates, Mercato, Mirdif City Centre, The Dubai Mall

Nike Al Ghurair Centre, Arabian Centre, BurJuman, Dubai Marina Mall, Dubai Marina Mall, Dubai Outlet Mall, Festival Centre, Ibn Battuta Mall, Mall of the Emirates, Mercato, Mirdif City Centre, Oasis Centre, The Dubai Mall, Uptown Mirdif

Nine West Al Ghurair Centre, Arabian Centre, BurJuman, Deira City Centre, Dubai Marina Mall, Dubai Outlet Mall, Festival Centre, Ibn Battuta Mall, Lamcy Plaza, Mall of the Emirates, Mercato, Mirdif City Centre, Reef Mall, The Dubai Mall, Uptown Mirdif

Noa Noa Mercato, Mirdif City Centre

Novo Dubai Marina Mall, The Dubai Mall

Nutrition Zone Ibn Battuta Mall, The Dubai Mall, Town Centre Jumeirah

Oasis Deira City Centre, Ibn Battuta Mall, Mall of the Emirates, Mirdif City Centre, The Dubai Mall

Okaidi Deira City Centre, Dubai Marina Mall, Festival Centre, Mall of the Emirates, Mirdif City Centre, The Dubai Mall

Omega Al Ghurair Centre, BurJuman, Deira City Centre, Festival Centre, Grosvenor House, Jumeirah Emirates Towers, Mall of the Emirates, Mercato, Mirdif City Centre, One&Only Royal Mirage, Souk Madinat Jumeirah, The Dubai Mall

Omega Boutique Wafi

THE One BurJuman, Dubai Outlet Mall, Jumeira 1 (Jumeira Theatre & Deli, Jumeira Rd), Mall of the Emirates, Wafi

Opera BurJuman

Opera Shoes Mall of the Emirates, The Dubai Mall, Wafi

Optifashion Mirdif City Centre, The Dubai Mall

OptiVision Al Khaleej Centre, BurJuman, Deira City Centre, Dubai Outlet Mall, Festival Centre, Mall of the Emirates, Mirdif City Centre, Palm Strip, The Dubai Mall

Organic Foods & Cafe The Greens (Emaar Business Park 2), Sheikh Zayed Rd and Village Mall (opening 2013)

Oriental Stores Al Khaleej Centre, Bur Dubai (Al Khor), Deira City Centre, Dubai Festival City, Ibn Battuta Mall, Jumeirah Centre, Mall of the Emirates, Mirdif City Centre, Deira (Al Sabkha)

Osh Kosh B'gosh Deira City Centre, Mall of the Emirates, The Dubai Mall

Oysho Festival Centre, Mall of the Emirates, Mirdif City Centre, The Dubai Mall

Pablosky Deira City Centre, Mall of the Emirates, Mirdif City Centre, The Dubai Mall

Pairs Deira City Centre, Mall of the Emirates, The Dubai Mall

Pal Zileri BurJuman, Deira, Mall of the Emirates, Mirdif City Centre, The Dubai Mall

Pan Emirates Ibn Battuta Mall, Al Barsha 1 (Nr Mall of the Emirates, Umm Suqeim Rd

Papermoon Town Centre Jumeirah

Paris Gallery Al Bustan Centre & Residence, Al Ghurair Centre, Arabian Centre, Burj Al Arab, BurJuman, Deira City Centre, Festival Centre, Hamarain Centre, Ibn Battuta Mall, Lamcy Plaza, The Dubai Mall, Town Centre Jumeirah, Wafi

Park n Shop Tecom (Al Shaffar Bldg), Jumeirah Lakes Towers (Al Shera Tower), Al Safa 1 (Al Wasl Rd)

Paspaley Atlantis The Palm, BurJuman, Mall of the Emirates, The Dubai Mall

Passion Arabian Centre, Lamcy Plaza

Patrizia Pepe Dubai Marina Mall, The Dubai Mall

Paul & Shark Dubai Marina Mall, Mall of the Emirates, The Dubai Mall

Paul & Shark Boutique BurJuman

Paul Smith BurJuman, Mall of the Emirates, The Dubai Mall

Peacocks Ibn Battuta Mall

Peak Performance Mall of the Emirates

Pepe Jeans BurJuman, Mall of the Emirates

Persian Carpet House Festival Centre, Jumeirah Beach Hotel, Le Royal Meridien Beach Resort & Spa, Mall of the Emirates, One&Only Royal Mirage, Souk Madinat Jumeirah, The Boulevard At Jumeirah Emirates Towers

Pet's Delight Arabian Ranches Centre, Emirates Hills, Mirdif (Nr Uptown Mirdif Park)

PH8 Dubai Marina Mall, Mirdif City Centre

Phat Farm Mall of the Emirates

Pierre Cardin BurJuman, Deira City Centre, Dubai Outlet Mall, Festival Centre, Ibn Battuta Mall, Mirdif City Centre, The Dubai Mall, Wafi

Pinky Furniture Al Barsha 1 (Nr Dubai American Academy)

Planet Nutrition Deira City Centre, Dubai Healthcare City, Dubai Marina Mall, Ibn Battuta Mall, Dubai Mall

Plug-Ins Al Ghurair Centre, Festival Centre, Mall of the Emirates, The Dubai Mall

PlusIT Ibn Battuta Mall

Porsche Design Atlantis The Palm, Dubai Airport, Mall of the Emirates, The Dubai Mall

Porsche Design SiS Mirdif City Centre

Pottery Barn Mirdif City Centre, The Dubai Mall

Pottery Barn Kids Mirdif City Centre, The Dubai Mall

Prada BurJuman, Mall of the Emirates

Premaman Arabian Centre, The Dubai Mall, Uptown Mirdif

Pride Of Kashmir Al Quoz (Interchange 4), Festival Centre, Grand Hyatt Dubai, Mall of the Emirates, Souk Al Bahar, Souk Madinat Jumeirah

Prima Gold Al Ghurair Centre, Burj Al Arab, BurJuman, Deira City Centre, Festival Centre, Gold Souk, Taj Palace Hotel Apartments, The Dubai Mall, The Westin Dubai Mina Seyahi Beach Resort & Marina

Prima Gold Jewellers Mall of the Emirates

Promod BurJuman, Deira City Centre, Dubai Marina Mall, Mall of the Emirates, Mercato, Mirdif City Centre, The Dubai Mall

Pull & Bear Deira City Centre, Mall of the Emirates, Mercato, Mirdif City Centre, The Dubai Mall

Puma Deira City Centre, Dubai Outlet Mall, Mirdif City Centre, The Dubai Mall

Pumpkin Patch Arabian Centre, Dubai Outlet Mall, Mall of the Emirates, Mirdif City Centre, The Dubai Mall, Uptown Mirdif

Pure Gold Al Fahidi Market, Al Souk Al Kabeer (Nr Emirates NBD), Al Ras (Nr Gold Souk Bus Station), Deira (Gold Center Bldg), Dragon Mart, Festival Centre, Gold Souk, Ibn Battuta Mall, Karama Complex, Mall of the Emirates, Mercato, Mirdif City Centre, Souk Madinat Jumeirah, The Dubai Mall

Pure Gold Jewellers Deira City Centre, Wafi

Q Home Decor Dubai Marina Mall, Mirdif City Centre, Oasis Centre, The Dubai Mall

Quiksilver Dubai Marina Mall, Festival Centre, Mall of the Emirates, The Dubai Mall

Rage Mall of the Emirates, The Dubai Mall

Ralph Lauren Bloomingdale's, BurJuman, Harvey Nichols, Mall of the Emirates, The Dubai Mall

Rasasi Al Manal Centre, Deira City Centre, Dubai Festival City

Rasasi Perfumes Arabian Centre, BurJuman, Festival Centre, Mall of the Emirates, Mirdif City Centre

The Raymond Shop Al Qusais, Bur Dubai (Abdulla Ibrahim Al Baker Bldg, Meena Bazaar), Deira (Nr Fish R/A), Karama Complex, Oud Metha (Nr Lamcy Plaza), Umm Hurair (Shop No 1, Zabeel Rd)

Raymond Weil Al Bustan Centre, Al Raffa (Al Futtaim Watches & Jewellery, Jhalid Bin Al Waleed), Al Nasr Square, BurJuman, Deira City Centre, Lamcy Plaza

Red Earth Bin Sougat Centre, Ibn Battuta Mall

Redtag Al Ghurair Centre, Al Wasl (Union Co-operative Society, Nr Shangri-la), Arabian Centre, Century Mall, Ibn Battuta Mall

Regal Textiles Al Bada'a, Al Satwa (Next to Al Maya Lal's Supermarket), Al Karama (Opp Al Attar Centre) Bur Dubai (Al Fahidi St), Bur Dubai (Cosmos Lane, Meena Bazaar), Bur Dubai (Murshid Bazaar)

Reina The Dubai Mall, The Village

Reiss Dubai Marina Mall, Galeries Lafayette, Mall of the Emirates, Mirdif City Centre, The Dubai Mall

Ride Bike Shop Al Quoz 1 (Nr Oasis Center, Shk Zayed Rd),Mirdif City Centre

River Island Deira City Centre, Ibn Battuta Mall, Mall of the Emirates, The Dubai Mall

Rivoli Arabian Centre, Atlantis The Palm, Deira City Centre, Dubai International Financial Centre (DIFC), Dubai Marina Mall, Festival Centre, Ibn Battuta Mall, (Jebel Ali Hotel), Jumeirah Beach Hotel, Jumeirah Centre, Lamcy Plaza, Mall of the Emirates, Mercato, Mirdif City Centre, Souk Madinat Jumeirah, Sunset Mall, The Dubai Mall, The H Hotel Dubai, The Westin Dubai Mina Seyahi Beach Resort & Marina, Wafi

Rivoli Arcade Dusit Thani Dubai, Grosvenor House, Jumeirah Emirates Towers, Movenpick Hotel Deira, Mövenpick Hotel Ibn Battuta Gate, One&Only Royal Mirage, Park Hyatt Dubai, The Address Downtown Dubai, The Address Dubai Marina

Rivoli Prestige Al Qasr, Burj Al Arab, BurJuman, Deira City Centre, Jumeirah Emirates Towers, Jumeirah Zabeel Saray, Mall of the Emirates

Rivoli Textiles Al Karama (Zabeel Rd), Satwa

Rivoli Textiles LLC Dubai Marina (Opp Marina Hotel Apartments)

Roberto Cavalli Mall of the Emirates, The Dubai Mall, Wafi

Rocco Barocco Dubai Marina Mall, The Dubai Mall

Rodeo Drive Al Bustan Rotana, Atlantis The Palm, Burj Al Arab, BurJuman, Dubai Outlet Mall, Festival Centre, Galleria Shopping Mall, Grand Hyatt Dubai, Grosvenor House, Holiday Centre Mall, Jumeirah Beach Hotel, Mall of the Emirates, Souk Madinat Jumeirah, The Boulevard At Jumeirah Emirates Towers, The Dubai Mall

Rolex Al Rigga (Twin Towers), Ahmed Seddiqi & Sons, BurJuman, (Capricorn Tower, Shk Zayed Rd), Deira City Centre, Grand Hyatt Dubai, Madinat Jumeirah, Mall of the Emirates, (Souk Murshid), The Dubai Mall, Wafi

Rossini Festival Centre, Wafi

Rossini Shoes Mercato

Roxy Dubai Marina Mall, Festival Centre, Mall of the Emirates, The Dubai Mall

Royal Gardenscape Al Quoz Industrial 4 (Nr Enoc Station & National Paints), Uptown Mirdif

Rugland Dubai Outlet Mall, Festival Centre, Lamcy Plaza

S*uce Bastakiya, Jumeirah Centre, Bastakiya, The Dubai Mall, The Village, Wasl Square

Sacoche Ibn Battuta Mall, Wafi

Sacoor Brothers Deira City Centre, Dubai Marina Mall, Dubai Outlet Mall, Festival Centre, Ibn Battuta Mall, Mall of the Emirates, Mirdif City Centre, The Dubai Mall

Sadek Music Deira (Burj Nahar, Nr Claridge Hotel), Ibn Battuta Mall, Souk Madinat Jumeirah, The Dubai Mall

Saks Fifth Avenue BurJuman

Salsa BurJuman, Deira City Centre, Festival Centre, Mall of the Emirates, The Dubai Mall

Salvatore Ferragamo Mall of the Emirates, The Dubai Mall

Samsonite BurJuman, Deira City Centre, Dubai Festival City, Dubai Outlet Mall, Mall of the Emirates, The Dubai Mall

Sana Fashion Abu Hail, Al Karama (Sheikh Rashid Rd)

Sanrio Al Barsha Mall, Bin Sougat Centre, Deira City Centre, Ibn Battuta Mall, Mercato, Mirdif City Centre, The Dubai Mall, Times Square

Scarabée Souk Madinat Jumeirah, Wafi

Sedar Al Bada'a (Al Diyafah Rd), Al Muraqqabat (Muraqqabat Rd), Al Quoz 3 (Shk Zayed Rd)

Sephora Deira City Centre, Dubai Marina Mall, Festival Centre, Mall of the Emirates, The Dubai Mall

Sharaf DG Al Mankhool (Al Gadhir Bldg, Mankhool St, Al Raffa), Al Wasl (Union Co-operative Society), Arabian Centre, Bur Dubai (Meena Bazaar, Al Fahidi St), Deira City Centre, Dubai Marina Mall, Deira (Gargash Centre, Al Nasser Square), Ibn Battuta Mall, The Dubai Mall, Times Square

Shoe Citi Arabian Centre, Deira City Centre, Dubai Outlet Mall, Mall of the Emirates, Uptown Mirdif

Shoe Mart Abu Hail (Nr Ministry of Youth & Sport, Al Quds St), Arabian Centre, Al Karama (CentrePoint), Bur Dubai (Nr Jumbo Showroom), Deira City Centre, Ibn Battuta Mall, Lamcy Plaza, Mall of the Emirates, Oasis Centre, Reef Mall, The Dubai Mall

Shoexpress Al Ghurair Centre, Ibn Battuta Mall, Mirdif City Centre, Oasis Centre

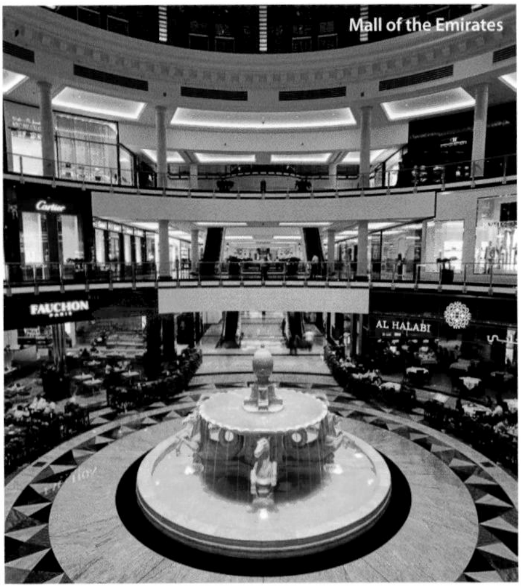

Mall of the Emirates

Singways The Walk, Jumeirah Beach Residence

Singways/Maison Decor Mall of the Emirates

Skechers BurJuman, Dubai Outlet Mall, Festival Centre, Ibn Battuta Mall, The Dubai Mall

Smash Festival Centre, Ibn Battuta Mall

Solaris Arabian Centre, Deira City Centre, Ibn Battuta Mall, Mall of the Emirates, Mercato, The Dubai Mall

Spinneys Al Ghurair Centre, Al Mankhool (Al Mankhool Rd, Nr Ramada Hotel), Al Mankhool (Nr Centrepoint), Al Safa 2 (Nr Umm Al Sheif Rd & Al Wasl Rd), Bin Sougat Centre, Business Bay (Business Bay Executive Towers), Dubai Marina (Marina Walk), Dubai MotorCity (Foxhill Bldg), Dubai Silicon Oasis (Silicon Mall Rd), Emirates Living (The Springs), Green Community (Souk Extra Ewan Residence), Ghusais 2 (Damascus St), Jumeira 1 (Jumeira Rd, Nr Jumeira Mosque), Mercato, Al Mamzar (The Square), Uptown Mirdif

Spinneys Market Al Barsha 2 (Souk Extra), Al Hudaiba (Al Mina Rd), Downtown Dubai (Emaar Residence), Downtown Dubai (Nr Al Manzil Hotel), Dubai Festival City (Nr American Universal School), Dubai Silicon Oasis, Emirates Living (1st Road, Meadows, Emirates Hills), Green Community, Ghusais 1, International City (France Cluster), Jumeirah Lakes Towers, Mirdif (Mirdiff Community Centre), Oud Metha (Nr Lamcy Plaza), Souk Al Bahar, Downtown Dubai (South Ridge)

Splash Al Karama, Al Bustan Centre & Residence, Al Ghurair Centre, Arabian Centre, Deira City Centre,

Dubai Outlet Mall, Ibn Battuta Mall, Mall of the Emirates, Mirdif City Centre, Reef Mall, The Dubai Mall

Spring Al Ghurair Centre, Arabian Centre, Festival Centre, Ibn Battuta Mall, Mall of the Emirates, Mirdif City Centre, Reef Mall, The Dubai Mall

Springfield Deira City Centre, Dubai Marina Mall, Festival Centre, Lamcy Plaza, Oasis Centre, The Dubai Mall

Stadium Deira City Centre, Dubai Marina Mall, The Dubai Mall

Steve Madden Arabian Centre, Mall of the Emirates, The Dubai Mall

Stradivarius Deira City Centre, Festival Centre, Mall of the Emirates, Mirdif City Centre, The Dubai Mall

Strandbags Ibn Battuta Mall, The Dubai Mall

Studio R BurJuman, Dubai Outlet Mall, Ibn Battuta Mall

Style Studio Arabian Centre, Lamcy Plaza, Oasis Centre, Reef Mall

The Sultani Lifestyle Gallerie Bur Dubai Festival Centre, Souk Al Bahar, The Dubai Mall

Sun & Sand Sports Ibn Battuta Mall

Sunglass Hut BurJuman, Deira City Centre, Dubai Outlet Mall**,** Mall of the Emirates

Superdry Deira City Centre, Mall of the Emirates, The Dubai Mall

Susan Walpole Armani Hotel Dubai, Atlantis The Palm, Dubai Duty Free, Dubai Marine Beach Resort & Spa, Dusit Thani Dubai, Jumeira Plaza, Mövenpick Hotel Ibn Battuta Gate, One&Only Royal Mirage, The Address Downtown Dubai, The Address Dubai Marina

Swarovski Al Ghurair Centre, BurJuman, Deira City Centre, Festival Centre, Ibn Battuta Mall, Mall of the Emirates, The Dubai Mall, Wafi

Swatch Al Ghurair Centre, Deira City Centre, Dubai Marina Mall, Festival Centre, Ibn Battuta Mall, Mall of the Emirates, Mirdif City Centre, Souk Madinat Jumeirah, The Dubai Mall, Wafi

Tag Heuer Al Ghurair Centre, Atlantis The Palm, BurJuman, Dubai Marina Mall, Festival Centre, Grosvenor House, Le Royal Meridien Beach Resort & Spa, Mall of the Emirates, Mirdif City Centre, Sunset Mall, The Dubai Mall, Wafi

Tanagra BurJuman, Deira City Centre, Mall of the Emirates, Wafi

Tavola Century Plaza, Emirates Living (Town Centre, Meadows), Mall of the Emirates, Mercato, Mirdif City Centre, Spinneys Centre (Al Wasl Rd), The Dubai Mall

Tchibo Dubai Outlet Malll, Ibn Battuta Mall, Mirdif City Centree, Oasis Centre, Uptown Mirdif

Ted Baker BurJuman, Deira City Centre, Dubai Marina Mall, Festival Centre, The Dubai Mall

Ted Lapidus BurJuman, Deira City Centre, Dubai Outlet Mall, Festival Centre, Ibn Battuta Mall, Lamcy Plaza, Mall of the Emirates, Mirdif City Centre, Wafi

Tehran Carpet House Souk Al Bahar

Tejori Gems Dubai Marine Beach Resort & Spa, Festival Centre, Gold & Diamond Park, Souk Madinat Jumeirah, The Dubai Mall

Thomsun Music Deira (Fish Roundabout), Deira (Sabkha Rd), Deira (Salahuddin St), Festival City, Ibn Battuta Mall, Mall of the Emirates, Mirdif City Centre, The Dubai Mall, Wafi

Tiffany & Co. Atlantis The Palm, BurJuman, Mall of the Emirates, The Dubai Mall

Timberland Arabian Centre, Dubai Outlet Mall, Ibn Battuta Mall, Mall of the Emirates, The Dubai Mall

Tod's BurJuman, Mall of the Emirates, The Dubai Mall

Tommy Hilfiger Al Ghurair Centre, BurJuman, Deira City Centre, Dubai Marina Mall, Dubai Outlet Mall, Festival Centre, Ibn Battuta Mall, Lamcy Plaza, Mall of the Emirates, Mercato, Mirdif City Centre, Oasis Centre, The Dubai Mall, Wafi

Topman Ibn Battuta Mall, Mall of the Emirates, Mirdif City Centre, The Dubai Mall

Topshop Ibn Battuta Mall, Mall of the Emirates, Mercato, Mirdif City Centre, The Dubai Mall

The Toy Store Al Ghurair Centre, Deira City Centre, Dubai Marina Mall, Ibn Battuta Mall, Mall of the Emirates, Mercato

Toys R Us Deira City Centre, Festival Centre, Times Square

Triumph Arabian Centre, Deira City Centre, Mercato

Tru Trussardi BurJuman, The Dubai Mall

Union Co-operative Society Al Barsha Mall, Al Mankhool (Shk Khalifa Bin Zayed Rd, Nr Sana Fashions Bldg), Al Rashidiya (Nr Rashidiya Police Station), Al Satwa (Satwa R/A, Nr Rydges Plaza), Al Twar (Al Nahda Rd), Al Wasl (Al Wasl Rd, Nr Safa Park), Al Wasl (Nr Shangri-la Hotel), Etihad Mall, Hor Al Anz East (Abu Hail Rd), Ras Al Khor (inside veg and fruit market),

United Colors Of Benetton Deira City Centre, Jumeirah Centre, Mall of the Emirates, The Dubai Mall

United Furniture Al Karama (Nr College of Islamic & Arabic Studies, Zabeel Rd), Al Quoz 3 (Nr Toyota Showroom & Oasis Centre, Sheikh Zayed Rd)

Valencia Deira City Centre, Mall of the Emirates, Oasis Centre, The Dubai Mall

Valentino BurJuman, The Dubai Mall

Valleydez Sunset Mall, Wafi

Vero Moda Festival Centre, Mall of the Emirates, Mirdif City Centre, The Dubai Mall

Versace BurJuman, Mall of the Emirates, The Dubai Mall, Wafi

Vertu BurJuman, Dubai Duty Free, Festival Centre, Grand Hyatt Dubai, Jumeirah Beach Hotel, Mall of the Emirates, The Boulevard At Jumeirah Emirates Towers, Trade Centre 2 (Rivoli Arcade, DIFC), The Dubai Mall, Wafi

Victoria's Secret Mall of the Emirates, Mirdif City Centre, The Dubai Mall

Vilebrequin Mall of the Emirates, Souk Madinat Jumeirah

Villeroy & Boch BurJuman, Deira City Centre, Dubai Outlet Mall, Mall of the Emirates, The Dubai Mall, Wafi

Vincci BurJuman, Deira City Centre, The Dubai Mall

Virgin Megastore BurJuman, Deira City Centre, Mall of the Emirates, Mercato, Mirdif City Centre, The Dubai Mall

Vision Express Arabian Centre, Dubai Marina Mall, Ibn Battuta Mall, Mall of the Emirates, Mirdif City Centre, The Dubai Mall

Wafi Gourmet The Dubai Mall, Wafi

Waitrose Dubai Marina Mall, The Dubai Mall

Wallis Arabian Centre, Ibn Battuta Mall, Mirdif City Centre, The Dubai Mall

The Watch House Arabian Centre, BurJuman, Deira, Festival Centre, Lamcy Plaza, Mall of the Emirates, The Dubai Mall

Whistles Mall of the Emirates

The White Company Deira City Centre, Festival Centre, Mall of the Emirates, Mirdif City Centre, The Dubai Mall, Wafi

Wizz Deira City Centre, Festival Centre, Ibn Battuta Mall, Mall of the Emirates, The Dubai Mall

Women'secret Deira City Centre, Festival Centre, Mirdif City Centre, The Dubai Mall

Woolworths Deira City Centre, Ibn Battuta Mall

XOXO The Dubai Mall

Yamamay Dubai Marina Mall, Mirdif City Centre, The Dubai Mall

Yas The Royal Name Of Perfumes Festival Centre, Ibn Battuta Mall, Mirdif City Centre, The Dubai Mall, Wafi

Yateem Optician Al Ghurair Centre, Al Souk Al Kabeer (Al Fahidi), Al Bada'a (2nd December St), Arabian Centre, Atlantis The Palm, BurJuman, Mall of the Emirates, Mirdif City Centre, Lamcy Plaza, Souk Madinat Jumeirah, The Beach Centre, The Boulevard At Jumeirah Emirates Towers, The Dubai Mall

Yellow Hat Nad Al Hamar (Nr Emarat Petrol Station), Times Square

Zak Electronics & Musical Instruments Al Karama (Nr Al Karama General Post Office), BurJuman, Deira (Nr Muraqabbat Police Station)

Zara BurJuman, Deira City Centre, Mall of the Emirates, Mirdif City Centre, The Dubai Mall

Zara Home Deira City Centre, Mall of the Emirates, Palm Strip, The Dubai Mall, The Walk at Jumeirah Beach Residence

Zawya Abu Hail (Al Zafrana Bldg), International City (Central Business District), Discovery Gardens (Zen 4, Bldg 19), Sheikh Zayed Rd (Al Manara St)

Going Out

GOING OUT

Dubai's gastronomic landscape is expansive. At one end of the spectrum, celebrity chefs, picturesque cocktail lounges and mammoth clubs compete for your hard-earned dirhams. At the other end, bargain ethnic eateries, drink-deal bars and plenty of bang-for-your-buck brunches are there to help at the end of the month. Dubai's social scene revolves around club nights, raucous brunches and laid-back shisha cafes, so expect to go out more than you ever did back home.

Dressing Up

Generally speaking, shorts and T-shirts are a no-no for Dubai's posher bars and restaurants, and even some pubs will frown at your beach-bum attire. While trainers aren't strictly outlawed it will depend on the whole ensemble, and many places don't let you in wearing filp-flops – even if they're nice ones. Dubai's dress code is on the smarter side – more beautiful than bohemian – so shine your shoes when you're stepping out.

Thursday and Friday nights are the big ones, with reservations required in the restaurants and international DJs packing out the clubs. During the week, you'll find drinks deals across the city and all manner of dining promotions, so the town is still buzzing. Since alcohol can only be served in hotels and sports clubs, chances are you won't have a 'local' on the corner. Instead, you might have a roster of four or five favourites within a 10 minute taxi drive. Most of the city's most popular restaurants are located in hotels for the same reason – but don't let the absence of a wine list deter you from exploring the many outstanding independent restaurants that Dubai has to offer.

The live entertainment scene lags behind other cities, but with the opening of new theatres and venues, and more big names such as Kanye and Kylie being lured over to perform, it is improving all the time.

Opening Hours

In general, cafes and restaurants close between 23:00 and 01:00, with bars and nightclubs split between those that close 'early' at 01:00 and those that go on until 03:00. The legal drinking age is 21, and it's best to avoid getting staggeringly drunk as it may land you behind bars. Most importantly, don't even think about getting behind the wheel of a car after drinking – Dubai maintains a strict zero tolerance stance on drink driving. Respect the laws and you'll have nothing to worry about – apart from your dwindling finances. Dubai certainly knows how to throw a party so don't forget your glad rags because over-the-top is par for the course in this town.

Ramadan Timings

During Ramadan, opening and closing times of restaurants change considerably. Because eating and drinking in public is forbidden during daylight hours, many places only open after sunset then keep going well into the early hours. Restaurants in some hotels remain open, but will be screened off from public view. Live entertainment is not allowed, so while some nightclubs remain open, all dancefloors are closed.

EATING OUT

Many of Dubai's most popular restaurants are located within hotels and leisure clubs, and their popularity is partly down to the fact that these are virtually the only outlets where you can drink alcohol with your meal. Almost all other restaurants are unlicensed. If you're the type who requires a glass of vino to make a meal complete, it's best to phone ahead to check whether the establishment serves alcohol. There's quite a hefty mark-up on drinks, with a decent bottle of wine often costing as much as your meal.

The city has some superb independent restaurants and cafes in areas such as Satwa and along Jumeira Road, offering a choice of mocktails or vast tea menus in the absence of alcohol.

Bottled water also seems to rocket in price in the five-star venues, and if you ask for water you'll often be given an imported brand, costing up to Dhs.40 a bottle. You should specify 'local' water when ordering, but even then you can expect to pay Dhs.10 or Dhs.20 for a bottle of water that costs less than Dhs.2 in the supermarket.

The Yellow Star

This yellow star highlights places that merit extra praise. It might be the atmosphere, the food, the cocktails, the music or the crowd, but any review that you see with the star attached is sure to be for somewhere that's a bit special.

Hygiene

Food and drink outlets are subject to regular checks by Dubai Municipality, and unclean outlets are warned to either scrub up or shut down. You can be fairly confident that restaurants within hotels and most independent restaurants meet basic health and hygiene requirements.

The city isn't immune to the odd food poisoning incident, however, so if a place looks like it might have some hygiene issues, it's best to avoid it. If you feel a restaurant you have visited could use an inspection, you can call the Municipality Food Control Department (800 900).

Food Allergies

If you suffer from any food allergies then do take extra care when eating out in Dubai's restaurants. The situation is improving, especially at some of the more ingredient-savvy eateries like MORE Cafe (04 323 4350) or Baker & Spice (p.493), for example. However, a lack of clearly-marked menus, and a serving culture that is trained to tell customers what they think they want to hear, can combine to form a dangerous scenario. Don't hesitate to inform servers about the severity of your allergies if you don't think they are catching the drift of your questioning.

Taxes & Service Charges

Look out for the small print at the bottom of your menu and you may spot the dreaded 'prices are subject to 10% service charge and 10% municipality tax'. In most hotel restaurants and bars, these extras are already included, but in an independent outlet they may appear as an additional charge. The 10% service charge is perhaps incorrectly named as often it isn't passed on to the staff, and you have no option of withholding it if you receive poor service. If you want to reward the waiting staff directly then the standard rule of a 10-12.5% tip will be appreciated, but give them cash if you can, or your tip may go straight into the till.

Vegetarian Food

Vegetarians should be pleasantly surprised by the variety available to them in Dubai's restaurants. Dubai is home to a large population from the subcontinent who are vegetarian by religion, and numerous Indian restaurants offer a range of cooking styles and tasty vegetarian dishes. Try Saravana Bhavan (p.535) and Aryaas (p.492) in Karama. In other restaurants (even in steakhouses), you'll often find at least one or two vegetarian options. Arabic cuisine, although heavy on meat-based mains, offers a great range of mezze that are mostly vegetarian.

Dubai's cafes are also great for adventurous and tasty vegetarian food. Of particular note are The Lime Tree Cafe & Kitchen (p.519), THE One (p.528), 1762 (p.484) and the Organic Foods and Cafe (p.417). For a special occasion, the extravagant Celebrities (p.499) offers fine dining and a completely separate vegetarian menu.

A word of warning: if you are a strict veggie, confirm that your meal is completely meat free. Some restaurants cook their 'vegetarian' selection with animal fat or on the same grill as the meat dishes. Also, in some places you may need to check the ingredients of the vegetarian items before ordering.

Cultural Meals

Bastakiya is a great place to eat while soaking up local culture. This traditional part of the city is best experienced by strolling through the streets, visiting the museums and dining at one of the many cafes. A cultural and culinary experience rolled into one.

Street Food

Shawarma is a popular local snack consisting of rolled pita bread filled with lamb or chicken carved from a rotating spit, vegetables and tahina sauce. You'll see countless roadside stands offering shawarma for as little as Dhs.3 each, and they make a great alternative to the usual fast-food staples. In residential areas, the small cluster of shops beside a mosque is often a good bet to find your local shawarma outlet. These cafes and stands usually sell other dishes, such as falafel (or ta'amiya), which are small savoury balls of deep-fried chickpeas, also sold separately or in a pita bread sandwich. Many offer freshly squeezed fruit juices for around Dhs.10. For a really unique version, check out Al Shera'a Fisheries Centre on Al Muraqqabat Road (04 227 1803) – the only place in town that offers fish shawarmas.

The Department of Tourism & Commerce Marketing works closely with the Emirates Culinary Guild and a few chefs to revive Emirati cuisine in Dubai. Truly local food has several distinct flavors, thanks to the country's trading past. Look out for tangs of cinnamon, saffron and turmeric along with nuts (almonds or pistachios), limes and dried fruit.

Independent Restaurants

While hotel restaurants tend to draw in the crowds, especially at the weekend, Dubai's independent choices are not to be missed. Areas like Oud Metha, Karama and the Jumeira strip are home to restaurants serving everything from authentic Arabic kebabs (Al Mallah, p.488) and tempting pad thai (Lemongrass, p.519) to crispy Peking duck (Lan Kwai Fong, p.518) and fiery Pakistani curry (Karachi Darbar, p.514). The point-and-cook concept restaurant China Sea is up with Dubai's very best eateries, while the back-to-basics curries at Ravi's have made it a Dubai institution. Whether you pop in for a hearty lunch or have a teetotal evening, you shouldn't ignore the affordable, culinary delights of these independents.

NIGHTLIFE

Bars, Pubs & Clubs

You can't expect authenticity from Dubai's pubs, but then when they're mostly in hotels, in the desert, in the Middle East, that shouldn't come as too much of a surprise. What you can look forward to is some inviting, friendly spots with a decent selection of draught and bottled beers, and reliably good bar grub. Many of these mostly English and Irish places are popular when there's a big game on. And they're all comfortable, raucous and smoky enough to feel like the real thing.

Cinemas

There are a number of cinemas around Dubai – many of them situated in shopping malls. The biggest cinemas include a 22-screen outlet in The Dubai Mall (Reel Cinemas), a 14-screen multiplex including VIP theatres at Mall of the Emirates (VOX Cinemas) and a 21-screen cinema at Ibn Battuta Shopping Mall (Grand Megaplex) – the latter has the region's first IMAX screen. There is also an IMAX theatre at Meydan in Nad al Sheba. New VOX Cinemas are due to open at Mercato and BurJuman. Aside from The Dubai Mall, which has an arthouse cinema called The Picturehouse, Dubai tends to show mainly mainstream films with multiple screenings.

Sporting Life

The glitz and glamour of Dubai's bars is all very well, but sometimes you just want a joint where you can catch the big match and enjoy a pint with your mates. These venues are recommended for supping and spectating: Champs (p.554), Boston Bar (p.552), Champions (04 607 7977), Double Decker (p.556), Girders (p.556), Nezesaussi (p.561), The Underground (p.565), The Locker Room (04 341 7750) and 25°55° Cafe Bistro (04 362 7900).

The Scene Club is a monthly film club that screens international independent films, followed by a Q&A with the director or producer (thesceneclub.com).

There are cinema annoyances – freezing air conditioning, people chatting to each other or talking on their mobile phones, and the heavy hand of the censor can all affect your experience. Also, the sound quality can be a little off and Arabic (as well as often French) subtitles cover the bottom of the screen. Grand Cinemas has addressed one problem by banning children under five years from attending screenings after 7pm.

A cinematic highlight is the Dubai International Film Festival (p.29) in December, which showcases a mix of mainstream, world and local cinema, from shorts to full features.

Cabana at The Address Dubai Mall

Grand Cinemas
Festival Centre Dubai Festival City **04 232 8523**
grandcinemas.com
Map **2 M9** Metro **Emirates**

Grand Cineplex
Nr Grand Hyatt, Al Garhoud Rd Umm Hurair 2
04 324 2000
Map **2 L8** Metro **Dubai Healthcare City**

Grand Megaplex Cinemas / IMAX
Ibn Battuta Mall The Gardens **04 366 9898**
grandcinemas.com
Map **1 G5** Metro **Ibn Battuta**

Lamcy Cinema
Lamcy Plaza Oud Metha **04 336 8808**
Map **2 K6** Metro **Oud Metha**

Reel Cinemas
The Dubai Mall Downtown Dubai **04 449 1988**
reelcinemas.ae
Map **2 F6** Metro **Burj Khalifa/Dubai Mall**

Reel Cinemas
Dubai Marina Mall Dubai Marina **04 449 1988**
reelcinemas.ae
Map **1 K5** Metro **Jumeirah Lakes Towers**

VOX Cinemas
Mall of the Emirates Al Barsha 1 **04 341 4222**
voxcinemas.com
Map **1 R6** Metro **Mall of the Emirates**

VOX Cinemas
Deira City Centre Port Saeed **04 294 9000**
voxcinemas.com
Map **2 N7** Metro **Deira City Centre**

VOX Cinemas
Mirdif City Centre Mirdif **04 284 0001**
voxcinemas.com
Map **2 P12** Metro **Rashidiya**

Alternative Screenings
While most of the cinema multiplexes only show big Hollywood movies, several bars and clubs put on screenings of older, foreign and independent films, usually early in the week and free of charge. Check out Movies Under The Stars at Wafi (04 324 4100), Movies & Munchies at Desert Palm (04 323 8888), or Poolside Movie Nights at Emirates Golf Club (04 417 9999) and the Dubai Polo and Equestrian Club (04 361 8111).

It is also worth keeping an eye on the local press for details of one-off screenings at some of the city's more progressive art spaces, such as The Jam Jar (p.254) and Shelter (shelter.ae).

Comedy Nights
Comedy nights in Dubai are popular with the expat crowd but events tend to be semi-regular, rather than weekly. The Laughter Factory organises monthly events, with comedians from the UK's Comedy Store coming over to play various venues throughout the Gulf. In Dubai these venues include Zinc (p.566) at the Crowne Plaza, the Mövenpick Hotel at JBR (p.244), and the Grand Millennium at TECOM (p.97). Keep an eye on thelaughterfactory.com for details of future shows.

There are also several one-off events featuring comedians from around the world, as well as local talent; some of these shows are organised by Dubomedy (dubomedy.com). Remember that a lot of comedy is regional, so unless you're familiar with the comedian's country, you might not get the joke.

Concerts & Live Music
Dubai hosts a number of concerts each year, and it seems to be attracting bigger and bigger names. Past acts to play here include J-Lo, Kylie, Robbie Williams, Mariah Carey and Muse. These big name acts usually play at outdoor venues such as the Tennis Stadium, Dubai Autodrome, Dubai Festival City, Dubai World Trade Centre Arena, the amphitheatre at Media City or the Sevens Stadium.

Rock fans enjoyed big acts such as Megadeth and Razorlight at the 2012 Gulf Bike Week, and the Emirates Airline Dubai Jazz Festival goes from strength to strength with performers including The Script, James Morrison, James Blunt, Jools Holland and Macy Gray. Sandance is a hugely popular music festival on Nasimi Beach at Atlantis The Palm, with past acts such as Rita Ora, Ellie Goulding, Stereophonics, Dizzee Rascal, Kaiser Chiefs and Soul II Soul.

In addition to artists at the height of their fame, Dubai also plays host to a string of groups that may be past their prime, but nonetheless provide good entertainment (think Rick Astley, Human League, Tony Hadley, Vanilla Ice and Snap!).

There's also been a recent rise in the number of alternative and slightly lesser-known (basically 'more cool') acts coming over for some sun, including Doves, Groove Armada, 2manydjs, Super Furry Animals and Soulwax.

If you don't mind travelling a bit, Abu Dhabi also attracts some huge names. The past few years have seen performances by Prince, Justin Timberlake, Beyonce, Kings of Leon, The Killers, Coldplay, Madonna and Jonas Brothers. Most of the concerts are held in the gardens of Emirates Palace (p.290) or at Yas Arena (yasisland.ae), next to Ferrari World.

Door Policy
Certain bars and nightclubs have a 'selective' entry policy. Sometimes the 'members only' sign on the entrance needs a bit of explaining. Membership is

usually introduced to control the clientele, but is often only enforced during busy periods. At quieter times, non-members may have no problems getting in. Large groups (especially those consisting of all males), single men and sometimes certain nationalities may be turned away without much of an explanation. You can avoid the inconvenience, and the embarrassment, by breaking the group up or by going in a mixed-gender group.

Some of the city's most popular hot spots, such as 360° (p.550), can be nearly impossible to enter on certain nights unless you're on the guest list. Several of the top clubs maintain electronic guest lists via Platinum List (platinumlist.net); you'll need to register with the website and then sign up for the events you want to attend. Pre-booking a table is another way to ensure entrance into a popular club. Keep in mind that table reservations usually come with a required minimum spend.

Dress Code

While many bars have a reasonably relaxed attitude towards dress code, some places will not allow you in if you are wearing shorts and sandals, while others require a collared shirt and have a 'no jeans or trainers' policy. In general, nightclubs are more strict, so dress to impress.

Under Age

The law in Dubai states that drinkers must be 21 or over. If you're lucky enough to look like you barely remember the 80s, make sure you carry some form of ID that shows your age – a passport or driving licence is best. Even if you think you're flattering your slightly wrinkled self, it's better to be safe than sorry. Otherwise you'll be on lemonade all night or, worse still, left outside alone.

Driving Under The Influence

Drinking and driving is illegal in Dubai. There is zero tolerance; if you are caught with even a hint of alcohol in your system you will be sent to prison. Be responsible and always take a taxi – they're cheap and plentiful – or book Safer Driver (saferdriver.ae) to take you and your car home. For more information on drink driving and the law, see p.134.

Parties At Home

There are several companies in Dubai that can do all the cooking, decorating and cleaning up for you, leaving you with more time to concentrate on your witty after-dinner anecdotes. All of the companies listed offer a complete service from event organisation to the hiring of performers and equipment rental. For a novel outdoor party idea, you can get your own shawarma stand set up in the garden, complete with shawarma maker. Several Arabic restaurants provide

Catch a movie

this service, which works out as a very reasonable and easy way to sustain hordes of party guests.

Also many popular Indian restaurants (such as Open House, p.464) offer catering services at great prices. You can order off the menu and specify the number of guests (although the general rule is reduce it by a few unless you want to be eating curry for a week). In addition to the specialist catering companies, many hotels and restaurants have catering departments. At times of year like Christmas or Thanksgiving, for example, most hotels offer packages that cover eveything from the turkey and the nut roast to all the trimmings.

Caterers

Depending on what you require, caterers can provide just the food or everything from crockery, napkins, tables and chairs to waiters, doormen and a clearing up service.

Cheeky Little Events

Specialises in parties for children, from babies through to teenagers, although hen parties or baby showers are just as doable. Not only looks after the catering, but the entertainment and decorations too.
Various locations **04 451 7201**
cheekylittleevents.com

ChoCo'a
ChoCo'a chefs offer a selection of cakes, pastries, Arabic delicacies and individually-designed specialty cakes and chocolate arrangements for birthdays, graduations, anniversaries and weddings.
Nr Mall of the Emirates Al Barsha 1 **04 340 9092**
chocoa.ae
Map **1 R6** Metro **Mall of the Emirates**

Decorative Cakes
Perfect for kids' parties, weddings or just about any event that requires a cake, this company can create an edible masterpiece in any design you ask of them.
Various locations **050 594 6708**
decorativecakes.piczo.com

Dish Catering & Events
With a promise to deliver 'food that steals the show', Dish caters modern cuisine for functions ranging from 20 to 700 people.
04 422 1613 dish.ae

Dubaipartyqueen
From corporate shindigs to money-no-object weddings, this company can arrange parties for all occasions and age groups.
dubaipartyqueen.com

Flying Elephant
Offers everything from entertainment for kids' parties to theme decorations and catering.
Sheikh Zayed Road Al Quoz **800 383 687**
flyingelephantuae.com
Map **1 U6** Metro **Noor Islamic Bank**

Harlequin Marquees & Event Services
Everything you need for an outdoor event, including marquees, tables, chairs, and even outdoor A/C units.
Nr Spinneys Warehouse Al Quoz Industrial 1
04 347 0110
harlequinmarquees.com
Map **1 U6** Metro **Noor Islamic Bank**

Indigo Entertainment
Offers an array of solutions for all private and corporate events, children's parties, holiday camps and family fun days.
City Tower 1 Shk Zayed Rd **04 331 8704**
indigouae.com
Map **2 H5** Metro **Emirates Towers**

Italian Chef At Home
Prepares personalised menus for dinners and lunches, prepared and served in your own home – and the kitchen is always left spotless!
Various locations **04 444 3627**
chefathomedubai.com

Lime Tree Cafe & Kitchen
Lime Tree prepares customised catering for your event, from canapes to full-on gourmet.
Nr Times Square Al Quoz Industrial 1 **04 325 6325**
thelimetreecafe.com

Marta's Kitchen
Specialises in canape-based and buffet style menus, from traditional home-cooked food to the most avant-garde innovative gastronomy.
Swiss Tower Jumeirah Lakes Towers **050 379 8002**
martaskitchen.com
Map **1 L5** Metro **Dubai Marina**

Open House
Catering service providing tasty Indian food, perfect for small to medium-sized parties.
Nr Pyramid Bldg Al Karama **04 396 5481**
Map **2 L5** Metro **Oud Metha**

Procat Catering Services
Large, professional catering outfit that is particularly suited to bigger catering jobs, such as large wedding parties or corporate catering gigs.
Al Khaleej Centre Al Mankhool **04 885 9990**
profms.com
Map **2 L4** Metro **BurJuman**

Safer Driver
If you've enjoyed a few drinks with dinner then leave the car and contact Safer Driver. You'll be breaking the law if you drive after even one drink, but this clever service means you avoid that and the hassle of picking up the car in the morning. Simply call 04 268 8797 with your location and the time you wish to be picked up. A driver will come to take you and your car home then be on his merry way.

Sandwich Express
Catering service specialising in sandwiches and salads.
Al Kawakeb Bldg, Shk Zayed Rd Trade Centre 2
04 343 9922
sandwichexpress.ae
Map **2 G6** Metro **Financial Centre**

Sweet Connection – The Gluten Free Kitchen
Sweet Connection is dedicated to developing recipes for coeliac disease sufferers and anyone who needs to follow a gluten-free diet: tasty breads, pizzas, cakes, cupcakes and biscuits.
Mayfair Bldg Dubai Investment Park 1 **050 876 3351**
sweetconnectiondubai.com
Map **1 F10** Metro **Jebel Ali**

Dial For Delivery

If the quantity and variety of restaurants in Dubai is astonishing, the number of places that offer takeaway and delivery is mind-blowing. From fastfood joints like Burger King and Subway, through the usual pizzerias, to homecooked specialties and fine-dining, you'll find it all. Fortunately, there are a number of websites that bring them all together – you can choose what type of cuisine you want, find who delivers locally, make your order and, in some cases, even pay online. Try dubai.foodonclick.com, roomservice-uae.com, casseroleonline.com, thesecretchef.me and 24h.ae.

Theatre

The First Group Theatre at Madinat Jumeirah and the theatres at DUCTAC are the city's main performance venues and between them offer a good range of shows from touring blockbuster stage shows to amateur productions. Cirque du Soleil has set up its impressive stage in Dubai each spring for the past few years and is always a big hit. It's also worth keeping an eye on small art spaces like Shelter (shelter.ae) and The Fridge (thefridgedubai.com) for one-off performances. If you don't mind travelling to get your theatre fix, Abu Dhabi National Exhibition Centre (adnec.ae) has hosted large-scale productions such as Lord Of The Dance. If you're keen to tread the boards yourself, check out drama groups (p.335) and acting schools.

Dubai Community Theatre & Arts Centre (DUCTAC)

In addition to rehearsal spaces, workshops, and exhibition halls, the complex features two fully equipped theatres. The Centrepoint Theatre can seat 543 people, while the Kilachand Studio Theatre has a capacity of 196 people. The theatres aim to present a variety of entertainment, from drama, opera and classical music to comedy and children's shows.
Mall of the Emirates, Al Barsha 1 **04 341 4777**
ductac.org
Map **1 R6** Metro **Mall of the Emirates**

First Group Theatre At Madinat Jumeirah

The theatre's 424-seater auditorium has witnessed an impressive list of performances. From 'treading the boards' classics to musicals and innovative comedy shows, make sure you keep your eyes open for what's coming into town next, and chances are you won't be disappointed.
Souk Madinat Jumeirah, Al Sufouh1 **04 366 6546**
madinattheatre.com
Map **1 R4** Metro **Mall of the Emirates**

DUCTAC

RESTAURANTS BY CUISINE

African
Tribes, Mall of the Emirates p.544

Afternoon Tea
Arcadia, The Monarch Dubai p.491
Karat, The Address Dubai Mall p.516
Lobby Lounge, The Ritz-Carlton Dubai p.519
Lobby Lounge & Terrace, The Ritz-Carlton DIFC p.519
Sahn Eddar, Burj Al Arab p.534
Sultan's Lounge, Jumeirah Zabeel Saray p.540

American
Applebee's, Shk Issa Tower, Shk Zayed Rd p.490
Caramel Restaurant & Lounge, DIFC p.499
Chili's, Jumeira Road p.502
Go West, Jumeirah Beach Hotel p.510
Gourmet Burger Kitchen, Mirdif City Centre p.510
Hard Rock Cafe, Festival Centre p.510
Johnny Rockets, Jumeira Rd p.514
Planet Hollywood, Wafi p.530
Plantation, Sofitel Dubai Jumeirah Beach p.530
Ruby Tuesday, The Dubai Mall p.534
Shooters, Jebel Ali International Shooting Club & Centre Of Excellence p.537

Argentinean
Gaucho, Dubai International Financial Centre p.508

Asian
Nomad, Jumeirah Creekside Hotel p.526
White Orchid Lounge, Jebel Ali Golf Resort p.546
Wild Ginger, ICONIC p.546

British
Alfie's, The Boulevard At Jumeirah Emirates Towers p.489
The Ivy, The Boulevard At Jumeirah Emirates Towers p.512
Rhodes Mezzanine, Grosvenor House p.531
Rivington Grill, Souk Al Bahar p.532
Titanic By Marco Pierre White, Melia Dubai p.543

Buffet
Al Muna, Mina A'Salam p.488
The Market Cafe, Grand Hyatt Dubai p.521
The Market Place, JW Marriott Hotel Dubai p.521
Meridien Village Terrace, Le Meridien Dubai p.523
Oceana Restaurant, Hilton Dubai Jumeirah p.526
Senses, Mercure Gold Hotel p.536
Spice Island, Crowne Plaza Dubai Deira p.538

Cafes
1762, DIFC p.484
Armani/Dubai Caffe, The Dubai Mall p.491
Bagels & More, Marina Diamond 3 p.493
Baker & Spice, Souk Al Bahar p.493
Balance Cafe, Oasis Centre p.493
Basta Art Cafe, Bastakiya p.494
Bo House Cafe, The Walk, JBR p.497
CafeM, Media One Hotel p.552
Cafe Ceramique, Town Centre Jumeirah p.498
Cafe Havana, Spinneys Centre p.498
Circle, Beach Park Plaza p.502
Counter Culture, Dubai Marriott Harbour Hotel p.502
Elements, Wafi p.504
Epicure, Desert Palm Dubai p.505
French Connection, Al Wafa Tower p.508
Gerard's, Magrudy's Mall p.510
Hey Sugar, The Village p.511
Jones The Grocer, Indigo Central 8, SZR p.514
Lime Tree Cafe & Kitchen, Jumeira Rd p.519
Madeleine Cafe & Boulangerie, The Dubai Mall p.520
THE One, Jumeira Theatre & Deli, Jumeira Rd p.528
Panini, Grand Hyatt Dubai p.529
Pergolas, Al Murooj Rotana p.530
Pronto, Fairmont Dubai p.531
Shakespeare & Co, Al Attar Business Tower p.536
Vienna Cafe, JW Marriott Hotel p.544

Chinese
The China Club, Radisson Blu Hotel p.502
China Times, Deira City Centre p.502
Da Shi Dai, Murjan, Jumeirah Beach Residence p.503
Dynasty, Ramada Hotel Dubai p.504
Hukama, The Address Downtown Dubai p.511
Lan Kwai Fong, Nr Lamcy Plaza p.518
Long Yin, Le Meridien Dubai p.519
The Noble House, Raffles Dubai p.524
Ping Pong, The Dubai Mall p.530
Royal China Dubai, DIFC p.533
Shang Palace, Shangri-La Hotel Dubai p.536
Summer Place, Habtoor Grand Beach Resort p.540
Zheng He's, Mina A'Salam p.550

Dinner Cruises
Al Mansour Dhow, Radisson Blu Hotel p.488
Bateaux Dubai, Nr British Embassy p.494
Tour Dubai, Nr British Embassy p.543

Emirati
Al Dahleez, Al Boom Tourist Village p.486
Al Fanar Restaurant & Cafe, Festival Centre p.486

European
25°55° Café Bistro, Dubai Marina Yacht Club p.484
Embassy Dubai, Grosvenor House p.504
Nineteen, The Address Montgomerie Dubai p.524

Far Eastern

Bamboo Lagoon, JW Marriott Hotel Dubai p.494
Beachcombers, Jumeirah Beach Hotel p.494
Chimes, Seven Sands Hotel Apartments p.502
Eauzone, One&Only Royal Mirage p.504
Indo Thai Asian, Radisson Royal Hotel p.512
The Noodle House, The Boulevard At Jumeirah Emirates Towers p.526
Veda Pavilion, Clubhouse Al Nafura p.544
Wok In, Movenpick Hotel Deira p.546
Wox, Grand Hyatt Dubai p.547
Yum!, Radisson Blu Hotel, Dubai Deira Creek p.547

Filipino

Max's Restaurant, Khalid Bin Al Waleed Rd p.522
Tagpuan, Karama p.541

French

AOC, Sofitel Dubai Jumeirah Beach p.490
Bistro Domino, Hotel Ibis Deira City Centre p.495
Bistro Madeleine, InterContinental Dubai Festival City p.495
Can Can Brasserie, The Ritz-Carlton DIFC p.498
Entrecôte Cafe de Paris, The Dubai Mall p.505
Imperium, Jumeirah Zabeel Saray p.512
La Petite Maison, DIFC p.517
Le Classique, Emirates Golf Club p.518
Le Metro, Park Regis Kris Kin Hotel p.518
Le Relais de L'Entrecote, Festival Centre p.519
Margaux, Souk Al Bahar p.521
Reflets Par Pierre Gagnaire, InterContinental Dubai Festival City p.531
Rostang, Atlantis The Palm p.533
St Tropez, Century Village p.538
STAY By Yannick Alléno, One&Only The Palm p.538

German

Brauhaus, Jumeira Rotana p.497
Der Keller, Jumeirah Beach Hotel p.504
Hofbräuhaus, JW Marriott Hotel Dubai p.511

Greek

Elia, Majestic Hotel Tower Dubai p.504

Indian

Amala, Jumeirah Zabeel Saray p.489
Antique Bazaar, Four Points By Sheraton Bur Dubai p.490
Armani/Amal, Armani Hotel Dubai p.491
Aryaas, Al Nakheel Bldg, Zabeel Rd p.492
Asha's, Wafi p.492
Ashiana, Sheraton Dubai Creek Hotel & Towers p.492
The Bombay, Marco Polo Hotel p.497
Dhow Ka Aangan, Dhow Palace Hotel p.504
Foodlands Restaurant, Nr Ramada Continental p.508
Gazebo, Nr Sharaf DG, Al Mankhool Rd p.508
Handi, Taj Palace Dubai p.510
Indego By Vineet, Grosvenor House p.512
India Palace, Al Hudda Bldg, Nr Al Tayer Motors p.512
iZ, Grand Hyatt Dubai p.512
Jaipur, Burj Residences, Tower 1 p.513
The Kebab Connection, Mercure Gold Hotel p.516
Khazana, Al Nasr Leisureland p.516
Mahec, Le Meridien Dubai p.520
Masala, Bab Al Shams Desert Resort & Spa p.521
Masala Craft, Century Village p.522
Nina, Arabian Court At One&Only Royal Mirage p.524
The Rupee Room, Marina Walk p.534
Sai Dham, Saleh Bin Lahej Bldg, Oud Metha Rd p.534
Saravana Bhavan, Nr Karama Park Square p.535
Signature By Sanjeev Kapoor, Melia Dubai p.537
Tiffinbites, The Walk, JBR p.542
Zafran, Mirdif City Centre p.547
Zaika, Al Murooj Rotana p.550

International

A La Grand, Grand Excelsior Hotel p.484
Al Dawaar, Hyatt Regency Dubai p.486
Al Forsan, Bab Al Shams Desert Resort & Spa p.486
Al Shindagah, Metropolitan Palace Hotel p.489
The Academy, Dubai Creek Golf & Yacht Club p.484
Anwar, Holiday Inn Bur Dubai Embassy District p.490
Après, Mall of the Emirates p.490
Arboretum, Al Qasr p.491
Armani/Lounge, Armani Hotel Dubai p.492
At.mosphere, Burj Khalifa p.492
AZ.U.R, Dubai Marriott Harbour Hotel & Suites p.493
Blades, Al Badia Golf Club By InterContinental Dubai Festival City p.496
Blue Flame, Jumeirah Creekside Hotel p.496
Blue Orange, The Westin Dubai Mina Seyahi Beach Resort & Marina p.496
The Boardwalk, Dubai Creek Golf & Yacht Club p.497
The Cavendish, Bonnington Jumeirah Lakes Towers p.499
The Cheesecake Factory, Mall of the Emirates p.500
Cascades, Fairmont Dubai p.499
Celebrities, The Palace At One&Only Royal Mirage p.499
Chalet, Nr Umm Suqeim Park, Jumeira Rd p.500
Channels, Media Rotana p.500
Chef's House, Radisson Blu Hotel, Dubai Media City p.500
Choices, Al Bustan Rotana p.502
Conservatory, Al Manzil Hotel p.502
Da Gama, Century Village p.503
The Deck, Ocean View Hotel p.503
Ember Grill & Lounge, The Address Dubai Mall p.505
Entre Nous, Novotel World Trade Centre Dubai p.505
The Farm, Al Barari, Nr Falcon City p.506
Farriers, The Meydan Hotel p.507
Fazaris, The Address Downtown Dubai p.507
Fire & Ice, Raffles Dubai p.507

Italian

Japanese

YO! Sushi, Mirdif City Centre p.547
Zuma, DIFC p.550

Korean

Mannaland Korean Restaurant, Al Mina Rd p.521
Seoul Garden Restaurant, Zomorrodah Bldg, Off Zaabeel Rd p.536
Sumibiya, Radisson Blu Hotel, Dubai Deira Creek p.540

Latin American

Asado, The Palace Downtown Dubai p.492
Beach House Cabana, Clubhouse Azraq, Shoreline Apartments p.494
El Malecon, Dubai Marine Beach Resort & Spa p.504
La Parrilla, Jumeirah Beach Hotel p.517
Pachanga, Hilton Dubai Jumeirah Resort p.528
Toro Toro, Grosvenor House p.543

Lebanese

Al Nafoorah, The Boulevard At Jumeirah Emirates Towers p.489

Mediterranean

Al Muntaha, Burj Al Arab p.488
Armani/Mediterraneo, Armani Hotel Dubai p.492
Ewaan, The Palace Downtown Dubai p.506
Finz, Ibn Battuta Mall p.507
Kaleidoscope, Atlantis The Palm p.514
La Villa, Pullman Deira City Centre Hotel p.518
Le Mistral, Grand Excelsior Hotel p.518
Majlis Al Bahar, Burj Al Arab p.520
The MED, Media One Hotel p.523
Mistral, Mövenpick Hotel Ibn Battuta Gate p.524
Roccha Restaurant, Rixos Bab Al Bahr, Al Marjan Island p.532
Thyme Restaurant, Oasis Beach Tower p.542
Trader Vic's, Festival Centre p.543
Vu's Restaurant, Jumeirah Emirates Towers p.545

Mexican

Cactus Cantina, Rydges Plaza Hotel, Satwa Roundabout p.498
El Chico, The Walk, JBR p.504
Maria Bonita Taco Shop & Grill, Nr Spinneys Centre, Umm Al Sheif St p.521
Maya By Richard Sandoval, Le Royal Meridien Beach Resort & Spa p.522

Middle Eastern

Al Basha, Habtoor Grand Beach Resort & Spa p.484
Al Dhiyafa, Habtoor Grand Beach Resort & Spa p.486
Al Diwan, Metropolitan Palace Hotel p.486
Al Hadheerah, Bab Al Shams Desert Resort & Spa p.486
Al Koufa Restaurant, Nr Al Nasr Leisureland p.488
Al Mallah, 2nd December St p.488
Al Safadi Restaurant, Al Kawakeb Bldg, SZR p.489
Amaseena, The Ritz-Carlton, Dubai p.490
Arabesque Cafe, Arjaan By Rotana Dubai Media City p.491
Automatic, The Beach Centre p.493
Awtar, Grand Hyatt Dubai p.493
Bastakiah Nights, Bastakiya p.494
Burj Al Hamam, Festival Centre p.497
Cafe Arabesque, Park Hyatt Dubai p.498
Chandelier, Marina Walk p.500
The Courtyard, Al Manzil Hotel p.503
Fakhreldine, Mövenpick Hotel & Apartments Bur Dubai p.506
Kabab-ji Grill, The Walk, JBR p.514
Kan Zaman Restaurant, Heritage & Diving Village p.514
Karam Beirut, Festival Centre p.516
Khan Murjan Restaurant, Wafi p.516
Levantine, Atlantis The Palm p.519
Mazaj, Century Village p.522
Mezza House, Yansoun 9 Souk Tamer Hind, Old Town p.523
NA3NA3, The Address Dubai Mall p.524
The Orchestra Restaurant & Cafe, Festival Centre p.528
Reem Al Bawadi, Nr HSBC, Jumeira Rd p.531
Wafi Gourmet, Wafi p.545
Wild Peeta, Deira City Centre p.546
Xennya Terrace, Holiday Inn Al Barsha p.547
Zaroob Restaurant & Cafe Lounge, Jumeirah Tower, Shk Zayed Rd p.550

Moroccan

Almaz By Momo, Mall of the Emirates p.489
Marrakech, Shangri-La Hotel Dubai p.521
Tagine, The Palace At One&Only Royal Mirage p.541

Pakistani

Karachi Darbar, Karama p.514
Ravi's, Nr Satwa Roundabout, Al Satwa Rd p.531

Persian

Al Borz, Al Durrah Tower, Shk Zayed Rd p.486
Pars Iranian Kitchen, Nr Chelsea Plaza Hotel p.529
Sarband, Century Village p.535
Shabestan, Radisson Blu Hotel, Dubai Deira Creek p.536
Shahrzad, Hyatt Regency Dubai p.536

Polynesian

Trader Vic's, Souk Madinat Jumeirah p.999

Portuguese

Nando's, Nr Crowne Plaza, Shk Zayed Rd p.524

Russian

Troyka, Ascot Hotel p.544

Cigar Bars

Karaoke Bars

Nightclubs

Pubs

Sports Bars

Wine Bars

VENUES BY LOCATION

Al Jafiliya

Chelsea Plaza Hotel

Nr Chelsea Plaza Hotel

Rydges Plaza Hotel, Satwa Roundabout

Al Karama

Abdul Aziz Mirza Bldg, Nr Karama Park Sq

Al Nakheel Bldg, Zabeel Rd

Karama

Nr BurJuman Centre

Nr LuLu Supermarket

Park Regis Kris Kin Hotel

Regent Palace Hotel

Shk Khalifa Bin Zayed Rd

Spinneys Bldg, Khalid Bin Al Waleed Rd

Zomorrodah Bldg

Al Khabaisi

Traders Hotel, Dubai

Al Manara

Indigo Central 8, Shk Zayed Rd

Al Mankhool

Dhow Palace Hotel

Majestic Hotel Tower Dubai

Ramada Hotel Dubai

Al Mina

Al Mina Rd

Mercure Gold Hotel

Al Muraqqabat

JW Marriott Hotel Dubai

Al Quoz 1

Oasis Centre

Al Raffa

Ascot Hotel

Melia Dubai

Nr Sharaf DG, Al Mankhool Rd

Al Rigga

Al Khaleej Palace Hotel

Hilton Dubai Creek
Glasshouse Brasserie, International p.510
Issimo Bar, Bar p.559
Table 9 By Nick & Scott, International p.541

Metropolitan Palace Hotel
Al Diwan, Middle Eastern p.486
Al Shindagah, International p.489
Sketch, International p.537

Radisson Blu Hotel, Dubai Deira Creek
Al Mansour Dhow, Dinner Cruise p.488
The China Club, Chinese p.502
Fish Market, Seafood p.507
La Moda, Italian p.517
Minato, Japanese p.523
Palm Grill, Steakhouse p.529
Shabestan, Persian p.536
Sumibiya, Korean p.540
Yum!, Far Eastern p.547

Sheraton Dubai Creek Hotel & Towers
Ashiana, Indian p.492
Creekside Restaurant, Japanese p.503
Vivaldi, Bar p.545

Taj Palace Dubai
Handi, Indian p.510
Sakura, Japanese p.534

Al Safa 2

Spinneys Centre
Cafe Havana, Cafe p.498

Al Satwa

Al Satwa Rd
Ravi's, Pakistani p.531

Al Shindagha

Heritage & Diving Village
Al Bandar Restaurant, Seafood p.484
Kan Zaman Restaurant, Middle Eastern p.514

Al Souk Al Kabeer

Bastakiya
Basta Art Cafe, Cafe p.494
Bastakiah Nights, Middle Eastern p.494

Al Sufouh 1

Al Qasr
Al Hambra, Spanish p.488
Arboretum, International p.491
Koubba Bar, Bar p.559
Pai Thai, Thai p.529
Pierchic, Seafood p.530

Arabian Court At One&Only Royal Mirage
Eauzone, Far Eastern p.504
Nina, Indian p.524
The Rotisserie, International p.533

Arjaan By Rotana Dubai Media City
Arabesque Cafe, Middle Eastern p.491

Le Meridien Mina Seyahi Beach Resort & Marina
Barasti, Bar p.551

Madinat Jumeirah
Segreto, Italian p.536

Media One Hotel
CafeM, Cafe p.552
M-Dek, Bar p.560
The MED, Mediterranean p.523
Z:ONE Lounge Bar, Bar p.566

Mina A'Salam
Al Muna, Buffet p.488
Bahri Bar, Bar p.550
The Wharf, Seafood p.546
Zheng He's, Chinese p.550

One&Only Royal Mirage
Jetty Lounge, Bar p.559
Kasbar, Nightclub p.559
The Rooftop Terrace & Sports Lounge, Bar p.562

Radisson Blu Hotel, Dubai Media City
Certo, Italian p.500
Chef's House, International p.500
Icon Bar & Lounge, Bar p.558
Tamanya Terrace, Bar p.564

Souk Madinat Jumeirah
Barzar, Bar p.551
Honyaki, Japanese p.511
Jambase, Bar p.559
Rivington Bar & Grill, Bar p.562
Trader Vic's, Polynesian p.999

The Palace At One&Only Royal Mirage
Beach Bar & Grill, Seafood p.494
Celebrities, International p.499
Olives, Italian p.528
Tagine, Moroccan p.541

Venues By Location

Oud Metha

Al Nasr Leisureland
Chi@The Lodge, Nightclub p.554
Keva, Bar p.559
Khazana, Indian p.516

Mövenpick Hotel & Apartments Bur Dubai
Fakhreldine, Middle Eastern p.506
Fountain Restaurant, International p.508

Nr Al Nasr Leisureland
Al Koufa Restaurant, Middle Eastern p.488

Nr Lamcy Plaza
Lan Kwai Fong, Chinese p.518
Lemongrass, Thai p.519

Saleh Bin Lahej Bldg, Oud Metha Rd
Sai Dham, Indian p.534

Palm Jumeirah

Atlantis The Palm
kaleidoscope, Mediterranean p.514
Levantine, Middle Eastern p.519
Nasimi Beach, Bar p.560
Nobu, Japanese p.526
Ossiano, Seafood p.528
Ronda Locatelli, Italian p.533
Rostang, French p.533
Saffron, International p.534
Seafire Steakhouse & Bar, Steakhouse p.535

Clubhouse Al Manhal, Shoreline Apartments
BidiBondi, Bar p.551

Clubhouse Al Nafura, Shoreline Apartments
Veda Pavilion, Far Eastern p.544

Clubhouse Azraq, Shoreline Apartments
Beach House Cabana, Latin American p.494

Jumeirah Zabeel Saray
Amala, Indian p.489
Imperium, French p.512
Lalezar, Turkish p.518
Sultan's Lounge, Afternoon Tea p.540
Voda Bar, Bar p.565
Voi, Vietnamese p.545

Oceana Beach Club
West 14th New York Grill & Bar, Steakhouse p.546

One&Only The Palm
STAY By Yannick Alléno, French p.538

Rixos The Palm Dubai
A La Turca Restaurant, Turkish p.484
White X Beach & Lounge, Nightclub p.566

Port Saeed

Deira City Centre
China Times, Chinese p.502
Wild Peeta, Middle Eastern p.546

Dubai Creek Golf & Yacht Club
The Academy, International p.484
The Boardwalk, International p.497
Aquarium Restaurant, Seafood p.490
Legends, Steakhouse p.519
QD's, Bar p.561

Hotel Ibis Deira City Centre
Bistro Domino, French p.495

ICONIC
Wild Ginger, Asian Subcontinent p.546

Park Hyatt Dubai
Cafe Arabesque, Middle Eastern p.498
The Thai Kitchen, Thai p.542
Traiteur, International p.544

Pullman Deira City Centre Hotel
Churchill's, Pub p.554
La Villa, Mediterranean p.518

At.mosphere

Where To Go For What

Dubai is a pick'n'mix of eateries, drinking spots and entertainment options vying to please a highly diverse audience. Whether you want a daytime binge of five-star cuisine, a raucous night out dancing to live music, an evening of brainteasers, or an early morning rendition of I Will Survive, you will find it all within Dubai's restaurants, cafes, pubs, bars and nightclubs.

Alfresco

Between late October and early May the weather in Dubai is perfect for alfresco dining and beachfront drinking. Popular spots for dinner with a waterfront view are: on stilts over the creek at The Boardwalk (p.497); overlooking the beach at Bussola (p.498); a collection of intimate restaurants at Century Village, including Da Gama (p.503) and Mazaj (p.522); the mix of cuisines by the water at Madinat Jumeirah, featuring the likes of Left Bank (p.559) and Zheng He's (p.550); on the terrace at Souk Al Bahar and neighbouring The Dubai Mall; and finally the streetside eateries of Marina Walk and The Walk, JBR (p.413).

Fish & Chips

You may not find a 'chippy' on every street corner in Dubai, but if you're really hankering for some good old fish and chips there are a few choices at your disposal. The Fish & Chips Room (04 427 0443) at JBR is popular, as is the nearby Bob's Fish & Chips on the other side of the marina. Both stay open until the wee hours of the morning too. The Fish & Chip Mirdif, 26C Street, near the mosque on 15 Street (04 288 1812) is a good option for Mirdif dwellers. The Irish Village (p.558), Barasti (p.551), The Boardwalk (p.497), the Dhow & Anchor (p.556) and Aprés (p.490) all deserve a special mention for the quality of their fish and chips. MORE Cafe (morecafe.biz) also has excellent fish and spicy chunky chips.

Dancing

There is a whole host of clubs to boogie the night away in (see p.550), as well as a few places for impromptu dance routines. A long-term favourite is Chi@The Lodge (p.554), which offers three rooms of music, plus an open-air garden where you can dance the night away. Nasimi Beach (p.560) at Atlantis hosts the popular Sandance beach parties throughout the cooler months, with the occasional pool party during the summer. Classy venues on the club scene include the Cavalli Club at the Fairmont Dubai and Republique at The Address Dubai Mall. For something a little more down and dirty, check out Rock Bottom (p.562) at the Regent Palace Hotel, Bur Dubai. For an eclectic music selection try Fridays at 360° (p.550), which regularly hosts international DJs. For entry before 20:00 on Fridays and Saturdays, you will need to get on the guest list at platinumlist.net.

Waxy O'Conner's

Late & Lively
In addition to the dedicated clubs listed in this chapter, Dubai's nightlife scene also includes several bars and restaurants which transform late evening into lively joints with hopping dancefloors. These include Barasti (p.551), Barzar (p.551), Boudoir (p.552), Buddha Bar (p.552), Clique (p.554), Malecon (p.504), Jambase (p.559), and The Warehouse (p.566).

Karaoke Bars
There are a few places in Dubai where you can show off your vocal abilities, or even just belt out a comedy version of Ice Ice Baby. Harry Ghatto's (p.558) in Emirates Towers is a popular haunt, with the small space filling fast, while the post-brunch karaoke sessions at Double Decker (p.556) range from the sublime to the ridiculous. For a unique night, try 'curryoke' at It's Mirchi (04 334 4088) in the Ramee Royal Hotel, Bur Dubai, which serves up Indian fare with an enormous multi-language song book. On the other side of the creek, Kisaku (p.516) is a good option, with private rooms for groups. Or sing your heart out at the Hibiki Music Lounge, a cosy karaoke lounge with three private rooms (p.558).

Ladies' Nights
Lucky ladies in this fair city can go out almost any night of the week and enjoy free drinks. Of course, this isn't a charitable venture by Dubai's bar scene; where ladies are drinking, the men and their wallets inevitably follow. Tuesday is the biggest ladies' night with many bars and pubs offering at least two free drinks. The most legendary venues are Oeno (p.561), Healey's Bar & Terrace (p.558) and Margaux (p.521), while Boudoir (p.552), Senyar (p.562) and Blends (04 436 7777) are very lady friendly, with free bubbly or cocktails nearly every night of the week. Icon Bar (p.558) is perfect for free post-work drinks straight from your office in Media City.

Quiz Nights
If you want to test your brain power and knowledge of useless trivia then head to one of Dubai's many quiz nights. Try Boston Bar (p.552) or Player's Lounge (04 398 8840) on Mondays, or Tuesdays at the Dhow & Anchor, Jumeirah Beach Hotel (p.240). If you don't mind fierce competition, give the quiz at the Arabian Ranches Golf Club (p.339) a go, or enter the Girders (p.556) quiz and enjoy some Scottish pub grub at the same time.

And The Rest...
Dubai is full of fun alternatives for when you need a break from the bar and restaurant scene. You can enjoy the slides and lazy river in between trips to the bar at Aquaventure at Atlantis The Palm (p.236), which offers a special rates for UAE residents. The ancient bowling alley at Al Nasr Leisureland (alnasrll.com) is the only one in the city that serves booze (at cheap prices too), and reservations can be made for large parties. For an especially memorable night out, you could charter a yacht from Dubai Marina Yacht Club. Dhs.1,500 will buy you two hours for up to 10 people and you can bring your own food and drink on board.

RESTAURANTS & CAFES

1762 — Cafe

Trendsetting sandwiches and stylish salads

A working lunch spot definitely, but this isn't fast food or food just to eat and run (although a selection of 'grab and go' goodies are available). Instead, 1762 has created a pleasant atmosphere to relax and enjoy the taste of artisan sandwiches, soups, salads and cakes. Its imaginative, deli-style menu features bursts of international flavours such as mango chilli chicken and wasabi labneh with salmon. And, as well as a daily-changing variety of salads, quiche and soups, there are homemade pies and pastries and desserts that are every bit as gourmet as the savoury menu.

Dubai International Financial Centre (DIFC)
Trade Centre 2 **04 800 1762**
1762.ae
Map **2 G6** Metro **Financial Centre**

25°55° Café Bistro — British

The sailing set's classic British fuel stop

A solid choice for good, wholesome, no-fuss food for breakfast, lunch or dinner. Whether you come to enjoy a pie and pint while watching the match or for a must-have full-English breakfast after a big night out, this bistro/pub/yacht club restaurant will satisfy your hunger. It's not about the location, although the terrace affords a stunning view overlooking the hedonistic marina, but rather about the hearty dishes. The roasts served on Saturdays and Sundays combine shared salads followed by slow roast prime beef ribs, rosemary marinated roasted lamb leg and cinnamon flavoured roasted pork leg with all the ubiquitous trimmings such as Yorkshire puddings, roast potatoes and root vegetables, as well as a selection of gravies.

Dubai Marina Yacht Club Dubai Marina **04 362 7955**
dubaimarinayachtclub.com
Map **1 K5** Metro **Jumeirah Lakes Towers**

A La Grand — European

Classy European fare hits Barsha

There are plenty of great independent restaurants and takeaways scattered throughout Barsha now, but if you'd like to sit down and tuck into something a little more refined, the choice is limited. A La Grand fits the bill pretty well. It's not Michelin star stuff, but it's good European food made using excellent ingredients and delivered to the table in a professional but friendly manner. The heartier meat mains are tasty and generous. The restaurant is open all day, has a good children's menu and also offers a good brunch.

Grand Excelsior Hotel Al Barsha 1 **04 444 9999**
grandexcelsior.ae
Map **1 R7** Metro **Mall of the Emirates**

A La Turca Restaurant — Turkish

Turkish all-day dining on The Palm

If flying to the Bosphoros for a quick food fix sounds a little too excessive, you can now find satisfyingly succulent kebabs at Rixos The Palm Dubai's new all-day dining restaurant A La Turca. Predominantly a buffet concept that serves up the usual mix of Middle Eastern dishes, there are a few surprising treats that shouldn't go untried. One example is the homemade Turkish thin crust pizza that is brought on a one metre-long platter to your table. Opt to eat outside and enjoy a laidback, alfresco dining experience where views of the cityscape create a unique backdrop to your meal.

Rixos The Palm Dubai Palm Jumeirah **04 457 5555**
rixos.com
Map **1 P3** Metro **Nakheel**

The Academy — International

Take the smooth with the rough at this golf cafe

A wide assortment of international appetisers, sandwiches, salads, main courses and beverages of all sorts is available in this snack bar overlooking Dubai Creek's golf course; a cheerful colour scheme fits in well with the view of luscious greens and happy golfers.

Dubai Creek Golf & Yacht Club Port Saeed
04 295 6000
dubaigolf.com
Map **2 M7** Metro **Deira City Centre**

Al Bandar Restaurant — Seafood

Tradition, seafood and camels by the creek

With an idyllic creekside location and good international seafood, Al Bandar is the perfect venue to ease visitors into the Arabian experience. It caters for a dress-down clientele, making a pleasant change from the usual five-star hotel feel. It's good value, and the nearby resident camels make for an excellent photo opportunity.

Heritage & Diving Village Al Shindagha **04 393 9001**
alkoufa.com
Map **2 M4** Metro **Al Ghubaiba**

Al Basha — Middle Eastern

Fine set menu options, with nimble belly dancers

Offers fine Lebanese food, with live music from 21:30. You can order al a carte, but the set menus are wide-ranging; wafer-thin pita, cheese rolls and grilled meat start from Dhs.220 per person up to Dhs.350 with prawn and lobster. A great spot to sit out on the terrace, dine on hearty grilled meats and watch the belly dancers perform.

Habtoor Grand Beach Resort & Spa Dubai Marina
04 399 5000
habtoorhotels.com
Map **1 L4** Metro **Dubai Marina**

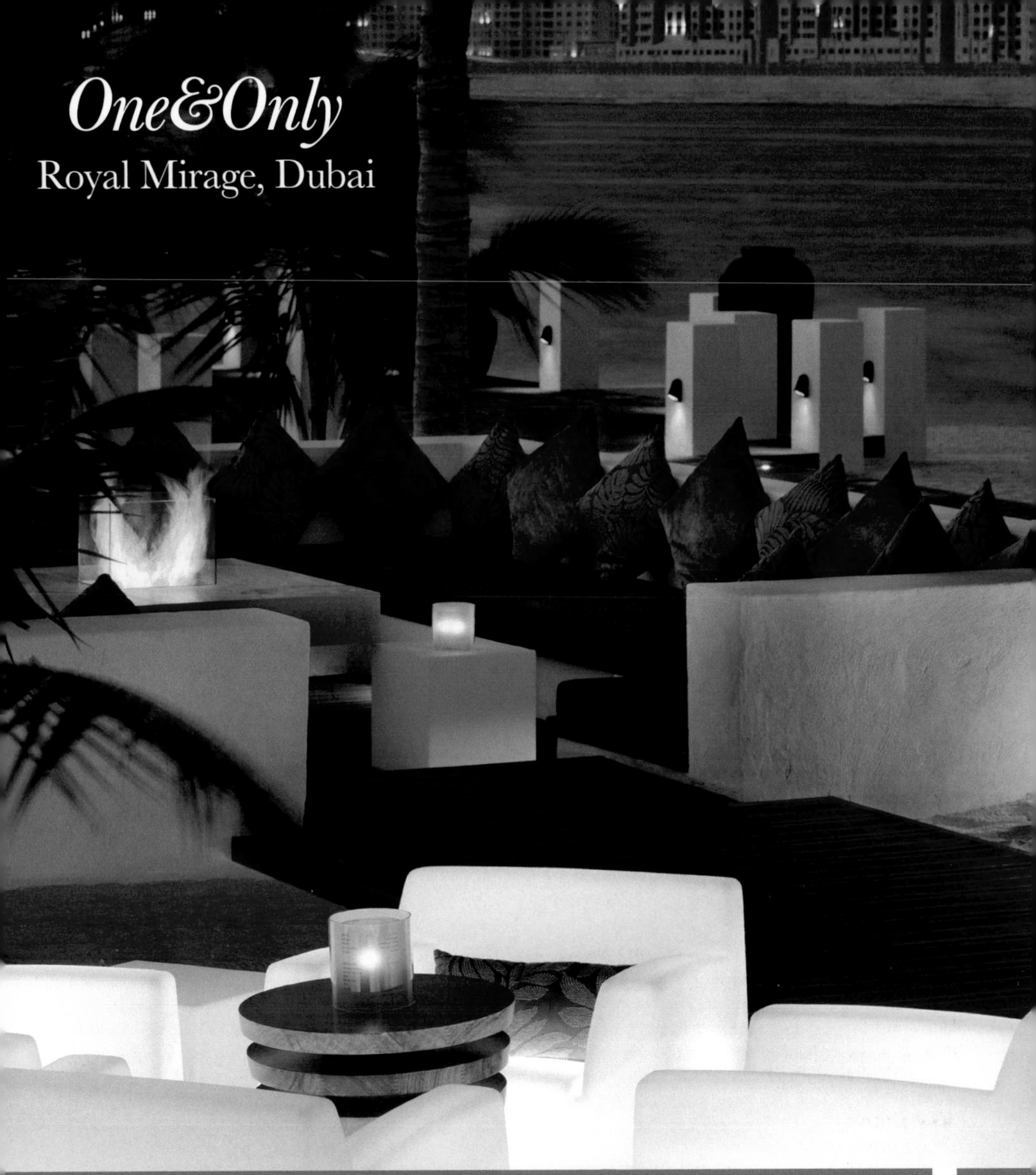
One&Only
Royal Mirage, Dubai

Al Borz — Persian
An ideal introduction to Iranian fare on SZR
Renowned as one of Tehran's best kebab houses, Al Borz serves up its famous kebabs and rich rice specialities in a family setting. A buffet lunch, large portions and moderate prices mean it's popular with Iranians and Persian food novices alike. Takeaway and delivery are available.
Al Durrah Tower, Shk Zayed Rd Trade Centre 1
04 331 8777
Map **2 H5** Metro **Emirates Towers**

Al Dahleez — Emirati
Cavernous shisha cafe with juices and Arabic grills
Packed nearly every night of the week, Al Dahleez serves some of the best shisha in Dubai, and its bizarre, faux-cavern interior is a great place to spend a few hours playing cards or backgammon. Large grilled sandwiches, traditional Arabic grills and fresh juices dominate the extensive menu.
Al Boom Tourist Village Umm Hurair 2 **04 324 3000**
alboom.ae
Map **2 L7** Metro **Dubai Healthcare City**

Al Dawaar — International
Quality buffet food that makes the world go round
Surprisingly sophisticated for a revolving restaurant, the decor here is minimalist and the buffet ample rather than over the top. Enjoy dainty starters, a la carte-style main dishes and an unrivalled dessert table, plus changing views over Deira and out to sea.
Hyatt Regency Dubai Corniche Deira **04 317 2222**
hyatt.com
Map **2 N4** Metro **Palm Deira**

Al Dhiyafa — Middle Eastern
Rustic decor and meat galore
Brass ceiling fans, the warm red glow from table lamps, and a tantalising aroma of roasting meats fill Al Dhiyafa. The buffet food themes change daily, and the splendid array of fresh, imaginative food remains constant, particularly the meat dishes.
Habtoor Grand Beach Resort & Spa Dubai Marina
04 399 5000
habtoorhotels.com
Map **1 L4** Metro **Dubai Marina**

Al Diwan — Middle Eastern
Fantastic cuisine with Arabic music
Enjoy traditional Lebanese food and belly dancing from 23:00 at this cosy restaurant. The selection of wine, Montecristo cigars and Beluga caviar provide a special treat, but the hummus Al Diwan and the oriental mixed grill are not to be missed.
Metropolitan Palace Hotel Al Rigga **04 227 0000**
habtoorhotels.com
Map **2 N6** Metro **Al Rigga**

Al Fanar Restaurant & Cafe > *p.487* — Emirati
Lose yourself in the old Arabian atmosphere
Ask to be seated in one of their majlis and wile away the hours sitting outdoors drinking Arabic tea and soaking up the unique atmosphere. In contrast, the indoor section reveals a bustling scene from the old town where you can take your pick and enjoy lunch or dinner in the Pearl Merchant's House, Bait Al Tawash (courtyard) or Souq, all of which conjure up images reminiscent of traders and architecture from the past. It's not just a spectacle – the Emirati food has plenty to admire. Start with koftat samak, a delicious crumbled and deep fried fish, combined with onion, coriander and special spices. The mains are mouthwatering, and you can take your pick from a selection of lamb, fish or chicken specialities, many of which come from their fabulous grill. Bring your experience to a close with local favourite lequimat. These delicious fried dough balls covered in date syrup are hard to resist.
Canal Walk Dubai Festival City **04 232 9966**
alfanarrestaurant.com
Map **2 M9** Metro **Emirates**

Al Forsan — Arabic
Magical atmosphere amid the desert dunes
A small but perfectly formed buffet offers Arabic and international dishes, while the a la carte option has a great selection for kids. The magical, Arabian atmosphere, helped by the rich decor and surrounding dunes, is worth the 45 minute drive from Dubai.
Bab Al Shams Desert Resort & Spa Bawadi
04 809 6100
meydanhotels.com

Al Fresco — Italian
A taste of Italy in the heart of Dubai
Great little Italian serving authentic pastas and risottos. Be sure to leave room for dessert; the tiramisu is delicious. The casual vibe in this cosy nook makes it perfect for alfresco dining with a big group of friends.
Crowne Plaza Dubai Trade Centre 1 **04 331 1111**
ichotelsgroup.com
Map **2 H5** Metro **Emirates Towers**

Al Hadheerah — Middle Eastern
Delightful dining: great food and entertainment
A traditional Arabic (including Emirati) buffet is served here, amid a variety of elaborate performances. Enjoy grilled seafood, meat and desserts; henna painting and shisha are available for an extra charge. The evening costs Dhs.425 per person Saturday to Thursday, and Dhs.495 on Fridays. Prices include water, soft drinks, Arabic coffee, an exciting visit to the onsite Heritage Museum, and camel, horse and pony rides.
Bab Al Shams Desert Resort & Spa Bawadi
04 809 6100
meydanhotels.com

Al Hambra — Spanish

Tasty dishes that fuse Andalusia with Morocco

A mariachi duo, exposed brickwork and vaulted ceilings set the mood at this excellent Spanish venue. The seafood paella served here is a must, but there are also some delicious tapas, rustic Spanish dishes and a few tasty options for vegetarians. The pricey menu may mean reserving this restaurant for those special occasions only.

Al Qasr Al Sufouh 1 **04 366 6730**
jumeirah.com
Map **1 R4** Metro **Mall of the Emirates**

Al Koufa Restaurant — Middle Eastern

Great food and live performances

In true Arabic style, Al Koufa comes alive around 23:00. Enjoy a great atmosphere, delicious fruit juices and excellent traditional Arabic food, including some lesser known and Emirati dishes, till the early hours. A charge of Dhs.30 covers the live performances.

Nr Al Nasr Leisureland Oud Metha **04 335 1511**
alkoufa.com
Map **2 L6** Metro **Oud Metha**

Al Mahara — Seafood

Superlative seafood in a submarine setting

Your visit starts with a simulated submarine ride 'under the sea', arriving at an elegant restaurant curled around a huge aquarium. The superlative fine dining menu is predominantly seafood – with gourmet delights such as Alaskan king crab and foie gras ravioli or poached Tsarskaya oysters – and boasts prices to match. Gentlemen are required to wear a jacket.

Burj Al Arab Umm Suqeim 3 **04 301 7600**
jumeirah.com
Map **1 S4** Metro **Mall of the Emirates**

Al Mallah — Middle Eastern

Fab Arabic fastfood at this no-frills institution

Watch the world go by in Satwa from this popular pavement Arabic joint, as you sample excellent shawarmas and some of the best falafel in Dubai. The 'Diana' and 'Charles' shakes are also recommended.

2nd December St Al Hudaiba **04 398 4723**
Map **2 J4** Metro **Al Jafiliya**

Al Mansour Dhow — Dinner Cruise

All aboard for traditional food and music

This two-hour creek trip features dinner aboard a traditional dhow operated by Radisson Blu. Great views, atmospheric oud music, a traditional buffet spread and shisha make this a memorable evening. The ship sails at 20:30, and costs Dhs.185 per adult.

Radisson Blu Hotel, Dubai Deira Creek Al Rigga **04 222 7171**
radissonblu.com
Map **2 M5** Metro **Union**

Al Muna — Buffet

Buffet bonanza in plush Madinat surroundings

Al Muna offers a mouthwatering buffet of international cuisine, as well as a 24-hour a la carte menu catering to those who want a more personal experience. Like everything in the Madinat, it comes in a nice posh package with elegant decor and an inviting terrace to match.

Mina A'Salam Al Sufouh 1 **04 366 6730**
jumeirah.com
Map **1 R4** Metro **Mall of the Emirates**

Al Muntaha — Mediterranean

Great views, reasonable dining at the top of the Burj

The breathtaking coastline view from this restaurant at the top of Burj Al Arab, 200m above sea level, goes some way to excusing the eccentric decor; thankfully, the Mediterranean menu is more appealing than the interior. Dishes like Atlantic lobster and sweetbread ravioli or 'wild sea bass three-ways' add a wonderful twist to simple flavours and ingredients. The beautifully presented dishes contribute to an evening of grandeur, but you may feel you're paying for the name more than anything else.

Burj Al Arab Umm Suqeim 3 **04 301 7600**
jumeirah.com
Map **1 S4** Metro **Mall of the Emirates**

Al Nafoorah — Lebanese

Busy Lebanese place that's perfect for group dining

Located in the heart of Dubai's business district, Al Nafoorah's large outdoor area makes it stand out against other Levantine options. Whether you go a la carte or choose one of the tasty set menus, you're in for a Middle Eastern culinary treat: the stuffed vine leaves are among the many highlights, while the meaty mixed grill is as tasty as anything you'll get in Beirut. The atmosphere strikes the fine balance between professional and relaxed to make this a great choice for business lunches or evening meals under the stars.

The Boulevard At Jumeirah Emirates Towers Trade Centre 2 **04 319 8088**
jumeirah.com
Map **2 H6** Metro **Emirates Towers**

Al Safadi Restaurant — Middle Eastern

No-frills dining where the food outshines the venue

Function rules over form at big and busy Al Safadi, but it's the high quality Arabic food that people come here for. Street-side tables are perfect for more relaxed dining, shisha and people watching. Another branch is on Al Rigga Road in Deira (04 227 9922).

Al Kawakeb Bldg, Shk Zayed Rd Trade Centre 2 **04 343 5333**
alsafadi.ae
Map **2 G5** Metro **Financial Centre**

Al Shindagah
International

Umm Ali's the word at this reliable restaurant

Expect bountiful buffets and consistently good food at this restaurant. During Ramadan the focus here shifts from international to delicious Middle Eastern treats (including its fabulous umm ali). The buffet costs a little over Dhs.100 a head and includes soft drinks, which makes it good value.

Metropolitan Palace Hotel Al Rigga **04 227 0000**
habtoorhotels.com
Map **2 N5** Metro **Al Rigga**

Alfie's
British

Great British food with a touch of class

A stylish, high-quality restaurant serving a best of British menu with a decor that whispers English gentleman. Starters are biased towards seafood from the simple – dressed Cornish crab, half a dozen oysters or Alfie's signature cured salmon – to the stylish, Welsh rarebit with asparagus and a fried egg, smoked haddock hash, or potted shrimps and smoked eel. Main courses are big on comfort, timeless and tasty with dishes such as fish and chips, grilled rib of beef with anchovy butter and chips, slow roasted rump of lamb, and traditional haggis with clapshot. In short, it's a gastro pub menu but with a great deal of elegant refinement and many classic finishing touches.

The Boulevard At Jumeirah Emirates Towers
Trade Centre 2 **04 319 8785**
jumeirah.com
Map **2 H6** Metro **Emirates Towers**

Almaz By Momo
Moroccan

A richly decorated restaurant, perfect for lounging

The subdued atmosphere inside this Moroccan restaurant is a contrast to the retail buzz outside. Settle down with a mocktail and enjoy its stews, tender lamb and fluffy couscous. With the tempting menu, you won't be going anywhere fast – the service is as laidback as the vibe. Located in Harvey Nichols, this is the ideal resting point during a shopping trip.

Mall of the Emirates Al Barsha 1 **04 409 8877**
altayer.com
Map **1 R6** Metro **Mall of the Emirates**

Amala
Indian

Indian that is another Jumeira gem

This restaurant serves authentic North Indian cuisine focusing on Mughalai curries, tandoori and biryani dishes with a contemporary new twist which is definitely a cut above the rest. Like the rest of the restaurants at Zabeel Saray, Amala oozes refined class with its dark brown and turquoise decor offset by a stunning water fountain centrepiece. The service is very attentive without being obtrusive, and with plenty of different options to choose from the a la carte menu, it's excellent value for money. Dishes can be ordered mild or as spicy as your palate can handle and washed down with a glass of wine. Afterwards you can enjoy a refreshing cocktail on the terrace.

Jumeirah Zabeel Saray Palm Jumeirah **04 453 0444**
jumeirah.com
Map **1 L3** Metro **Nakheel**

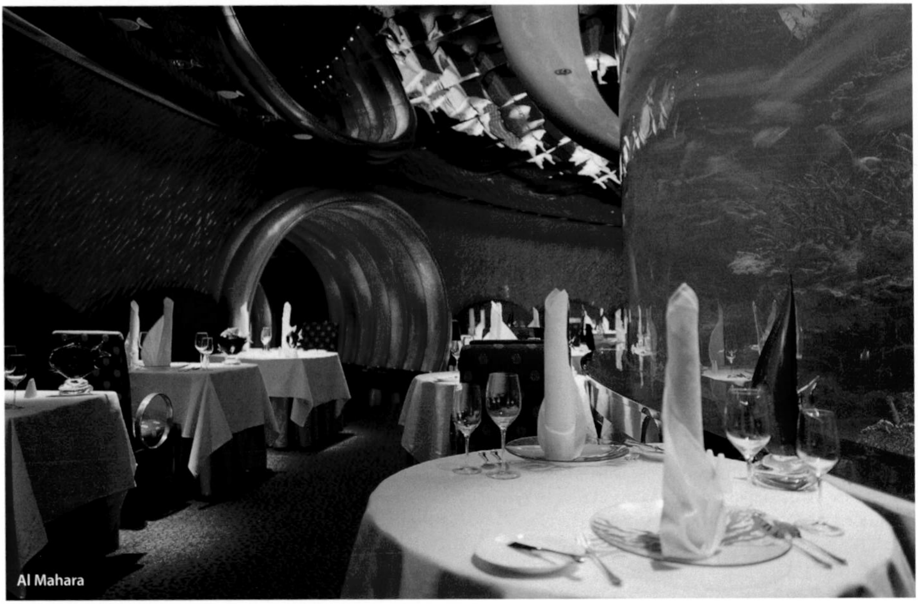

Al Mahara

Amaseena — Middle Eastern

Exotic Arabian dining under the stars

A torch-lit entrance, sounds of the oud, the aroma of shisha, and exotic belly dancing under the stars make this a truly magical Arabian experience. The food – which takes the form of an all you can eat Arabic buffet – is excellent, and you can sit in your own private majlis.

The Ritz-Carlton, Dubai Dubai Marina **04 399 4000**
ritzcarlton.com
Map **1 L4** Metro **Dubai Marina**

Amwaj — Seafood

Top food and service – a real fine-dining find

Amwaj is a Dubai must-visit. The service couldn't be more attentive nor unobtrusive, and the chef is an expert at combining seemingly contrasting flavours into dishes that work so well you'll find yourself licking the plate clean. Priding itself on perfectly prepared seafood, Amwaj's meat and vegetarian dishes are equally impressive.

Shangri-La Hotel Dubai Trade Centre 1 **04 405 2703**
shangri-la.com
Map **2 G5** Metro **Financial Centre**

Andiamo! — Italian

Enticing pizzas straight from the exciting oven

This chic, relaxed Italian features Miro-style lamps, with an abundance of mirrors, wood and stark colours, and an eye-catching pizza oven. The starters are pretty, delicious and generous while pizzas are thin, crispy, fresh and tasty. Prices are a little above average.

Grand Hyatt Dubai Umm Hurair 2 **04 317 2222**
restaurants.dubai.hyatt.com
Map **2 L8** Metro **Dubai Healthcare City**

Antique Bazaar — Indian

A musical extravaganza and a feast of curry

Antique Bazaar offers a full range of curried delights to an ever-present musical accompaniment. When in full swing, the live music show is a memorable cultural experience, but can detract from the great food. Arrive early for conversation, late to party.

Four Points By Sheraton Bur Dubai **04 397 7444**
antiquebazaar-dubai.com
Map **2 L5** Metro **BurJuman**

Anwar — Arabic

Family-friendly Arabic-inspired buffet

Located in the courtyard, this all-day dining venue serves up a decent buffet as well as an a la carte option. The buffet is mainly Arabic with a small spattering of Indian, pasta and seafood dishes, while the salad bar is very fresh and there's desserts aplenty.

Holiday Inn Bur Dubai, Al Hamriya **04 357 2999**
holidayinn.com
Map **2 M5** Metro **BurJuman**

AOC — French

Solid European cuisine and a knock-out terrace

The staff are friendly and the venue, especially the terrace, is excellent but the a la carte menu serves up largely European main courses rather than anything authentically French. The wine list and desserts do their best to return a touch of *oooh la la* to proceedings.

Sofitel Dubai Jumeirah Beach Dubai Marina
04 448 4848
sofitel.com
Map **1 K4** Metro **Dubai Marina**

Applebee's — American

Tex-Mex galore at this family-friendly favourite

An all-American family restaurant serving up huge portions of Tex-Mex, burgers, and crowd pleasers. Smiling staff, big screen TVs, and great kids' and dessert menus keep the whole clan happy. The Oreo milkshake is a fine way to end your calorie overload.

Shk Issa Tower, Trade Centre 1 **04 343 7755**
applebees.com
Map **2 H6** Metro **Emirates Towers**

Après — International

Party like you're on the piste at this après-ski spot

This cosy alpine ski lodge has a comfortable bar area and an unrivalled view of the Ski Dubai slopes. The varied menu offers wholesome fare including steaks, fondue and excellent pizzas. During the day, it's great for families and, at night, the laidback vibe and cocktail list encourage chilled dining and socialising.

Mall of the Emirates Al Barsha 1 **04 341 2575**
emiratesleisureretail.com
Map **1 R6** Metro **Mall of the Emirates**

Aquara — Seafood

Classy marina terrace spot to take in the yachts

Aquara is chic but understated, allowing the view of million-dirham yachts to speak for itself. It specialises in seafood, most of which is served with an Asian twist. Friday brunch is excellent. The centrepiece is the seafood bar with lobster, oysters, prawns, crab, clams, sushi and sashimi. A great terrace too.

Dubai Marina Yacht Club Dubai Marina **04 362 7900**
dubaimarinayachtclub.com
Map **1 K5** Metro **Jumeirah Lakes Towers**

Aquarium Restaurant — Seafood

Consistently good food in a swanky setting

This is one of Dubai's old time favourites, but despite its age, it still serves up tasty seafood dishes with a glorious view of the creek. If you can pull yourself away from the view, enjoy the well-priced menu inspired by the countries surrounding the Pacific Rim.

Dubai Creek Golf & Yacht Club Port Saeed **04 295 6000**
dubaigolf.com
Map **2 M7** Metro **Deira City Centre**

Arabesque Cafe — Middle Eastern

A quiet and classy Middle Eastern feast

Decorated in the style of a traditional Arabian palace – and enhanced by ornate lighting, plush, purple soft furnishings, traditional ornaments and decorative touches – this pleasant restaurant specialises in Middle Eastern fare. It's mainly a buffet format and there are deals to be had at the breakfast and lunch buffet, as well as the Friday brunch.

Arjaan By Rotana Dubai Media City Al Sufouh 1
04 436 0000
rotana.com
Map **1 M5** Metro **Nakheel**

Arboretum — International

Tempting variety in an impressive setting

Enjoy Asian, Middle Eastern and western salads and appetisers here before tackling the wide range of seafood, meat or pasta dishes and the fantastic desserts. The buffet (with a live-cooking station) is available at traditional meal times, or you can order a la carte throughout the day.

Al Qasr Al Sufouh 1 **04 366 6730**
jumeirah.com
Map **1 R4** Metro **Mall of the Emirates**

Arcadia — Afternoon Tea

A serving of high-class high tea

For an afternoon of refinery, the relaxing atrium at The Monarch is the perfect place to be ensconced with your scones. The high tea experience starts with a tower of sandwiches and a bottomless teapot, before moving on to scones and finally the patissier's platter – all for Dhs.120.

The Monarch Dubai Trade Centre 1 **04 501 8888**
h-hotel.com
Map **2 J5** Metro **World Trade Centre**

Armani/Amal — Indian

An Indian gem in the world's tallest tower

With its open kitchen and vaulted framework, this award-winning restaurant evokes a hip nightspot in a converted Indian marketplace. Orange and blue light shades brighten the muted Armani colour palette and the high-end Indian cuisine is just as vibrant. Outside, the terrace is a magical spot with views up the Burj Khalifa tower and down over the fountains – perfectly positioned to watch the fountain light show.

Armani Hotel Dubai Downtown Dubai **04 888 3888**
dubai.armanihotels.com
Map **2 F6** Metro **Burj Khalifa/Dubai Mall**

Armani/Dubai Cafe — Cafe

Armani by name, Armani by nature

Classy Italian dishes are served up with the kind of flair you'd expect from this cafe's designer namesake, and the surroundings live up to the label too. It's all about moody reds and dark wooden tones that create an ambience, which is at the same time welcoming and effortlessly stylish.

The Dubai Mall Downtown Dubai **04 339 8396**
Map **2 F6** Metro **Burj Khalifa/Dubai Mall**

Armani/Hashi — Japanese

A new Dubai must-do

Inside, the restaurant is beautifully elegant, but the prime seats are outside with the Burj's sky-piercing spire above you and the romantic Dubai Fountain in front. The service is refreshingly down-to-earth, yet the food is easily just as exquisite and out of the ordinary as the stunning surroundings.

Armani Hotel Dubai Downtown Dubai
04 888 3888
dubai.armanihotels.com
Map **2 F6** Metro **Burj Khalifa/Dubai Mall**

Armani/Hashi

Armani/Lounge — Italian
All-day dining with an Italian twist
Dine at any time of the day, but enjoy the traditional Italian Aperitivo experience from 18:30-20:00. Stimulate the appetite with an aperitif of your choice and accompanying canapes. Move on to a la carte options, accompanied by the soothing strains of the resident violinist and fantastic views of the Dubai Fountain.
Armani Hotel Dubai Downtown Dubai **04 888 3888**
dubai.armanihotels.com
Map **2 F6** Metro **Burj Khalifa/Dubai Mall**

Armani/Mediterraneo — Mediterranean
A sophisticated approach to a designer buffet
With muted tones and full length windows overlooking the Dubai Fountain, this restaurant is popular with hotel guests and those wanting to sample Armani's twist on classic Mediterranean dishes. A la carte options are available alongside the buffet and, surprisingly, the prices are far from outrageous.
Armani Hotel Dubai Downtown Dubai **04 888 3888**
dubai.armanihotels.com
Map **2 F6** Metro **Burj Khalifa/Dubai Mall**

Armani/Peck — Italian
Chic Italian deli where less is more
Black and white decor matches the simple, yet tasty, and beautifully presented Italian fare. Choose a la carte or try the 'sharing concept' set meal for a culinary journey through Italy. Pop into the upscale deli shop and take home imported and homemade pasta, desserts, cheeses, oils and other delicacies.
Armani Hotel Dubai Downtown Dubai **04 888 3888**
dubai.armanihotels.com
Map **2 F6** Metro **Burj Khalifa/Dubai Mall**

Armani/Ristorante — Italian
Substance and style at this signature restaurant
The Italian menu is dominated by truffles, whether sprinkled on your scallop starter, adding flavour to the creamiest risotto or even decorating your desert. Opt for the set truffle menu or mix and match classic with couture dishes, all served in your spacious booth.
Armani Hotel Dubai Downtown Dubai **04 888 3888**
dubai.armanihotels.com
Map **2 F6** Metro **Burj Khalifa/Dubai Mall**

Aryaas — Indian
A veggie thali feast of unbeatable value
This Indian chain has been serving up excellent fare since 1959, and, despite its prison-like austerity, the food is excellent. The house speciality is thali, small pots of different flavours into which you dip endless naan bread or rice. Around Dhs.15 will buy enough food to fill you up for the whole day.
Al Nakheel Bldg, Zabeel Rd Al Karama **04 335 5776**
Map **2 L6** Metro **Al Karama**

Asado — Latin American
Argentinean gem that really raises the steaks
A combination of moody lighting, passionate music, and a meat lover's dream menu cement Asado's top steakhouse position. Excellent meat and an enormous wine selection, with terrace views of Burj Khalifa thrown in, make this Argentinean restaurant something special.
The Palace Downtown Dubai Downtown Dubai **04 888 3444**
theaddress.com
Map **2 F6** Metro **Burj Khalifa/Dubai Mall**

Asha's — Indian
Atmospheric Indian with superstar status
Indian superstar Asha Bhosle has put a lot of love into this restaurant. Beautifully decorated, the quality of the atmospheric interior is equalled by the eclectic menu, which includes Indian classics, Asha's signature dishes, and some fusion choices. Great cocktails too.
Wafi Umm Hurair 2 **04 324 4100**
wafirestaurants.com
Map **2 L7** Metro **Dubai Healthcare City**

Ashiana — Indian
Top-notch curries and kebabs in an eclectic setting
Dimmed lights and live music set the tone for the ambling, relaxed Indian meal to come. The staff have perfected the art of subtle attentiveness, and the kitchen seems to nail each item on its vast menu, from seafood and mutton curries to more contemporary dishes and massive meats from the tandoor.
Sheraton Dubai Creek Hotel & Towers Al Rigga **04 228 1111**
sheratondubaicreek.com
Map **2 M5** Metro **Union**

Asmak — Seafood
Good prices and good seafood combine
Asmak's simple, calm blue and white decor hides a quaint little place with a talented chef who knows how to prepare succulent seafood as well as a variety of hot and cold mezzes. Guests can take a stroll to the seafood bar and select their fare and tell the chef how they want it prepared. The spicy garlic potatoes are a must-try but best avoided on any sort of romantic outing. Choose between indoor seating or alfresco dining on a beautiful wooden deck.
Century Village Al Garhoud **04 282 5377**
centuryvillage.ae
Map **2 N8** Metro **GGICO**

At.mosphere — International
World's highest restaurant with standards to match
The world's highest restaurant was always going to be big on the wow factor. But the wonder goes beyond the stupendous views, for this is a properly impressive

restaurant in its own right. The kitchen delivers on the lofty ambition with opulent menus of premium ingredients and exquisite presentation. The Grill is open for lunch and dinner and is the equal of any of the UAE's top restaurants both in excellence and price tag. The Lounge opens from midday to 02:00 for drinks and snacks; it is also home to the highest high tea in the world and is a more affordable option to enjoy the cuisine and the views. This really is the ultimate in high-end dining destinations – and has to be the finest sundowner spot anywhere.
Burj Khalifa Downtown Dubai **04 888 3828**
atmosphereburjkhalifa.com
Map **2 F6** Metro **Burj Khalifa/Dubai Mall**

Automatic — Middle Eastern
Fresh, tasty Arabic delights in a casual setting
This popular chain continues to serve high quality Arabic food in various locations in Dubai. The vast range of mezze is accompanied by mountainous portions of salad, and grilled meat, fish and kebabs. The atmosphere is minimalist but clean and bright, with family-friendly amenities and good service.
The Beach Centre Jumeira 1 **04 349 4888**
Map **2 G4** Metro **Emirates Towers**

Awtar — Middle Eastern
Stylish Arabian decor and moreish mezze
Gold-swathed booths and low lighting give the feeling of opulent Arabic elegance at this Lebanese restaurant. The starters and desserts steal the show from the mains, so load up your plate from an appealing selection of well-presented mezze. A belly dancer makes an appearance after 22:00.
Grand Hyatt Dubai Umm Hurair 2 **04 317 2222**
dubai.grand.hyatt.com
Map **2 L8** Metro **Dubai Healthcare City**

AZ.U.R — International
Good, honest food with a cracking terrace
Boasting a fantastic wooden floored terrace with great views of the Marina, AZ.U.R is a popular spot. You can dine alfresco all year round with fans in the scorching summer months and heaters in the winter. The menu is small but offers a decent selection of Spanish, Moroccan, French and Italian inspired chicken, vegetarian, meat and seafood dishes. The wine menu is on the generous side and beautifully complements the menu. Ask the staff about the soup and risotto of the day as these change on a daily basis. The restaurant is very child-friendly, offering high chairs as well as a kids' menu with favourites like fish fingers, chicken strips, pasta, sandwiches and ice-cream.
Dubai Marriott Harbour Hotel & Suites
Dubai Marina **04 319 4794**
azur.dubaimarriottharbourhotel.com
Map **1 L5** Metro **Dubai Marina**

Bagels & More — Cafe
Hearty, authentic American-style bagels
Take advantage of free Wi-Fi at this NYC-style deli along with your morning bagel and coffee, or enjoy a hearty lunch outside on the terrace. The bagels come in a myriad of flavours and are crammed with a host of delicious fillings from lox to pastrami – this is as close as it gets to a genuine New York bagel experience on our sandy shores.
Marina Diamond 3 Dubai Marina **04 430 8790**
Map **1 L5** Metro **Dubai Marina**

Baker & Spice — Cafe
Honest, wholesome, organic food
No two visits to Baker & Spice will ever be the same. The menu, based on the freshest organic ingredients sourced from local farmers, changes daily depending on what is available. What is constant, however, is the carefully prepared 'home-cooked' flavour of every dish, from breakfast to dinner. It's fresh, healthy and wholesome. You also have an unobstructed view from your table on the terrace to the Dubai Fountain dancing against the backdrop of the Burj Khalifa. Understandably, the terrace fills up quickly on a first-come, first-served basis, but you can wait your turn inside. Apart from an indoor dining area, there is also a market selling deli-style salads, home-made pickles and jams, and organic fruits and vegetables.
Souk Al Bahar Downtown Dubai **04 425 2240**
bakerandspiceme.com
Map **2 F6** Metro **Burj Khalifa/Dubai Mall**

Balance Cafe — Cafe
Healthy bites, Ayurvedic vibes and guilt-free cakes
Nutritionally balanced meals grace Balance Cafe's varied menu, which proves that healthy eating doesn't equal boring. The selection includes tasty dishes

Bagels & More

inspired by Mediterranean, Indian and Japanese cooking: choose between wraps, soups and sushi for light bites or opt for the heartier mains that include pasta, kebabs and barbecue grub. There's an emphasis on vegetarian dishes but meatier options like grilled prawns and lamb biryani are also available. Nutritional information is provided for all dishes.
Oasis Centre Al Quoz 1 **04 515 4051**
balance-wellness-centre.com
Map **2 L6** Metro **Noor Islamic Bank**

Bamboo Lagoon — Far Eastern
Grass-skirted singers and a brilliant buffet
Bamboo Lagoon's staggering range of exquisite fusion cuisine demands a repeat visit. The bottomless buffet with numerous stalls offers everything from sushi to curries and grills, and an abundance of oriental trappings dominate the decor. At 21:00 a band takes to the stage and grass-skirted singers serenade diners with Polynesian tunes and entertaining covers.
JW Marriott Hotel Dubai Al Muraqqabat **04 607 7977**
marriottdiningatjw.ae
Map **2 P6** Metro **Abu Baker Al Siddique**

Basta Art Cafe — Cafe
Atmospheric escape from the Bur Dubai bustle
This courtyard cafe and gallery offers quiet sanctuary amid busy and atmospheric Bastakiya. Sit on majlis-style cushions or under a canopy while choosing from the menu of hearty breakfasts, healthy salads and tempting paninis. Its sister outlet at Arabian Ranches has a similarly rustic-chic atmosphere.
Bastakiya Al Souk Al Kabeer **04 353 5071**
bastakiah.com
Map **2 M4** Metro **Al Fahidi**

Bastakiah Nights — Middle Eastern
Magical place celebrating local cuisine and culture
This spot offers a perfect amalgamation of great location and delectable food. Choose from the fixed menus or a la carte offerings – there's no alcohol on the menu, but you'd be a fool to let that put you off.
Bastakiya Al Souk Al Kabeer **04 353 7772**
bastakiah.com
Map **2 M4** Metro **Al Fahidi**

Bateaux Dubai — Dinner Cruise
More than just your average creek cruise
This sleek, glass-topped vessel offers four-course fine dining from a varied international menu, with five-star surroundings to match. Intimate lighting, with cosy tables and splendid views of the city, make for a top pick for romance or a special tourist treat. A bubbly Friday brunch is also available.
Nr British Embassy Al Hamriya **04 399 4994**
bateauxdubai.com
Map **2 M5** Metro **BurJuman**

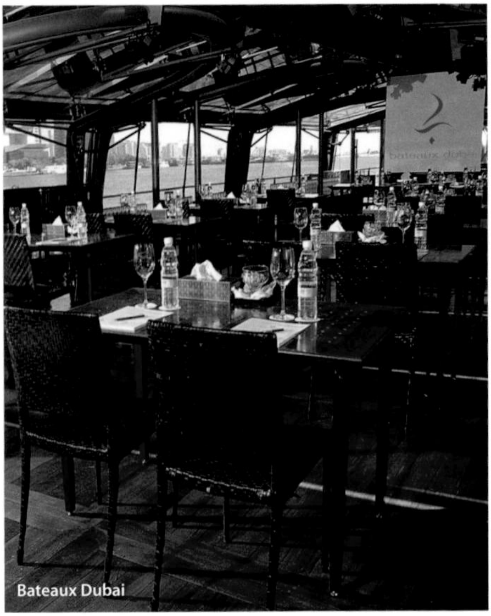
Bateaux Dubai

Beach Bar & Grill — Seafood
Seafood by the seashore for true romantics
Seafood lovers must make a trip to this opulent, romantic beach bar. Terrace tables are candle-lit, and the fresh fish is cooked simply but with style. There's seafood platters to share, and surf and turf options for people who simply can't pick just one dish.
The Palace At One&Only Royal Mirage Al Sufouh 1 **04 399 9999**
oneandonlyresorts.com
Map **1 M4** Metro **Nakheel**

Beach House Cabana — Latin American
Tapas and good times all the way
A good choice for a laidback evening spent with friends. Casual seating, hot and cold tapas, hearty mains, reasonable prices and a good cocktail selection add to the convivial feel.
Clubhouse Azraq, Shoreline Apartments Palm Jumeirah **04 361 8856**
emiratesleisureretail.com
Map **1 N4** Metro **Nakheel**

Beachcombers — Far Eastern
Decadent oriental cuisine in a memorable location
This breezy shack has an idyllic location right on the beach with fantastic views of the Burj Al Arab. Expect excellent far eastern buffets with live cooking stations for stir-fries and noodles. The Peking duck, curry hotpots and satay are highly recommended.
Jumeirah Beach Hotel Umm Suqeim 3 **04 406 8999**
jumeirah.com
Map **1 S4** Metro **Mall of the Emirates**

Bella Donna
Italian

Reasonably priced cuisine from a bygone era

Bella Donna has a vaguely 1920s feel. Its low-cost Italian fare includes homemade pasta and classic pizzas like the margarita or the more unusual capricciosa (with a cooked egg and potatoes). There is no kids' menu but there is plenty to keep them happy.

Mercato Jumeira 1 **04 344 7701**
binhendi.com
Map **2 F4** Metro **Financial Centre**

Benihana
Japanese

Great value Japanese with entertainment on tap

Dining at Benihana is an all-round pleasure. The quality is excellent, the staff are chatty and the prices are great. The seats of choice are around the teppanyaki grills, where the chefs cook your food to order, with side helpings of cheeky banter and cooking utensil trickery. For more intimate dining, opt for the terrace outside. Also at Al Bustan Rotana (04 282 0000).

Amwaj Rotana Dubai Marina **04 428 2000**
rotana.com
Map **1 K4** Metro **Jumeirah Lakes Towers**

Benjarong
Thai

Perfect Thai served in mediocre surroundings

The decor is in a regal Thai style, the food is deliciously concocted and perfectly presented, but the atmosphere is a little lacking. The menu is tempting though, with classics and a few inventive twists; if you love Thai food you'll certainly enjoy it.

Dusit Thani Dubai Trade Centre 2 **04 343 3333**
dusit.com
Map **2 G6** Metro **Financial Centre**

Bentoya Kitchen
Japanese

Quick, fresh and authentic bento on SZR

Bentoya's popularity with Dubai's Japanese expats vouches for the authenticity of its fresh, good quality maki, sushi and bento boxes. The teriyaki beef is particularly recommended. The compact, double storey restaurant is well-priced and ideal for a casual bite.

Al Kawakeb Bldg, Shk Zayed Rd Trade Centre 2
04 343 0222
bentoya.info
Map **2 G6** Metro **Financial Centre**

BiCE
Italian

High-end Italian is one of Dubai's best-loved

With dark woods, white table clothes, dim lighting, gold flourishes and serving trolleys displaying everything from aperitifs and olive oils to cheeses and fish, this restaurant could have stood unchanged for half a century. The old European feel is a far cry from the traditional trattoria style Italian bistro, but Italian this unashamedly is. Pizzas and pastas feature, but they're overshadowed – both in number and lip-licking descriptions – by imaginative meat cuts and, most of all, seafood dishes. If you're struggling to decide, the waiters make excellent suggestions (you may need guidance through the large wine menu too), or you could just opt for a fish from the trolley – cooked and served however you'd like it. Prices are fairly high but tables remain full even midweek, such is the quality of the fare and popularity of the location.

Hilton Dubai Jumeirah Resort Dubai Marina
04 399 1111
hilton.com
Map **1 K4** Metro **Jumeirah Lakes Towers**

BiCE Mare
Italian

Superb seafood at this intimate Italian

Sister to BiCE, the 'mare' signifies a seafood dominated menu of delicious dishes, both simple and complex, that bring fish lovers back time and time again. Dine inside and be entertained by the sultry jazz hands of the resident pianist or take in the splendid Dubai Fountain show from the terrace.

Souk Al Bahar Downtown Dubai **04 423 0982**
bicemare.com
Map **2 F6** Metro **Burj Khalifa/Dubai Mall**

Biella
Italian

Tasty Italian and a perfect shopping pit stop

An Italian staple in malls across town, put down your shopping and tuck into tasty favourites served by friendly staff. The extensive menu includes salads and pasta, but the pizzas top the bill. The terrace at the Wafi branch is a perfect spot to recharge on coffee and cake.

Wafi Umm Hurair 2 **04 324 4666**
pyramidsrestaurantsatwafi.com
Map **2 L7** Metro **Dubai Healthcare City**

Bistro Domino
French

Reasonably priced fare in low-key surroundings

A hearty selection of dishes is served here that will leave you warm, satisfied and wishing you were tucking into your meal in a rustic chateau. The tempting menu is an authentic mix of typical French dishes (including deliciously buttery escargot) and fabulously rich desserts.

Hotel Ibis Deira City Centre Port Saeed **04 292 5000**
ibishotel.com
Map **2 N7** Metro **Deira City Centre**

Bistro Madeleine
French

Reasonably priced fare in laidback surroundings

Say au revoir to pretence and settle in for some casual dining in a relaxed atmosphere. While it may not offer views of the Riviera, the Festival City waterfront promenade is a good alternative. The bistro hits the mark on French classics like duck confit, flavourful escargot and rich coq au vin. Aside from the a la carte

options, Bistro Madeleine also has a weekday 'quick lunch' special which includes a main course, soft drink, tea or coffee and a madeleine for just Dhs. 40; and the Thursday 'French Night' is a lovely buffet of cold cuts, cheeses, mains and dessert platter. With chirpy, cheerful and knowledgeable staff and prices that won't break the bank, this is bistro dining done right.
InterContinental Dubai Festival City
Dubai Festival City **04 701 1127**
diningdfc.com
Map **2 M9** Metro **Emirates**

Black Canyon — Thai

Good Asian with popular takeaway service

A combination of coffee shop and Far East fusion, Black Canyon serves up a wide variety of noodle and rice dishes, curries, soups and Thai specialities. It uses fresh ingredients without enhancers or preservatives and this certainly translates into the flavours. Has other branches at Festival Centre and Arabian Ranches, and offers a popular takeaway service.
The Walk, Jumeirah Beach Residence Dubai Marina
04 423 1993
salehbinlahejgroup.com
Map **1 K5** Metro **Jumeirah Lakes Towers**

Blades — International

Fine dining but child-friendly too, a parent's dream

Delicious Asian noodles, steaks and tasting platters feature prominently in this fine-dining eatery that also welcomes children with a healthy kids' menu and colouring books. Excellent service for all ages and not a chicken nugget or plastic toy in sight.
Al Badia Golf Club By InterContinental Dubai Festival City Dubai Festival City **04 701 1127**
albadiagolfclub.ae
Map **2 M10** Metro **Emirates**

Blue Elephant — Thai

Be transported to Thailand by this popular haunt

A stalwart of Dubai's Thai restaurant scene, it's changed little in the 15 years since opening – if it isn't broke why fix it? The restaurant is spacious; however it has plenty of split levels and quiet corners to make it intimate for small tables or large groups. The food is simply excellent. The choice, as you would expect from a Thai menu, is vast and the set menus offer a chance to sample a little of everything. Blue Elephant sticks to what it knows – pad thai, Thai curries, spring rolls, dim sum, sweet and sour and the like. Mixed amongst the traditional are some signature dishes and unique options such as the fresh lime seabass. The food may not have many frills but it is perfectly prepared and presented.
Al Bustan Rotana Al Garhoud **04 282 0000**
blueelephant.com/dubai
Map **2 N7** Metro **GGICO**

Blue Flame > *p.527* — International

Surf and turf menu is a match made in heaven

From steaks to seafood, the Jumeirah Creekside Hotel's signature grill restaurant combines an interactive experience with an extensive 'surf and turf' menu. With a focus on fresh local produce, the land and sea themed menu features a range of culinary delights, including twisted tuna, poached egg ravioli and a selection of the finest meats and seafood cooked fresh to order on the charcoal grill. For those who cannot decide which dish to go for, Blue Flame's inspiring 'meatelier' trolley offers a selection of Wagyu and Angus beef tenderloins, sirloins and rib eyes to choose from; there's also a personalised, interactive iPad beverage list. Be sure to make a return visit to the glass-walled cooking pod, where a master chef guides you through how to cook your very own dish – before you enjoy eating it!
Jumeirah Creekside Hotel Al Garhoud
04 230 8580
jumeirah.com
Map **2 M8** Metro **GGICO**

Blue Orange — International

Food from all around the world, around the clock

A lively open kitchen serves up breakfast, lunch and dinner at this 24-hour contemporary buffet restaurant. The menu is international: choose from dishes such as Japanese sushi, Arabic mezze, Chinese dim sum and Belgian waffles. Family-friendly and reasonably priced – and with all the theatrics of live cooking stations.
The Westin Dubai Mina Seyahi Beach Resort & Marina Al Sufouh 1 **04 399 4141**
westinminaseyahi.com
Map **1 M4** Metro **Nakheel**

Blue Elephant

Blue Rain — Thai

Fine-dining Thai restaurant that sticks with tradition

Modern and minimalist with a spectacular waterfall running down the outside of the building, Blue Rain is an impressive sight to behold. This fine-dining Thai restaurant has been causing a stir thanks to its authentic dishes, including a number of offerings which aren't found in standard Dubai Thai eateries. Blue Rain has managed to balance its menu for those dining on their own money, and those dining on accounts. At one end there are really affordable options, while at the other there are extravagant, pricey dishes perfect for impressing clients or flexing the company card. There are a couple of modern takes on authenticity – such as the inclusion of Wagyu beef in the red curry – but in terms of taste, everything is exactly as it should be – light and delicate and yet bursting with robust flavours.

The Ritz-Carlton, Dubai International Financial Centre Trade Centre 2 **04 372 2222**
ritzcarlton.com
Map **2 G6** Metro **Financial Centre**

Bo House Cafe — Cafe

Cafe fare in JBR's best spot

There's no shortage of casual eateries in JBR, but Bo House's enviable location between the street and shore sets the artsy cafe-cum-restaurant apart. Whether you turn up for shisha on the terrace or opt for lunch by the floor-to-ceiling windows, the beach view is unmatched. At Dhs.52, the English breakfast is not cheap, but you get a respectable serving of all the usual treats, as well as a glass of freshly squeezed juice of your choice. The Four Eggs (Dhs.36) dish stood out as the star of the menu: the filling portion came complete with a generous sprinkling of taste bud-teasing sumac. You'll have to resist the temptation to polish the whole plate if you want to save space for Bo House's homemade ice creams on your way out.

The Walk, Jumeirah Beach Residence Dubai Marina
04 429 8655
bohousecafe.com
Map **1 K5** Metro **Dubai Marina**

The Boardwalk — International

Fine menu in a prime creekside location

Stood on wooden stilts, overlooking the creek, Boardwalk's close-up water views are unmatched. The menu features an array of generous and well-presented starters and mains including seafood and vegetarian options. The restaurant doesn't take reservations but you can grab a drink at QD's (p.561) while you wait.

Dubai Creek Golf & Yacht Club Port Saeed
04 295 6000
dubaigolf.com
Map **2 M7** Metro **Deira City Centre**

The Bombay — Indian

A casual spot to enjoy tasty fare

An unassuming restaurant that packs quite a punch, The Bombay may not be widely-revered but it is a favourite destination for Indian food lovers who are in the know. The dishes are well-priced, generous and among the most authentic in the city, and the laid-back atmosphere lends itself to a convivial night out with friends.

Marco Polo Hotel Muteena **04 272 0000**
marcopolohotel.net
Map **2 P5** Metro **Salah Al Din**

Brauhaus > *p.553* — German

Beers, bratwurst and Bavaria abound at Brauhaus

Join German expats and those after authentic Bavarian food – and, of course, beer – in this casual spot. The semi-private booths are the choice spot to enjoy substantial portions of well-cooked schnitzels, bratwursts and sauerkraut. Top it all off with the huge selection of imported German bottled beers and draft ales and you'll be full-bellied and happy in no time.

Jumeira Rotana Al Bada'a **04 345 5888**
rotana.com
Map **2 J4** Metro **World Trade Centre**

Brunetti — Italian

The best things come in small packages

Accompany an authentic Italian brew with miniature sweet treats, savoury snacks and home-made gelati, sink into booth seats surrounded by faux-leather and retro prints, and enjoy the Aquarium views. One of The Dubai Mall's best, but it won't break the bank.

The Dubai Mall Downtown Dubai **04 339 8173**
brunetticaffe.com
Map **2 F6** Metro **Burj Khalifa/Dubai Mall**

Burj Al Hamam — Middle Eastern

Quality offerings from the Lebanese chain

Located at the Marina Promenade, the popular Lebanese franchise now offers diners the chance to experience Arabic cuisine with a waterside setting. Don't expect to find any fusion or twists on the menu, Burj Al Hamam is all about traditional Arabic fare at its very best. Portions are generous, so be careful when ordering mezzes because you will definitely want to save space for the mixed grill and seafood mains; the kastaleta (lamb chops) and kibbeh sajieh come highly recommended. Dessert selections are just as varied, with mahalabiyas to traditional Arabic pastries on offer. If you're not feeling so peckish then go alfresco, kick back with a shisha and take in the marina views… it's the closest slice of Beirut that you'll find in Dubai.

Festival Centre Dubai Festival City
04 232 9021
burjalhamam.com
Map **2 M9** Metro **Emirates**

Bussola — Italian
Beachside pizza and cocktails under the stars
Adventurous, delicious Sicilian-influenced pizzas served alfresco on a terrace by the sea – Arabia doesn't get much more Mediterranean than this. Upstairs the open-air deck offers a relaxed atmosphere, with more formality and a fuller menu downstairs. The desserts are excellent whatever floor you're on.
The Westin Dubai Mina Seyahi Beach Resort & Marina Al Sufouh 1 **04 399 4141**
westinminaseyahi.com
Map **1 M4** Metro **Nakheel**

The Butcher Shop & Grill — Steakhouse
Man-size portions of unadulterated meat
There is other meat on offer, but this is really all about steak, so pick your giant fillet, rump, T-bone, prime rib or rib-eye and tuck in. There's quality as well as quantity and, best of all, you can take home a few cuts from the in-house butchers counter complete with cooking tips. Also at The Walk, JBR and Mirdif City Centre.
Mall of the Emirates Al Barsha 1 **04 347 1167**
thebutchershop-me.com
Map **1 R6** Metro **Mall of the Emirates**

Cactus Cantina — Mexican
Burritos, margaritas and potential for a great night
The portions here are *muy grande*, with the emphasis leaning more toward the Tex than the Mex (refried beans and melted cheese with everything). The lively atmosphere is aided by a pumping soundtrack and energetic staff. Weekends see the joint jumping, with crowds attracted by meal deals and generously sized and priced jugs of margaritas.
Chelsea Plaza Hotel, Satwa Roundabout Al Jafiliya **04 398 2274**
cactuscantinadubai.com
Map **2 J5** Metro **Al Jafiliya**

Cafe Arabesque — Middle Eastern
Excellent Arabic in romantic, creekside surrounds
Whether you go buffet or a la carte, linger over a cold mezze spread, succulent wood-fired kebabs and fantastic Lebanese, Syrian and Jordanian dishes as you take in marvellous views of the creek. With romantic, soft lighting, the perfect evening awaits – finished with a stroll along the creek.
Park Hyatt Dubai Port Saeed **04 317 2222**
dubai.park.hyatt.com
Map **2 M7** Metro **GGICO**

Cafe Ceramique — Cafe
Typical cafe treats in a creative setting
Reserve this cafe for when you, or the kids, need to release your creativity. Turn up, choose an item and decorate it using the paints and stencils – it will then be glazed for collection at a later date. The menu has a good choice of light snacks, kids' choices and hot and cold drinks. It's also a popular choice for childrens' parties with special birthday menus. There's another branch in Festival Centre (04 232 8616).
Town Centre Jumeirah Jumeira 1 **04 344 7331**
cafeceramique.ae
Map **2 F4** Metro **Burj Khalifa/Dubai Mall**

Cafe Havana — Cafe
A step up from standard mall foodcourt offerings
Dotted all over Dubai, this chain offers consistently good cafe-style food with a Middle Eastern twist. Quality is high, prices reasonable and the service spot on. See website for branch listing.
Spinneys Centre Al Safa 2 **04 394 1727**
binhendi.com
Map **2 B5** Metro **Noor Islamic Bank**

Can Can Brasserie — French
Classy French fare in a stylish brasserie setting
Serves high-class brasserie fare in a stylish Parisian setting just steps away from the hustle and bustle of DIFC. Can Can Brasserie is a great lunch spot for financiers with a flair for all things French – classics from escargots to steak frites grace the menu, and busy executives can enjoy it all in just 45 minutes by choosing the excellent-value Business Lunch. The tomato tartelette is full of juicy flavour, while the poached organic salmon main strokes a fine balance of textures and tastes with a scrumptious herb crust, delicate cauliflower puree and earthy porcini mushrooms. Breakfast options range from croissants to heartier combos such as eggs benedict.
The Ritz-Carlton, Dubai International Financial Centre Trade Centre 2 **04 372 2222**
ritzcarlton.com
Map **2 G6** Metro **Financial Centre**

Cafe Ceramique

Caramel Restaurant & Lounge — American

Oozing urban cool

This is where those who work hard, come to play even harder. Stylish wooden furniture spills out from the bar on to the terrace, where trendy cabanas and warm lighting set the mood for stylish lounging. From the mac n cheese to the lobster tacos, expect high quality dishes with American flair. Prices are high, so dress your best.

Dubai International Financial Centre (DIFC) Trade Centre 2 **04 425 6677**
caramelgroup.com
Map **2 G6** Metro **Financial Centre**

Carluccio's — Italian

Tasty Italian with super fountain and Burj views

From the hearty carb dishes to the shelves laden with cookery books and deli produce, Carluccio's is a family-friendly slice of Italy. The modern white interior and alfresco dining are stylishly modern rather than cosy trattoria, while the terrace has great views of Dubai Fountain. Serving breakfast, lunch and dinner, outlets are also open at Mirdif City Centre (04 284 3728) and Dubai Marina Mall (04 399 7844).

The Dubai Mall Downtown Dubai **04 434 1320**
carluccios.com
Map **2 F6** Metro **Burj Khalifa/Dubai Mall**

Carnevale — Italian

Family-friendly Italian in the shadow of the Burj

Carnevale offers upmarket Italian food, swift service and views of the Burj Al Arab from the adjoining indoor terrace. Despite its exclusive, Venetian-themed interior, families and children are well catered for.

Jumeirah Beach Hotel Umm Suqeim 3 **04 406 8999**
jumeirah.com
Map **1 S4** Metro **Mall of the Emirates**

Casa Mia — Italian

Well-prepared Italian fare and a massive wine list

A quality restaurant, the standard Italian menu is nothing if not consistent, and the temperature-controlled wine cellar holds more than 400 Italian wines. Portions are suitably generous, and most of the dishes are available either as a main or a side, allowing you to deviate from your usual spag bol order and broaden your gastronomical horizons.

Le Meridien Dubai Al Garhoud **04 702 2506**
casamia-dubai.com
Map **2 N8** Metro **GGICO**

Cascades — International

Decent dining in a venue you'll fall for

Tumbling water features dominate the Fairmont hotel's breathtaking lobby where this international restaurant serves dishes to suit every palate and devilishly tempting desserts to finish. Head here for a trendy dinner, business lunch, extended brunch or an indulgent cocktail while elevator watching.

Fairmont Dubai Trade Centre 1 **04 311 8316**
fairmont.com/dubai
Map **2 J5** Metro **World Trade Centre**

The Cavendish — International

A hearty feed in JLT

With a daily buffet and a vast a la carte menu, it takes some time to decide which corner of the world to order from. Whether you opt for the succulent signature burger or delicious pasta dishes, you won't be disappointed. A bright and airy space, it's perfect for business breakfasts, lunches and dinners.

Bonnington Jumeirah Lakes Towers Jumeirah Lakes Towers **04 356 0600**
bonningtontower.com
Map **1 K5** Metro **Jumeirah Lakes Towers**

Celebrities — European

Well-crafted European dishes in a romantic setting

This elegant restaurant offers romantic views of softly lit gardens from tables peppered with rose petals and iridescent stones. The well priced European menu contains dainty but filling dishes such as sea-bass and baked rack of lamb, or try the tasting menu for Dhs.275.

The Palace At One&Only Royal Mirage Al Sufouh 1 **04 399 9999**
oneandonlyresorts.com
Map **1 M4** Metro **Nakheel**

Center Cut — Steakhouse

Serious restaurant for meat and grape lovers

On first arrival, Center Cut looks like a rather austere affair. However a warm welcome from the staff starts to melt the stiff atmosphere and the menu quickly makes up for the rest. This is very much a steakhouse, in cuisine if not in surroundings, with the first page of the menu adorned with a diagram of a cow and the cuts of meat. The drinks waiter arrives first with his trolley of delights to mix you a heady concoction from the impressive cocktail selection. The sommelier provides much-needed advice too. Appetisers include Atlantic salmon, scallops, foie gras and oysters while your main meal is all about the steaks. Choose from Australian or United States cuts with a selection of sauces and sides. There is also a lamb or chicken choice but not a fish in sight, so this really isn't a venue for non-carnivores. After your serving of meat you can indulge further with a chocolate nemesis or a trio of cheeses – if your arteries can take it.

The Ritz-Carlton, Dubai International Financial Centre Trade Centre 2 **04 372 2222**
ritzcarlton.com
Map **2 G6** Metro **Financial Centre**

Certo — Italian

Impressive menu with an eye-catching wine cellar

Certo's tasty, creative menu and floor-to-ceiling, glass encased wine cellar bring to life what would otherwise be a fairly non-descript business hotel restaurant. Excellent starters and mains combine with good, attentive service to make this one of the best Italians in the area.

Radisson Blu Hotel, Dubai Media City Al Sufouh 1
04 366 9111
radissonblu.com
Map **1 M5** Metro **Nakheel**

Chalet — International

Firm favourite of residents and tourists alike

Clean, modern and compact, this Beach Road eatery offers a culinary world tour with Chinese noodles and Indian curries, but the main draws are the sturdy Arabic offerings. Expect a clientele as eclectic as the menu but beware the unisex toilet.

Nr Umm Suqeim Park, Jumeira Rd Umm Suqeim 2
04 348 6089
Map **1 T4** Metro **First Gulf Bank**

Chandelier — Middle Eastern

Great outdoor venue, good food and shisha

Set in the lively Marina Walk, Chandelier has a modern interior and a great outdoor section overlooking the marina. The service is leisurely, but with an interesting mix of fare and a full range of mocktails and juices, no one really cares.

Marina Walk Dubai Marina **04 366 3606**
Map **1 K5** Metro **Dubai Marina**

Channels > *p.461* — International

Great, value-for-money, themed buffet dining

This all-day diner makes up for rather drab surroundings and a flat atmosphere with its great value buffets four nights a week. The spread is staggering, the desserts in particular, and the price (from Dhs.179 including house drinks) makes it a great option for big groups.

Media Rotana Tecom **04 435 0000**
rotana.com
Map **1 P6** Metro **Dubai Internet City**

The Cheesecake Factory — American

A large slice of comfort food

Famed for its large portions, the American restaurant chain serves up eye-poppingly large portions of comfort food – from avocado rolls to the indulgent mac n cheese burger. And then there's the cheesecake, more than 40 different types. It's certainly not good for the waistline, but this is the place to come if you want to have your cake and eat it!

Mall of the Emirates Al Barsha 1
Map **1 R6** Metro **Mall of the Emirates**

Chef Lanka — Sri Lankan

Dubai's best place to try Sri Lankan cuisine

Located just opposite LuLu's, this is a smart, clean, Sri Lankan restaurant offering good value and tasty food. Eat from the buffet for just Dhs.8 at lunch and Dhs.20 at dinner, or order a la carte for authentic dishes modified to your desired level of spiciness. The string shoppers (a tasty meal of circular steamed red rice), or the kingfish curry and koththu roti (chopped roti bread stir-fried with chicken, leeks, tomatoes and carrots), are highly recommended. Takeaway and delivery are available.

Nr LuLu Supermarket Al Karama **04 335 3050**
Map **2 L6** Metro **Al Karama**

Chef's House — International

Eat your way around Asia in Media City

As all-day diner restaurants goes Chef's House is a cut above the rest and the decor and service attest to this. A combination of beautiful colours such as red, black and creams provides the setting for six theme nights and a Saturday brunch from 12:30 to 15:30. The restaurant offers an extensive international buffet with live cooking stations where you can choose from a huge variety – from mouthwatering freshly prepared sushi to a must try chocolate fountain flanked by fruits, sweets, cakes and such waiting to be smothered in warm comforting chocolate, it's all there to tuck into. For the Saturday brunch, kids have their own room laid out for them complete with meals, jumping castles, face painting and games, all while under the watchful eyes of dedicated staff.

Radisson Blu Hotel, Dubai Media City Al Sufouh 1
04 366 9111
radissonblu.com
Map **1 M5** Metro **Nakheel**

Feast of Festivals

Dubai gastrophiles should look forward to the month of March as that's when the Taste of Dubai Festival 2013 hits the city. This three-day culinary tour-de-force sees Michel-starred and celebrity chefs from restaurants across Dubai showcase their skills at Dubai Media City. Taste some signature dishes, enjoy a cookery class, participate in beverage tastings and see world-famous chefs share their secrets live on stage. See tasteofdubaifestival.com for more information. Other foodie festivals include the International Fine Food Festival (ifffestival.com) at Meydan Grandstand, which features local and internationally sourced produce. Further afield, Gourmet Abu Dhabi (gourmetabudhabi.ae) is a 10-day festival that showcases world chefs and their culinary skills.

Arz Lebanon

Chandelier

Asado

Al Muntaha

Zuma

Chili's
American

Burgers, ribs and paraphernalia a-plenty

Around the world and all over Dubai, Chili's delivers its winning formula for inexpensive, all-American tucker in huge portions and in family-friendly surroundings. Takeaway and home delivery (04 282 8303) are also available. See website for locations.

Saleh Bin Lahej Bldg, Nr Welcare Hospital
Al Garhoud **04 282 8484**
chilis.com
Map **2 N7** Metro **GGICO**

Chimes
Far Eastern

Asian eatery that lures the locals

The minimal decor emits a delicious aroma that entices local residents in from outside, while visitors from further afield will be pleasantly surprised by its well-cooked curries, seafood, noodles and fried rice. If you're after substance rather than flair, you'll be more than happy with its delicious Singapore pepper mud crab, Thai green curry and nasi goreng.

Seven Sands Hotel Apartments Al Barsha 1
04 323 4211
chimesdubai.com
Map **1 R6** Metro **Mall of the Emirates**

The China Club
Chinese

A tucked-away place to duck in for Peking duck

A chic space, with subtle touches of authenticity, serving recognisable favourites and new creations. The Peking duck, carved at the table, is excellent. Lunchtimes (Dhs.95 for a tasting menu) and Friday brunches (Dhs.140 excluding alcohol) are great value.

Radisson Blu Hotel, Dubai Deira Creek Al Rigga
04 222 7171
radissonblu.com
Map **2 M5** Metro **Union**

The China Club

China Times
Chinese

Affordable Asian treats in a tranquil atmosphere

This restaurant brings you closer to China with its soothing music, water statues and flashes of red and black. Its tempting sushi bar is only a small part of the menu, which packs an assortment of dim sum, stir-fries and noodles. Also at Jumeira Plaza (04 344 2930).

Deira City Centre Port Saeed **04 295 2515**
binhendi.com
Map **2 N7** Metro **Deira City Centre**

Choices
International

Pleasant all-day dining restaurant

The comfortable, elegant dining areas at this all-day dining restaurant host a themed buffet each night of the week, including French, seafood and international. Unlimited beer, wine and soft drinks are included in the price; breakfast and lunch buffets are also served.

Al Bustan Rotana Al Garhoud **04 282 0000**
rotana.com
Map **2 N7** Metro **GGICO**

Circle
Cafe

The perfect venue to meet up for a girlie gossip

Light, bright and gloriously feminine, the decor at Circle suits its menu of yummy bagels, salads, smoothies and puddings. Walls are lined with mirrors and quirky photos, and there's even a resident goldfish. Also at Dubai Media City (04 391 5170/1).

Beach Park Plaza Jumeira 2 **04 342 8177**
circle-cafe.com
Map **2 D4** Metro **Business Bay**

Conservatory
International

A relaxing oasis at any time of day

Uncomplicated and reasonably priced, this buffet restaurant features European, Arabic and Asian flavours. Choose between the airy but stylish indoors and the atmospheric outdoor courtyard. Pile your plate with tasty morsels but remember to save room for the delicious desserts.

Al Manzil Hotel Downtown Dubai **04 428 5888**
almanzilhotel.ae
Map **2 F7** Metro **Burj Khalifa/Dubai Mall**

Counter Culture
Cafe

A top spot for breakfast or traditional brunch

Hot and cold breakfast buffet, juices, the sun shining on the terrace and a newspaper spread across the table… all weekends should start this way. The simple layout of this little gem is welcoming at any time of the day or night, and the food is deliciously unfussy. There's a wealth of choice and the friendliest of service.

Dubai Marriott Harbour Hotel & Suites
Dubai Marina **04 319 4793**
counter-culture.dubaimarriottharbourhotel.com
Map **1 L5** Metro **Dubai Marina**

The Courtyard — Middle Eastern

Atmospheric restaurant serving tasty Arabic treats

A typical selection of hot and cold mezzes, soups and mixed grills are served in this licensed, outdoor restaurant. Discounted mezze packages offer excellent value; alternatively, individual portions can be ordered for Dhs.18 each. A broad a la carte menu is also available if you fancy poultry, fish or steak.

Al Manzil Hotel Downtown Dubai **04 428 5888**
almanzilhotel.ae
Map **2 F7** Metro **Burj Khalifa/Dubai Mall**

Creekside Restaurant — Japanese

All-you-can-eat in an Asian-inspired setting

One of the best Japanese restaurants in the city, Creekside now runs 'theme nights' every day of the week. In other words, it has become an all-you-can-eat paradise. The restaurant's clean lines and bright interior make a great setting for large groups, and the food, though limited in variety, far exceeds the buffet norm.

Sheraton Dubai Creek Hotel & Towers Al Rigga
04 207 1750
sheratondubaicreek.com
Map **2 M5** Metro **Union**

Cucina — Italian

Great pizza and pasta in faux-Tuscan surroundings

A solidly traditional menu and a reasonably priced wine list make up for the faux-rural Tuscan decor. The pizzas are great and the pasta dishes are good Italian staples. Be sure to get there in time for the staff's renditions of Italian tunes.

JW Marriott Hotel Dubai Al Muraqqabat
04 607 7588
marriottdiningatjw.ae
Map **2 P6** Metro **Abu Baker Al Siddique**

Da Gama — International

Modern Portuguese with Mexican-Asian twist

Da Gama has a little bit of a split personality. The menu mixes traditional Portuguese dishes with Mexican favourites and Asian fusion options. Secondly there is the change of atmosphere from the family dining and relaxed shisha lounge outside to the dark, nightclub style bar inside (complete with dancefloor). Finally, the array of diners and drop-ins are equally eclectic, from tourists looking for an alfresco eatery to the mix of nationalities who come to hang out. Variety is definitely the spice of life, which is especially apparent with the tantalising selection of sweet and spicy delights including edamame, Asian duck salad, miniature burgers, succulent steaks, mixed quesadillas and fajitas. If you came for the promise of Portuguese perfection then try the espatada skewers.

Century Village Al Garhoud **04 282 3636**
centuryvillage.ae
Map **2 N8** Metro **GGICO**

Da Shi Dai — Chinese

Contemporary design and dim sum delights

Enjoy the 'lighter side of Chinese dining' with fresh and delicately arranged dishes like crystal prawns, kung po chicken and a selection for vegetarians. Alfresco dining, reasonable prices and fast, friendly service guarantee return visits.

Murjan, Jumeirah Beach Residence Dubai Marina
04 426 4636
da-shi-dai.ae
Map **2 Q13** Metro **Dubai Marina**

Celebrity Chefs

Does food prepared by famous hands taste better? To find out head to Frankie's (p.508) or Titanic (p.543) to sample Marco Pierre White's menu; Pierre Gagnaire's Reflets (p.531); Mezzanine (p.531) and Rhodes Twenty10 (04 316 5550) by Gary Rhodes; or Atlantis for Nobu Matsuhisa's offering (p.526). Enjoy fine dining at Giorgio Locatelli's Ronda Locatelli (p.533), Santi Santamari's Ossiano (p.528) and Jamie's Italian at Festival Centre (p.513). Michelin-starred chef Yannick Alléno has three venues at One&Only The Palm (p.538), and Sanjeev Kapoor has restaurants ranging from the pricey Signature (p.537) to the more affordable Khazana (p.516).

Da Vinci's — Italian

Reliable food and novel decor

This rustic trattoria features wholesome decor, with checked tablecloths and even a dummy pianist. The food is reliably hearty and straightforward; there are three-course lunch deals and early evening discounts, and the drinks are affordable.

Millennium Airport Hotel Dubai Al Garhoud
04 702 8888
millenniumhotels.com
Map **2 N8** Metro **GGICO**

The Deck > *p.242, 509, 557, 567* — International

Dine alfresco and enjoy the view

Enjoy the panoramic views of The Deck, where the stylish yet relaxed seating area overlooks the Palm Jumeirah and a stunning infinity pool. A tempting selection of bar snacks are available throughout the day – and breakfast is served here too. But the real draw is the a la carte menu of Ocean-meets-Arabic gourmet fare, including open ravioli of oxtail, grilled sea bass with artichoke, and courgette and saffron risotto. The Deck grill sharing platter with an assortment of fish, meat and Arabic rice is a specialty.

Ocean View Hotel, Jumeirah Beach Residence
Dubai Marina **04 814 5599**
jaresortshotels.com
Map**1 K4** Metro **Jumeirah Lakes Towers**

Der Keller — German

Der Keller *ist sehr gut* for German fare

From pretzels to schnitzels, frankfurters to fondue, the popular Der Keller delivers fine German cuisine and beer in a cosy pseudo-subterranean setting with a Burj view. Try to resist the fresh bread as the starters are as big as mains and the mains bigger than Austria.

Jumeirah Beach Hotel Umm Suqeim 3 **04 406 8999**
jumeirah.com
Map **1 S4** Metro **Mall of the Emirates**

Dhow Ka Aangan — Indian

Traditional decor, live music and excellent kebabs

Traditionally decorated in rich wood with many elaborate ornaments nailed to the walls, the atmosphere and live in-house music mingle well with the authentic food. Savour its range of biryanis, special curries and kebabs from the charcoal-smoked clay oven, plus excellent desserts.

Dhow Palace Hotel Al Mankhool **04 359 9992**
dhowpalacedubai.com
Map **2 L5** Metro **Al Karama**

Dynasty — Chinese

Chinese that's good enough, but doesn't dazzle

A mix of Szechuan, Cantonese and Peking dishes allows diners to explore China's culinary landscape. A choice of set menus lets novices experiment without committing to the comprehensive a la carte menu. Ultimately, the food and service don't match the superior setting.

Ramada Hotel Dubai Al Mankhool **04 506 1148**
ramadadubai.com
Map **2 L4** Metro **Al Fahidi**

Eauzone — Far Eastern

Stylish place for teppanyaki and sake

Dine beneath softly lit canopies overlooking a network of waterways for a truly romantic meal. The Thai and Japanese fusion dishes are best accompanied by an unusual sorbet such as chilli and raspberry, or some sake. Groups should try the teppanyaki station, from Dhs.250 per head.

Arabian Court At One&Only Royal Mirage Al Sufouh **04 399 9999**
oneandonlyresorts.com
Map **1 M4** Metro **Nakheel**

El Chico — Mexican

Feast on fine Mexican fare along The Walk

One of the most popular dining options on The Walk, this is proper Mexican overindulgence. Nachos served dripping with cheese are dunked into the fresh guacamole for starters, while burritos, fajitas and enchiladas filled to bursting point make the best main courses, although spicy chicken and steaks are also on the menu. The restaurant is unlicensed but its location along the buzzing JBR is great for a spot of people-watching.

The Walk, Jumeirah Beach Residence Dubai Marina **04 423 3828**
elchico.com
Map **1 K5** Metro **Jumeirah Lakes Towers**

El Malecon — Latin American

Salsa dancers, Cuban food and great drinks

Graffiti-covered turquoise walls and low lighting creates a sultry Cuban atmosphere that builds up during the evening, helped along by live music and Salsa dancers. Big windows overlook the glowing Dubai Marine lagoon, and Malecon's doors are constantly swinging, so it's a great place to start or end the night.

Dubai Marine Beach Resort & Spa Jumeira 1 **04 346 1111**
dxbmarine.com
Map **2 H4** Metro **World Trade Centre**

Elements — Cafe

Industrial art warehouse vibe in Wafi

Walls crammed with paintings give Elements the feel of an industrial art warehouse. Lunchtime is always busy thanks to the bargain three-course buffet, while the shisha terrace fills up in the evenings as diners dig into sushi, tapas, pasta and Arabic dishes.

Wafi Umm Hurair 2 **04 324 4252**
wafi.com
Map **2 L7** Metro **Dubai Healthcare City**

Elia — Greek

Great Greek treats packed with flavour

Sit inside the slightly over-air-conditioned dining area or, better still, out on the terrace, which manages to be serene despite looking out over Bur Dubai. The selection of Greek dishes is served with zesty olive oils, fluffy breads and include succulent meatballs and moreish dolma.

Majestic Hotel Tower Dubai Al Mankhool **04 501 2529**
dubaimajestic.com
Map **2 L4** Metro **Al Fahidi**

Embassy Dubai — European

Restaurant, vodka bar and club with opulent class

Three venues in one, comprising a sophisticated nightclub, elegant restaurant, and champagne and vodka bars. The decor is opulent: intricately tiled walls, baroque lamps, candlelit tables and floor-to-ceiling windows overlooking the Dubai Marina skyline all add to the luxurious feel. Modest in size, dining here is intimate making it a perfect romantic location. Fine-dining favourites including oysters, caviar (at Dhs.2,000 a pot for 50g), and foie gras all make appearances in the starter selections. For hearty appetites, the US prime beef wellington with a petite

jug of Madeira juice is a favourite – the meat tender, the pastry slightly crunchy. The desserts are the piece de resistance. The warm blackberry crumble is both sharp and sweet and the Devonshire clotted cream makes it a heavenly (if a little sinful) treat. It all comes with a hefty price tag (dinner for two without alcohol costs Dhs.500-600 per person) but, as a location to impress guests, it doesn't get much better.
Grosvenor House Dubai Marina **04 317 6000**
grosvenorhouse-dubai.com
Map **1 L5** Metro **Dubai Marina**

Ember Grill & Lounge — International
Popular grill restaurant with a warm ambience
This funky restaurant comprises an open kitchen, a glass-walled bar (the only licensed venue in The Dubai Mall) and a large dining room made intimate with booth seats and round tables. From simple grills to experimental creations, it's a pricey end to a shopping spree, but it certainly hits the spot.
The Address Dubai Mall Downtown Dubai
04 888 3444
theaddress.com
Map **2 F6** Metro **Burj Khalifa/Dubai Mall**

Entre Nous — International
Short on character but excellent value buffet
The restaurant has few distinguishing features, but excels with its value-for-money themed buffets. Fill your plate every day with tasty, high-quality fare from Dhs.129 (excluding drinks). The atmosphere is businesslike, but if you're in the neighbourhood, Entre Nous puts on a great spread.
Novotel World Trade Centre Dubai Trade Centre 2
04 332 0000
novotel.com
Map **2 H6** Metro **World Trade Centre**

Entrecôte Cafe de Paris — French
Like steak? Come here. Don't like steak? Move along
Steak-frites is the order of the day, in fact the only order, here; diners must simply decide on the grade and age of the steak, which comes bathed in a secret recipe sauce. Tokenistic lampshades and chandeliers, plus a waterfall muffling the shoppers' hum, mean you can tuck into your steak and almost forget you're in a mall.
The Dubai Mall Downtown Dubai **04 434 0122**
Map **2 F6** Metro **Burj Khalifa/Dubai Mall**

Epicure — Cafe
Gourmet deli that focuses on freshness
This licensed gourmet deli serves freshly baked bread and pastries, healthy fruit compotes, and a range of cooked breakfasts while you gaze out over the Desert Palm's swimming pool and polo fields or devour the day's newspapers. The staff take their time with the service, which makes it perfect for a lazy lunchtime of lounging. A delicious range of lunch dishes and light snacks are also available, along with excellent juices and hot drinks.
Desert Palm Dubai Warsan 2 **04 323 8888**
desertpalm.peraquum.com

Esca — Italian
Good value international and Italian buffet fare
Esca has a sharp, designer atmosphere, with a huge metallic oven behind the live cooking station. Food is buffet style, with international offerings for breakfast and lunch, while dinner is along an Italian theme. Outdoor dining is available.
Qamardeen Hotel Downtown Dubai
04 428 6888
qamardeenhotel.ae
Map **2 F7** Metro **Burj Khalifa/Dubai Mall**

Ember Grill & Lounge

ET Sushi — Japanese

Great pre-karaoke sushi venue

Don't let the uninspiring décor of ET Sushi fool you, they serve great sushi as well as some other Japanese dishes like gyosa (hand-made pan fried chicken dumpling), yaki tori (grilled chicken skewers), seabass with teriyaki sauce and seared tuna with soy sauce. Clientele can choose from the tasty freshly prepared colour-coded creations like sushi, sashimi, nigiri sushi and maki rolls direct from the conveyor belt that loops around oak wood tables or from the a la carte menu. The service is fast and smooth, and the staff and chef are always on hand to walk you through the menu. Don't forget to enjoy a bowl of miso soup in true Japanese tradition with your main meal instead of before or after. A must try is the chef's speciality: the exotic Shiroan desert which is made with white beans and served with green tea ice cream…yum. Finally, round off your meal by testing your vocal range with a spot of karaoke at Tokyo@The Towers upstairs.

The Boulevard At Jumeirah Emirates Towers Trade Centre 2 **04 319 8088**
jumeirah.com
Map **2 H6** Metro **Emirates Towers**

Ewaan — Mediterranean

The most archetypical Dubai shisha joint in town

Surrounding the palm-lined pool in the Arabian-themed Palace Hotel, the private cabanas at this shisha joint sit directly beneath the towering Burj Khalifa. Customers can stretch out on Arabic seating while a musician plays the oud and attentive staff serve up shisha and tasty mezze.

The Palace Downtown Dubai Downtown Dubai **04 888 3444**
theaddress.com
Map **2 F6** Metro **Burj Khalifa/Dubai Mall**

ET Sushi

The Exchange Grill — Steakhouse

A treat for meat lovers and fans of fine dining

The Exchange Grill at the Fairmont oozes quiet excess. If a business lunch with a client involves pushing the expense account boat out, then the outsized leather armchairs, modern art installations and a floor-to-ceiling chandelier should hit the right note. The menu strikes a balance between the classic and the innovative with the highlight being the prime aged Angus beef. Accompany lunch with a full bodied wine and wash it down with a brandy or two as the afternoon draws on. This is a business lunch Mad Men style.

Fairmont Dubai Trade Centre 1 **04 311 8316**
fairmont.com/dubai
Map **2 J5** Metro **World Trade Centre**

FAI — Thai

Posh surroundings and a pleasing menu

Book early and enjoy your meal on the veranda of this stylish restaurant and you'll be afforded a view of the Burj Lake and the fantastic fountain show. As you'd expect from a Palace eatery, the Thai dishes are packed with flavour and artfully presented.

The Palace Downtown Dubai Downtown Dubai **04 428 7888**
theaddress.com
Map **2 F6** Metro **Burj Khalifa/Dubai Mall**

Fakhreldine — Middle Eastern

Get your glad rags on for some stylish Lebanese

From the first dip into the creamy hummus to the last crumb of Arabic sweet, the quality is apparent and the bill isn't too painful. Choose from rarer Arabic dishes and old favourites as you watch the belly dancer.

Mövenpick Hotel & Apartments Bur Dubai Oud Metha **04 336 6000**
moevenpick-hotels.com
Map **2 K6** Metro **Oud Metha**

The Farm — International

Dubai's best kept secret

Located within the new uber-luxurious Al Barari residential area, The Farm serves wholesome, taste bud-tantalising treats. From sensational seafood creations such as saffron shrimp curry and chilli mussels to marvellous meat feasts like rib eye steak and honey glazed duck, pretty much every palate has been catered for. There is a generous Thai selection crossing soups, salads, starters and mains, and for calorie counters and the digestively-challenged there are gluten free and low fat options. Set hidden in an oasis of running water, frangipani trees and sprawling greenery, this idyllic sanctuary is perfect to while away hours over delicious dishes and exotic juices and freshly-made smoothies.

Al Barari, Nr Falcon City Nad Al Sheba **04 392 5660**
thefarmdubai.com

Farriers
International

Excellent buffet with a fabulous Friday brunch

Does Dubai really need another posh brunch? Yes, it does; if it's done Meydan-style with free-flowing bubbly, live jazz and a kids' club. During the rest of the week, dine in the bright, airy interior or on the track-side terrace sampling delicious signature dishes courtesy of vast interactive buffet stations.

The Meydan Hotel Meydan **04 381 3111**
meydanhotels.com
Map **2 E10** Metro **Business Bay**

Fazaris
International

Varied menu and a romantic Burj view setting

With 12 pages of mouthwatering dishes from Japan, south-east Asia, India, Arabia and the Mediterranean, this is a menu that tries to cater for everyone. Inside is cavernous and bright, while outside is more romantic, with views of The Palace hotel and the Burj Khalifa.

The Address Downtown Dubai Downtown Dubai **04 888 3444**
theaddress.com
Map **2 F7** Metro **Burj Khalifa/Dubai Mall**

Finz
Mediterranean

Cheerful seafood in Ibn Battuta's China Court

The open-to-the-mall setting means Finz won't win many romantic accolades, but come here if you want to choose from an eclectic mix of Portuguese, Italian, Spanish and South American fare. Seafood dominates the menu, while the signature beef espetada is great.

Ibn Battuta Mall The Gardens **04 368 5620**
Map **1 G5** Metro **Ibn Battuta**

Fire & Ice
International

Extreme concept venue, not for the conservative

A conceptual restaurant offering unusual dishes from two set menus: the seven-course Ice menu (Dhs.1,000) features the likes of foie gras on a bed of popping candy, and crab cakes with a bubble bath-type topping, while the Fire menu (Dhs.500) is a little tamer.

Raffles Dubai Umm Hurair 2 **04 324 8888**
dubai.raffles.com
Map **2 K7** Metro **Dubai Healthcare City**

Fish & Co
Seafood

Quirky fish & chips joint

This restaurant sticks to what it knows best: serving a vast menu covering everything from classic fish fingers to prawns, oysters, hammour and salmon. For the indecisive, there's a seafood platter and a single steak option for stubborn carnivores. Branches: Millennium Tower (04 343 9171), Sheikh Zayed Road (04 343 9171) and Al Ghurair City (04 227 0252).

Festival Centre Dubai Festival City **04 232 9522**
fish-co.com
Map **2 M9** Metro **Emirates**

Fish Bazaar
Thai

Exotic Asian fusion in chic alfresco setting

With an idyllic setting complete with its own stream, Fish Bazaar offers a tranquil haven tucked away from the bustling city. A tempting array of traditional Thai and Japanese dishes, plus a live cooking station at the seafood grill, ensures there really is something for everyone. If you fancy something a little different, opt for the sushi sandwich or create your own dish from the wide range of fresh seafood, vegetables and exotic spices.

Habtoor Grand Beach Resort & Spa Dubai Marina **04 408 4257**
habtoorhotels.com
Map **1 L4** Metro **Dubai Marina**

Fish Market
Seafood

Choose your seafood straight from the market stall

This novel restaurant lets diners pick raw ingredients from a large bank of fresh, raw seafood and vegetables. Choose anything from tiger prawns and Omani lobster to red snapper, and then request your cooking style preference. The food is not outstanding but the concept is entertaining.

Radisson Blu Hotel, Dubai Deira Creek Al Rigga **04 222 7171**
radissonblu.com
Map **2 M5** Metro **Union**

Five Dining > *p.553*
International

Buffet delights and a lively atmosphere

Lively, relaxed venue with a well-chosen buffet where the theme changes daily between favourites that include seafood and pasta. Well-priced, the ambience is more suitable for groups than romancing couples.

Jumeira Rotana Al Bada'a **04 345 5888**
rotana.com
Map **2 J4** Metro **World Trade Centre**

Flavours On Two
International

Dinner-brunch favourite with a new Flavour nightly

This stylish, busy 'dinner-brunch' venue focuses on a different global cuisine each night, including Mexican, Indian, British, seafood, Italian and Asian. The wide range of dishes includes cold starters, hot grills and delicious desserts. Free-flowing alcohol is included (Dhs.179 during the week or Dhs.189 at the weekend), or you can upgrade to champagne.

Towers Rotana Trade Centre 1 **04 312 2202**
rotana.com
Map **2 G5** Metro **Financial Centre**

Focaccia
Italian

Home-style decor and cooking in a casa setting

Book a table in the kitchen, library, dining room, or cellar of this homely Italian, or catch a glimpse of the sea from the terrace. Tasty pasta dishes dominate,

but save room for the delicious desserts. The brunch option has a wider menu with Iranian options.
Hyatt Regency Dubai Corniche Deira **04 209 1234**
restaurants.dubai.hyatt.com
Map **2 N4** Metro **Palm Deira**

Fogo Vivo > *p.243, 509, 557, 567* **Brazilian**
A speciality Brazilian steakhouse
Serving more than 20 different types of meat – many cooked 'live' in the open fire at the heart of the restaurant – this is a great place to come with family and friends. Novelties are delivered aplenty with a Brazilian 'cowboy' carving a variety of grilled meats at the table – show a green card for more meat, a red card to say that you're full! A fun and interactive way to enjoy the wonderful flavours of Brazilian cuisine.
Ocean View Hotel Dubai Marina **04 814 5599**
jaresortshotels.com
Map **1 K4** Metro **Jumeirah Lakes Towers**

Foodlands Restaurant **Indian**
High quality and low prices; a great independent
Among the many cheap and cheerful independent restaurants in town, Foodlands deserves a special mention thanks to the excellent quality and awesome array of Indian, Persian and Arabic dishes. The menu also features some surprises such as grilled lobster. The window into the kitchen will get your mouth watering suitably before your sizzling meal arrives.
Nr Ramada Continental Hotel Hor Al Anz **04 268 3311**
foodlands.com
Map **2 Q6** Metro **Abu Hail**

Fountain Restaurant **International**
Pub grub is served up in style
The sleek white walls, chocolate and purple furniture, together with colourful British food packaging positioned around the restaurant help create a very modern, stylish and authentic setting. The weekend brunch is a British feast, with typical pub grub expertly delivered. The menu offers buffet and a la carte options including a carvery, Lancashire hot pot, and fluffy beef and Guinness pie – but it is the sheer size of their signature fry-up that draws in the crowd. Large enough to feed a small family, this breakfast platter includes pork sausages, black puddings, tomatoes, sauteed potatoes, steak, bacon, baked beans, fried bread and mushrooms. Friendly staff will ensure each fry up is made to order, so the food is cooked to your own specifications. If by some good fortune you still aren't full, try the deliciously sweet treacle pudding for dessert. The premium package, including a selection of British drinking favourites, is Dhs.195.
Mövenpick Hotel & Apartments Bur Dubai
Oud Metha **04 336 6000**
moevenpick-burdubai.com
Map **2 K6** Metro **Oud Metha**

Frankie's **Italian**
Jockey-owned joint that's no one-trick pony
Grab a vodka Martini and pizza in the bar at this stylish joint, co-owned by Frankie Dettori and Marco Pierre White, then head into the main restaurant for Italian classics and new favourites such as duck ravioli. With a sultry interior, pianist and good Friday brunch, this is a classy establishment.
Oasis Beach Tower Dubai Marina **04 399 4311**
jebelali-international.com
Map **1 K4** Metro **Dubai Marina**

French Connection **Cafe**
Onsite bakery guarantees a great breakfast venue
Survey Sheikh Zayed Road as you relax in this cheerful cafe. Expertly prepared coffee and freshly baked pastries, breads and cakes top the menu which also offers a full English breakfast, salads and tasty sandwiches. Free Wi-Fi is available at this and the sister branch behind Spinneys next to BurJuman.
Al Wafa Tower, Shk Zayed Rd Trade Centre 1
04 343 8311
fcdubai.com
Map **2 F5** Metro **Financial Centre**

Gaucho **Argentinean**
This classy Argentinean venue means business
London favourite, Gaucho has made its second foray into international waters (the first being Beirut) here in Dubai. Ultra modern with cow hide upholstery and a black and white backdrop, it is set on two floors – upstairs is home to a lounge bar should you wish to dine informally, while downstairs houses the restaurant. The service is impeccable, beginning at your table where you are presented with a board carrying the various cuts of beef, each with its own comprehensive explanation on origin, taste and cooking recommendation courtesy of the highly knowledgeable and passionate staff. The food is quite simply perfection; try the Tira De Ancho, a spiral cut to share which is slow grilled with chimchurri, for a delicious twist on the traditional steak. This may be a special occasion restaurant but, after visiting, you'll find any excuse for a celebration.
Dubai International Financial Centre (DIFC)
Trade Centre 2 **04 422 7898**
gauchorestaurants.co.uk
Map **2 G6** Metro **Financial Centre**

Gazebo **Indian**
Indian food at its very best
Choosing from the vast menu is a challenge, but whether you order from the charcoal grilled specialities, mouthwatering curries and biryanis, fresh salads, tasty breads or deliciously sweet lassis and kulfis, you'll be served an authentic dish packed with flavour. The elegantly-clad staff are genuinely friendly

go for it
EXPERIENCE
THE FINEST BRAZILIAN GRILL

and the service is top notch. A great value Indian experience. See website for further locations.
Nr Sharaf DG, Al Mankhool Rd Al Raffa **04 359 8555**
gazebo.ae
Map **2 K4** Metro **Al Karama**

Gerard's — Cafe
Jumeira institution that draws yummy mummies
The courtyard setting gives this popular meeting spot and coffee house its unique atmosphere and there's also a good selection of croissants, pastries and chocolate covered dates; takeaway trade is brisk. Also at Al Ghurair Centre (04 222 8637).
Magrudy's Mall Jumeira 1 **04 344 3327**
Map **2 H4** Metro **Emirates Towers**

Giannino — Italian
A chic venue and an authentic Italian menu
The original Giannino's in Milan holds three Michelin stars and considers Giorgio Armani, David and Victoria Beckham and Justin Timberlake as regular clients, so the Dubai restaurant certainly has a lot to live up to. Set back from the hustle and bustle of The Walk at JBR, the chic decor and opulent setting certainly doesn't disappoint. The menu offers a wide selection of authentic Italian dishes lovingly prepared with ingredients sourced direct from Italy. The fabulous high ceilings, plush furnishing and impeccable lighting strikes the ideal balance between sophistication and cool, but it comes with a price tag to match.
Meydan Beach Dubai Marina **04 433 3777**
meydanbeach.com
Map **1 K4** Metro **Jumeirah Lakes Towers**

Glasshouse Brasserie — Mediterranean
Sophisticated atmosphere, good food and prices
Managed by the team behind Table 9, Glasshouse is a chic brasserie serving up Mediterranean cuisine at reasonable prices. Good for a business lunch or a lively group dinner, its interior is stylish with glass walls, dark woods and tasteful colours. On Mondays, drinks are one dirham with a two course meal.
Hilton Dubai Creek Al Rigga **04 227 1111**
hilton.com
Map **2 N5** Metro **Al Rigga**

Go West — American
Tex-Mex with a Wild West twist
A well-priced menu includes the signature Angus beef, which complements a big drinks menu. A band plays from 19:30 every night (except Sundays) so reserve a spot indoors or on the terrace if you fancy a dining experience with a Western twist.
Jumeirah Beach Hotel Umm Suqeim 3 **04 406 8999**
jumeirah.com
Map **1 S4** Metro **Mall of the Emirates**

Gourmet Burger Kitchen — American
Burgers at their best
This popular chain serves up a winning formula – good juicy meat, fresh produce, a diverse choice of toppings and sauces, and hearty portions of fries in trendy canteen-style settings. The delivery service has saved many a hungry couch potato. See the website for other locations around Dubai.
Mirdif City Centre Mirdif **04 284 3955**
gbkinfo.com
Map **2 P12** Metro **Rashidiya**

Hakkasan — Far Eastern
Trendy Chinese with spectacular decor
What works in London or NYC doesn't always translate to Dubai. Hakkasan is a textbook example of how it can be done. Using familiar Hakkasan elements like the neon bar and the 'cage' design, there are also new introductions, like the 'sunrise' bar and, spectacularly, the terrace – a tranquil Zen garden unlike anywhere else in Dubai. The Hakkasan favourites are on the menu; starters like crispy duck salad, soft shell crab and stewed wagyu beef steal most of the plaudits, although the dim sum defines melt in the mouth and the main courses – Pipa duck, sweet and sour pomegranate chicken, and spicy black pepper rib-eye – are best ordered to share. Expensive, but as good as dining gets in Dubai.
Jumeirah Emirates Towers Trade Centre **04 384 8484**
hakkasan.com
Map **2 H6** Metro **Emirates Towers**

Handi — Indian
Handi crafts a mean curry
An elaborate thali offers four curries and kebabs for Dhs.90, including biryani, salad, dessert and lassis. The lamb curry with cashew and cardamom is particularly good and biryani fans will love the individual copper pots sealed to keep the flavour in. Live music and private dining rooms add to the atmosphere.
Taj Palace Dubai Al Rigga **04 223 2222**
tajhotels.com
Map **2 N6** Metro **Al Rigga**

Hard Rock Cafe — American
Big on flavour, entertainment and portion sizes
This stalwart of affordable fun has a polished rocker vibe with dining options on the upper deck where friendly staff buzz between tables. The theme is big – big venue, big entertainment, big portions and big fun. Not to mention big on fried food. With live music, drinks in jugs and shared platters that require a huge appetite, it's perfect for a group night out. A nice change from the usual sophisticated Dubai eateries.
Festival Centre Dubai Festival City **04 232 8900**
hardrock.com
Map **2 M9** Metro **Emirates**

Haru Robatayaki — Japanese
An authentic Japanese experience on The Walk
Haru draws a crowd with its fresh, delicious, grilled robatayaki specialities. Bright lights, Japanese pop music and knowledgeable, friendly staff keep the feel upbeat. Also at the Green Community (04 885 3897).
The Walk, Jumeirah Beach Residence Dubai Marina **04 437 0134**
haru.ae
Map **1 K5** Metro **Dubai Marina**

Hey Sugar — Cafe
Your first stop for an indulgent sugar rush
Choose from the rainbow of delicious cupcakes, pair with a coffee or shake, and gorge yourself inside this tiny outlet. Giant and mini cupcakes are a great alternative to a traditional birthday cake. Takeaway and delivery are available. See website for details of other locations throughout Dubai.
The Village Jumeira 1 **04 344 8204**
Map **2 H4** Metro **Emirates Towers**

Hofbräuhaus — German
Super sausages and strudels in this brauhaus
From the sauerkraut to the white sausage with sweet mustard and the strudel, everything is top notch. Add in the great German beer, Bavarian garb for the staff and accordion music, and you have a fun night out.
JW Marriott Hotel Dubai Al Muraqqabat **04 607 7588**
marriottdiningatjw.ae
Map **2 P6** Metro **Abu Baker Al Siddique**

Hoi An — Vietnamese
Traditional Vietnamese with a western twist
Compact and stately, Hoi An's teahouse-inspired space is perfect for exploring the exotic Vietnamese flavours that come out of the kitchen. Although it's always busy, the ambience is one of hushed formality, making it a good choice for business deals and intimate dinners. Novices should opt for the set meal, in which each dish is explained by the well-informed staff.
Shangri-La Hotel Dubai Trade Centre 1 **04 405 2703**
shangri-la.com
Map **2 G5** Metro **Financial Centre**

Honyaki — Japanese
Top class sushi restaurant in a jaw-dropping location
With a breathtaking location – the terrace looks over the Madinat amphitheatre and waterways with the Burj Al Arab behind – it would be easy for Honyaki to rest on its laurels. What you get is actually a modern Japanese restaurant rooted in authenticity. The miso, sashimi and maki sound familiar but there are just enough twists (tekami cones topped with tasty deep fried onions, for example) to surprise and delight. And then, of course, there are the views. Lunch is quiet but still enjoyable; Honyaki comes to life in the evening when the maki is washed down with sake while the Burj twinkles nearby. Try the mochi ice cream, whether you've a sweet tooth or not.
Souk Madinat Jumeirah Al Sufouh 1 **04 366 6730**
jumeirah.com
Map **1 R4** Metro **Mall of the Emirates**

Horizon All Day Dining — International
Good value buffet with a great view
The open kitchen in the middle of the restaurant produces consistently impressive international cuisine, with well-priced theme nights throughout the week. With circular booths, as well as more conventional tables, there is always a quiet spot; outside, the shaded terrace is very popular when the weather is fair.
Amwaj Rotana Dubai Marina **04 428 2000**
rotana.com
Map **1 K4** Metro **Jumeirah Lakes Towers**

Hukama — Chinese
A fresh and fancy eatery offering well-cooked fare
More fine dining Chinese than comforting carb-fest, this sophisticated eatery offers glorious views of Burj Khalifa from its terrace, and a menu that consists of the usual and the unexpected (such as wontons on soy infused crushed ice).
The Address Downtown Dubai Downtown Dubai **04 888 3444**
theaddress.com
Map **2 F7** Metro **Burj Khalifa/Dubai Mall**

Hunters Room & Grill — Steakhouse
Stylish surrounds and succulent dishes
A veritable meat feast is offered at this restaurant, so come prepared for the hearty portions of fine steaks from North America, Australia and Brazil. The meat is tender, the selection on offer is broad and, as you'd expect from The Westin, the restaurant has a fresh contemporary vibe.
The Westin Dubai Mina Seyahi Beach Resort Al Sufouh 1 **04 399 4141**
huntersdubai.com
Map **1 M4** Metro **Nakheel**

Icho Restaurant — Japanese
High altitude, premium, Japanese dining
Icho sets aside Japanese minimalism with a sprawling venue spread over three floors of the Radisson Royal Hotel. The 49th floor is set up for traditional a la carte Japanese fare and is ideal if you're after a quieter, more intimate dining experience with the other half. Sit by the dedicated sushi bar or opt for a table by the floor-to-ceiling windows for some of the best panoramas of Sheikh Zayed Road. Alternatively, you can get up close to the chefs at the teppanyaki grills on the 50th floor as they sear, sizzle and juggle through either the set teppan menus or your selection of meats and veg.

While both floors may share the same menu, certain items are only available on the teppan floor. Cap off with a visit to the bar on the 51st floor for some signature sake cocktails and some laidback tunes.
Radisson Royal Hotel, Dubai Trade Centre 1
04 308 0000
radissonblu.com
Map **2 H5** Metro **World Trade Centre**

Il Rustico — Italian

Relaxed, unpretentious, with decent fare

It may not be classy, but Il Rustico is the type of Italian restaurant that doesn't need a special occasion. The pasta, pizzas and salads are all freshly made on the premises, and the desserts taste as good as they look. The wine list won't disappoint either.
Chelsea Plaza Hotel Al Jafiliya **04 398 2222**
chelseaplazahoteldubai.com
Map **2 J5** Metro **Al Jafiliya**

Imperium — French

International cuisine with a French twist

Zabeel Saray has the look and feel of a grand palace and Imperium – the all day-dining venue – could be its main hall. The restaurant is enormous but design elements – and a beautiful terrace – maintain some charm and intimacy. The restaurant is headed by Chef Jean Hurstel, a talented French chef whose skills in Parisian cuisine are transcended into the main courses produced in the kitchen. The beef bourgignon is deliciously tender and the gravy delightfully enriched with red wine. Each main course is served in a petite stainless steel pan, making it easy to pass the dishes around for guests to share. The buffet selection is more of an international affair with enough cuisine choices to satisfy most palates. Surprisingly for a high-end hotel, the price tag for such a meal is excellent. The a la carte menu will only set you back Dhs.175 per person.
Jumeirah Zabeel Saray Palm Jumeirah **04 453 0444**
jumeirah.com
Map **1 L3** Metro **Nakheel**

Indego By Vineet — Indian

Serves up one of Dubai's most upmarket curries

Run by Vineet Bhatia, the first Indian chef to win a Michelin star, it is little surprise to discover that this restaurant elevates Indian cooking to a fine art. Its red velvet armchairs and tastefully restrained decor make this an elegant dining restaurant where creativity and imagination run free. As both the menu and the prices should tell you, if you're looking for a madras and a pint, this isn't the right place. If you're looking for tandoori salmon and chocolate samosas, it is.
Grosvenor House Dubai Marina **04 399 8888**
grosvenorhouse-dubai.com
Map **1 L5** Metro **Dubai Marina**

India Palace — Indian

Mouthwatering food in atmospheric surrounds

Surrounded by elaborately carved wood and strains of traditional sitar music, you'll be transported back to the Moghul Dynasty. Cosy booths and private dining rooms make for an intimate scene. The food is excellent and diners are spoilt for choice. Visit the website for details of other locations.
Al Hudda Bldg, Nr Al Tayer Motors Al Garhoud
04 286 9600
sfcgroup.com
Map **2 N8** Metro **GGICO**

Indo Thai Asian Restaurant — Far Eastern

Elegant, Zen dining for delicious Asian cuisine

Just above the luminous lobby of the Radisson Royal Hotel sits Indo Thai. A spa-like restaurant featuring an elegant oriental chic design, its menu boasts a variety of authentic Indonesian and Thai cuisines. Elements of other well-known Asian dishes can be found and enjoyed as well. To have a taste of everything, order the Indo Thai platter for fresh springs rolls and skewers. While the servers uphold their beaming smiles they offer good knowledge of the menu, and are polite and professional throughout your entire stay.
Radisson Royal Hotel, Dubai Trade Centre 1
04 308 0000
radissonblu.com
Map **2 H5** Metro **World Trade Centre**

The Ivy — British

Ivy League indulgence in the heart of Dubai

Apart from the ultra-fashionable interior (all early 1900s chic with white tablecloths, plush leather seats, signature green serviettes, huge, tainted vintage-like mirrors and enviable artwork on the walls), the food and service is not half bad either. The Ivy, like its London sibling, serves predominantly British food (old favourites like liver and crispy bacon and confit pork belly) but also caters to those who fancy mixing it up a little with international dishes such as beef tataki and Scandinavian iced berries. Be sure to make a reservation. This is a busy, popular eatery with a fan-base that could have easily followed it all the way from London.
The Boulevard At Jumeirah Emirates Towers
Trade Centre 2 **04 319 8767**
theivy.ae
Map **2 H6** Metro **Emirates Towers**

iZ — Indian

Stylish setting for contemporary tandoori tapas

iZ's dark, contemporary interior is beautifully designed, complete with hardwood screens, sculptures and chic private rooms. The perfectly prepared Indian dishes are presented tapas style, with tandoori items served by the piece – ideal for

sampling several flavours or sharing. Signature dishes such as salmon tikka and murgh makhani are served alongside freshly baked naan and biryani, along with dal and curry dishes. Expect gourmet Indian cuisine that respects tradition.
Grand Hyatt Dubai Umm Hurair 2 **04 317 2222**
restaurants.dubai.hyatt.com
Map **2 L8** Metro **Dubai Healthcare City**

Jaipur
Indian

Northern Indian specialities to eat in or take out

Familiar dishes sit alongside delicious specialities from Rajasthan and northern India, and the friendly service sets a relaxing atmosphere. A busy delivery service means that the ingredients are always fresh, and an alfresco terrace offers great views of Burj Khalifa.
Burj Residences, Tower 1 Downtown Dubai
04 422 6767
royalorchidhospitality.com
Map **2 F6** Metro **Burj Khalifa/Dubai Mall**

Jamie's Italian
Italian

TV chef's place focuses on familiarity and quality

Unlike celeb chefs before him, Jamie Oliver has opted not to chase after the big bucks, but has gone for the mid-range and family markets with Jamie's Italian. The restaurant has a mix of industrial and chic, homely decor with vast dangling chandeliers. There's a mezzanine level, a busy main dining room and a cosy terrace on the Marina Walk where, tucked behind a garden trellis, you can enjoy a glass of vino with your tasty pumpkin risotto. The menu features some outstanding antipasti and a selection of tasty traditional and innovative pastas which come chunky and fresh – the rigatoni is big enough to lose a meatball inside, while the mains cover the usual suspects – a burger, steak and Jamie's signature baked fish parcel. Granted, it's a franchise, but it really feels as though some serious love and care has gone into this venture.
Festival Centre Dubai Festival City **04 232 9969**
jamieoliver.com
Map **2 M9** Metro **Emirates**

Japengo Cafe
International

Sushi, salads and sandwiches and a whole lot more

A Japanese-western hybrid menu that impresses with top-notch food in a neon bright, minimalist setting. The menu ticks all the boxes, ranging from sushi, noodles and rice classics such as nasi goreng to fish and chips, New York strip loin and Mexican taquitos. Other locations include Ibn Battuta, Mall of the Emirates, Palm Strip, Souk Madinat Jumeirah and Dubai Festival City; see website for details.
Mall of the Emirates Al Barsha 1 **04 341 1671**
binhendi.com
Map **1 R6** Metro **Mall of the Emirates**

Jigsaw
International

Good value buffets and international flavours

Located in the brand new Mövenpick Deira, Jigsaw is on a one-restaurant mission to bring variety to the dining scene in this part of town. Tuesday is Curry Night, Wednesday goes Mexican and, come the weekend, the airy restaurant hosts the international Market Grill Night where – in addition to grilled steaks and chicken – guests can feast on a selection of fresh salads and Lebanese-style sides, as well as hearty pasta dishes which are made to order. Innovative flavour combinations, such as chopped green olives and pine nuts in a tandoori-style paste, add an international twist to the otherwise standard buffet

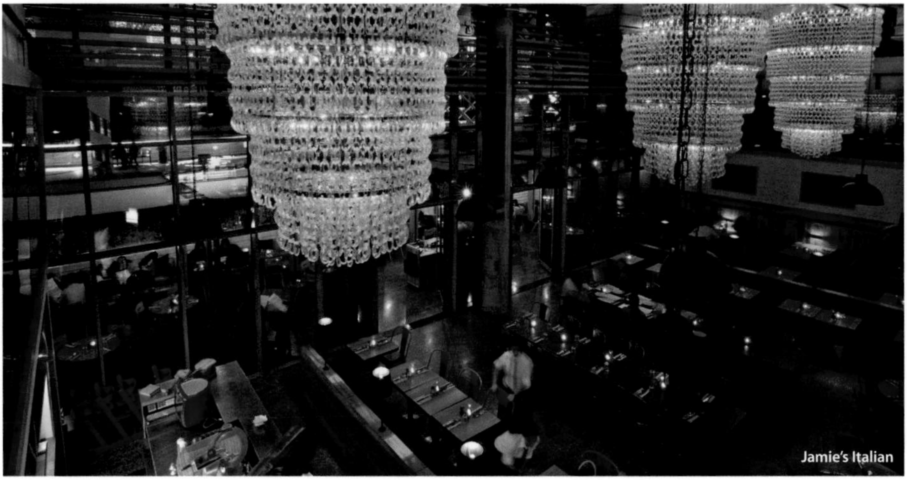
Jamie's Italian

fare. The dessert menu riffs principally on European classics, from panna cotta to pudding and chocolates, but it is the Indian sweet bites, made of cashew nuts, that really stand out.
Mövenpick Hotel Deira Muteena **04 444 0111**
moevenpick-hotels.com
Map **2 P6** Metro **Abu Baker Al Siddique**

Johnny Rockets — American
Retro American diner that guarantees a happy day
This 1950s inspired American diner, with its classic decor, red vinyl booths and coin-operated jukeboxes, transforms a casual family meal into a novelty experience. Fresh burgers, great milkshakes, reasonable prices, and impromptu outpourings of dance to Staying Alive by friendly, bow-tied staff will brighten up anybody's evening. See the website for other locations.
Juma Al Majid Centre, Jumeira Rd Jumeira 1
04 344 7859
johnnyrockets.com
Map **2 G6** Metro **Financial Centre**

Jones The Grocer — Cafe
Food heaven for all gourmet and cheese lovers
Don't be fooled by the name – this is more than a grocer, much more. In fact it's an emporium of homemade pastas, freshly baked breads, gourmet fresh and imported treats such as pestos and sweets, and a fromagerie of artisan cheeses. And that's just the deli. The urban chic cafe is not to be missed. Early risers can choose between crispy French toast drizzled with maple syrup for the indulgent, and mouthwatering classics such as eggs benedict or muesli yoghurt for the health conscious. Lunches range from hearty shepherd's pie to the warm yellow fin tuna pasta salad, all bursting with natural goodness and flavour. And the bakery section is overflowing with fresh croissants and bread. This is food as it should be. It's insanely good.
Indigo Central 8, Nr Times Square, Shk Zayed Rd
Al Manara **04 346 6886**
jonesthegrocer.com
Map **1 T6** Metro **Noor Islamic Bank**

The Junction — International
Buffet delights in Deira
The Junction's speciality is the buffet, with breakfast and lunchtime deals at reasonable prices, while weekend evenings feature a themed buffet. Friday is seafood and the prawns are recommended, with numerous methods of cooking on offer including battered, barbecue and tandoori.
Traders Hotel, Dubai Al Khabaisi
04 214 7272
shangri-la.com
Map **2 P6** Metro **Abu Baker Al Siddique**

JW's Steakhouse — Steakhouse
Everything you'd expect from a good steakhouse
Chefs can be seen cleaving huge chunks of meat in the open kitchen of this steak restaurant. It's a good introduction to the meat and seafood you'll soon enjoy from your leather armchair. Salads are prepared fresh at your table and the desserts are generous.
JW Marriott Hotel Dubai Al Muraqqabat **04 607 7977**
marriottdiningatjw.ae
Map **2 P6** Metro **Abu Baker Al Siddique**

Kabab-ji Grill — Middle Eastern
So-so venue, so good food
Although the inoffensive decor and laminated menus scream 'chain', the food at this JBR joint is excellent. The service is fast, and the prices won't make you flinch. Its take on fatoush is incredible, one of the best in Dubai, and the grills are juicy, especially the veal.
The Walk, JBR Dubai Marina **04 437 0122**
kabab-ji.com
Map **1 K5** Metro **Dubai Marina**

Kaleidoscope — Mediterranean
International cuisine in an airy Atlantis setting
Of the two buffet restaurants at Atlantis, this is the low-key option. A bright, sunny dining area draws in poolside crowds. A deli sandwich counter, a rustic Italian station, and offerings from Asia, India and Europe make this a well-rounded dining experience that is satisfying but not overwhelming.
Atlantis The Palm Palm Jumeirah **04 426 2626**
atlantisthepalm.com
Map **1 N1** Metro **Nakheel**

Kan Zaman Restaurant — Middle Eastern
Enjoy traditional Arabic fare by the creek
Kan Zaman offers an excellent Arabic menu and a chance to try some local food. Traditional Emirati dishes include local breads served either with honey and dates or cheese. Portions are large and prices are low – perfect for sharing. Quiet in the week, it's bustling at weekends. Dine outside on the large terrace or nab a seat on the rooftop balcony.
Heritage & Diving Village Al Shindagha **04 393 9913**
alkoufa.com
Map **2 M4** Metro **Al Ghubaiba**

Karachi Darbar — Pakistani
Perennial favourite for cheap, tasty, quality food
The simple decor, plain menus, and utilitarian settings may not pull visitors in off the street, but that's their loss. With Pakistani dishes on the menu, it offers a little something different to other restaurants from the subcontinent.
Karama Complex Al Karama **04 334 7272**
karachidarbargroup.com
Map **2 K6** Metro **Al Karama**

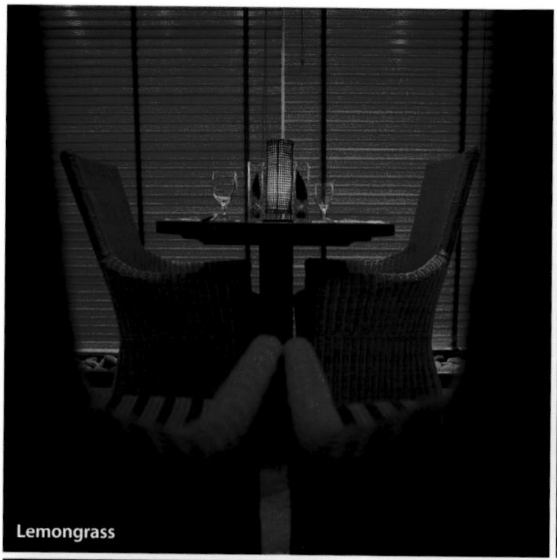
Lemongrass

Kiku

El Malecon

La Parrilla

Hoi An

Karam Beirut — Middle Eastern

A great introduction to Lebanese dining

This popular chain restaurant serves up classic Lebanese fare including mezza, grilled halloumi and mixed grill, and fresh baskets of flatbread are delivered throughout the meal. Inside, the restaurant's white tablecloth-covered tables are arranged in large groups which makes it very family-friendly. Outside, the view overlooks the yacht filled marina with the colourful ferris wheel in the background. Depending on the evening, live music can also be enjoyed from the floating stage. The ambience makes it easy to forget that the restaurant is attached to the mall, particularly as this is one of the few restaurants in the area that is licensed.

Festival Centre Dubai Festival City **04 232 8004**
karambeirut.ae
Map **2 M9** Metro **Emirates**

Karat — Afternoon Tea

Afternoon tea with style and size

Settle on an opulent, high-backed leather seat and choose from 26 teas before the four-course feast arrives. Devonshire cream scones are followed by finger sandwiches, miniature cakes, pastries and Arabic sweets. It's vast by any standard and, at Dhs.125, it's one not to be missed.

The Address Dubai Mall Downtown Dubai
04 438 8888
theaddress.com
Map **2 F6** Metro **Burj Khalifa/Dubai Mall**

The Kebab Connection — Indian

Top traditional food with a welcoming ambience

If you're prone to playing safe with a chicken tikka or the occasional balti, opt for the set menu at this licenced restaurant – it's a cracking introduction to the complex world of authentic Indian cuisine and the staff make for knowledgeable guides.

Mercure Gold Hotel Al Mina **04 301 9888**
accorhotels.com
Map **2 J4** Metro **Al Jafiliya**

Khan Murjan Restaurant — Middle Eastern

Atmospheric, and popular with a vibrant crowd

Located in the heart of the underground souk, the restaurant is set in an open courtyard and offers a range of Arabic dishes from across the region. The traditional architecture and aromas from the bread kiln oven creates a tranquil setting to fuel up in before exploring the souk. From fatayer to tagine barkook, (lamb simmering in spices and sweetened plum), and mosakaat al sultan (fried eggplant) to shawarma, the menu takes you from Turkey to Lebanon.

Wafi Umm Hurair 2 **04 327 9795**
wafi.com
Map **2 L7** Metro **Dubai Healthcare City**

Khazana — Indian

Celebrated cuisine from this Indian celebrity chef

Indian celebrity chef Sanjeev Kapoor's eatery specialises in cuisine from north India. Try the grilled tandoori seafood and gravy-based dishes, as well as the kebabs and Anglo-Indian novelties like 'British raj railroad curry'.

Al Nasr Leisureland Oud Metha **04 336 0061**
khazanadubai.com
Map **2 L6** Metro **Oud Metha**

Kiku — Japanese

Japanese diners flock to this sushi-teppanyaki joint

Kiku is regularly packed with Japanese guests. There is a choice of dining areas, from the traditional private tatami rooms to the teppanyaki bar, sushi counter and regular tables. The menu is diverse, and the set meals are particularly worth trying.

Le Meridien Dubai Al Garhoud **04 702 2703**
kiku-dubai.com
Map **2 N8** Metro **GGICO**

Kisaku — Japanese

Traditional Japanese in a unique setting

A mix of dining settings – from sitting at the sushi bar to chairs with no legs and standard tables for the unadventurous – add to the Kisaku experience. With celebrity chef Chitoshi Takahashi at the helm, the array of sushi and sashimi platters are of a very high standard and the service impeccable.

Al Khaleej Palace Hotel Al Rigga **04 223 1000**
Map **2 N5** Metro **Union**

The Kitchen — International

International food cooked before your eyes

The open kitchen is the centrepiece of this intimate spot, which serves a mix of Thai, Lebanese and European divided into styles of cooking – wok, charcoal grill, wood burning oven and tandoor.

Hyatt Regency Dubai Corniche Deira **04 317 2222**
restaurants.dubai.hyatt.com
Map **2 N4** Metro **Palm Deira**

Kosebasi — Turkish

Delve into the world of authentic Turkish cuisine

Let the friendly staff take you on a culinary tour of Anatolia with their excellent recommendations. The mezze, breads and kebabs all have a hint of familiarity, but are surprisingly different to standard Arabic fare, and good. The special Turkish pie with sauteed aubergines is a must. The pavement terrace is bustling while, inside, functionality is alleviated by bright mosaic tiles. Also at Mirdif City Centre (04 284 0285).

The Walk, Jumeirah Beach Residence Dubai Marina
04 439 3788
kosebasi.com
Map **1 K5** Metro **Dubai Marina**

Kris With A View — International

Affordable and swanky romance in Bur Dubai

If you are turned off by the price tag of a romantic night out at a rooftop restaurant, then you will be pleasantly surprised by Kris With a View. Dining on the top floor of the Park Regis Hotel, just across from BurJuman Centre, gives you a unique vantage point over the city without breaking the bank. The menu has dishes from a collection of Asian cuisines, and even more impressive is that the chefs from each region are onsite to ensure the dishes are properly prepared. The mango and long bean salad from the Thai menu is a popular pick that packs in a variety of flavours with a spicy kick. Order your dessert to be served at the adjacent wine bar so you can enjoy the live music and a great selection of wine.

Park Regis Kris Kin Hotel Al Karama **04 377 1111**
kris.ae
Map **2 L5** Metro **BurJuman**

La Moda — Italian

Simple Italian food in a lively setting

La Moda serves great Italian food, both unpretentious and generous in portion. The lively ambience and big tables make it perfect for an evening of pizza swapping with friends, while the small, pretty terrace is more romantic.

Radisson Blu Hotel, Dubai Deira Creek Al Rigga **04 222 7171**
radissonblu.com
Map **2 M5** Metro **Union**

La Parrilla — Latin American

Great steaks, worked off on a vibrant dancefloor

Well-known for its range of steaks in every conceivable cut and origin, La Parrilla's live band entices diners away from their tables and onto the dance floor for a post-dinner tango. The vibe is pure Argentina and the decorative cart wheels and traditional wooden furniture only add to the charm.

Jumeirah Beach Hotel Umm Suqeim 3 **04 406 8999**
jumeirah.com
Map **1 S4** Metro **Mall of the Emirates**

La Petite Maison — French

Lose yourself in fine wine and excellent cuisine

Typically Gallic, but not in a cliched French way, the cuisine here is simple and delicious, and lets the high quality fresh produce speak for itself. As the atmosphere picks up, the lighting turns down and the venue packs out, and it's easy to get carried away with your order. Of course, it comes at DIFC prices, but it's worth every dirham.

Dubai International Financial Centre (DIFC) Trade Centre 2 **04 439 0505**
lpmdubai.ae
Map **2 G6** Metro **Financial Centre**

La Veranda — Italian

Unpretentious fare that won't break the bank

This cosy restaurant serves large portions of inexpensive pizza, pasta and seafood alongside marina views. Children are well catered for with typical treats like burgers and fish fingers on the menu.

Jumeirah Beach Hotel Umm Suqeim 3 **04 406 8999**
jumeirah.com
Map **1 S4** Metro **Mall of the Emirates**

La Vigna — Italian

Kitsch Italian trattoria with tasty pizzas

Sitting somewhere between modern and kitsch, La Vigna looks like your typical Italian restaurant. The faux-Italian decor, complete with red and white checked tablecloths, Italian memorabilia, wooden beams and a large fire oven set the scene well for an Italian odyssey, if slightly on the cheesy side. While the food is standard Italian fare, the pizzas are without question the tastiest dish on the menu: large in size, with plenty of flavour and served piping hot. The outdoor seating is certainly La Vigna's best selling point. The prices are reasonable too, so if you do find yourself in Garhoud with a rumbling tummy, La Vigna is not a bad option at all.

Century Village Al Garhoud **04 282 0030**
centuryvillage.ae
Map **2 N8** Metro **GGICO**

Lalezar

La Villa
Mediterranean

Good spot for a working lunch

Warm yellow walls enclose beautifully appointed tables with fresh flowers, low-level lighting. The Business Lunch, served Saturday to Wednesday, is a hit with diners who can then round off their flavourful and filling meals with a winning dessert and choice of satisfying beverages.

Pullman Deira City Centre Hotel Port Saeed **04 294 1222**
pullmanhotels.com
Map **2 N7** Metro **Deira City Centre**

Lalezar
Turkish

The humble kebab gets the fine dining treatment

The soothing splendour of this opulent Ottoman restaurant fits well with the smart vibe at the Jumeirah Zabeel Saray. An exquisite, mosaic-tiled interior complete with gurgling fountain dresses up homely Turkish fare as fine dining. With an array of authentic mezze and intriguing beverages it is a perfect spot for a quiet lunch or romantic dinner, and it certainly serves the poshest kebab in town.

Jumeirah Zabeel Saray Palm Jumeirah **04 453 0444**
jumeirah.com
Map **1 L3** Metro **Nakheel**

Lan Kwai Fong
Chinese

Inexpensive and popular, so don't mind the decor

If you judge a good Chinese restaurant by the number of Chinese diners inside, then Lan Kwai Fong is worth exploring. Located between Lamcy Plaza and the Mövenpick Hotel, the restaurant's exhaustive menu includes a vast array of dim sum, clay pot, seafood, meat, duck and noodle dishes.

Nr Lamcy Plaza Oud Metha **04 335 3680**
Map **2 K5** Metro **Oud Metha**

MAHEC

Le Classique
French

Country-club dining with pianist and dress code

Le Classique, the dining equivalent of championship golf at Emirates Golf Club, asks gentlemen to dress in coat and tie. Beginning with beverages in the handsome lounge, patrons move into the lavish country club dining room. A pianist sings old standards, while the staff serve from a delicious menu.

Emirates Golf Club Emirates Living **04 380 2222**
dubaigolf.com
Map **1 M5** Metro **Nakheel**

Le Dune Pizzeria
Italian

Romantic desert dining, Italian style

Perfect for a romantic getaway, Le Dune Pizzeria brings the smells and tastes of rustic Italy to the heart of the desert. The welcoming antipasti buffet offers a taste of everything but save room for the tiramisu trio.

Bab Al Shams Desert Resort & Spa Bawadi **04 809 6194**
meydanhotels.com

Le Metro
French

All day dining with surprisingly delicious dishes

This large and slightly garish restaurant serves as the all-day dining restaurant for guests and is therefore not really on many expat's culinary radars. Shame, as the food at Le Metro is deceptively good. With an extensive menu that focuses more on French cuisine, you'll be sure to find quintessential favourites – snails with salad, oysters and croque monsieur – listed next to more international options. Be sure to ask one of the friendly waiters when the oysters were last imported from France. If you're lucky enough and they've just arrived, you won't be disappointed with their quality. Quiet yet atmospheric, the friendly ambience allows diners to linger over a tasty meal in an unpretentious setting. A three course meal for two will only set you back around Dhs.300, so for no-nonsense food, Le Metro wins hands down.

Park Regis Kris Kin Hotel Al Karama **04 377 1111**
staywellgroup.com
Map **2 L5** Metro **BurJuman**

Le Mistral
Mediterranean

Enjoy the taste of the Mediterranean

Le Mistral offers a range of tasty dishes that celebrate the traditional cuisines of a number of countries bordering the Mediterranean Sea, like Spain, France and Morocco. Think Spanish paella, Italian risotto with seafood and many more authentic dishes that are large on flavour – and portion size! The Mediterranean Touch for Lunch set menu is perfect for a hugely satisfying meal served with speed.

Grand Excelsior Hotel Al Barsha 1 **04 444 9999**
grandexcelsior.ae
Map **1 R6** Metro **Mall of the Emirates**

Le Relais de L'Entrecote — French

Meat eaters of the world rejoice

The most famous steak-frites bistro in Paris has come to Dubai (complete with wood panelling, paper tablecloths and cabaret posters). A Parisian institution since the 50s, it arrives as an antidote to all the choice on other menus. You see, this place has no choice, no menu; everyone gets salad and baguette followed by steak (with a 'secret-recipe' sauce) and chips — traditionally washed down with plenty of red wine. Portions are modest but, as is traditional in the original bistro, once you've finished your plateful the waitresses (in full French maids outfits) serve another helping, and another, and another, until you give up. All for Dhs.125. If you leave room for dessert, you will get a choice, and a menu of classic French puddings to complete the *ooh-la-la* experience.

Festival Centre Dubai Festival City **04 232 5208**
lerelaisdelentrecote.com
Map **2 M9** Metro **Emirates**

Legends — Steakhouse

Luxury dining by the creek

Relaxing atmosphere, deep comfortable seats and good quality food that includes a range of steaks and seafood, accompanied by an extensive wine list. The decor is modern, with a ceiling that stretches right to the top of the distinctive white sails. Golfers enjoy the portion sizes.

Dubai Creek Golf & Yacht Club Port Saeed
04 295 6000
dubaigolf.com
Map **2 M7** Metro **Deira City Centre**

Lemongrass — Thai

A sound favourite with Thai lovers

One of the better – and cheapest – Thai restaurants in Dubai, the menu offers a typical range of decently executed Siamese dishes. There's no alcohol, but the fruit mocktails compensate. The setting is bright, inviting and comfortable, and the service unobtrusive. Also at Ibn Battuta Mall (04 368 5616).

Nr Lamcy Plaza Oud Metha **04 334 2325**
lemongrassrestaurants.com
Map **2 K6** Metro **Oud Metha**

Levantine — Middle Eastern

Lavish Lebanese, complete with belly dancer

With a very high ceiling and large sweeping red curtains, Levantine is a lavish affair. Indulge in a banquet of classic Lebanese dishes as you watch a talented belly dancer make her rounds. Finish your meal by sharing a shisha in the upstairs terrace bar with relaxed floor seating and views of Dubai.

Atlantis The Palm Palm Jumeirah **04 426 2626**
atlantisthepalm.com
Map **1 N1** Metro **Nakheel**

The Lime Tree Cafe & Kitchen — Cafe

Wholesome food in a relaxed setting; a classic

A Dubai institution whose food nods towards Mediterranean cuisine, with roast vegetables, halloumi cheese and roast chicken paninis, as well as delicious salads, satay kebabs and quiches. Don't leave without sharing an enormous slice of the superlative carrot cake. Good alfresco options too. Also at Ibn Batutta Mall, Al Quoz and Media City.

Nr Jumeirah Mosque, Jumeira Rd Jumeira 1
04 349 8498
thelimetreecafe.com
Map **2 H4** Metro **World Trade Centre**

The Lobby Lounge — Afternoon Tea

Fine china and silver spoons; tea at its most refined

Tea at the Ritz is an exquisite experience. Delicate finger sandwiches and dainty pastries, succulent scones with clotted cream and a selection of jams, a fabulously colonial selection of teas and the fine china are all deliciously regal. It feels exclusive, but everyone is welcome.

The Ritz-Carlton, Dubai Dubai Marina **04 399 4000**
ritzcarlton.com
Map **1 L4** Metro **Dubai Marina**

Lobby Lounge & Terrace — Afternoon Tea

An afternoon delight in DIFC

Lofty ceilings, comfortable armchairs and cream coloured decor combine to create a calm environment that is perfect for an informal business meeting. The Lobby Lounge & Terrace offers a tasty afternoon tea menu with all the traditional trimmings. The bite sized raisin scones are delightfully buttery without being too rich, and the imported Wilkinson Jams from the English countryside are a nice touch. For a caffeine free lunch, try the African amber tea with hibiscus and vanilla, which is fruity and mild with a comforting aroma. High tea is served between 14:00-17:00 and costs Dhs.140 (excluding service charge).

The Ritz-Carlton, Dubai International Financial Centre (DIFC) Trade Centre 2 **04 372 2222**
ritzcarlton.com
Map **2 G6** Metro **Financial Centre**

Long Yin — Chinese

Great service, fantastic food and ambience to boot

From the warm welcome at the door to the delicious contemporary Cantonese and Szechwan cuisine – this is a real treat. Dishes include the incredibly tasty pork ribs with salt and pepper, and the Long Yin steamed platter (chicken wonton, chicken and prawns siomai), ideal for sharing. Ask the knowledgeable waiters for recommendations and you could be ordering minced beef soup with egg white, seafood fried rice, oriental fried egg noodles, beef Vietnamese style, Peking style

chilli prawns and a side of pak choi with garlic sauce. The food is well balanced, with an excellent drinks menu to accompany it. But the standout dish of the meal has to be the prawns with wasabi cream, a nice kick to a crunchy favourite.
Le Meridien Dubai Al Garhoud
04 702 2455
longyin-dubai.com
Map **2 N8** Metro **GGICO**

Luciano's — Italian

Poolside Italian serving up fantastic pizzas

Good quality dishes from across Italy are served at this reasonably priced poolside restaurant. The portions are generous and the starters deserve a special mention. The real star of the show, however, is the selection of thin-crust pizzas. When the weather is conducive, ask for a table outside underneath the fairy-light bedecked palm trees.
Habtoor Grand Beach Resort & Spa Dubai Marina
04 399 5000
habtoorhotels.com
Map **1 L4** Metro **Dubai Marina**

M's Beef Bistro — Steakhouse

An elegant, well-established steakhouse

The battle for the best steakhouse in Dubai is a fierce one; however, M's is a serious contender. What's great about this intimate restaurant is its commitment to food excellence. While the decor and ambience, whether inside or out on the terrace, is certainly pleasant, the real prize has to go to the food. From the splendid array of speciality bread through to the devilishly delicious desserts, every single mouthful is simply sublime. The country style terrine with walnut toast is the perfect start to a meal of pure indulgence. Naturally, the mains are all about the steaks, although there are some seafood and vegetarian options. Weigh up your appetite before ordering your melt-in-the-mouth New Zealand, Argentinean or American steak by the gram, not forgetting side dishes that include a superb gratin dauphinois. Leave room for the desserts, most notably the warm chocolate tart.
Le Meridien Dubai Al Garhoud
04 702 2455
msbeefbistro-dubai.com
Map **2 N8** Metro **GGICO**

Madeleine Cafe & Boulangerie — Cafe

French fare with a view to thrill

Tucked away from the mania of the Dubai Mall lies Madeleine Cafe & Boulangerie; a spacious cafe resembling a traditional Parisian restaurant. Clean wooden tables and chairs are accompanied by the ever-so-kitsch French ornaments that are dotted around the room. The menu offers casual French cuisine, focusing more on snack options including sandwiches, soups and crepes, and all portions are hearty and flavourful. Try their signature dessert 'Madeleine's' – a tray of freshly baked fairy cakes with a selection of pistachio, chocolate or lemon ingredients which make for a perfect coffee accompaniment. Madeleine's true piece de resistance is the spectacular view of the Dubai Fountain show, providing a truly memorable alfresco dining experience.
The Dubai Mall Downtown Dubai **04 438 4335**
madeleinecafe.com
Map **2 F6** Metro **Burj Khalifa/Dubai Mall**

MAHEC — Indian

Traditional Indian fare with a fine dining spin

Aiming to set itself apart from the crowd, and there's certainly no shortage of good Indian restaurants in Dubai, MAHEC reinterprets the cuisine with a modern, fine dining spin on staple classics. The emphasis here is not on portion size but on presentation, quality ingredients and paying homage to traditional cooking techniques. MAHEC's extensive menu caters to both vegetarians and non-veggies in equal amounts and, if you do have trouble narrowing down your meal, opt for the five-course gourmet set menu. Delicious. Notable selections include the chermoula prawns, spice crusted sea bream and lamb chop in truffle scented sauce. Reinvention does come at a price, which may detract casual curry seekers, but if you're looking for a meal less ordinary then you won't be disappointed. In case you're wondering, MAHEC stands for Modern Authentic Hindustani Evolved Cuisine.
Le Meridien Dubai Al Garhoud **04 217 0000**
mahec.diningdubai.com
Map **2 N8** Metro **GGICO**

Majlis Al Bahar — Mediterranean

Views to take your breath away, prices to match

Majlis Al Bahar offers front row seats to the iconic hotel's nightly light show. The meaty Mediterranean cuisine isn't exceptional but the mini barbecues are a novel attraction, and the salads are well executed.
Burj Al Arab Umm Suqeim 3 **04 301 7600**
jumeirah.com
Map **1 S4** Metro **Mall of the Emirates**

Manga Sushi — Japanese

Tokyo trendy with a decor unseen elsewhere

As the name suggests, this Japanese eatery is all about Japan's cult comics, from the large screen showing Manga movies to the artworks on the walls. You may feel like you've drifted into Tokyo, where traditional fare has a modern edge. If you're looking for something a little different, you'll find it here.
Beach Park Plaza Jumeira 2 **04 342 8300**
mangasushi.ae
Map **2 D4** Metro **Business Bay**

Mango Tree — Thai

Decent Thai tucker with tantalising views

Grilled specialities, plentiful seafood, and signature dishes from the Bangkok restaurant offer something different to standard Thai fare. The service is quiet but attentive and the beautifully designed location has some of the best views in Downtown Dubai.

Souk Al Bahar Downtown Dubai **04 426 7313**
Map **2 F6** Metro **Burj Khalifa/Dubai Mall**

Mango Tree Bistro — Thai

Mall dining for the gourmet foodie

Serving a delectable menu of Thai goodies in serene surroundings, this is a lovely respite from the crowds of shoppers. Pop in for a quick array of finger foods or relax for longer over a heartier meal – it's all expertly prepared and of a surprisingly high standard.

Mirdif City Centre Mirdif **04 284 3635**
Map **2 P12** Metro **Rashidiya**

Manhattan Grill — Steakhouse

Steaks and sophistication at this fine dining find

Soft lighting, plush seating, smooth music and an excellent selection of succulent steaks make this one of the finest fine-dining venues in town. There are seafood and vegetarian dishes on the menu too. It's pricey, but you certainly get what you pay for here.

Grand Hyatt Dubai Umm Hurair 2 **04 317 2222**
restaurants.dubai.hyatt.com
Map **2 L8** Metro **Dubai Healthcare City**

Mannaland Korean Restaurant — Korean

Authentic Korean, full of flavour and atmosphere

A real find, for a truly unique Dubai dining experience, this Korean restaurant in Satwa offers traditional floor seating and excellent, authentic food cooked right there at your table. Wash it all down with a teapot of 'special brew'. Great value too.

Al Mina Rd Al Mina **04 345 1300**
Map **2 J4** Metro **Al Jafiliya**

Margaux — French

Breathtaking views and belly-pleasing cuisine

Despite overlooking the Burj Khalifa and its huge fountain display, the undisputed star of the show remains the menu, which includes some great veggie options, steaks, fish, an interesting gold risotto and delicious penne, broccolini and juicy scallops; leave room for the cheesecake, arguably the best in Dubai.

Souk Al Bahar Downtown Dubai **04 439 7555**
margaux.ae
Map **2 F6** Metro **Burj Khalifa/Dubai Mall**

Maria Bonita Taco Shop & Grill — Mexican

Friendly neighbourhood Mexican, a tortilla thriller

Maria Bonita stands out as a friendly, well-worn neighbourhood eatery serving traditional Mexican and Tex-Mex dishes that include flavourful nachos, spicy quesadillas and meaty fajitas, served in a laidback atmosphere. Also at The Green Community (Casa Maria, 04 885 3188).

Nr Spinneys Centre, Umm Al Sheif St
Umm Suqeim 1 **04 395 4454**
mariabonitadubai.com
Map **2 B5** Metro **Noor Islamic Bank**

The Market Cafe — Buffet

A creative, fun twist on buffet dining

Wander from station to station selecting your style of food as well as your specific starters, mains, desserts and drinks. Mix and match or stay within the Italian, Asian, Arabic or international cuisines on offer. Great food and service; this restaurant mainly caters to hotel guests, but it is a good option for lunch if in the area.

Grand Hyatt Dubai Umm Hurair 2 **04 317 2222**
restaurants.dubai.hyatt.com
Map **2 L8** Metro **Dubai Healthcare City**

The Market Place — Buffet

Excellent all-you-can-eat with free-flowing drinks

Free-flowing drinks make revellers feel at home at this bistro-style restaurant – but it is the five-star food that distinguishes this buffet eatery, featuring several live-cooking stations and an impressive array of starters and desserts. This is a great place for group celebrations and is packed at the weekends.

JW Marriott Hotel Dubai Al Muraqqabat **04 607 7977**
marriottdiningatjw.ae
Map **2 P6** Metro **Abu Baker Al Siddique**

Marrakech — Moroccan

Tranquil surroundings and earthy flavours

Smooth arches and lamps add to an overwhelming sense of tranquillity, while a duo belts out traditional tunes on a small stage. Starters such as wedding pie with pigeon, crushed almonds and icing sugar are served on blue ceramics. For mains, try the lamb tagine with fluffy, fragrant rice. Afterwards, a light orange salad is the perfect ending.

Shangri-La Hotel Dubai Trade Centre 1 **04 405 2703**
shangri-la.com
Map **2 G5** Metro **Financial Centre**

Masala — Indian

Delicious Indian in a desert setting

Masala serves tasty versions of all the dishes you might expect, from the tandoor to curries and rices. Tables in alcoves surround a central kitchen from where the slapping of naan accompanies the sounds of tabla and sitar. You'd be well advised to arrive early and enjoy a desert sundowner.

Bab Al Shams Desert Resort & Spa Bawadi
04 809 6194
meydanhotels.com

Masala Craft — Indian

Authentic Indian that ticks all the boxes

No need to book a flight to India anytime soon. Just take a quick trip to Century Village, stroll through the myriad of restaurants along the walk and arrive at Masala Craft. You'll discover one of Dubai's most romantic and exotic Indian hideaways. They've put a modern twist on Indian décor inside Masala, but have remained authentic with low cushion seating and shisha. Invite a group to wine and dine on the outdoor terrace, and be treated like royalty as the waiters individually serve each dish to your plate. The smell of fresh baked tandoori breads and the taste of rich palak paneer lasooni with saffron phirni for dessert will surely trick your mind into thinking you really have landed in the spice land!

Century Village Al Garhoud **04 282 9626**
centuryvillage.ae
Map **2 N8** Metro **GGICO**

Max's Restaurant — Filipino

Filipino diner that's friendly and fun

This family diner is a favourite with the Filipino community. The decor is typical fast food diner complete with paper place mats, but the food is plentiful and tasty. It serves much loved Filipino favourites like speciality fried chicken served with rice or Kamote fries (sweet potato fries). The menu also boasts exotic sounding dishes like Kare-Kare (oxtail and tripe stew), Lumpiang Ubod (crabmeat sautéed with fresh coconut) and drinks like Sago't Gulaman (a drink made with tapioca balls and gelatin and sweetened with syrup), fresh Buko juice (young coconut juice served in its shell) and Buko Pandan Shake. If you're not the adventurous type, the sizzling tofu is definitely a worth a try. Although the cuisine is mostly Filipino, the clientele is varied. Serves certain dishes in kids' portions.

Spinneys Bldg, Khalid Bin Al Waleed Rd Al Karama **04 325 7797**
maxschicken.com
Map **2 L5** Metro **BurJuman**

Maya By Richard Sandoval — Mexican

Modern Mexican rivals Dubai's best

In a city of plenty, finding a restaurant that truly stands out can be difficult. Maya – from Richard Sandoval, a giant of the American restaurant scene – makes a distinctive splash. Even discounting the crepas con cajeta (not easy – it could be Dubai's most sumptuous dessert), what precedes is a masterclass in controlled abandon. The food is a tour of rural Mexico, from southern corn fields to coastal fishing villages, all reinterpreted through a prism of modern creativity. Spiciness is whispered rather than screamed and while you'll find fresh guacamole being whipped up at the table, there's not a fajita in sight; instead, dive into lobster with chili chipotle, langoustine tacos, or pan-seared corn-fed chicken on cilantro rice. The interiors are as lovely as the food, but you're best off heading for the terrace – the perfect place for great food washed down with plenty of margaritas.

Le Royal Meridien Beach Resort & Spa Dubai Marina **04 316 5550**
richardsandoval.com/mayadubai
Map **1 L4** Metro **Dubai Marina**

Mazaj — Middle Eastern

Strong, bold Lebanese fare at an affordable price

Nestled away in a corner, just by the entrance of Century Village, understated Mazaj is easy to overlook; though it's far from empty. Regular patrons keep Mazaj busy and lively so if you prefer a quieter, shisha free experience opt for a table inside. What the menu lacks in creativity it makes up for in variety, with a wide selection of hot and cold mezzes, mains, desserts and an extensive wine list from Lebanon's prized wineries. The sujuk and Kachtalieh are house specialities and come highly recommended! Servings are generous, service prompt, and venue laid back; Mazaj skips pretence to deliver strong, bold Lebanese fare at an affordable price.

Century Village Al Garhoud **04 282 9952**
centuryvillage.ae
Map **2 N8** Metro **GGICO**

Mazina — International

A good option for a family brunch

The Saturday brunch at Mazina is perfect for families who want a long, hearty lunch with the kids without them getting bored. This isn't your usual brunch, which for many of us is a good thing. You can relax in a laidback atmosphere enjoying a good variety of food whilst your young ones either bounce around on the inflatable castle or get competitive on the Wii. In the meantime you can make your way around the array of waist-expanding delights, from the never-ending salad choices to the dim sum options and wok favourites cooked from your selection. There is also a choice of roasts and an assortment of desserts that you simply have to make room for. It might not be a wild bunch; however, if your appetite is healthy enough and you want to treat the kids, Mazina is a solid option for a Saturday afternoon. And you can always head to the mall after to walk off your lunch.

The Address Dubai Marina Dubai Marina **04 888 3444**
theaddress.com
Map **1 K5** Metro **Dubai Marina**

The Meat Co. — Steakhouse

Meat and drink for steak fans

The terrace here offers excellent views of the Burj Khalifa while you decide which country you want your steak to come from, the cut and how you want it

basted. The meat is aged, ensuring plenty of flavour and, for many, this is one of the most consistently good steak joints in the city, although the prices are steep. Also has a branch at Souk Madinat Jumeirah (04 368 6040).
Souk Al Bahar Downtown Dubai **04 420 0737**
themeatco.com
Map **2 F6** Metro **Burj Khalifa/Dubai Mall**

The MED — Mediterranean

Sassy, cool Mediterranean with a fun brunch
On the eighth floor of Media City's latest hotspot, The MED serves up a fun, energetic and good value menu of Mediterranean classics, impeccably realised with just enough Gallic arrogance to reveal the chef's nationality. Head here on Fridays for a lively brunch.
Media One Hotel Al Sufouh 1 **04 427 1000**
mediaonehotel.com
Map **1 M5** Metro **Nakheel**

Medzo — Italian

A taste of the Amalfi coast in Wafi
Back with a new look and a new, longer menu, Medzo still delivers the same splendid gastronomy. Elegant white mix with chandeliers and dreamy drapes to create a more romantic atmosphere set to a soundtrack of soft piano. When the weather permits, the tree-shaded terrace completes the experience.
Wafi Umm Hurair 2 **04 324 4100**
pyramidsrestaurantsatwafi.com
Map **2 L7** Metro **Dubai Healthcare City**

Méridien Village Terrace — Buffet

Great outdoor buffet with different themed nights
Set in the middle of Le Meridien's outdoor dining area, the huge buffet switches nightly between culinary themes. Numerous live-cooking stations keep the food wonderfully fresh, and a great choice of drinks are replenished with alarming regularity. Only open in winter, this is one of the best buffets in town.
Le Meridien Dubai Al Garhoud
04 702 2455
meridienvillageterrace-dubai.com/
Map **2 N8** Metro **GGICO**

Mezza House — Middle Eastern

Popular Levant place with an atmospheric setting
This gem combines traditional themes with a modern style. Mezza House specialises in Levant cuisine, along with a few family signatures. Look out for Granny's potato chips and Nasso's chocolate. The fresh, zingy flavours are complemented by a welcoming atmosphere and delicious fruit cocktails, and the outdoor shisha lounge is the perfect place to round off your meal with Arabic coffee. It's good value too. Reservations for terrace dining are recommended. Lunch discounts (20% off bills over Dhs.200) are on offer in April and May, 12:00-17:00 weekdays.
Yansoun 9 Souk Tamer Hind, Old Town
Downtown Dubai **04 420 5444**
mezzahouse.com
Map **2 F6** Metro **Burj Khalifa/Dubai Mall**

Minato — Japanese

Authentic Japanese restaurant with live cooking
Dubai's oldest Japanese restaurant features intricately painted vases, rice paper doors and soft lighting, creating a personal yet traditional atmosphere. A sushi bar, private tatami rooms, and teppanyaki tables liven up pricey dishes, and weekly sushi buffets are served.
Radisson Blu Hotel, Dubai Deira Creek Al Rigga
04 222 7171
radissonblu.com
Map **2 M5** Metro **Union**

Miyako

Mistral
Mediterranean

Bountiful buffet at Ibn Battuta Gate

Open all day, this licensed buffet restaurant serves classic Mediterranean fare throughout the week, with special themed nights on Monday (grill) and Tuesday (seafood) for added variety. The starter and dessert stations display a staggering range, so you won't be going home hungry.

Mövenpick Hotel Ibn Battuta Gate The Gardens
04 444 0000
mistral.ae
Map **1 G5** Metro **Ibn Battuta**

Miyako
Japanese

Superb teppanyaki that will lure you back for more

Small yet chic, Miyako combines a laid-back ambience with a genuinely exciting menu. The speciality is a delicate seafood broth served in a paper bowl and heated over a naked flame, while the tender slivers of teppanyaki are excellent.

Hyatt Regency Dubai Corniche Deira **04 317 2222**
restaurants.dubai.hyatt.com
Map **2 N4** Metro **Palm Deira**

Mizaan
International

International cuisine and a worldly wine list

This hotel restaurant serves a range of international cuisine, from Indian and Thai curries to grilled Mediterranean vegetables, to guests and Dubai residents. The accompanying wine list is great value compared with similar venues in Dubai.

The H Hotel Dubai Trade Centre 1 **04 501 8888**
h-hotel.com
Map **2 J5** Metro **World Trade Centre**

Mosaico
Italian

Fine buffet, great for both high fliers and families

Open 24 hours a day, Mosaico blends Italian flavours with Spanish flamboyance. The Mediterranean buffet incorporates freshly prepared tapas, pastas and pizzas made to order, and honey-drizzled profiteroles. Polish it off with a glass or three of traditional Italian wine.

Jumeirah Emirates Towers Trade Centre 2
04 319 8088
jumeirah.com
Map **2 H6** Metro **Emirates Towers**

NA3 NA3
Middle Eastern

Stylish surrounds and a good selection of dishes

NA3 NA3 (pronounced 'na na') is a demure all-day dining restaurant. A tasty range of stews, salads and deserts are on offer as well as a live cooking station serving seafood, grilled meat and shawarmas.

The Address Dubai Mall Downtown Dubai
04 888 3444
theaddress.com
Map **2 F6** Metro **Burj Khalifa/Dubai Mall**

Nando's
Portuguese

Cheap, cheerful chicken with a kick

Famous for its peri-peri chicken, which ranges from mild to extra hot. The takeaway option is popular (extra points for the 'poultry in motion' slogan on the delivery bikes). Also at Al Ghurair Centre (04 221 1992), The Greens Centre (04 360 8080), Burj Residences (04 422 4882) and The Dubai Mall (04 434 0190).

Nr Crowne Plaza, Shk Zayed Rd Trade Centre 1
04 321 2000
nandos.ae
Map **2 H6** Metro **Emirates Towers**

Nina
Indian

First class Indian fare with a European accent

Flickering candles and heavy velvet curtains set the scene at the One&Only's stylish Indo-European option, Nina. If hearty curries and all-empowering fieriness is what you're after, you're better off looking elsewhere – the food at Nina brings diners on an altogether more refined culinary journey to India. Whet the appetite by sampling a selection of roti and naan with savoury pickles and salads such as seared tuna with mustard cress and lime vinaigrette. The spinach kofta is exquisite, as are the tandoori prawns served with lemon rice. Tangy Indian sauvignon blanc pairs nicely with the lighter dishes, while the deep-flavoured shiraz by Sula is a match with the meatier dishes, like the grilled lamb chop, shish kebab and tikka.

Arabian Court At One&Only Royal Mirage
Al Sufouh 1 **04 399 9999**
oneandonlyroyalmirage.com
Map **1 J4** Metro **Nakheel**

Nineteen
European

Fine-dining that puts the glamour into golf

The dark interior of the Montgomerie's flagship restaurant is lit by 70s kitsch lampshades, and subtle lights that single out your table. In contrast, the show kitchen is loud and proud. Choose from a range of rotisserie grills, and dive into the extensive wine list. Also serves a popular Saturday roast.

The Address Montgomerie Dubai Emirates Living
04 888 3444
theaddress.com
Map **1 L7** Metro **Nakheel**

The Noble House
Chinese

Chinese dishes elevated to works of art

High-backed chairs and a sunken ceiling, in an austere setting worthy of its Raffles home, make this Chinese restaurant a truly fine dining experience. Showcasing traditional dishes with a contemporary twist, the fine details of Chinese cuisine have been preserved well.

Raffles Dubai Umm Hurair 2 **04 324 8888**
raffles.com
Map **2 K7** Metro **Dubai Healthcare City**

The Boardwalk

Nobu
Japanese

Unreal sushi and sashimi made by the best

Nobuyuki Matsuhisa, the godfather of sushi, has upped the ante for Japanese food aficionados, who will love the exceptional quality, attention to detail and huge menu of sushi, sashimi and tempura. Despite its reputation, Nobu is not restricted to celebrities – as long as you can get a reservation.

Atlantis The Palm Palm Jumeirah **04 426 2626**
atlantisthepalm.com
Map **1 N1** Metro **Nakheel**

Nomad > *p.527*
Asian

Fresh Asian classics to suit your mood

There are so many sides to Nomad that it is difficult to sum up. Romantic waterside dining, cosy fireside lounging, upbeat DJ-side dancing, or relaxing poolside snacking – and it's a huge venue, so there's room for whatever mood you're in. Starters perfect for sharing include sushi and seafood tempura, while simple, reasonably-priced favourites such as nasi goreng and Singapore noodles complement a number of a la carte meat and fish dishes. The venue also hosts an Asian tapas wine bar, New York-style deli, an Asian pool grill, and a dim sum trolley.

Jumeirah Creekside Hotel Al Garhoud **04 230 8571**
jumeirah.com
Map **2 M8** Metro **GGICO**

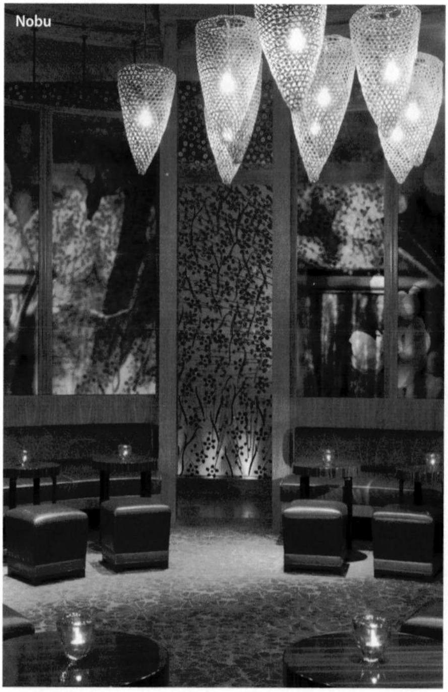
Nobu

The Noodle House
Far Eastern

Simple, tasty dishes and a laid-back set up

A refreshingly relaxed affair, just turn up and wait for the first available spot at one of the long communal tables. You order by ticking your desired dishes on the notepads (after some advice from the clued-up staff, if required). The mouthwatering food is well priced, with big portions of soups, noodles and stir-fries served up in record speed. The modern decor, open kitchen and zingy cocktails add to the vibrant atmosphere. Other branches are located in the Souk Madinat Jumeirah, which has the added bonus of a terrace for alfresco eating, The Dubai Mall, DIFC, Dubai Media City and BurJuman. Call 800 666353 for home delivery.

The Boulevard At Jumeirah Emirates Towers
Trade Centre 2 **04 319 8088**
thenoodlehouse.com
Map **2 H6** Metro **Emirates Towers**

The Observatory
International

Breathtaking views, sophisticated cocktails

It's all about the views at this atmospheric 52nd floor gastro-lounge. Spectacular 360° vistas over the Marina and The Palm accompany the concise (but tasty) menu, while the cocktails are excellent. Come just before sunset then stay for the evening to get the full benefit of the amazing panorama.

Dubai Marriott Harbour Hotel & Suites
Dubai Marina **04 319 4795**
observatory.dubaimarriottharbourhotel.com
Map **1 L5** Metro **Dubai Marina**

Oceana
Buffet

Cruise the world at this international eatery

The decor at Oceana is akin to glamorous dining rooms of 1930s cruise ships – lots of chrome and wood with Art Moderne furniture and lighting fixtures. Different nights feature different cuisines – choose from seafood, Arabic, French and Mexican.

Hilton Dubai Jumeirah Resort Dubai Marina
04 399 1111
hilton.com
Map **1 K4** Metro **Jumeirah Lakes Towers**

Okku
Japanese

Japanese fine dining in the UAE

There are more than 40 creative concoctions on Okku's innovative menu – dishes such as the flavoursome 'O' style hotate (seared scallops with figs in a truffle-wafu goma), and veal short rib shoyu-ni: a ginger-soy braised veal short rib that's so tender it falls off the bone with one light touch of a fork. Leave room for the signature foie gras kushiyaki or the 'O' style yellow tail carpaccio. Another highlight is the sushi bar.

The H Hotel Dubai Trade Centre 1 **04 501 8777**
okkudubai.com
Map **2 J5** Metro **World Trade Centre**

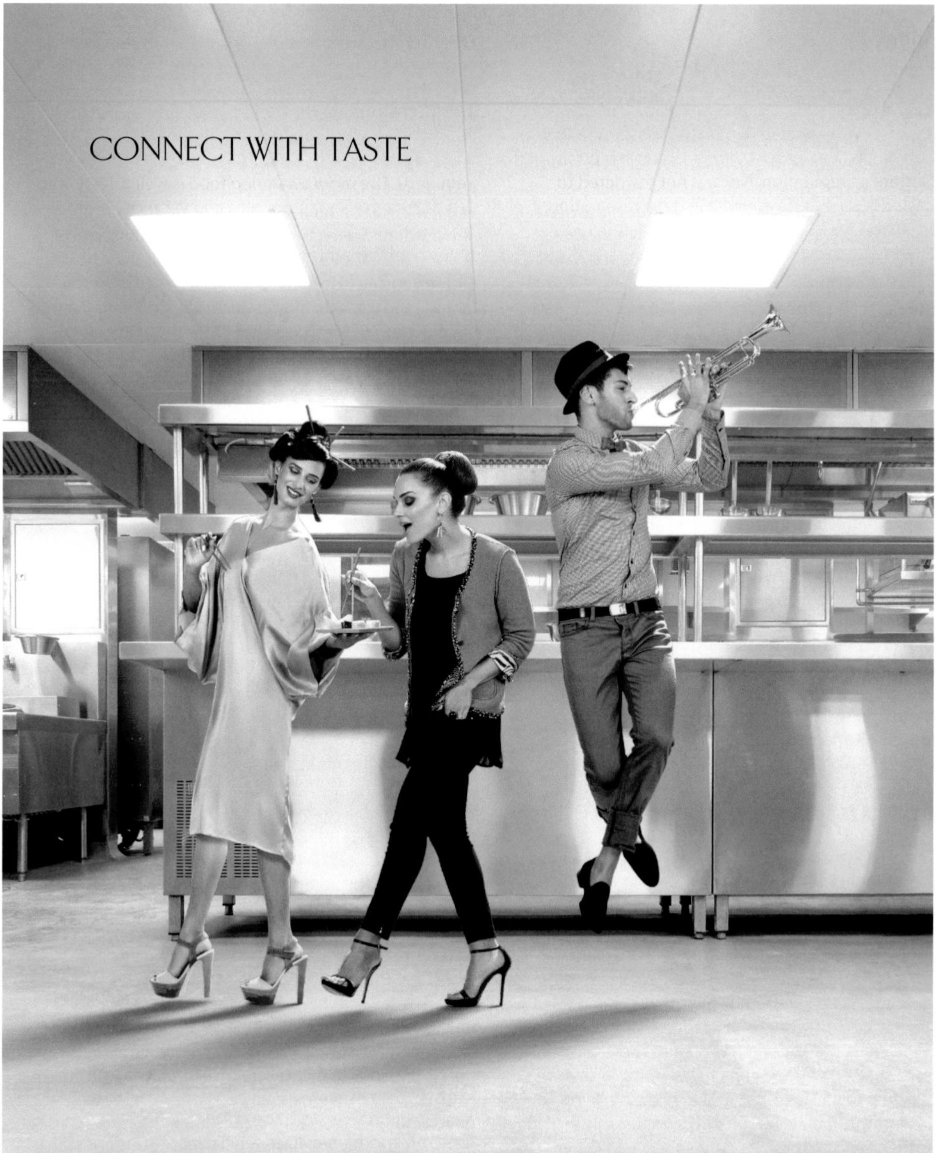
CONNECT WITH TASTE

Olives
Italian

Slip into Mediterranean mode at the One&Only

Sturdy wicker furniture, lots of archways, indoor foliage and white ceramic tiles on the walls help to set the scene in Olives. Pizzas and pastas are the stars of the Mediterranean menu, and there's a lovely outdoor terrace overlooking the gardens and pool area. Boasting a Riviera coastal cafe feel, this is the perfect place to feast on braised lamb shank with roasted garlic salad and an orange rosemary jus – the chef's signature dish.

The Palace At One&Only Royal Mirage Al Sufouh 1
04 399 9999
oneandonlyroyalmirage.com
Map **1 M4** Metro **Nakheel**

THE One
Cafe

This could be the one for funky cafe fans

Tucked away on the first floor of THE One furniture store, this funky cafe features an extensive menu that is imaginative, alongside some reliable classics. The food is high quality; the fresh juices are fabulous and the cakes outstanding. An all-day breakfast menu strays from the ordinary with brunch-ish offerings like banana French toast and a zaatar and halloumi omelette. As well as healthy options like quinoa, asparagus and feta salad there are more hearty offerings including the marinated lamb leg fillet. There's also a good kids' menu.

Jumeira Rd Jumeira 1
04 345 6687
theone.com
Map **2 H4** Metro **Emirates Towers**

The Orchestra
Middle Eastern

A pleasant culinary surprise

Open all day, this family restaurant is a meat lover's paradise serving succulent meat and chicken dishes, along with sandwiches. But if you want the real Orchestra experience, try the starter platter of mozzarella sticks, buffalo wings, fried calamari, spring rolls and barbecued flavoured potato wedges followed by the seafood mix platter. There's also a good selection for vegetarians, as well as a small selection of Italian dishes and a children's menu. In this musical-themed restaurant, comfortable brown leather chairs and solid wood tables beautifully complement the leather covered walls and cream sofas with subtle bronze tones and artfully displayed musical instruments. You can dine alfresco or smoke a shisha and enjoy the beautiful Marina Pavilion view by day or the twinkling lights of the fairground by night. Branches in BurJuman (04 352 8882), Deira (04 295 8010) and The Dubai Mall (04 339 9448).

Festival Centre Dubai Festival City **04 232 8232**
goodcouae.com
Map **2 M9** Metro **Emirates**

Orchid Restaurant
International

Standard dining for hotel guests and neighbours

For diners looking to escape the shopping frenzy of nearby The Dubai Mall, Orchid offers up standard international selections right from the hotel's in-room dining menu. Tucked away on the second floor, the restaurant has indoor and outdoor seating – both with ample flat screen TVs for cable news viewing. The outdoor option is nearby the hotel pool and the echoes of the Dubai Fountain show remind you just where you are. Non alcoholic beverages such as the lemon mint make a refreshing choice. Connected to Orchid is a small Starbucks stand for those in need of a quick 'pick me up'. While not a destination in its own right, Orchid does give those in the neighbourhood a decent meal away from the crowds.

Ramada Downtown Dubai Downtown Dubai
04 330 7330
ramadadowntowndubai.com
Map **2 F6** Metro **Burj Khalifa/Dubai Mall**

Ossiano
Seafood

Superb seafood from a three-starred Michelin chef

Santi Santamaria serves up delicate Catalan-inspired seafood dishes at this impeccable eatery. Glistening chandeliers and floor-to-ceiling views of the aquarium provide a formal but romantic setting to enjoy the incredible, and incredibly expensive, fare in.

Atlantis The Palm Palm Jumeirah **04 426 2626**
atlantisthepalm.com
Map **1 N1** Metro **Nakheel**

Pachanga
Latin American

A Latin American feast, ideal for meat lovers

Pachanga occupies two distinct areas; a lounge and a restaurant. The lounge is reminiscent of a private Cuban cigar room, furnished with brown leather chairs, encased cigar cupboards and varnished wooden panelling. In contrast, the restaurant is a palette of white and cream with Colonial style pillars lining the buffet area. Its Latin American fare includes signature dishes stretching from as far north as Mexico through to Argentina. On Tuesdays, Pachanga celebrates all things grilled with a Brazilian-style Churassco barbecue with succulent beef, chicken and lamb cuts served directly to your table on a giant skewer. The peppered rib-eye is particularly tender, juicy and cooked to medium-rare perfection. If that's not enough to satisfy your stomach, then the additional buffet counter including the mouthwatering chorizo sausage and the crispy breaded crab should ensure you crawl home in search of elasticated trousers. Churassco Tuesdays are a bit of a bargain, starting at Dhs.195.

Hilton Dubai Jumeirah Resort Dubai Marina
04 399 1111
hilton.com
Map **1 K4** Metro **Jumeirah Lakes Towers**

Pai Thai — Thai

Fantastic Thai cuisine in a truly romantic setting

You'll have a night to remember at Pai Thai, from the abra ride to the restaurant to the nouvelle Thai cuisine. The outdoor seating offers delightful views and the menu provides the odd twist on familiar favourites.

Al Qasr Al Sufouh 1 **04 366 6730**
madinatjumeirah.com
Map **1 R4** Metro **Mall of the Emirates**

The Palermo Restaurant — Seafood

Remote fine dining, great for special occasions

The Polo Club may be a drive away, but the quiet, elegant dining room and excellent food make it worth it. The original appetisers and quality meats and seafood will not disappoint. Perfect for an intimate meal or business dinner, it's an unexpected mini-break.

Dubai Polo & Equestrian Club Dubai Studio City
04 361 8111
poloclubdubai.com
Map **1 N13** Metro **Mall of the Emirates**

Palm Grill — Steakhouse

Classic steaks and classical music

Palm Grill cooks up juicy steaks in an open-plan kitchen to the accompaniment of a live pianist. The steaks are a tender delight, cooked precisely to order and big enough to satisfy the most ravenous meat lover – so time is required to savour each bite.

Radisson Blu Hotel, Dubai Deira Creek Al Rigga
04 222 7171
radissonblu.com
Map **2 M5** Metro **Union**

Panini — Cafe

Decent pit stop for lunch on the go

Set among the tropical indoor 'rainforest' in the impressive lobby of the Grand Hyatt, complete with lush greenery and jungle mist, Panini is a good place to meet up with friends or business associates for a lunch on the run. The food is nothing special but it is very convenient.

Grand Hyatt Dubai Umm Hurair 2 **04 317 2222**
dubai.grand.hyatt.com
Map **2 L8** Metro **Dubai Healthcare City**

Panorama — International

Amazing daytime views, mediocre food

Being located on the 43rd floor of any building on Sheikh Zayed Road offers the advantage of astonishing views. Panorama exploits the stunning scenery with seating along three different sides of the building. Although the dinner-time lighting is too bright inside to enjoy the panorama outside, the view can easily be enjoyed during the day during their breakfast buffet. There is nothing magical or impressive about the food: Panorama offers the hotel's room service menu. The typical international items are available here as well as a few special items like their surf and turf dish. Families looking to enjoy penthouse views without the usual formal ambience may find this family-friendly location to be a good fit. Although average in quality, the variety means everyone in the family should be able to find something they like.

Emirates Grand Hotel Trade Centre 2
04 323 0000
emiratesgrandhotel.com
Map **2 G6** Metro **Financial Centre**

Pars Iranian Kitchen — Persian

Traditional Iranian food and laid-back shisha vibe

This branch of Pars offers a traditional, laid-back atmosphere a million miles from the modernity suggested by the garish neon sign outside. The menu includes standard regional favourites such as mixed grills and mezze, while a delightful front garden, enclosed by a fairy light-entwined hedgerow, is home to soft, cushioned bench seats, perfect for shisha. Other locations include Mall of the Emirates and 2nd December Street in Satwa.

Nr Chelsea Plaza Hotel Al Jafiliya **04 398 4000**
Map **2 J5** Metro **Al Jafiliya**

Pax — Italian

Pick 'n' mix Italian with SZR views

Pax does traditional Italian dishes in less than traditional sizes to give punters a pick 'n' mix of tastes. It is a style they call bocconcini (little delicacies), and with appetisers starting at Dhs.15, and most mains costing less than Dhs.70, a hearty feed is not prohibitively expensive.

Dusit Thani Dubai Trade Centre 2 **04 343 3333**
dusit.com
Map **2 G6** Metro **Financial Centre**

Peppercrab — Singaporean

Authentic Singaporean fare, impeccable service

The minute you step onto the parquet rock polished floor and catch a glimpse of the feng shui tropical garden through the large floor to ceiling windows, you know you're in for a dining experience that will linger long after the meal. If you're looking for the ultimate Singaporean gastronomic experience, Peppercrab won't disappoint. Guests can watch the chef in action in the kitchen while the large seafood display tanks will keep the kids entertained. While it doesn't have a child's menu, it does serve smaller portions, and a kids' club is available during dining. The famous chilli pepper crab remains a must try. The wine menu is as generous in size as the rest of the restaurant.

Grand Hyatt Dubai Umm Hurair 2 **04 317 2222**
restaurants.dubai.hyatt.com
Map **2 L8** Metro **Dubai Healthcare City**

Pergolas
Cafe

A venue that changes to match the food

Perfect for a romantic evening, the international buffet is based around changing theme nights. The terrace is overlooked by fairytale architecture and the decor changes throughout the week to reflect themes, including seafood and 'Orient Express' evenings.

Al Murooj Rotana Trade Centre 2 **04 321 1111**
rotana.com
Map **2 G6** Metro **Financial Centre**

> **Stretch In Style**
>
> If you're feeling a bit flash (or are on a stag or hen party), you can rent a stretch Hummer, Lincoln or even Mercedes Limo Van from Dubai Exotic Limo(dubaiexoticlimo.com), Connection Chauffeur (uae-limousine.com) or Premier Limousines (premierdubai.com) so that you arrive at your destination in style. They are fully equipped with TV screens and a stereo system, with neon or leopard skin interiors, so you can make your journey as eventful as your destination.

Petals
International

Seafood delights enjoyed at a great height

One of the world's tallest hotels, the Rose Rayhaan stands proud on Sheikh Zayed Road. Its international all-day dining restaurant serves some good seafood, so take your pick and enjoy the view while it is poached, grilled or fried to your liking.

Rose Rayhaan By Rotana Trade Centre 2
04 323 0111
rotana.com
Map **2 G6** Metro **Financial Centre**

Pierchic
Seafood

Quite possibly Dubai's most amazing restaurant

Situated at the end of a long wooden pier that juts into the Arabian Gulf, Pierchic offers unobstructed views of the Burj Al Arab, which probably reflects in the heftier price tag. The superior seafood is meticulously presented and the wine menu reads like a sommelier's wish list.

Al Qasr Al Sufouh 1 **04 366 6730**
jumeirah.com
Map **1 R4** Metro **Mall of the Emirates**

Ping Pong
Chinese

Tip-top dim sum

Sleek and urban, Ping Pong is softened with dark wood and bench seating. An extensive dim sum menu offers steamed, baked and fried options and the flowering teas are a unique twist.

The Dubai Mall Downtown Dubai **04 339 9088**
pingpongdimsum.ae
Map **2 F6** Metro **Burj Khalifa/Dubai Mall**

The Pizza Company
Italian

Tasty pizza, tasty prices

Does exactly what the sign on the door says. If it's good old-fashioned, well-made pizza you're after, then The Pizza Company ticks all the boxes. There are pasta and salad options, but the 'grandma's own recipe' base makes pizza a bit of a no-brainer. Other branches on Al Rigga St and The Walk. Offers a good delivery service.

2nd December St Al Hudaiba **04 345 4848**
Map **2 J4** Metro **Al Jafiliya**

Planet Hollywood
American

Burgers and blaring decor – one for the kids

With bright colours, lots of space and friendly staff, this is a popular place to take the kids. The menu features huge, American-style portions, a kids' menu, plus a Friday brunch with movies, toys and face painting.

Wafi Umm Hurair 2 **04 324 4777**
planethollywoodintl.com
Map **2 L7** Metro **Dubai Healthcare City**

Plantation
Afternoon Tea

A welcome change to stuffy alternatives

The light, airy surrounds of Plantation's 'modern colonial' conservatory makes a pleasingly relaxed setting for afternoon tea or a light bite. As the lights of JBR's towers start to glow, it becomes a relaxed lounge bar, perfect for a dapper drink or a neat night cap.

Sofitel Dubai Jumeirah Beach Dubai Marina
04 448 4848
sofitel.com
Map **1 K4** Metro **Jumeirah Lakes Towers**

Prego's > *p.461*
Italian

A true Italian through and through

Prego's takes one cuisine for its buffet – Italian – and specialises in it. From soups with shavings of parmesan and an antipasti station laden with marinated vegetables, to hearty pastas and pizzas for mains, the authentic dishes are all extremely satisfying and expertly prepared.

Media Rotana Tecom **04 435 0000**
rotana.com
Map **1 P6** Metro **Dubai Internet City**

Prime Steakhouse
Steakhouse

A winning ticket, a regal steakhouse

A steakhouse should be judged on the quality of its steaks and Prime's Tajima Wagyu, USDA Black Angus and organic Rangers Valley are the best money can buy. Giant chandeliers, crisp white linen, tinkling ivories and an exceptional level of service combine with racecourse views to deliver an exceptional steakhouse.

The Meydan Hotel Meydan **04 381 3111**
meydanhotels.com
Map **2 E10** Metro **Business Bay**

Promenade French

Average fare, not savoir-faire

The selection of dishes from the a la carte menu of this French-style cafe is limited and the international buffet is basic. The mains are rather expensive, but the various cuts of meat and the seafood selection are cooked on the grill to specific requirements.

Four Points By Sheraton Bur Dubai Al Hamriya **04 397 7444**
starwoodhotels.com
Map **2 L5** Metro **BurJuman**

Pronto Cafe

Deli-style cuisine worthy of a lingering lunch

Fairmont's Pronto should not be pigeonholed into Dubai's lacklustre hotel cafe culture. Its deli-style cuisine is worthy of a lingering lunch, with sushi and Arabic selections, alcohol and incredible cakes. It also offers complimentary Wi-Fi.

Fairmont Dubai Trade Centre 1 **04 311 8316**
fairmont.com/dubai
Map **2 J5** Metro **World Trade Centre**

Ranches Restaurant & Bar International

Above-par golf restaurant out in suburbia

Set within the elegant golf club building, Ranches serves unpretentious fare in comfortable surroundings, with a focus on traditional British dishes like the excellent pies, served up with veg and mash. The outdoor terrace offers a more intimate dining experience overlooking the course. Tuesday is a popular quiz night, and there are themed buffets during the week.

Arabian Ranches Golf Club Arabian Ranches **04 360 7935**
arabianranchesgolfdubai.com
Map **1 Q13** Metro **Mall of the Emirates**

Rare Restaurant Steakhouse

A rare romantic treat amid green fields

Steaks, mostly 300 or 400 day grain-fed Australian beef, are the headline act, but alongside are some mouthwatering grilled fish, seafood and lamb options to tempt even the most ardent carnivores. Integrity and simplicity are key strengths of the grill menu, but you are encouraged to complicate things to your heart's content with an assortment of tasty sauces, sides, mustards and sea salts. The starters remain creatively impressive, and the service is slick but friendly. The atmosphere is a relaxed and tranquil sort of refinement and, of course, the peaceful, green views offer the same delicious respite from the hot, sandy desert surrounding the resort. The wine list is a tome, but a manageable one.

Desert Palm Dubai Warsan 2 **04 323 8888**
desertpalm.peraquum.com

Ravi's Pakistani

Great cuisine at this popular cheap eatery

Ravi's has legendary status among western expats, and is one of the cheapest eateries in town. This 24-hour diner offers a range of Pakistani curried favourites and rice dishes. The prices are cheap at double the price and the dishes keep punters coming back for more. The venue is basic and dining is available inside or outside.

Nr Satwa R/A, Al Satwa Rd Al Satwa **04 331 5353**
Map **2 J5** Metro **Al Jafiliya**

Reem Al Bawadi Middle Eastern

An Arabic favourite – great mezze, grills and shisha

Semi-isolated booths with thick Arabic cushions surround the perimeter, while tables lined with armchairs fill the dark, bustling dining area. The grills and mezze coming out of its kitchen are as appealing as the setting. There are five other locations in Dubai; see the website for details.

Nr HSBC, Jumeira Rd Jumeira 3 **04 394 7444**
reemalbawadi.com
Map **2 C4** Metro **Business Bay**

Reflets Par Pierre Gagnaire French

Parisian pomp with sculptured dishes

From the Michelin-starred grandfather of molecular gastronomy comes a magical, imaginative and highly conceptual dining experience. Bold purple carpet and pink chandeliers along with floor-to-ceiling mirrors and white tablecloths are the backdrop to a menu that strives to be a work of art.

InterContinental Dubai Festival City Dubai Festival City **04 701 1127**
diningdfc.com
Map **2 M9** Metro **Emirates**

Rhodes Mezzanine British

Impeccable food from the master of British fayre

Food is serious business at Rhodes Mezzanine. The atmosphere is elegant and refined if a little sombre and the decor is predominately a blank canvas, so food is the focus. It's the best of British cuisine in all its calorific glory. After an aperitif in the bar, your journey through Michelin perfection begins. With the amuse bouche and petit fours (British fare such as tomato soup and scones) your meal will undoubtedly stretch long, especially as you'll need time to let all the delicious heavy dishes digest. Whether you opt for seafood, steak or game, each dish takes classic ingredients and gives them an edge. Desserts are simple. The classic jam roly poly, bread and butter pudding, and sticky toffee pudding don't have a modern twist in sight. And tradition tastes very good.

Grosvenor House Dubai Marina **04 399 8888**
grosvenorhouse-dubai.com
Map **1 L5** Metro **Dubai Marina**

The Rib Room — International

A fine dining affair without the fuss

This classy fine dining venue serves a combination of delicious carnivorous creations and superb seafood selections in a modern dark wood panelled space with a choice of intimate booths or open plan seating. The decor has a classic, timeless quality and is the perfect backdrop to the main attraction – the food. Whether you opt for a prime cut, showcased raw steak, or go for one of the show-off shellfish dishes, it is all about constructing your perfect meal. The friendly staff will talk you through cooking styles, add-ons, sides and sauces so that your meal is as close to your personal taste as possible. And let's not forget the start and finish of this culinary hedonism – crab legs, oysters and scallops all make for splendid appetisers while the desserts tempt with all the right choices from chocolate fondant to a creme brulee duo.

Jumeirah Emirates Towers Trade Centre 2 **04 319 8088**
jumeirah.com
Map **2 H6** Metro **Emirates Towers**

Rivington Grill — British

Elegance and perfection to satisfy a sweet tooth

Straight out of London, this white tableclothed, intimate eatery brings the best in European cuisine with dishes sculptured to perfection. The menu deviates little from meats, as the name suggests, but they're cooked to perfection, presented beautifully and served up with sides so good they could do as main courses. The terrace is perfect for watching the Dubai Fountain displays and you'll want to linger once you've seen the dessert menu. The Rivington Bar & Grill is now open at Souk Madinat Jumeirah, including a standalone bar on the second floor serving British cocktails and beers on tap with regular promotions.

Souk Al Bahar Downtown Dubai **04 423 0903**
rivingtongrill.ae
Map **2 F6** Metro **Burj Khalifa/Dubai Mall**

Roccha Restaurant — Mediterranean

Arguably Palm Jumeirah's best kept secret

With the hotel being situated at the very end of the Palm Jumeirah, Rixos The Palm Dubai and its restaurants could be overshadowed by other five-star properties on the island. But its location is by no means a negative aspect – in fact, this results in the luxury hotel's dining experiences becoming more enjoyable. Roccha is an alfresco offering, serving sumptuous dishes ranging from seafood to chicken, all in a relaxed, friendly setting. With stunning views of the Palm Jumeirah and Dubai Marina, it's the perfect location for an elegant dinner followed by drinks.

Rixos The Palm Dubai, Palm Jumeirah
04 457 5555
rixos.com
Map **1 P3** Metro **Nakheel**

Rococo — Italian

The old world meets the new

The modern interior fuses with the traditional fare to leave a lasting impression. Black marble floors, deep purple walls, chandeliers and a magnificent sea view are juxtaposed with classic seafood and Italian dishes. Prices are higher than most nearby but so is the quality.

Sofitel Dubai Jumeirah Beach Dubai Marina
04 448 4848
sofitel.com
Map **1 K4** Metro **Jumeirah Lakes Towers**

Rodeo Grill & Bar — Steakhouse

A steak-lover's heaven, excellent wine to match

Smoke a Montecristo cigar, sip a cool draught ale, and choose your selection from the grill while you relax in the snug little bar where the chef works from an open kitchen. The steaks are exceptional, the desserts delightful and the wine list expansive (and expensive). Rodeo Grill doesn't represent a cheap night out, but in return you can expect the highest quality steaks served with sides such as silky smooth garlic mash, all served in uber-cool surroundings.

Al Bustan Rotana Al Garhoud
04 282 0000
rotana.com
Map **2 N7** Metro **GGICO**

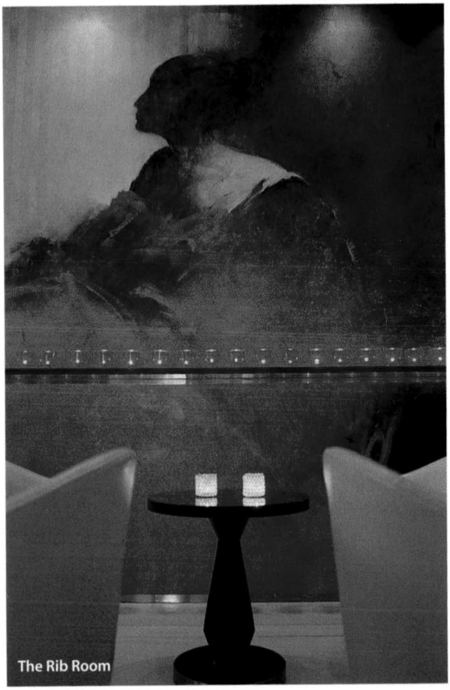
The Rib Room

Romano's Macaroni Grill — Italian

Italian treats for shoppers

Overlooking the aquarium at The Dubai Mall, this restaurant serves traditional, hearty Italian fare with a twist of creativity – it's just the ticket for anyone who's shopped till they've almost dropped and needs tasty sustenance quick smart. The pizzas are good but the pasta and, above all, risotto dishes here demand most attention. Until dessert, that is, when the famous tiramisu steals the whole show. Another branch is located at Festival Centre.

The Dubai Mall Downtown Dubai **04 330 8089**
salehbinlahejgroup.com
Map **2 F6** Metro **Burj Khalifa/Dubai Mall**

Ronda Locatelli — Italian

Popular Atlantis venue with a celebrity Italian chef

Giorgio Locatelli's cavernous restaurant seats hundreds in raised alcoves or at tables surrounding a huge stone-built wood-fired oven. The casual menu offers a good range of starters, pasta and mains, as well as a selection of small dishes that are perfect for sharing. A great comfort food venue.

Atlantis The Palm Palm Jumeirah **04 426 2626**
atlantisthepalm.com
Map **1 N1** Metro **Nakheel**

Rosso — Italian

A solid spot that you'll keep coming back to

Huge, pleasing portions, and a large open terrace make this contemporary Italian an attractive dining venue for groups and couples, while great drinks offers make it a popular post-work watering hole. Go steady on the starters to leave room for the liquid chocolate pudding.

Amwaj Rotana Dubai Marina **04 428 2000**
rotana.com
Map **1 K4** Metro **Jumeirah Lakes Towers**

Rostang — French

Traditional bistro fare from a Michelin-starred chef

Rostang's wood trim, leather bench seating and dim lighting perfectly mimic the decor of a 1930s bistro. Two-star Michelin chef Michel Rostang's seasonal menu, based on different French regions, is full of comforting dishes that shy away from experimentation and concentrate on preparation and presentation.

Atlantis The Palm Palm Jumeirah **04 426 2626**
atlantisthepalm.com
Map **1 N1** Metro **Nakheel**

The Rotisserie — International

Filling buffet in the grounds of the Royal Mirage

All-you-can-eat buffet with exquisite Arabic and Mediterranean dishes. Ranging from mezze to an excellent lamb tagine, the only problem is finding

Rodeo Grill & Bar

room to sample everything on offer. Ask for a table outside or by the window so you can enjoy the view.

Arabian Court At One&Only Royal Mirage
Al Sufouh 1 **04 399 9999**
oneandonlyresort.com
Map **1 M4** Metro **Nakheel**

Royal China Dubai — Chinese

Dim sum in a sophisticated environment

As you enter, a modern floor-to-ceiling glass bar greets you and offers up tempting cocktails to start the evening. Beyond the bar, the sizeable indoor dining room exudes Asian-chic and is filled with dark wood and red chandeliers. The picture-filled menu is helpful for previewing some of the more creative dishes and the staff can help guide you to the signature items such as fried taro and crispy chilli beef. Several set menus are available as well as plenty of a la carte options. The crispy aromatic duck is reason enough alone to visit Royal China – relax with a glass of wine while the waiter carves the duck meat and hand rolls each bite tableside. They also offer enjoyable outdoor seating; when weather permits this is a great place to enjoy impressive dim sum during the lunch hour.

Dubai International Financial Centre (DIFC)
Trade Centre 2 **04 354 5543**
royalchinadubai.com
Map **2 G6** Metro **Financial Centre**

Royal Orchid — Thai

Popular Thai restaurant by the marina

Similar to their counterpart in JBR, Royal Orchid serves up Thai, Chinese, and a few Mongolian dishes to hungry patrons. The exterior is classically Thai inspired, with comfy loungers on the terrace decking. The inside is slightly too bright to make for a romantic atmosphere but great for friends to relax and chat.

The prawn dishes are particularly succulent, but if you're in search of traditional Chinese fare, you'll be disappointed by the menu's selection. However, Royal Orchid's speciality dish, the magic wok, certainly shouldn't be missed. Chefs prepare your favourite meat, fish or vegetables in your chosen flavours and seasoning, and the hearty portion arrives at your table still sizzling. As a cheaper option, it's a welcome addition to Dubai Festival City's new line of restaurants, and a great place to dine by the waterfront.
Festival Centre Dubai Festival City **04 232 8585**
theroyalorchid.com
Map **2 M9** Metro **Emirates**

Ruby Tuesday — American
Burgers and booths in this kid-friendly joint
High quality Angus beef burgers and steaks are the speciality, and the affordable menu also includes ribs and seafood. There's a salad bar and kids' menu too.
The Dubai Mall Downtown Dubai
04 434 1442
binhendi.com
Map **2 F6** Metro **Burj Khalifa/Dubai Mall**

The Rupee Room — Indian
Excellent curry venue with live Indian music
Offers a wide selection of tasty north Indian dishes in relaxed surroundings. The glass-fronted kitchen allows you to keep an eye on the action and there is often a great trio of live musicians playing. There are a handful of tables outside offering marina views.
Marina Walk Dubai Marina **04 390 5755**
therupeeroom.com
Map **1 K5** Metro **Dubai Marina**

Ruth's Chris Steak House — Steakhouse
Steak, the stylish way
White leather sofas, red and dark panelling, and slick service are topped off with superior steaks cooked to precise temperatures and sizzling in butter, served with an extensive selection of accompaniments. The desserts too are excellent.
The Monarch Dubai Trade Centre 1 **04 501 8666**
ruthschris.ae
Map **2 J5** Metro **World Trade Centre**

Saffron — Asian
Buffet concept, Atlantis style: bigger and better
The sheer size and variety of the buffet stations are staggering. From sushi and Singaporean noodle soups to Sunday roasts and steaming dim sum, from wok-fried specialties to Malaysian rotis, there's lots to sample. Leave room for the dessert section, which features a chocolate fountain and ice cream stand.
Atlantis The Palm Palm Jumeirah **04 426 2626**
atlantisthepalm.com
Map **1 N1** Metro **Nakheel**

Sahn Eddar — Afternoon Tea
Definition of luxury: afternoon tea at the Burj
It may be an expensive cuppa, but this is the ultimate afternoon tea. It begins with a glass of bubbly and continues with course after course of dainty sandwiches and fine pastries. Sahn Eddar is on the first floor, but to make it really memorable you can go to the Skyview Bar to enjoy the stunning vistas (p.564).
Burj Al Arab Umm Suqeim 3 **04 301 7600**
jumeirah.com
Map **1 S4** Metro **Mall of the Emirates**

Sai Dham — Indian
Great vegetarian food in an impressive setting
With gold textured walls and stylish wooden furniture, the tardis-like interior of Sai Dham defies expectations from outside. Serving superb vegetarian food that 'celebrates purity', it uses only gentle spices, so the fresh taste of all ingredients comes through.
Saleh Bin Lahej Bldg Oud Metha **04 336 6552**
sai-dham.com
Map **2 K6** Metro **Oud Metha**

Sakura — Japanese
Sake and sushi in a memorable setting
Sakura offers one of Dubai's widest varieties of Japanese food, from sushi and teppanyaki to the less well-known shabu shabu. The two weekly buffet nights are excellent value. Seating is available at the cooking tables themselves, standard tables, or in one of the private tatami rooms – great for enjoying sake.
Crowne Plaza Dubai Trade Centre 1 **04 331 1111**
ichotelsgroup.com
Map **2 H5** Metro **Emirates Towers**

Sakura — Japanese
Sushi, pure and simple
From the Teppanyaki hot plate, where all manner of delicious cuts and veggies are orchestrated in a dramatic display of knife wielding, to the perfectly rolled sushi – you don't get much more Japanese than Sakura. Unlicensed but intimate, you can dine discretely or sit for the show at the Teppanyaki table.
Taj Palace Dubai Al Rigga **04 223 2222**
tajhotels.com
Map **2 N6** Metro **Al Rigga**

Salmontini Le Resto — Seafood
Abundance of salmon in sophisticated setting
Salmontini's chic interior is fashioned around large windows overlooking the mall's indoor ski slope. Choose from a selection of Scottish salmon, worked in every possible way (from smoked and grilled to cured and poached). There are some good all-inclusive deals.
Mall of the Emirates Al Barsha 1 **04 341 0222**
salmontini.com
Map **1 R6** Metro **Mall of the Emirates**

Sana Bonta — Italian

Bespoke menus and decent Italian fare

Sana Bonta's completely customisable Italian menu is a bit of a novelty, but will appeal to picky eaters and those who feel the need to take control. Separated into antipasti, pastas and pizzas, diners tick off the ingredients they want and wait for the results.

Dubai International Financial Centre (DIFC)
Trade Centre 2 **04 425 0327**
sanabonta.com
Map **2 G6** Metro **Financial Centre**

Sanabel — International

A fresh formula for all-day dining

Part buffet and part a la carte restaurant, Sanabel lets you have your fill of salads, mezze and dessert, but cooks your steak, swordfish or succulent shish kebab to your liking. It's good value for money and well laid out to break up the dining area, while the alfresco terrace offers views of the Jumeira coastline. It's a very promising start from the Pullman, and one worth going out of your way to investigate.

Pullman Dubai Mall of the Emirates Al Barsha 1
04 377 2000
pullman-dubai-malloftheemirates.com
Map **1 R6** Metro **Mall of the Emirates**

The Yellow Star

This yellow star highlights places that merit extra praise. It might be the atmosphere, the food, the cocktails, the music or the crowd, but any review that you see with the star attached is sure to be for somewhere that's a bit special.

The Sapphire — Thai

Delicious Asian specialities and stonegrill treats

Nestled at the back of the Century Village complex, The Sapphire provides an element of stylish serenity on an otherwise chaotic promenade. This bar-turned-grill dishes up a tasty blend of Asian and western cuisine with a talented new Japanese chef at the helm. The menu is substantial but signature stonegrill dishes remain de rigueur. Succulent Australian cuts that are served raw, come atop a stone plate that sizzles at 400 degrees, so that you can cook them how you like. Sauces, side dishes and vegetables complete each hearty portion. If you're less inclined to cook the meat yourself, the chef will prepare everything in the kitchen, with a number of other delicious Asian home-style dishes served straight to your table. The pad thai and Malaysian assam laksa are particularly zesty and flavourful.

Century Village Al Garhoud
04 286 8520
thesapphiredubai.com
Map **2 N8** Metro **GGICO**

Saravana Bhavan — Indian

Terrific thali at bargain prices

This is arguably the best of the area's south Indian restaurants. Saravana prefers elbow-to-elbow dining on tables decorated with only a bottle of mineral water. But what it lacks in decor it more than makes up for in service and the food. The menu is long but it's the thalis that draw big crowds – for around Dhs.12 you can get a plate packed with colour and incredible flavours. For authentic vegetarian breakfasts, and mouthwatering Indian lunches and dinners, this is fantastic value for money.

Abdul Aziz Mirza Bldg, Nr Karama Park Square
Al Karama **04 334 5252**
saravanabhavan.com
Map **2 L6** Metro **Al Karama**

Sarband — Persian

Tasty, cheap and atmospheric Iranian

Sarband serves up authentic tasty Iranian fare at very reasonable prices. This little Iranian gem with its rustic decor allows you to eat indoors or alfresco to enjoy a little people watching while you enjoy the no-fuss but mouthwatering delicious fare. If you're wanting to enjoy a taste of home cooked Iranian food you have to do it the authentic way by having a mix of dishes such as salad shirazi, mast khiar, kashk bademjan, mirza ghasemi, rice tagdig with ghormah sabzi and meat dishes served with saffron rice washed down with sekanjebeen (a mixture of syrup, fresh mint, cucumber and crushed ice) shared amongst your table guests. And round off the meal with a relaxing cup of Iranian tea served with mint and rose petals, or a glass of wine as the restaurant is fully licensed.

Century Village Al Garhoud
04 283 3891
sarbandrestaurant.com
Map **2 N8** Metro **GGICO**

Seafire Steakhouse & Bar — Steakhouse

Top seafood and steak at Atlantis

You get a warm feeling inside when you enter this New York-style eatery, where dinner starts with a list of extravagant sounding and delicious tasting appetisers. When it comes to the main, try to resist the succulent fillet, T-bone or the seafood grill – the Atlantis strip sirloin is one of the finest steaks you'll taste. Seafire is first and foremost for beef lovers, but the menu does try and cater to all with a selection of other red and white meats and seafood, and a few vegetarian options. The service is impeccable but refreshingly friendly, and the stylish dining room manages to retain an intimate feel despite its size.

Atlantis The Palm Palm Jumeirah
04 426 2626
atlantisthepalm.com
Map **1 N1** Metro **Nakheel**

Segreto — Italian

An Italian secret in the heart of Madinat

Candle-lit lamps lead you through the walkways to this hidden gem. Start the evening with a glass of prosecco on the terrace by the canal, then head into the stylish, modern interior. Segreto suits both dinner with friends and a romantic date. The food is aesthetically appealing, but the portions are more suited to a catwalk model than a rugby lad. But with pastas through to risottos all dressed in traditional Italian flavours, the chef gets it right every time

Madinat Jumeirah Al Sufouh 1 **04 366 6730**
jumeirah.com
Map **1 R4** Metro **Mall of the Emirates**

Senses — Buffet

A safe bet with live music and theme nights

Senses offers a relaxing contrast to the hustle and bustle of nearby Second December Street. The a la carte menu offers the expected pizzas and pastas as well as alcoholic beverages. The efficiently-sized buffet changes themes each evening, most popular being their carvery night. What sets Senses apart from other typical hotel lobby restaurants is the soothing live music played each night. Despite the sophisticated sounds the restaurant remains family friendly as well as reasonable on the wallet. Senses is a great choice if you are already in the area and looking for familiar international foods.

Mercure Gold Hotel Al Mina **04 345 9992**
accorhotels.com
Map **2 J4** Metro **Al Jafiliya**

Seoul Garden Restaurant — Korean

Private rooms with in-table barbecues

Each of the private rooms is equipped with a traditional Korean barbecue, which you can put to use by ordering a beef dish. Order as many of the small starters as you can, as they're all delicious. Cool ginger tea and a sweet melon dessert round off a delicious meal perfectly.

Zomorrodah Bldg, Off Zaabeel Rd Al Karama
04 337 7876
Map **2 L6** Metro **Al Karama**

Seville's – The Spanish Tapas Bar — Spanish

Drinks and tapas in a special atmosphere

Share tapas such as lightly battered calamari or tasty mussels, or feast on the heartier dishes available such as the excellent paella pans. Live music, which often has customers up dancing, adds to the buzzing ambience and the rustic decor has a cosy, homely feel. Reasonable prices help keep the atmosphere busy and the terrace creates a tranquil spot for alfresco dining.

Wafi Umm Hurair 2 **04 324 4777**
pyramidsrestaurantsatwafi.com
Map **2 L7** Metro **Dubai Healthcare City**

Sezzam — International

Large restaurant with a range of dining options

The open-plan concept is a little confusing, but once you've got the hang of it you can indulge in excellent, varied food. There are three kitchens: 'Bake' serves up pizzas, lasagne and roasts; 'Flame' offers grilled meats and seafood; and 'Steam' serves up Asian cuisine.

Mall of the Emirates Al Barsha 1 **04 409 5999**
kempinski.com
Map **1 R6** Metro **Mall of the Emirates**

Shabestan — Persian

The opulence of Persia in a traditional setting

This restaurant is as much about the decor as it is about the food. Ornate tables and chairs, decorative trinkets and traditional cooking stations combine to give a regal experience. The fresh breads epitomise the quality of food and the dishes are plentiful.

Radisson Blu Hotel, Dubai Deira Creek Al Rigga
04 222 7171
radissonblu.com
Map **2 M5** Metro **Union**

Shahrzad — Persian

Mouthwatering kebabs with live Persian music

Shahrzad's interior seems a bit dated, but the live Persian music and copper-clad open kitchen give it an exciting atmosphere. Start with the ash irishta noodle soup, and move on to the tasty appetiser platter before some of the best kebabs in town.

Hyatt Regency Dubai Corniche Deira **04 317 2222**
restaurants.dubai.hyatt.com
Map **2 N4** Metro **Palm Deira**

Shakespeare & Co — Cafe

Shabby chic decor and a good menu range

Uniquely eccentric, with a mix of floral designs with lace and wicker. The food is equally eclectic, combining Arabic, Moroccan and continental dishes with a splendid selection of sandwiches and smoothies. Visit the website for other locations.

Al Attar Business Tower, Shk Zayed Rd
Trade Centre 2 **04 331 1757**
shakespeareandco.ae
Map **2 G6** Metro **Financial Centre**

Shang Palace — Chinese

Dim sum and then some at this excellent Chinese

The food at Shang Palace is delicious and the knowledgeable staff will guide you through the huge menu. Tuck into shark fin soup, live seafood and dim sum while people-watching from the balcony overlooking the Shangri-La's bustling entrance, or take a quieter position inside the circular dining room.

Shangri-La Hotel Dubai Trade Centre 1 **04 405 2703**
shangri-la.com
Map **2 G5** Metro **Financial Centre**

Shiba — Japanese

A Japanese gem tucked away at The Meydan

Shiba's views along The Meydan Hotel and grandstand are impressive and its terrace sits just above the track itself. Lively during racing, it is parkside peaceful the rest of the time. Inside, the charismatic Japanese chef oversees sushi and robatayaki grill counters and geisha hostesses look after diners hidden behind screen doors and enjoying the secret sake bar.

The Meydan Hotel Meydan **04 381 3111**
meydanhotels.com
Map **2 E10** Metro **Dubai Healthcare City**

Shooters — American

Modern saloon that gives you its best shot

Modern western saloon with denim-clad waiters. Surprisingly quiet despite the gunfire from the five floodlit shooting ranges below. The menu is simple but considered, mainly offering fish and steak. King-size prawns and lobster tails are firm favourites.

Jebel Ali International Shooting Club & Centre Of Excellence Waterfront **04 814 5604**
jebelali-international.com
Metro **Danube**

Siamin Restaurant — Thai

Low-key Thai eatery on the quiet side of the Marina

The unlicensed Siamin is unlikely to draw the crowds from other parts of town, but as a quiet, local Thai venue for Marina east-siders it fits the bill. The interior is ornate and intimate, the service excellent, and the dishes well flavoured with some good sharing options.

The Radisson Blu Residence Dubai Marina
Dubai Marina **04 435 5000**
radissonblu.com
Map **1 K5** Metro **Dubai Marina**

Shang Palace

Signature By Sanjeev Kapoor — Indian

Indian modern cuisine with sparks of brilliance

Sanjeev Kapoor's latest Dubai restaurant bears all the hallmarks of its progressive and eclectic chef, with traditional Indian dishes given an innovative makeover. Samosas and bhajis take a back seat to such modern delights as tandoori wasabi lobster, basil pepper hammour tikka, paneer cooked in a butternut pumpkin and tomato sauce, and goat shanks simmered in kashmiri and chilli onion gravy. All the flavours of India are still there but international flavours such as wasabi, zataar and parmesan are thrown into the mix. Signature looks every inch the fine dining restaurant, with the pairing of white linen tablecloths and Indian silks in rich walnut tones adding a touch of contemporary elegance. But far from the décor, it's the creative menu that really makes Signature stand out from the plethora of excellent restaurants in Dubai.

Melia Dubai Al Raffa **04 386 8111**
melia-dubai.com
Map **2 K4** Metro **Al Karama**

Singapore Deli Restaurant — Singaporean

Authentic, home-style cuisine in a relaxed venue

From bowls of steaming noodles to traditionally cooked nasi goreng, the authentic dishes available at Singapore Deli Restaurant are consistently excellent. The casual atmosphere and home-style cooking draws a large crowd of regular customers who come for a taste of home.

Nr BurJuman Centre Al Karama **04 396 6885**
Map **2 L5** Metro **BurJuman**

Sketch — International

Artsy venue with a quirky menu

Dishes like fillet steak with spicy chocolate sauce and hammour with pea tzatziki lend a slight quirkiness to Sketch's menu. The atmosphere is enhanced by the incongruous spotlights, which cast the scarlet walls with a theatrical glow, making the whole place feel like it's run by a group of experimental artists. There's a good cocktail list too.

Metropolitan Palace Hotel Al Rigga **04 227 0000**
habtoorhotels.com
Map **2 N5** Metro **Al Rigga**

Smiling BKK — Thai

Cheerful Thai joint with a cheeky attitude

This outstanding Thai pad is a rare thing: a restaurant that serves great food with a slice of good humour. The cheekily named dishes are reasonable at around Dhs.30, but with gossip mag pages for place mats and ingenious theme nights such as 'sing for your supper', it's the atmosphere that sets Smiling BKK apart.

Nr Emarat, Off Al Wasl Rd Al Wasl **04 349 6677**
Map **2 E5** Metro **Burj Khalifa/Dubai Mall**

Spectrum On One — International
Possibly the biggest menu in Dubai

Divided into some of the world's most delicious regions – India, China, Thailand, Europe, Japan and Arabia – you need a good half hour to absorb the menu. The surroundings are spacious, with intimate spots for couples, room for groups to mingle and a tucked-away bar.

Fairmont Dubai Trade Centre 1 **04 311 8316**
fairmont.com
Map **2 J5** Metro **World Trade Centre**

Spice Island — Buffet
A Dubai favourite, great for kids

A trip to the Spice Island buffet creates a few dilemmas with so many cuisines begging to be picked up from the live cooking stations and cuisine divided areas. There's a choice of alcoholic and non-alcoholic packages, and the kids can hang out in a designated play area, where they can make you a dessert. Entertaining the adults is a singing trio, who pass around the tables and buffet area. It's all suitably informal and really good fun.

Crowne Plaza Dubai Deira Muteena **04 262 5555**
ichotelsgroup.com
Map **2 P5** Metro **Salah Al Din**

Splendido Restaurant — Italian
Classy Italian in intimate surroundings

Splendido offers a classy and intimate environment. Chef de Cuisine Corrado Pani originates from Sardinia, but has spent much of his life travelling around the world, and here he brings together some of the planet's best and most interesting ingredients to complement an authentic Italian/Mediterranean flavour. His speciality is the antipasta polpo arrosto – which is a tasty grilled octopus treat. If octopus does not tickle your fancy, then there is a huge selection of delicious pasta, seafood and meat options available on the a la carte menu. There are also buffet options for breakfast, lunch and dinner, all at reasonable rates, especially if you take advantage of one of the many specials, such as Friday Brunch (from Dhs.375 with alcohol) or the Business Lunch (from Dhs.125).

The Ritz-Carlton, Dubai Dubai Marina **04 399 4000**
ritzcarlton.com
Map **1 L4** Metro **Dubai Marina**

St Tropez — French
A hearty menu under the 'stars'

The portions here are generous and sure to please any appetite. The starters and salads are large enough to serve as a full meal or are the perfect size for sharing. The homemade pesto, featured on the fresh tomato and mozzarella salad, is just one example of the personal touches that set this kitchen apart. The main course options include lamb, chicken, seafood and their speciality – steaks. The Australian beef is hard to pass up, especially when complemented by your choice of fresh sauces. Satisfying your sweet tooth is not hard thanks to the many dessert choices. The popular outdoor seating alongside other Century Village diners is a great choice, while the tables inside offer more privacy and are set by candlelight amongst walls of vintage celebrities' photos. Either location is a pleasant place to enjoy the hearty menu and a drink.

Century Village Al Garhoud **04 286 9029**
centuryvillage.ae
Map **2 N8** Metro **GGICO**

STAY By Yannick Alléno — French
French dining with a contemporary twist

With three Michelin stars to his name, Yannick Alléno is a veteran when it comes to food and has brought his signature restaurant, STAY, to Dubai. The concept here is all about no-fuss, comfort French dining with a contemporary twist. Seasons dictate the menu on offer but signature favourites, such as the black angus beef fillet 'café de Paris', stay on and come highly recommended. Desserts take centre stage with an open Pastry Library allowing you to participate in the dessert making process. Strong flavours and quality ingredients though come at a price, making this a venue more suited for a special occasion than casual dining.

One&Only The Palm Palm Jumeirah
04 440 1030
oneandonlyresorts.com
Map **1 L3** Metro **Nakheel**

Stefano's — Italian
Classic Italian dishes in a relaxed alfresco setting

Dining tables and sofas fill Stefano's location near the beach at Marina Walk – these set the scene for a relaxing Italian retreat that offers excellent views as well as home-cooked, classic Italian cuisine. The menu includes traditional items, such as spaghetti and pizza, and pairs them with fresh juices and shisha. There are other branches in Al Barsha (04 340 3015) and Dubai Marina Walk (04 422 2632).

Marina Walk Dubai Marina **04 422 2632**
stefano-restaurant.com
Map **1 K4** Metro **Dubai Marina**

Stone Fire Pizza Kitchen — Italian
Traditional pizzas and successfully bizarre options

Serves arguably the most original pizzas in Dubai. Not only does it produce superb Italian fare from the freshest ingredients, but it also comes up with some bizarre combinations that raise pizza-eating to fine dining. The Norwegian salmon white pizza with caviar and avocado is a delectable example.

The Dubai Mall Downtown Dubai **04 330 8152**
stonefirekitchen.com
Map **2 F6** Metro **Burj Khalifa/Dubai Mall**

Spectrum On One

Sukhothai
Thai

Excellent food and a beautiful interior

With dark wood-panelled walls and authentic Thai artefacts, it's a great venue for a romantic occasion or a special treat. The extensive and expensive menu offers all the favourites and the seafood dishes are top notch. There's an outdoor area, but the beautifully decorated interior is unbeatable. The set lobster and crab menus are outstanding, with dishes such as stir-fried lobster in creamy red curry and wok-fried live Hong Kong crab with capsicum, ginger, and black mushroom, while the kids menu makes it an ideal venue for a family get-together.

Le Meridien Dubai Al Garhoud **04 702 2307**
sukhothaidubai.com
Map **2 N8** Metro **GGICO**

Sultan's Lounge
Afternoon Tea

Afternoon tea haunt with good snack menu

The interior of Sultan's Lounge is finely appointed for a Turkish-themed tea and coffee lounge, but the outlet is made by the large, relaxed terrace where comfy wicker chairs welcome weary bones. Sandwiches, soups and light bites, rather than hearty meals, dominate the menu; the real variety is reserved for teas and coffees. The English and Ottoman afternoon teas are hearty indeed, featuring all manner of savoury and sweet treats with jam and cream. Served up over views of the beach and The Palm Jumeirah, follow it with a shisha for a real Dubai experience.

Jumeirah Zabeel Saray Palm Jumeirah **04 453 0444**
jumeirah.com
Map **1 L3** Metro **Nakheel**

Sumibiya
Korean

Feasting fun at this eatery where you're the chef

Eating is a social affair at this yakiniku (Korean grilled meat) eatery, where diners use the gas grill in the middle of every table to sear, grill and charcoal bite-size morsels. It's informal, fun and tasty; if your food is overdone, you only have yourself to blame.

Radisson Blu Hotel, Dubai Deira Creek Al Rigga
04 222 7171
radissonblu.com
Map **2 M5** Metro **Union**

Summer Place
Chinese

Trendy Asian lounge in Dubai Marina

Summer Place is a terrific addition to the Habtoor Grand's collection of popular bars and restaurants. The venue includes a lounge, an indoor dining room flanked by custom aquariums, and outdoor seating with a view over The Palm. The decor, along with the DJ booth, set Summer Place as a great place to enjoy a cocktail and some Asian bites. The hors d'ouerve sampler platter is available with or without pork and is a great dish to accompany one of the menu's many

Sumibiya

creative cocktails. Those choosing a full sit-down dinner will have plenty to choose from, including deep-fried pork ribs, pan fried noodles, and a variety of dim sum. The spare rib beef with black bean sauce has a great combination of flavours and is particularly tender. There also is a private dining room with great views for those celebrating a special occasion.

Habtoor Grand Beach Resort & Spa Dubai Marina
04 399 5000
grandjumeirah.habtoorhotels.com
Map **1 L4** Metro **Dubai Marina**

Sumo Sushi & Bento
Japanese

Brilliant bento boxes that fit the bill perfectly

You can almost picture the Tokyo executives tucking into their lunch beside you in this little venue. Sticky beef atop rice and vegetables, with a little cup of green tea... it's simple, healthy stuff and, while Sumo might not win culinary awards, it does what it sets out to do very well indeed. In fact, the concept has proven extremely popular and it translates well to its other branches in Al Garhoud (04 283 0622), Media City (04 3911041) and Healthcare City (04 438 0661. Also available for delivery and pick-up

Town Centre Jumeirah Jumeira 1
04 344 3672
sumosushi.net
Map **2 F4** Metro **Burj Khalifa/Dubai Mall**

Sushi
Japanese

Simple name, simple concept – high-quality sushi

Artfully prepared in the open kitchen of this petite venue, sushi and sashimi portions are served up delightfully and your bill is determined by the number of pieces you feel like indulging in. The careful preparation and the melt-in-your-mouth morsels are of high quality.

Grand Hyatt Dubai Umm Hurair 2 **04 317 2222**
restaurants.dubai.hyatt.com
Map **2 L L8** Metro **Dubai Healthcare City**

Sushi Sushi
Japanese

Extensive Japanese in a convenient location

Sushi Sushi's location in the Century Village is perfect for a dinner stop before a late flight or during a night out at neighbouring Irish Village. The courtyard setting makes for a pleasant outdoor meal under the stars; an indoor dining room, complete with sushi conveyor belt, is a great alternative during the hot summer months. With a solid wine and liquour menu, starting off here for a drink on the comfy couches in a dim modern setting can easily transition into a tasty dinner. The sushi menu is impressive with a creative list of rolls as well as traditional sashimi plates. In addition to the namesake options, there are also plenty of grilled items, noodles, appetisers and snacks to choose from. Make sure to ask about the special rolls of the day from the sushi chef behind the counter.

Century Village Al Garhoud **04 282 9908**
centuryvillage.ae
Map **2 N8** Metro **GGICO**

Switch Restaurant & Lounge
International

Swish interior with a menu that really stands out

The space age, experimental interior by designer Karim Rashid gives this mall food outlet a touch of the wow factor, while the food is also very good. There's an exemplary seared tuna loin with citrus sauce, for example, beautifully presented goat's cheese tarts and a range of salads, mains and sandwiches that are all beautifully executed. This is a restaurant in a mall, rather than a mall restaurant.

The Dubai Mall Downtown Dubai **04 339 9131**
meswitch.com
Map **2 F6** Metro **Burj Khalifa/Dubai Mall**

Table 9 By Nick & Scott
International

Delectable and contemporary cuisine

Located in the space that once held Gordon Ramsay's Verre restaurant is a tempting British serving with chefs Scott and Nick at the helm. The menu is a mix of traditional favourites including venison and lobster, with a few less conventional dishes such as rabbit and pork knuckle to liven up the range. The service is impeccable, the food itself is delightful, and each dish is lovingly presented and bursting with flavour. But it's the added touches throughout the meal – the surprisingly delicious cauliflower cheese amuse bouche and the after dinner sweet stand – that makes an evening at Table 9 truly special.

Hilton Dubai Creek Al Rigga **04 212 7551**
table9dubai.com
Map **2 N5** Metro **Al Rigga**

Tagine
Moroccan

Atmospheric interior, melt-in-the-mouth dishes

Duck down and enter through the tiny carved wooden doorway into a beautiful Moroccan den of embroidered hangings, glowing lanterns and sultry music. The food is deliciously authentic, and the meat dishes so tender. The intimate cushioned booths are the best seats in the house.

The Palace At One&Only Royal Mirage Al Sufouh 1 **04 399 9999**
oneandonlyroyalmirage.com
Map **1 M4** Metro **Nakheel**

Tagpuan
Filipino

Home-style Filipino cooking at great prices

The tiny tables inside tiny Tagpuan fill up quickly, but the outside area on the terrace offers more space. Come here to try simple but tasty versions of Filipino home favourites including adobong pusit (squid), fried tilapia (fish) or pinakbet (mixed vegetables).

Karama Complex Al Karama **04 337 3959**
Map **2 K6** Metro **Al Karama**

The Talk Restaurant & Lounge
International

Dining that's just fine and a terrace to talk about

Mövenpick's buffet restaurant offers an ample selection with live cooking stations; the quality and service are good and the prices, fine, but the stakes are high on Dubai's all-inclusive scene and distinguishing diners may wonder where the wow factor is. Step outside to the stunning pool terrace and bar – and suddenly there's a whole lot more to talk about.

Mövenpick Hotel Jumeirah Beach Dubai Marina **04 449 8888**
moevenpick-hotels.com
Map **1 K4** Metro **Dubai Marina**

Teatro
International

A popular classic on the buzzing SZR strip

Perennially popular Teatro offers a fusion of tastes, with dishes from Japan, China, India and Europe. Whether you go for pizza, noodles, sushi or a curry, the food is guaranteed to please. There are great views over Sheikh Zayed Road, and a half-price discount if you order before 19:15. It's a residents' favourite so be sure to book in advance.

Towers Rotana Trade Centre 1 **04 312 2202**
rotana.com
Map **2 G5** Metro **Financial Centre**

Terra Firma Steakhouse — Steakhouse

A classy carnivore's dream with all the trimmings

Steakhouses are plentiful in Dubai and the competition is fierce. Terra Firma is no exception when it comes to the high standard set by its culinary counterparts and, thanks to its commendable attention to detail, they are a strong contender in the clash of the carnivorous kings. Set on the promenade of the Intercontinental Dubai Festival City and shaded from the public by high fences, the location is the first plus point. This is a modern restaurant with a masculine twist that sets the scene for the steaks to come. Fire sculptures and decking decorate the alfresco option while large booths and neutral tones create an elegant option inside. Following suit, the menu embraces simplicity of a really good steak, accompanied by a choice of sides – including steak toppers like lobster, multiple styles of spuds, various veggies and a selection of sauces.

InterContinental Dubai Festival City
Dubai Festival City **04 701 1127**
ichotelsgroup.com
Map **2 M9** Metro **Emirates**

Thai Chi — Thai

A double dose of Asia at this Thai-Chinese favourite

Choose from the Thai-inspired bamboo lounge or the regal dinner room straight out of China at this double-flavoured Asian. The menu features excellent appetisers, meats, poultry, seafood and vegetarian options from both the Thai and Chinese kitchens. The shared platters are favourites with the regulars.

Wafi Umm Hurair 2 **04 324 4100**
pyramidsrestaurantsatwafi.com
Map **2 L7** Metro **Dubai Healthcare City**

Toro Toro

The Thai Kitchen — Thai

Classy Thai place in the delightful Park Hyatt

Set around four live-cooking areas, the decor is stylish and modern with dark walls and teak wood floors contrasting well with the large soft lights. Although relatively small, the menu consists of a range of Thai delicacies prepared to maximise the rich, authentic flavours. Portions are perfect for sharing and the Friday brunch is a delight – more refined than most.

Park Hyatt Dubai Port Saeed **04 317 2221**
restaurants.dubai.hyatt.com
Map **2 M7** Metro **Deira City Centre**

Thai Terrace — Thai

A hidden gem straight from the alleys of Bangkok

This cheap and cheerful Thai eatery is a solid choice, especially if you happen to be in the Karama or Old Town area. Its renditions of favourites such as spring rolls and green curries are all very good, and the pretty outdoor seating area makes a pleasant spot to grab a budget bite.

Shk Khalifa Bin Zayed Rd Al Karama **04 396 9356**
Map **2 L5** Metro **Al Karama**

Thiptara — Thai

Fresh-from-the-tank seafood and Burj views

Expect fresh and spicy seafood at this quality Thai restaurant with enviable views overlooking the Burj Khalifa and the Dubai Fountain. There's a lively lobster tank from which to take your pick, while the wine list is extensive. All in all, it's a hard combination of great food and location – perfect for impressing visitors and business associates.

The Palace Downtown Dubai Downtown Dubai
04 888 3444
theaddress.com
Map **2 F6** Metro **Burj Khalifa/Dubai Mall**

Thyme Restaurant — Mediterranean

A bustling, family-friendly slice of Europe

Think heavy wood, cast iron fittings, chalk boards, open kitchens and oversized wine glasses, and you won't be a million miles away from this Mediterranean brasserie. It may not be unique in concept, but families, couples and groups tuck in noisily, and the multi-stage kitchen concept also works fantastically for the Friday brunch.

Oasis Beach Tower Dubai Marina **04 315 4200**
thethymerestaurant.com
Map **1 K4** Metro **Jumeirah Lakes Towers**

Tiffinbites — Indian

Modern take on Indian food in a buzzing setting

The JBR venue stands out for its glitzy pink decor, but the food is also decent and excellent value. The signature Tiffin dishes are a refreshing take on Indian classics from chicken tikka to lamb rogan josh, with

a host of vegetarian options thrown in. The light mains arrive in cute tin bowls, and are served with tasty vegetable sides and a bowl of rice. Buzzing yet unhurried, the friendly ambiance calls for lingering over shared street-style morsels and samosa bites, while people-watching. Takeaway is available, while ordering in is an option in the Dubai Marina area. The Mirdif City Centre branch (04 284 0305) also delivers to the Mirdif area.
The Walk, Jumeirah Beach Residence Dubai Marina **04 440 4952**
Map **1 K5** Metro **Dubai Marina**

Titanic By Marco Pierre White — British

Immerse yourself in the grandeur of fine dining

This chic, art deco styled restaurant is fine dining as it should be: a sommelier to guide you through your wine and food pairings; a knowledgeable waiter to talk you through the menu; and a maitre d' who really 'works' the room. Main courses lean heavily towards meat, well steak to be precise; there's no tricks – just spot-on cooking using the finest ingredients. Fish dishes are equally accomplished with classics such as lobster thermidor and magret of duck Marco Polo, all perfectly complemented by side orders of triple cooked chips (more chipper than chippie) or zucchini fritti. Titanic ticks all the boxes in terms of decor, service and menu. Quite simply put, it is a first-class place to eat. And in Bur Dubai that's not something you can say very often.
Melia Dubai Al Raffa **04 386 8111**
melia-dubai.com
Map **2 K4** Metro **Al Fahidi**

Tokyo@thetowers — Japanese

Modern dining with private rooms and lively tables

With elegantly partitioned tatami rooms, lively teppanyaki tables where chefs stage dramatic performances, and an eclectic menu, diners have enough options to keep things interesting. The private rooms all have traditional floor cushions and you can dine overlooking the mall if you need a view. Head to the sushi bar for colourful, imaginative and delicious creations, or the more intimate a la carte tables for a romantic dinner for two.
The Boulevard At Jumeirah Emirates Towers Trade Centre 2 **04 319 8088**
jumeirah.com
Map **2 H6** Metro **Emirates Towers**

Toro Toro — Latin American

Trendy new Latino-style haunt

If you've sampled the delights of Grosvenor House's Buddha Bar, then you'll find a similar air of sophistication at its sister restaurant. Entering the pan-Latin eatery is like stepping into a dramatic amphitheatre – giant bull sculptures flank the entrance and a two-storey fireplace lights the foyer. Everything about Toro Toro is sublime, from the supermodel hostesses who glide to your table to the eclectic menu choices. The menu is divided into three sections; from the sea, from the land and from the garden. Dishes are served tapas-style and each delicately prepared entree is served lovingly with influences from as far as Brazil to Peru. Try the churrasco selection. Lamb, Brazilian sirloin, and flame grilled chicken arrive on a long skewer and are dished up at your side. Wash down your feast with some of the best cocktails in town – the Salsa Fever sprinkled with chilli flakes is divine.
Grosvenor House Dubai Marina **04 399 8888**
grosvenorhouse-dubai.com
Map **1 L5** Metro **Dubai Marina**

Tour Dubai — Dinner Cruise

Dhow dining for something a bit different

For dinner with a difference, take to the creek on a traditional dhow. Majlis seating, regular and buffet dining and cocktail receptions all await. Alternatively, for a romantic evening, charter a personal dhow, complete with your own butler, roses for your partner, champagne, five-star dining and a limousine.
Nr British Embassy Al Hamriya **04 336 8407**
tour-dubai.com
Map **2 L6** Metro **BurJuman**

Trader Vic's — Polynesian

Exotic food blended with tropical cocktails

The winning combination of Trader Vic's notorious tropical drinks, exotic Asian menu and colourful South Pacific interiors arrives at Festival City. With a party-ready bar area that comes alive from happy hour onwards, and a plush dining room with a thatched outdoor terrace that welcomes romantic couples and

tokyo@thetowers

lively get-togethers alike, this is an exotic escape from city life. Enjoy signature starters such as the creamy crab rangoon wontons, mains including 'beef and reef' teriyaki and tasty banana fritters with coconut ice cream for dessert. The message is to eat, drink and be merry – all in equal measure. There are also branches at Crowne Plaza and Souk Madinat Jumeirah, and see Trader Vic's Mai-Tai Lounge (p.564) for an even livelier version.
Festival Centre Dubai Festival City
04 255 9000
tradervics.com
Map **2 M9** Metro **Emirates**

Traiteur — International

A brasserie menu in a fine dining setting
Previously a decadent mix of European dishes that required a bank loan, Traiteur has been reinvented as a French brasserie and is all the better for it. The elegant setting remains, with the terrace that commands impressive views of the marina and beyond. Traiteur is as much a feast for the eyes as for the palate, with an elevated show kitchen that positions the restaurant's chefs on stage. Wine lovers will also be won over, although with some of the bottles available, the bill can quickly stack up.
Park Hyatt Dubai Port Saeed **04 317 2222**
restaurants.dubai.hyatt.com/
Map **2 M7** Metro **Deira City Centre**

Tribes — African

African-themed restaurant oozing charm
The menu at this African eatery is as vast as the continent and features dishes from Morocco to South Africa and most places in between, so there's something to suit every taste. The decor sits somewhere between modern abstract and rustic Africa, which fits perfectly with the character of the menu. The staff are friendly; they know their menu inside out and they also have some notable musical talent to really ramp up the atmosphere. With delicious dishes such as Central African pie, peri peri sardines and spicy lamb rump, followed by melk tert or chocolate malva pudding with vanilla ice cream, moreish doesn't cover it. If you're planning a visit, be sure to bring your appetite.
Mall of the Emirates Al Barsha 1 **04 395 0660**
tribesrestaurant.com
Map **1 R6** Metro **Mall of the Emirates**

Troyka — Russian

Russian regulars served in an intimate surrounding
Troyka's old world charm creates an intimate mood to enjoy tasty cuisine. The Tuesday night buffet is all-inclusive and comprises time-honoured delicacies from Russian cuisine such as chicken Kiev and beef stroganoff. A band plays every night from 22:30 and an extravagant live Vegas-style cabaret begins at 23:30. Head here if not for the hearty fare, then for the traditional dancing, music and costumes.
Ascot Hotel Al Raffa **04 352 0900**
ascothoteldubai.com
Map **2 L4** Metro **Al Fahidi**

Urbano — Italian

Enjoy a front row seat for the Dubai Fountain
Whether you're looking for a well earned lunch after a morning's shopping, a short coffee break, or a family night out, Urbano makes for a great location. A pizzeria, trattoria and cafe, with an expansive terrace overlooking the Dubai Fountain, it serves traditional Italian dishes and a selection of international specialities. Busy both day and night, Urbano's relaxing but vibrant atmosphere attracts a wide range of clientele. It is best to book in advance if you want to guarantee an outdoor table at weekends or holidays. Unlike some of the surrounding restaurants with a Dubai Fountain view, Urbano offers value for money, with main courses starting from Dhs.55.
Souk Al Bahar Downtown Dubai **04 435 5777**
urbano.ae
Map **2 F6** Metro **Burj Khalifa/Dubai Mall**

Veda Pavilion — Far Eastern

Laidback post-beach hangout with amazing views
Chic yet comfortable, this is a great place to head to after a day at the beach. The substantial drinks list and affordable far eastern inspired menu are suited to casual lunches, dinners with groups of friends, or just a lazy beer on the poolside terrace, with views of the Burj Al Arab and the Arabian Gulf.
Clubhouse Al Nafura, Shoreline Apartments
Palm Jumeirah **04 361 8845**
emiratesleisureretail.com
Map **1 N4** Metro **Nakheel**

Vienna Cafe — Cafe

Austrian-style cafe in the middle of the JW Marriott
The wood panelling and delicate tablecloths are not readily associated with Deira, but it blends well with the grandeur of the JW Marriott. There is a good selection of food, from light salads to steaks, but the real draw is people-watching while enjoying a good cuppa or well-prepared coffee.
JW Marriott Hotel Dubai Al Muraqqabat **04 607 7977**
marriottdiningatjw.ae
Map **2 P6** Metro **Abu Baker Al Siddique**

Villa Beach — International

Probably the most upmarket beach shack ever
Mediterranean fare within cork-popping distance of the sea and Burj Al Arab. The wooden-decked terrace and hanging lanterns give it a laidback feel, but the quality is anything but. Delicious dishes include warm

Villa Beach

goat's cheese, prosciutto and figs, tender steaks and Bailey's tiramisu, and the service is top class.
Jumeirah Beach Hotel Umm Suqeim 3 **04 406 8999**
jumeirah.com
Map **1 S4** Metro **Mall of the Emirates**

Vivaldi — Italian

Romance on the creek, with great food and wine

Perched over the Dubai Creek, this is a clear contender for one of the most romantic restaurants in Dubai. Spectacular views from both inside the warmly lit restaurant and out on the terraces, an experimental Italian menu and a comprehensive wine list will have you coming back for more.
Sheraton Dubai Creek Hotel & Towers Al Rigga
04 207 1750
sheratondubaicreek.com
Map **2 M5** Metro **Baniyas Square**

Voi — Vietnamese

Vietnamese with a French accent

A welcome addition to a city where the number of Vietnamese restaurants can be counted on one hand. The kitchen here focuses on upscale Vietnamese with French influences, and the emphasis is on high quality fresh ingredients, making for light and refreshing dining. Seafood dishes are particularly impressive and, if you are feeling adventurous, go for the chef's tasting menu. The atmosphere is as opulent as the food, with ornately designed ceilings and walls centred around a crystal chandelier, and the dramatic all-white dining room is straight out of a palatial French film set. Voi is especially suited to a romantic night out, as several candle-lit outdoor tables overlook the resort's grounds.
Jumeirah Zabeel Saray Palm Jumeirah **04 453 0444**
jumeirah.com
Map **1 L3** Metro **Nakheel**

Vu's Restaurant — Mediterranean

European cuisine in a sophisticated setting

Enter Vu's on the 50th floor of the Jumeirah Emirates Towers and it's clear you've walked into a gem. Each table is neatly positioned to take full advantage of the impressive floor-to-ceiling views over Dubai. Service is impeccable, if a little on the serious side, and caters mostly to heavy pocketed out-of-towners or the wealthy set of Dubai. The menu is peppered with fine-dining favourites – fresh oysters, seared scallops and slow roasted pork belly, to name a few – each using the highest quality ingredients. The Wagyu beef is a favourite, served with a subtle hint of foie gras which melts in the mouth, giving a rich and creamy texture that complements the tender beef perfectly. While the atmosphere may compel guests to feel it appropriate to chat in hushed voices, it's difficult not to feel gastronomically satisfied by the time you leave.
Jumeirah Emirates Towers Trade Centre 2 **04 319 8088**
jumeirah.com
Map **2 H6** Metro **Emirates Towers**

Wafi Gourmet — Middle Eastern

A wide variety of delicious Arabic delights

Deliciously prepared traditional Lebanese dishes, along with pastries, sweets, ice creams, exotic juices and hot drinks, make Wafi Gourmet a great sustenance stop when on a shopping spree. Make sure you browse around the delicatessen and you're sure to leave with more bags than you arrived with.
Wafi Umm Hurair 2 **04 324 4433**
wafigourmet.com
Map **2 L7** Metro **Dubai Healthcare City**

Wagamama — Japanese

Modern Japanese dining done in a funky style

Modelled on a traditional Japanese ramen bar, with communal tables, Wagamama's streamlined design works well for a quick bite. Orders are immediately and freshly prepared. Also at Crowne Plaza and The Greens. Delivery is available.
Jumeirah Beach Residence Dubai Marina **04 399 5900**
wagamama.ae
Map **1 K4** Metro **Dubai Marina**

Wavebreaker — International

Relaxed beach bar perfect for sunset drinks

A beach bar that serves snacks, light meals, kids' meals, barbecue grills and a variety of cocktails and mocktails. It's a perfect place for a laidback afternoon, while at sunset, it's quiet, cool and the beach view is stunning, making you linger for more than just one of their sophisticated sundowners.
Hilton Dubai Jumeirah Resort Dubai Marina
04 399 1111
hilton.com
Map **1 K4** Metro **Jumeirah Lakes Towers**

West 14th New York Grill & Bar — Steakhouse

A winning recipe steakhouse

This Brooklyn-inspired, warehouse-style steakhouse is all about indulgence, but it's indulgence of a simple kind – high quality ingredients and the finest cuts of great tasting meat. Add a few signature frills, such as a steak knife menu and a whole trolley dedicated to condiments, plus a killer location, and you've got a new contender for the city's best steakhouse.

Oceana Beach Club Palm Jumeirah **04 447 7601**
west14th.ae
Map **1 N3** Metro **Nakheel**

Western Steak House — Steakhouse

Homely venue that serves up great food

Great for meat lovers to line their stomachs before a night on the town. It's an unpretentious venue that provides a refreshing change with its homely atmosphere and decor, serving up large portions of great quality fare in a comfortable setting.

Crowne Plaza Dubai Trade Centre 1 **04 331 1111**
ichotelsgroup.com
Map **2 H5** Metro **Emirates Towers**

The Wharf — Seafood

Excellent location, which you pay for

The Wharf faces the magical waterways of Madinat, and the outdoor deck and sailing paraphernalia are appealing. There's steak and a smattering of Arabic dishes on the menu, alongside plentiful pizza, and while the food is well presented, prices are a little steep. If you sit outside be prepared for the obsessive taking of photos and comings and goings of the abras.

Mina A'Salam Al Sufouh 1 **04 366 6730**
jumeirah.com
Map **1 R4** Metro **Mall of the Emirates**

White Orchid Lounge — Asian

Delightful eastern cuisine that's worth the trip

Some of the best eastern flavours in Dubai are served up at this contemporary Asian restaurant which focuses on Thai and Japanese dishes. Mix sushi platters and green curries, or try something from the teppanyaki table. The decor is styled on a Thai bamboo hut, there's a spacious outdoor terrace, and service is impeccable.

Jebel Ali Golf Resort Waterfront **04 814 5604**
jaresortshotels.com/Hotels/Home
Metro **Danube**

Wild Ginger — Asian

Simple pan-Asian makes for convenient pit stop

Employing the sleek but chic, simplistic designs of many other Asian restaurants and chains, Wild Ginger has an interesting location, perched on the top floor of the Iconic fashion store within Deira City Centre. The fusion dishes revolve predominantly around sushi, salads, soups and sizzlers, with a touch of tempura and side order of Szechwan for good measure. The smoothies and cocktails are excellent and reasonable prices combined with quick service pitches Wild Ginger as an attractive alternative to the usual mall foodcourt fare. It's not exactly a venue for a romantic meal out but, if you need to grab a bite before catching a film, or require some respite during a marathon shopping session and you want to avoid burgers and deep fried chicken without stretching the finances much further, then this would be a good option.

ICONIC Port Saeed **04 295 3511**
Map **2 N7** Metro **Deira City Centre**

Wild Peeta — Middle Eastern

Healthy eatery, locally owned and widely enjoyed

This Emirati-owned fusion shawarma restaurant created a huge buzz on its opening way back in 2009 thanks to its offering of fresh, healthy shawarmas, salads and juices, served by some of the friendliest staff in Dubai, and it has gone from strength to strength ever since, becoming a popular, laid-back haunt for anyone living or working near the creek. The Moroccan salad and Thai shawarma are both highly recommended and both takeaway and home/work delivery are available.

Deira City Centre Port Saeed **800 9453**
wildpeeta.com
Map **2 N7** Metro **Deira City Centre**

Wok In — Far Eastern

Excellent Asian offering surprising specials

The decor of Wok In may not provide any surprises – the traditional Asian blacks, reds and creams abound – but the open kitchen in the middle provides a great focus (you can choose to eat up at the counter if you

Wox

wish) and the revelations come thick and fast once food starts arriving. A mix between the conventional and the creative, even the dishes with traditional names have been given a contemporary twist. Spring rolls come with dipping sauces tasty enough to eat as soups, while the beef ribs are melt-in-the-mouth tasty in a Thai BBQ marinade. Noodle dishes take centre stage when it comes to the main course, although the fried rices should not be disregarded. It's very reasonably priced too.
Mövenpick Hotel Deira Muteena **04 444 0111**
moevenpick-hotels.com
Map **2 P6** Metro **Abu Baker Al Siddique**

Wox — Far Eastern

Watch your food sizzle and steam before tucking in
Sit at the noodle bar or one of the individual tables, place your order from the simple (but comprehensive) menu and watch the flurry of sizzling woks and steaming pots as your food is prepared in front of you. A no-frills culinary delight.
Grand Hyatt Dubai Umm Hurair 2 **04 317 2222**
dubai.grand.hyatt.com
Map **2 L8** Metro **Dubai Healthcare City**

Xennya Terrace — Middle Eastern

Great for guests who want an Arabic experience
Combining the best of Arabic and North African cuisine, this subtly decorated restaurant has private dining rooms which may be preferable to the packed-in main seating area. Traditional live music and dancing adds to the atmosphere.
Holiday Inn Al Barsha Al Barsha 1 **04 323 4333**
hialbarshadubai.com
Map **1 R6** Metro **Sharaf DG**

Yakitori House — Japanese

Authentic diner that draws a knowledgeable crowd
Laid out in the red and black style of a Japanese diner and with a huge menu of sushi, tempura, noodles, set meals, and the signature yakitori dish, this restaurant offers unrivalled choice.
Ascot Hotel Al Raffa **04 352 0900**
ascothoteldubai.com
Map **2 L4** Metro **Al Fahidi**

Yalumba — International

A taste of Australian nouvelle cuisine in Dubai
Hugely popular with the expat community, Yalumba is the only five-star establishment in Dubai that offers authentic Australian cuisine with a modern twist. Open for breakfast, lunch and dinner – except on Fridays – the Le Méridien Dubai eatery features an extensive menu of traditional specialities, as well as seafood and international dishes. Signature items include the eggs benedict with smoked salmon, or kangaroo tartar (definitely for those with a more adventurous palate). Yalumba is also known for its impressive seafood nights, with everything from lobster to sushi on offer for Dhs.219 per person. Brunch fans will also not be disappointed with the Friday feast, which consists of a grand selection of seafood, international buffet options and desserts, complemented by four types of world-class champagnes. At Dhs.499 per person, it certainly doesn't come cheap; plus it is disappointing that the option is not available for those who would prefer to dine sans alcohol. A word of warning: diners can get quite rowdy after a drink or five.
Le Meridien Dubai Al Garhoud **04 702 2328**
yalumba-dubai.com
Map **2 N8** Metro **GGICO**

YO! Sushi — Japanese

Fresh, fun sushi straight from the conveyor belt
Sushi addicts and first-timers will find something here, with both traditional and unconventional sushi available. Friendly staff explain the types of sushi on the conveyor belt, and the different coloured plates indicate the price of the dish. Branches are also in Dubai Festival City, BurJuman, Dubai Marina Mall, The Dubai Mall and DIFC.
Mirdif City Centre Mirdif **04 284 3995**
yosushi.com
Map **2 P12** Metro **Rashidiya**

Yum! — Far Eastern

International cuisine that's in Deira, but not dear
Catering to an especially busy lunch crowd, the focus is on fresh, high quality Asian food cooked swiftly. Good-sized dishes are offered from Thailand, Malaysia, Indonesia and other neighbouring countries, with healthy options highlighted on the menu for those who are body conscious. If you do intend to go for a group work lunch then it's a good idea to book in advance as it fills up fast.
Radisson Blu Hotel, Dubai Deira Creek Al Rigga **04 222 7171**
radissonblu.com
Map **2 M5** Metro **Union**

Zafran — Indian

Fine-dining Indian that's eclectic in every approach
Zafran's mall surroundings may seem mismatched to Michelin-starred chef Atul Kochar, the man behind the venture, but don't let that deter you. Opting for a private booth ensures a quiet and crowd-free affair while you tuck into classic Indian fare with contemporary twists – and an extensive mocktail and shakes list to wash it all down. There's another branch in Dubai Marina Mall (04 399 7357).
Mirdif City Centre Mirdif
04 284 0987
Map **2 P12** Metro **Rashidiya**

Let's Do Brunch!

Da Gama

Brunch may have been invented in the States, given kudos in New York, and be setting itself a place mat in the hipper centres of western Europe, but in this particular Middle Eastern city, it's a hobby, a social skill, a weekend institution. It's the calorific glue that holds the weekend together. Far from the genteel image of croissants, scrambled eggs and good coffee over the day's newspapers, brunch in Dubai is synonymous with triumphantly eating your own body weight in food and washing it down with free-flowing champagne. And all for a set price.

Having eaten and quaffed the entire day away, brunchers are renowned for then throwing themselves into misguided rampages around the city's nightspots, and suffering spirit-crushing hangovers the following morning. New arrivals are quickly asked whether they've been to a brunch yet, typically by an expat with more Dubai-years under their (loosened) belt, and a knowing glint in their eye. So why is this gluttonous sport so popular in Dubai?

This city's predominantly expat community probably has plenty to do with it. There are more work-hard, play-even-harder young singles looking to blow off steam and mingle, so Dubai has a more sociable culture than most. The fact that you boil alive if you venture outside for more than 10 minutes during at least three months of the year also helps keep people inside and ingesting at the weekends. Whatever the reason, brunch has become quite the art form; one which diners master by flexing their (softening) stomach muscles at the masses of competitive, creative and uniquely reasonable deals available from the city's fleet of five-star hotels.

Formerly purely a Friday fun-for-all, the pursuit is now spreading through the week, almost to the point where brunch becomes a round-the-clock way of living, rather than just a way of eating. If you want to throw yourself in at the deep end and push your liver to its very limits, head to Waxy's (p.566) on a Friday. Here, you can buy five drinks, a greasy breakfast buffet and carvery banquet (effectively lunch and dinner – 'linner'?), and a dignity bypass for a rock bottom price. Roll up at 17:00 and you'll find brunch victims rocking out to Bruce Springsteen or clinging to the walls for mercy. Also contributing to brunch's bad name are Double Decker (p.556), which offers a similar deal, and Spice Island (p.538) – a place that boasts the booziest of brunch deals: absolutely all-you-can-eat (from British breakfast to Chinese, Japanese, Mexican and Arabic) and drink for not

Brunch. You might think the word is self-explanatory: a portmanteau of 'breakfast' and 'lunch' – a meal you have between the two more accepted dining anchors. If so, you clearly haven't lived in Dubai that long.

much more than a basketful at Choithrams; while at Warehouse (p.566), the emphasis is more on the cocktails and music than the finger food.

Once you've flaunted your daytime partying prowess, you might want to prove your worth when it comes to tackling sheer food volume and variety. Friday brunch at JW Marriott lets you set up base in either The Market Place (p.521), Hofbrauhaus (p.511), or Bamboo Lagoon (p.494), then pilfer as much as you like from all three buffets. Then there's the other end of the brunching spectrum – namely, Spectrum on One (p.538). The deal at this Fairmont favourite epitomises Dubai's posh and pricey all-inclusive. For a higher fee, you can feed on the entire world (from Japan to Europe via India), swig a champagne flute all afternoon, and feel slightly classier about your splurge than your Waxy-going counterparts might. Al Qasr (04 346 1111), Seafire (p.535) and Armani/Hashi (p.491) are equally high-minded affairs, and while the fare at Yalumba (p.547) is top notch, its patrons typically set upon on its bounties with a little more relish. Similar can be said of the Bubbalicious Brunch at The Westin (p.249)

Somewhere in the middle of this brunch-ometer lies a trove of average-priced bargains that take the feasting mission slightly less seriously, and are therefore ideal for a laidback meal with chums or a family outing. Glasshouse (p.510) is a subtly sophisticated example, with a la carte options rather than the standard buffet relay, while MORE Cafe (04 323 4350) is ideal for a non-alcoholic brunch in the traditional sense: cakes, homemade breads, coffee and pancakes (with salads, curries and sandwiches in there somewhere as well).

Lotus One

Carter's (p.552) and Mazina (p.522) are both child-friendly, offering smaller portions and a less alcohol-orientated atmosphere, while Legends (p.519) serves up a tasty view of the creek along with its munch fest. If you're sick and tired of piling your plate with too many flavours, there are plenty more cuisine-specific brunches to be tasted too, such as the self-explanatory Thai Kitchen (p.542) and the deliciously Japanese Zuma (p.550). And so, there it is. Brunching in Dubai is as big as football in the UK, sumo wrestling in Japan and basketball in the US. So raise your fork and get stuck in.

Zaika — Indian

Atmospheric, classy Indian with great set menus

Intimate upmarket Indian set in a characterful split-level rotunda building. Private booths occupy the upper level while Buddha statues and candles sit among the tables downstairs. The a la carte selection is based on traditional Indian flavours, with some good set menu options. The large sweeping staircase keeps the restaurant intimate for romantic diners.

Al Murooj Rotana Trade Centre 2 **04 321 1111**
rotana.com
Map **2 G6** Metro **Financial Centre**

Zaroob Restaurant & Cafe Lounge — Middle Eastern

Old meets new in a Levant street-style restaurant

Recycled old world accessories and corrugated iron walls covered in graffiti and art accentuate Zaroob's street food theme, where the chefs, or 'masters', each work at a cooking station dedicated to one speciality. Delicious and generously portioned dishes starting at Dhs.5 mean you can eat your fill and have change left to buy pickles and cheeses from the on-site deli.

Jumeirah Tower, Shk Zayed Rd Trade Centre 2 **04 327 6060**
zaroob.net
Map **2 G6** Metro **Emirates Towers**

Zheng He's — Chinese

Deliciously inventive Chinese with great views

Zheng He's superb take on Chinese delicacies serves up exciting combinations of dim sum and mini starters, traditional dishes and marinated fish and stir-fried meats, with arguably the best duck in town. Wine is a little pricey but the view makes it worthwhile.

Mina A'Salam Al Sufouh 1 **04 366 6730**
jumeirah.com
Map **1 R4** Metro **Mall of the Emirates**

Zuma — Japanese

Stylish Japanese venue that draws the DIFC crowds

The stunning multi-level space is elegantly lit, with clean lines of wood and glass creating a restaurant and bar that has stepped straight out of London. It's buzzy, stylish and perfect for a first date or business lunch. Food arrives from the open kitchen and sushi bar artistically presented in classic Japanese style – like the decor, it is all about simplicity and flair. It's not cheap so if dinner is beyond your budget it's still worth going for a drink at the packed bar. The ebisu lunch menu, priced at Dhs.130, is an affordable treat, and the ebisu express (Dhs.72) is perfect for a speedy working lunch.

Dubai International Financial Centre (DIFC) Trade Centre 2 **04 425 5660**
zumarestaurant.com
Map **2 G6** Metro **Emirates Towers**

BARS, PUBS & CLUBS

360° Bar, Lounge & Club — Bar

Lazy lounging, rebellious partying, ocean views

This newly refurbished, two-tiered circular rooftop bar boasts all-round views of the Arabian Gulf and Burj Al Arab. House DJs spin at the weekends, and late afternoon loungers smoking shisha give way to scruffily chic stylistas supping cocktails as the tempo rises. Bartenders make a mean mojito, but for something sweeter, try the vanilla version of the classic Cuban cocktail. Open from 16:00 – and at weekends you'll need to get your name on the guestlist through platinumlist.ae.

Jumeirah Beach Hotel Umm Suqeim 3 **04 406 8999**
jumeirah.com
Map **1 S4** Metro **Mall of the Emirates**

The Agency — Wine Bar

Refurbished and refocused on wine

Shifted to the lobby of the Jumeirah Emirates Towers, The Agency has grown up; leaving the themed nights and ladies' nights to its sibling outlet at the Madinat Jumeirah. Here, The Agency is free to focus on its main offering: wine. There are 80 varieties of wines to test the palates of discerning oenophiles. These include a sommelier's selection and collection of Mondavi wines from California. Food offerings include cheese platters and a selection of light bites, though if you prefer something more substantial burgers from the adjoining Rib Room can be ordered. If you'd like to learn more about wines, The Agency also offers Grape Academy and Blind Tasting events, which should prep you enough to take on the wine quiz challenge.

The Boulevard At Jumeirah Emirates Towers Trade Centre 2 **04 319 8088**
jumeirah.com
Map **2 H6** Metro **Emirates Towers**

Bahri Bar — Bar

Cookie-cutter perfection in the shape of a bar

This might just be the perfect bar: stunning views of the Burj Al Arab and the sparkling ocean beyond grace the spacious terrace while, inside, lavish but comfortable furnishings create an intimate atmosphere. A selection of delicious drinks and nibbles, plus live music at the weekends, complete a picture of perfection.

Mina A'Salam Al Sufouh 1 **04 366 6730**
jumeirah.com
Map **1 R4** Metro **Mall of the Emirates**

Balcony Bar — Bar

Cocktails, vintage whiskies and leather armchairs

Dark, masculine wooden panelling and black leather armchairs dominate this sophisticated cocktail bar. The drinks list is extensive, and each cocktail is artfully

presented. For the extravagant pocket, there are some eye-wateringly expensive champagnes and vintage whiskies, while teetotallers can choose from a basic selection of booze-free beverages.
Shangri-La Hotel Dubai Trade Centre 1 **04 405 2703**
shangri-la.com
Map **2 G5** Metro **Financial Centre**

The Bar
Bar

A good spot to whet your whistle in Deira

Encased in glass and furnished with a mix of high tables, barstools and soft leather armchairs, the interior is unobtrusive and relaxed. The well-stocked bar dispenses interesting aperitifs and after-dinner liqueurs, as well as cocktails, wines and bottled beers.
Hyatt Regency Dubai Corniche Deira **04 317 2222**
restaurants.dubai.hyatt.com
Map **2 N4** Metro **Palm Deira**

Bar 44
Bar

An ideal place to start or end the evening

Good things come at high prices, or so it seems in this classy spot. From the bar's lofty location on the 44th floor, enjoy magnificent views of the Marina and the excellent selection of wine and cocktails.
Grosvenor House Dubai Marina **04 399 8888**
grosvenorhouse-dubai.com
Map **1 L5** Metro **Dubai Marina**

Bar Below
Bar

Hidden Marina bar that's yet to take off

A classy but quiet bar area tucked away at the back of Le Royal Meridien, dishing up good (but pricey) cocktails accompanied by run-of-the-mill tunes. While the large chandelier and classy decor do raise an eyebrow, Bar Below rarely draws a big crowd.
Le Royal Meridien Beach Resort & Spa Dubai Marina **04 399 5555**
leroyalmeridien-dubai.com
Map **1 L4** Metro **Dubai Marina**

Barasti
Bar

Beachside magnet for expat sun and fun hunters

Expats flock to lively beachside Barasti in flip-flops or their Friday finery – so arrive early if you want to avoid the queue. Stars of the underrated menu include particularly good seafood, ribs, steak and one of the city's best burgers. The view, big screens, split level seating, beach beds, live music and a friendly crowd make this a reliable spot for a good night out. And the weekend deals on food and beverages are a real bonus. Entry is free all day, every day, so you can spend the day on the beach and then head to the bar!
Le Meridien Mina Seyahi Beach Resort & Marina Al Sufouh 1 **04 318 1313**
barastibeach.com
Map **1 M4** Metro **Nakheel**

Barzar
Bar

Slick, urban-feel bar with a few surprises

This funky two-tiered bar hits the balance between laidback cool and noisy revelry, with the added attraction of live bands. Eclectic drinks, such as beer cocktails, are paired with more traditional offerings in the cocktail, lager and bar snacks departments.
Souk Madinat Jumeirah Al Sufouh 1 **04 366 6730**
jumeirah.com
Map **1 R4** Metro **Mall of the Emirates**

Belgian Beer Cafe
Bar

Laidback creekside brunch spot

The place to grab high-quality Belgium beers and classic moules-frites. There's a huge variety of beers to sample, while the hearty food is comfort eating at its best, with stews, sausages and meatballs served up in man-sized portions. The Festival City branch has a scenic terrace that perches over the Creek. The BBC, as it's affectionately known, runs a Friday brunch which is a laidback alternative to the scenes elsewhere.
Crowne Plaza Dubai Festival City Dubai Festival City **04 701 1127**
diningdfc.com
Map **2 M9** Metro **Emirates**

BidiBondi
Bar

Great local bar, if you're lucky enough to live there

Typically relaxed and informal, this Aussie bar on Palm Jumeirah has a beach diner feel complemented by poolside perches. The menu offers hefty burgers, salads, bar snacks, breakfast and kids' specials alongside a range of cocktails, beers and wines.
Clubhouse Al Manhal, Shoreline Apartments Palm Jumeirah **04 427 0515**
emiratesleisureretail.com
Map **1 N4** Metro **Nakheel**

Belgian Beer Cafe

Blue Bar **Bar**

A hidden gem for jazz fans

Dark wood, low lighting and a smoky atmosphere create the perfect setting for live jazz on Thursdays. Mingle with the business crowd from Trade Centre over post-work drinks and bar bites. There's live music on Wednesdays and Fridays as well.

Novotel World Trade Centre Dubai Trade Centre 2 **04 332 0000**

novotel.com

Map **2 H6** Metro **World Trade Centre**

The Boston Bar > *p.553* **Bar**

Post-work hangout with several theme nights

Slightly dingy but great for after-work drinks and watching sports. Theme nights include sports on Saturdays and Sundays, a tricky yet popular Monday quiz, Tuesday ladies' night, Wednesday two-for-one, Thursday ladies' night, and a Friday breakfast binge.

Jumeira Rotana Al Bada'a **04 345 5888**

rotana.com

Map **2 J4** Metro **World Trade Centre**

Boudoir **Nightclub**

Ladies' nights, big queues and Parisian decor

This exclusive spot can be difficult to get into, but once inside you'll be treated to a Parisian-style club with opulent fabrics, hypnotic tunes and moody lighting. The music varies through the week and there are drinks deals for ladies on most nights.

Dubai Marine Beach Resort & Spa Jumeira 1 **04 345 5995**

myboudoir.com

Map **2 H4** Metro **World Trade Centre**

Buddha Bar **Bar**

A flamboyant bar that attracts a glamorous crowd

Half restaurant, half bar, this nightspot never fails to impress with moody lighting, a huge Buddha statue and marina views. If the waiter can hear you over the funky Buddha bar beats, then order a sublime cocktail.

Grosvenor House Dubai Marina **04 399 8888**

grosvenorhouse-dubai.com

Map **1 L5** Metro **Dubai Marina**

Cabana **Bar**

The Dubai Mall's best kept secret

Cabana's Miami-cool pool bar and restaurant sits sweetly beneath the Burj Khalifa. Lounge on sunbeds and beanbags by the pool, or enjoy the privacy of a cabana, as you enjoy the eclectic, well-executed menu and a chilled soundtrack. It's the perfect setting for cocktails and Friday brunch is a lively occasion.

The Address Dubai Mall Downtown Dubai **04 888 3444**

theaddress.com

Map **2 F6** Metro **Burj Khalifa/Dubai Mall**

CafeM **Wine Bar**

Cheese and wine the easy way

Ideal for a business tete-a-tete during the day, CafeM takes on a bar atmosphere when the post-work crowd hits. From 19:00 to 22:00, on Sundays to Thursdays, enjoy unlimited wine and cheese for a bargain price. Great for a no-fuss night out with friends.

Media One Hotel Al Sufouh 1 **04 427 1000**

mediaonehotel.com

Map **1 M5** Metro **Nakheel**

Calabar **Bar**

Lively Latin lounge with views inside and out

A large sweeping bar, serving cigars and all manner of drinks from international brews to unique Latin American inspired cocktails, is the centrepiece of this chic lounge. Asian, Japanese and Arabic nibbles make a great accompaniment to sundowners on the terrace.

The Address Downtown Dubai Downtown Dubai **04 436 8888**

theaddress.com

Map **2 F7** Metro **Burj Khalifa/Dubai Mall**

Carters **Bar**

Gastro pub food; a good weekend watering hole

The oversized wooden ceiling fans, hunting trophies and colonial-style paraphernalia lend Carters a slightly 'themed' quality, but don't be put off. The food is decent gastro-pub fare, and the large bar and live music make this a popular place at the weekend.

Wafi Umm Hurair 2 **04 324 4100**

pyramidsrestaurantsatwafi.com

Map **2 L7** Metro **Dubai Healthcare City**

Cavalli Club **Nightclub**

Catwalk fashion comes first, substance second

Roberto Cavalli's leopard print and Swarovski encrusted nightspot is one of the city's places to be seen if you're part of the 'It' crowd. Earlier in the evening, the club houses a decent Italian restaurant that serves up some good Mediterranean fare, after which you can move to the cocktail and cigar lounge, wine bar, or even the boutique shop.

Fairmont Dubai Trade Centre 1 **04 332 9260**

cavalliclubdubai.com

Map **2 J5** Metro **World Trade Centre**

Chameleon Bar **Bar**

Vibrant bar, refreshment and entertainment on tap

Depending on when you visit, the mood at this stylish bar will be set by a live pianist or a hip DJ. Relax on comfy couches, or on bar stools, to enjoy the reasonably priced selection of cocktails and signature Chameleon drinks.

Traders Hotel, Dubai Al Khabaisi **04 265 9888**

shangri-la.com

Map **2 P6** Metro **Abu Baker Al Siddique**

Chameleon Club — Nightclub

The chameleon that tries to stand out

Flashy and flamboyant, this club makes no attempt to blend in. Entry is via a red carpet that delivers you into an elevator that takes you to the penthouse level. There, you are greeted by every colour of neon lighting imaginable as the floors, walls and ceilings are an ever changing pallete of colour. Supporting this visual explosion of light is a giant chameleon positioned over the bar with its tongue protruding over most of the dance floor. Although dining is an option, most patrons arrive from 23:00, in time for the techno to be turned up.

Byblos Hotel Tecom **050 113 5858**
chameleonclubdubai.com
Map **1 N6** Metro **Dubai Internet City**

Champs — Sports Bar

Pool, live music, sports, party-time atmosphere

Like any friendly local, this bar (formerly Aussie Legends) regularly hosts live bands and musicians. The small dance floor tends to kick off quite early at the weekends, and the pool table is popular. The grub is decent and the large TVs keep sports fans occupied.

Chelsea Plaza Hotel Al Jafiliya **04 398 2222**
chelseaplazahoteldubai.com
Map **2 J5** Metro **Al Jafiliya**

Chi@The Lodge — Nightclub

Fun night spot for up-for-it partygoers

Best in the winter when the vast garden dancefloor is open, Chi@The Lodge is always busy with its three or four different rooms of contrasting music, lots of seating, large screens and VIP 'cabanas'. The regular fancy dress and themed nights are hugely popular as is the annual Rugby Sevens afterparty that takes place here. It's easy to get taxis outside, there's a shawarma stand in the car park and entrance is free before 22:30 on most nights.

Al Nasr Leisureland Oud Metha **04 337 9470**
chinightclubdubai.com
Map **2 L6** Metro **Oud Metha**

The Cigar Lounge — Wine Bar

Classic and classy, one for the city's cognoscenti

Whether you're in the mood for post-work cocktails or pre-dinner drinks, this spot hits the mark. The view of the Burj Khalifa is worth the visit alone, but with an extensive selection of cocktails, a small but delicious menu of cheeses, tapas and sweets, and a chic atmosphere set to the soothing sounds of jazz, this is the perfect venue to make a night of it. The fine choice of cigars adds to the pleasing mix of old boys' charm and trendy sophistication.

The Address Downtown Dubai 04 436 8888
theaddress.com
Map **2 F7** Metro **Burj Khalifa/Dubai Mall**

Chinwaggery — Wine Bar

Casual, laid back venue for a chin wag.

Derived from an English phrase, have a chin wag, meaning an informal talk or chat, Chinwaggery is the perfect venue for a casual get together or after-work wind down. Though its name may be British inspired, Chinwaggery's decor and ambience takes its cue from across the Atlantic, New York style. The slick, elegant indoor lounge provides an intimate setting while an open air terrace, overlooking JBR, is ideal for group settings during cooler months. Food is not an afterthought and the extensive drinks menu also includes wine flight options to sample what's on offer. Amongst the hustle that is JBR, Chinwaggery is a laid-back hidden gem.

Mövenpick Hotel Jumeirah Beach Dubai Marina
04 449 8888
moevenpick-hotels.com
Map **1 K4** Metro **Dubai Marina**

Churchill's — Pub

Good for escaping your shopping significant other

While it might not be the kind of place you go out of your way to visit, this traditional English pub complete with TVs, pool table and dartboard has one distinct advantage – it is attached (via the Sofitel Hotel) to Deira City Centre, so when shopping loses its appeal you can nip in for a quick half. Also serves some standard but tasty British pub grub.

Pullman Deira City Centre Hotel Port Saeed
04 294 1222
pullmanhotels.com
Map **2 N7** Metro **Deira City Centre**

Cin Cin — Bar

As bling as Beyoncé in a diamond-coated catsuit

With a stylish backdrop of warehouse-high wine shelves, and walls fashioned like falling water, it's easy to get carried away ordering imaginative cocktails and fine wines, but brace yourself for the bill – this is expense account territory.

Fairmont Dubai Trade Centre 1 **04 311 8316**
fairmont.com
Map **2 J5** Metro **World Trade Centre**

Clique — Bar

Big tunes, big views, big prices

The latest spot in the financial district for nightowls, Clique is a minimalistic pool bar where the champagne flows and the clientele comes in size zero. Every weekend night, the DJs pump the latest house anthems out towards an incredible DIFC backdrop to a lively and up-for-it crowd.

Jumeirah Emirates Towers Trade Centre 2
04 319 8088
jumeirah.com
Map **2 H6** Metro **Emirates Towers**

The Agency

Lotus One

Sho Cho

Irish Village

Barasti

Crossroads Cocktail Bar
Bar

Refined Raffles bar with a new Sling twist

Home of the Dubai Sling, an imaginative mix of coriander, chilli, fig and lemon, and the drink of choice for surveying the nearby sparkling skyline. With extremely knowledgeable staff, well-executed bar snacks and a dizzying choice of drinks, you won't mind paying above-average prices for the experience.

Raffles Dubai Umm Hurair 2 **04 314 9888**
raffles.com
Map **2 K7** Metro **Dubai Healthcare City**

Cu-ba > *p.527*
Bar

Tranquil Creek atmosphere with a Cuban flavour

Hosted on the rooftop of Dubai's newest escape, the Jumeirah Creekside Hotel, Cu-ba overlooks stunning cityscapes and angles of the infamous creek. Relax on poolside loungers and enjoy fruity mojitos and rum-infused cocktails served with a menu of appetisers bursting with Cuban flavour to zest up your evening: marinated raw tuna, fried bananas, Cuban-style short ribs and more. The resident DJ plays soothing house tunes on weekdays, and alternative up-tempo beats on the weekend; for fans of the cigar, Cu-ba stocks a plethora of authentic Cuban cigars.

Jumeirah Creekside Hotel Al Garhoud **04 230 8582**
jumeirah.com
Map **2 M8** Metro **GGICO**

Dhow & Anchor
Pub

Good pub grub in a relaxed setting

Dhow and Anchor's bar is a popular spot, particularly during happy hour and sporting events – try the outdoor terrace if you are dining and enjoy glimpses of the Burj Al Arab. The menu includes the usual range of drinks and terrific curries, pies, and fish and chips. Head down on Tuesday night for the pub quiz.

Jumeirah Beach Hotel Umm Suqeim 3 **04 406 8999**
jumeirah.com
Map **1 S4** Metro **Mall of the Emirates**

Double Decker
Pub

The ultimate crowd-pleasing pub

Adorned with London transport memorabilia, this two storey bar serves upmarket pub grub including plenty of stodgy choices and tasty sharing platters. It is packed on Fridays with revellers attracted by its lively, bargain brunch. Weekly karaoke and ladies' nights plus big screen sports ensure there is something for everyone.

Al Murooj Rotana Trade Centre 2 **04 321 1111**
rotana.com
Map **2 G6** Metro **Financial Centre**

The Dubliner's
Pub

Perfect for watching sports, eating or telling stories

Cosy and lively, this Irish pub has a weekly quiz, good music and plenty of screens for watching sports. The menu is full of fresh, tasty and reasonably priced dishes. Save room for the Bailey's cheesecake.

Le Meridien Dubai Al Garhoud **04 702 2307**
diningatmeridiendubai.com
Map **2 N8** Metro **GGICO**

Eclipse Bar
Bar

Pulling out all the stops to attract a cool clientele

On the 26th floor, Eclipse is all about glamour, with red leather padded walls, marble tables and a huge bar serving hundreds of different cocktails. Humidor, liqueurs and elegant canapes appeal to the hip crowd.

InterContinental Dubai Festival City
Dubai Festival City **04 701 1127**
diningdfc.com
Map **2 M9** Metro **Emirates**

Fibber Magee's
Pub

Characterful Irish pub with all the essentials

Succeeding where many fail, Fibber's has the unpolished feel of a true pub. Televised sport, DJs, themed entertainment evenings (including the excellent Easy Tiger quiz on Tuesdays), great value food and drink promotions make it perennially popular.

Nr Crowne Plaza Hotel, Off Shk Zayed Rd
Trade Centre 1 **04 332 2400**
fibbersdubai.com
Map **2 H5** Metro **World Trade Centre**

Girders > *p.243, 509, 557, 567*
Pub

British pub with a Scottish theme

You're always assured a warm welcome at Girders, a traditionally British pub that makes a nod to Scotland and Ireland with a Gaelic-themed menu. This is a place to come to and enjoy traditional favourites such as the pub quiz, big-screen sporting action and a daily happy hour between 18:00 and 20:00. From the modern steel furnishings to the cosy fireplace, this is the perfect spot to enjoy the well-stocked bar, hearty dishes such as the full Scottish breakfast and shepherd's pie, and a lively atmosphere to boot.

Ocean View Hotel Dubai Marina **04 814 5599**
jaresortshotels.com
Map **2 K4** Metro **Jumeirah Lakes Towers**

The Gramercy
Pub

New York trendiness in the heart of DIFC

It could just be the pedigree that comes with the name but The Gramercy feels very cigars and whisky circa New York prohibition era. In reality, however, this fashionable gastro pub has rendered itself popular with the DIFC crowd looking for an after-work watering hole. The Gramercy has a buzzing atmosphere with the narrow space occupied by booths on one side, a long, New York lounge-style bar on the other, and a small stage for the jazz band. The menu is all encompassing, appealing to burger-

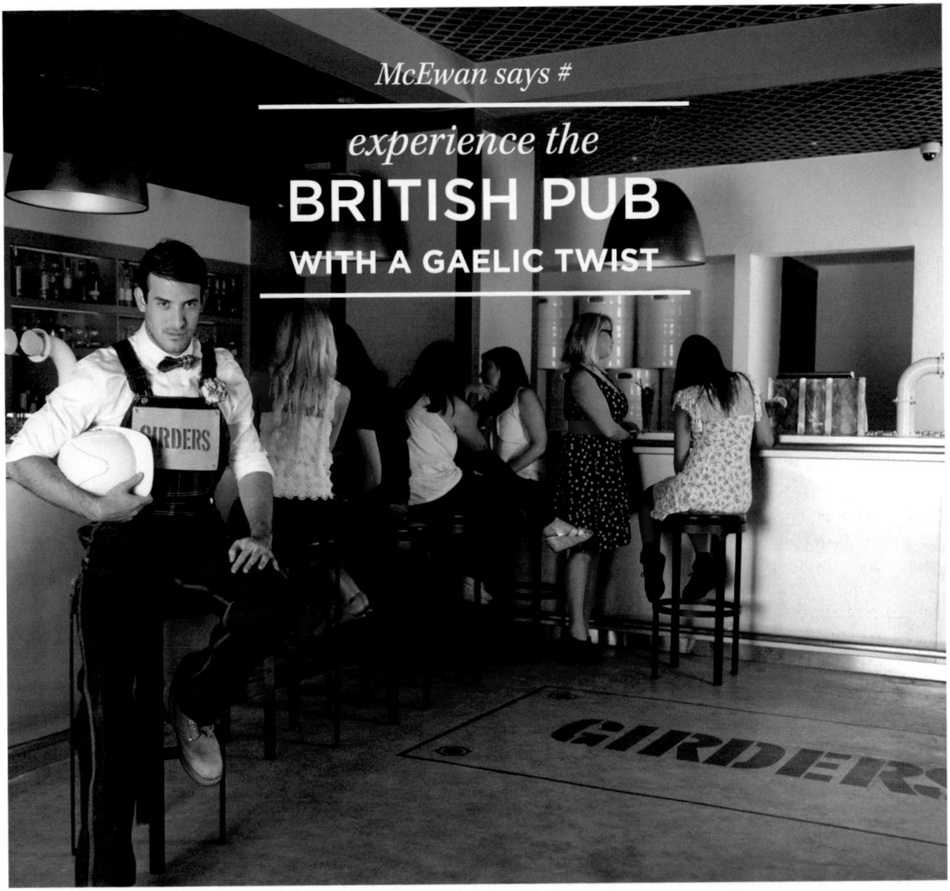
McEwan says #
experience the
BRITISH PUB
WITH A GAELIC TWIST
GIRDERS

hungry revellers as well as the more food savvy. While it's mainly a stomping ground for DIFC folk, the stellar band, impressive drinks menu and satisfying food are sure to draw crowds from outside the Downtown area.
Dubai International Financial Centre (DIFC) Trade Centre 2 **04 437 7511**
thegramercybar.com
Map **2 G6** Metro **Emirates Towers**

The Grandstand Bar — Pub

Sports pub with lots of flavour

Whether you're looking for good pub grub or you just want to watch the match, look no further than The Grandstand. Big screen TVs show the latest games, ladies can enjoy free mojitos every Monday between 18:00 and 21:00, while the menu includes substantial dishes like rib eye steak and bangers and mash, as well as a bar menu of nibbles. Something for everyone.
Park Regis Kris Kin Hotel Al Karama **04 377 1111**
staywellgroup.com
Map **2 L5** Metro **BurJuman**

Harry Ghatto's — Karaoke Bar

Release your inner singer at this fun karaoke joint

Karaoke at Harry Ghatto's calls for more of a group effort than a solo performance, so it's an ideal place to end a group night out. There's no stage to speak of, so creeping wallflowers have no excuse not to pipe up. Instead crooners and squawkers can hide in the comfort of the crowd as they sing along to numbers from Burt Bacharach to Beyoncé. There's a great drinks list and over 1,000 songs to choose from. If your dearly departing colleague is looking to leave a legacy, this is the perfect place to do it.
The Boulevard At Jumeirah Emirates Towers Trade Centre 2 **04 319 8088**
jumeirah.com
Map **2 H6** Metro **Emirates Towers**

Harvester's Pub — Pub

Middle-of-the-road English pub

The decor is exactly what you would expect from a themed English pub, as in fact is the drinks menu. What you come here for though is the pub-style menu which is classically hearty and tasty, with a chicken tikka masala that would put many Indian restaurants to shame.
Crowne Plaza Dubai Trade Centre 1 **04 331 1111**
ichotelsgroup.com
Map **2 H5** Metro **Emirates Towers**

Healey's Bar & Terrace — Pub

Fab gastro pub on the right side of the road

JLTers are happy to call Healey's their local – or maybe that should be their 'posh local', as Healey's makes for a welcome, upmarket bar experience compared to the rowdier McGettigan's (p.560) downstairs. The decor is clean and modern, the prices reasonable, and, should you get hungry, tasty gastro pub grub is on offer too. The terrace, with its panorama of new Dubai, is a lovely spot on which to enjoy a evening drink in the cooler months, while promotions like Wednesday's ladies' night sees the bar pack out.
Bonnington Jumeirah Lakes Towers Jumeirah Lakes Towers **04 356 0000**
bonningtontower.com
Map **1 K5** Metro **Jumeirah Lakes Towers**

Hibiki Music Lounge — Karaoke Bar

Sing your heart out for the lads, or just your friends

This cosy karaoke lounge features a small stage, comfy seating areas, and a central bar, plus three private rooms, with Japanese, Singaporean and Thai themes. Singers have around 8,000 songs to choose from, and it makes for a great night out. Happy hour is from 19:30 to 21:30 nightly.
Hyatt Regency Dubai Corniche Deira **04 317 2222**
restaurants.dubai.hyatt.com
Map **2 N4** Metro **Palm Deira**

The Hub — Bar

A cut above your average Irish or sports bar

The bar stocks a decent selection of bottled and draught beers, but it's worth making happy hour for some great drinks deals. Flat screen TVs show an array of live sport; friendly staff and a buzzing atmosphere add to the many reasons why you should make The Hub your regular haunt for the big game.
Sofitel Dubai Jumeirah Beach Dubai Marina **04 448 4848**
sofitel.com
Map **1 K4** Metro **Jumeirah Lakes Towers**

Icon Bar & Lounge — Bar

Slick after-work spot in the heart of Media City

The carefully styled ambience – red leather chairs, sequined drapes and expensive looking ceramics – pulls in the Media City crowds and is book-ended by big screens showing football. Bar snacks and great pizzas help keep the stamina up.
Radisson Blu Hotel, Dubai Media City Al Sufouh 1 **04 366 9119**
radissonblu.com
Map **1 M5** Metro **Nakheel**

The Irish Village — Pub

A small piece of Ireland in the heart of Dubai

A perfect spot to forget the city and enjoy a pint of the black stuff. This laid-back Irish pub offers both indoor and alfresco seating, managing to create an authentic pub experience complete with a sprawling beer garden. There's a good selection of pub grub on offer that comes in generous portions and at a reasonable price. For those seeking a more authentic experience

there's the option of traditional Irish fare including freshly baked soda bread, Irish stew and Bailey's cheesecake, which is not to be missed! Friendly staff will make you feel right at home, plus the chocolate box setting and chilled-out tunes make this a great venue all year round. Keep an eye on the website for regular concerts and events.
The Aviation Club Al Garhoud **04 282 4750**
irishvillage.ae
Map **2 N8** Metro **GGICO**

Issimo Bar — Bar

Enjoy a touch of James Bond in Deira
The long, narrow jazz bar has a retro-futuristic feel with stark chrome, black leather and large slanted Japanese-style panels. There's a superb selection of (pricey) martinis and cocktails, while the clientele is an interesting blend of moneyed hotel guests, Mafioso lookalikes, and hip young clubbers.
Hilton Dubai Creek Al Rigga **04 227 1111**
hilton.com
Map **2 N5** Metro **Al Rigga**

Jambase — Bar

Great fun jazz club-wedding reception mash up
A tempting drinks selection and generous portions of food is enough to kick off a good night at this Dubai favourite, but all this plays second fiddle to the storming live band that has everyone jostling for the dancefloor. The decor oozes a 50s jazz bar vibe, while the music is funky turn-of-the-century.
Souk Madinat Jumeirah Al Sufouh 1 **04 366 6730**
madinatjumeirah.com
Map **1 R4** Metro **Mall of the Emirates**

Jetty Lounge > *p.485* — Bar

Possibly the finest beachfront bar in the world
There are few bars that offer panoramas paired with chic beachside lounging to match those of Jetty Lounge. This gem is the perfect post-work hangout, or a delightful night cap venue. Order a summery mojito from the Hawaiian shirt-clad waiters, sample a few tasty appetisers such as mezze, Spanish ham and cheeses or Asian inspired platters, and listen to the sounds of chilled out beach tunes. If you feel like bar hopping, you can jump aboard a private boat that will take you to the sister hotel, One&Only The Palm, for more great sea views.
One&Only Royal Mirage Al Sufouh 1 **04 399 9999**
oneandonlyresorts.com
Map **1 M4** Metro **Nakheel**

Karma Kafé — Bar

Big Buddha's little sister
Inside this dark and very cool bar, an array of devilish cocktails are waiting to be discovered. The little sister of Buddha Bar (p.552), it shares the same stylish decor and funky feel, but its Burj Lake view is the trump card. The terrace is popular, so arrive early.
Souk Al Bahar Downtown Dubai **04 423 0909**
karma-kafe.com
Map **2 F6** Metro **Burj Khalifa/Dubai Mall**

Kasbar — Nightclub

Atmospheric club with an air of exclusivity
Kasbar combines the mystique and luxury of regal Arabia with the feel of an exclusive dance party. In keeping with the Arabian decor of the Royal Mirage, this is a sultry, candlelit nightclub perfect for liaisons, as well as dancing and chilling out.
One&Only Royal Mirage Al Sufouh 1 **04 399 9999**
oneandonlyresorts.com
Map **1 M4** Metro **Nakheel**

Keva — Bar

Perfect mix of dining, lounging and cocktails
A great spot for a pre-clubbing dinner or drink (thanks to its neighbour Chi, p.554), Keva's mix of open booths, bar stools and more formal dinner tables are busy with a well-dressed crowd. Its strapline 'eat play lounge' says it all; the European and Asian cuisine is as elegant as the interior of darkwood and splashes of red.
Al Nasr Leisureland Oud Metha **04 334 4159**
Map **2 L6** Metro **Oud Metha**

Koubba Bar — Bar

Ultra decadent, ultra cool and amazing views
One of the most stunning views in Dubai awaits from the terrace of this sumptuous cocktail bar. Just off the terrace is the Armoury Lounge, where you can indulge in Cuban cigars surrounded by wooden screens, lavish carpets, and antique Indian weaponry.
Al Qasr Al Sufouh 1 **04 366 6730**
jumeirah.com
Map **1 R6** Metro **Mall of the Emirates**

Left Bank — Bar

A taste of hip and a sip of swank
With its black wallpaper, red velvet booths and white leather couches, this bar feels like an exclusive spot in a cosmopolitan city. The stylish food and cocktails fit well with the swanky surroundings, and the 'small plates' menu begs to be explored with a cocktail in hand. There's a lower key version at Madinat Jumeirah.
Souk Al Bahar Downtown Dubai **04 368 4501**
emiratesleisureretail.com
Map **2 F6** Metro **Burj Khalifa/Dubai Mall**

Library Bar — Bar

Cocktails and cigars in an English country setting
With its dark wood, comfy sofas and dimmed lighting, the Library Bar could be a study in an English country house. The bar serves light bites,

main meals, a good range of cocktails and, of course, top quality cigars.
The Ritz-Carlton, Dubai Dubai Marina **04 399 4000**
ritzcarlton.com
Map **1 L4** Metro **Dubai Marina**

Loca — Bar

Tasty tex-mex that guarantees a good night out

This bar and restaurant has a Mexican flavour, serving up great cocktails and excellent fare that is a cut above standard tex-mex offerings. If your party of friends has got a thirst, bar tables now come with their own Heineken taps to ensure you're permanently topped up. Also has a lovely Friday brunch.
Dubai Marine Beach Resort & Spa Jumeira 1
04 346 1111
dxbmarine.com
Map **2 H4** Metro **World Trade Centre**

Shisha Spots

Shisha is a popular pastime in the region and you'll notice the fragrant scent of flavoured tobacco as you're walking around in the evenings. If you want to give it a try yourself, head to one of the following spots: Chandelier (p.500), The Courtyard (p.503), Kan Zaman (p.514), Barzar (p.551), and Sanctuary Pool Lounge (p.262). For more on shisha, see p.22.

Long's Bar — Bar

Looking for a party? Come along to Long's

A firm favourite with long time expats and glammed-up singles alike, Long's is often crowded and smoky but dull moments are not on the menu: there are plenty of happy hours and theme nights to enjoy. Serves decent pub grub too.
Towers Rotana Trade Centre 1 **04 312 2202**
rotana.com
Map **2 G5** Metro **Financial Centre**

M-Dek — Bar

Lively Media City pool lounge

A popular post-work drinks spot, the bar takes on an alfresco club atmosphere at weekends with a resident DJ. Sip champagne, sample cocktails and pass over the disappointing bar snacks as you laze on white sofa beds and take in the view of Dubai Marina.
Media One Hotel Al Sufouh 1 **04 427 1000**
mediaonehotel.com
Map **1 M5** Metro **Nakheel**

Magnum — Nightclub

For the young and hip, this is the place to be

From Edward Maya and Avicii to Ritchie Hawtin and Sven Vath, Magnum has all your favourite beats covered six days a week. Come in for tasty starters during ladies night on a Tuesday, receive free bubbly till midnight and relax in the trendy chic lounge to ultra-chill tunes. On Fridays, be sure to wear high tops or at least a comfortable pair of kicks, as DJ Nuthiya will have you breakdancing to rhythm and blues all night long. At Magnum they know Saturday usually means 'short changed' but not 'burnt out' so head down and receive 50% off on selected beverages and get footloose to the up-tempo beats pouring out of the speakers. Magnum also has an exclusive face card deal, which will knock 50% off your bill every time. Calling all young, chic Dubai residents – the new Magnum bar is the place to be.
Ramada Jumeirah Hotel Al Hudaiba **04 702 7000**
ramadajumeirah.ae
Map **2 J4** Metro **Al Jafiliya**

McGettigan's Irish Pub — Pub

Irish boozer with entertainment and atmosphere

This fairly cavernous bar is pretty rowdy all week. A far-cry from the old-fashioned 'Oirish t'bae sure' theme bar, there are plenty of stools, tables and nooks for drinkers and diners, with a menu that focuses on inexpensive but hearty fare over haute cuisine. Big matches are shown, the quiz is a hoot and there's regular live entertainment. The Guinness is well-kept and well-served, the Irish stew comes piping hot with a couple of doorstops of bread, and the singer kicks off with Dirty Old Town… what more do you want from an Irish boozer?
Bonnington Jumeirah Lakes Towers Jumeirah Lakes Towers **04 356 0560**
mcgettigansdubai.com
Map **1 K5** Metro **Jumeirah Lakes Towers**

Nasimi Beach — Bar

Party haunt on the beach

Located in the shadow of Atlantis The Palm, Nasimi Beach boasts a relaxed vibe. The restaurant's select menu features expertly prepared seafood and meat dishes and, as evening becomes night, superstar DJs take to the decks and the glamour levels soar. Not cheap, but a great Dubai experience.
Atlantis The Palm Palm Jumeirah **04 426 2626**
atlantisthepalm.com
Map **1 N1** Metro **Nakheel**

Nelson's > *p.461* — Pub

Busy British boozer in Barsha

Pitch up to this unpretentious bar if you want to watch football, tuck into traditional English dishes and enjoy some British banter. The bar in the centre resembles a typical Victorian pub, and punters can settle into large armchairs, prop themselves up on bar stools, or cluster around widescreen televisions.
Media Rotana Tecom **04 435 0000**
rotana.com
Map **1 P6** Metro **Dubai Internet City**

Neos **Bar**

Glorious views and '20s glamour on the 63rd floor

With a modern art deco design, Neos is the perfect place for that special occasion. Drag your eyes from the stunning skyline panorama to take in the extensive menu of well executed cocktails and small bites. With top notch service, dress smart, sit back and enjoy the pianist in this glamorous bar. Reservations are recommended for that coveted window seat.

The Address Downtown Dubai Downtown Dubai **04 436 8888**
theaddress.com
Map **2 F7** Metro **Burj Khalifa/Dubai Mall**

Nezesaussi Grill **Sports Bar**

Antipodean sports bar for the tri-nations crowd

Celebrating the sport and cuisine of the tri-nations, Nezesaussi is a popular sports bar with rugby paraphernalia and 13 big screens. Great food and a comprehensive menu offers appeal to more than just sports fans. Meaty mains include South African sausages, New Zealand lamb and Australian steaks.

Al Manzil Hotel Downtown Dubai **04 428 5888**
Map **2 F7** Metro **Burj Khalifa/Dubai Mall**

No. 5 Lounge & Bar **Bar**

Cigar bar with 'old boys club' flair

Not one for a raucous night out, this is a place to sip a nice malt whisky or expertly-prepared Martini while snacking on some of the poshest bar bites you'll find anywhere. Refined and ideal for an after-hours meeting or low-key catch-up.

The Ritz-Carlton, Dubai International Financial Centre (DIFC) Trade Centre 2 **04 372 2222**
ritzcarlton.com
Map **2 G6** Metro **Financial Centre**

Oak N Barrel **Pub**

A classic pub with a touch of sophistication

The deep leather chairs, mahogany bar counters and classical taps all add to the character of this traditional English pub. And whether you want to find a laid-back corner to enjoy a wide range of classic pub-style malt beverages or special cocktails, or order a light meal while watching live sports events, the choice is yours. Regular events include the pub quiz every Sunday, Spareribs & Steak Night, and the legendary Friday Roast Lunch. As well as a daily happy hour, there are special promotional nights for ladies and teachers.

Grand Excelsior Hotel Al Barsha 1 **04 444 9999**
grandexcelsior.ae
Map **1 R6** Metro **Mall of the Emirates**

Oeno Wine Bar **Wine Bar**

Stylish wine bar that's far from cheesy

The fine wines, 50-plus cheeses and excellent service set Oeno apart. The decor is stylish and the wine wall, complete with library-style bookshelf ladder, adds a sense of decadence. Food is served tapas-style, and Tuesday nights bring three free glasses of sparkling wine for ladies from 18:00 to 21:00.

The Westin Dubai Mina Seyahi Beach Resort & Marina Al Sufouh 1 **04 399 4141**
westinminaseyahi.com
Map **1 M4** Metro **Nakheel**

Oscar's Vine Society **Wine Bar**

A cosy hideaway for wine and cheese

Wine cask tables and dim lighting set the mood for indulging in full-bodied reds and ripe cheeses. Special dining offers throughout the week offer good value for great French dishes such as cassoulet and moules mariniere. Friendly bartenders and a 'cheese master' are happy to explain the selections.

Crowne Plaza Dubai Trade Centre 1 **04 331 1111**
ichotelsgroup.com
Map **2 H5** Metro **Emirates Towers**

QD's **Bar**

Location, location, location and a cocktail or two

Sitting so close to the water's edge that you can almost dip your toes into the creek, you can watch the passing abras as the sun sets over Sheikh Zayed Road from this charming and atmospheric locale. Elegant bar snacks accompany an excellent cocktail list and, as the night wears on, the live band keeps the shisha-smoking crowd entertained. This is an extremely laidback affair and lovely for it.

Dubai Creek Golf & Yacht Club Port Saeed **04 295 6000**
dubaigolf.com
Map **2 M7** Metro **Deira City Centre**

Rare The Place > *p.461* **Bar**

Location makes for an alternative nightspot

One of Tecom's best kept secrets. Reminiscent of a drawing room from the Versailles Palace, it's small but elegantly attired in baroque furnishings, and fuses old with new in a way that creates a unique theatrical atmosphere for guests to relax in and enjoy their night. Comprising three areas, Rare's main bar takes centre stage with two surrounding seating sections – a lounge space kitted out in comfy leather furniture, and a casual club area with dance floor. Operating as a

Club Rush

Got a 13-going-on-30 year old? Bored teens will love Club Rush at Atlantis – a teenage hang out with a mocktail and snack bar, chill out lounge, internet cafe, games room, dance floor and big sound system, and you'll love it too because it's supervised and alcohol-free. Birthday parties with a DJ are also available (04 426 1365).

bar/lounge in the evenings before turning into a fully lively nightclub after midnight, the venue offers nights suitable for everyone's taste – from house music to live jazz, and Arabic pop to R&B.
Media Rotana Tecom **055 505 7580**
Map **1 P6** Metro **Dubai Internet City**

Rivington Bar & Terrace > *p.456* Bar

A place to see and be seen
With five outdoor terrace areas, and unobstructed views across the Dubai skyline, it is one of the finest spots to enjoy a cosy drink with friends. And with regular wine and cheese nights, happy hour deals, and a classic British menu of nibbles, it's hard to refuse.
Souk Madinat Jumeirah Umm Suqeim **04 366 6464**
rivingtongrill.ae
Map **1 R4** Metro **Mall of the Emirates**

Rock Bottom Cafe Bar

Sweaty, messy, dirty: an essential Dubai experience
Your Rock Bottom experience depends on your time – or condition – of arrival. Early on, it draws a respectable-ish crowd enjoying the reasonably priced diner food or a game of pool, before undergoing a nightly transformation into the sweaty, heaving, hedonistic home of the legendary Bullfrog cocktail and a cracking cover band. So unique are its appeals, it seemed impossible to repeat elsewhere, but the second Tecom venue (04 450 0111) perfectly captured the spirit and the sweat.
Regent Palace Hotel Al Karama **04 396 3888**
rameehotels.com
Map **2 L5** Metro **BurJuman**

The Rooftop Terrace & Sports Lounge Bar

Kick back your kitten heels, relax under the stars
Rooftop is a hangout for the beautiful people, so expect to pay high prices for your tall drinks. That aside, views of The Palm are superb; cleverly placed Arabic cushion seats promote interaction between the clientele in one of the most chilled-out bars.
One&Only Royal Mirage Al Sufouh 1 **04 399 9999**
oneandonlyresorts.com
Map **1 M4** Metro **Nakheel**

Sanctuary Pool Bar

A chameleon of a bar
Head to Sanctuary's lofty poolside during the day to soak up some rays and enjoy relaxed light bites and cocktails with a storming view. At night, you can enjoy the chilled lounge ambience with simple cuisine and cracking cocktails – although sucking on a shisha pipe while sprawled out across a majlis is just as tempting.
Pullman Dubai Mall of the Emirates Al Barsha 1
04 377 2000
pullman-dubai.com
Map **1 R6** Metro **Mall of the Emirates**

Senyar Bar

A mismatch bar but great cocktails
This rather confused bar has a private lounge with widescreen TV, a mezzanine level with quirky furniture, a comfortable terrace, and a main room with a dated fibre optic bar – it may lack cohesion but the cocktails are executed expertly and are topped off with tapas-style bar snacks.
The Westin Dubai Mina Seyahi Beach Resort & Marina Al Sufouh 1 **04 399 4141**
westinminaseyahi.com
Map **1 M4** Metro **Nakheel**

The Yellow Star

This yellow star highlights places that merit extra praise. It might be the atmosphere, the food, the cocktails, the music or the crowd, but any review that you see with the star attached is sure to be somewhere that's a bit special.

Shades Bar

A chill-out lounge with a taste for good food
For relaxed poolside dining with a delightfully spacious and breezy terrace, Shades manages to come up trumps. Located on the fourth floor of The Address Dubai Marina, Shades is divided into two sections; the first is on a raised-deck platform, equipped with glass tables and wicker chairs. The other is a pristine lounging area with large white comfy sofas, perfect for pre-dinner drinks or shisha. The new weekend a la carte BBQ special is stripped of all pretentiousness, leaving simple, delectable dishes. Try the delicious seafood platters offering succulent jumbo prawns, or the juicy lobster tail – both cooked to perfection without completely scorching the outside layers. Though it's a little pricy at around Dhs.160, the courteous service, wonderfully relaxing atmosphere and sublime food make it money well spent.
The Address Dubai Marina Dubai Marina
04 436 7777
theaddress.com
Map **1 K5** Metro **Dubai Marina**

Sho Cho Bar

A terrace made for lounging and sipping cocktails
It may be a Japanese restaurant with delicate and imaginative dishes, but the huge terrace, not to mention the sunshine holiday vibe, is what attracts the beautiful clientele to this popular spot. The mix of house and trance music and a gorgeous view of the shoreline make this a must. And the cocktails add the perfect finishing touch.
Dubai Marine Beach Resort & Spa Jumeira 1
04 346 1111
sho-cho.com
Map **2 H4** Metro **World Trade Centre**

Walk The Walk

Got the munchies? Head to The Walk, Dubai's latest place to be that's packed with a multitude of restaurants and cafes.

One of the most popular areas in Dubai for going out is The Walk, the 1.7km pedestrian-friendly boulevard that lies between the JBR residential development and the beach. You won't find any fine dining establishments here, but that's not the main draw; crowds come for the atmosphere and the relaxed, alfresco eating and drinking.

In the cooler months, hundreds of people of all nationalities – families, friends, couples, tourists – stroll the strip before settling down at a table to sociably while the night away. There are dozens of cafes and restaurants on The Walk, serving up pretty much every popular cuisine available. If you can't decide what you're in the mood for, just go for a wander and you'll soon stumble upon something that takes your fancy.

Starting at the Dubai end of the strip, the first JBR court is Murjan. This is the more upmarket side of The Walk, where the designer boutiques and home accessory stores congregate. There's also a cluster of international options to choose from here: Da Shi Dai (Chinese); Umi Sushi (Japanese); Suvoroff (Russian); Scoozi (Italian-Japanese fusion); The Fish & Chip Room (British); and On The Border (Mexican). There's also a cigar lounge here, La Casa Del Habano, for a refined end to the evening.

The next court, Sadaf, has its main culinary treats tucked away up on the plaza level, including branches of the excellent Lebanese chain Automatic and fun burger-and-shake joint Fuddruckers. Wedged among the JBR courts is Oasis Beach Tower, which contains some popular (and, unlike the JBR outlets, licensed) restaurants, including Frankie's, Wagamama and Trader Vic's Mai-Tai Lounge. Next up come some of the newer The Walk offerings, such as New Zealand's 'healthy' burger chain, Burger Fuel, and the popular Canadian coffee and donuts chain Tim Horton's.

The delights of JBR

JBR continues with Bahar and Rimal courts, which feature a great stretch of alfresco eating. Packed tables spread out onto the wide pavement, and it is perhaps The Walk's busiest section in the evenings and for leisurely weekend breakfasts. Highlights include Il Caffé Di Roma, Paul, Le Pain Quotidien, The Butcher Shop and Grill, Sukh Sagar and El Chico.

Things descend into more of a fastfood frenzy by Amwaj and Shams courts, with a selection of the usual suspects – Hardee's, Cinnabon, KFC, Pizza Hut, Figaro's Pizza – plus decent breakfast spot Coco's. If the endless options along The Walk are not enough to satisfy your appetite, there are plenty more cafes and restaurants by the water at Marina Walk, while the beachfront hotels – Amwaj Rotana, Sofitel, Habtoor Grand, Le Royal Meridien, Ritz-Carlton, Hilton and Sheraton – house a more upmarket selection of higher-class restaurants and bars.

Siddharta Lounge By Buddha Bar — Bar

Buddha-Bar spin-off to impress and satisfy

Located on the fourth floor of the hotel, with its own entrance for outside guests, Siddharta boasts a sleek and contemporary interior, featuring ample lashings of plush white seating, gold accents and glam marble finishing, coupled with floor-to-ceiling windows that reveal stunning views of Dubai Marina. You'll be spoiled for choice with a posh snack menu that features a mouthwatering selection of Asian-Mediterranean specialities, including wagyu beef mini burgers with orange soy and crispy prawn spring rolls with tamarind dipping sauce. Drinks aren't cheap, but this is a place to be seen.

Grosvenor House Dubai Marina **04 399 8888**
grosvenorhouse-dubai.com
Map **1 L5** Metro **Dubai Marina**

Skyview Bar — Bar

Drinks at the top of the Burj: a Dubai must-do

A cocktail here can easily run into triple figures and you have to book well in advance – there's a minimum spend of Dhs.275 per person just to get in. But it is worth it for special occasions or to impress out-of-town visitors. The views are amazing, as you would expect. You can also take afternoon tea here (p.534).

Burj Al Arab Umm Suqeim 3 **04 301 7600**
jumeirah.com
Map **1 S4** Metro **Mall of the Emirates**

Studio One — Bar

Sport, beer and chips – sometimes it's all you want

Big burgers and greasy fries are the perfect accompaniment to a night in front of the big game at this sport watcher's paradise. TVs scattered around the bar provide a multi-screen sport marathon. The price of beer isn't off-putting, and the selection is good.

Hilton Dubai Jumeirah Resort Dubai Marina
04 399 1111
hilton.com
Map **1 K4** Metro **Jumeirah Lakes Towers**

Submarine — Nightclub

Underground dance music and an alternative vibe

Submarine has filled a bit of the alternative dance void that exists in the city. It doesn't start to fill up until midnight, and the spaceship-meets-submarine decor might miss the mark, but Submarine's DJs will quickly remind you how diverse club music can be.

Dhow Palace Hotel Al Mankhool **04 359 9992**
dhowpalacedubai.com
Map **2 L5** Metro **Al Karama**

Tamanya Terrace — Bar

Good views, not bad nibbles and decent drinks

Tamanya treats its patrons to panoramic views of Media City, including iconic landmarks like the Burj Al Arab, The World and The Palm islands. The clientele is a good mix of tourists and expats and the resident DJ spins tunes from house and funk to sultry Latin grooves. Unlike some bars, the music is just loud enough to enjoy without having to scream in your mates' ears all night. There are typical bar snacks if you're peckish, while Tamanya boasts a very good selection of cocktails at very reasonable prices. Guests can also choose wines from the Certo menu if the particular wine they want is not on the bar's menu.

Radisson Blu Hotel, Dubai Media City Al Sufouh 1
04 366 9111
radissonblu.com
Map **1 M5** Metro **Nakheel**

The Terrace > *p.461* — Bar

Rooftop chilling, media-style

This rooftop bar is the perfect alfresco drinking spot, with the option of perching at the long bar or relaxing in the garden style furniture. Food is served during the day but after 17:00 it is just drinks and shisha and the chill-out tunes of the resident DJ.

Media Rotana Tecom **04 435 0000**
rotana.com
Map **1 P6** Metro **Dubai Internet City**

Trader Vic's Mai-Tai Lounge — Bar

More of the same strong Trader Vic's cocktails

The livelier cousin of the Crowne Plaza and Madinat eateries (04 366 5346), this large bar is decked out in Polynesian style. Mai-Tai's totally tropical cocktail list is

Trader Vic's Mai-Tai Lounge

accompanied by tasty, if expensive, bar snacks and the spacious dancefloor provides a clubby feel.
Jumeirah Beach Residence Dubai Marina
04 399 8993
tradervics.com
Map **1 K4** Metro **Dubai Marina**

Two Guineas — Pub
No pretence British pub good for watching sport
A lively pub with walls lined with big screen TVs playing the latest sporting events. The menu consists of your typical British pub grub like bangers and mash, and fish and chips. While sipping on your ice cold beer, you can indulge in a game of pool in the separate pool room. The service is fast and friendly and the pub has a steady clientele of regulars making for a very pleasant, friendly and relaxed atmosphere, a kind of like where everybody knows your name type of place. Has a few theme nights like karaoke night on Saturday, Monday and Wednesday; Fiesta Festival from Sunday to Wednesday where you can select one of three lavish dishes for Dhs.59; and Branding night on Thursday where you can order as many drinks all night from a selected brand for only Dhs.99.
Holiday Inn Bur Dubai Embassy – District
Al Hamriya **04 357 2999**
holidayinn.com
Map **2 M5** Metro **BurJuman**

The Underground Pub — Pub
Football, beer, pub grub and the Tube
Themed on the Tube, the order of the day in this popular pub is (expensive) beer, burgers and ball sports which attract a large crowd of regulars. There are numerous screens to ensure you can get a good view of the live sports action, plus a dartboard and pool tables.
Habtoor Grand Beach Resort & Spa Dubai Marina
04 399 5000
grandjumeirah.habtoorhotels.com
Map **1 L4** Metro **Dubai Marina**

Uptown Bar — Bar
Shaken not stirred sundowners and fine views
The 24th floor location affords great terrace views of the Burj Al Arab and beyond, and the interior is classy enough – in a James Bond kind of way. An extensive menu of cocktails with price tags to match is complemented by tapas and bar snacks.
Jumeirah Beach Hotel Umm Suqeim 3 **04 406 8999**
jumeirah.com
Map **1 S4** Metro **Mall of the Emirates**

Vantage — Wine Bar
Elegant setting with impressive wine menu
The plush, purple interior of this wine bar offers an opulent, but intimate, setting to sample an extensive wine and cocktail list, while the terrace affords sweeping coast views. Arabic snacks dominate the menu, which also features a classic cheese platter.
Pullman Dubai Mall of the Emirates Al Barsha 1
04 377 2000
pullman-dubai.com
Map **1 R6** Metro **Mall of the Emirates**

Viceroy Pub — Bar
The stereotypical British pub-cum-bar
A familiar, pokey British pub with authentic tobacco smoke, a cast of middle-aged regulars and corner televisions tuned to different sports channels. It serves up reasonably priced, generously portioned British, Tex-Mex, Thai and Indian food with daily happy hours.
Four Points By Sheraton Bur Dubai Al Hamriya
04 397 7444
viceroypub.com
Map **2 L5** Metro **BurJuman**

Vintage Cheese & Wine Bar — Wine Bar
A cheese and wine aficionado's dream
Boasts an exclusive list of cold meat and cheese platters, costly vintages, burgundies and champagnes – but manages to retain the feel of a friendly local. The bar is small, so arrive early or very late to bag a sofa.
Wafi Umm Hurair 2 **04 324 4100**
pyramidsrestaurantsatwafi.com
Map **2 L7** Metro **Dubai Healthcare City**

Vista Lounge — Bar
Music, cocktails and a breathtaking backdrop
With fabulous views over the creek from the relaxed terrace, a romantically lit piano bar and a modern cocktail bar, Vista is a welcome addition to the 'other side of the creek'. It also has a small food menu serving mainly sandwiches and salads.
InterContinental Dubai Festival City
Dubai Festival City **04 701 1127**
diningdfc.com
Map **2 M9** Metro **Emirates**

Voda Bar — Bar
Ultra-chic bar with a Japanese flair
Futuristic and minimalistic, with a spacious floor plan that includes a handful of attractive white egg-shaped chairs and white leather sofas; there is a 15-page list of exotic Japanese inspired cocktails. The food served is specifically Japanese – beautifully presented and ideal for sharing. These delectable treats all come at a price and expect to pay around Dhs.60 per cocktail with sushi platters hitting the Dhs.115 mark. But the beauty of the bar and the delightful food bites ensure it is money well spent.
Jumeirah Zabeel Saray Palm Jumeirah **04 453 0444**
jumeirah.com
Map **1 L3** Metro **Nakheel**

Vu's Bar — Bar

Give your guests a slice of the high life

The doors open on to the 51st floor to reveal what feels like a private members' club, and the prices echo that suspicion. Through oddly-shaped windows you can glimpse fabulous views of Sheikh Zayed Road. The beer and wine lists are huge, but the cocktails steal the show.

Jumeirah Emirates Towers Trade Centre 2
04 319 8088
jumeirah.com
Map **2 H6** Metro **Emirates Towers**

Warehouse — Bar

Eat, drink and dance, all in one stylish venue

Warehouse, a restaurant-pub-wine bar-vodka bar-lounge club, is a stylish addition to the old-school side of the creek. There is a beer bar and garden on the ground floor serving fish and chips and the likes, while up the spiral staircase you'll find a dual-personality restaurant – half fine dining and half sushi – where the food is deliciously inventive. There is also an intimate nightclub should you want to continue the night.

Le Meridien Dubai Al Garhoud **04 702 2560**
diningdubai.com
Map **2 N8** Metro **GGICO**

Waxy O'Connor's — Pub

Not high society – but expect a great time

This faux Irish pub successfully staves off homesickness for party-hungry British and Irish expats...although Waxy's reputation draws expats from far and wide. Its legendary weekend brunch costs Dhs.85 for five drinks, a full English breakfast and then a carvery dinner. As you'd imagine, things can get more than a little raucous. At 18:00 the lights go down, the cheesy tunes start to play and the party starts. Popular for pub grub, pints and sport during the rest of the week too.

Ascot Hotel Al Raffa **04 352 0900**
ascothoteldubai.com
Map **2 L4** Metro **Al Fahidi**

The Whistler > *p.243, 509, 557, 567* — Bar

Cheese and wine – all in the best possible taste

Wine, cheese and a whole lot of luxury are what you'll find when you walk into The Whistler. Located on the 25th floor, this is the place to admire Dubai's sklyline and unwind. Let the sommelier advise you on the perfect pairing of fine cheese and wine, and enjoy a 'wine flight' – tasting a variety of red and white wines served using the popular Enomatic system. Live music from a saxophone player sets the ambient mood perfectly.

Ocean View Hotel Dubai Marina **04 814 5599**
jaresortshotels.com
Map **1 K4** Metro **Jumeirah Lakes Towers**

White X Beach & Lounge — Nightclub

Fantastic location: in and far removed from the city

Its fantastic location on the very furthest reach of Palm Jumeirah's eastern crescent is this venue's biggest draw. With views spanning the whole city, but with an island beach feel, White X manages to get the best of both worlds – a location both in and far removed from the city. The afternoon allows guests to sunbathe and soak in Jacuzzis on the beach, and early evening has a relaxed vibe great for lounging with a shisha on huge comfy sofas. Later on the DJ gets going and the place becomes a last-stop-of-the-night party spot. The drinks menu features a selection of tasty cocktails – the passion fruit mojito in particular

Rixos The Palm Dubai Palm Jumeirah **04 457 5555**
rixos.com
Map **1 P3** Metro **Nakheel**

XL Beach Club — Nightclub

Beach chic with a dash of late night decadence

With ample style and more than a pinch of decadence, XL Beach Club lives up to its grandiose name. Private cabanas and a shimmering pool set the scene, superstar DJs regularly spin the discs here and, once darkness falls, the chic outdoors venue plays host to some of the best parties in town. Stylish crowds, an eye-popping drinks list and lively vibes complete the picture. And, although things don't get going till late, it's worth the wait – this is partying under the stars at its finest.

Habtoor Grand Beach Resort & Spa Dubai Marina
04 399 5000
Map **1 L4** Metro **Dubai Marina**

The Z:ONE — Bar

Cool bar that warms up your evening

Ultra modern with a video wall and chic white decor, Z:ONE draws in the pre-party crowd with weekly theme nights: candy Martinis on Thursday, two-for-one cocktails on Sunday, and ladies' night on Tuesday. Other nights are lower key, ideal for a post-work wind down.

Media One Hotel Al Sufouh 1 **04 427 1000**
mediaonehotel.com
Map **1 M5** Metro **Nakheel**

Zinc — Nightclub

The slinky superclub experience

The soundtrack is modern, funky R&B, house and hip-hop, with Housexy (Ministry of Sound) and Kinky Malinki ferrying over their rostas of UK DJs. Design-wise, there are shiny flatscreens, lounge areas and glitzy mirrored walls, as well as a big dancefloor sectioned off by a mammoth bar.

Crowne Plaza Dubai Trade Centre 1 **04 331 1111**
ichotelsgroup.com
Map **2 H5** Metro **Emirates Towers**

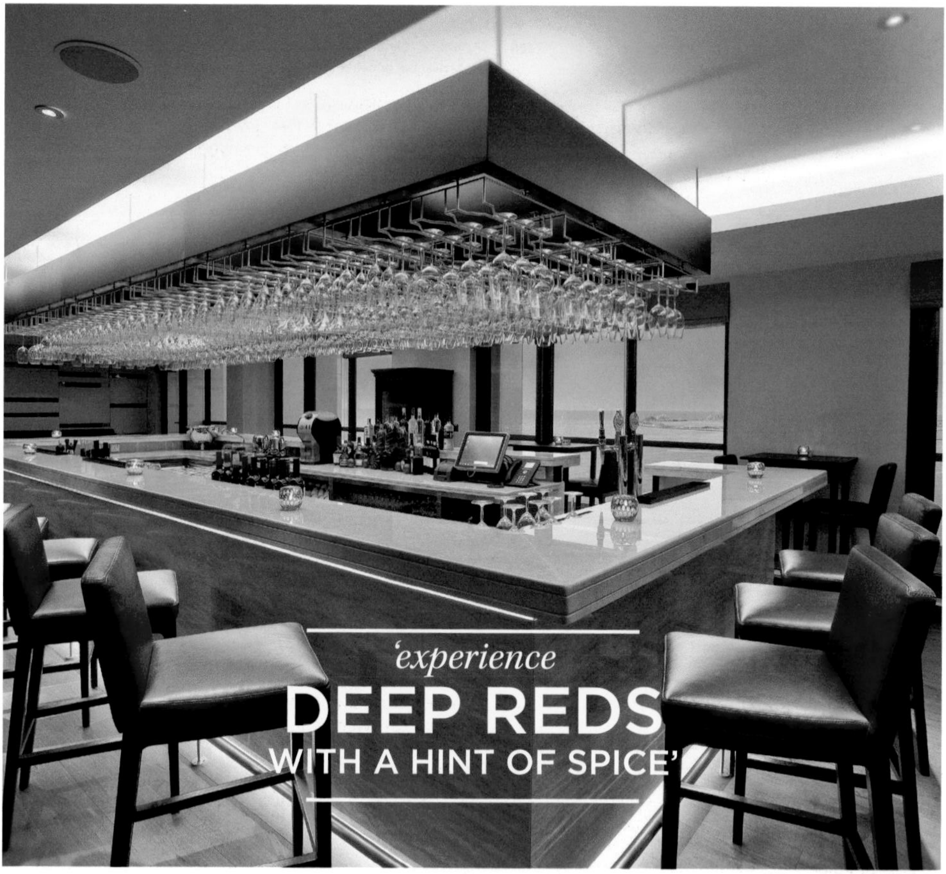
'experience
DEEP REDS
WITH A HINT OF SPICE'

# #

A

B

C

D

E

F

G

H

M

S

T

U

V

W

X

Y

Z

Explorer Products

Residents' Guides

Mini Visitors' Guides

Photography Books & Calendars

Check out ask**explorer**.com

Maps

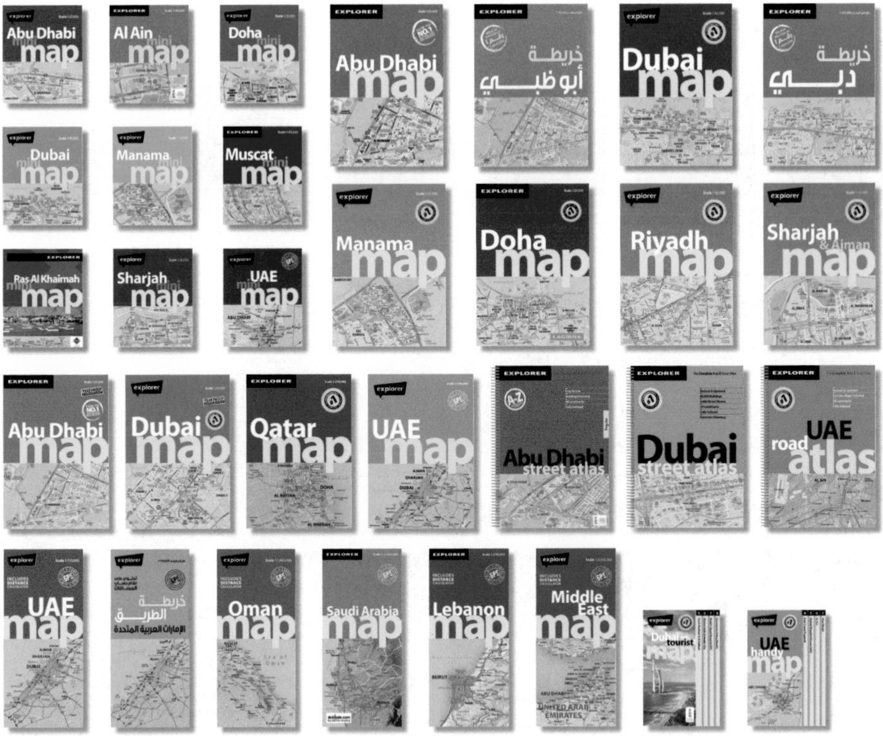

Adventure & Lifestyle Guides

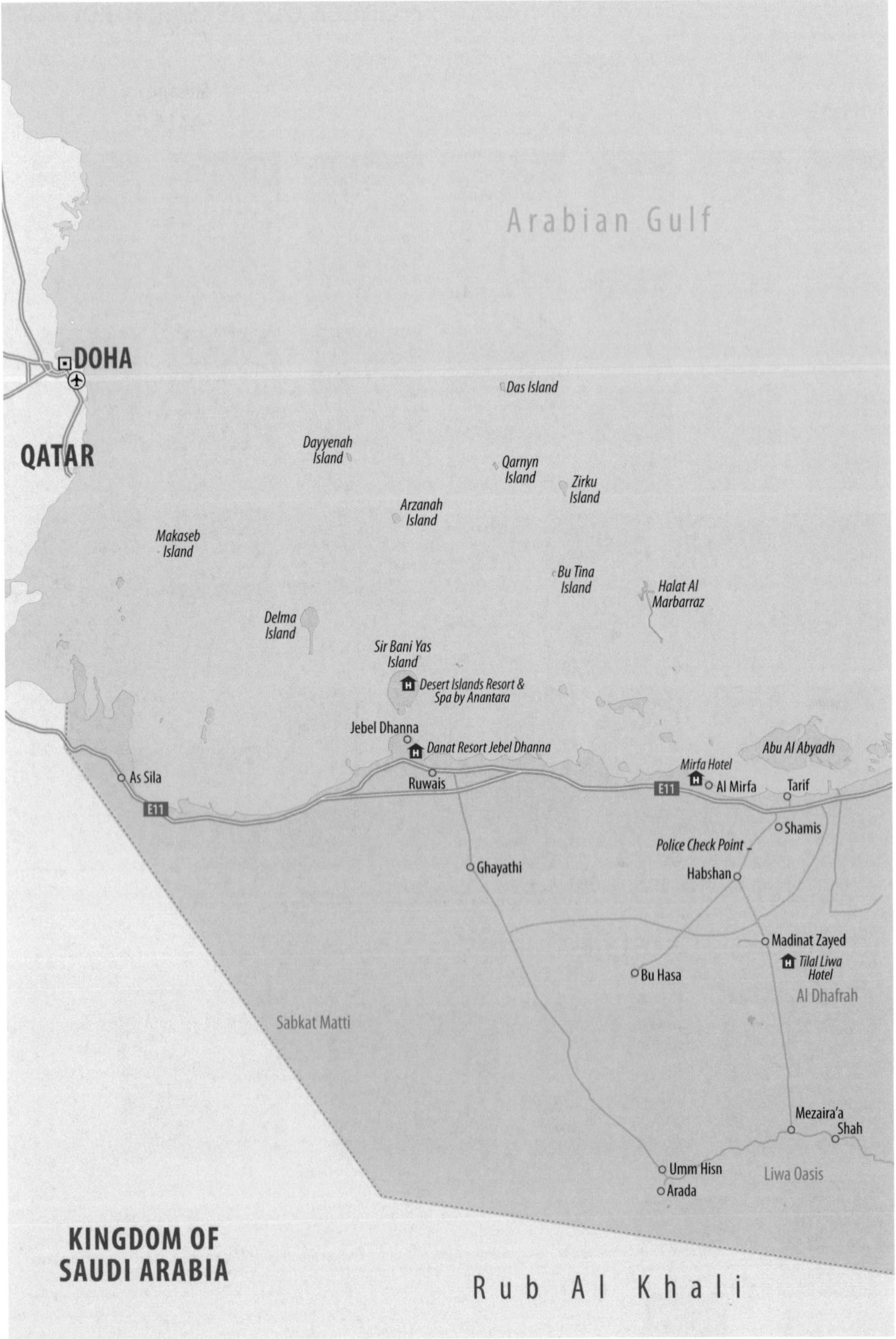
Arabian Gulf
DOHA
QATAR
Das Island
Dayyenah Island
Qarnyn Island
Zirku Island
Arzanah Island
Makaseb Island
Bu Tina Island
Halat Al Marbarraz
Delma Island
Sir Bani Yas Island
Desert Islands Resort & Spa by Anantara
Jebel Dhanna
Danat Resort Jebel Dhanna
Abu Al Abyadh
Mirfa Hotel
As Sila
Ruwais
E11
E11
Al Mirfa
Tarif
Shamis
Police Check Point
Ghayathi
Habshan
Madinat Zayed
Tilal Liwa Hotel
Bu Hasa
Al Dhafrah
Sabkat Matti
Mezaira'a
Shah
Umm Hisn
Arada
Liwa Oasis
KINGDOM OF SAUDI ARABIA
Rub Al Khali

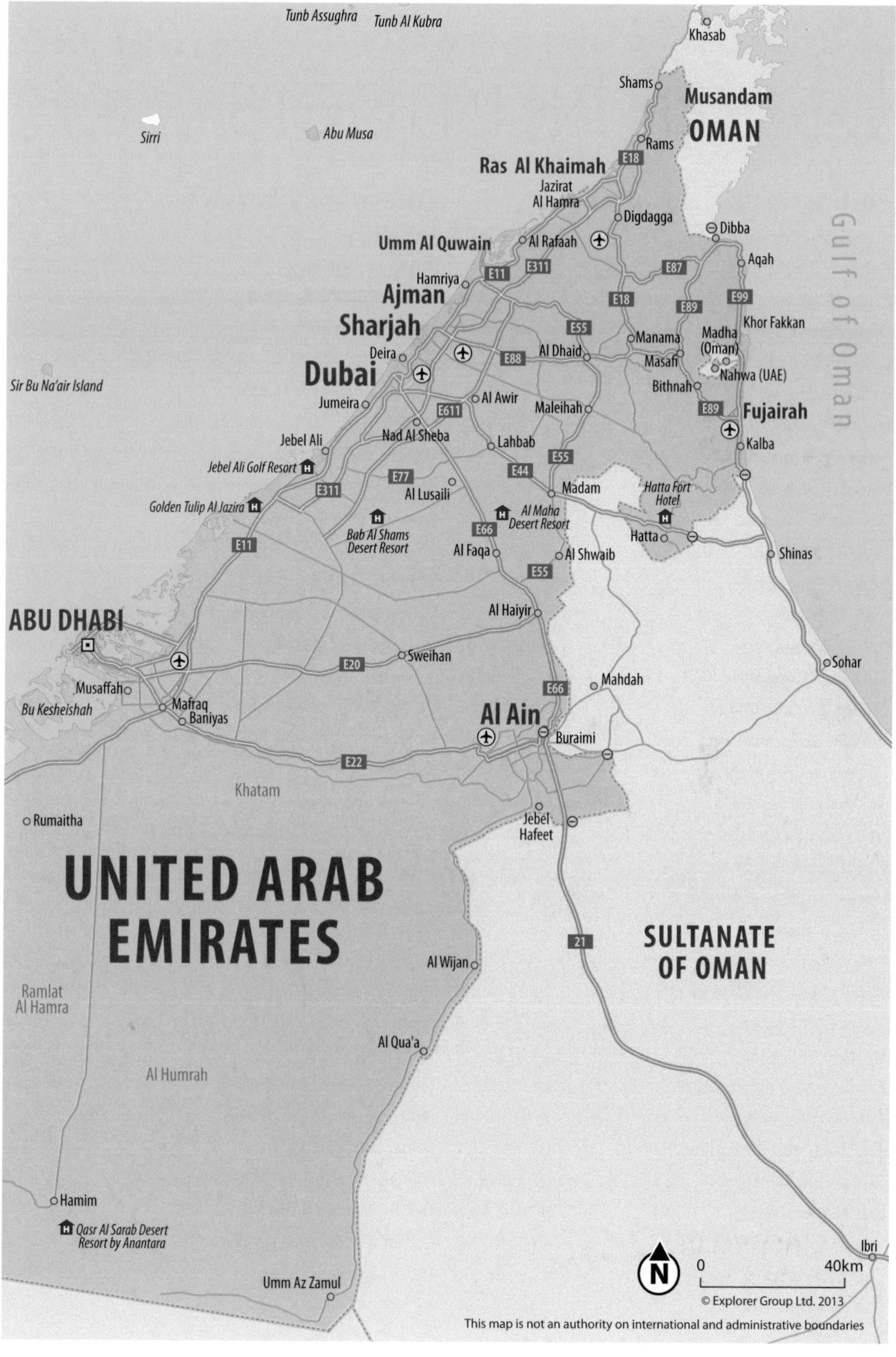
Tunb Assughra
Tunb Al Kubra
Khasab
Shams
Musandam
OMAN
Sirri
Abu Musa
Rams
E18
Ras Al Khaimah
Jazirat
Al Hamra
Digdagga
Dibba
Gulf of Oman
Umm Al Quwain
Al Rafaah
Aqah
Hamriya
E11
E311
E87
Ajman
E18
E89
E99
Sharjah
E55
Khor Fakkan
Deira
Manama
Madha
(Oman)
Al Dhaid
E88
Masafi
Dubai
Nahwa (UAE)
Sir Bu Na'air Island
Bithnah
Jumeira
Al Awir
E611
Maleihah
E89
Fujairah
Jebel Ali
Nad Al Sheba
Lahbab
Kalba
E55
Jebel Ali Golf Resort
E44
E77
Hatta Fort
Hotel
E311
Al Lusaili
Madam
Golden Tulip Al Jazira
Al Maha
Desert Resort
Bab Al Shams
Desert Resort
E66
Hatta
E11
Al Faqa
Al Shwaib
Shinas
E55
Al Haiyir
ABU DHABI
Sweihan
Sohar
E20
Mahdah
E66
Musaffah
Bu Kesheishah
Mafraq
Baniyas
Al Ain
Buraimi
E22
Khatam
Rumaitha
Jebel
Hafeet
UNITED ARAB
EMIRATES
21
SULTANATE
OF OMAN
Al Wijan
Ramlat
Al Hamra
Al Qua'a
Al Humrah
Hamim
Qasr Al Sarab Desert
Resort by Anantara
Ibri
N
0
40km
Umm Az Zamul
© Explorer Group Ltd. 2013
This map is not an authority on international and administrative boundaries

explorer

Useful Numbers

Embassies & Consulates

Australian Consulate	04 508 7100
Bahrain Embassy	02 665 7500
British Embassy	04 309 4444
Canadian Consulate	04 404 8444
Chinese Consulate	04 394 4733
Czech Embassy	02 678 2800
Danish Consulate	04 348 0877
Egyptian Consulate	04 397 1122
French Consulate	04 408 4900
German Consulate	04 397 2333
Indian Consulate	04 397 1222
Iranian Consulate	04 344 4717
Irish Embassy	02 495 8200
Italian Consulate	04 331 4167
Japanese Consulate	04 331 9191
Jordanian Consulate	04 397 0500
Kuwaiti Consulate	04 397 8000
Lebanese Consulate	04 397 7450
Malaysian Consulate	04 398 5843
Netherlands Consulate	04 440 7600
New Zealand Consulate	04 331 7500
Norwegian Consulate	04 382 3880
Omani Consulate	04 397 1000
Pakistani Consulate	04 397 0412
Philippine Consulate	04 220 7100
Qatar Consulate	04 396 0444
Russian Consulate	04 328 5347
Saudi Arabian Consulate	04 397 9777
Spanish Embassy	02 626 9544
South African Consulate	04 397 5222
Sri Lankan Consulate	04 398 6535
Swedish Embassy	02 417 8800
Swiss Consulate	04 329 0999
Thai Consulate	04 348 9550
US Consulate General	04 309 4000

Emergency Services

Ambulance	999
DEWA Emergency	991
Dubai Police Emergency	999
Fire Department	997

Police Services

Department for Tourist Security	800 4438
Dubai Police	04 609 9999
Al Ameen (for neighbourhood problems)	800 4888
Dubai Police Information Line	800 7777

Directory

Dubai International Airport Help Desk	04 224 5555
Flight Information	04 216 6666
Baggage Services	04 224 5383
Directory Enquiries (du)	199
du Contact Centre (mobile enquiries)	
From mobile	155
From any phone	055 567 8155
du Contact Centre (home enquiries)	04 390 5555
Directory Enquiries (Etisalat)	181
Etisalat Customer Care	101
Etisalat Information	144
International Operator Assistance	100
Mobile Phone Code (du)	052/055
Mobile Phone Code (Etisalat)	050/056
Speaking Clock	141
Dubai Meteorological Office	04 216 2218
Dubai Municipality Public Health Department	04 223 2323
Ministry Of Labour Hotline	800 665
Dubai Rent Committee	04 221 5555
Dubai Consumer Protection	600 54 5555
RTA Complaints Line	800 90 90
Salik	800 72545

Airlines

Aeroflot	04 222 2245
Air Arabia	06 508 8888
Air France	800 23823
Air India	04 227 6787
Air Mauritius	04 221 4455
Air New Zealand	04 335 9126
Air Seychelles	04 286 8008
Alitalia	04 282 6113
American Airlines	04 316 6116
Austrian Airlines	04 211 2538
Biman Bangladesh Airlines	04 2203 2029
British Airways	800 0 441 3322
Cathay Pacific	04 204 2888
China Airlines	02 626 4070
CSA Czech Airlines	04 294 5666
Cyprus Airways	04 221 4455
Delta Airlines	04 397 0118
Egypt Air	04 230 6666
Emirates	600 555 555
Etihad Airways	800 2277
flydubai	04 231 1000
Gulf Air	04 271 6207
Iran Air	04 224 0200
Japan Airlines	04 217 7501
KLM Royal Dutch Airlines	800 556
Kuwait Airways	04 228 5896
Lufthansa	04 373 9100
Malaysia Airlines	04 325 4411
Middle East Airlines	04 223 7080
Oman Air	04 351 8080
Pakistan International Airlines	04 223 4888
Qantas	04 316 6652
Qatar Airways	04 231 9921
RAK Airways	07 228 4875
Royal Brunei Airlines	04 334 4884
Royal Jet Group	02 575 7000
Royal Jordanian	04 294 4288
Saudi Arabian Airlines	04 229 6227
Singapore Airlines	04 316 6888
Swiss Air	04 381 6100

Hospitals

American Hospital	04 377 6644
Cedars Jebel Ali Int'l Hospital	04 881 4000
Dubai Hospital	04 219 5000
Iranian Hospital	04 344 0250
Latifa Hospital	04 219 3000
Medcare Hospital	04 407 9111
Mediclinic City Hospital	04 435 9999
Mediclinic Welcare Hospital	04 282 7788
Neuro Spinal Hospital	04 342 0000
Rashid Hospital	04 219 2000

24 Hour Pharmacy

Life Pharmacy	04 344 1122
IBN Sina Pharmacy	04 355 6909
Yara Pharmacy	04 222 5503

Taxi Service

Al Arabia Taxi	04 285 5566
Cars Taxi	800 227 789
Dubai Taxis	04 208 0808
Metro Taxi	600 566000
National Taxi	600 543322

Car Rental

Autolease Rent-A-Car	04 282 6565
Avis	04 295 7121
Budget Car & Van Rental	04 884 0022
Diamond Lease	04 885 2677
Dubai Exotic Limo	800 5466
EuroStar Rent-A-Car	04 266 1117
Hertz	800 437 89
Icon Car Rental	04 257 8228
National Car Rental	04 283 2020
Payless Car Rental	04 384 5526
Thrifty Car Rental	800 4694
United Car Rentals	04 285 7777

Road Service

Arabian Automobile Association (AAA)	800 8181
MESAR Roadside Assistance	050 204 5208

explorer

Dubai Explorer – 17th Edition
Edited by Carli Allan
Proofread by Lisa Crowther, Lidiya Baltova-Kalichuk
Data managed by Amapola Castillo, Derrick Pereira
Designed by Ieyad Charaf, Jayde Fernandes, Pete Maloney
Maps by Noushad Madathil, Zainudheen Madathil
Photographs by Pamela Grist, Pete Maloney, Derrick Pereira, Victor Romero

Publishing
Publisher Alistair MacKenzie
Associate Publisher Claire England

Editorial
Managing Editor – Consumer Carli Allan
Guides Editor Jo Iivonen
Deputy Guides Editor Stacey Siebritz
Managing Editor – Corporate Charlie Scott
Deputy Corporate Editor Lily Lawes
Digital Projects Editor Rachel McArthur
Web Editor Laura Coughlin
Production Assistant Vanessa Eguia
Editorial Assistants Amapola Castillo
Researchers Gayathri CM, Farida, Jagadeesh, Shalu M Sukumar, Suchitra P, Sreejith, Roja P

Design & Photography
Creative Director Pete Maloney
Art Director Ieyad Charaf
Designer Michael Estrada
Junior Designer M. Shakkeer
Layout Manager Jayde Fernandes
Cartography Manager Zainudheen Madathil
Cartographers Noushad Madathil, Ramla Kambravan, Jithesh Kalathingal
GIS Analysts Rafi KM, Hidayath Razi
Photography Manager Pamela Grist
Photographer Bart Wojcinski
Image Library Jyothin

Sales & Marketing
Group Media Sales Manager Peter Saxby
Media Sales Area Managers Laura Zuffova, Sabrina Ahmed, Bryan Anes, Adam Smith, Louise Burton, Matthew Whitbread
Business Development Manager Pouneh Hafizi
Corporate Solutions Account Manager Vibeke Nurgberg
Group Marketing & PR Manager Lindsay West
Senior Marketing Executive Stuart L. Cunningham
Group Retail Sales Manager Ivan Rodrigues
Retail Sales Coordinator Michelle Mascarenhas
Retail Sales Area Supervisors Ahmed Mainodin, Firos Khan
Retail Sales Merchandisers Johny Mathew, Shan Kumar
Retail Sales Drivers Shabsir Madathil, Najumudeen K.I., Sujeer Khan
Warehouse Assistant Mohamed Haji

Finance & Administration
Administration Manager Fiona Hepher
Accountant Cherry Enriquez
Accounts Assistants Sunil Suvarna, Joy Bermejo Belza, Jeanette Carino Enecillo
Admin Assistant & Reception Joy H. San Buenaventura
Public Relations Officer Rafi Jamal
Office Assistant Shafeer Ahamed
Office Manager – India Jithesh Kalathingal

IT & Digital Solutions
Digital Solutions Manager Derrick Pereira
IT Administrator R. Ajay
Database Programmer Pradeep T.P.

Contact Us

General Enquiries
We'd love to hear your thoughts and answer any questions you have about this book or any other Explorer product. Contact us at **info@askexplorer.com**

Careers
If you fancy yourself as an Explorer, send your CV (stating the position you're interested in) to **jobs@askexplorer.com**

Contract Publishing
For enquiries about Explorer's Contract Publishing arm and design services contact **contracts@askexplorer.com**

PR & Marketing
For PR and marketing enquiries contact **marketing@askexplorer.com**

Corporate Sales & Licensing
For bulk sales and customisation options, for this book or any Explorer product, contact **sales@askexplorer.com**

Advertising & Sponsorship
For advertising and sponsorship, contact **sales@askexplorer.com**

Explorer Publishing & Distribution
PO Box 34275, Dubai, United Arab Emirates
www.askexplorer.com

Phone: +971 (0)4 340 8805
Fax: +971 (0)4 340 8806